St. James Encyclopedia of Popular Culture

SECOND EDITION

St. James Encyclopedia of Popular Culture

SECOND EDITION

VOLUME 5

SUB–Z

INDEXES

Thomas Riggs

EDITOR

ST. JAMES PRESS

A part of Gale, Cengage Learning

Detroit • New York • San Francisco • New Haven, Conn • Waterville, Maine • London

St. James Encyclopedia of Popular Culture

Thomas J. Riggs, Editor

Product Manager: Douglas Dentino

Project Editor: Carol A. Schwartz

Editorial: Laura Avery; Dana Barnes; Erin Bealmear; Shawn Corridor; Matthew Derda; Jason Everett; Dana Ferguson; Jennifer Greve; Kristy Harper; Kristin Hart; Alan Hedblad; Andrea Henderson; Monica Hubbard; Jeff Hunter; Victor Ibarra; Reed Kalso; Kristin Key; Debra Kirby; Laurie Malashanko; Kim McGrath; Chelsea Merchan; Kathy Nemeh; Scot Peacock; Jennifer Wisinski

Rights Acquisition and Management: Christine Myaskovsky

Composition: Gary Leach

Manufacturing: Wendy Blurton

Imaging: John Watkins

Product Design: Kristine Julien

LIBRARY OF CONGRESS CATALOGING-IN-PUBLICATION DATA

St. James encyclopedia of popular culture / Thomas Riggs, editor ; with an introduction by Jim Cullen. -- 2nd edition.
p. cm. --
Includes bibliographical references and index.
ISBN 978-1-55862-847-2 (set) -- ISBN 978-1-55862-848-9 (vol. 1) -- ISBN 978-1-55862-849-6 (vol. 2) -- ISBN 978-1-55862-850-2 (vol. 3) -- ISBN 978-1-55862-851-9 (vol. 4) -- ISBN 978-1-55862-852-6 (vol. 5) -- ISBN 978-1-55862-853-3 (ebook)
1. United States--Civilization--20th century--Encyclopedias. 2. United States--Civilization--21st century--Encyclopedias. 3. Popular culture--United States--History--20th century--Encyclopedias. 4. Popular culture--United States--History--21st century--Encyclopedias. I. Riggs, Thomas, 1963- II. Title: Saint James encyclopedia of popular culture.

E169.1.J3 2013
973.9--dc23 2012049921

Gale, a part of Cengage Learning
27500 Drake Rd.
Farmington Hills, MI, 48331-3535

ISBN-13: 978-1-55862-847-2 (set) ISBN-10: 1-55862-847-9 (set)
ISBN-13: 978-1-55862-848-9 (vol. 1) ISBN-10: 1-55862-848-7 (vol. 1)
ISBN-13: 978-1-55862-849-6 (vol. 2) ISBN-10: 1-55862-849-5 (vol. 2)
ISBN-13: 978-1-55862-850-2 (vol. 3) ISBN-10: 1-55862-850-9 (vol. 3)
ISBN-13: 978-1-55862-851-9 (vol. 4) ISBN-10: 1-55862-851-7 (vol. 4)
ISBN-13: 978-1-55862-852-6 (vol. 5) ISBN-10: 1-55862-852-5 (vol. 5)

This title is also available as an e-book.
ISBN-13: 978-1-55862-853-3 ISBN-10: 55862-853-3
Contact your Gale, a part of Cengage Learning, sales representative for ordering information.

Printed in China
1 2 3 4 5 6 7 17 16 15 14 13

Contents

List of Entries

C

VOLUME 2

C *continued*

D

G

H

VOLUME 3

I

J

M

VOLUME 5

S *continued*

T

U

V

S

Suburbia

The development of suburbs—residential communities on the outskirts of cities—was one of the most dominant features of American life in the twentieth century. Far from being merely a way Americans organized their housing and ordered their landscape, the suburbs created an entirely new way of ordering American social life and culture. The result was a phenomenon known as *suburbia*, a term denoting not only a physical place but often a cultural and social mind-set as well. The rise of suburbia beginning in the nineteenth century had a major role in the development of American culture, extending long-cherished American beliefs in individuality and an agrarian ideal in new ways while simultaneously working to reshape both the American physical and social landscape.

ORIGINS

Although suburbia had its major impact during the twentieth century, it originated and developed in the nineteenth century. "I view great cities," Thomas Jefferson once wrote, "as pestilential to the morals, the health, and the liberties of man." Jefferson's antiurban view was shared by a growing number of people in the 1800s. As cities became crowded with people, bringing increased sanitation, transportation, and crime problems, those Americans who could afford to, namely the growing middle class, began moving to larger, single-family homes on the outskirts of major American cities. This was in direct opposition to European cities, where the middle and upper classes preferred to remain in the central city and poorer people were pushed to the outskirts. Prior to the mid-nineteenth century, work and home were closely intertwined, and cities reflected this mixture as well with residential buildings coexisting with commercial ones. As industrialization advanced, home and work became increasingly separated as men went off to work and women stayed home. New innovations in transportation, from ferries and omnibuses to steam railroads and horse-drawn streetcars, helped make this transition possible.

These new suburbs of the 1840s and 1850s contributed to the monumental shift in middle-class culture in key ways. New suburban homes became a measure of success for these middle classes, a way of telling the world they had arrived. Having money and success meant that the man of the house was able to move his family out of the increasingly grimy and dangerous city to a more pastoral, Edenic place separated from the world of work and commerce. It also allowed these families to reestablish at least a symbolic connection to Jefferson's agrarian ideal, where every family owned its own piece of land and thus remained independent—a key necessity for the success of liberty and, thus, the republic. With fewer people making their living in farming as the nineteenth century progressed, suburban homes with their often ornate gardens offered the closest approximation possible to this agrarian ideal.

The suburbs also contributed to the development of the cult of domesticity. Separated from the world of work in their suburban enclaves, women were placed at the center of the domestic world, caring for hearth and home, husband and children, a role exalted as one of supreme importance. Women were viewed as the centers of morality and the important transmitters of this morality to their children and ultimately to future generations. These ideals were not unique to the nineteenth century. The exaltation of the domestic sphere for women, the intense desire of Americans to own their own homes, the need to keep some kind of connection to the rural past in an increasingly urbanized present, the desire for social status, and the need for physical and economic security continued to find resonance within American culture throughout the twenty-first century.

Transportation factors again played an important role, from the development of streetcars in the late nineteenth century to the increasing dominance of the automobile after the 1920s and particularly after the development of the national highway system that began in the 1950s. Suburbs throughout the twentieth century continued to act as an increasingly attractive alternative to inner-city living for those who could afford it. Suburbs grew tremendously throughout the 1920s and 1930s, as bungalow houses and other styles sprang up one after the other on the more affluent sides of major cities around the United States. Throughout this period, suburbs remained closely tied to their urban cores, and their growth accompanied the larger process of urbanization occurring in the United States. In 1920 the number of people living in urban centers became a majority of the population (51.2 percent) for the first time.

With this increase in urban growth, developers across the country took advantage of the continuing desire for suburban living, buying up huge parcels of suburban land and developing them into neighborhoods and subdivisions. One of the most successful was J. C. Nichols of Kansas City, Missouri, whose Country Club District development played upon the deep cultural imperatives behind suburbanization. Nichols combined the lure of the new with the pastoral beauty of the past. His homes built during the 1920s had the most modern of conveniences: gas and electric service, the latest household appliances, and access to transportation connections. He set the homes amid a parklike setting, with generous set-back lines from the street, and ensured his development's success by enacting permanent deed restrictions that limited the extent to which residents could change their houses and yards.

Nichols also enacted racially restrictive covenants, ensuring that no resident sold his or her house to African Americans, Jews, or members of other minority groups. In doing so, he ensured that his development remained exclusive. His homes were expensive, and both he and his buyers made sure their investments did not decline in value. More importantly, these restrictions preserved the reason many people were moving to the suburbs in the first place: to avoid the problems (and peoples) of the cities and provide an environment in which they would not only be surrounded by the bounty of nature but also by their own kind of people. Nichols's formula, and success, proved a powerful example to developers across the country, who mimicked the restrictive covenants, design, and prestige of Nichols's Country Club District. Many similar developments sprang up across the United States during the 1920s.

RAPID POSTWAR GROWTH

The Depression of the 1930s and the collapse of the housing market brought a temporary end to the great wave of exclusive suburban developments, but suburbia, and the needs it served, was hardly finished. After World War II the United States experienced its greatest wave of suburban development. The same cultural factors that had influenced suburban development in the nineteenth and early twentieth centuries remained in the postwar period. One crucial difference was that as suburbia grew, it became available to a wider spectrum of Americans, reflecting the growth of the middle class during the postwar economic boom; however, it still remained largely closed to minorities. No longer were suburbs the exclusive domain of the well-to-do. Indeed, it is the 1950s that many associate with the suburbs, even though they existed long before, and continued long after, that decade. That association is the result of the vast cultural and social impact suburbia had on the United States in the postwar years.

The widening access to suburbia can largely be attributed to one man, developer William Levitt. Like his predecessor Nichols, Levitt's approach proved immensely successful, spawning an untold number of imitators. His idea was rather simple: he brought mass-production techniques and low prices to suburban housing just as Henry Ford had done in the automobile industry. Taking advantage of the great demand for housing and benefiting from federal government housing policies that provided mortgage guarantees for both developers and homeowners, Levitt purchased a large parcel of rural land in suburban Long Island, New York. There, he used mass-production techniques to construct more than 10,000 small, inexpensive homes. All were virtually identical, and all sold almost immediately.

Levitt's homes proved immensely popular with young couples eager to raise their new families in a comfortable and safe environment. The result was an almost instant community, called Levittown. With low initial and monthly payments for houses in such communities, many families could afford to leave the cities in greater and greater numbers for the relative space, comfort, and security of the suburbs. The result was "white flight," as urban whites moved out of the inner cities to escape the growing influx of black, Hispanic, and other minority groups. This population movement eventually took jobs, tax money, and a diverse population away from America's inner cities, contributing to the decline of cities across the country.

CULTURAL REPRESENTATIONS

But for those who could enjoy these new suburban developments, suburbia had a strong impact on American social life, so much so that the suburban lifestyle dominated American culture from the 1950s on. Television shows such as *Leave It to Beaver* (1957–1963) and *The Adventures of Ozzie & Harriet* (1952–1966) centered on white middle-class families in the suburbs. Their lives were idyllic ones, representing peace and harmony. The suburbs and their images on television also worked to promote a reworking of gender roles. Fathers were usually dressed in business suits and often shown coming home from work to discover the mishaps or other plot twists that had occurred during the day. Women were portrayed as homemakers content with baking cookies, making dinner, and caring for their children and husbands. This idyllic view of suburbia was not entirely incorrect, however, as the suburbs reinforced traditional notions of family and gender that had been challenged by working women during the World War II years. With the strict division of home from the world of work, suburbia in the 1950s and after continued trends that had begun in the mid-nineteenth century.

The suburbs also contributed to what many soon labeled the "culture of conformity." New suburban developments such as Levittown were filled with virtually identical houses and mostly white inhabitants. These new communities were soon filled by new families, many of them headed by young veterans eager to return to a normal life after the traumas of World War II, with similar backgrounds, experiences, needs, and ages. Group socialization and the adherence to established social norms were encouraged; individuality and isolation were not. Many found this new environment appealing, but critics soon began to criticize the social conformity demanded by the suburbs.

John Keats, in his book *The Crack in the Picture Window* (1956), attacked the conformity of suburbs as a "homogenous, postwar hell" of rigid social roles that produced an environment of mediocrity. Folksinger Pete Seeger sang in "Little Boxes": "Little boxes, on the hillside, little boxes made of ticky-tacky . . . little boxes all the same." Not only were the houses all the same, but the people's experiences were as well, living in identical social boxes that, as Seeger sang it, might well have been coffins.

Some later portrayals of suburbia focused on the restrictions and even a sort of creepiness regarding the formerly idyllic suburbs. *The 'Burbs* (1989) exploited the latent paranoia within the stereotypical sleepiness of suburbia, and *American Beauty* (1999) offered a cynical yet strangely optimistic characterization of the monotony associated with suburban life. Suburbs became a given setting for many television shows. Showtime's *Weeds* (2005–) manipulated the archetypal models of suburbia with its pot-dealing single mother lead character, while ABC's *Desperate Housewives* (2004–2012) reveled in the rivalries and secrets that percolated between neighbors.

EFFECTS AND TRENDS

In addition to its cultural impact, suburbs had a great impact on the American landscape and environment, encouraging the development of an automobile culture and suburban sprawl. Spread out away from cities, without access to older public transportation systems such as subways and rail lines, suburbanites depended on their cars for access to jobs in the city. This development was encouraged by the 1956 Federal Highway Act, which provided $25 billion to construct more than 40,000 miles of highways. It was the largest public works project in the history of the United States. In a culture that was already in love with the automobile, the suburbs encouraged even greater reliance on them. The result was suburban sprawl. Instead of tightly compacted centers where most services, entertainment, and employment were easily accessible on foot, suburbs encouraged all of these functions to spread out. Therefore, restaurants, stores, and other facilities each occupied their own buildings with parking surrounding them. Some were clustered in strip malls or enclosed shopping malls, but just as in the suburbs as a whole, all were geared to the need of the automobile.

Suburbia also encouraged the unique American social phenomenon of obsession with lawns and lawn care. Among the deeper ideological bases for suburbia was the need to re-create an Edenic natural setting that was believed to be superior to the concrete jungles of city life. Preserving the image of life in a garden, however, was difficult with so many houses so close together. As a substitute, Americans began to view their lawns as each contributing to a seamless expanse of grass that created as much of a parklike setting as possible. Maintaining this lawn became an important cultural imperative, as homeowners were responsible for keeping up their portion of the "park." Encouraged by magazines, advertising, seed companies, and often by homeowners associations' restrictive clauses that mandated proper upkeep of lawns, lawn care became a major suburban activity. In suburban developments during the warmer months, weekends were filled with the drone of lawn mowers. Competitions were held in neighborhoods to establish the "yard of the month," and people who refused to do their part were often shunned and occasionally sued for their noncompliance. The lawn obsession was also part of a larger cultural interest in outdoor life, and suburbs promoted such things as outdoor barbecues, swimming pools, and gardening.

MOVE TOWARD SELF-CONTAINED COMMUNITIES

While the classic 1950s image of suburbia still existed at the turn of the twenty-first century, suburbs in the 1980s and 1990s were in the midst of change. The biggest shift came in the relationship between suburbs and the cities they surrounded. By the 1980s many suburbs were beginning to evolve into self-contained communities, where people not only lived but also worked. In Orange County, California (outside Los Angeles); Cobb County, Georgia (north of Atlanta); Tysons Corner, Virginia (outside Washington, D.C.); and in similar communities across the country, suburbs became the locations for major office complexes that were home to thousands of workers. With their living and working needs now available in the suburbs, suburbanites found less and less need to travel to the downtowns of central cities.

These communities developed into their own small cities, which writer Joel Garreau labeled "edge cities." That trend, which historian Jon Teaford called "post-suburbia," was indicative of a new age in the history of suburbs. Although a relatively recent phenomenon, this shift may also portend a change in the ability of suburbia to fill certain cultural needs. With work and home sites now closer together, the role of suburbs as an idyllic retreat from the world of commerce had changed by the late 1990s, reversing a trend that began in the early nineteenth century. These developments, and the increasing concern over suburban sprawl, with its often negative effects on the environment and on what many were calling a loss of community in American life, were increasingly more noticeable by the end of the 1990s.

Over the course of the first decade of the 2000s, suburban demographics dramatically changed. No longer were suburbs the sanctuary of the white middle class. According to a 2010 report by the Brookings Metropolitan Policy Program, not only were metropolitan areas spreading out farther, but suburbs had also racially diversified, more broadly reflecting the population of the United States. By 2008 every racial demographic lived in suburbs, effectively blurring the racial divide that characterized earlier white flight. Additionally, the age and economic makeup of suburbs altered during this period. Due to the aging baby boomers, analysts projected that the growth of the senior population would occur most in suburbs. Suburbs also experienced the largest increase in poverty during the first decade of the twenty-first century.

Perhaps not surprisingly, the diversification of the suburbs was followed by an increase in the construction of gated communities. By 2001 more than seven million homes were part of gated communities. Gated communities were composed of predominantly white upper- and middle-class families. In *City of Quartz*, Mike Davis argues that the boundaries such communities erected further a membership-based elitism and racism that severs civic ties. Supporters of gated communities have suggested that these communities offer a greater sense of security and foster a close-knit community.

Following the housing boom in the late 1990s through the middle of the next decade, developers flooded the suburbs, leading to a mass amount of overbuilding of houses and condos. The recession that hit in late 2007 initiated a series of foreclosures, leaving a large number of homes abandoned and little demand or ability to purchase them. Urban areas attempted to revitalize their city centers, attracting a more affluent population but also increasing property values. As values continued to rise, affordable housing became more scarce and pushed lower-income families into the suburbs, where home prices were dramatically reduced due to the abundant supply.

The increasingly globalized economy, however, has given rise to what Wei Li describes as the "ethnoburb." Alongside the increased availability of homes, an increase in highly skilled workers immigrated to the United States. Abandoned suburban homes were highly attractive since they were often newly constructed and well maintained. The surrounding infrastructure provided ample opportunity for developing business, since many of the preexisting establishments had shut down or followed the exiting population. Ethnoburbs allowed for immigrants to maintain their cultural traditions while enjoying the perks of suburbia. The long-term effects of these changes on the historic roles suburbia has played in American social and cultural life remain to be seen.

Timothy Berg

SEE ALSO: The Adventures of Ozzie and Harriet*;* American Beauty*; Automobile; Baby Boomers;* Desperate Housewives*; The Fifties; Gated Communities; Highway System;* Leave It to Beaver*; Levittown; Malls; Seeger, Pete;* Weeds*; White Flight.*

BIBLIOGRAPHY

Blakely, Edward J., and Mary Gail Snyder. *Fortress America:*

Gated Communities in the United States. Washington, DC: Brookings Institution Press, 1997.

Brookings Institution Metropolitan Policy Program. *The State of Metropolitan America: Metros on the Front Lines of Demographic Transformation.* Washington, DC: Brookings Institution Press, 2010.

Davis, Mike. *City of Quartz: Excavating the Future in Los Angeles.* New York: Verso, 1990.

Duany, Andres; Elizabeth Plater-Zyberk; and Jeff Speck. *Suburban Nation: The Rise of Sprawl and the Decline of the American Dream.* New York: North Point Press, 2000.

Gans, Herbert. *The Levittowners: Ways of Life and Politics in a New Suburban Community.* New York: Pantheon, 1967.

Garreau, Joel. *Edge City: Life on the New Frontier.* New York: Doubleday, 1991.

Hayden, Delores. *Redesigning the American Dream: The Future of Housing, Work, and Family Life.* New York: Norton, 1984.

Hayden, Delores. *Building Suburbia: Green Fields and Urban Growth, 1820–2000.* New York: Vintage, 2003.

Jackson, Kenneth T. *Crabgrass Frontier: The Suburbanization of the United States.* New York: Oxford University Press, 1985.

Jenkins, Virginia Scott. *The Lawn: A History of an American Obsession.* Washington, DC: Smithsonian Institution Press, 1994.

Kruse, Kevin Michael, and Thomas Sugrue, eds. *The New Suburban History.* Chicago: University of Chicago Press, 2006.

Li, Wei. *Ethnoburb: The New Ethnic Community in Urban America.* Honolulu: University of Hawaii Press, 2009.

Mumford, Lewis. *The City in History: Its Origins, Its Transformations, and Its Prospects.* New York: Harcourt, Brace and World, 1961.

Nicolaides, Becky M., and Andrew Wiese, eds. *The Suburb Reader.* New York: Routledge, 2006.

Palen, J. John. *The Suburbs.* New York: McGraw-Hill, 1995.

Teaford, Jon C. *City and Suburb: The Political Fragmentation of Metropolitan America, 1850–1970.* Baltimore, MD: Johns Hopkins University Press, 1979.

Teaford, Jon C. *Post-Suburbia: Government and Politics in the Edge Cities.* Baltimore, MD: Johns Hopkins University Press, 1997.

Suicide

While suicide stems from complicated and often indeterminate reasons, the public is left to sort out the implications of what writer and chemist Primo Levi has called this "noninstinctive, unnatural choice." In the early part of the twentieth century, suicide was a taboo subject. Popular opinion held that madness was the most plausible explanation for such an act. When suicides were mentioned in the 1910s and 1920s, they were characterized in terms of trends: *Literary Digest* once reported of "rashes" of childhood suicides and again of college campus suicides. Suicide was seen as virtually a contagious disease.

Young people have always been at a higher risk for suicide, and this continues to be true in the twenty-first century. According to the National Institute for Mental Health, suicide was the third-leading cause of death for people between the ages of fifteen and twenty-four in 2007. Between the ages of fifteen and nineteen, males are five times more likely than females to commit suicide. Ethnically, the highest U.S. suicide rates occur among Native Americans and Alaskan Natives.

The stock market crash of 1929 brought the first widespread acknowledgement of suicide in the twentieth century, with instantly legendary images of despondent former millionaires leaping to their deaths. As some news accounts of the time would have had readers believe, a person walking through New York City had difficulty navigating the bodies littered on Wall Street. The crash was followed by a number of suicides, but according to John Kenneth Galbraith in *The Great Crash of 1929*, statistics suggest that the "suicide wave" of 1929 was largely a myth: "For several years before 1929, the suicide rate had been gradually rising. It continued to increase in that year, with a further and much sharper increase in 1930, 1931, and 1932—years when there were many things besides the stock market to cause people to conclude that life was no longer worth living." Nevertheless, the widely reported millionaire suicides expanded America's understanding of the causes of suicide to include not only madness but also great financial loss.

CELEBRITY SUICIDES

For decades, suicide receded into the shadows, until the 1962 death of movie star and sex symbol Marilyn Monroe. Events surrounding Monroe's death became fodder for gossip columns and investigative reports throughout the rest of the twentieth century and beyond. Instead of repudiating her for committing suicide, the nation shared her tragedy. Her death helped to spawn the growth of suicide hotlines, on which people in peril are encouraged to discuss their feelings with counselors. Monroe's well-publicized dependence on prescription drugs fueled the opinion that the pressures of celebrity became too much for her.

With the acceptance that the public might have contributed to Monroe's final act, suicide moved from private blame into the arena of shared responsibility. Unfortunately, statistics subsequent to her suicide also lend credence to the theory that suicides can be "contagious." According to Herbert Hendin in *Suicide in America*, "Just after Marilyn Monroe's death, the notes of a number of suicides linked their own deaths to her presumed suicide. . . . A sense of sharing the tragic death or suicide of someone famous . . . enables some people to feel that their death has a meaning it would otherwise lack."

Following Monroe's death, the pressures celebrities experienced were also linked to drug abuse and accidental overdoses. Other high-profile victims of the deadly combination of fame and drug abuse included comedian Freddie Prinze, who shot himself in 1977 at the age of twenty-two; comedian John Belushi, who died of a drug overdose in 1982; and grunge music pioneer Kurt Cobain, a heroin addict who shot himself in 1994.

The connection between a creative personality and suicide has seemed particularly strong among writers. The most prominent writer suicides of the twentieth century were those of Ernest Hemingway in 1961, Sylvia Plath in 1963, and Anne Sexton in 1974. Although Hemingway's suicide was attributed to poor physical and mental health, it seemed in keeping with his rugged, yet often despondent personality. The deaths of Plath and Sexton, however, seemed more tragic because those writers were comparatively young and healthy. Their deaths were especially indicative of the troubled female artist. As A. Alvarez writes of Sylvia Plath in *Savage God*, public perception perverted her death into "a myth of the poet as a sacrificial victim, offering herself up for the sake of her art." Her suicide intimated to the public that art has the power to destroy. Hunter S. Thompson, iconic American journalist, committed suicide on February 20, 2005. Although Thompson produced most of the work for which he is now famous in a short span ranging from the mid-1960s through the early 1970s, he became a celebrity for his hedonistic lifestyle and for his contempt of authority. In books such as *Hell's Angels: The Strange and Terrible Saga of Motorcycle Gangs* (1966), Thompson examined the radical fringes of American life, and he lived nearly as hard as the people he wrote about.

ACCUSATIONS AND IMPLICATIONS

Religious fervor, long attributed as a cause for mental instability and suicide, also showed its powers of destruction. When 914 followers of the Reverend Jim Jones committed mass suicide in Jonestown, Guyana, in 1978, suicide became inextricably linked to religious cults. Jones was seen as a charismatic brainwasher who convinced his members that their deaths were, according to him, "an act of revolutionary suicide protesting the conditions of an inhuman world." Subsequent cases confirmed the apocalyptic and suicidal nature of cults, most notably the deaths of the Branch Davidians in Texas in 1993 and the thirty-nine suicides among members of the Heaven's Gate cult in California in 1997.

The early 1990s saw rock and roll's Judas Priest and Ozzy Osbourne defend their music in separate court cases that blamed their songs for influencing teens to commit suicide. In both cases, the First Amendment rights of the musicians were upheld. Still, Osbourne's song "Suicide Solution" (1980)—as well as other songs such as "Goodbye Cruel World" by Pink Floyd (1979), books such as *Illusions* by Richard Bach (1977), and films such as *Dead Poets Society* (1989)—drew criticism for what some saw as glorifying the act of suicide.

DEATH WITH DIGNITY

In 1994 Oregon became the first state to pass a measure permitting physician-assisted suicide. The measure has withstood multiple repeal attempts. At the close of the twentieth century, physician-assisted suicide dominated the headlines, with purported "suicide doctor" Jack Kevorkian challenging laws across the country that made assisted suicide illegal. In 1998 he appeared on the news program *60 Minutes*, which aired a tape of him assisting a suicide. Kevorkian orchestrated the publicity stunt in an effort to force a Supreme Court ruling on the constitutionality of a person's "right to die." He was convicted of second-degree murder and served eight years in prison.

While Kevorkian's efforts did not lead to an overhaul of national policy, they did push the complex issue of suicide into the light of the shared public arena. Florida's supreme court upheld the state's law against assisted suicide in 1997, and in 1999 Alaska's supreme court upheld a similar ruling. In 2008 Washington State enacted a measure similar to Oregon's Death with Dignity Act, and the Montana Supreme Court held in 2009 that although the state constitution does not guarantee a right to assisted suicide, it does not prohibit physician-assisted suicide.

SUICIDE AND WAR

A permanent link between suicide and war was established in the American consciousness by the suicide attacks on the World Trade Center in New York on September 11, 2001. Although much of the world had dealt with the phenomenon of suicide attacks for years, it did not become a reality for Americans until 9/11. Following that fateful day, suicide attacks became increasingly normalized through reports from Afghanistan, Iraq, and Pakistan. Between 2001 and 2011 suicide attacks claimed 3,755 lives in Afghanistan, 4,681 in Pakistan, and 12,484 in Iraq. In addition to a military tactic, suicide has also been used as a means of protest. In 2010 Mohamed Bouazizi's self-immolation launched a series of protests across the Middle East and North Africa known as the Arab Spring.

There is also mounting concern about the rising rate of suicide among military veterans. According to a 2011 report by the Center for a New American Security, "service members took their own lives at a rate of approximately one every 36 hours." While the study suggests that there is not a direct correlation between war and suicide, it does conclude that war exacerbates prior existing conditions such as depression that could lead to suicide. Additionally, the military increased its efforts to diagnose and treat post-traumatic stress disorder (PTSD) associated with war.

ADOLESCENT SUICIDES

One of the issues that consistently garners public attention is the link between adolescent suicides and bullying. Often the victims are gay or are assumed to be gay, as was the case with four young people who committed suicide within a month in the fall of 2010. There are also those who are bullied simply because someone takes a dislike to them, as happened with Phoebe Prince in January 2010. The ubiquitous nature of cell phones, computers, and other devices has made cyberbullying a constant threat. In 2008 the mother of a teenage girl used MySpace to create a false male identity to entice and then taunt another teenager, who subsequently committed suicide. The adult was convicted only of computer fraud. In September 2010, Tyler Clementi, a Rutgers University student committed suicide by jumping off the Washington Bridge, ostensibly because his roommate, Dharun Ravi, secretly recorded his sexual encounters with an older man. In March 2012 Ravi was tried and convicted on fifteen counts of invasion of privacy. In response to these events and others, more than forty states passed laws against bullying, and schools were working to deal with the issue, although a variety of familial and social factors were also understood to be involved.

In 2011 the U.S. Centers for Disease Control and Prevention conducted a study that tracked suicide rates in relationship to the economy. The study found that the suicide rates in the United States dropped between 1990 and 2000 but then rose considerably during the economic downturn in the first decade of the 2000s. Despite growing concern about and attention paid to suicide, the rates seem to be increasing. Although there is no direct correlation between cause and effect, various social, psychological, and economic conditions are being taken into account.

Chris Haven

SEE ALSO: *Belushi, John; The Great Recession; Hemingway, Ernest; Hendrix, Jimi; The Internet; Joplin, Janis; Judas Priest; Mon-*

roe, Marilyn; 9/11; Osbourne, Ozzy; Pink Floyd; Plath, Sylvia; Presley, Elvis; Prinze, Freddie; Stock Market Crashes; Teenagers; Thompson, Hunter S.; War in Afghanistan; World Trade Center.

BIBLIOGRAPHY

Alvarez, A. *The Savage God: A Study of Suicide.* New York: Norton, 1990.

Cloud, John. "Bullied to Death." *Time*, October 18, 2010.

Durkheim, Emile. *Suicide: A Study in Sociology.* New York: Free Press, 1997.

Frayer, Lauren. "Study: US Suicide Rate Rises, Falls with Economy." AOL News, April 15, 2011. Accessed April 2011. Available from http://www.aolnews.com/2011/04/15/study-us-suicide-rate-rises-falls-with-economy/

Galbraith, John Kenneth. *The Great Crash 1929.* Boston: Houghton Mifflin, 1955.

Gutierrez, Peter M., and Augustine Osman. *Adolescent Suicide: An Integrated Approach to the Assessment of Risk and Protective Factors.* DeKalb: Northern Illinois University Press, 2008.

Harrell, Margaret C., and Nancy Berglass. "Losing the Battle: The Challenge of Military Suicide." Center for a New American Security, October 31, 2011. Accessed April 2012. Available from http://www.cnas.org/losingthebattle

Hendin, Herbert. *Suicide in America.* New York: Norton, 1982.

Hicks, Madelyn Hsiao-Rei; Hamit Dardagan; Peter M. Bagnall; et al. "Casualties in Civilians and Coalition Soldiers from Suicide Bombings in Iraq, 2003–10: A Descriptive Study." *Lancet*, September 3, 2011. Accessed April 2012. Available from http://www.thelancet.com/journals/lancet/article/PIIS0140-6736(11)61023-4/abstract

Joiner, Thomas E. *Myths about Suicide.* Cambridge, MA: Harvard University Press, 2010.

Kushner, Howard I. *Self-Destruction in the Promised Land: A Psychocultural Biology of American Suicide.* New Brunswick, NJ: Rutgers University Press, 1989.

Lester, David. *Patterns of Suicide and Homicide in the World.* Commack, NY: Nova Science Publishers, 1996.

Lester, David. *Encyclopedia of Famous Suicides.* Commack, NY: Nova Science Publishers, 1997.

Lester, David. *Making Sense of Suicide: An In-Depth Look at Why People Kill Themselves.* Philadelphia: Charles Press, 1997.

Sullivan, Ed *(1902–1974)*

Ed Sullivan, who could not sing, dance, or act, was television's greatest showman in its early years. For twenty-three years, from 1948 to 1971, he hosted America's premier variety show every Sunday night on CBS, on which he introduced an eclectic array of talent that ranged from opera singers to dancing bears to Elvis Presley and the Beatles.

Sullivan, a former newspaper columnist, appeared on the nation's television screens as a most untelegenic presence. He was everything that a professional television host is not supposed to be—awkward, stiff, and prone to frequent malapropisms. His real talent was behind the scenes, as a man who had his finger on the pulse of America's cultural tastes. He understood instinctively that a variety show should present acts that would appeal to the various demographic segments of its audience. Only on *The Ed Sullivan Show* could you see such diverse talents as Van Cliburn, Rudolf Nureyev, Robert Goulet, Richard Pryor, a plate spinner, and the Rolling Stones. With his distinctive nasal voice, Sullivan regularly promised audiences "a really big shew" and delivered by offering up virtually every form of twentieth-century entertainment.

EARLY LIFE AND CAREER

Edward Vincent Sullivan was born on September 28, 1902, in Harlem, New York, the son of a customs inspector. He was one of seven children (his twin brother, Daniel, died in his first year) and was raised in Port Chester, New York. Young Edward was a poor student, but upon graduating from high school he became a newspaper sports reporter. In 1932 he joined the *New York Daily News* as a Broadway columnist and soon came into contact with many figures in the entertainment industry.

While serving as emcee of the newspaper-sponsored Harvest Moon Ball dance contest in 1947, he was "discovered" by Worthington Miner, a general manager at CBS-TV, who asked Sullivan to host a planned variety series called *Toast of the Town.* The series debuted on June 20, 1948, reflecting from the beginning Sullivan's keen sense of diversity in programming. That initial episode featured Broadway's Richard Rodgers and Oscar Hammerstein, the rising comedy team of Dean Martin and Jerry

Ed Sullivan. *Ed Sullivan hosted his self-titled television variety show from 1947 to 1971.* HULTON ARCHIVE/STRINGER/ARCHIVE PHOTOS/GETTY IMAGES.

Lewis in their first TV appearance, classical pianist Eugene List, ballerina Kathryn Lee, a group of singing New York City firemen, and six June Taylor dancers (called the Toastettes). Within that single hour was something for everyone, from the highbrow to the most common man.

During his twenty-three-year run on CBS, Sullivan served as the cultural arbiter for much of middle America. He worked constantly to ensure that his audience witnessed the very best entertainment available, as he was deeply involved in all aspects of the show. He booked all the acts himself, helped edit each performer's material, and frequently juggled the show's running order. Some claimed he was a dictatorial taskmaster, but Sullivan took full responsibility for the success or failure of each week's episode.

In 1967 he revealed his show-business philosophy when he stated, "An audience will forgive a bad act but never bad taste." For a man who sought perfection in even his silliest performers, Sullivan always presented himself as a rather bumbling persona. An article in *TV Guide* once described him by writing: "Not since radio's Major Bowes have the airways been subjected to such a bumbling Barnum. Cod-eyed, cement-faced and so scaredy-cat stiff that he's been suspected of having a silver plate in his head, Sullivan has yet to complete gracefully the smallest gesture, unravel his vowels, or conquer a simple introduction." Sullivan's distinctive voice and mannerisms made him the target of many comics and impressionists, including John Byner and Will Jordan. While he may have been awkward, Sullivan knew his job was to introduce the talent and leave the stage so they could shine.

THE ED SULLIVAN SHOW

The format of Sullivan's show, which was retitled *The Ed Sullivan Show* in 1955, changed little over its many years. It was basically a filmed vaudeville show with acts chosen to appeal to the broadest possible audience. Guests from the world of the classical arts included violinist Itzhak Perlman, dancer Margot Fonteyn, and opera star Roberta Peters. For a rare TV appearance by diva Maria Callas, Sullivan staged a full scene from *Tosca*. Guests designed to attract more middle-class audiences included Broadway and movie stars, such as Richard Burton and Julie Andrews performing a scene from *Camelot*; songs by Barbra Streisand, Dinah Shore, and Eddie Fisher; and Henry Fonda reading Lincoln's Gettysburg Address.

Sullivan also was very fond of comics and often invited Borscht Belt veterans such as Alan King and Henny Youngman to perform. His most frequently returning comedy guests, however, were the Canadian team of Wayne and Shuster. For the youngsters in the audience, Sullivan was always sure to include a novelty act. These included acrobats, mimes, and animal acts. The specialty act most associated with Sullivan was the lovable Italian mouse puppet, Topo Gigio, who frequently exclaimed, "Hey, Eddie, kees-a-me goodnight!" Occasionally, Sullivan would devote an entire show to one subject, such as honoring the works of Irving Berlin, Cole Porter, and Walt Disney.

EVOLUTION OF THE SHOW

By the mid-1950s Sullivan became aware that American popular culture was changing drastically. He helped to promote racial diversity by showcasing black performers, such as Pearl Bailey, Nat King Cole, George Kirby, and Leontyne Price. Other television shows refused to present African American guests due to sponsor complaints. Furthermore, Sullivan began inviting rock-and-roll stars onto the show to raise its appeal to the demographically important teen audience. Elvis Presley made three memorable visits in 1956. Although cameras showed him from only the waist up on his last appearance to calm adult fears of the singer's swiveling pelvis, the fact that Presley was on the show seemed to legitimize rock to the adult audience.

On February 9, 1964, an appearance by the Beatles earned Sullivan his highest rating ever. That broadcast is considered a milestone event in television history. Throughout the 1960s more members of the counterculture appeared with Sullivan, such as Janis Joplin, Marvin Gaye, and the Rolling Stones. While he liked the ratings they brought, he was often uncomfortable with their attitudes and material. He had heated confrontations with the Doors and Bob Dylan over his attempts to censor their songs. Younger comedians like George Carlin, Woody Allen, and Bill Cosby were also more visible in the 1960s.

THE SHOW ENDS

After 1,087 episodes that presented more than 10,000 performers, *The Ed Sullivan Show* left the air on June 6, 1971. Sullivan died in October 1974. He and his variety program are monuments to a form of entertainment that no longer exists. Today, the mass television audience has nearly disappeared and has been dispersed with the advent of cable and more specialized programming. *The Ed Sullivan Show* provided one of the last opportunities for the entire family to gather around the tube and be entertained by a single program.

The show was immortalized by the hit Broadway musical *Bye, Bye Birdie* as the emblem of all that was good with television. For contemporary viewers it offered a rare opportunity to witness the performances of many of the twentieth century's greatest artists. As Harry Castleman and Walter Podrazik wrote of Sullivan in their 1989 book, *Harry and Wally's Favorite TV Shows*, "He was good because he was a good packager of entertainment. . . . He could spot talent, knew how to balance an hour program, and didn't waste time calling attention to himself. We could use more hosts like him now." Sullivan's legacy is enshrined in the many "really big shews" that entertained a generation.

Charles Coletta

SEE ALSO: *The Beatles; Borscht Belt; Carlin, George; Cole, Nat King; Cosby, Bill; The Doors; Dylan, Bob; Gaye, Marvin; Nureyev, Rudolf; Presley, Elvis; The Rolling Stones; Youngman, Henny.*

BIBLIOGRAPHY

Bowles, Jerry. *A Thousand Sundays: The Story of the Ed Sullivan Show*. New York: Putnam, 1980.

Brooks, Tim. *The Complete Directory to Prime Time TV Stars*. New York: Ballantine Books, 1987.

Castleman, Harry, and Walter Podrazik. *Harry and Wally's Favorite TV Shows*. New York: Prentice Hall, 1989.

Harris, Jay. *TV Guide: The First 25 Years*. New York: New American Library, 1980.

Ilson, Bernie. *Sundays with Sullivan: How the* Ed Sullivan Show *Brought Elvis, the Beatles, and Culture to America*. Boulder,

CO: Taylor Trade Publishing, 2010.

Marschall, Rick. *The History of Television.* New York: Gallery Books, 1986.

Sullivan, John L. *(1858–1918)*

Bare-knuckle prizefighter John L. Sullivan became a symbol of ethnic pride and working-class masculinity to the nineteenth-century Irish American community from which he emerged. Because of his boisterous claim that he could "lick any son of a bitch in the house" and his ability to back up those words, many Irish Americans saw in Sullivan a way to strike back at an unwelcoming American society. The working-class Irish cheered as Sullivan knocked out his Anglo-Protestant opponents, yet the fighter's popularity extended beyond ethnic and class identity: the rest of white America slowly accepted Sullivan as well. He emerged as the first national sporting celebrity, and his popularity brought a measure of respectability to the rough-hewn sport of boxing. When Sullivan began his career, bare-knuckle prizefights were against the law; by the time he quit, boxing matches were cultural events attended by all segments of society.

John Lawrence Sullivan was born into the Irish working-class community of Roxbury, Massachusetts, in 1858. Like many Irish immigrants, Sullivan's father worked as a hod carrier, which was the lowest paying of the new industrial jobs. As was the norm in his community, Sullivan moved into the industrial work at a young age. He did a variety of odd jobs but was unable to hold any down because of his tendency to get into fights with his fellow workers.

To support himself, Sullivan began to play baseball and box semiprofessionally. Complementing his boxing matches were fights in neighborhood theaters and movie halls. It was in one of these theaters, the Sullivan legend later suggested, that he first stood up and made his famous boast, "I'm John L. Sullivan and I can lick any son of a bitch in the house." Such claims, along with strongman demonstrations of lifting beer kegs above his head, soon earned him the nickname "Boston Strong Boy" and a reputation as an up-and-coming pugilist. On the strength of his reputation, Sullivan issued a challenge to Paddy Ryan, the reigning champion.

Middle-class society in nineteenth-century America frowned upon bare-knuckle prizefighting to the point that it was outlawed. Boxing was a working-class diversion, and the matches usually took place inside ethnic saloons. Champions often held questionable positions within the community, splitting their time between boxing, breaking up barroom scuffles, and brawling at the ballot box for the local political machines. Ryan was just such a champion, and by 1882 he could ignore the young challenger from Boston no longer and agreed to a bout. In February of that year, Ryan and Sullivan met for the first time in Mississippi City, Mississippi. Sullivan dominated the champion, knocking him out after nine rounds.

Now recognized as the heavyweight champion, Sullivan did not, as Ryan had, become political muscle. Instead, he issued his most famous and sweeping challenge: he offered $1000 to anyone (although he would not fight black opponents) in the United States who could last four rounds with him in a gloved match. With challengers lining up, Sullivan began a whirlwind tour of the United States. It was a carnival-like atmosphere, with juggling acts and vaudeville shows preceding his defeat of whoever challenged him. The flamboyance of his tour and his dominance in the ring caused his popularity to soar. Irish Americans across the country flocked to see the man who fought with both the colors of the United States and Ireland in his corner. Because Sullivan fought gloved matches, his bouts were legal and, thus, were attended by people who had never before seen prizefighting. Sullivan quickly became a cultural icon whose name and image appeared in advertisements and vaudeville shows.

Sullivan was still considered the heavyweight champion of boxing and, as such, was required to defend his title in a bare-knuckle fight. By 1889 Jake Kilrain was clamoring to get in the ring with him for a bare-knuckle bout. Kilrain had taken a path similar to Sullivan's, using his fists to rise out of the Irish working class. His impressive record, coupled with the debilitating effects of Sullivan's years of legendary drinking, resulted in even odds leading into the fight. On July 8, 1889, near Hattiesburg, Mississippi, the two men squared off in what would be the last-ever bare-knuckle championship bout. Despite his years of hard drinking and fights against weak challengers, Sullivan had trained himself back into shape. Under the scorching sun, Sullivan and Kilrain fought seventy-five rounds over more than two hours. When Kilrain was unable to start the seventy-sixth round, Sullivan was declared the winner.

Although Sullivan enjoyed a great deal of popularity outside his working-class community, not everyone embraced his displays of masculine aggression and violence. Parts of the American middle class, especially the emergent Irish American middle class, distanced themselves from the bruiser from Roxbury. Many cheered when "Gentleman" Jim Corbett, a man of breeding who had learned to box in a club instead of on the streets, knocked out Sullivan in twenty-one rounds in New Orleans, Louisiana, in September 1892 to earn the world heavyweight title.

From 1878 to 1905 Sullivan won thirty-one of thirty-five bouts, sixteen by knockout. He earned more than $1 million but spent it all. Later in life, Sullivan became an advocate of prohibition and delivered lectures on the topic. He is remembered as America's first big sports star, a man who paved the way for giants such as Babe Ruth, Muhammad Ali, and Michael Jordan.

S. Paul O'Hara

SEE ALSO: *Ali, Muhammad; Boxing; Corbett, James J.; Jordan, Michael; Ruth, Babe.*

BIBLIOGRAPHY

Gorn, Elliot J. *The Manly Art: Bare-Knuckle Prizefighting in America.* Ithaca, NY: Cornell University Press, 1986.

Isenberg, Michael T. *John L. Sullivan and His America.* Urbana: University of Illinois Press, 1994.

Summer, Donna *(1948–2012)*

Known as the Queen of Disco, Donna Summer was a singer and songwriter who became popular during the disco era of the 1970s. She was the first artist to have three consecutive double albums—*Live and More* (1978), *Bad Girls* (1979), and *On the Radio* (1979)—reach number one on U.S. music charts. She was also the first female artist to have four singles—"MacArthur Park," "Hot Stuff," "Bad Girls," and "No More Tears"—all reach number one within thirteen months. Over the course of her career, Summer crooned dozens of hits, created many platinum and gold albums, and earned many awards, including a Golden Globe Award and five Grammy Awards.

Summer was born LaDonna Andrea Gaines on December 31, 1948, and grew up in Boston. As a youth, she sang gospel in her church. She moved to Europe before finishing high school to accept a role in the stage version of the popular hippie musical *Hair.* She spent the next several years in Germany; married an Austrian actor named Helmut Sommer (the couple later divorced); took the stage name Donna Summer (a variation of her first name and an anglicized version of her husband's last name); and appeared in theater productions before beginning to work with two successful Munich producers, Giorgio Moroder and Pete Bellote, at their Musicland Studios. The duo made minor disco hits for the European dance-club scene that were quietly making their way to the underground nightclubs frequented by gays, blacks, and Latinos in New York City. Discos grew in popularity when a downturn in the economy made such clubs—with their $5 cover charge for an evening of entertainment—a preferable alternative to concerts.

Donna Summer. *Donna Summer was often called the "queen of disco" because of her many chart-topping dance hits in the 1970s.* FOTOS INTERNATIONAL/GETTY IMAGES.

Summer had two minor hits in Europe, then suggested to her producers that they record something similar to "Je t'aime . . . moi non plus," a breathy French hit from 1959 by Jane Birkin and Serge Gainsbourg. What they came up with was three minutes of Summer singing the words "love to love you, baby," a few other phrases, and a lot of moaning. When the track found its way to a party at the Los Angeles home of music producer Neil Bogart, who made a fortune in the 1960s with a record label that produced bubble-gum pop, his guests clamored to hear it over and over. He contacted Moroder and Bellote, asked them to make a longer version, and signed Summer to his new label, Casablanca.

FAME

Summer had a huge hit in the United States with "Love to Love You, Baby," and a debut album of the same name went gold. "It was a disc that spun day and night throughout the summer of 1975," wrote Albert Goldman in an article in the December 1977 issue of *Esquire.* "To the layman, it was just another catchy tune; to the initiate, it was the first unambiguous sign that we were in for another epidemic of the dancing sickness—that recurrent mania that sweeps over this country and Europe on an average of once every ten years." In an article in *Time* magazine, Jay Cocks observed that the song seems to signify "disco's coming-out party," the emergence of homosexual subculture into mainstream America. Goldman explained that the album was "the first frankly erotic album ever to achieve wide currency and airplay. Broadcasting the cries and moans of a woman enjoying intercourse may not sound like much of a breakthrough in this age of explicit sex and rampant pornography, but it must be borne in mind that phono-recording is the most oppressively censored medium in America."

Summer became a household name. For a time she had a constant bodyguard, since fans were known to trap her in elevators. She released a number of albums over the next few years, including two in 1976, *A Love Trilogy* and *Four Seasons of Love.* A less-discofied album, *I Remember Yesterday,* had a great hit the following year with "I Feel Love." The song is notable for what came to be known as the "galloping bass line," a thumping, backbone of drum-machine rhythm structure that became the staple of many disco hits. "Donna Summer snapped her choruses over booming rhythm tracks that moved the artfully tied construction boots of gay men and the teetery hetero platforms of the Saturday Night Fever disco hordes," wrote Gerri Hirshey in *Rolling Stone.* Summer's 1978 double-live album, *Live and More,* sold millions.

Summer made her film debut in the 1978 movie *Thank God It's Friday,* and in it she sings "Last Dance." While the movie received poor reviews, the single was a hit, shooting to the top of the music charts, and Summer received her first Grammy Award (Best Vocal Performance, Female) for the song. The album *Bad Girls,* released in 1979, features a blend of rock and disco—much of which she actually wrote herself—and garnered both good reviews and, again, huge sales. In 1980 she became the first artist signed by record industry executive David Geffen on his new label. Her work for Geffen includes *The Wanderer* (1980) and *She Works Hard for the Money* (1983). Her career slowed as the 1980s progressed: she made twelve albums in the ten years from 1974 until 1984 and only four albums in the nine years from 1985 until 1994.

AFTER DISCO

Summer kept a low profile after the death of disco but still enjoyed a cult following. In March 1998 she gave a benefit concert for New York City's Gay Men's Health Crisis at Carnegie Hall. "After nearly two hours of mature ovations and controlled excitement . . . the remarkably well-behaved audience could no longer be contained," wrote Larry Flick in *Billboard.* "As she began a salacious, guitar-drenched rendition of 'Hot Stuff,' fans rushed down the red carpeted aisles toward the stage."

In 2003 Summer published an autobiography titled *Ordinary Girl: The Journey*. In it she reveals that, in 1976, at the height of her career, she tried to commit suicide. The close call motivated her to seek help for depression. She also explains in her book that in the 1980s, when her career slowed, she was busy raising a family (she married her second husband, Bruce Sudano, in 1980). In 2004 she was inducted into the Dance Music Hall of Fame. Summer enjoyed a comeback in 2008 that included a featured performance on the television show *American Idol.* Her first album in seventeen years, *Crayons* (2008), met with success, as did singles "I'm a Fire" and "Stamp Your Feet." In 2008 *Billboard* magazine ranked Summer twenty-fourth on its list of 100 Hottest Artists of All Time. She performed at the Nobel Peace Prize Concert in Oslo, Norway, in 2009, honoring prize recipient U.S. President Barack Obama. Summer died of lung cancer on May 17, 2012.

Carol Brennan

SEE ALSO: American Idol*; Carnegie Hall; Disco;* Esquire*; Grammy Awards; Obama, Barack; Pop Music;* Rolling Stone*;* Saturday Night Fever*;* Time*; Top 40.*

BIBLIOGRAPHY

Cocks, Jay. "Gaudy Reign of the Disco Queen." *Time,* December 4, 1978, 93.

Flick, Larry. "Billboard Online's Donna Summer: A Benefit for the Gay Men's Health Crisis." *Billboard,* March 1998. Accessed April 5, 2012. Available from http://www.donna-tribute.com/articles/98/billbd.html

Goldman, Albert. "Disco Fever." *Esquire,* December 1977, 60–66.

Goldman, Albert. *Sound Bites.* New York: Turtle Bay Books, 1992.

Howard, Josiah. *Donna Summer: Her Life and Music.* Cranberry Township, PA: Tiny Ripple Books, 2003.

Jacobson, Mark. "Disco Dreams." In *Very Seventies: A Cultural History of the 1970s, from the Pages of Crawdaddy,* ed. Peter Knobler and Greg Mitchell. New York: Simon & Schuster, 1995.

Porter, Evette. "Awaiting the Diva." *Village Voice,* December 17, 1996, 61–62.

Rockwell, John. "The Disco Drum-Beating in Perspective." *New York Times,* February 25, 1979.

Rockwell, John. "Donna Summer Has Begun to Win Respect." *New York Times,* July 26, 1979.

Summer Camp

For more than a century, summer camps have provided millions of American children with their first taste of the world outside their family and neighborhood. The first commercial sleepaway camp was founded in 1876 in rural Pennsylvania, and its clients—elite Protestant boys from the Northeast—exemplified the industry's early reach. By the late nineteenth century, organizational camps were beginning to attract a broader range of middle-class and working-class boys. In the early twentieth century, the industry continued to broaden and diversify, serving girls as well as boys. At the industry's peak in the prosperous years following World War II, about one in six children attended camp.

Camp is still an important part of many American children's summers: while the traditional eight-week private camp is no longer as popular as it once was, in the early twenty-first century more than ten million children and adolescents between the ages of five and seventeen attend a wide variety of camps each summer. While day camps, short-term overnight camps, and specialty camps serve increasing numbers of children, many feature traditional activities that have varied little for generations: living in cabins with children of similar backgrounds; taking daily swims and engaging in other water and land sports, hikes, and overnight trips; doing arts and crafts; singing camp songs and roasting marshmallows around campfires. The industry has reflected disparate and changing goals, but the basic premise remains the same: that camps foster community life, personal development, and skill building, while providing retreats from the problems and dangers of the outside world.

AMERICAN ANXIETIES AND MODERN YOUTH

Summer camp is a distinctly American invention, whose origins reflect the aspirations and anxieties of late nineteenth-century middle- and upper-class life. First, as cities grew, particularly in the Northeast, industrialization and urbanization inspired some well-to-do men (and a few women) to travel to wilderness areas to experience the reinvigorating romance of nature and its fortification for urban life. Second, notions of child rearing among the upper and middle classes were in transition; as the birthrate among urban well-to-do families declined, parents devoted increasing resources toward providing a sheltered and longer childhood for their smaller families.

Acknowledging that children had their own peer cultures, adults expressed anxiety about how best to supervise and guide them. Rural children had traditionally helped their parents on farms during the summer, but increasing numbers of urban children and upper-class children had no set tasks over the long vacation. In addition, the first summer camps reflected the particular anxieties of their founders, a group of white middle- and upper-class Protestant men who worried about the effects of modernity upon elite boys' manliness. Youth leaders feared the enfeeblement of those who, they believed, ought to, by virtue of their class, lead the nation. Camp was to be an antidote to the "softness" of the modern work regime and vacations at resort hotels: a place where privileged boys would experience the toughening effects of outdoor life, albeit amid the safety of select peers and adult supervision.

Given that camps claimed to be an antidote to modern urban life, it is not surprising that they achieved their greatest popularity near the largest urban centers, particularly at lakes and mountains within a day's travel of the densely settled Northeast. While smaller camping districts—such as the Upper Midwest and the mountains of North Carolina—emerged in the early twentieth century, summer camps have always been most popular in the Northeast, where they first started. The Gunnery

Camp near Milford, Connecticut (1861–1879), has long been cited as the earliest camp model. It was not a separate camp but part of the summer term of a boarding school; for two weeks each summer, the boys lived in tents by the sea and simulated the life of soldiers.

Other early efforts included the North Mountain School of Physical Culture (1876–1878) northeast of Wilkes-Barre, Pennsylvania, which was advertised as a camp for "weakly boys," and the first church-sponsored camp, run by the Reverend George Hinckley of Hartford, Connecticut, during the summers of 1880 and 1881 near Wakefield, Rhode Island. Ernest Balch's Camp Chocorua, which ran from 1881 to 1889 on Asquam Lake, New Hampshire, was the first commercial organized camp. Chocorua provided a model that camps of all kinds would cite for years to come, in which children with similar family backgrounds lived together away from home, sharing leisure activities, chores, camp rituals and inside jokes.

Chocorua, like later camps, lauded the wilderness but took advantage of modern innovations. The boys made their own boats and did extensive chores around the grounds, but within a few years they were living in cabins instead of tents, and the camp had inaugurated a complex financial system to teach the boys about modern commerce. In general, while many camps started small, with a few tents and a rowboat, if they were successful they sheltered children from the wilderness that they extolled and provided comforts and improved recreational facilities as quickly as they could afford them. From the 1880s onward, innovations have run the gamut from electricity to miniature golf courses to film production, leading to countless discussions among camping professionals about what exactly makes a camp "campy."

THE EXPANSION OF THE CAMPING IDEAL

At the turn of the twentieth century, the field of camping expanded to benefit the poor as well as the rich. Progressive Era reformers worried particularly about the plight of new immigrant children growing up in city tenements, where poverty and overcrowding bred malnutrition and disease. Hoping both to assert a moral control over potentially unruly new Americans and to provide healthful and pleasurable activities in rural settings for needy youth, a variety of nonprofit and charitable organizations started their own camps. Settlement houses, church groups, and charitable organizations all sponsored short trips to the country for poor urban children. At the same time, camping opportunities for middle-class children grew as YMCAs, YMHAs, and their female counterparts began to work more intensively with children and adolescents. By the 1910s, reflecting new models of athletic girlhood, increasing numbers of girls' camps opened. New youth organizations such as the Boy Scouts, Girl Scouts, and Camp Fire Girls specifically exhorted children to camp outdoors. By the early twentieth century, boys and girls of many ethnicities and social classes were camping at their own facilities (as in other forms of commercial recreation, children of color experienced more limited camping opportunities).

As ideas about child rearing and recreation shifted over the course of the twentieth century, so did camps' daily routines. Most of the very early camps had a decidedly religious character. Protestants, and later Jews and Catholics, saw in camp a means to reinforce their religious communities. By the 1920s camping had expanded to serve a variety of interest groups, all of which saw in camping communal possibilities that transcended their individual political, religious, and social differences. Zionists, progressive educators, hiking enthusiasts, socialists, and military types all created camps in their own image. But they also were responsive to larger trends in children's recreation.

During World War I, many camps adopted military drill and army-style discipline. In the 1930s, influenced by the pedagogical theories of John Dewey, a countering discourse stressed creativity, social adjustment, and personality development. One enduring legacy is the place of Indian-style ritual. In the first years of the twentieth century, Ernest Thompson Seton's youth organization, the Woodcraft League, inspired many camps to "play Indian" by making teepees and totem poles, telling Indian stories by the campfire, and wearing moccasins and headdresses. Driven by nostalgia and desire for premodern "authenticity," many camps have continued to invoke Indian pasts.

Across the country, overnight camps flourished in the postwar years, as a generation of baby boomers grew to camping age. In 1948 the national umbrella organization, the American Camping Association, finally instituted national standards for camp accreditation, after decades of debate. But the years since have been rockier for the industry. Since the mid-1970s, more than 2,500 camps, or about one in five, have gone out of business. In the late 1960s and 1970s, camp owners found themselves competing against not only trips to Europe but also the anti-authoritarian youth culture of that era. Camps near major cities and tourist centers fell victim to high expenses and the temptation of camp owners to sell to real estate developers.

Since the 1980s, many traditional eight-week camps have inaugurated shorter sessions to accommodate parents who are scheduling their children's summers more tightly around competing interests, including joint custody issues and alternate family vacation plans. In addition, traditional camps now compete against newer specialty camps that focus on particular skills or provide specific experiences: computer skills, weight loss, gymnastics or soccer, and bike tours across the country. By the twenty-first century, about 75 percent of all camps were run by nonprofit groups and social service agencies, serving children of all economic classes and constituencies: this range includes Connecticut's Hole in the Wall Gang Camp for children living with cancer; Maine's Seeds of Peace for international youth from conflict-riven regions; and North Dakota's Kids on Fire, the evangelical camp profiled in the 2006 documentary *Jesus Camp*.

CAMPS IN THE POPULAR IMAGINATION

The popular image of the extended vacation at a private eight-week camp does not fully reflect the experience of most contemporary campers, for whom the average stay is one week at a nonprofit camp. But in the popular imagination, camps represent sites for children's adventurous "coming of age" rather than quick trips. In films such as *Meatballs* (1979), *Little Darlings* (1980), *Dirty Dancing* (1987), *Addams Family Values* (1993), and *Wet Hot American Summer* (2001), camps are a place where children and adolescents embark upon voyages of self-discovery, friendship, and loneliness; pranks of all kinds; and, if they are teenagers or counselors, sexual and romantic exploration. Camps continue to figure centrally in contemporary children's entertainment, such as the Disney Channel reality show *Bug Juice* (1998–2001).

For the adults who have attended them, camps often represent a nostalgic reminder of childhood. Over the past century, widely disparate groups have held in common the belief that rural spaces are healthier and safer for children and that camps in particular can be spaces of social transformation, in which adults can teach children the arts of acculturation and good citizenship (appropriate in regard to class, race, ethnicity, religion, politics, and gender) before returning them to their homes. Collectively, summer camps have shown an ability to change with the times and to accommodate different and sometimes diametrically opposed groups. They provide a window into the expansion of children's recreation over the past century and to the changes in the American social order that have enabled a widening range of communities to create children's leisure in their own image.

At times leisure took a back seat to ideology. Although summer programs such as weight-loss camps and band camps retained some of the elements of traditional summer camps, they were focused, goal-driven programs that were meant to deliver specific, long-term benefits. Fundamentalist groups used the summer camp model as a means to mold and temper adolescents. Ex-gay ministries like Exodus International routinely partnered with other Christian groups to recruit adolescents for summer retreats. The camps eerily mirror the comedy *But I'm a Cheerleader* (1999), in which a teenager is sent by her parents to a therapy camp to cure her homosexuality.

While not all religious-based camps target homosexuality, a rise in evangelical youth camps like Living Waters, Young Life, and Kids on Fire pointed to a dramatic shift in how the Religious Right targeted children. The 2006 documentary, *Jesus Camp*, revealed that evangelical organizations hope to combat the rise in secularism by immersing their youth in traditional Christian values. Secular groups such as Minnesota's Camp Quest began offering retreats in 1996; however, unlike its Christian-based counterparts, Camp Quest had only a dozen branches as of 2012.

Leslie Paris

SEE ALSO: *Baby Boomers; Boy Scouts of America; Camping; Fundamentalism; Girl Scouts; World War II.*

BIBLIOGRAPHY

Bond, Hallie E.; Joan Jacobs Brumberg; and Leslie Paris. *"A Paradise for Boys and Girls": Children's Camps in the Adirondacks.* Syracuse, NY: Syracuse University Press, 2006.

Deloria, Philip J. *Playing Indian.* New Haven, CT: Yale University Press, 1998.

Eells, Eleanor. *Eleanor Eells' History of Organized Camping: The First 100 Years.* Martinsville, IN: American Camping Association, 1986.

Gutman, Richard J. S., and Kellie O. Gutman. *The Summer Camp Memory Book: A Pictorial Treasury of Everything, from Campfires to Color Wars, You Loved about Camp.* New York: Crown Publishers, 1983.

Joselit, Jenna Weissman, and Karen S. Mittelman, eds. *A Worthy Use of Summer: Jewish Summer Camping in America.* Philadelphia: National Museum of American Jewish History, 1993.

Maynard, W. Barksdale. "An Ideal Life in the Woods for Boys: Architecture and Culture in the Earliest Summer Camps." *Winterthur Portfolio* 34 (1999): 3–29.

Miller, Susan. *Growing Girls: The Natural Origins of Girls' Organizations in America.* New Brunswick, NJ: Rutgers University Press, 2007.

Paris, Leslie. *Children's Nature: The Rise of the American Summer Camp.* New York: New York University Press, 2008.

Sandler, Lauren. *Righteous: Dispatches from the Evangelical Youth Movement.* New York: Viking, 2006.

Smith, Christian, and Melinda Lundquist Denton. *Soul Searching: The Religious and Spiritual Lives of American Teenagers.* New York: Oxford University Press, 2005.

Smith, Michael B. "The Ego Ideal of the Good Camper and the Nature of Summer Camp." *Environmental History* 11 (2006): 70–101.

Sun Records

Established in Memphis, Tennessee, in 1952 by visionary Sam Phillips, Sun Records revolutionized pop music. Phillips began what was originally called Memphis Recording Service to record blues artists, then started Sun as a home for some of them. In 1954 he recorded Elvis Presley, whose blending of musical genres had a major impact on the course of popular music. In his book on Sun, Colin Escott quotes Phillips on Elvis: "He sings Negro songs with a white voice which borrows in mood and emphasis from the country style, modified by popular music. It's a blend of all of them."

After selling Elvis's contract to RCA for $35,000, Phillips had the capital to continue work with such influential artists as Carl Perkins, Johnny Cash, Jerry Lee Lewis, and Charlie Rich. In 1969 Sun was sold to recording executive Shelby Singleton, who went about reissuing many of the label's important early recordings. Sun Records now has an online store where consumers can buy its classic recordings along with memorabilia.

Joyce Linehan

SEE ALSO: *Blues; Cash, Johnny; The Internet; Lewis, Jerry Lee; Pop Music; Presley, Elvis; Rich, Charlie; Rock and Roll.*

BIBLIOGRAPHY

Crouch, Kevin, and Tanja Crouch. *Sun King: The Life and Times of Sam Phillips, the Man behind Sun Records.* London: Piatkus Books, 2008.

Escott, Colin, and Martin Hawkins. *Sun Records: The Brief History of the Legendary Record Label.* New York: Quick Fox, 1980.

Escott, Colin, and Martin Hawkins. *Good Rockin' Tonight: Sun Records and the Birth of Rock 'n' Roll.* New York: St. Martin's Press, 1991.

Sundance Film Festival

The Sundance Film Festival helped revolutionize the world of American independent cinema by cultivating an audience for daring and innovative films and often catalyzing theatrical distribution deals for such films that otherwise would not have a chance for release. In 1981 actor Robert Redford, interested and concerned about the state of film in the United States, founded the Sundance Institute, an organization devoted to the support

Sundance Film Festival. *Sundance Film Festival director John Cooper, left, and Sundance Institute president Robert Redford speak at the festival's opening press conference in Park City, Utah, in 2010.* AP IMAGES.

and development of emerging screenwriters and directors. Quickly turning into a fertile ground for new artists (more than 300 filmmakers benefit annually from its various film, screenwriting, and cultural programs), the institute ballooned into the high-profile Sundance Film Festival, an annual winter event held in the quaint village of Park City, Utah, that is attended by more than 10,000 people. The festival runs for a period of ten days, screening international films, documentaries, short films, and American independent premieres—making the festival the preeminent showcase in the world for American independent films.

INDIES FIND A HOME

Understanding the importance of encouraging the spectrum of visions that film artists have, Redford and his institute have helped to enhance the quality of American films, along with giving an array of talented people the opportunity to develop and refine new work. The Sundance Film Festival has helped launch the careers of talented, eccentric actors and actresses that mirror its hip, young aesthetic, such as Lily Taylor and Parker Posey. Because of Sundance's widely publicized success stories of past participants, including Quentin Tarantino (*Reservoir Dogs*, 1992), Neil LaBute (*In the Company of Men*, 1997), and Debra Granik (*Winter's Bone*, 2010), and the diverse and bold style of the films it supports, the festival has attracted a great deal of attention in and out of Hollywood, making it one of the most talked-about events related to the film industry.

Studios tend to pursue more commercial scripts; stories that offer the guarantee of drawing in large audiences and funds. Scripts bought by large studios are often reworked without the original writer to match the studio's market-driven vision and not the artist's. But with Sundance and its persistent focus on risky choices that were pleasing audiences, celebrities and sleek studio executives armed with cell phones began to flood the Sundance Film Festival, giving it sudden prestige. As American audiences started to hunger for such stories, studio executives became more sycophantic toward their writers and directors. Wining and dining cutting-edge filmmakers during the course of the festival, they often kick-start careers that prove to be long-lasting.

Films screened at Sundance started a new trend toward dramatizing stories of a darker nature. Whether it be physical violence with an edge of black humor (Tarantino) or emotional violence (LaBute), people became drawn to films that explored different terrain and did not necessarily have happy endings. Large studio films tend to offer easy entertainment. Even when they are depressing, there can be excessive sentimentality that allows an audience to have an emotional release and leave the theater satisfied after having had a good cry. But the new wave of films and filmmakers that Sundance was producing did not do that. Instead, they offered worlds with little solace or answers, where characters were cruel to each other, as in LaBute's film *In the Company of Men* (which premiered at Sundance in 1997, launching his independent film career). It tells the story of disillusioned and bored corporate men who seduce a deaf woman in their office just so they can have the satisfaction of dumping her. It is important to tell these kinds of stories because they explore the intricate, often unhealthy, ways people relate to one another.

THE SUNDANCE BRAND

Sundance has even produced an "illegitimate offspring" in the form of "Slam Dance." Also held in Park City, it supposedly includes films that were rejected by Sundance, as well as others, and holds its festival concurrently with Sundance's. Slam Dance, too, has caught on, and now Hollywood executives have to divide their time between both festivals, always on the lookout for fresh, undiscovered talent. While Slam Dance is unaffiliated with the festival, the Sundance brand has moved beyond just the festival, starting as early as 1984, when the Utah Playwrights Conference became the Sundance Playwrights Lab. Redford teamed with Showtime and NBC in 1996 to launch the Sundance Channel, a cable network dedicated to independent film. In 1998 a film music program was added, while 2010 saw Sundance team with several U.S. government agencies to form FILM FORWARD, "an international cultural exchange program designed to enhance cross-cultural understanding, collaboration and dialogue around the globe by engaging audiences through the exhibition of film and conversation with filmmaker." Sundance's international reach continued in 2012 with the premier of Sundance London.

From a small festival of independent films in Utah, the Sundance Film Festival has grown into several important programs with six competition categories and seven out-of-competition areas, including the launch in 2010 of NEXT, which premiers low-budget films. For two weeks in winter, throngs of entertainment people flock to the little town of Park City to network and buy independent films, as the world watches via entertainment programs and the news. There is no restaurant, bar, or street corner in town that is without somebody affiliated with the film industry and ready to deal. The impact of Sundance remains strong, as proved in 2010, when films from the festival earned fifteen Oscar nominations, and in 2011 when forty-five films shown at the festival landed distribution deals.

Sharon Yablon

SEE ALSO: *Academy Awards; Cable TV; Celebrity; Hollywood; Movie Stars; Redford, Robert; Tarantino, Quentin.*

BIBLIOGRAPHY

Anderson, John. *Sundancing: Hanging out and Listening in at America's Most Important Film Festival.* New York: Spike, 2000.

Biskind, Peter. *Down and Dirty Pictures: Miramax, Sundance, and the Rise of Independent Film.* New York: Simon & Schuster, 2004.

Dargis, Manohla. "Still a Home for Directors, and Big Foot." *New York Times*, February 6, 2011, sec. L.

Mottram. James. *The Sundance Kids: How the Mavericks Took Back Hollywood.* New York: Faber & Faber, 2006.

Smith, Lory. *Party in a Box: The Story of the Sundance Film Festival.* Salt Lake City, UT: Gibbs Smith Publishers, 1999.

Zenovich, Maria. *Independent's Day.* DVD. New York: New Video, 2004.

Sunday, Billy *(1862–1935)*

A former professional baseball player with an entertainer's flair and a mastery of idiomatic language, Billy Sunday set the pace for modern evangelism. His tabernacle crusades of the early 1900s combined showmanship with fundamentalism and produced thousands of converts. His influence on the cultural dynamics of the country is incalculable, for, while many doubted the sincerity of Sunday's believers, his "Elmer Gantry" style would be copied by American evangelists throughout the twentieth century and beyond, serving to increase and cement the religious right as a significant force in society.

Born William Ashley Sunday on November 19, 1862, in a farmhouse near Ames, Iowa, Billy Sunday seemed an unlikely candidate for the ministry. While a stint in an orphanage instilled habits of honesty, he was also known to fight, drink, and chase women. He held a series of odd jobs until a baseball scout noticed his athletic abilities, and in 1883 he joined the Chicago White Stockings and enjoyed the boisterous life of a professional athlete.

One afternoon in 1886, while out with friends at a Chicago saloon, Sunday encountered an evangelistic group from the Pacific Garden Mission. Intrigued by their singing, he accepted an invitation to services and was soon converted. He joined the Jefferson Park Presbyterian Church a short time later. He continued to play baseball but gave up his habits of drinking and swearing and began giving inspirational talks to young fans. Sunday left baseball in 1891 to work for the Chicago YMCA. In 1893 he joined J. Wilburn Chapman's evangelistic services as an advance man, handling technical details for the revival

Billy Sunday. *Billy Sunday's charisma and showmanship as an evangelist in the early 1900s was adopted by other religious leaders throughout the century.* PICTORIAL PARADE/STAFF/ARCHIVE PHOTOS/GETTY IMAGES.

services. When Chapman retired in 1895, Sunday assumed his place and began a touring ministry.

Sunday's tabernacle crusades were conducted in temporary wooden structures with sawdust-covered floors. While the revival meeting was not new to America—the tradition stretched back to the Second Great Awakening of the early 1800s and the camp meetings on the frontier—Sunday added new elements to make his events successful. Careful planning went into the crusades, and teamwork was essential. A Sunday campaign resembled a vaudeville show as much as a mission; advance men promoted the coming attraction, secretaries made local arrangements, and bands and choirs were hired to provide entertainment. In 1909 Homer A. Rodeheaver, a song leader and trombone player, joined Sunday's troupe, and the tabernacle rang with music and excitement in the buildup to Sunday's explosive sermons.

Combining athletic gestures with colorful language, Sunday harangued his audiences about the need to get right with God. He defended the brevity of his visits by saying, "They tell me a revival is only temporary: so is a bath, but it does you good." He linked religion to patriotism and upright living, urging people to accept Christ as their savior and to signify their intention to convert by walking down the aisle and shaking Sunday's hand. Thousands did so. A New York campaign alone drew a million and a half people with 100,000 conversions. The weakness in his work was that he did not encourage people to join any specific church, and thus many of his converts never became committed to a particular faith.

Sunday did not avoid controversial issues or tone down his fundamentalist message in order to court popularity. He advocated Prohibition and wholeheartedly embraced the war effort, using religion to promote the sale of war bonds during World War I. He denounced modernism in religion, advocated the enactment of laws to ban the teaching of evolution in schools, and was a friend and adviser to conservative politicians. Unlike most evangelists, who settled down to become pastors or teachers in religious colleges, Sunday remained a fixture on the "sawdust trail." By his death on November 6, 1935, he had led more than 300 campaigns and claimed to have brought 300,000 souls to Christ.

By using the modern techniques of show business and linking religion not to intricate theology but to common language and experiences, Sunday established a unique American form of evangelism. Later leaders, most notably Billy Graham, would continue his practice of large-scale campaigns aimed at emotional conversions.

Tracy J. Revels

SEE ALSO: *Evangelism; Fundamentalism; Graham, Billy; Modernism; Prohibition; War Bonds; World War I.*

BIBLIOGRAPHY

Bruns, Roger. *Preacher: Billy Sunday and Big Time American Evangelism.* New York: W. W. Norton, 1992.

Dorsett, Lyle W. *Billy Sunday and the Redemption of Urban America.* Grand Rapids, MI: W. W. Eerdmans Publishing, 1991.

McLoughlin, William G., Jr. *Billy Sunday Was His Real Name.* Chicago: University of Chicago Press, 1955.

Sunday, Billy. *The Sawdust Trail: Billy Sunday in His Own Words.* Iowa City: University of Iowa Press, 2005.

Sunday Driving

Sunday driving, the practice of breaking the Sabbath by driving automobiles, especially during church services, stood as a symbol for what many believed was a nationwide decline in morality. For many Americans, the twentieth century marked an irreversible decline in everything they held dear. Uncontrollable "outside forces" seemed to be tearing apart families, destroying tight-knit communities, and eroding the foundations of morality on which previous generations had built their lives. Ministers around the country railed against these changes and identified the accoutrements of modernity as prime culprits. Telephones, radios, movies, and professional sports all received a measure of blame for corrupting the American spirit. To many people, however, nothing symbolized the degeneration of the modern era quite as well as the automobile, and to ministers facing declining church attendance, a particular cause for alarm was the increase in Sunday driving.

Ministers were not the only ones who believed that Sunday driving was cause for public concern. In a 1922 article in *Scribner's* magazine, Allen Albert claimed, "in good motoring weather I have attended Sunday-morning services from Waycross, Georgia, to Manistee, Michigan, and it would be hard to find any pews emptier anywhere." In her novel *Country People* (1924), Ruth Suckow illustrates the concern caused by the growing popularity of Sunday driving: "It was a wonder to Emma to sit on the porch on Sunday afternoons and count how many vehicles went by. But grandpa wouldn't even try to count. '*Ach*, no! no! no!' was all that he would say. This was all so wicked on Sunday!"

In Nashville, Tennessee, a 1923 ordinance forbade any business to sell gasoline, oil, or automobiles on Sundays and prohibited automobile service facilities from operating as well. "Everyone wanted to enjoy a Sunday outing in the automobile," editorialized the *Memphis (Tennessee) Tattler* in 1923, "but realized he was taking a big chance. He might run out of gas, have a puncture or break down miles away from home. Then the whole family would have to walk back."

Despite protests against Sunday driving, however, the practice always had many more advocates than opponents. Some people pointed out that automobiles could just as easily carry people to church as away from it. As *Motor Age* commented in 1919, "Even the farmer in the remotest rural district may wait until the last minute, jump into his car and go to church, attend services and be home in less than the time it used to take him to get there alone." Others, such as a writer for the *Christian Advocate* in 1920, rationalized that automobiles might encourage "many immoral practices," including "desecration of the Sabbath," but that "all good things are liable to abuse."

Some believed the freedom and mobility of automobiles would encourage religious celebration. "He . . . would take his religion out of doors, where God smiled and spoke to burdened business men," wrote a writer for *Christian Century* in 1928. "In serene solitude he would drive his car over smoky and smelly roads, oblivious of all but the deeper invisible realities. To the care-free accompaniment of the motor he would raise hymns of joy to the God of breeze and field."

And, of course, there were all of the Americans who simply disregarded protests from those who held onto older notions of morality. For better or for worse, Sunday driving became a standard feature of American culture—more notable for its unremarkable regularity than for the emotionally charged controversy it once provoked.

Christopher W. Wells

SEE ALSO: *Automobile; Radio;* Scribner's; *Television; The Twenties.*

BIBLIOGRAPHY

Berger, Michael. *The Devil Wagon in God's Country: The Automobile and Social Change in Rural America, 1893–1929.* Hamden, CT: Archon Books, 1979.

McCrossen, Alexis. *Holy Day, Holiday: The American Sunday.* Ithaca, NY: Cornell University Press, 2002.

Sunset Boulevard

A classic film noir, *Sunset Boulevard* (1950) is a cynical and decadent tragicomedy narrated, in gloomy noir fashion, by a dead man. Directed by Billy Wilder and populated by faded silent movie stars such as Gloria Swanson, Erich von Stroheim, and Buster Keaton, the film presents the story of Joe Gillis (William Holden), a weak-willed, materialistic scriptwriter. While trying to escape his creditors, Gillis happens upon the mansion of the wealthy, but slightly mad, silent movie star Norma Desmond (played by Swanson), who perpetually waits for a phone call from a studio that has long since forgotten about her. The handsome writer becomes a kept man who struggles to make it in the movie business only to fall prey to Norma as he tries to escape from her obsessive love for him.

In his biography *Billy Wilder*, writer Axel Madsen describes *Sunset Boulevard* as "a gnawing, haunting, and ruthless film with a dank smell of corrosive delusion hanging over it." And, indeed, typical of Wilder's sophisticated and cynical style, the film is a black comedy that addresses the casualties of the Hollywood dream machine—those obsessed by fame and success in the cruel world of the movie studios. The film is filled with stylish settings and wonderfully biting dialogue, and it has attained the status of a cult classic with quotable lines, the best known being "I'm ready for my close-up, Mr. DeMille." *Sunset Boulevard* has ranked as high as sixteenth in the American Film Institute's rankings of the best 100 American films of all time. Andrew Lloyd Webber created a Broadway musical version of the film, which opened in 1994.

Jeannette Sloniowski

SEE ALSO: *Broadway; Film Noir; Hollywood; Keaton, Buster; Lloyd Webber, Andrew; Movie Stars; The Musical; Silent Movies; Wilder, Billy.*

BIBLIOGRAPHY

Cooke, Grayson. "We Had Faces Then: *Sunset Boulevard* and the Sense of the Spectral." *Quarterly Review of Film and Video* 26, no. 2 (2009): 89–101.

Corliss, Richard. "The Authors-Auteurs." In *Talking Pictures: Screenwriters in the American Cinema.* New York: Penguin Books, 1975.

Madsen, Axel. *Billy Wilder.* London: Secker and Warburg, 1968.

Mundy, Robert. "Wilder Reappraised." *Cinema* 4 (1969): 14–19.

Taylor, Aaron. "Twilight of the Idols: Performance, Melodramatic Villainy, and *Sunset Boulevard.*" *Journal of Film and Video* 59, no. 2 (2007): 13–31.

Trowbridge, Katelin. "The War between the Words and Images—*Sunset Boulevard.*" *Literature Film Quarterly* 30, no. 4 (2002): 294–303.

Super Bowl

More than any other sporting event in America, the Super Bowl has truly become a cultural phenomenon. According to 2010 National Football League (NFL) figures, more than 106 million people in the United States alone watched the Super Bowl, and additional fans from 225 countries also watched the yearly extravaganza. The game has become, according to writer Michael Real (as quoted in Dona Schwartz's *Contesting the Super Bowl*), a "mythic spectacle," which "in the classical manner of mythical beliefs and ritual activities . . . is a communal celebration of and indoctrination into specific socially dominant emotions, life-styles, and values." The Super Bowl brings together several institutions: sports, television, advertising, and the American corporate culture. It also serves as an end-of-the-season celebration, glorifying revenues accumulated by team owners, advertisers, media outlets, and many other businesses that share in the tremendous profits generated by professional football.

AFL-NFL RIVALRY

The Super Bowl itself stems from a fierce rivalry between two football leagues. In 1960 the upstart American Football League (AFL) challenged the popular and well-established NFL. The AFL was well funded and soon began to contest the NFL in a bidding war for college players. In 1965 the AFL scored its first major coup when the New York Jets signed University of Alabama star quarterback Joe Namath. Namath's personality, media appeal, and on-field success gave the AFL an early degree of legitimacy. The AFL was also helped by a television contract. Under an exclusive deal with the American Broadcasting Company (ABC), each AFL team was paid $150,000—money that kept the league afloat during the difficult, early years of its existence.

In 1966 the AFL decided to further assert itself by attempting to sign established, veteran NFL players. When several of its stars signed lucrative contracts, the NFL found it had little choice but to accept the situation and started working on a merger of the two leagues. In June 1966 an NFL-AFL merger was announced. The merger called for a common draft of college players and a championship game—the Super Bowl—to start in 1967. The new league would be called the National Football League with the previous rivals split into two divisions: the National Football Conference (NFC) and the American Football Conference (AFC). The full merger would take place in 1970. The Super Bowl pitted the winners of the two conferences in one game in late January, following the regular season and a series of playoff games.

During the first few years of the new National Football League, the two conferences maintained separate identities and schedules. Initially then, the Super Bowl became a contest where the upstart AFL would try to prove its mettle against more established teams. As might be expected, in the first two Super Bowls (Super Bowls I and II), the NFL Green Bay Packers easily defeated their AFL opponents. Most believed it would take years before an AFL team would actually win a Super Bowl. Then, in Super Bowl III, the AFL champion New York Jets were matched against the powerful Baltimore Colts. Jets quarterback Broadway Joe Namath, on the eve of the contest in which the Colts were heavily favored, "guaranteed" a Jets victory. On January 12, 1969, the Jets stunned the sports world by defeating the Colts 16–7. The Jets victory finally gave the AFL its due and helped bring the two leagues together when the merger officially began the next year.

TELEVISION'S ROLE

Enhancing the merger of the two leagues in 1970 was a television package from ABC. For just more than $8 million each season, ABC agreed to televise thirteen prime-time games on Monday nights. Television revenues for the NFL totaled nearly $150 million. Overall, it meant that each of the twenty-six NFL teams in 1970 would receive about $1.7 million. The popularity of football stemmed primarily from its television exposure. During the 1970s television transformed football into America's premier spectator sport.

Before the 1973 season, Congress lifted TV blackouts on home games that were not sold out. While some predicted that this legislation would make it hard for some small market teams to fill the stands, that did not prove to be the case. Not only did TV viewing increase, but teams actually sold more tickets. And it was TV contracts—not single game sales—that became the meal ticket for the NFL. In 1978 the NFL signed the most lucrative sports TV contract ever. In January of that year, a Lou Harris poll found that 70 percent of the nation's sports fans followed football compared to 54 percent who followed baseball.

ADVERTISING

With the help of television, over the past few decades the game on the field has become just an ancillary part of the entire Super Bowl experience. More than anything else, the Super Bowl is about money and corporate advertising. This early February spectacle is the most lucrative sporting event in the United States and has become as much an advertising contest as a sports production. The NFL sold the broadcast rights for the 2010 Super Bowl for more than $4 billion of total revenues. At the Super Bowl itself, logo placement, advertising angles, and television commercials have taken on more importance than the outcome of the game. In fact, television commercials slated for the Super Bowl are often shown as news items on local broadcasts days before the game. There are even postgame telecasts that examine and evaluate the quality of Super Bowl commercials.

To demonstrate the serious connection between advertising and the Super Bowl, one need look no further than Anheuser-Busch's "Bud Bowl," which was a part of Super Bowl television broadcasts from 1989 to 1997. The Bud Bowl was a fictitious football game, played out in expensive commercial spots, between animated beer bottles of Budweiser and Bud Light. The Bud Bowl employed real announcers, and millions of dollars were spent to show these beer bottles running up and down the field attempting to score touchdowns. But the key to the Bud Bowl was Anheuser-Busch's promotions, which began at hundreds of retail outlets, months before the game itself. The beer company offered thousands of prizes that were tied into these advertising spots at the Super Bowl. Because of the advertising and prize giveaways, the final score of the Bud Bowl became more important than the results of the Super Bowl to many American television viewers. Anheuser-Busch even set up a toll-free number so potential prize winners could call and find out the final score of the Bud Bowl.

By 2010 thirty-second Super Bowl advertising spots were selling for well over $3 million. Yet the evidence indicates that those sums are well worth the price for American corporate advertisers. In 1990 the Gillette Company used the Super Bowl to introduce its new Sensor razor. Gillette spent more than $3 million on Super Bowl advertising to reach their male audience. By focusing its ads on Super Bowl Sunday, Gillette sold out its Sensor inventory through February and March following the broadcast, and the company was able to increase its market share by 35 percent in 1991. Evidence gathered by writer Phil Schaaf for his book *Sports Marketing* indicated that 66 percent of people tested recall Super Bowl commercials.

Money and corporate infiltration of the Super Bowl has also influenced the type of fans that attend the January event. In a sport that caters to the "average" fan during the regular season, few of those ordinary team boosters will ever have the opportunity to see a Super Bowl. Tickets are not sold to the general public—most go to corporate sponsors, celebrities, NFL owners and officials, other players, and news organizations. The look of a Super Bowl is far different from the look of a football game on a regular Sunday in October or November.

But a Super Bowl does bring in a great deal of money to a host city. The 2011 Super Bowl was reported to have had a $612 million economic impact in the Dallas region, according to a study commissioned by the North Texas Super Bowl XLV Host Committee. All but the first Super Bowl has been a sellout. At the 2011 event, tickets ranged from $200 for the plaza outside the stadium to $1,200 for club seats inside, a far cry from the $6 tickets one could buy for the first Super Bowl in 1967. Scalpers, or illegal ticket brokers, generally get four times that much for a Super Bowl ticket.

Tim Green, a former professional football player, writes in his book *The Dark Side of the Game* that "January is when the big money really starts to drop." Green is referring to the legal and illegal betting that accompanies the Super Bowl. The game is the most gambled-on sporting event in the United States. A person can lay a wager on just about any facet of the game: the first quarter score, which team will score first, which running back will get the most yards, the total score, or how many yards a particular quarterback will throw for. Millions of dollars of legal gambling goes on for each Super Bowl game—estimates for illegal gambling are much higher.

MEDIA EVENT

The Super Bowl is the most watched one-day event in the world. There is no worry about a rain-out and viewers represent a wide demographic range. The Super Bowl is also the second-biggest eating day in America—behind only Thanksgiving. In 1993 several national women's groups announced that Super Bowl Sunday was the worst day of the year for violence against women. Women's shelters claimed that hotlines were "flooded with more calls from victims [on Super Bowl Sunday] than on any other day of the year." Furthermore, a study released by Old

Dominion University in Norfolk, Virginia, showed that hospital admissions of women rose after games won by the Washington Redskins. While many subsequently questioned the links between domestic violence and the Super Bowl, the women's groups had scored a public relations coup by releasing their findings just before the Super Bowl, when national and world media attention was so focused on that event.

Additional evidence has shown that the Super Bowl brings out the worst in American sports fans. After Denver won its second consecutive Super Bowl in 1999, rowdy fans rioted in that city, overturning cars, breaking windows, and starting fires. One sports psychologist determined that testosterone levels of young males rose by 20 percent when their team won a big game. During the 1992 game between the Buffalo Bills and the Washington Redskins, American Indian groups used the Super Bowl media glare to call attention to what they believed were racist and demeaning uses of nicknames and mascots on professional sports teams. The Redskin team nickname was considered especially egregious to the American Indian Movement (AIM), and protestors ringed the stadium on Super Bowl Sunday, chanting slogans to voice their cause. Because of the media saturation in town for the Super Bowl, the AIM protestors appeared on television and were interviewed for national and international media outlets. While nothing came of the protests, AIM was able to get its message out and even forced the NFL to issue a statement about the team nicknames.

But perhaps the most spectacular Super Bowl television "event" took place during the 2004 halftime show when pop star Justin Timberlake removed a piece of singer Janet Jackson's top, momentarily exposing her right breast. Timberlake and Jackson maintained that the incident was accidental, calling it a simple "wardrobe malfunction." But the show was airing live, so millions of people witnessed the mistake before the network went to an awkward commercial break. It did not take long before videos started circulating on the Internet. The NFL, embarrassed by the incident, permanently banned MTV from conducting future halftime shows.

The Super Bowl has offered the American sports fan a plethora of heroic players and exciting teams: Joe Namath, Terry Bradshaw, Joe Montana, John Elway, Tom Brady, the Miami Dolphins, the Pittsburgh Steelers, the Dallas Cowboys, the New England Patriots, the Green Bay Packers, and the San Francisco 49ers. But player statistics and heroics have become overshadowed by economic, social, and cultural issues: Who will sing the national anthem? Who will perform at the half-time festivities? What television commercials will catch the attention of the American public? What political issues might arise this year? And what is the betting line on the game? These issues have turned the Super Bowl into more of a media event than a sporting contest.

David E. Woodard

SEE ALSO: *Advertising; Bradshaw, Terry; Brady, Tom; College Football; The Dallas Cowboys; Elway, John; Gambling; The Green Bay Packers; Jackson, Janet; Montana, Joe; MTV; Namath, Joe; National Football League (NFL); The Pittsburgh Steelers; Professional Football; Sports Heroes; Timberlake, Justin.*

BIBLIOGRAPHY

Briggs, Bill. "Super Bull!! Legends Are Forged on Super Bowl Sunday . . . So Are Big Fat Lies." NBC News, February 3, 2007. Accessed April 2012. Available from http://www.msnbc.msn.com/id/16877331/ns/business-us_business/t/super-bull/#.T2AYk8hCnDc

Duden, Jane. *The Super Bowl.* Parsippany, NJ: Crestwood House, 1992.

Gillette, Gary; Matthew Silverman; Peter Palmer; et al. *The ESPN Pro Football Encyclopedia.* New York: Sterling, 2007.

Green, Jerry. *Super Bowl Chronicles: A Sportswriter Reflects on the First 30 Years of America's Game,* 2nd ed. Indianapolis, IN: Masters Press, 1995.

Green, Tim. *The Dark Side of the Game.* New York: Grand Central Publishing, 1997.

Hanks, Stephen. *The Game That Changed Pro Football.* New York: Birch Lane Press, 1989.

Maher, Todd, and Bob Gill. *The Pro Football Playoff Encyclopedia.* New York: Maher Sports Media, 2011.

McGinn, Bob. *The Ultimate Super Bowl Book.* Minneapolis, MN: MVP Books, 2009.

Rosentraub, Mark S. *Major League Losers: The Real Cost of Sports and Who's Paying for It.* New York: Basic Books, 1997.

Schaaf, Phil. *Sports Marketing: It's Not Just a Game Anymore.* Amherst, NY: Prometheus Books, 1995.

Schwartz, Dona. *Contesting the Super Bowl.* New York: Routledge, 1998.

Weiss, Ann. *Money Games: The Business of Sports.* Boston: Houghton Mifflin, 1993.

Super Size Me

Inspired by the many lawsuits against fast-food corporations that claimed they were responsible for the massive weight gain and deteriorating health of plaintiffs, independent filmmaker Morgan Spurlock decided to document the effects of a fast-food diet—using himself as the experimental subject. *Super Size Me* (2004) is the resulting film. Spurlock's plan was to spend one month eating every meal at McDonald's, making sure to eat each item on the menu at least once. If, on ordering, a clerk asked him if he would like to "super size" his meal, enlarging his soda to 42 ounces and his french fries to 8 ounces, he would do it. He also cut his usual exercise routine to more closely resemble that of an average sedentary American.

At the outset of the project, Spurlock was examined by a general practitioner, a cardiologist, a gastroenterologist, a nutritionist, and a physiologist specializing in exercise. They found him to be an exceptionally healthy thirty-two-year-old man, standing 6 feet, 2 inches tall and weighing 185.5 pounds. Over the course of the ensuing experiment, Spurlock not only gains almost 25 pounds, but he also experiences depression, exhaustion, heart palpitations, decrease of sex drive, loss of liver function, asthma, and elevated cholesterol. His girlfriend and doctors express concern about continuing the experiment, but Spurlock refuses to quit. He shows symptoms of addiction and describes only feeling happy when he is eating.

Along with tracking the changes in his body, Spurlock travels around the country interviewing experts such as former surgeon general David Satcher and author John Robbins (*Diet for a New America*, 1987) and noting pertinent facts, such as that there are four McDonald's restaurants for every square mile in Manhattan. He also points out the ways the fast-food industry targets children with ad campaigns and toy giveaways, attracting a new generation to its addictive fare.

Perhaps because of a popular fascination with odd eating habits, upon its release in 2004 *Super Size Me* became one of the most popular feature documentaries in history, grossing almost $30 million. Though some critics claimed that the film was unscientific, unfair, and amateurish, audiences were mesmerized by Spurlock's odyssey. Even McDonald's responded. Though the giant chain denied any connection to *Super Size Me*, six weeks after the film's release, they eliminated the super-size option for meals and soon after added a number of more healthful menu options, including salads and fruit.

Super Size Me and other attacks on the fast-food industry provoked a backlash as well. In 2004 and again in 2005, the U.S. House of Representatives passed the American Personal Responsibility in Food Consumption Act (nicknamed the Cheeseburger Bill), making it illegal to bring suit against the fast-food industry for health problems caused by eating their food. Both times the bill failed to pass in the Senate. Other responses have included smaller-scale rebuttal documentaries by self-identified "McDieters," such as Soso Whaley's film *Me and Mickey D* and James Painter's *Portion Size Me*, both about losing weight by eating fast food. It also inspired *Super High Me* (2007), in which stand-up comedian Doug Benson chronicles the effects of thirty days of sustained marijuana usage on the human body as he simultaneously examines the ongoing debate over the use medical marijuana.

Tina Gianoulis

SEE ALSO: *Dieting; Fast Food; French Fries; Hamburger; McDonald's.*

BIBLIOGRAPHY

Gilbert, Anne. "*Super Size Me*." *Cineaste* 29, no. 4 (2004): 47.

Mello, Michelle M.; Eric B. Rimm; and David M. Studdert. "The McLawsuit: The Fast-Food Industry and Legal Accountability for Obesity." *Health Affairs*, November 2003. Accessed May 2012. Available from http://content.healthaffairs.org/content/22/6/207.full

Schlosser, Eric. *Fast Food Nation: The Dark Side of the All-American Meal.* New York: Harper Perennial, 2005.

Spurlock, Morgan. *Don't Eat This Book: Fast Food and the Supersizing of America.* New York: Berkley Trade, 2006.

Superman

The first and most important comic-book superhero, Superman looms large not only in comic books but also in all of twentieth-century popular culture. Among the few American characters instantly recognizable in virtually every corner of the globe, Superman is truly a pop culture icon. Certainly there is no purer representative of the fantastic possibilities inherent in the comic-book medium.

BIRTH OF A SUPERHERO

Superman sprang from the imagination of two Jewish teenagers growing up in Cleveland, Ohio, during the Great Depression. Jerry Siegel and Joe Shuster were both lower-middle-class sons of immigrants who believed in the American dream. Avid read-

Christopher Reeve as Superman. *Christopher Reeve starred as Clark Kent/Superman in the 1978 film adaptation of the iconic comic-book saga.* WARNER BROS/DC COMICS/THE KOBAL COLLECTION.

ers of science fiction and pulp magazines, the two youths aspired to write and draw their own adventure comic strip. In 1934, after several tryouts in their school newspaper, Siegel and Shuster hit upon the idea that they suspected would be a marketable comic strip.

In his striking red-and-blue costume with flowing red cape and red *S* emblazoned on his chest, Superman was the ultimate strongman, capable of achieving almost any physical feat. He was a fantastic being from a doomed alien planet (later revealed to be Krypton), come to apply the superhuman blessings of his native home in the service of his adopted world. And, perhaps most importantly, he assumed the persona of an undistinguished, mild-mannered newspaper reporter named Clark Kent. Unpretentious and seeking no glory, he was a superhero who would retreat into the anonymity of society when his spectacular deeds were accomplished. Here was the crucial point of reference for a Depression-era culture that extolled the virtues of the common man.

Superman was a brilliant creation—ingenious in its very simplicity and instantly accessible to a mass audience. It was, of course, not an entirely original concept. Superheroes of various sorts had a long history in popular myth and folklore. But the Superman/Clark Kent dichotomy was original as a contemporary expression of adolescent wish fulfillment. Siegel and Shuster, both of whom wore glasses and admitted to being shy, insecure, and unsuccessful with girls in high school, put much of themselves and their fantasies into the character. In truth, the essence of Superman's appeal was almost universal—especially to young males. Any boy or man who has felt in any way inadequate in a society of formidable male gender expectations has at times wished that he could transcend his human frailty as easily as Clark Kent removed his glasses.

Such a concept was destined to be a popular one with young people. But the middle-aged men who ran the newspaper syndicates failed to recognize Superman's appeal. After several years of failing to sell their idea to the newspapers, Siegel and Shuster reluctantly sold it to a fledgling comic-book company called Detective Comics (DC), for whom they had done some freelance work. As part of the contract, the two young men would write and draw the series as long as DC allowed them, but they also forsook all rights to the character in exchange for $130 ($10 per page for the thirteen-page story). It proved to be one of the most infamous contracts ever signed in the history of the U.S. entertainment industry.

SUPERMAN'S DEBUT

Superman debuted in the first issue of DC's *Action Comics*, dated June 1938. The cover of the classic issue, which fetches prices of more than $50,000 from collectors, showed the costumed hero lifting an automobile over his head as stupefied criminals flee in terror before him. It was a harsh image that DC's publishers feared would only confuse readers. But the audience responded positively and quickly. Only a few issues into publication, *Action Comics* became the best-selling comic book on the market, and the reason—confirmed by informal newsstand surveys—was obvious: Superman was a winning concept.

In later years Superman evolved into a character who was stoic, morally beyond reproach, and frankly rather humorless and dull. But Siegel and Shuster initially portrayed him as a feisty character who most closely resembled a super-powered, hard-boiled detective. He was a wise guy who took to crime fighting with an adolescent glee, routinely took time to mock and humiliate his adversaries as he thrashed them, and did not shrink from breaking the law when it stood in the way of true justice. It was a macho world into which only the glamorous reporter Lois Lane intruded. Although she had no time for the plain Clark Kent, she was, of course, infatuated with Superman, who rarely had time for her.

Siegel and Shuster cast their superhero as a populist champion of the oppressed, who defended common U.S. citizens from the evils of big money, political corruption, and greed in all its forms. As the United States drifted into World War II, Superman turned his attention to foiling spies and saboteurs on the U.S. home front, although his creators deliberately kept him away from the actual war so as not to upstage the real-life heroes in uniform.

COMIC-BOOK SUCCESS

At a time when most successful comic-book titles sold between 200,000 and 400,000 copies per issue, each issue of *Action Comics*—featuring only one Superman story—consistently sold around 900,000 copies. Mindful of these figures, DC featured the character in a second title, *Superman*, which established industry records by selling a staggering average of 1.3 million copies per bimonthly issue. The Superman phenomenon was not limited to comic books either. By 1941 Superman was featured in a syndicated newspaper strip, a series of short animated films produced by Paramount Pictures, and a highly popular radio show that opened with the immortal lines: "Faster than a speeding bullet! More powerful than a locomotive! Able to leap tall buildings in a single bound! Look! Up in the sky! It's a bird! It's a plane! It's . . . Superman!" Within a few short years of his comic-book debut, Superman had become a cartoon figure almost as widely recognized as Disney's Mickey Mouse.

The influence that Superman has had on the comic-book industry has been huge. Before his appearance comic books hardly constituted a medium distinct from newspaper comic strips. Most featured either reprinted newspaper strips or derivative variations of such strips. Superman was the first original character to exploit the fantastic creative possibilities of the comic-book medium—possibilities limited only by the imagination and skill of writers and artists. Images that would have been technically onerous or impossible to represent in motion pictures or radio could be easily adapted to the comic-book format. Superman's improbable adventures demonstrated this, and he single-handedly gave the comic-book industry a reason for being. Superman became the most widely imitated character in comic books, spawning a host of costumed superheroes from DC and its competitors. These superheroes established the comic-book industry as a viable commercial entertainment industry, and they have been the mainstay of comic books ever since.

Superman also established DC Comics as the industry's leading publisher. For a time, even his creators benefited financially from Superman's profits. But Siegel and Shuster saw diminishing returns for themselves even as their creation continued to generate massive revenue for the publisher. In 1947 they sued DC, trying to secure the profits that they claimed Superman should have earned them over the years. The court ruled against them, claiming that under the original 1938 contract, they had no rights to the character. For the next several decades they saw no royalties from the comic-book industry's most lucrative property. In the late 1970s, after the news media reported that Superman's creators were living in poverty, DC relented and paid them a yearly stipend for the remainder of their lives. A notorious tale well known to comic-book creators, the plight of Siegel and Shuster helped to rally writers and artists to push for new royalties and financial incentives, which the major publishers subsequently introduced in the 1980s.

THE SUPERHERO EVOLVES

Superman remained the most popular and best-selling comic-book character well into the 1960s. Under the close editorial direction of Mort Weisinger, Superman evolved into a character befitting his status as the elder statesman among superheroes. Abandoning all semblance of his rambunctious younger days, he became a staid, predictable, and paternalistic figure, always adhering to the strict letter of the law. He also gradually acquired an array of powers that made him almost invincible: flight; X-ray vision; telescopic vision; super-hearing; super-breath; the ability to move through time; the strength to move planets; and invulnerability to virtually everything except Kryptonite, the meteoric remnants of his native world Krypton.

Weisinger created a fairy-tale Superman mythos that incorporated Superman's youth (as Superboy in the midwestern town of Smallville), his friends (Lois Lane and Jimmy Olson were featured in their own comic books), villains such as Lex Luthor and Brainiac, and spin-off characters such as Supergirl and Krypto the Superdog. To overcome the creative limitations of the virtually omnipotent superhero, Weisinger also conceived a variety of imaginary stories that explored such questions as, "What if Superman had gone to another planet besides Earth?" and even "What if Superman had died?" These simple and entertaining stories were clearly aimed at children, and they sold well.

Airing from 1953 to 1957, the highly successful *Adventures of Superman* television series, to which Weisinger was a consultant, kept Superman in the public consciousness and served to promote his comic books to the new generation of baby boomers. In the mid-1990s an ABC television series called *Lois & Clark: The New Adventures of Superman* introduced the characters—played by Teri Hatcher and Dean Cain, respectively—to a new generation of viewers.

WANING POPULARITY

Superman's popularity among comic-book readers waned in the late 1960s. Faced by intense competition from Marvel's wave of more human superheroes such as Spider-Man, the Hulk, and the Fantastic Four, Superman's irreproachable Boy Scout image had become a commercial liability for new generations of young people grown expectant of antiestablishment trends in youth culture. By the mid-1970s the character's comic-book sales were at an all-time low, although his image remained the most lucrative comic-book licensed property for toys and other products. The pinnacle of the character's earning power came in the late 1970s and early 1980s in a series of major Warner Brothers *Superman* movies starring Christopher Reeve in the title role. Success in other media, however, did not translate into impressive comic-book sales, which continued to lag well behind those of trendy morally ambivalent superheroes such as the X-Men; the Punisher; and even DC's Batman, who began as a follow-up to Superman and proved to be far more adaptable to changing times.

The history of Superman in comic books during the last several decades of the twentieth century was largely shaped by DC's periodic attempts to revitalize the character by making him less super. In 1971 Superman's powers were halved. In 1986 DC contracted popular writer/artist John Byrne to rewrite Superman's origin, hoping to spark fan interest. Surely the most blatant of these efforts came in 1992 with the much-hyped "Death of Superman." The event produced a short-term boom in Superman's sales and concluded in the "Rebirth of Superman." In 1997 Superman got a radical new costume change. While nostalgic fans disapproved, DC responded that it had little choice but to try new things to reverse Superman's steady commercial decline.

POPULARITY REBORN

Superman's popularity in other media continued into the twenty-first century. There was no shortage of entertainment featuring the comic hero. The long-running television series *Smallville*, which followed the life of Clark Kent before he became Superman, aired from 2001 to 2011. In 2006 yet another Superman film was released: *Superman Returns* starred newcomer Brandon Routh as the man of steel. The film reportedly cost about $260 million to make and enjoyed strong, if not stellar, box-office returns.

Superman's legacy in the world of comic books continued as well, although with changes. In September 2011 DC Comics relaunched all its comic-book titles, including *Action Comics*. The new version of *Action Comics*, written by Grant Morrison, featured a Superman not in tights but in jeans, T-shirt, and the requisite cape. The new Superman was also a bachelor. The original *Action Comics* proved to have worth too, and in November 2011 a copy of the first issue of *Action Comics* sold at auction for a reported $2.16 million.

Superman's popularity throughout the decades might have waned, but that in no way diminished his significance. As the archetype for the superhero genre so intrinsic to U.S. comic books, he deserved his stature as the industry's de facto world ambassador. His presence was firmly etched into a global popular culture, encompassing motion pictures, television, advertising, music, and common language. And for the generations weaned on his adventures, Superman would forever remain the quintessential champion of truth, justice, and the American way.

Bradford Wright

SEE ALSO: *Baby Boomers; Batman; Comic Books; DC Comics; Disney (Walt Disney Company); The Great Depression; The Incredible Hulk; Marvel Comics; The Punisher; Radio; Spider-Man; World War II; The X-Men.*

BIBLIOGRAPHY

Daniels, Les. *DC Comics: Sixty Years of the World's Favorite Comic Book Heroes*. Boston: Little, Brown, 1995.

De Haven, Tom. *Our Hero: Superman on Earth*. New Haven, CT: Yale University Press, 2010.

Dooley, Dennis, and Gary Engle. *Superman at Fifty: The Persistence of a Legend*. Cleveland, OH: Octavia Press, 1987.

Feiffer, Jules. *The Great Comic Book Heroes*. New York: Dial Press, 1965.

The Greatest Superman Stories Ever Told. New York: DC Comics, 1987.

Jacobs, Will, and Gerard Jones. *The Comic Book Heroes*. Rocklin, CA: Prima Publishing, 1997.

Morrison, Grant. *Supergods: What Masked Vigilantes, Miraculous Mutants, and a Sun God from Smallville Can Teach Us about Being Human*. New York: Spiegel & Grau, 2011.

Supermodels

The word *supermodel* was first used in the 1940s and has endured to the present day, but the true supermodel phenomenon belongs to the 1980s and 1990s, when a few women epitomizing glamour and opulence captured the American popular consumer's imagination. For most of the era, the pantheon consisted of Cindy Crawford, Naomi Campbell, Kate Moss, Claudia Schiffer, Linda Evangelista, and Christy Turlington, six women who represented both the triumph of unadulterated image and the mass marketing of fashion.

Models had been famous before—Suzy Parker in the 1950s, Twiggy in the 1960s, Christie Brinkley and Janice Dickinson in the 1970s—but the "real" supermodels gained super-status by marketing themselves assiduously and commanding huge fees for themselves and their agents. Like most models, they tended to launch their careers in Europe, where the pay was relatively low but a girl (often as young as fourteen or fifteen) could accumulate photographs and develop a distinctive "look." Once in New York, the U.S. modeling capital, a girl hoped to sign or continue a relationship with a powerful agency such as Elite or Ford, where clients looked first. Models developed niches: Crawford was the confident sexual one, Moss the waif, Schiffer a Brigitte Bardot lookalike.

A SUPER APPEAL TO THE PUBLIC

The big six supermodels were lucky to enter the American scene at the moment in which fashion designers were changing their target market from the wealthy elite to the masses. When Calvin Klein began to advertise on television, billboards, and bus shelters, the subliminal message seemed to be that even common people could attract attention. At the same time, Hollywood actresses had deglamorized; now that they were more inclined to appear in jeans than in evening gowns and jewels, models stepped in to feed America's hunger for glitz. Yet, perhaps because supermodels had no real careers beyond posing and didn't even select the clothes or products they would wear, they were able to represent a product, an image, completely; in this regard they were forums for display, not fleshed-out personalities.

Advertisers focused on the big six (and a few slightly lesser lights, such as Elle MacPherson, Paulina Porizkova, Niki Taylor, and Tyra Banks) in part to show they could afford to: Hiring Turlington for seventy-two hours at a cost of $62,000 was a way for a company to display its success, confidence, and solvency. Then as now, models and supermodels alike made most of their money in advertising: Turlington's 1991 contract with Maybelline, for example, netted her hundreds of thousands of dollars for twelve days' work a year. The more prestigious assignments, including magazine covers such as *Vogue*, *Glamour*, and *Mademoiselle*, were comparatively unremunerative, though the exposure did help establish a model as a commodity. But a woman who had achieved supermodel status never had to worry: In 1995 Schiffer, then the industry's biggest wage earner, made $12 million from various jobs. In the eras of Reaganomics and, later, recession, such well-publicized paydays were part of a supermodel's allure.

MODEL DANGERS

The wild behavior that often accompanied the models' sudden wealth contributed to their mystique. Off the runway and out of the magazines, some of them danced and drugged the nights away with famous men. The careers of many would-be supermodels ended in financial ruin and despair. Psychologists Vivian Diller and Jill Muir-Sukenick, both former models, explained in *Psychology Today* that many in the business suffer from a "fragile personality that makes them potentially self-destructive . . . what we call 'extreme narcissistic vulnerability.'" Without a secure sense of and liking for herself, the authors argued, a girl might easily fall victim to exploitative agents, clients, drug dealers, and others who prey on the young and attractive. That situation has not changed. Models' ruination remains a popular subject of articles, books, and movies.

In the 1990s the public was primarily interested in the big six as images, not as women. While photographers and fashion designers achieved respect as artists, their models were considered merely muses or mediums for expression. Late in the decade, magazines started heralding "The Fall of the Supermodel," noting that reglamorized actresses were claiming many of the most prestigious modeling jobs and that consumers (in the words of superagent Katie Ford) had grown tired of "just seeing six people at the center of most magazines."

THE TWENTY-FIRST CENTURY SUPERMODEL

The word *supermodel* itself never went away. Magazines, merchandisers, and models themselves began applying it ever more liberally, even to women of comparatively moderate fame. Magazines such as *People* and *Us*, along with TV entertainment shows, have run features on models such as Alek Wek, Shalom Harlow, Adriana Lima, and model-actress Molly Sims, only some of whose names may remain familiar in coming years. Meanwhile, many of the original six and their circle have experienced a second act, largely by rebranding themselves as businesswomen and as adults. Moss secured more lucrative contracts than ever, and Turlington modeled for Maybelline again, this time touting products to counter the effects of aging. Several others popped up again as well—projecting calmer, more mature, even motherly images to appeal to a public who had grown older with them—though with correspondingly lower paydays for the modeling itself.

Image was not going to be enough to guarantee an enduring place in the popular imagination. In the century's first decade, certifiable supermodels included Gisele "the Body" Bündchen, highest-paid in the industry; Banks, who diversified into a talk show and the *Next Top Model* empire; and Heidi Klum, who produces and stars in popular shows such as *Project Runway*. Here is proof that overall, the term *supermodel* has come to designate merely "successful model" rather than "household name." Ultimately, the way to survive and be truly "super" has been to build a business rather than an image.

Susann Cokal

SEE ALSO: *Advertising; Banks, Tyra; Campbell, Naomi; Consumerism; Crawford, Cindy; Klein, Calvin; Moss, Kate.*

BIBLIOGRAPHY

Bellafante, Ginia; Georgia Harbison; and Belinda Luscombe. "The Runway Girls Take Off." *Time*, April 17, 1995, 66–68.

Gross, Michael. *Model: The Ugly Business of Beautiful Women.* New York: William Morrow, 1995.

Koda, Harold, and Yohannan Kohle. *The Model as Muse: Embodying Fashion.* New York: Metropolitan Museum of Art, 2009.

Kozar, Joy M. "Women's Responses to Fashion Media Images: A Study of Female Consumers Aged 30–59." *International Journal of Consumer Studies* 34, no. 3 (2010): 272–278.

Lieberman, Rhonda. "Supermodels." *Artforum* 31, no. 4 (1992): 8–9.

Marano, Hara Estroff. "Model Existence." *Psychology Today*, May 1, 1994, 50–58.

Parmentier, Marie-Agnès, and Eileen Fischer. "You Can't Always Get What You Want: Unsustainable Identity Projects in the Fashion System." *Consumption, Markets & Culture* 14, no. 1 (2011): 7–27.

Stein, Joel. "The Fall of the Supermodel." *Time*, November 9, 1998, 102–103.

Surf Music

Surf music, while not always about surfing, emerged out of the subculture created by surfers in Hawaii and California in the late 1940s and 1950s. Two distinct streams of surf music developed, one primarily instrumental, the other predominately vocal, each expressing a distinctive aspect of the surfer subculture. The sound was most prominent in the early and mid-1960s, when instrumental surf music was heard accompanying television shows such as *Hawaii Five-O* and vocal surf music by the Beach Boys topped the sales charts.

ORIGINS OF SURFING CULTURE

Although surfing as a form of recreation and sport developed in the nineteenth century as a Polynesian pastime, it was not until the early twentieth century that surfing caught on outside of Hawaii. Olympic swimming champion Duke Kahanamoku (who competed in the 1912 and 1920 Olympics) toured the mainland United States in the wake of his Olympic triumphs and created interest in surfing through exhibitions on both the East and West Coasts. Early in the twentieth century, surfboards were made usually of solid wood, but big-wave riders increasingly preferred hollow boards after Tom Blake introduced one in

The Ventures. *The Ventures scored a hit in 1964 with the surf-music staple "Walk, Don't Run."* MICHAEL OCHS ARCHIVES/GETTY IMAGES.

1928. Still, the lightest boards made of plywood weighed around fifty pounds, with big-wave boards weighing more than twice that. Blake introduced other design modifications, such as the addition of a tail fin, which aided in maneuvering.

World War II stalled surfing's development for the duration, then it transformed the sport as technological developments in plastic foams and resin revolutionized surfboard construction. Bob Simmons, a hydrodynamics student from Santa Monica, California, sandwiched polystyrene between two pieces of wood, wrapped the entire board in fiberglass, and sealed it with resin. The result was a lightweight, durable board that was shaped easily and could be maneuvered well with minimum experience. Postwar prosperity led to the development of local surfing communities in Southern California, Hawaii, and eastern Australia. For many of these surfers, dedication to the sport required them to maintain "open" work schedules that allowed them to hit the surf whenever it was good. This often meant many of them were unemployed or worked only during low periods in the surf. This preference for surf over employment, reinforced by traditional Hawaiian ideas of leisure, community, and nature, went against the grain of mainstream American postwar thinking, in which conformity and economic success were paramount.

Creating a counterculture of sorts, surfers not only promoted their sport but also a way of life. Tiki huts with palm-frond roofs began to appear on California beaches, with after-surf barbeques and campouts serving to bind this community together. *Surfer* magazine was created in 1960 to inform the surfing community of events, products, developments, and achievements. Surfing films portrayed spectacular rides from Hawaii and Australia to California and vice versa, but these documentaries, shot on 16-millimeter film, received little attention outside the surfing community. Bud Browne, the pioneer of the surf documentary, presented *The Big Surf*, *Hawaiian Surfing Movie*, and *Trip to Makaha*, all in the 1950s.

The surfing subculture was too small to have an impact on mainstream culture until writer Frederick Kohner penned a 1956 novel based on some of the exploits of his daughter Kathy on a Malibu beach, where she "hung out" with several prominent surfers, including Mickey Dora (one of the sport's first superstars), Billy Al Bengston (aka "Moondoggie"), and Terry "Tubesteak" Tracey. Tubesteak called Kathy a "girl-midget," as she was about five feet tall, and the name quickly transformed into "Gidget." The film *Gidget*, based on these stories, appeared in 1959, starring Sandra Dee and James Darren. Numerous sequels and knockoffs followed, such as *Gidget Goes Hawaiian* (1961), *Beach Party* (1963), and *Gidget Goes to Rome* (1963), *Muscle Beach Party* (1964), *Beach Blanket Bingo* (1965), and *How to Stuff a Wild Bikini* (1965).

THE DEVELOPMENT OF SURF MUSIC

The soundtracks for these movies were composed primarily of pop music with lyrics pertaining to the beach, but a new-sounding music also made an appearance in these films: surf music. Created by Dick Dale, "King of the Surf Guitar," surf music began as a musical attempt to re-create the sensation of riding a wave. Dale's combination of cascading licks, rapid playing, and a powerful bass line served as a perfect soundtrack for surf documentaries and occasionally turned up in Hollywood beach movies, but as with films based on surfing, the music also developed along two different lines. Surf music by instrumental groups such as Dick Dale and the Deltones, the Ventures, the Chantays, and the Surfaris found a devoted audience among surfers themselves, as did classic documentaries such as Bruce Brown's *The Endless Summer* (1964). Meanwhile, beach music by vocal groups such as Jan and Dean and the Beach Boys flooded the mainstream airwaves and, along with beach movies, represented the surfing subculture to most other Americans.

Instrumental surf music reached its widest audience with the Ventures' theme for the television series *Hawaii Five-O*. The group also had hits with "Walk, Don't Run" and "Perfidia" (both 1960). The Surfaris (from inland Glendora, California) are best known for their 1963 song "Wipe Out," characterized by the hysterical laugh and high-pitched exclamation "wipe out!" that opens the song. The Chantays reached number four on the sales charts with their classic "Pipeline," while Dick Dale and the Deltones continued their reign as the official cult band of the surf crowd with songs like "The Victor" (1964) and "Let's Go Trippin'" (1961).

These instrumentals took elements of popular music and transformed them by emphasizing the bass line and using the guitar as a melodic instead of rhythmic instrument. A good example of this is found in the Ventures' "Walk, Don't Run." Written and originally recorded by jazz guitarist Johnny Smith, who was inspired by a "walk, don't run" sign in a New York subway, the song was recorded by country guitarist Chet Atkins in 1957 as a lilting ballad. By adding a driving beat and bass line, the Ventures created a version that recalled elements of Atkins's guitar work plus jazz elements such as "bending" notes and a blue tonality, all with a rock-and-roll beat. The song peaked at number two on the sales charts in 1960, right behind another beach-inspired song, Brian Hyland's "Itsy Bitsy Teenie Weenie Yellow Polka Dot Bikini."

Despite the popularity of instrumental surf music, or perhaps because of it, vocal surf music became the more widely disseminated form of the genre. Although the music had little to do with the blazing guitars and heavy bass of Dick Dale and the Ventures, the lyrics of vocal surf music sought to capture the feel of the surfer subculture. "Surfin'" (1962), the first hit by a teen group from Hawthorne, California, called the Beach Boys, describes the dedication of surfers to their sport: "Surfin' is the only life, the only way for me." Written by non-surfer Brian Wilson and based mainly on stories from Beach Boy members and surfers Mike Love and Dennis Wilson, the songs of the Beach Boys presented an American youth market with an image of sunshine, beautiful girls, and surfing that was wholesome and superficial. In songs like "Surfin Safari'" (1962), "Surfin' USA" and "Surfer Girl" (1963), "Fun, Fun, Fun" and "I Get Around" (1964), "Help Me, Rhonda" and "California Girls" (1965), "Wouldn't It Be Nice" and "Good Vibrations" (1966), the leisure pursuits of young Southern Californians became a national industry.

Reinforced by other performers, such as Jan and Dean ("Surf City," 1963), and the beach movies of Frankie Avalon and Annette Funicello, the surfer subculture became a marketing tool used to sell not just entertainment but a whole range of products, such as clothing. Hang Ten, founded in 1961, produced clothing with its trademark symbol of two bare feet representing the act of hanging one's toes off the front end of a surfboard. Offshoot sports also developed, such as skateboarding, originally called "sidewalk surfing," and, in the 1980s, sailboarding.

Instrumental surf music witnessed a resurgence in the 1990s with the release of CD compilations of surf music and its use in new films such as Quentin Tarantino's *Pulp Fiction* (1994) and Bruce Brown's *The Endless Summer II* (1994), a sequel to the 1966 original. In addition, the television show *Hawaii Five-O* was revived in 2010, and CBS Music released a CD of the program's main theme and several original songs that artists recorded for the show. Among these were new versions of classic surf music.

Charles J. Shindo

SEE ALSO: *Atkins, Chet; Avalon, Frankie; The Beach Boys; Funicello, Annette;* Hawaii Five-O*;* Pulp Fiction*; Tarantino, Quentin.*

BIBLIOGRAPHY

Carroll, Nick, ed. *The Next Wave: The World of Surfing.* New York: Abbeville Press, 1991.

Chidester, Brian, and Domenic Priore. *Pop Surf Culture: Music, Design, Film, and Fashion from the Bohemian Surf Boom.* Santa Monica, CA: Santa Monica Press, 2008.

White, Timothy. *The Nearest Faraway Place: Brian Wilson, the Beach Boys, and the Southern California Experience.* New York: Henry Holt, 1994.

Survivor

The Mark Burnett–produced reality show *Survivor* premiered in the United States in 2000 to surprisingly high ratings and positive reviews, convincing CBS executives to air two seasons of the show each year since its third season. Originally created by Charlie Parsons of Great Britain for Swedish television in the late 1990s, the show pits a group of sixteen contestants against each other in a forty-day survival challenge set in a remote location, with the winner receiving a cash prize of $1 million. The premise has enjoyed worldwide popularity, but the American version has had the most successful run, with twenty-four seasons and a contract with CBS that will allow the show to continue at least through 2013.

With a motto of "outwit, outplay, outlast," *Survivor* emphasizes the contestants' evolving set of strategies and tactics for eliminating their competitors. Each season new heroes and villains emerge, and fans choose their favorite players based on cunning, skill, and personality. One of the most financially and critically successful reality programs of all time, *Survivor* is widely credited with initiating a wave of competition-based reality shows.

HOW IT WORKS

Survivor finds the contestants abandoned by boat or air in a secluded area, where they are met by the host, Jeff Probst, who separates the contestants into two to four teams (or "tribes") and explains the game's instructions. With no lodging provided, and only the barest necessities in the way of food and water readily available, the contestants must work as a team to set up camp and survive in extreme conditions, including heat and rain, while garnering rewards such as food, temporary respite from the grueling conditions, or immunity from elimination by winning challenges related to their survival. After each elimination challenge, the losing tribe must regroup in a "tribal council" and select a member to leave the tribe.

As the number of participants dwindles, the producers make adjustments by reassigning participants to other tribes or by merging tribes together. When only twelve participants remain, tribes are eliminated entirely and the contestants compete as individuals. At this stage, each eliminated contestant becomes part of a jury that determines the "ultimate survivor." The challenges continue until the final three contestants face the jury, which votes first to eliminate one of the three and then to choose a winner between the final two. Probst tallies the votes and names the winner on a live "reunion" show.

During the early stages of *Survivor*, the reward and immunity challenges provide each tribe the opportunity to develop as a team and learn the abilities of each individual. After the teams merge, the challenges become individual, with prizes and immunity the individual's goal. Many contestants then attempt to form alliances or otherwise manipulate the other contestants, a technique that is not only allowed but encouraged. The physical challenges test endurance, strength, and agility, with the winner being the one who remains in competition for the longest period of time. While the early team challenges are typically puzzle-oriented, they usually consist of physical and mental segments, with the team sharing the responsibilities based on each other's strengths. One of the individual challenges that is most popular with viewers consists of sampling local cuisine that is unusual to the contestants.

To maintain interest in *Survivor*, producers have introduced several new features to the show over the years, including hidden immunity idols and Exile Island. A hidden immunity idol allows its finder a measure of safety as long as the finder plays the idol before a tribal council vote. Exile Island allows eliminated tribe members the opportunity to play their way back into the merged tribe by defeating fellow eliminated members in challenges similar to the rewards and immunity challenges played during the course of the season.

KEYS TO RATINGS SUCCESS

Part of what makes *Survivor* a success is the producers' ability to choose contestants who appeal to the viewers. Several contestants have parlayed their popularity on the program into a show-business career. Some, such as Colby Donaldson (*Top Shots*) and Rob Mariano (*Around the World in 80 Ways*) have found success as hosts and stars of other programs; others have moved into the anchor role on newscasts or into behind-the-scenes production roles. Most continue to use their celebrity status to raise money for charities through sponsorships and appearances.

Several contestants have been injured or have been unable to compete due to illness. Contestants are not supposed to receive assistance from the crew, but when an injury occurs the host can intervene and call in medics who determine whether the contestant may continue. Despite this "no involvement" rule, Russell Hantz (runner-up of season nineteen and a notorious villain of the show) has stated that he followed the camera's progress to find immunity idols, and many other contestants have hinted that the conditions are not as harsh as they are portrayed to be and that they sometimes received assistance from the crew. In addition, some fans believe Probst asks leading questions during the tribal council in an attempt to influence voting.

During the show's run of more than twenty seasons on American television, the producers have often faced criticism about the "sameness" of the program. To rekindle viewer interest the producers have used devices such as "all-star" editions and "hero versus villain" themes to bring back old contestants who were fan favorites. And by changing locations each season, the show exposes viewers to a variety of unique cultures and locales. Different twists such as Exile Island and special immunity idols also help keep viewers interested. The formula appears to be working. *Survivor*'s large audience places it among the top twenty programs on television, despite a proliferation of copycat shows.

Linda Martindale

SEE ALSO: *Game Shows; Reality Television; Television.*

BIBLIOGRAPHY

Burnett, Mark, and Martin Dugard. *Survivor: The Ultimate Game.* New York: TV Books, 2000.

Gerrig, Richard J., ed. *The Psychology of "Survivor": Overanalyze, Overemote, Overcompensate: Leading Psychologists Take an Unauthorized Look at the Most Elaborate Psychological Experiment Ever Conducted—"Survivor"!* Dallas, TX: BenBella Books, 2007.

Smith, Matthew J., and Andrew F. Wood. *"Survivor" Lessons: Essays on Communication and Reality Television.* Jefferson, NC: McFarland, 2003.

Susann, Jacqueline *(1918–1974)*

Jacqueline Susann was a novelist who wrote only three works of fiction. Her first novel, *Valley of the Dolls*, is one of the ten most widely distributed books of all time. Susann is remembered as the first writer to become a media celebrity through her aggressive promotional appearances on television talk shows.

Born in Philadelphia in 1918, Susann moved to New York in 1936 to pursue a career in show business. In 1939 she married Irving Mansfield and worked as both a model and an actress, appearing on Broadway and in road company productions, including *The Women* in 1937. After fifteen years, however, she still had not hit it big in show business, and she turned to writing. In 1963 Bernard Geis Associates published her first book, *Every Night, Josephine!* about her beloved pet poodle. "According to [Geis], *Josephine!* was 'a modest success—number ten on the *Time* magazine best seller list, which isn't bad. I think we sold about thirty-five thousand to forty thousand copies,'" writes author Barbara Seaman in her book, *Lovely Me: The Life of Jacqueline Susann.*

In 1966 Bernard Geis Associates published Susann's second book and first novel, *Valley of the Dolls*, in which she channeled her show business knowledge into a combination of romance, lurid sex, and sensationalism, that, as the publishing blurb used to say, ripped the lid off the entertainment industry. The book quickly became a best seller, remaining number one on the *New York Times*' best-sellers list for a record-breaking twenty-eight

Jacqueline Susann. *Jacqueline Susann poses in her New York apartment in 1969, during the height of her celebrity.* © BETTMANN/CORBIS.

weeks and eventually selling more than thirty million copies worldwide. Susann and her press agent husband greatly helped the book become successful by launching the kind of hard-sell promotional campaign that had previously been exploited only by Hollywood. The first author to effectively exploit the television talk show circuit, Susann became as famous as her book. In a legendary media incident in 1969, she and author Truman Capote traded insults during separate appearances on the popular late-night television show *The Tonight Show Starring Johnny Carson*. Capote delivered his now infamous jibe that Susann reminded him of "a truck driver in drag."

In 1969 Simon & Schuster published Susann's second novel, *The Love Machine*. In 1973 William Morrow published her third and final novel, *Once Is Not Enough*. Each novel sold more than five million copies.

In late 1962, at the age of forty-four, Susann was diagnosed with breast cancer and had a mastectomy. Her illness was never announced publicly. Also concealed from the world at large was the fact that Susann and Mansfield's only son, Guy, was autistic. While Susann pushed the envelope with the content in her fiction, she adhered to what she perceived as the expectations of her era in real life, believing the public demanded celebrities who conformed to a positive, if manufactured, image, no matter what the actuality of their private lives. Susann lost her battle with breast cancer in September 1974.

ADAPTATIONS AND SEQUELS

Valley of the Dolls, a lurid, sudsy saga of three young women coping none too well with the challenges of show business, remains Susann's key work. Aside from its delirious camp excesses, the cult status of the 1967 film version (in which Susann briefly appears) was instantly certified when Susan Hayward replaced Judy Garland shortly after production commenced, and retrospectively by costar Sharon Tate's brutal murder by cult leader Charles Manson and his followers. Film critic Leonard Maltin called the film a "BOMB . . . terribly written, acted, and directed." Maltin also called an updated and expanded four-hour 1981 television remake "superior to the 1967 theatrical version." A 1970 in-name-only sequel, the equally cultish *Beyond the Valley of the Dolls*, directed by Russ Meyer, took Susann's hyperbole into the realm of deliberate (and violent) camp.

In late 1997 publisher Grove Press reissued the long-out-of-print *Valley of the Dolls*, peaking a mainstream Susann renaissance. The revival also included a New York City drag stage production of *Dolls*, and the trendy popularity of gay smart-set *VOD (Valley of the Dolls)* parties featuring jelly beans in the form of Susann's famous Valium pills (or "dolls").

In 1998 *Lovely Me: The Life of Jacqueline Susann* was made into a television movie titled *Scandalous Me: The Jacqueline Susann Story*. In 2000 Bette Midler and Nathan Lane starred as Susann and Mansfield in a film titled *Isn't She Great?* which flopped at the box office. In 2001 *Jacqueline Susann's Shadow of the Dolls* was published. Written by Rae Lawrence, who used notes for a sequel left behind by Susann, the novel picks up with the *Valley of the Dolls* characters in the late 1980s when they are older, although the only real change are the drugs of choice, now Valium and Xanax. In 2002 Marlo Thomas played Susann in the Broadway play *Paper Doll*. But perhaps the most bizarre manifestation of Susann-mania was an "interview" with the deceased author published in *Interview* magazine in October 1997 and based on a séance involving drag performer Lypsinka and a medium named Miss Eek.

Author and screenwriter Nora Ephron has commented on Susann's work:

> With the possible exception of *Cosmopolitan* magazine, no one writes about sadism in modern man and masochism in modern woman quite so horribly and accurately as Jacqueline Susann. *Valley [of the Dolls]* had a message that had a magnetic appeal for women readers: it described the standard female fantasy—of going to the big city, striking it rich, meeting fabulous men—and went on to show every reader that she was far better off than the heroines in the book. . . . It was, essentially, a morality tale.

Art Forum editor Sydney Pokorny gushed, "She's camp, she's glam, she's frivolous. . . . She understood the appeal of modern celebrity better than anyone else (except maybe [artist Andy] Warhol) . . . and on top of it all her heroines were always powerful, independent women. Jackie is a prophet of pop culture." Susann herself put it this way: "People who read me can get off the subway and go home feeling better about their own crappy lives, and luckier than the people they've been reading about."

Ross Care

SEE ALSO: *Broadway; Camp; Cancer; Capote, Truman; Carson, Johnny; Celebrity;* Cosmopolitan*; Garland, Judy; Hayward, Susan; Hollywood; Manson, Charles; Midler, Bette; The* New York Times*; Thomas, Marlo;* Time*;* The Tonight Show*; Valium.*

BIBLIOGRAPHY

Carvajal, Doreen. "Pink Trash—Camp and Glam and Still Badly Dressed, Jacqueline Susann Stages a Comeback." *New York Times*, July 27, 1997.

Korda, Michael. "Wasn't She Great?" *New Yorker*, August 14, 1995, 66–72.

Mansfield, Irving, and Jean Libman Block. *Life with Jackie*. New York: Bantam Books, 1983.

Seaman, Barbara. *Lovely Me: The Life of Jacqueline Susann*. New York: Morrow, 1987.

Twitchell, James B. *Carnival Culture: The Trashing of Taste in America*. New York: Columbia University Press, 1992.

Sushi

In the 1960s most people outside Japan thought of sushi as an exotic, even intimidating, delicacy. In the 1970s, however, the California roll, which combined crab and cucumber sticks with a West Coast favorite—the avocado—appeared, and by the 1990s sushi had become almost as popular in the United States as pizza and nachos. Sushi bars opened in U.S. cities and then in suburbs, and eventually shoppers could pick up prepackaged sushi in grocery stores. Over time many diners graduated from the California roll to explore the extensive array of dishes that went by the name of *sushi*.

All varities of sushi share one thing in common: a sticky short-grained rice mixed with sweetened vinegar. Beyond these basic ingredients sushi takes many forms. Probably the best-known style is *maki-zushi*, or rolled sushi. In this preparation the rice is laid on a layer of pressed black seaweed, called *nori*, and topped with other ingredients; it is then rolled into a cylindrical shape with the aid of a bamboo mat and sliced into portions. Fresh, uncooked slices of fish such as tuna, salmon, and yellowtail are often used in sushi, and some versions also include vegetables; others are completely vegetarian. The rolls may be thin or fat, or they may be shaped by hand into cones. The *nori* can be placed on the inside or the outside of the roll. Sushi is typically served with soy sauce for dipping, along with wasabi (a hot Japanese horseradish) and pickled ginger.

Among other popular styles of sushi are *nigiri-zushi*, in which the fish or other filling is placed on top of a mound of rice formed by hand, and *inari*, which is usually made of sushi rice wrapped in tofu and deep-fried. Japanese chefs often combine local ingredients to create regional specialties, and it was this tradition that led a Los Angeles chef to create the California roll.

The origins of sushi probably date back many centuries, but the version known today got its start as a casual, quickly prepared food in nineteenth-century Japan. It evolved into a gourmet delicacy, found favor in the United States, and then spread across other parts of the world. Today sushi is widely available, whether as an inexpensive snack, a satisfying meal, or a luxurious indulgence. The popularity of sushi, however, may be threatened as the supply of suitable fish becomes depleted because of overfishing and environmental changes.

Cynthia Giles

SEE ALSO: *Fast Food; Foodies; Gourmet Grocery Stores.*

BIBLIOGRAPHY

Corson, Trevor. *The Story of Sushi: An Unlikely Saga of Fish and Rice*. New York: Harper Perennial, 2008.

Dekura, Hideo; Brigid Treloar; and Ryuichi Yoshii. *The Complete Book of Sushi*. Boston: Periplus Editions, 2004.

Susskind, David *(1920–1987)*

David Susskind was one of the few successful television producers to also star in front of the camera. Throughout his long career he worked with numerous celebrities while producing television shows, movies, and plays, and he eventually hosted his own talk show that lasted for almost thirty years and earned multiple Emmy Awards.

Born in New York in December 1920, Susskind began his career in the late 1940s as an agent, eventually representing stars such as Jerry Lewis and Dinah Shore. After forming Talent Associates with Alfred Levy, he started to package live dramas before becoming a full-time producer in the mid-1950s. Over the course of more than thirty years, he produced hundreds of television dramas for such series as *The DuPont Show of the Month* (1957–1961) and *Armstrong Circle Theatre* (1950–1963); more than a dozen movies, including *Raisin in the Sun* (1961) and *Alice Doesn't Live Here Anymore* (1974); and numerous stage plays. Aspiring to be as dominant a figure in television as Cecil B. DeMille was in motion pictures, Susskind especially cherished prestige specials, and among his award winners were *The Ages of Man* (1966), with John Gielgud; *Death of a Salesman* (1966), starring Lee J. Cobb; and *Eleanor and Franklin* (1976), with Edward Hermann.

In 1958 Susskind became a celebrity in front of the camera when he obtained his own talk series, *Open End*, which was broadcast late at night and had unlimited time to examine an issue. The brash host liked to confront his guests, exemplified by his heated exchange with Soviet Premier Nikita Khrushchev. His often-controversial series, which was trimmed to two hours in the early 1960s, covered a wide range of topics, from such weighty issues as racism and organized crime to tabloid fare, including astrology and sex change operations. Retitled *The David Susskind Show* in 1967, the program continued for twenty years until its host's death in February 1987. In 2010 the first major biography of Susskind was published, portraying him as an intellectual, a womanizer, and a manic depressive. In a *New York Times* review of the book, Caryn James described Susskind as "one of television's loudest, most provocative lions."

Ron Simon

SEE ALSO: *Daytime Talk Shows;* Death of a Salesman*; DeMille, Cecil B.; Emmy Awards; Lewis, Jerry; Shore, Dinah; Television.*

BIBLIOGRAPHY

Asinof, Eliot. *Bleeding between the Lines*. New York: Holt, Rinehart, and Winston, 1979.

Battaglio, Stephen. *David Susskind: A Televised Life*. New York: St. Martin's Press, 2010.

Browne, Pat, and Ray B. Browne. *The Guide to United States Popular Culture*. Bowling Green, OH: Bowling Green State University Popular Press, 2001.

Gehman, Richard. "David Susskind Wants to Be Goliath." *TV Guide*, November 23, 1963, 15–19.

Swaggart, Jimmy *(1935–)*

A leading televangelist of the 1980s, Jimmy Lee Swaggart became an American celebrity whose rise and fall were both comic and tragic. The self-trained piano virtuoso's hot gospel stylings were barely distinguishable from the rock-and-roll standards performed by his cousin, Jerry Lee Lewis, a popular music icon. Instead of a recording career, Swaggart chose preaching, evolving a pulpit manner characterized by physical gyrations, abundant tears, and impassioned biblical declamations.

Scorning the bland sentimentality of other religious opinion makers, he rejected the ecumenical spirit of Billy Graham, the dean of late-twentieth-century evangelists. Always tough on sin, especially that of a sensual nature, Swaggart delivered fire-and-brimstone sermons. Though he imitated the southern tent evangelists of his youth, he learned to masterfully use media—first radio and later television. Often regarded as the most effective of the televangelists of the 1970s and 1980s, he had a blend of show business hucksterism and old-fashioned Holy Ghost revivalism that perpetuated a long tradition of American folk evangelism.

Born in 1935 near Ferriday, Louisiana, Swaggart was the son of a lay preacher in the charismatic Assemblies of God. Derisively called Holy Rollers in the early twentieth century, members of the denomination entered the middle class after

World War II. Their spirit-filled devotional style began to influence the older, mainline churches, both Protestant and Catholic.

Young Swaggart started preaching at age six, though he was not born again until two years later. Offered a recording contract around the time his cousin and best friend Jerry Lee was becoming famous, Swaggart vowed to use his musical talents only in the service of the Lord. He even asked God to strike him with paralysis should he ever perform "the devil's music." By the time he was twenty-three, he was regularly traveling the gospel-preaching circuit. His wife, Frances, remained a full partner throughout his ministry, and their two-year-old son grew up to become his father's lieutenant. Backcountry evangelism, always as much entertainment as religion, put Swaggart's temperament and talent to good use.

By 1964, despite success as a traveling preacher, he yearned for more respectability and was properly ordained by the Assemblies of God. He then took his "crusades" into cities. He inaugurated a gospel recording career and eventually sold more than fifteen million recordings. In 1973 he added a weekly television program, and by the end of the 1980s, his telecasts and publications were reaching a national audience of almost two million in fifty-three countries. Like other media preachers, Swaggart sought to anchor his operations, choosing Baton Rouge, Louisiana, as home base and building the Family Worship Center to seat 7,500. Perhaps to compensate for his own meager schooling, he followed the precedent of other celebrity preachers such as Aimee Semple McPherson and Oral Roberts by founding a Bible college to train Christian workers for domestic and foreign service.

Jimmy Swaggart. *Jimmy Swaggart appears confident at the end of a news conference in January 1989 at which he denied sex charges against him.* AP IMAGES.

Politically conservative and openly judgmental, Swaggart made enemies with his fierce and even personal attacks. Among his targets were Roman Catholics, lukewarm Protestants, social liberals, and fellow preachers with moral failings. He seemed oblivious to his own vulnerability when in early 1987 he caused a national scandal, which came to be known as Gospelgate, by accusing rival televangelist Jim Bakker of adultery. Though the charges were easily substantiated, it did not take long for Swaggart's enemies to publicly expose his engagement in a series of voyeuristic acts with a prostitute in a Louisiana motel.

Swaggart chose to own up to his wrongdoing by labeling it sin rather than inappropriate behavior. On February 21, 1988, he gave the premier performance of his life, speaking to a capacity audience at his Family Worship Center. His lips quivered as he weepingly apologized to his wife, his son, his daughter-in-law, and the Assemblies of God—which he attested "helped bring the Gospel to my little beleaguered town, when my family was lost without Jesus." Finally he apologized to Jesus himself and asked to be renewed by his cleansing blood.

The Assemblies of God eventually defrocked Swaggart as more of his transgressions surfaced. Nevertheless, his ministry continued throughout the 1990s, though his force was largely spent and the impressive evangelistic compound he built, in disrepair. As other televangelists made admissions of wrongdoing and were investigated for financial irregularities, the influence of the electronic church declined. Swaggart never regained his former popularity, and his career became part of twentieth-century religious lore. In 2004 he caused an international uproar when he stated in a televised sermon on same-sex marriage that he would kill any gay man who looked at him romantically, intimating that God would find such actions justifiable. He was subsequently forced to apologize for his statements.

Allene Phy-Olsen

SEE ALSO: *Bakker, Jim, and Tammy Faye; Gay and Lesbian Marriage; Gay Men; Gospel Music; Graham, Billy; Lewis, Jerry Lee; McPherson, Aimee Semple; Megachurches; Radio; Rock and Roll; Sex Scandals; Televangelism; Television; World War II.*

BIBLIOGRAPHY

Balmer, Randall. "Still Wrestling with the Devil: A Visit with Jimmy Swaggart Ten Years after His Fall." *Christianity Today*, March 2, 1998, 31–36.

Bauer, Susan Wise. *The Art of the Public Grovel: Sexual Sin and Public Confession in America*. Princeton, NJ: Princeton University Press, 2008.

Miller, Brett A. *Divine Apology: The Discourse of Religious Image Restoration*. Westport, CT: Praeger, 2002.

Nauer, Barbara. *Jimmy Swaggart: Dead Man Rising*. Baton Rouge, LA: Glory Arts, 1998.

Packard, William. *Evangelism in America: From Tents to TV*. New York: Paragon House, 1988.

Reid, Daniel G.; Robert Dean Linder; Bruce E. Shelley; et al. *Dictionary of Christianity in America*. Downers Grove, IL: Intervarsity Press, 1990.

Swaggart, Jimmy, and R. P. Lamb. *To Cross a River*. Baton Rouge, LA: Jimmy Swaggart Ministries, 1984.

Wright, Lawrence. *Saints and Sinners*. New York: Vintage Books, 1995.

Swann, Lynn *(1952–)*

During the late 1970s, a period when professional football players were joining the ranks of U.S. pop-culture icons, wide receiver Lynn Swann was at the peak of his highly successful nine-year career in the National Football League (NFL). Swann played on four Super Bowl–championship teams for the Pittsburgh Steelers when that team was dominating NFL play. His trademark was his ability to make acrobatic catches, especially at key junctures of important ballgames. Ironically, this athletic, gutsy player attributed his prowess on the gridiron to the skills he honed in the many dance classes he took as a youth, including ballet.

Swann, who was born in Tennessee and grew up in California, attended the University of Southern California, where he played on two Rose Bowl teams (including the 1972 championship team) and was a unanimous choice for first-team All-America honors in his senior year. The Pittsburgh Steelers selected him in the first round of the 1974 NFL draft.

Swann turned in a good performance as a rookie with the Steelers, where he led the NFL in punt returns and shared time at the receiver position. He became a starter in his sophomore season, and the team made the playoffs. In the American Football Conference (AFC) Championship game against the Oakland Raiders, Swann suffered a concussion that put in doubt his ability to play in the Super Bowl. Despite the risks, Swann decided to play, with spectacular results. He was named Super Bowl X's Most Valuable Player as Pittsburgh defeated the Dallas Cowboys 21–17, becoming only the third team ever to win back-to-back Super Bowls. Swann caught four passes for a total of 161 receiving yards. The highlight of the game was his catch of a 64-yard touchdown pass from quarterback Terry Bradshaw for a game-deciding score with just minutes remaining. Swann also made a diving 53-yard catch during the second quarter, a play that is considered by many to be one of the greatest in Super Bowl history.

The Steelers returned to the Super Bowl in 1979—once again against the Cowboys—with Swann catching seven passes for 124 yards, including an 18-yard touchdown pass from Bradshaw that was the decisive play in the Steelers' 35–31 victory The following year, his performance in Super Bowl XIV was the culmination of his best professional season, in which he caught sixty-one passes for a total of 880 yards and scored eleven touchdowns. In the third quarter of Pittsburgh's 31–19 Super Bowl victory over the Los Angeles Rams, Swann caught a 47-yard touchdown pass from Bradshaw in a play in which he leapt between two defenders to catch the ball before reaching the end zone.

Part of Swann's great success came from his being teamed with another wide receiver drafted in 1974, John Stallworth, who formed another threat at the wide-receiver position and kept other teams from focusing all of their attention on Swann. The two men gave Bradshaw an inviting choice of targets. As Swann notes in Lou Sahadi's *Super Steelers: The Making of a Dynasty*, "John [Stallworth] and I are both moving targets. It's just up to Terry to hit us. What's happened is that we developed a remarkable, almost undefinable rapport among the three of us."

The NFL's Man of the Year in 1981, Swann ranks second in Super Bowl receiving yards (364) and touchdowns (three) to San Francisco great Jerry Rice. During his playing career, he was named to the NFL Pro Bowl three times. He was considered for induction into the Professional Football Hall of Fame in Canton, Ohio, for thirteen consecutive years before he was finally voted in in 2001. Regarding Swann's initial failure to be inducted into the Hall of Fame, his teammate Joe Greene noted "Lynn Swann didn't have the stats, but he sure as heck had an impact. . . . He didn't play a long time, but he made an impact. . . . He played a lot of big games. I'm a great Lynn Swann fan. He deserves a lot more consideration."

Following his retirement from professional football in 1982, Swann worked as a sports broadcaster for the ABC network, covering football as well as a diverse array of other sports, ranging from rugby to dogsled racing. From 2002 to 2005 he served as the chair of the President's Council on Physical Fitness and Sports. Swann left broadcasting in 2006 to run for governor of Pennsylvania as a Republican candidate, an election he lost. He has also been active in a wide variety of charitable and other causes. He has served as the national spokesperson for the Big Brothers and Big Sisters of America since 1980 and on the board of trustees of the Pittsburgh Ballet Theater, for which he created a youth scholarship. Swann has also competed in several marathons and had a cameo as a television announcer in the 1991 movie *The Last Boy Scout.*

Jason George

SEE ALSO: *Ballet; Bradshaw, Terry; College Football; The Dallas Cowboys; National Football League (NFL); The Oakland Raiders; The Pittsburgh Steelers; Professional Football; Sports Heroes; Super Bowl.*

BIBLIOGRAPHY

Garner, Joe, and Bob Costas. *100 Yards of Glory: The Greatest Moments in NFL History.* New York: Houghton Mifflin Harcourt, 2011.

Sahadi, Lou. *Super Steelers: The Making of a Dynasty.* New York: Times Books, 1980.

Swatch Watches

The Swatch watch was released in 1983 as a response by the Swiss watch industry to the encroaching Japanese influence on the market for inexpensive, high-tech timepieces. The first Swatch was made of slim plastic with only fifty-one components, allowing it to be sold cheaply. By the 1990s the Swatch had become the most successful wristwatch brand of all time. The key to the popularity of Swatch was its collectibility. By rotating designs and discontinuing popular lines at key moments, the Swatch company was able to give their watches a cult status, especially among young people. Although the popularity of the watches was at its peak in the 1980s, Swatch has continued to remain successful into the twenty-first century by adding new varieties. These included Irony (a metal Swatch), Swatch SKIN Chrono (the world's thinnest watch), and Swatch Beat (featuring Internet Time).

Deborah Broderson

SEE ALSO: *Consumerism; Timex Watches.*

BIBLIOGRAPHY

Hall, John. *Bringing New Products to Market: The Art and Sci-*

ence of Creating Winners. New York: AMACOM, 1991.
Swatch AG. *Pop Swatch*. Biel, Switzerland: Author, 1994.

Sweatshirt

The humble gray cotton sweatshirt with fleece lining was one of the last garments to come out of the gym locker and into the realm of high fashion. This wonderfully practical sports cover-up was determinedly unglamorous: it was affiliated with no one sport in particular; its heavy cotton tended to lose shape over time and, unlike jeans, move away from sexual outline to a gray blob.

Technology, which around the early 1980s introduced just enough synthetic stretch (generally less than 5 percent) to maintain shape, collar, and cuffs without compromising the integrity and feel of cotton, breathed some life into the sweatshirt. In the early 1980s Norma Kamali made a woman's jumpsuit ensemble for day or evening in gray sweatshirt material; by 1986 Emporio Armani styling showed hooded sweatshirts with sports jackets; and in 1987 Quincy Jones appeared in an American Express advertisement in a short-sleeved sweatshirt. However, the sweatshirt may have never made it to the next level without actress Jennifer Beals, who wears cutup sweatshirts in the 1983 movie *Flashdance*. This sparked the do-it-yourself sweatshirt trends in the 1980s and early 1990s.

The variety of colors and the material's ability to be screen-printed with a logo have made it ubiquitous. Popular styles include zippers and hoods, and sweatshirt material has also been used to make other clothing items, such as skirts, pants, and blazers. Though they have become a staple piece of apparel, sweatshirts remain in the domain of informal or casual wear and are especially common among young people. In the early 2010s, the sweatshirt came under fire in the United States and United Kingdom because of its association with rebellion and rioting. It provoked further dialogue after the 2012 shooting death in Florida of an unarmed youth whose hooded sweatshirt was perceived to be threatening. Much like the meteoric rise in popularity of casual clothing such as jeans, sweatshirts have endured scandal, progress in manufacturing, and fashion evolution. In other words, the sweatshirt does not appear to be going away any time soon.

Richard Martin

SEE ALSO: *Armani, Giorgio; Flashdance Style; Hoodies.*

BIBLIOGRAPHY

Martin, Richard, and Harold Koda. *Jocks and Nerds: Men's Style in the Twentieth Century*. New York: Rizzoli, 1989.
Wilson, Denis. "A Look under the Hoodie." *New York Times*, December 23, 2006.

Swift, Taylor *(1989–)*

Taylor Swift is an American country singer whose crossover appeal made her a record-breaking star before she turned twenty-one. Her self-titled first album, which was released in 2006, claimed a position in the Top 10 on the Billboard 200 album chart and established Swift as a youthful singer of original and deeply personal songs. Her follow-up, *Fearless* (2008), held the number one position on that chart for more than two months, an achievement that led to her becoming the best-selling musical artist in any genre in 2008. Despite her success, Swift seemingly remains unjaded and squeaky clean. She has not fallen victim to the substance abuse problems and scandals that have derailed the careers of other young stars, leading some to mockingly christen her "Little Miss Perfect." But mothers accompany their daughters to her sold-out concerts, confident that Swift's lyrics will be PG, and seasoned music critics have deemed her "sweet and classy."

Swift was born on December 13, 1989, in Wyomissing, Pennsylvania. Exposed to a variety of musical genres, she was captivated by country music from her first LeAnn Rimes album. The music of the Dixie Chicks, Shania Twain, and Faith Hill only strengthened her attraction to the genre. Swift also wrote poetry from an early age, winning a national poetry contest in the fourth grade. By the time she was ten, she was performing at local fairs and festivals. Her first public performance of note came the following year, when she sang the national anthem at a Philadelphia 76ers basketball game.

Swift was serious enough about a career in music that her family had moved to Tennessee by the time she entered her teens. At fourteen she became the youngest staff writer in the history of Sony Tree music publishers. In 2005 she became the first artist signed by Big Machine Records, an independent label founded by Scott Borchetta, a former executive for DreamWorks Records.

In 2006 and 2007 her debut single, "Tim McGraw," stayed on the Billboard country chart for thirty-five weeks, reaching number six on the country singles chart. The song won critical praise for its song craft and for Swift's delivery. The album, which sold 39,000 copies the first week it was released, eventually claimed the number one spot on the top country albums chart and number five on the Billboard 200. It has been recognized as the longest-charting album (158 weeks) by a female country artist in the era of Nielsen SoundScan (a sales-counting system established in 1991). Swift wrote or cowrote with Liz Rose, an experienced song editor, all the songs on the album.

Her second album, *Fearless*, debuted in the top position on the album charts, selling more than half a million copies in its first week. The unparalleled success of the album, the first in music history to produce twelve Top 40 hits, made Swift the top-selling musical artist of 2008 and the first artist in the history of Nielsen SoundScan to have two albums (*Fearless* and *Taylor Swift*) in the Top 10 on the year-end album chart. Commercial success was accompanied by critical praise for her professional and honest songwriting.

The year following the release of *Fearless*, Swift garnered a string of honors. She became the youngest musical guest to host *Saturday Night Live*. The Academy of Country Music awarded her top honors for female vocalist, video ("Love Story"), and album (*Fearless*) and presented her with the Crystal Milestone Award, which is given for outstanding achievement in country music. (Swift is only the second artist to receive the prestigious award; Garth Brooks won it in 2007.) Awards from Country Music Television and Teen Choice followed, but it was her win for Best Female Video for "You Belong with Me" at the MTV Video Music Awards that proved history making in two ways. Swift was the first country singer in history to capture an MTV Video Music Award, but the significance of that moment was lost when Kanye West broke into Swift's acceptance speech, took the microphone from her, and announced that Beyoncé Knowles should have won the award for "Single Ladies."

Despite the furor surrounding the incident, it was scarcely more than a blip in Swift's career. In January 2010 *Fearless* won the Grammy for Album of the Year. At twenty she was the youngest artist to win that award. She also won Grammys for Best Country Album, Best Country Song ("White Horse," with cocomposer Rose), and Best Female Country Vocal Performance ("White Horse"). The following month, she made her feature-film debut in Garry Marshall's romantic comedy *Valentine's Day*. Her third studio album, *Speak Now*, was released in October 2010. Eleven songs from *Speak Now* charted on the Billboard Hot 100, setting a record for the greatest number of simultaneous entries to chart from a single album. She surpassed Barbra Streisand, Diana Ross, Mary J. Blige, Whitney Houston, and Janet Jackson to claim seventh place among women singers with the most Hot 100 hits.

At the 2011 Billboard Women in Music celebration, Swift became the youngest woman to be named the magazine's Woman of the Year, an award that annually honors "the achievements of a trailblazing female recording artist during the past 12 months and acknowledges her overall success and leadership in the music business." The award followed a year in which Swift had toured successfully worldwide and, according to Nielsen SoundScan, become the biggest-selling artist of the year in album sales. As of the end of 2011, she ranks among the top five in digital track sales. She has used her status to market cosmetics, fashions, and dolls and to raise money and awareness for clean water, literacy, and disaster relief.

Wylene Rholetter

SEE ALSO: *Brooks, Garth; Country Music; Houston, Whitney; Jackson, Janet; Knowles, Beyoncé; Marshall, Garry; MTV; Pop Music;* Saturday Night Live; *Streisand, Barbra; Top 40; Twain, Mark; West, Kanye.*

BIBLIOGRAPHY

Grigoriadis, Vanessa. "The Very Pink, Very Perfect Life of Taylor Swift." *Rolling Stone*, March 5, 2009, 44–51.

Roland, Tom. "How Sparks Fly." *Billboard*, December 2011, 22–26.

"Swift, Taylor." *Current Biography Yearbook, 2010*. New York: H.W. Wilson, 2010.

"Taylor Swift Named Billboard's Woman of the Year." *Billboard*, October 2001, 6.

Swimming Pools

Swimming pools have frequently reflected the greater social tensions in American society, often mirroring distinct dividing lines according to class, race, and ethnicity. In 1988 a local dispute in East Hampton, Long Island, received national attention. An affluent couple was threatening to sue their town for refusing them a permit to build a second swimming pool at their oceanfront home. While the dispute hinged on issues of zoning restrictions and environmental protection, the story was widely reported due to its almost comical justification of Thorstein Veblen's 1899 critique of the "leisure class." If one backyard pool is an emblem of comfort and leisure, two pools at an oceanfront home exemplify conspicuous consumption run amok.

At the same time, a different sort of swimming pool controversy was raging in Greenpoint, New York. Residents of this Brooklyn neighborhood bitterly disagreed about what should be done with the crumbling remains of the McCarren Park municipal pool. Some in the community, especially the Latino and African American residents, wanted the pool restored to its former splendor. Built in 1936, this enormous pool, which could accommodate 6,800 swimmers at a time, had served as a recreation resort for locals who were unable to afford membership at private pools. According to the *New York Times*, the pool had been "the hub of the working-class neighborhood's summertime social life." Other area residents, most of whom were white, wanted the pool closed permanently or rebuilt on a much smaller scale. They feared that such a large public pool would become a locus for urban crime.

These two episodes reveal the diverse and often discordant cultural meanings Americans attach to swimming pools. Private pools symbolize, sometimes in an extreme way, the "good life," connoting material comfort and leisure. Public pools, however, evoke distinctly different images. Some of the residents of Greenpoint associated public pools with urban decay and social disorder, while others associated a renovated pool with a rejuvenated and vibrant community life. These contradictory cultural meanings date back to the first swimming pools built in America and highlight some of the successes and failures of twentieth-century American society.

BEGINNINGS

Athletic clubs, colleges, and wealthy homeowners built the first private swimming pools in America during the Gilded Age. These pools were used for both sport and leisure, which at the time were the almost exclusive domain of the well-to-do. Early public swimming pools were built in and around large northern cities, serving distinct purposes for different segments of society. In 1897 Brookline, Massachusetts, opened the first municipal pool. Like most early public pools, it was located within a bathhouse. Progressive reformers and municipal leaders viewed these swimming pools as public health institutions and intended them to promote cleanliness among the nation's growing population of urban poor. Gradually, public pools evolved from baths to fitness institutions; they had become recreation and leisure facilities by the second decade of the twentieth century.

Social and cultural conflict dominated the history of swimming pools in America during the first half of the twentieth century. The vast majority of pools during this period were public. They were intensely contested civic spaces, and controversies raged over where pools should be built, who should be allowed to use them, and how they should be used. Debates over these issues reflected the dominant tensions in American society. These racial and class tensions, often obscured in other areas of life, appeared with striking clarity and definition at public pools, because Americans perceived them to be intimate and potentially hazardous spaces. Swimming in a pool necessitated exposing one's body; it brought swimmers visually and physically into intimate contact with one another. Swimming also exposed people to the dirt and disease of other swimmers. Consequently, the class, ethnic, and racial phobias that circumscribed and limited social interaction in general at this time became heightened at swimming pools.

In the early twentieth century, the social and cultural contests over swimming pools divided along class lines. A controversial proposal to build a swimming pool in New York's Central Park illustrates this class dynamic. John Mitchel, president of the board of aldermen, proposed the pool so that the city's poor, especially the children, would have a clean and cool place to bathe and play during the hot summer months. Without such a pool, these children had no place to swim except among the rats, garbage, and sewage in the East and Hudson Rivers. The mostly middle-class New Yorkers who opposed Mitchel's proposal were determined to maintain the park in its original form. A pool would "desecrate" the park, they feared, by transforming their oasis of genteel recreation into a popular amusement center. "No Coney Island, if you please, in that Park," one opponent pleaded.

These critics were also determined to protect the park's social landscape. "I have never been in favor of putting a swimming pool in Central Park," affirmed park commissioner Charles Stover. "I should consider it disastrous if the only swimming pool belonging to the city was put there. It would attract all sorts of undesirable people." Stover suggested instead that this swimming pool for the masses be built in a more appropriate location: "under the approaches to the Manhattan bridge." By keeping the swimming pool out of Central Park, New York's middle class defended their Victorian pastimes and reinforced the physical distance between themselves and their working-class neighbors.

TRANSITIONS

The late 1920s and early 1930s marked an important transition in the history of swimming pools. The number and popularity of public pools increased dramatically. Large northern cities doubled and even tripled the number of pools provided for residents, and southern cities and smaller communities began building municipal pools for the first time. The social contest over these pools changed as well: race replaced class as the most important distinction in determining patterns of discrimination. This racial contest, however, still occurred within a larger class context. Middle- and working-class blacks competed with working- and lower-middle-class whites for the use of public pools, while wealthy whites swam at private pools.

The pattern of the racial struggle at public swimming pools was closely tied to the size of the community and the region in which the pool was located. In the South, black Americans were excluded from using public pools entirely. In large northern cities, racial discrimination took the form of segregation. Such cities as New York, Chicago, and Boston largely avoided direct racial conflict and violence by providing separate pools for black residents. In smaller communities, however, black and white residents often competed over the use of a single pool. The dynamic of this struggle varied from town to town but generally involved exclusion, protest, and violence.

Pool Party. *Guests enjoy a pool party in Hollywood, California. Swimming pools at private homes have come to symbolize leisure and comfort in American life.* GENE LESTER/GETTY IMAGES.

Elizabeth, New Jersey, for example, opened its municipal pool in June 1930. By August of that year, a group of black residents had filed a complaint with the city, protesting their exclusion from the pool. The city's board of recreation commissioners ruled that blacks should have equal access to the facility. The pool remained tenuously integrated for two summers, but in 1933 black residents stopped using it because white swimmers continually harassed and assaulted them. In 1938 black residents tried to integrate the pool again but were once again subjected to the same abuse. Finally, the board closed the pool. It could no longer condone the discrimination and violence but was apparently unwilling to arrest the perpetrators.

POST–WORLD WAR II

The history of swimming pools fundamentally changed after World War II. America's rising economic tide, the increased rate of suburbanization, and racial desegregation combined to cause a dramatic increase in the number of private and residential pools. The economic prosperity of the postwar era, coupled with advances in pool construction, made backyard pools affordable to America's expanding middle class. In 1950 Americans owned only 2,500 private residential swimming pools; by 1970 they owned 713,000. During the same period, proliferating suburban communities often chose to build private swim clubs instead of public pools.

This general trend toward privatization was, at least partially, a response to the forced desegregation of municipal pools. During the 1940s black Americans won several important legal victories against communities with segregated swimming pools. One such community was Montgomery, West Virginia, which built a public pool in 1940 but did not open it. The city's elected officials faced a conundrum: They did not want Montgomery's black residents swimming in the pool, but they were reluctant to defy West Virginia's antidiscrimination statutes by openly turning them away. The city eventually leased the pool to a private nonprofit community association in 1946 for $1. The pool finally opened that summer, and the now "private" administrators had the legal right to deny admittance to blacks.

The African American residents of Montgomery quickly sued the city, arguing that leasing the pool to private interests did not relieve the city of its obligation to afford black citizens equal rights. The federal courts agreed: "Justice would be blind indeed if she failed to detect the real purpose in this effort of the City of Montgomery to clothe a public function with the mantle of private responsibility. 'The voice is Jacob's voice,' even though 'the hands are the hands of Esau.'" The court-ordered desegregation of Montgomery's pool, however, was a hollow victory for the city's black residents. In response to the court's decision, Montgomery closed the pool until 1961. White residents were apparently more willing to go without a community pool than to swim with their black neighbors.

Pool use continued to divide along racial lines in the 1970s and 1980s. Just as many white Americans chose to avoid living next to black Americans during this period by moving to restricted neighborhoods, they chose to avoid swimming with them by joining private swim clubs or building backyard pools. African and Latino Americans, many of whom continued to live in large cities, were left to swim at deteriorating public pools. Even most whites who remained in urban areas did not swim at public pools. As demonstrated by the Greenpoint controversy, some people did not want municipal pools in their neighborhoods at all.

The shift from public to private pools has, in some ways, transformed the quality of community life in America. Throughout much of the twentieth century, the public swimming pool served as a stage for public discourse. Community life was fostered, monitored, and disputed at these municipal institutions. The recent privatization of swimming, however, constitutes a retreat from public life. Private pools, especially residential ones, have stifled the public discourse that used to occur at community pools. Instead of swimming, chatting, and fighting with their neighbors at municipal pools, private pool owners have fenced themselves into their own backyards. The Greenpoint controversy reveals that public debate at and about municipal pools has not been silenced completely; however, too many controversies in contemporary America resemble the East Hampton dispute, demonstrating that people are frequently more eager to fight to get away from their communities than to become a part of them.

WATER PARKS

In the early twenty-first century, people around the world began flocking to water parks, which offer far more than traditional swimming pools. Water parks are amusement parks featuring a range of water-related activities, such as huge water slides and splash pools. Many water parks are designed around particular themes to make them attractive to tourists of all ages. Some are city owned, but most are privately owned. There are also indoor water parks located inside large hotels. The first water park, Wet 'N Wild, was built in Orlando, Florida, in 2004. By 2006 there were more than 1,000 in operation in the United States, and they attracted more than seventy-eight million visitors each year. At the time, there were only 600 water parks in existence in all other countries of the world combined.

There are safety issues involved at water parks, with typical injuries involving abrasions. For this reason, many pool surfaces and edges are lined with foam padding. The padding, however, increases the chance that bacteria may build up if water parks are not properly maintained and staff not sufficiently trained. In one study conducted of ten water parks (five indoor and five outdoor) in Wisconsin, health officials found that most bacteria was located in areas reserved for babies and small children. To reduce the likelihood of bacteria (such as *E. coli*, coliforms, and enterococci from fecal matter) entering the water, changing stations are usually placed inside nearby restrooms.

Jeffrey Wiltse

SEE ALSO: *Bathhouses; Central Park; Civil Rights Movement; Coney Island; Leisure Time; Suburbia; World War II.*

BIBLIOGRAPHY

Berners-Lee, Mike. *How Bad Are Bananas? The Carbon Footprint of Everything.* Berkeley, CA: Greystone Books, 2011.

Davis, Tracynda. "Water Quality of Modern Water Parks." *Journal of Environmental Health* 71, no. 9 (2009).

Jackson, Kenneth T. *Crabgrass Frontier: The Suburbanization of the United States.* New York: Oxford University Press, 1985.

Nasaw, David. *Going Out: The Rise and Fall of Public Amusements.* New York: HarperCollins Publishers, 1993.

Riess, Steven A. *City Games: The Evolution of American Urban Society and the Rise of Sports.* Urbana: University of Illinois Press, 1989.

Sugrue, Thomas J. *The Origins of the Urban Crisis: Race and Inequality in Postwar Detroit.* Princeton, NJ: Princeton University Press, 1996.

Van Leeuwen, Thomas A. P. *The Springboard in the Pond: An Intimate History of the Swimming Pool*, ed. Helen Searing. Cambridge, MA: MIT Press, 1998.

Williams, Marilyn Thornton. *Washing "The Great Unwashed": Public Baths in Urban America, 1840–1920.* Columbus: Ohio State University Press, 1991.

Wiltse, Jeff. *Contested Waters: A Social History of Swimming Pools in America.* Chapel Hill: University of North Carolina Press, 2007.

Swing Dancing

In the 1930s swing bands emerged at the forefront of American popular music, evolving from the jazz genre—which was primarily produced and listened to by African Americans—into music also patronized by urban whites. Long before baseball was integrated, the big swing bands—led by luminaries such as Duke Ellington, Benny Goodman, and Count Basie—brought together black and white musicians in a new social amalgam that decisively changed American culture.

Musically, swing offered rhythmic flexibility. Swing music is marked by a subtle swaying, living pulse, which came from musicians playing just ahead of the beat enough to be syncopated, or dragging behind it enough to be bluesy. Swing, notes historian Lewis Erenberg in *Swingin' the Dream: Big Band Jazz and the Rebirth of American Culture*, caused "a general revolution in the popular dance in the United States," as white youth took up the black dance innovations to banish whatever ballroom gentility remained in the Depression. After World War II swing grew increasingly fragmented and became less of a dance music and more of a concert music. Although bebop succeeded swing as the new wave of jazz innovation, it did not stimulate a new form of social dancing.

Harlem became the cultural capital of black America in the late 1920s, and it is there that swing dancing began, first appearing as the Lindy Hop. Originated among secret gangs in Harlem—which was quickly being populated by African Americans as whites departed—the steps were refined and made famous by dancers at Harlem's Savoy Ballroom. Lindy Hop refers to Charles Lindbergh's "hop"—his historic solo flight—across the Atlantic Ocean in 1927. Observing the acrobatics of some dancers at the Savoy, "Shorty George" Snowdon, a dance enthusiast, said, "Look at them kids hoppin' over there. I guess they're doin' the Lindy Hop." The swing combined steps from the shag, the Texas tommy, and vaudeville into a ballroom dance—a syncopated two-step or box step that accented the offbeat; the fundamental innovation of the dance was the "breakaway," when the partners spun away from each other and improvised a break. The acrobatic, or "air steps," were judolike variations in which partners would roll and flip each other over the back.

The Lindy Hop evolved into the jitterbug—a more acrobatic and almost "choreographed" version of the Lindy Hop. "The white jitterbug is oftener than not uncouth to look at," reported the *New York Times*, according to historian David Stowe in *Swing Changes: Big-Band Jazz in New Deal America*, "but his Negro original is quite another matter. His movements are never so exaggerated that they lack control, and there is an unmistakable dignity about his most violent figures."

Jitterbug enjoyed enormous popularity from 1936 until the end of the war. Every soda shop had a jukebox where teenagers could jitterbug after school. Eventually, in the late 1940s, the Lindy and jitterbug evolved into what came to be called "East Coast swing"—which had a rotating character, as the couple has no fixed relation to the room. An almost separate version of swing dancing developed on the West Coast, in which the two partners remain in a narrow slot on the dance floor. Even after swing was musically moribund, jitterbug remained the basic framework for couples dancing in the early days of rock and roll. It passed from the scene only after the twist had introduced the stand-alone form of dancing in the early 1960s.

In the late 1990s partnered social dancing began to make a comeback, with swing dancing an integral part of the revival. There was also a renaissance of swing and big band music—typified by groups such as the Royal Crown Revue and Big Bad Voodoo Daddy. Ballroom dance classes became extremely popular, particularly on college campuses. In the larger cities, ballrooms, dance clubs, and the larger dance teaching studios offered special nights of swing dancing. Contemporary social dancing reflected an extensive process of blending: for instance, hip-hop dance styles incorporated elements of the Lindy and jitterbug, and new swing styles showed a strong Latin influence.

Jeffrey Escoffier

SEE ALSO: *Basie, Count; Big Bands; Ellington, Duke; Goodman, Benny; Leisure Time; Lindbergh, Charles; Savoy Ballroom.*

BIBLIOGRAPHY

Erenberg, Lewis A. *Swingin' the Dream: Big Band Jazz and the Rebirth of American Culture.* Chicago: University of Chicago Press, 1998.

Stearns, Marshall Winslow, and Jean Stearns. *Jazz Dance: The Story of American Vernacular Dance.* New York: Macmillan, 1968.

Stowe, David W. *Swing Changes: Big-Band Jazz in New Deal America.* Cambridge, MA: Harvard University Press, 1994.

Swinging

Of all the social phenomena of the 1970s, one of the more taboo (and one of the most discussed) was *swinging*, sometimes called "partner swapping" or "wife swapping." Though few couples actually indulged in this practice, there were enough who did, or who knew about someone who did, to give the phenomenon widespread awareness. When the trend lost its popular buzz, however, swinging returned to what it had always been—the casual avocation of a group of hard-core enthusiasts.

There have always been so-called swingers throughout history. The Bible records plenty of incidents of men lying down with other men's handmaidens, and informal "clubs" devoted to extramarital experimentation have been around from the early days of the Republic. But the emergence of swinging as a loosely organized lifestyle coincided with America's sexual revolution in the 1960s.

THE ADVENT OF SWINGING IN AMERICA

Generally conducted at poolside parties and potluck dinners, partner swapping may have claimed as many as one million adherents during its heyday in the 1970s. Sometimes swinging involved couples placing ads in adult publications or choosing other couples they might like to pair up with. At other times, the encounters were purposely made random. One popular forum for selecting partners were key parties, in which the men tossed their car keys into a bowl and the women fished them out to determine with whom they would spend the night. The climate of sexual freedom espoused in such magazines as *Playboy* and *Penthouse* accelerated acceptance of the practice of swinging and eventually led to coverage in more mainstream publications as well.

Partner swapping even made it onto prime-time television. A 1971 episode of *All in the Family* traced the comic consequences of Edith Bunker's inadvertent reply to an ad from a pair of swingers. Vincent Gardenia and Rue McClanahan played the bewildered couple, who met up with the old morality in the form of Archie Bunker, America's avatar of sexual counterrevolution. But such downbeat portrayals of the lifestyle were the exception rather than the rule, as more people briefly flirted with the idea that maybe this open-marriage thing had some advantages to it after all.

An even surer sign that partner swapping had hit the mainstream came in 1973, when two members of the New York Yankees pitching staff swapped wives for the long haul. Lefties Mike Kekich and Fritz Peterson announced the spouse exchange in a bizarre press conference during spring training. The unique "trade" included the addition of the rest of their families: children, pets, and residences. (For the record, Kekich broke up with Marilyn Peterson soon after the switch, while Fritz Peterson remained married to the former Susan Kekich.) The high-profile swap briefly captured national headlines, but the fact that it did not scandalize baseball indicated just how much American sexual mores were changing.

SWINGING FOR A NEW GENERATION

The novelty of swinging eventually wore off, however. During the 1980s AIDS and sexually transmitted diseases made all but the most diehard believers of swinging reconsider the advantages of monogamy. With a conservative administration in Washington, promiscuity regained some of its negative stigma. Swinging once again became the private preserve of a little-publicized subculture. Still, during the 1990s, three million Americans were estimated to be swinging on a recreational basis. Facilitated by the Internet, and fueled by a reaction against the sexual moderation invoked during the AIDS era, sexual adventurousness was once again on the rise. House parties still provided a prominent medium for partner swapping, although a new wave of institutions, including affinity groups, travel agencies, and even bed and breakfasts, were catering to the burgeoning swinging lifestyle. In August 1997 more than 4,000 people attended a convention of the North American Swing Club Association in Palm Springs, California, where seminars were offered on such topics as "Recipes for a Successful Orgy" and "Growing Up with Kinky Parents."

The prevailing ethos at swinging encounters continued to be freewheeling sexual experimentation. But there were some changes from the wild and lawless 1970s. The spread of AIDS sensitized many partner-swapping enthusiasts to the primacy of good hygiene and a more judicious choice of partners. And society's growing acceptance of homosexuality allowed more swingers to experiment with same-sex partners. There was even a mini-wave of nostalgia for the old ways subsumed in the larger national wistfulness about the 1970s, as evidenced in such films as Ang Lee's *The Ice Storm* (1997), based on Rick Moody's novel of the same name. The film, whose harrowing climax occurs during a key party attended by its suburban Connecticut protagonists, captured the emotional sterility that allowed swinging to spread beyond a small hedonistic cult to briefly capture the fancy of middle-class America.

Though swinging was not a part of the mainstream in the first decade of the 2000s, it survived and, some believe, grew. A 2006 *Nightline* television special reported that the swinging lifestyle was on the rise, especially among affluent, middle-aged couples. The report investigated an increased interest in swingers clubs, vacations, and resorts. The Lifestyles Organization, a worldwide swingers organization, had a full-service travel agency that specialized in swinger travel to clothing-optional resorts. The report also put global swinger estimates at between four and eight million.

Curiosity and interest in "the lifestyle" spurred the continued appearance of swinging in the entertainment industry. Swinging played a role in episodes of such popular television series as *CSI: Crime Scene Investigation*, *Law & Order: SVU*, and *Criminal Minds*. Swinging's online presence remained steady as well, and there were a number of social networking sites dedicated to swinging, including iVoyeur and Swinger Social Network. It may be safe to conclude that as long as there is sex, there will be swingers.

Robert E. Schnakenberg

SEE ALSO: *AIDS;* All in the Family*; Baseball;* CSI*; The Internet;* Law & Order: SVU*; The New York Yankees;* Nightline*;* Penthouse*;* Playboy*; Sexual Revolution; Sitcom; Television.*

BIBLIOGRAPHY

D'Emilio, John, and Estelle B. Freedman. *Intimate Matters: A History of Sexuality in America*, 2nd ed. Chicago: University of Chicago Press, 1997.

Gould, Terry. *The Lifestyle: A Look at the Erotic Rites of Swingers.* Buffalo, NY: Firefly Books, 2000.

Michael, Robert T.; John H. Gagnon; Edward O. Laumann; et al. *Sex in America: A Definitive Survey.* New York: Warner Books, 1995.

Thomas, Patti. *Recreational Sex: An Insider's Guide to the Swinging Lifestyle.* Cleveland, OH: Peppermint Publishing, 1997.

Sykes, Wanda *(1964–)*

Comic Wanda Sykes was twenty-eight years old when she discovered her talent for making people laugh. Since then she has used her biting humor and brash delivery on the stand-up stage, on television, and in films, gaining recognition as one of the most original satiric wits of the twenty-first century. Never one to stand silent in the face of injustice, Sykes came out as a lesbian at a marriage equality rally in 2008, braving the risk of damaging her public career. Because her outspoken comedy routines had always attracted a liberal audience, however, most of Sykes's fan base remained loyal, and her gay and lesbian fans became even more vocal.

The daughter of an army colonel father and banker mother, Sykes was born in 1964 in Portsmouth, Virginia. She earned a bachelor of science degree at nearby Hampton University and went to work for the National Security Agency (NSA), a bureaucratic job that left her bored and unhappy. Always a joker, she first performed stand-up in 1987 in a local comedy contest and was soon doing her act in local clubs. In 1992 she quit her job at the NSA and moved north to work in the comedy clubs in New York. A job opening for rising comedy star Chris Rock led to her first big break, writing for the actor's Emmy-winning HBO comedy show, *The Chris Rock Comedy Show* (1997–2000).

Sykes's writing and performing skills and her irreverent humor have earned her three television shows: *Wanda at Large* on Fox (2003), *Wanda Does It* on Comedy Central (2004), and *The Wanda Sykes Show* on Fox (2009). She has also appeared in a number of films and comedy specials and has had recurring roles in several TV series, costarring in *The New Adventures of Old Christine* on CBS (2006–2010). She even did a stint as a football commentator on the HBO series *Inside the NFL*.

Though she had long had a large gay and lesbian following and had performed at gay pride festivals and on the gay-positive True Colors Tour, Sykes was very private about her personal life following her 1998 divorce from music producer David Hall. After the election in November 2008, however, when California voters approved Proposition 8 repealing gay marriage, Sykes took the stage at a Las Vegas marriage equality rally and announced that she was a lesbian. Sykes informed the crowd that she and her wife, Alexandra, had been married the previous October during a brief window of legality for same-sex marriage in California. She also stated that she was unable to keep silent in the face of attacks on gays such as Proposition 8.

Sykes seamlessly incorporated her lesbian identity into her act, remaining one of the most bluntly, candidly funny women in the entertainment industry. In 2009 she and Alexandra announced the birth of twin babies, Olivia Lou and Lucas Claude. In 2011 she became another kind of role model when, with typical straightforward irreverence, she publicly discussed her struggle with breast cancer, which resulted in a double mastectomy.

Tina Gianoulis

SEE ALSO: *Cancer; Gay and Lesbian Marriage; Las Vegas; Rock, Chris; Sitcom; Stand-Up Comedy; Television.*

BIBLIOGRAPHY

Karpel, Ari. "Black and Gay Like Me." *Advocate*, February 2, 2009, 54.

Talley, Lori. "Reality TV: In Her Sitcom Debut, Wanda Sykes Decided to Stick to What She Does Best—Be Herself." *Back Stage West* 10, no. 13 (2003): 1.

Tucker, Ken. "Magic Wanda." *Entertainment Weekly*, March 21, 2003. Accessed May 2012. Available from http://www.ew.com/ew/article/0,,432580,00.html

Sylvia

From its inception in 1978 to its finale in 2012, Nicole Hollander's comic strip, *Sylvia*, evolved to become a leading expression of postmodern feminism in satiric form. Appearing daily in newspapers coast to coast for some thirty years, Hollander's popular strip was also reprinted in many books, including such titles as *I'm in Training to Be Tall and Blonde* and *Ma, Can I Be a Feminist and Still Like Men?*

If the title character in Cathy Guisewite's *Cathy* strip represented the relationship struggles—romantic, parental, and interoffice—of a neurotic, thirty-something working woman, *Sylvia* portrayed a somewhat older, stouter, work-at-home woman comfortable with herself but at war with the foibles of contemporary society. Actually, Sylvia herself did not always appear in the strip that bore her name, a sly, surrealistic stream-of-consciousness in which Hollander applied her own witty touch to subjects both slight and substantial, from such comedy staples as pets and airlines to fresher ground like gender inequality and goddess spirituality. Sylvia was a plump, fiftyish advice columnist, as likely to be found conversing with her cats or a space alien as her nubile daughter Rita or her friend Beth-Ann. Like many of us, Sylvia also talked back to the media: when a commercial on the radio announced, "Spray N'Wash gets out what America gets into," bubble-bathing Sylvia responded, "Send some to El Salvador!"

Hollander had also worked as an art instructor and a book illustrator, but she found fame as a comic strip writer/artist when *Sylvia* was picked up for syndication by the Universal Press Syndicate in 1979. The increased visibility led inevitably to *Sylvia* books and a line of greeting cards; in 1981, another syndicate, Field Enterprises, bought the *Sylvia* rights and added a Sunday strip. For a time, Hollander incorporated herself as the Sylvia Syndicate and took over her own distribution. By the end of the 1990s, *Sylvia* was being distributed by the Los Angeles Times Syndicate, which later merged into Tribune Media Services. Despite being syndicated, Hollander retained the copyright on her daily creations. She was featured prominently in a PBS documentary about contemporary female comic strip artists.

In February 2010 the *Chicago Tribune* dropped Sylvia. The decision came as a blow to Hollander because it meant her creation no longer appeared in her hometown. She responded by starting a blog—www.badgirlchats.com—in the autumn of that year. On March 26, 2012, Hollander announced that she was retiring but that the blog would still feature strips from her decades of *Sylvia* archives.

Although there were recurring themes in *Sylvia*, there were no story lines; each day's strip was self-contained. Hollander's visual style was purposefully slapdash, in keeping with *Sylvia*'s cutting-edge humor. What distinguished the *Sylvia* strip was its celebration of the life of the mind of its heroine. As often as not, there was nothing happening in the strip per se except what Sylvia was imagining, in the fashion of a latter-day Little Nemo in Slumberland, except that she was wide awake both physically and ideologically. The strip's innovative fancies and conceits included "Menacing Supercops of the Future" such as the "fashion cop," policing errors of taste and style or the "love cop," seeking to break up incompatible couples or prevent them from forming; the eternally annoying "Woman Who Does Everything More Beautifully than You"; "Alien Lovers"; "Special Goddesses"; "The Woman Who Worries about Everything"; "The Cat Who Hypnotizes His Mistress"; "From the Diary of a Woman Who Never Forgets a Slight"; "Gender-Based Differences—How to Tell if You're a Gal or a Guy"; and "The Lonely Detective," in which Sylvia imagined herself a noirish Philippa Marlowe–type private eye tackling contemporary societal issues.

Popular culture was always a rich source for *Sylvia*'s satire. At times, her advice column was featured in the strip—she once addressed one of her troubled readers as "Dear disgusting wimp." Other gambits included Sylvia's proposals for TV game shows, such as the one in which recently divorced couples would have tried to guess each other's most annoying habits, or her extreme take-offs from *The Three Faces of Eve*, imagined dramas about women with three-way personality splits, one of which is always a housewife, as in "housewife, snake-handler, and educator" or "housewife, hair stylist, and brain surgeon." Considering that Hollander's *Sylvia* strip was always frankly feminist, multiethnic, multispecies, and unabashedly liberal in outlook, it was not surprising that it sometimes referred to current events, although the "ripped from the headlines" approach was never *Sylvia*'s prime focus as it has been for strips such as *Doonesbury*. In any given year, however, *Sylvia* managed to reflect—and have fun with—the mood of a small but hearty band of freethinkers as they warily eyed the shenanigans of the world at large.

Preston Neal Jones

SEE ALSO: *Advice Columns;* Cathy; *Comics;* Doonesbury; *Feminism.*

BIBLIOGRAPHY

Hollander, Nicole. *That Woman Must Be on Drugs: A Collection of Sylvia*. New York: St. Martin's Press, 1981.

Hollander, Nicole. *Mercy, It's the Revolution, and I'm in My Bathrobe*. New York: St. Martin's Press, 1982.

Hollander, Nicole. *Hi, This Is Sylvia: I Can't Come to the Phone Right Now, So When You Hear the Beep, Please Hang Up*. New York: St. Martin's Press, 1983.

Hollander, Nicole. *Sylvia on Sundays*. New York: St. Martin's Press, 1983.

Hollander, Nicole. *The Whole Enchilada: A Spicy Collection of Sylvia's Best*. New York: St. Martin's Press, 1986.

Hollander, Nicole. *Never Take Your Cat to a Salad Bar*. New York: Vintage Books, 1987.

Hollander, Nicole. *Tales from the Planet Sylvia*. New York: St. Martin's Press, 1990.

Hollander, Nicole. *Female Problems*. New York: Dell, 1995.

Hollander, Nicole. *The Sylvia Chronicles: 30 Years of Graphic Misbehavior from Reagan to Obama*. New York: New Press, 2010.

Horn, Maurice. *100 Years of American Newspaper Comics: An Illustrated Encyclopedia*. New York: Gramercy Books, 1996.

Syndication

Syndication refers to the sale or distribution of television programs that are offered to multiple markets for non-network exhibition. As a practice, syndication stands opposed to network broadcasting, in which the content and schedule are determined nationally for all affiliated stations. Syndication is composed of a variety of program types, including movies, first-run series, reruns of network programming, talk shows, game shows, foreign programs, and children's series. While syndication may resemble network distribution in that the same programs air over many separate outlets, the timing (the day of the week, as well as the hour of the day) may vary from location to location. Serving as a counterbalance to network control, syndication has developed from the simple sale of off-network programming in the early 1950s into a number of complex and varied business practices, including off-net, first-run, rerun, and barter syndication. Syndication is more than just the distribution of programs—its regulations and practices have played a major role in the development of contemporary television. From the Federal Communications Commission's (FCC) "Prime-Time Access Rules" (PTAR) and "Financial Interests and Syndication" (Fin/Syn) rulings to the programming of ultrahigh frequency (UHF), cable, and even entirely new networks, syndication has been one of the most debated—and most important—business and programmatic practices within the television industry.

BREAKING UP THE NETWORK MONOPOLIES

During the 1950s the television networks owned and controlled most of the programming they aired. The networks were able to present reruns of programs or sell the rights, even if they had minimal or no investment in the actual production. Networks defended this practice by arguing that they were equally responsible for the success of a series since they promoted, placed, and provided exposure for the program. This left them in the enviable position of taking a minimal financial risk in a show's production while at the same time enjoying long-term profit from its broadcast (and rebroadcast). Unable to risk the capital necessary to produce series on their own, many independent production companies disappeared during these early years, and by the 1960s, almost all programming was produced by the networks or movie studios. In an attempt to limit the networks' monopolization of television production, exhibition, and distribution, the FCC examined syndication and, in 1970 and 1971, instituted sweeping changes. The FCC's motivation was to reinvigorate local and independent production, and to accomplish this goal, it adopted the Fin/Syn and PTAR rulings.

The Fin/Syn rulings effectively ended network monopolies on syndication. Networks could no longer syndicate domestically and could sell a program internationally only if they had completely financed the production. Furthermore, networks were limited in the number of programs they could produce, thus creating greater dependence on outside production companies. The PTAR, meanwhile, limited prime-time network broadcasts to time slots from 7:00 p.m. to 11:00 p.m. in the top fifty television markets. In adopting these rules, the FCC hoped to open access to programming and encourage affiliates to air shows that were independently or locally produced. However, rather than create a resurgence in local programming, the PTAR led to the development of inexpensive programs that attracted significant audiences, such as the game shows *Wheel of Fortune* and *Jeopardy!* The FCC's decisions had tremendous economic ramifications that affected the television and movie industries alike. Given one year to divest themselves of their syndication services, networks sold these divisions. Such sales led to the formation of new companies such as Viacom, which was once a division of CBS but came to own Paramount Pictures and a television network (UPN).

THE GROWTH OF SYNDICATION

Syndication became increasingly important as television expanded and the new and independent UHF stations sought programming. With the expansion of non-network stations, syndicators found themselves in the enviable position of supplying content for a significant portion of the daily television schedule. Separated from the networks, the syndication industry became more profitable, powerful, and competitive, leading to new practices intended to make programs more economically attractive to affiliates. One such example is "barter syndication," which was designed to meet the needs of advertisers and affiliates alike. In this form of syndication, the distributor gives the program to affiliates free of charge in exchange for ad time on the program. By placing a program in enough markets around the country, the syndicator can sell commercials to national advertisers and keep the revenue as its payment. During the early days of UHF, stations needing to fill their schedules were cash-poor, and barter syndication offered them a way to gain programming without expending their limited capital. Eventually, as stations became more established, syndicators moved toward a combination of cash payments and ad time for their programs.

The most common form of syndication is "off-network syndication," which refers to programs that have already aired on network television. The cost of producing these programs is generally recouped during their network runs, which means most of the syndication revenue becomes profit. Anyone who grew up watching television after the 1960s is familiar with a host of programs—such as *Gilligan's Island*, *F Troop*, and *The Rockford Files*—that were (and still are) aired in this manner. With the growth of cable, entire networks, such as TV Land, have been built on the strength and popularity of off-network programming. A more recent trend has been "first-run syndication," which refers to programs that are syndicated when they are new. While there is more financial risk in this type of syndication—the costs are not absorbed through network exhibition—these programs offer tremendous control and profit potential to the producers. Programs that have been distributed in this fashion include *Baywatch*, *Star Trek: The Next Generation*, and a number of game shows. By the 1980s the emergence and success of "first-run syndication" led to a new type of inexpensive programming known as "reality programming," "trash," or "tabloid TV."

A FAR-REACHING IMPACT

With the rise of cable television in the 1980s, syndicators once again experienced an increased demand for programs. Following the growth of independent stations, the expanded cable market made syndication one of the most profitable businesses in television. This all began to change by the late 1980s, however, as production companies recognized the greater value of their programs. New networks also emerged, reducing the number of independent stations. The first blow came with the formation of the Fox network, which combined a number of previously independent stations and supplied them with regular network programming. By the end of the 1980s, syndicators experienced additional setbacks when the FCC eased syndication rules and policies, thus allowing networks more freedom to produce and distribute programming. This situation was further exacerbated by the development of two new networks (WB and UPN) that committed many of the remaining independents to network programming. Nevertheless, syndication remains a viable, powerful, and profitable method of television distribution.

In addition to the economic ramifications, syndication has created a unique cultural phenomenon: cross-generational exposure to television programming. Because of syndication, the beloved programs of one generation have remained popular with future generations. This speaks to both the nostalgia of the viewers and the timelessness of the programming. It is part of why television is unique.

James Friedman

SEE ALSO: Baywatch*; Cable TV;* Gilligan's Island*;* Jeopardy!*; Reality Television; Television;* Wheel of Fortune.

BIBLIOGRAPHY

The Economics of TV Programming and Syndication. Carmel, CA: Paul Kagan Associates, 1994.

Erickson, Hal. *Syndicated Television: The First Forty Years, 1947–1987*. Jefferson, NC: McFarland, 1989.

Head, Sydney W., et al. *Broadcasting in America: A Survey of Electronic Media*, 9th ed. Boston: Houghton Mifflin, 2001.

MacDonald, J. Fred. *One Nation under Television*. New York: Pantheon Books, 1990.

Sterling, Christopher H., and John M. Kittross. *Stay Tuned: A History of American Broadcasting*. Mahwah, NJ: Lawrence Erlbaum Associates, 2002.

T

Tabloid Television

During the 1980s the proliferation of popular television shows focusing on sex, crime, and gossip, such as *A Current Affair*, *Hard Copy*, and *Inside Edition*, led some media critics to fear that the lines between responsible journalism and sensationalism were being blurred. These tabloid television shows, so designated because of their resemblance to supermarket tabloid newspapers, relied on gossip, emotional appeals, checkbook journalism, staged reenactments, and home video footage. They also used sources that were barely credible. Such practices had an impact on mainstream broadcast journalism, which has been criticized for downplaying serious news in order to compete for viewers and advertising revenue.

Tabloid television began in earnest in 1986 when media magnate Rupert Murdoch created *A Current Affair* and placed it in syndication. The half-hour show featured anchorman Maury Povich, and its stories focused on sex, crime, and sleaze. At the height of its popularity, it had ninety million viewers in the United States. The show spawned a series of imitators, such as *Hard Copy* and *Inside Edition*, which for many people blurred the distinction between responsible journalism and gossip. In the 1990s events such as the O. J. Simpson murder trial and the death of Princess Diana offered much fodder for the purveyors of tabloid television.

The methods used by the producers of tabloid television are at odds with acceptable journalistic practice as defined by mainstream television news. Checkbook journalism, which is the practice of paying sources for interviews, is one of the most hotly contested. Mainstream journalists argue that this practice encourages sources to embellish their stories in order to make money. Reenactments of crimes or other activities is another method that critics say can mislead viewing audiences about actual events. Yet, even as the mainstream media condemned these practices, it began to engage in them as well.

One well-known example is the 1995 Simpson trial. Media coverage of the long, high-profile murder trial was continuous, and mainstream television employed tabloid practices to compete for viewers and ratings. A CBS news station in Los Angeles, for example, re-created the murders of Simpson's ex-wife and her friend for viewers, using computer modeling. In another example, the television show *Dateline* rigged the gas tanks on some Ford trucks to explode as a way of dramatizing their alleged danger. Some mainstream broadcasters also began citing tabloid reports as "news" in their own reports, justifying it with the disclaimer that they were reporting information, even though the accuracy of the information could not be verified. This sort of "peeping tom" journalism, which is reporting on what tabloid television shows are saying and even criticizing it, provides mainstream journalists with a way to present the same information but with reduced risk.

Author Matthew C. Ehrlich argues that this separation between mainstream and tabloid news is not concrete. In a 1996 article in *Journalism & Mass Communication Monographs*, he points out that the principal characteristics of tabloid television news have always been similar to the characteristics of investigative news. For example, both take a stand on the guilt or innocence of the particular parties involved, both take a moralizing tone, and both examine crime and sex. The only difference, Ehrlich argues, is that the mainstream media uses this material to inform and possibly rectify the world, while tabloid television uses the material merely to provide entertainment.

The zenith of tabloid journalism may have come in August 1997 with the death of Princess Diana, who died in a car crash while trying to evade paparazzi. In a statement made after her death, her brother Charles Spencer said, "I always believed the press would kill her in the end." Many people at the time criticized print tabloids for contributing to her death, because they were the organizations that paid outrageous amounts of money to paparazzi for her photograph. Tabloid television, while not as vilified, was criticized as well.

By the end of the twentieth century, tabloid television had lost much of its appeal for American audiences, and ratings were declining. Some of the disaffection with the genre was due to what critic Neal Gabler in *Life the Movie: How Entertainment Conquered Reality* insists is the result of tabloid television marginalizing itself through its own outrageousness. Some is due to the public reaction to Princess Diana's death. In the early twenty-first century, tabloid television still existed, but it was no longer as popular as it once was.

Mia Consalvo

SEE ALSO: Dateline*; Diana, Princess of Wales; Ford Motor Company; Media Feeding Frenzies; Simpson, O. J.; Tabloids; Television; Television Anchors.*

BIBLIOGRAPHY

Bishop, Ronald. "From behind the Walls: Boundary Work by News Organizations in Their Coverage of Princess Diana's Death." *Journal of Communication Inquiry* 23, no. 1 (1999): 90–112.

Ehrlich, Matthew C. "The Journalism of Outrageousness: Tabloid Television News vs. Investigative News." *Journalism & Mass Communication Monographs*, no. 155 (1996): 1–24.

Gabler, Neal. *Life the Movie: How Entertainment Conquered Reality*. New York: Knopf, 1998.

Krajicek, David J. *Scooped! Media Miss Real Story on Crime while Chasing Sex, Sleaze, and Celebrities*. New York: Columbia University Press, 1998.

Langer, John. *Tabloid Television: Popular Journalism and the "Other News."* New York: Routledge, 1998.

Smillie, Dirk. "Worst Blow to Tabloid TV May Be Falling Ratings." *Christian Science Monitor*, May 12, 1999.

Sparks, Colin, and John Tulloch, eds. *Tabloid Tales: Global Debates over Media Standards*. Lanham, MD: Rowman & Littlefield, 2000.

Tabloids

Tabloids were originally pint-sized newspapers specializing in the sensational. Once confined to so-called scandal sheets, or magazine-style newspapers that many people saw only in grocery store checkout lines, the subjects of sex and scandal seeped into the mainstream press and virtually all other media, including magazines, radio, television, and the Internet. By the end of the twentieth century, nearly all American journalism seemed affected by the spread of tabloid news as coverage of the personal foibles and problems of celebrities and politicians became commonplace. The line between the splashy press and the serious journal became blurred.

EARLY NEWSPAPERS

Once a proprietary name for a pill or tablet, the word *tabloid* came to be almost exclusively associated with sensational journalism. Later, *tabloid* described a newspaper about half the size of most broadsheets. Tabloids popularized the news by featuring bold pictorial coverage of sex escapades, murder and gore, sports, and scandals of all sorts, but especially those relating to the lives of the rich and famous. The word *tabloid* also sprouted offshoot words, such as *tabloidese* for the breezy writing style of many tabloids, *tabloidesque* to connote tabloid-type publications, and *tabloidization* to mean compression of stories or literature, according to *The New Shorter Oxford English Dictionary*.

To understand the incursion of tabloids and the tabloid style into the mainstream media, it is helpful to consider three eras of journalism: the early days of the media barons; the era of young, free-spirited reporters in the anything-goes years around the Roaring Twenties; and the electronic age when new forms of media mushroomed. Although *Vanity Fair* in its late twentieth-century incarnation dubbed the 1990s the "Tabloid Decade," the last several decades of the century could be called a tabloid age, as stories of murders, sex, scandal, and the once-private lives of public officials spread into every home through newspapers or the electronic media.

In the early years of U.S. journalism, power belonged to those who owned a printing press. There was no competition from radio, television, or other media in news coverage, advertising, or audience appeal. In the 1800s and early 1900s, the pulse of American journalism ticked away in New York City, where publishers found gold in what was called the "penny press"—a new form of American papers that produced eye-opening stories that were long on scandal and mayhem but short on analysis or depth. Building on the trend of sensationalized news in the penny press, publisher Joseph Patterson launched *New York Daily News* in 1919. The idea came to him after meeting Alfred Harmsworth, founder of the successful London tabloid the *Daily Mirror*. *New York Daily News* faced early struggles, but its compact size, low cost, and its irreverent language appealed to commuters. Imitators quickly followed, including the *New York Daily Mirror* (1924), *New York Evening Graphic*, and *Philadelphia Daily News* (1925).

The best-known promoters of mass-appeal newspapers were mogul William Randolph Hearst and his rival, Joseph Pulitzer. Hearst created a publishing empire of big-circulation newspapers, successful magazines, and a wire service (International News Service). His power extended to American foreign policy. When his headline-shouting newspapers published reports about Cuba's demands for independence from Spain, the articles helped bring on the 1898 Spanish-American War.

Hearst was in fierce combat for newspaper-circulation dominance with Pulitzer, a Hungarian-born newspaperman who bought and created newspapers, including the *St. Louis Dispatch* and the *St. Louis Post*, which he formed into the *Post-Dispatch*. Later, Pulitzer entered the New York journalism wars, buying the *World* in 1883 and four years later the *Evening World*. Pulitzer and Hearst battled furiously for readers through hyped-up news accounts that gave rise to the derogatory "yellow journalism" brand. During the 1920s both Hearst and Pulitzer extended their reach into tabloid enriched stories focusing on violence, celebrity gossip, and sex. After his death, however, Pulitzer's name became associated with high journalistic standards. Through his will, he endowed Columbia University School of Journalism and started the distinguished Pulitzer Prize for news excellence. Hearst too left a legacy of newspapers, magazines, and broadcast outlets.

HUNGRY REPORTERS

If Pulitzer and Hearst drove the popular-press wagons, the workhorses and talent pulling them were the reporters. In the early days, they were often a rough-and-tumble bunch who had little education but shared a knack for digging up stories and dirt and spinning a good yarn. Although they were poorly paid for their efforts, some of the nation's biggest literary figures of the twentieth century, such as Ernest Hemingway, got their start in newspapering.

What they lacked in college education, many of these young reporters of the 1920s made up on the streets and in the police stations of the nation. H. L. Mencken, the great Baltimore, Maryland, newspaperman, writer, and all-around curmudgeon, belonged to this breed. He wrote in 1941 of his early newspaper days:

> At a time when the respectable bourgeois youngsters of my generation were college freshmen, oppressed by simian sophomores and affronted with balderdash daily and hourly by chalky pedagogues, I was at large in a wicked seaport of half a million people with a front seat at every public show, as free of the night as of the day, and getting earfuls and eyefuls of instruction in a hundred giddy arcana, none of them taught in schools. . . . I was laying in all the worldly wisdom of a police lieutenant, a bartender, a shyster lawyer, or a midwife. And it certainly would be idiotic to say that I was not happy. . . . Life was arduous but it was

> gay and carefree. The days chased one another like kittens chasing their tails.

If there was one work of literature that encapsulated this wild and woolly journalism, it was the highly celebrated play *The Front Page* about newspapering in Chicago written by two former Chicago newsmen, Ben Hecht and Charles MacArthur. Hecht, who later gained fame as a screenwriter and author, recalled his early days as a newspaperman fondly, much as Mencken did, in his 1963 book about reporting days, *Gaily Gaily*. Hecht wrote: "I came to Chicago in 1910 at the age of sixteen and a half, and went to work immediately as a newspaper reporter on the *Chicago Journal*. I write of the five merry years that followed. As sang Bliss Carman: Oh, but life went gaily, gaily."

The essential trait among the memorable early newsmen, whether it was Damon Runyon, who wrote humorously of the guys and dolls of the underside of life, or sports writer and columnist Ring Lardner, it was the ability to spin a good yarn. During the early 1920s Gene Fowler, called "the last of the troubadours," was one of the best on Park Row (the Fleet Street of New York City, where many newspaper offices were located). A talented writer and gifted reporter, Fowler portrayed the news scene in his 1961 book of reminiscences of the 1920s:

> I still can see the incredibly fast flutter of bandit Gerald Chapman's small feet as he dies on the hangman's rope. I again can hear Queen Marie of Romania tell her lady-in-waiting to "get rid of that damned thing!" after the Dakota Indians have given Her Majesty a war bonnet. Once again I am present at Carnegie Hall as the addled Mayor Hylan makes his ghostwritten address of welcome to President Woodrow Wilson during the ceremony; but unthinkingly keeps his back turned to Mr. Wilson during the ceremony. I remember also the lean Irish statesman Eamon de Valera, clad in his long underwear and huge boxing gloves on his hands, as he spars with his bull-necked secretary in a sitting room at the old Waldorf.
>
> Even as I write, there unaccountably springs to mind an occasion when I asked Henry Ford about the sleep habits of his good friend [Thomas] Edison. Was it true, as legend had it, that Mr. Edison, like Napoleon, slept but four hours? Yes, said Mr. Ford, but Mr. Edison slept twice and sometimes three times a day! . . . Little things about big men. Or, if you will, big things about little men. . . . The stories of my day are no longer big in the public attention, or else have been chewed upon until the taste is gone.

There were scores of sensational and landmark stories in those days that were covered by the serious papers as well as tabloids, although more colorfully in the latter. There was the manslaughter trial of top comic film actor Fatty Arbuckle, who was acquitted of brutally assaulting a young actress while he was at the peak of his career, his fame second only to that of Charlie Chaplin. There was Charles Lindbergh's historic transatlantic flight and the later trial of Bruno Hauptmann for the kidnap-murder of the Lindbergh baby. There were riveting accounts of murders and prohibition, the constitutional amendment giving women the right to vote, elections, the Great Depression, and World Wars I and II.

POSTWAR JOURNALISM

After World War II, journalism started maturing and opening up its pages to previously untouched stories as competition grew from radio and the new medium of television. In the prewar days, for example, few Americans knew that President Franklin Delano Roosevelt was crippled from infantile paralysis, or polio. An unwritten rule in the press was to protect Roosevelt from being shown, described, or referred to as confined to a wheelchair or wearing braces to stand briefly, assisted by crutches. It was not until after Roosevelt's death in 1945 that his true condition became universally known.

During the postwar era, however, most of the misdeeds of celebrities were still confined to gossipmongers and a magazine called *Confidential*, which exploited the private lives of movie stars. Employing a host of private investigators and informants, *Confidential* encouraged its reporters to use surveillance equipment and to pepper their facts with suggestive phrases. The magazines' pressure forced the hand of many studios, who, in order to salvage the career of an actor like Rock Hudson, offered up stories on lesser known actors. In 1953, the *National Enquirer* followed suit, transforming from a broadsheet into a tabloid that focused on the gore associated with murders and violent crime. By 1967 owner Generaso Pope Jr. wished to sell the magazine in supermarket checkout lines; Pope softened the stories to focus on on paranormal activity, UFOs, and celebrity gossip in order to appease store owners. Joe Azaria and John Vader launched the *Globe* in 1954, and by the mid-1960s it rivaled the *National Enquirer*. Few newspapers followed up with front-page stories on material that the tabloids dug up. Major exceptions included the sensational trial and subsequent acquittal of dashing Hollywood actor Errol Flynn on a charge of rape on a yacht.

Stories of large public scope, rather than scandal, dominated traditional newspapers and television news. There were the assassinations of President John F. Kennedy, Martin Luther King Jr., and Senator Robert Kennedy; space travel; the civil rights movement; the Vietnam War; the Watergate scandal; and the resignation of President Richard Nixon. Then came scandals that forced themselves onto front pages by their very dramatic nature and the public stature of those involved, such as the accidental drowning of Mary Jo Kopechne, a young aide of Senator Edward Kennedy, after a car driven by Kennedy went off a small wooden bridge following a party on Chappaquiddick Island, Massachusetts, in 1969.

FOCUSING ON SCANDALS

The Chappaquiddick story was the first of a series of news reports about the exploits of Washington figures. Conspiracy theories sparked up around the event, allowing for the tabloids to exploit the event with sensationalized headlines. The most powerful congressman at the time, House Ways and Means Committee Chairman Wilbur Mills, splashed his way onto front pages after his girlfriend, a striptease artist nicknamed "The Argentine Firecracker," jumped unexplainably into the Tidal Basin in the wee hours after the married and very private Mills and the woman had spent an argumentative evening together. Another powerful congressman, Wayne Hays, made news when it became known he had hired a woman with whom he had an intimate relationship to work in his office as a secretary, although she later admitted she could not take shorthand or type. The presidential ambitions of Senator Gary Hart ended after reporters learned that the married candidate was socializing with a young woman. Especially damaging to Hart was a widely circulated photograph obtained by the *National Enquirer* of him and the woman together on a Miami, Florida, boat named *Monkey Business*. The public's thirst for stories revealing the sordid and complex lives of celebrities and politicians encouraged newspapers like the *Boston Herald* to switch to a tabloid format in 1981, and the *New York Observer* emerged as a leading cultural tabloid in 1987, notable for its pink pages and Candace Bushnell's social column that inspired HBO's *Sex and the City*.

The scope of news coverage was revolutionized again when cable television began filling twenty-four hours a day with nonstop news, talk, and gossip. "Television tabloid" programs such as *Hard Copy* and *Inside Edition* delivered exposés and inside scoops on celebrities. The mainstream press started paying attention. The *Washington Post*, for example, promoted a new gossip column. The mainstay *New York Times* even started running short pieces on celebrities.

In the 1990s scandals reported in mainstream media included Washington Mayor Marion Barry's conviction and sentencing on a drug possession charge after being caught on videotape smoking crack cocaine in a hotel room with a woman who was not his wife during a police raid. Tales of sex and other titillating topics started cascading. The Senate confirmed Clarence Thomas, a black jurist, as an associate justice of the U.S. Supreme Court, but not before a former aide, Anita Hill, testified that she had been sexually harassed by him. There was John Wayne Bobbitt, whose penis was cut off by his wife, Lorena Bobbitt, and who later became a pornographic film curiosity after his organ was surgically replaced. There was the rape trial and acquittal of Senator Edward Kennedy's nephew William Kennedy Smith.

No story to date had captured the public interest as did the nationally televised "trial of the century" in 1995 of O. J. Simpson, who was accused of stabbing his ex-wife, Nicole, and a young man, Ron Goldman, to death. The acquittal of the former professional football hero produced emotions across the country ranging from outrage to joy. For worldwide coverage, however, few stories could match the 1997 death of Britain's Princess Diana, who, along with her boyfriend and driver, was killed in an automobile crash after a high-speed chase by photographers through the streets of Paris. In the aftermath of her death, the United Kingdom and California, among other governments, enacted laws restricting the news gathering techniques used by paparazzis.

SCANDALS IN THE WHITE HOUSE

The unrestrained news coverage of the Simpson case and that of the death of Princess Di were matched if not surpassed by a scandal that unfolded in the late 1990s involving a young woman named Monica Lewinsky. Her story of sexual intimacy with President Bill Clinton in the Oval Office while she was a White House intern and President Clinton's persistent denials resulted in the impeachment of Clinton by the House of Representatives on charges of perjury and obstruction of justice. After much agonizing, the Senate, in only the second impeachment trial of a president in U.S. history, acquitted Clinton of the charges, thus leaving him in office.

The story of the Clinton presidency involved scandal even before he was elected. Voters elected him despite stories he had had an affair while Arkansas governor with a nightclub singer named Gennifer Flowers. That story, picked up by the mainstream media, was broken by a grocery-store tabloid, the *Star*, with the bold headline "My 12-Year Affair with Bill Clinton." By coincidence, it was the same publication that brought down Dick Morris, one of Clinton's top political advisers, during the 1996 Democratic convention by breaking the story that Morris had been conducting an extramarital affair with a Washington prostitute at a hotel near the White House.

Media revelations about Clinton's extramarital affair led defenders to point out that other presidents, going back to Thomas Jefferson and including Franklin Roosevelt and John Kennedy, had also had affairs. Pundits said future presidential candidates would be routinely queried on their sexual pasts. Where journalists once left the private lives of politicians alone, it appeared that the personal problems of politicians would no longer be off the record. There appeared to be no limits to the public's appetite for salaciousness and sensation, stimulated by stories of sex on daytime TV soap operas and in movies and now fed by newspapers, cable TV, and the Internet. The last years of the twentieth century saw the way paved for universal coverage of the foibles of the famous, profoundly changing the tone of American politics, largely because of the irresistible dynamics of tabloid journalism.

INFLUENCE OF THE INTERNET

In the early twenty-first century, the trend toward tabloid-type coverage continued unabated, fueled by increasing numbers of Internet news and opinion sites. As a result, tabloid newspapers, mainstream newspapers, television stations, and websites all competed by offering titillating stories. No one in the public eye was considered off limits anymore.

News organizations of all kinds were reporting tabloid-style news. For example, ABC News reported in 2006 that evangelical minister Ted Haggard was being accused of drug use and gay sex. In 2009 the *National Enquirer* broke the news of golf-icon Tiger Woods's extramarital affairs. The online publication Politico revealed in 2011 that presidential candidate Herman Cain was accused of past sexual harassment, and that same year the *Los Angeles Times* published reports that Arnold Schwarzenegger had fathered a child with his housekeeper before he became governor of California.

The pressure to compete and be first with a story led to a serious scandal in the United Kingdom in late 2011 and early 2012. Two tabloids owned by tycoon Rupert Murdoch came under investigation for having hacked into the mobile phones of people they were writing about. Although no evidence surfaced of similar practices in the United States, observers feared that the lust for salacious stories might tempt reporters into crossing the line of journalistic ethics. In the meantime, during the 2012 election campaign, media of all kinds continued to publish accusations of new—and long-past—scandals involving U.S. politicians.

Michael L. Posner

SEE ALSO: *Advertising; Anita Hill–Clarence Thomas Senate Hearings; Arbuckle, Fatty; Cable TV; Chaplin, Charlie; Civil Rights Movement; Diana, Princess of Wales; Edison, Thomas Alva; Ford, Henry; The Great Depression; Hearst, William Randolph; Hemingway, Ernest; The Internet; Kennedy Assassination; King, Martin Luther, Jr.; Lardner, Ring; Lewinsky, Monica; Lindbergh, Charles; Mencken, H. L.;* The National Enquirer*; The* New York Times*; Polio; Radio; Runyon, Damon; Schwarzenegger, Arnold; Sex Scandals; Simpson, O. J.;*

Soap Operas; Television; Vanity Fair*; Vietnam; The* Washington Post*; Watergate; Wire Services; Woods, Tiger; World War I; World War II.*

BIBLIOGRAPHY

Fowler, Gene. *A Reporter's Reminiscence of the '20s.* New York: Viking Press, 1961.

Greenberg, Gerald S. *Tabloid Journalism: An Annotated Bibliography of English-Language Sources.* Westport, CT: Greenwood Press, 1996.

Kamp, David. "The Tabloid Decade." *Vanity Fair*, February 1999, 62–82.

Mencken, H. L. *The Vintage Mencken*, ed. Alistair Cooke. New York: Vintage Books, 1955.

Morton, Paula E. *Tabloid Valley: Supermarket News and American Culture.* Gainesville: University Press of Florida, 2009.

Walker, Mike. *Rather Dumb: A Top Tabloid Reporter Tells CBS How to Do the News.* Nashville, TN: Nelson Current, 2005.

Tales from the Crypt

Tales from the Crypt was one of the most popular and notorious horror comic books of the early 1950s. Like other titles published by EC Comics, *Crypt* featured stories that explored the depravity of human nature and the hypocrisy of middle-class society. Brutality, bloodshed, and sadism were the norm in these stories, and—much to the horror of American parents—children loved it.

When the series became widely imitated by competing publishers, the proliferation of horror comics provoked a public backlash that led ultimately to a 1954 U.S. Senate investigation into the comic-book industry. Chastised publishers adopted a stringent Comics Code that year to police the industry and subsequently prohibited the publication of horror comic books such as *Crypt*. From 1989 to 1996 a television series titled *Tales from the Crypt* based on the comic books aired on the cable channel HBO.

Bradford Wright

SEE ALSO: *Cable TV; Comic Books; Comics Code Authority; EC Comics; Horror Movies; Television.*

BIBLIOGRAPHY

Barker, Martin. *A Haunt of Fears: The Strange History of the British Horror Comics Campaign.* London: Pluto Press, 1984.

Benton, Mike. *Horror Comics.* Dallas, TX: Taylor Publishing, 1991.

Booker, M. Keith, ed. *Encyclopedia of Comic Books and Graphic Novels.* Santa Barbara, CA: Greenwood Press, 2010.

Talk Radio

Credited with shaping presidential elections and blamed for creating a climate of intolerance, talk radio rose to prominence in the 1990s by offering Americans a free, unfiltered, and often national forum. Whether the issue was a pushy boss, a hapless sports team, or a downtown parking crunch, talk radio became a sort of watercooler for the masses. The rise also reflected the increasingly combative nature of American discourse, with on-air arguments; taunts; and racy, satiric routines often the key to a talk show's success. As ratings increased, so did the critics who believed that the radio hosts were, in part, to blame for the increasingly hostile environment that led to a series of high-profile incidents, including the terrorist bombing in Oklahoma City. Leading talk show hosts Howard Stern, G. Gordon Liddy, and Don Imus were branded "shock jocks" for their brash, obnoxious, and often controversial points of view.

As Howard Kurtz notes in *Hot Air*, "When White House chief of staff Leon Panetta wanted to attack Newt Gingrich, the strongest insult he could muster was to accuse the House speaker of acting like 'an out-of-control radio talk show host.'" But whether agitator or great equalizer, talk radio offers anyone with a telephone a chance to become part of the national debate. Its influence can be felt off the dial as well, with radio jocks writing best-selling books, starring in films, and being spoofed on comedy shows such as *Saturday Night Live*.

Don Imus. *Don Imus is known for combining humor with serious and sometimes controversial commentary on his syndicated radio talk show.* ROBIN PLATZER/CONTRIBUTOR/FILMMAGIC/GETTY IMAGES.

EARLY DEVELOPMENT

The emergence of talk radio was as much the result of technological advances as the need for an open forum. Although commercial radio came into being in the 1920s, the toll-free telephone lines and satellite hookups that encouraged the spread of the talk-radio format did not arise until sixty years later. In the early days of radio, before television, the best-known voices were those of comedians making the jump from the vaudeville stage, old-style newsmen, and sportscasters. The first true talk-radio host may have been celebrity interviewer Barry Gray, who began broadcasting out of New York City in the mid-1940s. Gray's show, however, lacked one key element: the caller. Jerry Williams, who went on the air in Boston in 1957, became the first to take calls.

In the late 1950s, equipment was introduced that made possible the seven-second delay, enabling hosts to put callers on the air without fear. Talk radio received a similar boost in the 1980s with the spread of satellite and digital-phone technologies, which made toll-free numbers more affordable for station managers. Emboldened by the fact that these calls were being made not only to a radio station but also in many cases a radio station in another time zone, callers embraced this new forum. They could yell at another human and risk nothing more than being cut off by the host.

In addition to technical limitations, talk radio had been held back by the 1949 Fairness Doctrine, which required equal time for opposing views. Ronald Reagan abolished the Fairness Doctrine in 1987, and talk radio grew rapidly. It spread from seventy-five stations nationwide in 1980 to 125 by 1987 and 1,350 by 1998.

From the start, talk radio proved a strong voice for political protest. Jerry Williams brought consumer advocate Ralph Nader onto the air to criticize automobile makers in the 1960s. Twenty years later, Williams led a repeal of a law requiring the mandatory use of seat belts in Massachusetts. In 1988 Congress wanted to vote itself a 51 percent pay raise. A nationwide network of talk show hosts, led by Detroit's Roy Fox, suggested that listeners send tea bags to Washington, D.C., to show their displeasure. More than 150,000 tea bags were dumped in front of the White House; Congress withdrew the pay raise. During the national health care debate in the early 1990s, a survey of members of Congress revealed that 46 percent of them found talk radio the most influential media source, whereas only 15 percent cited the *New York Times*.

KING AND LIMBAUGH

As talk radio gained stature, so did the voices behind it. In many cases, they belonged to failed disc jockeys who had tried in vain to fit into the more conventional music format. Larry King was a broadcasting veteran who first went on the air in 1960 in Miami, Florida. He later struggled with a gambling problem, had three bad marriages, and was eventually arrested for misusing $5,000 from a business associate. In 1978 King got what just about everyone in radio gets: a second chance. From the 12th Floor Studio in Crystal City, Virginia, he launched the first nationally broadcast radio show, talking from midnight to 5:30 a.m. The success of his show proved that national talk shows could make it. King eventually left radio for his nightly interview television talk show on the Cable News Network (CNN) and launched a regular column in *USA Today*, laying the foundation for the rise of the talk star.

Rush Limbaugh, a college dropout who had failed repeatedly as a rock-and-roll disc jockey, launched his talk show in the mid-1980s, immediately establishing himself as a conservative voice; his show went national in 1988. No matter that Limbaugh had not registered to vote for several presidential elections; he was courted by President George H. W. Bush as the 1992 elections approached. Seeking his on-air support, Bush invited Limbaugh to the White House and even carried the talk show host's bags. Limbaugh's influence was considered so widespread that an effort by Congress to bring back the Fairness Doctrine in the 1990s was quickly dubbed the "hush-Rush" bill by the *Wall Street Journal*.

Limbaugh's success provided ample fodder to talk radio's critics, and his on-air mistakes created a strong anti-Rush backlash. The *Flush Rush Quarterly* spurred much of it, reporting Limbaugh's errors. On the Reagan-era Iran Contra scandal, for example, Limbaugh stated: "There is not one indictment. There is not one charge." In reality, there had been fourteen persons indicted and eleven who had either pleaded guilty or been convicted.

STERN AND IMUS

Limbaugh's histrionics were mild compared to those of the freewheeling Howard Stern, the self-proclaimed "moron" of talk radio. Stern made no secret of his distaste for his profession. "Radio is a scuzzy, bastard industry that's filled with deviants, circus clown rejects, the lowest of the low," he said. On the air, he discussed his sexual fantasies, argued with his staff, belched, and complained about the size of his penis. Unlike many other talk shows, Stern attacked celebrity culture instead of celebrating it. He called Oprah Winfrey "a big dolt with an empty, oversized head" and Roseanne "a fat slob."

Stern also promoted a series of "B"-level figures, from Jessica Hahn, known for her affair with television preacher Jim Bakker, to Frank Stallone Jr., the less famous brother of Sylvester. Stern's reporter, "Stuttering" John Melendez, carried out further attacks on celebrity culture. Disarmed by the stutter, expecting another *Entertainment Tonight*–styled softball interview, celebrities were shocked when confronted by John's questions. When Gennifer Flowers held a press conference to address her affair with then-presidential candidate Bill Clinton, Stuttering John stole the show from the pack of mainstream reporters. "Gennifer," he asked, "did Governor Clinton use a condom?" When Alfred Sikes, chairman of the Federal Communications Commission (FCC), fined Stern's employer, Infinity, $1.7 million for allegedly broadcasting obscenities, the radio host responded, on the air, by saying that he hoped that Sikes would develop cancer.

If Stern and Limbaugh were considered too controversial by many, Don Imus eventually found a balance between shock radio and serious discourse. He was known in his early career for outrageousness and for substance abuse. After treatment for alcoholism in 1987, he changed the format of his show to include political discussion together with a mix of news, racy skits, and spoof songs. Imus found himself in line with the media elite, interviewing President Clinton at one point and regularly hosting serious news veterans such as Cokie Roberts, Dan Rather, and Tim Russert.

It is this range—from the serious to the frivolous—that talk radio proponents say makes the medium more powerful than the generally entertainment-focused programming on television talk shows. *Talkers* magazine reports that the top five issues on talk radio between 1990 to 1995 were the O. J. Simpson case, the 1992 elections, the Persian Gulf War, the Oklahoma City bombing, and the Los Angeles riots. But lest it be taken too seriously, *Talkers* also rated discussion of John Wayne Bobbitt, the man whose penis was surgically reattached after it had been cut off by his enraged wife, higher than debates on Bosnia and gays in the military.

NATIONAL PUBLIC RADIO

For those more interested in serious-minded talk, National Public Radio (NPR) emerged a decade before Limbaugh, Stern, and Imus, and it developed its own distinctive style, known in part for its lengthy reports and the breathy but understated delivery of its hosts. NPR made its debut on May 3, 1971, with its first broadcast of *All Things Considered*. That first broadcast reached a few hundred thousand listeners through only 104 public radio stations. Twenty-five years later, *All Things Considered* was reaching about sixteen million Americans through NPR's 520 member stations, all the while holding faithful to the wishes of its first director, Bill Siemering, who wanted "calm conversation, analysis and explication."

By the late 1990s, NPR had long established itself as a dependable voice, but the influence of hot talkers such as Limbaugh and Stern was still being debated. Limbaugh took credit for the Republican victories during the 1994 congressional elections and made the cover of *Time* magazine, which asked in its headline: "Is Rush Limbaugh Good for America?" By the end of 1996, however, President Clinton had won a second term and the conservative movement was attempting to rediscover its voice.

OUTLOOK

Nobody debated whether talk radio would survive. It had made stars of big mouths (Stern, Imus), political impresarios (Limbaugh, Liddy), shrinks and sex therapists (Dr. Laura Schlessinger, Dr. Judy Kuriansky), and even discarded politicians (former New York governor Mario Cuomo, former New York City mayor Ed Koch). In the opinion of many, the United States had become, as Howard Kurtz wrote, "a talk show nation."

Shock radio could go too far, as was demonstrated by the firing of Imus for calling members of the Rutgers University women's basketball team "nappy-headed hos" in 2007. In early 2012 the focus was on Limbaugh, whom columnist Maureen Dowd called "the puppet master of the Republican Party." Limbaugh, who appears daily on a three-hour talk show, took aim at Sandra Fluke, a student at Georgetown Law School who was lobbying the school to require that contraception be covered by campus insurance. On air, Limbaugh called her a "slut" and a "prostitute" and suggested that she put a video of herself having sex on the Internet if she wanted the public to pay for her contraception. The backlash was immediate, coming from both Democrats and Republicans. Even Imus weighed in against Limbaugh. Limbaugh offered what many felt was a token apology, and advertisers began dropping his program. In the days following his tirade, the Democratic Party raised $1.6 million to continue to fight the Republican "war on women."

Geoff Edgers

SEE ALSO: *Bakker, Jim, and Tammy Faye; Celebrity; CNN; Disc Jockeys;* Entertainment Tonight*; The Internet; Iran Contra; King, Larry; Limbaugh, Rush; Nader, Ralph; The* New York Times*; Rather, Dan; Reagan, Ronald;* Roseanne*; Satellites;* Saturday Night Live*; Schlessinger, Dr. Laura; Shock Radio; Simpson, O. J.; Stallone, Sylvester; Stern, Howard; Telephone; Television;* Time*;* USA Today*; Vaudeville; The* Wall Street Journal*; Winfrey, Oprah.*

BIBLIOGRAPHY

Colford, Paul D. *The Rush Limbaugh Story: Talent on Loan from God*. New York: St. Martin's Press, 1993.

Cox, Jim. *American Radio Networks: A History.* Jefferson, NC: McFarland, 2009.

Dowd, Maureen. "Have You No Shame, Rush?" *New York Times*, March 4, 2012.

Farhi, Paul. "Rush Limbaugh Apologizes Again, but Advertisers Continue to Sever Ties." *Washington Post*, March 5, 2012.

Fowler, Gene, and Bill Crawford. *Border Radio: Quacks, Yodelers, Pitchmen, Psychics and Other Amazing Broadcasters of the American Airwaves*. Austin: Texas Monthly Press, 1987.

Kurtz, Howard. *Hot Air: All Talk All the Time*. New York: Time Books, 1996.

O'Connor, Rory. *Shock Jocks: Hate Speech & Talk Radio: America's Ten Worst Hate Talkers and the Progressive Alternatives*. San Francisco: AlterNet Books, 2008.

Press, Bill. *Toxic Talk: How the Radical Right Has Poisoned America's Airwaves*. New York: Thomas Dunne Books, 2010.

Stern, Howard. *Private Parts*. New York: Simon & Schuster, 1993.

Wertheimer, Linda. *Listening to America: Twenty-Five Years in the Life of a Nation as Heard on National Public Radio*. Boston: Houghton Mifflin, 1995.

Talking Heads

From its early days, the band Talking Heads defied categorization. Playing in New York during the height of the mid-1970s punk scene, the preppy-looking trio became a punk band by association. Despite being musically different from their peers, the group shared a similar minimalist sound, a combination of energy and intelligence, and a self-conscious and unpretentious demeanor. Some critics described their intellectual approach as "art rock," though the term failed to capture the group's appeal. Talking Heads were cerebral, but they were eminently danceable too. Like the characters in their songs, the band's music dramatized the human predicament between head and heart.

EARLY CAREER

David Byrne (vocals and guitar), Tina Weymouth (bass), and Chris Frantz (drums) formed Talking Heads in 1975 after dropping out of the Rhode Island School of Design and relocating to New York. Their first single, "Love Goes to a Building on Fire," was released in early 1977, displaying the band's spare technique. The same year they signed to Sire Records, an independent label whose roster included punk legends the Ramones, releasing *Talking Heads '77*. The album saw the addition of keyboardist Jerry Harrison, a former graduate student at Harvard.

The album appeared to ecstatic reviews. The lyrics to "Don't Worry about the Government" celebrated civil servants and life's more mundane qualities: "My building has every convenience / It's going to make life easy for me." The song's simplicity was almost shocking in its honesty. Hardly a tentative songwriter, Byrne was also capable of writing tense songs such as "No Compassion" and "Psycho Killer." The latter, although not a hit single, brought the group widespread attention for its psychodrama: "I can't sleep 'cos my bed's on fire / Don't touch me I'm a real live wire."

The group's 1978 release, *More Songs about Buildings and Food*, began a long collaboration with producer Brian Eno, who essentially became the fifth member of the band. The album produced a Top 40 hit, a cover of soul singer Al Green's "Take Me to the River," providing a glimpse into the Heads' future commercial successes and forays into dance, funk, and international rhythms. The song also vindicated the band's commercial philosophy: "It wouldn't please us to make music that's impossible to listen to," Byrne said in *Rolling Stone*. "But we don't want to compromise for the sake of popularity. It's possible to make exciting, respectable stuff that can succeed in the marketplace."

EXPLORATION OF SOUND

The opening track on 1979's *Fear of Music*, "I Zimbra," had polyrhythmic arrangements that announced the group's new musical direction, but not everyone was paying attention. "Life during Wartime," one of the group's best-known songs, contained the line, "This ain't no disco," which some mistakenly interpreted to mean that Talking Heads were the new standard bearers for the antidisco movement. *Remain in Light*, which was released in 1980, was the realization of the polyrhythmic experiment in "I Zimbra." Augmented by a host of outside musicians, the album had the feeling of a free-flowing jam session yet was tightly structured and disciplined.

Remain in Light displayed funk and African influences at a time when many whites thought the term *black music* referred to several distinct musical forms, such as disco, funk, soul, and rhythm and blues. Although the first single "Once in a Lifetime" was not a huge commercial hit, National Public Radio in 2000 named it one of the most important American musical works of the twentieth century. In 1990 *Rolling Stone* ranked the album the fourth best of the 1980s and in 2003 named it the 126th greatest album of all time, the highest of any Heads release.

The next year found the band pursuing solo projects that continued their musical blends. Weymouth and Frantz's side project, *Tom Tom Club* (1981), contained a merger of new wave, dance music, and rap. The self-titled album included "Genius of Love," a song sampled by several R&B and rap artists of the 1990s. Byrne completed a score for *The Catherine Wheel*, a dance performance by Twyla Tharp that proceeded with *Remain in Light*'s sound. Byrne's next project was for an experimental theater piece called *Music for the Knee Plays* (1985), which employed traditional New Orleans brass band struts and funeral marches. His skill in working with other musical forms was hitting its stride.

The band's first album in three years was 1983's *Speaking in Tongues*. Eno was no longer sharing production chores, and the band had shed many of its guest musicians. Talking Heads had a hit with "Burning Down the House," reaching their peak of popularity with the 1984 film, *Stop Making Sense*. Directed by Jonathan Demme, the film documented the Heads' 1983 tour and won the National Society of Film Critics' Award for Best Documentary. The band had excelled in creating music videos such as "Once in a Lifetime," which featured Byrne dancing like a marionette. The group's interest in film peaked with 1986's *True Stories*, the soundtrack to the movie of the same name written and directed by Byrne.

BREAKUP AND LEGACY

By the late 1980s international musical styles were being adopted by mainstream artists such as Peter Gabriel and Paul Simon. Talking Heads recorded three albums after 1985, producing hit singles such as "And She Was" before unofficially breaking up in 1988. In 1996, at the peak of alternative music's popularity, the group re-formed as the Heads, without Byrne, and recorded *No Talking Just Head*. Byrne sued his former bandmates and asked for an injunction against the album's release. A settlement was reached shortly before the album's debut, and *No Talking* was released to generally abysmal reviews.

Byrne continued to tour, record, and pursue his interest in world music, launching his own label, Luaka Bop, dedicated to Brazilian music. He also published the book *Bicycle Diaries* in 2009 and was featured in the 2010 documentary *Ride, Rise, Roar* about his tour with Eno. Harrison focused on producing other artists, such as Violent Femmes and Crash Test Dummies. Frantz and Weymouth's band Tom Tom Club continues to record and tour. Unlike many bands from their era, the Talking Heads never got back together, although they played in 2002 at their induction into the Rock and Roll Hall of Fame.

Daryl Umberger

SEE ALSO: *Disco; Funk; Green, Al; New Wave Music; Punk; The Ramones; Rap; Rhythm and Blues;* Rolling Stone*; Simon, Paul; Top 40.*

BIBLIOGRAPHY

Bowman, David. *This Must Be the Place: The Adventures of Talking Heads in the 20th Century*. New York: HarperEntertainment, 2001.

Davis, Jerome, and Mark Rowland. *Talking Heads*. New York: Vintage/Musician, 1986.

Gans, David. *Talking Heads*. New York: Avon, 1985.

Gittins, Ian. *Talking Heads: Once in a Lifetime: The Stories behind Every Song*. Milwaukee, WI: Hal Leonard, 2004.

Hermes, Will. *Love Goes to Buildings on Fire: Five Years in New York That Changed Music Forever*. New York: Faber & Faber, 2011.

Reese, Krista. *The Name of This Book Is Talking Heads*. London: Proteus Books, 1982.

Reynolds, Simon. *Rip It up and Start Again: Postpunk 1978–1984*. New York: Penguin Books, 2006.

Tang

Tang instant beverage entered American popular culture in the 1960s with a remarkable journey to outer space. The vitamin-fortified drink was first marketed in the late 1950s as a healthful alternative to soda pop. After being chosen by the National Aeronautics and Space Administration (NASA) to be the drink of the astronauts, Tang flew on several flights in the 1960s and soon became a drink of choice for children hoping to emulate the feats of the astronauts. Despite the introduction of new flavors in addition to the classic orange, Tang's popularity diminished in the 1980s and 1990s along with America's excitement over the space program. By 2010 Kraft Foods was marketing Tang in both powder form and ready-to-drink bottles and had found sales growth for the brand in international markets. Tang was being sold in many different countries using local fruit flavors, but orange remained the most popular worldwide.

Angela O'Neal

SEE ALSO: *NASA.*

BIBLIOGRAPHY

Holland, Gini. *The 1960's.* San Diego, CA: Lucent Books, 1999.

Varnam, Alan H., and Jane P. Sutherland. *Beverages: Technology, Chemistry and Microbiology.* New York: Chapman Hall, 1994.

Tanning

In the late nineteenth century, high fashion dictated the maintenance of alabaster skin. Creamy white skin signified a person of privileged status, not an unfortunate sun-darkened field laborer. But as the industrial age dawned and laborers increasingly spent long hours in factories and the coal haze above city streets blocked the sun from reaching their tenement windows, the professional-managerial class, with its increased leisure time, embraced a culture of outdoor living. Furthermore, the consumer culture that emerged along with the products of the industrial age prompted a cultural shift toward an emphasis on appearance. Advertising, motion pictures, and the popular press inundated people with images of the body: images that emphasized the display of hedonism, leisure, and sexuality. A tan soon became a status symbol.

Tanning Salon. *Despite the overwhelming evidence of their negative effects, indoor tanning salons remain popular.* IV MIRIN/SHUTTERSTOCK.COM.

SUNTANNING IN FASHION

Fashion proved the greatest influence on the popularity of the suntan. Many learned about fashion through film; in the early 1920s Béla Balázs had noticed that film was a major influence in the cultural shift away from words and toward visual images that "drew attention to the appearance of the body, the clothing, demeanour, and gesture," according to Mike Featherstone in *Theory Culture and Society*. Douglas Fairbanks Sr. was among the first to popularize the suntan. In his films and publicity shots in the popular press, his bronzed skin became an emblem of his vigorous pursuit of outdoor activities. While other male celebrities quickly followed his lead, women, even Fairbank's wife, Mary Pickford, preserved their light skin.

Europe continued to dictate fashion at this time, so when fashion designer Coco Chanel returned from vacation with a deep bronze tan and began using tanned mannequins for her designs in the 1920s, tanning transformed into a cultural obsession in and of itself. Consequently, the deep-cut backs of women's dresses in the 1920s and 1930s required tanned skin for the wearer to be appropriately fashionable. The more revealing fashions became adornments for bronzed skin, and by 1946 women could tan their skin publicly in as little as a bikini.

The new sun worship prompted by fashion had support from science, which had begun to report the healthful benefits of sunshine at the turn of the twentieth century. Previous warnings about the sun's harmful effects on the skin gave way to new research that had proven the sun's healing qualities on such diseases as rickets and tuberculosis in the late 1800s. Articles announcing the healing benefits of heliotherapy and tanned skin proliferated. Antebellum health adviser William A. Alcott promoted the idea that "not a few individuals would be gainers in point of health, especially children and females, by being slightly tanned over their surface." Dr. Edwin E. Slosson reported in *Daily Science News Bulletin* in 1923 that, instead of being harmful, "it seems that ultra-violet and violet rays may be positively beneficial," according to *Literary Digest*, which featured a photo of babies at the beach with the caption: "Nothing is better for babies—or grown people either—than a good coat of tan, we have it on high scientific authority." And by 1929 an American article proclaimed that "the skin of a healthy man is brown, smooth, and sleek," according to Featherstone.

During the warm months, interest in sunbathing on beaches began in the interwar years and continued unabated into the early 1980s. But while many could sunbathe during the summer, only the wealthy could afford the cost of air travel, which allowed them to spend winters in sunny locations. There were few status symbols as obvious as tanned skin during the winter. *Newsweek* reported in 1966 that in the "jet age" the tan had become a status symbol that could "be worn like Brooks Brothers clothes as a sure sign of affluence." Tanned skin became synonymous with health, wealth, leisure, and style.

NEW WAYS TO TAN

"Nothing is as transient, useless, or completely desirable as a suntan," a prefeminist Gloria Steinem wrote in *The Beach Book* in 1963, adding, "What a tan will do is make you look good, and that justifies anything." Steinem perfectly captured the kind of zeal that fueled many hours of sunbathing. The desire for tanned skin prompted formulas for obtaining the perfect tan to abound. People coated themselves in baby oil and red iodine, believing this mixture would turn their skin a fashionable caramel brown color. Some smoothed on a purple peroxide foam that promised to speed the tanning time and bleach the body hair to enhance the depth of the tan's color by contrast. Others restricted their diets before tanning, eating vitamins and avoiding wine and spicy foods, to increase their chances of getting a coppery glow. Some even rubbed their skin with salt to tan faster. The truly fanatical sun worshippers lay inside aluminum coffins or ringed their necks with sun reflectors to ensure themselves an even tan.

The proliferation of tanning salons and tanning booths promised people of every class access to a year-round tan by the late 1970s. (Indoor tanning became one of the fastest-growing industries in North America, increasing 54 percent between 1986 and 1988, according to *U.S. News & World Report*.) People willingly sought out these seemingly ridiculous activities because, according to *Newsweek*, "only the result counts." An episode of the 1990s television sitcom *Seinfeld* highlighted the folly of these tanning strategies when the character Kramer coats himself in butter as he basks in the sun, only to appear and smell like a well-roasted turkey to his hungry friend Newman.

Any number of brands sought to capitalize on the craze for suntanned skin. The first branded suntan cream available in America was a Coppertone product made mostly of cocoa butter that was introduced in 1944. By 1945 Coppertone Suntan Oil was advertised with an "Indian Head seal" and the slogan "Don't Be a Paleface." But Coppertone's most enduring image—"Little Miss Coppertone"—debuted on Miami, Florida–area billboards in 1953. The illustration of the tanned young girl whose dog is pulling down her panties to display her white-skinned bare bottom soon graced billboards, advertisements, and product labels across the country. The little girl came to represent the youthfulness associated with tanned skin. If Little Miss Coppertone represented the youthfulness of tanned skin, Bain de Soleil Orange Gelée advertisements captured the sexual appeal of the suntan. The 1980s advertisements for the Bain de Soleil brand using the sultry and darkly tanned model Kriss Ziemer epitomized the glamour many hoped a tan would confer.

TANNING AND SKIN CANCER

While the hazardous effects of a sunburn and the detrimental effects of sunbathing on fair-skinned people had long been known, worries about tanning began to reach a wider audience by the 1970s as the incidence of skin cancer had begun to rise noticeably. Between 1930 and 1986 the Skin Cancer Foundation of the American Cancer Society figured that the incidence of melanoma had risen tenfold, from one in every 1,500 people to one in every 150. Research into the ill effects of sunbathing resulted in the proliferation of products to protect the skin from burning. The Coppertone Solar Research Center created and initiated the use of SPF factors—a standardized measurement of a sunscreen's ability to protect the skin and prevent sunburn—in sun lotions in 1972, but SPF numbers (2, 4, 6, 8) did not appear on product labels until 1977. And not until 1980 did the Skin Care Foundation grant Coppertone Supershade 15 an acceptance seal as an "effective aid in the prevention of sun-induced skin cancer."

When research in the 1980s revealed that most exposure to the sun occurs during childhood, Little Miss Coppertone began to promote sun protection over tanned skin for children. The first offering of SPF 30 formulas appeared in 1993, and by 1998 Coppertone had joined with the American Academy of Dermatology to promote the use of sunblocks in the "Block the Sun, Not the Fun" campaign, the first in-school sun safety program. By 1994 Little Miss Coppertone could be seen wearing a hat, sunglasses, and a T-shirt, when she was used to help promote the new ultraviolet (UV) index.

The scientific authority of the 1990s condemned tanning. Dr. Darrell Rigel, professor of dermatology at New York University, Manhattan, told *FDA Consumer Magazine* contributor Alexandra Greeley that "there is no such thing as a safe tan. Why does the body tan? Because the body is being injured by ultraviolet radiation that hits it. This causes the body to make melanin, a natural sun screen. So to get tan, you must get injured first." The American Cancer Society reported that by the late 1990s the incidence of malignant melanoma had risen to one in seventy-five and predicted that 44,200 people would be diagnosed with the disease in 1999, of which 9,200 would die, according to Charles Gandee in a 1999 *Vogue* article. The scientific community has linked the rise in the number of affluent young people afflicted with melanoma to air travel. Dermatologist Patricia Wexler told Gandee that the melanoma rate is higher in younger generations "because our parents didn't go to the Delano or the Hamptons or St. Bart's."

Despite the overwhelming evidence of the negative effects of the suntan, tanning product companies continued to promote the benefits of a tan. The Bain de Soleil brand began to use lightly tanned women in its ads but continued to promote products to help obtain deeply bronzed skin into the 1990s, as did many other brands. One significant change in the promotion of tanning products was the residual rhetoric about how "healthy" tanned skin looks. A 1999 radio ad for the Go Bronze sunless tanning lotion sold at the Bon Marché department store, for example, featured a woman saying that she wanted tan, healthy-looking skin too.

CHANGING IDEAS

Sunless tanning products could offer the "look" without the damage. Products that turned the skin a realistic tan color made the sunless tanning market more viable in the 1990s and early twenty-first century than it had been when the first sunless tanning products were introduced in 1960. These first products, including Schering-Plough Healthcare Products' Quick Tanning lotion, the first sunless tanning lotion, offered an orangish tan color that was easily identified as fake. Some fashion magazines, such as *Vogue*, furthered the interest in sunless tanning lotions by presenting articles about the harmful effects of the sun in the same issue that featured photos of bathing-suit-clad models covered in sunless tanning lotions frolicking on a sun-drenched beach.

Though by the late 1990s some continued to mimic the looks of actor George Hamilton, dubbed by *Newsweek* as the "Sultan of Suntan" for the year-round tan he has maintained for decades, there had been a steady increase in the number of people who Coppertone identified as "sun concerned"—a category based on sales of products with an SPF number 8 or higher—since the early 1980s. A 1994 survey by the American Academy of Dermatology reported that one-third of the respondents never sunbathed and always used a sunscreen, according to Greeley. And dermatologist Dennis Gross indicated that, in assessing his patients from the mid- to late 1990s, "the number of women who consider a tan desirable has gone from the majority to the minority," according to Gandee.

Aside from the medical reasons to curb suntanning, the sexual appeal of pale skin was beginning to gain followers with the admirers of such public figures as Gwyneth Paltrow, Nicole

Kidman, and Uma Thurman. In addition, *Elle* and other fashion magazines began to feature paler models for spring and summer issues. Despite these developments, skin cancer rates continued to be a problem. In 2012 the American Cancer Society predicted that there would be more than 75,000 cases of skin cancer that year, with nearly 12,000 deaths. The American Academy of Dermatology recommends using sunscreen with an SPF of at least 30. Other recommendations include wearing a hat, a shirt, and sunglasses for protection from the sun's harmful rays. With such warnings and guidelines becoming widely known, perhaps future historians may well look back on the fashionable suntan as an oddity of the twentieth century.

Sara Pendergast

SEE ALSO: *Advertising; Billboards; Cancer; Chanel, Coco; Consumerism; Fairbanks, Douglas, Sr.; Leisure Time;* Newsweek*; Pickford, Mary;* Seinfeld*; Steinem, Gloria;* Vogue.

BIBLIOGRAPHY

Adler, Jerry; Mariana Gosnell; Karen Springen; et al. "The Dark Side of the Sun." *Newsweek*, June 9, 1986, 60–64.

"The Advantage of Tan." *Literary Digest*, September 22, 1923, 27–28.

Alcott, William A. *The Home-Book of Life and Health; or, The Laws and Means of Physical Culture Adapted to Practical Use.* Boston: Phillips, Sampson, 1856.

American Cancer Society. *QuickFACTS: Melanoma Skin Cancer: What You Need to Know—NOW.* Atlanta, GA: American Cancer Society, 2012.

"Brown as a . . . " *Newsweek*, August 1, 1966, 58–59.

Featherstone, Mike. "The Body in Consumer Culture." *Theory Culture and Society* 1, no. 2 (1982): 18–33.

Gandee, Charles. "Safety in Numbers." *Vogue*, May 1999, 310–313, 339.

Greeley, Alexandra. "Dodging the Rays." Rockville, MD: Department of Health and Human Services, Public Health Service, Food and Drug Administration, 1994.

Harris, Marvin. "The Rites of Summer: History of the Sun Tan." *Natural History*, August 1973, 20–22.

Levine, Art. "A New Bronze Age for the Tanning Industry: Indoor Tanning Salons Take on Their Critics." *U.S. News & World Report*, September 8, 1997, 48.

Segrave, Kerry. *Suntanning in 20th Century America.* Jefferson, NC: McFarland, 2005.

Steinem, Gloria. *The Beach Book.* New York: Viking, 1963.

Sweet, Cheryl A. "'Healthy Tan'—A Fast-Fading Myth." Rockville, MD: Department of Health and Human Services, Public Health Service, Food and Drug Administration, 1990.

Tap Dancing

An indigenous American dance form that evolved as African and European dance traditions merged during the eighteenth and nineteenth centuries, tap dancing involves the production of syncopated sounds by a dancer's feet. Tap dancing has been a mainstay of virtually every type of popular performing arts entertainment in the United States, from minstrel shows to vaudeville, Broadway and Hollywood musicals, nightclubs, precision dance teams, and television variety programs. A remarkably adaptive dance form, tap has fused with and reflected the changing entertainment sensibilities of American audiences for more than 200 years. Tap routines figure prominently in children's dance recitals, and adult amateurs find tap dancing a fun form of recreation and exercise.

BEGINNINGS

Some trace the roots of tap back to the ships that transported enslaved Africans to America, where Europeans observed Africans' dancing and vice versa; however, the two dance traditions began to merge in a significant way on southern plantations. When a mid-eighteenth-century law forbade slaves from playing drums, African Americans increasingly used their feet to sound out rhythms when dancing. Their observation of the articulated foot actions of Irish step dancing and other European dances practiced by whites engendered a new hybrid dance form in which blacks imbued fancy footwork with sophisticated rhythmic sensibilities. Oftentimes owners entered slaves into contests that awarded prizes for the most daring or complex dancing. These challenges inspired individual creativity and competition, characteristics that continued to drive the development of tap dancing into the twentieth century and beyond.

Minstrel shows, the most popular form of American entertainment during the mid-nineteenth century, codified tap as a stage dance. The most esteemed practitioner was William Henry Lane, known as Master Juba, a free African American who was one of the few blacks allowed to perform onstage with whites. As new social dances sprang up around the turn of the twentieth century, performers incorporated them into the tap dance vocabulary. By 1910 attaching metal plates to the bottoms of shoe heels and toes became commonplace (previously dancers had worn wooden-soled shoes or had pounded nails or pennies into the leather soles).

VAUDEVILLE AND BROADWAY

The next important step in the advancement of tap dancing was vaudeville. Tap dancers, striving to earn a living in a business that depended on continuously pleasing and surprising audiences, invented myriad impressive maneuvers. Different categories of tap dancers evolved, including eccentric dancers, such as Ray Bolger, who sported a loose-limbed, rubbery movement style; comedy dancers, such as Bert Williams and George Walker, who danced as foils for each other; flash acts, such as the Nicholas Brothers, who added spectacular acrobatic tricks to their tapping; class acts, such as Charles "Honi" Coles, with elegant costuming and movements; and rhythm or jazz tappers, such as John W. Bubbles, who explored the complicated rhythms of jazz music.

By the 1930s tap-dancing chorus lines had become a prominent feature of Broadway and Hollywood musicals. Although musical theater stars such as Fred Astaire, Gene Kelly, Ann Miller, Eleanor Powell, Shirley Temple, and Bill "Bojangles" Robinson advanced the popularity and artistry of tap dancing, ensembles did little to fuel tap's artistic evolution. The art of tap dancing lies in the subtle nuances and complex rhythmic interchanges between the beat, music, and tapping sounds. When executed by large groups, the sounds must be simple; otherwise multiplication may cause muddiness.

HARLEM'S HOOFERS

The art of tap transformed at the Hoofers Club in Harlem, New York, as great African American male tappers staged dance challenges, pushing each other to hone and amplify their skills. In this style of tap dance, referred to as jazz or rhythm tap, the hoofer functioned much like a jazz musician. In contrast to the strictly choreographed theatrical style of tapping, rhythm tap emphasized improvisation, as dancers created their own steps and rhythms to the popular swing music of the era.

During the 1950s tap hibernated as performance outlets vanished. The Hoofers Club closed, and jazz tappers found that the crowded rhythms of bebop, the postwar form of jazz music, left no space for tap sounds. Rock and roll was too loud for tapping, and the age of movie musicals was ending. Nightclubs turned to comedy and music acts, ballet overtook Broadway, and vaudeville had long since died.

RESURGENCE

The tap revival began when a group of old-time hoofers appeared at the Newport Jazz Festival in the early 1960s and intrigued the public with their artistry. In 1969 a series of Tap Happenings held in Manhattan featured legendary jazz tappers. By the 1970s the rhythmic explorations of these early dancers were recognized as an integral part of the history of jazz music. Their work, and tap dancing in general, began to be viewed more seriously.

The 1970s was a nostalgic decade on Broadway and saw the reintroduction of tap dancing in musicals and numbers such as *No, No, Nanette* (1971), *Bubbling Brown Sugar* (1976), and "42nd Street" (1980). The 1974 release of Metro-Goldwyn-Mayer's *That's Entertainment!* reacquainted audiences with the tap dance stars of old Hollywood musicals. Although some African Americans had turned away from tap over concerns that it fostered black stereotypes, the resurgence of tap dancing was significantly stoked by white women who brought rhythm tap to the modern dance concert stage.

Beginning in the 1980s, the emergence of new tap dance stars put a contemporary urban posture on tapping, ushering in a revolutionary era for the art form. Actor, singer, and dancer Gregory Hines appeared in the Broadway musicals *Sophisticated Ladies* (1983) and *Jelly's Last Jam* (1991). In the film *Tap* (1989), he pioneered an electronic form of tapping, originally engineered by Broadway veteran Al Desio, whereby the dancer makes music through electronic transmitters built into the tap shoes. In 1989 Congress declared National Tap Dance Day to be May 25, Bojangles Robinson's birthday. During the next decade, dancer and choreographer Savion Glover fused tap with hip-hop sensibilities, wowing audiences with his fierce, heavy-footed style in the Broadway revue *Bring in 'Da Noise, Bring in 'Da Funk* (1996) and becoming recognized as a tap prodigy.

Called America's folk dance, tap dancing in the twenty-first century incorporates influences from world music and other percussive dance forms. Practiced internationally, contemporary tap features more women than ever before. Although dance critics consider it a serious art form, tap is most commonly performed within the context of popular entertainment.

Lisa Jo Sagolla

SEE ALSO: *Astaire, Fred, and Ginger Rogers; Ballet; Broadway; Hip-Hop; Hollywood; Jazz; Kelly, Gene; Minstrel Shows; Modern Dance; The Musical; Newport Jazz and Folk Festivals; Rock and Roll; Stepping; Swing Dancing; Television; Temple, Shirley; Vaudeville; Walker, George; Williams, Bert.*

BIBLIOGRAPHY

Ames, Jerry, and Jim Siegelman. *The Book of Tap: Recovering America's Long Lost Dance*. New York: David McKay, 1977.

Frank, Rusty E. *Tap! The Greatest Tap Dance Stars and Their Stories, 1900–1955*. New York: Da Capo Press, 1990.

Hill, Constance Valis. *Tap Dancing America: A Cultural History*. New York: Oxford University Press, 2010.

Knowles, Mark. *Tap Roots: The Early History of Tap Dancing*. Jefferson, NC: McFarland, 2002.

Stearns, Marshall, and Jean Stearns. *Jazz Dance: The Story of American Vernacular Dance*. New York: Schirmer Books, 1968.

Tarantino, Quentin *(1963–)*

Perhaps best known for writing and directing the Academy Award–winning film *Pulp Fiction* (1994), Quentin Tarantino was one of the most critically lauded film directors of the 1990s. In *Reservoir Dogs* (1992) he redefined the primary elements of the pulp genre—murder, drugs, sex, violence, and betrayal—by introducing self-consciously witty dialogue, formal inventiveness, and slick yet casual violence. As a result, he raised what had been traditionally judged as a "B" movie genre to an avant-garde art form. His style became a brand name in the film industry.

Born in Knoxville, Tennessee, on March 27, 1963, Tarantino was a movie-obsessed high school dropout and video clerk at the famous Video Archives in Los Angeles. He spent his spare time working on the screenplays that would become his later movies. Making connections through a job at a movie production company, CineTel, Tarantino was able to get the script for *True Romance* (1993) in front of director Tony Scott, who would go on to helm the project. Featuring what would come to be known as Tarantino's trademark profanity and violence, quirky performances from Christopher Walken and Dennis Hopper attracted the attention of both critics and audiences. The movie would become as renowned for its monologues as for its violence.

FILMS OF THE 1990s

Tarantino used the money he made from the sale of the *True Romance* script to finance his directorial debut in *Reservoir Dogs*—it helped that actor Harvey Keitel loved the script so much he was willing to star for a fraction of his usual salary. The film premiered at the 1992 Sundance Film Festival. Although its violence was blamed for the film's limited release and lack of box-office success, the movie was critically celebrated and became a cult favorite. *True Romance* was released the following year, cementing Tarantino's new celebrity status.

In 1994 Tarantino's movie *Pulp Fiction* was released to great acclaim. Starring Uma Thurman and Samuel L. Jackson, *Pulp Fiction* won the Palme d'Or at the Cannes Film Festival and was nominated for seven Academy Awards. It was the first indie film to break $100 million at the box office, and Tarantino won the Oscar for Best Original Screenplay with writing partner Roger Avary. In addition to Tarantino's trademark violence, nonlinear story line, and dialogue laden with pop culture references, the film featured a return to fame for actor John Travolta. While on the one hand lauded for his writing by the Academy, on the other hand Tarantino was infuriated to find that director and screenwriter Oliver Stone had rewritten parts of the script for *Natural Born Killers* (1994). Tarantino fought to have his name taken off the film and was ultimately credited with the story versus the screenplay.

The success of *Pulp Fiction* gave Tarantino carte blanche in Hollywood, and he became involved with all aspects of moviemaking. He acted in films such as *Desperado* (1995, director Robert Rodriguez's sequel to *El Mariachi*); *Destiny Turns on the Radio* (1995); and another Rodriguez movie, *From Dusk till Dawn* (1996), for which Tarantino also wrote the screenplay and produced. He also directed a segment of the collaborative production *Four Rooms* (alongside Rodriguez again). His own film *Jackie Brown* (1997), a tribute to 1970s blaxploitation films starring Pam Grier and based on a story by Elmore Leonard, was well received critically but did not satisfy fans looking for another *Pulp Fiction*–type film.

FILMS OF THE TWENTY-FIRST CENTURY

While working on *Pulp Fiction*, Tarantino and Thurman had discussed the idea of a film featuring a professional female assassin, and eventually Tarantino completed the script. The revenge epic was titled *Kill Bill* and would be split into two parts, *Kill Bill: Vol. 1* and *Kill Bill: Vol. 2*. An homage to the martial arts genre fused with the sensibility of a so-called spaghetti Western and plot elements of pulp novels, the movies have been both praised and derided for their pastiche style. The first film is heavy with stylized violence and sardonic brutality. The second movie leans more on the typical Tarantino dialogue with a little less swordplay. The film also features David Carradine in his most high-profile role since the 1970s. Chris Nelson, a makeup artist on the two films, reports that they used more than 450 gallons of fake blood during filming. Both films were hugely successful, with each grossing more than $65 million in domestic box-office revenue and more than $150 million worldwide.

Tarantino and director-friend Rodriguez had met at the Toronto Film Festival in 1992 when their debut films *Reservoir Dogs* and *El Mariachi*, respectively, were shown. After working together on several films in the 1990s, Rodriguez invited Tarantino to film a segment for his new project, *Sin City* (2005). This led to an even bigger collaboration, with the two directors putting together an homage to "B"-movie exploitation films with *Grindhouse* (2007), a combination of two feature-length movies: *Planet Terror*, a zombie picture starring Rose McGowan and directed by Rodriguez, and *Death Proof*, with Kurt Russell as a homicidal maniac who runs down girls with his car, directed by Tarantino. The films were shown as a package deal, complete with faux trailers between features—one of which would later be fleshed out into Rodriguez's *Machete* (2010). While well received by the critics, the feature combination flopped at the box office. The films were released separately in Europe.

INGLOURIOUS BASTERDS

After working for many years on a revisionist-history script about a guerrilla band of Jewish American Nazi killers during World War II, Tarantino finally produced *Inglourious Basterds* (2009). (He has consistently refused to explain the odd spelling of the title.) The collage of interlocking stories featured great performances from an eclectic cast, including Brad Pitt, Mélanie Laurent, Diane Kruger, Michael Fassbender, and Eli Roth. The movie was a huge success both critically and commercially, garnering more than $320 million worldwide at the box office. It was ultimately nominated for four Golden Globes and eight Oscars, and then-relatively unknown Austrian actor Christoph Waltz swept the Best Supporting Actor trophies at the Globes, the Oscars, and the Screen Actors Guild awards for his role as Colonel Hans Landa, the so-called Jew hunter.

Tarantino basked in his *Inglourious Basterds* success as the head of the jury at the 2010 Venice Film Festival and was roasted later that year at the Friars Club—Thurman made him drink out of her shoe, and Jeff Ross suggested that the name Tarantino is actually Italian for *plagiarism*. While the evening was lighthearted as expected, the event had been postponed from its original September date after Tarantino's longtime editor Sally Menke was found dead in the Hollywood Hills after going on a walk with her dog. Menke was nominated for Oscars for film editing for her work on both *Pulp Fiction* and *Inglourious Basterds*, and she and Tarantino were reported to have an extremely collaborative process.

Tarantino has repeatedly referred to his desire to film *Kill Bill 3* but has said that he wants at least ten years between the second and third films. No matter the movie, Tarantino's audiences are served a hearty dose of shallowness, ease, and familiarity combined with as much violence and sex as an R rating can indulge.

Adrienne Russell

SEE ALSO: *Academy Awards; "B" Movies; Blaxploitation Films; Cult Films; DiCaprio, Leonardo; Grier, Pam; Hollywood; Hopper, Dennis; Keitel, Harvey;* Kill Bill*; Leonard, Elmore;* Natural Born Killers*; Pitt, Brad;* Pulp Fiction*; Spaghetti Westerns; Stone, Oliver; Sundance Film Festival; Travolta, John.*

BIBLIOGRAPHY

Bernard, Jami. *Quentin Tarantino: The Man and His Movies.* New York: Harper Perennial, 1995.

Clarkson, Wensley. *Quentin Tarantino: Shooting from the Hip.* London: Piatkus Books, 1995.

Greene, Richard, and Mohammad, K. Silem, eds. *Quentin Tarantino and Philosophy: How to Philosophize with a Pair of Pliers and a Blowtorch.* Chicago: Open Court, 2007.

Tarbell, Ida *(1857–1944)*

One of the magazine *McClure*'s muckrakers, Ida Tarbell changed the oil business in America. A female journalist was not common at the turn of the twentieth century, especially one who exposed industry. From *McClure's* excerpts, Tarbell published *The History of Standard Oil* in 1904. In the two-volume work she revealed the many unfair business practices of Standard Oil and owner John Rockefeller. Called the Joan of Arc of the oil region, Tarbell became a whistleblower on the most powerful trust in America. The government broke up the Standard Oil Company in 1911.

Born in Pennsylvania to an oil baron father, Franklin Tarbell, she was the only female freshman to attend Allegheny College. After earning a degree in biology in 1880, she joined the staff at *McClure's* with muckrakers Ray Stannard Baker and Lincoln Steffens. Her inquiry into Rockefeller was not all from professional interest—her father invented wooden barrels to hold oil and attained great wealth but nearly went bankrupt when he failed to sell his business to Rockefeller. Tarbell's father's ultimate victory, however, would come when his daughter's *The History of Standard Oil* and its revelations led to the breakup of the largest corporation in America. In 1999 the *New York Times* listed *The History of Standard Oil* as the fifth (out of 100) most influential journalist work of the twentieth century.

Tarbell was also a historian. Her first major publication in 1895 was on Napoleon and Josephine Bonaparte. She wrote eight books on Abraham Lincoln, his relatives, and his family. In fact, until the release of Abraham Lincoln Papers in 1947, she was considered the measure of Lincoln history. Tarbell made her mark in an era when women journalists were often not taken seriously. In recent years, with the decline of the newspaper industry and the rise of Internet news reporting, many new works have come out to support the use of journalism to expose injustices. A recent biography of Tarbell has emphasized the importance of investigative journalism.

Scott Stabler

SEE ALSO: *Baker, Ray Stannard; Muckraking; The Rockefeller Family; Steffens, Lincoln.*

BIBLIOGRAPHY

Brady, Kathleen. *Ida Tarbell: Portrait of a Muckraker*. New York: Seaview/Putnam, 1984.

Somervill, Barbara A. *Ida Tarbell: Pioneer Investigative Reporter*. Greensboro, NC: M. Reynolds, 2002.

Tarbell, Ida. *The History of the Standard Oil Company*. New York: McClure, Phillips, 1904.

Weinberg, Steven. *Taking on the Trust: The Epic Battle of Ida Tarbell and John D. Rockefeller*. New York: W. W. Norton, 2009.

Tarkanian, Jerry *(1930–)*

Jerry Tarkanian—ever so appropriately nicknamed "Tark the Shark"—is both one of the most talented and controversial college basketball coaches in the history of the sport. His nineteen-year tenure at the University of Nevada–Las Vegas (UNLV), which began in 1973 after a five-season stint as head coach at Long Beach State, was highlighted by a quartet of appearances in the Final Four, a national championship in 1990, and an overall record of 509 to 105.

Throughout his UNLV career, however, Tarkanian was constantly in conflict with the National Collegiate Athletic Association (NCAA), the governing body of college sports. In the late 1970s, the NCAA placed the Runnin' Rebels' hoops program on two years' probation for recruiting violations. The school was also directed to suspend Tarkanian as coach for the same period. Tarkanian blocked his suspension with a court order, which was overturned by the Nevada Supreme Court. The ensuing legal battle went all the way to the U.S. Supreme Court, which in 1988 made a ruling that essentially upheld the injunction against the 1977 suspension and instructed the NCAA to follow due process in its disciplinary actions

Two years after UNLV won the national championship in 1990, the NCAA commenced another major investigation of Tarkanian. The coach resigned under pressure and again sued the NCAA, accusing the organization of trying to run him out of college basketball. The suit was settled in 1998, just before it was set to go to trial. Admitting no liability, the NCAA paid Tarkanian $2.5 million. "They can never, ever, make up for all the pain and agony they caused me," Tarkanian has said. "All I can say is that for 25 years they beat the hell out of me."

Tarkanian eventually signed on as the basketball coach of Fresno State, from which he had graduated in 1955, but the conflict surrounding him did not subside. In 1997 controversy swirled on campus when it was revealed that the Bulldogs had recruited a convicted wife abuser and that two of his players were accused of assaulting their girlfriends. The following year, two players were jailed on charges of grand theft and assault with a deadly weapon.

In 2002 Tarkanian retired from Fresno State and from coaching. On the upside, he had led the Bulldogs to six successive twenty-win seasons and finished his career with well over 700 NCAA Division 1 victories. On the downside, after leaving Fresno State, the NCAA placed the Bulldogs on probation for abuses committed during Tarkanian's tenure as coach. In the years following his retirement, he unsuccessfully attempted to win elected office. He was the 2006 Republican Party nominee for Nevada secretary of state but lost the election. Four years later, he failed in his bid to unseat U.S. Senator Harry Reid.

Despite all the hullabaloo attached to his name, Tarkanian remains a seminal figure in the sport of college basketball, where his unconventional style combined with his phenomenal success have left a deep and lasting impact on the game.

Rob Edelman

SEE ALSO: *Basketball; Las Vegas; National Collegiate Athletic Association (NCAA).*

BIBLIOGRAPHY

Harp, Richard, and Joseph McCullough. *Tarkanian: Countdown of a Rebel*. New York: Leisure Press, 1984.

Tarkanian, Jerry, and Terry Pluto. *TARK: College Basketball's Winningest Coach*. New York: McGraw-Hill, 1988.

Tarkanian, Jerry, and Dan Wetzel. *Runnin' Rebel: Shark Tales of "Extra Benefits," Frank Sinatra, and Winning It All.* Champaign, IL: Sports Publishing, 2006.

Valenti, John, and Ron Naclerio. *Swee'Pea and Other Playground Legends: Tales of Drugs, Violence and Basketball.* New York: M. Kesend, 1990.

Yaeger, Don. *Shark Attack: Jerry Tarkanian and His Battle with the NCAA and UNLV*. New York: HarperCollins, 1992.

Tarkington, Booth *(1869–1946)*

A prolific and versatile writer of mainstream fiction, (Newton) Booth Tarkington is remembered for his portrayals of middle-class life in Indiana during the late nineteenth and early twentieth centuries. His best-known works, *The Magnificent Ambersons* (1918) and *Alice Adams* (1921), were awarded the second and the fourth Pulitzer Prizes for fiction, respectively. The former was adapted for the screen by Orson Welles in 1942, and the latter is considered by critics to be Tarkington's finest accomplishment. A novelist, a playwright, an essayist, and briefly a politician, Tarkington produced a total of 171 short stories, 21 novels, 9 novellas, and 19 plays along with a number of movie scripts, radio dramas, and even illustrations over the course of a career that lasted from 1899 until his death in 1946. Having achieved a wide audience but not the lasting respect of critics, most agree that his finest work was done around the time of World War I.

EARLY LIFE

Born in Indianapolis to the sort of comfortably well-established family that he later popularized in his fiction, Tarkington dictated his first short story to his sister at the age of six, and by sixteen he had written a fourteen-act work on Jesse James. After graduation from Princeton, Tarkington moved to New York and labored futilely for five years to get his work published before turning to his own background for inspiration. Tarkington said, "I had no real success until I struck Indiana subjects." He later described his first book, *The Gentleman from Indiana* (1899), as "my emotional tribute to the land of my birth." A commercial success, it received only lukewarm comment from critics, many of whom labeled it an unrealistic romance. Thus was a general pattern set for Tarkington's career. A 1991 *Dictionary of Literary Biography* entry on Tarkington suggests, "Although he had more talent than most of his contemporaries, his work never quite achieved major significance, and he had to be content with a large rather than a discriminating audience."

Booth Tarkington. *Booth Tarkington was awarded the Pulitzer Prize for fiction for each of best known works,* The Magnificent Ambersons *(1918) and* Alice Adams *(1921).* HULTON ARCHIVE/STRINGER/ARCHIVE PHOTOS/GETTY IMAGES.

CAREER

In 1902 Tarkington married Laurel Louisa Fletcher and was elected to the Indiana House of Representatives as a Republican, though he was forced to vacate his seat a year later due to an illness. The couple spent most of the next decade traveling through Europe, but Booth's happiness, as well as his writing, were disrupted by bouts of excessive drinking and finally by divorce in 1911. One year later he married Susanah Keifer and took up his literary career again full time. In 1914 he began work on his "Penrod" stories, which recaptured boyhood life in the late nineteenth century.

In the postwar years, Tarkington's career reached its zenith with two Pulitzer Prizes. His prolific output was not accidental; by all accounts he was a literary workhorse, sometimes putting in eighteen-hour days of solid writing with little or no diversion until the task of the moment was complete. The popularity of his work during this period made him financially comfortable, and beginning in the 1920s Tarkington settled into what he called "the milk run"—summers at Kennebunkport, Maine, and winters in Indianapolis. Cataracts gradually diminished his sight, and in 1930 he went completely blind. Surgeries successfully returned part of his vision a year later, but his vitality was diminished. He turned primarily to children's stories in the final phase of his career, while also becoming a significant collector of art. He died in 1946 after an illness.

WORKS

The volumes that Tarkington completed over the course of the first half of the twentieth century form a documentary testament of industrialization, urbanization, and social flux in urban Middle America. Biographer James Woodress characterizes his body of work as "a paradigm of growth in the Midwest." In his fiction, Tarkington clearly expresses his distaste for the bustle and grime of urban life. *The Magnificent Ambersons* documents the incursion of the dirty streets, unkempt masses, and smoke-filled air of the industrializing metropolis into an idyllic nineteenth-century world. Part of the tragedy of the book is aesthetic, as the beautiful estate of the great family is vanquished by bland, utilitarian architecture and uncultured people. Yet, ironically, Tarkington chose to spend much of his adult life in the city whose fall he lamented in his fiction. Addressing this paradox, Tarkington said, "I belong here, I am part of it, and it is part of me. I understand it and it understands me. I would be out of touch with what I know best if I did not spend at least part of each year in Indianapolis."

In describing his style, an anonymous reviewer in the *North American Review* commented, "Mr. Tarkington is neither a realist, nor a romanticist, nor a localist, nor an impressionist, nor any special kind of literary artist, but simply a complete novelist." Tarkington himself fought the impetus to pigeonhole his work, vehemently rejecting the label of "romanticist" that some reviewers tried to force upon him. His literary heroes were Mark Twain and especially William Dean Howells. Dickinson quoted Tarkington on his wholesome, all-American tastes: "[He] admires all those things which every decent, ordinary, simple-hearted person admires" and "hates precisely those things hated by all honest, healthy, 'American,' people." Yet, Tarkington was nonetheless criticized by some conservative contemporaries for his critique of the American fascination with wealth, superficiality, and what he often referred to as "bigness" as ends in themselves, an overriding selfishness that he saw leading society toward mental and spiritual degeneration.

Tarkington lives on through his two Pulitzer Prize–winning novels, the "Penrod" stories, and Orson Welles's 1942 film adaptation of *The Magnificent Ambersons*. These are remembered for their sentimental and socially conscious renderings of boyhood and middle-class life in the American Midwest around the turn of the twentieth century. Tarkington is not considered a literary genius, despite the Pulitzers. Instead, his legacy is as one of the most popular writers of the first half of the twentieth century—a period in which he sold more than five million volumes.

Steve Burnett

SEE ALSO: *Best Sellers; Twain, Mark; Welles, Orson; World War I.*

BIBLIOGRAPHY

Chevalier, Tracy, ed. *Twentieth-Century Children's Writers*, 3rd ed. Chicago: St. James Press, 1989.

Dickinson, Asa Don. *Booth Tarkington: A Sketch*. Garden City, NY: Doubleday, Doran, 1928.

Fennimore, Keith J. *Booth Tarkington*. Boston: Twayne, 1974.

Greasley, Philip A. *The Authors*. Bloomington: Indiana University Press, 2001.

Martine, James J., ed. *Dictionary of Literary Biography*, vol. 9 of *American Novelists, 1910–1945*. Detroit, MI: Gale Research, 1981.

Mayberry, Susanah. *My Amiable Uncle: Recollections about Booth Tarkington*. West Lafayette, IN: Purdue University Press, 1983.

Tarkington, Booth. *The World Does Move*. Garden City, NY: Doubleday, Doran, 1928.

Woodress, James. *Booth Tarkington: Gentleman from Indiana*. Philadelphia: Lippincott, 1955.

Tarzan

Tarzan is one of the world's best-known literary characters. Created by author Edgar Rice Burroughs, he first appeared in the pulp fiction magazine *All-Story* in 1912. Also known as Lord of the Jungle, Tarzan went on to conquer other media, appearing in books, movies, comic strips, and comic books and on television and the radio.

Burroughs was born in Chicago on September 1, 1875. After graduating from the Michigan Military Academy in 1895, he remained at the academy as an instructor until the next year when he resigned to join the U.S. Army as a private. He wanted to become an officer and have a career in the army, but during a routine medical exam, army doctors discovered that he had a heart murmur, making him ineligible to serve as an officer. Burroughs left the army in 1897 and went on to hold a series of short-lived jobs. In 1911 he decided to try his hand at writing.

Burroughs wrote *Under the Moons of Mars*, a science fiction novel featuring hero John Carter. He submitted the manuscript to *All-Story* magazine, which liked it and published it as a serial from February to July 1912. The story was so successful that Burroughs kept writing, and his novel, *Tarzan of the Apes: A Romance of the Jungle* appeared in its entirety in the October 1912 issue of *All-Story*.

Tarzan is the son of Lord and Lady Greystoke, who are marooned on the African coast by the mutinous crew of the ship on which they had been traveling. Lord Greystoke builds a hut for himself and his pregnant wife, and it is there that Tarzan is born. His mother dies soon after his birth, and his father is later killed by an attacking band of great apes. A female ape named Kala, who had just lost her own offspring, adopts and raises the human child.

"The apes called him Tarzan, meaning white-skin," the comic strip version explains. "He grew up among them. He learned to speak their language and he lived as they lived in the trees." Somewhere along the way the wild child learns modesty and takes to wearing a sort of sarong, fashioned from a leopard skin. Later, after stumbling upon his family's hut, he discovers books and teaches himself to read. As his knowledge increases, the boy begins to suspect that he is no ordinary ape.

Burroughs was basically a fantasist and well aware that in a real-life situation, his little white-skinned hero would not have made it to his first birthday. But it was more fun ignoring reality. The novice author also had no idea of what Africa was really like. In the pulpwood version of *Tarzan of the Apes*, Burroughs included a tiger named Sabor in his animal cast. His editor failed catch this, and a reader wrote in and pointed out that "the tiger is not and never has been included in the fauna of the African continent."

A TYPICAL VICTORIAN HERO

Eventually Tarzan encounters other humans. He first meets natives, and the interactions are far from cordial. Then another group of mutineers arrives in his stretch of wilderness. This bunch had captured a group of treasure seekers led by Professor Porter; members of his group include his daughter, Jane, and Tarzan's cousin William Cecil Clayton, the present Lord Greystoke and Jane's suitor. Once Tarzan, now a full-grown young man, encounters Jane, he is smitten. He proceeds to rescue her and her friends and to arrange a jungle interlude, perfectly innocent, with her.

Eventually, however, Jane sails back to America, leaving her Jungle Lord behind. Tarzan, with the help of a new friend, establishes that he is the true Lord Greystoke. But when he follows Jane to her home, he becomes convinced that she actually loves Clayton. So rather than tell her or Clayton the truth, he delivers one of the great curtain lines in fiction: "My mother was an Ape. . . . I never knew who my father was."

Burroughs, who was influenced by Victorian fiction, created Tarzan as a typical Victorian hero, a fellow who is a gentleman to the core. And just as true fictional gentlemen such as Oliver Twist and David Copperfield who survive in the urban jungle of nineteenth-century London, Tarzan survives in the jungles of Africa and proves that he, too, is a gentleman. A gentleman, if he is honest and right thinking, cannot be kept from rising to his true rank in society. And Tarzan does just that, eventually winning his rightful title and marrying Jane.

The publication of *Tarzan of the Apes: A Romance of the Jungle* in *All-Story* was a success, and in 1914 it was published as a hardcover book. Burroughs went on to write a total of twenty-six Tarzan books, the majority of them serialized in pulp magazines, such as *Argosy* and *Blue Book*, prior to being published as books. In 1918 the silent movie *Tarzan of the Apes* was released, starring barrel-chested Elmo Lincoln. He was followed in the role by actors Frank Merrill, James Pierce (who married Burroughs's daughter Joan), and P. Dempsey Tabler. In the talkies of the 1930s, Buster Crabbe, Bruce Bennett (under his real name of Herman Brix), and Glenn Morris all took turns wearing the leopard skin.

The definitive Tarzan, however, was Johnny Weissmuller. Not an actor but a record-breaking swimmer, he was in his late twenties when he first took to the trees as Tarzan in *Tarzan the Ape Man*, which was released in 1932. W. S. Van Dyke directed the film, and Maureen O'Sullivan played Jane.

BEYOND MAGAZINES, BOOKS, AND MOVIES

The Tarzan in the movies is not the articulate gentleman of the novels. He is a rather primitive fellow not much more versed in human speech than an actual ape. "My lines read like a backward two-year-old talking to his nurse," Weissmuller once complained. The major reasons for making the screen ape-man less than fluent were probably Weissmuller's slightly flutey voice and his evident inability to deliver any line of dialogue containing more than a half dozen words with any conviction. For swimming, grappling with man and beast, rescuing Jane, and swinging from tree to tree on a vine, though, he had no equal. An assortment of others, usually athletes rather than actors, succeeded Weissmuller in the role in the more than fifty films created around the Tarzan character. Of all the Tarzan films, however, the 1984 *Greystoke: The Legend of Tarzan, Lord of the Apes*, best captures Burroughs's original vision of the character.

Tarzan came to the comic pages as a daily strip in 1929, with a Sunday page added in 1931. The dailies, for several years, were anonymous adaptations of Burroughs's novels. There were no dialogue balloons or sound effects, and the copy, set in type, ran below the pictures. Hal Foster, a seasoned advertising illustrator, drew the first sequences. Having little faith in comics and even less love for Tarzan, he soon dropped the project, and a less gifted artist named Rex Maxon took over drawing the daily and the Sunday. Burroughs, who had originally wanted pulp illustrator J. Allen St. John for the job, never thought much of Maxon's rendering of his hero or the jungle denizens.

Tarzan the Ape Man, ***1932.*** *A movie poster promises "thrills and excitement" from the 1932 movie* Tarzan the Ape Man, *the first of several movies starring Johnny Weissmuller as the Lord of the Apes.* MGM/THE KOBAL COLLECTION.

Since United Feature Syndicate had the final say, all Burroughs could do was write disgruntled letters to the editors there. These apparently had some effect, because Foster was eventually persuaded to come back and draw the Sunday Tarzan page.

Foster drew impressive and ambitious Tarzan pages, and he created ancient Egyptian civilizations surviving in contemporary Africa, Viking pirates, prehistoric monsters on the rampage, and even a foxhunt in rural England with equal ease. When he left the feature in the mid-1930s, Burne Hogarth replaced him. Subsequent artists include Bob Lubbers, Russ Manning, Gil Kane, and Gray Morrow.

United Feature Syndicate included reprints of *Tarzan* in the lineup of *Tip Top Comics*, launched in 1936, and subsequently in *Comics on Parade* and *Sparkler Comics*. Dell introduced original adventures in 1947 with artwork by former Disney artist Jesse Marsh. In later years both Marvel Comics and DC Comics tried, unsuccessfully, to make a go of a comic book devoted to the character. Tarzan's influence in the comics did not die with his strip; other comic strips used the character for comic effect, including *Calvin and Hobbes*, *The Far Side*, *Bizarro*, *Penmen*, *Non-Sequitur*, and *Mother Goose and Grimm*.

Burroughs's hero also appeared in Big Little Books, on the radio, and on television. Disney produced a full-length animated feature in 1999. In 2003 *Tarzan* the television series premiered on the WB network. In it Tarzan is uprooted from the jungle and living in New York City; Jane is a New York City police officer. The show was canceled after only eight episodes.

Ron Goulart

SEE ALSO: Argosy; *Big Little Books; Burroughs, Edgar Rice;* Calvin and Hobbes; *Comic Books; Comics; DC Comics; Disney (Walt Disney Company);* The Far Side; *Marvel Comics;* Pulp Fiction; *Pulp Magazines; Television; Weissmuller, Johnny.*

BIBLIOGRAPHY

Foster, Harold. *Tarzan in Color: Volume 1 (1931–1932)*. New York: NBM Publishing, 1992.

Goulart, Ron, ed. *The Encyclopedia of American Comics*. New York: Facts On File, 1990.

Porges, Irwin. *Edgar Rice Burroughs: The Man Who Created Tarzan*. Provo, UT: Brigham Young University Press, 1975.

Sampson, Robert. *Strange Days*, vol. 2, *Yesterday's Faces: A Study of Series Characters in the Early Pulp Magazines*. Bowling Green, OH: Bowling Green University Popular Press, 1984.

Taliaferro, John. *Tarzan Forever: The Life of Edgar Rice Burroughs, Creator of Tarzan*. New York: Scribner, 1999.

Tattoos

Tattoos are indelible patterns created by introducing pigments under the skin. Tattooing dates back to prehistory, and it has been practiced at times by almost all cultures for purposes that range from group identification to personal ornamentation, ritual marking, and artistic expression. A tattoo may be a simple shape or line composition or a complex image with a rich palette of colors. Some designs are deeply symbolic; others are merely decorative or sentimental, perhaps commemorating a special event or relationship. In modern times, tattooing has enjoyed periods of popularity but has also acquired negative connotations.

On the negative side, tattooing became a widespread practice among gangs and prison populations in twentieth-century America, and in Europe tattoos were used to identify concentration camp inmates during the Holocaust. Consequently, many people came to associate tattoos with criminality and barbarism. Beginning in the 1960s, however, tattooing began to be viewed as a form of self-expression. By the twenty-first century celebrities routinely revealed their body ink. Tattoo art was found in mainstream magazines and museums, and the culture of tattooing had become a popular subject for reality television. In part, the increasing acceptance of tattooing came from improvements in the art and science of it, which made the practice safer, less painful, and more aesthetically interesting.

TATTOO HISTORY

Apart from earlobe piercing, tattooing has become the most popular form of "body modification" in most parts of the contemporary world. Body modifications can be identified as far back as the Bronze Age, and along with tattooing, they include piercings of various body parts, scarification (patterns created by the formation of scar tissue), and reshaping of body parts (through stretching or constriction). Such practices were common not only in tribal cultures but also in early civilizations from Egypt to India to Central America, and they persisted in many populations well into later periods. However, body modification was explicitly forbidden by both Islam and Judaism and was regarded by official Christianity as a pagan practice. Thus, tattooing largely disappeared from Europe and the Middle East. European explorers eventually encountered body-modification practices on their journeys to new lands, and in the eighteenth century British sailors brought home the Polynesian practice of body marking called *tatau*.

Tatau soon became *tattoo*, and by the late nineteenth century this exotic practice had become highly fashionable among British and European nobility. In the United States, where Martin Hildebrandt had opened the first professional tattoo shop in 1846, many Civil War soldiers sought tattoos as symbols of patriotism or tokens of remembrance, and tattooing soon took on the status of a folk art. It remained a costly, time-consuming process, however, until Samuel O'Reilly introduced his electric tattoo machine in 1891. The new device made it possible to use a number of needles simultaneously for outlining as well as shading. With this technique, according to Margo DeMello in *Bodies of Inscription*, the "true Americana style of tattooing was born: strong black lines; . . . heavy black shading; and a dab of color."

As tattooing became faster and cheaper, the rich lost interest, but the range of American customers expanded. Most tattoos were copied from generic, often crude designs known as "flash." Multiple tattoos were usually unrelated flash emblems, placed randomly on the body. Some people, however, covered their bodies with patterns and images in order to find work in sideshows. In *Tattooed: The Sociogenesis of a Body Art* (2003), Michael Atkinson characterizes this as the "carnival/circus era," during which tattooing became better known to the public but also acquired associations with the carnival subculture of "freaks" and hustlers. The next period, according to Atkinson, was an aggressively masculine "working class era" that lasted from the 1920s through the 1950s and turned tattoos into badges of belonging for certain marginalized groups.

GOING MAINSTREAM

As tattooing migrated downward on the social and economic scales during the first half of the twentieth century, body ink was increasingly viewed by the middle class as a symbol of cultural deviance and by the social sciences as an indicator of pathological tendencies. In the mid-1960s, however, tattooing underwent not just a renaissance but a reinvention in what Atkinson calls the "rebel era." Tattoos emerged as part of the counterculture movement, signifying a rejection of mainstream social values and a return to a "primitive" experience. At first, the practice—like many other aspects of hippie life in the 1960s—provoked establishment outrage, but the idea of tattoos as a form of self-expression ultimately proved to be widely attractive. This was especially true among women, many of whom regarded tattooing as one way to reclaim the female body from patriarchal suppression. By the 1970s, as the rebel era gave way to the New Age era, experimenting with body art had begun to take on an element of middle-class chic.

At the same time, a new generation of tattooists, often with training in the visual arts, began to replace the unsophisticated, industrial ink work of their predecessors with more creative, subtle designs that were often developed on a much larger scale. As Clinton Sanders explains in *Customizing the Body: The Art and Culture of Tattooing*, "Congruent with their background and aesthetic orientations, the new tattoo artists [drew] images from diverse artistic sources," such as "fantasy/science fiction illustration, traditional Japanese styles, tribal designs, portraiture, and abstract expressionism." This more serious generation of tattooists also introduced an array of subtle ink colors, along with equipment and techniques that enabled greater precision. By the 1990s, fine-art tattooing was well established—and there was also an increasing emphasis on hygienic practices that reduce (but cannot entirely eliminate) the risks of infection associated with any procedure that breaks the skin barrier.

In the middle of the first decade of the 2000s, tattoo culture became familiar to viewers of cable television shows such as *Inked* (A&E) and *Miami Ink* (TLC), so there was little controversy when a tattooed Barbie doll hit the market in 2011. With such general acceptance, however, tattoos no longer serve as a means to provoke outrage or symbolize social rebellion. For many young people, other forms of "bodymod"—especially multiple piercings—have become the preferred way to proclaim ""outsider" status. Nevertheless, tattoos are in a special category. Piercings can be abandoned, and they convey little information about the person sporting them. Even abstract tattoos, on the other hand, depict a state of mind or point of view that becomes part of the body forever. Although advanced laser instruments have made it more feasible to remove tattoos, the process is still uncertain, uncomfortable, and costly. In most cases, the decision to become tattooed remains a commitment for life.

Cynthia Giles

SEE ALSO: *Barbie; Body Piercing; Cable TV; Hippies; New Age Spirituality; Reality Television; Television.*

BIBLIOGRAPHY

Atkinson, Michael. *Tattooed: The Sociogenesis of a Body Art*. Toronto: University of Toronto Press, 2003.

DeMello, Margo. *Bodies of Inscription: A Cultural History of the Modern Tattoo Community*. Durham, NC: Duke University Press, 2000.

Sanders, Clinton, and D. A. Vail. *Customizing the Body: The Art and Culture of Tattooing*. Philadelphia: Temple University Press, 2008.

Taxi

At the Sunshine Cab Company on the television series *Taxi* (1978–1983), everyone comes off a little angry for putting in long hours at an unrewarding job while yearning for something better. Everyone, that is, except Alex Reiger (Judd Hirsch), the only practical thinker in the entire garage, who declares in the initial episode, "Me? I'm a cab driver. I'm the only cab driver in this place." Like Ralph Kramden in *The Honeymooners*, each week the characters of *Taxi* would take a new chance at success only to return to the garage defeated but still hopeful about the future.

Taxi was not only one of the best situation comedies of the late 1970s, but it was also one of the most awarded and critically acclaimed. It won eighteen Emmys in its five-year run (winning the Outstanding Comedy Series Emmy the first three of those years) and helped to launch the careers of Danny DeVito and Christopher Lloyd.

The series came into existence solely on the track record of its writer-producers, James L. Brooks, Stan Daniels, David Davis, and Ed Weinberger, who had been behind the highly successful *The Mary Tyler Moore Show* and its spin-offs. The four men decided to leave the show's production company, MTM Enterprises, and form their own production unit at Paramount Studios, which they named John Charles Walters Productions, after a sign Weinberger had seen in an English pub. There was no such person at the company, but the name sounded dignified.

Wanting to get away from shows about white-collar female workers, Brooks decided to revive an idea he had with Davis of doing a show about taxi drivers, an idea once considered in conjunction with Jerry Belson (cocreator of the TV series *The Odd Couple*) before it was abandoned. The producers had persuaded MTM to purchase the rights to an article on cabbies by Mark Jacobson that ran in the June 21, 1976, issue of *New York* magazine. Grant Tinker of MTM agreed to sell the rights for the article to the new production company for the same amount he had purchased them—$1,500.

BLUE-COLLAR CHARACTERS

The part of Alex Reiger was written with Hirsch in mind, but after the failure of his series *Delvecchio*, Hirsch was reluctant to return to television until he read the show's first script. Although Reiger would sometimes be troubled by philosophical questions when not dispensing advice to the others, Louie De Palma (DeVito), the firm's disagreeable, dishonest dispatcher, never seemed to suffer from hurt feelings or a troubled conscience.

The De Palma character was originally a minor part until casting director Joel Thurm brought in DeVito, who walked into the office in character and quickly came to dominate the show just as he did the garage. By and large, the show resisted using gratuitous insults and wisecracks, with the exception of De Palma, who was given to saying things like, "Banta, sometimes I wish you were smarter just so you could see how dumb you are" or "Fill out this form, and I hope you fill it out better than you fill out your pants." De Palma provides the conflict and is the antagonist the other cabbies band against.

Taxi. Taxi *starred, from left, Danny DeVito as Louie De Palma, Judd Hirsch as Alex Reiger, Marilu Henner as Elaine Nardo, Tony Danza as Tony Banta, Andy Kaufman as Latka Gravas, and Christopher Lloyd as Rev. Jim Ignatowski.* PARAMOUNT TELEVISION/THE KOBAL COLLECTION.

Other characters went through changes as well. Tony Danza's Tony Banta character was originally supposed to be a punch-drunk Irish heavyweight rather than an unsuccessful young boxer, while Marilu Henner's Elaine Nardo character was supposed to be a tough-minded Italian woman in her thirties rather than a young divorced woman looking to make ends meet, but the producers altered the characters to fit the performers they selected.

The characters on the show were realistic, except for Latka Gravas (Andy Kaufman), the cheerful mechanic from a mythic foreign country, who was included because the producers had enjoyed Kaufman's stand-up act and wanted to incorporate the kind of material he did into the show. Other characters included an aspiring actor Bobby Wheeler (Jeff Conaway) unable to land a part, and Reverend Jim Ignatowski (Lloyd), a former hippie burnout and minister of the "Church of the Peaceful" who seemed off in his own world and had an infinite number of peculiarities. (Reverend Jim had been written as a one-shot and was recruited to become a regular the second season after the shy John Burns character—played by Randall Carver—was written out of the show.)

What makes the show a classic is the superior quality of the writing and acting that went into the series. *Taxi,* like *M*A*S*H,* found a way to bring humor to what would often be potentially tragic situations. The characters are often estranged from other family, and as coworkers they become friends, forming an unlikely family of their own. Hirsch was particularly adept at picking out subtle, perceptive nuances in his performances, while Kaufman, Carol Kane (who played Latka's wife Simka), and Lloyd were simply off-the-wall wacky and amusing. The entire cast was nominated for a Golden Globe Award in 1979.

CRITICAL SUCCESS

Left alone by the network and given a good time slot, *Taxi* started off as a resounding success, finishing its first two seasons in the top twenty. However, in the third season, ABC moved the series to Wednesday night and saw the ratings fall off. When it was moved to Thursdays the following season, it did even worse, falling to fifty-third place, and it was soon canceled despite its Best Comedy Series Emmy wins.

Strangely enough, Tinker left MTM in 1981 to become the head of NBC, where he promoted the idea of quality programming. He beat out a bid from HBO for giving the series a second chance, and *Taxi* was picked up by NBC for its fifth and final season. (DeVito recorded a promo as De Palma snarling, "Same time, better network!")

Unfortunately for the show's followers, the numbers remained low. The following September when the Academy of Television Arts and Sciences presented the series with three Emmys, Outstanding Lead Actor in a Comedy Series winner Hirsch quipped, "Don't they know we've been canceled?" In accepting his award, Hirsch declared, "If you can't get it out of your mind, and you got to keep giving laurels to us, then you should really put us back on the air." However, there was to be no second reprieve, although the series proved very successful in syndication.

Dennis Fischer

SEE ALSO: *Brooks, James L.;* The Honeymooners*; Kaufman, Andy;* The Mary Tyler Moore Show*;* The Odd Couple*; Sitcom; Television.*

BIBLIOGRAPHY

Garner, Joe. *Made You Laugh: The Funniest Moments in Radio, Television, Stand-Up, and Movie Comedy*. Kansas City, MO: Andrews McMeel, 2004.

Lovece, Frank, and Jules Franco. *Hailing* Taxi. New York: Prentice Hall, 1988.

Sorensen, Jeff. *The* Taxi *Book: The Complete Guide to Television's Most Lovable Cabbies*. New York: St. Martin's Press, 1987.

Waldron, Vince. *Classic Sitcoms: A Celebration of the Best in Prime-Time Comedy*. New York: Macmillan, 1987.

Taxi Driver

Taxi Driver captures the angst felt throughout America in the post-Vietnam era. Directed by Martin Scorsese, *Taxi Driver* (1976) is a psychological drama and a tale of alienation, displaced sexuality, and life in the big city. The film stars Robert De Niro, Harvey Keitel, Cybill Shepherd, Jodie Foster, Peter Boyle, and Albert Brooks. Scorsese's male protagonists tend to be energetic, violent, and driven toward public recognition; Travis Bickle, played by De Niro, is no exception. Travis is a Vietnam-era vet who yearns to "be somebody" but succeeds only in becoming increasingly deranged and lonely as the film progresses. Scorsese's cinematography and the cast's skillful acting make *Taxi Driver* an enduring portrait of one of America's most disconcerting periods.

Set in New York City, *Taxi Driver* traces the daily habits of Travis as he drives his cab through the city, working long hours to avoid the monotony of his life. The film opens with shots of De Niro's eyes looking at the world from behind the glass windshield of his cab, calling to mind his isolation from society, which becomes magnified with time. Travis's life changes when he falls for a political campaign manager named Betsy, played by Shepherd. Betsy's rejection of Travis instigates his obsession with guns and his fixation with the idea of rescuing a teenage prostitute he meets in his cab, played by Foster.

Travis simultaneously destroys his body with drugs, alcohol, and junk food, and yearns to get himself into shape and to get his life organized. These two poles of his personality are best illustrated by an infamous scene in which Travis has a standoff with his mirror image. Travis looks at himself in the mirror and utters the most frequently quoted lines in the film: "You talking to me? You talking to me? You talking to me? . . . Well I'm the only one here." This scene enacts the construction, rehearsal, and performance of masculinity. In the privacy of his own room, Travis practices the role of the type of man he would like to be and calls to mind the anxiety embedded in the process of striving for this masculine ideal in the American post-Vietnam era.

The score for *Taxi Driver* was written by Alfred Hitchcock's composer, Bernard Herrmann, and was completed the day before Herrmann died. While he collaborated with Hitchcock on many films, Herrmann is most famous for composing the soundtracks for *Psycho* and *Vertigo*. Like many of Hitchcock's films, *Taxi Driver* is a film about making movies. In a direct reference to Hitchcock, Scorsese appears in a shot at the beginning of the film. He later acts in a scene in which he and De Niro gaze at the silhouette of a woman through an apartment window (calling to mind Hitchcock's *Rear Window*). The cinematic spectator is continually addressed by shots of De Niro watching movies, films, projectors, the gazes of secret service men through photographic lenses, Travis's mirror, and the car window through which Travis experiences much of the world.

Scorsese grew up in an Italian American community in Little Italy. He entered a seminary after grammar school only to be asked to leave at the age of fourteen after falling in love with a girl. He attributes much of his cinematic fascination with issues of family loyalty, hierarchy, and spirituality to his early years in Catholic school. He made his first short film in high school and went on to study film at New York University. While most of Scorsese's earlier body of work deals with issues pertaining to Italian American identity, he began to turn his camera away from Little Italy later in life with films such as *Alice Doesn't Live Here Anymore* (1974), *The King of Comedy* (1983), *After Hours* (1985), *The Last Temptation of Christ* (1988), and *Kundun* (1997). This is not to say that Italian American themes have not played a continual role in Scorsese's work. His 1990s films, such as *GoodFellas* (1990) and *Casino* (1995), and standards such as *Raging Bull* (1980) and *Mean Streets* (1973) point to his continuing interest in exploring stereotypes of Italian Americans through Mafia narratives.

Kristi M. Wilson

SEE ALSO: *De Niro, Robert; Foster, Jodie;* GoodFellas*; Hitchcock, Alfred; Keitel, Harvey;* Mean Streets*;* Psycho*;* Raging Bull*;* Rear Window*; Scorsese, Martin;* Vertigo*; Vietnam.*

BIBLIOGRAPHY

Lourdeaux, Lee. *Italian and Irish Filmmakers in America: Ford, Capra, Coppola and Scorsese*. Philadelphia: Temple University Press, 1990.

Odabashian, Barbara. "Double Vision: Scorsese and Hitchcock." In *Social and Political Change in Film and Literature*, ed. Richard Chapple. Gainesville: University Press of Florida, 1994.

Page, Ken. "Going Solo: Performance and Identity in *New York, New York* and *Taxi Driver*." In *You Tarzan: Masculinity, Movies, and Men*, ed. Pat Kirkham and Janet Thumin. New York: St. Martin's Press, 1993.

Tamburri, Anthony Julian; Paolo A. Giordano; and Fred L. Gardaphé, eds. *From the Margin: Writings in Italian Americana*. West Lafayette, IN: Purdue University Press, 1991.

Taylor, Elizabeth *(1932–2011)*

Fame and notoriety attached themselves to Elizabeth Taylor very early in her life and never left her. It is more than likely that she will forever occupy a place in both cultural and social history as twentieth-century America's most celebrated woman—as well as one of its most beautiful—and certainly Hollywood's last genuine star in the great tradition. Whether in good films or bad, the pull of her magnetic presence continually drew hordes of fans, mesmerized by her screen persona and her offscreen life, which took on the aura of myth.

A national institution and a living legend, Taylor became the paradigmatic exemplar of media-driven notions of celebrity and an emblem of outrageous excess—conditions that defined her adult image. Her extraordinary, colorful, and, indeed, remarkable life made her an object of constant fascination to the public, among whom she variously evoked admiration or even

Elizabeth Taylor. *Elizabeth Taylor was presented with the Jean Hersholt Humanitarian Award at the 65th Annual Academy Awards ceremony in 1993 for her work as an AIDS activist.* KEVIN MAZUR/CONTRIBUTOR/WIREIMAGE/GETTY IMAGES.

worship, as well as periodically inviting derision or attracting moral outrage. The notoriety, however, that attached to her fabled marriages (seven husbands, eight weddings), her abundant wealth, her disappointments and tragedies, her many illnesses, her weight problems, and her battles with substance abuse served seriously to overshadow her acting achievements to the detriment of her professional reputation.

By the time she voluntarily retired from filmmaking after a character role as Pearl Slaghoople in *The Flintstones* (1994), her last film, Taylor had the longest postwar career of any actress in Hollywood. It was largely as undistinguished as it was lengthy, her abundance of talent and intelligence too often buried, as she herself observed with her customary candor, in a welter of mediocrity. Nevertheless, among her credits, the handful of good roles in worthwhile films rightfully earned her five Academy Award nominations and two Oscars, the French Legion d'Honneur, and the American Film Institute Lifetime Achievement award, while her eloquent campaigning for causes, notably in the field of AIDS research, brought her the Jean Hersholt Humanitarian Award from the Academy of Motion Picture Arts and Sciences.

CHILDHOOD ON THE LOT

Elizabeth Rosemond Taylor was born in Hampstead, London, on February 27, 1932, the daughter of American parents. Francis Taylor was an art dealer and his wife, Sara, was a socially ambitious former stage actress. Thanks to their influential connections, Elizabeth and her elder brother, Howard, enjoyed a privileged early childhood. To escape World War II, the Taylors returned to the United States in 1939, finally settling in Beverly Hills, California, where Francis opened a fashionable gallery in the Beverly Hills Hotel. With child and teen stars a popular fixture of Hollywood movies at that time, Sara was determined that her pretty, violet-eyed daughter would be one of them.

A shy child who loved animals, Elizabeth had no desire to become an actress but, in the grip of an iron-willed mother, found herself at age nine auditioning for MGM, who turned her down, and Universal, who took her on. She made her debut playing an objectionable brat with little to say in a poor comedy called *There's One Born Every Minute* (1942), after which the studio dropped her. She lived the natural life of a child again until late the following year when she made *Lassie Come Home* for MGM, beginning a contractual association with MGM that lasted until the early 1960s. The studio immediately lent her to Fox for a tiny role as the child who dies in *Jane Eyre* (1943), after which she was enrolled in the MGM schoolroom and appeared (mostly in small featured roles) in a string of films that were largely forgettable. It was the death of normality. Owned by the studio and controlled by her mother, Elizabeth did as she was told, her self-image gradually shaped by her movies, her adolescence a fantasy lived through the roles she played.

While training for her first major role—in *National Velvet*—twelve-year-old Elizabeth fell from her horse and sustained a spinal injury, the first of several such over the course of her life. When the film was released in 1944, her performance as Velvet Brown, who, disguised as a boy jockey, wins the Grand National, enchanted critics and audiences alike. Fresh, natural, and vivacious, the adolescent also revealed the beginnings of her great beauty that even the braces on Velvet's teeth failed to mar. Over the next few years Elizabeth was transformed from sparkling teenager to ripening, sensuous woman, with no intermediate stage. As the eponymous *Cynthia* (1947), her role sounded a perilous echo of her own life—an overprotected, overcontrolled teenager battling with her mother (Mary Astor) to gain adolescent freedoms; in *A Date with Judy* (1948) she was the sophisticated, sexy, and knowing teenager who sets out successfully to catch the man (Robert Stack, aged twenty-nine) earmarked for Judy (Jane Powell).

In a radio interview with Louella Parsons just before the release of *Cynthia*, the fifteen-year-old rising star, who had not yet been allowed a boyfriend, said that she wanted to be a great actress but added, with ironic prescience, "most of all, I want to snare a husband." Meanwhile, MGM sent her to England in late 1949 to play a wife—married to Robert Taylor—in *Conspirator*, a film whose only merit was to reveal the actress's burgeoning beauty, talent, and physical maturity. She was seventeen.

INCANDESCENT BEAUTY

All eyes were on the young Elizabeth Taylor by 1949, a year in which she made the cover of *Time* magazine; became engaged to the wealthy and eligible William Pawley Jr. in a blaze of publicity; broke the engagement when he demanded she give up the career to which she was now totally committed; and, on loan to Paramount, began work on *A Place in the Sun*. Under the guidance of director George Stevens, her performance marked a new seriousness in what was the most significant film of her career up to that point and one of the best she ever made. Taylor, at her most incandescent as the young heiress ensnared in a doomed love affair, starred opposite Montgomery Clift. Offscreen, they adored one another, but it was a hopeless situation for the deeply infatuated Taylor, who learned to settle for a close and enduring friendship with the homosexual Clift and fell in love with Nicky Hilton instead.

She met Hilton, heir to the hotel fortune, while filming *A Place in the Sun* and married him in May 1950. The extravagant "fairy-tale" wedding was glitteringly stage managed by MGM, as was the release of her new film, rushed out to coincide with her nuptials. The resulting publicity made *Father of the Bride*, in which Taylor starred as the about-to-be-wed daughter of Spencer Tracy and Joan Bennett, one of the studio's most profitable hits. The real-life, eighteen-year-old bride left on an extended European honeymoon during which she discovered that her husband was a neglectful, abusive, womanizing drunk. By December the marriage was over. Bruised and bewildered, Taylor went back to work, moved to her own apartment for the first time, and was squired by choreographer and director Stanley Donen. MGM disapproved and sent her to England in June 1951 to play a secondary role in *Ivanhoe*.

By the time she returned, *A Place in the Sun* had placed her firmly in the upper echelon of stardom, and she was in love with Michael Wilding, a British actor who was twice her age. Demonstrating the willful determination that became one of the hallmarks of her character, she virtually proposed to him, and they married in 1952. The couple had two sons, but their floundering marriage, doomed from the start by the inequity of age and status, was over by 1956, the release year of *Giant*, in which Taylor gave a fine dramatic performance opposite Rock Hudson and James Dean, and the year she began making *Raintree County*.

A lavish period drama that cast Taylor as a southern belle tormented in love, *Raintree County* (1957) brought the actress her first Oscar nomination. During filming, costar and friend Clift had the car crash that famously left its mark on his beauty. Taylor, who had been devastated by the death of her friend Dean in similar circumstances, was first at the scene, cradling Clift's bloody head in her lap. She remained his closest friend, and it was reportedly at her insistence that the by-then seriously drug- and alcohol-addicted actor was cast in *Suddenly, Last Summer* (1959)—the film that brought her an Oscar nomination for her performance as Katharine Hepburn's traumatized niece.

MARRIAGE AND SCANDAL

In 1957 Taylor was swept off her feet by the flamboyant producer and impresario Mike Todd (born Avrom Goldbogen), twenty-four years her senior. She converted to Judaism and married him in Acapulco in February 1957. The best man was Todd's great friend, crooner Eddie Fisher. August brought the premature and difficult birth of Liza Todd, and Taylor was warned that she could have no more children. (In 1964 Taylor, with Richard Burton, adopted a German-born daughter, to be known as Maria Burton.) In March 1958 Taylor had begun filming *Cat on a Hot Tin Roof* with Paul Newman when Todd's plane, *Lucky Liz*, crashed in a storm. A hysterical and grief-stricken Taylor emerged from sedated seclusion to complete the film, giving a performance of powerful depth as Tennessee Williams's unhappy Maggie the Cat and earning a well-deserved Oscar nomination.

Fisher provided solace in her grief. When he divorced his wife, Debbie Reynolds, to become Taylor's fourth husband, the star's sympathetic public, fueled by the tabloids, turned hostile, branding her a home wrecker. (In truth, the Fisher-Reynolds marriage had been in crisis for some time.) Fisher and Taylor married in a Las Vegas synagogue in May 1959, the year she was approached by Walter Wanger to play the title role in *Cleopatra*. Facetiously agreeing to consider the offer for a fee of $1 million, Taylor was astounded when Twentieth Century Fox agreed to this unprecedented and astonishing sum. But first she had a contractual obligation to fulfill at MGM.

The vehicle chosen for her was *Butterfield 8*, in which she played Gloria Wandrous, high-class hooker and nymphomaniac who pays for her sins by dying in the wreckage of her sports car. The moral climate and censorship rules of the time caused endless headaches in the search for compromise, resulting in a substandard and tacky film that, from the outset, Taylor was opposed to making. Despite the roller-coaster ride of her private life and her volatile temperament, she was no scarlet woman, and her eventual forced acquiescence represented a tough battle that the studio won. She costarred with Laurence Harvey and, at her insistence, her husband, Fisher. Despite the odds, Taylor, the throat scar from her recent surgery largely concealed, gave a convincing performance that, ironically, brought Taylor her first Oscar win, thought to have been awarded on a sympathy vote. (Co-nominee Shirley MacLaine famously remarked, "I lost to a tracheotomy.")

THE BURTON AFFAIR

In September 1960 Taylor arrived in London to begin work on *Cleopatra* for director Rouben Mamoulian. Her costars were Stephen Boyd (Antony) and Peter Finch (Caesar). By October Taylor was ill, and by November, her recurring infections led to the temporary shutdown of filming. She flew to Palm Springs, California, to recuperate and returned in January 1961 to resume work. Mamoulian had resigned and been replaced by Joseph L. Manckiewicz, who set to work on script changes. At this time, the *Motion Picture Herald* top ten box-office poll was announced, with Taylor at number one. While work on the script dragged on, the Taylor-Fisher retinue, installed at the Dorchester Hotel, lived like royalty, with "Queen" Elizabeth exhibiting the extravagance for which she became renowned. She had her favorite foods specially flown in from several corners of America, as well as from France and Italy and, while Manckiewicz rewrote the script, she shopped. The marriage to Fisher was not turning out to be a success.

On March 4, 1961, Taylor became dangerously ill and was rushed to the London Clinic, where emergency surgery was performed. For some days she hovered between life and death while the world (and Twentieth Century Fox) held its anxious breath, but she emerged from the clinic about a week later, having made, according to the surgeons, a miraculous recovery. Restored to favor by her adoring public, the world's most famous glamour icon departed to California for necessary rest and recuperation and collected her *Butterfield 8* Oscar while *Cleopatra* was once again shut down and rescheduled to shoot in Rome.

The Taylor-Fisher entourage—three children, several dogs and cats, and a large staff—arrived in Rome in September and took up residence at the Villa Papa, a seven-bedroom mansion set in 8 acres of gardens a few minutes from the Cinecittà studios. Delays in filming had brought cast changes, and the new Mark Antony, Richard Burton, was occupying a nearby villa with his family. Filming began on September 25, fraught with the problems of a half-finished script and uncompleted sets. Amid the chaos, Taylor remained calm and professional—and fell head-over-heels in love with Burton.

Their affair was the most protracted and public adultery that the modern world had yet to behold, and the world remained at once scandalized and transfixed by the affair for the best part of fourteen years in the face of the Taylor-Burton antics. The complexities of double divorce prevented the couple from marrying until March 1964, during Burton's Canadian season of *Hamlet*, by which time they had made *The VIPs* (1963) together. It was a feeble British film that cashed in shamelessly on the couple's notoriety, but worse was to follow with the risibly awful *The Sandpiper* (1965). Professionally, the liaison marked a period of decline for both of them. Their fees (never less than a million plus for Taylor) were grossly disproportionate to the quality of their joint ventures, with the shining exception of *Who's Afraid of Virginia Woolf?* This screen adaptation of Edward Albee's play revealed a hitherto unthinkable Taylor: blowzy, loud, passionate, and vitriolic as the embittered Martha, locked in a poisonous game with her husband, George. It was a tour de force, the finest work of her career, and her second Oscar was a fitting tribute to her committed and lacerating performance.

FAME AND EXCESS

Taylor and Burton, inescapably, were famous for being famous. They were also famous for their drinking binges, their rows, and their astonishing extravagances. They became a kind of traveling circus, buying an oceangoing yacht, several homes, priceless paintings, and jewelry. Burton bought his wife the Krupp diamond ($305,000), the historic "La Peregrina" pearl ($37,000), the Cartier diamond ($1.1 million), and the Shah Jahan yellow diamond ($900,000). By 1972 the marriage was in trouble, and 1973 saw the announcement of a separation and a failed attempt to reconcile. They were divorced in 1974, remarried on the banks of an African river in Botswana in 1975, and parted finally in 1976.

Between their endless travels and upheavals, Taylor had made numerous films, of which only *The Taming of the Shrew* with Burton and *Reflections in a Golden Eye* with Marlon Brando (both 1967) merited any real attention. At the end of 1976 she married John Warner, former secretary to the navy, and settled in Virginia to play the role of the loyal politician's wife. Her high-profile campaigning helped her husband get elected to the U.S. Senate, but she grew bored and put on weight. The couple separated in 1981. With her film career gradually petering out, Taylor took to the stage for the first time, playing Regina in *The Little Foxes* on Broadway and in London's West End (1981—1982). It was a brave stab at a medium for which she was totally untrained, but the public flocked to the show, and in 1983 she joined forces with Burton, playing Amanda to his Elyot in Noël Coward's *Private Lives* on Broadway. It was a risible exercise, really, but the public willingly paid inflated ticket prices to see the legendary pair.

In August 1984 Burton died of a cerebral hemorrhage. Taylor collapsed at the news but stayed away from the funeral for fear of causing a media stampede. She subsequently made a pilgrimage to Burton's family in Wales and attended a memorial service in London before returning to make a TV movie (one of several during the 1980s, among them *North and South* and *Sweet Bird of Youth*). The following year brought more grief with the news that her friend Rock Hudson was ill with AIDS. Her publicized visit to Hudson's bedside marked the beginning of her high-profile campaigning for AIDS awareness and research funds, and it became her primary occupation as her acting career wound down.

HER FINAL YEARS

Throughout the late 1980s, Taylor's name was romantically linked with numerous men, among them actor George Hamilton and the multimillionaire Malcolm Forbes. She made *Young Toscanini* (1988) in Italy for Franco Zeffirelli, which was shown at the Venice Film Festival but was barely released. It was her last major screen appearance. Alongside her AIDS work, she launched the first of her perfumes (the aptly named Passion) and gave attention to her children and grandchildren. She continued, however, to be dogged with illnesses of various kinds and, increasingly, relied on painkilling drugs. (According to biographer Donald Spoto, she suffered seventy-three illnesses, accidents, and injuries requiring hospitalization between 1947 and 1994.) Suffering the effects of drug dependency, she checked herself into the Betty Ford Clinic in 1988, where she met construction worker Larry Fortensky.

In October 1991, in a ceremony held at singer Michael Jackson's ranch, thirty-nine-year-old Fortensky became fifty-nine-year-old Taylor's seventh husband. It was a last act of personal folly, and the marriage was over by 1997, the year that she had an operation to remove a brain tumor. Once again people the world over waited anxiously for the outcome. Taylor emerged, shaven-headed, to continue crusading on behalf of the less fortunate, demonstrating the truth of her own words, spoken in a 1987 interview: "I have no plans to succumb. I am a survivor."

In 2000 she was honored in the land of her birth by being made a Dame of the British Empire. She and James Earl Jones gave a one-night benefit performance of the play *Love Letters* to raise more than $1 million for the Elizabeth Taylor AIDS Foundation in 2007. Taylor died on March 23, 2011, of complications from congestive heart failure. She was seventy-nine.

Robyn Karney

SEE ALSO: *Academy Awards; AIDS; Broadway; Celebrity; Celebrity Couples;* Cleopatra*; Clift, Montgomery; Dean, James; Divorce; Fisher, Eddie; Hepburn, Katharine; Hollywood; Hudson, Rock; Jackson, Michael; Lassie; MGM (Metro-Goldwyn-Mayer); Newman, Paul;* A Place in the Sun*; Studio System;* Time*; Tracy, Spencer; World War II.*

BIBLIOGRAPHY

Bragg, Melvyn. *Richard Burton: A Life*. Boston: Little, Brown, 1988.

Kashner, Sam, and Nancy Schoeberger. *Furious Love: Elizabeth Taylor, Richard Burton, and the Marriage of the Century*. New York: Harper, 2010.

Mann, William J. *How to Be a Movie Star: Elizabeth Taylor in Hollywood*. Boston: Houghton Mifflin Harcourt, 2009.

Peltason, Ruth A., ed. *Elizabeth Taylor: My Love Affair with Jewelry*. New York: Simon & Schuster, 2002.

Spoto, Donald. *Elizabeth Taylor*. Boston: Little, Brown, 1995.

Taylor, Elizabeth. *Elizabeth Taylor*. New York: Harper & Row, 1965.

Vermilye, Jerry, and Mark Ricci. *The Films of Elizabeth Taylor*. Secaucus, NJ: Citadel, 1976.

Walker, Alexander. *Elizabeth: The Life of Elizabeth Taylor*. New York: Grove Weidenfeld, 1990.

Taylor, James *(1948–)*

Blending folk, country, and blues to create a distinctive musical sound, James Taylor spearheaded the singer-songwriter movement of the 1970s. Born in Boston in 1948, Taylor began playing guitar at twelve and soon was performing at small folk gigs. Having struggled with depression at boarding school, at seventeen he checked himself into a mental hospital, where he graduated from high school. After moving to London in 1968, he was the first American artist signed to the Beatles' Apple Records.

His first album, *James Taylor*, was lauded by critics but sold poorly, and he returned to the United States in October 1968. In 1970 he had his first popular and critical success with *Sweet Baby James*, recorded in collaboration with singer-songwriter Carole King. The album and its single "Fire and Rain," which addressed Taylor's psychiatric struggles, reached high positions on the pop charts and earned Taylor several Grammy Awards. In 1971 he was featured on the cover of *Time* magazine as the "originator of the singer-songwriter era." Described in *Time* as "a blend of Heathcliffian inner fire with a melancholy sorrows-of-young-Werther look," Taylor was romantically linked to folksinger Joni Mitchell, though he married singer Carly Simon in 1972.

Throughout the 1970s and 1980s, he continued to release critically and commercially successful albums, refining his style while maintaining his superb musical craftsmanship. In the 1990s and the first decade of the 2000s he played to packed houses, and his albums *Hourglass* (1997) and *October Road* (2002) went platinum. He has continued to tour and to make frequent appearances at political and popular events, on talk shows, and on late-night television. After a 2007 appearance at the fiftieth anniversary of the Troubadour, he embarked in 2010 on a successful Troubadour Reunion Tour with King and musicians from his original band. Although he is known as the granddaddy of singer-songwriters, he remains a thoroughly contemporary musician and an ever-popular star.

Victoria Price

SEE ALSO: *The Beatles; Blues; Country Music; Daytime Talk Shows; Depression; Folk Music; Grammy Awards; King, Carole; Mitchell, Joni;* Time*;* The Tonight Show.

BIBLIOGRAPHY

Herbst, Peter. "James Taylor: The *Rolling Stone* Interview." *Rolling Stone*, September 6, 1979, 38–43.

"James Taylor: One Man's Family of Rock." *Time*, March 1, 1971, 39–45.

"James Taylor Online." GeekTV Network. Accessed March 2012. Available from http://www.james-taylor.com/

Taylor, Robert *(1911–1969)*

Typecast for most of his career as a handsome ladies' man, Robert Taylor became a top box-office attraction after his first major film in 1936, and he continued to star in big-budget movies for the next twenty years. The list of leading ladies who played opposite Taylor include some of the biggest stars of Hollywood's Golden Age: Irene Dunne, Loretta Young, Barbara Stanwyck, Joan Crawford, Greta Garbo, Jean Harlow, Hedy Lamarr, Ava Gardner, Greer Garson, Vivien Leigh, Norma Shearer, Katharine Hepburn, Elizabeth Taylor, and Deborah Kerr. Of his long association with MGM (Metro-Goldwyn-Mayer), Taylor said, "I stayed with one studio for twenty years, took what they gave me to do, did my work." Summarizing his treatment at the hands of movie critics, he said, "I never got raves, but neither did I get pans."

Born Spangler Arlington Brugh (a name dear to trivia buffs), the son of a physician in Filley, Nebraska, Taylor initially decided on a medical career, but acting in amateur productions in college soon led him in another direction. He enrolled in a Los Angeles drama school, where a talent scout saw him in a production of *Journey's End* in 1934. After a screen test, he was signed by MGM to a seven-year contract starting at $35 a week. In his first film he played a supporting role to Will Rogers in *Handy Andy* (1934). A succession of low-budget pictures followed, but in 1936 he moved to number four in the box-office ratings with the tearjerker film *Magnificent Obsession*, opposite Dunne. Taylor starred in the role of a playboy who becomes a respected surgeon in order to restore the sight of a woman he had blinded in an automobile accident. After the film was released, all of the most glamorous Hollywood leading ladies wanted to play opposite the handsome young actor.

Two other important films followed in 1936—Taylor starred with Stanwyck in *His Brother's Wife* and with Crawford in the historical drama *The Gorgeous Hussy*. His sudden appeal at the box office led MGM to cast him opposite Garbo in *Camille*. Comparing him with the uniquely talented Garbo, critics were almost unanimous in calling the pairing one of the great mismatches in cinema history. Studio executives pointed out, however, that in the important area of ticket sales, Taylor ranked number three in 1937, while Garbo was only number six. In 1937 Taylor played the more macho role of a secret service agent ordered by President William McKinley to join a gang of robbers to expose a powerful mob, in *This Is My Affair*, opposite Stanwyck as a saloon girl. Taylor and Stanwyck were married in 1939, a much-publicized Hollywood romance that lasted until 1952.

In the late 1930s, studios gave Taylor parts designed to draw more men to his pictures. He was the cocky, athletic young American in *A Yank at Oxford* (1938), a boxer in *The Crowd Roars* (1938), and he even starred in a Western, *Stand Up and Fight* (1939). Taylor's own favorite film was the romantic *Waterloo Bridge* (1940), in which he played a soldier who meets a ballet dancer (Leigh) during a London air raid.

His most expensive film was *Quo Vadis* (1951), in which he essayed the role of a Roman centurion, which Gregory Peck had turned down. In the lavishly made movie, shot in Italy, Taylor falls in love with a Christian beauty (Kerr), in a plot that threatens to throw both of them to the lions. The movie grossed $11 million, at that time the fourth-biggest moneymaker in history. Other big-budget spectacles followed: *Ivanhoe* (1952), *Knights of the Round Table* (1953), and *Valley of the Kings*, filmed in Egypt in 1954. In the next few years Taylor's popularity dwindled, and his contract with MGM ended, but he continued to work in minor films and in a television series called *The Detectives*. In his last movie, in 1968, he and Charles Boyer played secret agents in *The Day the Hot Line Got Hot*. He died the following year after a long struggle with cancer. Fellow actor Ronald Reagan, then governor of California, said at his funeral: "He was more than a pretty boy, an image that embarrassed him because he was a man who respected his profession and was a master of it."

Benjamin Griffith

SEE ALSO: *Celebrity; Celebrity Couples; Community Theater; Crawford, Joan; Dunne, Irene; Garbo, Greta; Gardner, Ava; Harlow, Jean; Hepburn, Katharine; Hollywood; Lamarr, Hedy; MGM (Metro-Goldwyn-Mayer); Movie Stars; Peck, Gregory; Reagan, Ronald; Rogers, Will; Stanwyck, Barbara; Taylor, Elizabeth; Television; The Western; Young, Loretta.*

BIBLIOGRAPHY

Jarvis, Everett G. *Final Curtain: Deaths of Noted Movie and Television Personalities*. New York: Carol, 1995.

Shipman, David. *The Great Movie Stars: The Golden Years*. New York: Hamlyn, 1973.

Shipman, David. *Cinema: The First Hundred Years*. New York: St. Martin's Press, 1993.

Tranberg, Charles. *Robert Taylor: A Biography*. Albany, GA: BearManor Media, 2011.

The Tea Party

In current usage, the term *Tea Party* refers to both a popular synthetic political movement and a political sensibility that has become an obsession of the American news media and a powerful influence within the Republican Party. Although there has been at least one National Tea Party Convention and many political activists have taken the name Tea Party to their groups as "chapters," the Tea Party is not an official organized political party. It lacks a charter, a central administration, a universally selected and acknowledged leadership, a system of funding that collects membership dues, a national membership roster, an agreed-upon platform, or anything else that might enable it to, in and of itself, nominate and run candidates for public office.

THE BOSTON TEA PARTY

The movement's name derives from a key event in the struggle of the thirteen British colonies on the Atlantic seaboard of North America. The goal of the Boston Tea Party of December 16, 1773, was either to achieve representation in the English Parliament equal to their economic importance or to form themselves into a separate sovereignty not subject to the English crown.

In Boston that evening, after a mass meeting chaired by Samuel Adams, a disciplined group of men dressed as Mohawk

Indians went to Boston Harbor, boarded three recently arrived ships of the East India Company, and tossed their entire cargoes of tea—342 chests in all—into the harbor. They were protesting not the import tax or duties, as is generally supposed, but the imposition of a monopoly on the importation of tea by a bill that was passed in the English House of Commons on April 27 of that year to save the East India Company from bankruptcy. The principle of "no taxation without representation," a feature of English political discourse since their Civil War in the mid-seventeenth century, and of American political agitation since the 1760s, was not, from the evidence of all surviving documents, directly invoked at any time during the incident.

RICK SANTELLI'S "RANT"

The Boston Tea Party has been mistakenly celebrated over the years by antitax protesters, especially during the "Tax Day" protests of the 1990s. On December 16, 2007, the anniversary of the original Boston Tea Party, supporters of Republican Congressman Ron Paul held a fund-raiser for his 2008 presidential campaign, which they called a "tea party." But the appropriation of the term really took off on February 19, 2009, when CNBC commentator (and former stockbroker) Rick Santelli, reacting to the Obama administration's Homeowners Affordability and Stability Plan, went on a self-described "rant" on the floor of the Chicago Mercantile Exchange. He said, among other things, "You know, the new administration's big on computers and technology. . . . How about this, president and new administration? Why don't you put up a website to have people vote on the Internet as a referendum to see if we really want to subsidize the losers' mortgages?" He added, "We're thinking of having a Chicago Tea Party in July. All you capitalists that want to show up to Lake Michigan, I'm gonna start organizing. . . . We're going to be dumping in some derivative securities. What do you think about that?"

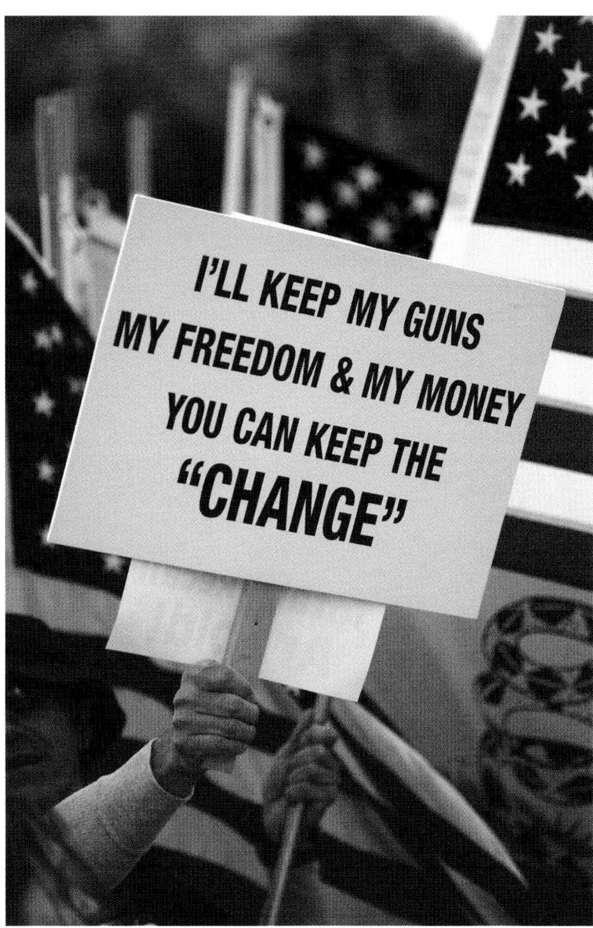

Tea Party Rally. *A protester at a Tea Party rally in Santa Monica, California, in 2009 holds a sign that summarizes the group's position on taxes, gun control, and the Obama administration.* DAVID MCNEW/GETTY IMAGES.

AMERICANS FOR PROSPERITY

Whatever else it was, Santelli's rant was not an explicit antitax protest. Nor was his proposed "tea party" an attempt, as the 1773 original was, to break a monopoly of any type. It was mostly a call for bankers, brokers, and financiers to organize a resistance to the bailout of their victims. But no sooner were the words out of Santelli's mouth—in fact, the same day—that a group called Americans for Prosperity (AFP) set up a Tea Party Facebook page and began organizing Tea Party events. Santelli and AFP deny any collusion, so it may be just a coincidence—or an illustration of the speed with which new phrases and ideas can be coined and distributed in the age of the Internet.

AFP is a section 501(c)(4) organization funded by billionaires Charles and David Koch of Koch Industries. In its charter, AFP states that its members are "committed to educating citizens about economic policy and a return of the federal government to its Constitutional limits." Its website says that AFP supports "cutting taxes and government spending in order to halt the encroachment of government in the economic lives of citizens by fighting proposed tax increases and pointing out evidence of waste, fraud, and abuse." AFP also opposes all efforts to establish the reality of climate change and any program for mitigating the change, but its main focus is antitaxation and, by extension, antigovernment.

THE TEA PARTY AND THE MEDIA

"The power of language is so great," wrote the late Underground Grammarian Richard Mitchell, in *Less than Words Can Say* (1979), "that it can call things into existence simply through naming them." Mitchell's words apply with stunning accuracy to the rise of the Tea Party. The role of the mainstream media—including the Internet, newspapers, television networks, and syndicated radio talk shows—in the rise of the Tea Party phenomenon cannot be overstated. Once Santelli and AFP had introduced the term *Tea Party* into the national electronic grid, the media distributed it to every television screen, front page, computer monitor, and radio in America and kept the words circulating constantly, packed in subliminal images and emotionally coded language.

The media's motives for promoting the Tea Party in this way certainly include the desire for immediate commercial advantage in the ruthless competition for public attention, but one should not rule out the possibility of other, less obvious agendas, not excluding partisan politics. Whatever their motives, the media's function have not been to provide a detailed description of the movement and the beliefs it embodies, still less to recruit members to the cause. The longer the media keeps the words *Tea Party* in the foreground of the public consciousness, always in conjunction with subtle references to the evils of big government, taxation, affirmative action, socialism, and the other fears of the uninformed and disaffected segments of the American citizenry, the more other individuals are drawn to the Tea Party banner.

The media also plays a crucial role in so-called "Tea Party events," which are actually pseudo-events. American historian Daniel J. Boorstin, who coined the term *pseudo event* in his seminal book *The Image, or What Happened to the American Dream?* (1962), defines a pseudo-event as one that is "not spontaneous, but comes about because someone has planned, planted, or incited it . . . planted primarily (not always exclusively) for the immediate purpose of being reported or reproduced," that has "ambiguous relation to the underlying reality of the situation" and is "usually . . . intended to be a self-fulfilling prophecy." Viewed through the lens of Boorstin's definition, of course, the Tea Party itself is revealed as a pseudo-event.

THE TEA PARTY AND THE GOP

Since the Tea Party first coalesced in the American consciousness, it has had considerable impact on the goals, direction, and leadership of the Republican Party. Many analysts assert that the Republicans won a majority in the U.S. House of Representatives in the 2010 national election on the strength of Tea Party support. Political operatives claiming to be Tea Partiers who can speak for the Tea Party, were able to influence a number of Republican primaries in favor of the more conservative candidate. Most of the Republican aspirants to the 2012 presidential nomination skewed their messages to some extent to conform to what they thought the Tea Party wanted. The Tea Partiers' conservative agenda includes the deregulation of all economic activity; recriminalization of abortion and homosexuality; overall reduction in government services—implicit in the antitax crusade—and the elimination of most, if not all, environmental protections.

Several celebrities and commentators have professed sympathy for the Tea Party and have offered themselves as spokespersons, including Glenn Beck and Ted Nugent. Among the Republican politicians who have overtly sought to carry the banner of the Tea Party are Ron Paul and his son Rand Paul, Sarah Palin, Dick Armey, Eric Cantor, and Michele Bachmann.

THE FUTURE OF THE MOVEMENT

How much of the above applies to both sectors of the Tea Party movement—the billionaire-funded pseudo-grassroots movement and the genuine populist sensibility—and how much applies to one or the other, remains to be seen. The fact that the goals of the former (chiefly the elimination of taxes and regulations) are often incompatible with the permanent interests of the latter (a safe and healthy life, financial stability, social order) has not yet had much impact on the progress of the movement. As the 2012 national election ground on, the Tea Party influence appeared to peak and wane. It remains to be seen whether the Tea Party will succeed in becoming a permanent feature of American political life.

Gerald Carpenter

SEE ALSO: *Beck, Glenn; The Internet; Obama, Barack; Palin, Sarah; Religious Right.*

BIBLIOGRAPHY

Foley, Elizabeth Price. *The Tea Party: Three Principles*. New York: Cambridge University Press, 2012.

Formisano, Ronald P. *The Tea Party: A Brief History*. Baltimore, MD: Johns Hopkins University Press, 2012.

Monbiot, George. "A Billionaires' Coup in the US." *Guardian*, September 23, 2011.

Rosen, Ruth. "The Tea Party and Angry White Women." *Dissent* 59, no. 1 (2012).

Skocpol, Theda, and Vanessa Williamson. *The Tea Party and the Remaking of Republican Conservatism*. New York: Oxford University Press, 2012.

Taibbi, Matt. *The Great Derangement: A Terrifying True Story of War, Politics, and Religion*. New York: Spiegel & Grau, 2008.

Zernike, Kate. *Boiling Mad: Inside Tea Party America*. New York: Times Books, 2010.

Teddy Bears

Most adults carry fond, even significant memories of their teddy bear, a possession integral to the childhood of all but the severely deprived in America and beyond. Although these days one can find stuffed toys representing every animal from an aardvark to a zebra, the figure of the bear remains the most popular choice among children and adults alike. By the latter part of the twentieth century, teddy bears had become something of an industry in the United States and Europe.

Both America and Germany lay claim to the invention of the teddy bear, each for good reasons. In fact, the teddy bear seems to be the product of a remarkable historical coincidence occurring in 1902. One part of the story starts in Mississippi, where President Theodore Roosevelt was on a hunting trip. One of his companions captured a black bear cub, tied a rope around its neck, and brought it to Roosevelt to shoot, but the president, seeing no sport in killing an exhausted, bound, and defenseless animal, declined.

A reporter traveling with the hunting party telegraphed the story to the *Washington Post*, which ran a front-page cartoon by Clifford Berryman the following day that showed Roosevelt refusing to shoot the bear cub with the caption "Drawing the line in Mississippi." In Brooklyn, New York, the cartoon was seen by Morris Michtom, the owner of a small novelty store, who had been trying unsuccessfully to sell a few stuffed toy bears made by his wife, Rose. Inspired by Berryman's cartoon, Michtom wrote to the White House, received permission to use the presidential name, and put the toys in his shop window with a sign reading, "Teddy's bears." The bears sold quickly, and the demand for more was so great that Michtom soon founded the Ideal Novelty and Toy Corporation and put "Teddy's bears" into mass production.

Meanwhile, thousands of miles away, in Germany, Richard Steiff was also in the grip of a big idea. While watching trained bears performing in a circus, he had the thought that a toy bear standing upright with jointed arms and legs might be a marketable commodity. He made some drawings of his conception and took them to his aunt, Margarete Steiff, a well-known toy and doll maker. She designed a stuffed bear based on her nephew's ideas and exhibited them at the 1903 Leipzig Toy Fair. European stores initially expressed no interest in the new toys, but an American buyer was enthusiastic and ordered several thousand for export to the United States. Consequently, the teddy bear may be said to have two birthdays, although the name is clearly owed to its American maker and the president who inspired it.

Today, teddy bears are big business; there are an estimated 2.5 million collectors in the United States alone. So significant has this "bear market" become, the industry now distinguishes between two kinds of teddy bears: toys and collectibles. Toy bears are distinguished by their soft stuffing, designed to make them "huggable," while collectible teddy bears are characterized by jointed arms and legs, firm stuffing, and a relatively unyielding exterior. Many experts regard Gund, Inc., as the premier maker of cuddly toy bears, but to collectors, Steiff still reigns supreme, with antique Steiff bears sometimes fetching in excess of $10,000 at auctions. In 2000 the oldest-known Steiff bear sold for £82,000, or approximately $130,000.

The popularity of the teddy bear soon spread beyond the United States to Britain and elsewhere, and some teddy bears are based on characters in universally loved children's stories by English writers. Winnie-the-Pooh, the honey-loving bear created by A. A. Milne in 1926, has been a perennial favorite, as has Paddington Bear, who first appeared in the 1950s storybook *A Bear Called Paddington* by Michael Bond and Peggy Fortnum. A stuffed Smokey the Bear has been around for decades to remind bear lovers that "only *you* can prevent forest fires." Teddy bears have also been based on human characters, both real and fictional, several with movie connotations. Thus, we have had such creations as "Humphrey Beargart" and the macho "Rambear."

Any popular collectible tends to spawn enterprises designed to feed it, and teddy bear collecting is no exception. For example, in 1997 the Build-A-Bear Workshop opened its first store, in St. Louis, Missouri, offering customers the opportunity to design their own personal teddy bears at a mall-based outlet. Other teddy-bear based products and services offered in the twenty-first century include mail-order catalogs devoted to bears and other bear products (such as T-shirts and posters), magazines for the teddy bear collector, bear calendars, teddy bear conventions, and innumerable websites devoted to commerce in stuffed bears.

Justin Gustainis

SEE ALSO: *Toys; Winnie-the-Pooh.*

BIBLIOGRAPHY

Bull, Peter. *The Teddy Bear Book.* New York: Random House, 1970.

Merrett, Alicia, and Ann Stephens. *The Complete Book of Teddy-Bear Making Techniques.* Philadelphia: Running Press, 1998.

Severin, Gustav. *Teddy Bear: A Loving History of the Classic Childhood Companion.* Philadelphia: Courage Books, 1995.

Waring, Philippa. *In Praise of Teddy Bears.* London: Souvenir Press, 1997.

Teen Idols

As long as there are teenagers, there will be teen idols. From the vintage "Frankie" Sinatra to Elvis Presley, from the Beatles to David Cassidy, from the New Kids on the Block to Justin Bieber, the names and faces may change with the decades, but the emotions that drive the phenomenon do not. Teen idols symbolize a rite of passage for preteens and early teens. They are ideal dream mates who fuel romantic fantasies and provide a safe release for hormonally charged emotions. After all, unlike flesh-and-blood boyfriends or girlfriends, teen idols make no demands. This cultural phenomenon primarily targets teen girls so that male teen idols have often been made to fit into a formulaic mold that is at once approachable and subtly sexualized in order to best appeal to this demographic.

CLASSIC TEEN IDOLS

Collectively, teen idols have long been dismissed as lightweight flashes in the pan. But in fact, many notable performers have passed through the teen idol ranks. Before becoming one of Hollywood's most prolific and acclaimed leading men, John Travolta was a popular pin-up, the result of his costarring role in the 1975 TV series *Welcome Back, Kotter.* The 1997 box-office blockbuster *Titanic* derived much of its drawing power from the casting of teen idol Leonardo DiCaprio. Pop-soul maestro Michael Jackson was a teen idol in the 1980s as well as in the previous decade when he was one of the Jackson Five. The Beatles were huge teen idols in the 1960s, as was Presley in the 1950s. In the 1940s females screamed for Sinatra.

Even those teen idols who did not successfully make a transition as their fans matured have continued to be regarded

David Cassidy, Teen Idol. *David Cassidy was one of many young, good-looking stars who won the hearts of teen girls in the 1970s.* MICHAEL OCHS ARCHIVES/GETTY IMAGES.

with affection. To their fans, they represent a special time in their lives. To the credit of these teen idols, they also left imprints on popular culture. For example, many of the icons of the 1950s—the decade in which the modern teen idol is rooted—became fixtures on the record charts. From late 1957 through 1963, young performers were responsible for more than a few number one hits, including Tab Hunter's "Young Love" and Frankie Avalon's "Venus," and many more tunes by teen idols climbed to the Top 5.

Just as Presley went from the recording studio to Hollywood, other teen idols made the leap to the big screen. These were major players during the final years of the so-called Hollywood "star system." Sandra Dee, who became a teen favorite with her depiction of the surfing-obsessed Gidget, went on to become a Top 10 box-office draw for the years 1960, 1961, 1962, and 1963—an astonishing feat, considering the list also included Doris Day, Cary Grant, Elizabeth Taylor, and Sinatra. Between 1959 and 1964 Fabian appeared in eight films, ranging from comedies to teen genre flicks to a John Wayne action adventure movie. Hunter clocked in nearly twenty films between 1950 and 1964.

Popular culture as we know it in the 2010s was only nascent in the early twentieth century, when increased media consumption gave rise to wider recognition of stars and, later, a cult of fandom. Back in the 1930s singer-actor Rudy Vallee induced swoons from schoolgirls when he performed while clutching a megaphone. But Sinatra is credited as the official pioneer of the teen idol movement. At age twenty-seven Sinatra had a skinny, vulnerable look. That look (which was adopted by many of his successors), combined with his lush romantic ballads, elicited mass hysterics and stampeding among teenage "bobby soxers" at his December 1942 performances at New York's Paramount Theater. When Sinatra later appeared at the Boston Armory, the seats were bolted down as a security measure. While teen idols did not originate in the 1950s, the economic stability in America after World War II engendered a vibrant youth culture and a new commercial market.

TUMULTUOUS IDOLS

In the 1950s the emergence of American teenage culture prompted another kind of hero worship. Before he cinched his eternal stardom with his 1955 death in a car crash, James Dean had come to symbolize the teenager in pain, with his angst-ridden performance in *Rebel without a Cause*. Presley had his own angst-ridden performances on-screen and in song, including the bravado *Heartbreak Hotel*. But Dean and Presley also summoned up a sense of looming danger. In Presley's case, his sexy stage antics and the fact that he was a white singer who sounded "black" made him anathema to authority figures.

A much safer alternative to rebellious idols was found in Charles Eugene Boone. Better known as Pat Boone, the performer from Nashville, Tennessee, emerged as the flip side of the coin that bore the imprints of Dean and Presley. Considering the era's controversy over rock and roll, it is significant that Boone rose to fame by singing cover versions of songs originally recorded by African Americans. His easygoing delivery and boyish charm helped to defuse the volatility of rock and roll. Furthermore, Boone did not exude sexual magnetism. It was Boone who set the stage for what transpired, following a Richter-scale shift in the world of rock and roll.

Denoting that upheaval was the U.S. Army's 1957 decision to draft Presley. Other significant careers also came to a standstill. Chuck Berry faced a prison term for having transported a minor over a state line for sexual purposes. Jerry Lee Lewis was blackballed because of his marriage to his thirteen-year-old cousin. Plane and car crashes took the lives of Buddy Holly, Ritchie Valens, and Eddie Cochran.

With the music world in transition, promoters moved in to provide an antidote—a new commodity to entice teenagers and their growing spending power. The idea was to cater to teenage desires without the erratic undercurrent or explosive passion that had made Presley an infamous household name. So the new teenage idol was created. It was no coincidence that, along with the lure of their talent—some of it legitimate, some wholly manufactured—the teen idols were exceedingly clean cut and attractive. Or that the male teen idols appeared vulnerable as opposed to predatory. After all, strong masculine qualities can be off-putting to young females. Thus, over the years, many teen idols have had an androgynous look.

TEEN IDOLS NEXT DOOR

Fabian and Avalon set the standards against which the 1950s teen idols were measured. Each had the engaging affability of the boy next door. And not coincidentally, both were managed by producer-promoter Bob Marcucci, who was teamed with Peter DeAngelis in Chancellor Records. The label was based in Philadelphia, a city that specialized in turning out teen idols.

In the *Rolling Stone Illustrated History of Rock & Roll*, Phil Spector—the legendary producer known for his work with girl groups, the Righteous Brothers, and the Beatles, and the "wall of sound" that backed their tunes—calls Philadelphia of the 1950s "the most insane, most dynamite, the most beautiful city in the history of rock and roll and the world." The city's thriving music industry included competing record labels and their respective producers and promoters. Their collective goal was to get their performers booked on the Dick Clark–hosted *American Bandstand*. As the premiere showcase for rock-and-roll performers, the show was essential to the careers of would-be teen idols.

When the pioneering rock-and-roll artists made their ascent, there were no national television shows devoted to rock and roll. The performers made their reputations after months or even years of touring. Prior to his famed appearances on *The Ed Sullivan Show*, Presley was a regional star, the result of having played the hinterlands. Only after becoming known regionally did he enjoy exposure on national TV variety shows. By contrast, later teen idols could become "overnight" successes as a result of a single carefully promoted TV appearance. Ricky Nelson's rise as a teen idol began when he sang a single song on his family's long-running series, *The Adventures of Ozzie and Harriet*. Tommy Sands was an unknown seventeen-year-old when he appeared in the NBC telecast of *The Singing Idol*, which generated 8,000 pieces of fan mail. Avalon, Bobby Rydell, and Fabian all owed their fame to *American Bandstand*.

MARKETING FABIAN

The rise and fall of Fabian stands as a cautionary chapter in the teen idol annals. Fabiano Forte was a fourteen-year-old boy literally sitting on his front porch when he was spotted by Marcucci, who was already managing Avalon. Though Fabian's father had just been taken away by ambulance after having suffered a heart attack, Marcucci was brazen enough to ask, "Say, kid, can you sing?" Fabian was not interested. After continuing to see the teenager in the neighborhood, including at the corner drug store where he worked, Marcucci returned to the family home. This time Fabian agreed to become a Marcucci protégé.

At the time Avalon was finally enjoying success as a singer—after having bombed with a trio of singles. But unlike Avalon, who could carry a tune and was an accomplished musician, Fabian had no natural musical prowess; in fact, he had failed his high school chorus class. But Marcucci persisted, taking the youth to a series of vocal coaches and introducing him to local audiences via sock hops. He also launched a major promotional campaign touting Fabian as "The Fabulous One." Still, despite several *American Bandstand* appearances, the teenager's initial records failed. "You gotta find this kid a hit record!" Clark told Marcucci. That hit turned out to be "I'm a Man," which Fabian lip-synched on a December 1958 show. The single climbed the charts and paved the way for additional hits, tours, and movie roles. But Fabian's fame and largely off-key singing also led to cruel barbs from the press, which left the teenager hurt and bewildered.

Ironically, Fabian garnered some of his best notices when he played a psychopathic killer in a 1961 episode of the TV anthology series *Bus Stop*. But the casting of the teen idol also generated controversy because teen idols of the day were not expected to have dimension as artists—they were not taken seriously by the very industry that created them. Thus, when times and tastes changed and his teenage fan base grew older, Fabian had to grapple to survive as a performer. In a 1979 interview for *New West*, Fabian said of his reign as an icon, "I was just a street-punk kid who got into all this because my father had a heart attack and the family needed money. I didn't know nothing. Sure I had girls—I was a healthy young man. But what all this teen idol stuff comes down to is business. Big business."

BUSINESS OF MAKING IDOLS

In the 1960s that big business was typified by the staggering success of the Beatles and the teen idols who followed in their wake. Foremost among the latter was the fabricated-for-TV group the Monkees. Selected from a casting call that drew more than 400 applicants, the group starred in their own series and a major movie and had nearly a dozen Top 40 hits, three of which went to number one. Integral to the success of Monkeemania, Beatlemania, and myriad other teen idol manias, was the teen fan magazine industry, which thrived during this era. A hybrid of the girls' magazines that debuted in the 1940s and early rock-and-roll magazines, these publications sold hundreds of thousands of copies per month.

Reflecting the relationship between the idols and publishing, teen fan magazine pioneer Charles Laufer once related how he honed in on the appeal of 1970s teen icon David Cassidy. It happened as he was watching an episode of TV's *Marcus Welby, M.D.* "A kid comes on, and he's got diabetes. I didn't know who he was, but he was raw-boned and vulnerable, and I thought, this kid's terrific. So I waited for the credits. The next day I came into the office and said, 'Who the hell is David Cassidy?'" Laufer tracked down Cassidy, who was about to begin work on the 1970s TV show *The Partridge Family*, about a family singing group. Laufer went on to publish the *Partridge Family* teen magazine and to oversee the group's fan club. Though it was a fictional group in which only two of the show's cast members—Cassidy and stepmother Shirley Jones—actually sang, the Partridge Family went on to have a number one hit with "I Think I Love You." The shag-haired Cassidy later called the group "the last gasp of innocence in America."

In truth, there have been many more gasps of innocence within the teen idol roll call. During the 1970s the roster included Cassidy's half-brother, Shaun Cassidy, as well as Donny and Marie Osmond, Robby Benson, and Andy Gibb. Among 1980s idols were Scott Baio, John Stamos, Menudo, and Debbie Gibson. The safe, sweet side of teen idoldom continued in the 1990s with actor Jonathan Taylor Thomas and singing groups such as Hanson, and in the first decade of the 2000s with Taylor Swift and Justin Bieber.

DARKER TEEN IDOLS

Another kind of teen idol—of the less-than-wholesome variety—has also thrived since the late 1970s. This type of teen idol is exemplified by the heavy metal group KISS, which became a potent teen idol force in the late 1970s despite the group's shock-value tactics. According to fan magazine publishers, kids rallied to the group's larger-than-life stage theatrics, as well as to the members' comic-book-like appearance. The band members' image made them seem more like fictional characters than real people and therefore threatening heavy metal artists. Madonna, meanwhile, was embraced in the 1980s as the enticing embodiment of the disobedient girl and a proud boy toy, something about which young females fantasize. In the 1990s that naughty but cool mantle shifted to the Spice Girls and their mantra espousing "girl power," while in the first decade of the 2000s Lady Gaga took over the role of pop culture's most provocative bad girl.

Of course, neither the Spice Girls nor Lady Gaga could have succeeded in a more modest era; by the same token Connie Francis would today be considered an anachronism. Teen idols are both a product and a reflection of their times. As with all products, their success or failure is indelibly linked to marketing as well as timing. The stakes are tantalizing because teen buyers make up a significant portion of the music-buying public.

TEEN IDOLS TODAY

Just as the teen idols of the 1950s were able to become overnight successes as a result of television, the current teen idols are able to become multimillionaires on the basis of synergy and mass marketing. That doesn't mean that television has lost its ability to create teen idols. The television show *Glee*, which began in 2009 and focuses on the experiences of a glee club at a fictional high school, has given rise to more than a few teen idols—including Chris Colfer and Lea Michele—with devoted fan bases. In the realm of reality television, the musical competition *American Idol*, which first aired in 2002, has also propelled young performers such as David Archuleta into the ranks of idoldom.

In the first decade of the 2000s two movie franchises based on best-selling books produced several teen idols. The first franchise was the *Harry Potter* series of eight movies based on J. K. Rowling's novels about a young wizard in Britain. These films made international celebrities of their three young stars: Daniel Radcliffe, Emma Watson, and Rupert Grint. Similarly, Robert Pattinson and Taylor Lautner, the two male stars of the *Twilight* movies about vampires and werewolves in the Pacific Northwest, gained a following of young women ready to swoon for them—and argue vehemently about the relative merits of *Team Edward* versus *Team Jacob*, terms that denote which fictional character a fan finds most adorable.

Another potent force in the marketing of teen idols in the twenty-first century has been the Internet. Justin Bieber, a

Canadian pop music star who gained global fame as a teenager, first came to public attention after his mother posted videos of his performances on the website YouTube. After Bieber released his first album, *My World 2.0* (2010), when he was only sixteen, the official video for the lead single "Baby" became the first video ever to receive more than 250 million views on YouTube. Bieber also uses social media such as Twitter to connect with his adoring fans, further bolstering his popularity.

The power of teen idoldom is not summed up merely by dollars and cents. "When you're talking about teen idols, you're talking about being godlike," said Bobby Sherman, a leading 1970s teen idol, in a 1979 interview for *New West*. But there are distinctions between the teen idol types. As explained by Sherman: "See, there's an A group and a B group. The A group is like the Beatles. They create a lifestyle which changes people. Then there's the B's, like I was. I was like a number in a system that was created in a succession of molds that perform well for their time and place."

Yet when the Beatles first arrived on the scene, they were perceived by the media to be no more than a fad. To young females, they were cause to celebrate en masse and to release sexual energy. The group's musical evolution and staying power could not have been foreseen. The same can be said of the young performers who carry on the teen idol tradition. Some may go on to achieve greatness. If not, they will doubtless live on in the scrapbooks and memories of the fans whose hearts and lives they touched.

Pat H. Broeske

SEE ALSO: The Adventures of Ozzie and Harriet*;* American Bandstand*;* American Idol*; Avalon, Frankie; The Beatles; Berry, Chuck; Bieber, Justin; Bobby Socks; Boone, Pat; Bubblegum Rock; Cassidy, David; Clark, Dick; Day, Doris; Dean, James; DiCaprio, Leonardo; Fabian; Fan Magazines; Francis, Connie;* Glee*; Grant, Cary; Harry Potter; Heavy Metal; Holly, Buddy; Hollywood; Hunter, Tab; The Internet; Jackson, Michael; The Jackson Five; KISS; Lady Gaga; Lewis, Jerry Lee; Madonna;* Marcus Welby, M.D.*; The Monkees; Movie Stars; Nelson, Ricky; The New Kids on the Block;* The Partridge Family*; Pop Music; Presley, Elvis;* Rebel without a Cause*; Rock and Roll; Rydell, Bobby; Safe Sex; Sex Symbol; Sinatra, Frank; Spector, Phil; The Spice Girls; Star System; Sullivan, Ed; Swift, Taylor; Taylor, Elizabeth; Teenagers; Television; Travolta, John;* Twilight*; Vallee, Rudy; Valens, Ritchie; Wayne, John;* Welcome Back, Kotter.

BIBLIOGRAPHY

Broeske, Pat H., and Cheryl A. Latuner. "Teenzine: A Loss of Innocence." *Los Angeles Times Sunday Calendar*, August 25, 1985, 42–46.

Brown, Peter Harry, and Pat H. Broeske. *Down at the End of Lonely Street: The Life and Death of Elvis Presley*. New York: Dutton, 1997.

Cartnal, Alan. "Teen Idols. The Truth! . . . About Shaun and Scott and Jimmy and Leif and Willie! . . . What They Think about Everything!" *New West*, January 1, 1979, 38–43.

"50 Years of Teen Idols." *People Weekly*, July 27, 1992, 42–128.

Firth, Simon; Will Straw; and John Street; eds. *The Cambridge Companion to Pop and Rock*. Cambridge, UK: Cambridge University Press, 2001.

Finn, Timothy. "Teen Idols Are the Profits of Today for Record Companies and Marketers." Knight Ridder/Tribune News Service, February 12, 1998, 21.

Halpern, Jake. *Fame Junkies: The Hidden Truths behind America's Favorite Addiction*. New York: Houghton Mifflin, 2007.

Lerner, Richard. "Teen Idols." *Parenting* 70, no. 9 (1995): 91.

Miller, Jim, ed. *The Rolling Stone Illustrated History of Rock & Roll*. New York: Rolling Stone, 1980.

Morgan, Thomas B. "Teen-Age Heroes: Mirrors of Muddled Youth." *Esquire*, March 1960, 65–68.

Shapiro, Marc. *Justin Bieber: The Fever!*. New York: St. Martin's Griffin, 2010.

Teenage Mutant Ninja Turtles

The Teenage Mutant Ninja Turtles cartoon characters—Leonardo, Raphael, Donatello, and Michelangelo—were one of the greatest cross-media phenomena of the 1980s and early 1990s. The Turtles, ordinary pets mutated into superheroes, began as an underground comic book created by cartoonists Peter Laird and Kevin Eastman in the mid-1980s as a spoof of such comics as the mutant X-Men and the grim, urban Daredevil. An instant smash, the Turtles soon branched out into other media, including films, an animated television series, multiple toy and merchandise tie-ins, and a live-action television program. The success came at the cost of their identity, however, as the original, funky nature of the Turtles comics became more cartoonish and child friendly to better facilitate their mass acceptance.

Jay Parrent

SEE ALSO: *Animated Films; Comic Books;* Daredevil, the Man without Fear*; Saturday Morning Cartoons.*

BIBLIOGRAPHY

Eastman, Kevin B.; Peter A. Laird; and Steve Lavigne. *Teenage Mutant Ninja Turtles: A Quarter Century Celebration*. Rockville Centre, NY: Metal Mammoth, 2009.

"Eastman & Laird & Their Pet Turtles." *Comics Sense*, July 1987, 50–52.

"Lights! Camera! Turtles!" *Comics Sense*, August 1989, 17–19, 50.

Teenagers

Although people between the ages of twelve and twenty have always existed, the social category we call "teenagers" did not reach widespread public consciousness until the turn of the twentieth century. During that period of thriving industrialization, numerous industries searching for the largest number of customers began to target older children as a demographic distinct from younger children, for whom most children's goods were created. As early as the late nineteenth century, for example, the fashion industry began to introduce separate styles for people in between the categories of child and adult, while book publishers addressed the same age group with new forms of literature, such as Louisa May Alcott's *Little Women* and the popular Oliver Optic adventure novels for boys. Such developments gradually introduced the American public to the idea that people in and around the teen years had needs and desires separate from those of younger children or adults.

HALL AND TEENAGE PSYCHOLOGY

In 1904 the psychologist G. Stanley Hall published *Adolescence: Its Psychology and Its Relations to Physiology, Anthropology, Sociology, Sex, Crime, Religion, and Education*. In it Hall described adolescents as people who experience "storm and stress" from the physical and psychological changes that accompany the onset of puberty and the entrance to adulthood. Teens, therefore, were considered likely to experience a rebellious period characterized by conflict with authority figures, mood swings, and a tendency toward risky behavior. Hall's book had a tremendous impact on the fields of education, child psychology, and public policy. The perception of the teenage years as a volatile "in-between" period that can make its inhabitants vulnerable to certain kinds of stresses became the dominant view of teens during the twentieth century and has continued in various forms to the present day.

The experiences of American adolescents have varied greatly according to race, ethnicity, and social class. High school attendance in the early twentieth century was a luxury not widely available to teens from working-class, minority, or immigrant families, many of whom had to get their "working papers" after completing the eighth grade so they could help support their families as wage earners. But the financial crisis of the Great Depression reduced the number of available jobs, leading to an increase in high school enrollments. In high schools, teens from various backgrounds were brought together in an institution that identified them as peers based on their age group, universalizing such experiences as school sports, proms, classes, and clubs. As more and more American teens found themselves unified under the heading of "high school students," more adults began to recognize teens as a distinct group and to develop an interest in teenage culture. By the late 1930s and early 1940s, numerous forms of popular culture—including films, stage plays, and radio programs, particularly comedies—focused on stories with teenage characters. This form of entertainment was popular with adults who were curious about the attitudes and activities associated with teenagers. It should be noted, however, that it was only white, middle-class youths who were celebrated as characters in popular culture.

As the American economy improved, teens were increasingly targeted as consumers of cultural goods aimed at their age group. The first mass-market magazine for teenage girls, *Calling All Girls*, debuted in 1941 and was soon followed by many others. Teens were recognized as trendsetters with their fashions, slang, and musical tastes. During the affluent 1950s, teens had more leisure time and more spending money than ever before, and numerous industries sought to tap that resource with an even greater array of teen-centered cultural products, including

Teenagers. *Teenage friends listen to records and drink sodas in the mid-1960s, well into the era in which their age group became an economic force carefully targeted by marketers.* © EWING GALLOWAY/CLASSICSTOCK/CORBIS.

teen movies, rock and pop music, and television programs. Their status as powerful consumers existed alongside their status, in adults' minds, as people to be worried about, because of their vulnerability to "storm and stress," as Hall would have put it. Throughout the twentieth century and into the twenty-first, teens have often been discussed in the news media as either the victims or perpetrators of various types of crimes and other rebellious activities, as well as being perceived as the driving force behind American popular culture.

TEEN IDOLS

Elvis Presley appeared on the scene in 1954, at a moment when middle-class teenagers were primed to respond to his working-class swagger and rhythm-and-blues–inflected music. Teen idols existed in some form prior to 1950. Frank Sinatra, for example, was mobbed by young women when he played a sold-out one-month engagement with Benny Goodman's orchestra at the Paramount Theatre on Times Square. Elvis mania far surpassed Sinatra in his prime, however, at least in part because he was aggressively marketed through his music and through movies, some of them based on his music. Further, Elvis was a teenager himself in the early 1950s, and the freedom implied in his hip-thrusting sexuality and status as an outsider in relation to adults appealed to both male and female teens.

Beatlemania, at its height slightly less than ten years post-Elvis, reflected, on the surface, a trend of safer entertainment marketed to teens. The teenage population had grown significantly during the late 1950s and early 1960s, and the fact that teenagers, as a group, had more money to spend resulted in teen interests playing a greater role in directing popular culture. The shaggy but still short mop tops, and the relatively innocent desires expressed by lyrics such as "I want to hold your hand," were more palatable to mainstream society than Elvis's tight clothes and pelvic thrusting had been. Still, while the Beatles were initially promoted as wholesome, their offstage behavior was often antiauthoritarian and, as such, appealed to a large number of teenagers, making the Beatles one of the most commercially successful acts in history.

Teen idols have come and gone in the decades since Beatlemania. In the mid-1980s, Duran Duran rose to prominence side-by-side with MTV, exploiting the new medium, which very specifically targeted a teenage demographic. "Boy bands" like Backstreet Boys and 'NSync, popular in the late 1990s, also enjoyed a teen idol status and, as some critics have argued, may have helped usher in more inclusive ideas about masculinity, some of which are obvious in more contemporary teen-targeted pop culture. *High School Musical*, for example, features a jock, played by Zac Efron, who also sings and dances. Predominantly African American hip-hop stars, while often considered outside the category of "teen idol," have also been influential in shaping teenage pop culture in the last several decades.

TEENAGE ANGST AND TEENAGE CRIMINALS

An oft-assumed component of teenage psychology is alienation, especially from previously loved and respected parents. Teenagers are often thought of as misunderstood and emotionally unstable individuals who are unable to conform to the rules of adult society. Holden Caulfield, hero of J. D. Salinger's influential 1951 novel *Catcher in the Rye*, is an iconic example of the teenager who is unable to cope with the transition from childhood to adulthood. He sees adults as "phonies," and while he aspires to make good and find a place for himself in the world, he also seems unable to stop himself from engaging in self-destructive behavior. This notion of teenage angst has been echoed throughout pop culture, typically in "bad boy" characters that are good at heart. While they often make mistakes, they are also frequently forgiven. It is assumed that bad choices are a part of being a teenager and not character based. Dylan from the original *Beverly Hills, 90210* television series fits this mold, as does Jess from *Gilmore Girls* and Shane Botwin from the Showtime comedy *Weeds*. Indie music, which has become increasingly popular since the 1980s, is also full of teenage angst. Interestingly, some commentators have noted that in real life, as opposed to fiction, many teenagers are able to navigate the physical and emotional changes of adolescence without undergoing any great degree of psychological stress. When driven or culturally conservative teenagers appear in pop culture, however, they are often played for laughs, as in the 1980s sitcom *Family Ties* character Alex P. Keaton, who wears suits, reads the *Wall Street Journal*, and obsessively plans his future, starting with admittance to Princeton.

In the 1990s fears about teenage angst turning into violent behavior rose to prominence in the national conversation with the flurry of publicity surrounding a number of school shootings, especially the one at Colorado's Columbine High School in 1999. These fears are, of course, part of a long history of fears about teenage criminality that become more pronounced when there's a sense in the culture at large that teenagers view their peers, and the media they consume, as more influential in their lives than are their parents. School shootings, as well as gang violence, have received extensive treatment in the news media since about 1990. This coverage has resulted in both productive discussions about factors that contribute to teen violence, including the role of violence in entertainment, and also largely unfair stereotypes about teenagers being violent and amoral. Many people have cited such stereotypes about young African American males as being at play in the 2012 shooting death of Trayvon Martin by neighborhood watch volunteer George Zimmerman.

DIGITAL TEENS

In the twenty-first century, digital media is omnipresent and has given many teenagers the chance to consume a wider variety of media, as well as to participate more fully in the production of pop culture. Digital cable, which is present in a large number of homes, provides a diversity of programming, including Spanish-language channels, Black Entertainment Television, and Logo, which caters to the LGBT (lesbian, gay, bisexual, transgender) community. Although surveys suggest that adults often view teenage media use in a negative light, social media such as Facebook and Twitter have allowed teenagers to connect in new ways, including to organize politically, as in the Occupy Wall Street movement and the Million Hoodie March. Young adult fiction has become increasingly popular and commercially successful, thanks in part to the Internet and e-books. Books are discussed in various online communities, and adult authors such as John Green and Libba Bray interact with their tech-savvy teen readers on YouTube and Twitter. Teenagers are also responsible for having created a large number of blogs, on a wide array of topics, including fashion, food, music, politics, and technology. Some of these blogs have garnered positive attention from mainstream media outlets and have generated income from advertising and sales.

Ilana Nash
Daisy Gard

SEE ALSO: *The Beatles; Boy Bands;* The Catcher in the Rye*; Consumerism; Facebook; Goodman, Benny; The Great Depression; Hip-Hop; Leisure Time; Presley, Elvis; Rock and Roll; Sinatra, Frank; Slang; Social Media; Teen Idols; Twitter; YouTube.*

BIBLIOGRAPHY

Allison, Emma. "Social Media Has Fed the Fever." *New York Times*, March 29, 2012.

Crace, John. "The Teen Bloggers Who Took Over the Internet." *Guardian*, September 8, 2009.

Nichols, Sharon, and Thomas Good. *America's Teenagers—Myths and Realities: Media Images, Schooling and the Social Costs of Reckless Indifference*. Mahwah, NJ: Lawrence Erlbaum Associates, 2004.

Palladino, Grace. *Teenagers: An American History*. New York: Basic, 1997.

Patten, Melanie. "90's Boy Bands Changed Our Tune on Manliness, Study Shows." *Star* (Toronto), May 13, 2010.

Rollin, Lucy. *Twentieth-Century Teen Culture by the Decades: A Reference Guide*. Westport, CT: Greenwood Press, 1999.

Tejano Music

During the 1930s and 1940s a music developed in the American Southwest that mirrored the cultural evolution of Hispanics in the region into Mexican Americans, a bicultural community formed by the first generation of Americans of Mexican descent to aspire for inclusion in Anglo-American life. Popular dance band ensembles catered to this generation's biculturalism by playing genres chosen from both the Latin and the American traditions: bolero, *danzón*, *guaracha*, and rumba alternating with boogie, swing, and fox-trot, among others. After World War II, a type of fusion of the traditions took place that developed into a distinctive sound, especially among the *orquestas* and *conjuntos* in Texas, where the largest Hispanic recording companies existed at that time. The result was a music that came to be known as Tejano. As a fusion music, Tejano organically developed over many decades as each generation of Mexican American musicians synthesized traditional Mexican and Tex-Mex sounds with the American popular music of its own era, including swing, country, jazz, rock, and hip-hop.

MEXICAN AMERICAN ORIGINS

As orchestras became more professional and ballroom dance circuits extended throughout the Southwest, Texas recording artists came into great demand and spread their new music through the southwestern United States and northern Mexico. Among the first prominent big bands was that of Beto Villa, from Falfurrias, Texas. Sometimes called the father of the Mexican American *orquesta*, Villa popularized a folksy, "country"-style polka that came to be known as "Tex-Mex," especially when compared with the more sophisticated urban sounds of *danzones*, *guarachas*, fox-trots, and swings. Villa's influence was so strong that many followers appeared throughout the Southwest. The most noteworthy was singer-saxophonist Isidro López, also from Texas, who is known for adding the working-class *canción ranchera* to the Tex-Mex repertoire. Balde González of Victoria, Texas, and Pedro Bugarín of Phoenix, Arizona, smoothed out the musical deliveries and broadened the repertoire of genres included in Tex-Mex.

The peak years for the Mexican American orquesta were the 1960s and 1970s, when Little Joe Hernández emerged as one of the greatest all-time performers and popularizers of Tex-Mex. Little Joe led a band made up of family members and friends under a series of names, and he struggled to get studios to record his music and radio stations in Texas to play it. Finally, he decided to form his own recording and distribution companies. Little Joe fused the Tex-Mex *ranchero* sound with American jazz and rock within the same musical number to achieve a unique bimusical sound that came to be called "La onda chicana" (the Chicano Wave).

Little Joe's first experiment in Chicano Wave occurred on his hugely successful 1972 album, *Para la gente* (*For the People*). Backing Joe and his brother Johnny's harmonic duet were the usual instruments of a well-organized Mexican American band of those years: two trumpets; two saxophones; a trombone; and a rhythm section of bass, electric guitar, drums, and keyboards. On the album, many of the arrangements were augmented with strings from the Dallas symphony—a novelty for Tex-Mex music—and interlacing jazz riffs. This historic album continued to be standard fare among dance bands in Mexican American communities for decades.

CROSSOVER ARTISTS

Texas was the center for Tejano music (*Tejano* comes from *Tejas*, which is Spanish for "Texas"), and dance bands and recording artists from there would tour north as far as Chicago and New York City and south as far Mexico City. The advent of three Spanish-language television networks further popularized the music in the Caribbean and South America. After peaking in the 1970s, Tejano threatened to fade because young people thought of it as the music of their parents, and recent immigrants wanted something more authentically Mexican. By the 1990s, however, a new wave of young Mexican American performers had surged to remake Tejano for the next generation, infusing it with the electric and urban sounds of rock and hip-hop to accommodate the more recent concentration of Hispanics in big cities and to appeal to bilingual fans across many popular music genres.

Perhaps the most widely known of these young Tejano stars was Selena Quintanilla-Pérez, who topped the Latin charts in the early 1990s and won the Best Mexican American Album Grammy for *Live* (1993). Selena (her stage name) won Tejano Music Awards for Best Female Entertainer or Vocalist from 1986 through 1995 and set attendance records at the 66,000-plus-capacity Houston Astrodome. When the twenty-three-year-old "Queen of Tejano" was killed in 1995, she was at work on her first crossover album, *Dreaming of You* (1995). Posthumously released with four songs in English, it sold 175,000 copies in one day to become the second-fastest-selling album ever by a female singer. After debuting at number one, it spent forty-nine weeks on the Billboard 200. In fewer than five months it became her second certified platinum album. The year after Selena's death, the Tejano Music Awards added a category for best Tejano crossover song.

CULTURAL PRESENCE

Tejano performers and producers acknowledge that their music, as strong and successful as it became, grew from limitations. Their names, heritage, and neighborhood roots prevented them from being just average rock stars, but they were as much American as Mexican, so they created their own genre and found their niche. It is an identity negotiation that parallels the lives of bilingual Americans. Selena made life on the border work for her. When Mexicans criticized her lack of fluency in Spanish, it only boosted her fan base among young Mexican Americans who were tired of hearing the same criticism from their older relatives.

Tejano music peaked in the mid-1990s. A PBS documentary, *Songs of the Homeland* (1995), portrayed its rise from immigrant roots to popular culture integration. The 1997 film biography *Selena* helped propel Jennifer Lopez to stardom. In 1998 the Grammy Awards added a category for Tejano music, which had previously been lumped into the broader Mexican American/Tejano category. This made room to honor other genres of Mexican American music, such as *norteño* and *ranchero*, which had been overshadowed by Tejano's recent dominance. By 2000 Latin American music had so grown in variety and popularity that the Recording Academy responsible for the Grammy Awards had spawned the Latin Recording Academy with its own Latin Grammy Awards and ceremony.

Nicolás Kanellos

SEE ALSO: *Country Music; Grammy Awards; Hip-Hop; Jazz; Long-Playing Record; Lopez, Jennifer; Public Television (PBS); Rock and Roll; Selena; Swing Dancing; World War II.*

BIBLIOGRAPHY

Peña, Manuel. "From *Ranchera* to *Jaitón*: Ethnicity and Class in Texas-Mexican Music." *Ethnomusicology* 29, no. 1 (1985): 29–55.

Peña, Manuel. *The Texas Mexican-Conjunto: History of a Working-Class Music*. Austin: University of Texas Press, 1985.

Peña, Manuel. *Musica Tejana: The Cultural Economy of Artistic Transformation*. College Station: Texas A&M University, 1999.

Pérez, Chris. *To Selena, with Love*. New York: Celebra, 2012.

San Miguel, Guadalupe. *Tejano Proud: Tex-Mex Music in the Twentieth Century*. College Station: Texas A&M University, 2002.

Telephone

The telephone is a device for conducting spoken conversations across any distance beyond the range of the unaided human ear or the unamplified human voice. It works by transferring the atmospheric vibrations of human speech into a solid body and by converting those vibrations into electrical impulses sent through a conducting medium—originally metal wires but then optical fibers and electromagnetic microwaves as well.

The word *telephone* is a compound of two Greek words, *tele*, meaning far, and *phone*, meaning sound. The instrument is probably the most widely used of all telecommunications appliances, with hundreds of millions of telephones in use all over the world. The telephone is also the archetypal electronic medium, in the sense of the word intended by communications theorist Marshall McLuhan—an "extension of man"—but its social impact is grossly understudied in favor of the more readily observable television. The telephone is small and unobtrusive, and its impact on the visible environment (except for the poles and wires) is minimal.

INVENTION

Notwithstanding a host of rival claimants, the traditional account of the telephone's invention by the Scottish-born Alexander Graham Bell (1847–1922) remains substantially the correct one. While the word *telephone* had been used to describe a device similar to a children's string telephone as long ago as the seventeenth century, and, although the general concepts on which the invention was based had been known for several decades, it was certainly Bell who experienced the sudden flash of insight that he immediately translated into a working model.

Bell and his assistant Thomas Watson (1854–1934) had been trying to develop not a telephone but something Bell called a "harmonic telegraph," by which he hoped to expand the bottleneck throttling communications traffic and permit the transmission of more than one telegraph message over a single wire at the same time. Bell's ideas involved a series of vibrating metal reeds (like those used in wind instruments). Of course, once he had developed that technology, his goal was, in fact, to discover a way to transmit all the sounds of the human voice via his harmonic telegraph.

On June 2, 1875, Bell and Watson were working at opposite ends of a line, and Bell heard the distinct sound of a plucked reed coming through the line. He ran to the next room and shouted to his assistant, "Watson! What did you do then? Don't change anything!" From that moment, it took only an hour or so more of plucking the reeds and listening to the sounds they made before Bell was able to give Watson instructions on making the first Bell telephone, which was capable of transmitting only the sounds of the human voice, not words. Bell and Watson worked through the summer of 1875, and in September Bell began to write the specifications for his basic patent, which was issued on March 7, 1876. (The famous "Mr. Watson, come here! I want you!" was spoken after the first patent was issued, when Bell and Watson were working on perfecting their transmitter.) Ultimately victorious, Bell had to defend his patent in more than 600 separate lawsuits.

The Bell Telephone Company, the first of its kind, was founded on July 9, 1877. That same July Bell married Mabel Hubbard and sailed to England to introduce his telephone there. Well before 1900, Watson, Thomas Edison, Emil Berliner, and others had worked with Bell's patented technology to produce a telephone that would remain largely unchanged throughout the twentieth century. The telephone has consisted of the same basic components throughout its history: a power source, switch hook, dialer, ringer, transmitter, and receiver.

SOCIAL IMPACT

The social impact of the telephone has been literally incalculable. Although the telegraph, patented by the painter and inventor Samuel F. B. Morse in 1840, enjoys pride of place as the first electric instrument to extend and greatly speed human communication, it never became a ubiquitous home appliance like the telephone—it was too complicated to use and required too much special knowledge (codes, key technique). All a person needed to know in order to use a telephone was how to talk and to listen; it was not necessary to be literate or to have more than a minimal mechanical aptitude. It was, moreover, next to impossible to gossip using a telegraph. Like a religion, telegraphy had its privileged class, the operators, and gossip passed most freely between equals, without going through an intermediary. Because the telephone enabled two people to exchange gossip directly, though they might be on opposite sides of the earth, the telephone, more than any other invention, has produced what McLuhan calls "the global village."

The telephone changed war and business and the whole gamut of public activities as well, but it did not transform them out of recognition the way it altered the fundamental relationship of one individual to another and of one individual to society. Warfare was altered by the invention of a new weapon, from the metal sword to the atomic bomb; business was altered by intellectual inventions, such as double-entry bookkeeping or speculation or advertising or market capitalism. Public life changed with the emergence of new institutions—the law, the republic, democracy, dictatorship—and in the twentieth century was being replaced by the television camera.

EFFECTS ON INTERPERSONAL RELATIONSHIPS

But the telephone began the seismic shift in sensibility described by Martin Pawley in his book *The Private Future*: "Western societies are collapsing not from an assault on their most cherished values, but from a voluntary, almost enthusiastic abandonment of them by people who are learning to live private lives of an unprecedented completeness with the aid of the momentum of a technology which is evolving more and more into a pattern of socially atomizing appliances." The telephone, which has been traditionally promoted as a means of bringing people together, of connecting them, is in fact the archetype of Pawley's "socially atomizing appliances." Scottish filmmaker Bill Forsyth gives a perfect example of this in his film *Local Hero* (1983). Actor Peter Riegert plays a character who wants to invite to dinner a girl standing less than 20 feet away from him on the other side of a glass partition—so he dials her extension. That is "the Private Future" in action.

Cordless phones, answering machines, cellular phones, call waiting, phones in automobiles, headset phones that free up both hands—all of these seem likely to increase a person's dissociation from the present and to hasten a withdrawal from the public sphere into "private lives of an unprecedented completeness." The dangers inherent in the disappearance of any meaningful public life should be obvious. The telephone poses a more immediate danger, however, because of its technology's effect on the human physiology.

As McLuhan observes in *Understanding Media*, the overloading of one sensory organ—as the telephone overloads the ear—results in the numbing of the others. People talking on the phone think they can see perfectly well what is happening around them and can react to it in a timely manner, but they cannot. A woman driving a large vehicle, about to negotiate a tricky left turn through a busy intersection while she chats on the telephone with a friend, has the illusion of being in two places at once—with the friend and in traffic—but is in fact nowhere at all. The friendship, however, is not in physical danger—the other vehicles approaching that intersection, along with their passengers, are in the gravest peril. By the end of the 1990s, legislation restricting the use of telephones in automobiles in the United States began to pass in several states. The whole concept of interdependence, of civic responsibility, is losing its force. The huge juggernaut of communications technology that was launched when Bell burst in on Watson and shouted "Don't change anything!" has changed everything.

CELLULAR PHONES

Use of the traditional landline telephone steadily declined since the introduction of the cell phone. According to statistics from the Centers for Disease Control and Prevention, U.S. households were steadily becoming completely wireless, and homes that still had a landline received the majority of their phone calls via their cellular phones. Cellular phones spread across the globe and were owned by every demographic. The ease of installing cellular towers as opposed to running miles of telephone cable provided residents with access to information, in particular to people living in remote or underdeveloped areas where the Internet was not available.

As the technology progressed, cellular phones broadened their capabilities. Initially used as a means of communication similar to traditional landline phones, mobile phones also offered the ability to text message—or send short written messages from phone to phone—which became a primary use. Phones were also being used as media players, cameras, video recorders, and a variety of other devices. Mobile technology quickly advanced in order to satisfy customers' needs. Companies began to offer smartphones, which used computer operating systems to enhance their capability. smartphones allowed users to check e-mail, browse the Internet, and run third-party applications (apps).

Computer company Apple was the first to introduce an app store, which offers various applications for use on mobile devices; the market proved to be a huge success, and other manufacturers established stores for their products. Initial apps included messaging, social media, and e-mail; however, consumer demand and innovation brought about games, GPS services, banking, and purchasing apps. Such increased capability has pushed the phone into new territory, moving it from a simple communication device into the realm of a personal computer.

Gerald Carpenter

SEE ALSO: *Apple Computer; AT&T; Cell Phones; Edison, Thomas Alva; E-mail; The Internet; McLuhan, Marshall; Smartphones; Social Media; Texting; Videos.*

BIBLIOGRAPHY

Blumberg, Stephen J., and Julian V. Luke. "Wireless Substitution: Early Release of Estimates from the National Health Interview Survey, July–December 2009." Centers for Disease Control and Prevention, May 2009. Accessed April 28, 2012. Available from http://www.cdc.gov/nchs/data/nhis/earlyrelease/wireless200905.htm

Casson, Herbert Newton. *The History of the Telephone*. Chicago: McClurg, 1910.

Coe, Lewis. *The Telephone and Its Several Inventors: A History*. Jefferson, NC: McFarland, 1995.

Fischer, Claude S. *America Calling: A Social History of the Telephone to 1940*. Berkeley: University of California Press, 1992.

Harlow, Alvin F. *Old Wires and New Waves: The History of the Telegraph, Telephone, and Wireless.* New York: D. Appleton-Century, 1936.

McLuhan, Marshall. *Understanding Media: The Extensions of Man.* New York: McGraw-Hill, 1964.

Pawley, Martin. *The Private Future: Causes and Consequences of Community Collapse in the West.* London: Thames and Hudson, 1973.

Prescott, George B. *Bell's Electric Speaking Telephone: Its Invention, Construction, Application, Modification, and History.* New York: Arno Press, 1972.

Stehman, Jonas Warren. *The Financial History of the American Telephone and Telegraph Company.* Boston: Houghton Mifflin, 1925.

Stern, Ellen, and Emily Gwathmey. *Once upon a Telephone: An Illustrated Social History.* New York: Harcourt Brace, 1994.

Televangelism

Since the beginnings of commercial radio, evangelical Christians have recognized the effectiveness of the broadcast media in disseminating their faith. By enabling them to reach new audiences as well as committed believers, broadcasting has provided evangelists with a means of building large and widespread followings. As a result, religious broadcasters have continually taken advantage of new technologies, from local radio programs in the early 1920s to twenty-four-hour cable television networks by the late 1970s. The use of television by evangelists as a medium for expressing their views proved to be an especially influential development during the last quarter of the twentieth century and into the new millennium, as conflicts between religious conservatives and mainstream popular culture grew. In this context, the term *televangelism* became widely adopted to describe the use of broadcasting to promote not only evangelical Christian beliefs but also a wide range of social and political views espoused by Christian fundamentalists.

The roots of contemporary televangelism can be traced to the 1950s, when evangelists such as Billy Graham, Rex Humbard, and Oral Roberts started to use television programs to spread their conservative Protestant beliefs. Most early examples of televangelism adopted a traditional format, concentrating on sermons, church services, and revival meetings, and operated on fairly small budgets. Early televangelist programming was also generally restricted to Sunday mornings and usually broadcast over a small number of stations covering a limited geographic area. Over time, however, technological changes and increasing resources allowed televangelists to reach much larger audiences. The advent of videotape, for example, provided an inexpensive and flexible means of distributing programs so that they did not have to be broadcast live or recorded on expensive motion picture film. The proliferation of television stations during the 1950s and 1960s provided a broader variety of outlets for televangelism, as did the subsequent expansion of cable television.

As a result of these innovations, televangelism underwent a major period of growth during the 1970s. Organizations like Pat Robertson's Christian Broadcasting Network and Jim Bakker's Praise the Lord (PTL) Satellite Network used local cable television systems, linked by satellite transmissions, to bring their programming to virtually all parts of the country and

Jimmy Swaggart Begs for Forgiveness. *Jimmy Swaggart begs for forgiveness as one of several televangelists whose personal misdeeds were exposed in the 1980s.* ROB NELSON/TIME LIFE PICTURES/GETTY IMAGES.

throughout the week—not just on Sundays. To take advantage of this increase in exposure, televangelists also adopted new programming formats, such as the talk show and newsmagazine, which had become staples of commercial television. The rapid growth in their operations also brought greater political influence to televangelists during the late 1970s and 1980s. With the conservative turn in American politics at this time and the rise of the Christian Right as a political force, prominent televangelists such as Jerry Falwell and Robertson found that broadcasting provided them with a powerful tool for publicizing their views and shaping the nation's political agenda.

Toward the end of the 1980s, however, televangelism went into a period of decline, primarily as a result of separate financial and sexual scandals involving both Bakker and Jimmy Swaggart, two leading religious broadcasters. Their sexual misconduct and Bakker's misappropriation of funds donated to the PTL Network exposed televangelism to increasing public criticism and suspicion. The core audience of the television evangelists did not turn away from them, but their broader influence within American society dropped, as did their television ratings. The failure of Robertson to win the Republican presidential nomination in 1988 also marked a downturn in the political influence of the conservative televangelists. Christian broadcasters responded to these trends by trying to broaden the appeal of their programming, experimenting with new formats and offering an increasing number of family-oriented programs without an explicit religious or political message.

Even so, televangelists who specialized in traditional preaching retained a presence throughout the early twenty-first century. Perhaps the most successful televangelist of the first decade of the 2000s was Joel Osteen of Lakewood Church in Houston, Texas. Despite having no college degree or formal theological training, Osteen took over as pastor of Lakewood Church following the death of his father, who was pastor before him. The younger Osteen quickly focused on increasing the church's media presence by advertising heavily and increasing its television airtime. Osteen's sermons tended to be simple and positive, emphasizing his main theme that "God wants us to have a better life." This idea was based on the "health and wealth" gospel of prosperity theology, a doctrine espousing that Christians were entitled to physical well-being and economic success. Even though his message was criticized as a diluted form of the Christian faith, his church experienced tremendous growth, and Osteen's books topped the best-sellers lists.

The propagation of web-based video sharing during the early twenty-first century once again shifted the way televangelists reached audiences. Websites such as YouTube offered preachers another inexpensive way to put their message out into the world. A preacher of some renown already, Osteen's videos averaged 200,000 views or more on YouTube. The medium was so valuable that websites like GodTube, a video-sharing platform specifically geared toward Christian videos, proliferated. In the 2010s such videos were an as-yet-emerging media format with seemingly limitless possibilities for distribution and viewership; the Internet was an ideal place for televangelism to reimagine itself.

Through their successful use of broadcasting and later Internet technology, televangelists have established a notable presence in American popular culture over the past several decades. Considerable disagreement exists over the size of their audiences, and a number of studies have suggested that televangelists have had more success in reinforcing the faith of existing believers than in reaching new converts. Nonetheless, televangelism has become a persistent feature of American media and, as such, has contributed substantially to the diversity of views that constitute American popular culture.

Roger W. Stump

SEE ALSO: *Bakker, Jim, and Tammy Faye; Cable TV; Fundamentalism; Graham, Billy; Moral Majority; Robertson, Pat; Sex Scandals; Swaggart, Jimmy; Television.*

BIBLIOGRAPHY

Armstrong, Ben. *The Electric Church*. Nashville, TN: Thomas Nelson Publishers, 1979.

Bruce, Steve. *Pray TV: Televangelism in America*. New York: Routledge, 1990.

Hadden, Jeffrey K., and Anson Shupe. *Televangelism, Power, and Politics on God's Frontier*. New York: Henry Holt, 1988.

Hadden, Jeffrey K., and Charles E. Swann. *Prime Time Preachers: The Rising Power of Televangelism*. Reading, MA: Addison-Wesley, 1981.

Osteen, Joel. *It's Your Time: Activate Your Faith, Achieve Your Dreams, and Increase in God's Favor*. New York: Free Press, 2009.

Schultze, Quentin J. *Televangelism and American Culture: The Business of Popular Religion*. Grand Rapids, MI: Baker Book House, 1991.

Television

At the same time that radio began to achieve commercial viability in the 1920s, the United States and Great Britain began experimenting with television, the wireless transmission of moving pictures. Although Great Britain was initially somewhat more successful, both countries experienced a lot of difficulty in the early stages. There were a variety of reasons for this adversity.

In the United States many people whose livelihoods were tied to radio were also responsible for developing television. Accordingly, they were in no hurry to see radio, a sure moneymaker, usurped by the new medium. In addition, the Great Depression greatly slowed the development of television in the 1930s. A tremendous amount of infighting also existed between potential television manufacturers and the Federal Communications Commission (FCC) in trying to establish uniform technical standards. And finally, just as it seemed as though television was poised to enter U.S. homes, the onset of World War II delayed its ascendancy until the war's end.

In the late 1940s and early 1950s, however, commercial television exploded on the U.S. market, forever changing the way products were sold, people were entertained, and news events were reported. In the years immediately following World War II, television quickly became the dominant medium in the United States. It influenced, shaped, and recorded popular culture in a way no other media was able to equal.

EARLY STAGES OF TELEVISION

There was no single inventor of television. Scientists had long been intrigued by the idea of transmitting images via wire. Among the early pioneers of television were Scottish engineer

John L. Baird, who is credited with inventing a mechanical television system in the 1920s. Inventor Vladimir Zworykin, who emigrated from Russia to the United States in 1919, got his first television system patent in 1923. He then developed a cathode-ray picture tube, which he called the kinescope, as well as an all-electronic camera tube, known as the iconoscope. In the late 1920s he went to work for RCA as the director of the company's Electronic Research Lab. In 1930 Philo Farnsworth obtained a patent for the first all-electronic television.

Although televisions first appeared on the market in 1939, there were virtually no stations and no established programming at that time. It was not until just after World War II that TV began its meteoric rise to media dominance. As John Findling and Frank Thackeray note in *Events That Changed America in the Twentieth Century*, in 1946 only 7,000 TV sets were sold. As television stations began appearing in an increasing number of cities, however, the number of sets sold rose dramatically. In 1948, 172,000 sets were sold; in 1950 there were about four million sets sold. By 1960 nearly 90 percent of U.S. homes had a television, a percentage that has only climbed since.

Before television the U.S. public had spent its leisure time in a variety of ways. But as each new station appeared in a particular city, corresponding drops would occur in restaurant business, movie-ticket demand, book and magazine sales, and radio listeners. By the early 1960s Americans were spending a large portion of their leisure time watching TV, a trend that has remained remarkably stable ever since.

Television originally only had twelve very high frequency (VHF) channels—2 through 13. In the late 1940s more than 100 stations were competing for transmission on VHF channels. Frequency overcrowding resulted in stations interfering with one another, which led to the FCC banning the issuance of new licenses for VHF channels for nearly four years. At the conclusion of the ban, stations receiving new licenses were given recently developed ultrahigh frequency (UHF) channels (14 through 83). Most TV sets, however, needed a special attachment to receive UHF channels, which also had a worse picture and poorer sound than VHF channels. Unfortunately, it was mostly educational, public access, and community channels that were relegated to UHF. Because of the FCC's ban, the three major networks—ABC, CBS, and NBC—were able to corner the VHF channels and dominate the television market until well into the 1980s.

TELEVISION ADVERTISING

Since its introduction into U.S. society, television has proven itself capable of holding its audience riveted to the screen for countless hours. As a result, people who saw television as a means through which to provide culturally uplifting programming to the public were gravely disappointed. Instead, TV almost immediately became an unprecedentedly effective means of selling products. Most of the public was not interested in educational programming, and if people did not watch, advertisers did not pay for airtime in which to sell their products. TV shows in the late 1940s followed the model established by the success of radio; single advertisers paid for whole shows, the most common of which were half-hour genre and variety shows. But in 1950 a small lipstick company named Hazel Bishop changed forever the way companies sold their products.

When Hazel Bishop first began advertising on TV in 1950, the company had only $50,000 a year in sales. In just two years of television advertising, and at a time when only about 10 percent of U.S. homes had televisions, that number rose to a stunning $4.5 million. As advertisers flocked to hawk their products on television, TV executives scrambled to find a way to accommodate as many companies as possible, which would result in astronomical profits for both the advertisers and the networks. Television executives realized that single product sponsorship was no longer effective. Instead, they devised a system of longer breaks during a show, which could be split up into thirty-second spots and sold to a much larger number of advertisers. Although this advertising innovation resulted in television's greatest period of profitability, it also led to advertising dictating television programming.

In the early 1950s television advertisers realized they had a monopoly on the U.S. public; they were competing with each other, not with other media, such as books or magazines. People watched regardless of what was on television. Advertisers discovered that what most people would watch was what was the least objectionable (and often the most innocuous) show in a given time slot, giving rise to the concept of Least Objectionable Programming. A TV show did not have to be good, it only had to be less objectionable than the other shows in the same time slot. Although more serious dramatic television did not entirely disappear, the majority of shows were tailored to create the mood advertisers thought would result in their consumers being the most amenable to their products. By the mid-1950s lightweight sitcoms dominated the U.S. television market. The relative success and happiness of television characters became easily measurable by the products they consumed.

Prior to the twentieth century, leisure time was a concept generally realized only by the wealthy. But as the middle class grew astoundingly fast in the post–World War II boom, a much larger population than ever before enjoyed leisure time, which helped contribute to television's remarkable popularity. Perhaps even more important was the rise of the concept of disposable income, money that people could spend on their wants rather than their needs. Advertisers paying for the right to influence how people might spend their disposable income largely funded television. As a result, television was ostensibly free prior to the late 1970s. Nevertheless, television's cost had always been high; it played perhaps the single largest role in contributing to the United States becoming a consumer culture unparalleled in world history. Countless television shows achieved an iconic stature in popular culture, but none had as powerful an effect on the way people lived their day-to-day lives as had commercials.

RADIO AND MAGAZINES REACT

By the mid-1950s it became clear that television's influence would not be confined to the screen. Other forms of media simply could not compete directly with television. As a result, they had to change their markets and formats in order to secure a consistent, although generally much smaller than pre-television, audience. Perhaps the most far-reaching consequence of the rise of television was that the United States went from being a country of readers to a country of watchers. Previously hugely popular national magazines such as *Collier's*, *Life*, and the *Saturday Evening Post* went out of business in the late 1950s.

Likewise, as television, an ostensibly more exciting visual medium than radio, adapted programming previously confined to the radio, radio shows quickly lost their audience. Magazines and radio stations responded similarly. Rather than trying to compete with TV, they became specialized, targeting a singular demographic audience. Simultaneously, advertisers grew savvier in their research and development and realized that highly specific consumer markets could be reached via radio and magazine advertising. Strangely, television's rise to prominence secured the long-term success of radio and magazines; their response to the threat of television eventually resulted in a much larger number of magazines and radio stations than had been available before television. In the late 1990s audiences could find a radio station or magazine that focused on just about any subject they might want.

HOLLYWOOD

Perhaps the industry struck hardest by the advent of television was the U.S. film industry. Hollywood initially considered TV an inferior market, not worthy of its consideration. In the late 1940s as many as 90 million people a week went to the movies. But television's convenience and easy accessibility proved to be great competition for Hollywood. By the mid-1950s the industry's movie audience had been reduced to half its former number. Hollywood never recovered as far as actual theater audiences are concerned. In fact, by the late 1990s only fifteen million people a week attended the cinema, even though the United States had twice the population it had in the late 1940s.

Hollywood, however, found a way to adapt. Rather than relying exclusively on box-office receipts, it learned to use television to its advantage. Beginning at the end of the twentieth century, after-market profits, including the money generated from pay-per-view; cable channels; premium movie channels; and, most of all, video sales and rentals, were just as important to a film's success, if not more so, than a film's box-office take.

In addition, television's media domination contributed greatly to blurring the lines between TV and Hollywood. Most Hollywood studios also produced TV shows on their premises. Furthermore, just as radio stars once made the jump from the airwaves to the silver screen, TV stars routinely progressed from the small screen to the movies. As a result, many celebrities could not be simply categorized in the way they once were. Too many stars had their feet in too many different media to validate singular labels. For example, Oprah Winfrey, a television talk-show maven, also had been involved in several successful books, promoted the literary careers of others, frequently appeared on other talk shows and news magazines as a guest, and acted in and produced a number of both television and Hollywood films. Television's unequaled cultural influence resulted in turning any number of stars who would have formerly been confined to one or two media into omnipresent multimedia moguls.

TELEVISION NEWS

If radio ushered in the era of broadcast journalism, then TV helped to further define and legitimize it. In addition, television newscasts changed the way people received and perceived news. By the late 1950s TV reporters had learned to take advantage of emerging technologies and use them to cover breaking news stories live. Television broadcasts and broadcasters grew to hold sway over public opinion. For example, public sentiment against the Vietnam War was fueled by nightly broadcasts of its seemingly senseless death and destruction. Journalist Walter Cronkite added further fuel to the growing fire of anger and resentment in 1968 when he declared on air that he thought the war in Vietnam was a "terrible mistake." When most U.S. citizens think of the events surrounding the assassinations of John F. Kennedy, Martin Luther King Jr., and Bobby Kennedy, as well as the civil rights movement, the first moon walk, the *Challenger* space shuttle disaster, the Gulf Wars, and the 1992 riots in Los Angeles after the Rodney King trial verdict, it is the televised images that often first come to mind.

Unfortunately, by the late 1990s many people came to rely on television news as their main source of information. In addition to nightly news and news-oriented cable networks, cheap-to-make and highly profitable newsmagazines such as *Dateline*, *20/20*, and *48 Hours* became TV's most common form of programming. Rarely did these shows feature news of much importance; instead, they relied on lurid and titillating reports that did nothing to enrich the public's knowledge of world events. Nevertheless, the broadcasts received consistently high ratings, thus ensuring the continuing flow of advertising dollars.

That most people relied on television for their information meant that most of them were underinformed; for full accounts of a particular story it was still necessary to seek out supporting written records in newspapers, magazines, and books. The problem with relying on television for information is, as Neil Postman writes in *Amusing Ourselves to Death*, "not that television presents us with entertaining subject matter but that all subject matter is presented as entertaining." Accordingly, it is Postman's contention that the U.S. public's reliance on TV for information is dangerous, for when people become "distracted by trivia, when cultural life is redefined as a perpetual round of entertainments, when serious public conversation becomes a form of baby-talk, when, in short, a people become an audience and their public business a comedy show, then a nation finds itself at risk."

POLITICS ON TELEVISION

Because of news broadcasting and the fact that television was the best way to reach the largest number of people, television helped shape U.S. politics in the second half of the twentieth century. Effective television advertising became crucial to the success or failure of nearly all national elections. Unfortunately, such advertising was rarely completely factual or issue oriented. Instead, most such advertisements were used to smear the reputation of a particular candidate's opponent. Perhaps the most famous example of such advertisements occurred in the 1988 presidential campaign, during which Republican George H. W. Bush ran a series of slanted and inflammatory spots about his Democratic opponent, Michael Dukakis.

Furthermore, the careers of several presidents became inextricably intertwined with TV. For example, President Ronald Reagan, a former minor movie star and television product pitchman, used his television savvy so effectively that he came to be known as the Great Communicator. Conversely, President Bill Clinton, whose initial effective use of television reminded some of John F. Kennedy's, became victim to his own marketability when in August 1998 he admitted in a televised speech to the nation that he had lied about his affair with a young intern named Monica Lewinsky. His admission, which was meant to put the incident behind him, instead spawned a virtual television cottage industry, with literally dozens of shows devoting themselves to continual discussion about his fate, which was ultimately decided in a televised impeachment trial.

Strangely, considering the man was wary of the medium, perhaps no politician's career was more tied to television than

Richard Nixon's. As a vice presidential candidate on Dwight Eisenhower's 1952 Republican presidential bid, Nixon came under fire for allegedly receiving illegal funding. A clamor arose to have him removed from the ticket. On September 23, 1952, he went on TV and delivered a denial to the accusations. More than one million favorable letters and telegrams were sent supporting Nixon; he remained on the ticket, and he and Eisenhower won in a landslide.

Conversely, only eight years later TV would play a role in Nixon losing his own bid for the White House. He agreed to a series of televised debates with his much more telegenic opponent, John F. Kennedy. Nixon's pasty face and sweaty brow may have cost him the election. Many historians believe that Kennedy won the debates as much by his more polished appearance and manner than by anything he said.

Nixon learned from his error. While again running for the presidency in 1968, he hired a public relations firm to run his campaign. The result was a much more polished, image-conscious, and TV-friendly candidate; he won the election easily. In the last chapter of his political career, broadcast and print media helped spur investigations into his involvement with the Watergate affair. The hearings were broadcast live on TV, which helped to turn public opinion against the president, who resigned from office as a result. One of the most famous images in the history of television is that of Nixon turning and waving to the crowd as he boarded the helicopter that removed him from power forever.

SPORTS AND ADVERTISING

Prior to World War II, baseball was widely recognized as the country's national pastime. Games were often broadcast live on the radio, and the country blissfully spent its summers pursuing the on-the-field exploits of larger-than-life figures such as Babe Ruth. After the war, however, other sports grew to prominence, largely because of television; beer; and, until 1970, cigarette advertisers, who saw in sports audiences a target market for their products. Individual sports such as golf and tennis grew in popularity, but team sports such as hockey; basketball; and, most of all, football had the greatest increases. By the late 1960s and with the advent of the Super Bowl, annually the most viewed broadcast in the United States, football surpassed baseball as the favorite pastime.

Because of their nature, team sports had a built-in drama that could escalate in intensity over the duration of a season. Spectators were drawn to the players in this drama, which resulted in athletes hawking products perhaps more so than any other cultural icons. In fact, as advertising revenues increasingly funded sports, athletes became perhaps the highest-paid workers in the United States. Basketball player Michael Jordan reportedly earned more than $30 million to play for the Chicago Bulls in the 1997–1998 season. In the fall of 1998 pitcher Kevin Brown signed with the Los Angeles Dodgers for a seven-year deal worth $105 million. Accompanying their paychecks was a rise in media scrutiny. Elite athletes were hounded by paparazzi in a way once reserved for movie stars and royalty. Such was the price of television fame in the United States.

Despite the ridiculous salaries and the accompanying out-of-control egos of many athletes and owners, it could be argued that television made sports better for most people. Seeing a game live at a venue remained thrilling, but TV, with its multiple camera angles and slow-motion instant replays, was by far a better way to actually see a game. In addition to better vision, all the comforts of home were available without the hassle of inclement weather, expensive tickets, heavy traffic, and nearly impossible parking.

And because of TV and its live transmission of sports, certain moments became a part of the collective cultural fabric of the United States in a way that never would have been possible without television. Heroes and goats achieved legendary status nearly immediately. The broadcasting of sporting events became just as important to U.S. culture as the televising of important political and social occasions. Although not particularly significant in their contribution to human progress, because of television certain images became just as much a part of U.S. culture's visual memory as the image of Neil Armstrong walking on the moon. These televised feats include San Francisco 49er Joe Montana's pass to Dwight Clark in the back of the end zone in the 1981 National Football Conference championship game to beat the Dallas Cowboys and the ground ball dribbling between Boston Red Sox first baseman Bill Buckner's legs in the sixth game of the 1986 World Series.

END OF THE CENTURY

As the twentieth century careened to a close and people in the United States prepared to embark on a new century, debates over television's inarguable influence continued to rage. Was TV too violent? Was television's content too sexually oriented? Had television news coverage become vacuous and reliant on the superfluous and tawdry? Was TV damaging children and contributing to the fraying of the country's social fabric? Regardless of the answers to these and countless other questions about television's influence, the inarguable fact was that television was the most important popular culture innovation in history.

Heroes and villains were coronated and vanquished on television. Sound bites as diverse in intent and inception as "where's the beef?" "read my lips," and "just do it" became permanently and equally ensconced in the national lexicon. Television was not without its flaws, but its accessibility and prevalence created what never before existed: shared visual cultural touchstones. As one, the U.S. public mourned the death of the Kennedy brothers, argued about the veracity of the Clarence Thomas/Anita Hill hearings, recoiled in horror as Reginald Denny was pulled from his truck and beaten, and cheered triumphantly as Mark McGwire hoisted his son in the air after hitting his sixty-second home run. For better or for worse, in the second half of the twentieth century television dominated and influenced the U.S. cultural landscape in an unprecedented fashion.

TWENTY-FIRST-CENTURY TELEVISION

Though television had infiltrated almost every home in almost every country by the end of the twentieth century, change was inevitable. People still turned to television as a primary source of information and entertainment, but in the twenty-first century there were more choices. The explosive growth of the Internet meant television viewers could turn to their computers to find entertainment and news, tailored to their individual interests, around the clock.

Access to television programming continued to evolve in the twenty-first century. Gone were the days when viewers sat down in front of their televisions and turned to one of the handful of available channels. In fact, most homes subscribed to cable, satellite, or some other form of feed that provided access to hundreds of channels. According to the National Cable & Telecommunications Association, there were more than fifty-eight million basic cable and forty-five million digital cable customers as of fall 2011.

With the increase in choice came an increase in demand, not in terms of a financial boost but in terms of demand from the consumer. The consumer could now dictate what to watch, as well as when and where to watch. On-demand options grew in popularity—consumers could record programs on digital video recorders to watch at their convenience, or they could take advantage of on-demand offers via their cable or satellite providers. They could also subscribe to streaming services, such as Netflix or Amazon-on-Demand, which streamed content directly to their computers or televisions. One of the more popular streaming services was Hulu, which launched in 2007 and offered free streaming of a number of movies and television programs via the Internet.

What did these changes mean for the television industry? Everything comes with a price. Services such as Hulu had free models, but there was a catch—viewers had to sit through a few ads here and there. In addition, many of the streaming services were based on paid subscription models. Still, many viewers relished the freedom to watch shows whenever and wherever they wanted and were willing to pay for such services.

In terms of programming, the major networks battled with cable networks for viewers. In the past, cable television aired movies or reruns of television series, but cable networks eventually began to produce original programming. Premium cable channels such as Showtime and Home Box Office found success with original shows such as *Sex and the City* and *The Sopranos*. Other cable networks, including FX, USA Network, Spike, and AMC, all began creating original programs. Programs on cable channels were not restricted by the same regulations as those on network television, so story lines could be somewhat edgier and language more colorful.

Though its glory days might be in the past, television remained as important in the twenty-first century as ever; it just was not quite the same. With TV embedded in every part of media—from computers and smartphones to tablets and e-readers—it was no longer confined to the box in the living room.

Robert C. Sickels

SEE ALSO: *Advertising; Anita Hill–Clarence Thomas Senate Hearings; Baseball; Basketball; Boston Red Sox; Cable TV;* Challenger *Disaster; Civil Rights Movement; Cronkite, Walter; The Dallas Cowboys;* Dateline*; Game Shows; The Great Depression; Gulf Wars; Hulu; Jordan, Michael; King, Martin Luther, Jr.; King, Rodney; Leisure Time; Live Television; McGwire, Mark; Montana, Joe; Netflix; Professional Football; Radio; Reality Television; Ruth, Babe; Sitcom; Soap Operas;* 20/20*; Vietnam; Winfrey, Oprah; World War II.*

BIBLIOGRAPHY

Abramson, Albert. *The History of Television, 1942 to 2000.* Jefferson, NC: McFarland, 2003.

Baker, William F., and George Dessart. *Down the Tube: An Inside Account of the Failure of American Television.* New York: BasicBooks, 1998.

Barnouw, Erik. *Tube of Plenty: The Evolution of American Television.* New York: Oxford University Press, 1990.

Caldwell, John Thornton. *Televisuality: Style, Crisis, and Authority in American Television.* New Brunswick, NJ: Rutgers University Press, 1995.

Comstock, George. *The Evolution of American Television.* Newbury Park, CA: Sage Publications, 1989.

Findling, John E., and Frank W. Thackeray. *Events That Changed America in the Twentieth Century.* Westport, CT: Greenwood Press, 1996.

Himmelstein, Hal. *Television Myth and the American Mind.* Westport, CT: Praeger, 1994.

Johnson, Steven. *Everything Bad Is Good for You: How Today's Popular Culture Is Actually Making Us Smarter.* New York: Riverhead Books, 2005.

Lotz, Amanda D. *The Television Will Be Revolutionized.* New York: New York University Press, 2007.

Postman, Neil. *Amusing Ourselves to Death.* New York: Penguin, 1985.

Spigel, Lynn, and Jan Olsson, eds. *Television after TV: Essays on a Medium in Transition.* Durham, NC: Duke University Press, 2004.

Stark, Steven D. *Glued to the Set: The 60 Television Shows and Events That Made Us Who We Are Today.* New York: Free Press, 1997.

Sturcken, Frank. *Live Television: The Golden Age of 1946–1958 in New York.* Jefferson, NC: McFarland, 1990.

Udelson, Joseph H. *The Great Television Race: A History of the American Television Industry 1925–1941.* Tuscaloosa: University of Alabama Press, 1982.

Television Anchors

According to television news legend Walter Cronkite, the term *anchorman* was invented by Sig Mickelson, the first head of the television and radio news department at CBS. It was expressly coined for use at the political conventions of 1952, the first campaign ever covered by modern television. These conventions were made coherent by one broadcaster who provided perspective on events and introduced reporters bringing news from various parts of the convention; in short, the man who anchored the broadcast.

In the United States and other developed countries around the world, television news anchors have become the de facto source of news for much of the public. With fewer people reading newspapers and more and more getting their information from television, TV news anchors on national and local newscasts have become the people the public turns to with the question, "What happened today?" Television news anchors, with their individual quirks and inflections, help to put a human face on the news. The power of the anchor to slant or comment on the news has been a source of concern for conservative and liberal critics alike. In totalitarian systems they are often seen as nothing more than the face of the government, reporting news that is generally patently false or propagandistic.

SETTING THE STANDARD

Cronkite set the standard for anchors in the United States during the period when he was known as the "most trusted man in

America." He was even urged to run for president at various times in his career. His sign-off, "And that's the way it is," rivaled Edward R. Murrow's "Good night and good luck" as the most popular signature piece of any news person in U.S. television history. Other significant news anchors of the 1960s included Chet Huntley and David Brinkley, who brought a partnership sensibility to the job that became a template for other newscasts. Their familiar signature—"Goodnight Chet. Goodnight David."—was often invoked in both comedy and drama.

The first television news anchors were used on weather reports and national and local television newscasts. Many of them had worked originally in radio, where the news format consisted of a reader announcing the news in sonorous and serious tones. This immediately translated to television, where a clock or sheet of paper could be used as props to make the set design appear serious. Early local television news instituted the anchor as the centerpiece of the show, delivering news, sports, and weather. It was only late in the 1960s that news programs began to have separate segments for different types of news, each presented by its own reporter. During this period the news anchor began to rise in prominence, since he (early anchors were exclusively male) was the person that attracted viewers to the channel. The most popular anchors were those who appeared trustworthy and serious.

CHANGING ROLES

In the 1970s feminism led to the installation of female coanchors on many newscasts. Soon the serious reading of the news was supplemented with repartee and chat among coanchors. News consultants, such as Frank Magid and Associates, helped to bring about a more scientific method of choosing news anchors based on demographic sensibilities and entertainment style. Men and women with telegenic looks and breezy ad-lib skills were used to attract viewers, while older newspeople with significant experience were usually retired or given reporting assignments in the field. Audiences seemed to want reporters they could trust, but they also preferred anchorpeople who entertained them.

The conflict caused by the changing role of the news anchor was probably best highlighted in *Network* (1976), Paddy Chayefsky's vivid send-up of the news industry, which presaged the merging of news and entertainment. In the film the news anchor, after suffering a mental breakdown, returns to the news desk only to entreat his audience to "get out of their chairs, go to the window and scream, 'I am as mad as hell and I'm not going to take it anymore!'" The anchor's complaint became a popular catchphrase for the universal frustration of modern life. Ted Baxter, the fictional news anchor on *The Mary Tyler Moore Show* (1970–1977), perhaps best exemplified the stereotype of the modern anchorman: the vacuous, handsome man, puffed up with self-importance and barely aware of the meaning of anything he read on the air. The theme was again taken up in the comedy *Anchorman: The Legend of Ron Burgundy* (2004), starring Will Ferrell and Christina Applegate, in which a female anchorwoman challenges the male-dominated field.

PROGRESS

While Barbara Walters became the first female television coanchor in 1976, it took three more decades before a woman was allowed to serve as the sole anchor of a nightly news program. In 2006 Katie Couric, a longtime cohost of the *Today* show, was hired to anchor the *CBS Evening News*; three years later Diane Sawyer was named host of *ABC World News*. The two represented a changing face in how the news was broadcast. Traditional evening news programs were losing their viewership because of the increased presence of cable news programs. Channels such as Fox, CNN, and MSNBC offered twenty-four-hour coverage and supplanted the network news channels' typical daily, one-hour formats. Additionally, cable news moved away from the Cronkite model and employed not only charismatic anchors but also ones who were pundits, effectively conflating news with entertainment.

After CNN, MSNBC, and Fox became commercial successes, a perpetual ratings war ensued between the three networks. Fox enlisted anchors and analysts Sean Hannity, Bill O'Reilly, and Greta Van Susteren, who offered a conservative viewpoint, precipitating a programming move that altered the entire landscape of television news. MSNBC adopted a liberal approach by hiring Chris Matthews, Keith Olbermann, and Rachel Maddow; CNN opted for the middle ground, running with Anderson Cooper and Wolf Blitzer. While not a new concept, business interests dictated who delivered the news, but the tone and slant of the news was forever changed by the cable news-as-entertainment model.

Jeff Ritter

SEE ALSO: *Brinkley, David; Brokaw, Tom; Cable TV; Chayefsky, Paddy; CNN; Cronkite, Walter; Feminism; Ferrell, Will; Fox News Channel; Huntley, Chet; Jennings, Peter; Maddow, Rachel;* The Mary Tyler Moore Show*; Murrow, Edward R.;* Network*; O'Reilly, Bill; Rather, Dan; Television; Walters, Barbara.*

BIBLIOGRAPHY

Cunningham, Liz. *Talking Politics: Choosing the President in the Television Age*. Westport, CT: Praeger, 1995.

Farnsworth, Stephen J., and S. Robert Lichter. *The Nightly News Nightmare: Television's Coverage of U.S. Presidential Elections, 1988–2004*. Lanham, MD: Rowman & Littlefield, 2007.

Fensch, Thomas, ed. *Television News Anchors: An Anthology of Profiles of the Major Figures and Issues in United States Network Reporting*. Jefferson, NC: McFarland, 1993.

Goldberg, Robert, and Gerald Jay Goldberg. *Anchors: Brokaw, Jennings, Rather and the Evening News*. Secaucus, NJ: Carol Publishing Group, 1990.

Marlane, Judith. *Women in Television News Revisited: Into the Twenty-First Century*. Austin: University of Texas Press, 1999.

Temple, Shirley *(1928–)*

Shirley Temple, Hollywood's quintessential child star during the 1930s and 1940s, became a diplomat in later years, serving as ambassador to Ghana and Czechoslovakia, and as the U.S. ambassador to the United Nations under her married name, Shirley Temple Black. But it is the diminutive moppet with golden ringlets and an engaging smile that older Americans remember from the Saturday afternoon matinees of their childhoods. Her unique appeal and immense popularity were without precedent and have never been equaled by the junior members of the Hollywood acting fraternity. The child star who acted, danced, and sang her way into the hearts of millions was like a beam of sunlight during the cloudy days of the Depression years.

In a series of box-office smashes, little Shirley Temple dispensed sweetness and light, beguiling her adult audiences and upstaging her adult costars in a series of films specially designed to capitalize on her qualities. Decades before the rise of film-product merchandising, Temple's popularity gave rise to a profitable industry in Shirley Temple products such as dolls, cutouts, and clothes, and her name has passed into common language as a synonym for smiling, curly-haired, doll-like little girls and as the name of a nonalcoholic cocktail served to children and teetotaling adults.

Temple made her first feature film appearance in 1932. She was awarded a special Academy Award "in grateful recognition of her outstanding contribution to screen entertainment during the year 1934" and was the number one box-office attraction in the United States and Britain from 1935 to 1938. During this time her salary rose to $100,000 per picture, but by the end of 1939—unable to keep advancing age at bay—Temple's career began its downward slide. She was eleven years old.

EARLY LIFE AND FIRST FILMS

Born in Santa Monica, California, on April 23, 1928, Temple was taken to dancing classes at age three by her ambitious mother, who pursued her daughter's film career, toting her around to various Hollywood studios. Her strategy was successful, and Temple was soon chosen for a series of one-reel movies called "Baby Burlesks," which led to her first small roles in feature films. In 1934 Fox Studios, in need of a tot to perform a song-and-dance number in *Stand Up and Cheer*, engaged her at $150 per week. Her performance in *Baby Take a Bow* (1934) led to a contract with Fox. Only weeks later *Little Miss Marker*, the first film under a two-picture deal that her mother had previously made with Paramount, was released and became a huge hit. Based on a story by Damon Runyon, this film catapulted the six-year-old Temple to stardom, becoming such a classic that it was remade several times.

As little Miss Marker, Temple was paired with Adolphe Menjou, the smooth veteran of many sophisticated screen liaisons. She plays the daughter of a gambler who, in debt to his bookie, dumps his small daughter on the man as "security" and disappears. Menjou plays the seemingly flint-hearted bookie, who softens under the influence of the charming child, reforming his ways and embracing the role of surrogate father. *Little Miss Marker* established the formula for a string of subsequent films—whose success rested on Temple's tiny shoulders—in

Shirley Temple. *Shirley Temple dances with Bill "Bojangles" Robinson in a scene from the 1935 film* The Littlest Rebel. **20TH CENTURY FOX/THE KOBAL COLLECTION.**

which an orphaned or, at the very least, motherless child is packed off by an inept or mildly villainous guardian to live with a reluctant relative. She quickly melts the icy heart of whichever aunt or grandfather she has been inflicted upon and never wants to leave but is reclaimed for purposes of exploitation by the original caregiver. After much effectively plotted—if less than believable—conflict, she is finally blissfully reunited with her loved ones.

THE LATE 1930s

After *Baby Take a Bow* Temple starred in *Now and Forever* (1934) for Paramount with Gary Cooper and Carole Lombard (he a jewel thief, she his mistress; Temple plays his motherless daughter). The year ended with *Bright Eyes* (1934), in which an orphaned Temple sings the hit song "On the Good Ship Lollipop." In 1935 she danced with Bill "Bojangles" Robinson in *The Little Colonel* and *The Littlest Rebel*. In *Our Little Girl* (1935) she successfully reunites her two estranged parents, and in *Curly Top* (1935), a loose retelling of *Daddy Longlegs*, she sings the hit song "Animal Crackers in My Soup" as she takes control of her adoptive playboy father's affairs, both professional and romantic.

And so it continued. Temple, remaining cute as a button, proved herself a real trouper, delivering her lines and dispensing wisdom to adults with unnerving authority and breaking effortlessly into song and dance with breathtaking ease. In *Stowaway* (1936) the eight-year-old impersonates Eddie Cantor, Al Jolson, and Ginger Rogers dancing with a Fred Astaire doll. The following year she starred in the film version of *Heidi* (1937); the role suited her to perfection, and the film won critical plaudits. In *Wee Willie Winkie* (1937), directed by John Ford, she successfully pulls off the revision of the original Rudyard Kipling character from a small boy to a young girl. This film—the tale of a child who becomes the mascot of a British army regiment in colonial India—was the most expensively produced of the Temple vehicles, with sentimentality taking second place to action. *Rebecca of Sunnybrook Farm* (1938), about an orphan who becomes a radio star, reprised Temple's career and remains an excellent introductory film for those who have never seen her.

THE 1940s

In 1939, after the successful *The Little Princess* and the less successful *Susannah of the Mounties*, Temple's popularity began to slip. In 1940, with her asking price now $300,000, she starred in Maurice Maeterlinck's *The Blue Bird*. Adapted by the author and filmed in color, it was the first Temple vehicle to lose money. At the end of the year her mother and the studio (now Twentieth Century Fox), who had long had an uneasy relationship, agreed to terminate Temple's contract. She returned to the screen via MGM, who did not know what to do with her, and after a feeble performance in *Kathleen* (1941), she went to United Artists and appeared in *Miss Annie Rooney* (1942). She disappeared for two years and came back in *Since You Went Away* (1944), a popular wartime family drama in which she plays third fiddle to Claudette Colbert and Jennifer Jones.

LATER LIFE AND POLITICAL CAREER

The world had changed, and so had Temple, now sixteen. She was rejected by a disappointed public unable to accept her transformation from dream child to attractive but ordinary teenager. Nine films between 1945 and 1949 (including *The Bachelor and the Bobby-Soxer*, 1947, with Cary Grant) and marriage at age seventeen to John Agar only accelerated her downward slide. Two comeback attempts with television series in 1958 and 1960 failed to generate any enthusiasm, and finally Temple retired from acting. After divorcing Agar, she married TV executive Charles Black in 1950, and as Shirley Temple Black entered Republican politics during the 1960s. Her 1967 congressional bid was unsuccessful, but she was appointed a U.S. representative to the United Nations in 1969, acted as the American ambassador to Ghana between 1974 and 1976, was the U.S. chief of protocol from 1976 to 1977, and served as ambassador to Czechoslovakia from 1989 to 1992. In 1972 she survived breast cancer and became one of the first women to speak openly about the disease and her mastectomy.

Once described by author David Thomson as "just a child leading her life under adult shadows . . . a Lilliputian moralist in ringlets, tap-dancing into your heart and then delivering the sententious message that sorts out confusion," Temple certainly had her detractors. There were those who found her unbearable and those who noted the shortcomings in her singing and dancing. Novelist and onetime film critic Graham Greene was famously sued for a review in which he asserted that she was an adult masquerading as a child. But to most, she was the perfect antidote to reality in a difficult era. As Temple herself later put it: "I class myself with Rin-Tin-Tin. At the end of the Depression people were perhaps looking for something to cheer them up. They fell in love with a dog and a little girl. It won't happen again." Temple published an autobiography, *Child Star, USA*, in 1988.

Robyn Karney

SEE ALSO: *Academy Awards; Astaire, Fred, and Ginger Rogers; Cancer; Cantor, Eddie; Child Stars; Colbert, Claudette; Cooper, Gary; Divorce; Ford, John; Grant, Cary; The Great Depression; Jolson, Al; Jones, Jennifer; Lombard, Carole; MGM (Metro-Goldwyn-Mayer); Runyon, Damon; Teenagers; Television; Toys; War Movies.*

BIBLIOGRAPHY

Black, Shirley Temple. *Child Star, USA*.New York: McGraw Hill, 1988.

Hammontree, Patsy Guy. *Shirley Temple Black: A Bio-Bibliography*. Westport, CT: Greenwood Publishing, 1998.

Reid, John Howard. *Your Colossal Main Feature Plus Full Support Program*. Raleigh, NC: Lulu Press, 2005.

Thomson, David. *A Biographical Dictionary of Film*. New York: Alfred A. Knopf, 1994.

Windeler, Robert. *The Films of Shirley Temple*. New York: Citadel Press, 1995.

The Temptations

While many believe the Temptations to be the best soul singing group of all time, this assessment of the band's accomplishments is limited, considering their substantial impact upon both the look and sound of popular music. The group was formed in Detroit, Michigan, in 1960 from the remnants of two previous bands—the Distants and the Primes. They soon became a major force in the success of Berry Gordy's Motown Records and have been referred to as the originators of the "Motown sound." Rising to popularity with other precedent-setting Motown performers such as Marvin Gaye, Martha and the Vandellas, and the Supremes, the group was at the center of a huge music explosion. During this period, AM radio was a multilayered media format that gave access and success to a large number of artists from rock, pop, country, soul, blues, and rockabilly music. Over the course of nearly forty years, the Temptations would have twenty-two members and earn three Grammy Awards. The group would place forty-three singles in the R&B Top 10 as well as earn fourteen R&B number one hits. As pop artists, the Temptations would hit number one four times and place fifteen sides in the pop Top 10.

Known for their lush harmonies, smooth onstage choreography, and a bold sense of fashion that made them immediately recognizable, the Temptations conquered pop, rock, R&B, and the soul music market during the course of a career that remains strong. From the start, the membership of the Temptations was ever changing. The Distants, a local Detroit outfit who recorded for the Northern label and released a single in 1959 ("Come On") included Elbridge Bryant, bass singer Melvin Franklin, and baritone Otis Williams. The Primes were a trio of transplants from Alabama comprising tenor Eddie Kendricks, Kell Osborne, and Paul Williams. It was Otis Williams who brought Kendricks and Paul Williams into the fold when the Primes broke up. Impressed by the Primes' use of choreography, Otis Williams wanted to incorporate that into the Distants' live performances. The Distants changed their name to the Temptations, and by 1961 they were signed to a Motown subsidiary, Miracle. While at Miracle the Temptations released several sides with only one achieving any commercial success: "Dream Come True," in 1962. By 1963 Bryant was out of the band and was replaced in 1964 by the notable tenor voice of David Ruffin.

EARLY HITMAKERS

At this point the Temptations began working with William "Smokey" Robinson. A songwriter of immeasurable talent and a producer who would go on to achieve his own success with the Miracles, Robinson gave the Temptations their first hit, "The Way You Do the Things You Do" (1964). It would be the first

The Temptations. *Known for their lush harmonies, smooth choreography, and fashion sense, the Temptations were one of Motown's most successful acts in the 1960s.* MICHAEL OCHS ARCHIVES/GETTY IMAGES.

of many Top 10 hits for the group. Their debut album, *Meet the Temptations*, was released that year. Also in 1964 the Temptations scored big with what would become their signature song, "My Girl"—another Robinson composition, which hit number one on both the pop and R&B charts. Crossing over as they did, in an era of racial strife and turmoil, made their accomplishments even more meaningful and paved the way for others to follow. Continuing this pattern, in 1966 they released another hit from the pen of Robinson, "Get Ready." Harder and edgier, "Get Ready" was of tremendous appeal to rock audiences. Two albums resulted from their early association with Robinson, *Sing Smokey* (1965) and *Gettin' Ready* (1966), which also contained the stunning, "Ain't Too Proud to Beg," another signature tune for the Temptations.

Moving on, the Temptations began working with producers Norman Whitfield and Brian Holland and also moved Ruffin into the lead vocal position, a spot Kendricks had filled admirably for some time. Ruffin's voice soared on well-known hits "Beauty's Only Skin Deep" and "(I Know) I'm Losing You" (both 1966). Together, Kendricks and Ruffin shared lead vocal duties on the classic romantic hit "You're My Everything," from the 1967 album *With a Lot o' Soul.* Ruffin pushed to have his name placed in front of the band's name, a request that resulted in his firing from the Temptations. He was replaced by Dennis Edwards, a former member of another band, the Contours. Edwards's voice was a perfect fit as the Temptations took their sound into a more psychedelic direction. His arrival also ushered in a time of change for the Temptations and their sound when he recorded the stinging lead vocal for "I Can't Get Next to You," the most significant cut from 1969's *Puzzle People.*

CHANGING INFLUENCES

With Whitfield in full control of production, the Temptations were moving away from the smooth, soulful love songs that had made them so successful. Tunes like "Cloud Nine" (1968), "Psychedelic Shack" (1969), and "Ball of Confusion (That's What the World Is Today)" (1970) were commentary on America's drug culture and politics. Changing their sound and style to fit into the world around them, the Temptations remained current, timely, and part of the mainstream. Furthermore, their influence carried over as rock and pop acts sought to emulate not only their moves but also their material.

By 1971 Kendricks was leaving the band. His swan song with the Temptations was "Just My Imagination," a mellow, flowing tune that showed off the group's skillful harmonies. Paul Williams, who suffered from alcoholism, also left around this time. Damon Harris and Richard Street joined the Temptations. Rumors of the band's demise circulated, but the Grammy-winning single "Papa Was a Rolling Stone," displaying vast expanses of instrumental work and Edwards's strong vocals, was a huge crossover hit that only seemed to underscore the versatility and tenacity of the group. Their album *All Directions*, released in 1972, put an end to the idea that the Temptations were about to disband, as did a Grammy Award for their album *Masterpiece* the following year.

After more lineup changes, the Temptations recorded their final project for Motown Records in 1976. *The Temptations Do the Temptations* signaled the end of an era as the act moved to Atlantic Records. Atlantic had designs on turning the Temptations into a disco act. Unsuccessful and dissatisfied, the Temptations returned to Motown and hit the charts once again in 1980 with the single "Power." A reunion tour and album followed in 1982. Ruffin and Kendricks joined the five current Temptations in what was a brief but glorious moment in time that included an impressive performance at Radio City Music Hall in New York City. But problems, both personal and professional, made it impossible for Ruffin and Kendricks to remain. In 1984 Ali-Ollie Woodson was on board as lead singer.

TRIUMPH AND TRAGEDY

Inducted into the Rock and Roll Hall of Fame in 1989 by the soul duo Daryl Hall and John Oates, the Temptations were formally acknowledged for their contribution to popular culture and to America's music. Yet their success was marked by tragedy all along the way. Original member Paul Williams died in 1973 of a self-inflicted gunshot wound. Ruffin passed away in 1991 of a drug overdose, and Kendricks succumbed to lung cancer in 1992. Another founding member, Melvin Franklin, lost his life in 1995 after a brain seizure. By the 1990s Otis Williams was the only original member left performing with the group, and he had spent years in court defending his right to use the Temptations name after Edwards left and formed a rival group. Publishing his autobiography in 1988, he carried on while Motown released a number of anthologies and greatest hits packages, including *Emperors of Soul* in 1994 and the critically acclaimed *Ultimate Collection* in 1996.

A 1990s renaissance of sorts caused renewed interest in the band. Romantic R&B singing acts of all racial persuasions looked to the work of the Temptations for inspiration. The group's sound was found in the work of chart-topping 1990s acts such as Boyz II Men, Babyface, and the Backstreet Boys. Further interest in the group was fueled by an NBC television movie, *The Temptations*, shown in two parts in November 1998. Based on Otis Williams's book, the miniseries focused on the classic Temptations lineup, the drama of their collective rise to fame and fortune, and the individual trials and tragedies of each member. The movie remains a cable TV staple, frequently shown on VH1. The 1998 release of a new CD, *Phoenix Rising*, also on Motown, refuted the idea that the Temptations were merely an oldies act resting on their laurels. Williams, along with tenor Ron Tyson, Barrington Henderson, Terry Weeks, and Harry McGilberry Jr., give credence to the original members' expression, "Temps forever."

Their 2000 release *Ear-Resistible* won the Temptations their third Grammy, and their 2006 version of the Supremes' "Reflections" earned a Grammy nomination. More members would join and leave the group, while spin-off groups featuring former members continue to tour, as does the official Otis Williams version. As noted by Hall and Oates when inducting the Temptations into the Rock and Hall of Fame, "they're still gigging on . . . and through all the trials and tribulations, through all the personal changes, and through all the personal problems and everything, you know they're still . . . still working." The Temptations' sound is everlasting; indeed, three of the group's songs are included in the Rock and Roll Hall of Fame's "500 Songs That Shaped Rock and Roll: "My Girl," "Ain't Too Proud to Beg," and "Papa Was a Rolling Stone."

Jana Pendragon

SEE ALSO: *Atlantic Records; Babyface; Boy Bands; Disco; Gaye, Marvin; Gordy, Berry; Grammy Awards; Hall and Oates; Made-for-Television Movies; Martha and the Vandellas; Motown; Pop Music; Rhythm and Blues; Robinson, Smokey; Rock and Roll; Ross, Diana, and the Supremes; Soul Music.*

BIBLIOGRAPHY

George, Nelson. *Where Did Our Love Go?: The Rise and Fall of the Motown Sound.* Urbana: University of Illinois Press, 2007.

Gordy, Berry. *To Be Loved.* New York: Warner Books, 1994.

Ribowsky. Mark. *Ain't Too Proud to Beg: The Troubled Lives and Enduring Soul of the Temptations.* Hoboken, NJ: John Wiley, 2010.

Williams, Otis, and Patricia Romanowski. *Temptations.* New York: Putnam, 1988.

The Ten Commandments

The annual network presentation of Cecil B. DeMille's 1956 epic film *The Ten Commandments* has been an American television standard every Easter for decades. Highlighted by Oscar-winning special effects, such as the spectacular parting of the Red Sea, *The Ten Commandments* vividly tells the biblical story of the life of Moses, with 1950s superstar Charlton Heston in the lead role. Featuring a cast of thousands, the three-plus-hour saga remains a perennial audience favorite, proving that larger-than-life spectacle continues to be among Hollywood's principal contributions to popular culture.

One of the most important early motion picture directors, DeMille helped define Hollywood's early cinematic style in silent films such as the classic 1915 melodrama *The Cheat*. Primarily a comedy director in his early career, DeMille made his first epic film, *The Ten Commandments*, in 1923. In this earlier version, DeMille interwove the biblical story with a modern-day parable of two brothers, one a saint, the other a sinner. Even with an exorbitant shooting budget, the film was a huge moneymaker for Paramount Pictures and made DeMille the top director of his day.

In the mid-1920s the director started his own studio, and his reputation reached legendary proportions. As noted in *Baseline*'s *Encyclopedia of Film*, "By the middle of the decade DeMille, with his Germanic swagger, boots and riding crop, had come to represent the archetypal director to the moviegoing public." After movies switched to sound, DeMille remained one of Hollywood's most bankable directors throughout the 1930s and 1940s, known for his sweeping historical epics.

In 1952 he directed *The Greatest Show on Earth*, which won the Oscar for Best Picture—DeMille's first. In 1955 rumors began circulating Hollywood that the legendary director was planning to remake his 1923 classic, *The Ten Commandments*. Everyone wanted to audition. As actor Vincent Price, who would be cast as Baka, the Master Builder of the Pyramids, recalled, "I think all of us, Eddie Robinson, myself, Judith Anderson, we all really wanted to be in a DeMille picture. We really felt that you couldn't call yourself a movie actor unless you had been in a DeMille picture! So we all took these sort of small, but rather arresting parts." Indeed, the cast was star-studded, with Charlton Heston as Moses, Yul Brynner as Ramses, and Anne Baxter as Nefretiri, and featuring Edward G. Robinson, Yvonne De Carlo, Debra Paget, Nina Foch, Judith Anderson, Vincent Price, and John Carradine. Bit players included future television stars Mike Connors and Robert Vaughn and musician Herb Alpert.

In *The Ten Commandments*, Golden Age Hollywood filmmaking meets the 1950s. As described by film critic Pauline Kael, "Charlton Heston is the highly athletic Moses; Anne Baxter is the kittenish princess who loves him; Judith Anderson is the sinister slave who knows the secret of his Jewish birth; Cedric Hardwicke is the likable old Pharaoh; Yul Brynner is the prince who beats Moses to the Egyptian throne; Edward G. Robinson is the traitor to the Jews; Debra Paget is the young slave old Robinson has got his eyes on. Stir them all together, throw in stone tablets, a whopping big Golden Calf, part the Red Sea, and you've got Cecil B. DeMille's epic—3 hours and 38 minutes of it. As old-fashioned hokum, it's palatable and rather tasty." Filmed in VistaVision, *The Ten Commandments* was nominated for seven Academy Awards, winning for Special Effects.

Both Hollywood and DeMille made better films than *The Ten Commandments*, but few have remained as popular for as long. A family favorite, a good old-fashioned epic, and a television tradition, *The Ten Commandments* has become a staple of American popular culture.

Victoria Price

SEE ALSO: *Academy Awards; Alpert, Herb, and the Tijuana Brass; Brynner, Yul; DeMille, Cecil B.; Heston, Charlton; Hollywood; Movie Stars; Price, Vincent; Silent Movies.*

BIBLIOGRAPHY

Barson, Michael. *The Illustrated Who's Who of Hollywood Directors: The Studio System in the Sound Era.* New York: The Noonday Press, 1995.

Birchard, Robert S. *Cecil B. DeMille's Hollywood.* Lexington: University Press of Kentucky, 2004.

Kael, Pauline. *5001 Nights at the Movies.* New York: Henry Holt, 1991.

Monaco, James, and the editors of *Baseline. Encyclopedia of Film.* New York: Perigee, 1991.

Shipman, David. *The Story of Cinema: A Complete Narrative History from the Beginnings to the Present.* New York: St. Martin's Press, 1982.

10,000 Maniacs

Formed under the name Still Life in rural Jamestown, New York, in February 1981, the band 10,000 Maniacs became noted for its melodic folk music and the wistful lyricism and distinct vocal patterns of its lead singer, Natalie Merchant. After releasing one EP and three albums, the group blossomed into prominence in the late 1980s on the strength of its single "What's the Matter Here?" The hit put the group in the Top 40 alongside friends R.E.M. Following the success of its fifth album, *Blind Man's Zoo* (1989), the band's participation in the MTV (Music Television) Inaugural Ball for President Bill Clinton in 1993, and its swan song performance on *MTV Unplugged* (1994), Merchant left to pursue a successful solo career. The remaining members of the band, guitarist Robert Buck, keyboardist Dennis Drew, and bassist Steve Gustafson, recruited an old collaborator, singer-violinist Mary Ramsey, releasing *Love among the Ruins* (1997) to critical praise, which marked a new chapter in the band's eventful career. After the death of Robert Buck in 2000, the remaining members went through a difficult series of disagreements and personnel changes, and they eventually reconstituted themselves successfully under the same name.

Scott Thill

SEE ALSO: *Alternative Rock; Folk Music; MTV; R.E.M.*.

BIBLIOGRAPHY

Shelters, Scott. "10,000 Maniacs Turn 30." *Jamestown (NY) Post-Journal*, September 3, 2011.

Tennis

A ball, a racket, and a net. The simplicity of tennis is one reason that its origins are difficult to pinpoint. At any one time, variations of the game were probably played in almost every country in the world. Some historians believe tennis was invented in the Middle Ages—it is mentioned in twelfth-century manuscripts—but exactly when and where are probably lost to antiquity. The word *tennis* is derived from the French word *tenez*, meaning "to hold." Certainly the French greatly enjoyed the game. By the sixteenth century, up to 2,000 *jeu-de-paume* (the name for the ball) courts had been built in France, though it is thought that every Western European country had courts at the time.

THE BASICS

Until perhaps the nineteenth century, tennis courts were walled, and the exact rules of the game may have differed from country to country, maybe even court to court. In 1858, however, a lawn court was constructed in England, and by 1873 an Englishman, Major Walter Clopton Wingfield, modernized and standardized the game. Calling his game *sphairistike* (Greek for "ball and stick"), Wingfield set the net at 4 feet, 8 inches high. The court was shaped like an hourglass, narrow at the net and wider at the baseline, and a game was played to fifteen points. This standardization was probably what increased interest in the sport. At about the same time, it spread to the United States and, soon after, other countries.

The early establishment of national championships in some of these countries spoke to the rapidly growing popularity of tennis. In 1877 Wimbledon, the British championship, was first played. It was at this time that the rectangular court was established and the current scoring system was widely adopted. A match usually consists of either the best of three or five sets, meaning the first player to capture two or three sets, respectively, wins. The first player to win six games takes a set. To win a game, a player must score four points; the first three points are successively called "15," "30," and "40" (originally "45"), and zero is referred to as "love." A player must win by two points, so a game continues until this happens; the terminology in extended play is "deuce" if the game is tied and "advantage" for the player holding a one-point lead.

Complicating matters, a player must have a two-game advantage to be declared the winner of a set. This sometimes leads to marathon play. An extreme example occurred at Wimbledon in June 2010, when John Isner and Nicolas Mahut played a set that was decided 70–68. In all, the match lasted a record eleven hours. To avoid such scenarios, most tournaments use tiebreakers.

MAJOR TOURNAMENTS

In 1881 the U.S. national championship (now the U.S. Open) was contested. Ten years later, the French national championship (now the French Open) began, and by 1905 the national championship of Australia (now the Australian Open) was being played. These four events, collectively known as the Grand Slam, are the most prestigious tournaments in tennis. In addition, there is the Davis Cup, first held in 1900 between the United States and England. It evolved into an international competition that now features well more than 100 countries.

Over the years in tennis, various court surfaces have been used, ranging from grass to clay to concrete to composition. Each surface accentuates a different aspect of the game, which adds to the diversity of the play. For example, the French Open is played on clay (a good surface for hitting ground strokes from the baseline at the back of the court), while Wimbledon uses grass (which magnifies the importance of volleying at the net).

MEN'S SUPERSTARS

Tennis in the twentieth century was highlighted by a string of great men's players. The 1920s were dominated by American Bill Tilden, who enjoyed great popularity. In the 1930s, 1940s, and 1950s, Ellsworth Vines, Fred Perry, Don Budge, Jack Kramer, Pancho Gonzales, and Lew Hoad were, at various times, either officially ranked number one or regarded as such. In the 1950s and early 1960s, a host of Australian players reached the top echelon, most notably Rod Laver. The late 1960s and the 1970s saw players such as Arthur Ashe, Stan Smith, Björn Borg, Jimmy Connors, and John Newcombe come to the forefront. The marquee names of the 1980s were Ivan Lendl, John McEnroe, and Boris Becker, while players such as Pete Sampras and Andre Agassi made names for themselves in the 1990s.

The first decade of the 2000s saw incredible achievements and rivalries. Swiss player Roger Federer was the best player in the world from 2003 to 2006, and in 2009 he established a record by winning his fifteenth Grand Slam title. The only player to consistently challenge Federer was Spain's Rafael Nadal, who dominated on the red clay of the French Open and also won a gold medal during the 2008 Olympics. Tennis analysts consider the 2008 Wimbledon final between Federer and Nadal to be one of the greatest matches of all time; it went five sets and nearly five hours before Nadal prevented Federer from winning his sixth Wimbledon title in a row. In 2011 Serbian Novak Djokovic established himself as a player for the ages, winning three of the four Grand Slams. With Federer, Nadal, and Djokovic on the scene, the early decades of the twenty-first century has been a golden era for men's tennis.

WOMEN'S SUPERSTARS

Women's tennis has also had its share of illustrious players. The list includes Suzanne Lenglen in the 1920s; Helen Wills and Helen Hull Jacobs in the 1920s and 1930s; Maureen "Little Mo" Connolly and Althea Gibson (the first to break the color barrier in tennis) in the 1950s; Margaret Court, Maria Bueno, and Billie Jean King in the 1960s; Evonne Goolagong, Chris Evert, and Martina Navratilova in the 1970s and 1980s; and Steffi Graf, Monica Seles, and Martina Hingis in the 1990s.

The twenty-first century has been a particularly interesting time, headlined by African American sisters Serena and Venus Williams. Between them, they have won nearly two dozen Grand Slam titles. This period has also been marked by a surge Russian women's tennis. Russian women have regularly appeared in the top ten, and Maria Sharapova and Svetlana Kzunetsova each has won multiple Grand Slams. Belgium has made its mark, too, as

Justin Henin and Kim Clijsters have also won a number of Grand Slams. Interestingly, both Henin and Clijsters retired for spells, only to come back again and continue to compete at high levels.

BATTLE OF THE SEXES

Professional tennis has been somewhat of a battle of the sexes. This was best illustrated by the appropriately termed Battle of the Sexes, held in the Houston Astrodome in 1973. The match pitted women's star Billie Jean King against former Wimbledon champion Bobby Riggs. Months earlier Riggs, a self-proclaimed "king of the chauvinist pigs," challenged the top-ranked women's player in the world to a tennis match. He wound up playing the second-ranked player, Margaret Court, and beat her 6–2, 6–1 in what was called the "Mother's Day massacre." This led to the King-Riggs match in front of 30,000 fans at the Astrodome and a worldwide television audience of fifty million. King beat Riggs in three straight sets and took home the $100,000 winner-take-all prize.

Although Riggs claimed to be a chauvinist, he probably did more for women's tennis than anyone in history. The ensuing publicity drew attention to the growing complaint from women's professionals that their prize money should be equal to men's, particularly since many female players felt their blend of finesse and power made their matches more enjoyable for spectators. The Women's Tennis Association, coincidentally founded the year of the King-Riggs match, has consistently worked toward greater equity in prize money. The U.S. Open led the way by offering equal prize money in 1973. The Australian Open followed suit in 2001, and the French Open and Wimbledon came on board in 2006 and 2007, respectively.

Lloyd Chiasson Jr.

SEE ALSO: *Agassi, Andre; Ashe, Arthur; Connors, Jimmy; Evert, Chris; Gibson, Althea; King, Billie Jean; Laver, Rod; McEnroe, John; Navratilova, Martina; Riggs, Bobby; Seles, Monica; Sports Heroes; Williams, Venus and Serena; Wimbledon.*

BIBLIOGRAPHY

Collins, Bud. *The Bud Collins History of Tennis: An Authoritative Encyclopedia and Record Book*. Chicago: New Chapter Press, 2010.

Cummings, Parke. *American Tennis: The Story of a Game and Its People*. Boston: Little, Brown, 1957.

Grimsley, Will. *Tennis: Its History, People and Events*. Englewood Cliffs, NJ: Prentice-Hall, 1971.

Lorimer, Larry. *The Tennis Book: A Complete A-to-Z Encyclopedia of Tennis*. New York: Random House, 1980.

Powell, Mike. *A Game to Love: In Celebration of Tennis*. New York: Abrams, 2011.

Schickel, Richard. *The World of Tennis*. New York: Random House, 1975.

Schwabacher, Martin. *Superstars of Women's Tennis*. Broomall, PA: Chelsea House, 1997.

Tennis Shoes/Sneakers

Although a nineteenth-century U.S. lexicographer described sneakers as "shoes with canvas tops and rubber soles," the vernacular meaning has come to include any shoe with natural or synthetic rubber soles. Uppers can be of leather, nylon, canvas, plastic, or combinations of these. Alternative names for sneakers include tennis shoes, gym shoes, plimsolls, felony shoes, cross trainers, boat shoes, athletic shoes, and running shoes. According to the National Sporting Goods Association, in 2010 sales for walking shoes totaled $4.26 billion; gym shoes/fashion sneakers were $3.58 billion; jogging/running shoes were $2.32 billion; and cross-training/fitness shoes were $2.12 billion.

DEVELOPMENT OF MODERN SNEAKERS

Modern sneakers have beginnings in various sports shoes. One ancestor is the expensive British upper-class footwear of the late 1800s, used for lawn tennis, cricket, and croquet, as well as at the beach. Worn by both sexes, these canvas or leather lace-up oxfords—or high tops—had rubber soles. By the end of the nineteenth century, they were priced for the average consumer. Field and track shoes are also forerunners in the industry. At the turn of the twentieth century, football and baseball players wore essentially the same shoe: leather high-topped lace-ups with leather soles and cleats. Major mail-order business Sears, Roebuck & Company sold leather shoes made specifically for runners as early as 1897.

Converse All Stars. *Considered the quintessential sneaker, Converse All Stars, which were first introduced in 1917, remain popular in the 21st century.* SANDRA BAKER/ALAMY.

For three decades beginning in 1900 not much changed in the sneaker business, but from the 1930s to the 1960s technical improvements were implemented that ultimately made sneakers trendy. The quintessential sneaker—the Converse All Star—premiered in 1917. In 1922 another mail-order business, Montgomery Ward, offered high- and low-top sneakers—for "work, play or everyday wear"—for children and adults. Paul Sperry introduced his wavy sole for boating shoes in 1935, and other shoemakers produced nonskid soles in patterns including diamonds, feathers, and chain links. Keds offered a variety of colored uppers, and sponge rubber, plastic foam, cushioned heels, and soles—all to add comfort—were later introduced.

In addition, it was in the 1940s and 1950s that Dassler Brothers (later split into Puma and adidas), Converse, Spalding, and other companies were gaining reputations as sports shoemakers. Also during this time sneakers, coupled with blue jeans, became symbols of youth. Adidas eventually made shoes with nylon uppers, and Velcro began to be used as a fastener in the 1960s. The 1970s pushed sneakers into the spotlight with the optimum shoe pursued by both consumers and manufacturers. Geoffrey Beene, Calvin Klein, and other designers transformed sneakers into fashion.

SPECIALTY SHOES

When jogging became a popular pastime, *Runner's World* magazine printed surveys comparing the qualities of shoes. The running fad of the late 1970s propelled shoe manufacturers such as Saucony, Brooks, and Etonic to develop anti-pronation devices on their shoes so that athletes would land flat-footed. Flared and elevated heels, in addition to soft molded and cantilevered soles, were some of the improvements designers offered. Bill Bowerman, a University of Oregon coach, created the waffle sole for added traction. With their popularity well established, by 1978 sneakers amounted to 50 percent of all shoes sold.

By the 1980s many shoe brands had become household words. The aerobic exercise trend of this time called for a new kind of shoe that Reebok pioneered. Nike joined in with a gas-filled midsole in the late 1970s and by the 1980s added windows in the sole to display this air. Hip-hop musicians soon adopted sneakers as part of their style and referenced them in their songs. In 1986 rappers Run-DMC issued "My adidas," an anthem to the Super Star model they wore without laces. That same year Reebok came out with a pump shoe for the excessive price of $175: the strong desire to be in vogue, coupled with an inability to afford expensive sneakers, even pushed a few young people to rob, and sometimes kill, others for their costly sneakers.

From the 1980s into the 1990s, the technologically crafted sneaker looked ready for space trekking. For example, L.A. Gear introduced flashing lights, straps, and intricate lacing systems, while Puma, New Balance, and other brands opted for sculptured, multicolored soles. With lighter materials, shoes could afford to be bulky, resembling moon boots more than sports shoes. Still, despite the style and technology, questionable labor practices of Southeast Asian manufacturers that were contracted to make shoes for brands such as Nike and Reebok eventually caused consumer boycotts. In response to those campaigns, the manufacturers agreed to make some reforms, although many critics contended that the changes were superficial.

While athletic styles were similar for males and females, nonsport sneakers were distinctively for women. Keds advertised low-heeled pumps with toe bows in 1917. Sequin sneakers, stitch-it-yourself needlepoint sneakers, and wedge-heeled satin sneakers were all products developed in the 1970s. About this time fashion designer Betsey Johnson created high-heeled sneakers, a style that would gain popularity in the 1990s, along with sneaker clogs. Another 1990s style, homemade platform sneakers, was copied by Converse and fashion designer Donna Karan, among others.

MODERN MARKETING

Meanwhile, new retail venues were created to meet the demand for sneakers. In the 1960s sporting goods stores sold athletic shoes with their low-tech siblings available in regular shoe shops. Specialty stores began to open. Department stores had designated athletic footwear and accessories sections. In shopping malls the Athlete's Foot; Foot Locker; and, exclusively for women, Lady Foot Locker, among others, sold only sneakers. By the late 1990s superstores such as Sneaker Stadium and the Sports Authority dotted the landscape. Nike owners Phil Knight and Bowerman, who had retail outlets as importers for Tiger (now Asics), opened Nike Towns, selling Nike shoes, apparel, and accessories.

Athletes' endorsements for sneakers were common after 1920. Chuck Taylor, whose signature was added to the Converse All Star in 1923, had directed basketball clinics for Converse and had been on the Akron (Ohio) Firestones professional basketball team. Northwestern University coach Arthur "Dutch" Lonborg lent his name to the 1932 Montgomery Ward basketball shoe. Jim Thorpe endorsed B. F. Goodrich's Chief Long Lance brand sneakers. Female endorsers in the 1970s included Chris Evert for Converse and Virginia Wade for ProKeds.

Endorsements, however, created mixed loyalties in the 1970s and 1980s. Some athletes wore favorite shoes with the logo of their endorser hiding the brand they wore. Others changed shoes during the course of a game, giving multiple endorsers equal time. But in the commodified culture of the 1990s, endorsements by athletes, such as basketball star Michael Jordan for Nike, propelled manufacturers into hero-selling machines. The lure of celebrity endorsements continued into the new century. Another basketball player, LeBron James, signed a huge deal with Nike in the first decade of the 2000s, while in 2012 rising star Derrick Rose of the Chicago Bulls signed a reportedly $260 million contract to endorse adidas.

During the first decade of the 2000s a new craze emerged for toning shoes—athletic shoes with an unstable, strongly curved sole. Manufacturers claimed such shoes required more work from the wearer, so that they burned more calories and toned their muscles more quickly. Some medical researchers, however, disputed those claims.

Also during the decade, the trend for minimalist shoes began to catch on with runners and more casual wearers. Barefoot shoes snugly fit all five toes like the fingers of a glove. These thin shoes provided little protection between the foot and the running surface. Advocates claimed that they offered a more natural running motion for the human foot. Those who were not ready to switch to barefoot shoes could buy minimalist running shoes, which had extremely lightweight construction. Although these new styles gained in popularity, industry experts warned that runners should take care to choose the shoe style that worked best for their particular stride and way of striking the ground.

In the future, technology may assist athletes in doing just that—choosing the shoe that works best for each individual's feet. Some product engineers predict that the day is coming when a person can go to a shoe store, choose a style, and then request customized changes, thus ordering a unique pair of shoes that no one else will own. Advances in computer-aided design and digital manufacturing brought the possibility of such customized footwear closer to reality, giving everyone a taste of what it is like to be a premiere athlete—at least in terms of one's sneakers.

ViBrina Coronado

SEE ALSO: *adidas; The Chicago Bulls; Department Stores; Evert, Chris; James, LeBron; Jeans; Jordan, Michael; Karan, Donna; Klein, Calvin; Malls; Nike; Rap; Run-DMC; Sears Roebuck Catalog; Sports Heroes.*

BIBLIOGRAPHY

Cheskin, Melvyn P. *The Complete Handbook of Athletic Footwear.* New York: Fairchild, 1987.

Smit, Barbara. *Sneaker Wars: The Enemy Brothers Who Founded adidas and Puma and the Family Feud That Forever Changed the Business of Sport.* New York: Ecco, 2008.

Strasser, J. B., and Laurie Becklund. *Swoosh: The Unauthorized Story of Nike and the Men Who Played There.* New York: Harcourt, Brace Jovanovich, 1991.

Vanderbilt, Tom. *The Sneaker Book.* New York: New Press, 1998.

Walker, Samuel Americus. *Sneakers.* New York: Workman Publishing, 1978.

Wolkomir, Richard. "The Race to Make a 'Perfect' Shoe Starts in the Laboratory." *Smithsonian*, September 1989, 94–104.

Tenuta, Judy *(1956–)*

Stand-up comedienne Judy Tenuta is the goddess of her own religion, "Judyism," and she encourages the "pigs" in her audience to worship her. Her performances may include accordion music, sadomasochistic play with audience members, and stories of dating the pope—all punctuated by her catchphrase, "It could happen!" In 1997 she hosted an Internet talk show, *The Princess of Pop Culture.* Her comedy albums include *Buy This, Pigs!* (1987), *In Goddess We Trust* (1995), and *A Space Goddessy* (2002). She has also appeared in movies such as *Material Girls* (2006) and *Going Down in LA-LA Land* (2011).

Christian L. Pyle

SEE ALSO: *The Internet; Stand-Up Comedy.*

BIBLIOGRAPHY

Tenuta, Judy. *The Power of Judyism.* New York: HarperPerennial, 1991.

Terkel, Studs *(1912–2008)*

Studs Terkel was born Louis Terkel in New York City. When he was eight, his family moved to Chicago, a city of raw, midwestern muscularity and deep jazz rhythms that sharply influenced his life and career. Terkel's parents ran a rooming house, which sparked his interest in diverse people, and his Jewish heritage brought with it a passion for social justice. His love of acting and jazz, combined with his urban, working-class environment, spawned his dual role as local radio personality and oral historian.

Though he graduated from college and law school at the University of Chicago, Terkel never practiced law. Instead, taking his nickname from Studs Lonigan, a famous literary character of the day, he succumbed to the lure of the stage, acting in radio and community theater productions and even in the exciting new medium of television. From 1949 until 1951 he had his own weekly show on NBC, *Studs' Place*, an innovative, improvisational situation comedy about "regular folks." Terkel took the show's loose, unscripted format from the jazz he loved.

In 1951 anticommunist fever was rising, and Terkel's television career was cut short when NBC discovered he had signed leftist petitions seeking reform on such controversial issues as rent control and segregation. With his typical stubborn conviction, he refused to renounce the petitions, and his show was canceled. His next step was to approach radio station WFMT with a proposal for an hour-long interview show. The station hired him and became Terkel's home for the next forty-five years, until his retirement in 1997.

During those years Terkel interviewed hundreds of politicians, writers, artists, and "regular folks," becoming in the process the quintessential "regular folk" himself. Dressed in his trademark uniform, a red-and-white-checked shirt and red socks,

Studs Terkel. *Studs Terkel used his radio work and writings to chronicle the varied experiences of "regular folks" in America.* CHICAGO TRIBUNE/CONTRIBUTOR/MCCLATCHY-TRIBUNE/GETTY IMAGES".

Terkel developed an interviewing style that was homey yet incisive, respectful yet downright curious. This combination made many people comfortable in revealing their insights and experiences to him.

His interviews with celebrities and politicians were sensitive and probing, often undressing sides of figures in popular culture that were previously concealed. Terkel ventured out across the United States with his show, interviewing ordinary people. Many of his fans would agree that he made his biggest contributions to society in these treks, in which he chronicled the impact of historical events on everyday life.

Terkel often quoted a poem by Bertolt Brecht:

When the Chinese wall was built, where'd the masons go for lunch?
When Caesar conquered Gaul, was there not even a cook in the army?
When the Armada sank, King Philip wept.
Were there no other tears?

It is these individuals whom history leaves out of its story who most deeply interested Terkel, and he strove to become their scribe. Beginning with *Giants of Jazz* in 1957, which extolled previously little-known black musicians, Terkel produced a series of books that gave voice to the experience of the "regular folks." In 1967 he wrote *Division Street America*, the first of his oral histories, quickly followed by an impressive list of titles, including: *Hard Times: An Oral History of the Great Depression* (1970); *Working: People Talk about What They Do All Day and How They Feel about What They Do* (1974); *American Dreams, Lost and Found* (1980); *The Good War: An Oral History of World War II* (1984); *The Great Divide: Second Thoughts on the American Dream* (1988); *Race: How Blacks and Whites Think and Feel about the American Obsession* (1992); *Coming of Age: The Story of Our Century by Those Who've Lived in It* (1995); *My American Century* (1997); *Will the Circle Be Unbroken?: Reflections on Death, Rebirth, and Hunger for a Faith* (2001); *Hope Dies Last: Keeping the Faith in Difficult Times* (2003); *And They All Sang: Adventures of an Eclectic Disc Jockey* (2005); *Touch and Go: A Memoir* (2007); and *P.S.: Further Thoughts from a Lifetime of Listening (2008).*

Each book depicts a multifaceted picture of the historical period or area of human experience it covers and the society that lived through it. Not interested in pat answers or definitive statements, Terkel took delight in the astonishing variety of human experience, and it is that delight he passes on to his readers, like a jovial host at a huge gathering. "Oral journalism is associated with me," Terkel once said, "and I like that, and it's true. Because it's the sound of the voice that I'd like to capture."

Terkel indeed captured the sound of hundreds of voices, previously unheard, but his own voice is apparent in his books as well, often merely in what he chose to write about. He often jokingly said that his red-and-white-checked shirt represented his politics. Terkel's ideological beliefs as a longtime socialist and his interest in working people went hand in hand. A resister of technology, he never used an electric typewriter or drove a car, preferring to take the bus to work. It was perhaps his down-to-earth style that contributed to his success in radio, a much less superficial and glamour-oriented medium than television. He expressed his concern over how high-tech media have affected interpersonal relations when he complained, "We are more and more into communications and less into communication." Terkel did his best to combat that trend by simply loving to listen to people talk about themselves.

Terkel died in Chicago on October 31, 2008. Like the lover of jazz that he was, he once requested that his epitaph be, "Curiosity did not kill this cat."

Tina Gianoulis

SEE ALSO: *Communism; The Fifties; Radio; Red Scare.*

BIBLIOGRAPHY

Baker, James Thomas. *Studs Terkel.* New York: Twayne, 1992.

Parker, Tony. *Studs Terkel: A Life in Words.* New York: H. Holt, 1996.

"Studs Terkel." The Old Globe. *Upstage Online*. Accessed March 31, 2012. Available from http://www.oldglobe.org/information/newsletter/2009/09newsletters/april-may_09_newsletter.html#studs

"Studs Terkel: Conversations with America." Chicago History Museum. Accessed March 28, 2012. Available from http://www.studsterkel.org/

Terkel, Studs. *Talking to Myself: A Memoir of My Times.* New York: Pantheon Books, 1977.

The Terminator

The Terminator is one of the most popular robots of film. There are actually many models of Terminator: the metal skeleton covered by human flesh (technically a cyborg) first seen in *The Terminator* (directed by James Cameron, 1984); the liquid metal, shape-shifting new T-1000 introduced in the sequel, *The Terminator 2: Judgment Day* (Cameron, 1991); a female terminator called T-X seen in *Terminator 3: Rise of the Machines* (directed by Jonathan Mostow, 2003); and the army of diverse models that appears in *Terminator Salvation* (directed by McG, 2009).

The Terminators of the first two movies were created by visual effects artist Stan Winston, following Cameron's designs. In the first film, the Terminator (played by Arnold Schwarzenegger) travels back in time from the near future to kill Sarah, the mother of the still unborn John Connor, who will become the guerrilla leader that fights the rebellious machines in a future war. In *Terminator 2*, this evil Terminator becomes the fatherly protector of mother and son, saving them from the murderous T-1000. The Connors also appeared in a short-lived television series called *Terminator: The Sarah Connor Chronicles* (2008–2009), which was set after the events in *Terminator 2* and focused primarily on the human characters.

The second sequel, *Terminator 3*, reprised the formula of time travel and conflict involving both killer and protector robots, and Schwarzenegger again starred in the film. *Terminator Salvation*, in contrast to the other movies in the franchise, focused exclusively on a future war between robots and humans occurring in 2018, and it did not feature Schwarzenegger.

The *Terminator* films have appealed to the popular imagination owing to their special effects and the magnetic presence of Schwarzenegger in the title role. In fact, Schwarzenegger became so identified with the Terminator that while he served as governor of California (2003–2011), he was often humorously referred to as the "governator."

Sara Martin

SEE ALSO: *CGI; Schwarzenegger, Arnold.*

BIBLIOGRAPHY

Decker, Kevin S., and Richard Brown, eds. *Terminator and Philosophy: I'll Be Back, Therefore I Am.* Hoboken, NJ: Wiley, 2009.

Jeffords, Susan. "Can Masculinity Be Terminated?" In *Screening the Male: Exploring Masculinities in Hollywood Cinema*, ed. Steven Cohan and Ina Rae Hark. New York: Routledge, 1993.

Mann, Karen. "Narrative Entanglements: *The Terminator.*" *Film Quarterly* 43 (1989–1990): 17–27.

Rushing, Janice Hocker, and Thomas S. Frentz. *Projecting the Shadow: The Cyborg Hero in American Film.* Chicago: University of Chicago Press, 1995.

Telotte, J. P. "The Exposed Modern Body: *The Terminator* and *Terminator 2.*" In *Replications: A Robotic History of Science Fiction.* Urbana: University of Illinois Press, 1995.

Terry and the Pirates

A popular and highly influential adventure strip, *Terry and the Pirates* was set in China and began in the autumn of 1934. It was written and drawn during its heyday by Milton Caniff. The cinematic layouts and the impressionistic inking style that Caniff perfected influenced a whole generation of comic strip and comic-book artists.

Terry Lee was just a boy when he arrived in China, accompanied by an avuncular adventurer named Pat Ryan. Almost immediately the pair was tangling with an assortment of pirates on land and sea. Among them was the quintessential femme fatale, the Dragon Lady. During World War II Caniff, who had been dealing with the Japanese invaders since the late 1930s, turned *Terry and the Pirates* into a fairly authentic chronicle of combat activities in the China-Burma-India theater. He left his strip at the end of 1946 to do *Steve Canyon. Terry and the Pirates*, taken over by George Wunder, continued until early in 1973.

Ron Goulart

SEE ALSO: *Caniff, Milton; Comic Books; Comics.*

BIBLIOGRAPHY

Caniff, Arthur Milton; Frank Engli; Pete Hamill; et al. *The Complete* Terry and the Pirates, *1937–1938.* San Diego, CA: IDW Publications, 2007.

Harvey, Robert C. *The Art of the Funnies.* Jackson: University Press of Mississippi, 1994.

Marschall, Richard. *America's Great Comic Strip Artists.* New York: Abbeville Press, 1989.

Tex-Mex Music

SEE: *Tejano Music.*

Texting

Texting, or text messaging, is the act of composing and sending a brief message using a cell phone and a service that allows the exchange of messages between cell phones. The term *texting* originally referred to sending messages only containing text, using a service called "short message service" (SMS). The *short* in short message service refers to the length of text messages, as they are limited to 160 characters. As technology advanced, *texting* also came to refer to sending messages containing images and video and audio files, using a service called "multimedia messaging service" (MMS).

A person who sends a text message is called a "texter." The message itself is called a "text." Text messaging is most often used between private cell phone users when voice communication is impossible, undesirable, or inconvenient. In some places, text messaging is significantly cheaper than placing a voice call.

The concept of text messaging has its origins in the pager. The one-way numeric pager (often called simply a "pager" or a "beeper") is a simple personal telecommunications device that can receive a message consisting of only a few digits, typically a phone number that the owner of the pager calls. Early instances of text messaging involved sending a series of digits to a pager that spelled a word when the pager was viewed upside down. For example, the numbers 07734 appear as the word *hello* when they are viewed upside down. The first instance of true text messaging via SMS is said to have occurred on December 3, 1992, when Neil Papworth, a test engineer for the British company Sema Group, used a personal computer to send the text message "Merry Christmas" via the Vodafone network to the phone of Richard Jarvis, a director at the Vodafone company.

Use of text messaging services grew slowly, with customers in 1995 sending on average less than one message per customer per month. By 2007, however, text messaging was the most widely used mobile data service, with 74 percent of all cell phone users worldwide actively using SMS. As the popularity of texting increased, the functionality of SMS expanded and improved, allowing users to send and receive news and emergency alerts, request emergency services, cast television votes, and make donations to various organizations.

Although the service proved beneficial, concerns about texting arose. Many car accidents occurred because distracted drivers were texting while driving. As a result, numerous U.S. states made texting while driving illegal. Cell phone usage in general has been cited as the number one cause of distracted driving. One notable texting-while-driving case in 2012 involved a teenager who fatally crashed after sending a text message every ninety seconds during her four-hour commute. Some cities have considered passing laws against walking while texting, citing an increase in car accidents caused by pedestrians who were not watching traffic.

Other concerns involve the texting phenomenon known as "sexting." This is the practice of sending sexually explicit or suggestive messages, called "sexts," sometimes accompanied by a photo or video. Once sent, these messages can be easily disseminated to others without the original sender's permission or knowledge. Of greatest concern in this matter are privacy issues and child pornography. If either the sender or recipient of sexually explicit material is a minor, he or she may be arrested for distributing child pornography, which is a felony.

While the long-term impact and possible consequences of texting are unknown, its growth in both popularity and functionality shows no signs of slowing. In his 2009 book *Txtng: The Gr8 Db8* (Texting: The Great Debate), author and linguist David Crystal adeptly articulates the sense of awe felt at the beginning of the twenty-first century: "Has there ever been a linguistic phenomenon which has aroused such curiosity, suspicion, fear, confusion, antagonism, fascination, excitement, and enthusiasm, all at once? And in such a short space of time. Less than a decade ago, hardly anyone had heard of [texting]."

Kim Keeline

SEE ALSO: *Cell Phones; E-mail; Pornography; Sexting; Smartphones.*

BIBLIOGRAPHY

Austin, Michael. "Texting while Driving: How Dangerous Is It?" *Car and Driver*, June 2009.

"Cellphone and Texting Laws." Insurance Institute for Highway Safety. Accessed June 1, 2012. Available from http://www.iihs.org/laws/cellphonelaws.aspx

Crystal, David. *Txtng: The Gr8 Db8*. Oxford, UK: Oxford University Press, 2009.

Lenhart, Amanda. "Teens, Smartphones & Texting." Pew Research Center, March 19, 2012. Accessed June 1, 2012. Available from http://pewinternet.org/~/media//Files/Reports/2012/PIP_Teens_Smartphones_and_Texting.pdf

Purcell, Kristen; Roger Entner; and Nichole Henderson. "The Rise of Apps Culture." Pew Research Center, September 14, 2010. Accessed June 1, 2012. Available from http://pewinternet.org/Reports/2010/The-Rise-of-Apps-Culture/Overview.aspx

Thalberg, Irving G. *(1899–1936)*

Irving Grant Thalberg may have been the most influential motion picture executive of his time. "The Boy Wonder," as he was called, was an expert in knowing what the public wanted and how to get it to them under budget. As head of production for Metro-Goldwyn-Mayer (MGM), he oversaw countless productions during his tenure, including *The Big Parade* (1925) and *Mutiny on the Bounty* (1935), although *The Good Earth* (1937) was the only picture for which he ever received on-screen credit as producer.

Despite suffering from a weak heart his entire life, Thalberg was a classic workaholic. He also personally oversaw the career of his wife, actress Norma Shearer. Thalberg was often quoted as saying, "Credit you give yourself is not worth having." The Thalberg Award, given by the Academy of Motion Picture Arts and Sciences, is named for him.

Jill A. Gregg

SEE ALSO: *MGM (Metro-Goldwyn-Mayer);* Mutiny on the Bounty.

BIBLIOGRAPHY

Flamini, Roland. *Thalberg: The Last Tycoon and the World of MGM*. New York: Crown Publishing, 1994.

Marx, Samuel. *Mayer and Thalberg: The Make-Believe Saints*. New York: Random House, 1975.

Robbe, Adrian. *Metamorphosis of Hollywood Filmmaking*. Raleigh, NC: Lulu, 2008.

Thomas, Bob. *Thalberg: Life and Legend*. New York: Doubleday, 1969.

Thanksgiving

A nationwide holiday in the United States since 1863, Thanksgiving plays a number of important roles in popular culture. It was customary in Europe to hold days of thanksgiving for successful harvests and for events such as military victories, deliverance from plagues, and royal births. The date and site of the first Thanksgiving in what is now the United States are still debated, but the most famous is the one held in October 1621 in Plymouth Colony. There, European immigrants, "the Pilgrims," and indigenous Wampanoag Indians celebrated the harvest season with a feast that included turkey. Throughout the colonial era, days of thanksgiving were common, especially in New England, but not universal or regular. Although national days of thanksgiving were proclaimed by the Continental Congress in 1777 and by President George Washington in 1789, there was no great public clamor for an annual festival until the nineteenth century.

Credit for getting Thanksgiving Day established as a nationwide holiday must go to Sarah Josepha Hale, the editor of an influential women's magazine (and author of the poem, "Mary Had a Little Lamb"), who lobbied legislatures and presidents from 1827 on. In 1863 President Abraham Lincoln proclaimed the last Thursday of November 1863 as a day of "thanksgiving and praise to our beneficent Father who dwelleth in the Heavens," and since then Thanksgiving has been an annual celebration.

Every year the U.S. president would proclaim which day would be Thanksgiving Day and traditionally that day was always the last Thursday of November. In 1939, however, President Franklin Delano Roosevelt, in response to businesspeople who complained that there was insufficient shopping time between Thanksgiving and Christmas, proclaimed Thanksgiving to be a week earlier. This continued for two more years but created such public outrage that in December 1941 Congress passed a joint resolution establishing Thanksgiving as the fourth Thursday of November every year.

Thanksgiving, as a nondenominational harvest festival, is part of the American civic religion, celebrated by people of all faiths as well as by those who are not religious. It is marked by Pilgrim pageants; the decoration of schools, churches, and shopping malls with harvest themes; proclamations by politicians voicing gratitude for the country's prosperity; and the televising of college and professional football games. Above all, it is a day that family members gather for a meal that traditionally includes turkey, stuffing, mashed potatoes, sweet potatoes, cranberries, and pumpkin pie. Americans abroad observe the day and duplicate this traditional meal as best they can wherever they are. The illustrator Norman Rockwell's depictions of this family feast have become American icons.

For most people Thanksgiving stands for family togetherness. Motion pictures, such as *Planes, Trains & Automobiles* (1987) and *Dutch* (1991), are stories of returning home, whatever the obstacles, for this holiday. The final scene of *Raising Arizona* (1987) is a dream sequence in which a dysfunctional and childless couple are blessed in the future by the arrival of children and grandchildren for a traditional Thanksgiving.

The celebration of Thanksgiving marks the launch of another holiday: Christmas. As early as 1889 a New York newspaper claimed that "as soon as the Thanksgiving turkey is eaten, the great question of buying Christmas presents begins to take the terrifying shape it has come to assume." Thanksgiving parades, especially Macy's Thanksgiving Day Parade in New York and the Hollywood Christmas Parade in Los Angeles, usher in the shopping season.

Gerry Bowler

SEE ALSO: *Christmas; Consumerism; Hollywood; Macy's; Parades.*

BIBLIOGRAPHY

Cohen, Hennig, and Tristam Potter Coffin, eds. *The Folklore of American Holidays*. Detroit, MI: Gale, 1987.

Gioia, Robyn. *America's Real First Thanksgiving: St. Augustine, Florida, September 8, 1565*. Sarasota, FL: Pineapple Press, 2007.

Hatch, Jane M. *The American Book of Days*. New York: Wilson, 1978.

Tharp, Twyla *(1941–)*

A leading choreographer of modern dance and ballet, Twyla Tharp rose to prominence during the dance boom of the 1960s and 1970s. Her choreography incorporates dance elements from rock and roll, blues, and jazz and has been set to the music of Jelly Roll Morton, Bix Beiderbecke, Fats Waller, Chuck Berry, the Beach Boys, and David Byrne. In the mid-1970s Tharp began to cross over into ballet choreography. *Push Comes to Shove* and *Nine Sinatra Songs* were the two finest works that grew from her collaboration with Mikhail Baryshnikov and the American Ballet Theater. Other important works are *The Catherine Wheel* and *In the Upper Room*.

Although her work continues to draw on modern dance, Tharp is arguably the most important ballet choreographer since George Balanchine. Her choreography can be seen in the movies, *Hair* (1979), *Ragtime* (1981), *Amadeus* (1984), and *White Nights* (1985). Since 2001 Tharp has choreographed and directed a series of Broadway productions based on the work of singers, songwriters, and composers. The productions include *Movin' Out* in 2001 with music by Billy Joel, *The Times They Are a Changin'* (2005), based on the music of Bob Dylan, and in 2010 the songs of Frank Sinatra in *Come Fly with Me*.

Jeffrey Escoffier

SEE ALSO: *Balanchine, George; Ballet; Baryshnikov, Mikhail; The Beach Boys; Beiderbecke, Bix; Berry, Chuck; Blues; Broadway; Dylan, Bob; Jazz; Modern Dance; Morton, Jelly Roll; Rock and Roll; Sinatra, Frank.*

BIBLIOGRAPHY

Siegel, Marcia B. *Howling near Heaven: Twyla Tharp and the Reinvention of Modern Dance*. New York: St. Martin's Press, 2006.

Tharp, Twyla. *Push Comes to Shove: An Autobiography*. New York: Bantam Books, 1992.

Tharp, Twyla; Don Mischer; Mikhail Baryshnikov; et al. *Baryshnikov Dances Sinatra and More: A Dance Creation by Twyla Tharp: The Little Ballet, The Sinatra Suite, Push Comes to Shove*. DVD. West Long Branch, NJ: Kultur International Films, 1984.

Theater

SEE: *Broadway; Community Theater; The Musical; Tony Awards.*

Them!

Them!, the first and best of the giant insect and arachnid subgenre of horror films, was directed by Gordon Douglas and released by Warner Brothers in 1954. The "Them" in the film are giant ants, which mutated because of atomic-bomb testing in the American Southwest. A scientist (Edmund Gwenn), his daughter (Joan Weldon), an FBI agent (James Arness), and a police officer (James Whitmore) lead the effort to find and destroy the migrating horde of ants before it is too late.

The film is characterized by a matter-of-fact approach. Early witnesses to the ants' existence are either semicatatonic, like the young girl who can say only "Them!" or the pilot (Fess Parker), who is placed in a psychiatric ward after claiming to have seen giant bugs. The climax, an all-out assault on the ant colony living in sewers in Los Angeles, is moody and frightening, especially by the standards of 1950s special effects.

Other films in this genre include *Tarantula* (1955), *The Deadly Mantis* (1957), *Beginning of the End* (1957), and *The Black Scorpion* (1957).

David Lonergan

SEE ALSO: *Horror Movies.*

BIBLIOGRAPHY

Halliwell, Leslie, and John Walker. *Halliwell's Film Guide*. New York: HarperPerennial, 1994.

Jones, Alan. *The Rough Guide to Horror Movies*. London: Rough Guides, 2005.

Parish, James Robert, and Michael R. Pitts. *The Great Science Fiction Pictures*. Metuchen, NJ: Scarecrow Press, 1977.

The Thing

John Carpenter's *The Thing* (1982) is one of the peaks of sci-fi horror cinema, comparable only to *Alien* (1979). Its premise is simple and effective. A group of American scientists working in Antarctica are stalked by a shape-shifting alien, which kills them one by one and then assumes the victim's physical and mental identity. This extraterrestrial creature has lain dormant for centuries, buried in the Antarctic ice, until a team of Norwegian scientists defrosts it. The originality of Carpenter's film, otherwise quite conventional as regards character development and plot structure, stems from the shape-shifting abilities of the alien. Suspense is consistently maintained throughout the film

The Thing. *Kurt Russell starred as a member of the scientific team that discover a shape-shifting alien in the Antarctic in the 1982 film* The Thing. UNIVERSAL/THE KOBAL COLLECTION.

because the creature's nature makes it impossible for the audience to predict the shape it will take next. Intense horror is achieved by each new manifestation of the Thing, based on the truly scary designs of special effects wizard Rob Bottin.

INSPIRATION

The Thing is actually a double adaptation. Its main inspiration is Christian Nyby's 1951 film *The Thing from Another World*, an adaptation of "Who Goes There?," a short story by John W. Campbell Jr., which was also the basis of Carpenter's version. Nyby's *Thing* is one of the many monster films produced in the 1950s, a vogue fueled by terrors related to the Cold War and its feared alien—that is to say, communist—invasion of America. The first *Thing* failed to truly frighten the audience because the horrific potential of Campbell's original shape-shifting alien could not be adequately realized on the screen. Producer Howard Hawks wanted to achieve what would be achieved thirty years later by special effects artist Rick Baker and director John Landis in *An American Werewolf in London* (1981): a complete on-screen transformation of human into horrific nonhuman creature. The rudimentary special effects available to Nyby and his crew made this utterly impossible, and they had to rely on the traditional man in a rubber suit, shaped in this case—its detractors claim—as a rather unimpressive giant carrot.

SPECIAL EFFECTS

After the success of Ridley Scott's *Alien*—a story loosely based on another sci-fi pulp tale about a hostile alien fond of invading human bodies—the time seemed ripe to face the challenge Hawks had failed to meet. By 1981 special effects had progressed far from the poor 1950s standards under the guidance of makeup pioneer Dick Smith. Two of his disciples, Rick Baker and Rob Bottin, had discovered the wonders of latex foam, a new, supple material invented by George Bau, which enabled them to turn their wild flights of fancy into actual sculptures and models. Baker and Bottin commenced a fierce competition for the position of king of special effects, beginning with a werewolf film on which they worked together, Joe Dante's *The Howling* (1981). Baker won the first round by reaping the first Oscar for Best Makeup thanks to his work in *An American Werewolf in London*, but the quality of Bottin's work for Carpenter's *The Thing* certainly did not lag behind Baker's.

CULT STATUS

The Thing is now a cult film. Its original release, however, was badly timed, for it coincided with that of Steven Spielberg's *E.T.* Audiences charmed by Spielberg's cute, homesick alien found little to enjoy in Carpenter's grim tale, which, in addition to horrific scenes of mutation, offers one of the most pessimistic endings on record. By the late 1990s, however, *The Thing* had been fully vindicated by devoted fans who carved a niche for Carpenter's film in the roll call of top horror films. Its newfound popularity could be accounted for by two main factors: the first factor, no doubt, is the quality of Bottin's extraordinary work, which aged well and is hailed by many contemporary monster-makers as seminal inspiration. The scene of the postmortem that reveals the bizarre, nightmarish shapes the alien can assume is one of the most terrifying metamorphoses ever filmed.

The other factor that contributes to the cult status of *The Thing* is the atmosphere of despair that surrounds Carpenter's doomed heroes. Unlike countless monster films that conclude with the victory of humankind and the destruction of the alien monster, the end of *The Thing* suggests that the monster is alive as one of the only two survivors—either the sensible black scientist Nauls (T. K. Carter) or McReady, the rugged white hero played by Kurt Russell. Suggesting that the monster might find its last refuge in an African American man may have come to seem provocative enough with the onset of political correctness; but even more provocative is the suggestion that it is perhaps the hero, with whom our sympathy has lain throughout the film, who is the monster. Very little hope is left for trust among human beings or for the survival of humankind. This bleak prospect awoke an echo of sympathy in the more pessimistic late 1980s and 1990s, when fears of nuclear annihilation or alien conquest were superseded by fears of more subtle invasions, such as that by the AIDS virus. Fortunately for the admirers of Carpenter's masterpiece, no trivializing sequel followed—doubtless because of its downbeat conclusion and poor box-office returns. However, in 2011 Universal Pictures released a new version of *The Thing* that the studio labeled a prequel to Carpenter's film. It received generally poor reviews and was not a box-office success.

Sara Martin

SEE ALSO: *Academy Awards;* Alien*; Cult Films;* E.T. The Extra-Terrestrial*; Hawks, Howard; Horror Movies; Scott, Ridley.*

BIBLIOGRAPHY

Cumbow, Robert C. *Order in the Universe: The Films of John Carpenter.* Metuchen, NJ: Scarecrow Press, 1990.

Muir, John Kenneth. *The Films of John Carpenter.* Jefferson, NC: McFarland, 2000.

Salisbury, Mark, and Alan Hedgcock. *Behind the Mask: The Secret of Hollywood's Monster Makers.* London: Titan Books, 1994.

Timpone, Anthony. *Men, Makeup and Monsters: Hollywood's Masters of Illusion and FX.* New York: St. Martin's Griffin, 1996.

The Third Man

The film *The Third Man* (1949) is remembered for its compelling tale of mystery, Anton Karas's haunting zither score, and the blend of expressionism's jagged angles and film noir's shadows in Robert Krasker's Oscar-winning cinematography. The film draws in the viewer right away, as Holly Martins (Joseph Cotten) arrives in postwar Vienna to visit his friend, Harry Lime (Orson Welles), only to find that Harry is dead. When Major Calloway (Trevor Howard) claims that Harry was a black marketeer, Holly begins to investigate his friend's mysterious death. He discovers that Harry is still alive and is as corrupt as Calloway claimed. Holly's conscience is torn between Calloway and the beautiful Anna Schmidt (Alida Valli), Harry's lover who urges Holly to remain loyal to his friend. The screenplay for this stirring mystery was cowritten by the great twentieth-century novelist Graham Greene.

Christian L. Pyle

SEE ALSO: *Cotten, Joseph; Film Noir; Welles, Orson.*

BIBLIOGRAPHY

Greene, Graham, and Carol Reed. *The Third Man.* New York: Simon & Schuster, 1968.

Slide, Anthony. *Fifty Classic British Films, 1932–1982: A Pictorial Record.* Mineola, NY: Dover Publications, 1985.

30 Rock

30 Rock, a behind-the-scenes parody of a comedy-sketch show, is the critically acclaimed brainchild of former *Saturday Night Live* (*SNL*) head writer Tina Fey. Since first airing in October 2006, *30 Rock* has been filmed mainly in Long Island City (in Queens) and only partly at NBC's Manhattan headquarters, 30 Rockefeller Plaza, for which the show is named and where most of the action is set. Although it is labeled as a sitcom, the individual scenes of each episode are filmed with a single camera, which gives the production the feel of a documentary. The result is a sharply edited, highly crafted lampoon of its parent network, NBC, and the sketch show *SNL*. In addition to Fey, executive producers include Lorne Michaels and Marci Klein (of *SNL*), Robert Carlock (*Friends*), David Miner, Jeff Richmond, and John Riggi. The show features an award-winning cast, including Fey, Alec Baldwin, Tracy Morgan, Jane Krakowski, and Jack McBrayer.

Originally conceived as a sitcom based on a news show, the *30 Rock* pilot evolved to focus on an *SNL*-like variety show called *The Girlie Show* (*TGS*). Fey plays Liz Lemon, *TGS*'s show-runner, who is professionally successful but privately is a hilariously neurotic wreck, her nerves frayed by her attempts to mediate the relationships between her boss, Jack Donaghy (Baldwin); the writing staff; and the show's talent. Much of the show's humor derives from Donaghy's paternalistic, often dismissive, interactions with the fraught Lemon. At one point he tells her, "If you were any other woman on earth, I'd be turned on right now." As the newly appointed executive of NBC, Donaghy restructures *TGS* by replacing "top girl" Jenna Maroney (Krakowski) with the audacious movie star, Tracy Jordan (Morgan), and renames the show *TGS with Tracy Jordan.* Jenna, who craves distinction and notoriety, is immediately impressed by her replacement's "street cred," and together the two stars look down on the rest of the staff. In one funny exchange, when Jenna complains to Tracy that one of the underlings has been acting haughty, Tracy responds, "But he is not famous. Why is the government allowing this?"

The supporting cast includes Kenneth (McBrayer), an overeager NBC page; Pete (Scott Adsit), *TGS*'s sometimes level-headed producer; and the *TGS* writing staff. Fey once described her *30 Rock* writers as a strategic blend of "four Harvard nerds, four performers turned writers, two regular nerds, and two dirtbags." The *TGS* writers fit this mold as well. Among them are the Harvard-educated and condescending "Toofer" (Keith Powell); Josh, a naive writer-impressionist (Lonny Ross, in seasons 1–4); and, among others, two "scumbags": lazy J. D. Lutz (John Lutz) and tactless Frank (Judah Friedlander), who broadcasts insults on his baseball caps. Also central to the ensemble are Cerie, Liz's young and unprofessional assistant (Katrina Bowden); Jack's adoring aide Jonathan (Maulik Pancholy); GE's septuagenarian CEO (Rip Torn); and Tracy's long-suffering entourage: Grizz (Grizz Chapman) and Dot Com (Kevin Brown). The show has had a host of guest stars and cameo appearances, including Matt Damon, Dean Winters, Steve Martin, Salma Hayek, Jennifer Aniston, Al Gore, Condoleezza Rice, Conan O'Brien, Julianne Moore, Brian Williams, and Oprah Winfrey.

Despite having a few initial detractors, *30 Rock* eventually won over most of the critics and has consistently ranked high on numerous "best of" lists throughout its run. In 2009 *Newsweek* named it the best TV comedy of the decade. Over the course of its first six seasons, *30 Rock* broke records for the number of Emmy nominations received by a comedy series in 2008 and 2009. Its award shelf includes Emmys in several categories, including Outstanding Comedy Series, Outstanding Writing for a Comedy Series, Outstanding Lead Actor in a Comedy Series, and Outstanding Lead Actress in a Comedy Series, as well as Golden Globes and guild prizes for producing and writing. In the face of such critical success, however, the show's ratings have been low. This is partly because NBC has scheduled it during Thursday night prime time against some of the competition's strongest shows. Fey, however, has joked of another possibility: "Let's face it, between Alec Baldwin and me there is a certain 50 percent of the population who think we are pinko Commie monsters."

It's more likely, however, that viewers have opted for shows with less sophisticated humor. According to the *New York Times*, critics prefer *30 Rock* to other prime-time comedy fare due to the "crackling chemistry" between Fey and Baldwin and the "snappy and sharp" acting of the rest of the cast. In 2009, *30 Rock* was placed in syndication on Comedy Central and WGN. NBC announced in 2012 that a shortened seventh season of *30 Rock* would be its last. At that time, five seasons had been released on DVD and were available for streaming on Netflix, ensuring that audiences would continue to enjoy the antics of Liz Lemon and the rest of the *TGS* cast.

Stephen P. Davis

SEE ALSO: *Baldwin, Alec; Cable TV; Damon, Matt; Emmy Awards; Fey, Tina; Martin, Steve; Netflix; O'Brien, Conan;* Saturday Night Live*; Sitcom; Television; Winfrey, Oprah.*

BIBLIOGRAPHY

Franklin, Nancy. "Sketchy Comedy: Tina Fey's *30 Rock.*" *New Yorker*, December 8, 2008.

Steinberg, Jacques. "*30 Rock* Lives, and Tina Fey Laughs." *New York Times*, September 23, 2007.

30 Rock Official Website. Accessed May 2012. Available from http://www.nbc.com/30-rock/

This Is Your Life

A human-interest show that presented documentary-style biographies of celebrities through the recollections and testimonials of colleagues, friends, and relatives, *This Is Your Life* was one of the most popular shows on radio and television during its lengthy run. Although occasionally lesser-known but accomplished guests appeared on the program, the show is best remembered for its surprise tributes to Marilyn Monroe, Jack Benny, Bette Davis, and other Hollywood stars.

Created by perennial host Ralph Edwards for radio in the 1940s, *This Is Your Life* came to television on October 1, 1952, as a half-hour series and lasted for nine seasons on NBC. On both radio and television, the show's format was the same. Edwards would appear to encounter the evening's guest by happenstance in or near the television studio. After a brief exchange of pleasantries, Edwards would announce "This is your life!" and the startled guest would be taken to the show's set, where his or her life story would unfold before a live studio audience. Reading from the *This Is Your Life* book, Edwards would recount the celebrity's childhood, school years, and rise to fame with a sentimental flare certain to elicit an emotional outpouring from both guest and audience. Edwards was so effective, in fact, that one show celebrating the life of educator Laurence C. Jones inspired his television audience to send $700,000 in contributions to a Mississippi college. The show's specialty, however, seemed to be orchestrating parades of long-lost teachers and friends whose appearance was sure to trigger tears from the honored guest.

From time to time a planned show would have to be scrapped because the celebrity learned of the project in advance, but for the most part Edwards was remarkably successful in his Candid Camera–style ruses, especially as the show was broadcast live until the 1959–1960 season. *This Is Your Life* did, however, tip off two guests: Lillian Roth, so that producers could obtain permission to discuss her successful struggle with alcoholism, and Eddie Cantor, who producers feared might experience a heart attack at too dramatic a surprise.

The show generated two spin-offs, a British version of *This Is Your Life* and, in 1953, *The Comeback Story*, which each week presented the inspiring tale of a faded star who was regaining fame and fortune. It also spun off several incarnations of itself. Edwards revived *This Is Your Life* in 1971, this time featuring the Nelson Riddle Orchestra, but the syndicated show lasted only one season. It reemerged for another try in 1983, and over the years several *This Is Your Life* specials have appeared on NBC, with Ralph Edwards hosting until 1993.

Despite its reputation for sentimentality and sensationalism, *This Is Your Life* proved to be a resilient formula for the surprise party, whether televised or not. Not only have television producers fit it into every decade's programming, if only for an evening, but also the words "This is your life!" have entered the popular imagination as a theme appropriate to almost any kind of party or celebration.

Michele S. Shauf

SEE ALSO: *Benny, Jack; Cantor, Eddie; Davis, Bette; Edwards, Ralph; Monroe, Marilyn.*

BIBLIOGRAPHY

Brooks, Tim, and Earle Marsh. *The Complete Directory to Prime Time Network and Cable TV Shows, 1946–Present*, 9th ed. New York: Ballantine Books, 2007.

McNeil, Alex. *Total Television*. New York: Penguin Books, 1996.

Thomas, Clarence

SEE: *Anita Hill–Clarence Thomas Senate Hearings.*

Thomas, Danny *(1914–1991)*

Although he later starred in the longest-running situation comedy in television history and became one of TV's top producers, Danny Thomas once denounced the new medium as a "workplace for idiots." He made this comment after spending two years hosting NBC's *All-Star Revue*, rotating with comedians Jack Carson, Jimmy Durante, and Ed Wynn. He quit the show in 1952 to return to the nightclub circuit. A year later he was back on the small screen, well on his way to becoming one of the icons of television's Golden Age.

Born Muzyad Yakhoob in Deerfield, Michigan, the fifth of nine children of Catholic immigrants from Lebanon, Danny's first experience in show business was selling candy at a burlesque theater. At age twenty he began singing on a Detroit radio station, and six years later he started a career in nightclubs, as a stand-up comic and master of ceremonies. His popularity steadily increased during the 1940s, leading to a brief career in films. In his two best-remembered films, he played pop composer Gus Kahn in *I'll See You in My Dreams* (1951) and the Al Jolson role in the remake of *The Jazz Singer* (1952).

In 1953 Thomas began developing a situation comedy for ABC. Discussing the project with writer Mel Shavelson, he explained that he wanted to stay home with his family in Los Angeles. As he wrote in his autobiography in 1990, "I was away on the road so much that they hardly knew me. They called me 'Uncle Daddy.'" Shavelson realized at once that they had a concept for a comedy show, featuring a nightclub entertainer trying to have a normal family life along with a career in show business. Thomas's wife, Rose Marie, suggested the title, *Make Room for Daddy.* While Thomas was on the road, the children took over his space in the home, and when he returned, they had to shift bedrooms and move their belongings to "make room for Daddy."

The show made its debut on ABC in September 1953, running for four seasons with its ratings near the bottom. The low ratings came despite the fact that the show won an Emmy as Best Situation Comedy Series in 1954, the same year Thomas won an Emmy for Best Actor Starring in a Regular Series. After the third season, Jean Hagen, Thomas's on-screen wife, quit the show and became the first leading character in a sitcom to die in the off-season. When the next season started, little Terry and Rusty were told, "Mommy's gone to Heaven."

The Danny Thomas Show. *The cast of* The Danny Thomas Show, *originally titled* Make Room for Daddy *when it debuted in 1953, included, from left, Marjorie Lord, Rusty Hamer, Danny Thomas, and Angela Cartwright.* MARTERTO PRODUCTIONS/THE KOBAL COLLECTION.

In 1957 the renamed *Danny Thomas Show* was moved to CBS and aired on Monday night in the 9 p.m. time slot. In the first episode Thomas had just married his new bride (Marjorie Lord), who arrived with a cute, precocious five-year-old stepdaughter, played by Angela Cartwright. Another popular character on the show was Thomas's Lebanese Uncle Tonoose, played by Hans Conried. Ratings immediately soared to the top ten, and the newfound audience remained loyal throughout the run of the series, which ended in 1964.

In 1967 a special, *Make More Room for Daddy*, aired on NBC. Two years later another special titled *Make Room for Granddaddy*, reuniting Thomas, Lord, Cartwright, Rusty Hamer, and Conried, proved so popular that it became a pilot for the 1970–1971 series on ABC. Thomas's "grandson," played by Michael Hughes, was introduced on that show. His real-life children also became important in show business; son, Tony, produced such hit shows as *Golden Girls* (1985–1992) and *Empty Nest* (1988–1995), and daughter, Marlo, starred in the hit series *That Girl* (1966–1971).

In the 1950s Thomas had branched out into production, forming partnerships first with Sheldon Leonard and later with Aaron Spelling. He became one of the most successful television producers of the 1950s and 1960s, whose blockbuster programs included *The Andy Griffith Show* (1960–1968), *The Dick Van Dyke Show* (1961–1966), *Gomer Pyle, U.S.M.C.* (1964–1969), and *The Mod Squad* (1968–1973).

In 1991 Thomas made a rare guest appearance on his son Tony's series, *Empty Nest.* A week later, his fans were stunned to learn that he had died of a heart attack. His later years were marked by his generosity in giving and raising money for his favorite charity, St. Jude's Hospital.

Benjamin Griffith

SEE ALSO: The Andy Griffith Show*; Emmy Awards;* The Golden Girls*;* The Mod Squad*; Sitcom; Spelling, Aaron; Television; Thomas, Marlo; Van Dyke, Dick.*

BIBLIOGRAPHY

Brooks, Tim, and Earle Marsh. *The Complete Directory to Prime Time Network and Cable TV Shows: 1946 to Present*, 6th ed. New York: Ballantine Books, 1985.

McNeil, Alex. *Total Television: A Comprehensive Guide to Programming from 1948 to the Present.* New York: Penguin, 1991.

Sackett, Susan. *Prime-Time Hits: Television's Most Popular Network Programs.* New York: Billboard, 1993.

Thomas, Isiah *(1961–)*

Before basketball great Isiah Thomas joined the National Basketball Association (NBA), he starred for two seasons at Indiana University. There he won All-American honors in 1981, led the Hoosiers to a national title, and was cited as the National Collegiate Athletic Association (NCAA) tournament's Most Valuable Player (MVP). Following that season, Thomas chose to leave school and turn pro. He was drafted in the first round by the Detroit Pistons and went on to play thirteen seasons in the NBA. The 6-foot, one-inch, 185-pound point guard became the captain and star of the Pistons, leading the team to three successive appearances in the NBA finals (1988, 1989, and 1990). In both 1989 and 1990, the Pistons emerged as champions. In 1990 Thomas was cited as the MVP of the finals. Between 1982 and 1993 he started in twelve successive NBA All-Star games and was the contest's MVP in 1984 and 1986.

In his time in the NBA, Thomas teamed with Joe Dumars to make up one of pro basketball's top backcourts. Upon his retirement after the 1993–1994 season, Thomas was the all-time scoring leader of the Pistons, with 18,822 points. He also was tops in assists (9,061), steals (1,861), and games played (979). One of the keys to his success was his mental approach to the game. "I've always believed no matter how many shots I miss," Thomas once said, "I'm going to make the next one."

Although Thomas left college before he graduated, he continued his studies at Indiana University, and in 1987 he earned a degree in criminal justice. Since his retirement, he has immersed himself in a range of basketball-related endeavors. "If all I'm remembered for is being a good basketball player," he declared, "then I've done a bad job with the rest of my life." However, many of his post-hoop undertakings have been fraught with controversy.

In 1994 Thomas became a part owner and vice president of the NBA expansion team the Toronto Raptors. He hoped to take over the team, but the deal, which involved majority owner Allan Slaight, fell apart. As a result, Thomas left the Raptors four years later and joined NBC as a basketball analyst. In 1999 he headed an investment group that purchased the Continental Basketball Association (CBA), a professional minor league, but the CBA declared bankruptcy and ceased operations two years later. Then, from 2000 to 2003, Thomas was head coach of the Indiana Pacers.

In late 2003 Thomas became president of basketball operations for the New York Knicks, but his tenure in New York was stormy. He was lambasted in the media and by Knicks fans for overspending on second-rate players; at the close of the 2005–2006 campaign, the Knicks had the highest NBA payroll but the second-worst league record. In 2006 he was, nevertheless, also named as the team's head coach—which led to further controversy when he reportedly instigated an on-court brawl in a game against the Denver Nuggets. Even though the Knicks failed to improve in the standings, team owner James Dolan signed Thomas to a multiyear contract. In 2008, however, as the Knicks were completing yet another dismal season, Donnie Walsh replaced Thomas as the team's president, and within weeks the decision was made not to retain Thomas as head coach.

In 2009 Thomas signed on as the men's basketball coach at Florida International University (FIU). The following year, Dolan, Walsh, and Thomas announced that Thomas was being hired as a consultant for the Knicks while he remained coach at FIU. Because the arrangement violated NBA bylaws, the announcement was quickly reversed; however, media reports circulated that Thomas remained connected to Dolan and the Knicks and that he even helped spearhead the 2011 trade that brought star forward Carmelo Anthony to New York.

Despite all of the contention that has tarnished Thomas's post-playing career, it does not diminish his accomplishments on the basketball court. In 1996 he was named one of the fifty greatest players in NBA history. The Pistons also retired his jersey number (11), and he was elected to the Naismith Memorial Basketball Hall of Fame in 2000.

Rob Edelman

SEE ALSO: *Basketball;* Hoosiers*; National Basketball Association (NBA); National Collegiate Athletic Association (NCAA); The New York Knickerbockers.*

BIBLIOGRAPHY

Challen, Paul. *The Book of Isiah: The Rise of a Basketball Legend.* Chicago: Login Publishers Consortium, 1996.

Challen, Paul. *From the Back Court to the Front Office: The Isiah Thomas Story.* Toronto, ON: ECW Press, 2004.

Thomas, Isiah. *The Fundamentals: 8 Plays for Winning the Games of Business and Life.* New York: HarperBusiness, 2001.

Thomas, Isiah, and Matt Dobek. *Bad Boys! An Inside Look at the Detroit Pistons 1988–89 Championship Season.* Grand Rapids, MI: Masters Press, 1989.

Thomas, Lowell *(1892–1981)*

A best-selling author, globe-trotting adventurer, and legendary broadcaster, Lowell Thomas traveled from the Arctic to the outback, covering stories ranging from World War I to Lawrence of Arabia. In all he authored fifty-five travel books. He began working in radio in 1930 and continued broadcasting until 1976. Although he worked for a variety of sponsors and two networks, he is best remembered for hosting CBS Radio News. His fifteen-minute nightly broadcast was rarely far from the top of the news ratings, and his sign-off is well remembered: "so long until tomorrow."

Chris Chandler

SEE ALSO: *Best Sellers;* Lawrence of Arabia*; Radio; World War I.*

BIBLIOGRAPHY

Dunning, John. *On the Air: The Encyclopedia of Old-Time Radio.* New York: Oxford University Press, 1998.

Lowell, Thomas. *Good Evening Everybody: From Cripple Creek to Samarkand.* New York: Morrow, 1976.

Lowell, Thomas. *So Long until Tomorrow: From Quaker Hill to Kathmandu.* New York: Morrow, 1977.

Thomas, Marlo *(1937–)*

Marlo Thomas is best remembered as the naively innocent and exhaustingly enthusiastic Ann Marie of the television series *That Girl* (1966–1971), for which she won a Golden Globe Award and received four Emmy nominations. She played an unmarried woman who was living alone in New York City, neither searching for a husband nor working as a domestic. The show was the model for later television series such as *The Mary Tyler Moore Show* (1970–1977) and *Murphy Brown* (1988–1998).

That Girl was more traditional than it claimed. Although Ann was largely on her own, her father and her ever-present boyfriend were never more than a phone call away when she found herself in one of her typical predicaments. Moreover, the show was less than realistic in portraying her economic situation. Although she worked at low-paying temporary jobs, the kind typically available to women of the period, she lived in a three-room apartment in a good neighborhood in New York City and dressed in the height of fashion.

After the series ended, Thomas became a producer and in that capacity won Emmy Awards for her work on *Free to Be . . . You and Me* (1974) and *The Body Human: Facts for Girls* (1980). She won a third Emmy for her role in *Nobody's Child* (1986). She has been a strong advocate for a variety of women's causes, founding the Ms. Foundation for Women with feminists Gloria Steinem, Patricia Carbine, and Letty Cottin Pogrebin in 1973. In 1980 Thomas married talk-show host Phil Donahue. Since then she has had a number of small stage and film roles and has appeared on televisions shows including *Ally McBeal* (1997–2002) and *Friends* (1994–2004). She also played the lead role in writer and director Elaine May's *George Is Dead*, which opened in Phoenix, Arizona, in 2009 and debuted on Broadway in 2011.

Chris Chandler

SEE ALSO: Ally McBeal; *Broadway; Donahue, Phil; Emmy Awards; Feminism;* Friends; The Mary Tyler Moore Show; Murphy Brown; *Steinem, Gloria; Television; Thomas, Danny.*

BIBLIOGRAPHY

Atholl, Desmond, and Michael Cherkinian. *"That Girl" and Phil.* New York: St. Martin's Press, 1990.

Thompson, Hunter S. *(1937–2005)*

Hunter S. Thompson represented life on the edge, even of the counterculture; he was the man who listed his religion as none, his politics as anarchist, and his hobby as collecting guns. He claimed membership in the American Civil Liberties Union, the National Rifle Association, and the National Organization for the Reform of Marijuana Laws, and he once ran for sheriff of Aspen, Colorado. Born in Louisville, Kentucky, the drug- and alcohol-abusing Thompson worked for the mainstream press in the late 1950s and early 1960s—*Time* magazine, the *New York Herald Tribune*, and the *National Observer*—before he became a voice of antiestablishment values, writing for *Rolling Stone* and inventing "gonzo journalism." He was even turned into a character in the comic strip *Doonesbury*.

Thompson wrote his first article for an alternative magazine in 1965, when the *Nation* asked him for a story about the Hells Angels; it was titled "The Motorcycle Gangs: Losers and Outsiders," and it led to his first book contract. Thompson spent a year with the Angels as a field study for *Hell's Angels: The Strange and Terrible Saga of the Outlaw Motorcycle Gangs* (1966). He was charged with separating fact from fancy, and in doing so he condemned the press for coverage that he felt misrepresented the biker club, merely repeating what law enforcement officials chose to say rather than learning the truth from the members. Thompson's book portrayed the Angels not as deliberate dropouts but rather as drug-using and alcohol-abusing men not fit for society. Perhaps the lowest point in the book was his description of an episode of gang sex with one woman. At the end of his time with them, some Angels who felt he was exploiting them for his own gain nearly stomped him to death.

GONZO JOURNALISM

The term *gonzo journalism* was reportedly first used in reference to Thompson's 1970 coverage of the Kentucky Derby for *Scanlan's* magazine. He claimed later that his writing process included no plan, draft, or revision but had evolved out of necessity when, unable to write, he merely ripped pages out of his notebook, numbered them, and sent them on to his editor. The result was "The Kentucky Derby Is Decadent and Depraved," a hilarious account of Thompson in Louisville. The article worked too well to have been assembled so randomly, but Thompson later proclaimed himself the inventor of a new type of nonobjective journalism.

Because of the titles of his next two books (both first published in *Rolling Stone*), *Fear and Loathing in Las Vegas: A Savage Journey to the Heart of the American Dream* (1972) and *Fear and Loathing on the Campaign Trail '72* (1973), "Fear and Loathing in . . . " became the trademark Thompson headline of many of his *Rolling Stone* articles. His book titles evoke some of the writer's character traits as well as his subject matter: *The Great Shark Hunt: Strange Tales from a Strange Time (Gonzo Papers, Volume One)* (1979); *The Curse of Lono* (1983): *Generation of Swine: Tales of Shame and Degradation in the '80s (Gonzo Papers, Volume Two)* (1988); *Songs of the Doomed: More Notes on the Death of the American Dream (Gonzo Papers, Volume Three)*

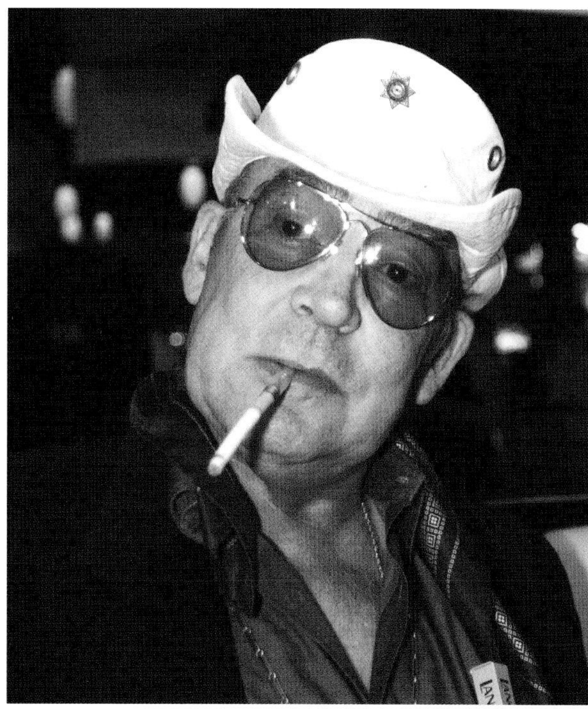

Hunter S. Thompson. *Hunter S. Thompson labeled his opinion-laden, irreverent, counterculture-influenced writing style as "gonzo journalism."* DENISE TRUSCELLO/CONTRIBUTOR/DENISE TRUSCELLO/CONTRIBUTOR/GETTY IMAGES.

(1990); *Better than Sex: Confessions of a Political Junkie (Gonzo Papers, Volume Four)* (1994); and *The Proud Highway: Saga of a Desperate Southern Gentlemen, 1955–1967* (1997).

The two *Fear* books helped establish Thompson as a writer with an attitude. *Fear and Loathing in Las Vegas* purports to be an autobiographical account of his failure to cover two events for a magazine because he spent more time on drug trips than on reporting. The character Raoul Duke, who represents Thompson, became "Uncle Duke" in Garry Trudeau's famous and long-running comic strip *Doonesbury*. More than twenty-five years after the book was published, it was made into a movie that received some good reviews but made only short stops in theaters.

BEYOND THE MAINSTREAM

Fear and Loathing on the Campaign Trail '72, a collection of articles Thompson wrote for *Rolling Stone*, reflects the author's continued abhorrence of the mainstream press while at the same time making him, rather than the candidates, the center of the reporting. *Boys on the Bus* (1973), by Timothy Crouse (another *Rolling Stone* writer), depicts how the press covered the 1972 presidential campaign and provides many stories about Thompson's nonjournalistic antics at the time. Crouse claims that when *Rolling Stone* dispatched him and Thompson to Washington to open a bureau, he was "to write the serious backup pieces, keep Thompson out of trouble, and carry the bail bond money." Thompson showed up on the campaign trail in sneakers, sunglasses, a Miami sports shirt, and a hunting jacket; everyone else in the press corps wore coats and ties. Crouse reports that Thompson was downright irreverent, offering to share his beer, Wild Turkey, and drugs and wondering aloud if he would have time to drop some acid at the next campaign stop. Eventually, however, many members of the press came to respect Thompson because he was able to write what they could not. While his colleagues were committed to objective reporting, he was able to express his own opinions in colorfully descriptive language.

Thompson continued to publish book collections of his journalistic pieces in a series called the Gonzo Papers. Meanwhile, he persisted in his outrageous behavior. "I'm afraid I've become addicted to my own adrenaline," he once said. In 2003 he published a memoir called *Kingdom of Fear: Loathsome Secrets of a Star-Crossed Child in the Final Days of the American Century*. Two years later, at the age of sixty-seven, he shot and killed himself at his home near Aspen, Colorado. The documentary film *Gonzo: The Life of Dr. Hunter S. Thompson* was released in 2008.

By turns funny, insightful, prophetic, and brutally satiric, Thompson's writing style has been badly imitated and never duplicated. Generally, those who followed him enjoyed his irreverent and rich writing, and, even after his death, he remained a larger-than-life example of the counterculture of the 1960s.

R. Thomas Berner

SEE ALSO: *Alternative Press; Beer; Comics;* Doonesbury*; Gangs; Hells Angels; Kentucky Derby; LSD; Marijuana;* The Nation*;* Rolling Stone*; Suicide; Tennis Shoes/Sneakers;* Time.

BIBLIOGRAPHY

Berner, R. Thomas. *The Literature of Journalism: Text and Context*. State College, PA: Strata Publishing, 1999.

Carroll, E. Jean. *Hunter: The Strange and Savage Life of Hunter S. Thompson*. New York: Dutton, 1993.

Crouse, Timothy. *The Boys on the Bus*. New York: Random House, 1973.

McKeen, William. *Hunter S. Thompson*. Boston: Twayne, 1991

Perry, Paul. *Fear and Loathing: The Strange and Terrible Saga of Hunter S. Thompson*. New York: Thunder's Mouth Press. 1993.

Seymour, Corey, and Jann Wenner. *Gonzo: The Life of Hunter S. Thompson*. New York: Little, Brown, 2007.

Thompson, Hunter S. *Kingdom of Fear: Loathsome Secrets of a Star-Crossed Child in the Final Days of the American Century*. New York: Simon & Schuster, 2003.

Vetter, Craig. "Playboy Interview: Hunter Thompson." *Playboy*, November 1974.

Whitmer, Peter O. *When the Going Gets Weird: The Twisted Life and Times of Hunter S. Thompson*. New York: Hyperion, 1993.

Thompson, John *(1941–)*

In 1984 Olympic and college basketball coach John Thompson Jr. became the first African American to guide a National Collegiate Athletic Association (NCAA) basketball team to the championship. Thompson coached the Georgetown University Hoyas team from 1972 through 1999, turning around Georgetown's abysmal record and making it a national powerhouse in the Big East Conference that he helped to charter in 1979. Under his leadership, the team compiled twenty-four consecutive winning seasons (excluding his first year there and his last two), beating its opponents in more than 70 percent of its games.

Thompson's student-athletes were known for their aggressive playing styles as well as for their commitment to academic achievement at their elite Catholic institution. The coach supervised both his players' scholarly progress and their outside friendships, rescuing some stars from the bad influence of drug dealers. His shoulder-resting trademark towel that he used on the court to wipe away his perspiration symbolized his hard-driven temperament. But he also kept a deflated basketball on his desk as a symbol to Georgetown players that there should be more to their lives than the game. After his coaching career, Thompson became the host of a talk show on ESPN radio that ran until the end of February 2012.

Frederick J. Augustyn Jr.

SEE ALSO: *Basketball; ESPN; National Collegiate Athletic Association (NCAA); Olympics; Talk Radio.*

BIBLIOGRAPHY

Porter, David L., ed. *Biographical Dictionary of American Sports: Basketball and Other Indoor Sports*. Westport, CT: Greenwood Press, 1989.

Porter, David L., ed. *African-American Sports Greats: A Biographical Dictionary*. Westport, CT: Greenwood Press, 1995.

Porterfield, Jason. *Basketball in the Big East Conference*. New York: Rosen Central, 2008.

Shapiro, Leonard. *Big Man on Campus: John Thompson and the Georgetown Hoyas*. New York: Henry Holt, 1991.

Thomson, Bobby *(1923–2010)*

Robert Brown "Bobby" Thomson played major-league baseball from 1946 through 1960. His name will forever be linked with the "shot heard round the world"—what many consider the most dramatic event in the history of American sports. On October 3, 1951, as a New York Giant, he belted a come-from-behind home run to win the National League pennant in his team's final at-bat. The home run capped a thrilling pennant race between the New York Giants and their bitter rivals, the Brooklyn Dodgers. In front of a national television audience, Thomson and the Giants reveled in their victory just as New York delighted in its place at the cultural center of a thriving postwar America. But Thomson's home run retained significance well beyond the 1950s. Beginning in the 1970s, as Major League Baseball increasingly cloaked itself in the garb of nostalgia, the shot heard round the world symbolized a simpler America, where an average guy who lived with his mother on Staten Island could drive to Manhattan one autumn afternoon and return home a hero.

BECOMING A GIANT

Thomson was born in Glasgow, Scotland, on October 23, 1923. At the age of two, he moved with his mother and five siblings to join his father, James, in New York. James was a cabinetmaker who had moved to America to seek a better living. The Thomsons would struggle financially throughout Bobby's youth on Staten Island. He first played professionally, without much success, in the Giants' minor-league organization in 1942. He then postponed his baseball career to join the U.S. Army Air Corps. After spending three years stationed in Victorville, California, he went to a Giants training camp for returning servicemen. The Giants assigned him to their Triple-A affiliate in Jersey City, where he played for one year.

After an outstanding rookie season with the Giants in 1947, Thomson showed only occasional flashes of brilliance. Critics accused him of having a nonchalant attitude that adversely affected his play. Despite having been named an All-Star in 1948 and 1949, by the end of the 1950 season it seemed Thomson was destined for an average career on a mediocre New York Giants team.

Bobby Thomson. *Bobby Thomson's "shot heard round the world" clinched the National League pennant for the New York Giants in 1951.* PHOTO FILE/CONTRIBUTOR/MAJOR LEAGUE BASEBALL/GETTY IMAGES.

THE SHOT HEARD ROUND THE WORLD

By the early part of the 1951 season, neither Thomson nor the Giants had improved. The Giants lost twelve of their first fourteen games. Over that period Thomson hit a dismal .193. Although the team recovered from their disheartening start, in early August they found themselves in distant second place, thirteen-and-a-half games behind the Brooklyn Dodgers. The press and most fans predicted that the championship would go to Brooklyn. But on August 11, the Giants started a sixteen-game winning streak fueled by Thomson's hot hitting, and they found themselves within reach of the Dodgers. They caught the Dodgers with one day left in the season, and after the season's final game, the two teams remained tied for first place. They split the first two games of a three-game playoff series, and the whole season came down to the third game: the winner would take the National League pennant and move on to the World Series.

The deciding game started inauspiciously for the Giants as they fell behind 4–1, due in part to Thomson's poor baserunning. Dodgers pitcher Don Newcombe appeared indestructible until the bottom of the ninth inning, when he gave up three base hits and the Giants closed the gap to two runs, with base runners on second and third. With the winning run coming to the plate and his pitcher clearly tiring, Brooklyn manager Charlie Dressen made a call to the bullpen for Ralph Branca. With one out, Thomson stepped into the batter's box. He watched Branca's first pitch blow past him for a strike. When the second pitch came in hard, high, and inside, Thomson lashed out at the ball, and it shot off his bat toward the left-field wall. Russ Hodges, the Giants announcer, called the action on WMCA radio: "There's a long drive . . . it's gonna be . . . I believe . . . the Giants win the pennant! The Giants win the pennant! The Giants win the pennant! The Giants win the pennant! I don't believe it! The Giants win the pennant!" Thomson claimed his feet never touched the ground as he circled the bases.

The shot heard round the world immediately gained legendary status, epitomizing the postwar optimism felt in New York and throughout America. The series was the first sporting event to be telecast live from coast to coast, and its dramatic finish affirmed New York's place as the de facto capital of a thriving American culture. New York sportswriter Red Smith captured the euphoric sense of disbelief. "Now it is done," he wrote. "Now the story ends. And there is no way to tell it. The art of fiction is dead. Reality has strangled invention. Only the utterly impossible, the inexpressibly fantastic, can ever be plausible again." Thomson's home run spoke for a city and a nation where the impossible had become the attainable.

AFTER THE GLORY

Thomson played solid baseball for eight more years, but he never recaptured the glory of 1951. Following the 1953 season, the Giants traded him to Milwaukee. He played briefly for several other teams before retiring in 1960 and settling in New Jersey with his wife, Elaine, and their three children, where he worked as a paper products salesman. He passed away in August 2010, at the age of eighty-six.

In the 1970s, amid salary disputes and escalating ticket prices, Major League Baseball began to market itself through nostalgia, attempting to connect the contemporary game to a mythical past. Thomson's homer became the crowning moment of that myth. The shot heard round the world symbolized a time of innocence and purity, when players played for the love of the game and the fans loved their players—a time when the tall, plodding, immigrant son of a cabinetmaker could swing a bat and become a hero. Nostalgia for this event also extends into the literary world; the famous home run is the opening scene of Don DeLillo's highly acclaimed 1997 novel *Underworld.*

Steven T. Sheehan

SEE ALSO: *Baseball; The Brooklyn Dodgers; Live Television; Major League Baseball; Radio; Sports Heroes; World Series.*

BIBLIOGRAPHY

Prager, Joshua. *The Echoing Green: The Untold Story of Bobby Thomson, Ralph Branca, and the Shot Heard round the World.* New York: Pantheon, 2006.

Robinson, Ray. *The Home Run Heard round the World.* New York: HarperCollins, 1991.

Rosenfeld, Harvey. *The Great Chase: The Dodgers–Giants Pennant Race of 1951.* Jefferson, NC: McFarland, 1992.

Thomson, Bobby; Lee Heiman; and Bill Gutman. *The Giants Win the Pennant! The Giants Win the Pennant!* New York: Zebra Books, 1991.

Thorogood, George *(1952–)*

George Thorogood's gritty blues-rock music brought a classic sound and working-class consciousness to the 1980s pop scene. Beginning as a blues guitarist in the vein of slide players such as Elmore James and Hound Dog Taylor, Thorogood and his group, the Destroyers, crossed over to a pop-rock audience in 1978 with their cover of "Move It on Over" by singer-songwriter Hank Williams Sr. In 1982 he released his major-label debut, *Bad to the Bone,* and its title track remains his best-known single, due in large part to its repeated exposure on MTV and its frequent use on television and film soundtracks.

Though his two subsequent albums, *Maverick* (1985) and *Born to Be Bad* (1988), went gold, his audience began to shrink by the end of the decade. His only major success in the 1990s was the single "Haircut," a rebellion against authority figures who urged the song's protagonist to "get a haircut, and get a real job." He continues to tour and record. Since the late 1990s he has released a number of compilations, live albums, and studio projects including *2120 South Michigan Avenue* (2011).

Marc R. Sykes

SEE ALSO: *Blues; James, Elmore; MTV; Pop Music; Rock and Roll; Williams, Hank, Sr.*

BIBLIOGRAPHY

Stambler, Irwin. *Encyclopedia of Pop, Rock & Soul.* New York: St. Martin's Press, 1989.

Stanton, Scott. *The Tombstone Tourist: Musicians.* New York: Pocket Books, 2003.

Thorpe, Jim *(1888–1953)*

Few would argue that Jim Thorpe is one of the most accomplished American athletes of the entire twentieth century. His time in the National Football League (NFL) and his Professional Football Hall of Fame enshrinement attest to this fact. There, it is noted that he was an "All-America halfback at Carlisle [and] 1912 Olympic decathlon champion. . . . First big-name athlete to play pro football, signing with the pre-NFL Canton Bulldogs in 1915. . . . Named 'The Legend' on the all-time NFL team. . . . Voted top American athlete of first half of 20th century." Additionally, Thorpe won Olympic gold in both the decathlon and pentathlon. That his medals were ingloriously

Jim Thorpe. *Jim Thorpe competes in the U.S. Olympic trials in 1912. He went on to win gold medals in the pentathlon and decathlon that year at the Olympic Games in Stockholm, Sweden.* TOPICAL PRESS AGENCY/STRINGER/HULTON ARCHIVE/GETTY IMAGES.

stripped away because he had briefly played professional baseball is one of the less than honorable deeds of the International Olympic Committee.

EARLY LIFE

James Francis Thorpe, a Sac and Fox Indian, was born in the Oklahoma Territory. His Indian name was Wa-tho-biuck (or "Bright Path"), and he, his twin brother, mother, and rancher father resided in a one-room cabin near the small town of Bellemont. Young Jim was a natural athlete who loved and excelled in all sports. His early life, however, was laden with disappointment and tragedy. When he was eight, his brother was stricken with fever and subsequently passed away, and five years later his mother died. In 1904, at age sixteen, he headed east to Pennsylvania's Carlisle Indian School. His small size—he was 5 feet 5 inches tall and weighed 115 pounds—prevented him from finding a spot on the Carlisle varsity football team. This frustration, coupled with the death of his father, resulted in declining grades, alienation, and eventual sequestering in the Carlisle guardhouse.

By his late teens, Thorpe had grown 5 inches, adding bulk and muscle. Pop Warner, Carlisle's legendary coach, first took note of his track-and-field skills and eventually recruited him for the football team. After starting out as a kicker, he became the starting halfback during the 1908 season, and his athletic career began to blossom. During that season his running, punting, place-kicking, and occasional passing guided Carlisle to a 10–2–1 record; Walter Camp, America's reigning football expert, cited him as a third-team all-American.

After playing professional baseball in the Carolina League, Thorpe returned to Carlisle and solidified his legend as an all-time-great college gridiron star. In 1911 he was involved in most of Carlisle's offensive plays. His 50- and 60-yard punts soared through the sky. In the year's penultimate contest, an 18–15 victory over Harvard, he carried the ball on 40 percent of all plays and kicked four field goals. Carlisle ended the campaign with an 11–1 record; the following season, Thorpe added to his luster by leading Carlisle to a 12–1 mark. In both years Camp cited him as a first-team all-American.

THE OLYMPICS

Perhaps Thorpe's greatest triumph came in the 1912 Olympics, held in Stockholm. He was set to compete in two punishing events: the pentathlon, made up of five track-and-field competitions (javelin throw, discus throw, running broad jump, 200-meter dash, and 1,500-meter race), and the decathlon, consisting of ten events (javelin throw, discus throw, long jump, high jump, pole vault, shot-put, 400-meter run, 1,500-meter run, 100-meter dash, and 100-meter hurdles). He won gold medals in each, and King Gustav of Sweden proclaimed that Thorpe was the "greatest athlete in the world."

Thorpe returned to the United States a bona fide hero. But the cheering was to be short-lived. A journalist soon discovered that Thorpe had played professional baseball. Therefore, he could not be classified an amateur athlete; only amateurs could compete in the Olympics. In a letter to the Amateur Athletic Union, Thorpe wrote, "I did not play for the money . . . but because I like to play ball. I was not wise to the ways of the world and I did not realize this was wrong and that it would make me a professional in track sports."

Back when Thorpe was in his athletic prime, it was a common practice for college athletes to pass their summers playing pro ball to pick up a few extra bucks. They played under assumed names—so no one was the wiser—and they could retain their amateur status. Had Thorpe done so, his indiscretion would have remained a secret. When confronted with the accusation that he had played ball for money, he was honest enough to admit the truth. Nevertheless, he was divested of his medals by the International Olympic Committee. This dishonor is particularly ironic considering that today professionals with million-dollar salaries are allowed to compete for Olympic gold. For the "crime" of playing pro baseball, Thorpe pulled down a salary of $25 to $30 a week.

PROFESSIONAL CAREER

Thorpe was to be the Bo Jackson and Deion Sanders of his day, as he went on to play major-league baseball and pro football. His debut in the majors came in 1913, when he patrolled the outfield for the New York Giants. From then through 1919 he played in 289 games, mostly for the Giants, but with brief stints in Cincinnati, Ohio, and Boston. In 1915 Thorpe made his pro football debut with the Canton Bulldogs. Between 1915 and 1928 he played halfback for the Bulldogs (where he spent the bulk of his career), Cleveland Indians, Oorang Indians, Rock Island Independents, New York Giants, and Chicago Cardinals. In 1916 he was the Bulldogs' starting halfback and head coach, guiding his team to an undefeated season. In 1920 he became the first president of the American Professional Football Association, the precursor of the NFL.

Thorpe was forty when he retired from football. For the next two decades he held various menial jobs—often, ironically, working under an assumed name because of the humiliation. He toiled as a "B"-movie actor in Hollywood. He accepted public speaking engagements in which he would be garbed in Native American gear as he discussed athletics and the plight of the American Indian. During these hard times, he also became an alcoholic.

HONORS AND AWARDS

In January 1950 the Associated Press surveyed 391 sportswriters and broadcasters to determine the greatest athletes of the first half of the twentieth century. Thorpe was cited as the top football player and bested Babe Ruth as the finest all-around athlete. A year later his life story was told in the Hollywood movie *Jim Thorpe—All American*, with Burt Lancaster in the title role. Thorpe died in 1953, after suffering his third heart attack. The following year his remains were placed in a mausoleum in Mauch Chunk, a Pennsylvania town of 5,000 located at the foot of the Pocono Mountains, which was summarily renamed for Thorpe.

Since his death his honors have multiplied. In 1955 the NFL's Most Valuable Player trophy was named for Thorpe; the trophy awarded to college football's top defensive player also was named for him. In 1958 he was admitted into the National Indian Hall of Fame, and in 1961 he was chosen for the Pennsylvania Hall of Fame. By 1963 he had become a charter inductee in the Professional Football Hall of Fame—and, when arriving at the hall, located in Canton, Ohio, one is greeted by a statue of Thorpe. Most importantly, in 1982—twenty-nine years after his death—Juan Antonio Samaranch, the new president of the International Olympic Committee, reestablished Thorpe's amateur status. The following year his children were presented with replicas of his Olympic medals.

Rob Edelman

SEE ALSO: *College Football; Lancaster, Burt; Olympics; Professional Football.*

BIBLIOGRAPHY

Bruchac, Joseph. *Jim Thorpe, Original All-American*. New York: Penguin, 2008.

Nardo, Don. *The Importance of Jim Thorpe*. San Diego, CA: Lucent Books, 1994.

Newcombe, Jack. *The Best of the Athletic Boys: The White Man's Impact on Jim Thorpe*. Garden City, NY: Doubleday, 1975.

Schoor, Gene, and Henry Gilfond. *The Jim Thorpe Story: America's Greatest Athlete*. New York: Messner, 1951.

Wheeler, Robert W. *Jim Thorpe: World's Greatest Athlete*. Norman: University of Oklahoma Press, 1979.

The Three Caballeros

Produced with the newly formed Office of Inter-American Affairs, Walt Disney Studios' animated film *The Three Cabelleros* (1944) presented stellar technical achievements, blending live action and animation in color on a scale never before achieved and putting the film years ahead of its time. Rooted in the World War II era, the film was among a series of features, beginning with *Saludos Amigos* (1943), that attempted to celebrate diplomatic relations between the United States and Latin America by erasing stereotypical images of Latin American culture: the untrustworthy womanizing lover, or *guerillero*; his lascivious female counterpart; and the stupid and lazy *poncho*.

These films are also noted for being the first concerted effort to use animation as an instructional medium for popular audiences and to atone for what Eric Smoodin describes in the book *Animating Culture* (1993) as "the previous sins of Yankee cultural chauvinism." Yet what started out as lessons in geography evolved into fantastical depictions of, as Smoodin notes, "geographies animated by imagination and desire."

The Three Cabelleros actually reveals more about the culture and ideologies of the United States than of Mexico and Brazil, the featured countries. Latin America is presented to the star of the film, Donald Duck, as a series of birthday presents. The movie constructs a tourist-based representation of Latin America's peoples and culture; Latin America's exotic pleasures and fun are offered for the delight of North America. The film renders the people of Latin America, particularly the women, homogeneous. The diversity of racial types on the continent is not presented—rather, the women are "recognizably" Latin American. This portrayal is linked directly to the hypersexual image of Latin American women popularized by 1940s-era singer and actress Carmen Miranda, notably in the film's Carmen Molina dance sequence with phallic cacti. Though the effort to present a truer vision of Latin America is made obvious, *The Three Cabelleros* reveals an underlying set of messages of American imperialism and racism.

Frances Gateward

SEE ALSO: *Animated Films; Disney (Walt Disney Company); Miranda, Carmen.*

BIBLIOGRAPHY

Barrier, Michael. *The Animated Man: A Life of Walt Disney*. Berkeley: University of California Press, 2007.

Maltin, Leonard. *The Disney Films*. New York: Crown Publishers, 1984.

Maltin, Leonard. *Of Mice and Magic: A History of American Animated Cartoons*. New York: Plume Books, 1987.

Smoodin, Eric. *Animating Culture*. New Brunswick, NJ: Rutgers University Press, 1993.

3-D

SEE: *New 3-D; Stereoscopes.*

Three Investigators Series

The Three Investigators series, a forty-three-volume set of mysteries for juvenile readers published by Random House between 1964 and 1987, features three teenage male amateur sleuths: Jupiter Jones, Pete Crenshaw, and Bob Andrews. Jupiter, a former child actor, is the group's leader; Pete the impulsive athlete; and Bob the reserved, studious type. Although the sleuths are amateurs, they are portrayed handling themselves in a thoroughly professional manner, including offering business cards and maintaining scrupulous files in their office, a trailer hidden in a junkyard owned by Jupiter's aunt and uncle. The office has several secret entrances, including a tunnel that can be accessed through a loose board on the junkyard fence. The three investigators use modern equipment in their investigations, including the telephone and portable tape recorders.

Film director Alfred Hitchcock served as a consultant to the Three Investigators at the beginning and end of each story. After Hitchcock's death in 1980, the series stopped using his name as a character, replacing him with a fictitious film director, Hector Sebastian, for new titles and paperback reprints of the first thirty volumes. The early volumes (1–9 and 11) were written by Robert Arthur Jr. (1909–1969), who served as an editor for *Alfred Hitchcock Magazine*, the author of many screenplays for *Alfred Hitchcock Presents*, and the compiler of several short-story collections bearing the director's name. The title pages of the Three Investigators books identify the authors of each volume. Most of the authors wrote under pen names, such as William Arden for Dennis Lynds, Marc Brandel for Marcus Beresford, Nick West for Kin Platt, and M. V. Carey for Mary Virginia Carey.

The three investigators were too young to drive, and in the early books they were chauffeured around their native Rocky Beach (near Hollywood, California) in a gold-plated limousine whose services they had won in the first volume. In later books their chauffeur returned to help the boys during his time off. This transportation complication made the Three Investigators series more believable to readers who were just a few years younger and facing the same problems. Because of the more realistic adventures experienced by the trio, librarians preferred these books over the mass-market—and old-fashioned—Hardy Boys books.

After the publication of the earlier volumes, Random House issued a new series of Three Investigators Crimebusters stories, but they were discontinued after a little fewer than a dozen paperback volumes had been published. In these stories, written by some of the same writers as the original series, Jupe,

Pete, and Bob are old enough to drive and hold down part-time jobs. The Crimebusters series has a modern theme with more action and violence, erasing the innocence of the original series. The Three Investigators series has proven popular in Germany, and several new stories were written specifically for that market in a series known in translation as the "Three Question Marks." Some of these stories have been translated into English.

After many years of proposals and failed options, the three investigators were featured in two motion pictures by Studio Hamburg of Germany. The films used English-speaking actors and were dubbed in German for their domestic market. The actors were Chancellor Miller as Jupiter, Nick Price as Pete, and Cameron Monaghan as Bob. Although the films used titles from the original books and retained many familiar elements, they are new stories intended to appeal to modern audiences. The first film, *The Three Investigators and the Secret of Skeleton Island* (2007), was filmed and set in Cape Town, South Africa. The second, *The Three Investigators and the Secret of Terror Castle* (2009), was filmed in Cape Town to represent Rocky Beach, California, complete with the Jones Salvage Yard and the secret hideout office.

James D. Keeline

SEE ALSO: *Best Sellers; The Hardy Boys; Hitchcock, Alfred; Hollywood.*

BIBLIOGRAPHY

"Juvenile and Young-Adult Mystery Fiction." In *Critical Survey of Mystery and Detective Fiction*, rev. ed., ed. Carl Rollyson. Pasadena, CA: Salem Press, 2008: 2067–2074.

T3I Readers' Site, accessed October 17, 2012. Available from http://3investigators.homestead.com/files/t3ihome.htm

The Three Stooges

Although they spent more than three decades making films, it was television that turned the Three Stooges into one of the most recognizable and beloved comedy teams in the world. Specializing in unsophisticated, violent slapstick, the Three Stooges slapped, poked, and generally abused each other in more than 200 short films between 1934 and 1958, when their shorts were released to television, to the delight of young baby boomers. By 2010 almost all of the Stooges' films had been issued in DVD format, once again bringing the comic trio to a whole new generation.

THE VAUDEVILLE YEARS

Formed in vaudeville in 1923, the team's original members were Moe Howard (born June 19, 1897, as Moses Horwitz; died May 4, 1975) and his brother Shemp (born March 17, 1895, as Samuel Horwitz; died November 23, 1955), who acted as sidekicks to their boyhood friend, comedian Ted Healy. In its early years the act was billed as "Ted Healy and His Stooges" and sometimes "The Racketeers." While various "stooges" moved

The Three Stooges. *The Three Stooges, from left, Larry Fine, Moe Howard, and Curly Howard, brought their brand of slapstick comedy to over 200 short films between 1934 and 1958.* NEW YORK DAILY NEWS ARCHIVE/CONTRIBUTOR/GETTY IMAGES.

in and out of the act, each virtually interchangeable with another, the addition of Larry Fine (born October 5, 1902, as Louis Feinberg; died January 24, 1975) in 1925 rounded out the troupe. For the next several years Healy's Racketeers were Moe, Larry, Shemp, and Fred Sanborn (1899–1961). Although there was very little that was innovative about the team's act—the physical comedy they performed was borrowed from old vaudeville slapstick—their success in vaudeville led them to Broadway in the late 1920s and to film in 1930, where this lineup supported Healy in the feature film *Soup to Nuts*. Although the film was not a hit, the Stooges found a warm audience.

In the meantime, a rift had grown between Healy and his players, as the trio of Moe, Larry and Shemp resented the pay inequity—they earned only one-tenth what Healy earned weekly. Such financial disagreements were exacerbated by Healy's problems with alcohol, which were worsening. The Stooges left Healy when he nixed a contract offered to them by Fox (to perform without Healy), striking out on their own as "Howard, Fine and Howard" while Healy hired new stooges to do the old act. Although Healy managed to convince Moe and Larry to return, Shemp left the act to pursue a career in feature films and was replaced by his younger brother Jerry (born October 1903 as Jerome Lester Horwitz; died January 18, 1952), who shaved his head and soon emerged as Curly, the most popular stooge. Signed to a one-year contract with Metro-Goldwyn-Mayer (MGM) studios in 1933, the Stooges appeared in feature films including *Meet the Baron*, *Dancing Lady* (with Joan Crawford), *Fugitive Lovers*, and *Hollywood Party*. But it was short films such as *Plane Nuts* (also 1933) that allowed them to reproduce their vaudeville act. When their contract was up, Healy stayed with MGM, while the Three Stooges went on as a trio, signing a deal with Columbia in 1934 for a series of two-reel comedies—a commitment that would end up lasting twenty-four years.

TAKING THE ACT TO HOLLYWOOD

It was during the early Columbia years that Moe, Larry, and Curly developed into recognizable characters, with hairstyles that scarcely changed over the decades: Moe's thick black mop with its evenly cut bangs was as much a fixture of the act as the two large tufts of curly hair that protruded from Larry's balding head and Curly's cue-ball dome. Moe assumed Healy's role as the leader (off camera as well as on), slapping, poking, or punching the childlike Curly or the hapless Larry. However, it was the bald and portly Curly who usually stole the show, delighting audiences with his masterful body language, which he exercised with his feet as much as his hands, sometimes dancing or spinning on the floor. Curly's high-pitched voice was also used to great effect by singing; barking; and, most of all, wisecracking—and his occasional defiance of the bossy Moe almost always resulted in more abuse.

The films generally followed a standard plot, which of course was merely a vehicle for their slapstick set pieces and verbal gags. In most films, the group would take on occupations such as plumbers, waiters, doctors, salesmen, soldiers, or businessmen, where they would proceed to make a mess of the situation. Although the tiniest disagreements would usually result in an exchange of slaps, pokes, and insults—a formula that was usually repeated several times in each film—in the end Moe, Larry, and Curly always stuck together in their efforts to resolve whatever problem they faced.

Working under directors such as Edward Bernds, Charlie Chase, Del Lord, and Jules White, the Stooges didn't write their own scripts, but their ad-libbing frequently survived the films' final cut. Highlights of their early years with Columbia include their World War II parodies of Adolf Hitler in *You Nazty Spy* (1940) and *I'll Never Say Heil Again* (1941). Such performances had personal resonance because of the Stooges' Jewish background but were nevertheless enhanced by Moe's striking transformation into the German füehrer. Although the trio appeared in occasional feature films, including *Start Cheering* (1938), *Time Out for Rhythm* (1941), and *Swing Parade* (1946), short subjects remained the principal format for their films.

With his health steadily deteriorating, Curly suffered a stroke while on the set of *Half-Wit's Holiday* in May 1946 and was forced to retire from the act. His brother Shemp returned from a solo career as a character comedian and rejoined the group. Although it was difficult to fill the shoes of the trio's most popular member, Shemp helped to sustain the group's success for the next decade, until his unexpected death in November 1955. Despite the loss of another brother, Moe chose to continue the act, with onetime burlesque star Joe Besser replacing Shemp. The Three Stooges had starred in Columbia's top-grossing short-subject series for many years, but the era of short-subject films was coming to a close by the early 1950s. With most major studios having phased out two-reelers, the Stooges' career with Columbia ended in 1958 when the studio closed its short-subjects department.

A NEW MEDIUM

Just as the act seemed on the verge of retiring, a new generation discovered a quarter century of face-slapping, nose-tweaking, eye-poking comedy with the release of seventy-eight Columbia shorts (featuring Curly) to television. Capitalizing on their renewed popularity, the group formed their own company, Comedy III Productions, and carried on making numerous personal appearances (which had always been their most lucrative source of income) and launching a line of merchandise and comic books. Meanwhile, by 1958 Joe Besser had been replaced by Joe DeRita, who became known as "Curly Joe," and the trio ventured into a series of feature films aimed primarily at children, including *Have Rocket, Will Travel* (1959), *Snow White and the Three Stooges* (1961), *The Three Stooges Meet Hercules* (1962), *The Three Stooges in Orbit* (1962), and *The Outlaws Is Coming* (1965). In 1965 the group produced live-action wraparounds for a series of five-minute animated cartoons.

The impact of the Three Stooges' comeback in the late 1950s and 1960s was part of a general renewal of interest in slapstick comedy. During this period many of the works of the Marx Brothers and Laurel and Hardy and the silent films of Charlie Chaplin were revived and found new television audiences. On the big screen, the success of high-budget feature films such as *It's a Mad, Mad, Mad, Mad World* (1963), *Those Magnificent Men in Their Flying Machines* (1965), and *The Great Race* (1965) was probably due in no small part to the Three Stooges' role in the renaissance of physical comedy. Long after the Three Stooges' demise, homage continued to be paid to Curly's antics, such as in cartoons like "Jabberjaw" in the 1970s.

Although they had retired by the end of the 1960s, the Three Stooges' popularity continued to grow in succeeding decades, weathering criticism from parents concerned with the group's excessive violence and from feminists offended by the Stooges' objectification of women. Though the Stooges themselves were gone, their production company, now changed from Comedy III to C3 Entertainment, continued to promote the Three Stooges brand in commercials and merchandise from T-shirts to computer screensavers. Over almost seven decades of national popularity, that brand had become so recognizable that millions of people in countries all over the world instantly understand the meaning of comparing local politicians to the Three Stooges. Even words from their act, such as "Soitenly!" and "Nyuk, nyuk," have remained part of the popular lexicon into the twenty-first century.

In 2000 ABC broadcast a film biography of the Stooges' rise to comic fame. Directed by James Frawley, the film starred Evan Handler, Paul Ben-Victor, and Michael Chiklis as Larry, Moe, and Curly. In 2008, having become famous in film, television, and DVD, the trio took their place in yet another media when Famous Frames Mobile Interactive made a deal with C3 to release five vintage Stooges shorts for play on digital devices such as smartphones and tablets. Around the same time, Peter and Bobby Farrelly began working on a new Three Stooges film; not a biopic this time, but a feature-length comedy showcasing the Three Stooges characters in a modern setting. After many problems in finding the right cast and production company, the film, titled simply *The Three Stooges*, opened in April 2012, with Sean Hayes, Chris Diamantopolos, and Will Sasso in the lead roles. The Farrelly brothers reasoned that the difficult economic times of the 2010s might, like the Depression and war years that gave birth to the Three Stooges, call for a little madcap humor.

Kevin O'Connor

SEE ALSO: *Chaplin, Charlie; Comic Books; Crawford, Joan; Feminism; Laurel and Hardy; The Marx Brothers; MGM (Metro-Goldwyn-Mayer); Screwball Comedies; Smartphones; Stand-Up Comedy; Television; Vaudeville; World War II.*

BIBLIOGRAPHY

Atkinson, Claire. "Why I Oughta . . . The Licensing Division behind One of the World's Most Beloved Brands." *Retail Merchandiser* 50, no. 4 (2010): 60.

Besser, Joe; Jeff Lenburg; and Greg Lenburg. *Not Just a Stooge.* Orange, CA: Excelsior Books, 1984.

Feinberg, Morris. *My Brother Larry: The Stooge in the Middle.* San Francisco: Last Gasp of San Francisco, 1984.

Hansen, Tom, and Jeffrey Forrester. *Stoogemania.* Chicago: Contemporary Books, 1984.

Howard, Moe. *Moe Howard and the Three Stooges.* Secaucus, NJ: Citadel Press, 1977.

Kurson, Robert, *The Official Three Stooges Encyclopedia: The Ultimate Knucklehead's Guide to Stoogedom.* Lincolnwood, IL: Contemporary Books, 1998.

Maurer, Joan Howard. *Curly: An Illustrated Biography of the Superstooge.* Secaucus, NJ: Citadel Press, 1985.

Scordato, Mark. *The Three Stooges.* New York: Chelsea House, 1995.

Seely, Peter, and Gail W. Pieper. *Stoogeology: Essays on the Three Stooges.* Jefferson, NC: McFarland, 2007.

Three's Company

Three's Company was the definitive mindless television sex comedy, speaking to a generation willing to escape from reality while sitting in front of the TV. Running on ABC from 1977 to 1984, the show reflected the swinging needs of the viewers and was the vehicle through which a major Hollywood blackballing took place.

Three's Company starred John Ritter as the pratfalling chef Jack Tripper; Joyce DeWitt as the sensible florist Janet Wood; and Suzanne Somers as the prototypical dumb, blond secretary (and minister's daughter) Chrissy (full name: Christmas) Snow. As the series opens, Janet and Chrissy need a third roommate for their Santa Monica, California, apartment. The morning after the going-away party for their last roommate, they find a man sleeping in their bathtub, and upon learning that he can cook, they let him move in. Nothing sexual ever goes on between the roommates, but not for Jack's lack of leering. While he is hitting on anything in a skirt, he has to pretend to be gay so that the landlord will allow the living arrangement, which was still a new idea in the 1970s.

Usually joining the trio at the local hangout, the Regal Beagle, is Jack's sleazy best friend Larry Dallas (Richard Kline). The landlords are impotent Stanley and sex-starved Helen Roper, played by Norman Fell (who also played an uptight landlord in the movie *The Graduate*) and Audra Lindley. Jack often has to distract Mr. Roper by coming on to him and disgusting him until he leaves; though it was never given a name, Jack's faux homosexuality manifests itself in limp wrists, simpering, and hissing. After the Ropers were spun off in 1979, Jack, Janet, and Chrissy's new landlord became Ralph Furley, a leisure-suited nebbish played by Don Knotts.

Three's Company was chock-full of pratfalls (Ritter's forte), double entendres, and misunderstandings. In a typical episode Jack gives a woman cooking lessons, but a roommate thinks he is giving "love lessons." The show became hugely popular and was featured on the cover of *Newsweek* in February 1978, with a staged shot of Somers with her lingerie falling off and Ritter leering over her shoulder, something that never happened on the show. Even the theme song (" . . . where the kisses are hers and hers and his . . . ") implied sex where there was none.

Three's Company made a celebrity out of the buxom Somers, who got her big break with a few seconds of screen time in George Lucas's *American Graffiti*, along with half a dozen other actors. In the summer of 1980, Somers asked her *Three's Company* producers for a share of the profits and a fivefold salary increase, from $30,000 to $150,000 per episode. The producers did not accept her request, and, making an example of her, held her to her contract for a final year. During the 1980–1981 season Somers appeared only in one-minute inserts at the end of each show, featuring Chrissy talking on the phone to one of the characters; it is explained on the show that Chrissy is tending to her sick mother in Fresno. The inserts were taped separately on a closed set. Soon Chrissy was written out of the show, and Somers found it hard to obtain a job in Hollywood.

Somers's first replacement, in the fall of 1980, was Chrissy's cousin, the blond and clumsy Cindy Snow (Jennilee Harrison). After a year Cindy moves out to go to school at the University of California at Los Angeles (UCLA) but still stops by on occasion. In the fall of 1981 lanky nurse Terri Alden (Priscilla Barnes) moves in. In 1984 Janet gets married; Terri moves to Hawaii; and Jack meets his true love, Vicky Bradford. Jack and Vicky spun off into *Three's a Crowd* (1985–1986), where they live together (Vicky does not believe in marriage) above Jack's restaurant. Jack's foil this time is Vicky's disapproving father, who also owns the building.

Most of the show's stars became indelibly associated with their roles (with the exception of Knotts, who will always be remembered as Barney Fife in *The Andy Griffith Show*). Somers did make a comeback, mostly by continuing to look good as she aged, which she owed to a product she will be forever associated with, the Thighmaster (and later, the Buttmaster). Besides exercise books and videos, she also wrote and spoke out about surviving abuse. Ritter died in 2003 at age 54, while starring in the hit TV sitcom *8 Simple Rules.*

Karen Lurie

SEE ALSO: American Graffiti*;* The Andy Griffith Show*;* The Graduate*; Hollywood; Sitcom; Television.*

BIBLIOGRAPHY

Brooks, Tim, and Earle Marsh. *The Complete Directory to Prime Time Network and Cable TV Shows 1946–Present*, 6th ed. New York: Ballantine Books, 1995.

Hamrick, Craig. *The TV Tidbits Classic Television Trivia Quiz Book*. New York: iUniverse, 2004.

McNeil, Alex. *Total Television*. New York: Penguin, 1996.

Somers, Suzanne. *After the Fall: How I Picked Myself Up, Dusted Myself Off, and Started All over Again*. New York: Crown Publishing, 1998.

Thurber, James *(1894–1961)*

Ohio-born satirical writer James Thurber was most noted for his ability to illustrate, through the use of humor, the frailties of human beings in a world seemingly dominated by forces of their own making. His primary media, the short story and his famous pen-and-ink cartoon sketches, have served as models for later critics and observers of the social scene who write in a casual style reminiscent of the *New Yorker*, which began publication in the 1920s and for which Thurber was a regular contributor. Much of his work, including his writings and drawings of animals, especially dogs, and the unforgettable Walter Mitty have become permanent fixtures in American literary folklore.

Thurber was born in Columbus in 1894, during a time when the United States was experiencing great change due to the forces of industrial development: explosive urban growth, immigration, labor upheavals, and the dizzying pace of technological advancement. All of these influenced Thurber's work. Thurber's poor eyesight—as a child his brother William accidentally shot him in the eye with a bow and arrow—prevented him from enjoying an active childhood and later in life rendered him legally blind. After a difficult start at Ohio State University, Thurber found his stride as editor of the school newspaper and literary magazine. While in college, he befriended future playwright and film director Elliott Nugent, with whom he would collaborate in New York in later years.

Thurber's writing career foundered from the start. He accepted a job as a reporter for the *Columbus Dispatch* after World War I, moved to Europe in the 1920s to write for overseas newspapers, then returned to the United States and wrote for the *New York Evening Post*. While living in New York, Thurber met author E. B. White, who introduced him to the editors of the *New Yorker*, a new magazine that hoped to capitalize on the Roaring Twenties image of the city by developing a smart, lighthearted, and slightly irreverent literary style. Thurber was hired as an associate editor, and then later managed to get himself "demoted" to a contributing author. The marriage of the *New Yorker* and Thurber was fortuitous: his articles and sketches graced the pages of the magazine for years to come and helped set the overall tone for the publication. Thurber and White collaborated on the 1929 best-selling book *Is Sex Necessary?*—a spoof on the sex-psychology books popular during the 1920s.

Thurber's use of humor to point out human shortcomings took several forms. His cartoons often depicted people struggling with the trials and tribulations of everyday life, especially in the face of modern technology that often made things more, rather than less, troublesome. Thurber believed that humans often unnecessarily complicated their lives through an excess of "abstract reasoning" instead of being practical. Thus, he always portrayed animals in a sympathetic light, commending their reliance on instinctive wisdom instead of the fuzzy reasoning of humans. Males were especially targeted for ridicule by Thurber; his cartoons often included spineless husbands being berated by their domineering and opinionated wives. In "The Secret Life of Walter Mitty," (1939) Thurber's most famous *New Yorker* story,

James Thurber. *James Thurber's cartoons, articles, and stories for the* New Yorker *magazine beginning in the 1920s brought him widespread fame.* KURT HUTTON/STRINGER/PICTURE POST/GETTY IMAGES.

he created a title character who escaped his meager, workaday world by becoming a larger-than-life hero in his daydreams, a gentle symbol of humanity's loss of direction and purpose in modern times. Thurber's work also found its way to the stage, as in *The Male Animal* (1940), a Broadway collaboration with Nugent, and *A Thurber Carnival* (1960), an off-Broadway revue in which Thurber himself performed.

Beset with alcoholism, rage, and blindness, Thurber's last years were not happy ones for him or his friends, and his personal problems were reflected in his creative output. In a piece for the *New York Times Book Review*, John Updike commented, "The writer who had produced *Fables for Our Time* and *The Last Flower* out of the thirties had become, by the end of the fifties, one more indignant senior citizen penning complaints about the universal decay of virtue." Still, Thurber is considered one of the twentieth century's most prominent humorous writers, with works that took many forms over the span of his career, including novels, short stories, articles, and sketches—almost all of them containing a strain of melancholia that is distinctly modern in style. A quotation from one of his many fables perhaps best describes Thurber's attitude: a dinosaur, talking to a human, remarked, "There are worse things than being extinct, and one of them is being you." Thurber was not a hater of humankind; he was a modernist who saw the limitations of man in a conspicuously optimistic age.

Jeffrey W. Coker

SEE ALSO: *Best Sellers; Broadway; The* New Yorker*; Updike, John; White, E. B..*

BIBLIOGRAPHY

Holmes, Charles S. *The Clocks of Columbus: The Literary Career of James Thurber*. New York: Atheneum Books, 1972.

Thurber, James. *Thurber's Dogs*. New York: Simon & Schuster, 1955.

Thurber, James. *A Thurber Carnival*. New York: Samuel French, 1962.

Thurber, James. *Vintage Thurber*, 2 vols. London: Hamish Hamilton, 1963.

Thurber, James. *My Life and Hard Times*. New York: HarperCollins, 1999.

Tierney, Gene *(1920–1991)*

After debuting as a teenage model and budding stage actress, Gene Tierney soon metamorphosed into one of Hollywood's most recognizable movie stars of the 1940s and 1950s. Her reputation relied on the promotion of her distinctive looks and physical elegance. Twentieth Century Fox founder Darryl F. Zanuck famously proclaimed her "unquestionably the most beautiful woman in movie history." With high cheekbones and unusually shaped eyes, Tierney, a New Yorker, was considered "exotic."

Studios cast Tierney in films that highlighted her mystique, such as *The Shanghai Gesture* (1941) and *The Egyptian* (1954). In seeming contradiction with her inscrutable features, Tierney's image also reflected her Swiss finishing-school poise and sophistication, garnering her the cosmopolitan title role in the film noir classic *Laura* (1944) and that of the love-obsessed femme fatale of *Leave Her to Heaven* (1945). Offscreen, Tierney's life embraced another incongruity. The popular star suffered well-publicized misfortunes and subsequent breakdowns, and her aura of graceful beauty came to signify tragedy.

Elizabeth Haas

SEE ALSO: *Film Noir; Hollywood;* Laura*; Movie Stars; Preminger, Otto; Zanuck, Darryl F.*

BIBLIOGRAPHY

Ellrod, J. G. *The Stars of Hollywood Remembered: Career Biographies of 82 Actors and Actresses of the Golden Era, 1920s–1950s*. Jefferson, NC: McFarland, 1997.

Lambert, Gavin. "Gene Tierney: Beverly Hills Backdrop for the Enigmatic Star of *Laura*." *Architectural Digest*, April 1992.

Tierney, Gene, and Mickey Herskowitz. *Self-Portrait*. New York: Wyden Books, 1979.

Vogel, Michelle. *Gene Tierney: A Biography*. Jefferson, NC: McFarland, 2005.

Tiffany & Company

Tiffany, a name long synonymous with elegance and style, owes its luster to the New York firm founded in 1837 by Charles Lewis Tiffany, which, since becoming Tiffany & Company in 1853, has provided the well-to-do with exquisitely crafted jewelry and home furnishings. Louis Comfort Tiffany, a brilliant and famous glass designer, founded Tiffany Studios in 1900 and succeeded his father as head of Tiffany & Company.

Tiffany's place in America's popular imagination was given a boost by Truman Capote's 1958 novel *Breakfast at Tiffany's* and the 1961 film of the same title, in which Audrey Hepburn as Holly Golightly accepts from her admirer a Tiffany-engraved toy Cracker Jack ring. No doubt the popularity of the girls' name Tiffany in the last decades of the twentieth century owes much to its associations with the beautiful creations of Tiffany & Company. In 2012, its 175th anniversary year, Tiffany was still thriving. The company reported that its worldwide sales for the previous fiscal year had been $3.6 billion.

Craig Bunch

SEE ALSO: Breakfast at Tiffany's*; Capote, Truman; Consumerism; Hepburn, Audrey.*

BIBLIOGRAPHY

Loring, John. *Tiffany's 150 Years*. Garden City, NY: Doubleday, 1987.

Loring, John. *Tiffany's 20th Century: A Portrait of American Style*. New York: Abrams, 1997.

Loring, John. *Tiffany Style: 170 Years of Design*. New York: Abrams, 2008.

Tijuana Bibles

It is surely no accident that illicit pornographic comic books, popularly known as Tijuana Bibles, thrived during the heyday of media censorship in modern America, roughly the mid-1920s to the mid-1950s. In the early decades of the twentieth century, movies, comic strips, and pulp magazines all had ample room for the naughty and risqué, but by the 1920s the pressures of social respectability were increasingly hemming in popular culture. The acceptance of the stringent Hays Code by Hollywood in 1934 was a significant turning point in this larger trend. Like girlie magazines and stag movies, Tijuana Bibles represented an escape from the Puritanism of mainstream culture. As the cartoonist Harvey Kurtzman, creator of *MAD Magazine*, once noted, "The obvious repression of sexual fantasy in [mainstream comic strips] brought its release in the little dirty books, or Tijuana Bibles."

Almost as ephemeral as washroom graffiti, Tijuana Bibles were anonymous in every sense imaginable. For the most part, no one knows who wrote them, who drew them, or who published them. The name *Tijuana Bible* plays off the fictitious foreign addresses that were given as the place of publication. In addition to erotic and exotic Mexico, Tijuana Bibles were said to be produced in Cuba and possibly in England and Canada as well. Some suggested that organized crime was behind these tawdry sex books. Cartoonist Will Eisner, best known for creating the masked crime fighter the Spirit, has frequently recounted the story of how, as a struggling artist in the 1930s, he was approached by a gangster who wanted him to draw Tijuana Bibles.

Despite their obscure origin, almost 1,000 separate Tijuana Bibles were published and managed to circulate throughout North America. "The distribution system was mysterious, but it worked," commented Kurtzman. comic-book historian Donald Gilmore, in the first scholarly study of the genre, notes that Tijuana Bibles were "conceived in dark attics, published in dingy garages on unnamed alleys, and distributed from the hip pockets of vendors across the nation . . . [but] accounted for a multi-million-dollar business in the tight economy of the Great Depression."

The earliest Tijuana Bibles of the 1920s and 1930s were comic strip parodies. Often deftly done imitations, these books featured such stars of the funny pages as Betty Boop, Popeye, Olive Oyl, Mickey Mouse, and Dick Tracy all engaging in activities forbidden in family newspapers. In positing a secret sex life for popular cultural icons, Tijuana Bibles both influenced and anticipated the work of such later cartoonists as Kurtzman, whose *Little Annie Fanny* started running in *Playboy* in the 1960s. The work of such 1960s countercultural cartoonists as Robert Crumb and S. Clay Wilson—who drew Disney-esque animals with earthly human appetites—also shows the influence of Tijuana Bibles.

By the early 1930s Tijuana Bibles had expanded from their origins as cartoon parodies and started featuring Hollywood celebrities such as Laurel and Hardy, Mae West, the Marx Brothers, and Clark Gable. These Tijuana Bibles played off the rumors of "Hollywood Babylon" that flourished in the tabloid press. Hollywood was shown as a happy playground of orgies and bisexuality. Noting the large number of strips featuring celebrities, cartoonist Art Spiegelman notes in *Tijuana Bibles: Art and Wit in America's Forbidden Funnies, 1930s–1950s* that Tijuana Bibles "were not overtly political but were by their nature anti-authoritarian, a protest against what [Sigmund] Freud called Civilization and Its Discontents. Here was a populist way to rebel against the mass media and advertising designed to titillate and manipulate, but never satisfy."

Some Tijuana Bibles were more explicitly political in one way: they featured such world figures as Adolf Hitler, Benito Mussolini, Joseph Stalin, Chiang Kai-shek, and even Whittaker Chambers (a Cold War spy who, a recent biography confirms, was a bisexual, just as he was portrayed in a Tijuana Bible from the late 1940s). As with the Hollywood strips, the politics of these Tijuana Bibles was implicitly antiauthoritarian, ridiculing the powerful by showing that they had base needs. Of course there was a limit to how subversive Tijuana Bibles could be. The main goal was to titillate, and the strips replicated the racial and ethnic stereotypes found in mainstream culture.

Artistically the quality of Tijuana Bibles varied greatly. Two talented cartoonists, "Doc" Rankin and Wesley Morse, have been identified and singled out by aficionados of the genre. In *Tijuana Bibles*, Bob Adelman praises Rankin's "graceful, articulate, Deco style" and Morse's "wonderful graphic flair." (Morse later went on to do *Bazooka Joe* comics.) Only a few other Tijuana Bible cartoonists, all of them anonymous, were as good as Rankin and Morse. The worst Tijuana Bibles were also among the worst comic books ever done: crudely drawn, illiterate, and mean-spirited.

With the decline of censorship in the mid-1950s, signaled by the emergence of *Playboy* in 1955, Tijuana Bibles lost their reason to exist. However, as with other trashy and throwaway bits of the past, Tijuana Bibles continue to have a nostalgic appeal. In the mid-1970s, novelist John Updike wrote that the type of pornography he "most missed" was "Popeye, Olive Oyl, and Wimpy fellating and gamahuching one another, in comic books circulating in southern Pennsylvania in the late 1940s." Not surprisingly, books reprinting Tijuana Bibles continue to roll off the presses.

Jeet Heer

SEE ALSO: *Bazooka Joe; Betty Boop; Cold War; Comic Books; Comics; Crumb, Robert; Disney (Walt Disney Company); Eisner, Will; Freud, Sigmund; The Great Depression; Hollywood; Laurel and Hardy;* MAD Magazine*; The Marx Brothers;* Playboy*; Pornography; Pulp Magazines; Tabloids; Updike, John; West, Mae.*

BIBLIOGRAPHY

Adelman, Bob; Art Spiegelman, Richard Merkin; et al. *Tijuana Bibles: Art and Wit in America's Forbidden Funnies, 1930s–1950s*. New York: Simon & Schuster, 1997.

Gilmore, Donald H. *Sex in Comics: A History of the Eight Pagers*. San Diego, CA: Greenleaf Classics, 1971.

Slade, Joseph W. *Pornography and Sexual Representation: A Reference Guide*. Westport, CT: Greenwood Press, 2001.

Timberlake, Justin *(1981–)*

Justin Timberlake first found fame as a member of the boy band *NSYNC. Unlike many of his bandmates and peers, however, he went on to become one of the most recognized and successful pop singer-songwriters of the early twenty-first century. He has also become known as an actor, a dancer, a record producer, an entrepreneur, and a philanthropist. His success in these various arenas has been both financial and critical. As of 2011 he had won four Emmys and six Grammy Awards.

Timberlake was born on January 31, 1981, in Memphis, Tennessee, and the city's eclectic music scene made a big impression on him as a child. Following early performances in his church choir, Timberlake won a charm pageant and sang at the Grand Ole Opry. He gained a foothold on the national stage when he competed on, but did not win, *Star Search* at the age of eleven. He soon joined the cast of Disney's *The All New Mickey Mouse Club*, where he met his future girlfriend Britney Spears; his future bandmate J. C. Chasez; and the future stars Christina Aguilera, Ryan Gosling, and Keri Russell. Between Mouseketeer skits and musical numbers, he adapted to the limelight.

At the age of fourteen, Timberlake and Chasez were recruited by music mogul Lou Pearlman to join the boy band *NSYNC. After the rise and fall of New Kids on the Block in the late 1980s and early 1990s, the teen-pop craze was resurgent, with the Pearlman-assembled Backstreet Boys leading the way. *NSYNC was designed to mimic Backstreet's success. The plan worked. *NSYNC's second album, *No Strings Attached* (2000), sold more than fourteen million copies, and Timberlake (known to his teen fans as JT) was the group's most recognizable member. The recognition was due in part to tabloid coverage of his relationship with, and break from, fellow teen superstar Spears.

*NSYNC's success owed much to Timberlake's strong work ethic as a songwriter and to his trademark falsetto. After the group's third album in 2001, JT struck out on his own. His first solo album, *Justified* (2002), sold more than seven million copies, won a Grammy for "Cry Me a River," and featured the hit single "Rock Your Body." After assisting with the Black Eyed Peas' hit "Where Is the Love?" he was again a tabloid darling. Then, during the halftime show of the 2004 Super Bowl, Timberlake's hand caused a "wardrobe malfunction" that flashed Janet Jackson's breast on live TV. Though many pundits doubted that the "malfunction" was truly an accident, the controversy quickly fizzled and Timberlake's success continued uninterrupted. His next album, *FutureSex/LoveSounds* (2006), broke the charts with "SexyBack" and won four Grammy Awards, thanks in part to a collaboration with the recording gurus Timbaland and Rick Rubin.

Between 2006 and 2012, Timberlake became one of the most sought-after actors in Hollywood, first by earning critical acclaim for parts in the 2006 films *Alpha Dog*, *Southland Tales*, and *Black Snake Moan*. The blockbuster *The Social Network* (2010) featured Timberlake playing Napster cofounder Sean Parker. Reviewer Mike Schulz wrote that Timberlake's acting showed "such dynamic energy and reptilian charm that he threatens to walk off with the picture." As a flood of dramatic and comedic roles opened up to him, Timberlake starred in the sci-fi drama *In Time* (2011), playing a man revolting against a tyrannical economic/time system. He contributed the voice of Boo Boo in *Yogi Bear* (2010), played the preppy target of affections in *Bad Teacher* (2011), and was the "friend" of Mila Kunis in *Friends with Benefits* (2011).

Especially memorable among his many TV appearances were his stints hosting *Saturday Night Live* (*SNL*) in 2003, 2006, 2009, and 2011. On two of those occasions, he pulled double duty as musical guest and host. His skits often placed him in self-effacing situations, emasculating costumes (tutu included), and sexually charged boy-band farce, most notably with the Emmy Award–winning (and viral YouTube hit) music video "Dick in a Box," co-created with *SNL* regular Andy Samberg and others. He concocted additional comedic magic in "history of rap" sequences for *Late Night with Jimmy Fallon*. In addition to performing, Timberlake has led the music label Tennman Records and invested in restaurants, the William Rast fashion label, and the networking site Myspace. His philanthropic interests range widely, including a number of celebrity golf tournaments that raise money for various causes in Tennessee.

Timberlake's appeal comes from serious talent and hard work as much as it does from limelight-cradled charisma, sex appeal, and the wielding of a falsetto that drives teenage fans into shrieking fits. Not only does his stage presence command attention, but he also appears genuinely at ease in any public situation, unlike so many other performers who barely conceal either stilted nerves or an insecure craving for approval when placed in unfamiliar situations. High-profile romance has also been a factor in Timberlake's fame, including entanglements with Spears, Cameron Diaz, Alyssa Milano, Scarlett Johansson, and Jessica Biel. Some infamous breakups notwithstanding, Timberlake is generally seen as a gentleman who entices but also warms hearts.

Stephen P. Davis

SEE ALSO: *Aguilera, Christina; Boy Bands; Emmy Awards; Grammy Awards;* Grand Ole Opry*; Hollywood; Jackson, Janet;* The Mickey Mouse Club*; Napster; The New Kids on the Block; Pop Music;* Saturday Night Live*; Spears, Britney; Super Bowl; YouTube.*

BIBLIOGRAPHY

Smith, Sean. *Justin: The Unauthorized Biography*. New York: Gallery Books, 2005.

Steinberg, Jacques. "Censored *SNL* Sketch Jumps Bleepless onto the Internet." *New York Times*, December 21, 2006.

Time

Published weekly without interruption since March 3, 1923, *Time* magazine was a new genre of publication that appeared in the United States after World War I and spawned many imitators at home and abroad. *Time* was the first mass-circulation magazine to offer a weekly digest of current events and commentary organized into departments and written in a breezy, idiosyncratic style. As the inaugural publication of a company that would become a publishing empire, *Time* quickly established itself as a "lengthened shadow" of one of its founders, who maintained close control over its content and used it to shape public opinion.

In its early issues *Time* contained conservative, Republican-oriented content, publishing highly favorable coverage of the presidential aspirations of Republicans Herbert Hoover, Wendell Willkie, and Dwight D. Eisenhower. Opinions expressed in the magazine were frequently at odds with those of Democratic president Franklin D. Roosevelt, even though founder Henry R. Luce gave his wholehearted support to the administration in the interest of national unity during World War II. *Time* was, however, one of the earliest and most vocal critics of the right-wing tactics of Senator Joseph McCarthy in the 1950s. In the early twenty-first century *Time* continued to maintain an important role as a leading American newsweekly, presenting the news objectively without any particular political emphasis.

In 1922 two friends, Henry R. Luce and Briton Hadden, founded *Time*. Luce was born and raised in China, the son of a Presbyterian missionary and the grandson of a Scranton, Pennsylvania, grocer. Hadden was a native of Brooklyn, New York, the son of a stockbroker and the grandson of a bank president. The two were schoolmates at the Hotchkiss School, and then they served together in a military-reserve unit during World War I. After the war, both attended Yale University, graduating in 1920. Luce won Yale's DeForest Prize for a speech he gave his senior year that was imbued with idealism and advocated American benevolent hegemony as "the great friend of the lame, the halt and the blind among nations, the comrade of all nations that struggle to rise to higher planes of social and political organization."

CONDENSED NEWS

It was while working together as reporters for *Baltimore News* in 1922 that Luce and Hadden hatched plans for a weekly magazine, which they originally wanted to call *Facts*. Earlier, while working briefly as a reporter for the *New York World*, Luce had proposed to Hadden an idea "for a magazine that comes out every Friday with all the news condensed so you and all the other rich millionaires commuting home for the weekend can catch up on the news that they have missed. How's that?" The two men quit their jobs at *Baltimore News* after three months, drew up a prospectus, convinced some wealthy friends to invest in their enterprise, and spent most of 1922 setting up editorial offices in New York and hiring a staff.

Among the part-timers listed on *Time*'s first masthead is Archibald MacLeish, who later became a well-known, Pulitzer Prize–winning poet. He wrote the Education section for $10 a week. For National Affairs editor, Luce hired Alan Rinehart, the son of novelist Mary Roberts Rinehart. In the days when gender roles were somewhat stratified, Luce and Hadden hired men as editors and reporters and women as researchers called "secretarial assistants."

Luce projected a first-year income of $155,000, most of it from 25,000 subscriptions at $5 each, and the remaining $30,000 from advertising. The fledgling publishers were disappointed when a mailing of 500,000 promotional pieces yielded only 6,000 subscribers. Another 5,000 were earmarked for newsstand distribution.

The folksy tone of a stockholders' report just before Christmas 1922 hardly suggests that the fledgling venture would grow within a generation into one of the world's most powerful media conglomerates: "*Time* knows well that the people that will help it most are those who are best satisfied with it. For that reason it does not desire to antagonize any of its stockholders by asking to do anything that is distasteful. From time to time summary requests will be made. . . . 'Give me a letter to this potential advertiser.' 'Get me 13 subscriptions.'"

Time's first issue, featuring a sketch of retiring House Speaker Joseph G. Cannon on the cover, was published on March 3, 1923. The thirty-two-page magazine carried a relatively steep newsstand price of fifteen cents. Only 9,000 copies sold, far less than the optimistic projection of 25,000. For the first year or so, both circulation and advertising revenue remained sluggish. When the magazine's first volume was completed, the publishers sent bound copies to charter subscribers. Among those who sent endorsements was Franklin D. Roosevelt, the unsuccessful vice presidential candidate in 1920, who wrote, "I do not think the articles are too brief—they are just about right in length and they are as unbiased as far as it is possible for red-blooded Americans to make them so."

AN IDIOSYNCRATIC STYLE

There was little original reporting in early issues, which were cobbled together with information from a variety of sources, including newspapers, wire-service reports, and speeches, rewritten in the inimitable *Time* style that was largely the brainchild of Hadden. The first issue defines what became the signature approach of *Time* over the years, with only minor variations: information organized into departments, such as national news, foreign news, the arts (and their subdivisions), books, religion, education, finance, and so forth. The first issue also features three light-humor departments: Imaginary Interviews, Point with Pride, and View with Alarm. Teams of writers and researchers, supplemented in later years by reporters and correspondents from bureaus around the world, wrote the articles. A brief *New York Times* notice heralding the launch of the publication was headlined "Time New Weekly—First Issue of Magazine Devoted to Summarizing Progress."

True to its mission as articulated by Luce and Hadden, the new magazine was designed to be read by busy millionaires and others in less than an hour, so columns were at first restricted to 7 inches. An unusual feature was the regular coverage of the number of lynchings in southern states. Author and former *Time* editor and executive Robert T. Elson, in his semiofficial two-volume history, *The World of Time Inc.*, quotes Luce as saying, "We were what would be called pro civil rights for Negroes from the beginning. One of the things in which we may have been useful is the fact that we tried to report every single lynching. We tried to print the exact story, without moralizing."

Time, especially in its earlier decades, is perhaps best known for the idiosyncratic style favored by Hadden, which has been variously termed "breezy," "arch," and "cute." It was notable for the liberal use of word coinages, especially portmanteaus or puns, as in describing a young would-be newspaper publisher as a "Hearstling"; for its resuscitation of words and allusions from classical Greek, such as *kudos* or *katabasis*; for its syntax bending, especially through the use of inverted word order, as in "Forth from the White House followed by innumerable attendants, Mr. and Mrs. Warren G. Harding set out" (their return, not surprisingly, was termed a katabasis); for its historical and literary allusions; and for its pomposity-deflating identification of subjects with their middle names, as in "Walter Percy Chrysler," or with nicknames in parentheses, as in "Bernarr ('Body Love') Macfadden." *Time* writers also pioneered in the stringing together of frequently alliterative adjectives, as when describing George Bernard Shaw as "mocking, mordant, misanthropic"; and in the uncanonical use of nouns as attributives, as in "Teacher Scopes." *Time*'s writers were clearly writing for an educated and well-read audience.

Elson suggests in his book that Hadden's admiration for Homeric Greek prompted him to pepper his copy with a plethora of hyphenated modifiers:

> At all times Hadden had by him a carefully annotated translation of the *Iliad*. In the back cover he had listed hundreds of words, especially verbs and the compound adjectives, which had seemed to him fresh and forceful. The classic ring of this vocabulary, which he frequently reviewed, served him as a tuning fork for the language that he wanted in *Time*.

Luce is credited for the popularization of several words. One is *tycoon*, a term previously used to describe a Japanese shogun. Luce used it to refer to American business moguls.

"BUSINESS IS OUR LIFE"

As a cost-saving measure, Luce and Hadden moved the editorial offices to Cleveland, Ohio, in 1925 but returned to New York City within three years. By the end of the 1920s, *Time* had published several sixty-page-plus issues and was reporting net profits of about $125,000 on total revenues of $1.3 million, with a circulation of 200,000. Newsstand sales doubled to 23,000 copies within a year. In 1928, with the selection of aviator Charles Lindbergh, *Time* initiated its custom of selecting a "Man of the Year"—hero or villain—that expanded over the years to included women; anonymous groups, such as the under-thirty generation; and objects, such as the personal computer. The Man of the Year philosophy echoed Luce's secular-evangelical belief that history is mightily shaped by individual will, a phenomenon he saw himself embodying as the most influential publisher of his time.

In February 1929 Hadden, then thirty-one, died of a streptococcal infection exacerbated by overwork, and Luce assumed greater day-by-day oversight of the magazine, confirming his reputation as a shrewd businessman as well as a savvy journalist. In the months before the stock market crash ushered in the Great Depression, *Time*'s tilt toward business had become quite evident. Within a month after Hadden's death, Luce said in a speech, with characteristic flourish, "Business is, essentially, our civilization; for it is the essential characteristic of our times. . . . Business is our life. It is the life of the artist, the clergyman, the philosopher, the doctor, because it determines the conditions and problems of life with which either artist or philosopher, let alone ordinary mortals, have to deal."

It thus struck some observers as strange that Luce packed the editorial staff of his new publication, *Fortune* (which debuted February 1930), with such imaginative writers as Archibald MacLeish, Dwight Macdonald, and Russell Davenport. "There are men who can write poetry, and there are men who can read balance sheets," said Luce. "The men who can read balance sheets cannot write. . . . Of necessity, we made the discovery that it is easier to turn poets into business journalists than to turn bookkeepers into writers."

Starting in the late 1920s, *Time* used the new medium of radio to expand its reach, while simultaneously shaping the way radio presented news and documentary material. In 1928 *Time* general manager Roy Larson and *Time* radio executive Fred Smith developed a ten-minute radio program, *Newscasting*, that presented news from the pages of the magazine. The next year they added another ten-minute program, *NewsActing*, in which actors, including Agnes Moorehead and Orson Welles, impersonated and directly quoted the subjects in the news accompanied by sound effects. In 1929 the two shows merged into one fifteen-minute program, called *The March of Time*. By 1931 the weekly show had expanded to a half hour and featured a narrator, known as "The Voice of Time," and dramatizations of news events. In an article for the January 1935 issue of *Tower Radio* magazine, Tom Carskadon wrote, "Listeners say [*The March of Time*] is the most vivid, the most real, the most significant program on the air. Radio experts call it the finest piece of out-and-out radio production on the air today."

Within a few years, a moving-picture-newsreel version was created, and the legend "Time Marches On" soon became a familiar sight on movie screens from coast to coast. Although, as Elson writes, "the method of *The March of Time* is no longer acceptable as journalism . . . TV, the modern film documentary, the new school of *cinéma vérité* owe much to its pioneering methods."

"IDEOLOGICAL DISTORTION OF THE NEWS"

Despite the success of its radio programs and other ventures, *Time* suffered through the Depression, especially given the huge start-up costs of *Life* magazine in 1936. In the period before the United States entered World War II, Luce had come to believe that Americans had a fateful role to play in world affairs and urged military aid to the beleaguered European allies. After Japan attacked the United States at Pearl Harbor in 1941, Luce committed *Time* to the cause of "absolute victory." He also threw his support to the Nationalist Chinese forces of Chiang Kai-shek, much to the consternation of *Time*'s correspondent in China, Theodore H. White, who later wrote the Pulitzer Prize–winning book *The Making of the President, 1960*. White broke with Luce when ordered to write flattering pieces about the man White called "China's somber tyrant." John Heidenry complained in his *New York Times* review of a 1995 book about Luce and White that Luce "believed that ideological distortion of the news was often preferable to objectivity, particularly where China and the Republican Party were concerned."

In the years following World War II, *Time* maintained a firm anticommunist tack, but it also was among the first publications to challenge the demagoguery of Wisconsin senator Joseph McCarthy. Still, during the 1950s and 1960s, *Time* was perceived as having a Republican bias—at least an "Eastern establishment" Republican bias. However, in 1964, *Time* endorsed the Democratic presidential candidate, favoring Lyndon B. Johnson over Barry Goldwater. Luce had retired as editor in chief earlier that year, handing over the reins to Hedley Donovan. At Luce's retirement, the firm that had started forty-some years earlier with an investment of $86,000 had grown into a conglomerate with revenues of more than $400 million.

In January 1990 Time Inc. and Warner Communication combined to form an even larger conglomerate, Time Warner. In the words of the *New York Times*, the merger brought together Luce's company "with its rich journalistic history and its aristocratic, traditional leadership" and Warner's "with its lucrative stable of movie, entertainment and cable television properties." During the 1980s the management of Time Inc. decided that it was time to de-emphasize the role of its magazines as future sources of revenue and corporate viability, leading some observers, such as author Richard M. Clurman, to worry about the future of its journalistic integrity. In his 1992 book, *To the End of Time: The Seduction and Conquest of a Media Empire*, Clurman concludes that "there are people in Time Warner who believe and act as if the purpose of business is only business."

AOL COMES AND GOES

In 1997 revenue at the publication increased 21 percent to about $94 million, and circulation rose slightly to 4.2 million, earning *Time* the designation "Hottest Magazine of '97" by *Adweek* magazine. In 1998 *Time* celebrated its seventy-fifth anniversary with a gala at New York's Radio City Music Hall. It invited all the men and women who had appeared on the magazine's cover to attend, resulting in a star-studded affair with guests that included President Bill Clinton, Russian ex-premier Mikhail Gorbachev, the Reverend Billy Graham, actress Sharon Stone, and author Toni Morrison. By the end of the twentieth century, managing editor Walter Isaacson restored some of the old luster of *Time*'s authority and credibility in a "post-magazine" era by leading the publication into the new-media era via its Pathfinder Internet service, by increasing science and technology coverage, and by planning *The Time 100* series on CBS Television.

On December 14, 2000, the U.S. government approved a merger between Time Inc. and America Online (AOL). The $111 billion deal was the biggest merger in American history, and it was considered a terrible idea by almost everyone not directly involved with the two companies. Other media giants, such as Disney and Microsoft, argued that the merger would give the combined company a media monopoly, and many academics and policy advisers agreed. Time Inc. brought a publishing empire to the deal that included magazines such as *Time, Life, Sports Illustrated, Health, People, Southern Living*, and *Fortune*; the Little, Brown publishing company; television networks such as HBO, CNN, and TBS; and a host of movie and music properties. AOL had a subscriber list of twenty-six million and the technology to transform the Internet. Federal Trade Commission (FTC) approval was contingent on the new company sharing that technology with other forms of media.

The new company, AOL Time Warner, was led by Steve Case from AOL as chairman and Gerald Levin from Time Warner as CEO. Within ten years, the naysayers were proved right in their assessment that the merger was bad business. AOL suffered greatly from the rise of broadband Internet connections that made dial-up connections obsolete. In 2008 Time Warner divested itself of AOL and put AOL shares up for public trading. For fiscal year 2011 Time Warner reported revenue of $29 billion.

Edward Moran

SEE ALSO: *CNN; Disney (Walt Disney Company);* Fortune*; Graham, Billy; The Great Depression;* Life*; Lindbergh, Charles; Luce, Henry; Microsoft; Morrison, Toni; The* New York Times*;* Newsweek*; Radio; Welles, Orson; World War I; World War II.*

BIBLIOGRAPHY

Carskadon, Tom. "*Time* Marches On." *Tower Radio*, January 1935, 24.

Clurman, Richard. *To the End of "Time": The Seduction and Conquest of a Media Empire.* New York: Simon & Schuster, 1992.

Elson, Robert T. *Time, Inc.: The Intimate History of a Publishing Enterprise 1923–1941.* New York: Atheneum, 1968.

Elson, Robert T. *The World of Time, Inc.: The Intimate History of a Publishing Enterprise 1941–1960.* New York: Atheneum, 1973.

Griffith, Thomas. *Harry and Teddy: The Turbulent Friendship of Press Lord Henry R. Luce and His Favorite Reporter, Theodore H. White.* New York: Random House, 1995.

Hamblin, Dora Jane. *That Was the Life.* New York: Norton, 1977.

Johnson, Sammye, and Patricia Prijatel. *The Magazine from Cover to Cover.* New York: Oxford University Press, 2007.

Reed, David. *The Popular Magazine in Britain and the United States of America 1880–1960.* London: British Library, 1997.

Roberts, Johnnie L. "All for One, One for AOL." *Newsweek*, December 25, 2000.

Tebbel, John. *The American Magazine: A Compact History.* New York: Hawthorn Books, 1969.

Tebbel, John, and Mary Ellen Zuckerman. *The Magazine in America: 1741–1990.* New York: Oxford University Press, 1991.

Vanderlan, Robert. *Intellectuals Incorporated: Politics, Art, and Ideas inside Henry Luce's Media Empire.* Philadelphia: University of Pennsylvania Press, 2010.

Wainwright, Loudon. *The Great American Magazine: An Inside History of "Life."* New York: Knopf, 1986.

Wood, James Playsted. *Magazines in the United States*, 3rd ed. New York: Ronald Press, 1971.

Times Square

Less of a square and more like two triangles located at the intersection of Broadway and Seventh Avenue in New York City, Times Square has been associated over the years with a series of seemingly opposite combinations: both high and low culture, glitz and grime, and exciting bright lights and seedy dark corners. The history of Times Square is a direct reflection of the history of Americans' relationship with their cities.

ORIGIN OF THE SQUARE

The origin of Times Square can be traced to the 1811 New York Commissioner of Streets and Roads' plan, which laid out the Manhattan grid above Fourteenth Street. The significance of this plan, and many others like it across the United States prior to and after 1811, is that the future growth of the American city was partitioned off and predetermined as easy-to-develop slices of land. This not only assured efficient exploitation but also brought about a sort of democratization of the city, which the older cities of Europe with their main squares, large cathedrals, and prominent town halls did not possess. By virtue of this new grid, every building was just as important as the next, at least in terms of location on the grid.

And so, the nineteenth-century American city gradually filled up its preplanned grid, creating uniform streets between often not-so-uniform buildings. American city dwellers of this time lived in cities because they wanted to; that is, because they preferred the orderly and paved conditions of the city over the often irregular and muddy conditions of the rural areas, the only other option at this time (before the suburbanization of America).

As New York expanded north from Fourteenth Street, the diagonal path of the former Indian trail known as the Bloomingdale Road (later Broadway) was so strong that it ignored the 1811 grid plan and cut right through it. As a result, at every intersection of Broadway with a north-south avenue, a "square" came into being: Union Square at Fourth (Park) Avenue, Madison Square at Fifth Avenue, Herald Square at Sixth Avenue, and Long Acre (Times) Square at Seventh Avenue.

In the 1890s live-performance theaters (or "legitimate theaters") began to locate themselves in and around Long Acre

Square: Oscar Hammerstein's 1895 Olympia Theatre on Broadway between Forty-Fourth and Forty-Fifth streets was one of the first and most famous. Others soon followed from their former locations below Twenty-Third Street, and the area became known as a theater district. At its peak in 1925, the vicinity of Times Square was home to approximately eighty legitimate theaters.

The story goes that because the city of New York had not yet installed street lighting as far north as Long Acre Square, theater owners took it upon themselves. Exploiting the new technology of electric lighting, the fronts of the new theaters became giant advertisements, spelling out the title of the play on offer and sometimes also the main players. Later, multiple-story-high advertisements for chewing gum, soft drinks, and other products appeared. The result was that, by about 1910, Broadway was dazzlingly lit up at night and became known as the Great White Way.

In 1904 Long Acre Square changed its name to Times Square after the completion of the New York Times Tower at Forty-Second Street and Broadway. The newspaper decided to celebrate the opening of its new building by counting down the last minutes of 1904 from the top of it. Two years later, the festivities grew to include the lowering of a ball at midnight. This event soon grew into the enormous annual party now held every year in Times Square.

A subway shuttle linking Times Square with Grand Central Station at Forty-Second and Park Avenue was opened in 1904. This was followed by an Interborough Rapid Transit (IRT) line (1918) and a Brooklyn-Manhattan Transit (BMT) line (1923), both with stops at Forty-Second Street—and thus another aspect of Times Square was born: a transportation hub, an interchange, a "Crossroads of the World." This nickname later was strengthened by an Independent Subway (IND) line stop (1932) and the New York City Port Authority Bus Terminal (1950) at Forty-Second Street and Eighth Avenue, and the first Lincoln Tunnel entrance/exit (1937) at Forty-Second and Tenth Avenue.

A CHANGING ENTERTAINMENT CENTER

The theaters (and their accompanying restaurants, bars, and hotels), the fantastic lights, and the busy transportation interchanges were all direct reflections of how the concept of "city" was portrayed in the minds of Americans at the turn of the twentieth century. The city at that time was a place of energy, excitement, and culture. It was the place to be, the place where anything could happen and where most things did. The theater represented high culture, and those who attended the performances were the elite. The lights, however, could be enjoyed by anyone, and Broadway, Times Square, and Forty-Second Street (it is difficult to separate them) at the turn of the twentieth century was a place to see and be seen.

With the arrival of talking movies in the late 1920s and the Great Depression of the 1930s, the character of the Times Square area began to change. It still remained a center for entertainment, but at that time both high and low culture were represented: live performance and musical comedy theaters on one side and burlesque houses and "movie palaces" on the other. In addition, in that time before plane travel became commonplace, New York City was a port of call for anyone traveling between Europe and America, especially during World War II, when most every American soldier passed through and spent some time at Times Square. It was a crowded and popular place, as exemplified by the estimated two million people who thronged Times Square on August 14, 1945, to read the official announcement of the Japanese surrender on the Times Building's "zipper" (news bulletin board).

In the years following World War II, the rise of television (which brought entertainment into the home, ending the need to go out) and city suburbs (which were clean, spacious, and safe) further strengthened the decline of Times Square and also the American city. The area began to take on vulgar associations, and its large-scale advertisements reflected this with block-long flashing neon gin bottles and 30-foot-high heads that puffed cigarettes boasting real smoke. The Forty-Second Street corridor became known not only for pornographic movies but also for its easy access to prostitution; by extension, it also became a place for illegal drug trading and street gambling.

Times Square. *A panoramic view of Times Square, an iconic symbol of New York City, flashes with lights from Broadway theaters and animated, brightly lit signs.* ANDREY BAYDA/SHUTTERSTOCK.COM.

To many city dwellers, the new burlesque houses, movie palaces, and general gawking crowds were an insult to the city but were part of a growing trend; it was changing from being a special place where special things happened to being an ordinary, common place associated with dirt and grime, overcrowded conditions, degeneracy, and crime—and, as a result, neglect and dereliction. After World War II the American city was not seen as a place to live. Instead, it was seen as a place to get away from—hence the growth of suburban communities, which paradoxically still depended upon the city as the place to work.

LATE TWENTIETH-CENTURY CHANGES

During the late 1970s and early 1980s, as foreshadowed by the 1967 replacement of the 1904 Times Building's original facade with blank marble panels, the Times Square area again dramatically changed. This time it was a physical, not social, change: from a mixture of different-sized theaters and commercial buildings into a wasteland of overscaled and faceless skyscrapers. Many famous turn-of-the-twentieth-century theaters were demolished to make way for new developments, which were carried out with the promise that they would "revitalize" Times Square, but all they really did was add to its density.

One of the reactions to this change of Times Square was the 1987 city ordinance that required new buildings to include "super" signage several stories high and with varying degrees of animation. In addition, a 1988 ruling gave "landmark" status to most remaining theaters in the area, following the general trend in New York and other American cities of building preservation by government intervention. At the same time, large-scale musical productions with hummable tunes and easy lyrics catering to a simpler audience than the typical live theater became successful at Times Square theaters.

Various urban planning development studies and inquiries were undertaken to ascertain if anything could be done for the area, but no consensus was reached. In 1992 the private Times Square Business Improvement District, composed of area property owners and residents, was established. This organization, similar to others set up across the United States at this time, was privately funded to undertake those duties normally associated with the city government: public safety, sanitation, community services, economic strategy, and tourism promotion.

The city ordinances concerning the aesthetics of future development, the listing of "historic" buildings, and the creation of private entities to do the city's job all had the goal of retaining a sort of street-life status quo, but at the expense of turning Times Square into a regulated and controlled public amusement park. This last stage reflects the state of the American city at the turn of the twenty-first century: the city as a place to visit, as one might visit an amusement park. As Americans began to not only live and work in the suburbs, they also began to realize that while the suburbs might be cleaner, more spacious, and safer than the city, they were also more boring. The city, at this point, became that preserved exciting piece of the past whose purpose was to be used when one wanted an urban experience.

In 1996 the next logical step along this road was taken as the Disney Corporation renovated the Amsterdam Theatre (1903), once home to *The Ziegfeld Follies*, for its own use in staging offerings such as *Beauty and the Beast* and *The Lion King*. Dick Clark's Rock 'n Roll New Year's Eve celebration of 1998 (his twenty-seventh), complete with its ever youthful and tanned host, was reportedly attended by half a million people and watched on television by an estimated 300 million. At that point, the only things missing were crying kids and the long lines for the rides.

Times Square made headlines of a different sort in 2010 as the location of an attempted terrorist attack. A Pakistani-born U.S. citizen parked a sport utility vehicle (SUV) containing a crude bomb in Times Square on the evening of May 1. A street vendor reported the SUV to the police because it was running and billowing smoke. The SUV contained an explosive device made of gasoline, propane, firecrackers, and alarm clocks, which failed to go off as planned. Days later, authorities arrested the perpetrator, Faisal Shahzad, as he attempted to fly out of the country. He was convicted in October 2010 and sentenced to life in prison.

For all its commercialization, Times Square remains one of the spots most associated with the vibrancy and never-say-die spirit of New York City. On Friday, September 9, 2011, more than 100 Broadway stars kicked off a weekend commemorating the tenth anniversary of the 9/11 terrorist attacks by performing the song "New York, New York" on the streets of Times Square. And at the end of December, Dick Clark—still showing the effects of an earlier stroke—led an estimated million revelers in counting down to the New Year for his last time (Clark died in April 2012). Ten years earlier, as the smoke from the Twin Towers cast a pall over the city, few people would have believed such joyful celebrations possible, but Times Square, like the city of New York, just keeps reinventing itself.

Christopher S. Wilson

SEE ALSO: *Advertising; Broadway; Burlesque; Clark, Dick; Disney (Walt Disney Company); The Great Depression;* The Lion King*; The* New York Times*; 9/11; Rodgers and Hammerstein; Sport Utility Vehicles (SUVs); Suburbia; World War II;* The Ziegfeld Follies.

BIBLIOGRAPHY

Dunlap, David W. *On Broadway: A Journey Uptown over Time.* New York: Rizzoli International, 1990.

Ellis, Edward Robb. *The Epic of New York City: A Narrative History.* New York: Coward-McCann, 1966.

Jackson, Kenneth T. *Crabgrass Frontier: The Suburbanization of America.* New York: Oxford University Press, 1985.

Rencoret, Francisco Javier. *New York City: The Edge of Enigma.* New York: Princeton Architectural Press, 1991.

Sagalyn, Lynne B. *Times Square Roulette: Remaking the City Icon.* Cambridge, MA: MIT Press, 2001.

Stern, Robert A. M.; Gregory Gilmartin; and John Massengale. *New York 1900: Metropolitan Architecture and Urbanism 1890–1915.* New York: Rizzoli International, 1983.

Stern, Robert A. M.; Gregory Gilmartin; and Thomas Mellins. *New York 1930: Architecture and Urbanism between the Two World Wars.* New York: Rizzoli International, 1987.

Stern, Robert A. M.; Thomas Mellins; and David Fishman. *New York 1960: Architecture and Urbanism between the Second World War and the Bicentennial.* New York: Monacelli Press, 1995.

Traub, James. *The Devil's Playground: A Century of Pleasure and Profit in Times Square.* New York: Random House, 2004.

Timex Watches

The introduction of the Timex watch in 1950 revolutionized the time-keeping industry. The relatively simple design, with fewer parts than other watches, made the Timex more durable, a feature that led to one of the world's most important advertising campaigns. Capitalizing on the country's growing fascination with television, Timex hired veteran newsman John Cameron Swayze to run an elaborate series of torture tests—live on Steve Allen's popular Sunday night program. Timex watches were smashed by jackhammers, sloshed through dishwashers, and strapped to world-class divers taking flops off the cliffs of Acapulco. By 1956 sales of the watch that "takes a licking and keeps on ticking" surpassed the five million mark.

One of the more famous commercials occurred in 1958, when Swayze strapped a Timex to an outboard motor. When the watch slipped off the propeller and disappeared into the tub of water, he had to promise to try again the following week. Timex decided to end the torture tests campaign in 1977 with a staged failure: an elephant stomped and crushed a watch. "It worked," Swayze quipped to the television audience, "in rehearsal."

In the 1970s Timex received stiff competition from digital watches and from imported watches from Asia. It survived by developing new products such as its "Ironman Triathlon" sports watch and the "Indiglo" luminescent watch face. As the company entered the twenty-first century it had some 7,500 employees on four continents.

Geoff Edgers

SEE ALSO: *Advertising; Allen, Steve; Ironman Triathlon; Television.*

BIBLIOGRAPHY

McDermott, Kathleen. *Timex: A Company and Its Community, 1854–1998*. New York: Timex, 1998.

Tiny Tim *(1932–1996)*

"Tiny Tim" was the last and most successful of many stage names adopted by singer and ukulele player Herbert Khaury. Born in New York, Khaury was a struggling performer as Darry Dover, Larry Love, Julian Foxglove, and Sir Timothy Thames, before being given a small part in the counterculture movie *You Are What You Eat* in 1968. He became modestly well known as Tiny Tim, the pseudonym he was currently employing, and received his first national exposure shortly afterward on NBC's *Rowan and Martin's Laugh-In*. His odd garb, odder stage presence, and falsetto renditions of old songs quickly made Tiny Tim a celebrity. His signature song (and 1968 hit) was "Tip-Toe thru' the Tulips with Me"; it was first recorded in 1929.

A frequent guest on *The Tonight Show*, Tiny Tim made history when he married "Miss Vicki" during the December 17, 1969, episode. The ceremony was witnessed by more than 20 million viewers in America—a daughter, Tulip, was born in 1971, and the couple divorced six years later.

Both in falsetto and a quivery baritone, Tiny Tim recorded hundreds of popular songs from the nineteenth and twentieth centuries and knew thousands more. He had probably performed a more varied repertoire of songs, in more venues, than any other singer of his generation. He died in Minneapolis, Minnesota, where he had moved with his third wife, "Miss Sue," on November 30, 1996.

David Lonergan

SEE ALSO: Laugh-In; The Tonight Show.

BIBLIOGRAPHY

"Deaths: Tiny Tim." *Billboard* 108, no. 50 (1996): 69.

Grimes, William. "Tiny Tim, Singer, Dies at 64; Flirted (Chastely) with Fame." *New York Times*, December 2, 1996, B12.

Hoffmann, Frank W., and William G. Bailey. *Arts & Entertainment Fads*. New York: Harrington Park Press, 1990.

"Unconventional Pop Figure Tiny Tim Dies." *Washington Post*, December 2, 1996, B4.

The *Titanic*

May 31, 2009, marked the end of an era. On that date Millvina Dean, the last survivor of the *Titanic*, died. Even as time passes, however, the myth of the ship refuses to die. April 15, 2012, was the hundredth anniversary of the sinking of the *Titanic*. Many commemorations were planned, including an anniversary cruise that took the same route as the ocean liner.

In the realm of popular culture, the *Titanic* has turned out to be more than just a ship that sank; it has become an icon of an era long past, as well as a contemporary phenomenon. It seems that each generation since the sinking has rediscovered the shipwreck in new books, movies, and even music.

THE VOYAGE AND ITS AFTERMATH

When the luxury ocean liner *Titanic* left Queenstown, Ireland, on April 11, 1912, the ship's fame was far different than it would become in just a few short days. The voyage of the *Titanic* was a tremendous news event all around the world. The *Titanic* was the largest and most luxurious liner of its time. People were thrilled with the improvements the industrial age had brought to daily life, and the *Titanic* seemed to be the ultimate realization of their dreams. When the *Titanic* was called "unsinkable," some saw the description as proof of human supremacy, while others saw it as a direct challenge to God.

When the *Titanic* struck an iceberg on April 14, 1912, and sank two hours later (on April 15), with more than 1,500 people losing their lives, the world also lost much of its innocence and faith in the supremacy of humankind. If this ship, so carefully planned and built to withstand anything, could sink on its maiden voyage, on what could society depend? Was the sinking a warning from God, as some religious leaders claimed? Was it meant to warn the public against the materialism of the Gilded Age, as some proposed? Would it reverse the progress brought about by the age of industry? As is often the case with tragedies, the event led to arguments on ideological perspective among many people. Religious leaders, for example, used the example of Ida Straus, who chose to remain with her husband on the ship, as an example to argue against divorce. Among some groups, women who survived were scolded for not following Mrs. Straus's example and remaining with their husbands to

***The* Titanic.** *The* Titanic *leaves the harbor in Queenstown, Ireland, on her maiden voyage in April 1912.* POPPERFOTO/CONTRIBUTOR/GETTY IMAGES.

perish. Both sides of the suffrage issue also used the *Titanic* tragedy to argue their case.

The sinking of the *Titanic* illuminated growing disparities in class around the world. In 1912 the world was marked by distinct social classes; it was a time when those with money were perceived as rarefied beings, somehow superior to others. Sailing on the *Titanic* were many people of immense wealth, such as John Jacob Astor and Benjamin Guggenheim. While neither man survived, many other first-class passengers did. When those numbers were compared to the number of steerage passengers rescued, an outcry arose against the privileged. Why did they seemingly have more right to be rescued than the others? While the Industrial Revolution continued, there was a backlash against progress and the wealthy. Change was in the air.

The tragedy also spawned increased efforts to launch rescue operations for those involved in water accidents. In the hope of averting a repeat of the event, the International Ice Patrol was founded by the nations of the North Atlantic. The official inquiries in America and Britain also produced changes in the laws regarding lifeboats and other safety issues. After its use on the *Titanic*, the Marconi wireless apparatus was popularized to send distress signals so that rescuers on land could receive messages regarding survivors.

In a media-saturated society, it is only appropriate that it would not take long before the *Titanic* tragedy became a popular commodity. From 1912 to 1913, at least 100 songs about the *Titanic* were published, including Leadbelly's recording of "Down with the Old Canoe." The first *Titanic* motion picture, *Saved from the "Titanic,"* starring survivor Dorothy Gibson, appeared just one month after the disaster and was filmed on the *Titanic*'s sister ship, the *Olympic*. Survivor Lawrence Beesley published his account, *The Loss of the S.S. "Titanic,"* six weeks after the tragedy. Additionally, articles appeared in *Scientific American* and other popular magazines of the time, and countless books were written about the sinking. *Futility*, the rediscovered 1898 novel by Morgan Robertson, told the story of a ship so similar to the *Titanic*, including its name, *Titan*, that many felt it had predicted the sinking of the *Titanic*.

After 1913 most of the interest in the *Titanic* died down rapidly. The great ship occasionally showed up again, mainly in motion pictures, including the British film *Atlantic* (1929) and the German film *Titanic* (1943). The German film, made during World War II, was a propaganda exercise with the only heroic person on the ship a fictional German crew member. In 1953 the United States finally produced its version of the story in true Hollywood style. Starring Barbara Stanwyck and Clifton Webb, *Titanic* was a melodrama with the shipwreck used largely as a background for the fictional story of an estranged couple who reconcile as the ship sinks.

REMEMBERING THAT NIGHT

By November 1955 the *Titanic* myth experienced its first resurgence. Walter Lord, a longtime student of *Titanic* lore, published his classic *A Night to Remember*, retelling the story of the *Titanic*'s short life. By January 1956 it had sold 60,000 copies; it has never been out of print since. Appearing two months after Lord's book, *Down to Eternity* by Richard O'Connor was received poorly.

Not to be left out of the picture, so to speak, a May 1955 episode of the popular *You Are There* television series dealt with the *Titanic*. A March 1956 teleplay about the ship, directed by George Roy Hill and narrated by Claude Rains, was shown on network television. In addition, motion pictures began appearing, including *Abandon Ship* (1957) and *A Night to Remember* (1958). The latter film, produced in documentary style, is regarded as the most faithful and accurate telling up to that time. Now a permanent part of popular culture, the story of the woman who was the most famous survivor of the *Titanic*, Margaret Tobin Brown, was chronicled in *The Unsinkable Molly Brown*. The story was first reproduced as a Broadway musical with Tammy Grimes (1960) as the title character and then in a motion picture starring Debbie Reynolds (1964). Both were huge successes and proved there was continued interest in the shipwreck.

The *Titanic* again slipped to semi-obscurity in the mid-1960s. It did, however, remain a popular subject for the occasional television show. In 1966 the premier episode of the television adventure show *The Time Tunnel* dealt with the disaster. A television miniseries, *S.O.S. "Titanic,"* starring David Janssen as John Jacob Astor, was produced in 1979. The ship also played an important role in fictional books such as Clive Cussler's *Raise the "Titanic"* (1976) and *The Memory of Eva Ryker* (1978), written by Donald A. Standwood.

DISCOVERING THE *TITANIC*

On September 1, 1985, Dr. Robert Ballard of the Woods Hole Oceanographic Institute and Jean-Louis Michel of the French IFREMER Institute returned the *Titanic* to the front pages when they located the wreck of the ship. It had long been a Holy Grail of sorts to those fascinated by it, and previous expeditions had tried unsuccessfully to locate the wreckage. Ballard became an instant celebrity and a vocal critic of those who wanted to salvage items from the ship. There were even those who wanted to try to raise the *Titanic*. Articles appeared in *National Geographic* and other magazines, and more books were published on the subject, including reprints of Lord's book. Documentaries such as *Secrets of the "Titanic"* (1986) soon began to appear, and it seemed that the event was taking on a mystical quality. There was even a video game, *Search for the "Titanic,"* appearing in 1989, which allowed players to finance and plan an expedition to locate the wreckage.

Interest remained high over the next few years as periodic new books and television specials kept the *Titanic* visible to the public. Much debate went on about whether to salvage any of the ship. Those who argued to salvage the vessel were concerned that time was of the essence and felt that artifacts would soon be all that was left of the event. Those against salvaging it, championed by Ballard, felt the wreck was a memorial and should be left alone. Eventually, the pro-salvage group won, and artifacts from the ship were brought to the surface.

On April 23, 1997, a new interpretation of the disaster appeared when *"Titanic": A New Musical*—a big-budget theater production—debuted on Broadway. In a theater season with few successes and even fewer legitimate hits, this musical was a smash; it won five Tony Awards, including one for Best Musical.

JAMES CAMERON'S *TITANIC*

Nothing, however, could prepare the world for the coming of the James Cameron 1997 film, *Titanic*. Amid rumor and innuendo regarding "the most expensive film ever made," the public waited for its release and a chance to judge it for themselves. When the release date was delayed and the film went way over budget, many predicted another disaster, this one of a business nature. Would it be a hit or the most expensive miss in motion picture history? It became obvious after the film's initial release that Cameron did not need to worry. *Titanic* became the largest-grossing movie ever made up to that time. It also tied Academy Award–winner *Ben Hur* (1959) (to be tied later by *The Lord of the Rings: The Return of the King*, 2003) for most trophies won, with eleven. The soundtrack from the movie became one of the best-selling movie soundtracks in history; the love theme from the movie, "My Heart Will Go On" performed by Céline Dion, quickly became a number one song. And the stars of the motion picture, Leonardo DiCaprio and Kate Winslet, both relatively unknown before the film, became superstars.

The public could not get enough of the film or the ship. Using life-size models and computer-generated images, the film was generally considered the most historically accurate, although some historians disagreed with liberties taken with some of the characters. The Edwardian hairstyles and wardrobe depicted sparked a fashion craze, and the blue diamond necklace that was a centerpiece of the plot became a best-selling piece of costume jewelry. *Titanic* museums even began to turn up in such places as Branson, Missouri.

THE FUTURE OF THE *TITANIC*

April 14, 2012, marked the 100th anniversary of the *Titanic*'s hitting the iceberg. To commemorate the centennial, events were held around the world. The cruise ship MS *Balmoral* replicated the *Titanic*'s route; a plaque with names of all of the ship's deceased was unveiled in Belfast, Ireland, where the ship was built; memorial services were held in Southampton, England, where the ship launched; and the National Geographic Channel featured a miniseries about the ship and its future underwater. Unfortunately the ship itself continues to deteriorate, between human visitors and the ravages of the ocean floor. Some experts believe the deck could collapse by 2040 and the ship itself could disappear by 2065. There have been more than 100 expeditions to the shipwreck's site, including one by Cameron in 2001. In 2010 Ballard returned to the site to complete a 3-D map of the wreckage before it disappears.

In the early twenty-first century, the *Titanic* continues to fascinate the public. There are faithful *Titanic* buffs who have read about and pondered the fate of the vessel for many years. Among them are members of the *Titanic* Historical Society, headquartered in a jewelry store in Indian Orchard, Massachusetts. Membership increases every time the ocean liner returns to the front page of the news, but it took a blockbuster film to make the *Titanic* a true cultural phenomenon among the general public. The *Titanic* remains a commodity to be bought and sold. Its sinking is a historic tragedy that will forever be a part of history and of popular culture.

Jill A. Gregg

SEE ALSO: *Academy Awards; Blockbusters; Broadway; CGI; DiCaprio, Leonardo; Hollywood; Leadbelly;* Lord of the Rings *Film Trilogy; The Musical;* National Geographic; *Rains,*

Claude; Scientific American*; Stanwyck, Barbara; Tony Awards; Winslet, Kate.*

BIBLIOGRAPHY

Ballard, Robert D., and Rick Archbold. *The Discovery of the "Titanic."* New York: Warner Books, 1987.

Ballard, Robert D., and Michael S. Sweeney. *Return to "Titanic."* Washington, DC: National Geographic, 2004.

Barratt, Nick. *Lost Voices from the "Titanic."* New York: Palgrave Macmillan, 2010.

Biel, Steven. *Down with the Old Canoe: A Cultural History of the "Titanic" Disaster.* New York: W. W. Norton, 1996.

Lord, Walter. *A Night to Remember.* New York: Holt, Rinehart, and Winston, 1955.

Lynch, Don. *"Titanic": An Illustrated History.* New York: Hyperion, 1992.

McCarty, Jennifer Hooper, and Tim Foecke. *What Really Sank the "Titanic."* New York: Citadel Press, 2008.

Spignesi, Stephen J. *The Complete "Titanic": From the Ship's Earliest Blueprints to the Epic Film.* Secaucus, NJ: Carol Publishing Group, 1998.

Wade, Wyn Craig. *The "Titanic": End of a Dream.* New York: Penguin Books, 1986.

TiVo

In January 1999, TiVo was introduced at the Consumer Electronics Show in Las Vegas as one of the first digital video recorders (DVRs). The device became synonymous with recording television, pausing live shows, and skipping commercials. Prior to 1999, the only way to record a television show was to purchase a VHS tape, put it in a VCR, and program the VCR each time a new tape was inserted. TiVo made the process of recording television much simpler. Plug in a box, subscribe to the service, and select a show; TiVo takes care of the rest. While many people have labeled TiVo a "souped-up VCR," the box actually contains a hard drive that saves shows just like downloading a file onto a computer.

TiVo enables users to pause or rewind live shows for up to half an hour. In addition, it easily fast forwards through a program's commercials or skips them entirely, although this second feature had to be programmed into the TiVo remote. According to Roger Allan for Electronic Design, "With TiVo, viewers never have to miss their favorite show, nor will they be bothered by phone calls or other interruptions. . . . Viewers can watch what they like when they choose, without videotaping." Not only did TiVo make recording convenient, but it also enabled people to control when they watched television instead of television dictating when they could watch certain programs.

Although other companies such as Pioneer and Philips introduced their own DVRs, TiVo's extra features set it apart. With an on-screen interactive guide to two weeks of show listings, it eliminates the need for printed TV listings. Subscribers can create a "Wishlist" by entering in a keyword; the system then records all shows having to do with that keyword. TiVo tapes "Suggestions" automatically based on shows already watched and rated, and with the "Season Pass" it records every new episode of a series regardless of time or channel.

It is perhaps TiVo's menu-driven interface that makes it the preferred DVR device. Howard Look, vice president for TiVo Studios, describes the desire of the company to set itself apart from the competition: "We could've taken the approach of building a unit with a high-tech 'geeky' interface," said Look. "Instead, we chose to make it very friendly and not intimidating. . . . We designed a user interface that works for everyone, including children and grandparents."

The company has faced some concerns about privacy because it sells aggregate user data. The data gives advertising companies general viewing information not associated with the users' names, which helps industry analysts determine what shows people watch—or do not watch—and whether people are skipping commercials. Due to competition from cable companies and several difficult lawsuits over patents, it has also had difficulty making a profit, despite having about two million subscribers in the United States in 2011, plus subscribers in several other countries.

During the early days of DVRs, consumers felt a strong brand loyalty to TiVo, partly fueled by its cute name and company mascot—a smiling television with antennae ears that dances on-screen when the system is first set up. While generic cable company DVR boxes have created significant competition for the TiVo, the company name has wormed its way into the vernacular, with people saying "TiVo it" rather than "record it." Brodie Keast, senior vice president and general manager for TiVo services, explains the continuing popularity of the device: "The TiVo service is really all about putting the consumer in control of their TV experience. It makes sure that TV fits into one's life instead of planning one's life around it."

Kim Keeline

SEE ALSO: *DVRs; Hulu; Netflix; Television; Videos.*

BIBLIOGRAPHY

Brosnan, John, and Kyle Copeland. *Beginning TiVo Programming.* Indianapolis, IN: Wiley/Wrox, 2007.

Grover, Ronald. "TiVo Wants to Be the Google of Television. How?" *Bloomberg Businessweek*, June 18, 2009.

Hansell, Saul. "TiVo Is Watching When You Don't Watch, and It Tattles." *New York Times*, July 26, 2006.

Krikorian, Raffi. *TiVo Hacks: 100 Industrial-Strength Tips & Tools.* Beijing: O'Reilly, 2003.

TMZ

Since its creation in 2005, TMZ has become the most popular website for celebrity news and gossip. With a presence on the Internet, television, and SiriusXM Radio, the news source is most famous for being the first to announce a variety of celebrity-related stories, including Michael Jackson's death in 2009. While similar sites focus on positive achievements of celebrities, TMZ concentrates on reporting "entertainment news in real time in an unvarnished way," according to its founder, Harvey Levin.

TMZ also offers photographs and video clips of spontaneous celebrity encounters, as well as music and film blogs and links to other entertainment websites. The website has provided live streaming of high-profile events, including Jackson's funeral. It was also the first website to post video of Paris Hilton's 2006 fender bender and obtain copies of Suri Cruise's birth certificate

(2006). On September 10, 2007, TMZ launched *TMZ on Television*, which features Levin and his crew discussing the stories that appear on their website. TMZ also has a webcast and a Sirius Radio program that encourages audience participation.

Levin, a former attorney and *People's Court* (1981–) reporter, serves as managing editor. He says that each story is fact-checked and reviewed by lawyers before it appears on the website. TMZ brands itself as a celebrity justice website to hold stars accountable for their misdeeds. Because TMZ can get the information online quickly, a celebrity's agent often has no time to talk to the press before a story is reported about his or her client.

By making requests under the Freedom of Information Act (1966) TMZ can obtain the arrest reports and other legal documents and offer updates as the situation changes. When the organization broke a story about Mel Gibson's 2006 DUI arrest, for example, it provided Gibson's mug shot and the arrest report, which contained anti-Semitic remarks. Because TMZ published the story so rapidly online, Gibson's agents had little time to spin the report, and his image suffered. Levin has stated that the company can share celebrity news and gossip quickly: "We're not doing things the same way as everybody else. We're a real, functioning newsroom that publishes on demand. We don't have time periods like TV shows and we don't have publishing cycles like newspapers and magazines have."

The website does not hide its investigating style or the manner it uses to obtain information. "We're not into doing these kind of wax figures on the red carpet [stories]," Levin has told the press. "We're not beholden to publicists. We've kind of created our own path here." Some critics question the professionalism of the organization, and Debbie Rowe, the mother of Jackson's two eldest children, filed a lawsuit against TMZ in 2010. Rowe's case alleged that the company broadcast stolen footage of an interview she did shortly after Jackson's death. Despite the criticism, TMZ continues to be popular among the growing number of Americans who cannot seem to get enough celebrity news.

Linda Martindale

SEE ALSO: *Celebrity; Gibson, Mel; Gossip Columns; Hilton, Paris; Hollywood; The Internet; Jackson, Michael; Radio; Satellite Radio; Television.*

BIBLIOGRAPHY

Cohen, Sandy. "Celebrity News Site Breaks Gibson Story." *USA Today*, August 1, 2006.

Epstein, Joseph. *Gossip: The Untrivial Pursuit.* New York: Houghton Mifflin Harcourt, 2011.

To Kill a Mockingbird

Harper Lee's novel *To Kill a Mockingbird* gives an accurate reflection of race relations in the southern United States during the 1930s. The novel, set around a single father and his two children in a small town in Alabama, contains a vast array of symbolism to intertwine the main plot with several subplots. Through her novel, Lee debunked the picture of quaint antebellum southern society with the realism of southern society. The timing of its publication, which denounced prejudicial attitudes, aligned with the early civil rights movement in the United States. This best-selling novel became a classic and required reading for many U.S. high school students. In 2007 Lee received the Presidential Medal of Freedom for her contributions to literature; the medal is the highest civilian honor in the United States.

Author Harper Lee was born in Monroeville, Alabama, in 1926. She spent four years at the University of Alabama and one year at Oxford University in England. She also attended law school, leaving six months short of finishing her course work to pursue a writing career in New York City. There she helped author Truman Capote, a childhood friend, research *In Cold Blood.* To earn money she took a job as an airline reservation clerk.

In 1960 Lee's novel *To Kill a Mockingbird* was published, and it was instantly successful. In 1961 the novel won the Pulitzer Prize. By 1962 a motion picture based on the book was released; it won three Academy Awards, including one for Gregory Peck as Best Actor. Also in 1962 Lee won the Paperback of the Year award from *Bestsellers* magazine for the best-selling paperback of the year.

Lee, a direct descendant of Confederate general Robert E. Lee, recommended to potential authors, "Write what you know and do so thoughtfully." She emphatically denied the her prize-winning work was autobiographical. The similarities it contains to her own life are striking, however. Her father, Amasa Coleman Lee, for example, was a lawyer.

The novel's symbolism and clarity make it a literary classic. It is narrated in the voice of a white six-year-old tomboy named "Scout" Finch. She lives with her older brother, Jem, and her father, Atticus Finch, in the small town of Maycomb, Alabama,

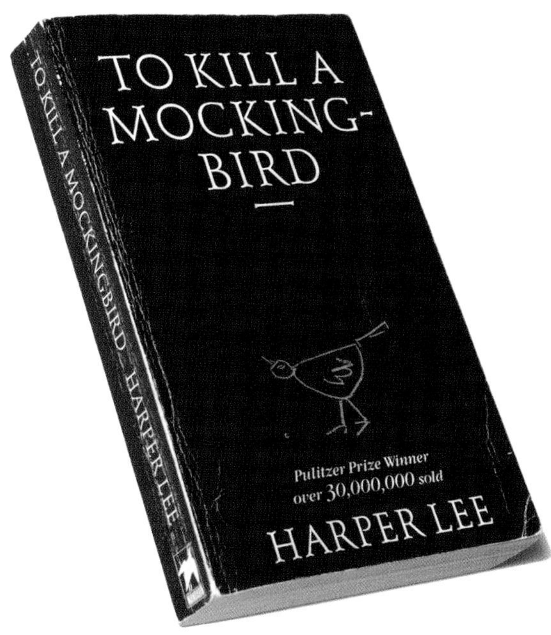

To Kill a Mockingbird. *The Pulitzer Prize–winning novel* To Kill a Mockingbird, *which portrays race relations in the South in the 1930s, is considered a literary classic.* CBW/ALAMY.

in 1930. The story centers on the alleged rape of the white Mayella Ewell, daughter of the wicked Bob Ewell, by Tom Robinson, who is black. Atticus serves as Robinson's attorney. The all-white jury finds Robinson guilty even after Atticus proves reasonable doubt of Robinson's guilt.

The novel portrays common stereotypical racist events of the time. Atticus faces taunts of "nigger lover" and "lawing for niggers." There also is the attempted lynching of Robinson. The perceived threat of blacks to white women and salvation embodied in white males are mocked.

Throughout the novel, Lee pursues various themes such as ignorance versus knowledge, cowardice versus heroism, and children versus adults. Courage versus cowardice is portrayed in Atticus's demeanor in a confrontation with Bob Ewell over Atticus's open disbelief of Mayella's accusation. The dispute also represents an old notion of racial cohesion that Ewell believes Atticus is breaking. Lee draws parallels of ignorance in her handling of characters Boo Radley and Robinson; they are both presumed guilty. Radley is the Finches' neighbor with an evil reputation, especially among the children, who fear him without ever having met him; he turns out to be a hero when he saves Scout and Jem from murder at the hands of Bob Ewell. Robinson dies while trying to escape prison, showing how the racist South endured and egalitarian measures floundered.

Explicitly symbolic is Jem's attempt to make a snowman during a rare Alabama snowfall. As he makes the snow into a ball, he rolls it to accrue more snow. While rolling the snowball, it picks up dirt, giving the snowman a dirty surface. The snowman signifies the superficiality of skin color.

To Kill a Mockingbird underscores many themes and represents a universal story from a regional perspective. The overall argument involves the obvious plea for justice while mocking the mores of southern society. It is Lee's only major published work. Although Lee faded back into the obscurity of Monroeville, her mark in literary persuasion endures. There have been several portrayals of Lee in films about Truman Capote; perhaps most famously, she was played by Sandra Bullock in the 2006 film *Infamous*.

Scott Stabler

SEE ALSO: *Bullock, Sandra; Capote, Truman; Civil Rights Movement; Peck, Gregory.*

BIBLIOGRAPHY

Johnson, Claudia Durst. *To Kill a Mockingbird: Threatening Boundaries*. New York: Twayne, 1994.

Lee, Harper. *To Kill a Mockingbird*. Philadelphia: Lippincott, 1960.

Shields, Charles J. *Mockingbird: A Portrait of Harper Lee*. New York: Henry Holt, 2006.

To Tell the Truth

To Tell the Truth was one of the most durable and popular panel quiz shows ever to appear on television, having a run of more than twenty years in both network and syndicated form. Along with *What's My Line?* and *I've Got a Secret*, *To Tell the Truth* was one of three similar shows introduced by Mark Goodson-Bill Todman Productions in the 1950s. These shows were designed to appeal to a relatively upscale television audience and to counter the effects of widely publicized quiz show payola scams. In the original version of *To Tell the Truth*, which ran from 1956 to 1968 on CBS, Bud Collyer was host, moderating a group of celebrity panelists that included Orson Bean, Polly Bergen, Kitty Carlisle, Peggy Cass, and Tom Poston. The show ran on prime time from 1956 to 1967 and in the daytime from 1962 to 1968.

The panelists' goal was to determine which one of three players was telling the truth about an unusual event or circumstance in which they were involved. All three claimed by affidavit to be the authentic truth-teller, and each panelist was given an opportunity to question the contestants individually for a designated amount of time. After the panelists completed their questioning and try to identify who is telling the truth, the host asked, "Will the real John Doe please stand up?" The contestants were awarded money based on their success in fooling the panel. Because the genuine contestant was not identified until the end of the question sessions, those in the home and studio audience were able to play along.

After the "real John Doe" introduced himself or herself, the impostors identified themselves to the panelists. The information disclosed in these introductions was almost as entertaining as the game itself, because the impostors were often struggling actors or individuals employed in careers that could not have been more dissimilar from that of the truth-teller.

To Tell the Truth had a second run in syndication from 1969 to 1978 with hosts Garry Moore (1969–1977) and Joe Garagiola (1977–1978). Bean, Cass, and Carlisle returned as panelists and were joined by Bill Cullen. Another short-lived version ran in syndication from 1980 to 1981 with host Robin Ward and regular panelists Cass and Soupy Sales. After a decade-long hiatus, the show returned in the fall of 1990 on NBC but lasted only one season. During that season the show had several hosts, including Alex Trebek, Lynn Swann, and series creator Mark Goodson. The show would go dark for another ten years, until a run in syndication in 2000 and 2001, when it was hosted by John O'Hurley, an actor best known as J. Peterman on *Seinfeld*. Carlisle was a guest panelist on one episode, making her the only cast member to have appeared in each version of the show.

All versions of *To Tell the Truth* were preserved, and the show appears in reruns. The longevity of the program (and others like it) probably had much to do with its extremely low production costs. The consistent appearance of familiar panelists also added to its popularity, since the personal style of each of the celebrities was part of the entertainment. Carlisle could be expected to make her appearance in a floor-length gown and feather boa, Cass would look erudite but down-to-earth in her horn-rimmed glasses, and Bean could be counted on to ask questions that revealed a font of obscure knowledge.

Sue Russell

SEE ALSO: *Game Shows; Goodson, Mark; Quiz Show Scandals; Sales, Soupy;* Seinfeld*; Swann, Lynn; Television;* What's My Line?.

BIBLIOGRAPHY

Brooks, Tim, and Earle Marsh. *The Complete Directory to Prime Time Network and Cable TV Shows, 1946–Present*, 9th ed.

New York: Ballantine Books, 2007.

DeLong, Thomas A. *Quiz Craze: America's Infatuation with Game Shows.* New York: Praeger, 1991.

Harris, Jay S., ed. *TV Guide: The First 25 Years.* New York: Simon & Schuster, 1978.

Schwartz, David; Steve Ryan; and Fred Wostbrock. *The Encyclopedia of TV Game Shows.* New York: Zoetrope, 1987.

Today

The longest-running early-morning network television program, the *Today* show premiered on NBC on January 14, 1952, just months after the first live coast-to-coast television broadcast in the United States. Aired live from New York at 7 a.m. Mondays through Fridays, the two-hour show—the prototype of the newsmagazine format—added a Sunday program in 1987 and a live Saturday program in 1992. By 2012, sixty years after its origin, the *Today* show was still relying on its original format: a combination of news; interviews with leading newsmakers; features on topics such as health, personal finance, and food; and entertainment segments.

PIONEER IN DAYTIME TELEVISION

Sylvester "Pat" Weaver, who developed *Your Show of Shows* and the *Tonight* show, created the *Today* show as a type of broadcast newsmagazine that could be watched in segments while viewers ate breakfast or prepared to go to work or school. It premiered when television sets were a rarity and early-morning broadcasting was unknown. In 1952 daytime television was still uncommon in many parts of the United States.

After a considerable search, the man Weaver chose to host the show was Dave Garroway, a relaxed, witty conversationalist who wore professorial horn-rimmed spectacles. His early experience as a radio newscaster, plus his wide audience gained on the variety show *Garroway at Large* over WMAQ-TV in Chicago, convinced Weaver he was the performer needed to attract and hold a nationwide audience that was just out of bed. Jack Lescoulie was picked to report sports as well as the amusing stories from the day's news, and Jim Fleming read a news summary every half hour. *Today* opened in its own studio in the RCA Exhibition Hall on West 49th Street in Manhattan, outfitted with a large plate-glass window that allowed passersby to see the show and be seen on camera. President Harry Truman, known for his morning walks, happened to lead his entourage by the *Today* window one morning when he was in New York and was stopped for a brief interview. During the show's first year, television critics complained of the program's slow pace and obsession with technological gadgets.

The show began making money in its second year, attracting larger audiences and luring thousands of children and their parents by adding J. Fred Muggs to the cast. Muggs was a strong-minded ten-month-old chimpanzee owned by trainers Buddy Menella and Roy Waldron. His unpredictable antics sometimes intimidated the staff but delighted the audience. Within the year J. Fred was making personal appearance tours and meeting his adoring fans. He became more difficult to handle each year and after five years gave way to a new chimp named Mr. Kokomo. The press release announcing his retirement said that Muggs was leaving to "extend his personal horizons."

Frank Blair became the show's newscaster in 1953 and remained on *Today* for twenty-three years, longer than anyone else connected with the program. That same year the show began to feature shapely young women as "*Today* girls," who read the temperature and a one-word description of the weather in major U.S. cities. The first of these was actress Estelle Parsons, followed by Lee Meriwether (Miss America of 1955), singer

Today, *1981.* *The personalities on the* Today *show in 1981 included, from left, critic Gene Shalit, anchors Jane Pauley and Tom Brokaw, and weatherman Willard Scott.* NBC/NBC NEWSWIRE/GETTY IMAGES.

Helen O'Connell, and actresses Betsy Palmer, Florence Henderson, and Maureen O'Sullivan. The only one of them to gain long-running status on the show was Barbara Walters, whose role was gradually expanded to that of coanchor. Walters, who had appeared on rival CBS's *The Morning Show* was originally hired by *Today* as a writer. Pressed into on-camera service during the events surrounding the assassination of President John F. Kennedy, she became a regular in 1963.

CHANGES AT ANCHOR

In July 1961 Garroway closed the show for the last time, giving his audience a smile, a raised open palm, and his trademark peace sign-off. He was replaced by John Chancellor, a veteran newscaster who was never comfortable in the show's format and left after fourteen months. Replacing Chancellor in October 1962 was Hugh Downs, who became the only television personality to have a regular position on all three of Pat Weaver's program creations: *Today*, *Tonight*, and *Home*. Downs had been Jack Paar's announcer and sidekick during the entire run of Paar's show (1957–1962). He continued to appear regularly on ABC's *20/20*, coanchoring the show with Walters in the late 1990s.

Frank McGee replaced Downs in October 1971, and Walters's growing stature on the program strained their relationship. Jim Hartz, hired with Walters's approval, replaced McGee (who died of bone cancer in 1974) and after a short stay was himself replaced by Tom Brokaw. When Walters left the show for a lucrative ABC contract in 1976, an extensive search was begun to replace her, and six candidates were tested on air: Cassie Mackin, Betty Rollin, Linda Ellerbee, Kelly Lange, Betty Furness, and Jane Pauley. Pauley, born in 1950, was only two years older than the show itself, but she won over all the contenders, and the new team of Brokaw, Pauley, and Willard Scott was able, in 1977, to bolster the show's declining ratings and maintain its number one rank among morning programs. Bryant Gumbel joined *Today* as a sportscaster in 1980 and became a cohost in 1982. By that time, the show no longer was the dominant force in the early morning. ABC's *Good Morning America*, which had previously beaten *Today* in the ratings for a few weeks in 1979, now won the ratings race consistently in 1982 and 1983, and in one week in 1983, the *CBS Morning News* nudged *Today* into third place.

During the 1980s the Gumbel-Pauley-Scott team increased the program's ratings and won the race against *Good Morning America* frequently until 1989, when a well-publicized incident sent the series into another decline. In February 1989 an interoffice memo in which Gumbel was harshly critical of Scott and movie critic Gene Shalit was leaked to the press, causing fans to express their loyalty by changing channels. The second move that proved unpopular with the viewers was the reduced role played by Pauley when Deborah Norville was added to the show as newscaster. Pauley announced her departure on December 28, 1989, but continued on other NBC shows, filling in for Brokaw on the *NBC Nightly News* and hosting her own prime-time series, *Real Life with Jane Pauley*.

Today's ratings plunged 15 percent in the spring of 1990, and *Good Morning America* was atop the charts again, but in April 1991 the popular Katie Couric was named cohost with Gumbel, and *Today* soon became dominant again. Couric had joined the show as its first national correspondent in June 1990 and had served as substitute anchor since February 1991. A native of Washington, D.C., and an honor graduate of the University of Virginia, Couric showed an intelligent, probing, but polite and friendly style in memorable segments of the show, including Hillary Rodham Clinton's first television interview as First Lady, General Colin Powell's farewell to his position on the joint chiefs of staff, Anita Hill's first interview after the crisis with Clarence Thomas, and General Norman Schwarzkopf's first interview after the Persian Gulf War. She also cohosted, with Dick Enberg and, later, Bob Costas, NBC's morning coverage of several Olympic Games.

Couric left the show in 2006, going to rival network CBS as the anchor of its evening news show. Meredith Vieira, a journalist who had previously been on ABC's *The View*, filled the coanchor seat from 2006 to 2011. After Vieira's departure, *Today* news anchor Ann Curry stepped up to take the coanchor job but was replaced by Savannah Guthrie in 2012.

Matt Lauer, a native of New York City, replaced Gumbel as coanchor of *Today* in January 1997, and the show continued to gain viewers. A graduate of Ohio University with a degree in communications, Lauer worked as coanchor of *Today in New York* for the city's NBC affiliate before joining the *Today* show's news desk in 1994. His frequent filling in for golfing buddy Gumbel led to an outpouring of cards and letters from fans throughout the nation, and Lauer was promoted to coanchor. Another factor in the show's continued high ratings was the moving of the show into a glass-walled, ground-floor production center in June 1994. Just as in the early days of the program, the crowd outside the window became a vital part of the *Today* show; the hosts frequently conduct on-the-spot interviews with visitors. *Today* continued to earn the top ratings through the first decade of the twenty-first century in spite of the multiple changes to its anchor team.

EXPANDING *TODAY*

In 2000 the show expanded its coverage to three hours, and in 2007 *Today* added another hour, making it the only four-hour national morning show broadcast. The fourth hour is hosted by a different team, Kathie Lee Gifford and Hoda Kotb. Other familiar faces on the 2012 *Today* show include Natalie Morales, news anchor, and Al Roker, weatherman, who together cohost the third hour.

In January 2012 the show celebrated its sixtieth anniversary by hosting an on-the-air reunion with as many of its past anchors as it could assemble. The *Today* show remains a window on the world for its viewers, with live shows originating from the Orient Express streaking across Europe, as well as from China, Russia, the French Riviera, Italy, the United Kingdom, Australia, South America, and Cuba.

Benjamin Griffith

SEE ALSO: *Anita Hill–Clarence Thomas Senate Hearings; Brokaw, Tom; Costas, Bob; Downs, Hugh; Gulf Wars; Miss America Pageant; Olympics; Paar, Jack; Television;* 20/20; *Walters, Barbara;* Your Show of Shows.

BIBLIOGRAPHY

Battaglio, Stephen. *From Yesterday to "Today": Six Decades of America's Favorite Morning Show*. Philadelphia: Running Press, 2011.

Castleman, Harry, and Walter J. Podrazik. *Watching TV: Four Decades of Watching Television*. New York: McGraw-Hill, 1982.

Kessler, Judy. *Inside "Today": The Battle for the Morning.* New York: Villard, 1992.

McNeil, Alex. *Total Television: A Comprehensive Guide to Programming from 1948 to the Present*, 4th ed. New York: Penguin Books, 1996.

Mink, Eric; Laurie Dolphin; and Christian Brown. *This Is "Today": A Window on Our Times.* Kansas City, MO: Andrews McMeel Publishing, 2003.

Toffler, Alvin *(1928–)*

Alvin Toffler, perhaps the most popular futurist in America, became a celebrity in the 1960s and 1970s for his predictions and suggestions for ways people could cope with the unprecedented rate of change initiated by new technologies. With the publication of his best seller *Future Shock* in 1970, Toffler became a household name and won many admirers in government and business. *The Third Wave* (1980) made him internationally known, and with *Powershift: Knowledge, Wealth, and Violence at the Edge of the Twenty-First Century* (1991) and *Creating a New Civilization: The Politics of the Third Wave* (1994), Toffler's fame grew widely. Since 1993 his wife, Heidi, has begun to share authorial credit with him, although he claims that she coauthored all of his previous books as well. Together they are known as the couple "who brought futurism to the masses," as Michael Krantz wrote in a 1996 article in *Time* magazine.

In *Future Shock*, Toffler argues that Americans were experiencing confusion and denial about the changes they were witnessing in society. He calls this "future shock," a concept he derived from the anthropological concept of "culture shock," which means the inability of members of primitive cultures to adapt to a more advanced culture. Very similarly, Toffler argues, Americans were growing unable to cope with the new culture that was coming into being as technology changed the way people worked and lived. Witnessing the social upheaval of the 1960s, Toffler believed that the mass hysteria of the protests and growing divorce and crime rates were signs that Americans were reaching a limit beyond which they could accept no more change. As remedies to future shock, Toffler argues that children should read more science fiction and that the study of the future should become a standard part of American education.

The main problem, according to Toffler, was that America was undergoing a fundamental shift from a Second Wave to a Third Wave society. The First Wave was the adoption of the agrarian way of life 10,000 years ago, the Second Wave was the urbanization and industrial revolution that began in the late seventeenth century, and the Third Wave that began after World War II he calls a "super-industrial revolution." This last phase of human development was fueled by the rise of technologies that were driven by knowledge rather than power derived from ownership of raw materials.

In *The Third Wave* he predicts that the personal computer would become a household item, three years before IBM (International Business Machines) introduced computers for home use. Toffler also believed that an information superhighway would become an important part of our everyday lives and that changes in our economy would effect a fundamental restructuring of our society; a "demassification" that would turn back some of the impact of centralization and standardization of the industrial era. Workers would return to the home, establishing living patterns similar in some ways to the First Wave of human development. The difference, however, is that people would be linked by new technologies that enabled them to communicate with others all over the world. And instead of having to purchase identical, mass-produced products, consumers would be presented with a growing number of choices as smaller industries became more feasible. In what became the focus of his two books of the 1990s, he predicted that the federal government would become less centralized as power shifted to small interest groups and local governments.

Finally, in their latest book, *Revolutionary Wealth: How It Will Be Created and How It Will Change Our Lives* (2006), the Tofflers argue that people can make money from the chaos of the changing economy and that new ways of creating value will help avoid a future of scarcity. For example, they coined the term *prosumer economy* to describe a new emphasis on unpaid work that greatly increases the quality of life.

LOOKING FORWARD TO CHANGE

Toffler looked forward to the changes that would take place, arguing optimistically that a more direct democracy, more varieties of family structure and home life, greater utilization of renewable energy resources, a decentralized government, and a more accessible media would result from the Third Wave, effectively eliminating social hierarchies. He attempted to ease the fears of Americans about the rapid rate of change. In *The Third Wave* he argues that "we are the final generation of an old civilization and the first generation of a new one. . . . Much of our personal confusion, anguish, and disorientation can be traced directly to the conflict within us, and within our political institutions, between the dying Second Wave civilization and the emergent Third Wave civilization that is thundering to take its place." His optimism about the positive effects this shift would have on the quality of life and his urgent message that we must prepare for these changes rather than impede their progress drew many disciples, most notably Ronald Reagan and Newt Gingrich. Ted Turner even claimed to have gotten the idea for CNN (Cable News Network) from *The Third Wave.*

The Tofflers' main goal has been to prepare people for the changes ahead and to make them more comfortable with the concept of change. They want Americans to abandon their nostalgia for small-town life, the nuclear family, and employment stability of the past and to embrace a future in which knowledge and flexibility will be the greatest assets. As Toffler told Charles Platt in *Dream Makers*, he wants to "open up the reader's mind to other ways of conceptualizing our political and social structures. I think that helps people adapt."

Anne Boyd

SEE ALSO: *CNN; Divorce; IBM (International Business Machines); The Internet; Reagan, Ronald; Science Fiction Publishing; Turner, Ted.*

BIBLIOGRAPHY

Cole, Patrick E., and Michael Krantz. "Cashing In on Tomorrow: A Generation after the Tofflers' *Future Shock*, Professional Prognosticators See Nothing but Blue Skies." *Time*, July 15, 1996, 52–54.

Judis, John B. "Newt's Not-So-Weird Gurus: In Defense of the Tofflers." *New Republic*, October 9, 1995, 16–23.

Platt, Charles. *Dream Makers: The Uncommon Men and Women Who Write Science Fiction*, vol. 2. New York: Berkley Books, 1983.

Toffler, Alvin. *Future Shock*. New York: Random House, 1970.

Toffler, Alvin. *The Third Wave*. New York: Morrow, 1980.

Toffler, Alvin, and Heidi Toffler. *Revolutionary Wealth: How It Will Be Created and How It Will Change Our Lives*. New York: Knopf, 2006.

Toga Parties

At the turn of the twentieth century, when poet Ezra Pound advised writers to "make it new," he was referring to the need for a new vision that would propel artists through a new century. However, as artists, intellectuals, writers, and other makers of culture turned to their crafts in order to create a new world, they found themselves peering at the past as much as the future. They looked not to the recent past, from which they wanted to free themselves, but to the ancient past of Greece and Rome. Homage to the classical world sometimes manifested itself in the toga party, which took place throughout the century and became particularly popular during the 1970s. Revising classical culture to modern sensibilities, toga parties represented not only youthful exuberance but also an underlying desire to maintain a link to the days of yore. (The name derives from the *toga*, a simple cloth wrap worn loosely around the body in imitation of the national garment of the early Romans.) Such parties played out the legendary excesses of the Roman god, Bacchus, the god of wine, and his Greek precursor, Dionysus.

It is not hard to see why the figure of Dionysus had such appeal in the twentieth century, when more open attitudes toward sexuality began to take hold. At the beginning of the century, "modern women" announced their modernity by cropping their hair short and wearing Greek bangs, and during the 1920s classical-style tunics became popular. One motto of the 1930s—"wine, women, and song"—was a direct call from the ancient rite of the Bacchanal, or Dionysian rites of spring. The call of the ancient Greeks and Romans was even heard at the White House of Franklin Delano Roosevelt in the early 1930s, when Eleanor Roosevelt hosted a great toga party in an attempt to poke fun at the politicians and news writers who viewed the president as a second Caesar.

The toga was revived with the 1978 film *Animal House*, which features a fraternity house toga party. Across the United States, students wrapped themselves in bed sheets draped like togas in attempts to imitate Greek and Roman figures and the Bacchanal. At times, John Belushi and other actors from *Animal House* would show up at such parties. Perhaps the most widely publicized, if not the largest, toga party was held at the University of Wisconsin, where 10,000 people attended, all wearing sheets draped like togas and many sporting garlands of flowers in their hair. Much as rock concerts of the 1960s defined that generation, toga parties became an identifying rite of passage for the generation of the 1970s.

During the 1990s toga parties were still known to take place, although largely as nostalgic gestures. Occasionally the idea of the toga party is still revived, and articles on how to make a toga out of a bed sheet have appeared in magazines and on the Internet, along with ways to serve grapes and alcohol in the mock tradition of the Greeks. However, by and large, the fad has died out. Toga parties are now popular mostly among undergraduates enrolled in courses focused on classical and foundational Greek and Roman literature.

Lolly Ockerstrom

SEE ALSO: Animal House*; Belushi, John; College Fads.*

BIBLIOGRAPHY

"About Toga Parties." eHow. Accessed December 2011. Available from http://www.ehow.com/about_4743658_toga-parties.htm

Hope, Thomas. *Costumes of the Greeks and Romans*. New York: Dover: 1962.

Marum, Andrew, and Frank Parise. *Follies and Foibles: A View of 20th Century Fads*. New York: Facts On File, 1984.

Tokyo Rose

During World War II, Allied forces in the Pacific, which were mostly American, were assailed by propaganda broadcasts from radio stations throughout the Japanese empire. Many of the broadcasters were women, and American soldiers and sailors collectively referred to them by the name "Tokyo Rose." The American Office of War Information concluded that none of

Tokyo Rose. *Tokyo Rose meets with American troops in the waning months of World War II.* MPI/STRINGER/ARCHIVE PHOTOS/GETTY IMAGES.

these women referred to herself as Tokyo Rose and that the name "Tokyo Rose" was "strictly a GI invention."

The Tokyo Rose broadcasters taunted the Allied soldiers by implying that their wives and sweethearts back home were being unfaithful to them. Some soldiers later claimed that Tokyo Rose announcers identified Allied units, predicted Japanese bombing raids, warned soldiers who were about to go into battle that they would be cut to pieces, and made otherwise demoralizing remarks.

There was one Tokyo-based program, known as *Zero Hour*, which consisted of musical numbers, readings of letters from Allied prisoners-of-war (POWs), and some news. A woman served as DJ for the musical portions of the program, and she interspersed the music with brief, and generally innocuous, commentary. The woman was an American named Iva Toguri d'Aquino. Although she never referred to herself as "Tokyo Rose" in her broadcasts—her moniker was "Orphan Ann"—she ended up being assigned the role of Tokyo Rose.

D'Aquino was born in the United States to Japanese parents. In 1941 she was in graduate school in the United States, studying to be a doctor, but she left the country for Japan to take care of a sick aunt. After the Japanese attacked Pearl Harbor and the United States was drawn into the war, she became stranded in Japan. While seeking work to support herself, d'Aquino got a part-time clerical job at NHK, the government radio service. She was noticed by Charles Cousens, an Australian POW who had been ordered by his Japanese captors to create radio propaganda aimed at the Allies. Cousens—who was later cleared of treason charges by Australian authorities—claimed that he tried to sabotage *Zero Hour* by making it useless as propaganda. As part of that plan, according to Cousens, he hired d'Aquino because she was anti-Japanese and had a bad radio voice. While she was working for Japanese radio, d'Aquino helped out many Allied POWs who were interned in the Tokyo area, giving them food and expressing pro-American sentiments.

Following the war two Hearst reporters looking for the famous Tokyo Rose were led to d'Aquino, who signed a contract giving various Hearst enterprises the exclusive rights to her story. In return, d'Aquino was promised $2000 (which for various reasons she never got). In the contract d'Aquino identified herself as "the one and original 'Tokyo Rose'" and gave numerous autographs identifying herself as Tokyo Rose. D'Aquino was stretching the truth, and it soon led her into serious trouble.

American authorities held d'Aquino in a Japanese prison for nearly a year while investigators tried to determine whether her broadcasts on behalf of Japan amounted to treason. Released in 1946 for lack of evidence, she wanted to return to the United States. The American Legion and noted broadcaster Walter Winchell were outraged that d'Aquino wanted to come back to the United States, and they demanded that she be arrested and tried. The public outcry convinced the Justice Department that d'Aquino's case needed to be reopened, and in September 1948 d'Aquino returned to the United States under military escort. The Federal Bureau of Investigation (FBI) arrested her when she arrived in San Francisco, California.

D'Aquino's trial began in July 1949. Of the eight charges against her, the jury found her guilty of only one charge of treason. D'Aquino was sentenced to ten years in prison, fined $10,000, and stripped of her American citizenship. Her sentence was later reduced for good behavior, and she was released in 1956 after serving six years. D'Aquino then moved to Chicago and went to work for her father, who owned and operated a mercantile shop, which she continued to run after his death in 1972.

Beginning around 1974 the Japanese American Citizens League (JACL) took an interest in d'Aquino's case. Then in 1976 media reports sympathetic to d'Aquino appeared. The jury foreman at her trial told *60 Minutes* that he thought d'Aquino was innocent of all charges. Articles in the *Chicago Tribune* indicated that two of the witnesses against her had lied. The JACL, the California legislature, conductor Seiji Ozawa, and soon-to-be Republican senator S. I. Hayakawa, among others, all supported d'Aquino receiving a presidential pardon, and in January 1977, just before his term of office came to an end, President Gerald Ford pardoned d'Aquino. The pardon restored d'Aquino's civil rights, including her American citizenship. In 2006 d'Aquino died of natural causes at the age of ninety.

Eric Longley

SEE ALSO: *FBI (Federal Bureau of Investigation); Radio;* 60 Minutes*; Winchell, Walter; World War II.*

BIBLIOGRAPHY

Chapman, Ivan. *Tokyo Calling: The Charles Cousens Case*. Sydney: Hale & Iremonger, 1990.

Duus, Masayo. *Tokyo Rose: Orphan of the Pacific*, tr. Peter Duus. New York: Kodansha International, 1979.

Harper, Dale P. "Personality: American-Born, UCLA-Educated Tokyo Rose Was Convicted of Treason against the United States." *World War II*, September 1994, 8, 67–69.

Howe, Russell Warren. *The Hunt for "Tokyo Rose."* New York: Madison Books, 1990.

Norton, Mary Beth, et al. *A People and a Nation: A History of the United States*, Vol. 2. Boston: Houghton Mifflin, 2003.

Uyeda, Clifford I. "The Pardoning of 'Tokyo Rose': A Report on the Restoration of American Citizenship to Iva Ikuko Toguri." *Amerasia* 5 (1978): 69–93.

Tolkien, J. R. R. *(1892–1973)*

Born in South Africa in 1892 to English parents and a resident of the United Kingdom from 1895 until his death in 1973, John Ronald Reuel Tolkien was one of the most prominent fantasy writers of the twentieth century. He is beloved for his epic fantasy trilogy, *The Lord of the Rings* (1954–1955), and its prequel, *The Hobbit* (1937). In his 1997 book *Defending Middle-earth: Tolkien, Myth, and Modernity*, Patrick Curry estimated worldwide sales of *The Lord of the Rings* at approximately fifty million copies—"probably the biggest-selling single work of fiction this century." *The Hobbit* has sold an estimated forty million copies, and Tolkien's books have been translated into more than thirty languages.

A 1997 survey of some 25,000 readers in England found *The Lord of the Rings* to be the runaway winner as the most important book of the past 100 years. Tolkien's popularity only increased with the release of three lauded, blockbuster live-action film adaptations of *The Lord of the Rings* between 2001 and 2003.

J. R. R. Tolkien. *J. R. R. Tolkien's academic studies of languages and literature are said to have greatly informed his own fiction writing.* HAYWOOD MAGEE/STRINGER/PICTURE POST/GETTY IMAGES.

ACADEME, LANGUAGES, AND WAR

In addition to his literary contributions, Tolkien was a prominent philologist. His academic career encompassed thirty-nine years, dating from his appointment in 1920 as Reader in English Language at Leeds University. He became the Rawlinson and Bosworth Professor of Anglo-Saxon at Oxford University in 1925 and held the prestigious Merton Professor of English position at Oxford from 1945 until his retirement in 1959. Tolkien's essay "*Beowulf*: The Monsters and the Critics" (1936) is regarded as a landmark scholarly work, as is his examination of regional dialect in the *Canterbury Tales*, "Chaucer as a Philologist" (1949). His critical edition of *Sir Gawain and the Green Knight* (1925), developed in collaboration with E. V. Gordon, is still taught today.

"There were not two Tolkiens, one an academic and the other a writer," asserts T. A. Shippey in his 2000 work, *J. R. R. Tolkien: Author of the Century*. "They were the same man, and the two sides of him overlapped so that they were indistinguishable—or rather they were not two sides at all, but different expressions of the same mind, the same imagination." Tolkien's academic research delved into ancient northern literatures and led him to learn such languages as Finnish, Gothic, Middle English, Old English, Old Norse, and Welsh. This research in turn shaped his fiction. In the U.S. foreword to the Ballantine edition of *The Lord of the Rings* (1966), Tolkien avers that his trilogy is "primarily linguistic in inspiration."

The blurring of Tolkien as an academic and a fantasy writer is nowhere more apparent than in his essay "On Fairy-Stories," first presented as the 1938 Andrew Lang Lecture at the University of St. Andrews and later expanded for the collection *Tree and Leaf* in 1964. Here, Tolkien demarcates a territory for fantasy that is distinct from stories that are presented as travelers' tales, dreams, or beast fables. Fantasy entails an act of sub-creation, namely, a secondary world separate from the primary world of everyday life. Secondary worlds must be internally consistent, thereby structuring a sense of "credible, commanding Secondary Belief." Central to fantasy are the elements of recovery, escape, and consolation. Tolkien coined the term "Eucatastrophe," which denotes the "sudden joyous 'turn'" that is the hallmark of fairy-tale happy endings.

Tolkien applied the precepts of "On Fairy-Stories" to the secondary world that occupied much of his life: Middle-earth. The genesis of Middle-earth was a poem written by Tolkien during his student days, based on a line from the Old English Advent poem "Crist," by Cynewulf: "Hail, Earendel, brightest of angels, over middle-earth sent to men." It sparked Tolkien's imagination and established the basis for a cosmology that began to emerge during World War I. As a lieutenant with the Lancashire Fusiliers, Tolkien was posted to France and fought in the Battle of the Somme. He later explained in a letter to his son, Christopher, that many of the early writings about Middle-earth were composed "in grimy canteens, at lectures in cold fogs, in huts full of blasphemy and smut, or by candle lights in bell-tents, even some down in dugouts under shell fire." These writings bore the title *The Book of Lost Tales*.

Tolkien returned to Oxford after a bout with trench fever and found sustenance in the English countryside. He was seized with the desire to create a mythology for England. Humphrey Carpenter quotes Tolkien on this point in his definitive biography, where the Oxford professor recollects how he "had a mind to make a body of more or less connected legend, ranging from the large and cosmogonic to the level of romantic fairy-story—the larger founded on the lesser in contact with the earth, the lesser drawing splendour from the vast backcloths—which I could dedicate simply: to England; to my country."

A small literary circle of Christian academics—The Inklings—acted as midwife for Tolkien's mythology. At Oxford, Tolkien regularly met with Owen Barfield, Charles Williams, and C. S. Lewis, whose *Chronicles of Narnia* would later adorn the lists of fantasy literature. The Inklings read aloud passages of their work, including a children's novel that Tolkien had been writing since one fateful day in the late 1920s, when he scribbled on the page of a blank exam book, "In a hole in the ground there lived a hobbit."

MIDDLE-EARTH

The Hobbit was published in 1937 to popular and critical acclaim. Set in Middle-earth, it narrates the adventures of Bilbo Baggins, a staid halfling who embarks on a quest with the wizard Gandalf and a party of dwarves to reclaim treasure stolen by the dragon Smaug. Along the way, Bilbo finagles a magic ring away from a twisted hobbit named Gollum. "Prediction is dangerous," ventured the *Times Literary Supplement*, "but *The Hobbit* may well prove a classic."

Bilbo's inheritance is at the heart of *The Lord of the Rings*, which approached completion in 1950. Frodo Baggins undertakes a perilous journey to Mount Doom in the land of Mordor, ruled by the dark lord, Sauron. There he must cast away Bilbo's ring, revealed by Gandalf to be the One Ring of Power lost by Sauron in the distant past. Humans, dwarves, and elves aid Frodo in his quest, while the War of the Ring ignites across Middle-earth. Tolkien unsuccessfully negotiated with Collins publishing house for the joint issuing of his epic with *The Silmarillion*, a revised version of *The Book of Lost Tales*. Allen and Unwin, publishers of *The Hobbit*, eventually agreed to publish *The Lord of the Rings* in three volumes—*The Fellowship of the Ring* (1954), *The Two Towers* (1954), and *The Return of the King* (1955).

Reaction to *The Lord of the Rings* varied. If some critics waxed rhapsodic, others derided Tolkien's work as medievalist pablum. The trilogy was received as an independent work, since *The Silmarillion* had languished unpublished for more than twenty years. The trilogy did not achieve widespread attention until 1966, following its U.S. publication by Ballantine Books in the wake of an unauthorized Ace Books paperback edition in 1965. It quickly vaulted to the top of the best-seller ranks and mushroomed into a full-blown cult phenomenon on college campuses during the 1960s and early 1970s.

The Silmarillion was finally published posthumously in 1977. Fans were perplexed by the lofty creation myth, biblical language, detailed genealogies, and almost complete lack of characterization. Critics were equally baffled until the scope of Tolkien's mythology was communicated via the editorship of his son, Christopher. *Unfinished Tales of Númenor and Middle-earth* appeared in 1980, followed by the twelve-volume opus of textual criticism, *The History of Middle-earth* (1983–1996).

LEGACY

Tolkien's popularity endures. Critics and worldwide audiences heartily embraced the live-action film trilogy adaptation of *The Lord of the Rings* between 2001 and 2003. In 2007 Christopher Tolkien completed editorial work on *The Children of Húrin*, a novel-like prequel to *The Lord of the Rings* set millennia before the birth of Bilbo and Frodo Baggins, and more than 900,000 copies were in print worldwide two weeks after publication. Combining connected narrative materials present in such sources as *The Silmarillion*, *Unfinished Tales of Númenor and Middle-earth*, and *The History of Middle-earth*, *The Children of Húrin* offers casual readers their most accessible glimpse into what scholars now call Tolkien's legendarium, the sprawling mass of notes and manuscripts that constitute a fictional frame for *The Hobbit* and *The Lord of the Rings*. A growing body of scholarship focuses on the legendarium, and an academic journal, *Tolkien Studies*, was founded in 2004. Hundreds of scholarly articles and books on Tolkien and his works now exist.

Tolkien's influence on fantasy and science fiction has been profound. His example of a consistent, detailed secondary world is now the norm for imaginative writing. He is furthermore credited with the rekindling of fantasy as a narrative art. Among his descendants are such contemporary novelists as George R. R. Martin and Robert Jordan. Tolkien has inspired a legion of lesser imitators as well, with the result being derivative, multivolume series boasting faux medieval European settings, fit to bursting with cookie-cutter elves, inns, wizards, and megalomaniac dark lords. Outside of fiction, the example of Middle-earth has been fundamental to popular tabletop and digital games such as Dungeons & Dragons, Warhammer Fantasy Battles, and World of Warcraft. If Tolkienesque fantasy seems hackneyed today, few of his successors come close to rivaling the width and depth of the Middle-earth cosmos.

Neal Baker

SEE ALSO: *Best Sellers; Lewis, C. S.;* Lord of the Rings *Film Trilogy; Science Fiction Publishing.*

BIBLIOGRAPHY

Anderson, Douglas A.; Michael D. C. Drout; and Verlyn Flieger. *Tolkien Studies*. Morgantown: West Virginia University Press, 2004.

Carpenter, Humphrey. *Tolkien: A Biography*. Boston: Houghton Mifflin, 1977.

Carpenter, Humphrey; J. R. R. Tolkien; and Christopher Tolkien, eds. *The Letters of J. R. R. Tolkien*. Boston: Houghton Mifflin, 1981.

Curry, Patrick. *Defending Middle-earth: Tolkien, Myth, and Modernity*. New York: St. Martin's Press, 1997.

Lewis, C. S. "A World for Children." Review of *The Hobbit*, by J. R. R. Tolkien. *Times Literary Supplement*, October 2, 1937.

Shippey, T. A. *The Road to Middle-earth*. Boston: Houghton Mifflin, 1983.

Shippey, T. A. *J. R. R. Tolkien: Author of the Century*. Boston: Houghton Mifflin, 2000.

Tolkien, J. R. R. "On Fairy-Stories." In *Tree and Leaf.* Boston: Houghton Mifflin, 1965.

Tom of Finland *(1920–1991)*

Tom of Finland's frankly pornographic drawings have enjoyed a vast popularity since the 1970s. His work has been exhibited worldwide, and even mainstream publishers have produced collections of his drawings. Tom of Finland is now considered, in the words of biographer F. Valentine Hooven, "the foremost name in gay erotic art." In his essay in *Out in Culture*, critic Nayland Blake defines him as "one of the gay world's few authentic icons," noting his influence on artists as different as Robert Mapplethorpe, Bruce Weber, and Rainer Werner Fassbinder. A few years before Tom's death, a foundation was established to preserve and perpetuate his work, and in the 1990s Tom of Finland's influence even extended to fashion when the name of the pornographer became a trademark for a line of men's clothing.

Tom of Finland was born Touko Laaksonen in 1920 in Kaarina, then a rural area in the southwestern part of Finland. In 1939, after graduating from high school, Laaksonen went to art school in Helsinki to study advertising, but he soon had to suspend his studies because of World War II. After the war he completed his degree and also learned to play the piano at the renowned Sibelius Institute. In these early postwar years, Laaksonen kept his "dirty drawings" (as he liked to call them) to himself and earned his living by working as a freelance advertiser during the day and by playing the piano at parties and cafés in Helsinki's bohemian districts in the evenings. It was not until 1957 that he decided to submit some of his less graphic drawings (which he signed as Tom of Finland) for publication in *Physique Pictorial*, an American muscle magazine. The editor was so enthusiastic about the submissions that the cover of the Spring 1957 issue featured a drawing by Tom of Finland.

During the late 1950s and the 1960s, Tom of Finland's drawings were published regularly in American and European magazines and were sold to private publications all over the world. However, homosexual art did not sell very well at the time, and Tom of Finland could not give up his advertising job any earlier than 1973, the year of his first European exhibition. Five years later he went to Los Angeles for the first American exhibition of his drawings. During this trip he met Durk Dehner, who was to become Tom of Finland's successful manager and the cofounder of the Tom of Finland Foundation. In 1981, after the death of his companion of twenty-eight years, Veli, Tom of Finland divided his life equally between Finland and the United States until his own death ten years later.

In 1987 the anthological volume *Tom of Finland. Retrospective* was published to such great success that companion volumes *Retrospective II* and *Retrospective III* were also produced. Each volume documents Tom of Finland's career, from the naturalist drawings of the late 1940s to the 1987 "safe-sex" poster urging the use of condoms to his mature work featuring perfect physiques, exaggerated poses, and improbable sizes.

The characters in Tom of Finland's drawings are mostly men in uniform (soldiers, policemen, sailors, lumberjacks, and bikers in leather) involved in homosexual sex of all kinds and in every (im)possible position. Their huge pectorals and muscles, their perfectly rounded bottoms, and their enormous penises point to the exaggerated maleness of Tom of Finland's men, an iconography that goes against the dominant representation of gay men as effeminate and is thus an important point of reference for the leather gay subculture. Tom of Finland's drawings also counteract the enduring stereotype of "the sad and unhappy homosexual": the men in them are clearly having a lot of fun and are proud of their sexual orientation. Tom of Finland once declared that when he started to draw, "a gay man was made to feel nothing but shame about his feelings and his sexuality. I wanted my drawings to counteract that, to show gay men being happy and positive about who they were." Even if some of Tom of Finland's drawings take place in prisons or police stations or depict sadomasochistic situations, there is always a strong sense of play underlying them, and drama never intervenes.

A complex network of looks takes place in most of his drawings. As Blake points out, Tom of Finland has challenged the framework of the single gaze of traditional pornography where the object presents itself passively to the eyes of the viewer. In his drawings there is an interaction of looks between the different characters, which complements the gaze of the viewer. Often the two men having sex in the foreground are observed by a third man in the background. Sometimes the characters even respond to the gaze of the viewer, as in the case of Tom of Finland's reelaboration of Michelangelo's *David* (commissioned by the conservative Italian film director Franco Zeffirelli). Tom of Finland's David, much better endowed than Michelangelo's, wears a defiant look on his face and seems to be telling the viewer: "I know what you're looking at."

Tom of Finland's oeuvre is a lot more than just a series of "dirty drawings." As other critics have pointed out, when the cultural history of the late twentieth century's gay liberation movement is written, Tom of Finland will have to be acknowledged as having created an effective iconography for part of the gay world.

Luca Prono

SEE ALSO: *Gay Liberation Movement; Gay Men; Pornography.*

BIBLIOGRAPHY

Blake, Nayland. "Tom of Finland: An Appreciation." In *Out in Culture: Gay, Lesbian, and Queer Essays on Popular Culture*, eds. Corey K. Creekmur and Alexander Doty. Durham, NC: Duke University Press, 1995.

Hooven, Valentine F. *Tom of Finland: His Life and Times*. New York: St. Martin's Press, 1993.

Hooven, Valentine F. *Tom of Finland : Life and Work of a Gay Hero*. Berlin: Bruno Gmünder, 2011.

Tom of Finland. Retrospective I–III. Los Angeles: Tom of Finland Foundation, 1988–1997.

Tom Swift Series

A popular series of forty boys' novels published by Grosset & Dunlap between 1910 and 1941, the Tom Swift books were mostly published under the pen name Victor Appleton, though they were produced by the Stratemeyer Syndicate, a book packager that created other popular juvenile literature. Attempts were made to revive the series over the years, once in the 1950s with the Tom Swift Jr. books and again in the 1980s, 1990s, and early twenty-first century, but the last three attempts were not as successful as the first two series.

TOM SWIFT

The hero of the first series was Tom Swift, a young inventor, portrayed as a plucky, ingenious figure who used modern technology and American know-how to create new devices and foil his rivals. An excerpt from an advertisement written by Edward Stratemeyer (1862–1930) for the first Tom Swift books characterizes the scope of this series: "It is the purpose of these spirited tales to convey in a realistic way the wonderful advances in land and sea locomotion and to interest the boy of the present in the hope that he may be a factor in aiding the marvelous development that is coming in the future."

The Stratemeyer Syndicate, which created more than 1,400 books between 1905 and 1985, devised the series concepts and hired writers to complete book-length stories from a limited outline in exchange for a flat-fee compensation ($75 for the first Tom Swift book in 1910). The writer hired to become Victor Appleton for the majority of the Tom Swift volumes was Stratemeyer's close friend Howard Roger Garis (1873–1962), who created the Uncle Wiggily stories and ghostwrote nearly 300 books for the syndicate. Stratemeyer and Garis worked closely to craft a series of adventure stories with inventions inspired by the real-world work of inventors who were mentioned in such magazines as *Scientific American*. Other writers involved on a limited basis for this series included W. Bert Foster, John W. Duffield, and Thomas M. Mitchell.

The early Tom Swift volumes featured existing vehicles, including a motorcycle and a motorboat that Tom acquired and improved with suggestions from his father, "the aged inventor," Barton Swift. Next, Tom helped others with their inventions: the *Red Cloud*, an airship designed by John Sharp, and a submarine built by his father. By the fifth volume (all five were published in 1910), Tom built his first invention, an alkaline battery for an electric car. Later inventions of note included his sky racer (1911), a revolutionary photo telephone (1914), a coast-to-coast airline express (1926), a motor home called a house on wheels (1929), and a device to allow radio listeners to see the performers on a silvery screen with his "talking pictures" (1928).

In most cases, Tom Swift's vehicles were bigger and faster than their real-world counterparts, which often did not become practical until much later. A typical story involved a discussion of an exotic locale or strange event by the main characters, Tom; Barton; Tom's chum Ned Newton; and their eccentric friend, Mr. Wakefield Damon, who "blessed" more than 1,200 items and parts of his body throughout the series. Tom and friends were usually dogged by rivals, including Andy Foger, the squint-eyed redheaded bully who seemed to be on the scene no matter how remote the locale.

TOM SWIFT JR.

The Tom Swift series generated a combined sales of more than six million volumes, so it is no surprise that in the early 1950s, the Stratemeyer Syndicate created a spin-off series, Tom Swift Jr., to try to reclaim part of the market share lost to the *Rick Brant* series (1947–1968), published under the John Blaine pseudonym. Work on the Tom Swift Jr. series was begun in 1951, and by 1952 a manuscript of the first volume was far enough along to receive comments by one of the syndicate's science consultants, Robert H. Snyder. Despite this early start, the first five books in the series would not be published until 1954, after rewrites.

Between 1954 and 1971 Grosset & Dunlap published thirty-three books about Tom Swift Jr. and his sister Sandra; pal Bud Barclay; and potential girlfriend, Phyllis Newton, daughter of Ned Newton from the original series. Tom Swift Sr. makes appearances as a middle-aged man who remains active in science and invention. While the original series had titles such as *Tom Swift and His Electric Rifle* (1911), the Tom Swift Jr. series used atomic, electronic, and outer-space themes, such as *Tom Swift and His Atomic Earth Blaster* (1954). For the Tom Swift Jr. series, plot took a backseat to title in the early development of a volume. Long lists of proposed titles were considered. Once a title was selected, a story idea would be devised to match it.

Victor Appleton II was said to have "inherited his wonderful storytelling ability from the original Victor Appleton" in dust jacket ads for the early books. It is hard to say whether the syndicate was referring to the ghostwriters or itself. While several writers wrote a volume or two, most of the newer series (volumes 5–7, 9–29) were written by James Duncan Lawrence (1918–1994), a syndicate ghostwriter who also wrote for a number of different media, including screenplays for television and radio, books, and comic strips.

The Tom Swift Jr. series inspired a Parker Brothers board game in 1966 and a Tom Swift Jr. activity book in 1978. A television pilot called "The Solar Sub" with Gary Vinson as Tom Jr. was filmed in 1958 but was not sold or aired.

TOM SWIFT III, IV, AND YOUNG INVENTOR

The Tom Swift Jr. series was discontinued in 1971 due to declining sales, which had more to do with the aging baby boomers than it did with the perceived problem of Tom's achievements being surpassed by a real-world NASA. At the close of the Tom Swift Jr. series, an anonymous memo laid the groundwork for yet another new Tom Swift series, this time set in the distant future when Tom Swift's inventions have become a reality. This new series contained science fiction stories of interplanetary space travel with titles such as *Terror on the Moons of Jupiter* (1981).

Very little in the way of invention was included in the stories, and little or no reference was made to the previous two series. Part of the reason for this was that the new group of ghostwriters had published science fiction books under their own names and because this series was published by Wanderer, a division of Simon & Schuster, which purchased the Stratemeyer Syndicate in 1984. The third Tom Swift series was discontinued at this time.

In 1991 Simon & Schuster decided to try the venerable name of Tom Swift again in a new series, published under its Archway imprint. Thirteen volumes were published, this time featuring Tom Swift in a contemporary setting with inventions again being the focus, as in *Cyborg Kickboxer* (1991) and *Death Quake* (1993). Two additional volumes by Franklin W. Dixon were combined adventures with the Hardy Boys. Overall this new series did not sell very well, and it was soon discontinued.

Following the introduction of first-person narrative Hardy Boys and Nancy Drew series, Tom Swift received similar treatment. Six volumes were published in this series between 2006 and 2007. The cover illustrations have a Manga-inspired style reflecting the publisher's perception of what would be popular with young readers.

All in all, Tom Swift appeared in 105 published stories in five series in fewer than 100 years. While the five series have not attracted many young readers, they remain remembered by a segment of adult collectors, many of whom grew up with the Tom Swift Jr. books.

James D. Keeline

SEE ALSO: *The Bobbsey Twins; The Hardy Boys; Nancy Drew; NASA; Parker Brothers; Science Fiction Publishing;* Scientific American*; Stratemeyer, Edward.*

BIBLIOGRAPHY

Dizer, John T., Jr. *Tom Swift and Company: "Boy's Books" by Stratemeyer and Others.* Jefferson, NC: McFarland, 1982.

Dizer, John T., Jr. *Tom Swift, the Bobbsey Twins, and Other Heroes of American Juvenile Literature.* Lewiston, NY: Edwin Mellen Press, 1997.

Garis, Roger. *My Father Was Uncle Wiggily.* New York: McGraw-Hill, 1966.

Johnson, Deidre. *Edward Stratemeyer and the Stratemeyer Syndicate.* New York: Twayne, 1993.

Johnson, Deidre, ed. *Stratemeyer Pseudonyms and Series Books: An Annotated Checklist of Stratemeyer and Stratemeyer Syndicate Publications.* Westport, CT: Greenwood Press, 1982.

TomKat

SEE: *Cruise, Tom.*

Tomlin, Lily *(1939–)*

Lily Tomlin, a gifted comedian, writer, and actress, emerged on American television in the late 1960s as a featured performer on the highly innovative and successful comedy variety series *Rowan & Martin's Laugh-In.* She became noted for her gallery of memorable characters—such as Ernestine the telephone operator and the sassy, five-year-old Edith Ann—and for her ability to transform herself into many vivid personae without costume changes or makeup. During the 1970s and 1980s she established herself as "America's reigning female comic genius" by appearing in a series of praised television specials, releasing a best-selling comedy album, and making a successful transition to the big screen. Known for her versatility, she occasionally appeared in dramatic roles for some of Hollywood's most respected directors.

In 1985 Tomlin scored her greatest artistic triumph with her one-woman Broadway smash hit, *The Search for Signs of Intelligent Life in the Universe*, a summary of a generation of social history through a series of character sketches. By the 1990s and into the new millennium, Tomlin was displaying her talents through series television, film, animation, and commercials. She has earned Tony and Emmy Awards, a Grammy, and an Academy Award nomination.

Mary Jean Tomlin was born on September 1, 1939, in Detroit, Michigan. From a young age she was a close observer of people. Raised by a factory worker and a housewife who had moved north from Paducah, Kentucky, in search of jobs during the Depression, Tomlin discovered a passion for theater while attending Wayne State University. She combined her desire to perform comedy with talents for observation and mimicry to find her own style as an entertainer. In his 1989 book *Lily Tomlin: Woman of a Thousand Faces*, author Jeff Sorensen writes of Tomlin's comedic evolution, "Unlike other comics who stick with one successful persona, she was determined to play as many parts as she could dream up. Characters impressions were what interested Tomlin; she had no intention of standing up and telling topical jokes on subjects." Tomlinson herself has said, "My comedy is actual life with the slightest twist of exaggeration. I construct compressed accuracy, a character essence that is as true as I can get it. I don't go for laughter. I never play for a joke *per se.* If the joke gets in the character's way, I take it out."

LAUGH-IN

Tomlin began her career while still in college, playing in Detroit coffeehouses, and eventually made her way to New York. After honing her routines at a Manhattan nightclub and in several off-Broadway productions, she landed a part on *Laugh-In* in

Lily Tomlin. *Lily Tomlin parlayed her early success as a sketch comedian into television and movie roles and a successful one-woman Broadway show.* JEFFREY MAYER/CONTRIBUTOR/WIREIMAGE/GETTY IMAGES.

1969. Tomlin became a celebrity during her tenure on the show, which aired from 1968 to 1973. She endeared herself to audiences by inventing characters embodying both humor and intelligence. The most recognizable of her zany personae was Ernestine the telephone operator, a nasal, overbearing woman who began her sketches with the catchphrase, "One ringy-dingy, two ringy-dingy, is this the party to whom I am speaking?" The wise-cracking Ernestine became so popular that AT&T offered Tomlin $500,000 to do a commercial, but she refused, stating that it would compromise the character's comedic integrity. One of Ernestine's best-known lines was, "We don't care. We don't have to. We're the Phone Company."

Another of Tomlin's legendary characters of the early 1970s was Edith Ann, an uninhibited, lisping five-year-old who sat in an oversized rocking chair as she discussed her life. Edith Ann concluded her observations with her trademark expression: "And that's the truth." Tomlin continued to generate memorable characters after she left *Laugh-In* to star in a series of comedy specials. Her most famous creations include Trudy the bag lady, Sister Boogie-Woman, and Mrs. Beasley. The great popularity of these and other characters transformed Tomlin into a national comedic phenomenon.

BREAKING INTO FILMS

Tomlin's range continued to expand as she moved beyond television. Her film debut came in 1975 when she was cast in Robert Altman's music industry epic *Nashville*. Her performance in the noncomedic role of Linnea, a devoted mother and gospel singer who has an affair with a rock star, earned her an Academy Award nomination. She followed this early screen success with parts in such acclaimed films as *The Late Show* (1977), *9 to 5* (1980), *All of Me* (1984), *Big Business* (1988), and *A Prairie Home Companion* (2006). The 1978 release of *Moment by Moment*, a romance that paired her with John Travolta, caused a setback on her career. Critics lambasted the film, and audiences ignored it. Tomlin bounced back in 1985 with her Broadway triumph, *The Search for Signs of Intelligent Life in the Universe*. She and writer Jane Wagner produced the acclaimed feminist look at the human condition that appealed to all audiences.

Tomlin continued to express her versatility into the 1990s, acting as a TV executive on the sitcom *Murphy Brown*, performing the voice of the teacher/bus driver on the animated educational show *The Magic School Bus*, and making many film and TV guest appearances. Two of her best characterizations during this period were those of an aging hippie in the film *Flirting with Disaster* (1996) and a murderous Christmas spirit in a 1998 episode of *The X-Files*. During the first decade of the 2000s she had recurring roles on several popular television dramas—*The West Wing* , *Desperate Housewives*, and *Damages*—and on the sitcom *Will & Grace*.

In 2001 Tomlin officially came out to the press as a lesbian. Although her longtime relationship with Wagner was widely acknowledged in Hollywood, she had not previously announced her sexual orientation to the public. In 2003 she was awarded the Mark Twain Prize for American Humor, one of the comedy world's highest honors.

Charles Coletta

SEE ALSO: *Altman, Robert; AT&T; Broadway; Coming Out;* Desperate Housewives*; Emmy Awards; Feminism; Grammy Awards; Hollywood;* Laugh-In*; Lesbianism; Sitcom; Stand-Up omedy; Television; Tony Awards; Travolta, John;* Will & Grace*;* The X-Files.

BIBLIOGRAPHY

Anderson, Christopher. *The New Book of People*. New York: Putnam, 1986.

Brooks, Tim. *The Complete Directory to Prime Time TV Stars*. New York: Ballantine Books, 1987.

Grace, Arthur. *Comedians*. New York: Thomasson-Grant, 1991.

LaRoche, Loretta. *Kick Up Your Heels . . . Before You're Too Short to Wear Them: How to Live a Long, Healthy, Juicy Life*. Carlsbad, CA: Hay House, 2007.

Sorensen, Jeff. *Lily Tomlin: Woman of a Thousand Faces*. New York: St. Martin's Press, 1989.

Tone, Franchot *(1905–1968)*

In the succinct words of film critic David Thomson, "Tone was perhaps all that Franchot had—that and Joan Crawford," the first of his four wives. Born the son of a wealthy industrialist in Niagara, New York, and educated at Cornell, Franchot Tone had a distinguished stage career, working with the Group Theater among others. His film career, although long and prolific (1932–1968), consigned him to roles as wealthy café-society sophisticates, weak cads, or the losing end of love triangles in archetypal romances of the 1930s and 1940s. In 1936 he received an Oscar nomination for his supporting role in *Mutiny on the Bounty* and married Crawford "after one of the most denied, affirmed, and re-denied romances Hollywood had ever witnessed," as one columnist commented.

Unhappy with his film roles, Tone returned to Broadway, starring in Ernest Hemingway's *The Fifth Column* in 1940 but was soon back in Hollywood. Although he lacked the necessary screen charisma for leading-man stardom, he worked with many of the top directors, including John Ford, Josef von Sternberg, and Billy Wilder. He made several films with Crawford and was with Jean Harlow in *Bombshell* (1933) and Bette Davis in *Dangerous* (1935). He gave his most memorable performances toward the end of his career and his life: the dying president in Otto Preminger's *Advise and Consent* (1962) and the grim Ruby Lapp in Arthur Penn's *Mickey One* (1965).

Benjamin Griffith

SEE ALSO: *Academy Awards; Broadway; Crawford, Joan; Davis, Bette; Harlow, Jean; Hemingway, Ernest; Hollywood;* Mutiny on the Bounty*; Preminger, Otto; von Sternberg, Josef; Wilder, Billy.*

BIBLIOGRAPHY

Bret, David. *Joan Crawford: Hollywood Martyr*. New York: Carroll & Graf Publishers, 2007.

Jarvis, Everett G. *Final Curtain: Deaths of Noted Movie and TV Personalities*. Secaucus, NJ: Carol Publishing, 1995.

Shipman, David. *The Great Movie Stars: The Golden Years*. New York: Crown, 1970.

The Tonight Show

NBC's venerable late-night talk show *The Tonight Show* has provided a unique window into the changing times and mores of contemporary American culture. Beginning in 1954 as *Tonight!* (later renamed *The Tonight Show*), its five principal hosts have used the program as a pulpit for nightly commentary on events both profound and piddling. Over the decades, the show has fluctuated wildly in terms of its influence and quality. At various times it offered groundbreaking comedy, scintillating conversation, and instructions for stylish living. Even Jay Leno's tepid, nonthreatening *Tonight Show* of the 1990s seemed somehow to reflect the tenor of its self-satisfied times.

STEVE ALLEN AND JACK PAAR

The first host of *The Tonight Show* was Steve Allen, a former disc jockey who had presided over a succession of Golden Age TV offerings. During his innovative three-year run as host, Allen established the program's basic format: a monologue followed by a comedy set piece and a series of conversations with celebrity guests. Allen also inaugurated the show's long-running practice of breaking in new stand-up comedians. Lenny Bruce and Mort Sahl were just two of the comedians who got their start slinging jokes at Allen's audience. In later years, such prominent entertainers as George Carlin, Richard Pryor, and Roseanne Barr would gain their initial national exposure on the program.

In 1956 NBC moved Allen onto *The Steve Allen Show* and briefly retooled *The Tonight Show*. That experiment failed, and the network eventually brought in Jack Paar, a garrulous game show host, as Allen's replacement. Beginning in July 1957, Paar brought a more erudite presence to *The Tonight Show*. He eschewed comedy skits for genteel conversation, often booking guests from the political arena. Robert F. Kennedy and Richard Nixon were two of the luminaries who chatted with Paar over the years.

Behind the veneer of a highbrow gabber, there was a darker side to Paar as well. He picked fights with notable figures in broadcasting, Walter Winchell and Ed Sullivan among them. On numerous occasions he threatened to quit the program, citing network interference and his own ennui with the late-night grind. Paar was the first of *The Tonight Show* hosts to cut his workweek down from five days to three. On February 11, 1960, he finally walked out on the program—literally, in the middle of a broadcast. He returned to his desk a few weeks later, but after a series of additional controversial incidents, Paar took his leave of *The Tonight Show* in March 1962.

"HEEEEERE'S JOHNNY!"

For the next six months guest hosts filled the command chair, and then Johnny Carson took on permanent hosting duties as Paar's successor. A glib magician from Nebraska, Carson brought a midwestern geniality, along with a sharp wit, to the hosting chores. He also introduced America to Ed McMahon, his second banana from the game show *Who Do You Trust*, to serve as announcer and sounding board. The pair would remain together on the program for the next thirty years, with McMahon's famous introduction, "Heeeeere's Johnny!" becoming a globally recognized refrain.

For a time Carson retained Paar's reliance on learned guests, though over the decades Hollywood glitz began to trump intelligent conversation. In a reflection of this shift, in 1972 the show moved from New York to Los Angeles, where *The Tonight Show* took on more of an adult urban contemporary feel. Hipsters such as Burt Reynolds and Hugh Hefner replaced the stodgier guests of the New York years. *The Tonight Show* became more popular than ever, as "Johnny" reveled in his shaman of late-night status.

The show's veneer of cool began to melt away in the 1980s, as *The Tonight Show* grew old along with its audience. Once the icon of hipness, Carson now seemed a mainstream fuddy-duddy, as edgier comics such as David Letterman and, later, Arsenio Hall began to steal some of his limelight. The nadir of *The Tonight Show* came with the 1983 installation of Borscht Belt fossil Joan Rivers as Carson's permanent guest host. Considered by many to be whiney and shrewish, Rivers alienated many of the show's loyal viewers—and eventually enraged her patron by jumping ship for her own, competitive late-night program. Carson replaced her in 1986 with Jay Leno.

JAY LENO AND CONAN O'BRIEN

In May 1991 Carson abruptly announced that he would be retiring in May the following year. NBC tapped Leno to replace him, surprising many who considered Letterman more talented and more deserving of the job. Leno took over the day after Carson signed off. A workaholic stand-up, Leno relied on his strong monologues to distract attention from what many considered his subpar interviewing skills. He seemed on the verge of losing control of the show when Letterman fielded a competitive program on CBS in 1993, but he rode back to the top of the ratings in 1995 largely on the strength of his jokes about the O. J. Simpson murder trial.

Leno kept *The Tonight Show* on top of the ratings throughout the mid-1990s and early in the first decade of the 2000s. Then in 2004, during the show's fiftieth anniversary celebration, Leno announced his impending retirement, effective at the end of a newly signed five-year contract. NBC announced that his replacement would be Conan O'Brien, a former writer for *Saturday Night Live* and *The Simpsons*, whose *Late Night with Conan O'Brien* had taken over Letterman's post–*Tonight Show* slot after his departure in 1993. O'Brien's gangly 6-foot, 4-inch frame; fire-red hair piled awkwardly above his pale, freckled face; and name ripped from the pages of Marvel comic books made him an unlikely candidate for late-night superstardom, but his ability to transform low-budget gags and potty humor into a kind of high-brow social commentary (a signature of his tenure with *The Simpsons*) made him a cult hero among college-age viewers and earned *Late Night* an Emmy for Outstanding Writing in 2007.

O'Brien's first *Tonight Show* aired on June 1, 2009, and featured an opening sequence that showed the new host making a frantic journey from New York (where *Late Night* was filmed) to Hollywood, where he used a bulldozer to gain entry to the *Tonight Show* studio. The sequence introduced viewers to O'Brien's self-deprecating, visually stimulating style, but it was also a fairly accurate depiction of his real-life struggle in taking over for his predecessor. In 2008 Leno had begun having second thoughts about retirement, and NBC, hoping to keep him from defecting to another network, offered him a new show that would air during prime time in the 10–11 p.m. time slot.

O'Brien's *Tonight Show* had a strong debut but steadily hemorrhaged viewers to the point that, by the time *The Jay Leno Show* premiered in September 2009, *Tonight Show* ratings were at an all-time low. *The Jay Leno Show* fared similarly, and by the end of 2009 the network began to panic. Many affiliates complained that Leno's show was a poor lead-in to their 11 p.m. newscasts, and poor ratings for the news meant poor viewer crossover into *The Tonight Show*. The powers that be decided a change was needed.

NBC executives announced a new schedule that would place a shortened version of *The Jay Leno Show* after local news programs at 11:35 p.m., bumping *The Tonight Show*'s starting time back to 12:05 a.m. The announcement infuriated O'Brien and his supporters, who felt that Leno and NBC had reneged on a long-standing promise and had not given the new host a chance to develop an audience over time. He refused to abide by the time change and, despite polls indicating overwhelming popular support for O'Brien as host, the network eventually agreed to a $45 million contract buyout, ending O'Brien's run on January 22, 2009, just seven months after his debut. O'Brien exacted a measure of revenge on the network by filling his final week of shows with bits featuring exorbitantly expensive props and racking up millions in licensing fees and eventually by launching a competing show, titled *Conan*, on TBS in 2010.

NBC and Leno fielded intense criticism over their conduct during the conflict. In one of the last episodes of *The Jay Leno Show*, fellow late-night host Jimmy Kimmel answered a question about the greatest prank he ever pulled by saying, "I told a guy that five years from now, I'm going to give you my show. And then when the five years came, I gave it to him, and then I took it back almost instantly. I think he works at Fox or something now." Even the notoriously mild-mannered Oprah Winfrey took Leno to task and forced him to admit that he told "a white lie" when he announced his retirement in 2004.

Nevertheless, Leno returned as host of *The Tonight Show* in March 2010 and managed to recover some of the show's total viewership despite losing nearly a quarter of O'Brien's viewers in the coveted eighteen- to forty-nine-year-old demographic. Whereas Leno once held seemingly insurmountable leads over his competitors, Letterman, Kimmel, and O'Brien have each managed to best *The Tonight Show* in this advertiser-friendly age range at one point or another after Leno's return. Additionally, Comedy Central's *The Daily Show with Jon Stewart* and *The Colbert Report* have captured a large share of the late-night audience, signaling that younger viewers may be tiring of Leno's vanilla-flavored humor. There is little doubt, however, that *The Tonight Show* remains a beloved franchise and an integral feature of America's pop culture landscape, one that will retain a place in the hearts, if not always the viewing schedules, of Americans for decades to come.

Robert E. Schnakenberg

SEE ALSO: *Allen, Steve; Bruce, Lenny; Cable TV; Carlin, George; Carson, Johnny; Celebrity; Colbert, Stephen; Emmy Awards; Hefner, Hugh; Hollywood; Kimmel, Jimmy; Leno, Jay; Letterman, David; O'Brien, Conan; Reynolds, Burt; Rivers, Joan; Sahl, Mort;* Saturday Night Live; *Simpson Trial;* The Simpsons; *Stand-Up Comedy; Stewart, Jon; Sullivan, Ed; Television; Winchell, Walter; Winfrey, Oprah.*

BIBLIOGRAPHY

Carter, Bill. *The Late Shift*. New York: Hyperion, 1995.

Carter, Bill. *The War for Late Night: When Leno Went Early and Television Went Crazy*. New York: Viking, 2010.

Sweeney, Don. *Backstage at the "Tonight Show": From Johnny Carson to Jay Leno*. Lanham, MD: Taylor Trade Publishing, 2006.

Tony Awards

The Antoinette Perry Award for Excellence in Theatre—"Tony," for short—has a unique history. At the beginning of World War II, actress Antoinette Perry (1888–1946) helped found the American Theatre Wing, an organization dedicated to entertaining American service personnel as they passed through New York City. At war's end, the Wing broadened its mission to "supporting excellence and education in theater" and, in 1947, presented its first awards for achievement in live theater. That event was a late-night dinner party, and the award recipients—who included legendary actresses Helen Hayes and Ingrid Bergman, along with noted playwright Arthur Miller and famed choreographer Agnes de Mille—were announced at midnight in a fifteen-minute radio broadcast.

On the other side of the country, the Academy of Motion Picture Arts and Sciences had been giving out Oscars in Hollywood since 1929. Its event, too, had started out as a local gathering of industry professionals, but movies were such a big part of American culture that the Academy Awards soon attracted national interest. "Oscar night" was broadcast for the first time on network television in 1953, following in the footsteps of the television industry's Emmy ceremony, which premiered on television in 1952. But it was not until 1967 that the Tony Awards debuted on network television—for just one hour.

That same year, the American Theatre Wing joined forces with the League of New York Theatres and Producers (now known as the Broadway League), and the Tony event, which had been held in hotel ballrooms for the first twenty years, moved to a new home in Broadway's vintage Shubert Theater. Although the theater community wanted to maintain a clear distinction between the realm of onstage performance and the very different cinematic medium celebrated by the Oscars, the Tony producers also wanted to publicize live theater by presenting a high-profile event. So over time, the televised Tony programs began evolving toward the model set by the Oscars and Emmys: a largely scripted show, with famous presenters, comedy skits, musical production numbers, and dramatic revelation of the winners. Although hosts for the Tony Awards have typically been theater veterans such as Angela Lansbury or Hugh Jackman, many Tony presenters are crossover celebrities, better known to the public for their television and film roles than for their theater credentials. In 1997 the ceremony moved from Broadway proper to the famed Radio City Music Hall, and in 2003 the broadcast on CBS was expanded to three hours.

From the beginning, the Oscars and the Tonys have represented two significantly different aspects of America's cultural identity: live performance versus film production; New York versus Los Angeles; and, to an extent, "art" versus "pop." There is also a practical difference in terms of familiarity, since productions eligible for a Tony Award must be staged in one of the designated Broadway theaters. Very few people actually see Tony-nominated productions in New York City, while a great many people see (or could see) the Oscar-nominated movies at the local multiplex or even at home. So it is not surprising that the Academy Awards draw much more popular interest. Over the years, however, Broadway theater has reached an increasingly large audience through touring productions, and some of the

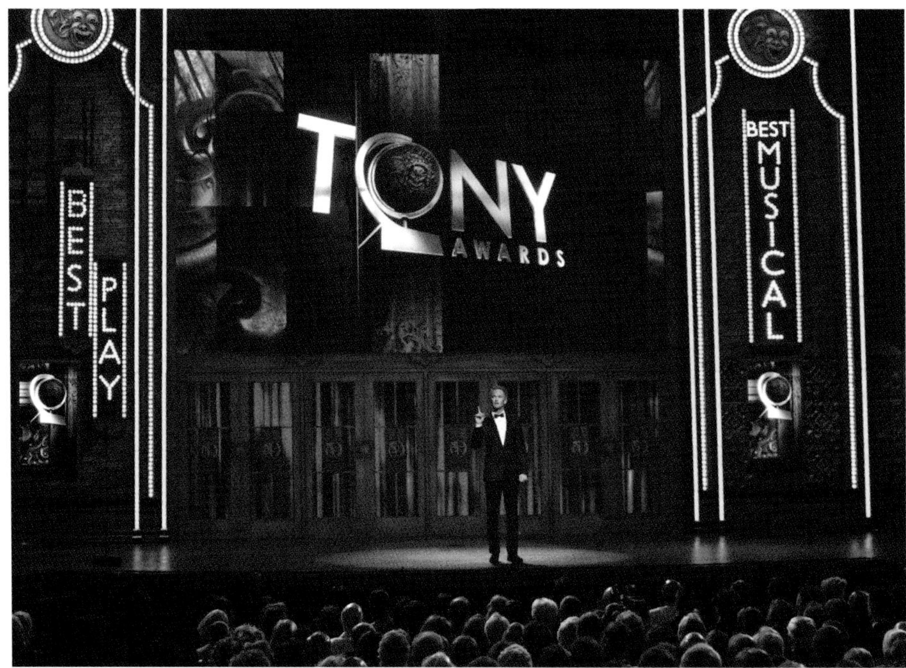

Neil Patrick Harris Hosts the Tonys. *Neil Patrick Harris hosts the television broadcast of the 65th Annual Tony Awards in New York City in 2011.* KEVIN MAZUR/WIREIMAGE FOR TONY AWARDS PRODUCTIONS/GETTY IMAGES.

most popular Broadway musicals and dramatic plays have been translated into film and television productions. In fact, four Tony-winning productions have been made into Oscar-winning Best Pictures: *My Fair Lady* (Tony, 1957; Oscar, 1964), *The Sound of Music* (Tony 1960; Oscar 1965), *A Man for All Seasons* (Tony, 1962; Oscar, 1966), and *Amadeus* (Tony, 1981; Oscar, 1984).

Tony Awards are given in two categories: plays, which includes both comedies and dramas, and musicals. In addition to the Best Play and Best Musical honors, which are given only to new works, there are also awards for the best revivals (new productions of older works) in each category. Performance awards are broken out by gender and category, (for example, Best Performance by a Leading Actress in a Musical), and there is a directing award in each category. In the musicals category, awards are given both for the best book (script) and the best score (music). There are also awards for costume design, scenic design, lighting design, and choreography, as well as special noncompetitive awards for lifetime achievement and humanitarian contribution.

In 2011 the Tony Awards ceremony moved back to its roots, broadcasting from a new home at Broadway's Beacon Theatre. In many respects, the event has become a theatrical production in itself rather than a communal gathering, but the awards still fulfill the original mission of the American Theatre Wing—to celebrate excellence and educate the public about live theater in America.

Cynthia Giles

SEE ALSO: *Academy Awards; Bergman, Ingrid; Broadway; Emmy Awards; Miller, Arthur; The Musical;* My Fair Lady*; Radio;* The Sound of Music*; Television.*

BIBLIOGRAPHY

Morrow, Lee A. *The Tony Award Book: Four Decades of Great American Theater.* New York: Abbeville Press, 1987.

Stevenson, Isabelle, and Roy A. Somlyo. *The Tony Award: A Complete Listing of Winners and Nominees of the American Theatre Wing's Tony Award with a History of the American Theatre Wing.* Portsmouth, NH: Heinemann, 2001.

Wilmeth, Don B., and C. W. E. Bigsby. *The Cambridge History of American Theatre: Vol. 3.* London: Cambridge University Press, 2000.

Tootsie

Named one of the top 100 American movies by the American Film Institute, *Tootsie* was the blockbuster romantic comedy of 1982. The 1980s saw the opening of several films featuring cross-dressing, including *Victor Victoria* (1982), *Yentl* (1983), and *Torch Song Trilogy (1988)*, but *Tootsie* was the one that garnered the most critical attention and popular acclaim. The American cultural obsession with cross-dressing surfaces in newspaper stories, television talk shows, children's tales, and movies. Anthropologists, literary critics, and historians all have paid a great deal of attention to cross-dressing, producing studies of hermaphrodites, boy actors, and the politics of camp. Cross-dressing and the treatment of cross-dressing raises, in a relatively concise if somewhat confusing fashion, questions of the construction of gender and sexuality. If a man can dress up successfully as a woman, does that mean that gender itself is merely a performance, albeit a culturally dictated one? What does it mean to "become a woman?" That is, what are our culture's definitions of femininity, and, by implication, masculinity?

Tootsie. *Dustin Hoffman, right, starred opposite Jessica Lange in* Tootsie. COLUMBIA/THE KOBAL COLLECTION.

Upon its release, *Tootsie* quickly became a focus for popular and critical debate of these questions. Both critics and popular audiences responded to the film's investigation of gender roles as well as its interrogation of what it means to be a woman and what it *could* mean to be a man.

BECOMING A WOMAN

In *Tootsie*, Dustin Hoffman plays Michael Dorsey, an out-of-work New York actor who dresses as a woman and calls himself Dorothy Michaels in order to land a role in a very successful soap opera, *Southwest General.* His character on the soap, named Emily Kimberley, becomes a fan favorite because of her improvised feminist protests on the set. Offstage, Hoffman falls in love with Jessica Lange, another actress in the show, who, thinking Hoffman is a woman, becomes his/her confidante. Finally, Dorothy unmasks, and the movie concludes with a stereotypically happy romantic ending. The guy gets the girl, and Michael understands the difficulties of being a woman. The movie shows that for Michael becoming a woman means more than simply shaving more often, wearing makeup, and donning pantyhose. In other words, while pretending to be Dorothy in order to make a living, he realizes that it's no easy game to live as a woman in our culture.

Michael Dorsey and Dorothy Michaels are familiar figures in Hollywood's long history of representations of male-female impersonators in movies such as *Easy Living* (1937), *Bringing Up Baby* (1938), *Some Like It Hot* (1959), *Victor/Victoria* (1982), and *Mrs. Doubtfire* (1993). In fact, Hoffman modeled Dorothy's mannerisms on Jack Lemmon's Daphne in *Some Like It Hot. Tootsie*'s appeal, however, lies in the way that it moves beyond the farcical transvestitism of its predecessors. The movie attempts to be social commentary, not just comedy. Hoffman's performance in the film does not resemble drag or camp but rather presents itself as a serious comment about playing a woman in contemporary American culture (just as it is serious business for Michael within the context of the movie).

EXPLORING GENDER ROLES

Tootsie quickly became the ground from which sprang feminist critiques of women in mainstream film, including analyses of positive and negative images of women and feminism in movies, as well as of the potential to co-opt the issue of feminism for enormous commercial profit. Many critics asserted that *Tootsie*'s lesson is that women are simply better than men—Dorothy, they argue, is not only more successful than Michael, she is also more sympathetic, empathetic, and observant. (Indeed, Hoffman's oft-repeated claim in interviews that playing Dorothy made him a better man, less prone to anger and more sensitive to others' needs, seems to attest to this interpretation.)

Since Dorothy is really a man, however, others have argued that the hidden message of the film is that men are actually better than women. After all, no matter whether one thinks that *Tootsie* destabilizes gender roles or reaffirms them, a man disguised as a woman seems to be better at being a woman than a real woman (as Teri Garr's character learns when she discovers that Michael has won the role of Emily over her). Many critics read the film as arguing that only a man can be tough and honest enough to express women's rights. In fact, the word *tootsie* has become slang among some literary and film critics for a man who claims his identity as a feminist even while maintaining a sexist understanding of women. The image of Hoffman in a long, red sequined dress operates simultaneously, it seems, as both an icon and a parody of feminism.

Although *Tootsie* is all about acting, in the end it is unclear whether or not the film implies that all gender roles are performances. Do the daily rituals of becoming a woman that *Tootsie* obsessively documents—tweezing eyebrows, applying mascara, shaving legs, applying nail polish, and fixing one's hair—mean the same thing for a man dressing as a woman as they do for a woman dressing up? There does not seem to be any question, for example, that Dorothy is *really* Michael (that is, that his masculinity is a performance). In addition, the film does not investigate the ways in which femininity is a performance that the "women" in the movie perform as well (or not as well) as the men.

"Genuine" gender roles are reasserted at the end of the movie, suggesting that cross-dressing or the understanding of gender as performance should take place only onstage, or for limited periods. In other words, one could read *Tootsie* as a slick (some would argue exploitative) poke at gender roles, whose conclusion leaves those roles finally intact (as a film that is, in the end, not good for women). And yet, such a reading might be too simplistic, for it denies what makes the film so popular in the first place—the basic ambiguity of cross-dressing itself. Whatever its deeper meanings, the film remains popular, still having a high rating on the website Rotten Tomatoes into the 2010s. In 2008 a special twenty-fifth anniversary edition of the movie was released on DVD and included a documentary on the making of the film.

Austin Booth

SEE ALSO: *Blockbusters;* Bringing Up Baby*; Feminism; Hoffman, Dustin; Hollywood; Movie Stars; Soap Operas;* Some Like It Hot.

BIBLIOGRAPHY

Garber, Marjorie. *Vested Interests: Cross-Dressing and Cultural Anxiety.* New York: Routledge, 1992.

Ginibre, Jean-Louis. *Ladies or Gentlemen: A Pictorial History of Male Cross-Dressing in the Movies.* New York: Filipacchi Publishing, 2005.

Showalter, Elaine. "Critical Cross-Dressing: Male Feminists and the Woman of the Year." *Raritan* 3, no. 2 (1983).

Top Chef

Top Chef is a one-hour reality show that features professional cooks squaring off in a series of weekly culinary challenges. The ultimate prize is the title of Top Chef and a cash award ranging from $125,000 to $200,000, depending on the season. The show follows contestants working in the kitchen, revealing how they adapt their skills and training to the various challenges presented. Each season of *Top Chef* is filmed in a different city, with the local culture and cuisine dictating the season's theme and the nature of its challenges. During season nine, for example, when the show was filmed in Texas, contestants were asked to create a savory dish from rattlesnake. Regularly ranked as the number one food show on cable TV, *Top Chef* debuted in 2006 and airs on the Bravo channel, a division of NBC Universal.

Critics have praised the series for featuring an ethnically diverse array of men and women, both as contestants and judges, and for challenging the long-established dominance of white male chefs. Padma Lakshmi, a renowned Indian American cookbook author, has served as *Top Chef*'s host since its second season. In order to qualify for the show, contestants must earn their living as cooks and must be working toward careers as chefs. The judges are a who's who of respected foodies. Expert chef Tom Colicchio, who was awarded the James Beard Foundation's coveted Outstanding Chef award in 2010, serves as the lead judge. Guest judges include Eric Ripert, Jacques Pepin, Lidia Bastianich, Hubert Keller, Michelle Bernstein, Anthony Bourdain, Ming Tsai, and Marcus Samuelson.

Each episode presents two tests for the "cheftestants," as they are called on the show. First, in the opening segment's Quickfire Challenge, contestants are given forty-five minutes to complete a task that tests their mastery of fundamental cooking skills. For example, they may be asked to prepare a dish using specific ingredients or to concoct a particular taste. Chefs who win the Quickfire Challenge are granted immunity from that episode's elimination challenge and advance automatically in the competition. Toward the end of the season, when it is no longer feasible to grant Quickfire winners immunity, the winners of the opening test are granted either a cash prize or an advantage in the Elimination Challenge, which is more elaborate and requires more time to complete.

Working individually or as part of a group, contestants in the Elimination Challenge are typically required to prepare several courses with several restrictions placed on their work. They may, for example, be given a tight budget for purchasing ingredients, or they may be forced to acquire what they need by going door-to-door. At the end of the Elimination Challenge, host Lakshmi asks the person determined to be the weakest chef to "please pack your knives and go." A closing video clip reveals the psychodrama of the exiting cheftestant, who typically puts a positive spin on the elimination and relates what went right or wrong to the TV audience. Each season cheftestants also compete in the Restaurant Wars segment, wherein they are divided into two groups and required to create the name, theme, decor, and menu for a restaurant within a set time and budget.

The show has served as a catalyst for the careers of numerous chefs, creating opportunities for contestants to open restaurants; endorse products; and, in some cases, star on other TV shows. Stephanie Izard opened the restaurant Girl & the Goat in 2010 after her participation in season four of *Top Chef.* Since its opening, her restaurant has received a James Beard Award nomination for Best New Restaurant, and the gourmet food magazine *Saveur* named it America's Best New Restaurant. Carla Hall, a finalist from seasons five and eight, became a co-host of ABC's *The Chew.* Season two runner-up Marcel Vigneron has a show on the SyFy channel show called *Marcel's Quantum Kitchen*, where his catering company produces experimental New Age foods, such as edible maps and bonbons in the shape of engagement rings.

Top Chef has also spawned two spin-offs: *Top Chef Just Desserts* and *Top Chef Masters.* The series also includes a number of special one-off episodes, such as "4 Star All Stars" and "Top Chef Holiday Special." International adaptations have appeared in Canada, Europe, and the Middle East.

Willie R. Collins

SEE ALSO: *Cable TV; Celebrity Chefs; Foodies; Game Shows;* Joy of Cooking*; Reality Television; Television.*

BIBLIOGRAPHY

Hyman, Gwen. "The Taste of Fame: Chefs, Diners, Celebrity, Class." *Gastronomica* 8, no. 3 (2008).

McKeever, Amy. "Profiling the Voltaggio Brothers." Eater, January 16, 2012. Accessed May 2012. Available from http://eater.com/archives/2012/01/16/profiling-the-voltaggio-brothers.php

Miller, Emily. *Top Chef: The Quickfire Cookbook*. San Francisco: Chronicle Books, 2009.

Miller, Emily. *How to Cook Like a Top Chef*. San Francisco: Chronicle Books, 2010.

Top 40

Top 40 is a listing of the forty most popular single records in the United States for a given week and is derived from radio station playlists and retail sales. The listing is based on trade magazines, including *Cashbox* and *Billboard*. Top 40 also is an AM radio format that consists of music, trivial talk, news, and promotions, including services, money, and goods given to listeners. Although Top 40 radio has undergone many changes over several decades, it remains a viable format. From 1956 to the present, Top 40 has provided Americans, especially those born in the 1940s, a musical smorgasbord served up through their favorite disc jockeys (DJs).

DJs were chosen on the basis of their voice, excitement, and sex appeal. The Top 40 format did not leave much room for personalities and for that reason did not appeal to some DJs. At first Top 40 was not aimed at a teenage market; instead, DJs, adhering to a playlist, entertained and did what was called "formula radio." However, Top 40 soon became a bridge from adult-oriented music to rock and roll and rhythm and blues as well as other styles. The youth market gravitated to Top 40, and the evolution of rock and roll contributed to its early success. By 1958 Top 40 stations had spread from the Midwest to the rest of the country.

ORIGINS

Although the Top 40 format originated in 1956, there were earlier developments in radio that helped in its formation. In 1935 *Your Hit Parade*, a program on NBC Radio, featured live performances of the most-liked songs based on sheet music, records, and airplay. In 1941 *Lucky Lager Dance Time*, a Los Angeles radio program on KFAC, first aired, playing hit records and devoting considerable airtime to the Top 10 songs. By 1949 KOWH, a radio station in Omaha, Nebraska, featured a playlist of popular records. The popular DJ Alan Freed produced the *Moondog's Rock and Roll Party* in 1951, introducing black music to a mostly white audience. In 1953 radio still held its own against television, with 96 percent of homes and the majority of cars having radios. Most Americans listened to radio on a daily basis or at least once per week. In 1953 the New Orleans, Louisiana, radio station WDSU played the Top 20. Top 40 became an expanded version of previous programs, including *Your Hit Parade* and *Lucky Lager Dance Time*, and was programmed over a full broadcast day with DJs and local advertisements.

The exact origin of the Top 40 is disputed, and there are several explanations of its beginning. One version holds that Top 40 began in the context of several bars in several cities, including Omaha and New Orleans as well as Dallas, San Antonio, and Houston, Texas. Another story credits the radio programmer Bill Gavin with having invented the Top 40 chart. Most scholars of radio, along with the DJ Dick Clark, however, believe that Top 40 began at a bar in Omaha, where, from 1953 to 1955, Todd Storz, operator of KOWH, devised the format. The story goes that Storz and his program director, Bill Stewart, were sitting in a bar in Omaha when they became aware that patrons played the same jukebox selections repeatedly over the course of four hours. When one of the patrons was asked why, she plainly responded, "I like 'em." Inspired by her response, Stewart developed a playlist of thirty songs based on the most-played records on the jukebox. Storz implemented this playlist at KOWH, and the ratings improved drastically.

Yet another explanation of Top 40's origins has Storz developing a radio program, called *Top 40 at 1450*, at his New Orleans station WTIX immediately after acquiring it in 1953. The program was developed in response to rival station WDSU's *The Top 20 at 1280* show. The DJ Bob Howard reasoned that if a list of twenty hits was satisfactory, then forty would be outstanding, and consequently he developed a show of forty selections called *Top 40 at 1450*. In 1955, following Howard's influence, Storz continued the concept at an Omaha radio station. Gordon McLendon, owner of KLIF in Dallas, also initiated the Top 40 format, including goofy promotions and jingles. By 1956 Top 40 had developed into a popular format.

PIONEERS

Several key individuals were considered pioneers of Top 40, with each bringing an innovation that became part and parcel to the format. McLendon, called "the Orson Welles of radio," was a creative talent, developing programming and promotional ideas that gave early Top 40 its form, vitality, and innovative jingles. In radio, jingles are the most reliable indicators for listeners remembering a station. Jingles existed before Top 40, but it was McLendon who hired a music director, who in turn employed a vocal group to record jingles designed for Top 40.

Mike Joseph and Chuck Blore were also two important programmers in early Top 40 radio. McLendon employed Blore as a DJ and a program director. Blore is credited with the concept of *color radio*, a term inspired by color television and a format developed in 1958 at KFWB in Los Angeles. Color radio was concerned not with ethnic diversity but rather with diversity in promotions, news, music, and a strong amusement and entertainment element. Joseph, a radio consultant, kept the industry focused on playing the hits and giving listeners what they wanted—always a central mission of Top 40 radio. Gavin, programmer for the *Lucky Lager Dance Time* programs heard on forty-eight western stations, monitored sales and combined these data with other statistics, creating the *Bill Gavin's Record Report* in 1958. This information base became the foundation on which the Top 40 playlist was created. The *Gavin Report* was an innovation in the radio business that gave statistics on various markets and that was essential to the development of Top 40.

In its early years, from 1956 to around 1962, Top 40 was democracy in radio. Musical categories including pop, rock and roll, country, rhythm and blues, novelty tunes, jazz, and movie soundtracks made the format and were played to a mass audience. For example, from a list of Top 40 singles, the following songs and artists were represented in the following categories in 1960: pop ("Save the Last Dance for Me," the Drifters), rock and roll ("It's Now or Never," Elvis Presley), country ("He'll Have to Go," Jim Reeves), rhythm and blues ("Finger Poppin' Time," Hank Ballard & the Midnighters), novelty tune ("Itsy Bitsy Teenie Weenie Yellow Polka Dot Bikini," Brian Hyland), jazz ("Georgia on My Mind," Ray Charles), and movie soundtrack ("Theme from *A Summer Place*," Percy Faith).

A clock, sometimes called a "hot clock" in the early days and now a computer readout with a written scenario, drives Top 40. DJs have to follow the clock religiously. Depending on its popularity, a song could be repeated every hour or every six hours. Top 40 has not been without criticism, and while the format purported to play what people wanted to hear and espouse democratic ideals, critics, including Columbia Records, accused DJs of relinquishing airtime and kowtowing to teenage tastes. Obviously during the course of its maturity, Top 40 changed in that each of the various subgenres of pop and rhythm and blues either now has its own radio format and niche market or no radio home at all.

The *disc jockey*—the term was coined by the record executive Jack Kapp in 1940—was the heart and soul of Top 40. A good DJ could imbue the staid format with a personality and an identity. Entertainers in their own right, the DJs of Top 40 radio would introduce and build up a song by talking while playing the instrumental introduction, finishing just before the vocal would start. This practice of talking up the song was called "hitting the post." While it is questionable whether DJs could accurately predict what records would become hits, Top 40 radio DJs always took credit for selecting certain hits. DJ Wolfman Jack takes a more conservative stance on the role of DJD making hits. "As long as I can remember there've been lists," he said. "Top 40 lists in the trade magazines, and in my life since 1960 I've been going by the goddamned charts. You didn't vary too far. There's no DJ alive who can make a record happen. All you can do is give it exposure." Many stations featured a pick hit based on a DJ's recommendation that actually turned out to be a hit.

DIVERSITY

The exposure of diverse musical styles, including African American popular music, owes much to the Top 40 format. By 1957, led by Chuck Berry and Fats Domino, a number of African American styles, from calypso to rhythm and blues, made the format, including records by Harry Belafonte, the Del Vikings (the first successful interracial group in rock and roll), the Drifters, Della Reese, Little Richard, the Coasters, Little Anthony and the Imperials, the Platters, Larry Williams, Roy Brown, Jimmy Reed, and Ruth Brown. The first Motown entry in the format was Barrett Strong's "Money," followed in succeeding years with records by the Supremes and the Four Tops, among others. Some of the most enduring rock and roll also debuted on the Top 40. In 1957 Jerry Lee Lewis, Buddy Holly and the Crickets, and the Everly Brothers all appeared on the Top 40.

While black popular music could be heard on Top 40 by the original performers of the music, the Top 40 format often played emasculated and watered-down versions of black popular music. "Cover" records had made their debut many years before Top 40. A narrow definition of *cover* referred to a successful song by a black artist that was later recorded by a white artist on a major label. The black bluesman Joe Turner's "Shake, Rattle and Roll" was recorded by Bill Haley and his Comets. "Sincerely" by the Moonglows, a black vocal group, was recorded by the McGuire Sisters. The covers in many instances climbed to the top of the charts, while the "authentic" originals were shut out. Eventually, the black originals began to outshine the covers, as Sam Cooke's "You Send Me" did over Teresa Brewer's version.

Top 40, according to radio consultant Guy Zapoleon, can be a format envisioned in four cycles, each lasting approximately ten years. Each cycle has three stages: birth, extremes, and doldrums. For example, Cycle 1 (1956–1963) encompassed pop, rock, R&B, dance, and country. Cycle 2 (1964–1973) embodied pop, rock, R&B, acid rock, soft rock, and country. Cycle 3 (1974–1983) adopted pop, rock, R&B, disco, adult/contemporary, and country. Cycle 4 (1984–1993) included pop, rock, R&B, rap/funk, adult/contemporary, and country.

When rap first broke into the pop charts, Casey Kasem, the originator of the countdown and *Casey's Top 40*, was credited with playing the hits. Other Top 40 stations, however, took a harder line; regardless of how rap songs charted, most Top 40 stations consistently avoided rap. As hip-hop increasingly became part of the cultural landscape, such artists as Kanye West, T.I., and Eminem found their way onto adult contemporary radio. Radio-friendly singles such as "Jesus Walks" by West, "My Name Is" by Eminem, "Can't Nobody Hold Me Down" by Sean "P. Diddy" Combs, "Hey, Ya!!" by OutKast, and "Give Me Everything" by Pitbull, helped solidify hip-hop's place in the rotation.

While Top 40 may have been democratic in its selection of playlists in that each song is evaluated on its on merit, the format was less so in terms of diversity in race and gender of Top 40 DJs, the majority of whom are white males. No satisfactory explanation exists as to why more female DJs or DJs of color were not employed in Top 40 radio. In 1964, after Top 40 had been in existence for more than nine years, several black DJs were hired, including Larry McCormick, reportedly the first African American DJ to work at KFWB in Los Angeles. In 1965 Chuck Leonard was hired for WABC radio in New York, and in 1969 Frankie Crocker was a Top 40 DJ on WMCA. In 1970 Walt Love was hired as a Top 40 DJ at KILT in Houston. In 1973 Yvonne Daniels, daughter of the singer-dancer Billy Daniels, broke gender and race barriers by becoming the first woman and first African American to be hired as a Top 40 DJ at WLS in Chicago.

DECLINE AND COMEBACK

By 1965 the DJ and program director Bill Drake experimented with programming ideas to transform KHJ in Los Angeles to a Top 40 station, devising the concept of "Boss Radio." This Top 40 format was copied by numerous stations across the country. By 1968 the listening audience for Top 40 had begun to erode from competition by FM "free form" (later called "progressive" rock) radio.

During most of the 1970s, Top 40 did maintain a smaller audience, even as the popularity of disco peaked in 1978. Although Top 40 regained some of its listening audience in 1983, by 1993 mainstream Top 40 had disappeared as new appellations, including rock and alternative, were added to Top 40 formats. The number of radio stations identifying themselves as Top 40 also dwindled from 578 to 441. Gavin noted that the strong competition experienced by Top 40 stations brought the ratings down. In addition to competition from other radio stations, Music Television (MTV), launched in 1981, was an immediate success with young viewers. MTV essentially did what Top 40 had purported to do all along—play the hits and give listeners what they wanted to hear.

In 1997 Top 40, fueled by such popular artists as the Spice Girls, made a comeback, and in its more than forty-five years of existence continued to be the best format for variety in music. The Top 40 radio format was a general standard that achieved intermittent success and impacted the music industry. It was a format and a system that monopolized playlists, dictating not only the songs radio listeners heard but also the frequency, the order, and the time of day of play and even to some extent the professional lives of the artists whose titles appeared on the list. Top 40 inherently became its own worst enemy because, as listeners matured, they developed preferences for certain types of music instead of the mélange of popular songs on the playlists. Radio stations began emphasizing light rock, classic soul and R&B, classical, and jazz in efforts to capture a particular segment of the market.

In spite of its vacillations, Top 40 has presented a diverse repertoire of songs that reflects the world of popular music. It has remained resilient in spite of its many changes. "Through forty years, [Top 40] had weathered . . . one competing format after another, one new technology after another, and all the shifts in fortune that society, culture, politics, and the economy can bring," observed noted writer and editor Ben Fong-Torres in *The Hits Just Keep on Coming.* By the beginning of the twenty-first century, Top 40 continued to be a viable format.

Willie Collins

SEE ALSO: *Ballard, Hank; Belafonte, Harry; Berry, Chuck; Charles, Ray; Clark, Dick; Cooke, Sam; Country Music; Disc Jockeys; Disco; Domino, Fats; The Drifters; Eminem; The Everly Brothers; Holly, Buddy; Jazz; Kasem, Casey; Lewis, Jerry Lee; Little Richard; Motown; MTV; Pop Music; Presley, Elvis; Radio; Rhythm and Blues; Rock and Roll; The Spice Girls; West, Kanye; Wolfman Jack;* Your Hit Parade.

BIBLIOGRAPHY

Fong-Torres, Ben. *The Hits Just Keep on Coming: The History of Top 40 Radio.* San Francisco: Miller Freeman Books, 1998.

Pollock, Bruce. *When Rock Was Young: A Nostalgic Review of the Top 40 Era.* New York: Holt, Rinehart and Winston, 1981.

Tora! Tora! Tora!

A 1970 motion picture recounting the attack on Pearl Harbor by the Japanese during World War II, *Tora! Tora! Tora!* was at the time of its release the second most expensive movie ever made, just behind *Cleopatra.* Based on the historic novels *Tora! Tora! Tora!* by Gordon W. Prange and *The Broken Seal* by Ladislas Farago, the film recounts what happened on both the American and Japanese sides. The title refers to the Japanese code word that signaled the launch of the attack.

The idea for making the film came from Elmo Williams, who was hoping for another financial triumph along the lines of *The Longest Day.* From the beginning it was planned as a film of monumental scale that would examine the events of Pearl Harbor in precise detail. A tremendous amount of research had been done by Prange and his staff at the University of Maryland. (Prange had been appointed by General Douglas MacArthur as the official historian of the Pacific war and had the advantage of being fluent in Japanese.) In order to further enhance the authenticity of the film, Akira Kurosawa, Japan's most famous and possibly greatest director, was hired to direct the Japanese scenes.

The production faced numerous problems. For example, apart from one destroyer, nothing was left of the original Japanese fleet, requiring the filmmakers to construct a Japanese aircraft carrier and a plywood battleship and have them sent to Japan for filming. With no Japanese Zeroes available, twenty-eight Vultee AT-6 aircraft were "stretched" six feet so that they would appear to be the same size and were then fitted with appropriate cowlings, windshields, and wheel skirts (with the result that parts were always falling off during flight).

Nor was there much left of the American fleet now that it had been mothballed. One floating battleship set alone cost $1 million to construct. The Fox miniature department built models of nineteen Japanese ships and ten American ships at a scale of three-quarters of an inch to the foot, thereby creating forty-foot "miniatures." They also had to build to scale the Battleship Row docks and surrounding land areas.

Tora! Tora! Tora! took two years to prepare under the supervision of Williams. American director Richard Fleischer was called in during the last six months of preparation before shooting was to begin. He met with Kurosawa and Williams in Hawaii. Williams wanted Kurosawa to cut several scenes from the script that he felt were extraneous. Kurosawa was reluctant but agreed. Kurosawa also felt it was important to depict the Japanese military as all spit and polish, formal, correct, and obsessed with protocol and ceremony, while Fleischer would

Tora! Tora! Tora! Tora! Tora! Tora! *dramatized the Japanese attack on Pearl Harbor.* **20TH CENTURY FOX/THE KOBAL COLLECTION.**

depict the American military as relaxed, laid-back, a bit sloppy, and casual.

Ultimately the producers of the film spent $25 million to reenact the attack on Pearl Harbor, more than the Japanese had spent to launch it. The attack itself was a complex sequence requiring smoke, flames, explosions, planes diving or bombing or crashing, torpedoes running; hangars, planes, and ships blowing up; anti-aircraft and machine guns firing; and actors in almost every shot.

The American sequences were scripted by Larry Forrester and starred Martin Balsam as Admiral Kimmel, Joseph Cotten as Secretary of War Stimson, E. G. Marshall as Lieutenant Colonel Bratton, James Whitmore as Admiral Halsey, and Jason Robards as General Walter C. Short. The Japanese sections were scripted by Hideo Oguni and Ryuzo Kikushima and starred Soh Yamamura as Admiral Yamamoto, Tatsuya Mihashi as Commander Genda, Takahiro Tamura as Lt. Commander Fuchida, Eijiro Tono as Admiral Nagumo, and Koreya Senda as Prince Konoye.

In Japan Kurosawa began to resent the intrusion of five American production people sent to oversee things. He insisted on shooting interior scenes from four o'clock in the afternoon to midnight. He did not like the American design of the prefabricated structure sent to Toeiga Studios to serve as his administration building. He cast the heads of several large corporations in bit parts (in hopes that they might finance his next film), and he insisted that everyone on the crew wear special *Tora! Tora! Tora!* jackets and regulation navy caps and salute the actors whenever one passed by.

When the first day of shooting came, set inside a shrine-room on board a battleship, Kurosawa decided it was the wrong shade of white and insisted that every member of the crew work to repaint it. He became obsessed with endless minor details while overlooking a major one, despite warnings from the Americans. The plywood battleship sent over from the United States was being constructed facing the wrong direction.

Soon the Japanese portions were falling far behind schedule. The studio became intolerant of the delays, and Kurosawa was receiving threats from politically important people who did not want the film to be made at all. (On his way to the set, Kurosawa would lie down on the floor of the limousine to avoid assassination.) As he became more abusive, his own crew started to turn against him. The story was released that illness forced him off the picture, but the truth was the studio had finally had enough and fired him. Two commercial Japanese directors, Toshio Masuda and Kinji Fukasaku, took over.

Perhaps it was because of the Japanese involvement, but the final film downplays the real reasons for the United States contemplating war with Japan before the attack. There is no mention of Japanese aggression in China or the much-publicized atrocities committed by the Japanese during their occupation. The film also fails to portray opposition to the war from within the ranks of the Japanese military.

Six servicemen were injured during the filming of the attack. After rumors circulated of naval carriers transporting props for the shoot, Representative John M. Murphy of New York proposed legislation to forbid the military from participating in commercial motion picture production.

The film is notable for how accurately it depicts the events, and it won an Academy Award for A. D. Flowers and L. B. Abbott for its spectacular battle effects. However, it did not prove to be the major league blockbuster its producers had hoped it would be, easily being eclipsed by the year's other great war epic, Franklin Schaffner's *Patton*. Many Americans did not like having to read subtitles during the Japanese portions of the film, and others feared that the Zero pilots would be made to seem heroic at the expense of American servicemen who struggled vainly to defend the base.

Dennis Fischer

SEE ALSO: *Cotten, Joseph;* Patton*; War Movies; World War II.*

BIBLIOGRAPHY

Fleischer, Richard. *Just Tell Me When to Cry: A Memoir*. New York: Carroll & Graf Publishers, 1993.

Iriye, Akira. *"Tora! Tora! Tora!" Past Imperfect: History According to the Movies*, ed. Mark Carnes. New York: Henry Holt, 1995.

Lassieur, Allison. *The Attack on Pearl Harbor: An Interactive History Adventure*. Mankato, MN: Capstone Press, 2009.

Prange, Gordon W. *At Dawn We Slept: The Untold Story of Pearl Harbor*. New York: McGraw-Hill, 1981.

Wohlstetter, Roberta. *Pearl Harbor: Warning and Decision*. Stanford, CA: Stanford University Press, 1962.

Tormé, Mel *(1925–1999)*

One of the most versatile entertainers of all time, Mel Tormé, known as the Velvet Fog, was one of America's most acclaimed vocalists as well as being a composer-arranger, a drummer, an actor in films and television, and a star performer on records and the live concert stage. The popular holiday classic "The Christmas Song" ("Chestnuts roasting on an open fire") is his best-known composition.

Born in Chicago, Tormé began his career at age four, singing on weekly radio broadcasts with the Coon-Sanders Nighthawks Band in 1929 and with Buddy Rogers and his band. When he was six he worked regularly with vaudeville units around Chicago, and at age nine he was cast as Jimmy the newsboy on the popular NBC radio soap opera *Song of the City*. Remaining as a regular on the show from 1934 to 1939, Tormé used his spare time to study drums and songwriting. At age fifteen he wrote his first hit song, "Lament to Love," which was recorded by Harry James in 1941. The following year he joined the Chico Marx Band in California as a singer and vocal arranger; he later replaced the group's drummer.

When the band broke up in July 1943, the young singer's career began to soar. He made his debut in a feature film with Frank Sinatra in RKO's *Higher and Higher*, followed shortly by *Pardon My Rhythm* and *Let's Go Steady*, minor musicals with a high school setting. These two films featured the Mel-Tones, a singing group formed by students from Los Angeles City College, featuring Tormé as lead singer and vocal arranger.

After serving in the army during World War II, Tormé signed a contract with MGM. There he played in *Good News* (1947), a popular college film starring June Allyson and Peter Lawford and featuring "The Varsity Drag." He also appeared in *Words and Music* (1948), with Mickey Rooney and Judy Garland. During the 1950s he recorded a string of hit records and toured widely on the concert stage as the leading singer of the new "Cool School" of jazz.

Making the transition to television in 1951, Tormé starred with Peggy Lee on *TV's Top Tunes*, a summer replacement for *The Perry Como Show*. For the next two years he hosted a daily talk show on CBS. During this time he was also frequently featured on television variety shows.

Tormé's career as a writer began in 1963 when producer George Schlatter hired him to write scripts for *The Judy Garland Show* on CBS. His experiences in coping with the unpredictable star of the show led him to write *The Other Side of the Rainbow* (1970), which was published by William Morrow and became a best seller. Tormé's autobiography, *It Wasn't All Velvet*, was published in 1988. He also wrote the foreword to Burt Korall's *Drummin' Men: The Heartbeat of Jazz, the Swing Years*, and the introduction to Bruce H. Klauber's *The World of Gene Krupa: That Legendary Drummin' Man*, both published in 1990.

His long career included appearances with most of America's best-known symphony orchestras. In 1982 Tormé won the Grammy Award as Best Male Jazz Vocalist for the album *An Evening with George Shearing and Mel Tormé*. He won another Grammy Award, also as Best Male Jazz Vocalist, in 1983 for the album *Top Drawer*. In 1984 he performed at the White House for the Reagans. As the aging superstar of pop music, Tormé won an even wider audience with frequent appearances as himself on the popular television comedy *Night Court* (1984–1992). In 1995 he appeared with the punk group the Ramones and the alternative rock group Mudhoney. He had a stroke in 1996, which finally ended his career. Tormé passed away in June 1999.

Benjamin Griffith

SEE ALSO: *Big Bands; Como, Perry; Garland, Judy; Grammy Awards; James, Harry; Krupa, Gene; Lee, Peggy; The Marx Brothers; MGM (Metro-Goldwyn-Mayer); Reagan, Ronald; Sinatra, Frank; Television; Vaudeville; World War II.*

BIBLIOGRAPHY

Balliett, Whitney. *American Singers: Twenty-Seven Portraits in Song*. New York: Oxford, 1988.

Friedwald, Will. *Jazz Singing: America's Great Voices from Bessie Smith to Bebop and Beyond*. New York: Da Capo Press, 1996.

Tormé, Mel. *It Wasn't All Velvet: An Autobiography*. New York: Viking, 1988.

Tormé, Mel. *My Singing Teachers: Reflections on Singing Popular Music*. New York: Oxford, 1994.

Mel Tormé. *Mel Tormé, pictured here with Nancy Sinatra, earned the nickname the "Velvet Fog" because of his smooth vocal style.* RON GALELLA/CONTRIBUTOR/GETTY IMAGES.

Touched by an Angel

Premiering in 1994, the television series *Touched by an Angel* chose an unusual formula to achieve success. In an age of dramatic television filled with tremendous violence and negativity, the series relied on spiritual faith, love, and redemption to send positive messages. The three main characters, all angels, include Monica (Roma Downey), her supervisor and mentor Tess (Della Reese), and Andrew (John Dye), the angel of death. The angels assist a wide range of different characters with their personal relationships and tackle many serious issues along the way, including AIDS, capital punishment, and teenage pregnancy.

Although the series focused on spiritual thoughts and did use the word *god*, it opted not to assert any specific religion or religious agenda. With little fanfare at first, *Touched by an Angel* consistently gained in popularity during the late 1990s to become a top-ranked and unique drama series. Still found in syndication, the series concluded in 2003 after a run of nine seasons and 213 episodes. Despite some controversy surrounding the show's cancellation, it remains one of the few television series focused on religious messages to achieve popularity in contemporary mainstream media. In 2011 star John Dye died of a heart attack at age forty-seven.

Randall McClure

SEE ALSO: *AIDS; Leisure Time; Syndication; Teenagers; Television.*

BIBLIOGRAPHY

Reese, Della, with Franklin Lett and Mim Eichler. *Angels along the Way: My Life with Help from Above*. New York: Putnam, 1997.

Williamson, Martha. *When Angels Speak: Inspiration from Touched by an Angel*. New York: Simon & Schuster, 1997.

Williamson, Martha, with David Seay. *In the Words of Angels:*

Twenty Inspiring Stories from Touched by an Angel.. New York: Simon & Schuster, 2001.

Williamson, Martha, and Robin Sheets. *Touched by an Angel.* Grand Rapids, MI: Zondervan Publishing House, 1997.

Tour de France

With its 100th anniversary taking place in 2013, the Tour de France bicycle race is the world's largest annual sporting event. With 12 million to 15 million roadside spectators and live broadcast coverage in sixty countries for the 2011 edition, its popularity is surpassed only by the World Cup and the Olympic Games. Spanning three weeks every July, it covers approximately 2,500 miles and is divided into daily stages that traverse France by various routes. The race pits some twenty teams of riders against mountain stages in the Alps and Pyrenees, flat stages in Brittany and Normandy, and individual time trials. The overall leader wears the illustrious yellow jersey, and the race finishes on the Champs Élysées in Paris.

BEGINNINGS

With the exception of the years encompassing World War I and II, the Tour has inspired fans every year since 1903. At that time magazine editor Henri Desgrange organized a long-distance bicycle race as a kind of publicity stunt designed to put his competitor and political rival, Pierre Giffard, out of business. The first race featured sixty riders (of which twenty-one finished the 292-mile course), with Italian-born Maurice Garin emerging as the overall winner. Garin was also the winner of the 1904 tour, but he and three other riders were disqualified for illegal use of cars and trains. Desgrange and the Tour organizers instituted a set of rule changes designed to increase supervision of the riders for the 1905 Tour, but, given the sheer number of competitors and distances covered, collusion, cheating, and scandal have been a prominent feature of the Tour ever since.

As bike manufacturers and other companies began to sponsor groups of riders in the 1910s and 1920s, providing them with a competitive edge by reserving the newest technologies for their teams alone, Desgrange became increasingly frustrated with the predictability of the results. In 1930 he removed commercial sponsorships from the event by stipulating that only teams representing their home country would be admitted and that all riders would use the same bicycles. He appeased the tour's sponsors by allowing a publicity caravan to trail the riders, and, as the sponsors employed increasingly carnivalesque tactics to capture spectators' attention, the caravan became nearly as popular an attraction as the race itself.

CONTROVERSY

The Tour retained the national team format until the 1960s, when bicycle manufacturers convinced organizers that they were on the verge of bankruptcy because of a lack of exposure. The 1962 Tour saw the return of sponsored trade teams, as well as the reappearance of widespread cheating controversies. One of the most successful riders in the history of the event, Jacques Anquetil of France, openly admitted to using amphetamines on his way to winning five Tours (1957, 1961–1964), and when the French government made performance-enhancing drugs illegal in 1965, the Tour resolved to implement drug testing beginning in 1966. Many riders protested the move, but when British rider Tom Simpson collapsed and died during a grueling climb on Mont Ventoux that was attributed to a combination of amphetamine use, dehydration, and exhaustion, the need for extensive anti-doping procedures became readily apparent.

Even some of the event's greatest heroes have been plagued by doping allegations. Belgian Eddy Merckx, considered by many to be one of the greatest riders of all time and the winner of five Tours (1969–1972, 1974), had been banned from competing in the Giro d'Italia (a similar race held in Italy) in 1969 after a controversial test found traces of stimulants in his system. Spanish cyclist Miguel Indurain, winner of five consecutive Tour championships (1991–1995), was accused of taking stimulants in 1994, but it was later revealed that the results were tainted by a legal asthma medicine he had taken.

The 1998 Tour became known for the so-called Festina Affair, when a Spanish team sponsored by watch manufacturer Festina was disqualified from the race after a team masseuse was found with hundreds of vials of the nearly undetectable growth hormone erythropoietin (EPO). This episode led to a lengthy investigation, with many other teams dropping out of the race to avoid doping allegations. The prevalence of performance-enhancing drugs during the Tour was brought to the public's attention like never before, and several major sponsors withdrew their contributions to the race.

U.S. RACERS

Victories by U.S. racers Greg LeMond (1986, 1989, and 1990) and Lance Armstrong (1999–2005) enhanced the event's profile in the United States toward the end of the twentieth century. LeMond, the first non-European to win the Tour de France, shocked the world by returning to his winning ways after a 1987 hunting accident left him with shotgun pellets embedded in the lining of his heart. Similarly, Armstrong overcame testicular cancer in 1996 and went on to become the only rider to have won seven consecutive Tour championships. His unprecedented success spawned doping accusations in both Europe and North America, though no conclusive evidence ever surfaced. In 2006 Armstrong's teammate Floyd Landis was stripped of his Tour victory after a drug test revealed abnormally high levels of testosterone. Landis denied the allegations for several years before finally admitting to steroid use in 2010 in a series of e-mails that also accused Armstrong of taking performance-enhancing drugs with his teammates. In 2012 Armstrong said he was done fighting the drug allegations against him, which meant he would be stripped of his seven victories, too.

Despite its long and sordid history with drug scandals, the Tour de France remains one of the most anticipated annual sporting events in the world. The race broadcast features spectacular views of the French countryside, throngs of dedicated cycling fans jockeying for a glimpse of their favorite racers, terrifying crashes, and heroic feats performed by some of the world's best endurance athletes using a technology that has changed little since its invention in 1885. Even with the specter of performance-enhancing drug use looming over the event, the excitement of watching riders reaching speeds in excess of 40 miles per hour in a final chase through the majestic Champs Élysées is nearly unmatched in professional sports.

Neal Baker

SEE ALSO: *Armstrong, Lance; Bicycling; Cancer; LeMond, Greg; Olympics; Sports Heroes; Television.*

BIBLIOGRAPHY

Delanzy, Eric. *Inside the Tour de France: The Pictures, the Legends, and the Untold Stories of the World's Most Beloved Bicycle Race.* Emmaus, PA: Rodale, 2006.

Fife, Graeme. *Tour de France: The History, the Legend, the Riders.* Edinburgh: Mainstream, 1999.

McGann, Bill, and Carol McGann. *The Story of the Tour de France: How a Newspaper Promotion Became the Greatest Sporting Event in the World,* 2 vols. Indianapolis, IN: Dog Ear, 2006–2008.

Sidwells, Chris. *A Race for Madmen: The Extraordinary History of the Tour de France.* London: Collins, 2010.

Thompson, Christopher S. *The Tour de France: A Cultural History.* Berkeley: University of California, 2006.

Walsh, David. *From Lance to Landis: Inside the American Doping Controversy at the Tour de France.* New York: Ballantine Books, 2007.

Whittle, Jeremy. *Bad Blood: The Secret Life of the Tour de France.* London: Yellow Jersey, 2007.

Town Meetings

Typically held once a year, town meetings bring citizens together to vote on decisions about local affairs, including ordinances, taxes, town officers, and local improvements. Most historians associate town meetings with the region and culture of New England, especially Massachusetts and Vermont. They symbolize a strong belief in political equality and direct democracy (versus the representative democracy of America's Constitution), which explains why town meetings continue today. Some historians and political scientists argue that town meetings are not truly democratic because citizens simply defer to an unspoken leadership when attending them. The meetings were repopularized by Bill Clinton's presidential campaign in 1992, and they became a staple of political campaigns and a tool that members of Congress use to meet with their constituents. In 2008 and 2009 the Tea Party movement came to national attention in part because its members regularly staged protests at such town hall meetings.

Kevin Mattson

SEE ALSO: *The Tea Party.*

BIBLIOGRAPHY

Bryan, Frank M., and John McClaughry. *The Vermont Papers: Recreating Democracy on a Human Scale.* Chelsea, VT: Chelsea Green, 1989.

Lockridge, Kenneth A. *A New England Town: The First Hundred Years: Dedham, Massachusetts, 1636–1736.* New York: W. W. Norton, 1985.

Mansbridge, Jane J. *Beyond Adversary Democracy.* New York: Basic Books, 1980.

Robinson, Donald L. *Town Meeting: Practicing Democracy in Rural New England.* Amherst: University of Massachusetts Press, 2011.

Toy Story

The first *Toy Story* film changed the animation industry when it was released on November 22, 1995. This joint venture between Pixar Animation Studios and Walt Disney Productions was the first fully computer-animated feature-length film. It follows the adventures of a toy cowboy, Woody (voiced by Tom Hanks), and a toy astronaut, Buzz Lightyear (voiced by Tim Allen). *Toy Story* became the second-highest-grossing film of that year and earned John Lasseter, who served as cowriter and director of the film, an Academy Award for Special Achievement. Woody and Buzz's adventures continued with the release of *Toy Story 2* in 1999 and *Toy Story 3* in 2010.

The critical and commercial success of the original *Toy Story* transformed the world of animation and computer-generated imagery (CGI). Within a few years of its release, Disney and other major studios abandoned traditional animation almost entirely in favor of computer animation, and the technology Pixar used to create the original *Toy Story* became an industry standard. In 2006 Disney bought Pixar outright and made Lasseter the head of animation for the whole company. The *Toy Story* franchise has made millions through merchandizing efforts, and *Toy Story 3* continued the tradition of critical success with glowing reviews and a nomination for an Academy Award for Best Picture. Woody, Buzz, and their friends have earned permanent cultural residence alongside such highly recognized and revered animated characters as Mickey Mouse, Bugs Bunny, and Snoopy.

Adrienne Furness

SEE ALSO: *Academy Awards; Animated Films; Bugs Bunny; CGI; Disney (Walt Disney Company); Hanks, Tom; Toys.*

BIBLIOGRAPHY

Kaplan, David A. "High Tech in Toon Town." *Newsweek,* December 3, 1995, 54–56.

"Pixar." *Marketing,* June 8, 2011, 18.

Stewart, James B. "A Collision of Creativity and Cash." *New York Times,* July 1, 2011.

Toys

Pushed out by a celebrity-driven popular culture and the virtual pleasures of game consoles in the twenty-first century, the beloved toys of the past, including blocks, erector sets, dollhouses, trains, tops, and tea sets, have been marginalized by media advertising that targets children not as imaginative players but as pop culture consumer imitators. Toys mirror cultural notions about family and child-rearing values while also resonating with a child's inner world of play. Thus, many contemporary toys mimic ideas found on television rather than creative possibilities found in a child's imagination. For example, children may be able to dress Barbie in a vast array of wardrobe options, but their choices are often prescribed by celebrities on television, computer, and movie screens.

Nevertheless, although twenty-first-century toy makers are more likely to be giant corporations than inventive artisans, the range of toys available in the 2010s has never been greater. Construction toys, such as Lego, remain extremely popular, while new materials and manufacturing techniques have made new kinds of toys possible, such as remote-control vehicles and semiautonomous robots. In their early days, in the 1980s, computer games were considered by many to be a damaging influence. As they have become more integrated into twenty-first-century life, when pitched at the right age level, they are increasingly seen as a benign if not beneficial presence in the playroom.

EARLY TOYS

Although toys have been around for thousands of years, the relationships among toys, children, and culture have shifted with the passing of time. Gary Cross, in *Kids' Stuff*, notes the discovery of 5,000-year-old dolls, balls, rattles, and ancient artifacts resembling smaller versions of adult tools and weapons. Many of these early toys and miniatures were made for religious rites or for the exclusive use of adults. Wooden Noah's arks and fashion dolls, for example, were favorite gifts of aristocratic women in the Middle Ages, whereas clay soldiers and knights were a source of entertainment for adult men. Eventually these "adult toys" were given to children. Brian Sutton-Smith, in his book *Toys as Culture*, explains that play and toys became a part of children's culture in the 1600s as a result of a decreased need for child labor combined with a new and related concern with controlling children's behavior. Play and toys began to be considered by such serious thinkers as John Locke and Jean Jacques Rousseau, who held that children were different than adults and needed protection and special activities, such as play, to progress.

Changes in American domestic life facilitated the introduction of toys into the home. Over the course of the nineteenth century, work was done with greater frequency away from the house and not by children, furthering the notion that children needed to be treated differently. Toys and children's books began to claim more importance in this new children's culture of the nineteenth century, for it was thought that they could provide for children's moral and intellectual development.

Developing industrial and technological capacities brought innovations to the making of toys; rubber, plaster, and sheet metal made toys easier to manufacture. Germany was the largest exporter of toys in the early nineteenth century and more than any other country was responsible for the modern world of toys. Just another dry good in the United States, toys offered gender-based play tools for boys and dolls for girls. After the Civil War, however, chain stores, such as Woolworth (1879) and Sears (1886), emerged and began to sell toys as gifts. Other stores, such as Macy's, designated specific sections of their consumer spaces for the sale of toys. FAO Schwarz opened in 1870 as a specialty retailer of toys.

THE ARRIVAL OF CHRISTMAS

Notions about the number of toys required in children's lives changed when Christmas became a legal holiday in the mid-nineteenth century, helped along by the popularization of Santa Claus in the 1823 poem "A Visit from St. Nicholas" by Clement Moore. The promise of Santa's arrival promoted an even larger children's market. Santa added a sense of mystery and a morality theme as "His List" told him who was "naughty or nice"; at the same time, this happy image of St. Nick served to disguise the crass commercialism of the Christmas spirit. Ultimately, indulging children became part of a family's status reinforced by new advertising and commercial interests.

Toys bought for boys in the early twentieth century reflected a fascination with industrialization and technology; early "industrial" toys include Lionel trains (1906), Moline Buddy trucks (1910), Gilbert Erector Sets (1913), Tinkertoys (1914), and Lincoln Logs (1916). These construction toys were the antecedent of Lego (1954), the very successful Danish Toy that allows children to follow a design or build their own creations. "Theodore Roosevelt and the Spanish American War set the stage for the development of numerous male-identified toys," explains David Brody in his dissertation "Fantasy Realized." The famous and durable teddy bear (based on Roosevelt's popularity) became a favorite, as well as the Daisy air rifle (1888), Admiral Dewey dolls, and the very successful yet racist Billikens (1912) with their Orientalized physical traits. In contrast, toys for girls reflected domestic life, featuring dolls and miniature kitchen appliances. Doll companies, such as E. I. Horsman and Effanbee, and manufacturers, such as Schoenhut and Steiff, produced the Patsy Doll (1924), Raggedy Ann, and other companion dolls.

EDUCATIONAL TOYS

In 1901 John Dewey wrote about the importance of toys fulfilling children's psychological needs. He ushered in a whole group of child experts in the twentieth century, including psychologist Stanley G. Hall and later the author of *Baby and Child Care*, Dr. Benjamin Spock, who promoted toys that fostered imagination and creativity. Educators, psychologists, and politicians soon had a great deal to say about child rearing and family values. Beginning in 1912, Maria Montessori began making parents aware of the importance of the objects children played with in terms of their ability to learn. Educational toys started to be promoted by a very aggressive *Parents* magazine (1926), whose subscribers were mainly mothers with expendable income. Urged on by such experts, parents grew interested in creating children who could navigate the more industrialized twentieth century with a greater sense of ease.

Noel Barrett, toy expert and star of PBS's *Antiques Road-Show*, is particularly impressed with a trend away from toys with religious associations toward such toys as mechanical banks, which adults could justify buying for their children because they taught thrift. Children were now considered a special and vulnerable group in society. Toys were meant to help prepare the young for success as Playskool (1928) and Fisher-Price (1930) sold more blocks, desks, and dollhouses. What was not considered by the child experts was how new developments within the realm of popular culture were impacting children's lives. As the celebrity glow of Roosevelt and Charles Lindbergh sold dolls and toy airplanes, toy makers began to look ahead to other venues for child-marketing connections.

In 1904 the Brown Shoe Company bought the exclusive rights to the popular comic strip character Buster Brown in an effort to sell more children's shoes at the World's Fair in St. Louis, Missouri. The scheme worked, and Buster also sold dolls and toys with both his and his dog's image on them. Later, radio characters, such as Little Orphan Annie, Tom Mix, and Jack Armstrong, sold cereal and advertised premium toys. In the 1940s Captain Midnight asked children to use their Ovaltine decoder to decipher secret messages. The Dionne Quintuplets sold dolls and cutouts, as did Shirley Temple and Charlie McCarthy.

DISNEY AND TOYS IN THE MEDIA

Walt Disney may have been the first to understand the monetary value of successful children's characters. Beginning in 1928, he transformed Mickey Mouse and others like him into dolls, toys, theme parks, movies, and billions of dollars. Even before the advent of television, Disney marketed Pinocchio dolls and Snow White coloring books. When he discovered the power of TV, he produced the incredibly commercial *Mickey Mouse Club* (1955). *The Wonderful World of Disney* was arguably the first infomercial aimed at children, highlighting upcoming Disney toys and theme park attractions.

Later, films of the 1980s and 1990s, such as *The Little Mermaid* (1989), *The Lion King* (1994), *Pocahontas* (1995), *Mulan* (1998), and *Tarzan* (1999), all had their own dolls, puzzles, and videotapes. The stories told are not Disneyfied just for dramatic reasons but very often are modified to sell more toys. They are intensely self-referential, with each medium, such as movie, TV show, or the toys themselves, encouraging involvement with the others. Each character becomes a brand that begs children to buy more. Indeed, the movies *Pocahontas* and *The Little Mermaid* feature irrelevant hair-brushing scenes designed to make their heroines more appealing for little girl doll play.

In the late 1940s television replaced radio as children's predominant form of entertainment. Beginning in 1947 under the title *Puppet Playhouse*, *Howdy Doody* was the first successful children's TV show. The selling of products related to the show began in 1949 when, according to Stephen Davis, author of *Say Kids! What Time Is It?*, a Howdy Doody comic book was produced to publicize the show. After millions of comic books were sold, property rights and merchandising became the focus of the program. Howdy soon began selling cards, dolls, and toys related to the characters on the show. Scripts were modified, and children reacted almost by instinct to anything that was promoted. Princess SummerFall WinterSpring, who was pushed onto the stage to provide a female character, helped sell little girls untold numbers of American Indian dolls and costumes. Television thus not only entertained children but shaped their consumer decisions.

Sensing the power of this new medium, both Hasbro, starting with Mr. Potato Head in 1951, and Mattel, with the Burp-Gun in 1955, made the decision to market on TV. As Stephen Kline points out in *Out of the Garden*, these marketing decisions revolutionized the toy industry. Up until the 1950s, yo-yos, toy tanks, Slinkys, Frisbees, play dishes, Silly Putty, and cap guns held their own as such companies as Marx and Ideal made their profits with efficient production techniques and a little Christmas advertising. Mattel's and Hasbro's decision now tied toys to electronic images, not Santa. Toy making became a year-round business, and the most highly promoted toys soon began to drive the others from the market.

Perhaps the most prominent of this new genre of toys was Barbie, created by Ruth Handler, the wife and business partner of Mattel executive Elliot Handler. Ruth created Barbie to fill a void in the girls' fashion doll industry. Originally discovered as a sex novelty toy in Europe, Barbie has the shape of a young woman, with long legs, a large bust, and a narrow waist. She reflects a teenage fantasy world, for she is beautiful and sexy, well dressed, and autonomous; Barbie has no parental ties. With her accessories and play environments, she stresses the virtue of consumerism. In Barbie's world consumerism means happiness.

While not really a TV series tie-in toy, Barbie was among the first toys to be heavily marketed by television. By the 1990s she was everywhere. Barbie's marketers used what Mattel called a "segmentation strategy" of not one Barbie doll but many, for different types of play. With an average of eight Barbies for every girl in the United States, Barbie was America's most successful commercial toy in the twentieth century.

In 1968 Lloyd Morrisett and Joan Ganz Cooney formed the Children's Television Workshop. Puppeteer Jim Henson was hired, creating such memorable characters as Big Bird, Cookie Monster, and Bert and Ernie. These amusing characters began selling letters of the alphabet, words, and prosocial values on *Sesame Street* but soon moved into dolls, toys, pajamas, and almost any other consumer good imaginable. There was even more merchandising as Henson's *Muppets* and their movies became blockbusters and Tickle Me Elmo became the most sought-after Christmas toy in 1996. At a ceremony following Henson's untimely death in 1990, his daughter told a Vassar College audience that the Muppets characters' bond with their audience was the company's most valuable asset.

The 1960s and 1970s were the height of old-time TV merchandising, as Hanna-Barbera, with *The Jetsons* and *The Flintstones*, and *Scooby Doo* continued the media success of children's television and licensed products. Still, the show came first, and the merchandising followed. This philosophy would change with the 1977 release of George Lucas's *Star Wars*. From the beginning, Lucas sought to promote the interrelation between the licensed products and the films, using the movies as a long commercial for the products and vice versa. Using the myth-creating principles of Joseph Campbell, Lucas formed a magical universe populated by such phenomenal characters as Luke Skywalker, Han Solo, and Princess Leia. These movies and their related products remained top sellers twenty years after their introduction and enjoyed a surge in sales with the release of each new Star Wars movie that appeared, well into the twenty-first century.

By 1980 Strawberry Shortcake's creators got this licensing message and acted quickly, according to Tom Engelhardt in "The Shortcake Strategy." American Greeting Cards surveyed young girls about the qualities they would find most appealing in a doll, and the toy maker Kenner introduced her at the Toy Fair in New York City. Strawberry Shortcake was pink and soft and spoke of her "berry" nice friends. After she was given her own TV special, $1 billion in products sold quickly.

My Little Pony and *The Care Bears* (both 1983) followed with more programming and merchandising. The toys and lunch boxes now came first. Children's groups were outraged by this type of activity, and a sympathetic Federal Communications Commission spoke out about television's obligation to children. However, the deregulation of the airwaves that proceeded under the administration of President Ronald Reagan (1981–1989) brought no guidelines concerning appropriate marketing to children. As a result, the after-school airwaves became filled with product-driven programs such as *Masters of the Universe*, *He-Man*, and other such shows.

The new Fox Children's Network and Nickelodeon began to impact not only children's Saturday mornings but their after-school time as well, with such shows as *The Rugrats* (1991) and *Mighty Morphin' Power Rangers* (1993). Programming now became a series of infomercials in which movies and live shows related to the program were promoted and every character or hideout was for sale. While networks worried about audience share during prime time, children's television advertising revenues continued to soar as new toys needed both program time slots and commercials to be successful.

While toy production in the 1990s was largely controlled by two major manufacturers—Mattel and Hasbro—the toy industry itself was undergoing a change. The cheap mass production of microchips in the 1970s had made possible the first game consoles, and with them the first virtual toys, notably *Pong* (1975), a simple tennis game with very basic graphics and no colors. The Atari 2600 home video game console was released in 1977 and, with record-breaking sales, was the most popular Christmas gift in the United States in 1979. Sales doubled the following year when Atari released a home version of the popular arcade game *Space Invaders*. By 1982 Atari had sold more than ten million game consoles and seven million units of *Pac-Man*, the highest-selling game cartridge.

Throughout the 1980s and beyond, as home computers were beginning to appear in households, the computer games market grew exponentially. The arrival of the Mario character, in Nintendo's *Donkey Kong* game in 1981, marked the beginning of a whole new toy market. In the form of game consoles, such as Sony's PlayStation, Microsoft's Xbox, and Nintendo's Wii and DS, as well as games on smartphones and other handheld devices, this market was worth an estimated $65 billion globally in 2011.

Cheap electronic components also made "computerized" physical toys possible. In 1996 the Japanese company Bandai released the Tamagotchi, a plastic key-fob-sized toy that responded to simple interactions. Depending on the amount of attention the toy received, it would grow through life stages—childhood, teenage years, and adulthood—thus encouraging its owner to keep playing with it. The falling cost of manufacturing objects, including the use of cheap plastics, made possible such toys as the Rubik's Cube, and remote-controlled vehicles and aircraft, once prohibitively expensive, became common. In the form of build-your-own robot kits, cheap electronics have fostered a revival of the kinds of constructive toys that seemed to be vanishing.

Mattel and Hasbro are huge global conglomerates locked in a bitter struggle for world toy dominance, swallowing up lesser manufacturers and mass producing toys that have brand and media recognition. Nowhere is this competition more apparent than in the toys handed out with children's meals in fast-food restaurants, which not only make the child keen to return to the restaurant but also publicize movies or other media. In 2011 Pixar's long-running *Toy Story* movie franchise went further, releasing a short *Small Fry* in which the character Buzz Lightyear is mistakenly swapped for a "Buzz Lightyear" toy in a fast-food restaurant.

Despite the dominance of media-driven branded toys, in the twenty-first century children still enjoy relatively simple, physical toys. Young children in particular continue to use Play-Doh, and active toys such as balls, bicycles, Frisbees, skateboards, and other outdoor games remain popular. Despite the frenzied media-driven promotion of toys, children—and adults—still want to play.

Michael Brody

SEE ALSO: *Advertising; American Girl Series; Amusement Parks; Animated Films; Baby Einstein; Barbie; Beanie Babies; Bicycling;* Buster Brown*; Cabbage Patch Kids; Christmas; Computer Games; Consumerism; Dance Dance Revolution; Department Stores; Dionne Quintuplets; Disney (Walt Disney Company); Electric Trains; Fast Food; Fisher-Price Toys;* The Flintstones*; Frisbee; Gameboy; GI Joe; Ginny Dolls; Hacky Sack; Hanna-Barbera; Henson, Jim;* The Howdy Doody Show*; Hula Hoop; Jack Armstrong; Legos;* The Lion King*; Lionel Trains; Little Orphan Annie; Lucas, George; Macy's;* The Mickey Mouse Club*; The Muppets; Pac-Man; Pokémon; Raggedy Ann and Raggedy Andy; Rubik's Cube; Sears Roebuck Catalog;* Sesame Street*; Skateboarding; Slinky; Smartphones;* Snow White and the Seven Dwarfs*; Spock, Dr. Benjamin;* Star Wars*; Teddy Bears; Television; Temple, Shirley;* Toy Story*; Video Games; Wii; Yo-Yo.*

BIBLIOGRAPHY

Brody, David. "Fantasy Realized: The Philippines, Orientalism and Imperialism in Turn-of-the-Century American Visual Culture." PhD diss. Boston University, 1997.

Brody, Michael. "The Wonderful World of Disney: Its Psychological Appeal." *American Imago* 33 (1976): 350–360.

Cross, Gary. *Kids' Stuff: Toys and the Changing World of American Childhood.* Cambridge, MA: Harvard University Press, 1997.

Davis, Stephen. *Say Kids! What Time Is It?* Boston: Little, Brown, 1987.

Engelhardt, Tom. "The Shortcake Strategy." In *Watching Television*, ed. Todd Gitlin. New York: Pantheon Books, 1986.

Fleming, Dan. *Powerplay: Toys as Popular Culture.* Manchester, UK: Manchester University Press, 1996.

Kline, Stephen. *Out of the Garden: Toys, TV, and Children's Culture in the Age of Marketing.* London: Verso, 1993.

"A Look at the $65 Billion Video Games Industry." Reuters, June 6, 2011. Accessed March 2012. Available from http://uk.reuters.com/article/2011/06/06/us-videogames-factbox-idUKTRE75552I20110606

Miller, G. Wayne. *Toy Wars: The Epic Struggle between G.I. Joe, Barbie, and the Companies That Make Them.* New York: Times Books, 1998.

Seiter, Ellen. *Sold Separately: Children and Parents in Consumer Culture.* New Brunswick, NJ: Rutgers University Press, 1993.

Sutton-Smith, Brian. *Toys as Culture.* New York: Gardner Press, 1986.

Winnicott, D. W. *Playing and Reality.* New York: Basic Books, 1971.

Tracy, Spencer *(1900–1967)*

Spencer Tracy, frequently defined by his peers as "an actor's actor," was the prime exemplar of understated acting in both comedy and drama. His unrufflable simplicity was deceptive, for beneath the surface of that craggy face and chunky frame would simmer anger, passion, compassion, or grief, as the role required. It is for his famous on-screen partnership with his legendary off-screen love, the redoubtable Katharine Hepburn, that Tracy remains best remembered, but his other achievements in a film career that spanned thirty-seven years and some seventy-three films were substantial.

Tracy was cast in a unique mold. He achieved leading-man status of the first rank without a vestige of glamour or movie-star good looks. His strikingly natural persona, combined with many of the characters he played, became a benchmark for solid values and dependability as he worked his way through a succession of priests, fathers, judges, and down-to-earth avenging angels. Avuncular, often gruff, and sometimes irascible (a reflection of his own temperament), there generally lurked an understanding heart beneath the rough exterior. Stern but kindly, often with a twinkle in his eye, Tracy was a rock of integrity who, but for graying hair and the lines of age that barely disturbed his familiar face, never essentially changed in either appearance or manner.

EARLY CAREER

Born in Milwaukee, Wisconsin, Tracy was the son of a truck salesman. He was educated at a Jesuit-run Catholic school and initially intended to enter the priesthood, but he later found he preferred dramatics and decided to become an actor. In 1922 he enrolled in the American Academy of Dramatic Arts in New York. After graduation he embarked on a succession of menial jobs until he eventually found work in a stock company. Gradually he made it to Broadway, where in 1930 his lead performance in a successful prison drama, *The Last Mile*, caught the attention of Hollywood director John Ford, who cast him as the lead in *Up the River*, a gangster film, that same year.

The next five years were spent under contract to Fox, where Tracy made a couple of films of interest, including *The Power and the Glory* (1933), but his best roles came among the frequent loan-outs to other studios, notably in the hard-hitting *20,000 Years in Sing Sing* (1932), made for Michael Curtiz at Warner Brothers. In this film, Tracy starred as a criminal who confesses to a murder of which he is innocent. The role gave the actor ample opportunity to display toughness and humanity in equal measure; indeed, during these early years, Tracy frequently was cast as a rough-hewn character either made good or gone bad.

Spencer Tracy. *Spencer Tracy starred in seventy-three films over the course of his nearly forty-year film career.* AP IMAGES.

Having married in 1923 and always a devout Catholic, a guilt-ridden Tracy courted unwelcome publicity in the early 1930s when his affair with actress Loretta Young was revealed in the scandal sheets. When in 1935 he was arrested for drunkenness, Fox fired him. MGM (Metro-Goldwyn-Mayer) hired him and in time provided fertile ground for a rich crop of roles that established Tracy as a star.

STARDOM AT MGM

His first major success at MGM was as the man who survives an unjust lynching and seeks vengeance in director Fritz Lang's powerful drama *Fury* in 1936. That same year he played a priest in *San Francisco* and earned his first Oscar nomination. He won the Best Actor Oscar in 1937 for his role as a Portuguese sailor protecting a young Freddie Bartholomew in *Captains Courageous* and in 1938 became the first actor to win two in a row when he was again voted best actor as Father Flanagan in *Boys Town*—the first of his biopics.

In 1942 the Tracy-Hepburn collaboration began with *Woman of the Year*, in which his sports reporter and her politician, wonderfully ill matched, fall in love. The film set the tone for the most successful and popular of their films together as competitive, witty, sometimes acidic, but always affectionate sparring partners in the battle of the sexes. In Frank Capra's political comedy *State of the Union* (1948), Tracy is a presidential candidate, Hepburn his estranged wife; in George Cukor's *Adam's Rib* (1949), they are married lawyers on opposite sides of an attempted-murder case; and in Cukor's *Pat and Mike* (1952), she is a sporting phenomenon, he a sports promoter of dubious connections who sets out to exploit her money-making potential. *Without Love* (1945), an uncertain romance from a failed Broadway play, sank without a trace (the only one to do so), whereas there were more serious but less popular excursions with Cukor's *Keeper of the Flame* (1942), Tracy impressive as a reporter destroying the reputation of a dead politician, and *Sea of Grass* (1947), a brooding drama with Tracy cast as a work-obsessed cattle tycoon.

In 1950 Tracy played the gruff, bumbling, and put-upon *Father of the Bride* to daughter Elizabeth Taylor, a huge hit directed by Vincente Minnelli that won him an Oscar nomination and was followed by a hit sequel, *Father's Little Dividend* (1951). But as quality roles grew rarer, so, correspondingly, did his memorable performances. The only truly noteworthy contributions to the 1950s were his political campaigner in John Ford's *The Last Hurrah* and his one-armed, dark-suited avenger in John Sturges's *Bad Day at Black Rock* (1955). Descending on a crumbling one-horse outpost to unearth a terrible secret and seek justice, an unconquerable, implacable, ironic, compassionate, and heroic Tracy was never better than in this superb Western morality tale. It earned him a third Academy Award nomination, and there was a fourth for *The Old Man and the Sea* (1958).

The 1960s brought the onset of illness. During his last years, Tracy grew increasingly moody and difficult to work with, and producers shied away from him. An exception was Stanley Kramer, and it was for him that the actor gave his impressive last three performances: a thinly disguised Clarence Darrow defending in an equally thinly disguised Scopes Monkey Trial in *Inherit the Wind* (1960); the presiding judge wrestling with the Nazi legacy in *Judgment at Nuremberg* (1961); and, in a last glorious reunion with Hepburn, another irascible, bewildered, and tenderhearted father in *Guess Who's Coming to Dinner?* (1967). Already very ill, Tracy died a few weeks after filming was completed.

Robyn Karney

SEE ALSO: *Academy Awards; Broadway; Capra, Frank; Cukor, George; Darrow, Clarence; Hepburn, Katharine; Hollywood; Lang, Fritz; MGM (Metro-Goldwyn-Mayer); Minnelli, Vincente; Movie Stars; Scopes Monkey Trial; Taylor, Elizabeth; Young, Loretta.*

BIBLIOGRAPHY

Curtis, James. *Spencer Tracy: A Biography*. New York: Knopf, 2011.

Davidson, Bill. *Spencer Tracy, Tragic Idol*. New York: Dutton, 1987.

Fisher, James. *Spencer Tracy: A Bio-bibliography*. Westport, CT: Greenwood Press, 1994.

Kanin, Garson. *Tracy and Hepburn: An Intimate Memoir*. New York: Bantam Books, 1972.

Loew, Brenda, ed. *Spencer Tracy, Fox Film Actor: The Pre-code Legacy of a Hollywood Legend*. Newton, MA: New England Vintage Film Society, 2008.

Tozzi, Romano. *Spencer Tracy*. New York: Galahad Books, 1973.

Trading Stamps

Trading stamps are small pieces of glue-backed colored paper, given in proportion to purchases made and redeemable for merchandise. They were first used in the United States in Schuster's Department Store in Milwaukee, Wisconsin, in 1890. Schuster's gave the stamps to customers paying in cash in an effort to limit credit use. The S&H Green Stamp Company attributes their invention to their founders (the Sperry and Hutchinson of "S&H") in 1896 as a way to "say 'thank you'" to customers and calls the trading stamps "America's first frequent shopper program and grandfather of marketing promotions such as frequent-flyer miles." The first S&H redemption center opened in 1897 as a kiosk. One of the earliest items in the catalog was a Bissell carpet sweeper; its modern counterpart was still in the catalog 100 years later.

The heyday of the trading stamp came during the 1950s and 1960s, when large numbers of Americans received the stamps with their groceries and exchanged filled books for a variety of household goods. At the height of stamp fever, S&H distributed its catalogs free in supermarkets and operated multiple redemption centers, the size of small shops, in towns all over the United States. They claim that in 1964 its catalog was the largest single publication in America.

S&H Green Stamps, Top Value, King Korn, Triple S, Gold Bell, and Plaid were among the most popular nationally circulated brands of stamps. Attesting to the pop chic of trading stamps, artist Andy Warhol painted a series of S&H green stamps posters along the lines of his famous Campbell Soup works.

As consumers opted for lower prices in lieu of stamps in the 1970s and 1980s, the movement waned but never disappeared. One of the last major grocery chains to carry the stamps was the Publix chain in Florida, which dropped them in favor of coupons and other promotions that were less costly to the store. A 1988 study in the *Journal of the Academy of Marketing Science* notes that a survey of retail stores showed that stores that gave trading stamps had significantly lower gross profit margins and net profit returns than stores that did not.

In the early twenty-first century, the consumer's persistent desire to be tangibly rewarded for patronage continued in other forms—frequent-flyer miles, the return of percentages of credit card purchases—but only a few retail establishments offered actual trading stamps. Although S&H continued to distribute stamps and offer merchandise catalogs, they began to offer "paperless green stamps" saved on an ID card and added automatically at the register. In addition to redemption for gifts in the catalog, the stamps could be used to save in the store, as coupons for entertainment, as frequent-flyer miles, or as donations toward a charity or community project.

Despite the near disappearance of trading stamps from stores, they still pop up in popular culture. For example, in a 2006 episode of the television show *Everybody Hates Chris* (2005–2009), one of the characters is obsessed with trading stamps. In a 2009 essay, film critic Roger Ebert refers to having used green stamps as a boy to acquire metal shelves for his science fiction collection. For Americans of a certain age, trading stamps remain a fond memory of their past.

Joan Leotta

SEE ALSO: *Consumerism; Siskel and Ebert; Warhol, Andy.*

BIBLIOGRAPHY

Judd, L. Lynn, and Bobby C. Vaught. "Three Differential Variables and Their Relation to Retail Strategy." *Journal of the Academy of Marketing Science* 16, no. 3 (1988): 30–37.

Trailer Parks

Films and television programs will feature certain "stock" devices to create a chosen visual and emotional environment. A frequent image in 1950s–1980s culture was a tightly packed row of homes, similar in style, each with a tiny fragment of land used for parking, storage, recreation, gardening, and decoration. The homes follow the model of the tight suburb, but they are not American ranch houses. The image is dominated by rectangular trailers, most having had the wheels removed or at least concealed with a trellis covering.

Early in its history, the trailer, or mobile home, was viewed as progressive and adventurous. By the end of the twentieth century, it was generally seen as the opposite of these American ideals. Today a director or producer incorporates the trailer park into a visual narrative most often to depict Americans locked in—spiritually and physically—to a lower economic class by social strictures. Some consider the trailer park to be America's modern tenement, yet the trailer park's existence also suggests

Trailer Park. *An aerial view captures the tight, monotonous confines of a trailer park, which has come to symbolize America's lower social and economic classes.* TIM ROBERTS PHOTOGRAPHY/ SHUTTERSTOCK.COM.

one of the nation's most democratic achievements—home ownership available to all classes.

The enlightened thought of Thomas Jefferson helped to make personal home ownership an American ideal. As they configured capitalist thought, economic philosophers and visionaries Adam Smith and Thomas Hobbes incorporated property value into the scheme by making personal land ownership possible within enlightened societies at the end of the 1700s. The owner could then increase the value by "improving" the property so that it would be sold for a higher price. This philosophy made up the foundation for Jefferson's dream of an agrarian republic, full of small property owners who each tended (and improved) his own land.

The American housing ideal has not ventured too far from these foundations over more than 200 years of development. Urban growth has provided alternative models—such as apartments and condominiums—but the ideal of the vast majority of Americans is to own a home. Rising home prices after 1950 forced developers to construct a new version of this ideal that would involve classes previously unable to own their own property. The effort to appeal to lower- and lower-middle-class American urges for home ownership bred the trailer park.

ON THE ROAD

The trailer grew out of Americans' early-twentieth-century impulse to travel the nation by automobile. The trailer-camper allowed travelers complete freedom to pull over at any time and enjoy the comforts of home. This travel filled an important void when services were few and allowed many Americans to reject the rapidity and regiment of train travel for the slow, wandering travel of the open road. Prior to the spread of hotels and following the proliferation of automobile ownership, roadside camping offered the most reliable form of comfort during travel. An autocamper's outfit was an instant hotel to which one had to add only water. "Just back off the main road," instructs one guide, "in a little grove of white birches on the bank of a noisy brook, which will furnish water and perchance, fish enough to fill the breakfast frying pan!"

While tents remained the most popular implement for car camping, the trailer grew in popularity from 1920 to 1950. By tent or trailer, car camping spread from fad to institution during this era, giving form to the autocamp: an open site in which campers pooled together. A unique culture rapidly grew out of such sites, particularly the male effort to assess and rate others' camping equipment and technology. Not dissimilar from the shared space of the modern trailer park, campers interacted with others whenever they left the cover of their tent or trailer. In the autocamps, the travelers discussed other sites, the road, and equipment. Out of such ingenuity, the "gypsy-trailer form" began standardized manufacture after 1920.

Cabin camping also grew in popularity during the interwar years; by 1935, however, the nation was most enthused with the evolving trailer technology. Between 1935 and 1937 popular articles included "Back to the Covered Wagon," "Nation of Nomads," "Tin-Canners," "Nomads of the Road," "Home of the Free," and the like. Futurists even began to predict that every American would soon live permanently in a cheap trailer. Their thinking revolved around the common sense of such mobility as well as the Depression-era thoughts of limiting waste. The trailer, after all, offered Americans the fulfillment of their most basic needs of shelter and safety, with few unnecessary frills.

Modernist thinkers rallied around this model as the wave for the standardized future—the geodesic dome with wheels. Such thinkers, however, overlooked Americans' unique cultural preferences. Those who could still afford nicer homes would want them, but the trailer offered possibilities for those of lesser means. As developers created standardized suburbs for the middle and upper-middle class from 1950 to 1980, the same drive for conformity and ownership fueled the construction of the first trailer parks. Now, of course, the sites were not intended for transients or campers who would take their trailer and leave in the morning; nor were they intended to be a person's long-term residence. The mobility behind the trailer park was economic: developers assumed young families would use them as a temporary home while saving for their suburban dream home.

TEMPORARY HOUSING

Used originally as temporary housing, trailer parks became noticeable to most Americans after World War II, when they were clustered around army posts and construction sites. By the late twentieth century, mobile home parks were no longer temporary aberrations on the landscape. While millions of Americans, most from young, blue-collar families, considered trailers to be their temporary homes, few architectural historians were willing to consider such mobile homes dwellings. Critics stress that the trailer is not architecture; instead, it is an industrial product, mass produced, low cost, and disposable. Bypassing craftspeople, the trailer comes out of a midwestern factory by truck almost ready for occupancy.

The attraction, of course, is the low cost of the trailer, compared to even the smallest house. Standardized suburban homes, such as the bungalow, have achieved dwelling status, but the mobile home remains without a place in our architectural lexicon. Most communities also exclude trailer parks from the mainstream, relegating them to the least desirable tracts of land, such as along rail lines, highways, or flood areas. Additionally, the odd transience of the trailer place it outside of taxation and even standard land ownership. The trailer park is not dissimilar from the autocamps of the early twentieth century: ordinarily, residents own their trailer but only lease or rent the plot on which it rests. The home, though, will normally remain at the site long after residents move.

The trailer park represents both the proliferation of American ideals of ownership to all economic classes and also a culture of exclusion and transience, starting young families on the track to owning their own homes while also divorcing them from enduring community connections. As the media reported the housing crisis of the 1970s, it also helped to create the enduring stereotypes of trailer parks. Townhouses and trailers were consistently presented as inadequate, makeshift substitutes for detached suburban dwellings. The new alternatives were posed as a threat to the postwar suburban ideal. In addition, hurricanes of the early twenty-first century seem to have been most destructive to residents of trailer parks.

Between 50 and 70 percent of American communities ban mobile homes from privately owned lots in residential neighborhoods. This restricts Americans who may only be able to afford a mobile home to reside within the lowly trailer park. More than half of the nation's mobile homes are sited in parks, surrounded by high walls required by local codes. It is likely that the trailer park, a construction of modern, industrial sensibilities, will remain "lower-class" squatter settlements into the future.

Brian Black

SEE ALSO: *Bungalow; Camping; The Great Depression; RV; Suburbia; World War II.*

BIBLIOGRAPHY

Belasco, Warren James. *Americans on the Road.* Cambridge, MA: MIT Press, 1981.

Hart, John Fraser; Michelle J. Rhodes; and John Morgan. *The Unknown World of the Mobile Home.* Baltimore, MD: Johns Hopkins University Press, 2002.

Hurley, Andrew. *Diners, Bowling Alleys, and Trailer Parks.* New York: Basic Books, 2002.

Jackson, John Brinckerhoff. *A Sense of Place, a Sense of Time.* New Haven, CT: Yale University Press, 1994.

Wallis, Allan D. *Wheel Estate.* Baltimore, MD: Johns Hopkins University Press, 1997.

Wright, Gwendolyn. *Building the Dream.* Cambridge, MA: MIT Press, 1981.

Tramps

The tramp, or hobo (the tramp's name for himself), refers to a wandering foot traveler, often a vagrant, thief, or beggar with no fixed abode or destination. The term *hobo*, originally meant to describe a migratory U.S. worker hitching rides on freight trains, disappeared as society increasingly controlled the outcast individuals who chose the itinerant or homeless life.

In the 1870s U.S. Civil War veterans and immigrants swelled the ranks of unemployed boys and men traveling from job to job, and the tramp menace alarmed newspaper editorialists and civic leaders concerned about the growing number of homeless vagrants descending on towns and cities. Tramps were often driven from town or sentenced to jail or the workhouse for vagrancy; even skilled craftsmen, such as itinerant or tramp printers, were unwelcome in small towns. Allan Pinkerton, the legendary U.S. detective, warned of the danger tramps posed in his 1878 book, *Strikers, Communists and Tramps.* But tramps found in the new railroad system the mobility to seek work in harvesting, lumberjacking, mining, or construction projects.

Hostility to the independent tramp may be found as early as St. Benedict's rule in 535 CE against the *girovagi*, or wandering monks, for whom religious life was but a pretense and who led their lives without restraint or obedience to church authority. The Elizabethan Poor Law of 1601 also condemned England's wandering, sturdy beggars, as did early U.S. courts. By 1700 Boston selectmen, for example, warned migrant strangers or vagabonds to leave town and refused them public charity.

By the Victorian era the hobo had become a fixture in the U.S. circus; perhaps the most famous hobo clown was Emmett Kelly (1898–1979), who portrayed Weary Willie the Hobo on television and in films such as *The Greatest Show on Earth* (1952). In silent movies Charlie Chaplin's Little Tramp was his signature character in seventy films, including *The Kid* (1921) and *The Gold Rush* (1925). Another famous tramp clown was Red Skelton's television character Freddie the Freeloader in the 1950s and 1960s.

In the theater of the absurd, Samuel Beckett's *Waiting for Godot* (1954; stage 1956) portrayed two pensive tramps on a country road musing about the nature of human existence. U.S. literature celebrated the romantic hobo or tramp life, from

Mark Twain's *Huckleberry Finn* (1884) to Beat generation writer Jack Kerouac's *On the Road* (1957) and *The Dharma Bums* (1958), as well as in folk music by the Industrial Workers of the World (the IWW, or Wobblies) and troubadours such as Woody Guthrie and Pete Seeger. Harry Kemp (1883–1960), the hobo poet, wrote autobiographical poems and narratives about his tramp adventures. But other works documented the grim reality of the hobo life, as in Jack London's *The Tramp* (1911) and George Orwell's *Down and out in Paris and London* (1933).

During the Great Depression of the 1930s, the number of tramps increased dramatically as more than a million homeless men, women, girls, and boys rode the rails and lived in hobo jungles in search of work or adventure. By that era reformers such as Father Edward Flanagan, who opened the Workingmen's Hotel and Boys' Town in Omaha, Nebraska, and Dorothy Day, who established the Catholic Worker Movement in New York, addressed serious social problems associated with tramping. By the 1980s homelessness was recognized as a major social issue in the United States when a rapid increase in people without adequate housing reached one million. Many of these contemporary tramps were young or mentally ill, unlike the older white alcoholic men found earlier in skid-row flophouse hotels.

In 1982 sociologist Douglas A. Harper published, *Good Company: A Tramp Life*, a book about his experiences living the life of a modern tramp. Harper recounts riding freight trains with men who did migratory farm work and lived in "hobo jungles." Soon after, this form of tramp existence disappeared as migratory work was taken over by Hispanic immigrants. The book was reissued in 2006 in a revised edition that contrasts the disappearing lifestyle of the tramp with modern urban homelessness, which has different causes and outcomes.

The movies *Boxcar Bertha* (1972) and *Ironweed* (1987) celebrate female hoboes. Hollywood featured hoboes in socially conscious movies including *Wild Boys of the Road* (1933) and *Sullivan's Travels* (1941), as well as later in *Joe Hill* (1971), *Emperor of the North* (1973), and *Bound for Glory* (1976). Most tramp songs glorify the freedom of the open road and the autonomy of the hobo life while overlooking its chronic poverty, hunger, violence, and insecurity.

The bum, a sedentary beggar who avoids work, is a variant of the tramp or hobo. This derogatory name originated in the German word *bummler*, or loafer. In the mid-1800s it meant a foraging soldier and later to loaf, beg, or wander like a vagabond or tramp. By the 1890s it referred to a hobo hitching a ride on a freight train. In the 1920s it came to mean ejection from a saloon via the bum's rush or inferior quality as in a bum job. By the 1960s it referred to resort habitués such as the beach bum or ski bum. In the twenty-first century, the tramp tradition survived in the annual National Hobo Convention at Britt, Iowa, and in the memory of the men and women who last rode the rails during the Great Depression.

Peter C. Holloran

SEE ALSO: *The Beat Generation; Chaplin, Charlie; Circus; The Great Depression; Hollywood; London, Jack;* On the Road*; Seeger, Pete; Skelton, Red; Television; Twain, Mark.*

BIBLIOGRAPHY

Brevada, William. *Harry Kemp, the Last Bohemian*. Lewisburg, PA: Bucknell University Press, 1986.

Flynt, Josiah. *Tramping with Tramps*. Montclair, NJ: Patterson Smith, 1972.

Gray, Frank. *The Tramp, His Meaning and Being*. London: Dent, 1931.

Harper, Douglas. *Good Company: A Tramp Life*. Boulder, CO: Paradigm Publishers, 2006.

Orwell, George. *Down and out in Paris and London*. New York: Harcourt Brace Jovanovich, 1933.

Transformers

In 1984 the Hasbro toy company launched a new product line: plastic action figures that could be converted from vaguely humanoid robots to functional mechanisms like vehicles or weapons. Beyond their clever design, these "Transformers" came with a background narrative. They were supposedly self-aware beings from Cybertron, engaged in a good-versus-evil battle between Autobots (led by the heroic Optimus Prime) and Decepticons (followers of the villainous Megatron). This complicated fictional universe was explained and expanded in an animated television program that ran for three years, as well as a Marvel Comics series (1984–1991) and an animated feature film (*Transformers: The Movie*, 1986).

The Transformers franchise has proved to be as wide ranging and persistent as the *Star Wars* and *Star Trek* franchises—and like those fan-driven phenomena, it has demonstrated international appeal. Hasbro originally adapted the Transformers from a Japanese toy line made by Takara, and the two companies continued to work together over the years in conceptualizing, manufacturing, and marketing. Although the Transformers universe varies in different countries, there are many common aspects, and fans gather annually at BotCon conventions in the United States, Canada, Japan, and Europe.

The success of Transformers was made possible by a 1984 change in the regulation of U.S. children's television programming, allowing products to be used as characters. Hasbro took advantage of the opportunity to combine novel toys with well-produced entertainment, also creating an innovative marketing campaign that made it fun to collect the toys and participate in the Transformers narrative. Although the first generation of Transformers was phased out of production in 1990, the shape-changing robots proved unstoppable. Through a series of creative reboots, Transformers evolved into an enduring international franchise.

Hasbro first tried a slightly updated version of the line in 1993, but Transformers: Generation Two was off-putting to original fans and failed to attract new ones. A 1996 relaunch attempt went in a completely different direction, with better luck. "Beast Wars: Transformers" introduced robots that were capable of changing their appearance to resemble real animals, and the new toy line was again paired with a popular animated series. The Beasts ended their run in 1999, and after another three-year hiatus, "Transformers: Armada" rebooted the franchise yet again. This version returned to the mechanical concept but introduced a new background narrative and a different set of adversaries. Several popular story arcs unfolded in the animated series, which ran from 2002 through 2003.

The next big development: a 2007 live-action film produced by the legendary Steven Spielberg. *Transformers* returned to the early narrative of Autobots and Decepticons, but

Transformers. *Shoppers check out shelves of Transformers action figures at a Toys "R" Us store in New York City.* DANIEL ACKER/BLOOMBERG VIA/GETTY IMAGES.

the robot characters were given a more alien appearance, and the film added a human-centered plot: teenager Sam Witwicky is on a quest for the powerful AllSpark, creator of the Transformers' robot race. Although critics were not enthusiastic about the film, its fast-paced story and well-done special effects proved popular with audiences. Sequels followed in 2009 (*Transformers: Revenge of the Fallen*) and 2011 (*Transformers: Dark of the Moon*), with action star Shia LaBeouf portraying Sam in all three films. The Transformers movies launched a new video game, new Hasbro toys, and a series of novels by noted science fiction author Alan Dean Foster.

Over the course of several decades, Transformers were themselves transformed from fairly simple toys to widely recognized cultural icons that represent the evolution of technology, the power of marketing, and the persistence of adolescent fantasy. Some commentators see a deeper—and perhaps darker—level of meaning in the franchise and its message. For example, Marc DiPaolo asserts in *War, Politics and Superheroes: Ethics and Propaganda in Comics and Film* that "the Transformers franchise is one of the most conservative superhero narratives in history." DiPaolo cites the lack of female characters, the "operatic" depiction of violence (especially in the live-action films), and a consistently militaristic worldview. From a different perspective, Jacqueline Wiegard's 2011 essay in *The Galaxy Is Rated G* suggests the live-action film develops a theme of heroic quest and depicts "the initiation of a young man into a modern world savior."

While the Transformers franchise appeals primarily to a juvenile audience, there is also a nostalgic attraction for adult men. As Dan Fleming and Damion Sturm observe in *Media, Masculinities, and the Machine*, "the boy can outgrow the toy as mere plaything but become a fan of Transformers (with its whole seductive meaning-making media system), and the man as 'toy collector' or moviegoer can share that field." All in all, the vivid integration of technology and violence, dramatized through a creative "play world," has created a franchise that successfully engages audiences across a spectrum of ages and interests.

Cynthia Giles

SEE ALSO: *Animated Films; Blockbusters; Comic Books; Comics; Marvel Comics; Movie Stars; Spielberg, Steven; Television; Toys; Video Games.*

BIBLIOGRAPHY

DiPaolo, Marc. *War, Politics and Superheroes: Ethics and Propaganda in Comics and Film.* Jefferson, NC: McFarland, 2011.

Fleming, Dan, and Damion Sturm. *Media, Masculinities and the Machine: F1, Transformers and Fantasizing Technology at Its Limits.* New York: Continuum, 2011.

Shook, John R., and Liz S. Swan. *Transformers and Philosophy: More than Meets the Mind.* Chicago: Open Court, 2009.

Wiegard, Jacqueline. "Inexplicable Utterances: Social Power and Pluralistic Discourse in *Transformers.*" In *The Galaxy Is Rated G: Essays on Children's Science Fiction Film and Television*, ed. R. C. Neighbors and Sandy Rankin, 123–137. Jefferson, NC: McFarland, 2011.

Traveling Carnivals

In American culture, the traveling carnival evokes all things seamy, dubious, and lurid. In their heyday in the 1930s, some

300 different traveling carnivals roamed the United States, offering a glimpse of mystery and excitement—and sometimes danger. It was the rare child who did not think of joining a traveling carnival or circus to escape a stultifying small-town environment. The carnival was the poor man's entertainment. An egalitarian institution, carnivals allowed equal-opportunity speculation and thus acquired a reputation for trickery and deceit—if not outright fraud. Due to America's developing network of train lines and highways, these carnivals were able to penetrate the most remote backwaters of the country. The carnival remains one of America's most enduring cultural institutions.

POPULAR ROOTS

The United States, being a young country, has long had fairly primitive tastes in entertainment. For the better part of the nineteenth century, entertainment in rural America consisted of traveling circuses and burlesque troops, vaudeville and magic-lantern shows, all traversing the country by train or by horse and buggy, offering temporary relief from the boredom of country life. The showmen were both exalted and disdained; occupants of an insular class, they were much maligned but envied for their carefree lifestyle. Cities contained a richer palette of diversions, but actors and showmen were no less scorned there. Dime museums that exhibited freaks of nature, magic acts, or flea circuses were a popular attraction.

In the latter half of the century, resort towns sprang up near urban centers to accommodate a growing middle class. Resort entertainment choices mirrored those of the city, with freak shows, burlesque, and primitive amusement parks relocating for the summer season. From these disparate entertainments, the traveling carnival emerged. It was an ad-hoc gathering of shows and concessions that traveled under the casual imprimatur of a manager or showman who handled the business end of things and was responsible for hiring and firing acts.

Most histories credit the 1893 Chicago World's Fair—which brought together the largest agglomeration of showmen ever assembled up to that point—with the traveling carnival's origination. Along the Midway Plaisance, an avenue at the fair's periphery, the freak shows; games of chance; burlesque; Wild West shows; and other, more unsavory, diversions assembled, and their close proximity led many of the showmen to compare notes on their business. "The showmen working the Midway Plaisance," writes Robert Bogdan in *Freak Show: Presenting Human Oddities for Amusement and Profit*, "not only shared the same grounds and experiences but even met to discuss common problems. . . . It was . . . in the area around Buffalo Bill's Wild West Show, that the idea for a collective amusement company was first discussed."

Otto Schmidt, a participant in these meetings, organized the Chicago Midway Plaisance Amusement Company, and he and his acts set out on a tour of the Northeast. The show featured thirteen attractions, some direct from the Midway Plaisance, but it failed due to poor organization and business practices and didn't even make it to its final booking, in New Orleans, Louisiana. Nevertheless, it provided the model for a new type of traveling amusement—part circus, part amusement park—and several showmen from Schmidt's troupe revamped the idea with success, going on to operate some of the first traveling carnivals.

From spring to fall of 1902, seventeen carnivals toured the United States. They pitched their tents in empty fields or vacant lots or were booked in conjunction with state and county fairs, these having become a welcome diversion for the small towns that served as the center of isolated farm communities. By 1905 there were forty-six traveling carnivals plying their trade. By 1937 an estimated 300 different shows traversed the country.

THE MIDWAY AND ITS ATTRACTIONS

The average carnival consisted of a circular avenue called the midway (the name derived from that of the avenue leading to the big top in a circus), ringed by the different attractions and circumscribing the rides and food vendors within a circular enclosure of colorful tents. Among the different attractions, a pre–World War II carnival would invariably include a model show, where naked (if the police could be sufficiently bribed) or scantily clad young women were exhibited behind a see-through fabric; a sex exhibit in which grift was especially common (anything even loosely associated with sex—fetuses preserved in formaldehyde, anatomical aids, or caged guinea pigs—could suffice); a palm reader; a dance pavilion; games of chance; food concessions; and, of course, rides.

The rides were usually owned and operated by the carnival's manager, and they provided a constant draw, an insurance against the vagaries of local jurisprudence—which often prohibited many acts from performing—or made grift a difficult and hazardous endeavor. Most carnivals would also include a free act, usually some spectacular daredevil stunt; for instance, a performer plunging off a tower into a small pool of water. This act was performed at the peak hour of carnival business, providing a climax and focal point to the day's events.

If the rides were the bread-and-butter of a carnival, games of chance were the jam. Extremely lucrative for the concessionaire, when the police would allow them, games of chance were in great part to blame for the carnival's dubious reputation and were a frequent source of animosity between the "townies" and the "carnies." The games were almost always rigged, with the "marks" being duped out of a considerable amount of cash. Where the police were vigilant, vendors laid off the grift. Where gambling was illegal or heavily frowned upon, the games paid off in "slum," or trinkets.

Every carnival featured a freak show, often called a "ten-in-one" or "string show," consisting of a number of different acts appearing in a single tent. The freak show provided the carnival with its air of mystery, and, although now moribund as an institution, it remains of abiding interest, with freak show paraphernalia commanding high prices by collectors. Most shows had at least one genuine *lusus naturae*—a fat woman, a living skeleton, Siamese twins—and a number of "made" acts. These ranged from outright frauds—a wild man of Borneo who might have grown up in Brooklyn or a mind reader who worked his dazzling clairvoyance by means of an elaborate code—to acts that were semi-legitimate. Tattooed men, torture acts, sword-swallowers, and snake charmers were the most common sort of acts, constituting a sort of middle class of the carnival world; they ranked slightly lower than nature's aristocrat, the freak, but far above the lowly wild man.

To attract an audience, a "talker," or quick-talking announcer, and several exhibitioners would gather on the "bally platform," giving short demonstrations and a "pitch." This was called "turning the tip." Once the tip had been turned—that is, lured into paying the entrance fee—they would be further induced to buy cheap merchandise—photos, pamphlets, and the like—and then to pay an additional fee to see the "blow-off," a genuine freak—a fat man or woman, a bearded lady, pinheads (microcephalics), or victims of other birth defects. A good blow-off could underwrite the operating expenses of a ten-in-one; therefore, freaks were a highly valued commodity.

Carnival life fostered an us-and-them attitude. You were either "with it" (in the know) or a mark. There was no middle ground, and sometimes pitched battles, deemed "clems" by the carnies, would erupt. Often small-town carnival goers were simply suspicious, and often the fights started after the games of chance had bled them dry. In 1930s small-town America, it was simply second nature to distrust the carnies. And yet, the lurid qualities of the carnival, the danger of being swindled, appear to have been part of the attraction. Carnival and carny alike were exotic, simultaneously feared and envied. The carnies' rejection of the "normal" world, of proper society, was an affront, but it was also an invitation. In the midst of the Great Depression, when the traveling carnivals were at their most popular, customers could still be counted on to spend their hard-earned pennies. Perhaps it was because escape from the hardship of everyday life had assumed a monumental importance for the hard-pressed citizenry.

DECLINE AND LEGACY

After World War II the number of carnivals in operation dropped substantially. No single reason can account for their precipitous decline. Perhaps it was that small-town audiences had become more sophisticated; perhaps changing social mores diminished the popularity of the freak show; or perhaps it was simply that society had become more regimented, and the escape carnivals represented had become anomalous. In addition, corporatism had invaded the carnival world. The result is today's pallid excuse for a carnival: no freak shows, games of chance that pay off in worthless trinkets, and not even a faint hint of danger or sex. The forbidden, as much a part of the carnival mystique as cotton candy or the smell of sawdust, had been excised from the carnival, and without the danger, the fun and excitement was simply less alluring.

But the image of the carnival remains powerfully alluring. Carnival paraphernalia—banners and promotional materials—are now highly sought after by collectors. In literature, as well, the carnival works its distinctive magic. By cleverly inverting the carnivalgoer's presumption of fraud, Charles G. Finney's novel *The Circus of Dr. Lao* (1935) tells of a traveling circus in which all the attractions are fantastically real, yet the townies fail to see past their suspicions. Katherine Dunn's best-selling novel *Geek Love*, about a family of carnival freaks purposefully deformed in utero, captured the public imagination in the late 1980s, becoming a best seller. Since Tod Browning's 1932 masterpiece, *Freaks*, the carnival has routinely appeared in motion pictures, and its appearance is usually a metaphor for subterfuge and betrayal. More recent films such as *Carny* (1980) treat the wayward carny with more affection, but one need only read David Foster Wallace's 1997 essay, "Getting Away from Being Pretty Much Away from It All," to comprehend the slightly sinister quality of the carnival and its workers. Jonathan L. Howard's novel *Johannes Cabal the Necromancer* (2009) plays off this sinister reputation as it weaves a tale of a sorcerer who must use a traveling carnival to entice 100 people to sell their souls to the devil in order to win back his own.

Carnivals conjure up a host of associations in American culture. Heirs to both the showmanship of Wild Bill Hickok and the entertaining mendacity of the snake-oil salesman, carnivals tap deeply into the American psyche: its restlessness, its love/hate relationship with conformity, and its attraction to all things criminal. The carnival was a nonjudgmental environment where the deformed, the drifter, and the outcast could find a place that would accept him or her unconditionally; it was a metaphor for freedom from troubles, escape from the mundane, and an invitation into a magical world where the rule is that things aren't always what they seem.

Michael Baers

SEE ALSO: *Best Sellers; Burlesque; Cody, Buffalo Bill, and His Wild West Show;* Freaks*; The Great Depression; Vaudeville; World War II; World's Fairs.*

BIBLIOGRAPHY

Bogdan, Robert. *Freak Show: Presenting Human Oddities for Amusement and Profit.* Chicago: University of Chicago Press, 1988.

Dunn, Katherine. *Geek Love.* New York: Knopf, 1989.

Finney, Charles G., and Boris Artzybasheff. *The Circus of Dr. Lao.* New York: Viking, 1935.

Gorham, Maurice. *Showmen and Suckers.* London: Percival Marshall, 1951.

Hall, Ward. *Struggles and Triumphs of a Modern Day Showman.* Sarasota, FL: Carnival, 1981.

Homberger, Francine. *Carny Folk.* New York: Citadel, 2005.

Mannix, Daniel P. *Memoirs of a Sword Swallower.* San Francisco, CA: V/Search, 1996.

McKennon, Joe. *A Pictorial History of the American Carnival.* Sarasota, FL: Carnival, 1972.

Wallace, David Foster. *A Supposedly Fun Thing I'll Never Do Again: Essays and Arguments.* Boston: Little, Brown, 1997.

Travolta, John *(1954–)*

There are many John Travoltas. One is the late-1970s star who rose to the dizzying heights of worldwide fame thanks to his roles in *Saturday Night Fever* (1977) and *Grease* (1978). Another is the actor whose waning popularity was reignited thanks to Quentin Tarantino's cult megahit *Pulp Fiction* (1994). In the late 1990s and early in first decade of the 2000s, Travolta continued to redefine himself as a versatile and prolific performer, adding a string of comedies, musicals, dramas, and action films to his impressive resume. Other facets of Travolta include his membership in the Church of Scientology—seemingly the secret of his perseverance against all odds on his road toward permanent fame—and his early image as a dancing and singing idol.

AN OVERNIGHT SENSATION

Travolta was born in Englewood, New Jersey, one of six children. His first taste of stardom came with his role as Tony Manero in John Badham's *Saturday Night Fever* (1977). This film coincided with Travolta's noted appearances in the TV series *Welcome Back, Kotter* (1975–1979) as high school troublemaker Vinnie Barbarino; the TV tearjerker *The Boy in the Plastic Bubble* (1976); and director Brian De Palma's film adaptation of the Stephen King novel *Carrie* (1976), in which Travolta played a sadistic classmate of the victimized heroine. *Saturday Night Fever*, the film that came to epitomize the booming disco culture of the 1970s, created a sweeping worldwide craze around Travolta—complete with countless dancing imitators vying for fame in Manero's famous cheap white three-piece suit. It also gave Travolta his first Oscar nomination (Best Actor). The second would come almost two decades later for his supporting role as Vincent Vega in *Pulp Fiction* (1994).

Among his many admirers, actress Bette Davis remarked that although Travolta was talented, he would not last. Davis's prophetic words proved accurate—at least for a while. Travolta followed the role of Tony Manero with the very popular Danny Zuko in *Grease* (1978)—a musical Travolta knew well from his early theater days. Thanks to *Grease* he became a teenage cult icon along with his costar Olivia Newton-John. Next came a starring role in 1980's *Urban Cowboy*. But the 1980s proved much less congenial to Travolta's supple talent, and he was relegated to a string of mediocre films that did poorly at the box office. The first signs of his renewed popularity came with the popular but insubstantial *Look Who's Talking* trilogy (1989, 1990, 1993), which was punctuated by Travolta's ineffectual resurrection of Tony Manero in Sylvester Stallone's *Staying Alive* (1983).

Just when Travolta seemed definitively condemned to playing uninspired roles like James Ubriacco of *Look Who's Talking* for the rest of his acting life, Tarantino stepped in, convincing his idol to play the philosophical, heroin-using hit man Vincent Vega. Travolta's return was but one of the ingredients that turned *Pulp Fiction* into a massive hit, and the film not only placed the tarnished star back into the top list of Hollywood stars, but it also garnered him a Best Supporting Actor Oscar nomination. With his professional rebirth, Travolta began working nonstop in a wide range of films. Notable performances from the late 1990s include an action villain in *Broken Arrow* (1996), gangster-cum-film producer Chili Palmer in the film adaptation of Elmore Leonard's *Get Shorty* (1995), a mechanic turned supernatural hero in *Phenomenon* (1996), an FBI agent in *Face/Off* (1997), and the Bill Clinton–inspired character Governor Jack Stanton in *Primary Colors* (1998).

BRANCHING OUT

Travolta remained active throughout the first decade of the new century as he continued to explore new film roles in a variety of movie genres. In 2000 he played an alien military official in *Battlefield Earth* (2000); although the film was a critical and commercial disaster, Travolta's enthusiastic performance earned the begrudging respect of some reviewers. In 2005 he reprised the role of Chili Palmer in *Be Cool*, another Leonard adaptation. Two years later Travolta returned to comedy in *Wild Hogs* (2007) as the leader of a pack of unlikely middle-aged bikers. That same year the actor dressed in drag to play Edna Turnblad in a remake of *Hairspray* (2007). In 2009 Travolta played opposite Denzel Washington in another remake of a film classic, *The Taking of Pelham 1-2-3*.

In January 2009 Travolta and his wife, actress Kelly Preston, suffered an unexpected tragedy when their sixteen-year-old son, Jett, died suddenly of a seizure. As Travolta later told interviewers, his Christian Science faith ultimately proved crucial in helping him weather the ordeal. By 2012 Travolta had once again returned to his busy acting schedule, joining the cast of *Savages* and *Gotti: In the Shadow of My Father*.

Travolta's enduring popularity, like that of many other major stars, is the result of a capricious combination of talent, adroit choosing of roles, luck, and the mysterious "X" factor, perhaps best defined as being in the right place at the right time. And finally, Tarantino's idolization of the actor appears to have been a crucial factor—without it, Travolta's career might not have gotten the boost it needed in order for him to roar back as a big-time star at the end of the twentieth century.

Sara Martin

SEE ALSO: *Celebrity; Celebrity Couples; Davis, Bette; Disco; Hollywood; Horror Movies; King, Stephen; Leonard, Elmore; Made-for-Television Movies; Movie Stars;* Pulp Fiction*;* Saturday Night Fever*; Sitcom; Stallone, Sylvester; Tarantino, Quentin; Television; Washington, Denzel;* Welcome Back, Kotter.

BIBLIOGRAPHY

Amis, Martin. "Travolta's Second Act." *New Yorker*, February 20–27, 1995, 212–216.

Andrews, Nigel. *Travolta: The Life*. London: Bloomsbury, 1998.

Bowles, Scott. "Travoltas Have 'Own Way' of Coping." *USA Today*, November 11, 2009.

Clarkson, Wensley. *John Travolta: Back in Character*. New York: Overlook Press, 1997.

Cohn, N. "Rebound for Glory." *Vogue*, October 1994, 191–192.

Collard, James. "John Travolta; What I've Learnt." *Times* (London), August 13, 2011.

James, Caryn. "As Praise Flows, Travolta Awaits His 3rd Comeback." *New York Times*, December 2, 2004.

John Travolta Official Website. Accessed February 2012. Available from http://www.travolta.com

Millea, H. "Stayin' Alive." *Premiere*, August, 1996, 54–60.

Schruers, F. "Travolta: The *Rolling Stone* Interview." *Rolling Stone*, February 22, 1996, 40–43.

The Treasure of the Sierra Madre

Released in 1948, *The Treasure of the Sierra Madre* is a classic adventure written and directed by John Huston. Set in Mexico, it was one of the first American movies to be filmed on location outside the United States. The film, with its themes of paranoia, greed, and duplicity, is deeply layered. It is an adventure story, an etiology of one man's mental disease, a subtle critique of capitalism, and an anthropologic study of the clash of cultures. Laced with disturbing psychological truths, it is precisely the fablelike quality of the film—the timeless and acute observation of human nature—that makes the film so remarkable. *The Treasure of the Sierra Madre* was nominated for the Academy Award for Best Picture but lost to Laurence Olivier's *Hamlet*. Huston won Academy Awards for Best Director and for Best Screenplay for the film, and his father, Walter Huston, who plays Howard, won an Academy Award for Best Supporting Actor.

In the film Fred C. Dobbs (Humphrey Bogart) is a drifter of dubious temperament, who dreams of the big score—he covets luxury but has not the patience or the perseverance to work for it. Audiences learn in the first scene that Dobbs is

The Treasure of the Sierra Madre. *Humphrey Bogart, left, and Tim Holt on the set of* The Treasure of Sierra Madre. WARNER BROS/THE KOBAL COLLECTION.

unscrupulous; he repeatedly panhandles from a wealthy American (played by John Huston) and then uses the money for such unnecessary luxuries as a haircut, lottery cards, and coffee. After teaming up with another young American, Bob Curtin (Tim Holt), and an aging prospector, Howard (Walter Huston), who has dazzled the younger men with stories of rich gold deposits in the surrounding mountains, he sets out on a quest for riches that will ultimately prove his undoing.

Curtin and Howard are basically decent, realistic individuals, and in one scene they and Dobbs discuss what they will do with their newfound wealth. Curtin dreams of buying a farm, and Howard plans to open a business to sustain him in his old age. Dobbs thinks only of the luxuries and women he will buy and of the people he will impress. The more gold they find, the further Dobbs descends into a delusional world—gold fever, as prospectors call it—in which his compatriots are mortal enemies. Every incident becomes proof of his partners' duplicity. For example, Dobbs becomes convinced Curtin is hunting for his stash, when in fact, he has unwittingly stumbled upon a gila monster and is trying to drive it off. Curtin dares Dobbs to put his hand under the rock. Dobbs hesitates, and Curtin kills the reptile.

Further evidence of Dobbs's evaporating morality is evidenced when an American, Cody (Bruce Bennett), who has followed Curtin back from a trip to restock supplies, wishes to join in their venture. Curtin, though unhappy, is amenable to the proposal, but Dobbs is adamantly opposed—he wants to kill the newcomer. It remains for Howard to cast his vote, and he reluctantly sides with Dobbs just as Mexican bandits—who had earlier waylaid the prospectors' train—stumble on the encampment, claiming to be *federales*. In the ensuing melee, Cody is killed, and the prospectors find a letter to his wife in his pocket. Curtin and Howard resolve to give a share of their gold to Cody's widow, but Dobbs abstains, saying, "You two must've been born in a revival meeting."

The Treasure of the Sierra Madre is a morality play, and Dobbs is its King Richard III, undone by his own instability. After Howard is temporarily separated from the two younger men, the last restraint on Dobbs's behavior is removed. Dobbs attacks Curtin, who manages to disarm Dobbs but then finds himself captive to Dobbs's psychosis, keeping watch over him until he can no longer stay awake. Dobbs seizes his chance and shoots Curtin. As Dobbs sits before the fire, he is consumed by his madness as the flames dance: "Conscience—what a thing—if you believe you got a conscience, it'll pester you to death . . . but if you don't believe ya got one . . . what can it do to ya?" Appropriately, Dobbs meets his fate at the hands of his brother in bestiality, Jefe, the bandit leader who kills him, seizes the burros and provisions, and discards the gold, which the bandits take for sand. The gold dust scatters in the wind. "O laugh, Curtin, old boy," cries Howard, when he and Curtin, who escaped death, find the empty bags. "It's a great joke played on us by the Lord or fate or nature or whoever you prefer . . . but whoever or whatever played it certainly had a sense of humor!"

In his book *The Movies on Your Mind*, psychiatrist Harvey R. Greenberg writes that *The Treasure of the Sierra Madre* "is much more than a clinical vignette of a diseased personality driven mad by gold. It is, by turns, the story of a young man's coming of age, of an aging man's search for his last resting place. It is a rousing adventure tale, a subtle commentary on the capitalist mentality." It is a testament to John Huston's ability as a storyteller and the breadth of his psychological insight that more than fifty years after its making, *The Treasure of the Sierra Madre* is still a powerful, convincing film. Dobbs is one of the most memorable antiheroes in film history, not because he is a villain, but because in his madness there lurks something all audience members recognize. Dobbs is a reminder that the real villain is most often within.

Michael Baers

SEE ALSO: *Academy Awards; Bogart, Humphrey; Huston, John; Olivier, Laurence.*

BIBLIOGRAPHY

Brill, Lesley. *John Huston's Filmmaking*. Cambridge, UK: Cambridge University Press, 1997.

Cooper, Stephen, ed. *Perspectives on John Huston*. Boston: G.K. Hall, 1994.

Greenberg, Harvey R. *The Movies on Your Mind: Film Classics on the Couch, From Fellini to Frankenstein*. New York: Dutton, 1975.

Madsen, Axel. *John Huston*. New York: Doubleday, 1978.

Miller, Gabriel. *Screening the Novel: Rediscovering American Fiction in Film*. New York: Frederick Ungar Publishing, 1980.

Pratley, Gerald. *The Cinema of John Huston*. South Brunswick, NJ: Barnes, 1977.

Thomas, Sam, ed. *Best American Screenplays 2*. New York: Crown Publishers, 1990.

Traven, B. *The Treasure of the Sierra Madre*. New York: Knopf, 1935.

Treviño, Lee *(1939–)*

In 1968 Lee Treviño became the first Mexican American to win a major professional golf championship at the U.S. Open. He also became the first player in history to shoot all four rounds of the event under par.

Born on December 1, 1939, in Dallas, Texas, and raised by his mother, who worked as a housekeeper, and his maternal grandfather, a gravedigger, Treviño got involved in golf because his family's four-room farmhouse overlooked the back of the Glen Lakes Country Club fairways. As a boy, Treviño studied the form of golfers on the course from his own backyard. He dropped out of school in the seventh grade and made his way into what was then an exclusively Anglo rich man's sport by working as a caddie and greenkeeper.

Treviño became a professional golfer in 1960, and by 1970 he was the leading money winner on the Professional Golfers' Association (PGA) tour. In 1971 he became the first player to win the U.S., British, and Canadian opens in a single year and was also the first Hispanic ever named PGA Player of the Year, Associated Press Athlete of the Year, and *Sports Illustrated* Sportsman of the Year. Among his other major tournament wins, he placed first yet again at both the British Open in 1972 and the PGA in 1974. He was awarded the Vardon Trophy for the fewest strokes per round four times in the 1970s; in 1980 he won once again, with a score of 69.73 for eight-two rounds, the lowest since Sam Snead in 1950.

Treviño was struck by lightning in 1974, and the resulting back problems and surgeries restricted his play in the early 1980s. He served as a TV sports commentator but came back to win the PGA in 1984 and the British Masters in 1985. Treviño retired from the PGA Tour in 1985, with more than twenty-five tour victories and total career earnings of more than $3 million (third highest at the time). He was elected to the Texas Sports, American Golf, and World Golf halls of fame. In 2000 *Golf Digest* ranked him as the fourteenth-greatest golfer of all time.

Nicolás Kanellos

SEE ALSO: *Golf; Sports Heroes;* Sports Illustrated.

BIBLIOGRAPHY

Kanellos, Nicolás. *The Hispanic American Almanac*, 2nd ed. Detroit, MI: Gale Research, 1997.

Trevino, Lee, and Sam Blair. *They Call Me Super Mex: The Autobiography of Lee Trevino*. New York: Random House, 1982.

Trevor, Claire *(1910–2000)*

Born in New York City and trained at the American Academy of Dramatic Arts and Columbia University, Claire Trevor sustained a long and prolific acting career that included more than 150 movies, 200 radio shows, 20 stage plays, and scores of television dramas. Trevor began her film career in 1933 in *Jimmy and Sally*. Playing a boozy moll in *Key Largo* (1948), she won an Academy Award as Best Supporting Actress. In 1956 she won an Emmy for Best Single Performance by an Actress for her role in the Producers' Showcase television drama, *Dodsworth*, with Fredric March. As late as 1987 she appeared in a motion picture *Breaking Home Ties*, based on Norman Rockwell images. Trevor died in 2000 in Newport Beach, California.

Benjamin Griffith

SEE ALSO: *Academy Awards; Emmy Awards; Radio; Rockwell, Norman; Television.*

BIBLIOGRAPHY

Shipman, David. *The Great Movie Stars: The Golden Years*. New York: Crown, 1970.

Shipman, David. *Cinema: The First Hundred Years*. New York: St. Martin's Press, 1993.

Trillin, Calvin *(1935–)*

Calvin Trillin, journalist and storyteller of the American scene, has introduced his readers to friends in unlikely places (such as Horse Cave, Kentucky), exposed several small-town scandals, and revealed a great many of his own idiosyncrasies along the way. Readers know a little about the way he thinks and a lot about the way he eats, from the pages of his self-titled "tummy trilogy," *American Fried* (1974), *Alice, Let's Eat* (1978), and *Third Helpings* (1983). Readers have also met his wife, Alice, who "has a weird predilection for limiting our family to three meals a day," and his two daughters, Abigail and Sarah, the lat-

Calvin Trillin. *Calvin Trillin's columns for the* New Yorker *and the* Nation, *as well as his novels and other writings, provide an interesting and sometimes highly personal take on American life.* ROBIN PLATZER/CONTRIBUTOR/FILMMAGIC/GETTY IMAGES.

ter of whom "refused to enter a Chinese restaurant unless she was carrying a bagel in reserve, 'just in case.'"

Because many of these pieces originated as columns in the *New Yorker* and other popular magazines, Trillin's cast of characters has become memorable, and regular readers anxiously await their latest escapades. Trillin enthusiasts have also developed an appetite for what he calls the "best barbecue in the world," available only in his hometown of Kansas City, Missouri. He writes about food not as an expert nor as a cook but as the owner of a prodigious appetite for foods that the doctor generally does not recommend.

Trillin's journalistic career began after his graduation from Yale in 1957 and a subsequent stint in the U.S. Army. From 1960 to 1963 he worked as an Atlanta, Georgia, correspondent for *Time* and labored in various departments until he was invited by editor William Shawn to join the staff of the *New Yorker.* Trillin's initial assignment for the *New Yorker* led in 1964 to his first book, *An Education in Georgia,* which chronicles the events surrounding the forced integration of the University of Georgia at Athens. Trillin continued to demonstrate his observational abilities in his regular *New Yorker* feature, "U.S. Journal," recording the experiences of ordinary American people in times of stress. Many of these articles later appeared in book collections such as *Killings* (1984), a compilation of short pieces on wrongful deaths and suicides, and *American Stories* (1991), which includes tales of crime interspersed with profiles of favorite Trillin characters, including Fats Goldberg, the formerly fat pizza baron who shuttles between New York and Kansas City, where he always stops for a chili dog at Kresge's.

Trillin is equally at home in many genres. His short satirical commentaries from the *Nation* are collected in *Uncivil Liberties* (1982) and *With All Disrespect: More Uncivil Liberties* (1985). He has also written fiction, including compilations of short stories "written for Alice" and a novel titled *Runestruck* (1977), the story of a pre-Columbian artifact discovered in a small town in Maine. He has tried his hand at light verse as well in *Deadline Poet* (1995). His more ruminative side is shown in memoirs such as *Remembering Denny* (1993), the story of a Yale friend who never lived up to his initial promise as a "golden boy" and eventually killed himself.

As a journalist, Trillin knows the value of a good lead, both as story idea and as reader enticement. Following are a few examples of the latter:

> Not long ago, I ran across a man who pulls his own teeth. ("Ouch," *With All Disrespect,* 55)

> Not long ago, I became preoccupied with the cost of the wristwatches worn by members of the New Jersey State Legislature. ("The Dark Side," *Uncivil Liberties,* 75)

> In my version of a melancholy walk on the waterfront, I find myself walking through a cold Atlantic mist along the docks of some East Coast city, wearing a turned-up trench-coat, making the best approximation of footsteps echoing on the cobblestones that can be expected from a man wearing crepe-soled shoes, and ducking into a passage that turns out to be the entrance to a gourmet kitchen-supply shop called something like the Wondrous Whisk—where I soberly inspect imported French cherry pitters and antique butter molds and Swedish meat slicers. ("Weekends for Two," *Alice, Let's Eat,* 155)

Trillin published the novel *Tepper Isn't Going Out* in 2002. Alice died in 2001, and he paid tribute to her in *About Alice* (2006). Throughout his career, much of his best humor has focused on politics, and he always has plenty to say about political candidates. Among his other favorite targets are presidents, particularly George W. Bush, as was evidenced in *Obliviously on He Sails: The Bush Administration in Rhyme* (2004) and *A Heckuva Job: More of the Bush Administration in Rhyme* (2006). In 2011 Trillin published a collection of forty of his essays that had previously appeared in the *New Yorker,* the *Nation,* and the *New York Times* in *Quite Enough of Calvin Trillin: Forty Years of Funny Stuff,* containing typical Trillin jabs at everyone from Bill Clinton and Barack Obama to Sarah Palin and Donald Trump. Like Kansas City barbecue, Trillin's writing can be addictive.

Sue Russell

SEE ALSO: *Barbecue; Foodies;* The Nation*; The* New Yorker*; Obama, Barack; Palin, Sarah;* Time.

BIBLIOGRAPHY

McClatchy, J. D. *Bright Pages: Yale Writers, 1701–2001.* New Haven, CT: Yale University Press, 2001.

Remnick, David, ed. *Life Stories: Profiles from the New Yorker.* New York: Random House, 2000.

Trillin, Calvin. *Alice, Let's Eat: Further Adventures of a Happy Eater.* New York: Random House, 1978.

Trillin, Calvin. *Uncivil Liberties.* New Haven, CT: Ticknor & Fields, 1982.

Trillin, Calvin. *With All Disrespect: More Uncivil Liberties.* New York: Ticknor & Fields, 1985.

Trillin, Calvin. *American Stories.* New York: Ticknor & Fields, 1991.

Trillin, Calvin. *Quite Enough of Calvin Trillin: Forty Years of Funny Stuff.* New York: Random House, 2011.

Trivial Pursuit

Trivial Pursuit can be credited with creating a whole new category of board games for adults as well as an entire industry of trivia games. On December 15, 1979, Canadian photographer Chris Haney and sportswriter Scott Abbott were inspired to create the game after competing against each other Scrabble. They had originally planned to call their game Trivia Pursuit until Haney's wife jokingly referred to it as Trivial Pursuit, and the name stuck.

The first 1,100 sets cost $75 each to manufacture. But after selling them to retailers for $15 a game, Haney and Abbott were in debt by early 1982. Then the U.S. game company Selchow and Righter became interested after hiring a public relations consultant who saw Trivial Pursuit's potential as a popular leisure-time diversion. After Selchow and Righter bought the rights to the board game, 3.5 million games were sold by late 1983. A year later the figure had jumped to twenty million. By the 1990s retail sales exceeded $1 billion, and the game was available in nineteen different languages and thirty-three countries. In 2008 Hasbro bought all rights to the game for $80 million.

There has been a Trivial Pursuit television show, and the game is available on the Internet. Since its debut in 1982, there have been dozens of variations of the game, many of them promotional tie-ins with movies or other aspects of popular culture, and Trivial Pursuit has become an essential part of the universal language of popular culture.

Frank Clark

SEE ALSO: *Board Games; Computer Games; The Internet; Leisure Time.*

BIBLIOGRAPHY

Butters, Patrick. "What Biggest Selling Adult Game Still Cranks out Vexing Questions." *Insight on the News,* January 26, 1998, 39.

Hasbro. *The Ultimate Trivial Pursuit Question & Answer Book.* New York: Puzzlewright, 2009.

Krance, Magda. "'Trivial Pursuit' Come to the U.S. to Take the Bored out of Games and the Profit Away from Pacman." *People Weekly,* September 19, 1983, 84–85.

"Let's Get Trivial." *Time,* October 24, 1983, 88.

Silver, Marc. "The Endless Pursuit of All Things Trivial." *U.S. News & World Report,* December 18, 1989.

Trixie Belden

"Schoolgirl shamus" Trixie Belden was featured in mysteries beginning with the first, *The Secret Mansion,* published by the Whitman Company in 1948, and concluding with the thirty-ninth, *The Mystery of the Galloping Ghost,* issued in 1986. Julie Campbell wrote the first six volumes. Then the new publisher, Golden Press, hired ghostwriters who used the pseudonym Kathryn Kenny. Thirteen-year-old Trixie lives in rural New York. She, her brothers, and her friends, all members of the club Bob-Whites of the Glen, usually solve thefts while participating in American and international adventures. Trixie appealed to teenage readers because her lifestyle and dreams were more familiar to them than were those of Nancy Drew. The Trixie Belden mysteries enabled readers to explore and solve problems vicariously. Set in a wholesome country environment, the stories are often didactic, criticizing wealthy socialites while praising the virtue of domesticity and self-sacrifice and reinforcing middle- and working-class values. In each book Trixie heroically rescues people or property from danger. Often impulsive and impatient, Trixie is always capable and honest; she works to earn money for such charity projects as UNICEF. Adult fans continue to collect the out-of-print books and sponsor Internet sites about the character and the stories.

Elizabeth D. Schafer

SEE ALSO: *Cherry Ames; Detective Fiction; Nancy Drew.*

BIBLIOGRAPHY

Mason, Bobbie Ann. *The Girl Sleuth: A Feminist Guide.* Old Westbury, NY: Feminist Press, 1975.

Trout, Robert *(1909–2000)*

Robert Trout was radio broadcasting's first true anchorman. The concept was purely a practical innovation: the networks' foreign correspondents and highly paid analysts were the stars, yet someone had to introduce their reports, kill time during technical problems, or read late-breaking bulletins as they poured into the studio. Trout was handpicked for this role as war clouds gathered over Europe in 1938, and gradually—broadcast after broadcast, day after day, crisis after crisis—he turned what had been a simple announcer's chore into a star role, creating the "broadcast news" institution that continues to this day.

Trout came out of local radio in Washington, D.C., where he had been assigned to introduce President Franklin Delano Roosevelt's "fireside chats." FDR was said to be so impressed with the young announcer's ad-libbing skill that he sometimes delayed the start of his talk a few seconds just to see how Trout would fill the time. The CBS network soon beckoned, even as the European situation worsened. The networks were beefing up their news operations, assigning correspondents to every major world capital; when the March 1938 German-Austrian crisis exploded, CBS brass picked Trout to sit in the studio, reading the late bulletins and introducing reports from the network's far-flung correspondents. And while the job could (and, on NBC, *was*) handled by any number of nameless staff announcers, Trout took the role at CBS and made it his own.

Broadcasting legend, of course, holds that the great innovation of that Austrian crisis was the invention of the "news roundup," the blending of several European correspondents' reports into a single live broadcast. Indeed, even the notion of CBS letting its own European staff speak on the air was an innovation in these pioneering days, but the idea of Trout holding the coverage together from New York, broadcast after broadcast—one steady, instantly identifiable voice speaking for the network over the long days or weeks of crisis—was equally revolutionary, and Trout seemed instinctively to understand the potential of his new role. His delivery was fast and facile, his manner urbane but not arrogant, his voice authoritative yet not pompous. By the time Germany invaded Poland in September 1939, it was impossible to imagine coverage of a major event without Trout at the CBS microphone, smoothly steering listeners from one event to the next, juggling shortwave reports and incoming bulletins while masterfully hitting every cue and station break.

Strangely, NBC never imitated this single "voice of authority"–type idea; even Trout's own bosses seemed not to realize what they had created. When CBS European chief Edward R. Murrow returned from his London posting in late 1941, the network brass sent Trout overseas—as a reporter. It was an obvious sign that they understood Trout's star status, yet the admittedly prestigious London assignment was ill advised at best. Trout acquitted himself adequately, but his absence from the New York studio deprived CBS of the central force that had spearheaded its crisis coverage for so long. Without him, CBS's coverage of the attack on Pearl Harbor seemed particularly disjointed and rudderless.

Robert Trout. *Robert Trout broadcasts from President Dwight D. Eisenhower's second inauguration in January 1957.* CBS PHOTO ARCHIVE/CONTRIBUTOR/CBS/GETTY IMAGES.

Having returned to New York by midwar, Trout turned the London job back over to Murrow and picked up right where he'd left off. It was Trout whose voice sounded across the nation just after 3:30 on the morning of June 6, 1944: "This means invasion!" he intoned, and America knew the D-day landings were officially under way. It was Trout whose leaden, disbelieving tones addressed the nation upon the unexpected death of President Roosevelt in April 1945, and it was Trout (after sleeping on a cot just outside the studio for several days so as not to miss the big moment) who told the world at 7 p.m. on August 14, 1945, "The Japanese have accepted our terms fully. . . . This, ladies and gentlemen is the end of the Second World War!"

Tougher times followed. Murrow again returned to New York, this time taking a job as chief of CBS's news operation. In 1946 Trout was given a real plum: his own nightly broadcast, a five-evening-a-week extravaganza sponsored by Campbell's Soup. It didn't last long. By 1948 Murrow realized he hated the executive suite, and Campbell's jumped at the chance to return the legendary broadcaster to the air . . . alone. Trout was off the show, a pill so bitter he resigned and defected to NBC for a time before patching things up and returning to CBS in the early 1950s.

And there he stayed, reporting everything from political conventions to the 1961 Alan Shepard spaceflight to a series of war-years retrospectives in the mid-1960s. His one big television break came in 1964, when low ratings and behind-the-scenes turmoil led CBS bigwigs to oust Walter Cronkite from the anchor chair, replacing him with Trout and Roger Mudd—a combination that was a blatant effort to copy the wild success of NBC's Huntley-Brinkley team. Trout and Mudd did no better against NBC, however, and viewer protests quickly guaranteed Cronkite's return to center stage.

Trout continued to work on radio, reporting on the political conventions into the late 1980s (more recently for ABC). He could always be counted on to reminisce about the war years or the glory days of network radio. He died on November 14, 2000.

Chris Chandler

SEE ALSO: *Brinkley, David; Cronkite, Walter; Huntley, Chet; Murrow, Edward R.; Radio; Television; Television Anchors; World War II.*

BIBLIOGRAPHY

Cox, Jim. *Radio Speakers: Narrators, News Junkies, Sports Jockeys, Tattletales, Tipsters, Toastmasters, and Coffee Klatch Couples Who Verbalized the Jargon of the Aural Ether from the 1920s to the 1980s—A Biographical Dictionary*. Jefferson, NC: McFarland, 2007.

Dunning, John. *On the Air*. New York: Oxford University Press, 1998.

Slater, Robert. *This . . . Is CBS*. Englewood Cliffs, NJ: Prentice Hall, 1988.

Sperber, A. M. *Murrow: His Life and Times*. New York: Bantam Books, 1986.

Trudeau, Garry

SEE: *Doonesbury.*

True Detective

True Detective, which started life as *True Detective Mysteries* in 1924, helped pioneer the American crime genre in the 1920s. Published monthly by Macfadden Publications, it featured true crime stories, making full use of the manners and language of the United States. The hard-boiled investigators in its pages represented a break from the European "Great Detective" tradition. Former police detective and novelist Dashiell Hammett, creator of the Sam Spade detective character, is among the crime writers whose work appeared in the pages of *True Detective*. Printed on cheap, grainy wood-pulp paper, *True Detective* was one of the first pulp magazines in the United States.

Robert E. Schnakenberg

SEE ALSO: *Hammett, Dashiell; Hard-Boiled Detective Fiction; Macfadden, Bernarr; Pulp Magazines.*

BIBLIOGRAPHY

Goodstone, Tony. *The Pulps*. New York: Chelsea House, 1970.

Panek, LeRoy. *Probable Cause: Crime Fiction in America*. Bowling Green, OH: Bowling Green State University Popular Press, 1990.

Winn, Dilys. *Murder Ink*. New York: Workman Publishing, 1984.

True Story Magazine

In 1919 the eccentric American publisher Bernarr Macfadden began publication of *True Story Magazine*. According to Macfadden, the magazine was inspired by personal letters of confession sent to him in his capacity as the editor/founder of *Physical Culture*. Sensing a widespread interest in the changing social/sexual codes of modern America, he put out a new magazine filled with firsthand accounts of social problems such as premarital sex, illegitimacy, adultery, unemployment, social relations, and crime (alongside slightly risqué movie stills of each story's most dramatic moments—the kiss, the temptation, the horrible realization).

The magazine personalized issues that were hotly debated in Jazz Age America (dancing, drinking, partying, petting) and offered a unique working-class perspective on issues that were not necessarily unique to the working class. Sensational, emotional, and controversial, *True Story* disseminated tales of sex, sin, and redemption that seemingly revealed the ubiquity of modern sexual and social irregularity. Most educated observers hated the magazine, figuring that it depicted the worst aspect of the revolution in manners and morals that occurred in the 1920s.

WIDE FOLLOWING

Workaday America loved the new confessional magazine. *True Story* became the publishing smash hit of the 1920s. One critic offered Macfadden a backhanded compliment when he noted that millions of Americans "wallow in the filth of his politely dressed confessions." Achieving circulation figures close to the two million mark by 1929, *True Story* easily matched the sales of traditional big sellers such as *Ladies' Home Journal* and the *Saturday Evening Post*. *True Story* (along with siblings *True Romance* and *True Experience* and competitors such as *True Confessions*) would maintain a large and devoted readership right into the twenty-first century.

The *True Story* that can be found in supermarkets in the new millennium, however, bears only a slight resemblance to the popular original. Macfadden lost control of his publication during the 1940s, but even by that time the magazine had come to represent a much more muted version of the original confessional genre. Over time *True Story* evolved into a magazine that told mild tales of women's sexual misadventure, tempered by strong doses of normative moral sermonizing. In the 1920s, the period in which *True Story* shocked middle-class Americans into a series of renewed (and somewhat successful) efforts at censorship, the magazine was an innovative, raunchy, working-class pulp that purveyed an eclectic range of stories designed to appeal to both a male and female audience.

WORKING-CLASS TALES

The popularity of *True Story* has too often been ascribed solely to its "sex sells" credo. In fact, in the 1920s the magazine offered the reader much more than titillating sex tales; it offered working-class Americans stories told in their own voice (the magazine accepted reader's personal stories). Although scholars have, and not without reason, scoffed at Macfadden's claims that his stories were both true and written by authentic working-class Americans, there is little question that his idea that stories of everyday working-class life were important was an original one. *True Story* argued, both explicitly and implicitly, that the story of modern working-class America was drama of epic proportions.

In its original guise, *True Story* told tales of how working-class men and women struggled to negotiate the changes wrought by modernity. The central premise of the magazine in those early days was the notion that "it is a new world . . . and it might be well to get ready for it." *True Story* claimed to help its readers make sense of the turbulent and changing mores that made up modern life and taught them how to safely embrace the emboldened society brought about by the Jazz Age. In short, *True Story* told tales of seemingly particular modern moral downfalls (drugs, crime, sex)—even if it did then offer up some patently old-fashioned and universal remedies for redemption (confess, make amends, walk a straighter path).

The importance of *True Story* lies in the ways in which it challenged the hegemony of middle-class publishing norms. Failing to apologize for the cheapness of his endeavor, Macfadden outraged Middle America (even as his product tempted its youth) by daring to elevate rowdy, raunchy, working-class youth into modern heroes. The magazine not only revealed and popularized the ways in which working-class youth flouted convention but also argued that its working-class antiheroes were the success stories of modern America. *True Story* valorized the lifestyles of the new American working class, with their extra dollars in their pockets, their love of material goods, and their desire for things previously denied. The magazine did not deny the realities of modern temptation; rather, *True Story* explicitly argued that it could teach working-class youth how to safely negotiate their path through modern life—through the vicarious (albeit entertaining) experience of stumbling, falling, and getting up again.

LOSING ITS RADICAL EDGE

As the 1920s progressed, *True Story* lost its radical edge. Macfadden, influenced by new marketing credos, sought to expand his advertising and his audience base. In order to achieve greater circulation figures and larger advertising revenues, he successfully transformed his confessional magazine into a women's publication. He achieved this transformation by erasing most of the men's stories, including advertising that targeted women, and—as a pander to conservative advertisers—toning down the content of the confessional stories.

By the 1930s *True Story* was a tamer version of the original confessional concept and a decidedly less exciting one. Although the magazine lost its male readership along with its male confessions, it did continue to offer one of the few working-class voices in the marketplace. That voice, however, was less raw, more conservative, and increasingly mediated by the concerns of advertisers and editors. *True Story* would barely change its format in the following seven decades. Although the transformation of the magazine into a women's romance magazine proved an effective survival strategy, the moment at which *True Story* was most vital, most alive, was undoubtedly during that time in the 1920s when Macfadden's confessional stories seemed to herald (terrifyingly and excitingly) the dawn of a raunchy modern American moment.

Jackie Hatton

SEE ALSO: *Advertising; Confession Magazines; Macfadden, Bernarr; The* Saturday Evening Post*; Tabloids; The Twenties.*

BIBLIOGRAPHY

Claussen, Dane S. *Sex, Religion, Media.* Lanham, MD: Rowman & Littlefield, 2002.

Ernst, Robert. *Weakness Is a Crime: The Life of Bernarr Macfadden.* Syracuse, NY: Syracuse University, 1991.

Hatton, Jacqueline Anne. *True Stories: Working-Class Mythology, American Confessional Culture, and* True Story Magazine, *1919–1929.* Unpublished PhD diss. Cornell University, Ithaca, NY, 1997.

Hersey, Harold. *Pulpwood Editor: The Fabulous World of the Thriller Magazines Revealed by a Veteran Editor and Publisher.* New York: Stokes, 1937.

Oursler, Fulton. *The True Story of Bernarr Macfadden.* New York: Copeland, 1929.

Trump, Donald

SEE: *The Apprentice.*

T-Shirts

Sex, work, and democracy together advanced the T-shirt as a clothing icon of the late twentieth century. Until the 1940s the T-shirt was exclusively an undershirt. U.S. sailors, in shipboard fraternity, worked in T-shirts, and during World War II they appeared on the July 13, 1942, cover of *Life* magazine and cavorted in the musical *South Pacific* (1943). The private world was now public, and the undershirt entered society, sometimes with the renegade image of Marlon Brando, other times with the innocent white shirt of James Dean. The T-shirt would not have the authority of the cut-and-sewn shirt with collar until the 1980s when Bruce Springsteen reinforced its proletarian roots while also identifying the T-shirt with the new 1980s masculinity of sex-object, gym-built male bodies.

Another factor that helped the T-shirt evolve from its status as an undershirt was the advent of printed T-shirts. Certain iconic T-shirts have come to be seen as emblematic of their era, such as the Che Guevara T-shirts that many wore to express the revolutionary ideals of the 1960s. Today, people wear printed T-shirts to show where they have traveled, to promote their interests and hobbies, to express loyalty to sports teams, and to support worthy causes. In 2011 T-shirts were even used to support a charitable cause in a record-breaking way: on November 13, for a fund-raising event, the owner of a T-shirt store in Iowa put on 247 T-shirts, breaking the previous world record.

Richard Martin

SEE ALSO: *Brando, Marlon; Dean, James;* South Pacific*; Springsteen, Bruce; Sweatshirt.*

BIBLIOGRAPHY

Harris, Alice. *The White T.* New York: HarperCollins, 1996.

Kidner, Lisa, and Sam Knee. *Vintage T-Shirts: More than 500 Authentic Tees from the '70s and '80s.* New York: Harper Design, 2006.

Tupperware

Perhaps no product line epitomizes post–World War II American suburbia as much as Tupperware plastic kitchen containers. Earl Tupper (1907–1983), inveterate experimenter from Harvard, Massachusetts, used his experience in 1937 working for du Pont to develop his own kind of plastic, which he used to make all types of products. In 1938 he founded the Earl S. Tupper Company, which had some success selling gas masks and signal lamp parts to the navy during World War II. But when he applied his flexible and durable material to civilian needs, Tupper achieved his greatest success.

THE PRODUCT

In 1945 Tupper trademarked his perfected plastic, Polyethylene-Tupper, or Poly-T, the "material of the future." Interested in women's daily lives (he experimented with designs for garter belt hooks and brassieres, for example), Tupper used this innovative material to create an entirely new line of housewares that revolutionized the way women dealt with food and other things in their kitchens. Up until this time, plastics such as Bakelite and celluloid were common materials but had limited uses—products made from them were either brittle or heavy and were not suitable for use with foods. In contrast, Tupperware was perfect in the kitchen. It came in many forms, including tumblers, bowls, pitchers, ice cube trays, butter dishes, and even cocktail shakers.

Tupperware Party. *Women attend a Tupperware demonstration in the 1950s. The company's direct-sales approach through in-home parties resulted in over $25 million in sales by its fourth year.* HULTON ARCHIVE/GETTY IMAGES.

Tupper's most famous and effective innovation, in 1946, was a set of storage canisters with resealable lids that could be "burped" to let out and keep out excess air. They were lightweight, airtight, indestructible, and waxy textured for a good grip. These canisters proved to be great improvements over the products most often used in the kitchen until then—the more common glass and metal containers, which were heavy, were not airtight, were prone to sweating from refrigerator condensation, and broke easily.

Tupper's plastic products were not only utilitarian but also materially seductive. The drinking tumblers came in many colors, including lime, raspberry, lemon, plum, and orange. The bowls were attractively shaped and could even be used to display fresh-fruit centerpieces. Tupperware was such an embodiment of postwar materialism that some of its pieces became part of the Museum of Modern Art's permanent collection in 1955 and were described as "carefully considered shapes . . . marvelously free of that vulgarity which characterizes so much household equipment." It is ironic that Tupper, such a pioneer bringing the modernity of his translucent plastic designs into the home, was an antiquarian at heart. He believed, nostalgically, in the traditional values of handcraftsmanship and manual labor, and his home was filled with antiques. In contrast the products he engineered and manufactured were truly "tomorrow's designs with tomorrow's materials."

THE PARTIES

While Tupper brought new materials and new forms into the domestic sphere, his products also introduced a new kind of sociability among women through private home sales. From 1950 on, Tupperware was marketed and distributed only by direct selling, through Tupperware parties, overseen by Tupperware Home Parties Incorporated, established in 1951 and also known as the Cinderella Company. These parties were actually commercial opportunities orchestrated as social events. A hostess would throw a party in her home, inviting friends and neighbors in order to provide firsthand demonstrations of the products (such as how to burp the storage canisters) and to give her guests a chance to purchase Tupperware items. Here women also played games and could win Tupperware prizes, and the hostess would try to recruit potential hostesses to give their own parties—all in exchange for Tupperware items for themselves.

This method of product distribution paradoxically offered women the freedom to be entrepreneurs while it emphasized their traditional domestic responsibilities as wives and mothers, giving them the chance to socialize on their own, yet in a way that channeled them into their standard gender roles. However ambiguous, Tupper's marketing strategy—overseen by saleswoman Brownie Wise until 1958—was clearly successful. In 1954 more than 20,000 women were dealers, distributors, and managers. In that same year sales topped $25 million and allowed Tupper to double the size of his manufacturing facility in Blackstone, Massachusetts. In 1958 he sold his interest in the company to Justin Dart of the Rexall Drug Company (which later became Premark).

Tupperware and the party system both successfully entered Britain in 1961. By 1979 there were more than 50,000 people selling over $700 million worth of Tupperware. In the 1980s Tupperware was sold in more than forty countries and carried product lines fitting specific cultural needs, such as the sushi saver in Japan. To bring it up-to-date, designer Morison Cousins redesigned Tupperware in the 1990s, giving it "Euro styling," with brighter colors and sleeker shapes. The company introduced Tupperkids, a line of children's toys, in 1994.

In 1995 the company spun off from Premark and renamed itself Tupperware Brands Corporation. Tupperware adapted to contemporary lives by producing microwave-safe containers and containers designed to prolong the shelf life of fresh produce.

After overhauling its product line, the company updated the way its parties were held to make them seem more like fun girls' nights out for working women. With the spread of the Internet, Tupperware also added the options of shopping online or holding an online Tupperware "party." During the early twenty-first century, Tupperware continued to update its image and introduced even sleeker, more modern-looking products.

Tupperware has continued to make gains around the world, especially in countries with developing economies. The company's website boasts that a Tupperware party starts somewhere in the world every 2.3 seconds. In 2010 the company reported annual sales of $2.3 billion. What is more, Tupperware is so familiar to Americans that, to many, it has become a generic word applied to all such plastic storage containers with resealable lids and also has come to symbolize the unique blend of domesticity, materialism, and superficiality that is seen to characterize life in the American suburb.

Wendy Woloson

SEE ALSO: *The Internet; Online Shopping; Plastic; Smithsonian Institution; Suburbia; World War II.*

BIBLIOGRAPHY

Clarke, Alison J. "Tupperware: Product as Social Relation." *American Material Culture: The Shape of the Field*, ed. Ann Smart Martin and J. Ritchie Garrison. Winterthur, DE: Henry Francis du Pont Winterthur Museum, 1997.

Clarke, Alison J. *Tupperware: The Promise of Plastic in 1950s America*. Washington, DC: Smithsonian, 1999.

Fenichell, Stephen. *Plastic: The Making of a Synthetic Century*. New York: HarperBusiness, 1996.

Kealing, Bob. *Tupperware Unsealed: Brownie Wise, Earl Tupper, and the Home Party Pioneers*. Gainesville: University Press of Florida, 2008.

Meikle, Jeffrey L. *American Plastic: A Cultural History*. New Brunswick, NJ: Rutgers University Press, 1995.

Turner, Ike and Tina

Formed in 1959 in St. Louis, Missouri, the partnership of Mississippi rhythm-and-blues musician Ike Turner and a young singer from Nutbush, Tennessee, named Anna Mae Bullock would result in one of popular music's most combustible sounds. Known for their impressive live performances, Ike (1931–2007) and Tina (1939–) Turner were an immediate crossover sensation who eventually released some twenty-nine albums on various labels. As significant as their contribution was to American black music, their sixteen-year union as the Ike and Tina Turner Revue also left an indelible impression upon rock and pop music the world over.

Supported by a full R&B orchestra and choreographed backup singers, Ike was bandleader, arranger, and producer for the duo. With a distinctive onstage style, the Ike and Tina Turner Revue created a whirlwind of sensation and emotion that inspired audiences and performers alike. Compatible with R&B, straight blues, Motown soul, and hard-core rock and roll, Ike and Tina shared bills with many top performers, including the Rolling Stones. While Ike was the competent instrumentalist and songwriter, it was Tina who created an enduring place within popular culture. As a woman and a performer of strength, grace, and spirit, she overcame poverty, self-doubt, and abuse in order to succeed personally and professionally.

Starting out as a piano player, Ike made history early on in 1951 when he played on the Sun Records session that produced one of the first rock-and-roll records ever recorded, Jackie Brenston's "Rocket 88." Picking up the guitar shortly thereafter, he became a busy session player who worked with blues greats Howlin' Wolf, Elmore James, and Otis Rush. It was at this time that he developed his distinctive stinging guitar style.

His own band, Ike Turner's Rhythm Kings, was the toast of East St. Louis, Illinois, when Bullock (Tina), the daughter of sharecroppers, met Ike for the first time. Tina joined Ike's touring band as a backup vocalist in 1956 when she was eighteen. By 1958 she was the star of the show. It was her lovely growl and wild, gospel accents that set her apart from other singers at the time. The high-energy performer filled the stage with her powerful presence and made every lyric of a song come to life. As sexual as she was talented, Tina was not simply a soul singer or an R&B vocalist: she was something new and different, and this captured the attention of white and black audiences.

As Ike and Tina Turner they recorded their first single in 1959 for Sue Records, "A Fool in Love." By 1960 this side was a number two hit on the R&B charts. Following up with "I Idolize You," "It's Gonna Work out Fine," and "Poor Fool," the Ike and Tina Turner Revue had five Top 10 hits on the R&B charts in less than three years. Their first album, *The Soul of Ike and Tina Turner*, was released in 1960 on Sue. Working for top labels such as Warner Brothers, Liberty Records, London, Hallmark, Valiant, Sunset, and United Artists, Ike and Tina released at least one project every year until their final album, *Nutbush City Limits*, was recorded in 1973. Their most successful project was *Workin' Together* (1970). Released on Liberty, this recording included Tina's version of "Proud Mary." Another highlight of their years together was working with producer Phil Spector, whose "wall of sound" production style dominated American pop music during the 1960s. This big sound complemented Tina's vocal prowess dramatically as is evidenced on *River Deep Mountain High*, released in 1966.

While Ike and Tina's stage union produced spectacular results and Tina had carved a name for herself as one of the premier women of rock and pop, their personal life together was hardly satisfactory. Ike was a taskmaster who insisted upon total control in everything, including his marriage. Using fear and Tina's own youthful inexperience against her, Ike finally married her in Mexico. After years of mistreatment and abuse, Tina left Ike in 1975, eventually divorcing him and rebuilding her career as a solo artist. In 1984, at the age of forty-five, she was once more an international sensation, making the charts again with her album *Private Dancer*. In 1985 she had a starring role in the popular Mel Gibson film *Mad Max beyond Thunderdome*, for which she also recorded the hit single "We Don't Need Another Hero."

The 1993 film *What's Love Got to Do with It?* chronicled Tina's rocky career and starred Angela Bassett along with Laurence Fishburne as Ike. Ike spent the 1980s battling drugs and legal problems. In 1991 Ike and Tina Turner were inducted into the Rock and Roll Hall of Fame, and EMI America released *Proud Mary: The Best of Ike and Tina Turner*, a twenty-three-track collection detailing their career from the early 1960s through the mid-1970s.

Tina released albums throughout the 1980s and 1990s, including *Break Every Rule* (1986), *Foreign Affair* (1989), and *Wildest Dreams* (1996). She gave what she called her farewell tour in 2000, but in 2008 she went back on the road in response to the demands of her fans. She also released a greatest-hits compilation called *All the Best* in 2004. Ike won his first solo Grammy for the record *Risin' with the Blues* (2006). He died in December 2007 at the age of seventy-six.

Jana Pendragon

SEE ALSO: *Blues; Grammy Awards; Howlin' Wolf; James, Elmore; Motown; Rhythm and Blues; Rock and Roll; The Rolling Stones; Spector, Phil; Sun Records; United Artists.*

BIBLIOGRAPHY

Ivory, Steven. *Tina!* New York: Putnam, 1985.

Mills, Bart. *Tina*. New York: Warner Books, 1985.

Turner, Ike, and Nigel Cawthorne. *Takin' Back My Name: The Confessions of Ike Turner*. London: Virgin Publishing, 1999.

Turner, Tina, and Kurt Loder. *I, Tina: My Life Story*. New York: Avon, 1986.

Wynn, Ron. *Tina: The Tina Turner Story*. New York: Macmillan, 1985.

Turner, Lana *(1920–1995)*

Nicknamed the "Sweater Girl," actress Lana Turner defined feminine sexuality during the World War II era. She portrayed an archetypal character in *The Postman Always Rings Twice* (1946), the first American film version of a James Cain novel and a seminal film noir, and helped reestablish the melodrama genre in the 1950s with her appearances in *Peyton Place* (1957) and *Imitation of Life* (1959). But Turner's importance is not rooted in her acting. She was a movie star in the old style—a product of the studio system, a glamour girl, a femme fatale.

Jean Mildred Frances Turner's film career began when she was seventeen years old and hired to be an extra in *A Star Is Born* (1937). MGM (Metro-Goldwyn-Mayer) gave her the name Lana, and studio publicity claimed she had been discovered by the editor of the *Hollywood Reporter* while having a strawberry soda at Schwab's drugstore (Turner later said she was drinking a Coke at the Top Hat Café). Her first significant role came in Mervyn LeRoy's *They Won't Forget* (1937), in which she played Mary Clay, a teenage girl who is raped and murdered twelve minutes into the film. In her most famous scene, Turner has no dialogue and simply walks across the screen wearing the tight sweater that inspired her nickname. The scene launched her career; critics wrote about "the girl in the sweater," and filmgoers sent fan letters to MGM.

Turner went on to make more than fifty films. In most of them she played a variation on one characterization: sexy but not quite slutty, strong but vulnerable. In 1945 she was one of the most highly paid actresses in Hollywood, and by the time she appeared in *The Postman Always Rings Twice* in 1946, she had already been a top box-office draw for several years. Still, the film provided her with her definitive role. In *The Films of Lana Turner*, Lou Valentino observes, "if Turner fans had to make a choice, *Postman* is the movie they would most elect to have time-capsuled." In it Turner plays the unhappy wife of a much older man who plots with a handsome young drifter to murder her husband. Because the Hays Code would not allow MGM to film a faithful adaptation of Cain's overtly sexual novel, director Tay Garnett dressed Turner in white for most of the film, which, according to Garnett, "made everything she did seem less sensuous. It was also attractive as hell. And it somehow took a little of the stigma off."

At the height of her popularity, Turner was a pervasive presence in American society. Children could buy Lana Turner paper dolls and coloring books. Her likeness was painted on airplane noses. There was a song titled "The Lana Turner Blues." Perhaps most significantly, Turner played a major role in defining the manner in which women would be portrayed in American popular culture. In the 1940s she appeared on magazine covers almost monthly. She endorsed beauty products and made the buxom look popular—in 1948, 4.5 million breast pads were sold to American women, who wanted to look like the Sweater Girl.

In the late 1950s Turner moved into melodramas. She received her only Academy Award nomination for *Peyton Place*, in which she played a widowed woman who becomes the subject of scandal when she is forced to reveal that her teenage daughter is illegitimate. In 1957 the signing of a sex symbol like Turner to the role of the mother made headlines. In *Imitation of Life*, Turner's most financially successful film, she played an actress and mother who arranges for an unemployed African American woman, Annie, and her daughter to live with her and act as her servants. As the two women's daughters grow older, Annie's daughter "passes" for white and grows ashamed of her mother.

Turner was married seven times, most notably to bandleader Artie Shaw and actor Lex Barker. In 1958 her daughter, Cheryl Crane, stabbed and killed Turner's boyfriend, mobster Johnny Stompanato. Turner survived the bad publicity surrounding Stompanato's murder and her daughter's trial with no visible damage to her career. She made ten more motion pictures after *Imitation*, and she appeared on television and onstage in the 1970s and 1980s. She died of throat cancer in 1995.

Randall Clark

SEE ALSO: *Academy Awards; Cancer; Celebrity; Celebrity Couples; Divorce; Film Noir; Hollywood; Mafia/Organized Crime; MGM (Metro-Goldwyn-Mayer); Peyton Place;* The Postman Always Rings Twice*; Sex Symbol; Shaw, Artie; Studio System; World War II.*

BIBLIOGRAPHY

Basinger, Jeanine. *Lana Turner*. New York: Pyramid, 1976.

Crane, Cheryl, and Cliff Jahr. *Detour*. New York: Arbor House, 1988.

Morella, Joe, and Edward Epstein. *Lana: The Public and Private Lives of Miss Turner*. New York: Citadel, 1971.

Parish, James Robert. *The Hollywood Book of Breakups*. Hoboken, NJ: John Wiley, 2006.

Root, Eric. *The Private Diary of My Life with Lana*. Beverly Hills, CA: Dove Books, 1996.

Turner, Lana. *Lana: The Lady, the Legend, the Truth*. New York: Dutton, 1982.

Valentino, Lou. *The Films of Lana Turner*. Secaucus, NJ: Citadel, 1976.

Wayne, Jane Ellen. *Lana: The Life and Loves of Lana Turner*. New York: St. Martin's Press, 1995.

Turner, Ted *(1938–)*

Ted Turner, a flamboyant southern entrepreneur and sportsman, first came to prominence in 1977 when, as the skipper of the winning yacht in the America's Cup race, he shocked the rather staid community of Newport, Rhode Island, with his wild celebrations and partying. Yet this notoriety masked the fact that he was also in the process of creating television's first "superstation," a local television station that, through the power of satellite communications, could broadcast its signal to cable-equipped households across the United States and ultimately around the world. In the process, he reinvented television-viewing patterns for most Americans and forced the major television networks to rethink their traditional broadcasting options. He also had an enormous impact on professional sports, owning both the Atlanta Braves baseball team and the Atlanta Hawks basketball team at different points in his career. Turner is also one of the most generous philanthropists in the entire world, and in 2009 he received the McCall-Pierpaoli Humanitarian Award.

Turner's career began quietly in 1970 when his company, Turner Communications, a small, family-owned and billboard-oriented advertising agency, merged with Atlanta's Rice Broadcasting and took over a controlling interest in local television station WTCG. During the first year of the Turner regime, *Georgia Championship Wrestling* became the station's most popular show. Ironically, news programming, for which Turner later became famous, received scant attention. At the time, serious news stories were, for the most part, treated tongue in cheek and more as entertainment than as a public service. To Turner, there seemed to be no such thing as good news, and he considered viewers to be much better off watching reruns of old television series than viewing dreary recounts of what went on in the world.

Ted Turner. *Ted Turner built a broadcast empire out of what was once a family-owned billboard advertising agency.* CINDY ORD/ CONTRIBUTOR/GETTY IMAGES ENTERTAINMENT/GETTY IMAGES.

Turner's purchase of the television station, however, led him to a development that turned the television industry on its head. He eventually discovered the existence of a communications satellite in a geosynchronous orbit over Earth that could be used on a twenty-four-hour basis. The technology was then in its infancy and relied on the National Aeronautics and Space Administration (NASA) for its positioning. It was not highly publicized and had consequently been underutilized by broadcasting entities, few of which saw the possibilities for global programming. However, to the flamboyant Turner, the idea of a small local station being able to send its signal all over the world made perfect sense.

Beginning with a tall television tower and a lone Earth station microwave dish maintained by one technician, Turner proudly proclaimed his operation to be the world's first "superstation." Offering an eclectic blend of movies, sports, reruns of discontinued television series, and original programming produced by a subsidiary company, the superstation achieved the status of a basic cable selection on most systems around the United States. Under Turner's direction, the station went from losing money to generating a profit. In 1979 Turner changed to name of WTCG to WTBS to reflect its corporate affiliation, and it became the primary revenue source financing the next components of the Turner empire.

CNN

Doing a flip-flop on his antinews stance, Turner expanded his broadcasting base the following year by creating the innovative Cable News Network (CNN), a twenty-four-hour news service carried by satellite to cable systems around the world. He correctly noted that the proliferation of cable programming had placed an emphasis on entertainment programming, ignoring the fact that continuous newscasting would be an ideal melding with cable since public interest was high and because the traditional networks dismissed twenty-four-hour news as too costly. To Turner, however, the financial risk was a gamble worth taking. He put CNN on the air in June 1980 by leveraging most of his holdings and routing all of the profits from WTBS and his other interests into the fledgling enterprise.

At first, critics and the major television networks regarded CNN as something of a novelty, dismissing the ambitious programming as "lightweight journalism" at best. However, the new network, with news bureaus around the world, began to get its reporters to breaking stories well before the established news organizations. By 1990 it had surpassed the networks with its on-the-spot coverage of the Persian Gulf War and established itself as the premier television news service in the United States. As a result, by the mid-1990s CNN had expanded its viewership to 140 countries around the world and had created such off-shoots as CNN Headline News and CNN International.

MOVIE LIBRARY

In 1986 Turner took another risk by purchasing the Metro-Goldwyn-Mayer (MGM)/United Artists (UA) motion picture studio in a complicated cash/stock transaction valued at approximately $1.5 billion. In order to finance his portion, he had to break up the studio and divest himself of a number of subdivisions to keep the money coming in. He immediately sold the UA portion of the studio back to financier Kirk Kerkorian, who had sold him the entire studio to begin with, and included MGM's film and television production and distribution. He sold the lot itself to television production entity Lorimar-Telepictures. He kept MGM's large library of motion pictures, which included the pre-1948 Warner Brothers and RKO films. Turner was now the owner of perhaps the largest library of filmed entertainment in the world, with sufficient material to keep WTBS going forever. He was also quick to seize on the option of marketing the films on video and leasing them to other networks.

Turner's next move was the controversial colorizing of many of the black-and-white films in his new library, raising the ire of film purists who were aghast at the thought of seeing such classics as *Casablanca* (1942) and *Citizen Kane* (1941) broadcast with computer-enhanced artificial color. Congress even got involved by holding hearings to determine authorship and copyright issues relating to film to see if the southern mogul actually had the right to modify the original artistic intent by introducing color. The issue was never resolved, but it did sensitize Turner to the issues involved. He and his company subsequently played a leading role in film preservation efforts in the United States.

Turner also established the Turner Classic Movie (TMC) cable channel in the early 1990s to air motion pictures in their original form with a knowledgeable host to introduce each one and talk about its production history. He launched the Cartoon Network in order to have a venue for showing all the Hanna-Barbera cartoons he had obtained.

PHILANTHROPIC INTERESTS

In addition, Turner played a leading role in a number of altruistic endeavors. He is an ardent environmentalist, and in the mid-1980s he became an antiwar activist. In 1985 he founded the Better World Society to produce film and television documentaries to educate people about such issues as pollution, hunger, and the perils of the arms race. A year later he introduced the Goodwill Games, a scaled-down version of the Olympic Games in an effort to promote brotherhood and world peace. In 1989 he created the Turner Tomorrow Award to provide an incentive for writers around the globe to come up with positive solutions to problems affecting the world.

In 1992 Turner turned his interest to Native American issues. He produced a number of documentaries and fact-based feature films on his TNT channel to show American history from the Native American point of view and to spotlight the contributions of indigenous Americans to the United States. In 1997, with his typical flamboyance, Turner pledged a gift of $1 billion to the United Nations to be distributed over the following decade. He emphasized, however, that the money had to be used for programs such as disease control, detecting and disarming landmines, UNICEF (United Nations Children's Fund), refugee relief, and peacekeeping.

Also in 1997 Turner merged his company with Time Warner to form the world's largest media company. Under the terms of the deal, Time Warner gained access to Turner's interests in cable and satellite television and, importantly, the rights to the library of pre-1948 Warner Brothers films, RKO films, and the MGM collection. In effect, Time Warner reclaimed its heritage and then some. The possibilities of commercial exploitation of the Turner materials in the Warner Brothers stores and fledgling theme parks with videos, new character licensing, and reissues of restored films is seemingly unlimited. In return, Turner became Time Warner's largest stockholder, with clout surpassed only by Chief Executive Officer Gerald Levin. Turner immediately began pressing the company to initiate an austerity program to reduce what he considered to be an untenable corporate debt approaching $17 billion. This included selling the corporate jets and consolidating redundant departments created by the merger.

PERSONAL STRUGGLES

While many people find Turner's unbridled ambition in the business world and his genuine concern for environmental and social causes to be an odd mix, his closest associates view it as an inevitable consequence of his unsettled childhood. As the son of an equally ambitious businessman, Robert Edward Turner II, who had seen his own parents lose their South Carolina home during the Great Depression, he was conscious of the value of a dollar. Turner's younger sister suffered from severe lupus and was very ill for several years before her death in 1958 at the age of seventeen. Then in 1963 Turner's father committed suicide after losing the family billboard advertising business due to debts. These combined experiences turned Turner away from organized religion but left him with an equally religious fervor to cure some of the ills of the world. "One should not set goals that he cannot reach," he told *Time* magazine in 1992. "I'm not going to rest until all the world's problems have been solved."

In 2001 Time Warner merged with AOL in what some experts have called one of the worst corporate mergers in American history (it demerged in 2009). Turner lost billions from the merger as his stock shares plunged when both the stock market and the dotcoms plummeted in the early twenty-first century. In 2006 Turner resigned from the AOL Time Warner board but retained thirty-three million shares of company stock. He is considered one of the largest landholders in the United States, and he divides his time between managing his Ted's Montana Grill restaurant chain and overseeing his many business and philanthropic interests. Married and divorced three times, the third time to actress and political activist Jane Fonda, Turner has five children.

Steve Hanson

SEE ALSO: *Cable TV;* Casablanca*;* Citizen Kane*; CNN; Environmentalism; Fonda, Jane; The Great Depression; Hanna-Barbera; MGM (Metro-Goldwyn-Mayer); NASA; Olympics; Television;* Time*; United Artists.*

BIBLIOGRAPHY

Andrews, Suzanna. "Ted Turner among the Suits." *New York*, December 9, 1996, 34.

Bart, Peter. "Ted's Trail of Tears." *Variety*, August 31, 1998, 4.

Bethell, Tom. "The Hazards of Charity." *American Spectator*, July 1998, 18.

Brands, H. W. *Masters of Enterprise: Giants of American Business from John Jacob Astor and J. P. Morgan to Bill Gates and*

Oprah Winfrey. New York: Free Press, 1999.

Dempsey, John. "Ted, Time: New Tower of Cable." *Variety*, July 22, 1996, 1.

Evans, Harold; Gail Buckland; and David Lefer. *They Made America: From the Steam Engine to the Search Engine; Two Centuries of Innovators*. New York: Little, Brown, 2004.

Goldberg, Robert, and Gerald Jay Goldberg. *Citizen Turner*. New York: Harcourt Brace, 1995.

Lowe, Janet. *Ted Turner Speaks: Insight from the World's Greatest Maverick*. New York: Wiley, 1999.

Meyer, Michael. "I Want to See What It's Like to Be Big." *Newsweek*, October 2, 1995, 62.

Miller, Judith. "What Makes Ted Turner Give?" *New York Times*, September 20, 1997.

Painton, Priscilla. "Man of the Year." *Time*, January 6, 1992, 35–39.

Range, Peter Ross. "The Demons of Ted Turner." *Playboy*, August 1983, 59.

Sharpe, Anita. "Not So Retiring: Used to Being Boss, Ted Turner Is Mulling His Time Warner Role." *Wall Street Journal*, November 27, 1995.

Turner, Ted, and Bill Burke. *Call Me Ted*. New York: Grand Central Publishing, 2008.

TV Dinners

Premade, frozen meals, dubbed "TV dinners" in the 1950s, have reflected changes in American culture for more than half a century. The first TV dinners were so named because they were meant to be eaten in front of the television, a relatively new technology in American homes in the mid-twentieth century. In 1955 Americans bought seventy million of the freezer-to-oven feasts, and five years later the number tripled to 214 million.

The proto-TV dinner, introduced in the 1930s, was a frozen Irish stew created by General Foods. In 1951 Swanson reached a larger market with manufactured potpies. The company followed three years later with their mass-marketed TV Dinners line. The first was turkey with cornbread dressing, peas, and sweet potatoes. Other varieties, such as Salisbury steak, ham, and chicken, quickly followed.

To satiate larger appetites, Swanson introduced Hungry Man meals in 1972, changing the name of their products to frozen dinners, but popular usage of the term *TV dinner* persisted. Food companies of the 1980s and 1990s reflected shifting tastes, emphasizing low-calorie yet upscale entrées with such names as Lean Cuisine, Budget Gourmet, and Le Menu. As microwave ovens became ubiquitous in American homes, TV dinners became even more convenient with shorter cooking times. In 2009 Schwan's Home Service put the TV back into TV dinner by introducing gourmet frozen dinners, such as chicken in curry sauce or polenta with braised meatballs, created by competitors on the reality television series *Top Chef* (2006–).

Wendy Woloson

SEE ALSO: *The Fifties; Frozen Entrées; Television;* Top Chef.

BIBLIOGRAPHY

"Better than TV Dinners?" *Consumer Reports*, March 1984, 126–127, 170.

Civitello, Linda. *Cuisine and Culture: A History of Food and People*. New York: Wiley, 2003.

I'll Buy That! 50 Small Wonders and Big Deals That Revolutionized the Lives of Consumers. Mount Vernon, NY: Consumers Union, 1986.

Stein, Joel. "TV Dinners Get Literal." *Time*, November 30, 2009. Accessed March 2012. Available from http://www.time.com/time/magazine/article/0,9171,1940692,00.html

Stern, Jane, and Michael Stern. *The Encyclopedia of Bad Taste*. New York: HarperCollins, 1990.

Vare, Ethlie Ann, and Greg Ptacek. *Patently Female: From AZT to TV Dinners: Stories of Women Inventors and Their Breakthrough Ideas*. New York: Wiley, 2002.

Volti, Rudi. "How We Got Frozen Food." *American Heritage of Invention and Technology*, Spring 1994, 47–56.

TV Guide

In 1953, when television was still a new and growing phenomenon on the American scene, the president of Philadelphia's Triangle Publishing, Walter H. Annenberg, conceived the idea of a national television magazine. Inspired by the wide circulation of a local magazine called *TV Digest*, Annenberg envisioned one central nationwide magazine with separate editions containing the different local television listings. Annenberg moved quickly, keeping the convenient digest size and adding glossy color photographs and articles. *TV Guide* was born on April 3, 1953, and remained the premier listing for television fanatics for half a century.

Beginning what was to be a tradition of exclusive reportage about television and its surrounding issues, the cover of the first issue showed one of the first photos of comedy queen Lucille Ball's new baby. The magazine was issued in ten editions, each geared to a different locality, and it sold more than 1.5 million copies. The idea had proved to be a good one, and *TV Guide* went on to become the best-selling weekly in the United States, with a circulation of more than thirteen million readers. The ten editions grew to 119 regional editions, and *TV Guide* became the name most often associated not only with television program listings but also with television journalism. Though perhaps not the most glamorous aspect of the television industry, *TV Guide* was certainly one of the most familiar.

INVENTING THE TELEVISION JOURNAL

During the publication's most successful years, the main office of *TV Guide* remained in Radnor, Pennsylvania, but the journal maintained a staff of more than 1,300, scattered in more than twenty bureaus around the country. Because *TV Guide*'s competition included the free television sections of local newspapers, the weekly needed to offer viewers something special, something not available in the local listings. To achieve this, the editorial staff of *TV Guide* developed a two-pronged approach: listings and articles.

To maximize the value of its program listings, *TV Guide* writers were assigned to cover individual television shows. Rather than using studio press releases, writers screened programs and even read scripts themselves to ensure that their descriptions of the shows were accurate. The National Features Department of the journal moved to New York City in 1991, to be even closer to the television industry there.

TV Guide's other approach to creating public demand for its product was its articles. Pages not filled with program listings contained photographs of stars, reviews of weekly programs and television movies, and feature articles. Some articles were predictable fluffy pieces highlighting the off-camera antics of sitcom casts or were interviews with current popular stars. Light though they may have been, these articles were often exactly what the television viewer wanted to see—alternate views of favorite shows and stars, as well as the critics' opinions of the shows they watched. But *TV Guide* took itself seriously as a television magazine too. The editorial staff aimed to present broad, objective reporting about what was on television as well as offer in-depth, provocative coverage about the TV industry itself and the effect of television on society.

The journal employed its own staff of distinguished reviewers and commentators and also sought outside contributors who would draw readers. Politicians such as John F. Kennedy and Gerald Ford and eminent writers including Joyce Carol Oates and John Cheever have been found in its pages along with names more commonly associated with the entertainment industry but no less distinguished, such as David Brinkley and Katharine Hepburn; even political activists including Gloria Steinem and Coretta Scott King have found their way into *TV Guide*. While printing the writing of such famous personalities was clever editorial policy on the part of a magazine eager to boost sales, appearing in such a popular magazine was also a smart move for a writer who wanted to be widely read.

COMPETING IN THE DIGITAL AGE

In 1988 *TV Guide* was sold to Rupert Murdoch, a flamboyant Australian entrepreneur associated with sensational journalism, who was accumulating a vast entertainment empire. The journal joined the London *Times*, the Fox television network, Twentieth Century Fox movie studio, Harper & Row publishers, and dozens of other publications and companies as part of Murdoch's News Corporation. Murdoch continued and expanded the *TV Guide* tradition of entertainment coverage that is both entertaining and thoughtful. Senator Paul Simon credited the *TV Guide* report on television violence for encouraging congressional hearings about the subject, and the Public Relations Service Council also acknowledged the magazine's role in prompting them to set ethical standards for video news releases. Along with the serious side of television reportage, Murdoch brought some of the flashy side of television to *TV Guide*. In 1999 the first annual *TV Guide Awards Show* was broadcast, with winners selected by reader vote.

In 1998 News Corp. sold *TV Guide* to Tele-Communication Incorporated (TCI), one of the major cable companies in the United States. Competing not only with the Sunday newspaper pullouts but also with new print competitors such as Time Inc.'s *Entertainment Weekly* and the cable on-screen guides, *TV Guide* saw its circulation began to slip. Attempting to marry the venerable *TV Guide* name with a cable presence, TCI launched the continuously running TV Guide Channel to inform viewers of programming and also an online *TV Guide* magazine to offer readers instant links to a variety of entertainment sites.

As 1999 drew to a close, ownership of *TV Guide* changed hands again when cable guide giant Gemstar International Group bought the magazine, cable channel, and web presence. The newly formed Gemstar-TV Guide continued to update the magazine and its offshoots, including an expanded fiftieth anniversary edition featuring different collectible covers in 2002 and a new full-size print format in 2005, but readership continued to fall. In 2007 Gemstar sold its *TV Guide* holdings to digital media corporation Macrovision, which hoped to consolidate its cable presence with the well-known TV Guide Channel.

In spite of the brand's efforts to update its approach to keep pace with new technology, *TV Guide* steadily lost ground, as more and more viewers relied on on-screen cable and satellite program guides. In only a year, Macrovision sold *TV Guide*, separating the print and digital formats. The cable channel and website were sold to Allen Shapiro and One Equity Partners for almost $300 million, while the print magazine, losing money and viewed as a liability, was sold to Open Gate Capital for only $1. In 2009 the TV Guide Channel and web journal were sold to Lionsgate, an independent film studio.

REBUILDING RELEVANCE

Open Gate tightened the magazine's budget by cutting and outsourcing jobs, eliminating thousands of free and discounted subscriptions, and building its advertising base. The new owners also transformed the magazine's content, minimizing the guide section and increasing the feature articles in an effort to once again provide unique entertainment coverage. On the digital front, Lionsgate worked to lift viewer ratings for the TV Guide Channel by including in its lineup films and TV series in syndication, such as *Will & Grace*, *Weeds*, and *Ugly Betty*.

As *TV Guide* changes with the times, it also offers a link to a simpler time—the early days of television when viewers, not yet inundated with entertainment, eagerly awaited news of the week's programs supplemented with pictures and stories about the stars. Viewers appreciated a journal that took the new medium as seriously as they did, and they devoured the magazine that was all about television, right down to the crossword puzzle. In the 1960s Marshall McLuhan envisioned a global community with television at its center. Television has no doubt been a huge force in modern culture, but not perhaps in the way he foresaw. By the twenty-first century, there were more television stations and more different kinds of programming than could have been imagined at the birth of the medium. Though there are hundreds of channel and program guides, *TV Guide* was the first and, to many American viewers, the only "real" guide to the exciting world promised by television. A glance back through the past issues of *TV Guide* provides a good chronicle of what television has been and what it has to say for itself.

Tina Gianoulis

SEE ALSO: *Ball, Lucille; Brinkley, David;* Entertainment Weekly; *Hepburn, Katharine; Oates, Joyce Carol; Sitcom; Steinem, Gloria; Television;* Weeds; Will & Grace.

BIBLIOGRAPHY

Ives, Nat. "*TV Guide* to Undergo Extreme Makeover." *Advertising Age* 76, no. 30 (2005): 3.

Kerwin, Ann Marie. "*TV Guide* Turns Gaze to Big Screen." *Advertising Age*, 69, no. 17 (1998): 62.

Peters, Jeremy W. "*TV Guide* Cuts Path to Relevance." *New York Times*, September 20, 2010, B1.

TV Guide Magazine Online. Lionsgate. Accessed May 2012. Available from http://www.tvguide.com/keywords/tv-guide-magazine

Twain, Mark *(1835–1910)*

Humorist and author Samuel Langhorne Clemens, better known by the pen name Mark Twain, rose from modest roots as a Hannibal, Missouri, typesetter to become an international celebrity whose satiric stories and novels, including *The Prince and the Pauper* (1881) and *A Connecticut Yankee in King Arthur's Court* (1889), poked fun at the foibles of frontier life and of Gilded Age society. He cultivated a homespun image as an American everyman, and his lecture tours—delivered wearing his trademark white flannel suit, in his inimitable heartland twang—drew crowds of thousands across five continents.

As one of the most influential realist writers of his age, and the first to come from the American interior, Twain reshaped the nation's literary landscape with hard-hitting vernacular works, most notably *Adventures of Huckleberry Finn* (1885), that challenged the era's dominant literary traditions and tackled such controversial subjects as African American slavery. Nobel Prize–winning novelist William Faulkner (1897–1962) hailed Twain as "the father of American literature." Another Nobel laureate, author Ernest Hemingway (1899–1961), wrote, "All modern American literature comes from one book by Mark Twain called *Adventures of Huckleberry Finn.*"

Although Twain's wide circle of close friends eventually included such luminaries as *Atlantic Monthly* editor and critic William Dean Howells (1837–1920) and Standard Oil executive Henry Huttleston Rogers (1840–1909), his literary work drew heavily upon his childhood along the Mississippi River. The author was born in Florida, Missouri, on November 30, 1835, two weeks after the passage of Halley's comet, but his family relocated to the port of Hannibal shortly after he turned four. He apprenticed as a printer at age thirteen and started his journalism career contributing humorous articles to a local newspaper operated by his brother, Orion.

After brief spells as a journeyman printer in Cincinnati, Philadelphia, and New York City, Twain—encouraged by legendary navigator Horace Ezra Bixby (1826–1912)—embarked on a career as a steamboat pilot. Twain's pseudonym, first adopted in 1863, derived from the pilot's term for water that stood 2 fathoms (12 feet) deep. When the American Civil War brought steamboat traffic on the Mississippi River to a halt in 1861, Twain accompanied his brother to the Nevada Territory, where the latter served as secretary to the governor.

Twain's first major literary success occurred with the publication of his short story "The Celebrated Jumping Frog of Calaveras County" in the New York–based *Saturday Press* in 1865. The tale of colorful gambler Jim Smiley and his frog Dan'l Webster introduced Twain as a spokesman for the common man and became the title work in a collection of twenty-seven stories and sketches published in 1867. He followed this with two comedic travel volumes: *Innocents Abroad* (1869), which drew upon his experiences on a group tour of Europe and the Middle East, and *Roughing It!* (1872), based upon the author's adventures in Nevada and Hawaii.

However, it was the publication of Twain's second novel, *The Adventures of Tom Sawyer* (1876), that finally established him as the dominant realist writer of the day. The following year he used his keynote address at Boston's Brunswick Hotel, upon the seventieth birthday of poet John Greenleaf Whittier (1807–1892), to confront the literary status quo directly. He satirized the era's three most prominent guardians of orthodox literary tradition—Ralph Waldo Emerson (1803–1882), Oliver Wendell Holmes Sr. (1809–1894), and Henry Wadsworth Longfellow (1807–1882)—to their faces and symbolically announced the dawn of a new literary age. With the subsequent publication of *Huckleberry Finn*, Twain tackled the controversial theme of race relations in a coarse, straightforward manner that shocked many contemporary sensibilities.

During his later years, Twain suffered significant personal and professional setbacks. His favorite daughter, Susy, died of spinal meningitis in 1896 at age twenty-four, followed by his wife, Olivia, in 1904, and his youngest daughter, Jean, in 1909. He also lost much of his fortune with an ill-fated investment in a mechanical typesetting machine, the Paige compositor. These misfortunes are reflected in the darker tone of many of his later works, including *The Man That Corrupted Hadleyburg* (1900). He fell increasingly under the influence of a devious young secretary, Isabel Van Kleek Lyon, and suffered bouts of severe depression as Twain's middle daughter, Clara, and Lyon fought over control of his affairs. When a journalist inquired after Twain's health in 1897, he famously remarked, "The report of my death was an exaggeration." The author actually died of heart disease on April 21, 1910, as Halley's comet passed by Earth again on its seventy-six-year cycle.

While humorist Artemus Ward (1834–1867) had previously introduced comedic regional writing to national audiences, Twain was the first American author to establish this genre as serious literature. Along with poet Walt Whitman (1819–1892) and novelist Herman Melville (1819–1891), he carved a place for the voices of ordinary Americans in their national literature.

Jacob M. Appel

SEE ALSO: *Faulkner, William; Hemingway, Ernest.*

BIBLIOGRAPHY

Emerson, Everett. *Mark Twain: A Literary Life*. Philadelphia: University of Pennsylvania Press, 2000.

Loving, Jerome. *Mark Twain: The Adventures of Samuel L. Clemens*. Berkeley: University of California Press, 2010.

Powers, Ron. *Mark Twain: A Life*. New York: Free Press, 2005.

Trombley, Laura Skandera. *Mark Twain's Other Woman*. New York: Alfred A. Knopf, 2010.

Twain, Shania *(1965–)*

Born Eilleen Regina Edwards on August 28, 1965, in Windsor, Ontario, Shania Twain became one of the best-selling female country artists of all time. Her rags-to-riches story is the stuff from which country lyrics are woven. However, unlike other female country greats, such as Dolly Parton and Taylor Swift, whose self-penned hits are often autobiographical, Twain has not overtly mined her life for her songwriting. Her songs are sometimes sassy and sometimes poignant, and they often boast what some critics have called a feminist edge. Revelations about her personal life and musical ambition came in a frank autobiography and a popular reality television show.

Twain was only two when her parents separated, and she moved with her mother and sister to Timmins, Ontario, where Sharon Edwards met and married Jerry Twain, an Ojibwa Indian, who adopted his wife's daughters. In a life marked by poverty, the young Eilleen found sanctuary in music. By her early teens, she was performing locally on television shows and after midnight in a hotel bar. Sharon and Jerry Twain were killed in an automobile accident when the singer was twenty-one, leaving her responsible for three younger siblings.

Twain's voice provided the means for her to support herself and her younger brothers and sister. While she was employed as a singer at the Deerhurst Resort in Huntsville, Ontario, she adopted the stage name Shania, an Ojibwa word meaning "I'm on my way." However, it was not until her youngest sibling was old enough to be independent that the singer focused on her dream. A demo tape eventually led to a contract with Mercury Nashville. Twain's self-titled debut album in 1993 created little stir. The video of "What Made You Say That," however, captured the attention of the British producer Robert John "Mutt" Lange, who had successfully worked with a long list of stars, including AC/DC, Céline Dion, and Bryan Adams.

Lange contacted Twain, and the two of them began writing songs together. A few months after their first meeting, the couple was married. Lange produced his wife's second album, *The Woman in Me* (1995), which became the all-time best-selling recording by a female country artist. The album debuted in the top position on the Billboard country album chart. Eight songs from *The Woman in Me* charted on the singles chart, and four of them—"Any Man of Mine," "(If You're Not in It for Love) I'm Outta Here," "You Win My Love," and "No One Needs to Know"—topped the charts. Twain, newly christened "the Cinderella of country music," was at last on her way.

The Woman in Me won a Grammy for Best Country Album, and the Academy of Country Music recognized it as Album of the Year. Its pop sound, combined with Twain's sexy image, established the singer as a country star tailored for MTV fans. Her third album, *Come on Over* (1997), cemented Twain as a crossover success and made her an international star. Twelve of the sixteen Twain-Lange songs were released as singles; three ("You're Still the One," "Honey, I'm Home," and "Love Gets Me Every Time") reached number one. "You're Still the One" also reached number one on the adult contemporary chart and earned Twain Broadcast Music Inc. (BMI) Songwriter of the Year for both pop and country in 1999. Another song, "Man! I Feel Like a Woman," garnered the singer a contract with the cosmetics company Revlon, which used the song in an ad campaign.

A separate cut for the European market increased Twain's fan base in the United Kingdom and in Europe. Her world tour ran for eighteen months and solidified Twain's position as a major artist. At the end of 1999, Twain was financially and artistically secure enough to retreat to Switzerland, where she and Lange had established residence. Her son, Eja, was born in 2001.

Up!, Twain's fourth album, was released in 2002. Although it produced a single, "Forever and for Always," that resulted in BMI Songwriter of the Year Awards in the United States and the United Kingdom, it failed to equal the record-breaking success of the two previous albums. Still, it sold around 5.5 million copies.

After *Up!*, Twain maintained a low profile, seemingly content to live mostly out of the spotlight. That privacy ended in 2008, when her divorce from Lange over his infidelity became fodder for the tabloids. In 2011 Twain married Frédéric Thiébaud, a Swiss Nestlé executive and the former husband of Lange's alleged lover.

The trauma of Twain's divorce affected her voice. She was diagnosed with dysphonia, a squeezing of the voice box by the surrounding muscles. Her efforts to recover as a woman and an artist served as the focus of *Why Not? With Shania Twain*, an hour-long series that ran for two months on the Oprah Winfrey Network. The *New York Times* described the reality show as "part episodic biography, part comeback tale and part confrontation therapy." Twain released a memoir, *From This Moment On*, in May 2011, the same month that her TV show debuted. Also in 2011 she agreed to perform sixty shows per year for the next two years, beginning December 1, 2012, at the Colosseum at Caesars Palace in Las Vegas. The show is titled "Shania Twain: Still the One."

Wylene Rholetter

SEE ALSO: *Country Music; Divorce; Grammy Awards; MTV; Pop Music; Television; Winfrey, Oprah.*

BIBLIOGRAPHY

Caramanica, Jon. "A Country Star in Search of Her Voice." *New York Times*, May 6, 2011.

Dam, Julie K. L., and Alexis Chiu. "Shania Twain: 'I Have a New Lease on Love.'" *People*, May 23, 2011.

Erlewine, Stephen Thomas. "Shania Twain." CMT. Accessed February 2012. Available from http://www.cmt.com/artists/az/twain_shania/bio.jhtml

Hedegaard, Erik, and Kurt Markus. "Shania Twain." *Rolling Stone*, September 3, 1998, 52–58.

"Shania Twain Speaks Out." Oprah.com, May 3, 2011. Accessed May 2012. Available from http://www.oprah.com/oprahshow/Shania-Twain-Speaks-Out/1

Twain, Shania. *From This Moment On*. New York: Atria, 2011.

Tweens

One of the most recently recognized demographic groups, *tweens* inhabit an imprecise space between childhood and the teen years. Though often defined as representing ages ten through fourteen, tweenhood can start as early as eight. The term *tween* was used as early as the 1940s (some trace the word to the 1954 fantasy classic *The Lord of the Rings* by J. R. R. Tolkien), but it did not explode into common parlance until the late 1990s. Then, as advertisers realized that the growing preteen population had an enormous influence on family spending, tweens were singled out as an important new market. Capitalizing on the vulnerabilities of early adolescence, commercials for everything from cosmetics to automobiles began to focus on the new tween consumer.

Although teenagers seem always to have been a well-established subculture, the concept of the teenage years as a distinct part of life is fairly new. Nineteenth-century teenagers entered adulthood straight from childhood. A separate teen culture began to appear in the 1920s with the rise of the automobile, which gave young people unprecedented independence, and the emergence of separate high schools, which brought them together in large groups. The term *teen* gained wide use in the late 1940s, much as *tween* did in the late 1990s, when marketers realized that the large population of young adults represented sales and profits.

Like their post–World War II teen forerunners, modern tweens were born into a fast-moving world of enormous and often frightening changes. Rapid technological advancements and an increasingly permissive media have resulted in a push to grow up, and tweens acutely feel the pressure to appear and to act older. Hectic daily agendas of schoolwork, extracurricular activities, lessons, and social interaction mimic adult schedules and adult stress at younger and younger ages. By the time children reach their tween years, most have learned about—either firsthand or from instruction—divorce, childhood sexual abuse, domestic violence, AIDS, drug use, sexuality, and many other worrying subjects they may not yet be emotionally prepared to handle. Experts such as William Damon, director of the Stanford University Center on Adolescence, are concerned about the tween rush to adulthood. "What we're seeing is a superficial sophistication," Damon has said. "There's been no increase in the values that help a kid get through the confusion of life in a steady, productive way."

However, when marketers of products, services, and media realized during the late 1990s that the tween population had surpassed twenty-seven million, they responded by launching products and ad campaigns aimed at the new demographic and in doing so helped mold tween identity. Tweens wanted to appear older, so new lines of tween cosmetics were introduced. Tweens wanted to fit in and be cool, so clothing designers and shoe manufacturers began aiming at the tween population. Tweens were, however sophisticated, still children, so toy companies focused on them as well, creating such products as Mattel's Generation Girl dolls that claimed to be more grown up than Barbie. Even food products, such as Tang breakfast drink and Chef Boyardee canned ravioli, were given new twists to make them seem modern and trendy to appeal to tweens. Advertisers found that children in this age group exerted a powerful influence over how their parents spent money, so they began aiming even auto ads at the tween viewer. Though many viewed girls as the major tween consumers, tween boys were also targeted as likely purchasers of skateboards, video games, and fashionably baggy clothes.

A wealth of media is directed toward the tween audience. *Teen People*, *Cosmo Girl*, *Discovery Girls*, *Boys' Life*, and *Tiger Beat* are only a few of the magazines for preteen readers. On cable television, the Disney Channel features a lineup of tween favorites, such as *Hannah Montana*, *Wizards of Waverly Place*, and *Phineas and Ferb*. Films such as *High School Musical* and its sequels (2006, 2007, and 2008) offer glamorized versions of adolescent life, drawing packed tween crowds.

Twenty-first century tweens also create their own media on social networking websites, such as Facebook, YouTube, and Twitter, where they may follow tweets from such pop idols as Miley Cyrus and the Jonas Brothers. For many middle-class tweens, cell phones, laptops, and tablet computers are indispensable social tools, allowing constant texting and video chat updates among friends.

Although their population has dipped a bit, the tween demographic continues to be strong into the 2010s, with a tween population of twenty-three million predicted for 2020. As tweens continue to explore the unknown territory of approaching adulthood in an increasingly fast-paced world, advertisers try to predict and mold their needs and desires.

Tina Gianoulis

SEE ALSO: *Advertising; Barbie; Cell Phones; Child Stars; Consumerism; Cyrus, Miley / Hannah Montana; Facebook;* High School Musical*; The Jonas Brothers; Laptops; Social Media; Tang; Teen Idols; Teenagers; Television; Texting; Toys; Twitter; Video Games; YouTube.*

BIBLIOGRAPHY

Hymowitz, Kay S. *Ready or Not: Why Treating Children as Small Adults Endangers Their Future—and Ours.* New York: Simon & Schuster, 1999.

Kantrowitz, B., and P. Wingert. "The Truth about Tweens." *Newsweek*, October 18, 1999, 62.

Phillips, Debra. "Tween Beat." *Entrepreneur*, September 1999, 126.

Siegel, David L.; Timothy J. Coffey; and Gregory Livingston. *The Great Tween Buying Machine: Marketing to Today's Tweens.* Ithaca, NY: Paramount, 2001.

Tweety Pie and Sylvester

The first pairing of Sylvester the sputtering cat and Tweetie (later Tweety or Tweety Bird) the wide-eyed canary came in "Tweetie Pie" (1947), directed by Friz Freleng, and it made history by winning an Academy Award. The duo would go on to appear in more than 40 Warner Brothers cartoon shorts by 1962, earning their studio another Academy Award for "Birds Anonymous" (1957) and several other Oscar nominations through the years. Generations of Americans have grown up watching Sylvester's classic, ever-thwarted attempts to catch Tweety. Originally voiced by Mel Blanc, Sylvester's sloppy "sufferin succotash" and Tweety's baby-voiced "I tawt I taw a puddy tat" made them two of the most easily identified characters in cartoons.

A number of Warner Brothers cartoons featuring a predator unable to catch his prey appeared and gained popularity in the 1940s, including such classic pairings as Elmer Fudd and Bugs Bunny and the Road Runner and Wile E. Coyote. Other studios created similar cartoons, one of the earliest examples being MGM's Tom and Jerry. Many of these cartoons, like Sylvester and Tweety, survived into the twenty-first century. Few characters, however, have attained the status Sylvester and Tweety enjoy.

Primarily responsible for uttering his taglines ("I tawt I taw a puddy tat! I did! I did taw a puddy tat!" and "You bad old puddy tat!") and looking cute, Tweety isn't known for his superior wit or intelligence. Then again, the little canary is consistently able to get away from the larger, faster Sylvester. Tweety is beloved because he does always get away from Sylvester and also because he is so cute—bright yellow with big blue eyes and a baby voice. Many people find him irritating for the same reasons. Either way, Tweety is one of the most recognized and imitated characters in cartoons.

Whereas Tweety is not known for his intelligence, Sylvester is known for his decided lack thereof. He generally goes barreling into situations, never considering the possibilities or consequences. After Sylvester dresses up in a dog suit and ends up being thrown into the back of the dog catcher's truck with a group of mangy mutts, he takes off his costume and shouts, "But I'm a cat!" Sylvester's son, Junior, is so ashamed of his father that he generally walks around with a paper bag over his head. Sylvester's only virtue may be his dogged persistence. With a combination of stupidity, audacity, and sputtering temper, he defies the image of the cat as smart, cool, and collected. He continues to be, along with the likes of Bugs Bunny and Daffy Duck, one of Warner Brothers's most popular characters.

Both Sylvester and Tweety had appeared in other cartoons before being paired for "Tweetie Pie," but since that first pairing, Tweety has appeared almost exclusively with Sylvester. Other regular characters added spice to the Sylvester and Tweety cartoons, including Granny, Tweety's owner and protector, and a bulldog, who, in his general dislike for cats, often saves Tweety from Sylvester's schemes. Junior first appeared in "Pop 'Im Pop" (1950). Sylvester has had other adventures, appearing in cartoons with Speedy Gonzales, the world's fastest mouse, and Hippety Hopper, the baby kangaroo. Sylvester even made a cameo appearance as the Grand Duke in "The Scarlet Pumpernickel."

As many of their counterparts did, the Sylvester and Tweety cartoons began as "curtain-raisers" in theaters. A 1949 U.S. Supreme Court ruling that declared it illegal for studios to demand that theaters book a cartoon, newsreel, or live-action short in addition to hit films marked the beginning of the end of curtain-raisers. The advent of television and waning public interest in movies made it difficult for studios to recover the costs of creating a cartoon short. Some less expensive cartooning methods were developed, but, ultimately, cartoon shorts had to make the move to television or perish. Sylvester and Tweety made this transition, culminating in a self-titled repackaging of their older cartoons as well as other Warner Brothers shorts that premiered on CBS in 1976. Sylvester and Tweety shorts appeared into the twenty-first century on various programs on network and cable stations.

The characters' popularity continued unabated through the 1990s. Sylvester and Tweety were reincarnated in a new cartoon series, *Sylvester and Tweety Mysteries*, in 1995 on the WB television network, and the duo returned to theater screens in 1996, appearing in *Space Jam* with legendary basketball player Michael Jordan. The cat and canary have been seen endorsing products such as Miracle Whip dressing and MCI long distance. In 1998 the United States Post Office honored Tweety and Sylvester with a 32-cent postage stamp. Sylvester and Tweety appear prominently in products from clothing to cups to clocks sold by Warner Brothers Studios.

Warner Brothers's marketing of the characters is no small part of their fame, which has continued into the twenty-first century, but Sylvester and Tweety have an appeal that goes beyond marketing. Sylvester is not the cat we might expect, Tweety isn't as innocent as he appears, and their interactions make great comedy. With Sylvester and Tweety, it is always the unexpected that makes audiences laugh. When people have seen the cartoons repeatedly and are still laughing, Sylvester and Tweety Pie's continuing popularity seems to be assured.

Adrienne Furness

SEE ALSO: *Academy Awards; Animated Films; Blanc, Mel; Bugs Bunny; Jordan, Michael; MGM (Metro-Goldwyn-Mayer); Saturday Morning Cartoons.*

BIBLIOGRAPHY

Friedwald, Will, and Jerry Beck. *The Warner Brothers Cartoons.* Metuchen, NJ: Scarecrow Press, 1981.

Lawson, Tim and Alisa Persons. *The Magic behind the Voices: A Who's Who of Cartoon Voice Actors.* Jackson: University Press of Mississippi, 2004.

Lenburg, Jeff. *The Encyclopedia of Animated Cartoons.* New York: Facts On File, 1991.

Woolery, George W. *Children's Television: The First Thirty-Five Years, 1946–1981: Part 1: Animated Cartoon Series.* Metuchen, NJ: Scarecrow Press, 1983.

Twelve-Step Programs

Twelve-Step programs are addiction-recovery treatments modeled on the techniques of Alcoholics Anonymous (AA). Manifestations of the self-help and social collectivist movements of the nineteenth century, AA and similar organizations represent a form of secularized religion, involving both Christian and Eastern philosophical principles. The Twelve Steps are a series of behavior-modification principles that appeal to a higher power, take action through personal inventories, make amends to others, and spread the message. Beginning with alcoholism, the treatment philosophy has been applied to gambling, eating disorders, drug addictions, sexual disorders, physical health problems, and a variety of other damaging compulsive behaviors, with varying degrees of success and not without some controversy.

HISTORICAL BACKGROUND

Dr. Benjamin Rush, a prominent physician in the early years of the United States (and signer of the Declaration of Independence), held that alcoholism was a disease, with abstinence its only cure. Nineteenth-century industrialization and resulting prosperity, however, encouraged a renewed belief in restraining moral attributes such as hard work, respectable behavior, and personal responsibility. Such values were embraced by the new middle class in England and appealed to other classes as well. Scottish author Samuel Smiles enshrined what he called a "gospel of work" in a series of best-selling books that included *Self-Help* (1859). This book, which was based on a series of self-improvement lectures that Smiles gave to young men, taught that financial success and personal happiness were based entirely on individual initiative and faith in God.

The self-help movement of Smiles spread across the Atlantic to the rapidly industrializing United States and influenced a generation of American self-help activists, including physician John Harvey Kellogg. In 1876 Kellogg was hired to supervise the Seventh Day Adventists' Health Reform Institute, located in Battle Creek, Michigan. Beyond the breakfast cereal he helped invent as a health food, Kellogg became the most prominent self-help health advocate in the world. He spread, popularized, and helped make nearly universal the Adventist notion that individuals are responsible for and can do something about their physical and spiritual health.

ALCOHOLICS ANONYMOUS

During the early twentieth century, an American Protestant evangelist named Frank N. D. Buchman established the Oxford

Group, a religious movement that encouraged conversion experiences through confession, restitution, and self-survey. It attracted two converts with severe drinking-related problems, New York City stockbroker William Griffith Wilson, or "Bill W." as he was later known to his AA friends, and Akron physician Robert Holbrook Smith, or "Dr. Bob." The pair adapted the principles and practices of the Oxford Group in tandem with the well-known self-help health dogma of Kellogg to the issue of controlling drinking. Previously, alcoholism had been treated as a matter for moral persuasion, institutionalization, or law enforcement. Bill W. and Dr. Bob's new program consisted of helping, talking to, or otherwise maintaining contact with other drunkards to engage in spiritual activity. On June 10, 1935, Dr. Bob had his last drink, marking the official start of Alcoholics Anonymous.

The circles of recovering alcoholics in AA grew slowly at first. The noble experiment of Prohibition, which ended in 1933, had changed the culture of alcoholism in American society. All-male saloons died with the introduction of Prohibition in 1920, replaced by mixed-sex drinking that continued after 1933. Gone was the fraternity of men supporting each other in and out of alcoholism. Prohibition forced drinking undercover, into homes, hotel rooms, and other places where it had not been common previously. Bootleg beverages, especially beer, were often weak or reduced with other substances so that they could be consumed in greater quantities.

The end of Prohibition meant the return of alcoholic beverages to their traditional strengths, a reality to which many drinkers could not adjust. Coupled with enticing stories in the press, advertisements promoting drinking as sophisticated and glamorous, and the abundant use of alcohol in Hollywood movies, alcoholism gradually increased in the years during and after the Great Depression. There were more than 100 members of AA by 1939, the same year that the Twelve-Step program was published in the book *Alcoholics Anonymous* (the "Big Book," as it is known in the movement). A national AA service office was established in New York City in 1940, and the *Saturday Evening Post* gave the AA and the Twelve-Step program its first extensive national publicity in 1941.

THE TWELVE STEPS

Bill W. wrote the Twelve Steps in a burst of inspiration during 1938 and 1939, but they were based on debate among members and reflected the collective nature of the organization and its religious underpinnings. Although the original version was written in the stilted language of the day, subsequent editions of the Big Book have kept the original wording. The founders described themselves as "average Americans," but most were male, Protestant, white, and middle class. Their perspective reflected their environment, although their view that alcohol was not in itself bad—but that some individuals were unable to drink only in moderation—differed from the view of the temperance movement that had flourished in the same socioeconomic class.

The first step of the Twelve-Step program is that a person has to admit powerlessness in his or her addiction. AA maintains that a person needs to have "hit bottom," experiencing a totally powerless situation, before redemption is possible. At Twelve-Step meetings (in which members are introduced on the anonymous, first-name basis pioneered by AA), testimonials of near destruction are given by new and old members alike. In step two, the member has to express the crucial element of belief: adherence to a Power greater than himself or herself. Only with faith can the member move on to step three (turning his or her life over to God [the higher power, according to the member's understanding]), step six (being ready to have God remove defects of character), and step seven (asking God to remove shortcomings).

Steps six and seven, together with step four (the making of a moral inventory), step five (the admission to another person of past wrong-doings), and steps eight and nine (the listing and making of amends to people who had been wronged), are called the action steps. The action steps say nothing about drinking, for in AA parlance, "liquor was but a symptom." Following steps ten (continuing inventory taking and wrong-doing admission) and eleven (the improvement of one's knowledge of God through prayer and meditation), step twelve is a resulting "spiritual awakening," which permits the member to spread the Twelve-Step method to other addicts and maintain the practice of the principles in everyday life. In AA's conception, helping other alcoholics is considered the best means by which to maintain an individual's own continued sobriety. It also perpetuates the AA organization and spreads the Twelve-Step concept.

CRITICISM AND OUTLOOK

The Twelve-Step program continues to be a focus of debate. Experts argue that it is difficult to evaluate recidivism rates of participants in a Twelve-Step program because of their anonymity. The reported numbers vary, but it is safe to say that a significant percentage of members drop out of the program in their first year, and, according to AA statistics, about 30 percent of members have been sober less than one year. AA's insistence that alcoholism is a disease counters more recent research that alcoholism is a behavior without physical cause.

AA has been criticized by feminists and minorities who argue that the organization is oppressive as a result of the language in the Twelve Steps and that the Twelve Steps are constraining, repressive, and foster codependence. They also argue that AA literature does not allow for discussion of social issues, such as discrimination and poverty, which often affect individual drinking patterns. The Twelve-Step's focus on God, or a "higher power," has been criticized by those who see it as running afoul of the doctrine of the separation of church and state, especially when AA cooperates with law enforcement officials in mandating AA treatment for convicted offenders. The AA's Protestant Christian roots has led to criticism that it is in itself a form of religion, or at least a quasi-religious or cult organization such as Transcendental Meditation or Scientology, an allegation AA denies. Research conducted over the past thirty years suggests that people with even fairly significant levels of alcohol dependence can learn to moderate their drinking, a view at odds with AA's longtime insistence that alcoholics cannot control their drinking.

From its modest beginnings, AA has grown into a worldwide organization of about two million members. Fellowship continues to be organized on a local level with no dues payable. Contributions for expenses are accepted from those attending meetings only. Affiliation of the AA or its local groups with churches, political organizations, or other official institutions is barred by the AA Twelve Traditions, another seminal document. More than 200 other organizations have developed their own versions of the Twelve-Step program, including Al-Anon (the organization for members of the families of alcoholics founded in 1951), Narcotics Anonymous, Gamblers Anonymous, Overeaters Anonymous, Debtors Anonymous, Augustine

Fellowship Sex & Love Addicts Anonymous, Survivors of Incest Anonymous, and Cocaine, Nicotine, and Co-Dependents Anonymous.

The AA meeting format, with members' accounts of desperate experiences and the "Hi, I'm so-and-so" introduction, have been the object of lampoons and parodies. Nevertheless, many experienced therapists agree that any form of treatment for addictive behavior is most likely to show a higher rate of success if the patient joins a Twelve-Step organization such as Alcoholics Anonymous. In the face of the omnipresent social problem of alcoholism and its detrimental effects on children and families, the growing social acceptance of gambling and tolerance of compulsive gamblers, and an ever-increasing variety of other addictive behaviors, Twelve-Step programs provide adequate substitutes for a dependent way of life.

Richard Junger

SEE ALSO: *Cocaine/Crack; The Great Depression; Prohibition; The* Saturday Evening Post.

BIBLIOGRAPHY

Alcoholics Anonymous. *Alcoholics Anonymous: The Story of How Many Thousands of Men and Women Have Recovered from Alcoholism.* New York: Alcoholics Anonymous World Services, 2001.

Kurtz, Ernest. *A.A. The Story: A Revised Edition of Not-God: A History of Alcoholics Anonymous.* San Francisco: Harper & Row, 1988.

Makela, Klaus, et al. *Alcoholics Anonymous as a Mutual-Help Movement: A Study in Eight Societies.* Madison: University of Wisconsin Press, 1996.

Padwa, Howard, and Jacob Cunningham. *Addiction: A Reference Encyclopedia.* Santa Barbara, CA: ABC-CLIO, 2010.

Rotgers, Frederick; Marc F. Kern; and Rudy Hoeltzel. *Responsible Drinking: A Moderation Management Approach for Problem Drinkers.* Oakland, CA: New Harbinger Publications, 2002.

Rudy, David R., and Arthur L. Greil. "Is Alcoholics Anonymous a Religious Organization? Meditations on Marginality." *Sociological Analysis* 50 no. 1 (1988): 41–51.

Thomsen, Robert. *Bill W.* New York: Harper & Row, 1975.

The Twenties

The 1920s were a period of rapid industrial growth, economic prosperity, and cultural change. Due mainly to the automobile industry, building and road construction, the development of the radio and advertising industries, and the emergence of "the new woman," the 1920s are often seen as the first "modern" decade, in which the major characteristics of the twentieth century emerged. Tensions between ideas of modernity and accepted traditional values characterize the popular culture of this decade.

Following American involvement in the First World War, the 1920s witnessed an emphasis on domestic concerns such as the economy and the cultural values of American society. The economic boom of the 1920s, best illustrated by Henry Ford's dominance of the automobile industry through the use of interchangeable parts in automobile production, led to a high standard of living for many Americans as wages increased while working hours decreased. This was possible mainly through the increased mechanization of industry and production on a massive scale.

Ford's River Rouge plant in Michigan, in which raw materials were processed and parts were fabricated and assembled all under Ford's control, illustrates the strengths of the 1920s economy. Ford produced an automobile that required little in highly paid skilled labor and could be sold at a relatively cheap price. The automobile industry, in turn, fueled growth in related industries such as construction, glass, rubber, oil, and tourism. This boom created an American economy in which industrial production, for the first time, outpaced consumer demand. In order to accommodate this increase in production, corporations turned to advertising as a way to increase demand. Advertisements created a positive image for a corporation or product by implying various benefits resulting from the product's purchase. Employing popularized ideas about the expression of desires taken from Sigmund Freud's theories of sexual repression leading to neurosis, advertisers sought to exploit the desires of the consuming public by emphasizing the benefits of consumption.

SELF-EXPRESSION IN THE ARTS

The emphasis on expression over repression went beyond the realm of advertising and can be seen in the popular culture of the 1920s. From novels such as F. Scott Fitzgerald's *The Great Gatsby* (1925) and Sinclair Lewis's *Babbitt* (1922) to the increasingly frenetic sound of jazz music and new dances such as the Lindy Hop (named after famous flyer Charles Lindbergh), American popular culture reflected a modern sense of ethics and values focused on individual pleasure and expression. Even all-American celebrities such as Douglas Fairbanks Sr. and Mary Pickford were challenged by more sexually expressive personalities such as Rudolph Valentino and Greta Garbo. This more modern approach to popular culture was reinforced by modern media such as the radio, phonographs, and sound film. Both the form and content of 1920s popular culture demonstrated a sense of modernity.

In literature, the 1920s were characterized by the writings of what Gertrude Stein called "the lost generation." Writers such as Fitzgerald, Lewis, Ernest Hemingway, John Dos Passos, T. S. Eliot, Ezra Pound, E. E. Cummings, and Sherwood Anderson critiqued American society, especially the traditions and values of rural life, or in their words, "the village." These writers were disillusioned by their involvement in the First World War, and this disillusionment is reflected in their writings. It was a lost generation, according to Malcolm Cowley in *Exile's Return: A Literary Odyssey of the 1920s* "because it was uprooted, schooled away, and almost wrenched away from its attachment to any region or tradition."

But the "lost generation" writers were not the only significant writers during the 1920s. Women like Edna St. Vincent Millay attempted to capitalize on the less repressive atmosphere of the 1920s by flaunting sexual expression in their poetry and life, and African American writers such as poets Langston Hughes and Countee Cullen and novelists Claude McKay, Jean Toomer, and Zora Neale Hurston joined artists such as Aaron Douglas and Augusta Savage in leading the "Harlem Renaissance."

This greater mainstream acceptance of African American culture is also reflected in the growing influence of jazz on

The Jazz Singer. *A poster promotes Al Jolson starring in* The Jazz Singer. *Jazz became the most popular form of music during the 1920s.* WARNER BROS/THE KOBAL COLLECTION.

American popular music, a phenomenon that emerged during World War I. The military's forced closure of Storyville, the red-light district in New Orleans, forced many jazz musicians out of Louisiana northward in search of other opportunities, and war mobilization provided greater contact between races at military installations and wartime manufacturing plants. These two factors led black musicians to adapt black blues and jazz to the expectations of a white audience.

Jazz spread first among younger audiences, mainly due to its spontaneous nature and its association with chaotic dancing, and critics denounced it as unmusical, intoxicating, and immoral. Despite these objections, jazz became the most popular form of music during the 1920s, dominating the radio airwaves and record sales and even influencing movies such as *The Jazz Singer* (1927). As jazz music became more popular, it also became more standardized, organized, and arranged. What had once been music that emphasized improvisation throughout a piece became a highly structured, formulaic genre in which improvisation was limited to specific breaks in the arrangement of jazz "riffs." What had been "hot" jazz, by musicians such as Louis Armstrong and His Hot Five, became "sweet" jazz at the hands of band leaders like Guy Lombardo and his Royal Canadians, or "symphonic" jazz, in the words of Paul Whiteman. Whiteman's orchestra debuted George Gershwin's *Rhapsody in Blue* in 1924, subtitled "for jazz band and piano." The work was primarily symphonic with jazz motifs. These orchestras and large bands developed what would become Big Band swing music in the 1930s and 1940s.

THE SILVER SCREEN

Like jazz music, motion pictures also gained greater acceptance during the 1920s as they moved out of working-class storefront nickelodeons into grand movie palaces attracting a middle-class and middle-brow audience. In the various conflicts between traditional values and modernity, movies challenged accepted middle-class values. According to Robert Sklar, in his book *Movie-Made America: A Cultural History of American Movies*, "movies came to be seen as offering values distinctly different from those of middle-class culture, and providing greater opportunities for ethnic minorities than other economic sectors." Not only was the movie industry dominated by recent immigrants, the films themselves (being silent in the early 1920s) were easily adapted to a variety of immigrant cultures and easily understood by immigrant audiences. As the audience for movies grew, so did the respectability of movies as an art form and acceptable leisure activity.

The movie industry portrayed a changing America through the opportunities it created for a more heterogeneous population and the attractions it held for a mass audience. But the movies themselves presented the values of modern America while at the same time reinforcing traditional middle-class values. Two of the most popular male stars illustrate this point. Valentino, in his short career before his sudden death in 1926, embodied the modern, passionate, and sexually expressive male of the 1920s in such films as *The Sheik* (1921) and *Blood and Sand* (1922), while Fairbanks, in *The Mark of Zorro* (1920), *Robin Hood* (1922), and *The Thief of Bagdad* (1925), embodied the traditional, robust, athletic, all-American male. Both men became celebrities and helped to cultivate the studio star system in which performers became the major commodity used in selling a movie to the public.

The 1920s witnessed the consolidation of the power of the studios, especially Paramount Studios under Adolph Zukor, which was the largest of the silent film producers. Metro-Goldwyn-Mayer was created by theater owner Marcus Loew, who bought and combined Metro Picture Company with Samuel Goldwyn's Picture Company under the direction of Louis B. Mayer. Chafing under the influence of powerful producers and studio executives, director D. W. Griffith and actors Charlie Chaplin, Fairbanks, and Pickford formed the United Artists Corporation in 1919 to distribute individually produced films and thereby avoid the formal structure of a studio. Each of these companies controlled several aspects of film production, distribution, and exhibition, yet the greatest change in Hollywood film occurred at the fledgling Warner Brothers Studio when it purchased and began producing films with the Vitaphone (sound-on-disc) technology in 1926. With the premiere of *The Jazz Singer* in 1927, the silent era ended. Within a few years, sound film production outpaced silent film.

In many ways, the silent era in popular culture ended earlier with the spread of radio technology in the 1920s. From amateurs broadcasting in basements and garages to fully formed and regulated networks after the Radio Act of 1927, the radio industry developed into Americans' most used and trusted source of news, information, and entertainment. The 1920s were a decade of growth for the radio industry, not only in its technical aspects but in regards to programming as well. Radio stations learned what worked well on radio and what did not.

The most attractive aspect of radio for the audience was its immediacy. Broadcasts of sporting events such as boxing matches and baseball games, political conventions and election returns, band performances from big-city ballrooms, and news reporting all became mainstays of the radio industry. Radio also found itself the new home of variety entertainment after the decline of vaudeville. The most popular radio comedy, the *Amos 'n' Andy Show* , featured white vaudevillians Freeman Gosden and Charles Correll portraying two black southerners whose simple ways and common misunderstandings provided the humor for the show.

The pervasive nature of radio reinforced, to a national audience, many regionally held stereotypes, especially of minorities. Many people believed what they heard on the radio, not only because it was capable of presenting news upon its occurrence but also because the radio produced a certain form of intimacy in which the listener identified with the broadcast in ways unlike other forms of media. The presence of a radio set within one's home and the necessity of the listener to create images from the sounds presented resulted in each listener creating a very personal program, unique and individual. This transformation in communications and entertainment, through its immediacy and national appeal, reinforced the feeling that the 1920s were the start of the "modern" era.

RESISTING MODERNITY

This modern shift in social and cultural values did not take place unopposed. Several social movements can be explained as a revolt against the changes occurring in American society. Nativism, Prohibition, and counterrevolution were attempts to save traditional values in the face of change. Nativism came in three basic forms. All, however, expressed a deep discomfort with the changes occurring in American society and mainly with the changes occurring as a result of immigration.

Antiradicalism was a form of nativism in which people who disagreed with the government were seen as undesirable. The attacks on foreigners during and after World War I in such notable instances as the Palmer raids and the unfair trial of anarchists Nicola Sacco and Bartolomeo Vanzetti were all part of this fear of radicals, especially in the wake of the Bolshevik Revolution in Russia in 1917. Fear of radicals spilled over into a fear of non-Protestants, especially Jews and Catholics. Michigan and Nebraska passed laws prohibiting parochial schools. This fear of others translated into fierce support of white Anglo-Saxon Protestants. In 1916 Madison Grant wrote *The Passing of the Great Race* in which he described the hierarchy of races, with whites being at the top, and distinguished between whites by dividing Europeans into three main groups—Mediterraneans, Alpines, and Nordics—with Nordics being the superior group. Belief in the inferiority of Asians, Africans, and southern and eastern Europeans led to the passage of the National Origins Act of 1924 in which immigration quotas were designed to increase the number of nordic immigrants while decreasing all others; this also meant the complete exclusion of Asian immigrants and small quotas for southern and eastern European immigrants.

The most dramatic example of nativism during the 1920s can be seen in the revival of the Ku Klux Klan. Unlike the post–Civil War era, when the purpose of the Klan was to intimidate African Americans, the 1920s Klan advocated white supremacy over blacks, Jews, Catholics, and any immigrants who were not white Anglo-Saxon Protestants. The modern Klan used expert advertisers for promotion and recruitment of new members. By 1923 more than three million Americans were members of the Klan, with the strongest Klan organizations in the Midwest and the West.

In January 1919 the Eighteenth Amendment was passed, prohibiting the manufacturing, selling, or transporting of intoxicating beverages in the United States. The Volstead Act of 1919 defined intoxicating beverages as anything with more than 0.5 percent alcohol. The move toward Prohibition was yet another attempt to return America to what many perceived as its past. Saloons had proliferated in the late nineteenth and early twentieth centuries. Many people viewed this development as an expression of change, of encroaching foreign influence. Halting the process of change meant reinforcing and retaining traditional values.

Part of the attack on things foreign and things new was the attack on science, especially in those areas where scientific theory and practice conflicted with deeply held religious beliefs, such as in the case of the theory of evolution and the belief in creationism. In 1925 the state of Tennessee passed a law prohibiting the teaching of evolution in public schools and colleges. In a test case in July 1925, schoolteacher John T. Scopes was tried under this law in Dayton, Tennessee. The case became a national sensation. The American Civil Liberties Union hired the famous trial lawyer Clarence Darrow to argue against the law, while the state got William Jennings Bryan (the populist Democrat and three-time presidential candidate) to argue its side. The "monkey trial," as it was known, argued over the issue of evolution versus creationism, but in the end the judge ruled that the only thing that mattered was the fact that Scopes did teach evolution and therefore was guilty. He was fined $100, which was suspended by the state supreme court. It was a victory for the antimodernists, but it would be their last one. A few days after the trial ended, Bryan died, and with him died much of the 1920s fundamentalist movement.

Each of these social movements (nativism, prohibition, and antievolutionism), seen in conjunction with the rapid spread of automobiles, economic prosperity, and the radio and film industries, illustrates the conflicted state of American culture during the 1920s.

Charles J. Shindo

SEE ALSO: *Advertising;* The Amos 'n' Andy Show*; Anderson, Sherwood; Armstrong, Louis; Automobile; Chaplin, Charlie; Creationism; Cullen, Countee; Darrow, Clarence; Fairbanks, Douglas, Sr.; Fitzgerald, F. Scott; Ford, Henry; Ford Motor Company; Garbo, Greta; Goldwyn, Samuel; Harlem Renaissance; Hemingway, Ernest; Hughes, Langston; Hurston, Zora Neale; Jazz;* The Jazz Singer*; Ku Klux Klan; Lewis, Sinclair; Lindbergh, Charles; Lombardo, Guy; McKay, Claude; Millay, Edna St. Vincent; Movie Palaces; Movie Stars; New Orleans Rhythm and Blues; Phonograph; Pickford, Mary; Prohibition; Radio; Scopes Monkey Trial; Silent Movies; United Artists; Valentino, Rudolph; Whiteman, Paul; World War I.*

BIBLIOGRAPHY

Cowley, Malcolm. *Exile's Return: A Literary Odyssey of the 1920s.* New York: Penguin, 1976.

Dumenil, Lynn. *The Modern Temper: America Culture and Society in the 1920s.* New York: Hill and Wang, 1995.

Goldberg, Ronald Allen. *America in the Twenties.* New York: Syracuse University Press, 2003.

Hentoff, Nat, and Albert J. McCarthy, eds. *Jazz: New Perspectives on the History of Jazz.* New York: Da Capo Press, 1959.

Nash, Roderick. *The Nervous Generation: American Thought, 1917–1930.* Chicago: Ivan R. Dee, 1990.

Sklar, Robert. *Movie-Made America: A Cultural History of American Movies.* New York: Vintage Books, 1975.

24

The acclaimed Fox TV espionage and counterterrorism series *24* ran for eight seasons between 2001 and 2010, winning two Golden Globes, including Best Television Series—Drama in

24. *Kiefer Sutherland, front, led the cast of 24, which followed twenty-four hours in the action-packed life of agent Jack Bauer over the course of a season.* FOX-TV/THE KOBAL COLLECTION/RAPOPORT, AARON.

2004, and multiple other awards. It is widely regarded as one of the greatest TV shows of all time. Kiefer Sutherland, who plays Jack Bauer, the show's lead, was nominated for seven Emmys, winning Outstanding Lead Actor in a Drama Series in 2006. Each season has a total of twenty-four episodes that combine to portray one twenty-four-hour day, in real time. A typical hour involves Bauer and his team racing against the clock to foil a terrorist plot, conspiracy, or impending catastrophe, as Bauer also tries to resolve a personal issue. In the series premiere, for example, his daughter goes missing while he is trying to prevent the assassination of a U.S. senator.

The first episode of *24* aired on November 6, 2001, less than two months after the terrorist attacks that destroyed the World Trade Center in New York City. Set in a secretive Counter Terrorism Unit (CTU) in Los Angeles, the show's emphasis on conspiracy theories and terrorism meant that it connected immediately with the mood of the nation. A ticking clock that is often visible on-screen adds tension to an already fast-paced and action-packed format. Crucially, the real-time element of the show also includes the advertising breaks, so the audience misses events that occur during the breaks. Split screens, showing action taking place simultaneously, increase the amount of information the viewer must take in and quicken the pace even further. As *Time* magazine wrote in its review of the first episode, "Forget sleeping through this one—you won't even want to blink. *24* is the most distinctive, addictive new TV series this season. . . . It's drama for the age of information overload."

The show's unusual format, its violent action, and the high-tension plotting made it one of the most popular TV shows, but the key element in its success was the character of Jack Bauer. The role revived Sutherland's career; the former star of teen movies was transformed, in *24*'s first season, into an uncompromising tough guy who is also trying to save his marriage. That season ended with Bauer holding his dead wife in his arms, a shocking twist that gave the character vulnerability that returned in later episodes.

Bauer's methods are often brutal. As Clive James explained for BBC Radio, "Bauer would drive a Humvee through your bedroom wall to disarm your alarm clock." In addition to his involvement in solving terror plots, detonating nuclear weapons, and saving the world from war, Bauer's emotional state is an important part of the series. He is often in despair at the end of the twenty-four-hour period; in addition to the death of his wife in the first season, season three ended with Bauer weeping after being forced by terrorists to execute his boss, Ryan Chappelle.

24 was frequently criticized for its violent story lines, which often depicted Muslim groups in a negative way, or Middle Eastern governments holding the United States to ransom. As the seasons passed, many of the plotlines became predictable—the kidnapping of Bauer's daughter is repeated more than once—while Bauer himself is frequently imprisoned, only to stage a daring escape. But its most controversial plot points are those involving torture, which was often justified in the show because it enabled Bauer and his agents to acquire crucial information as quickly as possible.

Writing in the *New York Times*, Adam Green noted that in season five torture ceased to be an occasional shocking event and became central to the show. At a time when American forces in Iraq were under investigation for alleged torture in Abu Ghraib, and when the waterboarding of terror suspects at Guantánamo Bay was a hot topic in the news, the show's seemingly casual depiction of torture concerned many critics. West Point military academy even went as far as to ask the show's producers to tone down torture scenes because it was feared that new military recruits were adopting *24*'s apparent moral position, justifying torture on national security grounds.

The popularity of *24* in the aftermath of the 9/11 terrorist attacks is perhaps not surprising. In its paranoia, violence, and the troubled morality of its lead character, the show perhaps reflected an age in which the difference between "good guys" and "bad guys" lay in their motivations rather than their actions.

Chris Routledge

SEE ALSO: *Emmy Awards; Gulf Wars; 9/11; Television.*

BIBLIOGRAPHY

"The 50 Greatest TV Shows of All Time." Empire. Accessed April 2012. Available from http://www.empireonline.com/50greatesttv/default.asp?tv=6

Green, Adam. "Normalizing Torture on *24*." *New York Times*, May 22, 2005.

James, Clive. "The Clock's Ticking on Torture." BBC News, March 30, 2007. Accessed April 2012. Available from http://news.bbc.co.uk/1/hi/magazine/6510593.stm

Poniewozik, James. "Television: The Time of Their Lives." *Time*, November 12, 2001

23 Skidoo

Though commonly associated with the Roaring Twenties, the popular catchphrase "23 skidoo" actually originated around the turn of the twentieth century. Its origin has been credited to two contemporaneous sources: telegraphic code and *The Only Way* (1899), a Broadway adaptation of Charles Dickens's Victorian novel *A Tale of Two Cities* (1859).

In the final act of *The Only Way*, an old woman solemnly intones the number of victims on their way to the gallows, with special emphasis on number twenty-three, the play's protagonist. The cry "twenty-three!" was soon taken up by Broadway habitués. In telegraphic code, "23" is an abbreviation for "Away with you!" The word *skidoo*, a derivation of "skedaddle," was soon added to "23" for the edification of those who had not seen the play or were unfamiliar with telegraphic code. For the next twenty years, the expression, or one of its variants, was commonly heard among students and young sophisticates. It ordinarily meant "Get lost," but was frequently used without any precise meaning. By the end of the 1920s, "23 skidoo" had fallen out of common usage, though it has proved to be more enduring than other catchphrases from that period.

Michael Baers

SEE ALSO: *Slang; The Twenties.*

BIBLIOGRAPHY

Mathews, Mitford W. *A Dictionary of Americanisms on Historical Principles*. Chicago: University of Chicago Press, 1951.

Partridge, Eric. *A Dictionary of Catch Phrases, American and British, from the Sixteenth Century to the Present Day*. New York: Stein and Day, 1986.

20/20

With the premiere on June 6, 1978, of its program *20/20*, the ABC television network launched its first news magazine. The network, which was experiencing difficulties in the late 1970s, was undertaking a major initiative to revise its news programming under the tutelage of its newly appointed president, Roone Arledge. Arledge targeted a number of ways in which ABC could improve its news division with the goal of attracting the average American viewer rather than news junkies. One result of this push was *20/20*, which was based on the success of the CBS program *60 Minutes*. Since its premiere in 1968, *60 Minutes* had enjoyed significant popularity as a distinctive means to present news through the use of longer segments and nontraditional news time slots.

The first *20/20* program was hosted by *Time* magazine critic Robert Hughes and former *Esquire* editor Harold Hayes. The kick-off story featured a report on rabbit abuse at greyhound tracks, and it failed to attract critical enthusiasm. The initial reviews ranged from "dizzyingly absurd" from the *New York Times* to "the trashiest stab at candy-cane journalism yet" from the *Washington Post*. Arledge immediately realized that the program's concept had to be reworked if it was to succeed. He rearranged the show's focus and introduced a new anchor, the longtime *Today*-show personality Hugh Downs. Under the beloved Downs, *20/20* thrived and took on a consumer focus. In 1984 Arledge decided to bring in Barbara Walters, who was considered a rising star at ABC and who had also been a *Today*-show personality. The pairing of the two anchors was a hit with viewers, and through their work on *20/20* Downs and Walters earned a place among the most respected journalists on television.

20/20 has featured countless groundbreaking and exclusive interviews with world-famous figures drawn from many different areas of public life. They have included politicians, stars in show business, sports figures, and even criminals. Among the most memorable interviewees have been Cuban leader Fidel Castro; Bill and Hillary Clinton, appearing at the height of the Whitewater controversy; Olympic diving champion Greg Louganis, who revealed for the first time that he was stricken with AIDS and had been HIV-positive when he competed in the 1988 Olympics; and former White House intern and presidential paramour, Monica Lewinsky. Also contributing to the success of *20/20* with viewers has been its numerous health-related stories, including one concerning Downs as he underwent a procedure on his knee.

Encouraged by the strong showing of *20/20*, ABC has created other news magazines over the years. With NBC's *Dateline* airing up to four times per week, in 1997 ABC decided to increase the showings of *20/20* to several nights a week. Although this change in programming met with some success, the network made a more radical move for the 1998–1999 season by combining all of its news magazines (including *PrimeTime Live*) under the *20/20* brand. Airing at least three times weekly, *20/20* expanded its original consumer focus to embrace the investigative pieces and hard journalism that had characterized *PrimeTimeLive* and to include more feature segments on the top news stories of the day. Downs and Walters were no longer the sole anchors of the expanded program but shared responsibilities with several other top ABC journalists, notably Sam Donaldson, Diane Sawyer, Charles Gibson, and Connie Chung. The show eventually returned to its once-a-week Friday evening format, and Barbara Walters, after a number of coanchor experiments, left the show in semiretirement in 2004 but returned frequently with high-profile interviews and reports. Elizabeth Vargas of ABC news became coanchor alongside John Stossel. Stossel eventually left for a new show on the Fox network, and in 2009 Chris Cuomo assumed the cohost position alongside Vargas. The program continued to draw large audiences with high-profile interviews and cutting-edge stories.

Alyssa L. Falwell

SEE ALSO: *AIDS; Arledge, Roone;* Dateline*; Lewinsky, Monica; The* New York Times*;* 60 Minutes*; Television; Television Anchors;* Time*;* Today*; Walters, Barbara.*

BIBLIOGRAPHY

Gunther, Marc. *The House that Roone Built: The Inside Story of ABC News*. Boston: Little, Brown, 1994.

Gutgold, Nichola D. *Seen and Heard*. Lanham, MD: Lexington Books, 2008.

Twiggy *(1949–)*

Arguably the very first "supermodel," England's Twiggy became an international star in the mid-1960s, bringing the world an idealized image of a youthful "Swinging London" and, for better or worse, heavily influencing popular conceptions of femininity. On the one hand, the 91-pound, saucer-eyed Twiggy (born Lesley Hornby) was a positive celebration of androgyny and a radical break from the insistence in the 1950s that female sex symbols possess curvaceous figures. Conversely, some critics have argued that Twiggy's slight physique helped push standards of thinness too far, leading many young women toward personal dissatisfaction with their bodies and, in some cases, anorexia.

After saturating the pages of fashion magazines at the end of the 1960s and appearing in a handful of early 1970s films, notably Ken Russell's *The Boyfriend*, Twiggy adopted the last name Lawson and remained out of the limelight for a time. She hosted the television show *Twiggy's People* in 1998, and she served as a judge on the reality-television show *America's Next Top Model* from 2005 to 2007. As that assignment illustrates, Twiggy's influence on the fashion industry never truly waned—svelte boyishness has recurred as a theme in female models for decades.

Shaun Frentner

SEE ALSO: *Androgyny; Reality Television; Supermodels; Television.*

BIBLIOGRAPHY

DeLibero, Linda Benn. "This Year's Girl: A Personal/Critical History of Twiggy." In *On Fashion*, ed. Shari Benstock and Suzanne Ferriss, 41–58. New Brunswick, NJ: Rutgers University Press, 1994.

Pepper, Terence; Robin Muir; and Melvin Sokolsky. *Twiggy: A Life in Photographs*. London: National Portrait Gallery, 2009.

Twiggy. *Twiggy: How I Probably Just Came along on a White Rabbit at the Right Time, and Met the Smile on the Face of the Tiger*. New York: Hawthorne Books, 1968.

Twilight

Author Stephenie Meyer has repeatedly said that the idea for her best-selling *Twilight* series came to her in a dream. The official saga includes four books: *Twilight* (2005), *New Moon* (2006), *Eclipse* (2007), and *Breaking Dawn* (2008). The first book in the series had a generous initial print run of 75,000 copies and gained momentum and word-of-mouth attention in its first year, spending endless weeks on best seller lists. By the time *New Moon* was released, Meyer was being mobbed at readings and signing events. *Eclipse* and *Breaking Dawn* were immediate best sellers, with a great deal of media coverage and fans flocking to midnight release parties. In 2008 the series sold more than twenty-seven million copies.

THE SAGA'S PLOT

The story centers on teenager Bella Swan, an introverted nonconformist who begins a tortured love affair with a vampire when she moves from her mother's house in Arizona to her father's house in dreary Forks, Washington. In *Twilight*, Bella meets and falls in love with Edward Cullen, a vampire masquerading as a high school student. Characterized by a gothic tone and lengthy passages of description, the novel focuses on Bella's obsession with Edward, the passion both of them fight, and the circumstances that conspire to keep them apart. In *New Moon* Edward leaves Bella because he believes he is a danger to her, and while he's gone, Bella reluctantly falls in love with Jacob Black, a Native American from the region who turns out to be a werewolf. This romantic triangle becomes the focus of the rest of the series, as Edward and Jacob alternately battle for Bella's affections—which never stray far from Edward—and declare uneasy truces to protect her. Finally, in *Breaking Dawn*, Edward and Bella get married, Bella almost dies giving birth to a half-vampire baby, and then she becomes a vampire herself.

The series is notable for breaking with some traditional vampire mythology. In Meyer's universe, for instance, vampires avoid the sun not because it will destroy them but because their skin sparkles in sunlight. Edward lives with a family of vampires that do not drink human blood, although they struggle against the continuous temptation. Like many vampire novels, though, the books' themes address the line between love and obsession, referencing the tortured and doomed lovers in William Shakespeare's *Romeo and Juliet* and Emily Brontë's *Wuthering Heights*. Bella feels compelled to follow Edward at almost any cost to herself. Her association with him leaves her injured and near death on more than one occasion, and her obsession causes her to shun normal activities and relationships with her peers.

COMPARISONS AND CRITIQUES

The *Twilight* saga continues the tradition of using vampires to explore themes of romance and sex, long a subgenre of adult romance fiction, that began with Bram Stoker's *Dracula* (published in 1897), was popularized through the writings of Anne Rice in the 1980s and 1990s, and became a solid part of the teen literature landscape with the success of Annette Curtis Klause's *The Silver Kiss* in 1990. The *Twilight* phenomenon has led to a paranormal romance craze in the teen market, helping bolster such series as *The Vampire Diaries* by L. J. Smith (which was developed into a television program in 2009) and *The House of Night* series by P. C. and Kristin Cast. The series' adult readership brought renewed attention to Charlaine Harris's long-standing *Sookie Stackhouse* series about the romance between a psychic and a vampire, leading HBO to adapt the series into the

Twilight *Fans Mob Robert Pattinson.* *Robert Pattinson greets a throng of* Twilight *fans at a promotional event in Madrid, Spain, in 2009.* EDUARDO PARRA/FILMMAGIC/GETTY IMAGE.

television show *True Blood* in 2008, which has become a pop culture phenomenon in its own right.

While the series is undeniably popular, it has also come under a great deal of criticism. Critics comment on Meyer's flowery, repetitive, and overlong writing style. Others express concern about Bella as a character, citing her passivity and the way the books repeatedly praise and reward her for sacrificing herself and her needs for her boyfriend. In the final book, Bella allows Edward to pressure her into marriage right after her high school graduation. After the wedding, when she has sex with him for the first time, the act is depicted as violent and results in a pregnancy that Bella continues even though it threatens her life and ultimately almost kills her. Supporters of the series talk about Bella and Edward's relationship as a safe fantasy for teens not yet ready for a real sexual relationship, as the couple does not consummate their relationship until the final book and Edward is wealthy, strong, and completely devoted to Bella.

GLOBAL IMPACT

Production began on the first *Twilight* movie before Meyer finished writing the series. The first film was released in 2008, starring Kristen Stewart as Bella, Robert Pattinson as Edward, and Taylor Lautner as Jacob. It made more than $69 million in its opening weekend, exceeding its $37 million budget by a margin that surprised many in and out of the film industry. Subsequent films were released in 2009 and 2010, and then the final book was adapted into a two-part film released in 2011 and 2012. The success of the films turned its stars into overnight celebrities stalked by tabloids, and fans have turned seeing the films into events on par with the book releases.

The *Twilight* series continues to impact audiences as the books are translated and published beyond the English-speaking world and the films are released worldwide. The story has been adapted into a graphic novel, and Meyer has released portions of a novel written from Edward's point of view. In 2010 Meyer released a novella, *The Short Second Life of Bree Tanner*, that follows a minor vampire character from *Eclipse*. The books and films are discussed endlessly in critical and academic circles as well as by die-hard fans and detractors, and the series has attracted a sizable adult fan base, causing an increase in the number of adults reading teen books of all types. The *Twilight* series has helped transform dark fantasy and horror from a genre that boasted a small cult following into a mainstream genre staple.

Adrienne Furness

SEE ALSO: *Best Sellers; Blockbusters; Cable TV; Celebrity; Dracula; Goth; Hollywood; Movie Stars; Teenagers; Vampires.*

BIBLIOGRAPHY

Adams, Lauren. "Bitten." *Horn Book Magazine*, January/ February 2010, 58.

Dargis, Manohla. "Edward, You May Now Bite the Bride." *New York Times*, November 17, 2011.

Grossman, Lev. "It's Twilight in America." *Time*, November 23, 2009, 52.

The Twilight Zone

Created by the visionary writer Rod Serling, *The Twilight Zone* proved both a landmark of televised science fiction and a powerful touchstone in the pop cultural consciousness of the United States. The black-and-white anthology series, which ran on CBS from 1959 to 1964, generated lukewarm ratings when it was originally broadcast but has grown in public estimation over time. Over the course of its five-year network run, *The Twilight Zone* explored themes never before examined on television. It exposed the talents of a generation of character players, such as Jack Klugman, William Shatner, and Robert Duvall, who would go on to become household names for subsequent portrayals. It also cemented the legacy of its creator, who at the time was known principally as the author of socially concerned live dramas.

THE SHOW'S TONE

Serling created *The Twilight Zone* to serve as a forum for his commentary about technology, conformity, discrimination, and a whole host of other issues. Frustrated by his inability to explore these topics in mainstream dramas in the face of censorship by network executives and skittish advertisers, he hoped that the show's science fiction anthology format might allow him to introduce a little liberal orthodoxy to viewers without alarming the executives in control. But if Serling was in it for the advocacy, the show's other creative collaborators consistently pulled it back into the realm of traditional fantasy. This dialectic proved good for all parties concerned.

The Twilight Zone premiered on October 2, 1959. Its introductory episode, "Where Is Everybody?," established the tone and creative parameters of the series. In it, a young man in air force garb finds himself in a seemingly deserted town. After increasingly frantic attempts to locate its inhabitants, he breaks down in despair. Only at the end is it revealed that the man is an astronaut being subjected to an experiment in an isolation booth and that the proceedings have been a hallucination.

In countless subsequent installments, *The Twilight Zone* would rely on this same formula of an ordinary human being suddenly beset by extraordinary circumstances. Quite frequently there was an unexpected twist at the denouement that cast the strange events in a new or supernatural light. To provide context and codify the cosmic significance of the events, Serling himself provided opening and closing narration, usually on camera in an immaculate Kuppenheimer suit.

SERIES' WRITERS

To supply these dark melodramas from week to week, *The Twilight Zone* relied upon a stable of writers seasoned in the macabre arts of science fiction and fantasy. Along with Serling, short-story veterans Richard Matheson and Charles Beaumont formed a creative troika that was responsible for much of the series' high-quality teleplays. Matheson's scripts tended toward more hard-science content, such as the classic "Little Girl Lost," about a child who vanishes through her bedroom wall into another dimension. Beaumont crafted some of the show's more horrific installments, such as the gothic gem "The Howling Man," in which a traveler in Europe happens upon the devil being kept locked up in a cell in a monastery. Other important contributors to the series included George Clayton Johnson, Montgomery Pittman, Earl Hamner Jr., Reginald Rose, and Ray Bradbury.

It was the workaholic Serling, however, who took on the bulk of the creative burden. All told, Serling would write 92 of the 156 broadcast episodes. His influence over the show was especially keen during the first three seasons,

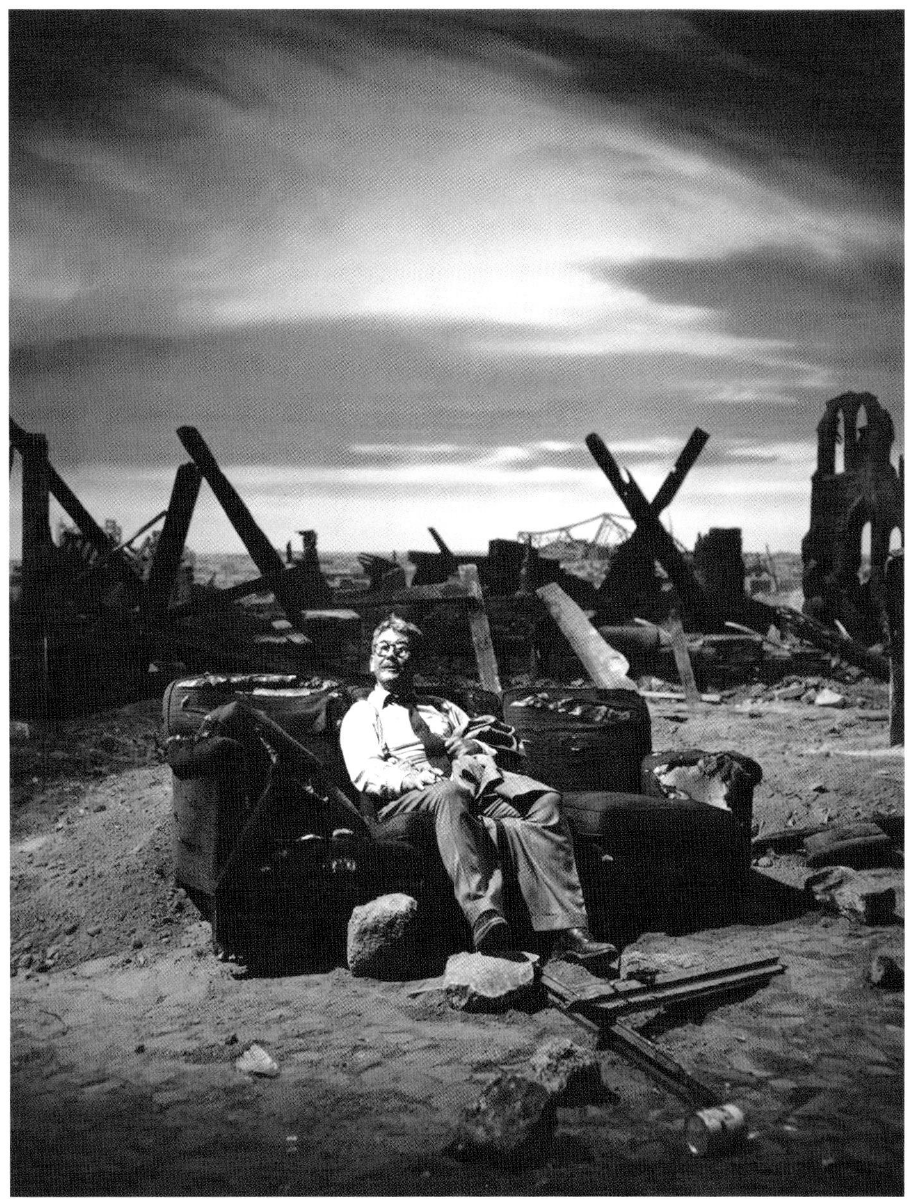

Twilight Zone. *Burgess Meredith plays the last man left alive after a nuclear explosion in a 1959 episode of* The Twilight Zone *titled "Time Enough at Last."* CBS PHOTO ARCHIVE/CONTRIBUTOR/ GETTY IMAGES.

when he personally penned some of the program's signature installments. "Eye of the Beholder" addresses people's perceptions of beauty through the eyes of a bandaged and disfigured young woman whom viewers see revealed in a shocking climax. "Mirror Image" explores the nature of identity when a woman waiting in a bus station is suddenly confronted by her exact double. And the chilling "The Obsolete Man" touches on Cold War themes in relating the last days of a librarian of the future condemned to death for defending the utility of books.

Episodes like these allowed Serling to fulfill his vision of commenting on existential and political themes without incurring the wrath of advertisers and network executives. But the show's social concern also emboldened him to write all too pontifically at times, a problem that was exacerbated by his heavy workload. Too many of his episodes were written in a rush of sanctimony, with long, windy speechifying from the central characters on the major issues of the day. Even the many gems could not spare the program from lukewarm public interest.

POOR SHOWING

The Twilight Zone was never a hit in the ratings and was in danger of cancellation by CBS almost from the start. At the end of the third season, the network elected to expand the show to an hour in hopes that that might change its fortunes. The quality of the scripts suffered, however, with many seeming interminably padded at the new running time. After a desultory fifth season, during which most of the series best creative talent left, the show was finally canceled.

The Twilight Zone may have ended in 1964, but its influence continued to grow. Many of the show's writers, such as Matheson, took their talents to the big screen. Others remained to work in television. Hamner, who wrote several episodes for *The Twilight Zone* set in the rural backwoods, went on to create *The Waltons*, the long-running cornpone drama on CBS.

Fittingly, Serling remained the busiest of all. He cowrote the screenplay for *Planet of the Apes* in 1968, among other theatrical ventures. He also released a series of short-story adaptations of his classic *Twilight Zone* teleplays. Serling's talents, however, remained best suited for the small screen. He hosted a very *Twilight Zone*–like anthology series, *Night Gallery*, from 1970 to 1973, but network interference eventually drove him out of the medium altogether. He died following complications from open heart surgery on June 28, 1975.

RERUNS AND MOVIE

Long after its network run had ended, *The Twilight Zone* remained a staple of syndicated reruns nationwide. Often aired late at night, it gave the creeps to a whole new generation of insomniacs who had not been around for the initial airings. The show's appeal was so broad that in 1977 *Saturday Night Live* could do a parody of it (with Dan Aykroyd doing a dead-on Serling) that had the audience howling with recognition. Serling's widow even launched a *Twilight Zone* magazine featuring new fiction in the tradition of the series. The time seemed ripe for a major revival of the franchise.

All did not work out as planned, however. In 1983 a *Twilight Zone* movie was released to much anticipation. In keeping with the spirit of the series, producer Steven Spielberg had opted for an anthology format, composed of three remakes of classic *Twilight Zone* installments and a fourth, all-new story. Up-and-coming directors Joe Dante (*The Howling*, 1981), John Landis (*An American Werewolf in London*, 1981), and George Miller (*Mad Max 2: The Road Warrior*, 1981) were brought in to helm three of the segments, with Spielberg handling the fourth.

Despite all that talent, however, and the best efforts of screenwriter Matheson, the result was a tepid mishmash that bombed at the box office. Each of the three remakes was markedly inferior to the original, while Landis's segment, the lone original story, was a sanctimonious misfire, dismissed by the show's aficionados as an unintentional parody of Serling. The fact that actor Vic Morrow was beheaded during filming did little to enhance the picture's public relations cachet and embroiled Landis in a career-threatening lawsuit.

NEW SERIES

Somewhat more successful—artistically, if not commercially—was a new *Twilight Zone* television series, launched in 1985 on CBS. The new show boasted a stellar lineup of creative talent, from Bradbury, Stephen King, and Harlan Ellison on the writers' side to directors such as William Friedkin, Dante, and John Milius. Actor Charles Aidman, who had appeared in two original *Twilight Zone* episodes, assumed Serling's post as narrator/moral contextualizer. A number of topflight episodes were produced, such as Ellison's brilliant "Paladin of the Lost Hour," that recaptured the spirit of the old series. Budget cuts, network interference, and low ratings, however, eventually took their toll, and the series was mothballed for good in 1989.

The UPN network launched yet another version in 2002 with actor Forest Whitaker as host. The show not only dealt with current events but also featured remakes of classic episodes, such as "Monsters Are Due on Maple Street." The show lasted one season but, like the original, was seen in reruns and on DVD.

In 2003 *The Twilight Zone* was ranked number twenty-six in *TV Guide*'s list of the fifty "most entertaining or influential television series in American pop culture." A year later *TV Guide* named the show the eighth most important cult TV show as "a series so unusual that they inspire what can be only called worship." The show's fiftieth anniversary in 2009 brought more acclaim and attention, including a collection of short stories titled *Twilight Zone: 19 Original Stories on the 50th Anniversary* (2009) and a collection of graphic novels from Walker Books for Young Readers.

Four decades after its network debut, *The Twilight Zone* continued to intrigue both the general public and fans of the science fiction/fantasy genre. The phrase "Twilight Zone kind of feeling" entered the popular lexicon as a term for the series' quintessentially eerie sensation of otherworldly alienation. Marathon airings of the episodes generated powerhouse ratings for local syndicated stations, making the syndication package a prized possession within the broadcast industry. Its viability into a second millennium ensured that Serling and his unique vision would remain a permanent marker on the U.S. pop cultural landscape.

Robert E. Schnakenberg

SEE ALSO: *Aykroyd, Dan; Bradbury, Ray; Cold War; Duvall, Robert; Graphic Novels; King, Stephen;* Planet of the Apes*;* Saturday Night Live*; Science Fiction Publishing; Serling, Rod; Spielberg, Steven; Syndication; Television;* TV Guide*;* The Waltons.

BIBLIOGRAPHY

Brode, Douglas, and Carol Serling. *Rod Serling and "The Twilight Zone": The 50th Anniversary Tribute*. Fort Lee, NJ: Barricade Books, 2009.

Presnell, Don, and Marty McGee. *A Critical History of Television's "The Twilight Zone," 1959–1964*. Jefferson, NC: McFarland, 1998.

Stanyard, Stewart. *Dimensions behind "The Twilight Zone": A Backstage Tribute to Television's Groundbreaking Series*. Toronto: ECW Press, 2007.

Wolfe, Peter. *In the Zone: The Twilight World of Rod Serling*. Bowling Green, OH: Bowling Green State University Popular Press, 1997.

Zicree, Marc Scott. *"The Twilight Zone" Companion*. New York: Bantam, 1989.

Twin Peaks

With a quirky mixture of murder mystery, soap opera, film noir, and the avant-garde, *Twin Peaks* rewrote the formula for prime-time television drama in the early 1990s. Created by U.S. filmmaker David Lynch (*The Elephant Man, Blue Velvet, Lost Highway*), *Twin Peaks*, a character-driven show sporting a cast of more than 100, used intricately interwoven subplots to keep viewers tuned in. This unconventional epic revolves around the murder of Laura Palmer, small-town beauty queen, and the investigating FBI agent whose dreams and quasi-Buddhist methods reveal the Black Lodge, a surreal waiting room inhabited by the personification of pure evil known only as BOB. *Twin Peaks* was canceled in 1991 after only thirty episodes.

Tony Brewer

SEE ALSO: Blue Velvet; *Lynch, David.*

BIBLIOGRAPHY

Barney, Richard A. *David Lynch: Interviews*. Jackson: University Press of Mississippi, 2009.

Chion, Michel. *David Lynch*. London: British Film Institute, 1995.

Lynch, Jennifer. *The Secret Diary of Laura Palmer*. New York: Pocket Books, 1990.

Twister

Invented by Reyn Guyer, Twister is a game in which several players reach over, under, and across each other to place their hands and feet on colored circles on a large vinyl game board. Named "Twister" by Milton Bradley, the game was demonstrated on *The Tonight Show* in 1966. While Eva Gabor was on her hands and knees, show host Johnny Carson stood over her and reached for another circle; the sexual innuendo and close physical contact made for controversial television and helped attract American youths to the game. Twister sold thirteen million games in its first year. In 1987, at the University of Massachusetts at Amherst, 4,160 contestants set a record for the number of simultaneous Twister players. In 2011 Twister entered the world of interactive video games with a version for Xbox Kinect in which players twist their bodies into required shapes to pass to the next level.

S. Naomi Finkelstein

SEE ALSO: *Board Games; Carson, Johnny; Milton Bradley;* The Tonight Show*; Toys; Video Games; Xbox Kinect.*

BIBLIOGRAPHY

Hoffman, David. *Kid Stuff: Great Toys*. New York: Chronicle Books, 1996.

Twitter

Since its introduction in 2006, Twitter has become one of the most popular and dynamic communication tools of the twenty-first century. Part social networking site, part microblogging service, Twitter is the engine of a vast online space known as the "twittersphere" or "twitterverse," where users post and read short text-based messages of 140 characters or less called "tweets."

RAPID EARLY GROWTH

Sometimes described as the SMS (short message service) of the Internet, Twitter gained popularity in 2007 when it was used as part of the South by Southwest festival, a film and music festival held annually in Austin, Texas. Screens set up at the conference allowed people to see the messages being sent by other users in real time. Twitter rapidly gained worldwide popularity, with more than 300 million users as of 2011, and it generated more than 300 million tweets and handled more than 1.6 billion search queries per day.

In a 2009 *Time* article, Steven Johnson described the simplicity of Twitter as a medium: "As a social network, Twitter revolves around the principle of followers. . . . If you follow 20 people, you'll see a mix of tweets scrolling down the page: breakfast-cereal updates, interesting new links, music recommendations, even musings on the future of education." On the choice of the service's name, founder Jack Dorsey said, "It was just perfect. The definition was 'a short burst of inconsequential information,' and 'chirps from birds.' And that's exactly what the product was." Twitter has from its start been criticized as a place for banal commentary from the self-absorbed. To fight the negative image of tweeting, the company changed its question for status updates from "What are you doing?" to "What's happening?" in 2009.

Tweets are publicly visible by default, although senders can add restrictions to their accounts. However, most users can follow anyone they wish, and most messages are visible to anyone, including those who are not subscribed to Twitter. Users can tweet via the Twitter website; via compatible external applications for use on smartphones or web-enabled devices such as iPads; or, in certain countries, via text messages. Because users are forced to write a message no longer than 140 characters, many people use URL-shortening services such as bit.ly or TinyURL and hosting services such as Twitpic to make it easier to link to websites or content with short web addresses. Because URL-shortening services hide the destination address, spam links have proliferated on Twitter because it is easy to fool a user into clicking.

Although all wording in a tweet is searchable (making information on a certain topic or event easy to find), users can facilitate a search by including *hashtags*—words prefixed with a "#" sign, which makes that word a link to all tweets using that hashtag. Users also communicate by preceding a user name with "@" to notify the named users that the message relates to them. This allows users to engage in conversations with other users or recommend people for their followers (sometimes called "tweeps") to read. Traditionally, Twitter users recommend new people to follow on Fridays by using the hashtag #FF (for "follow Friday"). On April 16, 2009, celebrity Ashton Kutcher (@aplusk) became the first user of Twitter to accumulate more than one million followers, beating news outlet CNN (@CNN) in the "Million Followers" contest. "I find it astonishing that one person can actually have as big of a voice online as what an entire media company can on Twitter," Kutcher said after reaching the milestone.

ENABLING REVOLUTION

But Twitter is not just a vehicle for publicity, marketing, celebrity gossip, and individual navel gazing. It has also proved remarkably effective as a tool for grassroots organization and social protest—from the so-called green revolution in Iran following the 2009 elections to the massive, sustained public demonstrations that led to the overthrow of the governments of Tunisia and Egypt in 2010 and 2011, respectively. The governments of Iran and Egypt blocked the service in retaliation. Other countries such as China have taken preemptive action to avoid such Twitter-facilitated uprisings by making the service illegal, and in January 2012 Twitter itself announced that it would comply with a number of governments by blocking tweets deemed offensive or inflammatory in certain countries, while making those tweets available to users elsewhere.

In emergency situations some people use the service as a simple way to get out a constant stream of recent information, although Twitter's well-deserved reputation for outages due to overuse precludes this usage from being efficient. Its biggest use is probably as a virtual water cooler where tweets are exchanged about the latest pop culture event, from the season finale of a favorite show to a celebrity sighting. Conferences, television shows, and bloggers now use hashtags and other Twitter techniques to direct conversations about their brands, hoping to use the power of social media to expand their reach and engage more consumers.

Like the closely related texting, Twitter has faced criticism that it affects people's writing abilities, concentration, and relationships. Certainly many people spend time with their nose to a cell phone or computer screen, and "texting thumb" (a soreness caused by the overuse of the thumb, the digit that many people use to type on a cell phone) has appeared as a term in some newspapers. However, Twitter is a tool that is still at the beginning of its popularity. It could die off, as its critics hope, or it could revolutionize the way people interact and share news and information. Perhaps, as Jonathan Zittrain, professor of Internet law at Harvard Law School has argued, "the qualities that make Twitter seem inane and half-baked are what makes it so powerful."

Kimberlee Diane Keeline

SEE ALSO: *Blogging; Cell Phones; CNN; Facebook; The Internet; iPad; Kutcher, Ashton; Smartphones; Social Media; Texting.*

BIBLIOGRAPHY

Barkhorn, Eleanor, and Kevin Fallon. "What the 2010 Twitter Top Trending Topics Tell Us about Pop Culture." *Atlantic Monthly*, December 14, 2010.

Cohen, Noam. "Twitter on the Barricades: Six Lessons Learned." *New York Times*, June 20, 2009.

Cross, Mary. *bloggerati, twitterati: How Blogs and Twitter Are Transforming Popular Culture*. Santa Barbara, CA: Praeger, 2011.

Diaz-Ortiz, Claire. *Twitter for Good: Change the World One Tweet at a Time*. San Francisco: Jossey-Bass, 2011.

Hansell, Saul. "Advertisers Are Watching Your Every Tweet." *New York Times*, July 16, 2009.

Johnson, Steven. "How Twitter Will Change the Way We Live." *Time*, June 5, 2009.

Parmelee, John H., and Shannon L. Bichard. *Politics and the Twitter Revolution: How Tweets Influence the Relationship between Political Leaders and the Public*. Lanham, MD: Lexington Books, 2012.

2 Live Crew

2 Live Crew, the primary progenitors of a hip-hop subgenre called Miami Bass, will probably be better remembered for their important legal battles than for their music. Their sexually explicit songs that objectified women and featured relatively simple bass-driven beats drew the attention of many conservative law-enforcement officials in their hometown of Miami as well as elsewhere. 2 Live Crew's legal perils during the late 1980s and early 1990s opened up debates about censorship and made them unwitting proponents of free speech.

Foreshadowing the legal battles over intellectual property that dogged the group a few years later, the group's first legal confrontation involved the appropriation of the name "Luke Skywalker" as a stage name by the group's leader (born Luther Campbell, December 22, 1960). Lucasfilm, the owner of the *Star Wars* trilogy trademark, promptly sued 2 Live Crew when they began to find aboveground exposure and their second album, *Move Somethin'* (1987), had reached number 68 on the Billboard pop chart. As a result, Campbell's stage and record company names were shortened to "Luke" and "Luke Records." The album that gained the most attention, though, was *As Nasty as They Wanna Be* (1989), which reached the pop album charts' Top 40 and spawned a hit single, "Me So Horny." In spite of or perhaps partly because of its many detractors, from law-enforcement officials and right-wing Christian groups to music critics, *As Nasty as They Wanna Be* sold over two million copies.

Enraged by the explicit content of 2 Live Crew's music, an attorney named Jack Thompson launched an all-out war against the group, culminating in a Broward County, Florida, judge deeming the album obscene under state law in March 1990. Soon after, a record store owner in Ft. Lauderdale, Florida, and another in Huntsville, Alabama, were arrested by local sheriff departments for violating obscenity laws. Around the same time, 2 Live Crew was arrested for performing songs from *As Nasty as They Wanna Be* in a Florida nightclub, and alternative band Too Much Joy, when visiting in the same area, was arrested for performing songs from that album in an act of protest. These events escalated into a full-scale debate within the media over free speech and First Amendment protection, with radio and television talk show pundits arguing over 2 Live Crew's social and musical merits.

The two record store retailers were eventually acquitted, as were 2 Live Crew and Too Much Joy. In one case, a jury even sought to deliver their "not guilty" verdict as a rap. In May 1992 the 1990 Florida obscenity ruling was reversed by the U.S. Court of Appeals for the Eleventh Circuit, and the U.S. Supreme Court refused to hear an appeal. But 2 Live Crew's legal woes were not over, as they faced another suit over the unauthorized sampling of Roy Orbison's "Oh Pretty Woman." The owners of the song's copyright, Acuff-Rose, argued that 2 Live Crew's use of the song devalued the original's worth. After a protracted legal battle, the U.S. Supreme Court ruled in 1994 that 2 Live Crew's sampling constituted legal fair use under copyright law. In a time dominated by easy access to digital recording and transferring technology, this was seen as a significant ruling by legal scholars.

After the *As Nasty ss They Wanna Be* scandal, 2 Live Crew milked the wave of publicity for a couple of minor hit albums

2 Live Crew. *The members of 2 Live Crew included, from left, Chris Wong Won, Luther Campbell, David Hobbs, and Mark Roth.* MICHAEL OCHS ARCHIVES/STRINGER/GETTY IMAGES.

in 1990 and 1991 (*Banned in the USA* and *Sports Weekend*). Soon after, however, the group's mainstream success fizzled, and the original lineup disbanded. Luke became a solo artist, periodically releasing albums on his own label. In 2010 the group reunited for an evening when they were recognized at the seventh annual VH1 Hip Hop Honors.

Kembrew McLeod

SEE ALSO: *Hip-Hop; Orbison, Roy; Rap;* Star Wars.

BIBLIOGRAPHY

Campbell, Luther. *As Nasty as They Wanna Be: The Uncensored Story of Luther Campbell of the 2 Live Crew*. Kingston, Jamaica: Kingston Publishers, 1992.

Price, Emmett George. *Encyclopedia of African American Music*. Vol. 2. Oxford, UK: Greenwood Press, 2010.

Shabazz, Julian L. D. *The United States of America vs. Hip-Hop*. Hampton, VA: United Brothers, 1992.

2001: A Space Odyssey

In 1964 film director Stanley Kubrick approached science fiction writer Arthur C. Clarke seeking a plot for "the proverbial good science fiction movie." They worked together to craft a story inspired by Clarke's short story "The Sentinel," in which an astronaut discovers a mysterious pyramid on the moon. As Clarke wrote a novel derived from their script, Kubrick created a unique movie that continues to amaze and frustrate viewers, the 1968 MGM film *2001: A Space Odyssey*.

SYNOPSIS

The film presents an abbreviated and speculative version of human evolution. The story opens at "The Dawn of Man" as prehuman man-apes discover a large, upright black slab. The apes are drawn to the monolith as it sings to them. After this, one ape, Moon-Watcher (Daniel Richter), discovers that a bone can be used as a club and learns how to use the club's power to acquire food and to dominate the emerging ape society. The setting shifts in one of the most famous cuts in film history: Moon-

2001: A Space Odyssey. *Keir Dullea plays astronaut Dave Bowman in Stanley Kubrick's science fiction cult classic* 2001: A Space Odyssey. MGM/THE KOBAL COLLECTION.

Watcher tosses his club into the air; as it falls, the club suddenly transforms into a spaceship sliding through space.

The plot now focuses on Heywood Floyd (William Sylvester), an official with the National Astronautics Council, who is traveling to the moon to investigate a mysterious black monolith discovered there. The monolith had obviously been created by intelligent extraterrestrial beings and was deliberately buried in a lunar crater. When Floyd arrives at the monolith, it emits a piercing shriek.

The setting shifts again to the *Discovery*, a spaceship en route to Jupiter. The ship carrying three scientists in suspended animation is staffed by astronauts Dave Bowman (Keir Dullea) and Frank Poole (Gary Lockwood) and the HAL 9000 computer (voice of Douglas Rain). After a mysterious equipment failure, Dave and Frank become suspicious of the supposedly infallible HAL. The astronauts conspire to disconnect HAL, but the all-seeing computer learns of their plot. HAL murders the sleeping scientists, sets Frank adrift in space, and traps Dave outside the ship. After he manages to reboard the *Discovery* via an airlock, Dave dismantles HAL's memory, reducing the computer to infancy and, finally, death.

As HAL's red eye goes black, a video begins to play in which Floyd explains the *Discovery*'s secret mission. The moon monolith's shriek had been a transmission aimed at Jupiter, and the *Discovery* had been sent in search of the signal's destination. In the film's final segment ("Jupiter and beyond the Infinite"), Dave flies a pod toward a monolith floating in space near Jupiter and is transported through a star gate (depicted as a psychedelic lightshow) into a surreal, symbolic world where he ages and dies in ornate but sterile white rooms. His death seems to produce a celestial fetus, the next stage in human evolution.

RESPONSE FROM CRITICS

The film polarized the critics; their responses tended to be either strongly positive or strongly negative. The film was daringly different from other major studios' big-budget releases. It did not have a clear story line or a central protagonist. There was little dialogue, and it was deliberately innocuous. Overall *2001* presented a cold universe in which humans behave like passionless automatons and in which the most sympathetic character is the homicidal computer HAL.

Some critics heralded *2001* as a step forward in the art of filmmaking. For example, Mike Steele, reporting in the *Minneapolis Tribune*, called *2001* a step "closer to the purity of the film" and away from a sequential story line imposed by literary aesthetics. Other critics found the movie to be a confusing muddle. In the *Village Voice*, Andrew Sarris deemed the movie a "thoroughly uninteresting failure" and the ending "an exercise in mystifying abstract fantasy in the open temple of High Art." As *2001* found its audience, several critics who had panned it wrote second reviews to reassess the movie's merits under a different set of criteria. Sarris, however, wrote a second review only to say that his opinion had not changed.

Despite the confusion and disfavor of many viewers, *2001* quickly gained the status of a "cult film," a movie that inspires fanatical devotion in a relatively small audience. For science fiction fans it is a realistic depiction of space travel. No other movie in the genre before or since has remained so true to the laws of physics. For film buffs it presents a dazzling experiment with the elements of filmmaking. Although viewers accustomed to conventional American movies may bemoan the long sequences of play with sight and sound, which do not advance a linear plot, lovers of the filmmaker's art delight as a spaceship and a space station waltz to Johann Strauss's *The Blue Danube*.

For devotees of the hallucinogenic drug culture, the surreal imagery, particularly in the final segment, was "The Ultimate Trip" promised by the tagline of a 1974 rerelease. The film remains an active part of the popular imagination and is often imitated, referenced, and parodied in various media. In the 1996 film *Independence Day* for example, David Levinson (played by Jeff Goldblum) opens his laptop, and HAL's red eye appears on its screen.

UNANSWERED QUESTIONS

Kubrick succeeded in offering the "proverbial good science fiction movie" because *2001* addresses universal, eternal questions: What is the meaning of life? What is the nature of God? What is the destiny of humanity? Are we alone in the universe? What is the relationship between humans and their machines? One of the aspects of the movie that frustrates viewers is that Kubrick provides no clear answers to these questions, but the nature of the questions is that they are unanswerable. As Clarke put it, "If you understood *2001* completely, we failed. We wanted to raise far more questions than we answered."

The film poses ancient questions in a relatively new language, science, and in a new medium, film. The extraterrestrial monoliths seem to be guiding human evolution; thus, they serve as a metaphor for the hand of God or destiny. However, *2001* explores theological issues outside of the framework of any religion or established mythology. The film forces its audience to rethink the assumptions such a framework might provide.

Perhaps the most memorable ingredient of *2001* is HAL, the fullest development of the film's sequence of human tools that begins with the bone club. One of the major issues of science fiction has been whether a machine capable of independent thought would be "human." In *2001* HAL is a terrifying monster, but he also seems to be more human than the humans. The audience cannot help but find the computer sympathetic as he begs for his life and it becomes apparent that he only killed out of fear. As interaction with computers increasingly becomes a part of everyday life, HAL remains a powerful symbol of both the peril and the promise of artificial intelligence.

Fans have noticed that if each letter of HAL is replaced by the next letter in the alphabet, HAL becomes IBM (Clarke denies that this was intentional). In 1997 (the year HAL was supposedly created), David Stork published a collection of essays, *Hal's Legacy: 2001's Computer as Dream and Reality*, in which scientists explore how close current technology comes to creating a HAL 9000.

Christian L. Pyle

SEE ALSO: *Clarke, Arthur C.; Conspiracy Theories; Cult Films; IBM (International Business Machines); Kubrick, Stanley; LSD; MGM (Metro-Goldwyn-Mayer); NASA.*

BIBLIOGRAPHY

Agel, Jerome, ed. *The Making of Kubrick's "2001."* New York: New American Library, 1970.

Bizony, Piers. *"2001": Filming the Future.* London: Aurum Press, 1994.

Clarke, Arthur C. *The Lost Worlds of "2001."* New York: New American Library, 1972.

Clarke, Arthur C., and Stanley Kubrick. *2001: A Space Odyssey.* New York: New American Library, 1968.

Coyle, Wallace. *Stanley Kubrick: A Guide to References and Resources.* Boston: G. K. Hall, 1980.

Geduld, Carolyn. *Filmguide to "2001: A Space Odyssey."* Bloomington: Indiana University Press, 1973.

Stork, David G., ed. *Hal's Legacy: 2001's Computer as Dream and Reality.* Cambridge, MA: MIT Press, 1997.

Whittington, William. *Sound Design & Science Fiction.* Austin: University of Texas Press, 2007.

Tyler, Anne *(1941–)*

Anne Tyler, a novelist who has received much critical and popular acclaim, is known for her insightful, often comic depictions of family relationships and ordinary life. Her novels, the best of which include *Dinner at the Homesick Restaurant* (1982), *The Accidental Tourist* (1985), and *Breathing Lessons* (1988), have won the Pulitzer Prize and the National Book Critics' Circle Award. (*The Accidental Tourist* was adapted into a film.) More recent works include *A Patchwork Planet* (1998), *Back When We Were Grownups* (2001), and *The Beginner's Goodbye* (2012). A longtime resident of Baltimore, Maryland, where she often sets her novels, Tyler is viewed by many as a southern novelist, largely because of her concern with family, home, and place.

James Schiff

SEE ALSO: *Best Sellers.*

BIBLIOGRAPHY

Bail, Paul. *Anne Tyler: A Critical Companion.* Westport, CT: Greenwood Press, 1998.

Croft, Robert W. *An Anne Tyler Companion.* Westport, CT: Greenwood Press, 1998.

Evans, Elizabeth. *Anne Tyler.* New York: Twayne, 1993.

Petry, Alice Hall. *Understanding Anne Tyler.* Columbia: University of South Carolina Press, 1990.

Petry, Alice Hall, ed. *Critical Essays on Anne Tyler.* New York: G. K. Hall, 1992.

Salwak, Dale, ed. *Anne Tyler as Novelist.* Iowa City: University of Iowa Press, 1994.

Stephens, C. Ralph, ed. *The Fiction of Anne Tyler.* Jackson: University Press of Mississippi, 1990.

Tyson, Mike *(1966–)*

Born in Brooklyn and educated in the pugilistic arts on the New York streets, Mike Tyson became history's youngest world boxing champion at age twenty and an ex-con by age thirty. From the start of his professional career in 1985, he displayed contradictions of character that drew controversy. An efficient powerhouse of a fighter, he suffered from an inability to control his anger, which sidelined his career more than once. When he bit off pieces of an opponent's ears during one heated match, many thought it was the end of his boxing career. However, he proved as skilled at comebacks as at knockouts, and even after his retirement from boxing in 2006, he has continued to appear on film and television as one of the world's most awe-inspiring and enigmatic athletes.

EARLY LIFE AND CAREER

Raised in a poor African American household by a single mother on welfare, Tyson was both powerfully built and filled with rage. He made money by mugging and purse snatching, and by the time he was thirteen, he had been arrested thirty-eight times. He ended up at the Tryon School for Boys in Catskill, New York, where he met ex-boxer Bobby Stewart, who recognized the tough youngster's fighting talent. Stewart introduced Tyson to Cus D'Amato, a visionary trainer who had worked with boxing champions Floyd Patterson and José Torres, and D'Amato soon began honing Tyson's natural talent.

Even with a champion trainer, Tyson's amateur career was only mildly distinguished. He competed in trials for the 1984 Olympics and earned a place on the team as an alternate. But in 1985, when he entered the professional arena, he proved he could steamroll opponents. For the next four years he won every fight he entered, most with knockouts and most in the first round. By 1986 he was world heavyweight champion.

Mike Tyson. *Despite the demise of his boxing career and his tumultuous personal life, Mike Tyson has maintained his celebrity.* JASON LAVERIS/CONTRIBUTOR/FILMMAGIC/GETTY IMAGES.

Two years later, at the height of his glory days, he married actress Robin Givens, and the couple received an onslaught of attention from tabloid and television reporters. The fairy-tale union did not last long. Givens confessed in a television interview with reporter Barbara Walters that Tyson abused her and that life with him was "pure hell," and the couple divorced in 1989.

CONTROVERSY AND DEFEAT

In 1990 "Iron Mike" suffered his first professional defeat. Displaying the inconsistency fans would later come to expect of him, the heavyweight champ lost his title to Buster Douglas, a virtual unknown with 50–1 odds. Disaster struck again in 1992 when Tyson was convicted of rape and sentenced to six years in prison. Although he persistently denied the charge, he served three years in a minimum-security facility and converted to Islam.

Tyson emerged from lockup, declaring he was a changed man and immediately resuming his boxing career. He continued to win matches, often within an embarrassingly short time. Fans who paid up to $1,500 to watch him fight the hopelessly outclassed Peter McNeeley in 1995 were disgruntled when the fight lasted less than a minute and a half. By 1996 Tyson had regained the World Boxing Council and World Boxing Association heavyweight titles, and working with flamboyant boxing promoter Don King, he negotiated one of the most lucrative boxing contracts in history, with the Las Vegas MGM Grand Hotel and Showtime Entertainment Television.

But the comeback success did not last long. The boxing world and the public reeled in shock and disgust when he lost control in a 1997 rematch with Evander Holyfield, who had previously beaten him, and bit off pieces of both of Holyfield's ears. Ear-biting jokes became a television staple, and Tyson's boxing license was suspended for life. However, after eighteen months of therapy and anger counseling, he approached the boxing commissions in New Jersey and Nevada with assurances that he had mended his ways. Both organizations voted him mentally fit, and he returned to the ring.

However, he continued to be plagued by the consequences of his uncontrolled rage. In 1999 he was sentenced to another year in jail for violating parole by assaulting two motorists after an automobile accident. Released after just three and a half months, he continued his string of impressive knockouts in 2000 and 2001, despite being noticeably out of shape and several steps slower than he was in his prime. His 2002 heavyweight championship bout with Lennox Lewis was steeped in prefight theatrics: Tyson notoriously proclaimed, "I want to eat his children," and the two brawled at a press conference designed to promote the event. A record pay-per-view television audience tuned in to see Lewis knock out a visibly drained Tyson in the eighth round.

A NEW FACE

Following a painful divorce from second wife Monica Turner, Tyson retuned to the ring in 2003 to face Clifford Etienne. Although he knocked out Etienne in forty-nine seconds, it was his new tattoo—a tribal design that covered the left side of his face—that made headlines. Amid rumors of his declining mental state and dwindling finances, he filed for bankruptcy in August 2003 and embarked on a series of unsanctioned and exhibition fights in mid-decade to pay his outstanding debts.

After retiring in 2006, he was arrested for DUI near his home in Phoenix, Arizona, and began treatment for various drug addictions. He emerged calmer and more stable than he had been in years, becoming a vegan and spending much of his time tending to racing pigeons, a hobby of his since his teenage years. His gentler, more subdued persona brought him renewed attention late in the decade as the subject of director James Toback's critically acclaimed documentary *Tyson* (2008). The former fighter also made a celebrated cameo appearance in the hit film *The Hangover* (2009) and its 2011 sequel and signed a deal for an Animal Planet network reality show about pigeon racing, *Taking on Tyson* (2011).

But tragedy struck in May 2009 when his four-year-old daughter Exodus suffocated after being accidentally tangled up in exercise equipment. Tyson's ability to handle the heartbreak without resorting to drug use or profanity-laden public tirades indicated to some that he was becoming a new man. He married girlfriend Lakiha Spicer in a private ceremony just two weeks after Exodus's death, and the couple renewed their vows in a more joyous celebration in 2011.

Over two decades of an intense and dramatic boxing career, Tyson fought only 217 rounds. Out of 58 fights, he won 50, 44 of which ended in knockouts. He was inducted into the International Boxing Hall of Fame on June 12, 2011. The press and the public have tended either to glorify him as the poor kid who made good or to demonize him as a thug and a felon. His method of channeling his deep anger at life into boxing have garnered him unprecedented success and deep ignominy. Five-foot, 11 inches and weighing around 220 pounds, Tyson's incongruously soft and high voice hints at a gentle core overlaid by years of depression, defensiveness, and rage. Perhaps this ambiguous combination of qualities is what keeps the public coming back for the next chapter in the "Iron Mike" saga.

Tina Gianoulis

SEE ALSO: *Boxing; Cable TV; Divorce; Holyfield, Evander; Las Vegas; Olympics; Reality Television; Sex Scandals; Tabloid Television; Tabloids; Tattoos; Television; Walters, Barbara.*

BIBLIOGRAPHY

Cashmore, Ernest. *Mike Tyson: Nurture of the Beast*. Oxford, UK: Polity, 2005.

Hoffer, Richard. *A Savage Business: The Comeback and Comedown of Mike Tyson*. New York: Simon & Schuster, 1998.

Jordan, June. "Requiem for the Champ." *Progressive*, February 1992, 15.

Kluck, Ted. *Facing Tyson: Fifteen Fighters, Fifteen Stories*. Edinburgh: Mainstream, 2008.

Rendall, Jonathan. *Scream: The Real Mike Tyson*. London: HarperSport, 2006.

Samuels, Allison, and Mark Starr. "Will He Get Up?" *Newsweek*, June 30, 1997, 80.

U

Ueckers, Bob *(1935–)*

No baseball player built more around a lifetime batting average of .200 than sportscaster/humorist Bob Uecker. The former catcher for three National League teams—dubbed "Mr. Baseball" by Johnny Carson—parlayed his limited on-field abilities into a lucrative second career, becoming visible through his play-by-play commentary, roles in sitcoms and movies, and series of commercial endorsements. "Anybody with ability can play in the big leagues," he once remarked. "But to be able to trick people year in and year out the way I did, I think that's a much greater feat."

A Milwaukee native, Uecker was signed by the hometown Braves (National League pennant winners in 1957 and 1958) for $3,000. "That bothered my dad at the time," Uecker later joked, "because he didn't have that kind of money to pay out." Contrary to his public persona, Uecker actually hit very well in the Braves' minor league system, batting over .300 in three different seasons. In 1962 he joined the parent Braves, where he was used for his defensive skills.

During the 1964 season, Uecker was traded to the St. Louis Cardinals and was part of a World Series team. "I made a major contribution to the Cardinals' pennant drive," he told Johnny Carson. "I came down with hepatitis. The trainer injected me with it." Before the first game of the World Series, Uecker stole a tuba from a Dixieland band and used it to catch outfield flies during batting practice. Teammate Tim McCarver later credited Uecker's infectious humor with the Cardinals' upset win over the Yankees in the series: "If Bob Uecker had not been on the Cardinals, then it's questionable whether we could have beaten the Yankees." Uecker practiced play-by-play commentary by broadcasting into beer cups in the Cardinals' bullpen. ("Beer cups don't criticize," he later observed.) Although Uecker's offensive skills were weak, he had his greatest batting success, ironically, with the top pitcher of his generation, Sandy Koufax. Uecker was traded to the Philadelphia Phillies in 1966 and retired a year later.

In 1971 Uecker was hired to do play-by-play for the new Milwaukee Brewers team in the American League. He quickly became a fan favorite for his self-deprecating humor as well as his observant commentary. In 1976 he was picked to announce games for ABC's *Monday Night Baseball* program, where he was paired with the ubiquitous Howard Cosell. Cosell, who possessed a large vocabulary and thinly veiled contempt for baseball, was a worthy companion for the unpretentious Uecker. When Cosell asked Uecker to use the word *truculent* in a sentence, Uecker quickly replied, "If you had a truck and I borrowed it, that would be a truck-you-lent." Uecker also became a favorite guest on Johnny Carson's *The Tonight Show*.

Uecker enjoyed popularity as a commercial spokesman for Miller Lite beer in the 1970s and 1980s, poking fun at his athletic inability. In the most famous spot, Uecker was shown in the stands touting Miller Lite while waiting for his complimentary tickets from the team management ("I must be in the front row!"). As the commercial faded to black, Uecker was seen in his free seats—in the uppermost part of the upper deck.

Uecker published a best-selling autobiography titled *Catcher in the Wry* in 1982. From 1985 to 1990, he costarred on the popular ABC situation comedy *Mr. Belvedere*, in which his irreverent sportswriter character proved a perfect foil for Christopher Hewitt's title role of a stuffy, English-born butler. In 1989 he enjoyed his greatest success in *Major League*, a surprise movie comedy hit, as Harry Doyle, the comical announcer for the woebegone Cleveland Indians. Uecker's ironic play-by-play—when Charlie Sheen's pitches land ten rows up in the grandstand, Uecker remarks, "Jusssst a bit outside"—chronicles the Indians' improbable rise to clinch the American League pennant.

Uecker returned to network baseball coverage in 1997, joining Bob Costas and Joe Morgan on NBC's broadcasts of playoff and World Series games. Again, Uecker's self-effacement played well off the erudition of both his colleagues. When asked to describe his greatest moment as a player, Uecker said with pride, "Driving home the winning run by walking with the bases loaded." He was inducted into the National Radio Hall of Fame in 2001 and received the Ford C. Frick Award for broadcasting in 2003 from the National Baseball Hall of Fame, where he accepted the award with a speech that reportedly had George H. W. Bush crying with laughter. The Milwaukee Brewers celebrated Uecker's 50th year in baseball in 2005 by placing the number *50* next to the retired numbers of former stars Paul Molitor and Robin Yount in the team's Ring of Honor.

Andrew Milner

SEE ALSO: *Advertising; Baseball; Beer; Carson, Johnny; Cosell, Howard; Costas, Bob; Radio; Television;* The Tonight Show.

BIBLIOGRAPHY

Green, Lee. *Sportswit*. New York: Harper & Row, 1984.

Shatzkin, Mike. *The Ballplayers: Baseball's Ultimate Biographical Reference*. New York: Arbor House/William Morrow, 1990.

Smith, Curt. *The Storytellers*. New York: Macmillan, 1995.

Uecker, Bob, with Mickey Herskowitz. *Catcher in the Wry*. New York: Putnam, 1982.

UFC/Mixed Martial Arts

Mixed martial arts (MMA) is a combination of multiple styles of hand-to-hand combat, including grappling and striking, that stems from a variety of cultures and disciplines. Some of the martial arts forms implemented are boxing, Brazilian jiu-jitsu, judo, karate, kickboxing, kung fu, tae kwon do, and wrestling. One of the first mixed forms of martial arts was exhibited in the ancient Greek Olympics in a sport called "pankration," which loosely translates to "all powers." Many mixed forms of martial arts have developed since that time, but several key predecessors stand out as inspiration for the contemporary sport of mixed martial arts.

INTRODUCTION TO THE UNITED STATES

The French kickboxing style savate, the Hawaiian hybrid form of kajukenbo, and Bruce Lee's jeet kune do are all examples of hybrid martial arts that combine multiple forms for overall effectiveness. The person credited with bringing mixed martial arts to the United States is Royce Gracie, whose uncle Carlos developed a mixed style of Brazilian jiu-jitsu called Vale Tudo in the 1920s and initiated a series of competitions known as the "Gracie Challenge" when he boasted that he could beat any contender.

Royce Gracie moved to the United States in the 1980s and invited his older brother, Rorion, to help him teach martial arts. Rorion helped organize the first Ultimate Fighting Championship (UFC) tournament in Denver, Colorado, on November 12, 1993, with entrepreneur Art Davie and filmmaker John Milius. Similar events had been held in Japan since 1989, but this was the first U.S. event, with eight competitors, fewer rules, and no time constraints. Among the athletes competing for the $50,000 prize were savate champion Gerard Gordeau, grappler Ken Shamrock, renowned kickboxer Patrick Smith, and Vale Tudo practitioner Royce. Royce won the competition, beating three of his opponents in only five minutes. The pay-per-view event drew more than 86,000 viewers.

As MMA gained popularity throughout the 1990s, more rules were introduced, time constraints were instituted, and more competitions were held. At one point there were multiple MMA competitions, including contests held by the Ultimate Fighting Championship, Strikeforce, Affliction Entertainment, and Japan's Pride Fighting Championship. Eventually the UFC dominated the market and absorbed much of its competition, but it allowed Strikeforce to operate as a distinct entity and run different fight cards. In 2001 a set of MMA rules was developed by the Association of Boxing Commissions that defined medical considerations and prohibited substances; established different weight classes; regulated fight lengths; and standardized the method for determining a winner by knockout, submission, or point count.

MMA drew instant criticism from public officials who deemed the sport brutal, dangerous, and violent. One of the main critics was Senator John McCain, a former navy boxer, who called for an immediate boycott of the sport, likening it to "human cockfighting." Despite public perception, as of 2012 there have only been two recorded deaths in sanctioned American matches, occurring in small venues in Texas (2007) and South Carolina (2010). Medical studies have been inconclusive and, at times, contradictory, but most indicated that boxing may be more dangerous than MMA due to the amount of striking blows that can cause traumatic brain injuries. As the sport gained popularity, controversy died down and UFC gained cultural acceptance on the same level as boxing, wrestling, and martial arts.

Strikeforce held the first women's match in 2006, and by 2009 female competitions were included as a part its main event fights. In spite of women's success on the Strikeforce card, UFC has maintained that its bouts will remain strictly male. The UFC Hall of Fame was established in 2003 and as of 2012 has eight inductees: Mark Coleman, Randy Couture, Royce Gracie, Matt Hughes, Charles Lewis, Chuck Liddell, Dan Severn, and Shamrock.

UFC AS ENTERTAINMENT

In 2005 Spike TV launched a reality TV show called *The Ultimate Fighter*, where unsponsored MMA fighters vie for a six-figure UFC contract. The accessibility of the show took the sport from an occasional pay-per-view event to a regular, weekly format that skyrocketed its popularity. In 2011 the UFC signed a seven-year contract with Fox to promote more than sixty events on their prime-time and cable channels, including *The Ultimate Fighter*, live MMA events, and various other special programming.

As of 2012 UFC programming is shown in 130 countries worldwide. Since the first UFC in 1993, there have been more than 200 UFC-sponsored events held in forty-six U.S. states and more than ten countries. In a testament to the sport's popularity, there are nearly a dozen video games; hundreds of different action figures; and countless trading cards, music albums, and fight DVDs. MMA fighters such as Liddell and Roger Huerta have appeared on the covers of *Sports Illustrated* and *ESPN Magazine*. Liddell also made a cameo appearance on HBO's *Entourage* (2004–2011), picking a fight with one of the show's main characters. Nigel "The UK Hammer" Hudson appeared on MTV's *Jackass* (2000–2002) series, knocking out Ryan Dunn in the ring. UFC competitor Quinton "Rampage" Jackson made the leap to the big screen when he was cast in the movie remake of *The A-Team* (2010) as B. A. Baracus, a role originally played by Mr. T.

In 2009 the reality TV show *Bully Beatdown*, hosted by UFC fighter Jason "Mayhem" Miller, premiered on MTV. The show pits real-life bullies in the ring against professional fighters to earn up to $10,000 if they can last two rounds. The unexplained twist is that the bullies have to give the money to their victims, who are watching the entire scene unfold. The history of UFC/MMA has also been covered in four documentaries focusing on the sport: *Jens Pulver: Driven* (2011), *Once I Was a Champion* (2011), *Cagefighter* (2012), and *History of MMA* (2012). Fictional MMA films include Bruce Lee's final film, *Enter the Dragon* (1973), *Blood and Bone* (2009), and *Warrior* (2011).

Ron Horton

SEE ALSO: *Boxing; Cable TV; ESPN;* Jackass*; Kung Fu; Lee, Bruce; Martial Arts; MTV; Olympics; Reality Television;* Sports Illustrated*; Toys; Video Games.*

BIBLIOGRAPHY

Gerbasi, Thomas. *UFC Encyclopedia*. Indianapolis, IN: DK/Brady Games, 2011.

Kraus, Erich, and Bret Aita. *Brawl: A Behind-the-Scenes Look at*

Mixed Martial Arts Competition. Toronto: ECW Press, 2002.

Snowden, Jonathan, and Kendall Shields. *The MMA Encyclopedia*. Toronto: ECW Press, 2010.

Whiting, Jim. *A New Generation of Warriors: The History of Mixed Martial Arts*. Mankato, MN: Capstone Press, 2010.

UFOs (Unidentified Flying Objects)

The concept of the unidentified flying object (UFO), ostensibly the vehicle of choice for alien visitors from outer space, originated in the United States in the 1940s. Over the course of the following decades, the concept of UFOs continued to attract a sizable cult of adherents, who were stimulated by the phenomenon's embodiment of both antigovernment social protest and romantic secular humanism.

The first mass sightings in the United States of flying objects of unknown origin occurred in 1896 when a number of people from California to the Midwest reported seeing mysterious aircraft. According to reports, they were dirigible-like machines that featured a host of intense colored lights. Two additional waves of sightings were reported in 1909 and 1910. During World War II several Allied pilots claimed to have spotted glowing objects that paced their airplanes. By and large, people attributed the reported sightings to optical illusions, misinterpreted or unknown natural phenomena, or top-secret military vehicles not known to the public.

EARLY FERVOR

A rash of sightings between 1947 and 1949 radically recast public perceptions of UFOs. A celebrated incident in which pilot Kenneth Arnold allegedly intercepted nine saucerlike objects flying at incredible speeds over Mount Rainier in Washington State put UFOs on the front pages of newspapers across the country. A landmark *True* magazine article by Donald Keyhoe titled "The Flying Saucers Are Real" postulated that UFOs, such as those encountered by Arnold, were actually extraterrestrial spaceships. Pulp magazines and Hollywood producers seized upon this image, and, not long after the publication of the article in 1949, the UFO as an alien vehicle became the dominant public interpretation of these phenomena. The shift in public perception was accompanied by a massive increase in the number of UFO sightings.

The government quickly became involved, inaugurating committees to investigate the sightings. The U.S. Air Force's Project Sign, which began its work in 1948, concluded that UFOs were real but were easily explained and not extraordinary. UFOs, the committee concluded, were not extraterrestrial spaceships but rather astronomical objects and weather balloons. Amid the growing public obsession with UFOs, a second project, Grudge, published similar findings but engendered little public belief.

The CIA-sponsored Robertson panel, named after H. P. Robertson, a director in the office of the secretary of the U.S. Defense Department, convened in January 1953 and drastically changed the nature of the involvement of the air force in the UFO controversy. Before this time, the government had sought the cause of sightings. The Robertson panel charged the air force with keeping sighting reports at a minimum, and the air force never again conducted a program of thorough investigations in regard to UFOs. The main thrust of its efforts became public relations, and government officials embarked on a series of educational programs aimed at reducing the gullibility of the

UFOs in 1952 Massachusetts. *Mysterious lights hover in the sky over Salem, Massachusetts, in July 1952, a time when many reports of UFOs were made across the United States.* AP IMAGES.

public on matters related to UFOs. This policy remained largely unchanged over the following decades.

Much to the government's consternation, adherents to the extraterrestrial theory formed a host of organizations that disseminated the beliefs of the UFO community through newsletters and journals. Among these groups were the Civilian Saucer Committee, the Cosmic Brotherhood Association, and the Citizens against UFO Secrecy. Some of the larger organizations funded UFO studies and coordinated lobbying efforts to convince the U.S. Congress to declassify UFO-related government documents.

In the eyes of many UFO fanatics, government officials were conspiring to shield information on extraterrestrial UFOs for fear of mass panic such as that following Orson Welles's famed *War of the Worlds* radio broadcast that many listeners mistook for an actual attack on the United States. The government-conspiracy theory took many forms, ranging from the belief in secret underground areas—most notably the mythical Area 51 in Nevada where, allegedly, alien bodies recovered from UFO crashes were preserved—to the concept of "men in black," government officials who silenced those who had come in contact with UFOs and aliens.

EVOLVING PERCEPTIONS

As the UFO craze continued through the 1970s, a host of reputable citizens stepped forward to say that they had witnessed a UFO. For example, Jimmy Carter, while governor of Georgia, made a report of an incident in southern Georgia several years earlier in which he and a group of people had seen an unidentified object in the air that changed colors. Although the object was unidentified, he did not believe that it had anything to do with extraterrestrial aliens nor that extraterrestrials have come to the earth.

The form of the UFO myth changed shape somewhat in the 1980s and 1990s. Individuals began to claim that they not only had seen UFOs but also had been abducted by aliens who performed experiments on them while onboard the spacecraft. Most such individuals offered distinct remembrances of having sperm and eggs removed from their bodies by alien doctors, presumably so that human reproduction could be studied in extraterrestrial laboratories. A 1997 poll indicated that about 50 percent of adult Americans believed in alien abduction theories, and abduction came to supersede sightings of "lights in the sky" as the dominant image associated with UFOs.

In 1997 tens of thousands of visitors flocked to Roswell, New Mexico, in observance of the fiftieth anniversary of the Roswell Incident, in which the government purportedly covered up the existence of a crashed extraterrestrial UFO. Tragically, that same year the Heaven's Gate UFO cult committed mass suicide as part of an effort to gain the attention of a UFO that they believed existed in association with the Hale-Bopp comet. Like other believers in UFOs, the cult placed its hopes and fears about the world in the idea of disk-shaped alien spaceships, but, as scholar Curtis Peebles aptly notes in *Watch the Skies! A Chronicle of the Flying Saucer Myth*, "We watch the skies seeking meaning. In the end, what we find is ourselves."

CULTURAL SIGNIFICANCE

UFOs and aliens have become an indelible part of popular culture. Movies, from *The Day the Earth Stood Still* (1951) to *Close Encounters of the Third Kind* (1977), have long portrayed extraterrestrial visitations via spaceships, and television series such as *The X-Files* and *Unsolved Mysteries* have capitalized on public interest with weekly narratives on encounters with aliens and UFOs. A number of Hollywood's biggest blockbusters, including the box-office smashes *Independence Day* (1996), *Contact* (1997), and *Men in Black* (1997), are standard UFO and alien fare.

Scholars believe that the UFO myth contains religious-like elements that do much to explain its massive appeal. In postulating the existence of superhuman beings by promising deliverance through travel to a better planet and by creating a community fellowship engaged in ritualized activities such as the various UFO conventions popular with believers, the UFO myth embodies much of popular religious belief. At the same time, the UFO myth, with its government-conspiracy dimensions, resonates with an American public increasingly distrustful of its government. UFO "flaps," periods of high numbers of UFO sightings, have corresponded to a number of broadly defined crises in government faith, among them the McCarthy hearings, the Vietnam War, and Watergate.

The search for explanations of UFOs has continued into the twenty-first century, and people still debate whether the Roswell Incident or Area 51 have had anything to do with visitors from other planets. In 2011 the British government released 8,500 pages of formerly classified documents in its files related to supposed UFO sightings. One report concerned six UFOs that had been observed at the same time in 1967. After one was blown up and another taken for analysis, the UFOs were found to be the result of a student prank. Nevertheless, 5 percent of alleged sightings of UFOs in Great Britain have never been explained. The controversy thus persists, and individuals around the world continue to disagree over the existence of UFOs and whether or not they are carrying aliens from outer space.

Scott Tribble

SEE ALSO: *Blockbusters;* Close Encounters of the Third Kind*;* *Conspiracy Theories; Cults;* The Day the Earth Stood Still*;* *Hollywood;* Independence Day*; McCarthyism; Radio; Roswell Incident; Vietnam;* War of the Worlds*; Watergate; Welles, Orson; World War II;* The X-Files.

BIBLIOGRAPHY

Bader, Christopher D.; Frederick Carson Mencken; and Joseph O. Baker. *Paranormal America: Ghost Encounters, UFO Sightings, Bigfoot Hunts, and Other Curiosities in Religion and Culture.* New York: New York University Press, 2010.

Bennett, Jeffrey. *Beyond UFO: The Search for Extraterrestrial Life and Its Astonishing Implications for Our Future.* Princeton, NJ: Princeton University Press, 2008.

Brown, Bridget. *They Know Us Better than We Know Ourselves: The History of Politics of Alien Abduction.* New York: New York University Press, 2007.

Bullard, Thomas E. *The Myth and Mystery of UFOs.* Lawrence: University of Kansas Press, 2010.

Jacobs, David Michael. *The UFO Controversy in America.* Bloomington: Indiana University Press, 1975.

Keyhoe, Donald. *The Flying Saucers Are Real.* New York: Fawcett Publications, 1950.

Peebles, Curtis. *Watch the Skies! A Chronicle of the Flying Saucer*

Myth. Washington, DC: Smithsonian Institution Press, 1994.

Sagan, Carl, and Thornton Page, eds. *UFOs—A Scientific Debate*. Ithaca, NY: Cornell University Press, 1972.

Saler, Benson; Charles A. Zeigler; and Charles B. Moore. *UFO Crash at Roswell: The Genesis of a Modern Myth*. Washington, DC: Smithsonian Institution Press, 1997.

Statt, Nick. "A Brief History of Unsolved Encounters." *Popular Science*, October 2011, 44.

Uggs

In the late 1990s a sheepskin boot without a heel or an arch became a prominent feature of the American style landscape. Reminiscent of Eskimo boots, Uggs actually hailed from the hardy Australian outback, where they protected ranchers from biting cold and sizzling heat because of their unique twin-faced sheepskin construction. (*Ugg* is a generic Australian term for sheepskin boot.) Oddly, given their origins, Uggs are most popular among women and teen girls. If the Ugg is ugly, as some say, it is an ugly duckling that grew into an extraordinary swan of a success story for Deckers Outdoor, the company that bought the brand in 1995.

Deckers acquired the California shoe company Ugg Holdings in 1996 and rapidly turned the Ugg boot into a gold mine through savvy and intensive marketing. Oprah Winfrey featured the boots five times on the "favorite things" segment of her popular talk show, and many movie stars have been snapped by paparazzi while donning the curious sheep-farm work boots. Due to such consistent and influential exposure, Uggs typically represent 92 percent of Deckers' sales. The company, which also makes popular brands such as Crocs and Teva, has seen sales increase 30 percent per year since it bought Ugg. Deckers' stock has risen by an astounding 2,400 percent during that same period.

The extraordinary success of the boot made Deckers CEO Angel Martinez cautious. In anticipation of the inevitable day when people stop buying Ugg boots, he has indicated that the company wants to broaden Ugg brand identification to include sandals and slippers. Yet after almost twenty years the Ugg boot appears to be the kind of golden fleece that every company wishes it had. As long as consumers discern the hidden beauty of Uggs, the humble sheepskin should continue to sell for Deckers.

Isabel Istanders

SEE ALSO: *Advertising; Celebrity; Crocs; Winfrey, Oprah.*

BIBLIOGRAPHY

Abkowitz, Alyssa. "Deckers Finds Its Footing with UGGs." *Fortune*, August 19, 2009.

La Monica, Paul R. "Behind the Brand: The Golden Fleece." CNNMoney, November 22, 2010. Accessed May 2012. Available from http://money.cnn.com/2010/11/22/markets/thebuzz/index.htm

Uncle Miltie

SEE: *Berle, Milton.*

Underground Comics

Underground comics (or "comix," with the *X* understood to signify X-rated material) include strips and books heavily dosed with obscenity, graphic sex, gory violence, glorification of drug use, and general defiance of convention and authority. All are either self-published or produced by very small companies that choose not to follow the mainstream Comics Code. Some undergrounds are political, carrying eco-awareness, antiestablishment messages and general revolutionary overtones. Others are just meant for nasty, subversive fun. All have elements of sensation and satire.

The origins of underground comics can be traced to the so-called Tijuana Bibles of the 1930s and 1940s: illegally produced eight-page minicomics that depict mainstream comic strip characters (such as Popeye, Mickey Mouse, and Dick Tracy) getting drunk and having sex. The legacy of underground comics is the alternative and independent comics of the 1980s and 1990s.

1960s ORIGINS

Underground comics truly came into their own during the 1960s, thanks to the talents of such artists and writers as Robert "R." Crumb, Gilbert Shelton, and S. Clay Wilson. The first underground strips appeared in underground papers including *East Village Other* of New York; *Barb* of Berkeley, California; the *Free Press* of Los Angeles; and the *Fifth Estate* of Detroit, Michigan. The first recognizable underground comic book is *God Nose (Snot Reel)* put out by Jack "Jaxon" Jackson in 1963. Undergrounds proliferated in the mid- and late 1960s, with printing and distribution by such companies as Rip-Off Press in San Francisco, Print Mint in Berkeley, and Kitchen Sink Enterprises in Milwaukee, Wisconsin. These companies sold their books not through newsstands but through head shops.

The first issues of Crumb's *Zap* (1967) were a milestone in underground comics. *Zap* features the catchy "Keep on Truckin'" image and introduced such characters as the hedonistic guru Mr. Natural and the outwardly proud but inwardly repressed Whiteman. Crumb's intense and imaginative artwork, strange and often shocking images, unsparing satires, and unflattering self-confessions still remain perhaps the most impressive work in the history of underground comics. His very popular comics and illustrations have become widely available in compilations, anthologies, and even coffee table books. The artist's life and work are the subject of the 1995 documentary film *Crumb*.

Shelton found his greatest success with his *Fabulous Furry Freak Brothers* comic, more than a dozen issues of which have been infrequently published since the first issue in 1968. The Freaks include Phineas, Freewheelin' Franklin, and Fat Freddy (the most popular of the three), who are fun-loving hippie buddies out looking for sex, drugs, and rock and roll—especially drugs. The comic also features the adventures of Fat Freddy's cat, who must sometimes fight off suicidal cockroaches in Freddy's apartment. Shelton also writes and draws the superhero parody strip "Wonder Wart-Hog."

Wilson holds the distinction of being the most perverse and most disgusting of any underground comic artist. His work is filled with orgies and brawls, molestations and mutilations. His characters are usually pirates, lesbians, motorcycle gangs, or horned demonic monsters. All his characters are drawn in anatomically correct detail, complete with warts, nose hair, sweat, saliva, and wet, rubbery genitalia. Comics featuring his work include *Zap* and *Yellow Dog*.

OTHER IMPORTANT ARTISTS AND WRITERS

Other important and popular underground artists and writers include Kim Deitch, whose playful and humorous work has appeared in the *East Village Other* and *Gothic Blimp Works*; Greg Irons, whose frightening, bony faces and horror stories have been featured in *Skull*; Rick Griffin, whose psychedelic-organic art has been printed in *Zap*, on countless posters, and on some of the more famous Grateful Dead album covers; Victor Moscoso, whose space-time distortions show the influence of M. C. Escher; George Metzger, who was the most important science fiction–fantasy underground artist with his dreamy *Moondog* book; and Richard Corben (later famous for the Den series in *Heavy Metal*), whose fleshy, muscular, scantily clad men and women have appeared under the pseudonym "Gore" in *Slow Death* and *Death Rattle*.

Mainstream artists who got their start with early undergrounds include Bill Griffith (*Zippy*) and Art Spiegelman (*Maus*, covers for the *New Yorker*). There have been few women in underground comics, but notable exceptions include Trina Robbins and Lee Marrs, both of whom worked as artists, writers, and editors. Robbins edited *It Ain't Me Babe Comix*—the first all-women comic—in the early 1970s.

In the 1960s and 1970s, the most popular underground sex comics were *Snatch Comics*, *Jiz Comics*, *Big Ass Comics*, *Gay Comics*, *Young Lust*, and *Bizarre Sex*. Popular pro-drug comics included *Freak Brothers*, *Dope Comix*, and *Uneeda Comix*. Among the popular political compilations were the antipollution *Slow Death* and the antigovernment *Anarchy Comics*. Small print runs and low distributions kept most of these comics away from the eyes of civil and political authorities. There were some notable legal battles, however, the most significant of which erupted in 1969 over *Zap Comics* issue 4, which features Crumb's infamous "Joe Blow" story about an incestuous, sadomasochistic family orgy. A New York State judge ruled the comic obscene and therefore illegal, holding the publisher Print Mint liable for fines.

Another significant legal battle took place between cartoonist Dan O'Neill and Walt Disney Productions over the comic-book series *Air Pirates Funnies*, which depicted graphic cartoons of Disney characters engaged in sexual acts and drug use. O'Neill went to the trouble of smuggling copies of the comic book into Disney's headquarters with the intent of infuriating board members and inciting a lawsuit. O'Neill's hope was to bring forth a legal discussion of parody and to render parody immune to copyright infringement laws. The lawsuit dragged on until the parties settled in 1980, with O'Neill agreeing he would never again copy a Disney character.

When head shops died out in the early 1970s, many underground comics vanished entirely, the survivors becoming available only through mail order. With the dawn of comic specialty shops in the early 1980s, undergrounds once again had a place on the shelves. In the 2010s reprints and compilations of early undergrounds are found alongside conventional mainstream books.

The influence of underground comic books and the openness of comics specialty shops helped make possible the so-called alternative or independent comics that flourished in the 1980s and that continued to reach wide audiences into the twenty-first century—so much so that makers of such comics began to hold a yearly Alternative Press Expo in 1994 and continued into the 2010s. Some of the most popular alternatives of the late 1980s and 1990s were *Love and Rockets* by the Hernandez brothers, *Yummy Fur* by Chester Brown, and the compilation *Weirdo, Raw*. Alternative comics published into the first decade of the twenty-first century include *Bitchy Bitch* by Roberta Gregory, *Hate* by Peter Bagge, and *Black Hole* by Charles Burns. *Cerebus* by Dave Sim and *Eightball* by Dan Clowes were still being published in the early 2010s. Also, in the early twenty-first century the publisher Drawn and Quarterly produced an annual showcase anthology of several artists. Like the early undergrounds, these new books are uncompromising in their treatment of sex and violence and often hold skeptical and subversive undertones. Most alternatives avoid the extremism of their 1960s and 1970s predecessors, but without these earlier books, the widely read and widely praised alternative books would not have been possible.

Dave Goldweber

SEE ALSO: *Comic Books; Comics Code Authority; Crumb, Robert; Escher, M. C.; Graphic Novels;* Maus; *Pornography; Tijuana Bibles;* Zap Comix.

BIBLIOGRAPHY

Adelman, Bob, ed. *Tijuana Bibles: Art and Wit in America's Forbidden Funnies*. New York: Simon & Schuster, 1997.

Eisner, Will; Bill Griffith; Malcolm Whyte; et al. *Zap to Zippy: The Impact of Underground Comix*. San Francisco: Cartoon Art Museum, 1990.

Estren, Mark James. *A History of Underground Comics*, 3rd ed. Berkeley, CA: Ronin, 1993.

Juno, Andrea, ed. *Dangerous Drawings: Interviews with Comix and Graphix Artists*. New York: Juno, 1997.

Kitchen, Denis, and James Danky. *Underground Classics: The Transformation of Comics into Comix*. New York: Abrams, 2009.

Pilcher, Tim, and Gene Kannenberg Jr. *Erotic Comics: A Graphic History from Tijuana Bibles to Underground Comix*. New York: Abrams, 2008.

Sabin, Roger. *Comics, Comix & Graphic Novels*. London: Phaidon, 1996.

Unforgiven

Of his 1992 film *Unforgiven*, director and star Clint Eastwood said, "the movie summarized everything I feel about the Western." Despite this, the film sparked considerable debate about exactly what it had to say about the Western. Some critics have portrayed the film as an anti-Western that tore down the icons of the genre, while others have insisted that it was simply a continuation of the genre with slight variations. Whatever deeper meanings the film may have intended, it meant for many, including the filmmakers, a restoration of the genre. Not only did the film give a needed career boost to actors like Eastwood, Gene Hackman, Morgan Freeman, and Richard Harris, but it also was credited with revitalizing the Western. Interestingly, the film was touted by some critics as the final word on the Western.

Indeed, none of the Westerns released in *Unforgiven*'s wake has matched the impact of Eastwood's dark, brooding film. Certainly none matched its critical and commercial success. It broke box-office records, not only for a Western, but for an August release, and won four Academy Awards: Best Picture, Best Director, Best Supporting Actor (Hackman), and Best Editing.

These accomplishments were all the more remarkable given the state of the genre. Within the film industry, the Western was largely considered dead and gone, and earlier attempts to resuscitate it had been tepidly received, with the exception of Kevin Costner's 1990 Western-of-a-sort, *Dances with Wolves*. David Webb Peoples penned the *Unforgiven* script (originally titled "The Cut-Whore Killings") in 1976, but it had attracted only slight interest. Francis Ford Coppola had optioned the script, but he allowed the option to lapse. Eventually it was picked up by Eastwood, who sat on the script for some time, claiming that he needed to age into the lead role of William Munny.

At the beginning of the film, Munny is a struggling hog farmer raising two young children. A prologue scrolling across the screen tells of a less domestic Munny, a drunk, an outlaw, and a killer, now reformed, according to Munny, by his wife, who has just died. But Munny's reputation brings to the ranch the Schofield Kid (Jaimz Woolvett), who lures Munny away in pursuit of a bounty on two cowboys involved in the mutilation of a prostitute. Munny, in turn, recruits his partner from the old days, Ned Logan (Freeman). What follows is the story of their search for the cowboys and their conflict with the law in Big Whiskey, Wyoming—specifically with brutal sheriff Little Bill Daggett (Hackman). The killings of the cowboys are pivotal. The first to die is Davey Boy, whose main crime is that he was on the scene when the prostitute was attacked. This is a drawn-out, painful scene in which Munny shoots the cowboy from a distance: the cowboy's life slowly ebbs while he calls out to his friends for water. Logan is too rattled by the murder to continue in pursuit of the other cowboy. The Schofield Kid, finally living up to his bravado, kills the second cowboy, who is using an outhouse at the time. The Kid is reduced to tears by the horror of his deed and realizes that he is not the Billy the Kid figure he has pretended to be.

The final scene is one that critics have found more troubling; it could have come out of an Old West penny dreadful. Munny confronts Daggett and his deputies, single-handedly killing five armed men. Munny's attack is motivated by vengeance against those who killed his friend. This, combined with the incredible odds against him, seems to turn Munny into a kind of mythological force for vengeance. But this approach works against the film's earlier attempt to define him as very human and fallible. Furthermore, given the unpleasantness of the earlier killings, the scene is tainted, for viewers, with the knowledge that, as Munny puts it, "It's a hell of a thing killing a man." The final scene, it can be argued, does not come off quite the way it might have in a more traditional Western.

Unforgiven employs many of the genre's clichés, while simultaneously undercutting the comfort that comes with them. This had been done before, particularly in the spaghetti Westerns of Sergio Leone, but where those presented a parody of the Western myth with almost cartoonish violence, the violence in *Unforgiven* is decidedly more realistic. Moreover, many earlier Westerns were brightly lit, but the action in *Unforgiven* is often shrouded in darkness and haze.

Eastwood dedicated the film to Leone and Don Siegel, acknowledging them as mentors. *Unforgiven* is certainly in the tradition of the spaghetti Western, but Eastwood carried that tradition to a new level. Putting his own spin on the genre, he redefined the Western for an era in which the invented heroics of the past seemed less convincing than they had in the heyday of the genre. *Unforgiven* reflects the skepticism of its time, when the old John Ford adage "when the legend becomes fact, print the legend" does not quite hold up any more. Eastwood's film suggests that legend is a frail thing and that perhaps truer things have a way of showing through.

Marc Oxoby

SEE ALSO: *Academy Awards; Eastwood, Clint; Hackman, Gene; Leone, Sergio; Spaghetti Westerns; The Western.*

BIBLIOGRAPHY

McVeigh, Stephen. *The American Western*. Edinburgh: Edinburgh University Press, 2007.

O'Brien, Daniel. *Clint Eastwood: Film-Maker*. London: Batsford, 1996.

Schickel, Richard. *Clint Eastwood: A Biography*. New York: Knopf, 1996.

Smith, Paul. *Clint Eastwood: A Cultural Production*. Minneapolis: University of Minnesota Press, 1993.

Unidentified Flying Objects

SEE: *UFOs (Unidentified Flying Objects).*

Unitas, Johnny *(1933–2002)*

The best-known names on the gridiron often are quarterbacks. In the 1990s such media darlings as Joe Montana and Steve Young, Dan Marino, John Elway, and Brett Favre earned the bulk of National Football League (NFL) fame; the marquee names during the following decade included Ben Roethlisberger, Drew Brees, Tom Brady, and Eli and Peyton Manning. None of these superstar signal callers, however, has anything on Johnny Unitas—otherwise known as "Mr. Quarterback," "The Golden Arm," and simply "Johnny U."—who played for the Baltimore Colts between 1956 and 1972. In his prime, Unitas was the league's most renowned, respected, and feared quarterback. As noted in his enshrinee data at the Pro Football Hall of Fame, he was a "legendary hero," and an "exceptional field leader [who] thrived on pressure."

Johnny U.'s career is defined by a combination of luck, persistence, and hard work. He was born John Constantine Unitas in Pittsburgh, Pennsylvania, and began his quarterbacking career as a sophomore at St. Justin's High School when the first-string signal caller broke his ankle. He had a scant seven days to master his team's complete offense. As he neared graduation, the lanky six-footer with the signature crew cut hoped to be offered a scholarship to Notre Dame but was denied his wish as the school determined that he probably would not add weight to his 145-pound frame. Instead, he attended the University of Louisville, graduating in 1955.

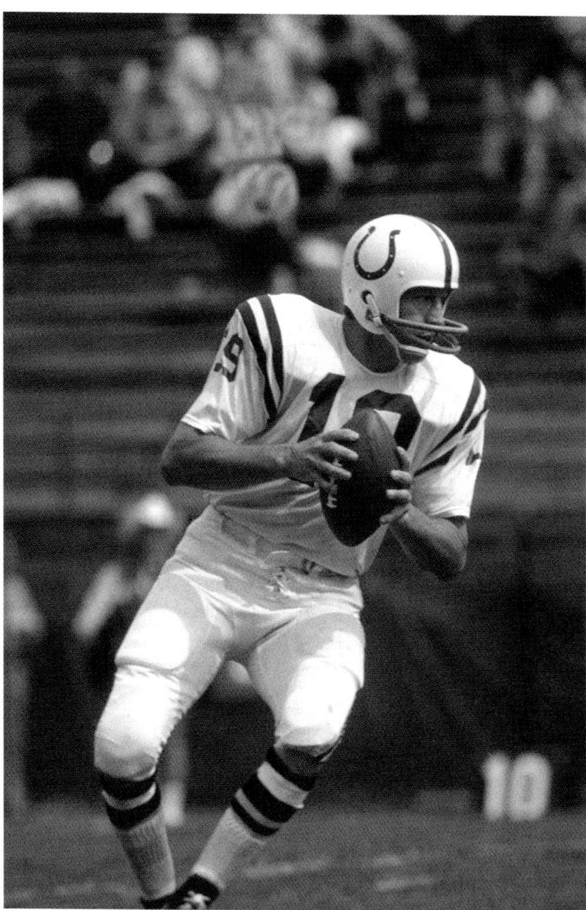

Johnny Unitas. Johnny Unitas led the Baltimore Colts to three NFL championships and one Super Bowl win in his stellar career. FOCUS ON SPORT/CONTRIBUTOR/GETTY IMAGES SPORT/GETTY IMAGES.

While he was no luminary on the college gridiron, Unitas nonetheless was drafted in the ninth round by the Pittsburgh Steelers. Unfortunately, the team was overloaded with signal callers—and its coach, Walt Kiesling, believed Unitas was "not intelligent enough to be a quarterback"—and so he was denied a slot on the Steelers' roster. Unable to hook up with another NFL team, he settled for working on a construction gang and a spot on the semipro Bloomfield Rams, where he earned $3 per game. Fortuitously, the Baltimore Colts called him in early 1956 and invited him to try out the following season. He was signed to a $7000 contract and played for the Colts for the next seventeen years before finishing his career in 1973 with the San Diego Chargers.

Unitas was the Babe Ruth, Michael Jordan, and Wayne Gretsky of quarterbacks. Upon his retirement, he held the NFL records for pass attempts (5,186) and completions (2,830), throwing for 40,239 total yards and 290 touchdowns, tossing touchdown passes in 47 consecutive games, and having twenty-six 300-yard games. He also threw for 3,000 yards or more in three seasons and piloted his team to three NFL championships (in 1958, 1959, and 1968) and one Super Bowl title (in 1971). Unitas was one of the stars of what is arguably the greatest game in NFL history: the Colts' 1958 title victory over the New York Giants, a 23–17 overtime win in which he completed 26 of 40 passes for 361 yards. Down 17–14 in the final minutes of the fourth quarter, he marched the Colts 85 yards; with seven seconds remaining on the clock, Steve Myhra booted a 20-yard, game-tying field goal. Then in overtime, Unitas spearheaded his team 80 yards on twelve plays, with Alan Ameche rushing for the game-winning touchdown.

AWARDS

Unitas was a five-time All-NFL selection, a three-time NFL Player of the Year, a ten-time Pro Bowl pick—a record for quarterbacks that was only broken in 2009 by Brett Favre—and a three-time Pro Bowl Most Valuable Player (MVP). He was named the Associated Press's Player of the Decade for the 1960s, and in 1999 the *Sporting News* ranked him number 5 on its list of the "100 Greatest Football Players," and ESPN ranked him number 32 on its list of the "50 Greatest Athletes of the 20th Century." Unitas was one of four quarterbacks—the others are Otto Graham, Sammy Baugh, and Joe Montana—named to the NFL's 75th Anniversary Team, and he was inducted into the Pro Football Hall of Fame in 1979. Since 1987 the Johnny Unitas Golden Arm Award has been presented to the top senior college quarterback.

In retirement, Unitas sported a crooked index finger on his passing hand, a souvenir of his playing career. He was fiercely proud of his reputation as a hard-nosed competitor who once declared, "You're not an NFL quarterback until you can tell your coach to go to hell!" He also has noted that playing in the NFL of the 1990s would be "a piece of cake. The talent's not as good as it once was." Also, defensive backs "used to be able to come up and knock you down at the line of scrimmage. If you tried to get up, they'd knock you down again, then sit on you and dare you to get up." Such defense is not allowed today, as many new rulings since Unitas's time have been instituted to protect a quarterback from injury.

Many fans believe that Unitas should not be blamed for his team's shocking 16–7 loss to Joe Namath and the underdog New York Jets in Superbowl III—the game that established the upstart American Football League as a real rival of the NFL. For most of the season, Unitas had been plagued by a sore elbow. Earl Morrall, who had replaced Unitas in training camp and was the league MVP, started the game for the Colts. In the first half, the Jets' secondary intercepted three of his passes. Unitas, the aging, injured veteran of the football wars, heroically came off the bench in the fourth quarter to complete 11 of 24 passes, for 110 yards. Unfortunately, the Colts could muster only a single touchdown. "I always tell people to blame [Colts coach Don] Shula for that," he once observed, "because if he had started me in the second half, I'd have got it."

Unitas succumbed to a heart attack on September 11, 2002, while exercising at a physical therapy center in Timonium, Maryland. A little over a month after his death, a 13-foot statue of the quarterback in a throwing pose was unveiled on the north side of Ravens Stadium, the home of the Baltimore Ravens (which came into existence in 1996, replacing the departed Colts).

Rob Edelman

SEE ALSO: *Brady, Tom; College Football; ESPN; Gretzky, Wayne; Jordan, Michael; Montana, Joe; Namath, Joe; National*

Football League (NFL); The Pittsburgh Steelers; Professional Football; Ruth, Babe; Shula, Don; Sports Heroes; Super Bowl.

BIBLIOGRAPHY

Callahan, Tom. *Johnny U: The Life and Times of John Unitas.* New York: Crown Publishers, 2006.

Fitzgerald, Ed. *Johnny Unitas: The Amazing Success Story of Mr. Quarterback.* New York: Nelson, 1961.

Sahadi, Lou. *Johnny Unitas: America's Quarterback.* Chicago: Triumph Books, 2004.

Towle, Mike. *Johnny Unitas: Mister Quarterback.* Nashville, TN: Cumberland House, 2003.

Unitas, Johnny, and Ed Fitzgerald. *Pro Quarterback, My Own Story.* New York: Simon & Schuster, 1965.

Unitas, Johnny, with Harold Rosenthal. *Playing Pro Football to Win.* Garden City, NY: Doubleday, 1968.

United Artists

Founded in 1919 by Douglas Fairbanks Sr., Charlie Chaplin, Mary Pickford, and D. W. Griffith, United Artists (UA) began as a distributor and financier of independent films. It was not a studio and never had stars under contract. UA was a unique entity in the early history of Hollywood, never losing sight of its goal: to make and distribute quality work.

The idea for United Artists began in 1918 when Fairbanks, Chaplin, Pickford, and cowboy star William S. Hart were traveling around the country selling liberty bonds to help the World War I effort. The four were talking about the rumors they had heard of possible studio mergers, and they began to discuss the possibility of forming their own company to protect them from the loss of control and lower salaries this might cause. Hart eventually bowed out, but he was soon replaced with the world's premier director, Griffith. When the company was officially formed in February 1919, many felt that "the idiots had taken over the asylum."

EARLY SUCCESS

The company was an immediate success. UA brought audiences hits such as Griffith's *Broken Blossoms or The Yellow Man and the Girl* (1919); Pickford's *Pollyanna* (1920); Fairbanks's *Robin Hood* (1922); and Chaplin's masterpiece, *The Gold Rush* (1925). With such quality work, UA's only problem in the early years was providing enough product to meet the demand of the audiences.

UA began courting other stars to have their work distributed through the company. While many declined, some of the top stars of silent films agreed, including Gloria Swanson, Norma Talmadge, and Buster Keaton. The company also brought in Joseph Schenck as a partner and chairman of the board in 1924. He secured producers like Samuel Goldwyn, Walt Disney, and Howard Hughes, all of whom added to the roster of successful films released through UA.

UA was temporarily hurt by the advent of "talking pictures." While initially there were hits such as *Coquette* (1929), for which Pickford won an Academy Award, as "talkies" became more the rule than the exception, the company found its product in less demand. One notable exception was *Hell's Angels* (1930), produced by Hughes. After silent screen star Greta Nissen had to be replaced, Hughes introduced to the screen the sex symbol of the 1930s, Jean Harlow. The result made *Hell's Angels* one of UA's biggest hits.

But UA was beginning to lose some of its creative talent as Griffith, Disney, Schenck, and others left. The company managed, however, to stay afloat with hits such as *The Scarlet Pimpernel* (1935), *Dodsworth* (1936), and *Algiers* (1938). The star founders of UA had all but faded by this time. Griffith was gone, Fairbanks was dead, and Pickford's career was over, although she was still a stockholder in the company. Chaplin continued to be successful, however, particularly with *Modern Times* in 1936.

A CHANGING HOLLYWOOD

UA fell on hard times in the 1940s. The hits were fewer, and more creative forces such as David O. Selznick and Alexander Korda left the company. In 1950 a syndicate led by Arthur Krim and Robert Benjamin took over operations. As the old studio system died, Hollywood changed. Soon the independents, including UA, had the upper hand. The old production code and puritanical limits to motion picture making were also disappearing. One of the first and biggest reasons for this was Otto Preminger's *The Moon Is Blue* (1953). UA released the film without the seal of approval from the Production Code Administration. Despite this, or perhaps because of it, the film was a box-office and critical success. The 1950s, however, marked the end of an era at UA for another reason. By 1956, founders Chaplin and Pickford gave in to pressure and sold their shares in the company. UA then had a public stock offering in 1957.

Following the public sale of UA, *The Apartment* (1960) was released and won five Academy Awards, signaling a prosperous time for the studio. In 1961 UA announced what turned out to be a brilliant decision: the company was going to release seven James Bond films, all of which went on to be big hits. The spy series proved to be one of the most successful in motion picture history.

If a motion picture company is to stay afloat, it must, in some way, reflect changes in society. Things were clearly changing with the Vietnam War, the generation gap, and the beginning of the sexual revolution. UA continued its success throughout the 1960s with violent and controversial hits such as *The Dirty Dozen* (1967) and *The Wild Bunch* (1969). In the late 1960s, UA experienced the first of many shakeups in ownership when in 1967 Transamerica took over the company. By 1969 millionaire Kirk Kerkorian was the largest shareholder. While UA continued to have hits, including *One Flew over the Cuckoo's Nest* (1975), many were not happy with the way the company was being run. In 1978 several executives, including Krim and Benjamin, resigned from the company to form Orion Pictures.

In November 1980 UA released a film that has become known as one of the biggest box-office disasters in motion picture history—*Heaven's Gate*, which lost $40 million. In 1981 MGM (Metro-Goldwyn-Mayer) bought UA, and the company became MGM/UA. The company continued to be sold and resold throughout the 1980s, and in the 1990s it no longer existed in its original form.

In the first decade of the 2000s, UA, which remained part of MGM, continued to change with each sale of its assets. It was remade into a distributor of "art-house" films such as *Bowl-*

ing for Columbine (2002) and *Hotel Rwanda* (2004). In 2005 a group that included the companies Comcast and Sony bought MGM/UA for $4.8 billion. In 2006 actor Tom Cruise and his partner, Paula Wagner, announced plans to create United Artists Entertainment LLC with MGM. Cruise served as an occasional star and producer. In 2008 Wagner left UA, which signaled more changes within the organization. UA then served as only a coproducer for a few films with MGM.

In 2010 MGM entered Chapter 11 bankruptcy proceedings and emerged with Spyglass Entertainment heads Gary Barber and Roger Birnbaum at the helm. Creditors overwhelmingly approved the deal that gave them control of the studio. With this latest incarnation of MGM, the future of UA is unknown. Despite this, UA will be remembered for its part in changing the face of Hollywood, for offering more control to the creative forces of motion pictures and less to the businesspeople. In addition to producing many hit films throughout the years, UA is largely responsible for the way in which the motion picture industry evolved as the studio system began to fade.

Jill Gregg Clever

SEE ALSO: *Academy Awards; Chaplin, Charlie; Cruise, Tom;* The Dirty Dozen*; Fairbanks, Douglas, Sr.; Goldwyn, Samuel; Griffith, D. W.; Harlow, Jean; Hollywood; Hughes, Howard; James Bond Films; Keaton, Buster; MGM (Metro-Goldwyn-Mayer);* One Flew over the Cuckoo's Nest*; Pickford, Mary; Preminger, Otto; Selznick, David O.; Silent Movies;* The Wild Bunch*; World War I.*

BIBLIOGRAPHY

Balio, Tino. *United Artists: The Company That Changed the Film Industry.* Madison: University of Wisconsin Press, 1987.

Bergan, Ronald. *The United Artists Story.* New York: Crown, 1986.

Unser, Al *(1939–)*

Al Unser Sr., one of the foremost names in the sport of auto racing, is known primarily for his remarkable success at the Indianapolis 500. He comes from a long line of auto racing Unsers. In fact, it can be argued that no other family has left such an indelible mark on a sport as the Unser family has left on auto racing: Al's brother Jerry was national stock-car champion in 1956 but was killed in 1959 while on a practice lap at Indianapolis. The two surviving brothers, Al and Bobby, went on to win a total of seven Indianapolis 500 races. Al's son, Al Unser Jr., is successful in his own right, having twice won at Indianapolis. Al Sr.'s nephews Johnny and Robby have also competed in the Indianapolis 500.

Al Unser Sr. was born in Albuquerque, New Mexico, on May 29, 1939. At age eighteen he began competitive auto racing with modified roadsters before progressing to midgets, sprints, stock cars, sports cars, Formula 5000, Championship Dirt Cars, and IndyCars. His dominance in the sport is illustrated by his placement in the national standings: third in 1968; second in 1969, 1977, and 1978; first in 1970; and fourth in 1976. He is one of the few drivers who can boast a career that spans five decades.

However, most drivers of Unser's generation are judged by their success at Indianapolis, where Unser ranks third in total number of 500 starts and is tied for second in the total number of races that he led at Indy. Although A. J. Foyt was the first driver to win four times at Indianapolis, Unser matched that feat in 1987. Rick Mears is the only other driver to do so since. In 1988 Unser surpassed the long-standing record for the most laps led during a career at the 500, having achieved a staggering total of 625.

In addition to winning Indianapolis four times (1970, 1971, 1978, and 1987), Unser won the Pocono 500 and the Ontario 500 twice each. When he won at Indianapolis, Pocono, and Ontario all in the same year (1978), he achieved the unique distinction of sweeping this "Triple Crown" of IndyCar racing. The 1970 season was perhaps his most remarkable of all, with ten wins on ovals, road courses, and dirt tracks to capture the national championship. Unser also won the prestigious "Hoosier Hundred" four years in a row, making him a dirt-car champion, and had his share in the Unser family dominance of the Pikes Peak Hill Climb, taking back-to-back victories in 1964 and 1965.

Even as Unser approached the end of his career, he was still able to win two more national championships, in 1983 and in 1985. His main competitor in 1985 was his own son, who lost to his father by only one point. At the age of forty-six Unser enjoyed the distinction of becoming the oldest IndyCar champion. He was inducted into the Motorsports Hall of Fame of America in 1991 and the International Motorsports Hall of Fame in 1998.

Al Unser Sr. *Al Unser holds the trophy for winning the International Race of Champions in 1978.* RACINGONE/CONTRIBUTOR/ISC ARCHIVES/GETTY IMAGES.

Unser, an avid snowmobile enthusiast, retired to his home in New Mexico. The Unser name has been used to market everything from die-cast race cars to bobble heads to computer games. He appeared on the TV series *Home Improvement* as well as other TV movies and documentaries, including his 2002 appearance on *ESPN SportsCentury*.

James H. Lloyd

SEE ALSO: *Automobile; Computer Games; ESPN; Extreme Sports; Foyt, A. J.;* Home Improvement*; Indianapolis 500; Leisure Time; Sports Heroes; Stock-Car Racing; Television; Toys; Unser, Bobby.*

BIBLIOGRAPHY

"Al Unser." Motorsports Hall of Fame. Accessed December 2011. Available from http://www.mshf.com/hof/unser_al_sr.htm

Bentley, Karen. *The Unsers*. New York: Chelsea House, 1996.

Dregni, Michael. *The Indianapolis 500*. Minneapolis, MN: Capstone Press, 1994.

Walker, Mark H. *Official ABC Sports Indy Racing: Road to the Indianapolis 500 Official Strategies and Secrets*. San Francisco: Sybex, 1998.

Unser, Bobby *(1934–)*

The Unser family has produced many superb race-car drivers, including Bobby Unser, who recorded thirty-five IndyCar victories and two United States Auto Club (USAC) national driving championships during a career that spanned thirty-two years.

Robert William Unser was born in Albuquerque, New Mexico, on February 20, 1934, and began racing at the age of fifteen. The dream of most race-car drivers at the time was to drive in the Indianapolis 500; Unser won there in 1968, 1975, and 1981. In addition to IndyCars, he claimed victories in sprint cars, stock cars, and midget racers. He won the Pikes Peak International Hill climb thirteen times. After retirement Unser won USAC's Fast Masters Tournament for drivers over the age of fifty. He was inducted into the Motorsports Hall of Fame of America, the International Motorsports Hall of Fame, and the National Sprint Car Hall of Fame.

During the height of his career, race cars and other toys were marketed with his name, including a Johnny Lightning model of the car in which Unser won the 1975 Indy 500. In the 1990s Unser worked for ABC Sports and was one of the most respected color commentators for the sport of motor racing. He also appeared in the TV series *Coach* (1989–1997) and *The American Sportsman* (1965–1982). In addition, Unser was seen in a variety of documentaries and TV movies, including *ESPN SportsCentury* (2001–2002).

James H. Lloyd

SEE ALSO: *Automobile; ESPN; Indianapolis 500; Leisure Time; Sports Heroes; Stock-Car Racing; Television; Toys; Unser, Al.*

BIBLIOGRAPHY

Scalzo, Joe, and Bobby Unser. *The Bobby Unser Story*. New York: Doubleday, 1979.

Unser, Bobby. *Winners Are Driven: A Champion's Guide to Business and Life*. Hoboken, NJ: John Wiley, 2003.

Walker, Mark H. *Official ABC Sports Indy Racing: Road to the Indianapolis 500 Official Strategies and Secrets*. San Francisco: Sybex, 1998.

Updike, John *(1932–2009)*

Considered by critics to be one of the most significant American writers of the latter half of the twentieth century, John Updike is best known for his series of Rabbit novels (*Rabbit, Run*, 1960; *Rabbit Redux*, 1971; *Rabbit Is Rich*, 1981; and *Rabbit at Rest*, 1990), which chronicles four decades of American culture through the eyes of Everyman protagonist Harry Angstrom. In the minds of many readers, Updike's depictions of everyday life and the stifling atmosphere of marriage vividly capture the emptiness of Middle America. Prolific and versatile, he published more than fifty volumes, including novels, short stories, essays, reviews, poems, memoirs, and drama.

THE VOICE OF MIDDLE AMERICA

Updike was born in Reading, Pennsylvania, on March 18, 1932, and grew up in the small town of Shillington, Pennsylvania. He later lived on a family farm in nearby Plowville. Through early academic success, Updike earned a scholarship to Harvard, where he continued the writing and drawing he had begun as a child. Following graduation from Harvard, he spent a year in Oxford, England, studying drawing on a fellowship, and two years in New York City working as a staff writer for the *New Yorker*.

John Updike. *John Updike is known for both his rich writing style and his astute examination of various aspects of American life in his novels, essays, and criticism.* DAVID LEVENSON/CONTRIBUTOR/GETTY IMAGES ENTERTAINMENT/GETTY IMAGES.

In 1957 Updike and his young family, which would grow to four children by 1960, left New York City and moved to the small town of Ipswich, Massachusetts. Big-city life had proved to be too distracting, expensive, and overwhelming. By returning to a small town, Updike found an atmosphere that would allow him to experience firsthand the middle-class life that would become the great subject of his work.

In Ipswich, Updike began publishing books, beginning with a volume of poetry, *The Carpentered Hen* (1958); a first novel, *The Poorhouse Fair* (1959); and a collection of stories, *The Same Door* (1959). Most of his early work, written between the early 1950s and mid-1960s, depicts and lyrically celebrates a mythically endowed Pennsylvania that the author knew intimately from childhood. His most famous novel, *Rabbit, Run*, about the angst and entrapment of early married life, went on to sell more than 2.5 million copies following its appearance in 1960. Before he turned thirty, he had established himself as one of his generation's foremost writers.

A NATIONAL SENSATION

Updike's break with his early work came in 1968 with the publication of the novel *Couples*, set in a small New England town and dealing with the adulterous interactions of a circle of ten couples. *Couples* was the author's first and only book to top the best-seller list, and it also landed Updike on the cover of *Time* magazine (he would appear there again in 1982). Over the subsequent decade, he became America's best-known chronicler of marriage and adultery, producing such works as *A Month of Sundays* (1975), *Marry Me* (1976), and *Too Far to Go* (1979). During this same period, Updike divorced his first wife, to whom he had been wed for twenty-three years, and remarried.

The next phase of Updike's writing was signaled by the publication of *The Coup* (1978), one of the most radical departures of his career. Set in a fictional African country and told from the perspective of a black African leader in exile, *The Coup* was a breakthrough novel, demonstrating that Updike could extend his vision beyond suburban adultery or a Pennsylvania boyhood. He wrote some of his finest and most exuberant fiction during the late 1970s and early 1980s, including *Problems and Other Stories* (1979), *Rabbit Is Rich*, and *The Witches of Eastwick* (1984). In addition, he emerged as one of America's finest and most prolific literary critics through the publication of his award-winning tome *Hugging the Shore* (1983), a collection of essays and reviews.

Updike's later novels, such as *Roger's Version* (1986), an intellectually demanding novel about a divinity professor and his battle with a computer scientist; *Rabbit at Rest*; and *Toward the End of Time* (1997), reveal his concerns with aging and display a bleakness and detachment that stand in contrast to the lyrical celebration of much of his early work. *Roger's Version* also signaled the increasing use of research in his writing, to the extent that he began appending bibliographies to his novels. More heavily intertextual and loaded with information, these novels reveal a more erudite author. The theme of death, explored in *Rabbit at Rest*, also reappears in the novella "Rabbit Remembered," published in *Licks of Love* (2001). This novella closes out the Rabbit series by focusing on the surviving members of Rabbit's family, who are still haunted by his memory on the verge of the new millennium.

ASSESSING UPDIKE'S INFLUENCE

Despite his large following, Updike has had his share of critics. Some have argued that while he was a brilliant verbal performer, he allowed himself to be carried away by his prose, to the point that his language became excessive in description and detail. In addition, some have found his graphic depictions of human sexuality to be gratuitous, and several feminist critics have accused him of misogyny.

In 2009 Updike died in Danvers, Massachusetts. He is considered by many to be America's greatest poetic novelist—a master of metaphor, scene, description, and image. With his verbal gifts, his eye for detail, and his lyrical love of the surface world, he created moments and scenes of extraordinary beauty and freshness. Like Walt Whitman, the great nineteenth-century poet, Updike attempted to celebrate and sing about America, delighting in its textures and surfaces, its objects and gestures. His subject, in his own words, is "the whole mass of middling, hidden, troubled America," and the purpose of his books, which together form "a continental *magnum opus*," is "the hymning of this great roughly rectangular country."

James Schiff

SEE ALSO: *Best Sellers; The* New Yorker.

BIBLIOGRAPHY

Baker, Nicholson. *U & I: A True Story*. New York: Random House, 1991.

Broer, Lawrence R., ed. *Rabbit Tales: Poetry and Politics in John Updike's Rabbit Novels*. Tuscaloosa: University of Alabama Press, 1998.

Detweiler, Robert C. *John Updike*. Boston: Twayne, 1984.

Greiner, Donald J. *John Updike's Novels*. Athens: Ohio University Press, 1984.

Luscher, Robert M. *John Updike: A Study of the Short Fiction*. New York: Twayne, 1993.

Newman, Judie. *John Updike*. New York: St. Martin's Press, 1988.

Olster, Stacey. *The Cambridge Companion to John Updike*. New York: Cambridge University Press, 2006.

Rodgers, Bernard F., Jr., ed. *John Updike*. Critical Insights. Ipswich, MA: Salem Press, 2011.

Schiff, James. *John Updike Revisited*. New York: Twayne, 1998.

Upstairs, Downstairs

The original five seasons of *Upstairs, Downstairs* (1971–1975) have been watched by an estimated one billion people in forty countries since it was first broadcast on *Masterpiece Theatre* during the 1974 season. Produced by London Weekend Television, the initial sixty-eight episodes follow the wealthy Bellamy family and their servants from 1903 until the aftermath of the 1929 stock market crash. Rigorous period detail, distinguished acting, and the equal time given to lower-class characters are hallmarks of the series. In depicting the erosion of the British class system throughout the Edwardian era, *Upstairs, Downstairs* bolstered the reputations of British television around the globe and public television in the United States. The series not only garnered high ratings for PBS but also won seven Emmy Awards and helped to ensure the success of *Masterpiece Theatre* as a PBS showcase synonymous with quality. Three additional hour-long episodes set in 1936, which were produced by BBC Wales and broadcast in 2010, received six Emmy Award nominations.

Neal Baker

SEE ALSO: *Emmy Awards;* Masterpiece Theatre*; Public Television (PBS).*

BIBLIOGRAPHY

Floyd, Patty Lou. *Backstairs with "Upstairs, Downstairs."* New York: St. Martin's Press, 1988.

Franklin, Nancy. "Back in Service." *New Yorker*, April 18, 2011, 126–127.

Marson, Richard. *Inside Updown: The Story of "Upstairs, Downstairs."* Bristol, UK: Kaleidoscope, 2005.

O'Flaherty, Terrence. *Masterpiece Theatre: A Celebration of 25 Years of Outstanding Television.* San Francisco: KQED Books, 1996.

Urban Legends

Popularly coined in 1981 in the book *The Vanishing Hitchhiker: American Urban Legends and Their Meanings* by Jan Harold Brunvand, urban legends have been part of the American cultural landscape for years. As Brunvand later explained in 2001, "Urban legends are all those bizarre, whimsical, 99 percent apocryphal, yet believable stories that are 'too good to be true.'" Nevertheless, people often believe them to be true despite contrary evidence.

Urban legends often take the form of anecdotal morality tales spun into elaborate narratives and typically involve elements of horror and/or humiliation. The tales range from the cartoonish story about a child who blew up from ingesting a mixture of Pop Rocks and Coca-Cola to the more sinister accounts of alligators from the New York sewers making their way into people's apartments via their toilets. Many of the creepiest and most grotesque urban legends detail violence perpetrated against teenagers and young adults. One popular urban legend tells the story of a teenage babysitter who calls the telephone operator to report a series of disturbing phone calls she has been receiving. The operator, in turn, informs the girl that the calls have been coming from inside the home where she is sitting. There are many variations of the story of the college student who, after taking a drink from a stranger in a bar, wakes up in a warm bath and notices that a kidney or some other vital organ has been extracted. Many urban legends are sexually explicit. Perhaps the most common of these is the story that details one of any number of Hollywood male heartthrobs going to an emergency room in the wee hours of the morning to have a gerbil removed from his anus.

Some urban legends originate from retellings of traditional legends or from purposeful mixings of real details with outright fantasy. Their story-based structure coupled with the teller's claims of authenticity help to pass off the legend as true. The narrator may claim that it happened to her, to her friend, or to this guy she knows. Many include messages or unspoken morals, like to beware of strangers or to check your car's backseat. The more sexually explicit legends seem to warn people of what some consider to be deviant sexual behavior. Urban legends are said to occur locally, yet the same basic stories are told over wide geographic areas. Tales involving razors in apples or spiders hatching from a spider bite have been told across generations and continents. Like other folklore, urban legends change, disappear, and reappear over time, but scholars are uncertain why some spread more than others.

Once the stuff of newspaper columns and word-of-mouth diffusion, urban legends are now grist for electronic media, including Snopes.com, the self-purported Internet resource for legends, rumors, and hoaxes, and Scambusters.org. Social media sites have become a new medium by which urban legends gain traction. In 2010 the story of a heroic flight attendant who combats racism by giving an African American a seat in first class resurfaced on Facebook. First circulated via e-mail in 1998, versions from 2010 and subsequent years altered the airline from British Airways to TAM or United and, in at least one version, substituted an irate Muslim man for the racist white woman and an elderly woman reading her Bible for the black man. A month after the attacks of September 11, 2001, an e-mail rumor spread, stating that women had died from anthrax-laden perfume samples they received in the mail. The rumor morphed to include almost any product sample, but Tide became the primary target. By 2012 thousands of e-mails, text messages, Facebook updates, and Tweets warned consumers that there was anthrax in Tide detergent samples. One recent study by Pamela Donovan suggests that urban legends transmitted electronically by such means as the Internet—particularly common "crime legends" that concern such fears as organized gang activity, abduction of children from malls and amusement parks, and theft of bodily organs for transplant—appear to gain more frequency during increased times of crisis, when individuals' fears about safety heighten, such as after September 11, 2001.

There are many sources that dispel urban legends. For example, the popular television show *Mythbusters*, which scientifically tests some legends, has debunked famous anecdotes—such as the possibility of someone being buried alive or the ability of a penny to kill someone when dropped from a skyscraper. Between 1999 and 2007, the Centers for Disease Control and Prevention hosted a health-based "hoaxes and rumors" web page to combat the slew of rumors and myths, from toxic rat droppings to HIV-contaminated needles left in coin-return slots and theater seats. Politically motivated lies are dispelled at the Annenberg Public Policy Center's nonpartisan website, factcheck.org. Yet despite the accessibility of these resources, our gullibility and our desire for good stories help spread urban legends and "believable" hoaxes rapidly through word of mouth as well as a variety of different media.

Stephen P. Davis

SEE ALSO: *E-mail; Facebook; Horror Movies; The Internet; 9/11; Serial Killers; Twitter.*

BIBLIOGRAPHY

Bennett, Gillian, and Paul Smith, eds. *Urban Legends: A Collection of International Tall Tales and Terrors.* Westport, CT: Greenwood Press, 2007.

Best, Joel, and Gerald T. Horiuchi. "The Razor Blade in the Apple: The Social Construction of Urban Legends." *Social Problems* 32, no. 5 (1985): 488–499.

Brunvand, Jan Harold. *The Vanishing Hitchhiker: American Urban Legends and Their Meanings.* New York: Norton, 1981.

Brunvand, Jan Harold. *Encyclopedia of Urban Legends.* New York: Norton, 2002.

Donovan, Pamela. *No Way of Knowing: Crime, Urban Legends, and the Internet.* New York: Routledge, 2004.

Lynch, Aaron. *Thought Contagion: How Belief Spreads through*

Society. New York: Basic Books, 1996.

Roeper, Richard. *Urban Legends: The Truth behind All Those Deliciously Entertaining Myths That Are Absolutely, Positively, 100% Not True!* Franklin Lakes, NJ: Career Press, 1999.

Turner, Patricia A. *I Heard It through the Grapevine: Rumor in African-American Culture*. Berkeley: University of California Press, 1993.

U.S. One

Running from Fort Kent, Maine, to Key West, Florida, U.S. One served as the site and symbol for East Coast travel for much of the twentieth century. Stretching 2,377 miles, Route One got its name in 1925—when federal highway numbering began—as a recognition of the road's history as the primary conduit for passengers, commerce, information, and culture along the Atlantic seaboard. Much like Route 66, Route One became a popular site for exploring "local color" and roadside excursions. In 1938 the Federal Writers' Project of the Works Progress Administration published a popular guidebook highlighting distinctive landmarks, historical sites, and even local foods found along the route. Although still in active use, U.S. One has lost much of its traffic to newer interstate highways that allow travel at faster speeds.

Justin Nordstrom

SEE ALSO: *Automobile; Highway System; Route 66.*

BIBLIOGRAPHY

Jaffe, Eric. *The King's Best Highway: The Lost History of the Boston Post Road, the Route That Made America.* New York: Scribner, 2010.

Malcolm, Andrew, and Roger Straus. *U.S. 1: America's Original Main Street.* New York: St. Martin's Press, 1991.

USA Today

Debuting during an era when most newspapers saw sharp circulation declines, *USA Today* became the first successful

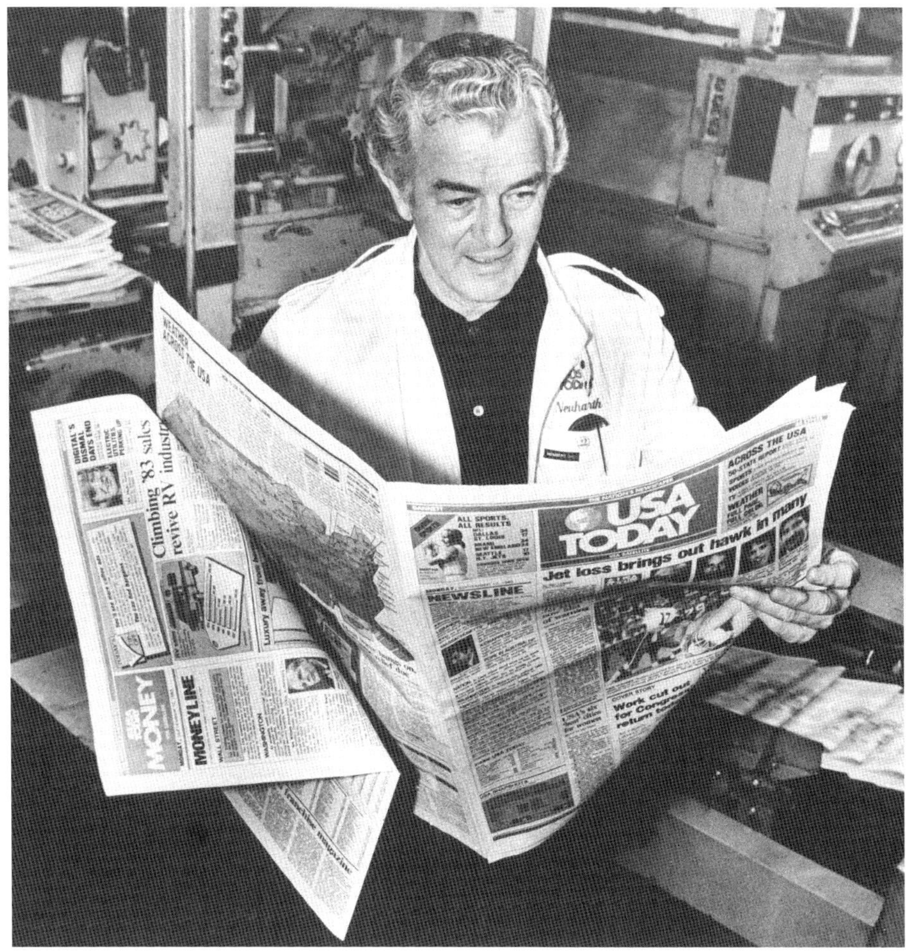

USA Today *Expands into New England in 1983.* *Allen H. Neuharth reviews the first issue of* USA Today *printed in New England on September 12, 1983, marking the newspaper's expansion into that part of the United States.* AP IMAGES.

national daily general-interest newspaper in the 1980s. Its stylish innovations, originally lampooned and mocked, were eventually adopted by most of the newspaper industry.

USA Today was the brainchild of Allen H. Neuharth, who became chairman of the Gannett newspaper chain during the 1970s. He began his publishing career in 1952 by starting a statewide sports newspaper in his native South Dakota. He joined Gannett in the 1960s by creating a statewide daily in Florida. He helped lead the company from its initial holdings in small, upstate New York newspapers to a more national base. During his tenure at Gannett, the publisher bought the Louis Harris and Associates polling organization. Upon being named chairman of Gannett in 1979, Neuharth began developing the idea of a national daily newspaper.

FILLING A NEED

In December 1980 Gannett began a satellite information system, which allowed publishing plants on the East and West Coasts to simultaneously publish the same information from one satellite. Neuharth insisted that there was also a growing market for a national newspaper. By the early 1980s, the rise of business travel meant that millions of people on business trips were tired of reading out-of-town newspapers and wanted a standard newspaper from one city to another. A Neuharth associate said, "When [a traveler] wakes up in the morning his first thought is, 'What city am I in?' . . . The local newspaper doesn't mean a thing to him."

Neuharth oversaw the development of the new newspaper, which was introduced in select markets on September 15, 1982, but did not saturate the entire country until late 1983. *USA Today*'s staff had a dilemma as the deadline for the first edition neared, when three breaking news stories jockeyed for top coverage: Lebanese president-elect Bashir Gemayel was assassinated; a plane crash in Spain killed fifty-five; and American-born Princess Grace of Monaco had died in an automobile accident at age fifty-three. The newspaper's editors spent much of September 14 on the streets and in offices in suburban Washington, D.C., determining that the public was most interested in Princess Grace's death because, as Grace Kelly, she had been a major American film star during the 1950s.

As a result, *USA Today*'s inaugural front page trumpeted the death of "America's Princess," relegating Gemayel's death to one paragraph on page one. Significantly, the coverage of the plane crash emphasized the "miracle" of 327 surviving passengers, not the fifty-five dead. The new paper was roundly castigated by media critics and competing newspapers for focusing on celebrity over international politics. In 1997 a subsequent *USA Today* editor, David Mazzarella, admitted that he would have led with the plane crash, featured a larger story on the assassination, and merely played Kelly's death as a small page one feature.

CRITICISM AND EDITORIALS

Criticism of *USA Today* began almost immediately. "A national daily newspaper seems like a way to lose a lot of money in a hurry," media analyst John Morton wrote upon *USA Today*'s debut. Complaints started with the newspaper's design. It was sold in vending machines designed to resemble television sets, leading critics to accuse the newspaper of coverage as shallow as television's. Unlike established newspapers, *USA Today* used flashy national commercials in its first years, with celebrities from Willard Scott to Willie Mays and Mickey Mantle promoting the newspaper. Many derisively compared *USA Today* to fast food, calling it "McPaper." The newspaper ran full-color photographs at a time when color photography was prohibitively expensive for many newspapers and was viewed as too garish by many editors. The *New York Times*, for example, was known as "the Gray Lady" for its steadfast black-and-white pages.

The back of the news section was a full-page, full-color weather map, while most of its rivals printed a small, black-and-white map of the weather on an inside page. Sections titled "News," "Money," "Sports," and "Life" had only one story jump from the first page to the inside. Neuharth and his editors made a conscious decision to replace long newspaper stories with shorter pieces, accompanied by sidebars, and employed numerous charts and tables. The paper's motto became, "An economy of words. A wealth of information." Each section also published polls every day and invariably referred to "America" in its news stories as "the USA."

In an editorial mission statement in *USA Today*'s first issue, Neuharth wrote that he wanted his newspaper "to serve as a forum for better understanding and unity to help make the USA truly one nation." Each section of his paper was a deliberate attempt to fulfill this belief. The news section featured a state-by-state breakdown of top news stories, giving readers a cross section of news events from across the country. The daily editorial was frequently accompanied by a differing viewpoint. The newspaper also developed a middle-of-the-road op-ed section, with regular national commentary from veteran journalists Richard Benedetto and Walter Shapiro. More politically pointed opinion makers, such as conservative writer Cal Thomas, tended to fare less successfully as the newspaper adopted a populist, rather than elitist, approach. One 1999 editorial, published after the Modern Library's list of the top 100 American novels of the twentieth century, maintained that the truly great novels were the most commercially successful ones, not the most critically or intellectually acclaimed works.

FINANCE AND SPORTS

USA Today's Money section (symbolized by a green title) introduced a regular feature, "Ad Watch," wherein popular television commercial campaigns were analyzed, not by ad executives but by focus groups of average American viewers. Eventually *USA Today* ran Ad Watch features to judge commercials produced for the Super Bowl. The newspaper also began running annual public service campaigns during preparation for filing IRS (Internal Revenue Service) forms, as well as during college admissions and financial aid seasons.

The paper's Sports section had the most far-reaching impact upon the newspaper industry. It published daily notes on all professional sports. For instance, during football season it introduced a Top 25 ranking for college sports (the Associated Press and UPI lists had previously gone only to twenty), in addition to Super 25 lists for high school sports. Major-league baseball coverage featured expanded box scores, offering play-by-play accounts on how every run in each major-league game was scored and extensive, week-by-week, team-by-team statistical charts. The expanded sports coverage was welcomed by Rotisserie League team owners, who rated their teams on how the players they owned performed day by day.

In 1991 *USA Today* introduced a successful weekly spin-off devoted to baseball. In both incarnations, the paper successfully challenged the *Sporting News*, which since 1886 had provided weekly coverage of baseball and other major sports. Significantly, the only major national daily newspaper formed after *USA Today*'s debut was a sports newspaper. The *National*, edited by former *Sports Illustrated* senior writer Frank Deford, debuted in 1989. Despite a roster of nationally known columnists and a series of high-profile scoops, the *National* lost its investment and folded within two years.

The Sports section also supplied *USA Today* with its greatest professional controversy. In 1992 *USA Today* sportswriters learned that tennis great and political activist Arthur Ashe was suffering from AIDS (acquired immunodeficiency syndrome), which had resulted from a tainted blood transfusion in 1983. An extremely private person, Ashe had told no one but family and close friends of his condition. The reporters contacted Ashe and told him they were planning a story on his health. Ashe responded by holding an emotional press conference, where he made his AIDS status public. *USA Today* came under intense criticism from inside and outside the journalism community. Many observers felt that the newspaper had violated Ashe's privacy and had engaged in emotional blackmail, while others (such as Phil Mushnick) maintained that Ashe's health was a legitimate news story. They argued that by coming forward and admitting he had AIDS rather than staying silent, he was able to raise both awareness of and financial support for the disease. Ashe lost his battle with the disease in early 1993.

LIFE AND CRITICISM

USA Today's Life section included a weekly column by radio and television talk show host Larry King, written much in the style of legendary gossip columnist Walter Winchell. King recommended movies and books, while also making occasional political commentary and discussing events in his personal life, most memorably his heart surgery, frequent marriages, and the birth of his son in 1999, when King was sixty-five. The Life section featured annual high school and collegiate Academic All-Stars, honoring the brightest students in the nation. *USA Today*'s television coverage included nightly listings for national cable channels several years before more traditional newspapers acknowledged cable's growing presence. The newspaper initiated a list of top box-office films, which was widely imitated by other venues, and provided complete Nielsen ratings for all prime-time television series. The Life section also developed one of the most respected book review sections in the country, with lengthy book reviews from freelancers and a best-seller list (eventually listing the Top 150 books) drawn from national bookstore chains. This was in opposition to the *New York Times* best-seller list, which listed only the top fifteen books and kept its listing methodology secret.

Cynicism toward the press grew during the 1980s and 1990s, fueled by political scandals, perceived ideological and cultural bias, and paparazzi reporting tactics (including those implicated in Princess Diana's 1997 death). Neuharth saw his newspaper's role as helping to alleviate the cynicism. The idiosyncratic Neuharth, whose autobiography *Confessions of an S.O.B.* included commentary from his two ex-wives, embarked on a cross-country "BusCapade" during 1987, visiting each of the fifty states. Neuharth celebrated the down-home common sense of average Americans from the heartland, as opposed to out-of-touch politicians and academics from the East and West Coasts. Some dismissed Neuharth's trek as a mere publicity stunt, but others appreciated his willingness to meet with his readers.

SUCCESS AND PRAISE

After a decade of losing money, *USA Today* finally turned a profit in 1993. The management spent their newfound profits on emphasizing editorial content over presentation. Executive editor Bob Dubill acknowledged that *USA Today*'s editors were "following TV. . . . Now, we're trying to lead TV." Within a fifteen-month span in 1996 and 1997, *USA Today* added an additional twenty-five reporting and editing slots to an editorial staff of 440. Publisher Tom Curley noted that many seasoned editors had returned to reporting beats. "We've taken some from the back room and put them on the street." Having begun in 1982 with only two domestic bureaus, by the late 1990s *USA Today* had four domestic bureaus and several foreign bureaus. That move coincided with the closing of many domestic and international news bureaus by the major television networks.

By the mid-1990s much of the early criticism of *USA Today* had abated. Media critic Ben Bagdikian (author of *The Media Monopoly*), who in 1982 called *USA Today* a "mediocre piece of journalism [presenting] a flawed picture of the world every day," recanted fifteen years later. "It has become a much more serious newspaper. . . . I don't think it's a joke anymore." Veteran Washington reporter David Broder said, "*USA Today* has become a pretty damn good newspaper. They are spending money, and it is making a difference. And they are everywhere." John Morton, who had initially criticized Neuharth's venture, said in 1997, "There is no question that they are a success. . . . You are less likely to find a front page article on some silly topic than on more serious issues. They have made it a more serious vehicle than it ever has been." Thomas Frank of the *Baffler*, while attacking the daily's middlebrow mindset, readily conceded that "*USA Today* is arguably the nation's most carefully edited and highly polished newspaper," concluding that it "has charted the course that almost every paper in the country is presently following." In 1997 even the Gray Lady began running color photographs in every section of its daily editions (the *Washington Post* followed suit two years later).

The circulation of most daily newspapers declined in the 1980s and 1990s, and New York, Philadelphia, Dallas, and Los Angeles all lost papers. *USA Today*, on the other hand, enjoyed the second-highest circulation of any paper in the country, with 1.62 million readers as of March 31, 1997. Analysts hailed *USA Today*'s strategies that maintained its circulation base by appealing to common demographic interests. Some, however, lamented that *USA Today* simply pandered to its readership's preexisting tastes rather than helping its audience cultivate new ones. Others maintained that the paper treated its readers as consumers, not public citizens, and were upset that Neuharth denied any professional obligation as a newspaper publisher to call for sustained political and social change.

Neuharth retired from Gannett in 1989 upon his sixty-fifth birthday and helped found the Freedom Forum, a media think tank that produces a quarterly magazine, *Media Studies Journal*. He wrote that the forum's principles were based upon "free press, free speech, and free spirit." In 1997 the forum opened the Newseum, directly across the street from *USA Today*'s Arlington, Virginia, headquarters. The Newseum hosts seminars; is the backdrop for the Cable News Network (CNN) media analysis program "Reliable Sources"; and features many interactive media displays, allowing visitors to generate their own news broadcast or select from newspapers across the country. More than one million visitors toured the Newseum within its first three years, and in 1999 it began a coast-to-coast tour that, like the BusCapade, visited each of America's fifty states. In 2008 the Newseum relocated to a brand-new building on Pennsylvania Avenue in Washington, D.C.

By the early twenty-first century, *USA Today* was ranked the top newspaper in America in print sales, reporting a circulation of 2,528,437 in 2006. It slid to second behind the *Wall Street Journal*, however, when digital copies were factored in. The new century also saw the newspaper expand its base of operations to include book publishing. Choosing to partner with small specialized companies, *USA Today* inked deals in 2007 with Nolo Press, Sterling Publishing, Sports Publishing, Andrews McMeel, Multimedia, and Mead Westvaco. The deal with Nolo included a twelve-book series of business and legal guides. *USA Today* and Sports Publishing agreed to copublish *25 Years of USA Today*. The Mead-Westvaco agreement involved publishing a year-in-a-box multipuzzle calendar, while the Multimedia deal led to the publication of a Sudoku puzzle magazine. The contract with Andrews McMeel concerned publication of both puzzles and a calendar. *USA Today* added smartphone and Internet TV apps in the early 2010s, providing free access to its print content.

Andrew Milner

SEE ALSO: *Advertising; AIDS; Ashe, Arthur; Kelly, Grace; King, Larry; Mantle, Mickey; Mays, Willie; The* New York Times*; The* Sporting News*; Super Bowl; The* Washington Post.

BIBLIOGRAPHY

Hartman, John K. *The "USA Today" Way: A Candid Look at the National Newspaper's First Decade, 1982–1992.* Mount Pleasant, MI: Author, 1992.

Kinsella, Bridget. "USA Today Extends Brand to Books." *Publishers Weekly*, May 28, 2007.

Neuharth, Allen. *Confessions of an S.O.B.* New York: Doubleday, 1989.

Prichard, Peter S. *The Making of McPaper: The Inside Story of "USA Today."* Kansas City, MO: Andrews, McMeel & Parker, 1987.

Stamm, Michael. *Sound Business: Newspapers, Radio, and the Politics of New Media.* Philadelphia: University of Pennsylvania Press, 2011.

Usher *(1978–)*

Known for his smooth vocals and sensual ballads, R&B superstar Usher Terry Raymond IV was born in Chattanooga, Tennessee, in 1978. He and his younger brother were brought up by a single mother. Jonetta Patton was a choir director, and by the age of six Usher was already singing in the church choir. When he was twelve, his mother moved the family to Atlanta, Georgia, where musical opportunities were greater. Usher began entering local talent shows. Within two years, he had signed a recording contract with LaFace Records, releasing his first self-titled album in 1994. That album did little more than get him noticed, but he was on his way with the release of *My Way* in 1997. The singles "You Make Me Wanna" and "Nice and Slow" reached the top of the R&B charts, and the latter crossed over to become a pop hit as well. By the end of the decade, Usher had achieved superstar status.

The 1990s were a time of growth for Usher. He had a recurring role on R&B singer Brandy's television vehicle *Moesha* (1996–2001), but his focus was always on music and broadening his appeal to reach a wider audience. Usher also worked hard at heightening his playboy image. He entered the twenty-first century at the top of his profession. His 2001 release of *8701* produced two number one hits—"U Remind Me" and "U Got It Bad"—and garnered him his first two Grammy Awards. The album sold 4.7 million copies. In 2002 Usher appeared as Marvin Gaye in the television show *American Dreams*.

The year 2004 proved to be Usher's year. His fourth album, *Confessions*, sold a million copies within a week of its release and eventually sold 9.7 million units. The endeavor was somewhat of a departure for Usher since it included a collaboration with Atlanta rappers Lil Jon and Ludacris. Within six weeks of its release, the trio's "Yeah" rose to number one, where it remained for twelve weeks. In May "Burn" unseated "Yeah" from the top position and remained there for the next eight weeks. At the end of 2004 Usher's "Yeah" and "Burn" were the top-selling songs of the year. It was the first time since 1964, when the Beatles had won the top two spots, that any singer had managed the feat.

Confessions remained at the top of the Billboard 200 for nine weeks. Sasha Frere-Jones of the *New Yorker* described the album as "a diverting, glossy series of apologies and whispery shouts," yet Usher brought home eleven Billboard Music Awards, including Artist of the Year. The fruits of 2004 carried over into the following year, and Usher won three more Grammy Awards, winning the top spots for Contemporary R&B Album for *Confessions*, Best R&B Performance by a Duo or Group for "My Boo" with Alicia Keys, and Best Rap/Sung Collaboration for "Yeah" with Lil Jon and Ludacris. That same year, Usher appeared in the film *In the Mix*, for which he received less than stellar reviews. He made it to Broadway in 2006, appearing as the shyster Billy Flynn in the musical *Chicago*.

Usher married his stylist and longtime friend Tameka Foster in 2007 and became the father of two, Usher Terry Raymond V and Naviyd Ely Raymond. The couple's split two years later was public and acrimonious. Both the marriage and the divorce played a large part in Usher's musical development. As a newlywed, he released *Here I Stand*, which sold 1.2 million copies and went platinum. Chronicling his somewhat more sedate life, *Here I Stand* revealed a more serious singer than the one who had been known for his overtly sexual lyrics. The divorce in 2009 led to *Raymond v. Raymond* (2010), which included the hits "Papers," the buzz single that rose to number one on Billboard's Hot R&B/Hip-Hop Songs; "Hey Daddy (Daddy's Home)"; "There Goes My Baby"; and the party jam "Lil Freak," which all climbed the charts simultaneously.

Usher became co-owner of the National Basketball Association's Cleveland Cavaliers in 2005. He also lent his name to fragrances for both males and females. He devoted considerable time to the New Look Foundation, which provides opportunities for inner-city youths. One of his wisest investments turned out to be promoting Canadian pop sensation Justin Bieber, who had been discovered by Usher's business partner, Scooter Braun, when he stumbled upon a Bieber video on YouTube. After signing with Usher's label, Bieber became his protégé. In spring 2010 *Raymond v. Raymond*, which sold 329,000 copies in its first week, edged out Bieber's *My World 2.0*, which sold 291,000 copies.

Elizabeth Rholetter Purdy

SEE ALSO: *Bieber, Justin; Broadway; Celebrity; Divorce; Grammy Awards; The Musical; National Basketball Association (NBA); Pop Music; Rap; Rhythm and Blues; YouTube.*

BIBLIOGRAPHY

Caulfield, Keith. "Usher's Third Number One; Bieber's Second Week Spike." *Billboard*, April 17, 2010.

Frere-Jones, Sasha. "Usher 2.0." *New Yorker*, June 2, 2008.

Mitchell, Gail. "Usher a Single Man." *Billboard*, March 13, 2010, 14.

"Usher.biography." Bio True Story. Accessed March 2012. Available from http://www.biography.com/people/usher-38321

U2

The band U2 has enjoyed immense commercial and critical success over a career in rock and roll that has spanned more than three decades. The membership of the band has remained unchanged since singer Bono (born Paul Hewson, 1960–), guitarist The Edge (David Evans, 1961–), bassist Adam Clayton (1960–), and drummer Larry Mullen Jr. (1961–) began performing together when they were students at Mount Temple Comprehensive School in Dublin in 1977. Their early efforts were characterized more by energy and enthusiasm than skill, but years of persistence paid off in 1980 when the group signed with the fledgling label Island Records. Their first single, "11 O'Clock Tick Tock," and first album, *Boy*, were released the same year. The music and lyrics on that first album contain elements that became signatures of the group's work: a guitar-driven sound, anthemic songs, and sociopolitical commentary.

BUILDING A FOLLOWING

While *Boy* and the follow-up, *October* (1981), brought U2 attention, particularly in the United States, their breakthrough came with 1983's *War*. The album's politically motivated songs—such as "Sunday Bloody Sunday," about the sectarian violence in Ireland, and "New Year's Day," a powerful antiwar anthem—have more in common lyrically with the politically charged songs from the 1960s and 1970s than with the fare from the conservative 1980s. However, a humming guitar sound that combines the most accessible elements of punk and new wave touched a nerve with contemporary rock audiences and propelled the album to number one on UK music charts and into the Top 10 in the United States.

U2's follow-up, *The Unforgettable Fire* (1984), was eagerly anticipated, but rather than give fans what they wanted—another collection of anthemic rock songs—they made an arty album of ambient and orchestrated experimentation. Still, the album's first single, "Pride (In the Name of Love)," is much like the signature tracks from the first two albums and was the band's biggest hit to date. "Pride" is considered by many sources, including *Rolling Stone* and *Spin*, to be one of rock's greatest songs. In 1985, the editors of *Rolling Stone* named U2 "the Band of the 1980s."

ROCK SUPERSTARS

It was *The Joshua Tree* (1987) that made U2 iconic. The band had headlined Amnesty International's "A Conspiracy of Hope" tour in 1986, resulting in its increased commitment to human rights issues. This new awareness, coupled with Bono's developing skills as a songwriter, helped to shape the new album. Encompassing such universal themes as the abuse of power and the resiliency of the human spirit, the album also examines the American political landscape from an Irish perspective. *The Joshua Tree* topped the Billboard charts for nine weeks, produced two number one singles ("With or without You" and "I Still Haven't Found What I'm Looking For"), earned the Grammy for Album of the Year, and sold more than fifteen million copies. It transformed U2 from a band that played 20,000-seat concert venues into one that could sell out the largest arenas in the world.

U2's fascination with America continued through 1987 and 1988. On the advice of Bob Dylan, Bono listened to early rock and roll, black gospel, Appalachian folk music, classic country ballads, and delta blues. The result was *Rattle and Hum* (1988), the title of a double album, book, tour, and black-and-white documentary that includes concert footage from the band's 1987 tour of North America. Sales of the album were modest, and the documentary provoked a backlash among American viewers who felt the band came off as arrogant and self-involved. The band announced at a New Year's Eve concert in 1989 that it would take some time off and, in Bono's words, "dream it all up again."

UPS AND DOWNS

The dream must have seemed more like a nightmare at times as the group gathered at Hansa Studios in Berlin in October 1990 to record *Achtung Baby*, its seventh studio album. The need to present a less pompous, self-righteous image was clear, but disagreement about the musical means to accomplish this goal created tensions and conflicts among the band members that were almost severe enough to cause a breakup. The four moved past their disagreements, however, to craft an album that is more varied lyrically and musically than U2's earlier efforts. A sense of idealism permeates the album, but the overall effect is more personal and less polemical. *Achtung Baby* topped the charts in the United States and other countries; won another Grammy; sold more than eighteen million copies worldwide; and featured a single, "One," that rivals "Pride" in the group's canon. *Achtung Baby* joined *The Joshua Tree* as one of the most acclaimed albums of all time.

For their subsequent "Zoo TV Tour" (1992–1993), U2 reinvented their live show. Whereas they had previously played on unadorned stages, the "Zoo TV" shows featured extravagant multimedia effects. There were large screens showing video clips and flashing bits of text, as well as, controversially, live satellite feeds from the ongoing war in Sarajevo. U2's next album, *Zooropa* (1993), was a product of the tour. It and its follow-up, *Pop* (1997), which is heavy on dance rhythms, drew mixed reviews. More significantly, attendance at U2 concerts began to dwindle.

BACK ON TOP

Deciding the time had come for another look at who they were, U2 withdrew for a break, again almost splitting up in the struggle to redefine themselves before releasing *All That You*

Can't Leave Behind in 2000. It sold more than twelve million copies and won seven Grammys, including Best Rock Album. It is the only album to have singles win the Grammy for Record of the Year in consecutive years: "Beautiful Day" in 2000 and "Walk On" in 2001.

No Line on the Horizon (2009), U2's twelfth album, took two years to make. Although it debuted at the top of the charts in thirty countries, sales were disappointing by U2 standards. Nevertheless, the group's massive, two-year "360° Tour," named for the staging configuration that allowed the audience to surround the stage, was the highest-grossing ($736 million) and best-attended (7.2 million tickets sold) tour in history.

Wylene Rholetter

SEE ALSO: *Alternative Rock; Dylan, Bob; Rock and Roll; Stadium Concerts.*

BIBLIOGRAPHY

"Bono." *Current Biography Yearbook, 2009.* New York: H.W. Wilson, 2009.

Gundersen, Edna. "Revisit U2's Dark, Dramatic *Achtung Baby.*" *USA Today*, October 26, 2011. Accessed February 2012. Available from http://www.usatoday.com/life/music/news/story/2011-10-26/u2-documentary-achtung-baby-reissue/50919390/

Hiatt, Brian. "U2 Revisit *Achtung Baby* and Plan for the Future." *Rolling Stone*, November 10, 2011, 15–18.

Johnson, Fred. "U2, Mythology, and Mass-Mediated Survival." *Popular Music & Society* 27, no. 1 (2004): 79–99.

Stokes, Niall. "U2's U.S. Landscapes; Ireland's Political Rockers, on Tour and on Target." *Washington Post*, September 20, 1987.

V

Valdez, Luis *(1940–)*

Luis Valdez is considered to be the father of Chicano theater. He is the instigator of the contemporary Chicano theatrical movement and its most outstanding playwright. Valdez has distinguished himself as an actor, a director, a playwright, and a filmmaker. However, it was in his role as the founding director of El Teatro Campesino, a theater of farm workers in California, that his efforts inspired young Chicano activists across the country to use theater as a means of organizing students, communities, and labor unions.

EARLY ACTIVISM

Luis Valdez was born June 26, 1940, into a family of migrant farm workers in Delano, California. The second of ten children, he began to work the fields at age six, following the crops. Although his education was constantly interrupted, he nevertheless finished high school and went on to San Jose State College, where he majored in English and pursued his interest in theater. While there he won a playwriting contest with his one-act work *The Theft* (1961). In 1963 the San Jose State Drama Department produced his play *The Shrunken Head of Pancho Villa.*

After graduating from college in 1964 Valdez joined the San Francisco Mime Troupe and learned the techniques of agitprop (agitation and propaganda) theater and Italian commedia dell'arte, both of which influenced his development of the basic format of Chicano theater: the one-act presentational *acto.* In 1965 Valdez enlisted in Cesar Chavez's mission to organize farm workers in Delano into a union. It was there that Valdez brought together farm workers and students and formed El Teatro Campesino to dramatize the plight of the farm workers. The publicity and success gained by the troupe led to the spontaneous development of a national Chicano theater movement.

In 1967 Valdez and El Teatro Campesino left the unionizing effort to expand their theater beyond agitprop and farm worker concerns. Since that time Valdez and the theater have explored most of the theatrical genres that have been important to Mexicans in the United States, including religious pageants, vaudeville with the down-and-out *pelado* (underdog) figure, and dramatized *corridos* (ballads). The type of socially engaged theater that El Teatro Campesino pioneered led to the creation of a full-blown theatrical movement in fields and barrios across the country.

For more than three decades El Teatro Campesino and Valdez have dramatized the political and cultural concerns of Hispanics, initially among workers and their supporters and later among students in universities and the general public through stage, television, and film. In establishing the canon of what *teatro chicano* should be, Valdez and El Teatro Campesino published their *actos* in 1971 with a preface in which Valdez outlined their theatrical principles: (1) Chicanos must be seen as a nation with geographic, religious, cultural, and racial roots in the Southwest; (2) *teatros* must further the idea of nationalism and create a national theater based on identification with their Amerindian past; (3) the organizational support of the national theater must be from within and totally independent; and (4) "teatros must never get away from La Raza. . . . If the Raza will not come to the theater, then the theater must go to the Raza. This, in the long run, will determine the shape, style, content, spirit and form of *el teatro chicano.*" Valdez and his theater did expand by taking Chicano theater to Broadway and more commercial venues and by moving into commercial cinema and television.

ACTIVISM THROUGH THEATER

During the late 1960s and the 1970s El Teatro Campesino produced many of Valdez's plays, including *Los Vendidos* (1967), *The Shrunken Head of Pancho Villa* (1964), *Bernabé* (1970), *Dark Root of a Scream* (1971), *La Carpa de los Rasquachis* (1974), and *El Fin del mundo* (1976). In 1978 Valdez broke into mainstream theater in Los Angeles, with the Mark Taper Forum's production of *Zoot Suit,* and in 1979 with the Broadway production of the same play. In 1986 he had a successful run of his play *I Don't Have to Show You No Stinking Badges* at the Los Angeles Theater Center.

In *Bernabé,* one of Valdez's most poetic plays, a young village idiot is transformed into a natural man by his marriage to La Tierra (the Earth) and his subsequent death. Employing Aztec mythology and symbols in a tale about contemporary barrio characters, the play explores the pre-Columbian heritage of Chicano society. The Mayan theme of "death is life and life is death" was developed here and continued to appear in Valdez's later works. The writing of *Bernabé* marked the beginning of Valdez's search for the meaning of Aztec and Mayan legends, history, and philosophy but revealed the influence of Spanish playwright Federico García Lorca, who also strove to elevate the country folk to heroic and mythic stature.

Valdez's screenwriting career began with early film and television versions of Corky González's poem "I Am Joaquín" (1969) and with his own *Los Vendidos.* Later, he wrote a film adaptation of *Zoot Suit* (1981). However, his real incursion into major Hollywood, California, productions and success came with his writing and directing of *La Bamba* (1987), the screen biography of Chicano rock-and-roll star Ritchie Valens. Other screen plays include *Corridos* (1987) and the successful television movies *La Pastorela* (1991) and *The Cisco Kid* (1994).

Valdez's plays, essays, and poems have been widely anthologized. He has published several collections of plays: *Luis Valdez—Early Works* (1990), *Zoot Suit and Other Plays* (1992), and *Mummified Deer and Other Plays* (2005). Valdez's awards include an Obie (1968); Los Angeles Drama Critics Awards (1969, 1972, and 1978); a special Emmy Award (1973); the San Francisco Bay Critics Circle Award for Best Musical (1983); a Presidential Medal for the Arts (1983); and honorary doctorates from San Jose State University, Columbia College, and the California Institute of the Arts. He was one of the founding faculty members of California State University–Monterey Bay, which opened in 1995.

Nicolás Kanellos

SEE ALSO: *Broadway; Chavez, Cesar; Emmy Awards; Hollywood; "La Bamba"; Labor Unions; Valens, Ritchie; Vaudeville.*

BIBLIOGRAPHY

Broyles-González, Yolanda. *El Teatro Campesino: Theatre in the Chicano Movement.* Austin: University of Texas Press, 1994.

Elam, Harry Justin, Jr. *Taking It to the Streets: The Social Protest Theater of Luis Valdez and Amiri Baraka.* Ann Arbor: University of Michigan Press, 2001.

Kanellos, Nicolás. *The Hispanic American Almanac.* Detroit, MI: Gale, 1997.

Kanellos, Nicolás, and Claudio Esteva Fabregat, eds. *Handbook of Hispanic Cultures in the United States.* Houston, TX: Arte Público Press, 1994.

Wood, Jamie Martinez. *Latino Writers and Journalists: A to Z of Latino Americans.* New York: Facts On File, 2007.

Vallee, Rudy *(1901–1986)*

One of the most popular American singers in the 1920s and 1930s, Rudy Vallee became a sought-after supporting actor in Hollywood films, an important pioneer in radio variety shows, and much later a musical comedy star on Broadway.

Born Hubert Prior Vallée in Island Pond, Vermont, he was a self-taught drummer in his high school band. In 1919 he began a self-study of the clarinet and saxophone, frequently spending six to eight hours a day practicing, and within a year he was performing publicly at the Strand Theater in Portland, Maine. After a year at the University of Maine, he transferred to Yale in the fall of 1922, where he earned tuition by playing his sax at country clubs and college dances. While playing with the Yale Collegians, he began using a handheld megaphone to amplify his crooning, light-tone voice. The megaphone—similar to the ones used by cheerleaders—became his trademark and was soon copied by other vocalists.

In 1924 Vallee dropped out of Yale and went to London, where he played sax at the Savoy Hotel with Vincent Lopez and the Savoy Havana Band. Returning to Yale, he continued his studies and graduated with a BA in philosophy in 1927. Moving to New York City, Vallee formed a small band called the Connecticut Yankees, consisting of two violins, two saxophones, and a piano. The primary purpose of the orchestra was to accompany their leader's suave but somewhat nasal vocals. An engagement at the Heigh-Ho Club in Manhattan in 1928 brought Vallee his first real fame. He was soon broadcasting on radio as many as twenty-five times a week, beginning each one with "Heigh-ho, everybody, this is Rudy Vallee." His sudden success brought him engagements at New York's Paramount and Palace theaters.

Vallee and the Connecticut Yankees went to Hollywood to film *The Vagabond Lover* in 1929, returning immediately to New York for more radio work and regular appearances at Villa Vallee, a nightclub he owned. He soon evolved a busy routine, starting with daily shows at the Paramount and other theaters, then nightly shows at the Villa Vallee, and three broadcasts, along with recording sessions and filming musical short subjects.

In 1929 Vallee also began broadcasting a weekly one-hour variety show on NBC radio. Stars such as Fred Allen, Jack Benny, Edgar Bergen, and Kate Smith made their debuts on *Vallee's Fleischmann Hour* and later became radio stars themselves. Other outstanding guests included George Gershwin, George Burns and Gracie Allen, Eddie Cantor, Red Skelton, and Fanny Brice. Vallee also invited black performers, rarely used on network shows, to appear, including Bill "Bojangles" Robinson, Maxine Sullivan, and Fats Waller. At its peak, the show featured America's top stars. On December 13, 1934, for example, Vallee broadcast from Radio City Music Hall, featuring announcer Jimmy Wallington; guests Henry Fonda and June Walker playing a scene from *The Farmer Takes a Wife*; and interviews with Cole Porter, Buck and Bubbles, William S. Hart, and Bea Lillie.

After ten years Vallee ended his popular radio show. In 1942 he played the bumbling millionaire in one of director Preston Sturges's best films, *The Palm Beach Story*, starring Claudette Colbert. After World War II began, Vallee joined the U.S. Coast Guard Service and led a forty-piece band on an extensive tour. He then returned to radio in 1944, broadcasting for two years with costar Monty Woolley. Hollywood beckoned in 1947, and Vallee played light comedy and character roles in such films as *The Bachelor and the Bobby-Soxer* (1947), with Cary Grant and Myrna Loy; *I Remember Mama* (1948), with Irene Dunne; *Unfaithfully Yours* (1948), with Rex Harrison; and *The Beautiful Blonde from Bashful Bend* (1949), with Betty Grable. From 1961 to 1964 he played in the Broadway musical *How to Succeed in Business without Really Trying*, and his final film was the Hollywood version of that show in 1967.

Benjamin Griffith

SEE ALSO: *Benny, Jack; Bergen, Edgar; Brice, Fanny; Burns, George, and Gracie Allen; Cantor, Eddie; Colbert, Claudette; Dunne, Irene; Fonda, Henry; Grable, Betty; Grant, Cary; Hollywood; Loy, Myrna; Porter, Cole; Radio; Skelton, Red; Smith, Kate; Sturges, Preston; The Twenties; World War II.*

BIBLIOGRAPHY

Lackmann, Ronald. *The Encyclopedia of American Radio: An A–Z Guide to Radio from Jack Benny to Howard Stern.* New York: Facts On File, 2000.

Parish, James Robert, and Michael R. Pitts. *Hollywood Songsters: Singers Who Act and Actors Who Sing: A Biographical Dictionary.* New York: Routledge, 2003.

Quinlan, David. *Quinlan's Film Stars.* Washington, DC: Brassey's, 2000.

Ragan, David. *Who's Who in Hollywood, 1900–1976.* New Rochelle, NY: Arlington House, 1976.

Valens, Ritchie *(1941–1959)*

The Latino teen-rock sensation Ritchie Valens had a brief but brilliant career. Most famous for his song "La Bamba," a rock-and-roll version of a traditional Mexican ballad, Valens fused different kinds of music together to form his own remarkable style. Influenced by some of the biggest names in rock and roll, including Elvis Presley, Bo Diddley, and Little Richard, he earned himself the nickname "The Little Richard of San Fernando." Although his career was cut short by a fatal plane crash, Valens wrote and recorded songs that would influence future generations of rock musicians, including the Beatles and Led Zeppelin.

Born Richard Stephen Valenzuela in the San Fernando Valley suburb of Pacoima, California, Ritchie received a Catholic upbringing despite money being tight. As a child, he made himself a guitar out of a cigar box and a broom handle and strung it with household string. His home life gave him a grounding in traditional Mexican mariachi music played by his relatives, and the radio exposed him to the rhythm-and-blues sound. In 1956 Ritchie joined a band called the Silhouettes, which performed at hops around the San Fernando Valley area. The Silhouettes were a multiracial band featuring two African Americans; a Japanese American; and Ritchie, a Mexican American. After various reshuffles in the band, Ritchie sang lead vocals and played the guitar.

Ritchie Valens. *Ritchie Valens's promising music career was cut short by his death in a 1959 plane crash, an event that has come to be known as "The Day the Music Died."* AP IMAGES.

Bob Keane of Del-fi Records discovered a sixteen-year-old Ritchie at one of the San Fernando garage hops. Once Keane saw how audiences responded to the band's charismatic lead singer, he gave him a recording contract. Keane changed the young artist's name to Ritchie Valens—a catchier, Anglicized version of his real name. Valens's first hit was a rock-and-roll number "Come on Let's Go," which he wrote himself. It reached number forty-two on the U.S. charts. In October 1958 Del-fi released "La Bamba" with a love song titled "Donna" on the other side. Valens wrote this love song about his high school sweetheart, whose father had forbidden her to go out with a Mexican. It turned out to be the more successful track, selling more than one million copies and reaching number two on the U.S. charts. "La Bamba" only climbed as high as number twenty-two.

Keane found Valens an unorthodox musician to work with; he would make up songs and then forget them, or he would base a whole song on just eight guitar chords and two lines of lyrics. Nevertheless, the pair successfully recorded a large number of songs in Keane's basement studio at his home in Silverlake, California. Keane wanted to get Valens out on the road since his major talent was in performing. He assessed that Valens's combination of toughness and shy vulnerability dazzled his teenage audiences.

Valens's final tour was called "The Winter Dance Party." He headlined with Buddy Holly and the Big Bopper. Valens, with the success of "Donna" under his belt, was not obliged to play low-profile concerts in the Midwest but reportedly did so out of loyalty to his fans. The weather was bitterly cold and the heating had broken on their tour bus. Holly chartered a plane with space for himself, his guitarist, and the Big Bopper. Valens could not cope with the subzero temperature levels and talked Holly's guitarist into tossing a coin for the last seat. Valens won the toss. The plane crashed shortly after takeoff in a field outside of Fargo, North Dakota. All aboard were killed. The occasion was dubbed by the press as "The Day the Music Died."

Had he lived longer, Valens possibly would have become one of the most significant musicians of the 1960s. In *Time Passages: Collective Memory and American Popular Culture*, cultural critic George Lipsitz writes, "Valens' tragic death at the age of seventeen deprived the Los Angeles Chicano community of its biggest star, and it cut short the career of one of rock and roll's most eclectic synthesizers." Valens's talent lay in his ability to mix radically different types of music: black rhythm and blues, white folk music, and Mexican mariachi songs—the sounds that surrounded him as he grew up in postwar California. Despite being the only musician of Mexican ancestry to make it in the mainstream pop scene, Valens regarded himself as first and foremost American. He did not speak Spanish and had to be coached for singing the Spanish lyrics of "La Bamba."

In 1987 a biopic called *La Bamba*, made by the Chicano film director Luis Valdez, was released, regenerating interest in Valens's music and demonstrating how his music continues to touch young people.

Candida Taylor

SEE ALSO: *The Beatles; Big Bopper; Diddley, Bo; Folk Music; Holly, Buddy; "La Bamba"; Led Zeppelin; Little Richard;*

Mariachi Music; Pop Music; Presley, Elvis; Rhythm and Blues; Rock and Roll; Valdez, Luis.

BIBLIOGRAPHY

Cullen, Jim. *The Art of Democracy: A Concise History of Popular Culture in the United States.* New York: Monthly Review Press, 1996.

Lehmer, Larry. *The Day the Music Died: The Last Tour of Buddy Holly, the Big Bopper and Ritchie Valens.* New York: Schirmer Trade Books, 2004.

Lipsitz, George. "Cruising around the Historical Block." *Time Passages: Collective Memory and American Popular Culture.* Minneapolis: University of Minnesota Press.

Stambler, Irwin. *The Encyclopedia of Pop, Rock and Soul.* New York: St. Martin's Press, 1974.

Valentine's Day

Valentine's Day, February 14, is a day consecrated by custom to the celebration of romantic love. The observance dates back to medieval times, but in twentieth-century America, Valentine's Day—like other occasions that are linked to sentiment, such as Mother's Day—has become a ritual appendage of consumer culture. Attempts to link Valentine's Day and its emphasis on worldly love to an early martyr (or pair of martyrs) of the Christian church have been discredited, and historians have come to attribute the connection between romance and February 14 to Geoffrey Chaucer (1340?–1400), the English poet and author of *The Canterbury Tales.*

In his work *The Parliament of Foules,* Chaucer wrote: "For this was on Seynt Valentynes Day, Whan every foul cometh ther to chese his make." Throughout the late Middle Ages and the early modern period, Valentine's Day was an occasion for declaring one's affections or using divination to determine the identity of one's lover or future spouse. Sleeping on a pillow to which five bay leaves were pinned, for example, would produce a dream in which a lover would be revealed. Observances of the day could be elegant and courtly or a raucous and vulgar charivari (mock serenade, usually of newlyweds). The first Valentine's Day cards were handmade, but by the early nineteenth century, printed cards were common in England. When this fashion was exported to the United States in the 1840s, a veritable Valentine mania broke out.

The industrialized world of the early 1800s suffered from a shortage of holidays. Where once the feasting and fasting days of the Christian year had provided the occasion for a host of holidays, festivals, and fairs, the Enlightenment and the industrial revolution had, in the names of efficiency and the economy, produced a calendar almost empty of special days. (In 1761 there were forty-seven bank holidays in England; by 1834 there were only four.) By popularizing and commercializing Valentine's Day in the United States, the merchant class reshaped, romanticized, and tamed the day for its own purposes. Valentine's Day (and slightly later, Christmas) demonstrates how business could profit from creating new meaning for an old holiday.

Printing companies were not the only ones to profit from the new popularity of the day. Other business interests rapidly attached themselves to the successful annual marketing of romance. Confectioners sold candies and chocolates in great quantities, while florists, jewelers, photographers, and makers of pens, pins, and knickknacks of all kinds found they could increase sales by linking their product to Valentine's Day. Women and children were prime targets for this commercialization of sentiment.

In the twentieth century the Valentine's Day industry grew even more vast. By the 1990s sales of candy for the occasion had risen to more than $600 million; seventy million roses are given on the day; restaurants are filled with couples seeking romantic dining; and over a billion cards are exchanged every year in the United States alone, with school children leading the way. Hallmark Cards, the largest American manufacturer, produces thousands of different designs, which are changed annually. Most of these cards are plainer than they once were, shorn of the peacock feathers, real lace, and jewels that once adorned those of the nineteenth century. It is interesting to note that Valentine cards were not always necessarily sent as straightforward declarations of love. A widespread custom was the anonymous sending of insulting or sarcastic cards, often aimed at women to keep them in their place, and comic or satirical, even vulgar, cards are still bought and sent.

Valentine's Day is celebrated in song and film as synonymous with romantic love. It is a day for dances and gala balls, the advertising of "honeymoon suites" for married couples whose ardor may have waned over the years, and for decorating public places with heart shapes pierced by the arrow of an often visible and cherubic Cupid. Over the years the holiday has spread beyond England and America to Europe, Asia, and other English-speaking countries such as South Africa and Australia, and production and sales of Valentine cards have become a worldwide phenomenon.

Gerry Bowler

SEE ALSO: *Christmas; Greeting Cards; Mother's Day.*

BIBLIOGRAPHY

MacDonald, Margaret Read. *The Folklore of World Holidays.* Detroit, MI: Gale Research, 1992.

Schmidt, Leigh Eric. *Consumer Rites: The Buying and Selling of American Holidays.* Princeton, NJ: Princeton University Press, 1995.

Valentino, Rudolph *(1895–1926)*

"The Great Lover" was the nickname given to Rudolph Valentino when he became a motion picture star in 1919. While the moniker is still synonymous with the actor, his last name alone is sufficient to evoke the same picture, that of a handsome, suave man who is irresistible to women. His female fans copied styles from his movies, and some men copied his hairstyles. During his brief stardom, he was often the butt of criticism from men. Despite this, women of the era literally fainted at the sight of him and worshipped him at the altar of their local movie theater.

For someone who had such a profound effect on popular culture during his lifetime, Valentino came from rather humble beginnings. He was born in Castellaneta, Italy, with the impossible name Rodolfo Alfonzo Raffaello Pierre Filibert Guglielmi di Valentina d'Antonguolla. His father, Giovanni, was a veterinarian who died of malaria in 1906. The young Valentino longed to become a cavalry officer, but his family felt that after the death of his father he needed a better-paying career to help take care of the family. His mother was finally persuaded to allow him to apply to the Royal Naval Academy, but he failed the physical. Eventually Rudolph attended the Royal Academy of Agriculture, where he graduated with honors. He planned to become a gentleman farmer, but fate had other plans.

After graduation, Valentino went on a trip outside Italy and proceeded to lose all his money gambling. To ease the family's embarrassment, he was sent to America on the U.S.S. *Cleveland* in 1913. After some difficult times in New York, Valentino began to find work as a taxi dancer (essentially a dancer for hire). Shortly thereafter, he got a job with millionaire Cornelius Bliss as a gardener. Unfortunately, he was soon fired when he wrecked a motorcycle owned by his employer.

Unemployed again, Valentino received help from a friend who was the head waiter at Maxim's Restaurant. He was hired for a position as a dancer there. He later met and was signed as a partner to dancer Bonnie Glass, who was replacing her previous partner, Clifton Webb (soon to be an actor). After Glass retired, Valentino danced with another partner, Joan Sawyer, on the vaudeville circuit. However, he soon grew tired of touring and resolved to give up dancing and become a farmer in California. To get there, he took a part in a play called *The Masked Model*, which was to tour the West Coast. Unfortunately the play closed in Utah, but he was paid with a ticket to San Francisco.

HOLLYWOOD

Once in California, Valentino met Norman Kerry, Mary Pickford's leading man, who persuaded him to try his luck in Hollywood. By 1917 he had made his first screen appearance as an extra in *Alimony* and had played several villains in other films. A chance meeting with screen star Mae Murray resulted in work on two of her films. It was this exposure that led to more work in Hollywood.

While working on *Once to Every Woman* in 1920, Valentino impulsively married actress Jean Acker. Acker locked him out of her room on their wedding night, and they separated before the marriage was ever consummated. This would ultimately become a source of embarrassment for studio executives when Valentino became a sex symbol. Despite their brief marriage, Valentino and Acker remained good friends to the end of his life.

Valentino made an important fan with his next project, *The Eyes of Youth* (1919), by catching the attention of June Mathis, head scenarist for Metro Studios. At the time Mathis was working on *The Four Horsemen of the Apocalypse*, based on the novel by Vicente Blasco-Ibáñez. Mathis was convinced that Valentino was the perfect actor for the part of Julio. Studio

Rudolph Valentino. *Rudolph Valentino, left, appears with Vilma Banky in a colorized still from the 1926 film* The Son of the Sheik. © MICHAEL NICHOLSON/CORBIS.

executives were not as impressed, but after much lobbying by both Mathis and Valentino, he was given the part. During early footage Valentino so impressed Mathis and director Rex Ingram that they expanded his part, and a star was born. From his first appearance in the film, when he tangos with Beatrice Dominguez, he enthralled the audience. Details of the film were copied by fans: the tango became a dance craze, men copied his slicked back hair, and women copied the bolero costume he wore.

If Valentino had expected the studio heads to respond to his popularity by giving him better parts and paying him accordingly, he was wrong. He appeared in several more films, such as *Camille* (1921) and *The Conquering Power* (1921), but executives refused his demand for a raise and then declined to renew his contract when it expired. Valentino eventually signed a new contract with the Famous Players-Lasky Paramount Studio and began filming *The Sheik* with Agnes Ayres. This film cemented his stardom. It would be almost impossible to imagine the kind of hysteria that greeted him after this film was released in 1921. Audiences were much less sophisticated and blasé in the early days of film than in the twenty-first century, and pandemonium reigned whenever Valentino made an appearance.

Valentino experienced a good year in 1922 with the release of the original *Blood and Sand* and *The Young Rajah*. That year he was also granted an interlocutory divorce from Acker. Unfortunately, he neglected to wait a year before marrying Natacha Rambova (Winifred Hudnut) in Mexico. When he returned to California, he was arrested and jailed for bigamy before being fined $10,000 and released. The resulting scandal actually increased Valentino's popularity instead of ruining him. He and Rambova remarried in 1923 after waiting the required year.

In 1924 he filmed several pictures, including *Monsieur Beaucaire* and *The Eagle*. For the film *The Hooded Falcon*, he grew a beard that not only infuriated his fans but also angered the Barbers of America Organization, which threatened to boycott his films. Needless to say, he shaved the beard. Unfortunately, Rambova had tremendous influence over Valentino's career but did not have the best taste when it came to selecting projects for him. His image began to tarnish, at least among the male half of the audience. Rambova bought him a slave bracelet, which he wore constantly, and began choosing projects for him that made his androgynous qualities appear more feminine. She was eventually barred from working in any capacity on his films. Shortly thereafter, Rambova left him, and the couple eventually divorced.

AN UNTIMELY DEATH

In 1926 Valentino starred in *The Son of the Sheik*, supposedly a sequel to his earlier hit film. His most steady date in this, the last year of his life, was eccentric Polish actress Pola Negri. According to some sources, Negri saw him off on a train to New York for the East Coast premiere of *Son of the Sheik*. It was the last time she would see Valentino alive. On August 15 he became seriously ill and was taken to the hospital. He was diagnosed with a perforated ulcer and underwent surgery. The surgery went well, and Valentino appeared to be on his way to a full recovery. Unfortunately, peritonitis set in, and the infection spread throughout his body; he died on August 23, 1926.

The events surrounding the viewing of the body and the funeral took on a circuslike atmosphere—it was likely the first celebrity funeral to cause such chaos. There were riots in the street near the Campbell's Funeral Parlour; approximately 100,000 people viewed the body. Rumors also began circulating about Valentino's death, the most persistent being that he was murdered, possibly by a jealous husband. And that wasn't the only drama surrounding the Great Lover's death. Negri, never one to give up an opportunity for publicity, claimed she and Valentino had been engaged, though the validity of this allegation was never proven. She mourned her lover by ordering a huge blanket of flowers spelling out her name, which was then draped over the casket.

The funeral service in New York was conducted at St. Malachi's Church, with more than 6,000 people in attendance. Valentino's body was then transported by train back to California—crowds of people gathered as the train passed through each town. The service in California took place at the Church of the Good Shepherd in Hollywood. Only 300 people attended this second funeral. The day following the funeral, 5,000 people visited the mausoleum. Valentino was buried in a crypt borrowed from Mathis. When she died two years later, her husband, Sylvano Balboni, solved the problem of what to do with Valentino's body by selling his adjoining crypt to the Valentino family. Valentino was then moved to his final resting place above Mathis's mother.

In 1927 a commemorative service was attended by faithful fans. This tradition continued for many years—there were active Valentino fan clubs well into the twenty-first century. Annual appearances of the so-called Lady in Black also helped keep Valentino's name alive. For more than fifty years she appeared, dressed in black with a veil covering her face, to bring red roses to his grave on the anniversary of his death. Speculation concerning the identity of this mystery woman varied. Some believed her to be engaged in some kind of publicity stunt, with various women allegedly playing the part. Others thought she might be a brokenhearted lover who could not forget him. The truth of the story was never established, and the lady eventually disappeared.

For women of the Jazz Age of the Roaring Twenties, Valentino was the first sex symbol of the dangerous kind. He represented all that was enticing to repressed women, who had only recently started to make gains in emancipation by getting the vote. Despite his short life, he represented something women had not dared long for in the Victorian and Edwardian eras. In spite of rumors that surfaced many years after his death regarding his sexual orientation and that of his ex-wives, the effect Valentino had on the 1920s cannot be minimized or overlooked.

Jill A. Gregg

SEE ALSO: *Celebrity; Hollywood; Movie Stars; Pickford, Mary; Sex Symbol; Silent Movies; The Twenties.*

BIBLIOGRAPHY

Botham, Noel, and Peter Donnelly. *Valentino: The Love God.* New York: Ace Books, 1977.

Leider, Emily W. *Dark Lover: The Life and Death of Rudolph Valentino.* New York: Faber & Faber, 2003.

Morris, Michael. *Madam Valentino: The Many Lives of Natacha Rambova.* New York: Abbeville Press, 1991.

Scagnetti, Jack. *The Intimate Life of Rudolph Valentino.* New York: Jonathon David Publishers, 1975.

Tajiri, Vincent. *Valentino.* New York: Bantam Books, 1977.

Walker, Alexander. *Rudolph Valentino*. New York: Stein & Day, 1976.

Valenzuela, Fernando *(1960–)*

Few baseball players have captured the popular imagination as Fernando Valenzuela did in the summer of 1981, when the word *Fernandomania* came into the English lexicon, as the young left-hander with the incredible screwball astounded the baseball world by tossing five shutouts during an eight-game winning streak to start the season. In a career that lasted from 1980 to 1997, Valenzuela was known almost as much for his burly physique and unorthodox windup as for his effectiveness and durability.

Valenzuela was born in Etchohuaquila, in the Mexican state of Sonora, about 350 miles south of the Arizona border. The youngest of twelve children, Fernando, by the age of sixteen, was earning $80 a month as a pitcher in the Mexican leagues. Beating out the Yankees by half a step, the Los Angeles Dodgers bought the left-hander's contract from Puebla for $120,000 in 1979. The following year, Valenzuela, making his debut with the Dodgers, pitched eighteen scoreless innings (too few to be eligible for rookie status) during the season's final weeks.

In 1981 twenty-year-old rookie Valenzuela exploded on the baseball scene. Fernandomania began in Los Angeles soon after the screwball-throwing left-hander started the season with a shutout, and it spread across the North American continent as Valenzuela managed to notch seven more victories (including four more shutouts) before registering his first loss. Although the league caught up with him in the second half of a strike-torn season, Valenzuela nevertheless finished the year as baseball's strikeout king, while also boasting the league's second-highest win total (thirteen) and an impressive 2.48 ERA (earned run average). In his first full season in the major leagues, the young man from Mexico had led his team to a World Series championship, while winning the National League's Rookie of the Year and also its Cy Young Award in an unprecedented achievement.

Valenzuela's face appeared on the covers of numerous sports magazines in the summer of 1981, while he charmed the sports world with his modesty, his eyes-to-the-sky windup, and his virtual ignorance of English. His age also kept people guessing, as many observers supposed that he was significantly older than his twenty years. Although Valenzuela went on to have a successful career with the Dodgers, Fernandomania faded by season's end. Afterward he was just a very good pitcher—good enough to win nineteen games in 1982 and register a league-leading twenty-one victories in 1986. Along the way he received baseball's first million-dollar salary arbitration award, in 1983.

Valenzuela pitched for the Dodgers for eleven seasons, during which he won 141 games while losing 116. He appeared in six All-Star games, including an epic performance in 1986 when he struck out five consecutive hitters, tying a record set in 1934 by fellow screwballer Carl Hubbell. One of Valenzuela's most appealing features was his durability, as he led the league in complete games in three seasons and twice in innings pitched. During the 1980s he was also one of the league's most consistent strikeout pitchers, finishing among the top five for seven years in a row. During the late 1980s his career began to be hobbled by shoulder soreness—an ailment no doubt caused by a decade of subjecting his arm to the strain of throwing his famed screwball. In addition to being a star hurler during his years with the Dodgers, Valenzuela was recognized for his excellent defense and a dangerous bat.

His years with the Dodgers were capped by a no-hitter on June 29, 1990, but his career was thrown into doubt after the Dodgers released him the following spring. For the next seven years Valenzuela bounced from team to team, including a stint in the Mexican leagues in 1992. Although his comebacks always seemed to draw a fair amount of attention, they were rarely successful (his thirteen wins and eight losses in San Diego in 1996 being the only exception), as he managed to compile a meager record of only thirty-two wins and thirty-seven losses during his post-Dodger career.

With 173 career victories, Valenzuela retired as the leading Mexican-born pitcher in major-league history. Spanish-speaking Dodger fans still enjoy Valenzuela as a commentator for the Spanish-language broadcasts. While it is doubtful that he will make the National Baseball Hall of Fame, he was named to the Hispanic Heritage Baseball Museum in 2003 and selected as one of the starting pitchers in Major League Baseball's Latino Legends project in 2005. Despite his considerable achievements with the Dodgers, he is nevertheless best remembered for setting the baseball world on its ear during his rookie season, the spring and summer of 1981.

Kevin O'Connor

SEE ALSO: *Baseball; Major League Baseball; The New York Yankees; Sports Heroes; World Series.*

BIBLIOGRAPHY

"'El Torro' Charges Ahead after 20 Years." *Christian Science Monitor*, April 20, 2001, 12.

Freedman, Lew. *Latino Baseball Legends: An Encyclopedia*. Santa Barbara, CA: Greenwood, 2010.

Littwin, Mike. *Fernando!* New York: Bantam, 1981.

McNeil, William F. *Dodger Chronicles*. Pittsfield, MA: W. F. McNeil, 1993.

McNeil, William F. *The Dodgers Encyclopedia*. Champaign, IL: Sports Publishing, 1997.

Sahadi, Lou. *The L.A. Dodgers: The World Champions of Baseball*. New York: Quill, 1982.

Thorn, John, and Pete Palmer, eds., and David Reuther. *Total Baseball*. New York: Warner, 1989.

Valium

Valium is the brand name for diazepam, an antianxiety medication. It debuted on the prescription drug market in the United States in 1963 and quickly became a widely prescribed tranquilizer. The name *Valium* comes from a Latin word that means "to be strong and well."

Developed by Leo Sternbach in the New Jersey labs of pharmaceutical giant Hoffmann-La Roche, Valium is classified as an anxiolytic or anxiety-dissolving drug. Sternbach also synthesized the tranquilizer Librium, which went on the market in 1960. Hoffmann-La Roche developed Librium to compete with Miltown, a rival company's popular tranquilizer. The drug companies marketed these drugs to middle-class Americans, many of whom were unlikely to visit a psychologist or psychiatrist for nonthreatening depression or anxiety disorders because of the stigma attached to mental illness. Valium, stronger than Librium and less bitter in taste, acts on the limbic system, the part of the brain that regulates emotional response and reaction. Because it is so potent, it can be formulated into much smaller doses than Librium, and unlike other tranquilizers, it soothes without inducing drowsiness.

"Some Roche executives did not expect much of [Valium], but a couple of them tried it on postmenopausal mothers-in-law whom they found insufferable, and were delighted by its calming effects," wrote Gilbert Cant in a 1976 article in *New York Times Magazine*. Doctors cautioned patients not to operate heavy machinery or drive a car while taking Valium and warned about mixing it with alcohol since the effects of both substances on the central nervous system are doubled when they are ingested together. Part of Valium's appeal lay in the belief that it was nonaddictive, and unlike other tranquilizers, it was almost impossible to take a lethal dose.

By 1974 doctors had written 59.3 million prescriptions for Valium, which meant that Hoffmann-La Roche had cornered 81 percent of the tranquilizer market in the country. A *Vogue* magazine article titled "Danger Ahead! Valium—The Pill You Love Can Turn on You," published the following year, extensively quoted Marie Nyswander, a New York City psychiatrist, who warns of Valium's addictive properties: "Probably it would be very hard to find any group of middle-class women in which some aren't regularly on Valium," she declared. Cant insisted that Valium had become the most profitable drug in history and questioned whether it had been "overmarketed" by Hoffmann-La Roche. Tellingly, only about 10 percent of Valium prescriptions in 1974 were written by mental health professionals; 60 to 70 percent were written by family doctors, gynecologists, or pediatricians. "Women, mostly those over 30, outnumber male users of Valium by 2/12; to one," Cant pointed out.

Valium also began to appear for sale illegally around 1975, the same year overall tranquilizer use in the United States peaked. In 1978 an estimated 20 percent of American women were taking Valium; doctors prescribed nearly 2.3 billion pills in that year alone. Still considered relatively harmless despite warnings by naysayers, Valium became so pervasive that it entered the vernacular. It was jokingly referred to as "Executive Excedrin" and made its way into comic scenes in movies, such as Alan J. Pakula's *Starting Over* (1979), as well as in films directed by Woody Allen and plays written by Neil Simon. According to his autopsy report, Elvis Presley had Valium in his system when he died in 1977.

ALARM BELLS

The 1979 best seller *I'm Dancing as Fast as I Can* did much to alert the public to Valium's dangers. Its author, Barbara Gordon, was a successful, educated Manhattan career woman who became hooked on the drug over a nine-year period. She had to be hospitalized when she stopped taking it because of the withdrawal symptoms. Reports of "rebound insomnia" from even light Valium use began to appear in the press, and Senate subcommittee hearings later that year garnered widespread media coverage. Joseph Pursch, director of the Alcohol Rehabilitation Service at the Naval Regional Medical Center in Long Beach, California, from 1973 to 1980, testified about the dangers of Valium.

Physicians began publicly confessing that they had become addicted to the free Valium samples mailed to them by Hoffmann-La Roche. An executive of the company defended the drug before the Senate subcommittee and asserted that its abuse was not the fault of Hoffmann-La Roche. Instead, he blamed the doctors who overprescribed it and insisted that some patients will become addicted to almost any substance. A physician also spoke on behalf of Hoffmann-La Roche argued that "to imply that the medicine is dangerous or highly addictive is not only incorrect, but it is a great disservice to millions of people whose lives are already troubled," according to *Time* magazine.

As a compromise, the Food and Drug Administration (FDA) forced Hoffmann-La Roche and other tranquilizer manufacturers to include the statement "Anxiety or tension associated with the stress of everyday life usually does not require treatment with an anxiolytic (antianxiety) drug" in the drug information provided to physicians. This requirement was effective in the summer of 1980. In 1981, however, a report on the possible link between Valium use and the rapid growth of cancer cells negatively affected the drug's popularity with the general public. The author of the study, David Horrobin, claimed he was forced out of his job with the University of Montreal because of his findings and his attempts to make them public. In 1985 Hoffmann-La Roche's patent for Valium expired, further impacting the company's sales of the drug.

By the early twenty-first century, antidepressants had resumed their place at the top of the list of prescription drugs. In 2007 doctors wrote 233 million prescriptions, and many patients were using multiple drugs. While the use of Valium has declined drastically since its heyday, the drug is still creating controversy. In 2007 the Associated Press revealed that water supplies in cities around the country are regularly contaminated with pharmaceutical products such as Valium. In Philadelphia, researchers identified fifty-six separate pharmaceuticals in the water that was being piped into homes. Because of established links between the use of antidepressants and suicide in young people, doctors no longer prescribe Valium for anyone under the age of eighteen. When they prescribe it for adults, they inform their patients that, contrary to earlier opinions, the side effects of Valium are numerous and can range from confusion, hallucinations, and seizures to aggression, hostility, and problems with the kidneys, breathing, and vision.

Carol Brennan

SEE ALSO: *Allen, Woody; Cancer; Depression; Presley, Elvis; Simon, Neil; Suicide;* Time*;* Vogue.

BIBLIOGRAPHY

Baenninger, Alex. *Good Chemistry: The Life and Legacy of Valium Inventor Leo Sternbach*. New York: McGraw-Hill, 2004.

Barber, Charles. "Drugged-Up Nation." *Nation*, June 12, 2008.

Cant, Gilbert. "Valiumania." *New York Times Magazine*, February 1, 1976, 34–44.

"Danger Ahead! Valium—The Pill You Love Can Turn on You." *Vogue*, February 1975, 152–153.

"The Drugging of America." *Science News*, February 25, 1978, 119.

Kent, Letitia. "Leo Sternbach: The Tranquil Chemist." *SciQuest*, December 1980, 22–24.

Mayers, Morton. *Happy Accidents: Serendipity on Modern Medi-*

cal Breakthroughs. New York: Arcade Publishers, 2007.

"Tranquil Tales." *Time*, September 24, 1979, 78.

"Valium Abuse: The Yellow Peril." *Newsweek*, September 24, 1979, 66.

"Valium Alarm." *Time*, January 19, 1981, 74–75.

"Yellow Light for Tranquilizers." *Time*, July 21, 1980, 53.

Vampires

No creature haunting European society's collective imagination has proven more enduring, more compelling, or more alluring than the vampire. But it was only with his transformation from emaciated, plague-carrying *nosferatu* (literally, "not dead") to suave, sexually appealing antihero that the vampire's status as pop cultural icon was cemented. Authors and poets ranging from Lord Byron, Johann Wolfgang von Goethe, Charles Baudelaire, and Joseph Sheridan Le Fanu to Edgar Allan Poe, H. G. Wells, Stephen King, and Anne Rice have made contributions to vampire lore. Vampires have starred on the page and onscreen.

Dracula, the best-known and most resilient vampire, has appeared in numerous films, and the teen vampire romance *Twilight* films have grossed more than $1.5 billion worldwide. On television, vampires have starred in dramas (*Kindred: The Embraced*, 1996, and *Blood Ties*, 2006), sitcoms (*The Munsters*, 1964–1966), soap operas (*Dark Shadows*, 1966–1971), and countless made-for-television movies. On the radio, Orson Welles's portrayal of Dracula for *The Mercury Theatre* in 1938 became an instant classic. In addition, vampires have been made the subject of such cultural castoffs as stamps, comic books, lunchboxes, breakfast cereals, cartoons, role-playing games, and do-it-yourself makeup kits—in short, just about anything capable of sustaining an image or supporting a narrative.

Bela Lugosi as Count Dracula. *Bela Lugosi makes Count Dracula a suave and sophisticated vampire in the 1931 film* Dracula. UNIVERSAL/THE KOBAL COLLECTION.

In pre-Christian times, the vampire was a regular in Middle European folklore. Typically portrayed as an unkempt peasant with terrible breath and a craving for the blood of farm animals, his taste underwent a profound change in the seventeenth century—instead of sheep and oxen, he began turning to members of his own family in search of nourishment. This shift in sensibility most likely occurred because distraught villagers needed a face to attach to deadly plagues infecting their neighbors.

THE VAMPIRE ENTERS LITERATURE

The vampire entered the literary realm by way of German Gothicism: in Heinrich August Ossenfelder's "The Vampire" (1748), Gottfried Bürger's *Lenore* (1773), and Goethe's *The Bride of Corinth* (1797), the once-shy bloodsucker slowly made the transition to sexual predator. But the first truly modern vampire appeared in John Polidori's extended revision of a fragment written by the English poet Lord Byron in 1816; amazingly, it was during the same session of storytelling at a villa near Geneva that Mary Shelley conceived the plot of *Frankenstein*. In Polidori's *The Vampyre* (1819), the dashing Lord Ruthven quenches his thirst with the blood of attractive young women. To cash in on Ruthven's surprising popularity, a number of plays, burlesques, and operas were quickly brought to stage in France, Germany, and England.

With the publication of James Malcolm Rymer's 868-page penny dreadful, *Varney the Vampire, or the Feast of Blood*, in 1847, the vampire became a pop culture phenomenon. Many elements of Varney's comic-book adventures were appropriated by Bram Stoker for use in his celebrated gothic novel, *Dracula* (1897). Female vampires also came into their own around this time; Le Fanu's novella *Carmilla* (1871) recounts a destructive lesbian affair, a theme exploited years later in such films as *Dracula's Daughter* (1936), *The Velvet Vampire* (1971), and *The Hunger* (1983), as well as in the homoerotic vampire fantasies of novelist Rice.

In preparation for his novel, Stoker read everything he could find on vampires at the British Museum. He was fascinated by stories of Vlad the Impaler, a fifteenth-century Romanian prince with a penchant for staking his victims. This real-life Dracula (Vlad's father was a member of the paramilitary group "Dracul") provided Stoker with a historical basis for his monster. *Dracula* effectively synthesized the vampire legend's major motifs (including shape shifting, mind control, avoidance of daylight, lack of reflection, and talismans such as garlic and crosses) and moved the Count out of his castle and into a bustling urban locale. Stoker's rendition of the vampire as a sexual oppressor roaming the streets of London tapped into the public's fear of serial killers such as Jack the Ripper, who less than ten years earlier had murdered five women in the city's East End.

VAMPIRES ON FILM

In 1922 German director F. W. Murnau brought the folkloric vampire back to life with his silent expressionist masterpiece,

Nosferatu: A Symphony of Horror. Max Schreck stars as Graf Orlock, a gaunt, bald, ratlike vampire who bears almost no resemblance to Bela Lugosi's suave, aristocratic Count Dracula. Four years before gracing the silver screen in Tod Browning's 1931 classic, *Dracula*, the Hungarian-born Lugosi established his reputation as the world's leading vampire by starring in a Broadway production of Stoker's tale (a half century later, Frank Langella would play the Count in a successful New York revival). Lugosi's exotic accent, distinctive mannerisms, and sinister charm captivated audiences, and Universal Studios contracted him to reprise his role in a slew of horror films.

Celluloid vampires suffered from burnout until 1958, when Christopher Lee reprised the role of the Count in Hammer Films' elegant bloodfest, *Horror of Dracula*. Numerous sequels, also starring Lee, soon followed. Other notable vampire pictures include Carl Dreyer's *Vampyre* (1932); Roman Polanski's *Fearless Vampire Killers* (1967); a 1972 blaxploitation film titled *Blacula*; Werner Herzog's remake of *Nosferatu* (1979); campy satires by Mel Brooks and Andy Warhol; a porno titled *Dracula Sucks* (1978); Francis Ford Coppola's big-budget rendition of *Bram Stoker's Dracula* (1992); a 1994 adaptation of Rice's *Interview with the Vampire*; the iconic *Buffy the Vampire Slayer* (1991), which became a long-running TV series; and a 2010 spoof of the genre titled *Vampires Suck*. Vampires even turned up in such unlikely genres as science fiction (*Lifeforce*, 1985), Westerns (*Billy the Kid vs. Dracula*, 1966), and historical dramas (*Abraham Lincoln: Vampire Hunter*, 2012).

Vampire iconography has exerted a powerful influence on communal style and behavior. A whole "Gothic" youth culture, complete with all-black clothing, somber music, and atmospheric nightclubs, arose as an offshoot of punk in the 1970s, and an underground cult of real-life blood drinkers has steadily increased in numbers. The socially revealing image of vampire as obsessive blood-junkie has been presented in such films as *Deathdream* (1974), *Martin* (1976), and *The Addiction* (1995). While the first vampires may have been irredeemable monsters, the trend in the twenty-first century has been toward normalizing vampires. Modern vampires just want to be like everyone else, as in the series *Being Human*, in which a vampire, a werewolf, and a ghost learn to get along as roommates.

TEENAGE VAMPIRES IN LOVE

The outlaw status of vampires gives them a potent appeal for teenage audiences, and at the turn of the twenty-first century a number of young adult vampire novels appeared. The most popular of these were L. J. Smith's *The Vampire Diaries*, two trilogies published between 1991 and 2011, and Stephenie Meyer's *Twilight* series, published 2005–2010. Both series blend the uncertainties of teenage romance with the dangers of the vampire life. Beginning in 2008 the *Twilight* novels were made into a popular series of movies, and the sleepy coastal town of Forks, Washington, where the books and films are set, became a mecca for teenage fans. In 2009 the CW network premiered *The Vampire Diaries*, a highly rated series based on Smith's novels. An even longer novel series is *The Southern Vampire Mysteries*, more than ten books written by Charlaine Harris beginning in 2001 and made into the HBO series *True Blood* in 2008.

There are many reasons for the vampire's enduring popularity. While most monsters are portrayed as ugly, even grotesque, vampires are often handsome or beautiful. They are surrounded by large and arcane bodies of knowledge concerning their origins, powers, and weaknesses. Foreign, well-traveled, aristocratic, charming, and even magnetic, they possess an undeniable erotic appeal. What is more, they are subversive, challenging traditional ideas about death, religion, science, sexual mores, and patriarchy. And lest we forget, they have what we all want: money, power, sexual attractiveness, and above all eternal youth.

Steven Schneider

SEE ALSO: *Blaxploitation Films; Blockbusters; Broadway; Brooks, Mel;* Buffy the Vampire Slayer*; Cable TV;* Dark Shadows*; Dracula; Frankenstein; Goth; Hollywood; Horror Movies; Lugosi, Bela; Made-for-Television Movies; Pornography; Radio; Sitcom; Teenagers;* Twilight*; Warhol, Andy; Welles, Orson.*

BIBLIOGRAPHY

Carter, Margaret L., ed. *The Vampire in Literature: A Critical Biography*. Ann Arbor, MI: UMI Research Press, 1989.

Carter, Margaret L. "The Vampire." In *Icons of Horror: An Encyclopedia of Our Worst Nightmares, Vol. 1*, ed. S. T. Joshi. Westport, CT: Greenwood Press, 2006.

Dresser, Norine. *American Vampires: Fans, Victims, and Practitioners*. New York: Norton, 1989.

Levine, Elana, and Lisa Parks, eds. *Undead TV: Essays on "Buffy the Vampire Slayer."* Durham, NC: Duke University Press, 2007.

Melton, Gordon. *The Vampire Book: The Encyclopedia of the Undead*. Detroit, MI: Visible Ink Press, 1999.

Pirie, David. *The Vampire Cinema*. New York: Crescent Books, 1977.

Silver, Alain, and James Ursini. *The Vampire Film: From Nosferatu to Bram Stoker's Dracula*. New York: Limelight, 1993.

Twitchell, James. "The Rise and Fall of Dracula." In *Dreadful Pleasures: An Anatomy of Modern Horror*. New York: Oxford University Press, 1985.

Waller, Gregory. *The Living and the Undead: From Stoker's "Dracula" to Romero's "Dawn of the Dead."* Urbana: University of Illinois Press, 1986.

Van Dine, S. S. *(1888–1939)*

The "Golden Age" of the detective novel is generally considered to have been the years between World Wars I and II. S. S. Van Dine's first Philo Vance detective novel, *The Benson Murder Case* (1926), is often cited as the book that began this era. Although there were only twelve Vance novels and his popularity fell as quickly as it rose, Vance was by far the best-selling mystery character of his time.

Born Willard Huntington Wright in Charlottesville, Virginia, Van Dine first became known as an editor and a literary critic for the *Los Angeles Times* and then for *Smart Set* magazine. By the 1930s his following as a mystery writer was already beginning to fade. He began writing for motion pictures and contributed a chapter to *The President's Mystery Story*, published by Franklin D. Roosevelt, in 1935.

Jill A. Gregg

SEE ALSO: *Detective Fiction.*

BIBLIOGRAPHY

Anderson, George Parker. *American Mystery and Detective Writers*. Detroit, MI: Thomson Gale, 2005.

Loughery, John. *Alias S. S. Van Dine*. New York: Scribners, 1992.

Van Dyke, Dick *(1925–)*

Dick Van Dyke is best known as a television comedian of the 1960s and 1970s, but his career has included everything from Broadway to motion pictures to drama, in which he has excelled by portraying likable and sensible characters. His most successful role was as the star of *The Dick Van Dyke Show*, an Emmy Award–winning sitcom that appeared on CBS from 1961 to 1966; he played the role of Rob Petrie, the head writer for the fictional *Alan Brady Show* who lives with his wife (played by Mary Tyler Moore) and son in suburban New Rochelle, New York. The show was unusual for a sitcom of the period in that it allowed its star to portray a TV dad, both at home and at work, while offering an insightful, behind-the-scenes glimpse of a television sitcom from the inside out.

ENTERTAINER AND EMCEE

Van Dyke, son of a trucking agent, was born in West Plains, Missouri, on December 13, 1925. His younger brother, Jerry, also became a comedian. It was while he was serving in the U.S. Air Force during World War II that Van Dyke began performing in shows; one of his buddies, Byron Paul, later became his personal manager. After a failed attempt, with a friend, to start an advertising agency after the war, Van Dyke formed a comedy pantomime act, *The Merry Mutes*, with another friend, Philip Erickson. "Eric and Van" broke up in 1953, and Van Dyke continued to appear solo in nightclubs around the country until he became emcee of two daytime programs for an Atlanta, Georgia, television station: *The Merry Mutes Show* and *The Music Shop*.

Dick Van Dyke. *Dick Van Dyke's versatility as an actor, comedian, and dancer was the basis of his popularity in the 1950s and 1960s.* MICHAEL OCHS ARCHIVES/GETTY IMAGES.

In 1955 he originated a variety program, which he called *The Dick Van Dyke Show*, for a New Orleans, Louisiana, television station, and he went to New York as emcee for CBS's *The Morning Show*, following in the footsteps of Walter Cronkite and Jack Paar. Van Dyke was also emcee of *CBS Cartoon Theater* in 1956 and NBC's *Laugh Line* in 1959.

Disappointed with CBS's refusal to offer him a daily show, Van Dyke appeared as a guest performer on a variety of television shows, including *The United States Steel Hour*, but it was on Broadway that he had his first major starring role. From April 1960 to October 1961, he attracted much critical and popular attention and won a Tony Award for the role of Albert Peterson in the musical comedy *Bye Bye Birdie*.

TELEVISION SITCOM STAR

A month after leaving that cast, he debuted as TV writer Petrie in his own weekly TV sitcom, *The Dick Van Dyke Show*, which premiered on October 3, 1961, with Van Dyke and Moore as the leads and Rose Marie, Morey Amsterdam, and Richard Deacon in supporting roles. The episode's title, "Head of the Family," was the title of the pilot episode made earlier by writer-producer Carl Reiner, who cast himself in the leading role—Johnny Carson was also briefly considered for the part—until Reiner agreed that Van Dyke was a better choice. Reiner, who appeared on the show in the role of Alan Brady, based many of the episodes on his own experience as a writer for the 1950s comedy series *Your Show of Shows*. *The Dick Van Dyke Show* was also a vehicle for the relatively unknown Moore, who had appeared mostly in commercials before assuming the role of Petrie's wife.

The Dick Van Dyke Show stands as an icon to the times, a mirror for the world of television in the early 1960s and for the suburban lifestyle that was then somewhat more idyllic than it would become in later years. The show was popular largely because of Van Dyke's ability to both play light, sophisticated, domestic comedy and engage in clownish, farcical pratfalls. The stories endure because they present believable characters in unusual but ultimately explainable situations. The producers and cast deliberately ended production after just five seasons, and so the quality of this series remains consistently high throughout; it won fifteen Emmys in five consecutive years.

FILM ACTOR AND MORE

Beginning in the 1960s Van Dyke starred in a number of memorable films. He reprised his Broadway role in a film adaptation of *Bye Bye Birdie* (1963) and then played the chimney sweep alongside Julie Andrews in *Mary Poppins* (1964). He next starred in *Lt. Robin Crusoe U.S.N.* (1966) and *Divorce American Style* (1967), after which he played an eccentric inventor in *Chitty Chitty Bang Bang* (1968). In the 1971 satire *Cold Turkey*, he tried a different type of role—that of a minister in a town undergoing withdrawal symptoms as residents try to give up smoking for a month to win a bounty from a tobacco company.

Reiner and Van Dyke were reunited in *The New Dick Van Dyke Show* in 1971 by a CBS network anxious to try to recapture the viewers and quality of their first sitcom a decade earlier. By this time *The Mary Tyler Moore Show* had become a hit; the trend was toward the sophisticated, more adult comedies, much like the original *Dick Van Dyke Show* had been. In *The New Dick Van Dyke Show*, Van Dyke was cast in the role of Dick Preston, the host of a local talk show in Phoenix, Arizona, and a happily married family man with a loving young daughter and a college-aged son. For the final twenty-four episodes, the scene shifted to Hollywood, as Preston accepts a major role in a daytime soap opera. This venue seemed a more deliberate attempt to duplicate the earlier show, with its faster pace and more emphasis on behind-the-scenes banter among the performers, writers, and producer.

Despite these devices, *The New Dick Van Dyke Show* was not overly popular with audiences and was almost canceled by the network, until a flap over an episode in which the Prestons' teenage daughter accidentally walked in on them while they were having sex. Though the bedroom scene was not shown on camera, the network refused to air the episode as it was filmed, and because of this, Reiner quit. It was after his departure that the show's setting moved to Hollywood, and the show's new soap-opera situation, plus publicity over the earlier controversy, helped raise its ratings somewhat. By 1974 Van Dyke decided not to continue the show, which nevertheless still won an Emmy. He returned to television later in the 1970s with a briefly running variety show called *Van Dyke and Company*. This won another Emmy for him.

Following this program, Van Dyke continued to make occasional movies and is well known for a series of public-service announcements aimed at fire safety for children that advised them to "Stop, Drop and Roll." He, along with Pearl Bailey and Hermione Gingold, supplied voices for the children's movie *Tubby the Tuba* (1977), and he appeared as the star of *The Runner Stumbles* (1979) and in the supporting cast of *Dick Tracy* (1990). In the early 1990s Van Dyke reappeared before television audiences as the "chairman" of *Nick-at-Nite*, the cable network program that shows reruns of classic TV shows including his own 1960s series.

Around this time he also appeared in episodes of the show *Jake and the Fatman* and in several television movies. His most notable role in this period was that of Dr. Mark Sloan in the hour-long CBS-TV dramatic series *Diagnosis Murder* (1993–2002). In this show Dr. Sloan is portrayed as a Los Angeles crime-solving physician with a police detective son, played by Van Dyke's real-life son, Barry. The program captured a strong following and benefited from a new writing team, which allowed it to grow and expand. Despite its serious subject, *Diagnosis Murder* was directed with a playful and human feel that reflected Van Dyke's combination of sophistication and humor.

Van Dyke continued film and TV work into the twenty-first century. A 2004 special, *The New Dick Van Dyke Show Revisited*, reunited much of the original cast. He returned to drama with three murder mysteries for the Hallmark channel, in 2006, 2007, and 2008. The hit 2006 film *Night at the Museum* saw Van Dyke return to the big screen. The actor is still most often seen on television; he's appeared on seemingly every TV talk show and most documentaries about TV comedy, such as *Pioneers of Television*, which appeared on PBS in 2008, and *Make 'Em Laugh: The Funny Business of America* in 2009. Van Dyke's unique style and likability made him a perfect comedic pioneer of the small screen.

Frank E. Clark

SEE ALSO: *Amsterdam, Morey; Animated Films; Broadway; Cable TV; Carson, Johnny; Cronkite, Walter; Dick Tracy; Emmy Awards;* Laugh-In*; Marie, Rose;* Mary Poppins*;* The Mary Tyler Moore Show*; Paar, Jack; Public Television (PBS); Reiner, Carl; Sitcom; Television;* Your Show of Shows.

BIBLIOGRAPHY

Castleman, Harry, and Walter J. Podrazik. *Harry and Wally's Favorite Shows: A Fact-Filled Opinionated Guide to the Best and Worst on TV*. New York: Prentice Hall Press, 1989.

Marc, David, and Robert J. Thompson. *Prime Time, Prime Movers: From "I Love Lucy" to "L.A. Law"—America's Greatest TV Shows and the People Who Created Them.* Boston: Little, Brown, 1992.

McNeil, Alex. *Total Television: A Comprehensive Guide to Programming from 1948 to the Present*, 3rd ed. New York: Penguin Books, 1991.

Putterman, Barry. *On Television and Comedy: Essays on Style, Theme, Performer and Writer*. Jefferson, NC: McFarland, 1995.

Van Dyke, Dick. *My Lucky Life in and out of Show Business: A Memoir*. New York: Crown, 2011.

Waldron, Vince. *Classic Sitcoms: A Celebration of the Best in Prime-Time Comedy*, 2nd ed. Los Angeles: Silman-James Press, 1997.

Waldron, Vince, and Dick Van Dyke. *The Official "Dick Van Dyke Show" Book: The Definitive History and Ultimate Viewer's Guide to Television's Most Enduring Comedy*. New York: Applause, 2001.

Van Halen

The rock quartet Van Halen exploded into the American mainstream in 1978 with an eponymously titled debut album that soon went platinum, thanks to its blend of musical experimentation and an old-fashioned rock-and-roll aesthetic. Named for Eddie Van Halen, the group's guitar virtuoso, the band has an image that promotes a hedonistic lifestyle and immediately captures the imagination of many young fans. *Spin* magazine, in its October 2000 issue, celebrated the "The 100 Sleaziest Moments in Rock" by putting Van Halen singer David Lee Roth on the cover. The band is notorious for its road antics, including the famous "contract rider" demanding no brown M&Ms. The group's reputation should not overshadow its music, influence, and legacy, however. Drawing from traditions of southern blues, European baroque, and 1980s America, the band over the years has weathered major lineup changes and stylistic reinvention to remain one of the nation's most innovative musical groups.

EARLY YEARS

Coming together in Pasadena, California, in the mid-1970s, Van Halen was one of the first of the new wave of West Coast hard rock and heavy metal bands that had grown up on and would eventually replace such British acts as Black Sabbath and Led Zeppelin. The band's first incarnation centered on Alex and Eddie Van Halen, sons of an accomplished Dutch musician. The boys' intense classical training helped them produce distinctive and innovative music in an era when many metal bands were surrendering to formula. The band added Michael Anthony as bass player and David Lee Roth as vocalist and gigged locally under the name Mammoth before choosing to call itself Van Halen.

Van Halen paid its dues in the highly competitive Los Angeles music scene, where it was discovered first by Gene Simmons of the band KISS and later by a Warner Brothers executive. Its debut album, with Roth's lewd, growling vocals on such songs as "Dance the Night Away" and "Runnin' with the Devil," grounded the band firmly in blues and heavy metal traditions, while Eddie Van Halen's creative guitar work, showcased on the extended pseudoclassical solo "Eruption," appealed to other traditionalists.

The band's next five albums all went multiplatinum, even when the band experimented with organs, synthesizers, saxophone, and a cappella crooning, as on 1982's *Diver Down* and 1984's *1984*. The latter album showed the band's more lighthearted, pop-friendly approach, as with the single "Jump" and its video, which took advantage of Roth's high-kicking manic stage presence. In 1985, at the height of the band's popularity, Roth left the group to pursue a moderately successful solo career. Van Halen continued with new lead vocalist Sammy Hagar, already well known from his work with Montrose and as a solo performer. The band released four hugely successful albums with Hagar at the helm, maintaining its exuberance while adding a nuance of socially meaningful music, as with "Right Here, Right Now," a powerful song and carefully crafted video about taking care of one's own life in the midst of problems abroad. In 1996 Hagar left and Van Halen responded by releasing live and greatest-hits albums and attempting a reunion with Roth at the 1996 MTV Music Video Awards. Van Halen resurfaced in 1998 with new lead vocalist Gary Cherone. "Without You," the first single with this new lineup, debuted at number one on the Billboard charts.

Cherone's contribution lasted only one tour and album (*Van Halen III*). After time off, the band returned in 2004, with Hagar as vocalist, recording new songs, undertaking a world tour, and releasing a greatest hits album. In 2007 Hagar was ousted, as was bassist Anthony when Roth rejoined the band for a reunion tour and Eddie's son, Wolfgang, took over bass duties. Induction into the Rock and Roll Hall of Fame occurred in 2007, but not without the usual Van Halen controversy. All the current band members stayed home, leaving Anthony and Hagar to accept the award and perform. After more years off, the band released the album *A Different Kind of Truth* in 2012 and embarked on another world tour. The album won universal praise with a review in *USA Today* noting, "this is the true kick in the butt that arena rock desperately needs."

RECOGNITION

It is Eddie Van Halen who has been recognized as the force behind most of the group's music. In 2011 *Rolling Stone* named him the eighth greatest guitarist of all time, noting that "Eddie is a master of riffs." *Guitar World Magazine* named his solo in "Eruption" as the second greatest guitar solo of all time. In his unending quest for superb sound, he rewired amps, assembled guitars backward, converted arias and concertos into searing solos, and tapped the fret board of his instrument with both hands at once. His solo on Michael Jackson's smash hit "Beat It" gave the song a hard edge, a certain legitimacy in a decade where dance and heavy metal fought for control of the airwaves. From the beginning, his technical mastery and innovation set new parameters for the iconic guitar hero.

As a tribute to his skill, in the Xbox 360 game *Guitar Hero 2*, a player earned an "Eddie Van Halen" for playing 500 consecutive notes. In 2009 the whole band joined the game with the release of *Guitar Hero: Van Halen*. While often making headlines for their infighting and lifestyle, as noted in their official biography at the Rock and Roll Hall of Fame, "Van Halen reinvigorated hard rock during a period of doldrums by bringing youthful, West Coast bravado and blistering virtuosity to the genre."

Colby Vargas

SEE ALSO: *Black Sabbath; Electric Guitar; Heavy Metal; Jackson, Michael; KISS; Led Zeppelin; MTV; Rock and Roll; Stadium Concerts; Video Games.*

BIBLIOGRAPHY

Christe, Ian. *Everybody Wants Some: The Van Halen Saga.* Hoboken, NJ: John Wiley, 2007.

Considine, J. D. *Van Halen!* New York: Quill, 1985.

Hagar, Sammy, and Joel Selvin. *Red: My Uncensored Life in Rock.* New York: !t Books, 2011.

Kitts, Jeff, ed. *"Guitar World" Presents Van Halen: Eddie Van Halen in His Own Words.* Milwaukee, WI: Hal Leonard Publishing, 1997.

Morison, Buzz. *The Mighty Van Halen.* Port Chester, NY: Cherry Lane Books, 1984.

Roth, David Lee. *Crazy from the Heat.* New York: Hyperion, 1997.

Shearlaw, John. *Van Halen: Jumpin' for the Dollar.* Port Chester, NY: Cherry Lane Books, 1984.

Walser, Robert. *Running with the Devil: Power, Gender, and Madness in Heavy Metal Music.* Hanover, NH: Wesleyan University Press, 1993.

Zlozower, Neil. *Van Halen: A Visual History, 1978–1984.* San Francisco: Chronicle Books, 2008.

Van Vechten, Carl *(1880–1964)*

In the course of his lifetime, Carl Van Vechten was a music, dance, and literary critic; a novelist; and a photographer. He was an early aficionado of ragtime and jazz, and during the Harlem Renaissance of the 1920s he wrote numerous articles in support of the movement. In his fifth and best-known novel, *Nigger Heaven* (1926), he meant to portray life in Harlem, New York, in a realistic and sympathetic fashion. Although controversial, the book was generally praised by white critics; it was condemned and dismissed by black critics because of its ill-chosen title. Van Vechten sought to ensure that the African American contribution to American culture would be recognized and appreciated in perpetuity by founding, in 1941, the James Weldon Johnson Memorial Collection at Yale University.

Laural Weintraub

SEE ALSO: *Harlem Renaissance; Hughes, Langston; Jazz; Modern Dance; Modernism.*

BIBLIOGRAPHY

Kellner, Bruce. *Carl Van Vechten and the Irreverent Decades.* Norman: University of Oklahoma Press, 1968.

Lueders, Edward G. *Carl Van Vechten.* New York: Twayne, 1965.

Smalls, James. *The Homoerotic Photography of Carl Van Vechten: Public Face, Private Thoughts.* Philadelphia: Temple University Press, 2006.

Vance, Vivian *(1909–1979)*

In the early days of television, when millions of Americans viewed small-screen stars as personal friends, Vivian Vance became the nation's most celebrated neighbor. Vance, a Broadway veteran with credits for *Voice of the Turtle* and Jerome Kern's *Music in the Air*, rocketed to stardom as Lucille Ball's landlady and confidante on the immensely popular *I Love Lucy* show. Her character, Ethel Mertz, by nature homespun and pragmatic, wavers just enough in her resolve to be cajoled into participating in the hair-brained schemes of Ball's antic Lucy Ricardo. She also struggles to pump life into her happy but conventional existence with husband Fred (William Frawley). Vance proved to be Ball's ideal foil; their interaction helped make the sitcom the country's number one show from 1951 to 1957.

Vance's perennial good cheer on screen masked her personal frustrations and several bouts with mental illness. She resented the ease with which the public accepted her as Ethel. "Ethel is a frump," she lamented. "She's frowsy, she's blowsy, and talks like a man." Vance also grew increasingly dissatisfied with costar Frawley; he was twenty-five years her senior and she complained, "He should be playing my father." Remarkably, the public remained entirely ignorant of the backstage feud between Frawley and Vance. Even after the secret leaked during the 1960s, an increasingly suburban America continued to view Fred and Ethel as representatives of a bygone era of neighborliness. Ironically, Vance's efforts on the *I Love Lucy* show helped popularize television, then a fledgling medium, and went a long way toward breaking down the traditional social patterns which Fred and Ethel Mertz represented.

Jacob M. Appel

SEE ALSO: *Arnaz, Desi; Ball, Lucille; Frawley, William;* I Love Lucy.

BIBLIOGRAPHY

Andrews, Bart. *Lucy & Ricky & Fred & Ethel: The Story of "I Love Lucy."* New York: Dutton, 1976.

Karol, Michael. *Lucy A to Z.* iUniverse, 2004.

McClay, Michael. *I Love Lucy: The Complete Picture History of the Most Popular TV Show Ever.* New York: Warner Books, 1995.

Wyman, Ric B. *For the Love of Lucy: The Complete Guide for Collectors and Fans.* New York: Abbeville Press, 1995.

Vanilla Ice *(1968–)*

White rapper Vanilla Ice burst onto the music scene in 1990 with his hit single "Ice Ice Baby," a danceable tune with a bass line lifted from the David Bowie/Queen collaboration "Under Pressure." The single, from the album *To the Extreme*, became the first rap song to reach number one on the pop singles chart, where it stayed for sixteen weeks.

Robert Van Winkle was born on October 31, 1968, in Dallas, Texas. He dropped out of high school and pursued break dancing and competitive motocross. In 1985 he began performing in local clubs, perfecting his dancing and rapping. "Ice Ice Baby" was first released in 1989 but did not receive much attention until the subsequent video gained a following. Critics often slammed Vanilla Ice for his rip-off of black culture, but apologists credited him with bringing rap to a larger audience. His popularity lasted just a few months—long enough to earn him a starring role in the movie *Cool as Ice* but not long enough to propel sales of his subsequent albums beyond a small core of dedicated fans.

After battling drugs and depression, Vanilla Ice regained his celebrity status via appearances on reality shows such as *The Surreal Life* (2007) and its spin-offs. He continued to release albums, albeit to little fanfare, and in 2010 appeared at a music festival arranged by Sony to promote the PlayStation music game series *SingStar*. In 2012 his home improvement show *The Vanilla Ice Project* returned for its second season on the DIY Network.

Tom Pendergast

SEE ALSO: *Bowie, David; Cable TV; DIY/Home Improvement; MTV; Pop Music; Rap; Reality Television; Television; Video Games.*

BIBLIOGRAPHY

Bego, Mark. *Ice, Ice, Ice: The Extraordinary Vanilla Ice Story.* New York: Dell, 1991.

Vanilla Ice. *Ice, by Ice.* New York: Avon, 1991.

Vanity Fair

The original *Vanity Fair* magazine, superbly edited by the inimitable Frank Crowninshield from 1914 to 1936, was the epitome of élan during the 1910s and 1920s. A unique amalgam of art, literature, humor, fashion, and social commentary, the periodical attracted a loyal audience and became the model of sophisticated success in the publishing industry, even after it was felled by the Great Depression of the 1930s. Revitalized some fifty years later, the *Vanity Fair* of the late twentieth century became a slick, celebrity-driven monthly that guided U.S. popular culture among the upwardly mobile. Amid the celebrity mania of the late twentieth century, *Vanity Fair* served as the bible of the stars.

Vanity Fair's emergence during the 1910s as a smart

Vanity Fair ***Magazine, 1916.*** *An elegant watercolor by Rita Senger graces the cover of an issue of* Vanity Fair *magazine in 1916. The magazine was targeted at the sophisticated urban leisure class during its heyday in the 1910s and 1920s.* © CORBIS.

magazine aimed at the urban leisure class was the direct result of a number of changes occurring in the United States in general and in the publishing business in particular. Following the Civil War, the country underwent many sweeping metamorphoses, among which was a gradual shift from a rural society to an urban one. Smart magazines surfaced as the population became gentrified during the second half of the nineteenth century, with rural communities diminishing and cities expanding. People in the United States began to conceive of themselves as a cultured nation with a swelling upper middle class that reveled in its newfound wealth.

According to George H. Douglas, "smart magazines were written and edited for the leisured classes (although not necessarily for the very rich)—for sophisticated urbanites, for the kind of person who was well traveled, well read, well acquainted; for people who wanted to be entertained, but on an exalted plane." He adds:

> [These magazines were] general magazines intended for the entertainment of cultural elites . . . rooted in . . . contrivances of humor, of gaiety, of urbanity, of high style and fashion. The rich, it seemed, were not usually interested in "uplift," in the birthpangs of reform and good works; as often as not they enjoyed the demimonde, even low life; they wanted to hear about the lives of actors, poets, of theater people, pugilists, polo players. They loved gossip and scandal.

INNOVATIONS AND BEGINNINGS

Major changes in the printing process during the 1880s and 1890s made faster typesetting and printing possible, allowing for more publications of higher quality. After the halftone process, chromolithography, and rotogravure printing were invented, magazines took on a new glossy format, filled with full-page color illustrations and advertisements. The vast changes in advertising, which metamorphosed from simple classified-type ads to colorful images and slogans thought out by prestigious firms, contributed to the evolution of a whole new kind of magazine, leading to an era that Douglas calls "a renaissance or high-water mark of the American magazine with many new giants entering the field, and many older ones becoming bigger and more affluent than they would have dreamed possible before. By the 1890s, magazines had become big business."

Entering a field that already included the *Saturday Evening Post*, *Ladies' Home Journal*, and *Harper's Magazine*, the first of these smart magazines was aptly called the *Smart Set* and was subtitled "A Magazine of Cleverness." A huge success during the first decade of the twentieth century, this literary and artistic monthly catering to cosmopolitan café society became a model periodical, featuring the writing of such brilliant young literary figures as H. L. Mencken and George Jean Nathan, who later became its joint editors. The *Smart Set* established the tone for all the smart magazines that followed.

CROWNINSHIELD AT THE HELM

Vanity Fair, the quintessential smart magazine, came into being by a rather circuitous route. In the 1890s a publication by the same name had a limited success in New York as a peekaboo magazine of dubious quality. In 1913 Condé Nast, a successful entrepreneur who had his first success in the publishing field with *Vogue*—a high-tone, women's fashion magazine—bought another fashion rag called *Dress*. He then purchased the rights to the name *Vanity Fair* and in 1913 put out the first issue of *Dress and Vanity Fair* to limited success. It stumbled around for a year without finding its niche, until Nast brought in his friend Crowninshield as editor. In March 1914 Crowninshield's *Vanity Fair* found its way to the newsstands, where it made a big splash.

In his first editorial Crowninshield wrote, "*Vanity Fair* has but two major articles in its editorial creed: first, to believe in the progress and promise of American life, and, second, to chronicle that progress cheerfully, truthfully, and entertainingly. . . . At no time in our history has the wonder and variety of American life been more inspiring, and, probably as a result of this, young men and young women, full of courage, originality, and genius are everywhere to be met with." With these young people as both audience and contributors, Crowninshield set about to create a magazine that would chronicle the cutting edge in art, literature, drama, sport, film, and dance.

Crowninshield himself was in his early forties, raised and educated in Europe. Although he was of aristocratic background, he was also a workingman who had been the editor of a number of top magazines. He was a devotee of modern art, helping to organize the Armory Show as well as owning a superb art collection himself. Thus, he knew how to appeal to the upper classes, the intelligentsia, and the avant-garde. Under Crowninshield *Vanity Fair* contained the writing of such diverse young talents as Edna St. Vincent Millay, Edmund Wilson, P. G. Wodehouse, E. E. Cummings, and Aldous Huxley, as well as more established writers such as F. Scott Fitzgerald. The magazine also featured art by Pablo Picasso, Henri Matisse, and Jacob Epstein and photography by Edward Steichen. As Cleveland Amory writes in his introduction to an anthology of the magazine:

> *Vanity Fair* was a pioneer in so many areas that it can be said to be a significant yardstick of American culture. Not only did it publish many pieces by first-rate writers and artists before—and after—they became known, but it set a new standard for photography and picture journalism. Another thing it did "first" was to give due recognition to Negro personalities and artists.

FINDING AN AUDIENCE

Although *Vanity Fair* never had an overwhelming subscriber base, the magazine succeeded largely by being unique and using its charm, wit, insouciance, and aesthetically appealing look to attract a loyal following. For young writers it was the place to work, even if it paid less than other magazines. Dorothy Parker, Robert Benchley, Robert E. Sherwood, and Edmund Wilson all found their start at *Vanity Fair*. A conversation piece among the Smart Set, *Vanity Fair* was the place to find out who was who and what was what, from articles on silent movie stars and dashing polo players to photographs of French poets and English royalty. There were essays by D. H. Lawrence and Harry Houdini; poems by Theodore Dreiser and Amy Lowell; paintings by Raoul Dufy and August Renoir; and, of course, Miguel Covarrubias's wonderful caricatures. Regular features included the yearly hall of fame, a popular section on men's fashion, humorous sketches, and theater reviews.

Throughout the Roaring Twenties, *Vanity Fair* was the most successful of the smart magazines, but when the Great Depression hit in 1929, it began to slip from favor. As the U.S. public struggled to make ends meet, advertisements were withdrawn, and fewer and fewer people wanted to read about café society. By 1936 Nast decided to merge *Vanity Fair* into *Vogue*, calling it a "heartbreaking decision." For more than forty-five years, all that remained of the magazine was a memory.

REBIRTH

In 1982, two years into the glamorous excess of the Ronald Reagan years, Condé Nast Publications decided to reissue *Vanity Fair* as an upscale publication for the elite of the 1980s. The new *Vanity Fair* hoped to follow the format of the original smart magazines. Initially, however, it floundered, and many believed the magazine would never be able to live up to the verve, wit, and genuine charm of its forebear.

In 1984 Tina Brown, the young University of Oxford graduate who had resurrected London's *Tatler*, was brought in to punch up the publication. Brown immediately put her mark on *Vanity Fair*, bringing in top writers from around the world by paying them unheard-of six-figure contracts. She turned her staff into stars and the magazine into a money earner. Under Brown the second incarnation of *Vanity Fair* became a slick publication with a celebrity buzz. Its approach, however, was formulaic. Filled with seductive advertisements for luxury products; photographs of movie stars; and articles about the rich, the famous, or the bizarre, the new *Vanity Fair*'s audience purported to be the Eighties Smart Set. In fact, the magazine became a mass-market publication aimed at the entire upwardly mobile population of the United States.

During the late 1980s and early 1990s, the covers of *Vanity Fair* seemed to feature many of the same actors in various poses—Demi Moore in multiple states of nudity, Tom Cruise with a sly smirk or a toothy grin, Arnold Schwarzenegger clothed or unclothed, all shot with Annie Leibowitz's unerring lens. But by the mid-1990s, with Brown departed for the *New Yorker*, *Vanity Fair* began to compete with more cutting-edge magazines, such as *Interview*, by featuring cover stories about young Hollywood. Where once *Vanity Fair* had signaled mainstream success, the magazine became a star maker, as cover stories about Matthew McConaughey, Matt Damon, and Renée Zellweger brought these young actors to the attention of the mainstream and boosted their status in Hollywood. If the original *Vanity Fair* set a sophisticated standard for U.S. culture, its second incarnation became the quintessence of late-twentieth-century popular culture—slick, global, and all about money and fame.

By the early twenty-first century, *Vanity Fair* was reporting that it had 6.7 million regular subscribers. The magazine was also maintaining a strong presence on the Internet, with apps available for a variety of electronic devices in order to provide widespread easy access to the magazine. Despite its continued popularity, *Vanity Fair* was not without its critics. The magazine came under attack in May 2009 for an article written by Mark Bowden in which he accused Arthur Sulzberger, the publisher of the *New York Times*, of being childish and basically incompetent. Other newspapers rallied to Sulzberger's defense, insisting that labeling Sulzberger was both unfair and inaccurate.

Victoria Price

SEE ALSO: *Advertising; Benchley, Robert; Cruise, Tom; Damon, Matt; Dreiser, Theodore; Fitzgerald, F. Scott; The Great Depression; Houdini, Harry; Me Decade; Millay, Edna St. Vincent; Moore, Demi; The* New York Times*; The* New Yorker*; Parker, Dorothy; Picasso, Pablo; Schwarzenegger, Arnold;* USA Today*;* Vogue*; The* Wall Street Journal*; Wodehouse, P. G.*

BIBLIOGRAPHY

Amory, Cleveland, and Frederic Bradlee. *"Vanity Fair": A Cavalcade of the 1920s and 1930s*. New York: Viking Press, 1960.

Carter, Graydon. *"Vanity Fair," the Portraits: A Century of Iconic Images*. New York: Abrams, 2008.

Davis, Mary E. *Classic Chic: Music, Fashion, and Modernism*. Berkeley: University of California Press, 2006.

Douglas, George H. *The Smart Magazines: 50 Years of Literary Revelry and High Jinks at "Vanity Fair," "The New Yorker," "Life," "Esquire," and "The Smart Set."* Hamden, CT: Archon Books, 1991.

Handelman, David. "Media Circus: Run for Cover!" Salon, December 11, 1997. Accessed April 28, 2012. Available from http://www.salon.com/1997/12/11/media_26/

Mitchell, Deborah. "Is Anna Wintour Really Worth a Million Bucks?" Salon, October 27, 1997. Accessed April 28, 2012. Available from http://www.salon.com/1997/10/27/27money/

Neuharth, Al. "Is the Press Unfair? *Vanity Fair*'s a Great Example." *USA Today*, April 24, 2009.

Vardon, Harry *(1870–1937)*

Golf's first international celebrity, Harry Vardon may be best remembered for something he popularized but did not invent: the overlap golf grip that bears his name. There was much more to Vardon, however, than the grip. In 1896 he became the first Englishman to win the British Open, and he followed by winning the prestigious tournament in 1898, 1899, 1903, 1911, and 1914. Vardon added the U.S. Open to his list of major championships in 1900, at which time he was arguably the most famous golfer in the world. Although a bout with tuberculosis in 1903 affected his health, his game remained strong. Vardon's legacy is also tied to the Vardon Trophy, given to the golfer with the lowest scoring average each year on the Professional Golfers' Association Tour.

Lloyd Chiasson Jr.

SEE ALSO: *Golf; Sports Heroes.*

BIBLIOGRAPHY

Atha, Anthony. *World of Golf: The History, the Classic Players, the Major Tournaments*. New York: Smithmark, 1997.

Browning, Robert. *History of Golf*. Norwalk, CT: Classics of Golf, 1985.

Concannon, Dale. *Golf: The Early Days*. New York: Smithmark, 1995.

Gibson, Nevin H. *The Encyclopedia of Golf*. New York: A. S. Barnes, 1958.

Grimsley, Will. *Golf: Its History, People and Events*. Englewood Cliffs, NJ: Prentice-Hall, 1966.

Howell, Audrey. *Harry Vardon: The Revealing Story of a Champion Golfer*. London: Stanley Paul, 1991.

Varga Girl

During World War II the Varga Girl pinup, with her long legs, narrow waist, and ample bosom, was a major military morale booster. As Jamie Malanowski notes in her 1994 *Esquire* article, the Varga Girl image "hung in billets and on bulkheads, was unfolded in foxholes, and was lovingly imitated on fuselages throughout Europe and the Pacific." Above all, the Varga Girl was timely. According to a 1996 article by Jeanne Meyerowitz in *Journal of Women's History*, her success derived from the confluence of a world war, the coming of age of "mass culture," and changing sexual mores. Drawn by Alberto Vargas, she was part of a new set of myths, which social theorist Leo Löwenthal of the neo-Marxist Frankfurt School called a by-product of twentieth-century capitalism. Mass culture, according to Löwenthal, was manufactured in assembly-line style by agents of mass media communication and was widely distributed.

Thousands of servicemen treasured the Varga Girl pinup. They were the pleased consumers of a product ingeniously distributed by *Esquire* magazine, which along with *Life* and *Reader's Digest* had been designated as wartime "morale boosters." The upbeat image of the Varga Girl provided a counter to the unpleasantness of the war and the loneliness of the trenches. As novelist Kurt Vonnegut observes in his introduction to *Varga: The Esquire Years*, "The American male's capacity to make do with imaginary women gave our military forces a logistical advantage I have never seen acknowledged anywhere."

CREATING THE VARGA GIRL

The Varga Girl and her predecessor, the Petty Girl, evolved from the more modestly clad Gibson Girl. Both girls were also directly related to the women drawn by Raphael Kirchner for the turn-of-the-century avant-garde publication *Le Parisien*. The airbrush technique used by George Petty and Vargas allowed the impression of flawless women, suggestively clad and sultry looking. In 1940, after Petty objected to the high-handed manner of *Esquire*'s publisher David Smart, he was replaced by Vargas. The Varga Girl (without the final *s*—a name suggested as more "euphonious" by Smart) became a monthly staple in *Esquire* and in the popular Varga Calendar.

Although appreciated by a significant portion of the U.S. male population, the pinup stirred controversy in the areas of sexuality, gender exploitation, cultural representation, mass (popular) culture, and consumerism. According to Meyerowitz, "The proliferation in the mass media of sexual representations of women is arguably among the most important developments in twentieth century popular culture."

There was strong resistance to these cultural developments. In 1943 the U.S. Post Office brought charges of obscenity against *Esquire*, specifically citing a number of Varga Girl illustrations. At the trial, one female witness asserted that the pinups and other cartoons in the magazine exploited and demeaned women, while another female witness argued that the Varga images "beautifully portrayed" the female form. *Esquire* won the suit and a lot of free publicity. Even today, the debate about whether erotic representations of women celebrate or degrade women is part of the discourse of feminists, lesbians, sexual libertarians, and antipornography and free-speech advocates.

THE ARTIST: ALBERTO VARGAS

The Varga Girl was the work of Peruvian-born illustrator Alberto Vargas (1896–1982). Educated in Europe, Vargas was influenced by the work of Jean-Auguste-Dominique Ingres and Kirchner. When he arrived in New York in 1916, he was struck by the confident, vivacious women he saw. For a time he worked for producer Florenz Ziegfeld and once said that from Ziegfeld he learned the difference between "nudes and lewds." He later worked as an illustrator and set designer for several major Hollywood studios. In 1939, after Vargas walked out in solidarity with union advocates at Warner Brothers, he was blacklisted. A year later Smart hired Vargas for a pittance, and without the right to royalties for his own work. Like Petty, Vargas was eventually driven to sue Smart. Vargas lost on appeal (he maintained that the judge was bribed), and he was enjoined from using the trademarked name "Varga."

In the mid-1950s *Playboy*'s Hugh Hefner hired Vargas to resurrect the Varga Girl under the artist's own name. The Vargas Girl appeared in *Playboy* regularly until it was eclipsed by more prurient fare. *Playboy* pushed the envelope by using photography to convey a new image of the desirable woman. According to Hugh Merrill in *Esky: The Early Years at Esquire*, whereas *Esquire*'s images had been "grounded" in burlesque shows patronized by the upper classes, *Playboy* had its cultural roots in the movies, an art form accessible to the masses. Photos of actress Marilyn Monroe graced the first issue of *Playboy*.

Eventually Vargas's idealized depictions gave way to centerfold photography that left nothing to the imagination. Yet according to Merrill, Vargas's work had helped set the stage for this change. In the 1940s the center of glamour had moved from New York City (the stage) to Hollywood (the movies). As Merrill notes, the "new cinematic standard of beauty of the 1950s did not come from nowhere. It was a real-life extension of the imaginary women in the Vargas paintings of the 1940s." Some of these paintings had even been showcased in the film *DuBarry Was a Lady* (1943).

Personally, Vargas was quite different from the sexually heady atmosphere he worked in. He was an unassuming, courtly gentleman, born during the Victorian era, who was devoted to his wife, Anna Mae. Yet Vargas's girls remain embedded in the collective psyche of the generations of the 1940s and 1950s, and they also remain as one of the cultural signifiers of those eras.

Yolanda Retter

SEE ALSO: *Consumerism;* Esquire*; Feminism; Gibson Girl; Hefner, Hugh; Hollywood;* Life*; Monroe, Marilyn; The Pin-Up;* Playboy*; Pornography;* Reader's Digest*; Sex Symbol; Sexual Revolution; Vonnegut, Kurt, Jr.; World War II;* The Ziegfeld Follies.

BIBLIOGRAPHY

"Alberto Vargas." Artists Galleries: N–Z. Accessed November 15, 2011. Available from http://www.thepinupfiles.com/vargas1.html

Buszek, Maria Elena. *"Pin-Up Grrrls: Feminism, Sexuality, Popular Culture*. Durham, NC: Duke University Press, 2006.

Malanowski, Jamie. "Vivat, Vivat, Varga Girl!" *Esquire*, November 1994, 102–107.

Merrill, Hugh. *Esky: The Early Years at Esquire*. New Brunswick, NJ: Rutgers University Press, 1995.

Meyerowitz, Jeanne. "Women, Cheesecake and Borderline Material: Responses to Girlie Pictures in the Mid-twentieth

Century U.S." *Journal of Women's History* Fall (1996): 9–35.

Vargas, Alberto, and Reid Austin. *Vargas*. New York: Harmony Books, 1978.

Vonnegut, Kurt. Introduction to *Varga: The Esquire Years: A Catalog Raisonné*. New York: Alfred Van der Marck Editions, 1987.

Variety

Variety, a weekly trade newspaper focusing on theater and film, has been a bible of the entertainment industry since the turn of the twentieth century. Founded in 1905 by Sime Silverman, a former vaudeville critic for a New York newspaper, *Variety* has origins that can be traced to a dispute between Silverman and a former editor, who asked the critic to soften a scathing review. Silverman promptly quit and set about launching *Variety*, whose distinctive, trademark *V* was designed by his wife on a nightclub tablecloth.

A PIONEERING PUBLICATION

In its early days, *Variety* became embroiled in a feud with the powerful Keith-Albee theater chain over what the paper considered the chain's stranglehold over vaudeville entertainment in the United States. The newspaper supported protests by a group of actors called the White Rats of America, a fledgling performers' union modeled after the Water Rats, a similar organization in London. Keith-Albee replied by forbidding its actors and agents to read or advertise in the publication, and it warned music publishers to withdraw their advertisements or face a blacklist of their songs in the chain's theaters. A famous editorial on March 28, 1913, established Silverman as a crusading editor in the tradition of "Dana, Pulitzer, and Bennett," wrote one show-business historian. *Variety*'s support for these unionization activities laid the groundwork for what would become today's Actors' Equity Association.

Variety reached its peak of popularity during the golden age of vaudeville in the 1920s and 1930s. "There were only two media" at that time, noted Syd Silverman, who was once heir apparent to his father's dynasty. "Legit theater and vaudeville." Known as the industry paper of record, along with its primary competitor, the *Hollywood Reporter* (established in 1930), *Variety* specialized in coverage of Broadway and off-Broadway theater in New York. For many years, it was the only trade publication to provide crucial data in the form of weekly box-office reports for stage productions.

Variety should not be confused with the more West Coast–oriented *Daily Variety*, founded by the elder Silverman in 1933. *Daily Variety*'s readership has traditionally been vastly different, made up of a select demographic of upper-income entertainment executives residing almost exclusively in Los Angeles. *Variety*'s readership, in contrast, has been scattered throughout the United States, Europe, and the rest of the world.

A DISTINCTIVE VOICE

During its heyday in the 1920s and 1930s, *Variety* affected a light and breezy style with its own slang and locutions, giving it a distinctive voice not unlike the *Guys and Dolls* patter of Damon Runyon and other Broadway denizens. Two of its most famous headlines during this period are considered journalistic classics of wit and brevity: on October 30, 1929, the day after the stock market crash, its banner headline read, "Wall Street Lays an Egg," after the slang term for a failed theatrical production; on July 17, 1935, a front-page report on the unpopularity of vapid films in small midwestern towns was headlined, "Sticks Nix Hick Pix." *Variety* peppered its prose with hundreds of examples of theatrical argot and invented terms, such as *boff* for a hit show, *cleffer* for a songwriter, *deejay* for a disc jockey, *strawhat* for a summer-stock company, and *whodunit* for a mystery show. *Variety* rarely used the word *talkies* to describe motion pictures with sound, instead preferring its own term, *talkers*. The publication referred to television in its early days as "video" and helped popularize the term *Tin Pan Alley* as a description of New York City's songwriting district.

NEW CHALLENGES

The popularity of new media took its toll on *Variety* in the latter part of the twentieth century, and its theater coverage began to seem less relevant in a world dominated by motion pictures, television, and video. In 1987 Syd Silverman made a difficult decision. After eighty-two years of family ownership, he resolved to sell his father's publication (along with *Daily Variety*) to Cahners Publishing Company, a subsidiary of the British-based Reed International. The sale was valued at approximately $56.5 million, and Cahners, which already published some fifty-two trade magazines, quickly set about making massive internal changes to resuscitate the paper.

Following the sale, Silverman announced that the publication's day-to-day editorial responsibilities would be handed over to Roger Watkins, a former general manager of *Variety* in London. The magazine, it soon became clear, was about to be ushered into a new era of corporate media. Within months, *Variety*'s staff was moved from the cramped, theater-district offices it had inhabited since 1919 to sparkling new cubicles on Park Avenue South. One editor even noted that some *Variety* reporters had still been "banging out stories" on vintage Underwood manual typewriters. All this would change under the Cahners management, which advised staff members of new dress codes—coats and ties for men—to go with the publication's spiffy corporate look. Other changes included a consolidation of staff members in the East Coast and West Coast offices of *Variety* and *Daily Variety*, a move that ruffled more than a few feathers; the sister publications were long known for harboring bitter rivalries and jealousies over story assignments and advertising accounts. Despite these changes, at least one *Variety* institution remained unchanged: columnist Army Archerd, who had written the "Just for Variety" column since the 1950s and was described by gossip writer Liz Smith as "a throwback to Walter Winchell, without the ego" and the paper's "most treasured asset."

THE PETER BART YEARS

Perhaps the most controversial shift came about with the 1989 hiring of Peter Bart as editor of *Variety*—he became editorial director of both *Variety* and *Daily Variety* in 1991. Because Bart had once been a studio executive, there was much speculation as to whether he could maintain an objective stance toward the industry that had long provided his bread and butter (and caviar). Even the *New York Times* and the *Washington Post* entered the debate, asking in one headline if Bart was simply "too solicitous of the industry he covers." The *Post* highlighted what became known as the "Patriot Games" incident as an especially egregious example of Bart's lack of journalistic boundaries. The incident occurred following *Variety*'s acerbic review of the Paramount film *Patriot Games* (1992), written by veteran critic Joseph McBride. Not only did Bart dash off an apologetic letter to Martin Davis, chairman of Paramount, following the review, he also demoted McBride to reviewing children's movies. McBride resigned soon afterward. Bart's supporters countered that *Variety* was, after all, a trade paper, with some 80 percent of its subscriber base and 50 percent of its ads coming from studios. It was no secret, they maintained, that the publication was mutually dependent upon, and accountable to, the entertainment industry.

In the 1990s the entertainment industry continued to share a cozy relationship with its chief trade publications, *Variety* and *Daily Variety*. Buoyed by increasing revenues and profits, *Variety* established several new ventures. In September 1997, it began publishing *Variety Junior*, a five-times-per-year paper covering the children's entertainment business; in November of that year, it reintroduced *On Production*, a paper about the making of film, television, and commercials; and in January 1998 it debuted its variety.com website. In May of that year, *Daily Variety* also began a five-days-per-week New York edition known as *Daily Variety Gotham*, which ran news about Broadway and the publishing and entertainment businesses while continuing its heavy coverage of the Hollywood film industry. Bart said that *Variety* hoped to attract another 14,000 subscribers with the new edition. In 1997 the *New York Times* reported that *Daily Variety* had advertising revenues of $27 million, up from $12 million in 1992. Furthermore, according to the report in the *Times*, the combined profit of *Variety* and *Daily Variety* increased from $2 million to $20 million during that period.

TRYING TO STAY RELEVANT

In the first decade of the 2000s, however, the increasing popularity of blogs and other Internet sites devoted to the entertainment industry began to eat away at *Variety*'s and *Daily Variety*'s readerships. The print version of *Daily Variety* shrank considerably, both in terms of ad revenues and the number of pages it published. Its circulation dropped from a high of 35,700 to about 24,700 in 2009.

Bart resigned his editorial post in 2009. Responding to Internet speculation that he had been forced out because of the decline of *Variety*'s various print publications, Bart said, "There was a stipulation that I could step down at my twenty-year mark if I wanted, and I did. . . . The speculation on these blogs that there are intrigues behind this move is surreal." He was replaced by Timothy Gray, who has been working as the editor of *Daily Variety* since 2005.

Kristal Brent Zook

SEE ALSO: *Broadway; Hollywood; The* New York Times*; Vaudeville; The* Washington Post*; Winchell, Walter.*

BIBLIOGRAPHY

Bart, Peter. *Boffo!: How I Learned to Love the Blockbuster and Fear the Bomb*. New York: Miramax, 2006.

Carmody, Deirdre. "Technology Opens Doors for Cahners Magazine." *New York Times*, July 19, 1993.

Fabrikant, Geraldine. "Executive Editor Is Appointed at *Daily Variety*." *New York Times*, August 16, 1991.

Green, Abel, and Joe Laurie Jr. *Show Biz: From Vaude to Video*. New York: Henry Holt, 1951.

Mathews, Jay. "The Protective Paws of *Variety*'s Top Dog." *Washington Post*, April 26, 1993.

Peterson, Iver. "For *Variety*: A New York State of Mind." *New York Times*, March 16, 1998.

Pogrebrin, Robin. "That's Entertainment: *Variety* Goes Bi-coastal." *New York Times*, February 3, 1998.

Smith, Liz. "Tricks of the Trade." *Vanity Fair*, April 1995, 118–121.

Sragow, Michael. "Execs, Checks, Sex, FX." *New York Times Book Review*, February 21, 1999, 28.

Vaudeville

Vaudeville, a collection of disparate acts (comedians, jugglers, and dancers) marketed mainly to a family audience, emerged in the 1880s and quickly became a national industry controlled by a few businesspeople, with chains of theaters extending across the country.

The term *vaudeville* originates either from the French Val de Vire (also Vau de Vire), the valley of the Vire River in Normandy known as the location of ballads and comic songs, or from the French name for urban folk songs, *voix de ville*, or "voice of the city." By the late nineteenth century, entertainment entrepreneurs adopted the exotic title of "vaudeville" to describe their refined variety performances. Whereas variety shows had a working class, masculine, and somewhat illicit reputation in the nineteenth century, early vaudeville innovators eliminated blue material from performances, remodeled their theaters, and encouraged polite behavior in their auditoriums to attract middle-class women and their children in particular. This pioneering process of expansion and uplift laid the foundation for the establishment of a national audience for mass-produced American culture.

It is difficult to define the content of vaudeville entertainment because it was so eclectic. The average vaudeville bill, which usually included between nine and twelve acts, offered something for everyone. Indeed, vaudeville primarily provided an institutional setting for attractions from other show business and sports venues of the day. Circus acrobats, burlesque dancers, actors from the legitimate dramatic stage, opera singers, stars from musical comedies, baseball players, and famous boxers all made regular appearances on vaudeville. Vaudeville bills also featured motion pictures as standard acts around the turn of the twentieth century, providing one of the key sites for the exhibition of early films.

VAUDEVILLE ACTS

Despite the diversity and cultural borrowing at the heart of vaudeville, this industry had its own aesthetic, standard acts, and stars. It featured a rapid pace, quick changes, and emotional and physical intensity; the personality of individual performers was paramount. Vaudeville demanded immediacy (performers tried to draw an outward response from the audience very quickly), as opposed to the more reserved, intellectual response advocated in the legitimate theater. On the vaudeville stage, the elevation of spectacle over narrative and the direct performer-audience relationship contrasted with legitimate drama's emphasis on extended plot and character development and the indirect (or largely unacknowledged) relationship between performers and the audience. Further, players retained creative authority in vaudeville acts, often writing their own routines, initiating innovations in the acts, and maintaining their own sets, while in the legitimate theater directors were gaining power over productions.

Standard acts included the male-female comedy team, in which the woman usually played the straight role and the man delivered the punch lines. One such pair, Thomas J. Ryan and his partner (and wife) Mary Richfield, starred in a series of sketches about the foibles of Irish immigrant Mike Haggerty and his daughter Mag. Many women, such as Nora Bayes and Elsie Janis, rose to stardom in vaudeville as singing comediennes. Perhaps the most famous singing comedienne was Eva Tanguay. Famous for her chunky physique; frizzy, unkempt hair; and two left feet, she earned huge salaries for her sensual, frenetic, and often insolent performances. Her hit songs included "I Don't Care" and "I Want Someone to Go Wild with Me." W. C. Fields and Nat Wills were among the many tramp comedians who became headliners in vaudeville, and Julian Eltinge, a man who excelled in his portrayal of glamorous women, led the field of female impersonators in vaudeville.

Between approximately 1880 and 1905 most vaudeville bills included at least one and as many as three acts of rough ethnic comedy. Joe Weber and Lew Fields, well-known German (also called Dutch) comedians, spoke with thick accents and fought each other vigorously onstage, while Julian Rose succeeded in vaudeville with his comic monologues about a Jewish immigrant's mishaps. Kate Elinore joined the male-dominated ranks of slapstick ethnic comedy with her portrayal of uncouth Irish immigrant women. Vaudeville also was the main outlet for blackface comedy following the decline of the minstrel show. However, it was not only white performers who donned the black mask; black comedians like the well-known Bert Williams also wore blackface to fit the caricature of a "shiftless darky."

EVOLUTION OF MASS-MARKET CULTURE

Vaudeville's styles and standards were embedded in the social and political changes of the era. Bold women like Tanguay reflected (and energized) women's increasing rejection of Victorian codes of conduct around the turn of the century. Women on stage, who sometimes championed divorce and women's suffrage, and women who flocked to the exciting environment of vaudeville theaters participated in the expansion of public roles for women. Ethnic themes and caricatures in comedy sketches provided a crude code of identification in cities that were becoming more diverse as immigration increased in late nineteenth century. Vaudeville's ethnic comedy addressed anxieties about immigration, including the xenophobia of native-born Americans as well as tensions surrounding upward mobility and assimilation within immigrant families.

Although many vaudeville performances were titillating and impertinent, the emphasis on propriety and respectability in the major vaudeville circuits was, according to Robert Allen,

Vaudeville Theaters. *Vaudeville theaters with large marquees promote their shows to passing patrons.* © BETTMANN/CORBIS.

author of *Vaudeville and Film, 1895–1915* and *Horrible Prettiness: Burlesque and American Culture*, "another chapter in the history of the consolidation of the American bourgeoisie." Administrators such as Benjamin Franklin Keith emphasized the opulence of their theaters; their well-mannered patrons; and the clean, even educational acts onstage; their mixed audience seemed to be led by the middle classes.

Vaudeville entrepreneurs drew most of the raw material for their entertainment from nineteenth-century popular theater, namely the heterogeneous offerings in the minstrel show, concert saloon, variety theater, and dime museum. In fact, vaudeville theater managers often remodeled concert saloons and dime museums into new vaudeville establishments. Concert saloons and variety theaters (terms often used interchangeably) combined bars with cheap (or free) amusements in connected rooms or auditoriums. These largely disreputable institutions were smoky, noisy, and crowded, where patrons were likely to be drunk; waitresses, jostling among the men, were often willing to sell sex along with liquor.

Tony Pastor, after running one of the few respectable concert saloons on the Bowery (a street in New York City well known for its tawdry amusements), opened a "variety" theater. He eliminated the smoking, drinking, and lewd performances that had previously characterized variety entertainment within the setting of the concert saloon. Pastor's variety theater, one of the most successful and famous establishments of its kind between 1880 and 1890, was a pivotal establishment in the early history of vaudeville because other entrepreneurs copied his reform efforts to popularize variety as "vaudeville."

Keith, the most powerful vaudeville innovator, adopted Pastor's philosophy in his efforts to make dime museums in Boston into respectable vaudeville establishments. Whereas Pastor operated only one theater, Keith eventually mass produced vaudeville for a nation. Born on January 26, 1846, Keith began his career in popular entertainment as a circus performer and promoter in the 1870s and then opened a dime museum in Boston in 1883. Many dime museums, a combination of pseudoscientific displays and stage entertainment, were housed in storefronts in inexpensive urban entertainment areas and attracted working-class and lower-middle-class audiences. Keith, with his colleague Edward F. Albee (also previously a circus performer), worked to remove the working-class reputation of the dime museum.

At the museum they displayed circus "freaks" for an admission charge of ten cents, and they soon opened a second-floor theater where they presented a series of singers and animal acts—their first vaudeville bill. Keith touted his clean variety and dramatic stage productions, such as a burlesque of Gilbert and Sullivan's *HMS Pinafore*, to draw more middle-class patrons to his theaters. After combining light opera with variety acts in the late 1880s and early 1890s, Keith eventually offered exclusively vaudeville after 1894.

BIG TIME VS. SMALL TIME

Vaudeville theaters, depending on whether they were classified as "big time" or "small time," served different clientele. With expensive interior designs and stars who demanded high salaries, big-time theaters had higher production costs and, consequently, more expensive admission prices than small-time vaudeville did. Big-time theaters were also more attractive to performers because these theaters offered two shows a day and maintained one bill for a full week. Small-time theaters, on the other hand, demanded a more grueling schedule from performers who had to offer three to six shows a day and only stayed in town for three or four days, as small-time theaters maintained a single bill for only half a week. For performers, according to Robert Snyder in *The Voice of the City: Vaudeville and Popular Culture in New York*, "small time was vaudeville's version of the baseball's minor leagues." Small-time theaters catered primarily to working-class or immigrant audiences, drawing particularly from local neighborhoods, rather than attracting middle-class shoppers and suburbanites who would frequently arrive at big-time theaters via trolleys and subway lines.

One of the leaders of small-time vaudeville was Marcus Loew, who began to offer a combination of films and live performances in rundown theaters in 1905. Over the next decade he improved his existing theaters and acquired new ones, establishing a circuit of 112 theaters in the United States and Canada by 1918.

CONSOLIDATION OF CONTROL

Whereas before 1900 vaudeville theaters were owned independently or were part of small chains, after 1907 the control of vaudeville rested in the hands of a few vaudeville magnates, including Keith. In 1923 there were thirty-four big-time vaudeville theaters on the Keith Circuit, twenty-three owned by Keith and eleven others leased by Keith. F. F. Proctor and Sylvester Poli each controlled chains of theaters in the East, and Percy G. Williams and Martin Beck, the head of the Orpheum circuit, had extensive vaudeville interests in the West. Another vaudeville organization, the Theater Owners' Booking Association, catered to black audiences in the South and employed black performers, including the great blues queens "Ma" Rainey and Bessie Smith.

During the first decade of the twentieth century, big-time vaudeville in the United States was consolidated under the guidance of Keith largely because of his extensive control of booking arrangements. In 1906 he established a central booking office, the United Booking Office (UBO), to match performers and theaters more efficiently. Performers and theater managers subsequently worked through the UBO to arrange bookings and routes. The UBO had tremendous leverage over performers because it was the sole entryway to the most prestigious circuit in the country; if performers rejected a UBO salary, failed to appear for a UBO date, or played for UBO competition, they could be blacklisted from performing on the Keith circuit in the future.

When *Equity*, a trade publication for actors, surveyed the history of vaudeville in 1923, it emphasized the power of central booking agencies, including the UBO: "It is in the booking office that vaudeville is run, actors are made or broken, theaters nourished or starved. It is the concentration of power in the hands of small groups of men who control the booking offices which has made possible the trustification of vaudeville."

Vaudeville performers tried to challenge the centralized authority of vaudeville through the establishment of the White Rats in 1900. Initially a fraternal order and later a labor union affiliated with the American Federation of Labor, the White Rats staged two major strikes, in 1901 and 1917. The White Rats never won any lasting concessions from vaudeville theater owners and managers, and the union was defunct by the early 1920s.

The leaders of vaudeville organized theaters into national chains, developed centralized bureaucracies for arranging national tours and monitoring the success of acts across the country, and increasingly focused on formulas for popular bills that would please audiences beyond a single city or neighborhood. In these ways, vaudeville was an integral part of the growth of mass culture around the turn of the century. After approximately 1880 a mass culture took shape in which national bureaucracies replaced local leisure entrepreneurs; mass markets superseded local markets; and new mass media (namely magazines, motion pictures, and radio) targeted large, diverse audiences.

VAUDEVILLE'S DECLINE

Vaudeville began to decline in the late 1920s, falling victim to cultural developments such as the movies that it had initially helped promote. There were a few reports of declining ticket sales (mainly outside of New York City) and lackluster shows in 1922 and 1923, but vaudeville's troubles multiplied rapidly after 1926. Around this time many vaudeville theaters announced that they would begin to advertise motion pictures as the main attractions, not the live acts on their bills; by 1926 there were only fifteen big-time theaters offering straight vaudeville in the United States. The intensification of vaudeville's decline in the late 1920s coincides with the introduction of sound to motion pictures. Beginning with *The Jazz Singer* in 1927, the innovation of sound proved to be a financial success for the film industry.

In 1928 Joseph P. Kennedy, head of the political dynasty, bought a large share of stock in the Keith-Orpheum circuit, the largest organization of big-time theaters in the country. Kennedy planned to use the chain of theaters as outlets for films he booked through his Film Booking Office (FBO), which he administered in cooperation with Radio Corporation of America (RCA). Two years later Kennedy merged Keith-Orpheum interests with RCA and FBO and formed Radio-Keith-Orpheum (RKO). Keith-Orpheum thus provided the theaters for the films that were made and distributed by RCA and FBO. The bureaucratic vaudeville circuits had worked to standardize live acts and subsume local groups into a national audience, but vaudeville did not have the technology necessary to fully develop a mass-production enterprise. As Snyder concludes, "A major force in the American media had risen out of the ashes of vaudeville."

Vaudeville was also facing greater competition from full-length revues, such as the Ziegfeld Follies. Whereas vaudeville bills often included spectacular revues as a single act on the bill, full-length revues increased in popularity after 1915, employing vaudevillians and stealing many of vaudeville's middle-class customers along the way. Between 1907 and 1931, for example, there were twenty-one editions of the Follies. Such productions, actually reviewed as vaudeville shows through the early twentieth century, used thin narratives (such as a trip through New York City) to give players the opportunity to do a comic bit or song-and-dance routine, borrowing the chain of intense performances from the structure of a vaudeville bill.

Just as the revue borrowed vaudeville performers and expanded on spectacles that had been popular as part of a vaudeville bill, the motion picture industry also incorporated elements of the vaudeville aesthetic. Vaudeville performers such as Eddie Cantor, the Marx Brothers, Bert Wheeler, Robert Woolsey, and Winnie Lightner took leading roles in film comedies of the 1920s and early 1930s. They brought some of vaudeville's vigor, nonsense, and rebelliousness with them to the movies. Motion pictures, therefore, drew on the traditional acts of vaudeville and, with the aid of technology, perfected vaudeville's early efforts at mass marketing commercial leisure. Vaudeville had helped create a world that made it obsolete.

Vaudeville helped recast the social and cultural landscape of the United States at the turn of the twentieth century. From a scattered array of commercial amusements, vaudeville helped build a national system of entertainment. From a realm of raunchy, male-dominated popular entertainment, vaudeville crafted a respectable culture that catered to the female consumer. From a fragmented theatrical world, this entertainment industry forged a mass audience, a heterogeneous crowd of white men and women of different classes and ethnic groups. Vaudeville was thus a key institution in the transition from a marginalized sphere of popular entertainment, largely associated with vice and masculinity, to a consolidated network of commercial leisure, in which the female consumer was not only welcomed but pampered.

M. Alison Kibler

SEE ALSO: *Blackface Minstrelsy; Cantor, Eddie; Fields, W. C.; The Marx Brothers; Minstrel Shows; Rainey, Gertrude "Ma"; Smith, Bessie; Williams, Bert;* The Ziegfeld Follies.

BIBLIOGRAPHY

Allen, Robert Clyde. *Vaudeville and Film, 1895–1915: A Study in Media Interaction*. New York: Arno Press, 1980.

Allen, Robert Clyde. *Horrible Prettiness: Burlesque and American Culture*. Chapel Hill: University of North Carolina Press, 1991.

Bernheim, Alfred. "The Facts of Vaudeville." *Equity* 8 (1923): 9–37, 13–37, 33–41, 19–41.

Cullen, Frank; Florence Hackman; and Donald McNeilly. *Vaudeville, Old & New: An Encyclopedia of Variety Performers in America*, 2 vols. New York: Routledge, 2007.

Gilbert, Douglas. *American Vaudeville: Its Life and Times*. New York: Dover Publications, 1963.

Jenkins, Henry. *What Made Pistachio Nuts?: Early Sound Comedy and the Vaudeville Aesthetic*. New York: Columbia University Press, 1992.

Kibler, M. Alison. *Rank Ladies: Gender and Cultural Hierarchy in American Vaudeville*. Chapel Hill: University of North Carolina Press, 1999.

McLean, Albert Forbes. *American Vaudeville as Ritual*. Lexington: University of Kentucky Press, 1965.

Snyder, Robert W. *The Voice of the City: Vaudeville and Popular Culture in New York*. New York: Oxford University Press, 1989.

Staples, Shirley. *Male-Female Comedy Teams in American Vaudeville, 1865–1932*. Ann Arbor, MI: UMI Research Press, 1984.

Vaughan, Sarah *(1924–1990)*

Known alternately as Sassy, the Incomparable, and the Divine One, Sarah Vaughan was among a handful of legendary jazz singers who brought the same level of creativity and musician-

Sarah Vaughan. *Sarah Vaughan's career as a performer and recording artist spanned fifty years.* DAVID REDFERN/STAFF/REDFERNS/GETTY IMAGES.

ship to the vocal line that her colleagues brought to sax, bass, and drums. Vaughan was one of the first singers to be associated with the progressive sounds of bebop in its earliest incarnation. "It's Magic," "Make Yourself Comfortable," "Broken-Hearted Melody," "Misty," and "Send in the Clowns" are among her best-known songs.

Vaughan was born in Newark, New Jersey, in 1924 to musically gifted parents. Her father played guitar, and her mother sang in the choir of their Baptist church. As a young girl, Vaughan was a serious student of piano, and she often served as organist for the church. Throughout her career she maintained these skills, along with her love for sacred music. She took an early interest, however, in jazz, music considered by some to be sinful. As a teenager she sometimes sneaked out with a girlfriend to witness the burgeoning music scene in Newark and New York City. After watching her friend take a prize in a talent contest at Harlem's Apollo Theater, Vaughan decided to give the contest a try. Her rendition of "Body and Soul" took first place and launched her musical career.

On the recommendation of singer Billy Eckstine, one of her earliest admirers and a lifelong friend, Vaughan accepted her first professional singing job with the Earl Hines big band in 1943. Eckstine left the band and began a new one with some of the greatest names in jazz: Charlie Parker, Dizzy Gillespie, Miles Davis, and Kenny Dorham. Vaughan came onboard in 1944. During her early days in the music business, Vaughan was known for her shyness and lack of physical glamour. With her very dark skin, her unspectacular figure, and her pronounced overbite, she lacked the beauty-queen allure of Lena Horne, but she quickly earned the respect of her musical colleagues. If any single jazz singer personified the capacity of the human voice to behave like a horn, it was that of the versatile and inventive Vaughan. Carl Schroeder, one of her pianists in the 1960s and 1970s, said of Vaughan, "She could walk the line between the melody and improvisation exactly the way a great saxophone player could."

BECOMING A LEGEND

Vaughan was grateful for the camaraderie of the boys in the band. Their good times together softened some of the difficulties of life on the road for black musicians in an era when racial segregation and bias remained the norm. She was less fortunate in matters of romance. She was often drawn to flashy, aggressive men who ultimately "did her wrong," both personally and professionally. Showing no interest in the business side of her career, she always told her associates, "I sing. I just sing." She liked to have a manager with her on the road to take care of all the incidentals of bookings and hiring of personnel, and she believed there was no better person to do the job than the one with whom she shared her bed. On several occasions her lack of interest in practical matters lost her a great deal of money as romances soured.

Vaughan maintained an active career on the road and in clubs like New York's famous Café Society from the 1940s through the 1960s. During these years, she recorded many of her landmark albums, which often featured potentially commercial pop songs to offset the commercial riskiness of straight-ahead jazz. The album *Sarah Vaughan and Count Basie* (Roulette, 1960) was named by critic Len Lyons as one of the 101 best jazz albums. Like many jazz musicians, Vaughan suffered through rock's encroachment on the commercial music scene, but she maintained a loyal cadre of fans. In her later years, her venues moved from the club to the concert stage, where she performed as guest soloist with several major symphony orchestras. She was particularly proud of the artistic relationship she developed with conductor Michael Tilson Thomas.

According to jazz historian Martin Williams in *The Jazz Tradition*, "Sarah Vaughan had an exceptional range (roughly of soprano through baritone) . . . a variety of vocal textures, and superb and highly personal vocal control. Her ear and sense of pitch were just about perfect, and there are no 'difficult' intervals for Sarah Vaughan." The same abilities that many found praiseworthy were seen as problematic to others. Vaughan was frequently taken to task by critics for allowing her facility for vocal pyrotechnics to obscure the lyrics of the great American popular standards in her repertoire. This criticism may have been exacerbated by the nature of the competition. Vaughan carried on most of her musical career in the shadow of Ella Fitzgerald, whose supreme gift among many was a precise and natural diction that made her the ideal singer for the sophisticated and witty lyrics of contemporaries Ira Gershwin, Cole Porter, and Lorenz Hart. But where Fitzgerald offered an almost childlike clarity, Vaughan offered dramatic highlights and greater emotional depth.

Regardless of the competition, Vaughan was an American legend. In 1981 she won an Emmy for Individual Achievement for her performance of Gershwin tunes on a PBS special in which she was accompanied by the New Jersey Symphony. In

1982 her CBS recording of *Gershwin Live!* garnered a Grammy for Best Jazz Vocal Performance, Female. In 1988 she was inducted into the American Jazz Hall of Fame; the following year she was named National Endowment for the Arts jazz master. Vaughan's final studio recording was a scatting duet with Fitzgerald on the Quincy Jones album *Back on the Block*. It was the only time that Vaughan and Fitzgerald ever performed together.

Vaughan often joked with friends that she was born in "Excess" (as opposed to "Essex") County, New Jersey. She was in fact prone to excess in many areas of her life: she smoked two packs of cigarettes a day (to the astonishment of fellow singers), loved a good cognac, and dabbled in cocaine. Nevertheless, she kept up a rigorous schedule of performances and recording dates well into her sixties. She was diagnosed at that time with an advanced stage of lung cancer and died a few months later at the age of sixty-six. Leontyne Price sent a message of sympathy to the First Mount Zion Baptist Church in Newark, New Jersey, where the funeral was held. Rosemary Clooney and Joni Mitchell were among those who attended a memorial service at Forest Lawn on the West Coast. Carmen McRae released the album *A Tribute to Sarah* in 1991. In January 2011 contemporary jazz singers Mary Stallings and Jane Montheit paid tribute to Vaughan over a two-night period at Lincoln Center.

Sue Russell

SEE ALSO: *Apollo Theater; Clooney, Rosemary; Davis, Miles; Eckstine, Billy; Emmy Awards; Fitzgerald, Ella; Gillespie, Dizzy; Horne, Lena; Jazz; Mitchell, Joni; Parker, Charlie; Porter, Cole.*

BIBLIOGRAPHY

Gates, Henry Louis, Jr., and Cornel West. *The African-American Century: How Black Americans Have Shaped Our Country*. New York: Free Press, 2000.

Gourse, Leslie. *Sassy: The Life of Sarah Vaughan*. New York: Scribner, 1993.

Gourse, Leslie. *Louis' Children: American Jazz Singers*. New York: Cooper Square Press, 2001.

Kirchner, Bill. *The Oxford Companion to Jazz*. New York: Oxford University Press, 2000.

Lyons, Len. *The 101 Best Jazz Albums: A History of Jazz on Records*. New York: William Morrow, 1980.

Williams, Martin. *The Jazz Tradition*, rev. ed. New York: Oxford University Press, 1983.

Vaughan, Stevie Ray *(1954–1990)*

The most influential guitarist of his generation, Stevie Ray Vaughan was able to play with power and soul, bringing blues into mainstream rock and helping spark the blues revival of the 1980s. He combined the power of Albert King with the flamboyance of Jimi Hendrix to create a style easily accessible to a generation of young fans and copycat guitar players.

EARLY YEARS

Vaughan was born in Dallas, Texas, into a family that included brother Jimmie, three and a half years his senior. Jimmie would later gain fame as the founder and guitarist of the Fabulous Thunderbirds, and he was Stevie Ray's earliest musical influence because of his record collection. The brothers soaked up Albert, B. B., and Freddie King; Kenny Burrell; Albert Collins; Lonnie Mack; and Jimmy Reed. By the age of eight, Stevie Ray was playing hand-me-down guitars from his brother. As a teenager Vaughan fell under the spell of Hendrix. He would later take Hendrix's 1960s psychedelic twist on blues and reinterpret it for the youth of the 1980s. Vaughan's cover of the Hendrix song "Voodoo Chile (Slight Return)" became a high point of his live shows.

After playing in several Dallas bands, Vaughan dropped out of school and moved to Austin in 1972, where a large blues scene was developing. Vaughan continued to play in various bands until forming his own group, Double Trouble, named for an Otis Rush song, in 1978. The original lineup included singer Lou Ann Barton, but as Vaughan gained confidence in his vocal abilities, the group was pared down to a power trio that included Tommy Shannon on bass and Chris Layton on drums. Double Trouble quickly rose to the top of the Austin music scene.

VAUGHAN'S CAREER TAKES OFF

Vaughan's reputation spread to R&B producer Jerry Wexler, who viewed a performance in 1982. Wexler, considerably impressed, used his pull to get Vaughan booked at the Montreux Jazz Festival in Switzerland, a feat almost unheard of for an unsigned artist. One member of the Montreux audience was British rocker David Bowie, who asked Vaughan to play on his *Let's Dance* album and join his 1983 world tour. Vaughan added some stunning Albert King–tinged licks to the album but pulled out of the tour due to money disputes and other quarrels. He returned to Austin and resumed playing the club circuit.

Another audience member at Montreux was Jackson Browne, who offered the use of his studio for the band to record a demo tape. The tape eventually found its way to John Hammond Sr., the legendary talent scout and producer who had discovered Bob Dylan, Bruce Springsteen, Aretha Franklin, and Billie Holiday. "He brought back a style that had died, and he brought it back at exactly the right time," Hammond said in *Stevie Ray Vaughan: Caught in the Crossfire*. "The young ears hadn't heard anything with this kind of sound."

Hammond produced the band's first album, *Texas Flood*, released by Epic Records in 1983. Although peaking only at number thirty-eight on the Billboard album charts, the record went gold with more than 500,000 copies sold. Vaughan's 1984 follow-up, *Couldn't Stand the Weather*, sold over one million copies and spent thirty-eight weeks on the Billboard top 200 album chart. Organist Reese Wynans joined Double Trouble for the 1985 release *Soul to Soul*.

ADDICTION AND REHABILITATION

Vaughan had always boosted his performances by using cocaine and alcohol, but his newfound success exacerbated the problem. Now that he was selling out concerts, his cocaine habit was no longer constrained by a lack of money in his bank account. As long as he was able to perform onstage, he was able to get anything he wanted before and after a show. In 1986 all-night mixing sessions for the *Live Alive* double-live album coupled with constant touring pushed Vaughan's drug abuse over the edge. After collapsing onstage during a London concert in October, it seemed Vaughan was headed for an early death like his idol, Hendrix.

Vaughan was determined to survive his addictions, entering a rehabilitation clinic and joining Alcoholics Anonymous. After a few months of treatment, he emerged a new man. Double Trouble's 1989 album *In Step* was the band's most focused and critically acclaimed release, selling more than one million copies and winning a Grammy Award for Best Contemporary Blues Album. Days after winning the award, Vaughan appeared on MTV's *Unplugged* program, showcasing his acoustic guitar mastery.

Vaughan's live performances were infused with a new vigor, and he was at the top of his game. His next project was an album with his older brother, Jimmie, called *Family Style*, recorded during the summer of 1990. The brothers planned to tour together in support of the album. Before the release of *Family Style*, Vaughan began a tour with Eric Clapton and Robert Cray. Buddy Guy, Bonnie Raitt, Jeff Healey, and brother Jimmie joined in for an appearance at Alpine Valley Music Theater in East Troy, Wisconsin, on August 25 and 26. The concert on the 26th concluded with Vaughan, Jimmie, Clapton, and Guy dazzling the crowd of 25,000 with "Sweet Home Chicago." Afterward, a helicopter carrying Vaughan and three members of Clapton's entourage to Chicago crashed into a fog-shrouded hillside near the theater. All aboard were killed. The accident was blamed on pilot error.

POSTHUMOUS RECOGNITION CONTINUES

Family Style was released on September 25 and broke the Top 10 on the Billboard album chart. The album was a departure for Vaughan, who showed more restraint than on his solo efforts. His career appeared to be moving into a more mature phase, demonstrated in songs like "Tick Tock," which showcased Vaughan's vocals rather than his guitar. *Family Style* won a Grammy Award for Best Contemporary Blues Album, and the instrumental "D/FW" won for Best Rock Instrumental.

Vaughan's death sparked interest in his earlier albums as well, and each quickly shot over one million in sales. *The Sky Is Crying*, an album of previously unreleased outtakes and masters, was released in 1991 and won two more Grammy Awards. Vaughan was inducted into the Blues Hall of Fame in 2000, and *Rolling Stone* ranked him number seven on its list of the "100 Greatest Guitar players of All Time" published in 2003. Various live recordings, reissues, and retrospectives continue to be released, proving Vaughan's enduring legacy. The twentieth anniversary of Vaughan's death was commemorated in July 2010 by a remastered two-disc release of Vaughan and Double Trouble's second album *Couldn't Stand the Weather*, featuring a mix of originals and outtakes as well as a previously unreleased live concert from 1984.

In addition to the various posthumous honors and album releases that have carried on Vaughan's legacy, the MusiCares Map Fund—which offers addiction recovery treatment to members of the music community—presents an annual award named in Vaughan's honor to a musician who gives back to the community.

Jon Klinkowitz

SEE ALSO: *Blues; Bowie, David; Clapton, Eric; Electric Guitar; Hendrix, Jimi; King, Albert; King, B. B.; King, Freddie; Rock and Roll.*

BIBLIOGRAPHY

Hopkins, Craig L. "Stevie Ray Vaughan: Day by Day, Night after Night: His Early Years, 1954–1982." New York: *Backbeat*, 2010.

Hopkins, Craig L. "Stevie Ray Vaughan: Day by Day, Night after Night: His Final Years, 1983–1990." New York: *Backbeat*, 2011.

Kitts, Jeff; Brad Tolinski; and Harold Steinblatt. "Stevie Ray Vaughan." *Guitar World Presents Stevie Ray Vaughan*. Wayne, NJ: Music Content Developers, 1997.

Leigh, Keri. *Stevie Ray: Soul to Soul*. Dallas, TX: Taylor Publishing, 1993.

Patoski, Joe Nick, and Bill Crawford. *Stevie Ray Vaughan: Caught in the Crossfire*. Boston: Little, Brown, 1993.

Rhodes, Joe. "Stevie Ray Vaughan: A White Boy Revives the Blues." *Rolling Stone*, September 29, 1983.

VCRs

SEE: *Videos.*

Veganism

An offshoot of vegetarianism, veganism is the practice of abstaining from all animal products (including meat, fish, eggs, and dairy) in one's diet and, in some cases, all consumer goods made from animal by-products whatsoever. Although use of the term *vegan* to describe vegetarians who also avoid dairy and eggs did not become common until after Donald Watson and Elsie Shrigley formed the British Vegan society in 1944, the morality of egg and dairy consumption had been under debate by vegetarians in North American and Western Europe since the early 1900s and among Eastern religious groups (particularly Jainism) for centuries. A 2008 study by the Vegetarian Resource Group estimated that there were around one million vegans in the United States alone. As a testament to veganism's increasing popularity in the twenty-first century, former president Bill Clinton announced in 2011 that he had adopted a vegan diet after a series of health scares related to high cholesterol.

Like strict vegetarians (as opposed to dairy- and milk-eating vegetarians), vegans oppose the consumption of animal flesh and other goods that come directly from the bodies of animals. In addition, strict vegans avoid food products such as honey, gelatin, and whey, as well as animal-based materials like leather, wool, goose down, and lanolin wax. One type of veganism, known as "raw" veganism, also avoids any plant matter that has been cooked at a temperature above 118 degrees Fahrenheit, the temperature at which a number of enzymes and nutrients inherent in vegetables begin to dissolve.

While some twenty-first-century vegans adopt the diet for health reasons alone, many early vegans did so primarily out of an ethical or religious concern for the well-being of all living creatures. This ethical concern is linked to the Sanskrit term *ahimsa*, meaning "nonharming or nonkilling," and the American Vegan Society adopted the motto "ahimsa lights the way" at its founding in 1960. As such, vegans have a long (and, for some, controversial) history of working in solidarity with animal rights groups like People for the Ethical Treatment of Animals (PETA). In a 2010 interview, comedian and talk show host Ellen

DeGeneres cited her horror at images of industrial farming in the documentary *Earthlings* as the reason she committed to a vegan diet. In addition to speaking out on animal rights, DeGeneres promoted veganism on her online blog "Going Vegan with Ellen."

Veganism offers its adherents a number of health benefits, such as lower cholesterol and blood pressure; a reduced chance at certain types of cancer, including colon, prostate, and breast cancer; and higher levels of certain vitamins such as vitamins A and E. However, as with all vegetarian diets, vegans must find other sources of protein to maintain their health, which can be found in a variety of beans, nuts, and processed vegetable proteins, including tofu, tempeh, and seitan. In addition, a vegan-specific health concern is the lack of vitamin B_{12}, a substance that naturally occurs in animal products such as meat, eggs, and dairy. B_{12} deficiency can lead to a number of health problems, including depression, anemia, and heart disease. Children and teenagers are particularly susceptible to the dangers of B_{12} deficiency, and health practitioners urge young vegans to closely monitor their B_{12} levels and suggest that vegans of all ages make food fortified with B_{12} a central part of their diet.

Jacob Schmitt

SEE ALSO: *Vegetarianism; Vitamins.*

BIBLIOGRAPHY

Davis, Brenda, and Vesanto Melina. *Becoming Vegan: The Complete Guide to Adopting a Healthy Plant-Based Diet.* Summertown, TN: Book Publishing, 2000.

Torres, Bob. *Vegan Freak: Being Vegan in a Non-vegan World.* Colton, NY: Tofu Hound Press, 2005.

Winograd, Jennifer, and Nathan J. Winograd. *All American Vegan: Veganism for the Rest of Us.* Los Angeles: Almaden Books, 2011.

Vegetarianism

Though it became especially prominent in the United States during the health food craze of the 1960s and 1970s, vegetarianism—loosely defined as an adherence to a plant-based diet—has been practiced around the globe for several millennia. Accordingly, the motivations for choosing a vegetarian diet are varied; some do so for religious or ethical reasons, others in pursuit of increased personal health or for environmental principles. Vegetarianism is far more than a passing diet fad—a 2008 study by *Vegetarian Times* magazine placing the number of vegetarians in the United States at 7.3 million, with a further 22.8 million people following a "vegetarian-inclined" diet. It is, for many, a lifestyle that influences their decision-making process on everything from what food to eat to what clothes to wear and even where to live.

Instances of vegetarianism have been discovered in almost every civilized society on record. Some ancient Egyptians are said to have abstained from eating meat as far back as 3200 BCE. The Greek philosopher Pythagoras (c. 570–495 BCE) was such an outspoken advocate of the meatless diet that most vegetarians were known as "Pythagoreans" until the formation of the British Vegetarian Society in 1847. Along with the Pythagoreans, a number of religious groups have practiced vegetarianism as a method of reducing animal suffering and attaining a greater sense of oneness with the world, including Buddhism, Hinduism, and Jainism. Even some Christians have adopted a vegetarian diet based on biblical passages such as Genesis 1:29, which reads, "And God said, 'Behold, I have given you every herb bearing seed which is upon the face of all the earth, and every tree in the which is the fruit of a tree yielding seed; to you it shall be for meat.'"

During the Renaissance, Leonardo da Vinci adhered to a meat-free diet in response to the brutal killing of animals for food or sport, as did a number of poets and artists in the eighteenth and nineteenth centuries, including Percy Bysshe Shelley, Charlotte Brontë, Leo Tolstoy, and Henry David Thoreau. In the twentieth century, vegetarianism became associated with a wide variety of social movements, including nonviolent political resistance inspired by Mohandas Gandhi and the "grow your own" imperative during the food shortages caused by World War II. Also during the twentieth century, people became increasingly aware of the conditions that industrial food products were prepared in and their toll on the ecosystem. By the time Frances Moore Lappé's influential book *Diet for a Small Planet* (1971) was published, vegetarianism had become a popular choice for those seeking a more humane, less environmentally damaging alternative to meat eating.

There are a number of different varieties of vegetarianism. A "strict" vegetarian eschews all forms of animal protein, including eggs and dairy. (A more militant form of strict vegetarianism, veganism, goes so far as to avoid all animal by-products in food and clothing.) A more common form of vegetarianism in the United States is lacto-ovo-vegetarianism, which allows for the consumption of eggs and dairy but not fish, poultry, or meat. A number of semivegetarian diets are also popular, including pescatarianism (which allows the eating of fish, dairy, and eggs) and pollotarianism (which allows poultry and fish). So-called flexitarians, who occasionally eat meat but opt for plant-based foods as much as possible, have become increasingly abundant in the twenty-first century, as a number of studies extolling the benefits of a vegetarian diet have been released.

Vegetarianism offers its practitioners a wide range of benefits. They have been shown to be at lower risk of a number of health concerns, including obesity, hypertension, diabetes, high cholesterol, and even certain types of cancer. A vegetarian diet is also shown to reduce a person's environmental impact: a 2009 study published in the *American Journal of Clinical Nutrition* found that the nonvegetarian diet required 2.9 times the amount of water and 2.5 times the amount of energy to produce than the vegetarian diet. Furthermore, according to a 2007 study by the National Institute of Livestock and Grassland Science in Tsukuba, Japan, for every kilogram (2.2 pounds) of beef produced, an amount of carbon dioxide equivalent to taking about a 160-mile drive is released into the atmosphere. A vegetarian diet, therefore, is not only sustainable, but it also contributes to a cleaner environment and better air quality. In the 2010s vegetarian options were easily accessible for many Americans: more than 10,000 vegetarian-friendly restaurants are listed on community-maintained dining guide VegGuide.org, and vegetarian protein sources such as soy, tempeh, and seitan are widely available in grocery stores across the country. Such availability has made vegetarianism in its many forms an increasingly attractive option for a wide range of people looking to improve their health and the health of their planet.

Jacob Schmitt

SEE ALSO: *Cancer; Environmentalism; Foodies; Veganism; Vitamins.*

BIBLIOGRAPHY

Lappé, Frances Moore. *Diet for a Small Planet.* New York: Ballantine Books, 1971.

Marlow, Harold J. "Diet and the Environment: Does What You Eat Matter?" *American Journal of Clinical Nutrition* 89, no. 5 (2009): 1699S–1703S.

Maurer, Donna. *Vegetarianism: Movement or Moment?* Philadelphia: Temple University Press, 2002.

Puskar-Pasewicz, Margaret. *Cultural Encyclopedia of Vegetarianism.* Santa Barbara, CA: Greenwood, 2010.

Robbins, John. *The Food Revolution: How Your Diet Can Help Save Your Life and Our World.* Berkeley, CA: Conari Press, 2001.

Spencer, Colin. *Vegetarianism: A History.* New York: Four Walls Eight Windows, 2002.

Walters, Kerry S. *Ethical Vegetarianism: From Pythagoras to Peter Singer.* Albany: State University of New York Press, 1999.

Velez, Lupe *(1908–1944)*

Lupe Velez starred in several successful films for RKO Radio Pictures in the late 1930s and early 1940s, including the *Mexican Spitfire* series. Despite her on-screen charisma and gift for comedy, the Mexico-born Velez is best remembered for her tumultuous love life. She had stormy and often violent relationships with actors Gary Cooper and Johnny Weissmuller (of *Tarzan* fame), to whom she was married for five years. A onetime nightclub performer, Velez made her first appearance in a full-length film opposite Douglas Fairbanks Sr. in *The Gaucho* (1927). By the 1940s, moviegoers' tastes had begun to change, and Velez's star faded. In 1944, she was impregnated by bit actor Harald Maresch, who would not marry her. Velez, a devout Catholic, would not have an abortion, and Hollywood of that era did not tolerate unwed mothers. She took what she felt was the only way out and committed suicide in December 1944.

Jill A. Gregg

SEE ALSO: *Abortion; Cooper, Gary; Fairbanks, Douglas, Sr.; Sex Scandals; Suicide; Tarzan; Weissmuller, Johnny.*

BIBLIOGRAPHY

Conner, Floyd. *Lupe Velez and Her Lovers.* New York: Barricade Books, 1993.

Parish, James Robert. *Hollywood Divas: The Good, the Bad, and the Fabulous.* Chicago: Contemporary Books, 2003.

Shipman, David. *Great Movie Stars: The Golden Years.* London: Warner Books, 1989.

Velveeta Cheese

Introduced by Kraft Foods in 1928, Velveeta is a cheese food product that is a blend of Colby and cheddar cheeses with emulsifiers and salt. The ingredients are heated until liquefied; squirted into aluminum foil packaging; and then allowed to cool into half-pound, one-pound, or two-pound bricks. Velveeta is part of a uniquely American group of highly processed foods, including such favorites as Spam and Jell-O, that have become the building blocks for a remarkably inexpensive though nutritionally dubious popular cuisine.

Revered for its plasticlike meltability, Velveeta is a favored topping for macaroni, omelets, and grilled sandwiches, though some prefer to eat it sliced. The single most popular brand of processed cheese, Velveeta products were purchased by some 34 percent of all American households in 2010. Some of the most requested Velveeta recipes developed by Kraft include those for Cheese Fudge and Cheesy Broccoli Soup. In the 1980s several preflavored Velveeta cheeses were introduced, including Mexican Salsa and Italian. In an effort to keep up with changing tastes, Kraft introduced Velveeta shredded processed cheese food in 1987, Velveeta Light in 1991, and pepper-jack flavor in 2006. The company also developed Velveeta Shells and Cheese and "Cheesy Skillets," prepackaged meals that require only the addition of meat while cooking.

David Marc

SEE ALSO: *Fast Food; Jell-O.*

BIBLIOGRAPHY

Weaver, Phyllis. "Velveeta Chronicles: A Food Memoir." In *Food and the Memory: Proceedings of the Oxford Symposium on Food and Cookery, 2000,* ed. Harlan Walker. Devon, UK: Prospect Books, 2001.

The Velvet Underground

In an oft-repeated declaration, Roxy Music cofounder Brian Eno once said that the Velvet Underground sold only a few records but everyone who bought their albums started a band. While Eno's claim is hyperbole, the avant-garde guitar stylings the Velvet Underground developed in the second half of the 1960s were revolutionary. Their music shaped the sound and attitude of the New York Dolls, the Modern Lovers, R.E.M., Suicide, Television, David Bowie, Patti Smith, Sonic Youth, Galaxie 500, Yo La Tengo, and countless other post-punk and indie-rock bands. Each of the Velvet Underground's periods—including their innovative noise, beautifully sparse neo-folk, and straightforward rock phases—laid the blueprint for an entire subgenre of rock and roll. And while the Velvet Underground did not sell many records by commercial standards, their influence has been widespread enough to secure their entry into the Rock and Roll Hall of Fame in 1996.

In the early-to-middle part of the 1960s, rhythm guitarist Lou Reed met lead guitarist Sterling Morrison and bassist/violist John Cale, and the three—along with percussionist Angus MacLise—began playing at Lower Manhattan poetry readings and happenings under various names, including the Warlocks, Falling Spikes, and the Primitives. As the Primitives, the group recorded a number of commercial dance-oriented singles for Pickwick Records, the company for which Reed was a staff songwriter. When Reed and Cale met, Cale was playing in an avant-garde group founded by famed minimalist La Monte Young, and the two became intrigued by the idea of bringing

Velvet Underground at Rock and Roll Hall of Fame Induction. *Members of the Velvet Underground, from left, Maureen Tucker, Martha Morrison (attending for her late husband, Sterling Morrison), John Cale, and Lou Reed, pose backstage after their induction into the Rock and Roll Hall of Fame in 1996.* AP IMAGES.

avant-garde concepts to rock and roll. In 1965 MacLise left and was replaced by Maureen "Moe" Tucker, who became known for her peculiar standup style of primitive drumming.

THE WARHOL INFLUENCE

The Velvet Underground soon began playing a regular gig at Greenwich Village's Cafe Bizarre—an engagement that abruptly ended when they launched into their screeching "Black Angel's Death Song" immediately after being told by the management never to play it again. Before the group was fired, it impressed pop art Svengali Andy Warhol, who invited them to play at a series of his film screenings called Cinematique Uptight and later in a multimedia spectacle called The Exploding Plastic Inevitable. During this time, Warhol arranged for European chanteuse/aspiring movie star Nico to sing with the Velvet Underground for the Exploding Plastic Inevitable, something that caused a certain amount of resentment among members of the band.

In 1966 Warhol took the band into the studio. These sessions resulted in the album *The Velvet Underground and Nico*, which had a Warhol-designed banana on the cover. The album featured three songs sung by Nico, as well as Reed's infamous drug song "Heroin." The monotone voices of Nico and Reed, combined with lyrics about sadomasochism, hard drugs, and death, made this album extremely uncommercial, particularly during a time dominated by the positive vibes of hippie flower power.

Rather than going a more commercial route on its second album, the group instead followed its muse (and a path that was driven by the ingestion of extreme amounts of amphetamines) by making *White Light/White Heat* (1968). This uncompromisingly noisy creation—whose lyrics deal with prostitutes, sailors, and other sundry topics, and which culminates with a seventeen-minute jam called "Sister Ray"—is too dissonant to be heavy metal and too heavy to be psychedelic.

GOING THEIR SEPARATE WAYS

After a long power struggle with Reed, Cale quit the group and was replaced by Doug Yule, who played only bass (the group never had another violist). Reed radically changed the group's direction with *The Velvet Underground* (1969), which almost uniformly features pretty, quiet songs such as "Pale Blue Eyes" and "Candy Says." Next the band recorded what would be called their great "lost" album, a series of demos that their label refused to release. Their last studio album, *Loaded* (1970), contains the oft-covered classics "Rock and Roll" and "Sweet Jane." Released by Atlantic Records after the band's commercially unsuccessful three-album stint at Verve Records, *Loaded* is the Velvet Underground's most conventional album, partially because of Tucker's absence from many of the recording sessions due to her pregnancy. (Doug Yule's little brother, Billy Yule, filled in on drums.) Reed quit the group before the album was mixed, and he claims that two songs—"Sweet Jane" and "New Age"—were significantly changed by Doug Yule and the rest of the group. (Reed's original vision was later restored on the 1995 Velvet Underground box set *Peel Slowly and See.*)

The group continued to tour without Reed, but Morrison and Tucker eventually quit, too, before Doug Yule put the name to rest in 1973 after releasing what amounted to a solo album, *Squeeze*. Morrison went on to teach English at the University of Texas and drive a tugboat in his spare time. Tucker raised a family and released a number of critically praised solo albums. Cale also released numerous solo albums and produced important albums by Jonathan Richman's Modern Lovers, Patti Smith, the Stooges, Squeeze, and Nico. In fact, the Cale-produced Nico solo albums, *Desert Shore* (1970) and *Marble Index* (1969), are considered classics. While all the members of the Velvet Underground have maintained a substantial cult following, Reed has maintained the highest profile, most notably with his 1972 hit "Walk on the Wild Side." Reed even played at the White House in front of President Bill Clinton and a number of foreign dignitaries in 1998.

In 1993 the group patched up its differences and did a brief tour of Europe (sans Nico, who died in a bicycle accident in 1988), resulting in the live recording *Live MCMXCIII* (1993). However, their egos soon clashed, and they again went their separate ways before recording a planned studio album. Morrison died in 1995, which put an end to speculation that the group might again record under the Velvet Underground moniker. In 2004 *Rolling Stone* ranked the Velvet Underground nineteenth on its list of the 100 most influential rock and roll artists of all time.

Kembrew McLeod

SEE ALSO: *Hippies; Indie Music; Pop Art; Reed, Lou; R.E.M.; Rock and Roll;* Rolling Stone*; Warhol, Andy.*

BIBLIOGRAPHY

Bockris, Victor, and Gerard Malanga. *Up-Tight: The Velvet Underground Story.* New York: Quill, 1983.

DeRogatis, Jim, with Bill Bentley. *The Velvet Underground: An Illustrated History of a Walk on the Wild Side.* Minneapolis, MN: Voyageur Press, 2009.

Heylin, Clinton. *From the Velvets to the Voidoids: A Pre-punk History for a Post-Punk World.* New York: Penguin, 1993.

Thompson, Dave. *Beyond the Velvet Underground.* New York: Omnibus, 1989.

Zak, Albin. *The Velvet Underground Companion: Four Decades of Commentary.* New York: Schirmer Books, 1997.

Ventura, Jesse *(1951–)*

With his surprise election as governor of Minnesota in 1999, former professional wrestler Jesse "The Body" Ventura (original name James Janos) captured the attention of the entire country. Representing the Reform Party, Ventura parlayed his gift for gab, celebrity status, and public disgust with "politics as normal" into a victory at the polls to become an instant icon of popular culture. Following his election, he was asked to appear on countless talk shows, became the subject of both serious news analyses and numerous jokes, and was even included as a *Doonesbury* character. The A&E cable channel quickly put together an episode of *Biography* and two networks started work on TV movies about him. In addition, humorist and fellow Minnesotan Garrison Keillor penned a Ventura satire called *Me* about a loutish loud wrestler who becomes governor.

Ventura's diverse background includes time as a U.S. Navy Seal, TV broadcaster, radio talk show host, and a successful eleven-year stint in professional wrestling. He was nicknamed "The Body" because of his impressive physique, but when a blood clot forced his early retirement from the ring, it was his talent behind the microphone as a color commentator, coupled with a penchant for boas and outrageous costumes, that garnered him an impressive fan base, first with World Wrestling Federation (WWF) and later with World Championship Wrestling (WCW). His charisma led to roles in films such as *Predator* (1987), *The Running Man* (1987), and *Batman & Robin* (1997).

As typifies late twentieth-century American popular culture, the road to politics was only a step away. Ventura was not the first celebrity elected to office, but it is difficult to imagine Arnold Schwarzenegger—Ventura's former workout partner—being elected governor of California in 2003 without the precedent set by Ventura's victory. What Ventura lacked in legislative accomplishment, he made up with controversy and self-promotion. Casting the press as the "heel" and himself as the "babyface," Ventura used what he learned in wrestling to "get over" with the voters. Most of the controversies were related to Ventura's outside ventures, such as serving as guest referee at a WWF pay-per-view taking place in Minnesota to his stint as color commentator for the ill-fated XFL. Near the end of his term as governor, Ventura faced a high disapproval rating, and he cited personal reasons for opting not to run for reelection.

While governor, Ventura penned the political autobiography *Ain't Got Time to Bleed* (1999) and a political critique, *Do I Stand Alone?* (2000)—both *New York Times* best sellers. In 2008 he coauthored a political memoir titled *Don't Start the Revolution without Me!*

Ventura's career after his term as governor was characterized by hits and misses. He had a short-lived talk show on MSNBC and appeared on other talk shows, always flirting with the idea of again running for public office, including president of the United States. Ventura hit it big with the investigative TV program *Conspiracy Theory with Jesse Ventura*, which began airing on truTV network in 2009. The premiere, according to truTV, drew 1.6 million viewers, a record for a new series on the network. Although in wrestling he was known as "The Body," Ventura has shown a keen calculating mind to gain the attention of the American public.

Patrick Jones

SEE ALSO: *Batman; Cable TV;* Doonesbury*; Keillor, Garrison; Schwarzenegger, Arnold; Television; World Wrestling Federation.*

BIBLIOGRAPHY

Barnes, Dana R. "Jesse Ventura." *Notable Sports Figures.* Detroit, MI: Gale, 2004.

Gray, Paul. "Body Slam." *Time*, November 16, 1988.

Hauser, Tom. *Inside the Ropes with Jesse Ventura.* Minneapolis: University of Minnesota Press, 2002.

Keillor, Garrison. *Me.* New York: Viking, 1999.

Lentz, Harris M. *Biographical Dictionary of Professional Wrestling.* Jefferson, NC: McFarland, 1997.

Tapper, Jake. *Body Slam: The Jesse Ventura Story.* New York: St. Martin's Press, 1999.

Ventura, Jesse. *I Ain't Got Time to Bleed: Reworking the Body Politic from the Bottom Up.* New York: Villard Books, 1999.

Ventura, Jesse, and Dick Russell. *Don't Start the Revolution without Me!* New York: Skyhorse, 2008.

Versace, Gianni *(1946–1997)*

As a boy, Gianni Versace observed his mother's dressmaking studio in Reggio Calabria, Italy; as a man, he moved to Milan, Italy, to design for various companies from 1972 to 1977 before establishing his own business in 1978. Versace was a consummate dressmaker, but his influence on the fashion industry transcended his designs. He rocked the fashion world in many ways, including featuring provocative models, packing runway shows with celebrities, dressing famous men and women such as Elton John and Princess Diana, and creating body-conscious clothing for the most self-confident clients. His body-exposing black safety-pin dress, worn by actress Elizabeth Hurley to a London movie premiere, was the most photographed dress of 1994. Leather and metal-mesh dresses from his last collection in 1997 referred to Byzantine art but clung to the body.

Versace was a flamboyant, larger-than-life figure. He conceptualized fashion as media and went about creating Cinderella fantasies for the 1980s and 1990s. However, it all ended tragically. In July 1997 a serial killer named Andrew Cunanan murdered Versace on the steps of his Miami, Florida, mansion for reasons that remain unknown. In the wake of his death, his sister, Donatella Versace, took over as head designer for the Versace label.

Richard Martin

SEE ALSO: *Diana, Princess of Wales; John, Elton; Serial Killers.*

BIBLIOGRAPHY

Martin, Richard. *Gianni Versace.* New York: Metropolitan Museum of Art/Abrams, 1997.

Martin, Richard. *Versace.* New York: Universe, 1997.

Vertigo

Released in 1958, *Vertigo*, which combines a complex story line with equally complex cinematography, is often singled out as Alfred Hitchcock's most important film. It debuted Hitchcock's now famous combination of forward zoom and reverse tracking. This unique method, along with other creative and technical complexities of the film, exerted a tremendous influence on an entire generation of filmmakers, especially the French New Wave. *Vertigo*'s presence is felt in films as diverse as *Jules et Jim* (1962), *High Anxiety* (1977), *Body Double* (1984), and *Twelve Monkeys* (1995).

Vertigo was unavailable for decades because its rights, along with those of four other films, were left by Hitchcock as a legacy to his daughter. It was rereleased in 1984 to much popular and critical acclaim. Because Hitchcock's films are so popular and are so creatively and technically complex, they complicate the distinction between high and low art.

Vertigo. *James Stewart, left, and Kim Novak starred in Alfred Hitchcock's* Vertigo. FOTOS INTERNATIONAL/CONTRIBUTOR/MOVIEPIX/GETTY IMAGES.

Vertigo is a complex psychological thriller—it opens with San Francisco police detective Scottie Ferguson letting a fellow officer fall to his death during a rooftop chase of a suspect. After the accident, Ferguson is hired by an old friend to investigate the friend's wife, Madeleine, who believes herself to be the reincarnation of a turn-of-the-century belle, Carlotta. Madeleine reenacts Carlotta's suicide by jumping off a mission bell tower while Scottie stands by helplessly, paralyzed by his vertigo.

The remainder of the film details Scottie's nervous breakdown and his discovery of a woman named Judy who bears an uncanny resemblance to Madeleine. Scottie re-creates Madeleine in Judy, forcing Judy to adopt Madeleine's makeup, clothing, hairstyle, and speech. When Scottie realizes he has been the dupe of a complex murder plot, he attempts to cure himself of his vertigo by revisiting the scene of Madeleine's death. Although he is able to conquer his vertigo, Scottie is nevertheless unable to save Judy, who falls to her death.

The overwhelming critical and popular response to *Vertigo*'s rerelease raises the question of why the film is such a vital text for film criticism and theory. The film itself has been interpreted in a variety of ways: as an allegorical tale of man's descent into the underworld in search of a lost love; as a psychological parable of guilt, obsession, and repression; and as an experiment in generic collage, drawing on the conventions of realism, fantasy, and the women's film. Together with *Rear Window*, *Vertigo* has often been discussed as a document of late 1950s culture, as a portrayal of the alienation and rootlessness of the 1950s, as well as of the constructions of 1950s femininity. It is these latter issues—the representation of women and the relationships among power, sexuality, and gender—that have garnered the most critical attention.

Hitchcock is frequently understood as a misogynist whose films entice audiences to participate in sadistic fantasies about women (such as Scottie's efforts to make over Judy into Madeleine, despite Judy's plea that he love her the way she is). Certainly Hitchcock's films are both fascinated by and horrified by women's (potential) power. Hitchcock's films can also be read, however, as exposures of the mechanisms of patriarchy—*Vertigo* can be read, for example, as a critique of the ways in which femininity in our culture is largely a masquerade and a male construct.

Hitchcock's films are central to film theory and feminist criticism because they are all about scopophilia—voyeurism, fetishism, and the interrelated questions of epistemology, identification, and spectatorship. One of the most important essays of feminist film criticism, Laura Mulvey's 1974 essay "Visual Pleasure and the Narrative Cinema," uses readings of Hitchcock's *Rear Window* and *Vertigo* to argue that classic Hollywood movies inevitably transform women into passive objects of male voyeurism and sadism. Mulvey's essay also claims that Hitchcock's female characters both represent and assuage male spectators' anxieties and desires, whereas female spectators are trapped into a masochistic identification with the female victims onscreen.

Later feminist film critics also turned to *Vertigo* as a central text. Tania Modleski, for example, uses *Vertigo* to elaborate upon the notion of the female spectator. She argues that identification is a more complex mechanism than heretofore considered and suggests that the female spectator is implicated in a split position, identifying with both the passive female object and the active male subject. Hitchcock himself seems to suggest this position when, in a pivotal scene in the movie, we see things from Judy's point of view as well as Scottie's. Indeed, it is *Vertigo*'s multiple points of view, and thus of knowledge and of identification, that suggest that the movie's appeal lies in its very ambivalence toward women and their potential to upset the male spectator's position.

Austin Booth

SEE ALSO: *Feminism; Hitchcock, Alfred; Hollywood; Novak, Kim;* Rear Window*; Sexual Revolution; Stewart, Jimmy; Suicide.*

BIBLIOGRAPHY

Modleski, Tania. *The Women Who Knew Too Much: Hitchcock and Feminist Theory*. New York: Methuen, 1988.

Mulvey, Laura. "Visual Pleasure and Narrative Cinema." *Screen* 16 (1975): 6–18.

Sloan, Jane. *Alfred Hitchcock: A Guide to References and Resources*. New York: G. K. Hall, 1993.

Viagra

Viagra, a "little blue pill" produced by the pharmaceutical company Pfizer Inc., became the first oral medicine approved for male impotence by the U.S. Food and Drug Administration (FDA). Its approval in March 1998 set off a worldwide demand and sent Pfizer stock soaring. Hardly a day went by when newspapers, radio, and television did not have stories of the Viagra craze. The pill, which sold by prescription for about $10 each retail, was taken by men with sexual problems about an hour before they expected to have sexual activity. Their performance during the sex act improved dramatically. The drug, chemically named sildenafil, had been used unsuccessfully as a medicine for heart problems. When some heart patients reported to doctors they were getting erections after taking the pill, it was developed to treat sexual impotence. It has since been hailed as a miracle pill by enthusiastic users, including eighty-six-year-old *Playboy* magazine founder Hugh Hefner, who called it "the best recreational drug on the market."

Clinical studies of about 4,000 men with erectile dysfunction showed that up to 72 percent reported they had successful

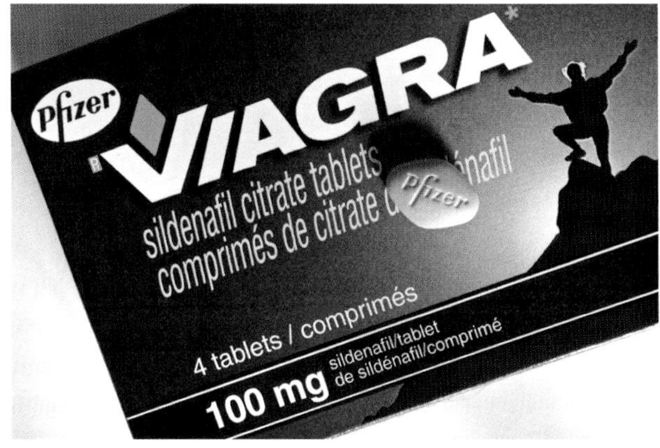

Viagra. *Viagra, an oral medication used to treat male impotence, was originally created by Pfizer as a type of heart medicine.* DAVID WEI/ALAMY.

intercourse after using Viagra, against 23 percent of men who took a placebo. Viagra works by improving the blood flow to the penis. More specifically, it inhibits the effects of an enzyme that acts to reverse erections after sex. Before Viagra came along, men with erectile problems had to forgo sex or rely on mechanical devices such as a small pump to produce an erection, surgical penile implants, or medicines injected directly into the penis.

Once the Viagra craze spread, so did reports of problems associated with taking the pill. Some men reported problems with their vision, seeing green or blue. There were stories of dizziness and headaches or upset stomachs. Men with heart problems who took nitroglycerin or nitrates were warned not to use Viagra because it could act to reduce blood pressure. By late 1998 the FDA issued warnings that Viagra could be hazardous to some men with heart ailments and that using the pill could lead to heart attacks or strokes. The agency said that although Viagra was still considered safe and effective, it posed potential problems for men with very high or very low blood pressure, so that patients should get careful examinations before taking the pill.

The FDA also said that 130 reported deaths of men who had taken Viagra could not be attributed directly to the drug. The average age of those who died was sixty-four, and many of the men had had serious health problems aggravated by sexual activity, which ended in heart attacks or strokes. "The people who died had underlying cardiovascular problems," Dr. Lisa Rarick, director of an FDA division, told reporters during late 1998. She added that men with heart problems should ask their doctors, "Is sex good for me?" By the time of the warning some six million prescriptions had been written for about three million men.

The underlying demand for Viagra could be linked to a major study published in 1999 by the *Journal of the American Medical Association* of the sexual habits of nearly 5,000 people, the largest such study since the report of biologist Alfred Kinsey some fifty years earlier. The new research revealed that sexual problems were widespread in the United States. On the basis of personal interviews with 1,749 women and 1,410 men, the research showed that about two out of five women and one out of three men had some form of sexual dysfunction.

The clamor for Viagra in other countries spurred some swindlers to peddle pills made to look like Viagra. Yet cashing in on demands for a silver bullet to cure sex problems was not new. The search for a magic potion that could produce erections on demand has gone on for centuries, encouraging charlatans who sold bogus remedies to unwitting, desperate men. Among the miracle cures thus ballyhooed have been underwear electrified to stimulate the penis, rhinoceros horns pounded into powder, and tiger penises made into soups.

Heavily marketed, Viagra seemed to be everywhere. Former U.S. presidential candidate Bob Dole appeared in Viagra ads in the late 1990s. He purportedly had been part of the drug's clinical trial and was impressed with its efficacy. The mass marketing of Viagra, along with the drug's somewhat uncomfortable connotations, inevitably led to jokes and parodies. Dole even parodied his Viagra ads in a Pepsi commercial. *Saturday Night Live* did a Viagra skit that featured actor Christopher Walken, and even public radio show *A Prairie Home Companion* made jokes about Viagra.

Despite the mockery, Pfizer continued to rake in profits from the drug: in 2011 the manufacturer reported Viagra sales of $1.98 billion. Competitors produced alternatives to Viagra, including Cialis and Levitra, but in terms of sales, none could hold a candle to the little blue pill.

Michael L. Posner

SEE ALSO: *Pepsi-Cola;* Saturday Night Live.

BIBLIOGRAPHY

Katzenstein, Larry. *Viagra: The Potency Promise.* New York: St. Martin's Press, 1998.

Loe, Meika. *The Rise of Viagra: How the Little Blue Pill Changed Sex in America.* New York: New York University Press, 2004.

Morgentaler, Abraham. *The Viagra Myth: The Surprising Impact on Love and Relationships.* San Francisco: Jossey-Bass, 2003.

Vaughan, Susan C. *Viagra: A Guide to the Phenomenal Potency-Promoting Drug.* New York: Pocket Books, 1998.

Victoria's Secret

Perhaps given a boost by the openness of the sexual revolution, the Victoria's Secret retail chain almost single-handedly redefined America's conception of lingerie beginning in the early 1980s. Despite the secrecy promised in the franchise's moniker, each of its stores replaced the modest, tucked-away, department-store displays of women's undergarments with an openly luxurious atmosphere that re-created a nineteenth-century boudoir. At the same time, Victoria's Secret decidedly built its image with a fairly conservative, middle-class shopper in mind and avoided any connotations of sleaziness that lingerie may carry. While some critics have contested the sometimes reactionary portrait of femininity developed in the store's designs and advertising campaigns, Victoria's Secret helped women of all shapes and sizes, if not tax brackets, feel that sensuality need not be limited to models and celebrities.

Victoria's Secret was launched through the personal vision of entrepreneur Roy Raymond, an ambitious graduate of Stanford University who found himself dissatisfied working in the lower rungs of large corporations. Raymond's brainchild came to him in the mid-1970s as the result of his own experiences of buying lingerie for his wife. A shy man by nature, Raymond found himself made uncomfortable by the probing glances of lingerie salespeople in department stores and, moreover, thought the wares of such stores were either excessively frilly or blandly conservative. Believing that many men and women alike shared in his desire for a middle ground between these two poles, Raymond decided to embark on the risky venture of creating his own boutiques.

In 1977 he borrowed a total of $80,000—half of it from his parents—and opened the doors of the first Victoria's Secret in a shopping center in the southern outskirts of San Francisco. Decorated to resemble a popularized Victorian bedroom, the premiere outlet was furnished with opulent Oriental rugs and period vanities whose drawers housed fittingly plush bras and panties made by designers such as Vanity Fair and Warner's. Although subsequent stores were less customized than Raymond's prototype, this balance of seduction and "classy" charm continued to rule the sensibilities of Victoria's Secret.

In its first year of business, the San Francisco store had amassed sales of an impressive $500,000, allowing Raymond to expand Victoria's Secret into four new locations, in addition to a headquarters, a catalog, and a warehouse. His creative vision was not equaled by financial mastery, however, and in 1982 he was forced to sell Victoria's Secret to the Columbus, Ohio–based conglomerate The Limited for the relatively slight sum of $1 million. Although it was already a nationally known fashion enterprise, The Limited chose to keep the personalized image of Victoria's Secret intact, albeit in a mass-produced, cost-efficient manner. Rapidly expanding into the terrain of America's malls throughout the 1980s, Victoria's Secret blossomed from a handful of stores to more than 400 and solidified its exclusive image by appending its own label to all of its offerings as a brand name. In addition to volume growth, the company was able to vend a widened range of products with the aid of a popular mail catalog issued eight times annually. While corsets, teddies, and silk pajamas remained at the hub of the Victoria's Secret wheel, home shoppers could also buy apparel, swimwear, and perfumes—such as Wild English Gardens and Heather's Embrace—all under a single banner promising both middle-class refinement and daring sexuality.

By the early 1990s Victoria's Secret had become the largest American lingerie outfitters, easily surpassing both the higher-priced Cacique chain and the racier Frederick's of Hollywood. However, despite the fact that the company had topped the billion-dollar mark, its growth showed signs of stagnation. In 1993 Grace Nichols took over the executive helm from former president Howard Gross and immediately addressed allegations that the quality of Victoria's Secret's merchandise did not match its elevated price tags. In addition, Nichols placed added emphasis upon an older age group as the company's target concern. Nevertheless, while Nichols stressed that thirty- to forty-year-old women need not feel out of place in sexy underwear, the company's advertising campaigns continued to exclusively portray younger models with svelte, busty figures. Indeed, some critics saw the Victoria's Secret formula of femininity as a limitation to the majority of American women and argued that the company's image (highlighted in design series such as their English Lace line) implicitly promoted an overly bourgeois conception of "good taste."

Whatever class and gender ramifications Victoria's Secret might have entailed, the company grew once again under Nichols's care throughout the 1990s, as millions of women—and men—continued to fill out their fantasies with the satin-lined aid of offerings such as the Angels bra series; fantasy bras—gem-studded brassieres that were priced in the millions; and, perhaps Victoria's Secret's single biggest contribution to the public imagination, the uplifting Miracle Bra. The company continued its success with publicity-generating promotions such as the Victoria's Secret fashion show, which launched in 1995 as a live show in New York. In 1999 the show was streamed live on the company's website and in 2001 began being broadcast annually on television. In 2011 Victoria's Secret reported annual sales of more than $6 billion.

Shaun Frentner

SEE ALSO: *Bra; Consumerism; Department Stores; Frederick's of Hollywood; Malls; Online Shopping.*

BIBLIOGRAPHY

Farrell-Beck, Jane, and Colleen Gau. *Uplift: The Bra in America*. Philadelphia: University of Pennsylvania Press, 2002.

Schwartz, Mimi. "A Day in the Life of Victoria's Secret." *Mademoiselle*, April 1990, 238–239.

Woodman, Sue. "Victoria Reigns Again." *Working Woman*, September 1991, 77.

Workman, Nancy V. "From Victorian to Victoria's Secret: The Foundations of Modern Erotic Wear." *Journal of Popular Culture*, Fall 1996, 61–73.

Vidal, Gore *(1925–2012)*

Thanks to the broadcast media, which continually gives public platform to the curmudgeonly wit and iconoclastic political observations of Gore Vidal, he became one of those rare authors who is as famous for what he says as for what he writes. Considered to be one of the most promising members of the generation of writers emerging from World War II (a group that included his archrival and frequent sparring partner, Norman Mailer), Vidal first made his mark with a fairly well-received novel based on his army experiences, *Williwaw*, in 1946. He followed up with two more books, the second of which, *The*

Gore Vidal. *Gore Vidal's work as a novelist, screenwriter, and commentator made him a prominent voice in the worlds of literature, entertainment, and politics.* JEFFREY MAYER/CONTRIBUTOR/WIREIMAGE/GETTY IMAGES.

City and the Pillar (1948), stirred waves of controversy because of its frank treatment of homosexuality. "Not until that third book," Vidal has recalled, "did I begin to get bored with playing safe."

Yet since those years, "playing safe" is a charge that has never been leveled against Vidal. After the literary slump that followed *The City and the Pillar*, he supported himself by writing television plays, finding in that infant medium a success that he was able to transpose to Broadway. This in turn led to screenwriting assignments, and in due time Vidal was able to return, though with mixed success, to novel writing. His most notorious book was 1968's story of transsexuality, *Myra Breckinridge*, a personal favorite of the author's.

While penning historical novels and essays, Vidal also kept himself in the public eye through frequent TV interviews, appearances on talk shows, and even the occasional film role. In his TV appearances, his gadfly manner and contentious political views entertained and, some would say, enlightened the public in a forum denied to most other scribblers. Vidal even ran for public office and, though never elected, was one of those unsuccessful candidates—Barry Goldwater, Vidal's political opposite, was another—whose views nonetheless had an influence upon the electorate.

WRITINGS

The man who would later rechristen himself Gore Vidal was born Eugene Luther Vidal at West Point, New York, on October 3, 1925. While his parents divorced soon after his birth, Vidal was close to his blind paternal grandfather, Thomas Pryor Gore, Oklahoma's first senator. Young Vidal read the Congressional Record and constitutional history to his grandfather, a formative experience that instilled political ambitions in the lad. As a young man, he decided to forgo attendance at Harvard for a stint in the military, a decision he claims never to have regretted. Indeed, it was the army that provided fodder for Vidal's first novel and for his most successful teleplay, the satirical *Visit to a Small Planet*, which concerns the misadventures of an alien from outer space who wants to start a war because, he says, "it's the one thing you people down here do *really* well."

Planet made a successful transition from TV to stage, as did Vidal's trenchant melodrama about rivalry between would-be presidential candidates at their party's convention, *The Best Man*, which became a much lauded film starring Henry Fonda. But Vidal was so displeased with the rewriting and the miscasting of Jerry Lewis in the film version of *Planet* that he disowned the movie. (Subsequently, Vidal would be equally displeased with the film version of *Myra Breckinridge*, and he would also sue to have his name removed from Bob Guccione's infamous production of *Caligula*.) Vidal was responsible for the screenplay of his friend Tennessee Williams's play *Suddenly, Last Summer* and made some major, although uncredited, contributions to the script of *Ben-Hur*. (To the annoyance and denials of Charlton Heston, Vidal insisted that he persuade director William Wyler to insert a homoerotic subtext into the film's key relationship between Judah Ben-Hur and his boyhood friend, Messala.)

POLITICS

Vidal, who once criticized the United States as "the land of the dull and the home of the literal," nevertheless always wanted to be its president. He ran for representative in New York City in 1960 and sought the Democratic nomination for senator of California in 1982, losing both battles but nevertheless winning many converts to his somewhat extreme positions (such as his proposal to tax church income). Although he dabbled with science fiction in one of his novels (*Messiah*, 1954), most of his latter-day books were historical novels, including *Julian* (1964), *Burr* (1973), and *Lincoln* (1984). *The Smithsonian Institution* (1998), in which time travel allows the protagonist to meet past political figures, manages to combine both the science fictional and the historical.

Vidal was always a staunch opponent of party politics, describing himself as a proponent of America but not of its politics. His writings during the early twenty-first century, including the highly regarded *Imperial America: Reflections on the United States of Amnesia* (2004), largely focused on his criticism of the George W. Bush administration, which he referred to as overtly expansionist and overly concerned with multinational, industrial oil rights. After that publication, Vidal published a memoir titled *Point to Point Navigation* (2006) and continued to make media appearances.

There was a time in Vidal's own history when his public spats with other literary figures, such as Truman Capote and William F. Buckley Jr., led to much-publicized lawsuits. In the case of his feud with Mailer, it even led to flung drinks and fisticuffs. (Covering the 1968 Democratic Convention for ABC-TV, the unlikely team of Vidal and Buckley ended up calling each other, respectively, "crypto-Nazi" and "queer.") Vidal in his later years, however, could hardly be said to have mellowed. "There is no warm loveable person inside," he proclaimed. "Beneath my cold exterior, once you break the ice, you find cold water." Vidal died on July 31, 2012.

Preston Neal Jones

SEE ALSO: Ben-Hur*; Broadway; Buckley, William F., Jr.; Capote, Truman; Daytime Talk Shows; Fonda, Henry; Gay Men; Heston, Charlton; Lewis, Jerry; Mailer, Norman; Television; Williams, Tennessee; World War II.*

BIBLIOGRAPHY

Altman, Dennis. *Gore Vidal's America*. Cambridge, MA: Polity, 2005.

Parini, Jay, ed. *Gore Vidal: Writer against the Grain*. New York: Columbia University Press, 1992.

Vidal, Gore. *The Essential Gore Vidal*, ed. Fred Kaplan. New York: Random House, 1999.

Vidal, Gore, and Robert J. Stanton, eds. *Views from a Window: Conversations with Gore Vidal*. Secaucus, NJ: L. Stuart, 1980.

Video Games

When the basic "electronic tennis" game, Pong, first appeared in American bars in 1972, it created a sensation that has since been replicated by the 1990s karaoke boom in Japan and the arrival of apps on smartphones and tablet computers in the early twenty-first century. In relative terms, of course, Pong was as fun and innovative in the 1970s as any video game now, but the basic principles of video gaming have remained the same—score the points, beat the enemy, come back for more. Based on the success of Pong, other games were developed, leading to the introduction of home game consoles by Atari and Nintendo throughout the 1970s and 1980s; the idea was that players would slot their favorite arcade game cartridges into the console and play the games through their television set—hence *video* rather than *computer* games. But the term has come to cover the main aspect of the medium: playing sight-and-sound games through any convenient screen.

A number of Pong imitators popped up in both the arcade and home gaming markets. After the release of George Lucas's blockbuster movie *Star Wars* in 1977, battling aliens became the rage in the first popular coin-operated machines, such as Space Invaders, Asteroids, and Galaxians, giving players a more varied and richer gaming experience. The success and appeal of the initial wave of games enticed other manufacturers to develop games. Video arcades sprouted up in shopping malls and became a favorite hangout for teenagers and young adults. In some sense the arcade boom that began in 1978 took the group appeal out of video gaming. People were still taking part in a mass fad, perhaps, but they were also cutting themselves off from others, with the distinction that while Pong required a human opponent, battling against pixilated aliens just pitted the player against the machine. Breakout (1976) may have introduced a puzzle element, and Pac-Man (1980) offered a maze race, but video games were essentially based on the same principle: "your" pixels blasting, avoiding, or racing against "their" pixels.

With the introduction of Donkey Kong in 1981, however, there was an attempt to make a "story" as attractive as the "action." The player had a character to portray, in this case that of a boy rescuing a princess from an ape monster, as opposed to the previous standard of the player as "thing"—a tennis racquet, a spaceship, or Pac-Man. Since 2000 increased computing power, better graphical capabilities, and consoles connected to the Internet have made gaming environments more realistic and have made playing them a social activity.

GAME EVOLUTION

Spurred by the success of Space Invaders, Asteroids, and Pac Man, Atari dominated the home video market during the early 1980s. Atari's success, however, was short-lived. The company's biggest failure came with 1982's adaptation of *E.T.* By all accounts it was a colossal failure, leaving Atari on the brink of bankruptcy. Moreover, a host of competitors such as Mattel and Coleco and the rise of home computers began to eat into Atari's market share. People's interests in gaming were also evolving, with the narrative adventure game ushering in a new wave of graphics and concepts. By exploiting this kind of narrative appeal, Nintendo was able dominate the console market throughout the latter half of 1980s. Its 8-bit Nintendo Entertainment System (NES), released in North America in 1985, took away the market from the Atari 2600, even managing to compete with the personal computer (PC) boom—in fact, it is estimated that by 1990 Nintendo consoles were in a third of American homes.

Part of the success of Nintendo in the 1980s was the blanket marketing of its games. Nintendo specialized in humanizing its games by populating them with characters as appealing as Mickey Mouse or Ronald McDonald, hence the introduction of Mario, the cute Italian American plumber who has saved the princess in as many imaginative variations on the platform game formula as possible. Mario first appeared in the Mario Bros. coin-op in 1983, and the NES Super Mario Bros. became the "greatest video game" of its generation in 1985, only to be surpassed by Super Mario Bros. 3 in 1989. Today Mario, Luigi, and friends battle Bowser on the Nintendo Wii and DS platforms.

The 1990s saw a battle between Sega, Nintendo, and Sony, all of which produced 16-bit and then 32-bit consoles. The Sega Saturn, which replaced its Mega Drive in 1994, put Nintendo temporarily out of the race, ending the domination established with Super Mario World (1991) for the Super NES. The arrival of Sony's PlayStation was a milestone: PlayStation, which came to dominate the market in America, Japan, and Europe, made games trendy, fun, violent, and often intelligent enough to appeal to "children" of all ages, from three to thirty-three and beyond.

The PlayStation also managed to follow the PC route into adventure gaming, combining speed and strategy with "filmic" production values. Between 1993 and 1998, Doom (1993) and Wipeout 2097 (1996) became instant classics, and for a growing number of PlayStation fans, the Tomb Raider and Final Fantasy series became ways of life. The arrival of 64-bit computing brought with it three-dimensional (3-D) gaming. Nintendo released the Nintendo 64 in 1996 along with the 3-D Super Mario 64 game. Movie tie-ins such as *Goldeneye* (1997) exploited the power of these consoles to produce filmlike realism. In 2000 the PlayStation 2 launched and soon became the best-selling console of all time. It remained on sale in various forms more than a decade later and supported some iconic games of the decade, including series such as the Grand Theft Auto driving game, Resident Evil, and Metal Gear Solid.

CONTINUING ADVANCES

In the first decade of the 2000s the PlayStation 2 competed with Nintendo's GameCube and Microsoft's Xbox for control of the gaming market. This period also saw the arrival of online gaming, in which gamers play against others or in teams. Gaming had become a popular activity, but it was still limited to a young, mostly male audience that was prepared to put in long hours working toward the end of a complex narrative game. That changed with the 2006 launch of the Nintendo Wii. At launch the Wii offered simple sports games, but its selling point was its wireless motion controllers, which detected motion in three dimensions and could be used as tennis rackets and golf clubs to hit virtual balls. The Wii was a huge hit with families and casual gamers, outselling the Xbox and PlayStation 2 combined in 2007. By the end of 2011, despite having fairly limited hardware, the Wii had sold almost ninety-five million units.

The Wii introduced a new audience to video gaming, but as the decade drew to a close a new kind of video game environment became popular. Mobile gaming had always had a small part of the market, but the release of the Nintendo DS and the PlayStation Portable (PSP) in 2004 were the first shots in a fierce battle. When Apple opened up its iPhone platform to software developers in 2008, portable gaming became the dominant video game market. Games such as Flight Control (2009), Doodlejump (2009), and Angry Birds (2009) were talked about in mainstream media as excited casual gamers clamored for the latest releases.

Portability made video gaming an everyday activity for millions of people worldwide. While consoles that take advantage of large television screens to present stunning graphics remain a major part of the market, the ubiquity of handheld devices and the presence of games on mobile phones and tablet computers on several software platforms make them compelling to users. The violence and gore some video games have led to concerns about their effect on children and young adults, but for the most part gaming has moved toward a more wholesome, fun experience. As video games have matured as a genre, they have acquired the range, and in some cases the artistic expressiveness, of film, literature, and theater.

Stephen Keane

SEE ALSO: *Apple Computer; Computer Games; The Internet; Laptops; Leisure Time; Lucas, George; Mario Brothers; Microsoft; Online Gaming; Pac-Man; Smartphones;* Star Wars*; Wii; Xbox Kinect.*

BIBLIOGRAPHY

Bukatman, Scott. *Terminal Identity: The Virtual Subject in Postmodern Science Fiction.* Durham, NC: Duke University Press, 1993.

Donovan, Tristan. *Replay: The History of Video Games.* East Sussex, UK: Yellow Ant, 2010.

Jones, Steven G. *CyberSociety.* Thousand Oaks, CA: Sage, 1995.

Melissinos, Chris. *The Art of Video Games: From Pac-Man to Mass Effect.* Welcome Enterprises, 2012.

Trushell, John. "Interactive Games and Other Fairy Tales: Or, Player(s) in Search of Authority." *Foundation: The International Review of Science Fiction* 70 (1997): 58–70.

Videos

By late 1987 more than half of American households owned a videocassette recorder (VCR). The small device had quickly entered the home and taken its place alongside the television as the premiere electronic consumer item. While the rise of the VCR was unprecedented, it pales in comparison to the speed, quality, and ease of use of subsequent innovations, including the digital video disc (DVD); digital video recorder (DVR); and the Internet, which allows users to download videos straight to their computers, televisions, or smartphones in mere minutes.

EARLY TECHNOLOGY

As with many other consumer products, videocassette recording technology had a long development period, one that dovetailed with the development of other forms of media. Necessary innovations came in the first half of the twentieth century. Dr. Fritz Pfleumer received a 1928 German patent for the deposition of magnetic powders on paper or plastic backing media. The German companies Allgemeine Elektricitäts-Gesellschaft (AEG) and BASF produced quantities of magnetic tape between 1934 and 1944 exclusively for German radio broadcasting stations.

In 1944 American corporation 3M began its own experiments with magnetic coatings, but it was not until after World War II that John T. Mullin, a U.S. electronic specialist, went to Germany and returned home with four Magnetophon recorders. These audiotape recorders were scrutinized, rewired with parts from the United States, and finally demonstrated before the Institute of Radio Engineers in 1946. Mullin joined the Ampex Electric Corporation and introduced the first successful American audiotape recorder in 1948. Although other American companies, including RCA, experimented with videotape recording during the late 1940s and early 1950s, Ampex, due largely to its advanced research in audiotape recording, was able to develop the first feasible professional videotape recorder—the VR-1000, which premiered in 1956, weighing 900 pounds and sporting a price tag of $75,000 a unit.

The vast majority of VR-1000 recorders were purchased by stations and studios affiliated with one of the three major television broadcasting companies—ABC, NBC, and CBS—which employed them in the retransmission, delay, and temporary archiving of programming. Technological innovations during the 1950s largely served the ends of professional engineers and included enhancements in mobility, advanced editing capability, and color recording. CBS was the first network to broadcast from videotape, presenting *Douglas Edwards and the News* in 1956 using Ampex recorders.

The technique of using video quickly diminished the need for live broadcasting. Stations could provide uniform "clock-times" for shows coast to coast, functionally eliminating differences introduced by time zones and the erratic adoption of daylight saving time in some regions. Videotape recording also freed performers from the anxiety of live performances. Errors could be corrected and retaped as in film production, and the possibility of the rerun was created. Recording technology allowed the networks to concentrate on technical quality and the consolidation of viewing markets. Little attention was paid to the development of a viable consumer videotape recorder, although videotape's impact on television viewing was already felt.

CONSUMER RECORDERS

The 1960s marked the beginning of consumer videotape recording. The high cost of the Ampex VR-1000 provoked Japanese manufacturers into developing a domestic alternative. Research began at Sony as early as 1953, but no significant gains were made until the Japanese company Toshiba developed a helical-scanning recording head in 1959. Helical-scanning technology, the basis of the VCR, used a videotape wound around a spinning, drumlike recording head, a novel method that avoided restrictions imposed by Ampex's numerous patents. In 1961 the Victor Company of Japan (JVC) introduced an improved dual helical-scan head. These innovations allowed for an increased recording quality with a slower tape transport, resulting in decreased tape use and cost savings. Yet these early units were inferior in image quality and unacceptable for broadcast use.

In 1958 the Society of Motion Picture and Television Engineers (SMPTE) adopted standards for the manufacture of videotape recorders, thus potentially allowing any manufacturer to enter the marketplace. The early 1960s also saw the use of transistorized electronic components, resulting in more compact recorders and potential portability, though the latter was not recognized in the consumer market—the 1963 Neiman Marcus Christmas catalog offered the gigantic $30,000 Ampex VR-1500 videotape recorder/entertainment center. In 1965 Sony introduced the helical-scan, black-and-white, reel-to-reel CV-2000, which used an extremely compact 1/2-inch tape (as compared to the 2-inch tape of the Ampex VR-1000). The CV-2000 was briefly offered as a consumer model, though marketers later emphasized its sale to broadcast and industrial markets. By 1967 Ampex claimed to have sold 500 recorders for home use, and by 1968 a number of consumer machines were available in the $800 to $4,000 price range, though most of these, including Cartrivision, failed to capture a significant home market because of high price or technical shortcomings.

Significant inroads were finally made when Sony introduced the 3/4-inch-tape U-Matic VCR to the American market in 1972. The development of the videocassette served as a significant leap beyond older reel-to-reel tape formats and completely removed the need for a skilled engineer/operator. Although consumers resisted the notion of a home videocassette recorder, broadcast engineers began to use the Sony U-Matic for news reportage, an area that was still dominated by film recording. The 1968 Mexico City Olympic Games were covered by at least one older-generation Ampex videotape recorder, and in 1974 a U-Matic was used to document President Richard Nixon's historic trip to Moscow.

BETAMAX

In 1975 Sony released the 1/2-inch Betamax recorder/television combination ($2,300) and followed it with the 1976 Betamax stand-alone model ($1,300); each was capable of recording one hour of programming. Whereas the U-Matic tape was the size of a large hardcover book, the Betamax cassette was the size of a paperback. The smaller size coupled with improvements in tape media and recording method left Betamax (*beta* being a Japanese term for a calligraphic stroke so rich that it completely covers the material below; in this case, where the video signal completely saturates the tape) strongly poised to enter a market already cluttered with competitors. The result was revolutionary.

Betamax launched its U.S. marketing program in fall 1975. The pitch was simple: "Any time is prime time." This was a "time-shift machine," one capable of recording a single program while the user watched another and of beginning a preset recording even when the user was not at home. A total of 55,000 home VCRs were sold by the end of 1976, 160,000 by the end of 1977, and more than 400,000 by the close of 1978.

According to a trade magazine poll in January 1977, 40 percent of Americans knew what a Betamax was. Yet according to a 1979 Nielsen poll, the total number of households in the United States owning VCRs was only 475,000, a mere 0.5 percent of the total homes owning televisions. Although other polls placed the number much higher, the situation was not yet considered threatening by the majority of the commercial broadcast executives. Sales of prerecorded videocassettes hovered at approximately one tape for every two VCRs. Sales of blank videocassettes continued to climb sharply, prompting some in the industry to ask what these tapes were being used for.

HOME VIDEO

In 1977 RCA introduced the Video Home System (VHS) VCR, which was capable of recording two hours of programming on its cassette. This increase in allowable recording time was followed by a two-hour Betamax recorder in 1977. RCA responded with a four-hour VHS in 1977, and in 1979 released a six-hour model. Stiff competition erupted between the two incompatible formats, although sales of prerecorded material continued to stagnate. By the end of the 1970s VHS had captured an increasing percentage of the VCR market and furthered its domination in the 1980s when production of the Betamax recorder was discontinued.

Although JVC and other manufacturers rushed to augment their models with features such as stop-action and pause, it was not until Sony's introduction of the Betascan in 1979 that the VCR threatened to severely alter the viewing patterns of American households. By allowing the viewer of recorded broadcast material to "scan" across the tape while simultaneously viewing it, Betascan users could easily skip commercial advertisements. This feature was rapidly incorporated into JVC's 1979 VHS model.

In 1984 a major Nielsen survey stated that 36 percent of the respondents used the stop or pause feature of their VCR to eliminate commercials from shows they were both watching and taping. Nearly half said that they frequently used the fast-forward capability to skip taped commercials. Debate raged over what this meant for the future of commercial viewing. Some analysts adopted an almost apocalyptic tone, saying that the VCR would mean the end of viable commercial broadcasting. Others took the more modest stance that while VCRs increased the difficulties of directing commercials at specific target audiences (children or female homemakers, for example), they potentially opened an entirely new group of viewers for their programming. While television viewing did decrease on Friday and Saturday evenings as viewers turned to other prerecorded materials or shows taped earlier in the week, the overall time spent viewing television increased from six hours and ten minutes in 1977 to seven hours and twelve minutes in 1987.

PRERECORDED VIDEO

Sales of prerecorded materials got off to a slow start. Andre Blay founded the Video Club of America in 1977, offering a slim catalog of fifty films on video, mostly licensed from Twentieth Century Fox; none of the titles was more recent than 1973 and all had been sold to television networks. Blay's Club was the first serious offering of prerecorded feature films at a time when adult films constituted the vast majority of publicly available videocassettes. Warner Home Video began releasing prerecorded videotapes of Hollywood films in 1980. Starting with a very modest forty-one titles in the first year, Warner increased its output as consumer demand climbed.

Warner Brothers, like other film producing companies, originally expected that consumers would purchase these recordings outright. Much to the companies' chagrin, stores sprouted up that offered to rent titles to viewers instead. These middlemen were perceived as a potential threat, much like television production companies had considered the VCR itself. Copyright was, for them, the right to completely dominate and control the marketing and distribution of their programming and films. MCA/Universal Studios and Walt Disney Productions attempted to sue Sony in 1976 just after the release of the Betamax recorder in the United States. The case wound its way through the federal court system until the Supreme Court decided in January 1984 that "neither the consumers who tape television programs for their own use nor companies that make and sell video recorders violate Federal copyright law." In light of the Betamax case, film companies opted for the creation of licensing agreements over expensive litigation, which paved the way for a widespread increase in available titles.

In the 1980s video made itself felt in other ways. The cable station Music Television (MTV) was launched in August 1981 with the appropriately titled "Video Killed the Radio Star" by the Buggles. It soon became a force in the music industry and a serious creator of youth culture. Performers, once content with the studio/radio/tour mode of production and promotion, had to consider visual elements often unrelated to the music itself.

In 1983 Sony introduced the Betamovie camera, the first camcorder. Although Sony had introduced the bulky PortaPak several years earlier, the Betamovie was the first truly portable video camera. Largely due to the public's penchant for creating documentary home movies, camcorder sales increased throughout the 1980s, eventually displacing the traditional 8-millimeter film camera in that role. Although never as ubiquitous as the VCR, the video camera enjoyed a higher profile in the late 1980s and 1990s. Through television shows such as *America's Funniest Home Videos* and the increasing use of amateur footage in news broadcasts, videotaped events became common viewing. Their importance would perhaps become most clear as the public witnessed the tapes of the Rodney King beating and the Los Angeles riots of 1992.

DVD AND INTERNET

DVDs were introduced in 1997 but did not supplant VHS tapes until 2003 due to the initial cost of DVD players and the minimal amount of titles readily available on DVD. Broadening the technology of the compact disc, DVDs transformed the home video market, offering more storage space and better visual and audio quality than VHS tapes.

The small size of the DVD enabled companies like Netflix to offer mail-order subscription rental services. Netflix initially offered a single rental subscription, but the company changed to a flat-rate unlimited rental service in 2000. Netflix integrated an online streaming option to its services and expanded its catalog to such an extent that physical stores like Blockbuster all but collapsed. The company experienced a downfall of its own in 2011 when it announced that it would offer its streaming and mail subscriptions as two separate plans. In response to the consumer uproar, which caused the company to lose subscribers as well as some of its catalog, Netflix backed down from this plan. Video-on-Demand services and copycat subscription services from companies like Amazon, Blockbuster, and Wal-Mart offered consumers additional options. Similarly, automated rental kiosks, such as Redbox and Blockbuster Express, offered customers the convenience of renting DVDs and Blu-ray from numerous locations, including grocery stores, large retail stores, convenience stores, and pharmacies. Unlike its competitors, however, the kiosks did not require a subscription; the customer simply rented the movie with a credit card. By 2012 Redbox kiosks outnumbered Blockbuster Express locations and purchased its struggling competitor.

The proliferation of technology coupled with the Internet have provided consumers with a host of home entertainment choices. TiVo and other DVR systems gave consumers the ability to record and watch television at their convenience. Gaming consoles like Microsoft's Xbox 360 and Sony's PlayStation 3 included video playback, Internet capability, and video downloads. Websites such as YouTube, Hulu, and Vimeo allow Internet streaming of a variety of content. In 2004 Vimeo started as an outlet for independent filmmakers and fans and has since morphed into a full-service platform for creative work.

In 2005 YouTube began offering registered users the ability to upload video content. YouTube's allure resided in its democratic fan-based system. At first it was a haven for videos showing small clips of babies, pets, random strangers, and celebrity missteps. As its popularity grew, people began to generate content specifically for YouTube. The site provided a platform for almost every stripe of would-be celebrity. Pop-sensation Justin Bieber was discovered via YouTube, and the YouTube channel *Smosh* was featured in *Time* magazine's 2006 Person of the Year issue. Additionally, shows on the site such as *Ask a Ninja* and *lonelygirl15* created fictional celebrities, with *lonelygirl15* altering the way the public interacted with YouTube. The success of Hulu, which offers movies and films from Fox, NBC, and Disney, pushed YouTube to contract with CBS, MGM, and Lionsgate in 2008 to upload entire films and television shows.

Videos have become synonymous with home entertainment and family leisure time. As technology developed, toy manufactures experienced a loss in sales as people spent more money on electronic equipment and video services. Consumers had greater control on how and when they interacted with entertainment. Internet and mobile devices such as the iPod and iPhone altered the way many people interacted with videos, since it was no longer necessary to watch a movie from the couch. In some ways, the increased mobility and convenience provided for greater access and cultural knowledge; however, in other ways it decreased social interactions, allowing people to construct private zones of entertainment.

Vance Bell

SEE ALSO: *Amazon.com;* America's Funniest Home Videos; *Compact Discs; DVRs; Hollywood; Hulu; The Internet; King, Rodney; Leisure Time; Microsoft; MTV; Netflix; 1968 Mexico City Summer Olympic Games; Radio; Television; TiVo; Video Games; Viral Videos; Wal-Mart; World War II; YouTube.*

BIBLIOGRAPHY

Barlow, Aaron. *The DVD Revolution: Movies, Culture & Technology.* Westport, CT: Praeger, 2005.

Burgess, Jean, and Joshua Green. *YouTube: Online Video and Participatory Culture.* Cambridge, MA: Polity Press, 2009.

Cover, Rob. "DVD Time: Temporality, Audience Engagement and the New TV Culture of Digital Video." *Media International Australia* 117 (2012): 137–148.

Cubitt, Sean. *Timeshift: On Video Culture.* New York: Routledge, 1991.

Frith, Simon; Andrew Goodwin; and Lawrence Grossberg, eds. *Sound and Vision: The Music Video Reader.* London: Routledge, 1993.

Hall, Doug, and Sally Jo Fifer. *Illuminating Video: An Essential Guide to Video Art.* New York: Aperture, 1990.

Lardner, James. *Fast Forward: Hollywood, the Japanese, and the Onslaught of the VCR.* New York: W. W. Norton, 1987.

Marlow, Eugene, and Eugene Secunda. *Shifting Time and Space: The Story of the Videotape.* New York: Praeger, 1991.

Vidor, King *(1894–1982)*

During his forty-year career, Texas-born pioneer film director King Vidor adapted as necessary to commercial considerations. His personal vision, and his concern with the problems of society and the individuals within it, resulted in two silent masterpieces and a handful of significant sound films. Both his wives, Florence Vidor and Eleanor Boardman, were leading silent stars.

Vidor established his reputation with a powerful antiwar statement in *The Big Parade* (1925) and secured it with *The Crowd* (1928). This profoundly realistic examination of struggle and alienation in the big city revealed a virtuoso use of the camera. His eclectic tastes and wide interests informed the watershed all-black musical *Hallelujah* (1929), the huge hit *The Champ* (1931), and the Depression drama *Our Daily Bread* (1934). Later work ranged from *Stella Dallas* (1937) and *The Fountainhead* (1949) to Westerns *Duel in the Sun* (1946) and *Man without a Star* (1955), as well as the epic *War and Peace* (1956). A five-time Academy nominee, he retired in 1959 and received an honorary Oscar in 1979 for "incomparable achievements as a cinematic creator and innovator."

Robyn Karney

SEE ALSO: *Academy Awards; The Great Depression; The Musical; War Movies; The Western.*

BIBLIOGRAPHY

Brownlow, Kevin. *Behind the Mask of Innocence: Sex, Violence, Prejudice, Crime: Films of Social Conscience in the Silent Era.* London: Jonathan Cape, 1990.

Finler, Joel W. *The Movie Directors Story.* New York: Crescent Books, 1985.

Stevens, George, Jr. *Conversations with the Great Moviemakers of Hollywood's Golden Age at the American Film Institute.* New York: A. A. Knopf, 2006.

Vidor, King. *A Tree Is a Tree.* New York: Harcourt, Brace, 1953.

Vidor, King. *King Vidor on Film Making.* New York: Daniel McKay, 1972.

Vietnam

American involvement in Vietnam began in the mid-1950s as the French, defeated on the battlefield by the communist Viet Minh, began to withdraw all military forces from their former colony. Fearing a vacuum that the communists might attempt to fill, the United States helped establish the Republic of Vietnam in the southern half of the country. In the face of North Vietnam's determination to unite all of Vietnam under its control, a series of U.S. administrations provided support to the South Vietnamese government. That support included economic and military aid under President Dwight D. Eisenhower, military advisers under President John F. Kennedy, combat troops under President Lyndon Johnson, and finally the invasions of Cambodia and Laos under President Richard Nixon.

PROTEST AND POLICY

As the commitment to Vietnam grew, so did protest within the United States. Americans, many of them college students, op-

Vietnam War. *Viet Cong prisoners of war are escorted through a rice field by a U.S. soldier in 1968.* MPI/STRINGER/ARCHIVE PHOTOS/GETTY IMAGES.

posed the war on moral grounds, frequently extending their opposition to the selective service system, whereby young men were drafted into military service. Other (often older) Americans, motivated by patriotism, anticommunism, or the conviction that their leaders knew best, supported the war effort and often disdained those who protested. The nation was thus polarized as it had not been since the Civil War a century earlier. Eventually a variety of factors—including U.S. combat casualties, the knowledge that racism and classism were playing a part in the drafting of young men to serve in Vietnam, and the lack of significant military progress—eroded much of the support for the war. Nixon gradually disengaged and withdrew most American troops in 1973. Under his "Vietnamization" policy, all fighting was turned over to the South Vietnamese army, which, Nixon said, was fully capable of achieving victory. South Vietnam fell to the communists in April 1975.

Vietnam first entered American popular culture through articulation of what became known as the domino theory. At a press conference in April 1954, Eisenhower was asked by a reporter to assess the importance of French Indochina for American national security. Eisenhower replied, "You have a row of dominoes set up, you knock over the first one, and what will happen to the last one is the certainty that it will go over very quickly. So you could have the beginning of a disintegration that would have the most profound influences."

The image of falling dominoes as a metaphor for the consequences of a communist victory in Vietnam was a compelling one, and many leaders who followed Eisenhower made use of it in policy discussions. It was endorsed by Kennedy, Johnson, and Nixon as well as their surrogates and spokespersons. Scholars and pundits debated the domino theory's merits in print and in person, and it even showed up in an episode of the popular late-1960s television show, *The Monkees*, in which the four musicians have an arrangement of dominos set up on a table. One of them says, "Look, Southeast Asia," and pushes the first domino over, with predictable results for the others.

FICTIONAL ACCOUNTS

One of the earliest literary discussions of Vietnam also appeared during Eisenhower's time with William Lederer and Eugene Burdick's 1958 book *The Ugly American*. Less a novel than a collection of loosely related stories, it is a stinging indictment of U.S. diplomacy throughout Asia—especially in the fictional country of Sarkhan, a thinly disguised Vietnam. The book depicts U.S. diplomats throughout the region as ignorant, incompetent political hacks who spend their time at embassy cocktail parties while communist agents move among the people, speaking their language, pretending to respect their culture, and gaining their allegiance. Several scholars claim that *The Ugly American* inspired Kennedy, who had read and endorsed the book when it first appeared, to create the Peace Corps. Others contend that reading it led Kennedy to transform a small, neglected U.S. Army unit called the Special Forces into those fabled champions of counterinsurgency, the Green Berets.

That elite commando force is also the subject of one of the few fictional works about Vietnam written while the United States was militarily engaged there: Robin Moore's *The Green Berets* (1965). Although the book was published during the Johnson administration, it was Kennedy who gave Moore permission to accompany a Special Forces "A" team to Vietnam but stipulated that the author must first go through Special Forces training. The resulting book was hugely popular, inspiring a song and a motion picture.

The film, John Wayne's 1968 production *The Green Berets*, was blatant propaganda on behalf of the war and against its critics. Wayne, whose right-wing sympathies were well known, starred, directed, and installed his own son as producer. The Pentagon, on Johnson's orders, lent Wayne immense amounts of military equipment and charged him cut rates for its use. In return the Defense Department had approval rights on the script, and it was not displeased with the result. The film glorifies the Special Forces, vilifies the Viet Cong, and portrays the war's American opponents as uninformed and misguided. The music that accompanies the film's opening credits is a choral version of Barry Sadler's "The Ballad of the Green Berets." Sadler, a Special Forces noncommissioned officer (NCO), wrote the song while serving in Vietnam and later saw his recording of it reach number one on the singles chart.

DOCUMENTARIES

In addition to using Wayne's film to influence public opinion on the war, the Johnson administration also produced a film of its own. *Why Vietnam?* was released in 1965 by the Defense Department, and a copy was made available for loan to any school, club, or civic organization that was interested in screening it. The forty-minute documentary was done in the melodramatic, end-of-the-world style of Frank Capra's *Why We Fight* films that was effective in the 1940s. But 1960s audiences often found the approach hokey. In addition, the historical perspective that the film used for its rationale for U.S. involvement in Vietnam was not only one-sided but at times simply untrue, as when the film's narrator claimed that the planned 1954 national plebiscite that would have united Vietnam was sabotaged by the communists in the North. In truth South Vietnam was responsible, with U.S. concurrence.

A very different documentary was released in 1974, just as the war was nearing its end. *Hearts and Minds*, directed by Peter Davis, was an uncompromising indictment of American involvement in Vietnam. The winner of an Academy Award for Best Feature-Length Documentary, the film uses juxtaposition. It portrays, for example, Nixon justifying his "Christmas bombing" of 1972 followed by footage of a Hanoi hospital destroyed in that bombing and interviews with Vietnamese peasants to show the devastating damage that the United States inflicted on Vietnam.

TURNING POINT

News coverage, especially on television, was of vital concern to the several U.S. administrations that waged war in Vietnam. It was believed, not without reason, that the focus and tone of the news might well have an effect on public support for the war. Consequently, civilian and military officials tried to influence the coverage, emphasizing some aspects, downplaying others, withholding some, and lying about more than a few. These efforts at news management were fairly successful for several years; many journalists, print and electronic, produced stories that were generally favorable to the American goals in Vietnam and the ways those goals were pursued.

The Tet offensive changed everything. At three o'clock in the morning Saigon time on January 30, 1968, the traditional Lunar New Year truce was broken when Viet Cong and North Vietnamese army units simultaneously attacked targets all across South Vietnam. The U.S. government had been trying to convince Americans that communists in Vietnam were weak and barely able to put up a resistance. Furthermore, the violence taking place in Vietnam had not really been brought home to Americans at that time. However, a number of images arising out of this campaign found their way into America's living rooms: dead Viet Cong on the grounds of the U.S. embassy in Saigon, the walls of which had never before been breached; the head of the South Vietnamese national police, General Loan, drawing his pistol and shooting a bound Viet Cong prisoner in the head; a U.S. Army major, explaining the devastation of a hamlet called Ben Tre by saying, "We had to destroy the village in order to save it."

Tet marked a turning point in media coverage of the war. Reporters, who had listened for months to the claims of American officials that the Viet Cong were defunct, now grew cynical in the face of clear evidence to the contrary. News stories began to be more critical of the "official" version of events. CBS news anchorman Walter Cronkite, who polls showed to be the most trusted man in America, said on television that he thought the war to be hopelessly stalemated and that the United States should negotiate with the communists.

THE WAR AT HOME

Meanwhile, U.S. antiwar protesters were receiving media coverage too, and much of it was unsympathetic. News reports tended to focus on the most dramatic or shocking aspects of antiwar activity. If 500 people demonstrated peacefully and three others burned a U.S. flag, the latter group would almost certainly be featured on the evening news. Further, as antiwar protests became more common, many journalists declined even to cover them unless they involved large numbers of people or were likely to turn violent. Astute demonstrators thus learned how to draw media attention through destructive or shocking behavior; however, the very acts that brought them news coverage also alienated most of the middle-class audience watching or reading at home.

Although many popular musicians of the period appeared oblivious to the war, there were some, particularly folk artists, who became known for their antiwar material: Joan Baez, Pete Seeger, Phil Ochs, and Barbara Dane were prominent among these. Other individuals and bands recorded at least one song critical of the war effort, including Country Joe McDonald's "Feel Like I'm Fixin' to Die Rag"; the Animals' "We Gotta Get out of This Place"; Buffalo Springfield's "For What It's Worth"; the Association's "Requiem for the Masses"; Barry McGuire's "Eve of Destruction"; the Doors' "Unknown Soldier"; and Crosby, Stills, Nash, and Young's "Ohio."

But there was reaction against protest, even on the radio. Some country artists, in particular, whose fan base tended to be more conservative than that of rock or folk musicians, recorded songs that were supportive of the war, critical of protesters, or both. These included two Merle Haggard records, "Okie from Muskogee" and "The Fightin' Side of Me," as well as Maybelle Carter's "I Told Them What You're Fightin' For," Johnny Wright's "Hello, Vietnam," and Dave Dudley's "Vietnam Blues."

POSTWAR BOOKS AND FILM

Although the war's end in 1975 also brought a halt to the musical battle being waged over the airwaves, most other aspects of American popular culture continued to find the Vietnam conflict a worthy subject. One of these manifestations involved memoirs: a number of veterans published personal accounts of their experiences in the war, including Tim O'Brien's *If I Die in a Combat Zone* (1973), Ron Kovic's *Born on the Fourth of July* (1976), Michael Herr's *Dispatches* (1977), and William Broyles's *Brothers in Arms* (1986). A number of oral histories from veterans were also collected and published, such as Al Santoli's *Everything We Had* (1981) and *To Bear Any Burden* (1985), Wallace Terry's *Bloods: An Oral History of the Vietnam War by Black Veterans* (1987), and Kathryn Marshall's *In the Combat Zone: An Oral History of American Women in Vietnam* (1984). The postwar period also saw no shortage of novels about the conflict in Vietnam. Some of the most important are O'Brien's books *Going after Cacciato* (1978) and *The Things They Carried* (1990), James Webb's *Fields of Fire* (1978), Winston Groom's *Better Times than These* (1978), John Del Vecchio's *The 13th Valley* (1982), and Philip Caputo's *Indian Country* (1987).

The dearth of war-related motion pictures made while the conflict was in progress was more than made up afterward. Ted Post directed 1978's *Go Tell the Spartans*, a bleak look at the early days of American "advisers" in Vietnam that suggests the seeds of American defeat were planted early in the struggle. The same year, Michael Cimino's *The Deer Hunter* won the Best Picture Oscar for its story of three friends whose service in Vietnam changes them in markedly different ways. A year later Francis Ford Coppola's *Apocalypse Now*, a near-epic film injected with a heavy dose of surrealism, premiered. Surrealism also permeates the second half of Stanley Kubrick's 1987 film *Full Metal Jacket*, which follows a group of young men from the brutality of marine corps boot camp to the terrors of their deployment in Vietnam. Two other important films, Oliver Stone's *Platoon* (1986) and John Irvin's *Hamburger Hill* (1987) take a more realistic approach, emphasizing the individual tragedies of young men's lives wasted in a war they do not understand.

In addition to the differing film depictions of the actual fighting in the Vietnam War, two subgenres of Vietnam War films emerged. One focuses on the figure of the Vietnam veteran, made crazy by the war, who brings his deadly skills home and directs them against his countrymen. Though many cheap exploitation films were based on this premise, using it as an excuse to revel in blood and explosions, two more complex treatments appeared. Martin Scorsese's *Taxi Driver* (1976), in which Robert De Niro offers a compelling portrait of the psychologically disintegrating Travis Bickle, and Ted Kotcheff's *First Blood* (1982), in which a former Green Beret named John Rambo, played by Sylvester Stallone, is pushed beyond endurance by a brutal police chief who pays a high price for his callousness, offer interesting insights into the lasting wounds war inflicts on soldiers.

The second subgenre of Vietnam War films posited that some Americans remained prisoners in Vietnam after the end of the war and required rescue. The first of these films, 1983's *Uncommon Valor*, stars Gene Hackman and downplays the exploitative aspects of its premise. But other films flaunted the same premise, most notably the Chuck Norris vehicle *Missing in Action* (1984) and its two sequels, *Missing in Action 2: The Beginning* (1985) and *Braddock: Missing in Action III* (1988). The most lurid example of this subgenre is Stallone's *Rambo: First Blood Part II* (1985). Stallone's crazed ex–Green Beret character is released from prison to undertake a rescue mission of Americans held prisoner in Vietnam. Despite being betrayed, captured, and tortured, he manages to free the captive GIs and mow down scores of Vietnamese soldiers and their Russian advisers, thus symbolically "winning" the Vietnam War for the United States.

TELEVISION

In addition to films, television shows and made-for-TV movies about the struggle in Vietnam appeared in the postwar era. *The A-Team*, which premiered in 1983, was based on the notion that a group of Special Forces troopers were framed for a bank robbery and sent to prison while serving in Vietnam. They escaped en masse and became fugitives. In order to pay the bills while on the run, they hired themselves out as mercenaries but only, of course, for a good cause. The show's scripts were generally as improbable as its premise, but George Peppard (who played the leader of the team, which included the impressively muscled but diction-challenged Mr. T as B. A. Baracus) led his group of virtuous vigilantes through five seasons of mayhem before cancellation of the show in 1987.

As *The A-Team* left television, a more serious drama about an army platoon in Vietnam during the late 1960s called *Tour of Duty* debuted. Although the show had an ensemble cast, its prominent character was Sergeant Zeke Anderson (Terence Knox), an experienced combat leader who often took up the slack left by the unit's "green" lieutenant. Although sometimes prone to clichés, the show dealt with the Vietnam experience fairly realistically, given the limitations of TV drama. It lasted three seasons and was canceled in 1990. Another serious show about combat in Southeast Asia also began in 1987. *Vietnam War Story* was an anthology show, with a new cast of characters each week on the line of the previous decade's *Police Story* and *Medical Story*. The plots were supposedly based upon real incidents, and many of the scripts were penned by actual Vietnam veterans. Despite these efforts at verisimilitude, the show endured for only one season.

China Beach (1988–1991) may be the best television series about the Vietnam War. Its setting was a military hospital complex in Danang during the 1967–1969 period. The ensemble cast of characters was large, including doctors and nurses, soldiers and marines, USO singers and prostitutes. But the show's main character and moral center was army nurse Colleen McMurphy (Dana Delaney). McMurphy volunteered for both the army and Vietnam and, although horrified by the realities of combat casualties, did her best as a nurse and a human being. Mixing comedy and drama, the show explored the relationships between the people of the China Beach facility and showed how such relationships can be created, changed, or destroyed by a war.

A large number of made-for-TV movies have been made about various facets of the Vietnam War. A few of the more interesting productions include *The Forgotten Man* (1971), in which Dennis Weaver plays a Vietnam veteran, presumed dead for years but actually a prisoner of war (POW), who returns home to find his wife remarried, his job gone, and his old life irrevocably lost. *When Hell Was in Session* (1979) tells the harrowing true story of Commander Jeremiah Denton's seven-year imprisonment as a POW in Hanoi. A similar tale is told in *In Love and War* (1987), about the captivity of Commander James Stockdale and his wife's efforts to have him released.

Friendly Fire (1979) details the story of a couple whose son is killed in Vietnam under mysterious circumstances. Their efforts to determine how he died bring them up against a wall of bureaucratic indifference. *The Children of An Loc* (1980) tells the true story of an American actress (Ina Balin, who plays herself) struggling to evacuate children from a Vietnamese orphanage during the fall of Saigon in 1975. One of the most affecting efforts was the HBO production *Dear America: Letters Home from Vietnam* (1987), based on Bernard Edelman's book of the same name. It combines the reading of actual letters with news footage and music of the period to tell the tale of the Vietnam War from the perspective of the men and women who lived it.

By the early twenty-first century, the Vietnam War had become part of the American cultural identity. It continued to affect the ways in which wars were carried out in Afghanistan and Iraq. It also influenced the cynicism of the American public and press and placed restraints on the things that governments could do without being held accountable. Younger veterans, some of them sons and grandsons of Vietnam veterans, were coming home with a new set of injuries and problems that served to heighten the impact of Vietnam. While Vietnam veterans had never been treated as heroes the way younger veterans are, many were still bearing the scars of the war, which many of them had entered as draftees rather than volunteers.

One of the ongoing problems faced by Vietnam veterans is the health impact of exposure to Agent Orange, a tactical herbicide used to clear vegetation in Vietnam. Agent Orange, which was discontinued in 1970, has been linked to cancer, skin conditions, birth defects, heart disease, respiratory problems, Parkinson's disease, Hodgkin's disease, type 2 diabetes, and a host of other conditions. While the government does not officially recognize the exposure of Vietnam veterans to Agent Orange, the Department of Veterans Affairs insists that anyone serving in the area between January 9, 1962, and May 7, 1975, may have been exposed. Consequently, all veterans who have been diagnosed with one of the diseases associated with Agent Orange are eligible to apply for benefits.

Justin Gustainis

SEE ALSO: *Academy Awards;* The A-Team*; Baez, Joan; Buffalo Springfield; Capra, Frank; The Carter Family; Communism; Cronkite, Walter; De Niro, Robert;* The Deer Hunter*; The Doors; The Draft; Flag Burning; Haggard, Merle; Kent State Massacre; Kubrick, Stanley; Made-for-Television Movies; The Monkees;* Platoon*; Protest Groups; Rambo; Scorsese, Martin; Stallone, Sylvester; Stone, Oliver; Student Demonstrations;* Taxi Driver*; Wayne, John.*

BIBLIOGRAPHY

Anderegg, Michael, ed. *Inventing Vietnam: The War in Film and Television*. Philadelphia: Temple University Press, 1991.

Anderson, David L., ed. *The Columbia History of the Vietnam War*. New York: Columbia University Press, 2010.

Daddis, Gregory A. *No Sure Victory: Measuring U.S. Army Effectiveness and Progress in the Vietnam War*. New York: Oxford University Press, 2011.

Department of Veterans Affairs. "Agent Orange." Accessed March 2012. Available from http://www.publichealth.va.gov/exposures/agentorange/

Franklin, H. Bruce, ed. *The Vietnam War in American Stories, Songs, and Poems*. Boston: Bedford Books, 1996.

Hershberg, James G. *Marigold: The Lost Chance for Peace in Vietnam*. Washington, DC: Stanford University Press, 2012.

Kalb, Marvin, and Deborah Kalb. *Haunting Legacy: Vietnam*

and the American Presidency from Ford to Obama. Washington, DC: Brookings Institution Press, 2011.

Lanning, Michael Lee. *Vietnam at the Movies.* New York: Fawcett Columbine, 1994.

Philips, Kimberley L. *War! What Is It Good For?: Black Freedom Struggles and the U.S. Military from World War II to Iraq.* Chapel Hill: University of North Carolina Press, 2012.

Rowe, John Carlos, and Rick Berg, eds. *The Vietnam War and American Culture.* New York: Columbia University Press, 1991.

Wachsberger, Ken. *Insider Histories of the Vietnam Era: Underground Press.* East Lansing: Michigan State University Press, 2011.

Young, Alvin L., and Paul F. Cecil. "Agent Orange Exposure and Attributed Health Effects in Vietnam Veterans." *Military Medicine*, July 2011.

The View

The brainchild of journalist Barbara Walters, *The View*, an ABC morning talk show, began in 1997 as a low-budget experiment but developed over time into a respected venue for discussion of American culture and politics. Often controversial, the program features a multigenerational panel of five women who talk with guests, express personal opinions, and comment on current events. Although there are segments covering entertainment, health, fashion, sex, and other lifestyle topics, the show is best known for spirited disagreements among the panel members and for frank confrontations with some guests. As executive producer, Walters typically appears on the program several times a week, but the position of moderator has passed through several hands—from the journalist Meredith Vieira (1997–2006) to the entertainer Whoopi Goldberg, who took over in 2007.

According to her memoir *Audition* (2009), Walters based her original concept for *The View* on two inspirations: the Sunday-morning news program *This Week with David Brinkley* and a daytime program called *Girl Talk*, hosted by Virginia Graham from 1962 to 1969. Walters obtained a reluctant go-ahead from ABC, and with her coproducer Bill Geddie, observed women conversing informally in small groups, searching for just the right combination of ages, temperaments, and opinions. They selected Vieira, the attorney Star Jones, the comedienne Joy Behar, and—for a "youth" representative—the twenty-three-year-old Debbie Matenopoulos. The show's freewheeling approach developed from the chemistry of these five panelists. The moderator prepared introductory remarks, but the on-screen discussion was unscripted and unrehearsed, and the panelists often spoke very personally about their lives.

As the popularity of the show grew and *The View* hosted increasingly important guests, the panelists attracted more attention. Matenopoulos acquired a reputation for being "ditzy" and was quietly let go after a year. The more serious Lisa Ling took her place but left in 2002 to become a reporter for *National Geographic*. Her replacement in the youth slot became the panel's most provocative, polarizing, and resilient member, Elisabeth Hasselbeck, who was a former contestant on the reality show *Survivor*, the wife of professional football player Tim Hasselbeck, and an outspoken political conservative. Walters, who continued to appear in a journalistic role on prime-time ABC news programs, always maintained political neutrality on *The View*, but Vieira, Jones, and Behar were unabashed liberals, so Hasselbeck was expected to provide a useful balance.

Hasselbeck's support of President George W. Bush led to on-screen clashes during his presidency, and tension definitely rose on *The View* during the 2004 election. There were other challenges as well, including Vieira's departure in 2006 to become cohost of the *Today* show on the NBC television network. More problematic, however, were personal changes for Jones, whose insistence on concealing the fact she had undergone gastric bypass surgery made the other panelists uncomfortable. Jones was also promoting a book and planning an extravagant wedding, leaving little time for *The View*, and many viewers became uncomfortable with her apparent self-absorption. For this reason, according to Walters, ABC decided not to renew Jones's contract, although the network wanted to ensure a positive departure. Jones chose instead to make a public break and surprised the panel with an on-air announcement. She later accused Walters of dishonesty and asserted that she had been let go because of previous disagreements with the controversial personality Rosie O'Donnell, newly hired as Vieira's replacement.

This unpleasantness made headlines, but the openly gay O'Donnell added an interesting perspective to the panel, along with a new energy, and at first the reconfigured ensemble worked well. Soon, however, the outspoken O'Donnell was engaged in public feuds with the colorful mogul Donald Trump, the conservative commentator Bill O'Reilly, and—most dramatically—her copanelist Hasselbeck. These highly publicized events made the program seem dysfunctional and overly political to many viewers, and in 2007 O'Donnell left *The View*.

The next moderator was the actress Goldberg, who established a more easygoing atmosphere. The comedienne Sherri Shepherd also joined the panel, adding a conservative, religious perspective. Political discussions once again took center stage during the 2008 election, with both Cindy McCain (wife of the Republican candidate) and Michelle Obama (wife of the Democratic candidate) appearing separately as cohosts.

The View continued to develop a role in the nation's political dialogue, leading Democratic strategist Kiki McLean to tell a *Los Angeles Times* reporter in 2010 that "*The View* is definitely a show that makes it on to the agenda of staff meetings when you're doing strategic planning, particularly for national campaigns." Although there have been attempts to duplicate the show's formula, *The View* continues to be a unique force in daytime television and a landmark in the history of women's programming.

Cynthia Giles

SEE ALSO: *Daytime Talk Shows; Goldberg, Whoopi; O'Donnell, Rosie; O'Reilly, Bill;* Today; *Television; Walters, Barbara.*

BIBLIOGRAPHY

Dale, Timothy M., and Joseph J. Foy, eds. *Homer Simpson Marches on Washington: Dissent through American Popular Culture.* Lexington: University of Kentucky Press, 2010.

Gold, Matea. "*The View* Gets Political—Viewers Love It." *Los Angeles Times*, February 8, 2010.

MacManus, Susan A. "Voter Participation and Turnout: Female Star Power Attracts Women Voters." In *Gender and Elections*, ed. Richard L. Fox and Susan J. Carroll. Cambridge, UK: Cambridge University Press, 2010.

Walters, Barbara. *Audition: A Memoir.* New York: Vintage Books, 2009.

Villella, Edward *(1936–)*

A critically acclaimed principal dancer with the New York City Ballet during the 1960s and 1970s, Edward Villella brought a virile athleticism to classical ballet that challenged the stereotype of the effeminate male dancer and popularized ballet and its male stars among the general public. His passionate energy and exceptional technique inspired the great neoclassical choreographer George Balanchine to create many ballets and roles for Villella, including *Tarantella* (1964) and the "Rubies" section of *Jewels* (1967). Committed to increasing Americans' awareness of ballet, Villella also danced in Broadway musicals; performed at President John F. Kennedy's inauguration; and appeared frequently on television, in variety and arts programs, and once, as himself, in an episode of the situation comedy *The Odd Couple.*

Injuries forced Villella to stop performing by 1986, when he became founding artistic director of the Miami City Ballet, a post from which he said he would retire in 2013. Under Villella's leadership, the Miami City Ballet evolved into a leading interpreter of the Balanchine repertoire and, with its prominent inclusion of Latino dancers, brought an ethnic diversity to the American ballet stage that reflected demographic changes in American society at large.

Lisa Jo Sagolla

SEE ALSO: *Balanchine, George; Ballet; Broadway; The Musical;* The Odd Couple*; Sitcom; Television.*

BIBLIOGRAPHY

Villella, Edward, and Larry Kaplan. *Prodigal Son: Dancing for Balanchine in a World of Pain and Magic.* New York: Simon & Schuster, 1992.

Wakin, Daniel J. "Bitter Departure for Miami's Ballet Patriarch." *New York Times,* November 13, 2011.

Viral Videos

A viral video is a video that becomes extremely popular very quickly via the process of Internet sharing, typically through video-sharing websites such as YouTube, social media sites such as Facebook, and e-mail. These videos are posted like any other, but due to particularly entertaining or gripping material, they are spread rapidly from viewer to viewer—like a virus—often resulting in millions of views. Many of the videos that "go viral" are short comic clips of spontaneous interactions recorded by amateur videographers, such as a giggling baby or a sneezing panda. However, viral videos can also include professionally produced material from published sources, such as the television show *Saturday Night Live* (1975–) and the sketch comedy website Funny or Die.

One of the earliest viral videos, circulated in 2000, took poorly translated dialogue from a Japanese video game and set it to music with photos of the phrase "all your base are belong to us" appearing in various formats (on store signs, shaved into someone's hair). However, the term *viral* was not coined until 2009, when it was used to describe the rapidly gained popularity of the video "David after Dentist," featuring a young boy's reaction to anesthesia after oral surgery (which by 2012 had been viewed more than 111 million times).

In his 1976 book *The Selfish Gene,* Richard Dawkins coined the term *meme* to indicate "a unit of cultural transmission." By 2012 the term was commonly applied to media spread through the Internet, including viral videos. Memes, Dawkins argued, spread through humans who also copy and modify them, causing them to evolve. Some videos, such as "keyboard cat," gained importance through repetition and imitation. The original video was a simple clip of a shirt-wearing cat whose owner manipulated the cat's arms to pretend it was playing the piano; the video's true popularity and meme status, however, stemmed from the thousands of videos recorded as creative responses. Some users, for instance, integrated the keyboard cat into their own videos, having the cat "play them off" (functioning much as a hook would to remove a bad performer in vaudeville theater).

The rapid and wide distribution of some videos has led to fame for their makers. In 2007 young songwriter Tay Zonday crooned an original song, "Chocolate Rain," and uploaded it to YouTube. The video eventually became popular enough to warrant Zonday's appearance in a Dr. Pepper commercial. Similarly, the 1987 Rick Astley hit "Never Gonna Give You Up" was re-popularized in the first decade of the 2000s as part of an Internet prank. Internet forum users would post a link to other Web content, claiming it related to the topic being discussed; instead browsers would be redirected to Astley's music video. The prank was called a "Rickroll." The viral joke's popularity resulted in a "live Rickroll," when Astley interrupted the 2008 Macy's Thanksgiving Day parade to perform his hit.

Sudden celebrity had its drawbacks for some, particularly those not initially seeking fame. A poignant example is the so-called Star Wars Kid who recorded himself reenacting a scene from *Star Wars* (1977) using a golf-ball retriever as a light saber and providing his own sound effects. The boy faced harassment after the video was leaked to the public in 2002. His family sued the schoolmates who distributed the video and eventually received a financial settlement.

Because of viral videos' potential to reach large, diverse audiences, marketing departments and political organizations have embraced the concept of viral videos. In 2012 the nonprofit organization Invisible Children released a thirty-minute documentary titled *Kony 2012* about the plight of child soldiers in Africa. The video was released on March 5, 2012, and by March 30 it had been viewed more than eighty-six million times, attracting the attention of international media outlets. Although there was a backlash of criticism against the organization for the views expressed in the video, the exposure yielded by its rapid dissemination facilitated dialogue about a previously unknown issue and about the potential uses of social media.

Issues of copyright law have increasingly complicated the dissemination of viral videos. Although many include original content filmed by their producers, those featuring copyrighted material have faced legal action from the original producers, who often claim that the postings constitute copyright infringement under the Digital Millennium Copyright Act.

By the 2010s viral videos had supplanted TV show synopses as the main topic of water-cooler conversation. Having seen a viral video allowed individuals to laugh at the same sneezing panda or discuss U.S. foreign policy together. The very existence of viral videos is a testament to the power of social networks and to the public's ravenous consumption of media, even in an era when the amount of information available to individuals far exceeds their capacity to consume it.

Kim Keeline

SEE ALSO: *E-mail; Facebook; The Internet;* Saturday Night Live*; Videos; YouTube.*

BIBLIOGRAPHY

Dawkins, Richard. *The Selfish Gene*. New York: Oxford University Press, 1976.

Grossman, Samantha. "'Kony 2012' Documentary Becomes Most Viral Video in History." *Time*, March, 12, 2012.

Tryon, Chuck. *Reinventing Cinema: Movies in the Age of Media Convergence*. New Brunswick, NJ: Rutgers University Press, 2009.

Wallsten, Kevin. "'Yes We Can': How Online Viewership, Blog Discussion, Campaign Statements, and Mainstream Media Coverage Produced a Viral Video Phenomenon." *Journal of Information Technology & Politics* 7, no. 2 (2010): 163–181.

Weng, L.; A. Flammini; A. Vespignani; et al. "Competition among Memes in a World with Limited Attention." *Scientific Reports* 2 (2012): 335.

Vitamin B_{17}

SEE: *Laetrile.*

Vitamins

Apart from their actual health benefits, vitamins have played an important role in the American consciousness, providing the arena for a struggle between competing systems of knowledge: the positivist authority of "normal science," with its controlled experiments and research protocols, versus the anecdotal evidence and personal experiences of ordinary consumers. Since antiquity it has been commonly known that there is a connection between diet and health, but it was not until the early 1900s that specific vitamins were isolated and accepted by the public as essential to well-being. What began as an exercise in public health became big business. In 2010 retail sales of vitamins and nutritional supplements exceeded $3 billion in the United States, with surveys showing more than 40 percent of Americans using vitamins on a regular basis. The story of vitamins demonstrates, in the words of the social historian Rima Apple, that "science is not above commerce or politics; it is a part of both."

Vitamins. *The sale of vitamins and other nutritional supplements has become big business in the United States.* MARIE C FIELDS/SHUTTERSTOCK.COM.

EARLY MARKETING STRATEGIES

The term *vitamins* (originally spelled *vitamines*) was coined shortly before World War I by Casimir Funk, a Polish American biochemist who was among the first to investigate the role of these substances in combating deficiency diseases such as rickets. By the mid-1920s, three vitamins had been identified (vitamin A, vitamin C, and vitamin D), as had the vitamin B complex. Even then manufacturers were quick to seize on the public's interest in vitamins as an angle for promoting their own products. Red Heart trumpeted the vitamin D content of its dog biscuits; Kitchen Craft declared that because its Waterless Cooker cooked foods in their own juices, none of the mineral salts and vitamins was poured out with waste water.

Particularly compelling were the appeals to "scientific mothering" in ads for such products as Squibb's cod-liver oil ("the X-RAY shows tiny bones and teeth developing imperfectly"), its competitor H. A. Metz's Oscodal tablets ("children need the vital element which scientists call vitamin D"), Cream of Wheat, Quaker Oats, and Hygeia Strained Vegetables. Pharmaceutical firms likewise targeted mothers in periodicals such as *Parents* magazine and *Good Housekeeping*, with the publishers' blessings: "An advertiser's best friend is a mother; a mother's best friend is 'The Parents' Magazine,'" proclaimed the publication's advertising department, while the director of the Good Housekeeping Bureau generously promised clients that all products advertised in the magazine, "whether or not they are within our testing scope, are guaranteed by us on the basis of the claims that are made for them."

Harry Steenbock, a researcher at the University of Wisconsin, discovered in 1924 that ultraviolet irradiation of certain foods boosted their vitamin D content, thus providing an alternative source to wholesome but distasteful cod-liver oil. The Wisconsin Alumni Research Foundation was created to protect Steenbock's patents and to license his process to manufacturers. Ironically, half a century later Senator William Proxmire of Wisconsin would spearhead a congressional campaign that led the Food and Drug Administration (FDA) to reclassify most vitamins as foods rather than drugs.

APPEALS TO SCIENTIFIC AUTHORITY

The scientific reasons advanced for taking a particular vitamin were often compelling. In the late 1700s, fresh fruit, rich in vitamin C, had been dramatically shown to be a preventive for scurvy, the cause of many shipboard deaths on long sea voyages. Captain James Cook added citrus to the diet of his crew on his three-year circumnavigation of the globe, during which only one of his seamen died. (Cook's limes, which became a staple of shipboard diet throughout the British navy, gave rise to the slang term *limeys* for Englishmen.) However, widespread consumption of a vitamin for its original purpose sometimes created partisans for its benign effects in another area, as when the Nobel laureate Linus Pauling advocated high dosages of vitamin C in the 1970s as a therapy for the common cold and subsequently proposed that it could even play a role in curing cancer.

The appeal to scientific authority helped to legitimate vitamin consumption, but as vitamins became popular science and as demand grew, other marketers became eager players. From the 1930s on, there was increasing competition between health professionals (physicians and pharmacists) on the one hand and grocers on the other. Trade journals for the druggists repeatedly stressed the profitability in vitamins and the desirability of keeping consumers coming back to the drugstore for their supplies (and discouraging them from buying vitamins in the general marketplace). The grocers (and later the health-food stores) and their public wanted to keep vitamins readily available and affordable. There were skeptics as well, including the FDA, whose own claim to scientific legitimacy had the force of law and which attempted to regulate vitamin marketing in order to prevent what it often saw as fraudulent claims and medical quackery.

Often, however, when the FDA frustrated the demand for dietary supplements with its regulatory impediments, it aroused an endemic populist distrust of big government and fierce resentment of a professional pharmaceutical and medical establishment seen as monolithic or even conspiratorial. In the late decades of the twentieth century, the public found a willing ally in Congress, which received no fewer than 100,000 phone calls during debate on the Hatch-Richardson "Health Freedom" proposal of 1994. The proposal reduced the FDA's "significant scientific agreement" standard to "significant scientific evidence" for labeling claims, so long as they were "truthful and non-misleading," and shortened the lead time for putting new products on the market. With sixty-five cosponsors in the Senate and 249 in the House, the bill passed handily.

Guidelines for the use of vitamins and other supplements continually change as more research becomes available. For example, in 2010 the Institute of Medicine called for an increase in the recommended dietary allowance of vitamin D. Also, in the 2010s some researchers reported that there was no evidence that taking supplements (rather than gaining vitamins and minerals from food) was helpful in any way. In fact, some studies seemed to indicate that taking supplemental doses of certain vitamins—notably A, E, and beta carotene—correlated to a slightly increased risk of death.

In spite of those findings, sales of supplements remained high. The chain store General Nutrition Centers (GNC), which sells vitamins, dietary supplements, and sports nutrition products, has grown rapidly since the 1980s and in the early 2010s had more than 4,800 locations in the United States. One of its most popular product lines was sports supplements, including protein products to help athletes gain muscle mass and energy drinks and snacks to use during and after workouts. GNC not only sells nutritional products but also manufactures its own brand.

Nick Humez

SEE ALSO: *Dieting;* Good Housekeeping.

BIBLIOGRAPHY

American Entrepreneurs' Association. *Health Food/Vitamin Store*, 2nd ed. Irvine, CA: Entrepreneur Group, 1993.

Apple, Rima D. *Vitamania: Vitamins in American Culture*. New Brunswick, NJ: Rutgers University Press, 1996.

Funk, Casimir, and H. E. Dubin. *Vitamin and Mineral Therapy: Practical Manual*. New York: U.S. Vitamin Corp, 1936.

Harris, Florence LaGanke. *Victory Vitamin Cook Book for Wartime Meals*. New York: William Penn Publishing, 1943.

Mindell, Earl, and Hester Mundis. *Earl Mindell's New Vitamin Bible*, rev. ed. New York: Grand Central Life & Style, 2011.

Pauling, Linus. *Vitamin C and the Common Cold*. San Francisco: W. H. Freeman, 1970.

Richards, Evelleen. *Vitamin C and Cancer: Medicine or Politics?* New York: St. Martin's Press, 1991.

Takton, M. Daniel. *The Great Vitamin Hoax*. New York: Macmillan, 1968.

Vogue

The first illustrated fashion magazine grew out of a weekly society paper that began in 1892. *Vogue* magazine's inauspicious start as a failing journal did not preview the success that it would become. In 1909 a young publisher, Condé Nast, bought the paper and transformed it into a leading magazine that signaled a new approach to women's magazines. In 1910 the once small publication changed to a bimonthly format, eventually blossoming into an international phenomenon with nine editions in nine countries: the United States, Australia, Brazil, Great Britain, France, Germany, Italy, Mexico, and Spain.

Following through on the vision of Nast, *Vogue* has continued to present cultural information; portraits of artists, musicians, writers, and other influential people; and current fashion trends. Since its inception the magazine has strived to portray the elite by serving as an example of proper etiquette, beauty, and composure. *Vogue* not only contributes to the acceptance of trends in the fashion and beauty industries but also provides a documented history of the changes in cultural thinking, actions, and dress. A glance through *Vogue* from years past helps to document the changing roles of women as well as politics and cultural ideas throughout the twentieth century. The influence of *Vogue* over many generations of women is demonstrated by its many imitations, including *Cosmopolitan*, *Glamour*, and *Mademoiselle*, which have all sought to claim part of the growing market of women's fashion magazines. Despite the abundance of such magazines, no other publication has been able to achieve the lasting influence and success of *Vogue*.

EARLY HISTORY

Vogue incorporated photography into its layout in 1913. Under the direction of editor-in-chief Edna Woolman Chase (1914–1951) and art director Dr. Mehemed Fehmy Agha, *Vogue* reinvented its image several times. During the Great Depression and World War II, circulation soared. Readers looked to the magazine to escape from the reality of the hardships in their lives. In the midst of the Great Depression fashions reflected the glamour of Hollywood, with movies exerting an enormous influence on the ideas of fashion and beauty. Photographers Edward

Steichen, Cecil Beaton, and Baron de Meyer emphasized this glamour by presenting their models in elaborate settings.

Additionally *Vogue* began focusing on more affordable, ready-to-wear clothing collections. During the war, images of fashions within the magazine emulated the practicality of the era. Different, more durable and affordable fabrics and simple designs became prominent. The magazine demonstrated that even in difficult circumstances women still strove for the consistency of caring for everyday concerns regarding fashion and beauty. Balancing the lighter features, ex-*Vogue* model and photographer Lee Miller's images of the liberation of Europe also provided a somber and intellectual view of the war. This element of the magazine kept readers involved and informed of the realities of the war.

POSTWAR

Under the supervision of editor-in-chief Jessica Daves (1952–1963) and Russian émigré Alexander Liberman, who served as art director (1943–1962) and editorial director of Condé Nast Publications (1962), simplicity of design prevailed in *Vogue* after World War II. One main component of the reformatting undertaken by Daves and Liberman was the hiring in 1943 of photographer Irving Penn, who, along with Richard Avedon, modernized fashion photography by simplifying it. Penn used natural lighting and stripped out all superfluous elements; his images focused purely on the fashions. Penn and other photographers also contributed portraits of notable people, travel essays, and ethnographic features to the magazine. Thoughtful coverage on the issues of the day, in addition to the variety of these stories and supplementary columns—including "People Are Talking About," an editorial consisting of news regarding art, film, theater, and celebrities' lives—counterbalanced the fashion spreads that showcased the seasonal couture collections. *Vogue* became multifaceted, appealing to readers across several economic and social strata.

As an editor-in-chief with theatrical style, Diana Vreeland (1963–1971) brought a cutting-edge, exciting quality to the magazine. Vreeland, famous for coining the term *youthquake*, focused on the changing ideas of fashion in the 1960s. Under her hand *Vogue* became even more fashion-oriented, with many more pages devoted to clothing and accessories. Imagination and fantasy became the ideals to portray within the pages of the magazine. Clothes were colorful, bright, revealing, and filled with geometric shapes that played with the elements of sex and fun. Additionally, during this era models no longer became merely mannequins but were personalities. The photographs depicted the models in action-filled poses, often outside of a studio setting. The women became identifiable; Suzy Parker, Penelope Tree, Twiggy, and Veruschka became household names and paved the way for Cindy, Claudia, Christy, and Naomi, the supermodels of the 1980s and 1990s.

Collaborating with photographers such as Helmut Newton, Sarah Moon, and Deborah Turbeville, editor-in-chief Grace Mirabella (1971–1988) also brought a sensual quality to the magazine; the blatant sexualized images from the 1960s became more understated, although no less potent. Tinged with erotic and sometimes violent imagery, the fashion layouts featured clothing with less of an exhibitionist quality; apparel became more practical. Filling the fashion pages were blue denim garments and easy-to-wear attire. Mirabella, in keeping with this practicality, adapted the magazine to a monthly publication. At this time *Vogue* also shrank in cut size to conform to postal codes. As a result each page was packed with information; *Vogue* became a magazine formulated for a society filled with working women on the go.

Vogue celebrated the end of the twentieth century by introducing *Vogue en Español* in Latin America. By the early twenty-first century the magazine had an annual readership of 1,248,121 worldwide. The average reader was an employed (64 percent) female (89 percent) who had attended college (64 percent) and had an annual income of at least $63,094 a year. Much of the focus continued to be on expanding *Vogue*'s foreign base with new Greek, French, Japanese, Portuguese, and Chinese editions.

The tradition of *Vogue* as a publication that covers all aspects of each generation continued. Under the guidance of Anna Wintour, editor-in-chief beginning in 1988, the magazine expanded beyond only reporting cultural and political issues and presenting fashion trends; it validated new designs and designers. *Vogue* continually sought, presented, and promoted new ideas regarding clothing, accessories, and beauty products while continuing to entertain, educate, and guide millions of women.

Jennifer Jankauskas

SEE ALSO: *Campbell, Naomi; Condé Nast;* Cosmopolitan; *Crawford, Cindy; The Great Depression; Supermodels; Twiggy;* Vanity Fair; *World War II.*

BIBLIOGRAPHY

Davis, Mary E. *Classic Chic: Music, Fashion, and Modernism.* Berkeley: University of California Press, 2006.

Devlin, Polly. *Vogue Book of Fashion Photography.* London: Thames and Hudson, 1979.

Hively, Evelyn Helmick. *Darling Ro and the Benet Women.* Kent, OH: Kent State University Press, 2011.

Jobling, Paul. *Fashion Spreads: Word and Images in Fashion Photography since 1980.* New York: Berg, 1999.

Kazajian, Dodie, and Calvin Tomkins. *Alex: The Life of Alexander Liberman.* New York: A. A. Knopf, 1993.

Lloyd, Valerie. *The Art of Vogue Photographic Covers: Fifty Years of Fashion and Design.* New York: Harmony Books, 1986.

Volkswagen Beetle

The phenomenal success of Volkswagen's diminutive two-door sedan in the American automobile market in the 1950s and 1960s was a classic example of conventional wisdom proven false. Car manufacturers in Detroit, Michigan, and their advertising agencies marketed large, comfortable cars with futuristic styling and plenty of extra gadgets. Futuristic rocket fins were in, and the more headlights and tail lights, the better. "Planned obsolescence" was built in: the look and feel of each year's models were to be significantly different from those of the previous year.

But throughout the 1950s, there was a persistent niche market in foreign cars, particularly among better-educated drivers who thought that Detroit's cars looked vulgar and silly and who were appalled by their low gas mileage. Most European imports got well over 20 miles per gallon to an American automobile's 8. The German manufacturers of the Volkswagen (VW) claimed that their "people's car" got 32 miles per gallon traveling at 50 miles an hour. Moreover, it was virtually impossible to tell a 1957 VW from a 1956 one—or, indeed, from the 1949 model, of which just two had been imported, by way of Holland. (The first VW "Transporter"—called a microbus in America—arrived in 1950.)

DESIGN AND PRODUCTION

To be sure, VW's sedan looked odd—rather like a scarab, which is why it was soon dubbed the "Beetle"—but it worked. Its rear-mounted, air-cooled, four-cylinder 1,200 cubic centimer engine proved extremely durable, with some owners reporting life spans in the high hundreds of thousands of miles. The cars had been designed so that they could be maintained by the owner, and many of them were, particularly by young owners who bought them used. And the microbus, with the same engine as the Beetle and a body only slightly longer, could hold an entire rock band and its instruments and still climb mountains. (It became so closely associated with the hippie movement that when the leader of the Grateful Dead died, VW ran an ad showing a microbus with a tear falling from its headlight and the headline "Jerry Garcia. 1942–1995.")

Developed by Dr. Ferdinand Porsche, the car had been ordered by German citizens for the first time in 1938 under the name "KdF-Wagen" (KdF stood for *Kraft durch Freude*, or "strength through joy"). But war broke out the following year, and the factory at Wolfsburg switched over, for the duration, to making a military version, the Kübelwagen (bucket/tub car), and an amphibious sibling, the Schwimmwagen, until Allied planes bombed operations to a standstill. After the war VW rebuilt its factory and resumed production, first under the British occupying forces and subsequently under Heinrich Nordhoff, VW's CEO until his death in 1968.

ICONIC AD CAMPAIGNS

From their modest beginnings, sales of imported VWs in America grew steadily. In 1955 the company incorporated in the United States as Volkswagen of America. In 1959 it hired a sassy new advertising agency, DDB Needham, which had already raised eyebrows with its "You Don't Have to Be Jewish to Love Levy's Real Jewish Rye" campaign. DDB's first ad featured three columns of dense type explaining the advantages of buying the VW sedan, broken up only by three photos—all of the car.

It soon became apparent that people already knew what the Beetle looked like (and had looked like for ten years), that it got great mileage, and that it cost less than anything from Detroit ($1,545 new in 1959, still only $2,000 in 1964). What they needed was a reason to identify with a nonconformist automobile. So DDB switched to ads containing very little copy; a picture of the car; a very short, startling headline in sans serif type; and a lot of white space. One DDB headline was "Ugly is only skin-deep." Another simply read "Lemon." A third, turning one of Madison Avenue's favorite catchphrases of the day on its head, said "Think Small." Indeed, almost all of DDB's VW ads were the conspicuous antithesis of conventional auto advertising.

The 1969 ad "Where are they now?" showed 1949 models of six cars—a Beetle and five made by companies that had gone

1965 Volkswagen Beetle. *The compact, rounded design of the Volkswagen Beetle stood in stark contrast to the large, angular look of most American cars in the 1950s and 1960s.* SSPL/GETTY IMAGES.

out of business. A slightly different ad campaign shifted to true stories of satisfied customers with unusual angles: the rural couple who bought a VW after the mule died and the Alabama police department that got a VW sedan for its meter patrol.

WHAT'S OLD IS NEW AGAIN

Although VW lost some of its market share in the 1970s once Detroit, spurred by the 1973 OPEC oil embargo, began concentrating on cars that were less ostentatious and got better mileage, the company continued to make Beetles until the end of the decade, when antipollution standards were passed that neither the sedan nor the microbus could meet. Although production of Beetles in Germany and the United States ceased in 1978, they still continued to be turned out elsewhere, notably in Mexico. Meanwhile, restored Beetles in the United States continued to command prices up to $7,000 (still a bargain compared to $15,000 for the cheapest new cars from Detroit) in the early 1990s.

When VW introduced a "concept car" at the 1994 Detroit Motor Show that looked remarkably like the old Beetle, response was so enthusiastic that the company went ahead and put its "Concept 1" into production at the same Mexican plant as the VW Golf (and powered by the same water-cooled engine, now under the front hood). The first new Beetles arrived in the United States in 1998 heralded by nostalgic advertising produced by Arnold Communications in Boston in a reprise of the DDB style, but with even less body copy: a picture of the sedan above headlines such as "Roundest car in its class" and "Zero to 60? Yes." One ad read simply "Think small. Again." Although not as popular as the original, the new Beetle lasted for more than a decade. In 2010 it was announced that more than a million had been sold. In 2011 Volkswagen announced plans to produce a third-generation Beetle.

Nick Humez

SEE ALSO: *Advertising; Automobile; The Grateful Dead; Hippies; World War II.*

BIBLIOGRAPHY

Addams, Charles, and Herb Valen. *Think Small.* New York: Golden Press, 1967.

Burnham, Colin. *Air-Cooled Volkswagens: Beetles, Karmann Ghias Types 2 & 3.* London: Osprey, 1987.

Darmon, Olivier; Rémi Noël; and Éric Holden. *30 Ans de Publicité Volkswagen.* Paris: Hoëbeke, 1993.

Hiott, Andrea. *Thinking Small: The Long, Strange Trip of the Volkswagen Beetle.* New York: Ballantine Books, 2012.

Keller, Maryann. *Collision: GM, Toyota, Volkswagen and the Race to Own the 21st Century.* New York: Currency Doubleday, 1993.

Nelson, Walter Henry. *Small Wonder: The Amazing Story of the Volkswagen.* Boston: Little, Brown, 1965.

Sloniger, Jerry. *The VW Story.* Cambridge, UK: Patrick Stephens, 1980.

von Sternberg, Josef *(1894–1969)*

Although there are other achievements for which to salute film director (and screenwriter, producer, and occasional cinematographer) Josef von Sternberg, his reputation has come to rest indissolubly on his most famous creation, Marlene Dietrich. After making *Underworld* (1927) and *The Docks of New York* (1928), two near masterpieces of the late silent era, von Sternberg was invited to Berlin to film *The Blue Angel* (1930). There he found Dietrich and cast her as the predatory Lola-Lola.

Von Sternberg brought Dietrich to Hollywood and turned her into an international screen goddess of mystical allure in six exotic romances, beginning with *Morocco* (1930) and ending with *The Devil Is a Woman* (1935). In this last and most baroque of Sternberg's films, his sensual imagery and atmospheric play of light and shadow on fabulous costumes and inventive sets found its fullest expression. Once parted from Paramount and his star, he endured a slow decline, but at the height of his success, this Viennese-born son of poor immigrant Jews (the "von" was acquired), who had served a ten-year apprenticeship as an editor, was acknowledged as Hollywood's outstanding visual stylist and undisputed master technician.

Robyn Karney

SEE ALSO: *Dietrich, Marlene; Hollywood; Movie Stars; Silent Movies.*

BIBLIOGRAPHY

Bach, Steven. *Marlene Dietrich: Life and Legend.* New York: Morrow, 1992.

Baxter, John. *Von Sternberg.* Lexington: University Press of Kentucky, 2010.

Finler, Joel W. *The Movie Directors Story.* New York: Crescent Books, 1985.

von Sternberg, Josef. *Fun in a Chinese Laundry.* New York: Macmillan, 1965.

Vonnegut, Kurt, Jr. *(1922–2007)*

American novelist, short-story writer, and essayist, Kurt Vonnegut Jr. was a rare example of an author whose prestige was equal among both general reading audiences and avant-garde critics. Author of such innovative works as *Cat's Cradle* (1963) and *Slaughterhouse-Five* (1969), Vonnegut was known primarily for his highly imaginative plots, his blending of historical fact with elements of the fantastic, and his scathing satirical eye. He is generally associated with the Black Humorists, a group of American authors who came to prominence during the 1950s and 1960s and included such figures as Thomas Pynchon, Joseph Heller, and John Barth. Vonnegut's literary output spans the six decades following World War II and engages the most salient social, political, and philosophical issues of this tumultuous era.

A PROLIFIC STORY WRITER

November 11, 1922, is the date of Kurt Vonnegut's birth, a birthday he considers significant for its coincidence with Armistice Day celebrations noting the end of World War I. Raised in Indianapolis, Indiana, among a culturally prominent family descended from German immigrant Free-Thinkers of the 1850s, the young author-to-be developed attitudes that would see him through the coming century of radical change. Pacifism was one such attitude; another was civic responsibility; a third was the value of large extended families in meeting the needs of nurture for both children and adults.

The first test of these attitudes came in the 1930s—during the Great Depression—when his father's work as an architect came to an end (for lack of commissions) and his mother's inherited wealth was depleted. These circumstances forced Vonnegut into the public school system, where, unlike his privately educated older brother and sister, he was able to form close childhood friendships with working-class students, an experience he says meant the world to him. Sent off to college with his father's instruction to "learn something useful," Vonnegut joined what would have been the class of 1944 at Cornell University as a dual major in biology and chemistry with an eye toward becoming a biochemist. Most of his time, however, was spent writing for and eventually becoming a managing editor of the university's independent student-owned daily newspaper, the *Cornell Sun*.

World War II interrupted Vonnegut's education, but for a while it continued in different form. In 1943 he avoided the inevitable draft by enlisting in the U.S. Army's Advanced Specialist Training Program, which made him a member of the armed services but allowed him to study mechanical engineering at the Carnegie Technical Institute and the University of Tennessee. In 1944 this one-of-a-kind program was canceled when Allied Commander Dwight D. Eisenhower made an immediate request for additional men. Prepared as a rear-echelon artillery engineer, Vonnegut was thrown into combat as an advanced infantry scout and was promptly captured by the Germans during the Battle of the Bulge. Interned as a prisoner of war at Dresden, he was one of the few survivors of that city's firestorm destruction by British and American air forces on the night of February 13, 1945, the event that becomes the unspoken center of *Slaughterhouse-Five*, named after the underground meat locker where the author took shelter. Following his repatriation in May 1945, Vonnegut married Jane Cox and began graduate study in anthropology at the University of Chicago.

Kurt Vonnegut Jr. *Kurt Vonnegut was known for his often humorous take the social, political, and philosophical issues that America faced from World War II into the first decade of the twenty-first century.* SYLVAIN GABOURY/STAFF/FILMMAGIC/GETTY IMAGES.

In the years immediately following the war, Vonnegut worked as a reporter for the City News Bureau, a pool service for several of Chicago's daily newspapers. Unable to get his thesis topics accepted and with his first child ready to be born, Vonnegut left Chicago without a degree and began work as a publicist for the General Electric (GE) Research Laboratory in Schenectady, New York, where his older brother Bernard was a distinguished atmospheric physicist. There Kurt drew on his talents as a journalist and student of science to promote the exciting new world where, as GE's slogan put it, "Progress Is Our Most Important Product."

Yet this brave new world of technology rubbed the humanitarian in Vonnegut the wrong way, and soon he was writing dystopian satires of a bleakly comic future in which humankind's relentless desire to tinker with things makes life immensely worse. When enough of these short stories had been accepted by *Collier's* magazine that he could bank a year's salary, Vonnegut quit GE. Moving to Cape Cod, Massachusetts, in 1950, he thenceforth survived as a full-time fiction writer, taking only the occasional odd job to tide things over when sales to publishers were slow.

Throughout the 1950s and into the early 1960s, Vonnegut published short stories in *Collier's*, the *Saturday Evening Post*, and other family-oriented magazines, sending material to the lower-paying science fiction markets only after mainstream journals had rejected it. Consistently denying that he was a science fiction writer, the author instead used science as one of many elements in common middle-class American life. When his most representative stories were collected in 1968 as *Welcome to the Monkey House*, it became apparent that Vonnegut was as interested in high school bandmasters and small town tradespeople as he was in rocket scientists and inventors of cyberspace; indeed, in such stories as "EPICAC" and "Unready to Wear," the latter behave like the former, with the most familiar of human weaknesses overriding the brainiest of intellectual concerns.

POSTWAR MOVE TO NOVELIST

Vonnegut's career as a novelist began as a sideline to his short-story work; low sales and weak critical notice for these books made them far less remunerative than placing stories in such high-paying venues as *Cosmopolitan* and the *Post*. It was only when television replaced the family weeklies as prime entertainment that he had to make novels, essays, lectures, and book reviews his primary source of income, and until 1969 these earnings were no better than any of Vonnegut's humdrum middle-class characters could expect. When *Slaughterhouse-Five* became a best seller, however, all this earlier work was available for reprinting, allowing Vonnegut's new publisher (Seymour

Lawrence, who had an independent line with Dell Publishing) to mine this valuable resource and further extend this long-overlooked new writer's fame.

It is in his novels that Vonnegut makes his mark as a radical restylist of both culture and language. *Player Piano* (1952)—in which a revolution against technology takes a similar form to that of the ill-fated Ghost Dance movement among Plains Indians at the nineteenth century's end (one of the author's interests as an anthropology scholar)—rewrites GE's view of the future in pessimistic yet hilarious terms. *The Sirens of Titan* (1959) is a satire of space opera, its genius stemming from the narrative's use of perspective—for example, the greatest monuments of human endeavor, such as the Great Wall of China and the Palace of the League of Nations, are shown to be nothing more than banal messages to a flying saucer pilot stranded on a moon of Saturn, whiling away the time as his own extraterrestrial culture works its determinations on earthy events. *Mother Night* (1961) inverts the form of a spy-thriller to indict all nations for their cruel manipulations of individual integrity, whereas *Cat's Cradle* (1963) forecasts the world's end not as a bang but as a grimly humorous practical joke played upon those who would be creators. With *God Bless You, Mr. Rosewater* (1965), Vonnegut projects his bleakest view of life, centered as the novel is on money and how even the most philanthropic attempts to do good with it do great harm.

By 1965 Vonnegut was out of money; to replace his lost short-story income and supplement his meager earnings from novels, he began writing feature journalism in earnest (collected in 1974 as *Wampeter* and *Foma & Granfalloons*) and speaking at university literature festivals, climaxing with a two-year appointment as a fiction instructor at the University of Iowa. Here, in the company of the famous Writers Workshop, he felt free to experiment, the result being (in an age renowned for its cultural experimentation) his first best seller, *Slaughterhouse-Five*.

Ostensibly the story of Billy Pilgrim, an American prisoner of war survivor of the Dresden firebombing, the novel in fact fragments six decades of experience so that past, present, and future can appear all at once. Using the fictive excuse of "time travel" as practiced by the same outer space aliens that played havoc with human events in *The Sirens of Titan*, Vonnegut recasts perception in multidimensional forms, his narrative skipping in various directions so that no consecutive accrual of information can build. Instead, the reader's comprehension is held in suspension until the very end, when the totality of understanding coincides with the reality of this actual author finishing his book at a recognizable point (the day in June 1968 when news of Robert Kennedy's death is broadcast to the world). *Slaughterhouse-Five* is thus less about the Dresden firebombing than it is a replication of the author's struggle to write about this unspeakable event and the reader's attempt to comprehend it.

INTERNATIONAL LITERARY FAME

The 1970s and 1980s saw Vonnegut persevere as a now-famous author. His novels became less metaphorical and more given to direct spokesmanship, with protagonists more likely to be leaders than followers. *Breakfast of Champions* (1973) grants fame to a similarly unknown writer, Kilgore Trout, with the result that the mind of a reader (Dwayne Hoover) is undone. *Slapstick* (1976) envisions a new American society developed by a U.S. president who replaces government machinery with the structure of extended families. *Jailbird* (1979) tests economic idealism of the 1930s in the harsher climate of post-Watergate America, whereas *Deadeye Dick* (1982) reexamines the consequences of a lost childhood and the deterioration of the arts into aestheticism. Critics at the time noted an apparent decline in his work, attributable to the author's change in circumstance: whereas he had for the first two decades of his career written in welcome obscurity, his sudden fame as a spokesperson for countercultural notions of the late 1960s proved vexing, especially as Vonnegut himself felt that his beliefs were firmly rooted in American egalitarianism preceding the 1960s by several generations.

Galápagos (1985) reverses the self-conscious trend by using the author's understanding of both biology and anthropology to propose an interesting reverse evolution of human intelligence into less threatening forms. *Bluebeard* (1987) and *Hocus Pocus* (1990) confirm this readjustment by celebrating such protagonists as the abstract expressionist Rabo Karabekian and the Vietnam veteran instructor Gene Hartke, who articulate America's artistic and socioeconomic heritage from a position of quiet anonymity.

That Vonnegut remained a great innovator in both subject matter and style is evident from his later, better developed essay collections, *Palm Sunday* (1981) and *Fates Worse than Death* (1991), and his most radically inventive work, *Timequake* (1997), which salvages parts of an unsuccessful fictive work and combines them with discursive commentary to become a compellingly effective autobiography of a novel. His model in both novel writing and spokesmanship was Mark Twain, whose vernacular style was Vonnegut's own test of authenticity. As Vonnegut says in *Palm Sunday*, "I myself find that I trust my own writing most, and others seem to trust it most, too, when I sound most like a person from Indianapolis, which is what I am."

Vonnegut's later works include *God Bless You, Dr. Kevorkian* (1999), a collection of fictional interviews that originally aired as radio pieces on New York's WNYC, and the essay collection *A Man without a Country* (2005), edited by Daniel Simon. Vonnegut died on April 11, 2007, after suffering severe brain injuries incurred by a fall. Several volumes of his writings appeared in the years following his death. Notable posthumous titles include *Armageddon in Retrospect: And Other New and Unpublished Writings on War and Peace* (2008), *Look at the Birdie: Unpublished Short Fiction* (2009), and *While Mortals Sleep* (2011). The first major critical biography of Vonnegut to be published after his death, *And So It Goes: Kurt Vonnegut: A Life* by Charles J. Shields, appeared in 2011. That same year Melville House published *Kurt Vonnegut: The Last Interview and Other Conversations* (2011), edited by Tom McCartan.

Jerome Klinkowitz

SEE ALSO: *Best Sellers;* Cosmopolitan*; The Draft; The Great Depression; Pynchon, Thomas; Radio; The* Saturday Evening Post*; Science Fiction Publishing; Television; Twain, Mark; Vietnam; Watergate; World War I; World War II.*

BIBLIOGRAPHY

Allen, William Rodney. *Understanding Kurt Vonnegut.* Columbia: University of South Carolina Press, 1991.

Ambrose, Stephen E. *Citizen Soldiers.* New York: Simon & Schuster, 1997.

Broer, Lawrence R. *Sanity Plea: Schizophrenia in the Novels of*

Kurt Vonnegut. Tuscaloosa: University of Alabama Press, 1994.

Gates, David. "Kurt Vonnegut, 1922–2007." *Newsweek*, April 23, 2007.

Klinkowitz, Jerome. *Vonnegut in Fact: The Public Spokesmanship of Personal Fiction*. Columbia: University of South Carolina Press, 1998.

Merrill, Robert, ed. *Critical Essays on Kurt Vonnegut*. Boston: G. K. Hall, 1990.

Mustazza, Leonard. *Forever Pursuing Genesis: The Myth of Eden in the Novels of Kurt Vonnegut*. Lewisburg, PA: Bucknell University Press, 1990.

Sears, Laurence. "And So It Goes." *Christian Science Monitor*, December 1, 2011.

Smith, Dinita. "Kurt Vonnegut, a Modern Twain, Dies." *International Herald Tribune*, April 13, 2007.

Yarmolinsky, Jane Vonnegut. *Angels without Wings*. Boston: Houghton Mifflin, 1987.

Wagner, Honus *(1874–1955)*

In 1936 Honus Wagner, "the Flying Dutchman," became one of the first five players to be inducted into the National Baseball Hall of Fame. When the Pittsburgh Pirates shortstop retired in 1917, he had accumulated more stolen bases, total bases, runs batted in (RBIs), hits, and runs than any player to that point. He also hit over .300 for seventeen consecutive seasons, while winning the National League batting title eight times. In 1909 Wagner, a nonsmoker, asked for his American Tobacco Company baseball card to be recalled because he objected to being associated with tobacco promotion; the recalled card sold for $451,000 during a 1991 auction. He died in Carnegie, Pennsylvania, at the age of eighty-one.

Nathan R. Meyer

SEE ALSO: *Baseball; Baseball Cards; Major League Baseball.*

BIBLIOGRAPHY

Hageman, William. *Honus: The Life and Times of a Baseball Hero.* Champaign, IL: Sagamore Publishers, 1996.

Hittner, Arthur D. *Honus Wagner: The Life of Baseball's "Flying Dutchman."* Jefferson, NC: McFarland, 1996.

Yolen, Jane, and Jim Burke. *All Star!: Honus Wagner and the Most Famous Baseball Card Ever.* New York: Philomel Books, 2010.

Wagon Train

One of television's most illustrious Westerns, *Wagon Train* wedded the cowboy genre to the anthology show format. Premiering in 1957, when the Western first conquered prime time, *Wagon Train* told a different story each week about travelers making the long journey from St. Joseph, Missouri, to California during the post–Civil War era. Such guest stars as Ernest Borgnine and Shelley Winters interacted with series regulars: the wagon master (first played by Ward Bond, then by John McIntire); the frontier scout (first Robert Horton, then Scott Miller and Robert Fuller); and the lead wagon driver (Frank McGrath).

Inspired by director John Ford's film *Wagon Master* (1950), the hour-long series (expanded to ninety minutes during the 1963–1964 season) was shot on location in the San Fernando Valley and produced by MCA, which gave the episodes a cinematic sheen. For three years *Wagon Train* ranked a close second to the television series *Gunsmoke* (1955–1975) before becoming the most popular series in America during the 1961–1962 season. The show ended in 1965 after 284 episodes.

Ron Simon

SEE ALSO: Gunsmoke*; Television; The Western.*

BIBLIOGRAPHY

Cawelti, John. *The Six-Gun Mystique.* Bowling Green, OH: Popular Press, 1984.

MacDonald, J. Fred. *Who Shot the Sheriff? The Rise and Fall of the Television Western.* New York: Praeger, 1987.

West, Richard. *Television Westerns: Major and Minor Series, 1946–1978.* Jefferson, NC: McFarland, 1987.

Waits, Tom *(1949–)*

In the 1970s, when many Americans were listening to soft rock or punk, Tom Waits's music and lyrics were unique, depicting the archetypal neighborhood barfly with nostalgic pathos. Like a time-warped beatnik, the singer-songwriter debuted in 1973 with *Closing Time* and followed with several acoustic jazz/folk albums throughout the 1970s. His gravelly, bygone, bittersweet voice became one of the most distinctive in popular music.

In the 1980s and 1990s he revved up his stage persona and electrified his music for his semiautobiographical *Big Time* (1988), a stage cabaret, album, and feature-length video. He released two critically acclaimed records during the 1990s: *Bone Machine* (1992) and *Mule Variations* (1999). The former won a Grammy for Best Alternative Album and the latter, a Grammy for Best Contemporary Folk Album.

His dark, gin-soaked tonality made him a mainstream figure, as did his regular appearances in movies and on soundtracks. In films he has typically played either himself or a gruff palooka as in *The Outsiders* (1983), *Down by Law* (1986), *Ironweed* (1987), and *Short Cuts* (1993). In the late 1990s and the first decade of the 2000s he appeared in a number of movies, notably director Terry Gilliam's *The Imaginarium of Doctor Parnassus* (2009).

During the early twenty-first century, Waits has continued to record albums such as *Bad as Me* (2011). He has collaborated with musicians ranging from experimental composer Philip Glass to hip-hop duo N.A.S.A. In 2011 he released a book of poems titled *Hard Ground,* which juxtaposed his writing with photographs of the homeless taken by portraitist Michael

O'Brien. Waits was inducted into the Rock and Roll Hall of Fame in 2011.

Tony Brewer

SEE ALSO: *Electric Guitar; Folk Music; Grammy Awards; Jazz; Pop Music; Punk; Rock and Roll.*

BIBLIOGRAPHY

Humphries, Patrick. *Small Change: A Life of Tom Waits*. New York: St. Martin's Press, 1990.

Maher, Paul. *Tom Waits on Tom Waits: Interviews and Encounters*. Chicago: Chicago Review Press, 2011.

Walker, Aaron "T-Bone" *(1910–1975)*

Jazz and blues streams have flowed side by side, and their confluence reflects the symbiotic melding of the genres. The musical crosscurrents of Aaron "T-Bone" Walker bridge these two streams; he was equally at home in both jazz and blues. He performed with jazz musicians such as Johnny Hodges, Lester Young, Dizzy Gillespie, and Count Basie. Walker and Charlie Christian, in their teens, both contemporaneously developed the guitar in blues and jazz, respectively. Walker linked the older rural country blues—à la Blind Lemon Jefferson—and the so-called city classic blues singers, such as Ida Cox and Bessie Smith of the 1920s, to the jazz-influenced urban blues of the 1940s; he also linked the older rural folk blues to the virtuoso blues.

Walker has no antecedent or successor in blues—he was the father of electric blues as well as one of the first to record electric blues and to further define, refine, and provide the musical language employed by successive guitarists. His showmanship—playing the guitar behind his back or performing a sideways split while never missing a beat or note—influenced Elvis Presley's act. Walker clearly influenced scores of musicians, including Chuck Berry, Freddie and Albert King, Mike Bloomfield, and Johnny Winter. "In a very real sense the modern blues is largely his creation. . . . Among blues artists he is nonpareil: no one has contributed as much, as long, or as variously to the blues as he has," notes blues historian Pete Welding in a Blue Note reissue of his work.

Aaron Thibeaux Walker (T-Bone is a probable mispronunciation of Thibeaux) was born on May 28, 1910, in rural Linden, Texas, but his mother, Movelia Jimerson, moved the

Aaron "T-Bone" Walker. *"T-Bone" Walker performs in London, England, in 1967.* DAVID REDFERN/STAFF/REDFERNS/GETTY IMAGES.

family to Dallas in 1912. His musical apprenticeship was varied and provided rich opportunities that prepared him for his role as showman and consummate artist. Walker was a self-taught singer, songwriter, banjoist, guitarist, pianist, and dancer. His mother was a musician, and her place served as a hangout for itinerant musicians. Her second husband, Marco Washington, was a multi-instrumentalist who led a string band and provided young Walker the opportunity to lead the band in street parades while dancing and collecting tips. At the age of eight, Walker escorted the legendary Blind Lemon Jefferson around the streets of Dallas, and at fourteen he performed in Dr. Breeding's Big B Medicine show. He returned home only to leave again with city blues singer Ida Cox.

While in school, Walker played banjo with the school's sixteen-piece band. In 1929 he won first prize in a talent show, which provided the opportunity to travel for a week with Cab Calloway's band. But it was during his engagement with Count Bulaski's white band that Walker fortuitously met Chuck Richardson, a music teacher who tutored Walker and Charlie Christian. Walker began earnestly honing his guitar techniques and, at times, also jammed with Christian. Unfortunately, he could not escape the pitfalls of "street life" during his musical apprenticeship and began gambling and drinking; he would later become a womanizer. In his teens he contracted stomach ulcers that continued to plague him throughout his career.

Walker first recorded for Columbia Records in 1929 as Oak Cliff T-Bone. The two sides were titled "Wichita Falls" and "Trinity River Blues." By 1934 Walker had met and married Vida Lee; they were together until his death. Walker and his wife moved to Los Angeles, where he played several clubs as a singer, a guitarist, a dancer, and an emcee. His enormous popularity quickly secured him a firm place in the Hollywood club scene. When he complained to the management that his black audience could not come to see him, the management integrated the club. His big break came with Les Hite's Band, with whom he recorded "T-Bone Blues" in 1939–1940 and performed on both East and West coasts. Ironically, Walker did not play guitar on this recording; he only sang. From 1945 to 1960, he recorded for a number of labels and became one of the principal architects of the California Blues. Some of his songs that have become classics of the blues repertoire are "Call it Stormy Monday," "T-Bone Shuffle," "Bobby Sox Blues," "Long Skirt Baby Blues," and "Mean Old World."

Walker was a musician's musician; his musicality was impeccable. His phrasing, balance, melodic inventions, and improvisations carried the blues to a higher aesthetic level than had been attained before. He serenaded mostly women with his songs of unrequited love, and the lyrics often gave a clue to the paradox of his own existence, as evidenced in "Mean Old World": "I drink to keep from worrying, baby, I smile to keep from crying / That's to keep the public from knowing just what I have on my mind."

Because Walker's recordings were made prior to the coming of rock and roll, he missed out on the blues revival that Joe Turner and other blues artists enjoyed. His records never crossed over into the popular market, and his audience was primarily African American. While the Allman Brothers recording of his song "Call It Stormy Monday" sold millions, his version was allowed to go out of print. From the mid-1950s to the early 1970s, the balance of his career was played out in small West Coast clubs as one-nighters. Although he did tour Europe in the 1960s and was a sensation in Paris, there were few opportunities to record. The Atlantic album titled *T-Bone* was inducted as a Classic of Blues Recordings in the Blues Foundation Hall of Fame in 2009. Walker suffered a stroke in 1974, and on March 16, 1975, he died. More than 1,000 mourners came out to grieve the loss of this great musician.

Willie Collins

SEE ALSO: *The Allman Brothers Band; Basie, Count; Berry, Chuck; Blues; Calloway, Cab; Celebrity; Cox, Ida; Gillespie, Dizzy; Hollywood; Jazz; King, Albert; King, Freddie; Presley, Elvis; Rhythm and Blues; Smith, Bessie.*

BIBLIOGRAPHY

Dance, Helen Oakley. *Stormy Monday: The T-Bone Walker Story.* Baton Rouge: Louisiana State University Press, 1987.

Stanton, Scott. *The Tombstone Tourist: Musicians.* New York: Pocket Books, 2003.

Walker, Aida Overton *(1880–1914)*

Aida Overton Walker dazzled theater audiences in the early twentieth century with her original dance routines, her enchanting singing voice, and her penchant for elegant costumes. One of the premier African American women artists of her time, she popularized the cakewalk and introduced it to English society. In addition to her attractive stage persona and highly acclaimed performances, she won the hearts of black entertainers for her numerous benefit performances near the end of her tragically short career and for her cultivation of younger women performers. She was, in the words of the *New York Age*'s Lester Walton, the exponent of "clean, refined artistic entertainment."

Born in 1880 in Richmond, Virginia, Aida Overton grew up in New York City, where her family moved when she was young and where she gained an education and considerable musical training. At the tender age of fifteen, she joined John Isham's Octoroons, one of the most influential black touring groups of the 1890s, and the following year she became a member of the Black Patti Troubadours. Although the show consisted of dozens of performers, she emerged as one of the most promising soubrettes of her day. In 1898 she joined the company of the famous comedy team Bert Williams and George Walker and appeared in all of their shows—*The Policy Players* (1899), *The Sons of Ham* (1900), *In Dahomey* (1903), *Abyssinia* (1906), and *Bandanna Land* (1908). Within about a year of meeting, Walker and Overton married, and before long they were one of the most admired and elegant African American couples onstage.

While her husband supplied most of the ideas for the musical comedies and Williams enjoyed fame as the "funniest man in America," Walker quickly became an indispensable member of the Williams and Walker Company. In *The Sons of Ham*, for example, her rendition of "Hannah from Savannah" won praise for combining superb vocal control with acting skill that together presented a positive, strong image of black womanhood. Indeed, onstage she refused to comply with the plantation image of black women as plump mammies, happy to serve; like her husband, she viewed the representation of refined African American types on the stage as important political work.

A talented dancer, Walker improvised original routines that her husband eagerly introduced in the shows; when *In Dahomey* was moved to England, she proved to be one of the strongest attractions. Society women invited her to their homes for private lessons in the exotic cakewalk that the Walkers had included in the show. After two seasons in England, the company returned to the United States in 1904, and it was Walker who was featured in a *New York Herald* interview about their tour. At times, Walker's husband asked her to interpret dances made famous by other performers—one example being the "Salome" dance that took Broadway by storm in the early 1900s—which she did with uneven results.

Walker enjoyed a decade of nearly continuous success with the Williams and Walker Company, but her career took an unexpected turn when her husband collapsed on tour with *Bandanna Land*. Initially he returned to his boyhood home of Lawrence, Kansas, where his mother took care of him. In his absence, Walker took over many of his songs and dances to keep the company together. In early 1909, however, *Bandanna Land* was forced to close, and she temporarily retired from stage work to care for her husband, now seriously ill. No doubt recognizing that he likely would not recover and that she alone would have to support the family, she returned to the stage in Bob Cole and J. Rosamond Johnson's *The Red Moon* in autumn 1909, and she joined the Smart Set Company in 1910. She also began touring the vaudeville circuit as a solo act. Less than two weeks after her husband's death in January 1911, she signed a contract to appear as a costar with S. H. Dudley in another all-black traveling show.

Although still a relatively young woman in the early 1910s, Walker began to develop medical problems that limited her ability to perform. As early as 1908 she had begun organizing benefits to aid such institutions as the Industrial Home for Colored Working Girls, and after her contract with Dudley expired, she devoted more of her energy to such projects, which allowed her to remain in New York. She also took an interest in developing the talents of younger women in the profession, hoping to pass along her vision of black performance as refined and elegant. She produced shows for two such female groups in 1913 and 1914—the Porto Rico Girls and the Happy Girls. She encouraged them to work up original dance numbers and insisted that they don stylish costumes onstage.

When Walker died suddenly of kidney failure on October 11, 1914, the African American entertainment community in New York went into deep mourning. The *New York Age* featured a lengthy obituary, and hundreds of shocked entertainers descended on her residence to confirm a story they hoped was untrue. Walker left behind a legacy of polished performance and model professionalism. Her demand for respect and her generosity made her a beloved figure in African American theater circles.

Susan Curtis

SEE ALSO: *Cakewalks; Vaudeville; Walker, George; Williams, Bert.*

BIBLIOGRAPHY

"Aida Overton Walker Is Dead." *New York Age*, October 15, 1914, 1.

Hill, Constance Valis. *Tap Dancing America: A Cultural History.* New York: Oxford University Press, 2010.

Riis, Thomas L. *Just before Jazz: Black Musical Theater in New York, 1890–1915.* Washington, DC: Smithsonian Institution Press, 1989.

Walker, Alice *(1944–)*

Alice Walker won the Pulitzer Prize and the American Book Award for her 1982 novel *The Color Purple*. By that time she was already a well-established and published writer, but it was the Pulitzer that brought her international recognition. Her books have since been translated into more than two dozen languages. Steven Spielberg's 1985 film adaptation of *The Color Purple* and a 2005 musical adaptation, which ran on Broadway for three years, brought her to the widespread attention of mainstream audiences. Both the book and the film were controversial, and Walker's fame was accompanied by severe criticism.

In *The Same River Twice: Honoring the Difficult* (1996), a book containing essays, journal entries, letters, and her original, never-used screenplay for the film, Walker addresses the criticism that the film was not true to her book: "Though *The Color Purple* is not what many wished, it is more than many hoped, or had seen on a movie screen before." She acknowledges that she was hurt by the accusations that she hated black men and had portrayed them in stereotypical and demeaning ways. Although Walker openly advocates black sisterhood, she also adamantly advocates the spiritual survival of all black people,

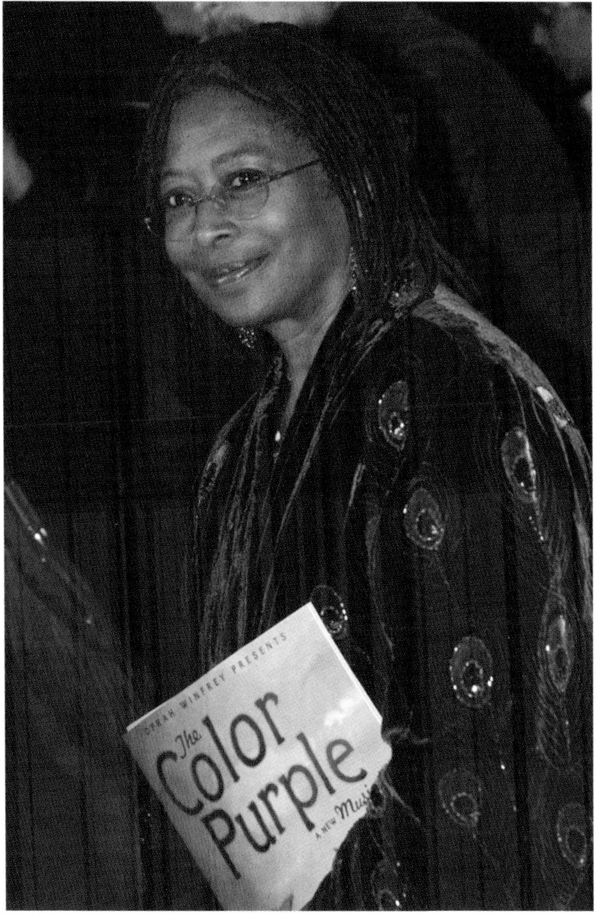

Alice Walker. *Alice Walker attends opening night of the Broadway stage version of* The Color Purple *in 2005.* BRUCE GLIKAS/ CONTRIBUTOR/FILMMAGIC/GETTY IMAGES.

men and women. It is this preoccupation, to use her own term, that motivates her life and her life's work of writing and activism.

Writing became important to Walker at an early age as a survival mechanism. Born Alice Malsenior Walker on February 9, 1944, in Eatonton, Georgia, she was the eighth child of Willie Lee and Minnie Lou Grant, southern sharecroppers. Walker has described the houses in which her family lived while she was growing up as "shabby" and "crowded," and she therefore spent a great deal of time out of doors; her writing is partly rooted in her need for space. When she was just eight years old, one of her brothers accidentally shot her in the eye with a BB gun, which blinded her in that eye and left her physically and emotionally scarred. She writes poignantly in "Beauty: When the Other Dancer Is the Self" of how, years later, her young daughter Rebecca helped her to see herself as "beautiful, whole and free." She also describes how fear of losing sight in the other eye enabled her to imagine life more fully, replete with its injustices and its beauty. As she put it, she "dashed about the world madly . . . storing up images against the fading of the light."

WRITING

Walker's novels are concerned with the plight of women, particularly black women, in twentieth-century America. The 1976 novel *Meridian*, for example, demonstrates her determination to revise the image of African American women by exploring the important roles they played in the civil rights movement of the 1960s, the success of which has historically been attributed to men. Her work does not only depict injustice but attempts to demonstrate how tribulations and joy often coexist. *The Color Purple* depicts a troubled young African American women named Celie who is attempting to make her own way in the state of Georgia in the 1930s but finds her choices limited by the racism of white society and the misogyny of black culture.

Critics have often focused on the themes of homosexuality and violence in *The Color Purple*, and the novel has frequently come under attack by censors for its explicit descriptions of sex, violence, and sexual violence. However, Walker juxtaposes images of rape, incest, and other forms of physical and emotional abuse with examples of love, loyalty, pleasurable and empowering sex, parental joy, and the communal bonding of men and women. Indeed, it was the characters' stories of joy and sorrow, rather than the negative depictions of black men, that helped keep *The Color Purple* on the *New York Times* best-seller list for twenty-five weeks. Similarly, in *Possessing the Secret of Joy* (1992), also a best seller, Walker simultaneously attacks the practice of female genital mutilation and depicts the beauty of love and sex between the young African woman Tashi and her American husband, Adam, both of whom appeared in *The Color Purple*.

Although it largely explores the oppressions and triumphs of black women, the collection of essays *In Search of Our Mothers' Gardens* (1983) holds interest for anyone who, like Walker, thinks black women are "fascinating creatures." Black and white women have praised its significant contribution to their own feminist enterprises. In these essays Walker speaks for generations of women whose stories were told through everyday work such as quilting, gardening, and cooking rather than through the written or spoken word. At the outset she defines the term *womanish*, suggesting that it may be particularly useful in helping black women talk about their feminism in culturally specific ways. Still, throughout these essays she provides a space for white feminists to discover the commonalities of women's oppression by emphasizing her belief that we are all part of one larger life story.

ACTIVISM

Walker has been active in politics since the 1960s, when she worked for the civil rights movement registering black voters in the American South and participating in the March on Washington in 1963. In more recent years she has been vocal in her support of liberal causes, protesting the Iraq War and criticizing Israel's treatment of Palestine. In 2011 Walker made headlines for referring to the United States and Israel as "terrorist organizations," criticizing the Israeli blockade of Gaza and America's military interventions in the Middle East.

It is also partly because of her dedication to the spiritual survival of her people generally and to black women specifically that the life and work of Zora Neale Hurston have been recovered. Hurston was a black woman writer and anthropologist who participated significantly in the Harlem Renaissance. In making a personal sojourn to Florida to find and mark Hurston's grave site, Walker helped restore dignity to a woman whose contributions to African American literature and culture are manifold but who died in poverty and obscurity.

While none of her subsequent work has been as popular as *The Color Purple*, Walker remains a prolific writer. She has published eight novels, including *Now Is the Time to Open Your Heart* (2005), as well as numerous collections of poetry, essays and short stories and several children's books. She continues to write about controversial issues, regardless of criticism, and remains popular because the issues are most often those that affect everyday people—ranging from the Million Man March and O. J. Simpson to repressed female sexuality and the need for struggle. She has said that she writes about controversial issues out of love, not hate, a reflection of her belief, as she expresses it in the preface to *The Same River Twice*, that "art is the mirror, perhaps the only one, in which we can see our true collective face. We must honor its sacred function. We must let art help us." In her critically acclaimed nonfiction meditation on the 9/11 bombings, *Sent by Earth* (2001), Walker reiterates this message, saying that hatred of all sorts can be resolved and dissipated only by love.

Jacquelyn Y. McLendon

SEE ALSO: *Best Sellers; Broadway; Civil Rights Movement; Gulf Wars; Harlem Renaissance; Hurston, Zora Neale; Million Man March; The Musical; 9/11; Simpson, O. J.; Spielberg, Steven.*

BIBLIOGRAPHY

Gates, Henry Louis, Jr., and K. A. Appiah, eds. *Alice Walker: Critical Perspectives Past and Present.* New York: Amistad, 1993.

Walker, Alice. *The Color Purple.* New York: Harcourt Brace Jovanovich, 1982.

Walker, Alice. *In Search of Our Mothers' Gardens: Womanist Prose.* San Diego, CA: Harcourt Brace, 1983.

Walker, Alice. *The Same River Twice: Honoring the Difficult.* New York: Scribner, 1996.

Walker, Alice. *Sent by Earth: A Message from the Grandmother Spirit after the Attacks on the World Trade Center and the Pentagon.* New York: Seven Stories Press, 2001.

Walker, George *(1873–1911)*

George Walker won fame at the turn of the twentieth century as the comedy half of the African American team of Williams and Walker. Up-to-date costuming, quick urban wit, and the character of the strutting dandy became the trademarks of his onstage persona. Walker's collaboration with Bert Williams resulted in one of the most popular black comedy teams to appear in successful musical comedy productions in the early 1900s. Beyond his personal fame, Walker also devoted great energy to the professionalization of black theater and performance. He served as a model to younger performers, and his efforts to form black professional organizations helped establish and maintain artistic and ethical standards for those working on the stage. Moreover, Walker's ambitious productions demanded scores of singers and dancers who gained employment and valuable stage experience.

Walker's humble beginnings did not predict the central role he would play in the black acting fraternity of the early twentieth century. Born in Lawrence, Kansas, in 1873, he began his career as part of a medicine show. The show made its way westward to San Francisco, where in 1893 Walker met and teamed up with Williams. The two formed a vaudeville act and toured with a succession of minstrel troupes, medicine shows, and traveling vaudeville shows until finding themselves stranded and unemployed in Chicago in the mid-1890s.

By this time the pair had polished an act in which Williams played the straight man and Walker supplied the comic punch lines, so they continued from Chicago on to New York. There they made a splash in a bit sketch in Victor Herbert's otherwise unsuccessful *Gold Bug* (1896) and attracted the attention of producers of other comedy revues. They joined such prominent white acts as McIntyre & Heath and Helena Mora in the Hyde Show but left it in 1897 to join an all-black company in Will Marion Cook's *Clorindy*. The show did not succeed, but the experience convinced Williams and Walker to seek the services of a professional management team. After reaching an agreement with Hurtig & Seamon, Williams and Walker starred in a string of musical comedies that put them at the center of the New York entertainment scene.

Under Hurtig & Seamon's management, Walker and Williams appeared in a variety show, *A Lucky Coon*, and three musical comedies that featured fuller plots, opportunities to act as well as sing and dance, and double-edged comedy that appealed to black and white audiences alike. In 1899 Walker married a talented singer and dancer, Aida Overton, who had joined the company a year earlier. His wife became a featured player in all the subsequent Williams and Walker musical comedies.

Although productions such as *The Policy Players* (1899) and *The Sons of Ham* (1900) enjoyed considerable success, it was Williams and Walker's *In Dahomey* (1902) that brought them national and international fame. The opening of this show on February 18, 1903, marked the first time a full-length African American musical comedy in three acts appeared on a Broadway stage. Following a run of fifty-three performances, the show traveled to England, where it remained for two seasons. A successful command performance at Buckingham Palace assured the show's success in London. Upon returning to the United States, the Williams and Walker company took *In Dahomey* on tour in America for the 1904–1905 season.

Disagreements with their managers led to a break, and the two comedians signed with Melville B. Raymond and organized the extravagant production *Abyssinia* in 1905. Although Williams was a more popular and perhaps more talented performer, Walker supplied the main ideas for this production, which featured avant-garde lighting effects, elaborate props, and elegant costumes for the entire cast. In their final show, *Bandanna Land* (1907), Walker fell ill. He was forced to retire from show business in the middle of the 1908–1909 season. He died in 1911.

Shortly before his retirement, Walker helped found the Frogs, an organization for African American professional entertainers. Similar to the Lambs, the more famous white actor's social club, the Frogs intended to promote "social intercourse between the representative members of the Negro theatrical profession." Under Walker's leadership, the Frogs maintained club rooms in Harlem, New York; organized occasional events such as the "Frolic of the Frogs," which featured prominent black acts, dining, and dancing; and represented a standard of excellence in stage work to which younger entertainers were encouraged to aspire. Walker devoted the last years of his career to this organization.

Upon his death he was remembered by Lester Walton at *New York Age* as a "dominating force in the theatrical world more because of the service he rendered the colored members of the profession, more because of the opportunities he created than for the types he originated." Although adored for his famous stage smile, his insistence on fashionable costuming, and his practiced—and oft-imitated—dandy strutting on stage, Walker set his sights higher than personal fame in Jim Crow America of the early 1900s. His chief aim, according to Walton, was "to elevate the colored theatrical profession, and the race as well." To an extent, he realized this dream, but his death also marked the beginning of the rapid decline of black musical comedy in pre–World War I America.

Susan Curtis

SEE ALSO: *Broadway; Medicine Shows; The Musical; Vaudeville; Walker, Aida Overton; Williams, Bert.*

BIBLIOGRAPHY

Curtis, Susan. *The First Black Actors on the Great White Way.* Columbia: University of Missouri Press, 1998.

Riis, Thomas Laurence. *Just before Jazz: Black Musical Theater in New York, 1890–1915.* Washington, DC: Smithsonian Institution Press, 1989.

Walton, Lester A. "Death of George W. Walker." *New York Age,* January 12, 1911, 6.

Walker, Junior, and the All Stars

Junior Walker and the All Stars were a rhythm-and-blues band that produced several smash hits for the Motown label in the 1960s with an untutored, earthy sound that went against type for Motown but provided the first of a new kind of hit for the recording-industry giant. The group's leader, Junior Walker, whose real name was Autry DeWalt II (1931?–1995), was born in Blytheville, Arkansas. As a young man he lived around South Bend, Indiana, where he met guitarist Willie Woods. During the mid-1950s the two performed in a group called the Jumping

Jacks. Walker, only a fair singer, was soon regarded as one of the best saxophonists of his generation.

By the late 1950s Walker and Woods had moved to Battle Creek, Michigan, and linked up with organist Vic Thomas and drummer James Graves. The four called themselves the All Stars, supposedly after a fan yelled out that every player was a star in this band. There was considerable truth in that statement, both because all four men were consummate R&B musicians, and because their relaxed, jam-session approach gave each player a chance to show his stuff. Years later, Grateful Dead guitarist Jerry Garcia would specifically cite "Cleo's Mood," the mid-1960s instrumental tune penned by Willie Woods, as an inspiration for the Dead's give-and-take jams.

The All Stars became very popular in Michigan clubs around 1960. In 1962, while they were performing at El Grotto, they were discovered by Johnny Bristol, at that time a recording artist for Tri-Phi Records in Detroit. Bristol strongly suggested that the group meet Tri-Phi president Harvey Fuqua. Fuqua himself was a former R&B performer; as one of the Moonglows, he had released a number of hits during the 1950s for Chicago's Chess Records. By 1962 he was president of both the Tri-Phi and the Harvey labels in Detroit; his wife owned Anna Records, and his brother-in-law, Berry Gordy, was the head of Motown, among the very few black-owned record labels of any size in the country. Fuqua quickly signed Junior Walker and the All Stars to his Harvey label. Over the next year the band released three

Junior Walker and the All Stars. *Junior Walker and the All Stars topped the R&B charts in 1965 with "Shotgun," a single that also made the pop Top 10.* FRANK DRIGGS COLLECTION/CONTRIBUTOR/ARCHIVE PHOTOS/GETTY IMAGES.

singles (but no hits), including "Twistlackawanna" and "Good Rockin' Tonight," the latter a cover of Elvis Presley's 1954 Sun label single (itself a cover of the Wynonie Harris version from 1948).

Fuqua's money troubles led him to fold his two companies and become a producer and talent scout for Gordy. Although Junior Walker and the All Stars did not receive a contract with Motown automatically, they did soon after thanks to Fuqua's recommendation. Gordy used the All Stars to launch his new, more R&B-oriented label, Soul.

In 1964 the band released "Monkey Jim," a song that sank without a trace, but its March 1965 single, "Shotgun," exceeded everyone's expectations. "Shotgun" started off literally with a bang: a gunshot that got its listeners' full attention right away. The song was a classic R&B tune that quickly went to number one on the R&B charts; more surprisingly, it also spent several weeks in the pop Top 10, peaking at number four. This performance was never surpassed by later All Star releases. Most of their fifteen hit records would do significantly better on the R&B charts, because that was the music they played. Two of these fifteen hits went to number one, and nine more singles reached the Top 10. Junior Walker and the All Stars had a dozen hits on the Billboard pop charts though only two ever made it to the Top 10. Unlike the typical middle-of-the-road Motown product, Junior Walker's singles were unabashedly rough and tough.

The strongest pop singles by the All Stars, after "Shotgun," were "(I'm a) Road-Runner," written and produced by Holland, Dozier, and Holland, the trio most responsible for the hits by the Supremes; "How Sweet It Is (To Be Loved by You)," from the same team; and "What Does It Take (To Win Your Love)," a ballad produced and cowritten by the band's old associates Bristol and Fuqua, by that time colleagues in Motown's production department. "What Does It Take" was a different sort of song for the All Stars, slow and dreamy by comparison with their usual output, but it was their only record to equal "Shotgun" on the charts. "Shotgun" itself was written by Autry DeWalt II (when the All Stars performed, he was Junior Walker, but when he copyrighted his creations, he kept his original DeWalt name).

The All Stars had a reasonably successful career by Motown standards, releasing fifteen charted singles (and several albums) over a seven-year period. The band had no further charted singles after 1971 but continued to tour on Motown-sponsored revues. Walker remained active as a performer, playing with a variety of sidemen, and in 1988 Walker appeared in the comedy film *Tapeheads*. In the 1990s his son Autry DeWalt III was a frequent drummer with the band.

Much of the music of the All Stars was underappreciated by the audiences of their day, and some of it was not heard at all. Among professional musicians, though, the band is held in higher esteem than many other groups with greater popular reputations. Walker died of cancer in Battle Creek on November 23, 1995, one of the great musicians of his generation. That same year he was inducted into the Rhythm and Blues Hall of Fame and in 2002, Walker's "Shotgun" was inducted into the Grammy Hall of Fame.

David Lonergan

SEE ALSO: *Gordy, Berry; The Grateful Dead; Motown; Presley, Elvis; Rhythm and Blues; Ross, Diana, and the Supremes.*

BIBLIOGRAPHY

George, Nelson. *Where Did Our Love Go? The Rise and Fall of the Motown Sound.* New York: St. Martin's Press, 1985.

Nite, Norm N. *Rock On Almanac*, 2nd ed. New York: HarperPerennial, 1992.

Whitburn, Joel. *The Billboard Book of Top 40 Hits*, 6th ed. New York: Billboard Books, 1996.

Walker, Madam C. J. *(1867–1919)*

Madam C. J. Walker revolutionized the African American hair-care industry with her entrepreneurial, organizational, and marketing strategies. Along the way, she became the first African American female millionaire.

Born Sarah Breedlove in 1867 in Delta, Louisiana, Walker moved to St. Louis, Missouri, twenty years later in search of better social and economic opportunities. Widowed with a two-year-old daughter, she struggled financially but was determined not to spend her entire life as a domestic. After Walker moved to Denver, Colorado, in 1905, her hair began to fall out, and she experimented with several formulas until she stopped her hair loss. This encouraged her to develop and market her own product, the "Walker hair-grower," to black women throughout the Denver area. As she later said to a reporter from the *Kansas City Star*, "Some of the remedy was grown in Africa, but I sent for it, mixed it, put it on my scalp, and in a few weeks my hair was coming in faster than it had ever fallen out. I tried it on my friends; it helped them. I made up my mind to begin to sell it."

The product was extremely successful in Denver, so Walker and her new husband, Charles Joseph Walker, began to market it throughout the United States, South America, and the Caribbean. She soon developed an array of hair-care products for blacks that became known simply as the "Walker System" and included shampoo, the "hair-grower," and a hot iron. Her method made coarse hair straight and silky.

To sell her products, Walker hired black women (known as "Walker agents") who went door-to-door dressed in white blouses and black skirts. This canvassing was supplemented by an intense advertising campaign in black newspapers and magazines across the country. Readers could hardly miss her ads, which, like her products, carried her portrait. Later she established beauty parlors and beauty schools to acquaint people with her products, and she also built factories and laboratories that manufactured her goods.

In spite of her business acumen, Walker was often criticized in the African American community for trying to make black women look white. However, she insisted that her products were not "straighteners" but rather a formula for a healthy scalp and manageable hair. Walker moved her company to Indianapolis, Indiana, in 1910 and then to New York City as her gross revenues began to exceed $1 million annually. She lived extravagantly, with massive real estate investments in and around New York City. Nevertheless, she also supported a large number of black philanthropic endeavors, including the National Association for the Advancement of Colored People.

Thanks to the pioneering of Walker, the black hair-care industry now generates billions of dollars. Hair-care companies that had ignored the African American consumer began to develop and market products akin to Walker's. Walker died at age fifty-one after a brief illness.

Leonard N. Moore

SEE ALSO: *Consumerism; Hairstyles.*

BIBLIOGRAPHY

Bundles, A'Lelia Perry. *Madam C. J. Walker*. New York: Chelsea House, 1991.

"Madame C. J. Walker." In *Epic Lives: One Hundred Black Women Who Made a Difference*. Detroit, MI: Visible Ink Press, 1993.

Stille, Darlene R. *Madam C. J. Walker: Entrepreneur and Millionaire*. Minneapolis, MN: Compass Point Books, 2007.

Walkman

The personal portable cassette player—known universally as the "Walkman," regardless of manufacturer—was the most important electronics product of the 1980s. Bought by millions worldwide, it dramatically changed the way people listened to music, and its convenience and small size dictated the shape and function of the next generation of digital technology. Manufacturer Sony's hunch was right: Americans did buy them in the millions, and the Walkman became one of those products that everybody owned, like a television, radio, or VCR.

Sony Walkman. *The Walkman personal cassette player, first introduced by Sony in 1979, was a must-have electronic device for music fans in the 1980s.* INTERFOTO/ALAMY.

EARLY TECHNOLOGY

The introduction of the Philips compact tape cassette in 1963 was an important technological step in the size reduction of talking machines. The newer machines used transistorized, solid-state amplifiers that took up far less room than vacuum tubes. The size of the cassette tape recorder was continually reduced in the 1960s until it resembled that of a paperback book. This was considered small enough for a portable unit.

Not small enough, however, for Masuru Ibuka of Sony, who wanted an even smaller stereo unit for his personal use—one that he could put in his coat pocket. The company he cofounded had made a profitable practice of reducing the size of electronic consumer goods. Starting with reel-to-reel tape recorders, radios, and then televisions, Sony had managed to find an unexpectedly large market for scaled-down versions of appliances that most families already owned. Sony's engineers took the path of a battery-operated cassette player that used highly efficient earphones instead of a loudspeaker. All the parts of the player were improved and reduced in size.

Ibuka and his partner Akio Morita were the leading proponents of the miniature tape player within Sony, where there was considerable resistance to the idea. Why would anyone want to own a tape player that was just slightly larger than the cassette tape it played? Ignoring the advice of their marketing department, the leaders of Sony took a chance with a product that the experts predicted would never sell.

INTRODUCTION OF THE WALKMAN

In 1979 Sony introduced its Soundabout cassette player, which was later called the Walkman. Although the innovative elements of the Soundabout system were praised, it was initially treated as something of a novelty in the audio industry. Priced at $200, it was not a realistic product for the mass market. Although it sold very well in Japan, where people were used to listening to music on headphones, sales in the United States were not encouraging. Sony's engineers reduced the size and cost of the machine and introduced the Walkman II in 1981. It was 25 percent smaller than the original version and had 50 percent fewer moving parts. Even more enticing to consumers was that its price dropped considerably.

The Walkman opened up a huge market for tape players. Americans were enjoying a more active lifestyle and embraced the concept of portable music, even if they had to sacrifice sound quality for portability. But as Sony developed the product, especially the earphone speakers, its fidelity and stereo reproduction improved drastically. It took about two years for Sony's Japanese competitors, including Matsushita, Toshiba, and Aiwa, to bring out portable personal stereos. Sony remained ahead of the competition by constant innovation: Dolby noise-reduction circuits were added in 1982, and a rechargeable battery feature was introduced in 1985. The machine grew smaller and smaller until it was hardly larger than the audio cassette it played.

In the ten years following the introduction of the Walkman, Sony sold fifty million units, including twenty-five million in the United States. Its competitors sold millions more. They were manufactured all over the Far East and came in a broad range of sizes and prices, with the cheapest model selling for around $20. Those who doubted the appeal of a personal tape recorder were silenced by the variety of uses that only a Walkman could provide. Waterproofed versions were marketed to those who enjoyed water sports, and there were special durable models for tennis players and runners. While sitting in a crowded subway car or jogging through a park, one could enjoy high-fidelity recorded sound.

Although a tribute to the semiconductor and the ingenuity of Japanese engineering, the Walkman was not only significant in the way it worked but also in what it represented: it was an evolutionary step in a process that began about 100 years earlier when pioneers of recorded sound began to reduce the size and cost of their machines. The Walkman was a significant product of portability resulting from the demands of an on-the-move, industrial society. It established a one-on-one relationship between people and their machines, changing the way they heard recorded sound and listened to music. The sound from the headphones of a portable player is intimate and immediate compared to the sound coming from the loudspeaker of a home stereo. Recording studios even began to mix the balance of their master recordings to suit the reproduction characteristics of Walkman headphones.

At the end of the twentieth century, the Walkman's dominance of the portable audio market was unchallenged, and its future seemed secure. Yet within its revolutionary concept were the seeds of its decline. Portability had become one of the most desirable features of audio equipment, and the search for smaller and smaller players led to an important advance in audio technology that completely overshadowed the Walkman in less than a decade. The size of the Walkman was determined by the size of the media it was designed to play, and thus each model conformed to the shape of a cassette tape or compact disc. But digital recording provided many more options for a recording medium, especially recording to magnetic memory, which could come in any shape.

In 1992 Sony introduced a recordable disc, called the Mini Disc (MD). Wafer-thin and about 3 inches square (comparable to the size of the computer floppy disk), the MD could hold approximately seventy-five minutes of music. The MD Walkman was the smallest Sony had made up to this point, and the company had high hopes that this format would replace the cassette. But Sony decided to make its Adaptive Transform Acoustic Coding (ATRAC) system a proprietary technology that dissuaded other companies from adopting it. Consequently, unlike the cassette and CD formats that came before it—which were quickly standardized and widely adopted—the MD was not copied by other manufacturers.

MP3 TECHNOLOGY

As a longtime manufacturer of audio equipment, Sony saw the future in new media that could be sold in stores and handled by the consumer. However, other manufacturers, especially those in the personal computer industry, felt no need to be shackled to individual records or discs and built the recording medium directly into the player. Using the widely adopted MP3-encoding system and tiny hard discs, companies such as Diamond introduced digital players at the end of the 1990s that were far smaller and could contain much more music than any Walkman. With the acceptance of online music stores such as iTunes, downloading of MP3 digital files became legal and widespread, and the MP3 player became the Walkman of the twenty-first century. Nevertheless, both its design and global audience were established years before by the Sony Walkman.

Andre Millard

SEE ALSO: *Cassette Tape; Compact Discs; iPod / iTunes; Leisure Time; MP3; Paperbacks; Radio; Television; Tennis.*

BIBLIOGRAPHY

Alderman, John. *Sonic Boom: Napster, MP3, and the New Pioneers of Music.* Cambridge, MA: Perseus, 2001.

Gould, William. *VGM Business Portraits. Sony.* Lincolnwood, IL: VGM Career Horizons, 1997.

Millard, Andre. *America on Record: A History of Recorded Sound.* New York: Cambridge University Press, 1995.

Morita, Akio; E. Reingold; and M. Shimomura. *Made in Japan: Akio Morita and Sony.* New York: Dutton, 1986.

Wall Drug

A rest stop at Wall Drug in South Dakota is a passport to a truly egalitarian social setting. It is a place that not only relieves highway tedium but also enables friendly interaction with other people from all walks of life. These qualities, however, were not foreseen in its humble origins.

For summer travelers driving endless hot hours across the Great Plains, an offer of free ice water cannot possibly be ignored. This simple but effective advertising gimmick was the savior of a small shop threatened with extinction by the hard times of the Great Depression. It was the brainchild of Ted and Dorothy Hustead, who had owned the establishment for five years without seeing much in the way of profit. In 1936 they put up some signs along the highway, and visitors started pouring in; they were still arriving in droves by the beginning of the twenty-first century. The tiny drug store located off Interstate 90 in downtown Wall, South Dakota, has expanded, evolving into several blocks of representational Wild West architecture, where shaded arcades of shops share space with motel and restaurant facilities. The store still serves free ice water.

Robert Kuhlken

SEE ALSO: *Advertising; Dime Stores/Woolworth's.*

BIBLIOGRAPHY

Jennings, Dana C. *Free Ice Water: The Story of the Wall Drug.* Aberdeen, SD: North Plains Books, 1975.

"Wall Drug." Accessed January 12, 2012. Available from http://www.walldrug.com

The *Wall Street Journal*

The *Wall Street Journal* has long had one of the highest total average circulations of any daily newspaper in the country. Once referred to by U.S. President Harry Truman as "the Republican bible," the *Journal* is noted not only for espousing politically conservative opinions but also for being a leader in innovative writing styles. The *Wall Street Journal* was acquired by Rupert Murdoch's international media conglomerate News Corp. in 2007 and subsequently underwent numerous changes. From a publication that began as a handwritten sheet of business news, more than a century later the *Journal* remained a highly regarded multisection newspaper that has been awarded more than thirty Pulitzer Prizes.

BEGINNINGS

The *Journal* was founded in 1882 by Charles H. Dow (1851–1902) and Edward D. Jones (1856–1920) as part of Dow Jones & Company. For the first fifty years of its existence, the *Journal* played second fiddle to the company's profitable news ticker service. During that period it was not uncommon for *Journal* reporters to trade in stocks that they reported. This was a common journalistic practice but presented a conflict of interest that William Henry Grimes (1892–1972) ended when he became the managing editor in 1934. Grimes, who would win the *Journal*'s first Pulitzer Prize in 1947, established policies that made the newspaper independent of sources. It reported more freely and confidently on business news and was more highly regarded by its readers.

KILGORE'S INFLUENCE

The person who ultimately shaped the modern *Wall Street Journal* was Barney "Bernard" Kilgore (1908–1967), who replaced Grimes in 1941. At the time, the *Journal* published two editions, the regular edition and the Pacific Coast edition. It was Kilgore's goal to make the paper national, meaning that a reader in Los Angeles would get the same paper as readers in Miami, St. Paul, Houston, and New York City. Folding the Pacific Coast edition into the regular edition was one of Kilgore's first steps in that direction. Kilgore's vision paid off when communications satellites made it easier for the newspaper content to be distributed to regional printing plants, from where printed newspapers could then be delivered. This system of distribution and printing became a model that other newspapers such as *USA Today* and the *New York Times* later followed.

Many of the changes that Kilgore made remained part of the *Journal* into the twenty-first century. He had a great influence on the paper's writing style, for example. He told reporters to write for readers, not for bankers and other newsmakers. Before Kilgore became managing editor, he had been a highly regarded writer for the paper. When reporters once complained to President Franklin Roosevelt that they could not understand the federal budget, he replied: "Read Kilgore in the *Wall Street Journal*; he understands it." Kilgore's axiom that reporters should write for the readers, not the people being written about, became conventional wisdom throughout the newspaper industry.

Kilgore decreed that not all stories had to be written in the inverted pyramid style—that is, with the most important information at the beginning of the story and the least important at the end. Instead, he not only encouraged reporters to produce in-depth stories that did not depend upon yesterday's news but also broadened the topics about which reporters could write about. In his mind, any story could be a business and economic story with the proper framing. Reporters produced not only company profiles but also stories on social trends, which some editors viewed as whimsical or off the wall. Under his watch, the *Journal* built its circulation and increased profits.

An offshoot publication of the *Journal* was the *National Observer*, which was created by Kilgore in 1962 and lasted until 1977. The *National Observer* was, in effect, the *Journal*'s Sunday paper or weekly magazine, and it was filled with analyses and features. It was such a different paper that among its early staff writers were nontraditionalists such as Tom Wolfe, who was later a force in the New Journalism movement, and Hunter S. Thompson, whose first major success was *Hell's Angels*, a work based on an article he had written about the infamous motorcycle gang.

LATER DEVELOPMENTS

After going online in 1996, the *Wall Street Journal* solidified its presence to become one of the largest paid-subscription newspaper websites, and in 2007 it expanded to add major foreign-language editions of the paper. The printed *Journal* began a weekly edition for all subscribers in 2005. In 2006 it placed advertising on its front page for the first time, and to save on printing costs it decreased the width of the paper (as other newspapers had done) from 15 inches to 12 inches. In 2007 the Dow Jones Company, and with it the *Wall Street Journal*, was bought for $5 billion by News Corp. under the control of Rupert Murdoch (1931–).

Critics were fearful that News Corp.'s acquisition of the *Journal* would compromise the paper's integrity. As the owner of several conservative media outlets, Murdoch was rumored to exercise influence over the reporting by his companies. While agreements were made that editorial decisions at the *Journal* would not be made without independent editors' consent, many other changes took place under Murdoch's control. The most significant modification was that front page headlines shifted from business-centric subjects to more generalized topics. This shift put the *Journal* in direct competition with other prominent daily papers in the United States. The addition of color photographs and graphics and the release of a revamped weekend edition in 2010 were other efforts made under New Corp.'s control to update the *Journal* and to make it appealing to a broader audience. By the early 2010s Murdoch and News Corp. were mired in controversy and litigation. Among the many charges levied against Murdoch, the only claim pertaining to the *Wall Street Journal* was the inflation of circulation reports in 2010.

Since the mid-twentieth-century, the *Wall Street Journal* had been expanding its purview beyond the limits of a merely financial daily newspaper. By the twenty-first century, the *Journal* had become more of a general interest paper than a strictly business publication. In the 2010s the *Wall Street Journal* was published in a number of editions, including *Wall Street Journal Asia*; *Wall Street Journal Europe*; and editions in Chinese, Japanese, Spanish, and German. Once a sister publication to a number of Dow Jones business-related newspapers and magazines, including Murdoch-owned *Barron's* and *SmartMoney*, as well as *Financial News* and Marketwatch.com, under its most recent leadership the remodeled *Journal* was more akin to publications like the *Washington Post* and the *New York Times*. With the fate of its owner in the balance, however, the future look and scope of the *Wall Street Journal* was unknown.

R. Thomas Berner

SEE ALSO: *Hells Angels; The* New York Times*; Thompson, Hunter S.;* USA Today*; The* Washington Post*; Wolfe, Tom.*

BIBLIOGRAPHY

Dealy, Francis X. *The Power and the Money: Inside the Wall Street Journal.* Secaucus, NJ: Carol Publishing Company, 1993.

Ellison, Sarah. *War at the Wall Street Journal: Inside the Struggle to Control an American Business Empire.* New York: Houghton Mifflin Harcourt, 2010.

Scharff, Edward E. *Worldly Power: The Making of the Wall Street Journal.* New York: New American Library, 1986.

Smith, Rebecca, and John R. Emshwiller. *24 Days: How Two Wall Street Journal Reporters Uncovered the Lies That Destroyed Faith in Corporate America.* New York: Harper Business, 2003.

Tofel, Richard J. *Restless Genius: Barney Kilgore, the Wall Street Journal, and the Invention of Modern Journalism.* New York: St. Martin's Press, 2009.

Wallace, Sippie *(1898–1986)*

Born Beulah Thomas in Texas, Sippie Wallace was an influential blues singer-songwriter who began her professional career as a teenager. After moving to Chicago in 1923 with her husband, Matt Wallace, and brothers (with whom she wrote and performed), she garnered a recording contract with OKeh Records. Known for her risqué lyrics ("I'm a Mighty Tight Woman"), African American– and female-based subject matter ("Women, Be Wise"), and rough phrasing, Wallace recorded much of her best music for OKeh between 1923 and 1927. Her music, like much of the blues of the 1920s and 1930s, articulated the experience of being female, black, and poor. However, Wallace was more than an entertainer—she conveyed a sense of understanding and empathy to her black listeners (though, ironically, this was often exploited in marketing aimed at whites).

Wallace disappeared from the blues scene for nearly forty years, but she resurfaced during the blues revival in the 1960s, recording several new albums between 1966 and 1986. As one of the genre's most stirring voices, she helped to write, sing, and shape twentieth-century American popular culture. She especially influenced singer-songwriter Bonnie Raitt, who has recorded many of Wallace's songs.

Deborah M. Mix

SEE ALSO: *Blues; Raitt, Bonnie.*

BIBLIOGRAPHY

Bogdanov, Vladimir; Chris Woodstra; and Stephen Thomas Erlewine. *All Music Guide to the Blues.* Milwaukee, WI: Hal Leonard Corporation, 2003.

Davis, Angela Y. *Blues Legacies and Black Feminism.* New York: Pantheon Books, 1998.

Harrison, Daphne Duval. *Black Pearls: Blues Queens of the 1920s.* New Brunswick, NJ: Rutgers University Press, 1988.

Sippie: Sippie Wallace Blues Singer and Song Writer. Videocassette (VHS). Directed by Michelle Paymar and Roberta Grossman. New York: Rhapsody Films, 1982.

Wallace, Sippie. *Complete Recorded Works, Vol. 1 (1923–25) and Vol. 2 (1925–45).* Compact disc. Vienna: Document Records, 1995.

Wal-Mart

With 4,400 retail stores spread across the United States and $419 billion in sales (as of April 2012), Wal-Mart had become

Wal-Mart. *Since the first Wal-Mart store opened in 1962, the discount giant has become a ubiquitous presence on the retail scene.* CARO/ALAMY.

an instantly recognizable and ubiquitous component of American popular culture. There are few places remaining in the United States that are beyond a short drive to a Wal-Mart. With upward of 50,000 different items on the shelves and racks of a typical store, Wal-Mart forever changed the way Americans shop.

The phenomenal success of Wal-Mart was the direct result of the vision and energy of its founder, Sam Walton. His motivation and charisma shaped a company that helped to establish discount merchandising as the major form of retail operation in the United States. His highly personal management style and folksy, down-home demeanor were instrumental in assembling a fiercely loyal workforce and maintaining high employee morale. Customers noted a marked difference in the quality of service after Walton's death, and low morale led to a major class-action lawsuit and the formation of a quasi union. In the twenty-first century, company officials have focused on global expansion. Between 2005 and 2011 the number of stores outside the United States grew from 1,587 to 5,200.

WALTON'S FIVE & DIME

Samuel Moore Walton was born in 1918 near Kingfisher, Oklahoma, into a farming family. He grew up in Missouri, graduating in 1940 from the University of Missouri with a degree in economics. After a short stint making $85 a month as a manager trainee for the J. C. Penney Company, Walton served in the army during World War II, attaining the rank of captain.

Walton launched his illustrious career in retailing with the purchase of a Ben Franklin variety store franchise in Newport, Arkansas, where he began his practice of high-volume, discount merchandising. From there he moved to bigger stores in several locations, calling his newly formed chain "Walton's Five & Dime." He depended on regular newspaper advertising and special sales promotions. He also began experimenting with self-service shopping, stationing clerks only at checkout counters. His stores became larger and more numerous. With his brother "Bud" as a business partner, by 1962 "Walton's Family Centers" had become the largest independently operated chain of variety stores in the country.

A key strategy in the rapid expansion of Walton's stores was one that became a model for success throughout the later Wal-Mart boom: placing new stores in small towns, based on the realization that consumer power there, represented by relatively small but concentrated populations, was more than adequate to support a large variety store. Early on, Walton formed his notion that a big store in a small town could be lucrative and capable of intercepting the flow of shoppers traveling to larger cities for major purchases. By establishing initial occupation of these smaller market niches, any threat of subsequent competition could be stifled. Although ready and willing to actively test his idea, Walton failed to find interested investors or franchise affiliation. Still determined, he went heavily into debt to finance the establishment of the first Wal-Mart in Rogers, Arkansas, which opened on July 2, 1962. The business prospered during the 1960s, first with several new stores opening in other locations in Arkansas and then extending into neighboring states. By the end of the decade, however, the need for expansion capital coaxed Walton into incorporation and sale of public stock.

EXPANSION

Walton set a course for rapid enlargement of his new Wal-Mart venture, fearing that if he did not crack the market offered by small towns, some other discount store would beat him to it. From thirty-eight stores in 1971, the chain grew to 276 outlets by 1980, most within a 300-mile radius of the firm's Bentonville, Arkansas, headquarters. Yet the greatest growth was yet to come. In the early 1980s Walton acquired several other retail chains. Transforming those stores into Wal-Marts allowed for quick saturation of new territories, particularly in the Deep South. At mid-decade, there were nearly 900 Wal-Marts in twenty-two states. For new construction, the prevailing expansion plan never wavered from the proven small-town location strategy. He further increased profits by capturing market shares in the suburbs of large cities.

Overall, the growth and expansion of Wal-Mart occurred in three phases. Until the mid-1970s, stores were tightly clustered around the northwestern Arkansas operational hub. The second phase, through 1980, produced regional expansion into neighboring states, while in the third phase, Wal-Marts were established throughout the United States.

Walton once described his management style as "MBWA"—management by walking around. He maintained a rigorous schedule of unannounced store visits, which always included Walton's own cheerleading drill and time for chatting with employees at every level. He acknowledged that human resources were the key to Wal-Mart's success, and he maintained a people orientation from the beginning that never wavered or waned. Hard work was always rewarded, with bonuses given for good ideas and stock options and profit-sharing incentives offered to all personnel. Walton himself worked sixteen-hour days and expected his corporate executives to do likewise.

The egalitarian tone of upper management was legendary, symbolized by the lack of assigned parking at corporate headquarters, even for Walton's old pickup truck. The company nurtured several programs aimed at giving back to the community. There were college scholarships for employees' children, as well as local high school students. With the stated purpose of stemming the tide of jobs leaving the country, there was the much-touted "Buy American" campaign (though as critics pointed out, Wal-Mart purchased domestically only if that was the cheapest price available). His recipe for prosperity evidently worked. By the late 1980s, *Forbes* magazine had placed Walton at the top of its list of the richest people in America for three years running.

In 1987 Wal-Mart ranked fourth among general retail chains, trailing Sears, Kmart, and J. C. Penney's; in that year alone, the company opened 121 new stores. Its board of directors included the then-First Lady of Arkansas, Hillary Rodham Clinton. In 1988 Walton stepped down as chief executive officer, though he still maintained an active voice in corporate plans and operations. The company he built had become a national icon. The new decade promised continued success and further expansion, and on a single day—January 30, 1991—Wal-Mart opened thirty-six new stores. Later that year Wal-Mart passed both Sears and Kmart to become the nation's leading retailer. Walton died on April 5, 1992, but the retailing spectacle he engineered remained firmly entrenched in American culture.

INNOVATIONS

Wal-Mart instituted a number of important and far-reaching technical innovations that serve as exemplars of retail trade management techniques in this country. In 1977 a companywide computer system was installed that grew in sophistication and applications until its database was second in size only to that of the federal government. Wal-Mart also pioneered the use of UPC bar code scanning, not only at the checkout counter but also at the backroom receiving area, which allowed for quick and accurate inventory data analysis. A satellite-based network, which initially cost $20 million, became the largest privately owned system in the country, allowing for regular and instantaneous communications among staff at all stores and management personnel at headquarters.

Wal-Mart also gained an edge on competition by vertically integrating the processes of wholesale purchasing and distribution of merchandise. Walton set up a series of centrally located distribution centers that received bulk shipments in large quantities from vendors and suppliers, often by rail. Through a process known as "cross-docking," the goods were then loaded on a fleet of company-owned trucks bound for individual stores, usually the same day. These distribution centers, full of automatic conveyor belts and often as large as 25 acres in area, did not actually function as warehouses but rather as facilitators that allowed for rapid transfer of products from a wholesale to a retail mode. The distribution centers served the growing network of retail locations at an approximate ratio of one distribution center per 100 stores. The company also assumed control of all departments within stores, including the jewelry, pharmaceutical, and automobile service sections that had previously belonged to outside contractors leasing floor space.

The success of Wal-Mart was emblematic of changing retail trends in the United States and paralleled the rise of discount merchandising. The economies of scale involved with bigger and more numerous stores, bulk purchasing directly from manufacturers, and high-volume sales enabled rapid growth and soaring profits even as individual item markups were reduced and savings passed on to customers. The public was quick to respond. As traditional department stores declined in consumer appeal, the large variety outlet promising low prices took over. The year Wal-Mart opened its first store—1962—was also the same year that Kmart, Woolco, and Target first opened stores. However, it was Wal-Mart that most successfully negotiated the transition from shopping center and mall-based retailing to one-stop shopping. Sales and service were guided by a pair of slogans displayed prominently in every store: "We sell for less" and "Satisfaction guaranteed." The "store greeter," often a senior citizen, is a fixture at the entrance to every store.

CHALLENGES

The amazing spread of Wal-Marts across the American landscape has not been without controversy. Several locations have actually welcomed the new neighbor, finding that their own business community has prospered from the increased consumer traffic. Much more commonly, however, local communities perceived the giant store on the edge of town as a threat to main-street merchants unable to compete with the bulk purchasing power of a national chain. Charges of unfair labor practices barely fazed the infamously nonunion shop. For all its self-congratulatory stance on promoting environmental issues and being green, the company has also been criticized for its use of veiled threats and other heavy-handed tactics in dealing with local zoning laws and environmental regulations. Opposition in large cities such as New York, Philadelphia, and Washington, D.C., managed to derail Wal-Mart's expansion plans in those cities.

In the early years of the twenty-first century, Wal-Mart faced a wave of employee discontent. Over a ten-year period, employee Betty Dukes and 1.5 million other women fought a class-action lawsuit concerning perpetual sexual discrimination all the way to the Supreme Court. The court finally heard *Dukes v. Wal-Mart Stores, Inc.* in June 2011, but in a split decision, the justices dismissed the suit on a technicality. The women had argued that local managers exercised their discretion to perpetually pay women less than men, but the court refused to hear the argument. Even justice Ruth Bader Ginsburg, who had argued sex discrimination cases before coming to the court, determined that the strategy used in the case was faulty.

In the faltering economy of the recession that arrived after late 2008, Wal-Mart continued to draw customers who could no longer afford to shop at higher-priced stores. According to critics, the company's profits are often amassed to the detriment of their employees, who make an average of $8 an hour. Many of them are forced to depend on government assistance for food and health care. The United Food and Commercial Workers union has established the Organization United for Respect at Wal-Mart (OUR Walmart) to lobby the retail giant for better wages and working conditions. By early 2012 thousands of employees in thirty states had joined the organization.

Robert Kuhlken

SEE ALSO: *Consumerism; Department Stores; Dime Stores/Woolworth's; Kmart; Malls.*

BIBLIOGRAPHY

Brunn, Stanley D., ed. *Wal-Mart World: The World's Biggest Corporation in the Global Economy.* New York: Routledge, 2006.

Featherstone, Liza. *Selling Women Short: The Landmark Battle for Worker's Rights at Wal-Mart.* New York: Basic Books, 2004.

Fishman, Charles. *The Wal-Mart Effect: How the World's Most Powerful Company Really Works—And How It's Transforming the American Economy.* New York: Penguin Press, 2006.

McInerney, Francis, and Sean White. *The Total Quality Corporation: How 10 Major Companies Turned Quality and Environmental Challenges to Competitive Advantage in the 1990s.* New York: Truman Talley Books, 1995.

Moreton, Bethany. *To Serve God and Wal-Mart: The Making of Christian Free Enterprise.* Cambridge, MA: Harvard University Press, 2009.

Ortega, Bob. *In Sam We Trust: The Untold Story of Sam Walton, and How Wal-Mart Is Devouring America.* New York: Times Business, 1998.

Schneider, Mary Jo. "The Wal-Mart Annual Meeting: From Small-Town America to a Global Corporate Culture." *Human Organization* 57, no. 3 (1998): 292–299.

Trimble, Vance H. *Sam Walton: The Inside Story of America's Richest Man.* New York: Dutton, 1990.

Vance, Sandra Stringer, and Roy Vernon Scott. *Wal-Mart: A History of Sam Walton's Retail Phenomenon.* New York: Twayne, 1994.

Woodman, Spencer. "Labor Takes Aim at Walmart—Again." *Nation*, January 23, 2012.

Walters, Barbara *(1931–)*

About her career as a television news journalist and interviewer, first lady of the news Barbara Walters has said, "I was the kind nobody thought could make it. I had a funny Boston accent. I couldn't pronounce my Rs. I wasn't a beauty." Walters did make it, even in the often superficial, looks-obsessed world of network television. Partially because of the feminist movement of the early 1970s, and partially because of her drive and versatility, Walters not only made a place for herself in television news, but she also became one of the most powerful women in the medium. Through her disarmingly personal approach to interviewing both heads of state and celebrities, she also changed the way the news was presented on television.

DAUGHTER OF A NIGHTCLUB OWNER

Barbara Walters was born, however unwillingly, into show business. Her father, Lou, was a nightclub owner who ran the Latin Quarter, a chain of popular clubs in New York, Boston, and Florida. Though celebrities were a part of her everyday life growing up, the girl who was to become a nightly visitor in the homes of millions of Americans wanted nothing more than to be normal. But that was denied her when her father suddenly went bankrupt and suffered a heart attack. In her yearbook from Sarah Lawrence College, Walters is pictured in a cartoon as an ostrich with its head stuck in the sand, but she was forced to face the world early.

Barbara Walters. *Barbara Walters has been a fixture of television news as a reporter, anchor, and host for more than fifty years.* CINDY ORD/CONTRIBUTOR/GETTY IMAGES ENTERTAINMENT/GETTY IMAGES.

To help her parents and developmentally disabled sister out of their financial troubles, she went to work, first as a secretary, then as a writer on such television shows as *Jack Paar* and *The Dick Van Dyke Show*. In 1961 she got a job as a writer and researcher for the *Today* show, and in 1964 she moved in front of the camera when she was promoted to "Today Girl," a title reflecting the sexist atmosphere prevailing in television at the time. But sexism notwithstanding, Walters was on her way to being a serious television journalist. In 1972 when President Richard Nixon changed U.S. policy and paid an official visit to the People's Republic of China for the first time since their revolution, Walters was the only woman to cover the trip.

She continued to make history and created a buzz of controversy in 1976 when ABC signed her to a five-year contract for $1 million per year. She was given the job of coanchor on the nightly news, sitting at the desk with longtime television news broadcaster Harry Reasoner. The industry and the country were shocked at the idea of a woman receiving so much money—twice the salary of venerable CBS news legend Walter Cronkite. When Walters went to work as the first woman to anchor the evening news, she encountered considerable ridicule, dismissive attitudes, and outright hostility. Reasoner himself was not happy to be working with her and let it show. *Time* magazine dubbed Walters the "Most Appalling Argument for Feminism." Even when she proved her journalistic skills by hosting the first joint interview with President Anwar Sadat of Egypt and Prime Minister Menachem Begin of Israel, viewers just did not seem to respond to her. The flagging ABC News ratings did not rise, and Walters was removed from the news desk in 1979 and given a new job—correspondent on the news magazine show *20/20*.

Walters soon rose to cohost *20/20* with Hugh Downs, and the show expanded from Friday nights to air editions on Wednesday and Sunday nights as well. Sunday nights she co-hosted with Diane Sawyer, another pioneering woman television journalist. In an industry that is more likely to capitalize on competition among women for high-visibility positions, the pairing of the two female anchors was unusual and refreshing.

ART OF THE INTERVIEW

Though her credentials as a news journalist are impressive, it is as an interviewer that Walters will be remembered. She has created dozens of "Barbara Walters Specials" and "Most Fascinating People" shows, which have aired at prime audience-grabbing times, such as following the Academy Awards show and on New Year's Eve. In each special she interviews several celebrities and over the years has delved into the personal lives of political figures, timeless icons of entertainment, and flashes in the pan. Her interviews have become such a television standard that it is not clear whether Walters interviews those who have made it or whether one has not really made it until one has been interviewed by Walters.

The interviews are incisive and revealing. Bill Geddie, producer of the Walters specials, says of her, "She has a way that has matured over the years of getting people to say things on the air that they never thought they were going to say." Often opening with the intimate aside, "I have to ask," Walters has elicited surprisingly personal revelations from such public figures as Cuban leader Fidel Castro; Russian President Vladimir Putin; entertainment superstar Cher; and, in one of the highest-rated news shows ever, Monica Lewinsky, center of a 1998 presidential scandal. Walters herself attributes much of her success as an interviewer to her devotion to her disabled sister, Jacqueline. Growing up so close to the difficulties her sister faced gave her an empathy and compassion she was able to use throughout her career.

In 1997 Walters branched out into another television standard—the talk show. Following her introduction "I've always wanted to do a show with women of different generations, backgrounds, and views," *The View* introduced a new format—the multihost talk show. The first cohosts were journalist Meredith Vieira, lawyer Star Jones, comic Joy Behar, and model Debbie Matenopoulos, frequently joined by Walters for the usual talk show fare: a few celebrities, a few writers of self-help books, and some lightweight chat about current news-making events. *The View* was originally advertised by Walters as "Four women, lots of opinions, and me—Barbara Walters." Though one suspects that Walters's separation of herself from the "four women" was not accidental, on *The View* she was looser and more relaxed—called "B. W." by her colleagues and allowing herself to be teased and, occasionally, put on the spot.

The View has remained a staple of the morning lineup for more than fifteen years, with many changes in the panel of hosts—by 2012 only Behar remained of the original cast. Frequent boisterous arguments are a staple of the show, and Walters has occasionally been called on to apologize for her co-hosts' volatile behavior, as in 2010 when Behar and Whoopi Goldberg walked off the set during a heated exchange with conservative Fox News anchor Bill O'Reilly.

DRAWING FIRE FROM CRITICS

Walters's distinctive style has often been parodied with a ruthlessness that indicates what an icon she herself has become. Probably the most famous send-up was performed by the late Gilda Radner on the early *Saturday Night Live* (*SNL*) show. With stiffly flipped hair and exaggerated lisp, Radner's "Baba Wawa" became almost as familiar to viewers as Walters herself. Later *SNL* crews also have parodied Walters's *The View*. Though hurt by the mockery at first, Walters soon learned that it was a measure of her own popularity, and she even invited the *SNL* cast to perform their parody on an April Fool's edition of *The View*.

Whereas satire may be considered a tribute, Walters still has her critics. She has been called aggressive and overbearing, common charges leveled at successful women in male-dominated businesses, and some have questioned her tactics for getting interviews. Many have criticized her for confusing news and entertainment. A standing joke in the industry revolves around her *touchy-feely* interviewing style, falsely attributing to her the question "If you were a tree, what kind of tree would you be?" In 1981, during an interview with actress Katharine Hepburn, Hepburn herself stated that at that point in her life she felt like a tree. Following her thought, Walters asked, "What kind of tree are you?" Hepburn responded that she felt like an oak, and the question moved forever into the archive of jokes about Walters.

In the early 2000s Walters began to slow the pace of her busy career. She left her position as coanchor on *20/20* in 2004, though she continued to appear regularly as a contributor. In 2010 she announced her last Oscar-night *Barbara Walters Special*. Reflecting on her life and career, she wrote her memoir, *Audition*, published in 2008. The book, like her approach to news broadcasting, is a combination of personal revelation, analysis, and gossip, both about herself and about the many celebrities she has known, from heads of state to media stars.

Walters will be remembered for many firsts and onlys. Her critics have blamed her for bringing too much entertainment into the news, but, for better or worse, she has been pivotal in creating the face of television news at the turn of the twenty-first century, a blend of fact, entertainment, and personality. There is no doubt that every woman in television news owes a debt to the girl whose college yearbook pictured her as an ostrich but who could not keep her head in the sand.

Tina Gianoulis

SEE ALSO: *Cronkite, Walter; Daytime Talk Shows; Downs, Hugh; Goldberg, Whoopi; O'Donnell, Rosie; Paar, Jack; Radner, Gilda; Television;* Today; 20/20; *Van Dyke, Dick;* The View.

BIBLIOGRAPHY

Buck, Joan Juliet. "A Good Run." *Vogue*, March 2008, 578.

Fox, Mary Virginia. *Barbara Walters: The News Her Way.* Minneapolis, MN: Dillon Press, 1980.

Lemann, Nicholas. "I Have to Ask." *New Yorker*, May 12, 2008, 112.

Malone, Mary. *Barbara Walters: TV Superstar.* Hillside, NJ: Enslow Publishers, 1990.

Oppenheimer, Jerry. *Barbara Walters, An Unauthorized Biography.* New York: St. Martin's Press, 1990.

Remstein, Henna. *Barbara Walters.* Philadelphia: Chelsea House, 1999.

Walters, Barbara. *Audition: A Memoir.* New York: Knopf, 2008.

Walton, Bill *(1952–)*

Despite an injury-plagued career, Bill Walton at his brief peak was compared to some of the greatest centers in National Basketball Association (NBA) history. In addition to his on-court contributions—which include leading the Portland Trail Blazers to an NBA championship in 1977 and serving as a key reserve during the Boston Celtics' 1986 championship season—Walton's outspoken political views and colorful personal life have kept him in the spotlight.

Walton began his career playing for the University of California at Los Angeles (UCLA) in the early 1970s, where he won three consecutive College Player of the Year Awards. In the 1973 National Collegiate Athletic Association (NCAA) championship game against Memphis State, Walton hit an unbelievable twenty-one out of twenty-two shots. During Walton's college career UCLA won eighty-six of ninety games and two national championships, one in 1972 and another in 1973. He holds the record for highest career field goal percentage in NCAA tournament play, having hit almost 69 percent of the shots he attempted from 1972 to 1974.

While his play on the court was outstanding during his college career, Walton also began to attract attention for his political views at UCLA. He was arrested during his junior year at an anti–Vietnam War rally, and he issued a public statement criticizing President Richard Nixon and the Federal Bureau of Investigation. Walton was also an avid fan of the rock group the Grateful Dead, frequently attending their concerts.

Although Walton's long history of injuries had already reared its head during his high school and college careers—he suffered a broken ankle and leg and underwent knee surgery while playing at Helix High School in La Mesa, California—he was nonetheless the first player chosen in the 1974 NBA draft by the Portland Trail Blazers. While he played impressively during his first two seasons, injuries limited him to approximately half of the possible games he could have played in during that time.

It was during the 1976–1977 season, however, that Walton really came into his own, scoring nearly nineteen points per game and leading the league in rebounding and blocked shots. The Trail Blazers reached the NBA Finals against Philadelphia that season but lost the first two games of the best-of-seven series. Largely due to Walton's spectacular play, however, the Blazers won the next four games, capturing the NBA championship in six games. It was only the second time in NBA history a team overcame a two-games-to-none deficit in the finals to win the title. Walton was named the Most Valuable Player (MVP) of the series, setting NBA Finals single-game records for defensive rebounds and blocked shots.

The following season, 1977–1978, Walton played even more impressively, earning the league's MVP Award as the Blazers won fifty of their first sixty games. Injuries, however, kept him out of the final twenty-four regular season games. Walton attempted to come back in the playoffs, but it was discovered that the navicular bone in his left foot was broken. Without him, the Blazers lost in the playoffs to the Seattle Supersonics.

Walton was traded to the San Diego Clippers following the 1978–1979 season, after an extremely acrimonious parting with the Trail Blazers, which he accused of providing poor medical advice. He missed most of his first two seasons with the Clippers, drawing criticism from his teammates and fans, who felt the team had erred in signing Walton to a lucrative long-term contract. Although his health improved and he was able to play fairly extensively in the 1983–1984 and 1984–1985 seasons, the Clippers never rose above mediocrity, and Walton never had the chance to repeat his playoff successes with Portland.

After his contract with the Clippers ran out, Walton contacted several of the league's top teams, seeking to find out if they needed a reserve center. Fortunately for him, the Boston Celtics, a championship contender, needed a big man of Walton's caliber to provide them with greater depth. He joined the team for the 1985–1986 season. The pickup paid incredible dividends for the Celtics, as Walton played in all but two of the team's eight-two regular season games and every playoff game. While his numbers were modest, he made a major contribution to the team's 67–15 record, as he provided scoring, rebounding, passing, defense, and high energy during his time on the court. Walton received the league's Sixth Man Award, given to the top reserve player in the league. The Celtics—with Walton backing up frontcourt legends Kevin McHale and Robert Parish—breezed through the playoffs that season, defeating the Houston Rockets in six games. The following season, however, injuries limited him to only ten games, after which he retired.

Walton became a television announcer in 1991 for NBC and has served as an analyst for basketball, volleyball, and other sports. He also worked as an announcer for the Los Angeles Clippers and ESPN. Walton retired from broadcasting in 2009 because of back problems. He was named to the Naismith Memorial Basketball Hall of Fame in 1993. In 1996 he was named one of the fifty greatest players in NBA history. Walton, who studied law at Stanford University during his breaks from basketball, lives with his wife in San Diego, California. His son

Luke was drafted by the Los Angeles Lakers in 2003 and was traded to the Cleveland Cavaliers in 2011.

Jason George

SEE ALSO: *Abdul-Jabbar, Kareem; Basketball; Bird, Larry; The Boston Celtics; The Grateful Dead; National Basketball Association (NBA); National Collegiate Athletic Association (NCAA); Vietnam; Wooden, John.*

BIBLIOGRAPHY

Halberstam, David. *The Breaks of the Game.* New York: Alfred A. Knopf, 1981.

Walton, Bill, and Gene Wojciechowski. *Nothing but Net: Just Give Me the Ball and Get out of the Way.* New York: Hyperion, 1995.

The Waltons

From 1972 to 1981 the Depression era returned to America through the popular television series *The Waltons.* For nearly a decade American viewers embraced *The Waltons* into popular culture as a symbol of past family values that were largely absent in American television programs.

Earl Hamner Jr., creator of *The Waltons*, grew up an aspiring writer in the Blue Ridge Mountains of Schuyler, Virginia. His early novel *The Homecoming* (1970) was a literary recollection of his own Depression-era childhood, of which he speaks fondly: "We were in a depression, but we weren't depressed. . . . We were poor, but nobody ever bothered to tell us that. To a skinny, awkward, red headed kid who secretly yearned to be a writer . . . each of those days seemed filled with wonder." In 1970 Lorimar Productions approached Hamner to create a television special based on *The Homecoming*, and hence, the Walton family made its television debut. Against the advice of reviewers and network executives who had little faith in the appeal of family programming, CBS took a chance and placed *The Waltons* in a Thursday night prime-time slot. To the surprise of many, the series not only held its own, but it also maintained a number eight position in the ratings for years to follow.

For viewers concerned with the growing number of television shows whose content often included violence or sexually oriented themes, the Walton family offered a refreshing option. Representative of Hamner's own family, members of the large Walton clan were richly endowed with a common thread of love, pride, and responsibility, yet each uniquely contributed to the depiction of rural America from the Depression era to World War II. This ideal family was headed by proud patriarch and millwright John Sr. (Ralph Waite); his wife, Olivia, a loving and devout Christian mother (Michael Learned); and the prolific writer and boy-next-door, John-Boy (Richard Thomas). There was Mary-Ellen, the headstrong nurse (Judy Norton); the musically talented Jason (Jon Walmsley); the lovely Erin (Mary McDonough); and Ben, the budding entrepreneur (Eric Scott). Along with these eight were aspiring aviator Jim-Bob (David W. Harper); Elizabeth (Kami Cotler), the youngest Walton; and the grandparents—Grandpa Zeb, the beloved woodsman (Will Geer), and tenacious Grandma Esther (Ellen Corby). Added to this numerous collection of distinctive individuals was a large cast of vibrantly colorful and richly developed supporting characters.

While critics of *The Waltons* accused the show of being sugarcoated and unrealistic, a glance at some of the thematic content might prove otherwise. Among the issues and events that were dealt with in the series were rural poverty; bigotry; the *Hindenburg* disaster; the bombing of Pearl Harbor; the death of a family member; draft evasion; and, of course, the human cost of war. Reflecting on this popular misconception, Thomas in a 1995 interview said, "One of the common errors in describing the show is that it was all so nice, everyone was nice. It's just not true. Everyone in the show could be foolish, everyone was hotheaded. John-Boy was always confronting people. . . . It was not this very sweet little family."

The family's unifying force, however, and perhaps the focal point of the show's broad demographic appeal, was that family members always maintained a high level of respect for one other, finding genuine joy in living while nevertheless working out the internal and external conflicts that defined their daily lives on Walton's Mountain. Perhaps, too, *The Waltons* fulfilled a desire in post-1960s America to return to a simpler time when families still ate supper together at the kitchen table; the general store was the social and economic hub of a community; and, at the end of a hard but honest day, familiar voices in the darkness of a white clapboard farmhouse could be heard to say, "Good night, John-Boy." The series spawned six reunion movies during the 1980s and 1990s, and in the 2010s reruns of the original program were still being shown on cable stations.

Nadine-Rae Leavell

SEE ALSO: *The Great Depression; Television; World War II.*

BIBLIOGRAPHY

Hamner, Earl, Jr. *The Homecoming.* New York: Random House, 1970.

Keets, Heather. "Good Night, Waltons." *Entertainment Weekly.* August 20, 1993.

Person, James E., Jr. *Earl Hamner: From Walton's Mountain to Tomorrow.* Nashville, TN: Cumberland House Publishing, 2005.

War Bonds

War bonds are a method of financing war that reduces demand for goods and services by taking money out of circulation through investment in the bonds. This provides funds to underwrite a war. Modern warfare is an expensive business and must be financed carefully; a government risks triggering inflation by increasing demand for goods. One method of avoiding this outcome is to raise taxes to finance the war, but such methods risk making a war unpopular. Through the more popular method of selling war bonds, citizens in effect invest in the war effort of their government just as they might invest in stocks. Selling war bonds lessens the need for tax increases.

During World War I the U.S. government raised $5 billion through the sale of Liberty Bonds. Mass rallies to sell the bonds featured celebrities such as Douglas Fairbanks Sr. Nonetheless, when most Americans talk about war bonds, they are generally referring to the bonds sold during World War II. In part this is because the efforts of World War I involved a good deal of compulsion rather than persuasion. During that war schoolchildren were badgered, courts imposed illegal fines on those not

War Bonds. A poster by N. C. Wyeth urged Americans to buy war bonds during World War I. BUY-ENLARGE/CONTRIBUTOR/ARCHIVE PHOTOS/GETTY IMAGES.

owning bonds, and the houses of nonpurchasers were painted yellow. World War II bonds are probably better remembered simply because, by then, mass media had expanded considerably and the scale of the media campaign was greater.

War bonds were but one of the means at the government's disposal to regulate the wartime economy. During World War II the cost of living in the United States increased significantly. Most of this increase occurred before 1943, when the government put strict price controls in place through the Office of Price Administration. The Revenue Act of 1942 established the modern American tax structure, which saw the tax base increase fourfold and introduced tax withholding. Through these measures, the government raised about 50 percent of its costs during the war. This was a considerable accomplishment compared with the 30 percent raised during World War I and 23 percent during the Civil War. During World War II war bonds raised approximately $150 billion, or a quarter of the government's costs.

According to historian John Blum, Secretary of the Treasury Henry Morgenthau said he wanted "to use bonds to sell the war, rather than vice versa." Morgenthau believed that there were quicker and easier ways for the government to raise money than through bond issues but that it would increase people's stake in the war effort if they bought bonds. Many businesses promoted war bond purchases. Entertainment industry figures lent their celebrity to bond drives. Singer Kate Smith sold $39 million worth of bonds in a radio session on September 21, 1943. Hollywood stars went on bond-selling tours, and pin-up girl Betty Grable auctioned off her stockings. Comic-book publishers DC and Marvel carried advertisements and columns urging their readers to tell their parents to buy bonds and purchase ten-cent defense stamps themselves. Covers of Batman and Superman comics appealed to readers to buy war bonds to "Keep Those Bullets Flying."

War Bonds were a relatively effective measure in reducing inflation and financing the war. Moreover they served as a means of popularizing the war by giving noncombatants a direct stake in its outcome. As sound fiscal policy, the measure of their worth can be judged by the inflationary pressures unleashed by President Lyndon Johnson's decision to finance the Vietnam War, which cost $150 billion, by printing more money rather than raising taxes or selling bonds.

Ian Gordon

SEE ALSO: *DC Comics; Fairbanks, Douglas, Sr.; Grable, Betty; Marvel Comics; Smith, Kate; World War I; World War II; Wyeth, N. C..*

BIBLIOGRAPHY

Blum, John Morton. *V Was for Victory: Politics and American Culture during World War II.* New York: Harcourt Brace Jovanovich, 1976.

Jones, John Bush. *All-Out for Victory!: Magazine Advertising and the World War II Home Front.* Waltham, MA: Brandeis University Press, 2009.

Perrett, Geoffrey. *Days of Sadness, Years of Triumph: The American People, 1939–1945.* Madison: University of Wisconsin Press, 1985.

Polenberg, Richard. *War and Society: The United States, 1941–1945.* Philadelphia: J. B. Lippincott, 1972.

War in Afghanistan

On the morning of September 11, 2001, al-Qaeda terrorists hijacked four jetliners with the intention of hitting American seats of power. American Airlines flight 11 crashed into the North Tower of New York's World Trade Center at 8:46 a.m. Sixteen minutes later United Airlines flight 175 bombed the South Tower. At 9:37 American Airlines flight 77 crashed into the Pentagon in Washington, D.C. The fourth plane, United Airlines flight 93, crashed into the ground in Shanksville, Pennsylvania, brought down by passengers who had taken over the plane. At the end of the day, nearly 3,000 people were dead as a result of the combined attacks, which soon came to be known as "9/11." Two days previously, al-Qaeda operatives disguised as journalists had assassinated Ahmad Shah Massoud, the commander of Northern Alliance forces in Afghanistan. Outraged Americans subsequently learned that al-Qaeda terrorists had been working closely with Taliban forces in Afghanistan to bring down Western nations, particularly the United States.

Terrorism was rampant in the twentieth century. In 1993 the World Trade Center had been the site of an earlier terrorist attack in which six people were killed and 1,042 wounded. In 1998 al-Qaeda had bombed American embassies in Kenya and Tanzania. The United States formally requested that the Taliban surrender al-Qaeda leader Osama bin Laden. The request was denied, as was a post-9/11 request. In response, the United States, with the full cooperation of its allies and the United Nations Security Council, went to war with Afghanistan as part of an international war on terror. On May 1, 2011, a small team of Joint Special Operations Command forces working with the Central Intelligence Agency (CIA) stormed a compound in Abbottabad, Pakistan, and killed bin Laden, achieving what many Americans felt was some measure of justice for the victims of 9/11 and their families and for the American people as a whole.

AFGHANISTAN

Located in south-central Asia and bordered in part by Iran and Pakistan, which have long histories of international terrorism, Afghanistan is slightly smaller than Texas. A brief period of democracy in the 1970s was ended by a coup and a communist countercoup that led to decades of civil war. In 1996 the Taliban, a Pakistani-sponsored movement, wrested control of the Afghan government. Among the population of 30,419,928, the Pashtun (42 percent) and the Tajik (27%) are the largest ethnic groups. Eighty percent of the population is Sunni Muslim, and the remainder is mostly Shia Muslim. The Afghan people are vulnerable to a variety of physical and political influences. The area is subject to earthquakes, floods, and droughts. Living conditions are among the poorest in the world, and Afghans have a per capita income of only $1,000 per year and an unemployment rate of 35 percent. Only 12.13 percent of the land is arable, but 78.6 percent of the workforce is involved in subsistence farming and herding. It is estimated that Afghanistan has unexploited mineral assets of between $1 trillion and $3 trillion.

Afghanistan leads the world in infant mortality (121.63 deaths per 1,000 live births) and maternal mortality (1,400 per 100,000). Women give birth to an average of 5.64 children. Almost one-third of all children under the age of five are underweight. Sixty-one percent of rural Afghans and 22 percent of urban residents lack access to safe drinking water, and 70 percent of rural and 40 percent of urban inhabitants have no sustained access to improved sanitation. Thus, incidences of diseases such as hepatitis A, typhoid fever, malaria, and rabies are high. Females are largely uneducated, attending school for an average of seven years, as compared to eleven years for males. Less than 13 percent of females are literate, but 43.1 percent of males are able to read and write.

THE WAR

On October 7, 2001, less than a month after the 9/11 attacks, the United States and Great Britain conducted the first bombing of Taliban strongholds in Iraq. Anti-Taliban forces consisted of Special Operations Forces, CIA operatives, American air power, Afghanistan's Northern Alliance, and friendly Pakistani tribes. By November 13, Taliban fighters had abandoned Kabul, and local officials agreed to establish an interim government. By January 2002 the North Atlantic Treaty Organization (NATO)–

led International Security Assisted Force had arrived in Afghanistan. Although combined forces succeeded in chasing both al-Qaeda and the Taliban out of Afghanistan, bin Laden and Mullah Omar both escaped, along with key operatives. The United Nations led the effort to stabilize the Afghan government. Following the establishment of a new constitution, democratic elections were held in 2004 (president) and 2005 (national legislature). Legislators consisted chiefly of local warlords and strongmen.

Even though Operation Enduring Freedom was considered successful, Afghanistan continued to be the scene of organized Taliban resistance. By 2005 American forces were concentrated in Iraq, and Iran had joined its longtime rival in fighting their common enemy, the United States. Thus, the Taliban was aided and abetted by Iran.

As the war in Iraq subsided in 2008, American forces again turned their attention to Afghanistan. In September President George W. Bush dispatched 4,500 more American troops to the country. That month proved to be the most violent since 2001, with at least 120 American and 104 NATO troops killed. By early 2009 Barack Obama, who had succeeded Bush as president, announced that he would not support a war without end in Afghanistan and began accelerating existing efforts to facilitate the eventual conclusion of the conflict. Obama's deployment included 10,000 marines under orders to eradicate the Taliban. Other NATO countries beefed up their forces by 17,000 troops. October turned out to be an extremely deadly month, with fifty-eight Americans killed, bringing the war's total to 849.

International leaders agreed that Afghanistan needed to be able to stand on its own and established 2014 as a target for withdrawal of international troops. Hamid Karzai was reelected president in 2009, but the election was marred by widespread Taliban attacks and accusations of voter fraud. American troops in Afghanistan reached 103,700 by December, but Obama announced that he would begin withdrawing them in 2011. He began a staged withdrawal in December 2011 and announced plans for the withdrawal of another 23,000 troops by the end of the summer of 2012. Obama faced reelection in November 2012, making the war's outcome heavily dependent on American political events.

CULTURAL IMPACTS

The protracted wars in Afghanistan and Iraq have taken enormous tolls, and military personnel have taken the brunt of the impact. In addition to those who died on foreign soil and those who returned with physical or psychological injuries, a new generation of Americans, some observers claim, has been imbued with a disregard for the sanctity and inherent dignity of all human life. That claim appeared to be amply justified on March 11, 2012, when thirty-eight-year-old Sergeant Robert Bales allegedly opened fire on sixteen sleeping Afghan civilians. Bales was serving his fourth tour of duty in the area. Old friends of Bales came forward to identify him as a considerate and gentle soul, but investigators learned that he had a previous arrest record. Blame for the attacks was leveled at the leadership of Joint Base Lewis-McChord in Washington State, where Bales was stationed. Reports surfaced that a base psychiatric team frequently overrode diagnoses of post-traumatic stress disorder and returned troubled soldiers to active duty.

Evidence that the war was having a far-reaching impact accompanied the knowledge that so-called war porn was becoming widespread. Videos of graphic violence became readily available on websites such as GotWarPorn.com and YouTube. The first videos had been released by military officials, but soldiers began taking their own videos, which became increasingly sophisticated as clips were spliced together and music added. Like regular porn, war porn is rated according to levels of violence. The onset of war porn is considered to be 2003, when graphic images of Iraqi prisoners being tortured and abused at Abu Ghraib Prison near Baghdad were first released. As violence accelerated in both Afghanistan and Iraq, war porn became bloodier, depicting headless corpses and unattached body parts. In Polk County, Florida, Christopher Wilson was charged with 300 misdemeanors and one felony count associated with trading regular porn with soldiers in exchange for war porn that he then published on his website. The website was shut down, but Wilson was not incarcerated.

As the wars in Afghanistan and Iraq dragged on, President Bush's approval ratings dropped. Bush and his advisers blamed the media for overplaying bad news from the war zones. A 2010 study by Sean Aday, who analyzed war reporting by NBC and Fox News, revealed that both networks had actually underplayed the bad news. Fox, which is owned by media mogul Rupert Murdoch, was predictably more supportive of the Bush administration than was NBC. A number of studies have found that Afghanistan virtually disappeared from the news once the United States expanded the war on terror to Iraq. Cynthia Tucker noted in the *Atlanta Journal-Constitution* on April 27, 2003, that Bush had not allotted any money in his budget to fulfill his promise to allocate $3.3 billion for restoring stability to Afghanistan.

Network commentators also noted the lack of attention. On CBS, Dan Rather labeled the Afghanistan War "all but forgotten," and Susan McGinnis reminded her morning audience that there was another war going on outside Iraq. In January 2002 nightly newscasts had devoted 106 minutes to the war in Afghanistan. A year later coverage had dropped to only eleven minutes. By March it had declined to sixty seconds.

While there has been an influx of memoirs and journalist accounts of the wars in Afghanistan and Iraq, there has been a dearth of fiction written about either war, even though the war in Afghanistan has lasted longer than World War I and World War II put together. While some observers insist that it takes distance from wars before definitive fiction begins to appear, Matt Gallagher of the *Atlantic* points out that in 1920, shortly after the end of World War I, John Dos Passos published *Three Soldiers*; Norman Mailer published *The Naked and the Dead* only three years after World War II ended in 1945; and Ronald Glasser published *365 Days* (1971) while the United States was still involved in Vietnam.

Despite the lack of fiction, there have been movies that depict the war in Afghanistan in various guises. *Taxi to the Dark Side* (2007) presents an unflinching examination of the Bush administration's policy on torture as told through the eyes of a taxi driver who is mistakenly arrested and then beaten to death by American soldiers in Afghanistan. *Restrepo* (2010), which was codirected by American author Sebastian Junger (*The Perfect Storm*) and British photographer Tim Hetherington, follows the lives of American soldiers stationed in a remote area of Afghanistan. The film won the Grand Jury Prize as the best documentary at the Sundance Festival. Most recent war films have dealt with the war in Iraq rather than the one in Afghanistan.

Elizabeth Rholetter Purdy

SEE ALSO: *Gulf Wars; 9/11; Obama, Barack; Vietnam; War Movies; World War I; World War II.*

BIBLIOGRAPHY

Aday, Sean. "Chasing the Bad News: An Analysis of 2005 Iraq and Afghanistan War Coverage on NBC and Fox News Channel." *Journal of Communication* 60, no. 1 (2010).

Caldwell, Dan. *Vortex of Conflict: U.S. Policy toward Afghanistan.* Stanford, CA: Stanford Security Studies, 2011.

Central Intelligence Agency. "Afghanistan." *World Factbook.* Accessed March 2012. Available from https://www.cia.gov/library/publications/the-world-factbook/geos/af.html

Collins, Joseph J. *Understanding War in Afghanistan.* Washington, DC: National Defense University, 2011.

Cordesman, Anthony H. *The Lessons of Afghanistan: War Fighting, Intelligence, and Force Transformations.* Washington, DC: CSIS Press, 2002.

Cordesman, Anthony H. *The War after the War: Strategic Lessons of Iraq and Afghanistan.* Washington, DC: CSIS Press, 2004.

Gallagher, Matthew. "Where's the Great Novel about the War on Terror?" *Atlantic,* June 14, 2011.

Hoskins, Andrew. *Televising War: From Vietnam to Iraq.* New York: Continuum, 2004.

Kreps, Sarah E. *Coalitions of Convenience: United States Military Intervention after the Cold War.* New York: Oxford University Press, 2011.

Lebovic, James H. *The Limits of U.S. Military Capability: Lessons from Vietnam and Iraq.* Baltimore, MD: Johns Hopkins University Press, 2010.

Nacos, Brigitte L.; Yaeli Block-Elkon; and Robert Y. Shapiro. *Selling Fear: Counterterrorism, the Media, and Public Opinion.* Chicago: University of Chicago Press, 2011.

Ramirez, Jessica. "Carnage.com." *Newsweek,* May 10, 2010.

Robertson, Lori. "Whatever Happened to Afghanistan?" *American Journalism Review* 25, no. 5 (2003).

Thussu, Daya Kishan, and Des Freedman, eds. *War and the Media: Reporting Conflict 24/7.* Thousand Oaks, CA: Sage, 2003.

Tyler, Patrick. *A World of Trouble: The White House and the Middle East—From the Cold War to the War on Terror.* New York: Farrar, Straus & Giroux, 2009.

Williams, Brian Glyn. *Afghanistan Declassified: A Guide to America's Longest War.* Philadelphia: University of Pennsylvania Press, 2012.

War in Iraq

SEE: *Gulf Wars.*

War Movies

As long as films have been made, war movies have been a significant genre, with thousands of documentaries, propaganda films, comedies, satires, or dramas reminding moviegoers of the deep human emotion and violence of the combat experience. Throughout the twentieth century and into the twenty-first, war movies both reflected and manipulated changing popular attitudes toward war. Some of the films, especially those created during wartime, were created as propaganda, elevating to an extreme the patriotism and heroism of soldiers and the glory attained in battle. Still others take on the subject of war only to criticize it, usually via a graphic depiction of the cost of war in terms of human lives.

EARLY DAYS

War has interested filmmakers from the first days of cinematic technology. J. Stuart Blackton's 1898 film *Tearing Down the Spanish Flag* is considered not only the first fictional U.S. war movie but also the first propaganda film. Set on an anonymous rooftop in Cuba during the Spanish-American War, this short film depicts a uniformed American soldier (played by Blackton himself) removing the Spanish flag and replacing it with the U.S. flag. Then the film cuts to a title card stating, "Remember the *Maine.*" Blackton's film was quickly followed by reenactments of the sinking of the *Maine* and other battles of the Spanish-American War. Even though the film is only a few minutes long, it managed to capture the contemporary popular imagination and established the foundation for war movies in the twentieth century.

WORLD WAR I: ROMANTICIZED PROPAGANDA

Most U.S. films made during World War I consisted of propaganda films either encouraging or, after 1917, supporting U.S. involvement in the European conflict. Most of these films romanticized the war, showing enlistment as a glorious, patriotic duty and emphasizing the power and importance of male bonding. Early World War I films often dealt with U.S. citizens volunteering for the French, British, or Canadian armies. Later films showed U.S. troops as the deciding factor in the European victory.

D. W. Griffith directed many of the key World War I propaganda films. Film historians credit Griffith with inventing many modern film techniques, and his impact on the history of the war movie is even more direct. For example, in his 1915 Civil War epic *The Birth of a Nation,* Griffith used cross-cutting techniques within battle scenes to shift from large-scale images of fighting to more intimate moments focusing on the film's main characters. Such techniques allowed future filmmakers to develop individual characters within a larger historical context of the war. Griffith's key World War I film was *Hearts of the World* (1918), shot partially under war conditions in France. In this polemical prowar film, Erich von Stroheim was cast as an evil and lustful German officer (a role he would repeat in numerous later films) who attempts to rape and brutally beat Marie (Lillian Gish). The film's anti-German sentiment is so strong that Gish's boyfriend is willing to kill her in order to save her from such a violation at the hands of the enemy. This depiction of Germans as unrepentantly evil would influence not only later World War I films but World War II films as well.

Few war movies appeared in the years immediately following the 1918 armistice. The propaganda of the wartime films was no longer necessary, and the American public seemed inclined to focus on domestic affairs. Three movies in the 1920s, however, brought about a resurgence of interest in World War I: *The Big Parade, What Price Glory?,* and *Wings.*

ADVERSARIES, AIR DRAMAS, AND ANTIWAR SENTIMENTS

The Big Parade (King Vidor, 1925) is credited with reviving the war film genre as well as being the first to realistically depict the war experiences of American soldiers. The plot, which follows a group of men from their enlistment through the conflict, would become standard in later World War II films.

Raoul Walsh's 1926 comedy-drama *What Price Glory?*, based on the Laurence Stallings and Maxwell Anderson stage play, follows two marines, Captain Flagg and Sergeant Quirt, as they engage in their own personal rivalry over the same woman while fighting in France. Though the film version does temper the antiwar sentiment of the original play, the film's comedy is sharply contrasted with its graphic and shocking depictions of battle scenes. Later war movies would often capitalize on what Jeanine Basinger in *The World War II Combat Film* calls the "Quirt-Flagg relationship" by focusing on two adversarial characters serving in the same platoon.

Wings (William Wellman, 1927), which won the first Academy Award for Best Picture, introduced a new subgenre of war films: the air drama. Director Wellman used his war experiences as a pilot for the Lafayette Flying Corps and the Army Air Service to create realistic aerial scenes that were accomplished by mounting cameras on the fighting planes and by using camera operators in other aircraft, instead of using rear projection effects. The realism and excitement of these scenes would be surpassed later in *Hell's Angels* (Howard Hughes, 1930), a film that cost nearly $4 million and that took longer than three years to make what turned out to be some of the most spectacular flying scenes ever filmed.

Unlike *The Big Parade*, these latter two films do not make a profound statement about the war, and their popularity was based primarily on sheer spectacle and excitement. John Monk Saunders, a veteran pilot and the original writer of *Wings*, would later write such air dramas as *Ace of Aces* (J. Walter Ruben, 1933), *The Dawn Patrol* (Howard Hawks, 1930; remade by Edmund Goulding, 1938), and *The Eagle and the Hawk* (Stuart Walker, 1933). These air dramas openly criticized the senseless waste of the war and starkly represented the mental strain suffered by pilots, while still remaining true to the adventurous nature of the subgenre.

The strongest antiwar statement made following World War I came in Lewis Milestone's 1930 adaptation of Erich Maria Remarque's novel *All Quiet on the Western Front*. This film begins with young German men enthusiastically volunteering to fight for their country. They quickly learn, however, that this war has nothing to do with honor and glory, and the mental breakdown and violent deaths of these soldiers are depicted in graphic detail. The realism of the battle scenes, including the image of two disembodied hands clutching a barbed wire, accounts for the film's continued status as one of the great war movies of the twentieth century. The final shot of Paul Bäumer (played by Lew Ayres), dying as he reaches for a butterfly just outside his trench, remains one of the most haunting and effective images in any war film. Even after World War II, the Great War served as the setting for profound antiwar commentary, including Stanley Kubrick's *Paths of Glory* (1957) and Dalton Trumbo's *Johnny Got His Gun* (1971).

WORLD WAR II: AMERICAN HEROISM

As America entered World War II, however, Hollywood needed to reverse this antiwar sentiment by creating films that demonstrated American heroism and success in the earlier war. In *Sergeant York* (Hawks, 1941), actor Gary Cooper's Alvin York, who went from devout pacifist to America's greatest war hero, provides a counterimage to the one created in such films as *All Quiet on the Western Front. Sergeant York* also showed the potential for individual heroic achievement and served as significant propaganda for the U.S. war effort.

World War II films generally have a clearly defined sense of good and evil. As in the films made depicting World War I, the enemies were presented not as complex human beings but most often as two-dimensional caricatures, designed to generate hate and loathing in the audience. Most movies created during the war years focused on the adventure and glory of warfare, as well as the strength of both the U.S. military and the American spirit. In addition, the majority of World War II films had a romantic subplot. The female love interests were either sweethearts pining away at the home front; nurses, AWACs, or reporters serving some military duty; or European, usually French, women whom the GIs meet while on leave. Often the movies follow soldiers from enlistment or training to combat. These formulas were sometimes mixed in with several variables, such as military branches or European or Pacific locales, to create a variety of successful films.

Surprisingly, given their underlying message, most of the early World War II combat films made in 1942 and 1943, such as *Wake Island* (John Farrow, 1942) and *Bataan* (Tay Garnett, 1943), focused more on catastrophic American defeats than on the victories. *Wake Island*, the first large-scale combat film of World War II, closely follows a group of soldiers until they are all killed in the ensuing battle. Both movies received the support of the U.S. government, and despite showing terrible defeats, these films mobilized popular support for the war and proved to be useful propaganda tools.

Few figures are more synonymous with the war movie than John Wayne. Just as in his Westerns, Wayne represented the ideal of American masculinity in a persona that exemplified the hard, determined, yet compassionate soldier. Such a persona is evident in such wartime films as *Flying Tigers* (1942), *The Fighting Seabees* (1944), *They Were Expendable* (1945), and *Back to Bataan* (1945) and in postwar films like *Sands of Iwo Jima* (1949), *Flying Leathernecks* (1951), and *In Harm's Way* (1965). These films follow the basic formulas of World War II movies, and Wayne repeated the same basic character in each. Although Wayne was criticized in later years for such repetitive, formulaic performances, he himself became an iconic hero, and his films were tremendous successes and morale boosters.

POST–WORLD WAR II

As World War II came to a close, such movies as *The Story of G.I. Joe* (William Wellman, 1945) and *A Walk in the Sun* (Lewis Milestone, 1945) moved away from the patriotism and heroics of films made in the earlier years of the war and toward a more realistic depiction of American soldiers in battle that emphasized the human cost of war over the glory of victory. Wellman continued to demythologize warfare in the 1949 film *Battleground*, which received an Academy Award nomination for Best Picture. These three films follow similar episodic plots focusing on a group of American soldiers, many of whom are killed through the course of the movie. In the opening of *A Walk in the Sun*, narrator Burgess Meredith (who also stars as famed war correspondent Ernie Pyle in *The Story of G.I. Joe*) describes the ethnic, class, and cultural diversity of his platoon:

> There was Tyne, who never had much urge to travel. Providence, Rhode Island, may not be much as cities go, but it was all he wanted, a one town man; Rivera, Italian American, likes opera and would like a wife and kid, plenty of kids; Friedman, lathe operator and amateur boxing champ, New York City; Windy, minister's son, Canton, Ohio, used to take long walks alone and just think; . . . Sergeant Ward, a farmer who knows his soil, a good farmer; McWilliams, first aid man, slow, Southern, dependable; Archimbault, platoon scout and prophet, talks a lot but he's all right; Porter, Sergeant Porter, . . . he has a lot on his mind; . . . Tranella speaks two languages: Italian and Brooklyn.

This conventional Hollywood platoon became a stereotype in the American war movie with an ensemble cast. But in these early examples, this broad demographic representation was used to emphasize the impact of the war on America as a whole.

Following World War II, Hollywood war films began to examine the complexities of warfare, exposing the fallibility and brutality of military authority by addressing the mental strain inflicted on war's participants and by showing the enemy as complex, human, and sympathetic. Gregory Peck's character, General Frank Savage, in *Twelve O'Clock High* (Henry King, 1949) is shown to be a vulnerable hero suffering a mental breakdown during the war. In *From Here to Eternity* (Fred Zinnemann, 1953), the enemy is not the Axis powers but the bullying, violent, murderous military authorities such as Ernest Borgnine's Fatso. In *The Caine Mutiny* (Edward Dmytryk, 1954), Humphrey Bogart's emotionally unstable Captain Queeg proves to be more of a danger to his men than any enemy is. In *The Bridge on the River Kwai* (David Lean, 1957), the Japanese prison camp commander is portrayed as a man caught between his sense of duty and honor for his country and his sympathy and respect for the prisoners.

This is not to say that the tradition of heroic war movies did not continue. Films such as *To Hell and Back* (Jesse Hibbs, 1955)—the story of Audie Murphy (played by himself), America's most decorated war hero—as well as *The Great Escape* (John Sturges, 1963) and *The Dirty Dozen* (Robert Aldrich, 1967) continued to show the more adventurous and exciting side of World War II. But into the 1960s and 1970s, in films such as *The Longest Day* (Ken Annakin, 1962) and *Patton* (Franklin J. Schaffner, 1970), Hollywood filmmakers increasingly delved into a critical examination of American militarism, reflecting the general disillusion of Americans as the Vietnam conflict escalated.

CONTEMPORARY TAKES ON WORLD WAR II

In 1998 the release of two World War II movies, *Saving Private Ryan* and *The Thin Red Line*, raised to a new level the realistic violence depicted in the war movie. Steven Spielberg's *Saving Private Ryan*, winner of five Academy Awards, follows a fairly standard plot. A small group of soldiers is sent on a mission to find one man lost in France during the Normandy invasion. The first thirty minutes of the movie, showing the mass slaughter that occurred in the opening minutes of the invasion of Omaha Beach, contain what some consider the most graphically violent and disturbing combat scenes presented in a fictional film. Terrence Malick's *The Thin Red Line* is equally violent, but this film about the invasion of Guadalcanal focuses more on the contrast between combat and the introspective moments available to soldiers during the lulls in battle. Both films rely on new developments in special effects and camera technology that allow for even more graphic and realistic depictions of military violence.

Contemporary filmmakers focused on World War II movies continue to choose between the stereotypic propaganda-like stance—such as Michael Bay's 2001 *Pearl Harbor*, which was panned by critics but continued to draw audiences despite its jingoistic clichés and historical gaffes—and taking a more critical, realistic look at war's effects on soldiers, as Clint Eastwood did in his pair of World War II films in 2006: *Flags of Our Fathers* portrays the cost of war on American soldiers, and *Letters from Iwo Jima* does away with the stereotype of the faceless foe, showing audiences that Japanese soldiers were faced with the same senseless brutalities. After criticizing Eastwood's *Flags of Our Fathers* for its lack of African American protagonists, Spike Lee told the story of four African American "Buffalo" soldiers in *Miracle at St. Anna* (2008).

With other, newer wars taking center stage for both filmed propaganda and the more introspective analysis, World War II has also become the setting for more purely fictional explorations in film, in movies such as Quentin Tarantino's *Inglourious Basterds* (2009), an irreverent rewrite of history in which a band of Jewish American soldiers assassinates Adolf Hitler and Joseph Goebbels; and Amit Gupta's *Resistance* (2011), which takes place in a hypothetical Nazi-occupied Britain.

KOREA BECOMES THE BATTLEFIELD

Of the more than fifty films made between 1951 and 1963 about the Korean War, most presented the enemy as one-sided villains, and few moved beyond the standard clichés of the Hollywood World War II films. Two exceptions appeared early in the war. Samuel Fuller's *Fixed Bayonets!* and *The Steel Helmet*, both released in 1951, take a harsh, uncompromising, and realistic look at the stress suffered by soldiers while keeping to the standard plot that follows a diverse platoon through the conflict. The characters in Fuller's films are often plagued with doubts and fears, and they are more concerned with the struggle to survive than with any potential acts of heroism.

Robert Altman's 1970 film *M*A*S*H*—later made into a TV series that ran from 1972 to 1983—tells the story of a Korean War field hospital, yet critics have suggested that its true subtext was the conflict in Vietnam, going on at the time of the film's airing.

AMERICA IN VIETNAM

The controversy surrounding the Vietnam conflict caused Hollywood to shy away from it as a subject for war films while the conflict was ongoing. The only exception is John Wayne's 1968 directorial debut, *The Green Berets*, which he codirected with Ray Kellogg. This film largely consists of Cold War propaganda justifying U.S. presence in Vietnam. Wayne transferred his World War II movie persona to this film, a persona that was clearly the product of another time. While the movie was a box-office success, it stands out as an anomaly in the development of the Vietnam War film, which, in the late 1970s and 1980s, would approach the war much more critically.

The Deer Hunter (Michael Cimino, 1978) and *Apocalypse Now* (Francis Ford Coppola, 1979) were among the first films to criticize the Vietnam War from a combat perspective. Both films contain graphic images of the most horrifying, and often surreal, aspects of the war. The Russian roulette scenes in *The Deer Hunter* show the extremes of mental and physical torture suffered by American prisoners of war, and the scene in *Apocalypse Now* where Colonel Kilgore orders a helicopter raid on a Viet Cong village so his men can surf on a nearby beach illustrates the extreme level of absurdity in this war. The senselessness of the Vietnam War would be addressed later in Stanley Kubrick's *Full Metal Jacket* (1987), a film that ends with a platoon spontaneously singing the *Mickey Mouse Club* theme in unison.

One of the most successful Vietnam War movies was Oliver Stone's 1986 Academy Award winner, *Platoon*. While this film does have a strong antiwar message, it follows a fairly standard war-movie plot, following the experiences of a naive young volunteer (played by Charlie Sheen) as he becomes increasingly disillusioned by the fighting. The movie also follows a clear good-versus-evil binary, but instead of the United States representing good and the Viet Cong representing evil, these moral forces are represented by two U.S. sergeants. Tom Berenger's Barnes brutally terrorizes a native village early in the film, while Willem Dafoe's Elias strongly resists this descent into barbarism and tries to maintain high moral standards in an immoral environment. The success of *Platoon* resulted in a spate of Vietnam War films in the late 1980s, but their numbers never reached the level and density that occurred during World War II and the Korean War. In addition, most Vietnam War movies made after 1978 engage in some level of criticism of the war, and none present themselves as the straightforward adventures that appeared in films about the earlier wars.

WAR IN THE DESERT

While Vietnam movies tended to be based on fictional screenplays—the real war having been shown nightly on U.S. television screens, in contrast to later Middle Eastern conflicts (the Gulf, Somalia, Iraq, Afghanistan)—today's filmmakers have divided their subject matter between fictional explorations and actual battles drawn from soldiers' (and reporters') memoirs. Winner of two Academy Awards, Ridley Scott's *Black Hawk Down* (2001) dramatized for audiences an actual U.S. Ranger and Delta Force mission in Somalia. Audiences can envision the Gulf War from the standpoint of an actual marine in Sam Mendes's *Jarhead* (2005; based on a memoir) and contrast that with the fictional black comedy of *Three Kings* (David O. Russell, 1999).

As certain segments of the American public became critical of the lingering U.S. military engagements in Afghanistan and Iraq, filmmakers who try to address this have faced a varying reception. For example, *In the Valley of Elah* (Paul Haggis, 2007; based on a true story), was released in the early days of the War in Iraq and presents an unflinching look at the cost of soldiering on young men's mental well-being. Despite many positive reviews, the film did not find much of an audience, as ultimately the movie suggests that the United States is not just a country at war abroad but also at home. Brian De Palma's bold *Redacted* (2007) depicts a version of the Iraq War that Americans are not hearing about at home. The movie offers a fictionalized account of an actual rape and murder of a young Iraqi girl by American soldiers, presenting to audiences the footage that exists but is not shown by the American media, which often edit coverage to present citizens with a more palatable conflict.

Green Zone (Paul Greengrass, 2010) received positive reviews for its critical take on the political rhetoric and false claims about the weapons of mass destruction that were the impetus for the War in Iraq, but the movie also had the cachet of a $100 million action-film budget. In contrast, Kathryn Bigelow's *The Hurt Locker* (2009; based on a reporter's fictional retelling), produced for only $15 million, portrays the effects of the Iraq War without taking political sides. This story of a bomb unit in Iraq—in particular, one soldier's inability to face the less-overtly stressful world at home—went on to win six Academy Awards and outperformed all the other Iraq/Afghanistan war films that had been made at the time (including *Elah*, *Stop-Loss* (Kimberly Peirce, 2008), and *Lions for Lambs* (Robert Redford, 2007).

Another approach to films focusing on the Middle Eastern conflict has been to look solely at the psychological effects of war, as it hits those back at home—whether via veterans home on leave, as seen in *The Lucky Ones* (Neil Burger, 2008), *Stop-Loss*, and *Brothers* (Jim Sheridan, 2009), or as experienced by the families of soldiers killed in action, in movies such as *Grace Is Gone* (James C. Strouse, 2007), *The Messenger* (Oren Moverman, 2009), and HBO's *Taking Chance* (Ross Katz, 2009).

In general, pre-Iraq-era films made during wartime emphasize glory, honor, and patriotic values, and it is only in the years following the wars that these values have been analyzed and criticized. As filmmaking technology has changed and improved throughout the twentieth and twenty-first centuries, U.S. filmmakers have achieved greater levels of realism in war movies, and these films collectively have enhanced and influenced Americans' awareness of the conditions of war. In addition, contemporary filmmakers have been more willing to be openly critical of the politics behind military actions. While this approach may garner a strong critical reception, it does not necessarily attract a broad audience or bring big box-office returns.

Andrew J. Kunka

SEE ALSO: *Academy Awards;* All Quiet on the Western Front*; Altman, Robert;* Apocalypse Now*;* The Birth of a Nation*; Bogart, Humphrey;* The Bridge on the River Kwai*; Cooper, Gary;* The Deer Hunter*; Eastwood, Clint;* From Here to Eternity*; Gish, Lillian; Griffith, D. W.; Gulf Wars; Hawks, Howard; Hollywood; Hughes, Howard; Kubrick, Stanley; Lee, Spike;* M*A*S*H*;* The Mickey Mouse Club*;* Patton*; Peck, Gregory;* Platoon*; Redford, Robert; Scott, Ridley; Spielberg, Steven; Stone, Oliver; Tarantino, Quentin; Vidor, King; Vietnam; War in Afghanistan; Wayne, John; World War I; World War II.*

BIBLIOGRAPHY

Basinger, Jeanine. *The World War II Combat Film: Anatomy of a Genre*. New York: Columbia University Press, 1986.

Dick, Bernard F. *The Star-Spangled Screen: The American World War II Film*. Lexington: University Press of Kentucky, 1985.

Dittmar, Linda, and Gene Michaud, eds. *From Hanoi to Hollywood: The Vietnam War in American Film*. New Brunswick, NJ: Rutgers University Press, 1990.

Doherty, Thomas. *Projections of War: Hollywood, American Culture, and World War II*. New York: Columbia University Press, 1993.

Karlin, Wayne. *War Movies: Journeys to Vietnam: Scenes and*

Out-takes. Willimantic, CT: Curbstone Press, 2005.

Langman, Larry, and Ed Borg. *Encyclopedia of American War Films*. New York: Garland, 1989.

Quirk, Lawrence J. *Great War Films*. New York: Citadel, 1994.

Rubin, Steven Jay. *Combat Films*. Jefferson, NC: McFarland, 1981.

Suid, Lawrence H. *Guts & Glory: Great American War Movies*. Reading, MA: Addison-Wesley, 1978.

War of the Worlds

Broadcast on October 30, 1938, Orson Welles's Mercury Theatre radio dramatization of H. G. Wells's *War of the Worlds* engendered a mass panic in which millions of Americans believed they were being invaded by Martians; in so doing, the broadcast dramatically demonstrated the nascent power of mass media in American culture.

The Mercury Theatre group, headed by the twenty-three-year-old Welles, had built a small national audience with its weekly radio adaptations of literary classics such as Joseph Conrad's *Heart of Darkness*. Welles, his partner John Houseman, and writer Howard Koch collaborated on the hour-long scripts. The trio nearly scrapped their *War of the Worlds* adaptation; Koch's faithful approximation of the novel did not translate well in rehearsals. The group decided to stick with the project after reworking the script to mirror a news broadcast. Nevertheless, as group members and even Welles himself later recalled, the feeling in the studio on the day of the broadcast was that *War of the Worlds* would not be a successful production.

DRAMA BECOMES REAL

The show commenced at 8 p.m. that Halloween eve, following an introduction by a CBS announcer that presented Wells's novel as the subject of the forthcoming dramatization. In the first ten minutes of the broadcast, Welles masterfully built dramatic tension by juxtaposing fireside-chat-styled meditations on renewed American prosperity with increasingly frequent news bulletins on atmospheric disturbances detected by astronomers across the United States.

Just as thousands of listeners switched over from the more popular Charlie McCarthy show (a less than compelling singer had just been introduced), Welles's group delivered a frantic news report from the small town of Grovers Mill, New Jersey, where Martians had landed: "A humped shape is rising out of the pit. I can make out a small beam of light against a mirror. What's that? There's a jet of flame springing from that mirror, and it leaps right at the advancing men. It strikes them head on! Good Lord! They're turning into flame!" As the broadcast followed the progress of the Martians up the East Coast, the reports became even more dire. "[People] are falling like flies," Welles reported. "No more defense. Our army wiped out . . . artillery, air force, everything wiped out. This may be the last broadcast." An actor portraying the secretary of the interior informed listeners that President Franklin Delano Roosevelt had declared a national emergency.

As the dramatization continued, thousands of Americans panicked. In Pittsburgh a man found his wife in the bathroom, clutching a poison bottle and yelling, "I'd rather die this way than like that." And, in a favorite story of Welles's, actor John Barrymore, upon hearing the broadcast, took to his backyard, where he unleashed his Great Danes from their doghouse with the admonition: "Fend for yourselves!" It has been estimated that 12 percent of the radio audience heard the broadcast, and more than half that number took it seriously; by sociologist Hadley Cantril's account, which was published in a landmark contemporary study sponsored by the Rockefeller Foundation, more than a million people were frightened by Welles's broadcast. Cantril's demographic survey placed the strongest currents of fear among less educated people and poor southern populations.

Welles concluded his broadcast with a restatement of the fictionality of the presentation ("The Mercury Theatre's own radio version of dressing up in a sheet and . . . saying 'Boo!'" as Welles put it), but the hysteria continued well into the night. CBS was inundated with calls, newspaper switchboards were jammed, and mobs continued to crowd the streets of New York and northern New Jersey. When the truth became apparent, public hysteria turned into ire directed at CBS. Hundreds threatened lawsuits against the network, and the Federal Communications Commission promised a full-fledged inquiry. As calmer heads prevailed, the public furor died down, and Welles became an overnight sensation; many of his biographers claim that without the celebrity engendered by the *War of the Worlds* broadcast, he might never have been able to bring his craft to Hollywood, where he became a celebrated director with films such as *Citizen Kane* (1941) and *The Magnificent Ambersons* (1942).

THE POWER OF RADIO

The *War of the Worlds* episode highlighted the emerging influence the mass media had on the American public. It demonstrated the power of the media to form and shape opinion in American culture and the passive willingness on the part of the public to place its faith in the legitimacy of sound and image. Ironically, *War of the Worlds* represented one of radio's final assertions of dominance within the media sphere; by the 1950s, television had replaced radio as the supreme force in mass culture.

Scholars assert that Welles's broadcast was so widely believed because it struck a particular chord with Americans in the years before World War II. The show aired just after the Munich crisis, to which Welles alluded at the outset of the broadcast, and the recent international conflict may have influenced some to believe that the reported invasion was not extraterrestrial at all. Sociologists have also located the show's resonance in the latent anxiety of the general population, engendered by years of economic depression. "On the surface, the broadcast was implausible and contradictory, but that didn't matter," asserted Joel Cooper. "In that one instance, people had an immediate explanation for all the unease and disquiet they had been feeling. And suddenly, they could do something. They could gather their families. They could run."

War of the Worlds has remained a vibrant part of American popular culture into the twenty-first century. In 1953 Byron Haskin produced a Hollywood film inspired by the Wells novel, and from 1988 to 1990 a syndicated television series inspired by the film enjoyed a successful run. In 1978 musician Jeff Wayne released a musical version of *War of the Worlds*, which was revived in 2011 featuring three-dimensional special effects.

In 1988, the fiftieth anniversary of the broadcast, public radio stations across the United States aired an ambitious remake

Average net paid circulation for September exceeded
Daily---1,800,000
Sunday-3,150,000

Copyright 1938 by News Syndicate Co., Inc. Reg. U. S. Pat. Off. NEW YORK'S PICTURE NEWSPAPER Entered as 2nd class matter, Post Office, New York, N. Y.

Vol. 20. No. 109 New York, Monday, October 31, 1938★ 48 Pages 2 Cents IN CITY LIMITS | 3 CENTS Elsewhere

FAKE RADIO 'WAR' STIRS TERROR THROUGH U.S.

—Story on Page 2

(NEWS foto)

"War" Victim

Caroline Cantlon, WPA actress, listening to this radio in West 49th St., heard announcement of "smoke in Times Square." Running to street, she fell, broke her arm.

(By Associated Press)

"I Didn't Know". Orson Welles, after broadcast expresses amazement at public reaction. He adapted H. G. Wells' "War of the Worlds" for radio and played principal role. Left: a machine conceived for another H. G. Wells story. Dramatic description of landing of weird "machine from Mars" started last night's panic.

—Story on page 2.

War of the Worlds ***Panic.*** *The panic that ensued after the* War of the Worlds *broadcast was front-page news in New York and across the United States.* NEW YORK DAILY NEWS ARCHIVE/CONTRIBUTOR/NEW YORK DAILY NEWS/GETTY IMAGES.

of *War of the Worlds* starring Jason Robards and featuring the Oscar-winning sound effects of Randy Thom; the citizens of Grovers Mill commemorated their town's role in the historic broadcast with a four-day festival that culminated with the unveiling of a bronze statue of Welles at a microphone and a rapt family gathered around its radio.

THE INVASION CONTINUES

In 2005 a heavily hyped updating of *War of the Worlds* by Steven Spielberg earned almost $600 million in the first year of its release, and in 2008 C. Thomas Howell directed a straight-to-DVD sequel, *War of the Worlds 2: The Next Wave*. The decade also saw *War of the Worlds* video games and phone apps, including the paradoxically named *War of the Worlds: Minigame Adventure*, and a postmodern fascination with monsters inspired the somewhat redundant 2009 novel *The War of the Worlds: Plus Blood, Guts, and Zombies* by Eric S. Brown and H. G. Wells.

While Wells's novel became a prototype of the alien invasion genre, the public's reaction to the radio broadcast has also become a media archetype. Writers have explored the phenomenon in a wide range of genres, from children's literature such as *Aliens Are Coming: The True Account of the 1938 "War of the Worlds" Radio Broadcast* by Meghan McCarthy (2006) to graphic novels such as *The Broadcast* by Eric Hobbs and Noel Tuazon (2010). Journalists frequently compared the Y2K panic, fueled by a fear that computer glitches at the turn of the millennium would devastate society, to that generated by the Welles's radio show. In Belgium, journalists on the state RTBF broadcasting network cited the Welles broadcast as inspiration for their convincing 2006 hoax in which they announced that Flanders had declared its independence and that the Belgian royal family had fled the country. *It Came from Mars*, a 2010 play by U.S. playwright Joseph Zettelmaier, was based on the public reaction to the 1938 radio show.

Up until his death in 1985, Welles would never reveal whether he had anticipated the massive misinterpretation of his radio drama. Whether intended as a hoax or not, however, the landmark *War of the Worlds* broadcast demonstrated the American public's preference for reading media's sound—and later its images—as truth rather than fiction.

Scott Tribble

SEE ALSO: *Academy Awards; Barrymore, John; Charlie McCarthy;* Citizen Kane*; The Fifties; Halloween; Hollywood; Radio; Radio Drama; Spielberg, Steven; Television; Video Games; Welles, Orson; World War II; Y2K.*

BIBLIOGRAPHY

Baughman, James. *The Republic of Mass Culture: Journalism, Filmmaking, and Broadcasting in America since 1941*. Baltimore, MD: Johns Hopkins University Press, 1992.

Brown, Robert J. *Manipulating the Ether: The Power of Broadcast Radio in Thirties America*. Jefferson, NC: McFarland, 1998.

Cantril, Hadley. *The Invasion from Mars: A Study in the Psychology of Panic with the Complete Script of the Famous Orson Welles Broadcast*. Princeton, NJ: Princeton University Press, 1940.

Flynn, John L. *War of the Worlds: From Wells to Spielberg*. Owings Mills, MD: Galactic Books, 2005.

Higham, Charles. *Orson Welles: The Rise and Fall of an American Genius*. New York: St. Martin's Press, 1985.

Thomson, David. *Rosebud: The Story of Orson Welles*. New York: Alfred A. Knopf, 1996.

Wells, H. G., and Glenn Yeffeth, ed. *"War of the Worlds": Fresh Perspectives on the H. G. Wells Classic*. Dallas, TX: BenBella Books, 2005.

War on Drugs

The *war on drugs* is a phrase that refers to the U.S. government's campaign to stop the import, production, sale, and use of illegal drugs. Efforts include severe penalties for people who possess drugs and who sell drugs and increased border patrols to prevent drugs from entering the country. Community programs, television spots, and crime-watch programs educate citizens on the dangers of drug use and abuse. The government also created drug-free school zones and increased penalties for drug crimes involving weapons.

The U.S. government first enacted drug laws in 1914 with the Harrison Narcotics Act, which taxed narcotics and required licensure for those who dispensed drugs. The Marihuana Tax Act of 1937 categorized marijuana as a narcotic for taxation and legislation purposes. The U.S. Congress first introduced mandatory prison terms for drug use and sale with the 1956 Narcotics Control Act.

Prior to the 1914 Harrison Narcotics Act, highly addictive opiates were the primary ingredients in widely used elixirs. Drug users were mostly middle-class women, and their addiction was not seen as a societal problem. The Civil War (1861–1865), however, brought the subject of addiction to the forefront. When physicians treated injured soldiers with morphine, they developed an addiction referred to as "soldier's disease."

As long as drug abuse was confined to nonthreatening social classes, public knowledge and debate were minimal. In 1900 society pitied drug addicts. They were considered unfortunate citizens with medical problems. By 1920, however, drug users had become known as drug fiends, immoral outcasts who spread their addictive disease to everyone they touched.

Antidrug campaigns were frequently prejudicial in nature. Opium use had been common in China since 1825 when the British introduced it as a means of leveling out the trade imbalance. Thus, early U.S. antidrug campaigns blamed Chinese immigrant laborers who were working on the railroad in California for bringing opiates into the country and for encouraging Americans to smoke opium. In the South, antidrug campaigns were leveled at African Americans, maintaining that they had developed superhuman strength after sniffing cocaine.

In other areas of the country Mexicans were blamed for marijuana's popularity. In 2006 authorities discovered a one-half-mile-long tunnel that began in Tijuana, Mexico, and stretched across the border to a warehouse in the United States. Two tons of marijuana were seized at the Tijuana end, and another 200 pounds were found at the warehouse in the United States.

Legislation and antidrug campaigns helped to contain drug use until it became mainstream in the 1960s. Cocaine use rose in the 1970s, but it was generally considered nonaddictive by the medical community. In 1971 President Richard M. Nixon officially declared a war on drugs, coordinated drug policies and legislation, and provided federal funds for education and prevention. In 1973 he created the Drug Enforcement Administration (DEA) to coordinate the efforts of all government agencies.

COCAINE AND MARIJUANA

Cocaine use peaked in the United States in 1982 with 10.4 million users, and by the mid-1980s the thrust of the antidrug campaign was on crack cocaine, an inexpensive form of the drug that was created by boiling powdered cocaine with water and baking soda to form rocks that could be chipped off and sold. In 1984 First Lady Nancy Reagan took on the war on drugs as her pet project, launching a "Just Say No" campaign and helping to focus attention on the issue. In 1986 the war on drugs gained momentum upon the sudden death of twenty-two-year-old Len Bias, a star basketball player with the University of Maryland who was chosen by the Boston Celtics as the number two pick in the National Basketball Association (NBA) draft a mere forty hours before his death. Americans, sports fans in particular, were stunned by the Maryland medical examiner's report that listed Bias's cause of death as "cocaine intoxication." Bias's death made headlines nationwide and sparked a movement toward stricter drug laws.

Despite the lack of proof that a national drug use epidemic existed, Americans bought the media portrayal of the "crack baby" and inner-city drug busts. In reality, so-called crack babies were sometimes the result of poverty and malnutrition. Because crack cocaine tended to be associated with inner cities, young African American males were targeted as the primary perpetrators.

By the mid-1980s Congress and most state legislatures enacted mandatory prison sentences based on the weight or quantity of a drug found on a person. The majority of federal and state drug offenders incarcerated in the 1990s were low-level sellers and dealers. High-level traffickers and other dealers with information to share traded information for lenient sentences.

The campaign against crack cocaine was so intense that the Anti-Drug Abuse Act of 1986 set severe penalties for drug possession and sale, including life in prison and property forfeiture. Other measures designed to curtail the use and sale of drugs included denying convicted ex-drug offenders social programs, such as government-backed college loans and grants and welfare assistance. The Comprehensive Crime Control Act of 1984 allowed police to enter homes and cars and conduct searches and seizures without a warrant. Many critics argued that this practice violated basic personal liberties. In the 1990s critics of the war on drugs stated that American drug policies had failed to put a dent in the drug trade. The U.S. government spent billions of dollars each year to improve border interdiction, increase the number of drug arrests and convictions, and build more prisons to house drug offenders.

The war on drugs also affected the availability, legalization, and decriminalization of medical marijuana. Critics argue that prohibition increases crime, deepens social and class conflict, and defies basic democratic ideals. It increases health problems by denying treatment to and incarcerating addicts. It tears families apart by incarcerating small-time users and sellers for long prison sentences. It promotes poverty by denying welfare and educational assistance to ex-offenders and their dependents and increases recidivism. Critics relate issues such as AIDS (acquired immunodeficiency syndrome), street-level dealers, and gang warfare to drug prohibition rather than drug use.

As early as 1994, a study undertaken by the U.S. Sentencing Commission revealed that while two-thirds of crack cocaine users were either white or Hispanic, 84.5 percent of those convicted for possession were African American. The commission recommended changing laws to bring sentencing for crack cocaine possession and dealing in line with those of powdered cocaine use and dealing. However, it was not until 2011 under a retroactive application of a new Fair Sentencing Act that crack cocaine violators had sentences reduced, and many prisoners were released early after judges reviewed their cases.

Debra Lucas Muscoreil

SEE ALSO: *AIDS; Cocaine/Crack; LSD; Marijuana; National Basketball Association (NBA).*

BIBLIOGRAPHY

Bogazianos, Dimitri A. *5 Grams: Crack Cocaine, Rap Music, and the War on Drugs*. New York: New York University Press, 2012.

Cooper, Edith Fairman. *The Emergence of Crack Cocaine Abuse*. New York: Novinka Books, 2002.

Gray, Mike. *Drug Crazy: How We Got into This Mess and How We Can Get Out*. New York: Random House, 1998.

Lindesmith, Alfred R. *The Addict and the Law*. Bloomington: Indiana University Press, 1965.

Musto, David F. *The American Disease: Origins of Narcotics Control*. New Haven, CT: Yale University Press, 1973.

Provine, Doris Marie. *Unequal under the Law: Race in the War on Drugs*. Chicago: University of Chicago Press, 2007.

Schmidt, Susan, and Tom Kenworthy. "Cocaine Causes Bias' Death, Autopsy Reveals: Dose Said to Trigger Heart Failure, Criminal Inquiry to Be Pressed." *Washington Post*, June 25, 1986. Accessed May 26, 2012. Available from http://articles.latimes.com/1986-06-25/sports/sp-20106_1_len-bias

Shohov, Tanya, and Frank Lamazi, eds. *War on Drugs: Issues and Development*. New York: Novinka Books, 2004.

"A Social History of America's Most Popular Drugs." PBS. Accessed May 23, 2012. Available from http://www.pbs.org/wgbh/pages/frontline/shows/drugs/buyers/socialhistory.html

Wisotsky, Steven. *Beyond the War on Drugs: Overcoming a Failed Public Policy*. Buffalo, NY: Prometheus Books, 1990.

Warhol, Andy *(1928–1987)*

Andy Warhol was a renowned pop artist in the 1960s and is considered one of the most important artists of the twentieth century. His boundless and apparently effortless creativity expressed itself in many forms: he was a commercial designer, painter, printmaker, filmmaker, and publisher.

AMERICANIZING POP ART

Although Warhol was intentionally obscure about his background, he was born Andrew Warhola in remote Forest City, Pennsylvania, the son of a Czech Roman Catholic immigrant miner. In 1946, after his father's early death, Warhol enrolled in Pittsburgh's Carnegie Institute of Technology as an art student. At the time, he worked as a window decorator in a department store. By 1950 he had graduated, shortened his name to Andy Warhol, and moved to New York City, where his reputation as a designer quickly blossomed. Besides working on graphics for such magazines as *Vogue* and *Harper's Bazaar*, he won awards for his advertising designs, particularly those for I. Miller shoes. During these years Warhol dyed his hair the signature silver color that he would maintain for the rest of his life.

In 1960, the year Warhol began to paint, he created groundbreaking works of pop art, a movement that had originated in England in the early 1950s. Lord and Taylor's department store on Fifth Avenue displayed enlargements of his paintings of the Dick Tracy comic strip in 1961. The seminal "New Realists" exhibition at the Sidney Janis Gallery solidified his position as the leading pop artist. After 1964 he was represented by the New York dealer Leo Castelli (1907–1999), who handled most of the pop artists' work.

Warhol quickly became notorious for his paintings of Campbell's soup cans, first exhibited at the Ferus Gallery in Los Angeles in 1962. Straightforward renderings of row upon row of the cans, these images were not publicity gambits but important avant-garde works, signaling a major change in the nature of art. Pop art was a cool reaction to the passionate—and, in the pop artists' minds, emotionally excessive—art of the abstract expressionists who then dominated the art scene. The soup cans were painted in the same spirit as Marcel Duchamp's "readymades": ordinary objects transformed into artworks by virtue of the artist's selecting and recontextualizing them. Warhol was forced to defend the paintings as legitimate art when Campbell's Soup Company sued him for copyright infringement. The corporation later decided that the paintings were good advertising.

FROM PAINT TO PRINT

In 1963, inspired by the Brillo soap pad boxes he had seen in supermarkets, Warhol ordered 100 wooden boxes from a carpenter and stenciled the sides with exact imitations of the Brillo graphic. For sale at $300 each, the boxes created great excitement at Manhattan's Stable Gallery exhibit the following year. When they were shipped to a Toronto gallery, however, their status as art was denied: Warhol's dealer had to pay merchandise duty to have them delivered.

With these works and others, Warhol had abandoned painting in favor of more anonymous techniques such as photo silk screening. "I want to be a machine," he said in 1962, subverting the idea of art as unique and handmade. Turning to Hollywood for his subjects, he used Marilyn Monroe as a motif in several silk-screened works, including *Gold Marilyn Monroe* (1962; held at the Museum of Modern Art [MOMA] in New York City). Rendered in the cheap-looking, off-register style of shoddy reproduction, these artworks suggest that Monroe's manufactured persona had overwhelmed her identity as a person.

Celebrities became a major theme in Warhol's works. Throughout the rest of the 1960s and the 1970s, he created images of athletes, politicians, and entertainers such as Elvis Presley, Troy Donahue, Jackie Kennedy Onassis, Elizabeth Taylor, and Chairman Mao Zedong. As in the Monroe images, the colors are often garish and off register. One series from this period is titled "Ten Portraits of Jews of the Twentieth Century." Warhol's fascination with iconic luminaries was reflected in the gossipy celebrity magazine he founded in 1969, *Inter/View* (later renamed *Andy Warhol's Interview* and then simply *Interview*). He was also captivated by historic artists. Like other artists of the 1980s who appropriated imagery from past art, Warhol made a series of paintings, drawings, and prints based on famous works by Botticelli and Leonardo da Vinci.

Partially in response to the civic strife of the 1960s, Warhol created his Death and Disaster series. Such works as *Car Crash*, *Race Riot*, and *Electric Chair* involve the stark reproduction of newspaper photographs, saturated with color and often replicated within the same frame. These artworks protest the media's callous and repetitious coverage of traumatic events, which, the artist believed, creates a numbing apathy in viewers.

MASS PRODUCTION

In 1964 Warhol established "The Factory," a rented Manhattan attic that became a mass-production studio. Here, assistants made series of prints under his detached guidance, churning out thousands of works. Often, Warhol clipped photographs from magazines and newspapers and had his helpers silk-screen them. The very name *factory* challenged the notion of an artist's studio as a place of inspiration and individual creation. In this spirit Warhol once said that anybody "should be able to do all my paintings for me." The Factory became nearly as notorious for its personnel as for the art that was produced there. Critic Robert Hughes once described its silver-papered walls as a home for "cultural space-debris, drifting fragments from a variety of Sixties subcultures (transvestite, drug, S & M, rock, Poor Little Rich, criminal, street, and all the permutations) orbiting in smeary ellipses around their unmoved mover." Shy and inhibited himself, Warhol seemed to be a voyeur of the hybrid subculture he created. In his role as funky entrepreneur, Warhol opened a nightclub with the thoroughly 1960s-sounding name the Exploding Plastic Inevitable, whose house band was the Velvet Underground. Its leader, Lou Reed, is now regarded as a soulful guru of heroine culture and a musical pioneer of punk and new wave music.

In a decade racked by assassinations, Warhol himself was shot on June 3, 1968, by Valerie Solanis, a former Factory groupie turned militant feminist. The only member of a group called S.C.U.M. (Society for Cutting Up Men), Solanis later claimed that she shot Warhol because of the power he had over her life.

FILM, FAME, AND VIDEOTAPE

Warhol also experimented in film during the 1960s, making several movies that have become classics of minimalist cinema and film history. They are typically outrageously boring and amateurish—qualities for which they were admired—in their recording of the spontaneous exhibitionism of his Factory "actors." *Eat* (1963) shows artist Robert Indiana eating a mushroom. *Empire* (1964) is composed of an eight-hour shot of one side of the Empire State Building; the changing light is the only action. *Film Culture* magazine awarded Warhol its 1964 Independent Film Award. In 1965, at his first solo exhibition at the Philadelphia Institute of Contemporary Art, he made it known that he had given up painting to concentrate on filmmaking.

In all, Warhol collaborated on more than seventy-five films. His highly regarded *Chelsea Girls* (1966) was the first underground film to be shown at a conventional commercial theater.

On a split screen, viewers watched a quirky documentary revealing the comings and goings of Warholian "superstars" in two different hotel rooms. *Four Stars* (1966–1967) used three projectors simultaneously on one screen and ran for more than twenty-four hours. The horror film *Andy Warhol's Frankenstein* opened in 1967. Homosexual themes were the focus of *My Hustler* (1965), *Bike Boy* (1967), and *Lonesome Cowboys* (1968).

Warhol enlisted Paul Morrissey, a production assistant and occasional cameraman at the Factory, to film and direct many of his movies; Morrissey's participation was intended to give the works a greater sense of structure and professionalism and to make them more appealing to a popular audience. Briefly interested in video, Warhol broadcast a private cable television show in the 1980s called "Andy Warhol TV."

As both his work and life indicate, Warhol was genuinely obsessed with celebrity, particularly Hollywood stardom. In the 1970s and 1980s he wholly gave himself over to the popular media. He was often seen at Manhattan's trendy disco Studio 54 and attended nearly every opening and award ceremony, escorting Brooke Shields, Bianca Jagger, Elizabeth Taylor, and the designer Halston to various events. He appeared almost nightly on *Entertainment Tonight*. Not only attracted by the celebrity of entertainers, Warhol also courted rising young artists, such as the graffiti artists Keith Haring (1958–1990) and Jean-Michel Basquiat (1960–1988).

THE WARHOL LEGACY

Like his films, Warhol's untimely death seemed banal: he died of complications after a fairly routine operation on February 22, 1987. The auction of his possessions, in itself a cultural event, revealed that he had been an impassioned collector. His extensive collection of folk art had once been exhibited at MOMA. His influence as an arbiter of taste continued even after his death; all manner of kitschy art and furnishings from his estate influenced the retro styles of the late 1980s and 1990s. Beginning in the 1990s his unique persona and biography (particularly those years when the Factory was active) was expressed in popular culture in many different forms. Several successful films feature a Warhol character. In *Basquiat* (1996, directed by Julian Schnabel), a vivid depiction of the 1980s New York art scene, rock star David Bowie plays a convincing Warhol. Oliver Stone's *The Doors* (1991) features Crispin Glover as the artist, and in Mary Harron's *I Shot Andy Warhol*, he is played by Jared Harris. Guy Pearce acted his character in *Factory Girl* (2006; directed by George Hickenlooper), a movie about the life of Warhol superstar Edie Sedgwick.

The Andy Warhol Foundation, established in 1987, controls Warhol's artworks and their reproduction. It is recognized as one of the largest grant-giving organizations for the visual arts in the country. In the decades since his death, his works have risen dramatically in value on the art market, commanding prices comparable to works by the most famous figures in art history, including Pablo Picasso, Vincent van Gogh, and Jackson Pollock. In 2008, for example, Warhol's *Eight Elvises* (1963), composed of repeating images of Presley dressed as a cowboy, sold for $100 million.

The meaning of Warhol's art has been endlessly debated; it is alternately seen as tremendously deep and mind-numbingly superficial. The artist often mystified interviewers by affecting a profound detachment—often to the point of boredom. In one early interview he explained, "If you want to know all about Andy Warhol, just look at the surface of my paintings and films and me, and there I am. There's nothing behind it." Warhol will always be associated with those aspects of 1960s popular culture that involve outrageous behavior, a sensationalist media, and the art world as glitzy big business. His most famous pronouncement, "In the future everybody will be famous for fifteen minutes," still seems to be an accurate observation about the media's insatiable appetite for creating quickly consumable subjects.

Mark B. Pohlad

SEE ALSO: *Abstract Expressionism; Advertising; Bowie, David; Cable TV; Capital Punishment; Celebrity; Consumerism; Department Stores; Dick Tracy; Empire State Building;* Entertainment Tonight*; Frankenstein; Gay Men; Graffiti; Halston; Haring, Keith; Hollywood; Horror Movies; Kitsch; Minimalism; Monroe, Marilyn; Movie Stars; New Wave Music; Onassis, Jacqueline Lee Bouvier Kennedy; Picasso, Pablo; Pollock, Jackson; Pop Art; Presley, Elvis; Punk; Race Riots; Reed, Lou; Rock and Roll; Schnabel, Julian; Stone, Oliver; Studio 54; Taylor, Elizabeth; Television; The Velvet Underground; Videos;* Vogue.

BIBLIOGRAPHY

Bockris, Victor. *The Life and Death of Andy Warhol*. New York: Bantam Books, 1989.

Francis, Mark; Margery King; and Hilton Als, eds. *The Warhol Look: Glamour, Style, Fashion*. Boston: Little, Brown, 1997.

Hackett, Pat, ed. *The Andy Warhol Diaries*. New York: Warner Books, 1989.

Honnef, Klaus. *Andy Warhol, 1928–1987: Commerce into Art*, tr. Carole Fahy and I. Burns. Cologne, Germany: Benedikt Taschen, 1993.

Hughes, Robert. "The Rise of Andy Warhol." *New York Review of Books*, February 18, 1982, 6–10.

Koch, Stephan. *Stargazer: The Life, World and Films of Andy Warhol*. New York: Rizzoli, 1991.

Koestenbaum, Wayne. *Andy Warhol*. New York: Viking/Penguin, 2001.

Michelson, Annette, ed. *Andy Warhol (October Files)*. Cambridge, MA: MIT Press, 2001.

Ratcliff, Carter. *Andy Warhol*. New York: Abbeville Press, 1983.

Shanes, Eric. *Warhol*. London: Studio Editions, 1993.

Tretiack, Philippe. *Andy Warhol*. New York: Universe Books, 1997.

Watson, Steve. *Factory Made: Warhol and the 1960s*. New York: Pantheon, 2003.

Washington, Denzel *(1954–)*

Handsome, intelligent, and stylish, Denzel Washington is among the leading African American film stars of his generation. Washington is the natural heir to Sidney Poitier, the first film star to have demonstrated that an African American could become a heartthrob and a top box-office draw in the United States. Unlike his celebrated predecessor, however, Washington's on-screen persona is characterized by a distinctly modern edge; he often plays morally ambivalent—and at times violent—characters. From his early breakthrough roles in *Glory* (1989) and *Malcolm X* (1992) to his dark, complex portrayals of criminals in such films as *Training Day* (2001) and *American Gangster* (2007), Washington has demonstrated a rare combination of versatility and dramatic range throughout his acting career, earning two Oscars along the way. In the first decade of the 2000s he also began to earn recognition for his work as a director and producer while continuing to explore new, often risky avenues for his considerable performing talents.

Denzel Hayes Washington Jr. was born in Mount Vernon, New York, on December 28, 1954. After receiving a BA in journalism from Fordham University, he studied acting at San Francisco's American Conservatory Theater. During his early career he worked primarily onstage and in television, receiving praise for his portrayal of Dr. Philip Chandler in the popular hospital series *St. Elsewhere* (1982–1988). Around this time Washington earned his first significant screen role, playing George Segal's black illegitimate son in *Carbon Copy* (1981). Six years later his portrayal of South African political activist Steve Biko in *Cry Freedom* (1987) brought him stardom and an Oscar nomination for Best Supporting Actor.

In the late 1980s Washington began to emerge as a major new African American star. His portrayal of Private Trip, an embittered but courageous runaway slave, in *Glory* earned him both a Best Supporting Actor Oscar and a Golden Globe Award. Over the next several years, the full scope of Washington's acting range became apparent, as he starred in a number of acclaimed dramatic and comedic roles. Notable films from the early 1990s include *Mo' Better Blues* (1990) and *Mississippi Masala* (1991). A turning point in his young career came when he played the title role in Spike Lee's *Malcolm X* (1992). Washington's performance as the controversial civil rights leader earned him a nomination for Best Actor at the 1993 Academy Awards. That same year he played key roles in three major films: he demonstrated his lighter side as Don Pedro in Kenneth Branagh's adaptation of William Shakespeare's *Much Ado about Nothing* (1993), starred opposite Julia Roberts in the legal thriller *The Pelican Brief* (1993), and played attorney Joe Miller in the landmark film *Philadelphia* (1993).

Washington spent the remainder of the 1990s expanding his already considerable body of acting work. He played private investigator Ezekiel "Easy" Rollins in the film adaptation of Walter Mosley's *Devil in a Blue Dress* (1995) and held lead roles in *The Preacher's Wife* (1996) and *He Got Game* (1998). In 1999 Washington once again received Oscar consideration—this time for his portrayal of Rubin "Hurricane" Carter, an African American boxer wrongly convicted of murder, in the biopic *The Hurricane* (1999). Two years later Washington earned his first Best Actor Oscar for his role as corrupt detective Alonzo Harris in *Training Day* (2001). In 2002 Washington made his directorial debut with the psychiatric drama *Antwone Fisher*; he also produced the film and played the role of Dr. Jerome Davenport.

As the decade progressed, Washington continued to explore new territory with his acting. Highlights from these years include the roles of Detective Keith Frazier in Spike Lee's *Inside Man* (2006) and the part of Frank Lucas in the biopic *American Gangster* (2007). In 2007 Washington also directed and starred in *The Great Debaters*. In 2012 he played rogue CIA agent Tobin Frost in the espionage thriller *Safe House* (2012); he also served as executive producer of the film. Even after more than two decades of box-office success, however, Washington remains committed to pursuing new film challenges. "I'm not ready for any memoirs yet," he told Alex Clark of the *Observer* in 2012. "The story's not told. Not yet. No. Too early. I'm living life—I don't want to write about it."

Frances Gateward

SEE ALSO: *Academy Awards; Boxing; Celebrity; Civil Rights Movement; Hollywood; Lee, Spike; Malcolm X; Movie Stars; Poitier, Sidney; Roberts, Julia;* St. Elsewhere*; Television.*

BIBLIOGRAPHY

Brode, Douglas. *Denzel Washington: His Films and Career.* Secaucus, NJ: Carol Publishing Group, 1997.

Clark, Alex. "Denzel Washington Is One of Hollywood's Heaviest Hitters, Breathing Life into Everything from Civil-Rights Heroes to Cold-Hearted Killers." *Observer* (London), February 12, 2012.

Simmons, Alex. *Denzel Washington.* Austin, TX: Raintree Steck-Vaughn, 1997.

Simon, Leslie. "Why Denzel Washington (not Tom Cruise) Is the New Paul Newman." *Film Comment* 34 (1998): 72–75.

Washington Monument

The Washington Monument is a tall, slender obelisk that towers above the Mall in the U.S. capital, dominating the skyline. A grateful public supported its construction in the nineteenth century to commemorate the first president of the United States, George Washington. Architect Robert Mills won a competition in 1836 with his proposal for a 600-foot obelisk and circular temple at the base. The monument was completed in 1884 without the temple and 45 feet shorter than Mills's design.

Unlike the capital's other presidential monuments, the Washington Monument is abstract, with no images or words; its power comes from the simple beauty of its form. It has been largely uncontroversial, which is unique for a political monument. Also, unlike the nearby Lincoln Memorial, the Washington Monument has not been the site of any significant political events. Instead, it has stood for more than a century in quiet solemnity as a proud testament to the person Americans consider the father of their country.

Dale Allen Gyure

SEE ALSO: *March on Washington.*

BIBLIOGRAPHY

Liscombe, Rhodri Windsor. *Altogether American: Robert Mills, Architect and Engineer.* New York: Oxford University Press, 1994.

Savage, Kirk. *Monument Wars: Washington, D.C., the National Mall, and the Transformation of the Memorial Landscape.* Berkeley: University of California Press, 2011.

Scott, Pamela, and Antoinette J. Lee. *Buildings of the District of Columbia.* New York: Oxford University Press, 1993.

The *Washington Post*

The *Washington Post* is the newspaper of the nation's capital. Among Washington, D.C.'s several daily papers, the *Post* is the oldest in continuous print and has the widest circulation. In addition to its print circulation, the Internet presence of the *Post* has expanded its viewership manifold in the twenty-first century. With more than 100 years in print, the *Post* has garnered hundreds of accolades, including nearly fifty Pulitzer Prizes. The newspaper has long been a leader in reporting on national politics and a frontrunner of investigative journalism.

The story of the *Washington Post* is really the story of three family members and one outsider who, over a period of four decades, took a somnolent and bankrupt newspaper in the capital of the United States and turned it into an icon of good journalism. The four people are Eugene Meyer; his daughter, Katharine Meyer Graham; her husband, Philip Graham; and the man Katharine hired as executive editor, Ben Bradlee. It is also the tale of two Pulitzer Prizes, the yin and yang of the *Post*'s rise to fame.

A RISKY INVESTMENT

The *Washington Post* was founded in 1877 by Stilson Hutchins and was undistinguished for a good part of its first century. Eugene Meyer bought the bankrupt paper for $825,000 at an auction in 1933, a time when there were four more substantial dailies in Washington and the city's premier paper was the *Star*. The *Post*'s early history under Meyer suggested a disastrous future because the paper continued to lose upward of $1 million per year. Nevertheless, Meyer, who was independently wealthy, stuck with the paper, saying, "In the pursuit of truth, the newspaper shall be prepared to make sacrifices of its material fortunes, if such course be necessary for the public good." His daughter would later show the same resolve for the good of truth and to the paper's benefit.

The daughter, however, did not start out to become a newspaper publisher. When Katharine Meyer graduated from the University of Chicago in 1938, she went to work as a reporter for the *San Francisco Examiner*. Within a year, however, her father ordered her home to work at the *Post*, although not with the intention that she would be groomed as his successor. In 1940 she married Philip Graham. Katharine immediately took on the role of dutiful wife. Eugene Meyer was appointed president of the World Bank in 1946, whereupon he made Philip Graham publisher of the *Post*. Meyer became chairman of the board.

Philip Graham, following in his father-in-law's footsteps, got very involved in politics and became something of a kingmaker, creating complications for reporters who were trying to cover all sides of a story, not just the boss's side. Shortly after Graham took over, Bradlee, then a young reporter, resigned from the *Post* and joined the Washington bureau of *Newsweek*. The *Post* continued to prosper, and Meyer bought out and shut down another daily paper in Washington, reducing the number of dailies to three. After Meyer died in 1959, Philip Graham became president and chairman of the board of the Post company. In 1961 the *Post* purchased *Newsweek* magazine.

Two years later Philip Graham killed himself—he suffered from bipolar disorder—and Katharine Graham was thrust into the role of publisher of her late father's newspaper. She became the first woman to head a nationally recognized publication, and she was a quick study. Realizing that she needed to put her own team in place, she hired Bradlee and put him on the fast track to become executive editor.

RISE IN STATURE

The *Post* lived in the shadow of the *New York Times*, which had a much longer tradition of journalistic greatness. The *Times*, a paper that covered the federal government thoroughly, was a direct competitor for the *Post*. In 1971 the *Times* started to publish a series of stories about a top-secret report that became popularly known as the Pentagon Papers, in effect, scooping the *Post* in its own backyard. The *Post* rose to the occasion, got its own copy of the papers, and published parts unavailable to the *Times*, thereby regaining its dignity and also showing a measure of journalistic skill not seen before. When the federal government, through the courts, temporarily enjoining both papers from publishing, the papers united, taking to the U.S. Supreme Court their fight for the right to publish and to maintain a sacred constitutional principle that the government does not have the right to censor. The newspapers won in late June 1971.

The *Post* reached national stature on its own a year later when it began almost exclusive coverage of a break-in at the Democratic National Committee in a building called the Watergate. Essentially it was a local police story that took on added importance when the *Post* discovered that some of the Watergate burglars had worked for the Committee to Re-elect the President (CREEP). Not only was the story great, but also the *Post*'s methodical unraveling of the machinations of President Richard Nixon's henchmen set newer standards for reporting. Two young reporters, Bob Woodward and Carl Bernstein, sometimes aided by an unidentified source in the executive branch who became known as Deep Throat, dug through records and interviewed hundreds of people to produce a series of stories that helped lead to President Nixon's resignation and to the *Post*'s 1973 Pulitzer Prize. (In 2005 it was revealed that Mark Felt, a high-ranking FBI agent, was Deep Throat.) The *Post* endured tremendous pressure to back off the story (its material fortunes were threatened), but Graham stood by her embattled newsroom and was eventually vindicated.

It has become part of the lore that Woodward and Bernstein brought down a president, but that overlooks all that was going on around the president at the time. For example, one Watergate burglar, threatened by a judge with a long jail sentence, turned state's evidence on his friends. Then there was a Senate committee investigating what went on, and eventually the House Judiciary Committee approved articles of impeachment. There was also the revelation that Nixon had taped many of his Oval Office conversations, and when the Supreme Court ruled that Nixon had to yield the tapes, he resigned. The *Post* did not single-handedly bring down the president, but if it had ignored the break-in story, the other facilitators might not have assumed their important roles.

The *Post* became a victim of its own hubris in 1981 when it published a story about an eight-year-old boy named Jimmy who supposedly used heroin. It was a dramatic story written by a young reporter named Janet Cooke that appeared on the front page. The story created a controversy not because the *Post* had published it but because the paper had not tried to help the boy; there was also churning inside the *Post* because the story had been published on the word of the reporter—no one asked for her sources, and there was none of the double-checking that had made the Watergate reporting an exemplary effort. It was only after the reporter won a Pulitzer Prize that other journalists started to check her credentials and discovered that she had lied about her education and her degrees. Cooke eventually revealed that "Jimmy" was fictionalized and actually an amalgamation of several street children Cooke had met. The *Post* returned the Pulitzer, and Cooke resigned.

The *Post* continued its exemplary ways throughout the remainder of the twentieth century. Ironically, none of the newspapers that circulated in Washington when Meyer purchased the bankrupt *Post* survived beyond 1981. The *Post* has continued, by necessity, to change with the times in order to survive. In 1996 it went online with a website, offering its content free to the public. Due to the increased availability of news and media on the Internet during the early twenty-first century, all print media in the United States saw slipping circulation and declining advertising revenue. Like many newspapers in the Internet age, the *Washington Post* has had to bow to the economics of the new journalism.

To mitigate its financial woes, the Washington Post Company sold the hemorrhaging *Newsweek* in 2010 for $1 and its debts. The *Post* also ran its first front-page advertisement in 2010. Despite its losses, as of 2009 the paper still had more than half a million subscribers, making it the fifth-largest paper in the United States. Through all of the challenges presented to it over the years, the *Washington Post* has proven itself, time and again, a superb newspaper in a difficult age for journalism.

R. Thomas Berner

SEE ALSO: *The* New York Times*;* Newsweek*; Watergate.*

BIBLIOGRAPHY

Bradlee, Ben. *A Good Life: Newspapering and Other Adventures.* New York: Simon & Schuster, 1996.

Graham, Katharine. *Personal History.* New York: Alfred A. Knopf, 1997.

Graham, Katherine. *Katherine Graham's Washington.* New York: Vintage, 2003.

Kelly, Tom. *The Imperial Post: The Meyers, the Grahams and the Paper that Rules Washington.* New York: William Morrow, 1983.

Kindred, Dave. *Morning Miracle: Inside the "Washington Post": A Great Newspaper Fights for Its Life.* New York: Doubleday, 2010.

Povich, Shirley. *All Those Mornings . . . At the Post.* New York: Public Affairs Books, 2006.

Roberts, Chalmers M. *The "Washington Post": The First 100 Years.* Boston: Houghton Mifflin, 1977.

Sherman, Scott. "Donald Graham's *Washington Post.*" *Columbia Journalism Review*, September/October 2002.

Watergate

On June 17, 1972, a security guard at the Watergate complex in Washington, D.C., discovered a piece of tape on the lock of the door that led to the Democratic National Committee headquarters, a discovery that set off a chain of events that would ultimately bring down the presidency of Richard Milhous Nixon. Afterward, Americans would wonder why Nixon and those around him risked so much on such a minor event while Nixon led in the election polls and the Democratic Party was in disarray. Indeed, Nixon would go on to win the election that November by a landslide.

The break-in at the Watergate was only part of a larger campaign designed by Nixon supporters to rattle Democratic candidates and tarnish the reputation of the whole party, which included harassment of Democratic candidates, negative campaign ads, two separate break-ins at the Democratic National Committee headquarters, and an additional break-in at the office of Daniel Ellsberg's psychiatrist. Ellsberg had offered up the Pentagon Papers for public consumption, detailing the strategy—or lack thereof—for America's position in Vietnam.

Theodore H. White, chronicler of presidents from Dwight Eisenhower to Ronald Reagan, points out in *Breach of Faith* that the Watergate break-in was riddled with mistakes. G. Gordon Liddy, adviser to Nixon, had been given $83,000 from Nixon's Committee to Re-elect the President (CREEP) to provide the necessary equipment for the break-in. When the tape was placed over the lock, it was placed horizontally rather than vertically, which made it more noticeable. The tape had been spotted earlier in the day and removed by a security guard, yet it was replaced in the same position. As only outside personnel were used for the break-in, they were easy to spot as not belonging in the complex. The electronic surveillance equipment purchased

Nixon Leaves the White House. *Richard Nixon boards the presidential helicopter as he leaves the White House for the last time after his August 9, 1974, resignation speech in the wake of the Watergate scandal.* ROLLS PRESS/POPPERFOTO/CONTRIBUTOR/POPPERFOTO/GETTY IMAGES.

by Liddy was inferior and had no cutoff between those conducting the actual break-in and those listening in a hotel across the street. When the break-in was discovered, the police were led to E. Howard Hunt and Liddy in the hotel across the street. Furthermore, all participants had retained their own identification papers.

Instead of being honest with the American public and taking his advisers to task, Nixon immediately became embroiled in a cover-up that would slowly unravel over the following two years—leading to Nixon's resignation in August 1974. As the facts surrounding the break-in were made known, it was revealed that the Nixon presidency had been involved in serious manipulation and abuse of power for years. It seemed that millions of dollars coming from Nixon supporters had been used to pay hush money in an ill-advised attempt to hide the truth from Congress and the American people. Nixon, it was discovered, truly lived up to his nickname of "Tricky Dick."

THE INVESTIGATION UNFOLDS

During the investigation, the names of Nixon's advisers would become as well known to the American people as those of Hollywood celebrities or sports heroes. Chief among these new celebrities were John Ehrlichman, Nixon's domestic affairs adviser, and Bob Haldeman, the president's chief of staff. Both would be fired in a desperate attempt to save the presidency. Another major player was John Dean, the young and ambitious counsel to the president. John Mitchell, the attorney general, and his wife, Martha, provided color for the developing story. Rosemary Woods, the president's personal secretary, stood loyally by as investigators kept demanding answers to the questions "what did the president know?" and "when did he know it?" The answers to those two questions provided the crux of the investigation. If it had been proved that Nixon was the victim of overenthusiastic supporters rather than a chief player in the scenario, his presidency could possibly have survived. When Nixon learned of the break-in was integral to understanding his part, if any, in the subsequent cover-up.

In the early days of the Watergate investigation, most media reported the break-in as a minor story with little national significance. However, two aggressive young reporters who worked for the *Washington Post* began to dig deeper into the background surrounding the actual crime. Aided by an informant who was identified at the time only as Deep Throat, Carl Bernstein and Bob Woodward uncovered one of the major stories of the twentieth century and became instrumental in forcing the first presidential resignation in U.S. history. (In 2005 it was revealed that Mark Felt, a high-ranking FBI agent, was Deep Throat.)

THE TAPES

As Congress began to hold congressional hearings, Alexander Butterfield, a Nixon presidential aide, revealed that a complex taping system had been installed to record conversations in the Oval Office, Camp David, the Cabinet rooms, and Nixon's hideaway office. Nixon's distrust of others would prove to be his own undoing. He fought to maintain control over the tapes and went so far as to fire a number of White House officials in what became known as the "Saturday Night Massacre." The Supreme Court did not accept Nixon's argument that the tapes contained only private conversations between the president and his advisers and, as such, were protected by executive privilege. From the moment in 1974 that the court in *United States v. Nixon* ordered the president to release the tapes, it was widely accepted that Nixon had lost the presidency.

The tapes released contained eighteen minutes of silence that have never been explained. In 1996 the lawsuit of historian Stanley I. Kutler and the advocacy group Public Citizen resulted in the release of more than 200 additional hours of tape. In *Abuse of Power: The New Nixon Tapes*, Kutler writes that the new information reveals that Nixon was intimately involved both before and after Watergate in abuses of power. A taped conversation on June 23, 1972, proved that Nixon and Haldeman talked about using the CIA to thwart the FBI investigation into the cover-up. When the *New York Times* published the Pentagon Papers, Nixon told his advisers: "We're up against an enemy conspiracy. They're using any means. We're going to use any means." This conversation helps illustrate Nixon's paranoia and his adversarial relationship with the American citizenry. It also points out his belief in his own invincibility.

IMPEACHMENT

In mid-1974, after Nixon had been named an unindicted coconspirator in the Watergate affair, the House of Representatives approved three articles of impeachment. These charges arose from months of listening to those involved in the Nixon presidency and Watergate cover-up explain the machinations of the Nixon administration in televised public hearings. To save themselves from serving time in prison, most Nixon cohorts were willing to implicate higher-ups. Ultimately, Hunt, Liddy, James McCord, and four Cuban Americans from Miami were convicted and served time in jail.

Until the final days of his presidency, Nixon insisted that he would survive. When he recognized that it was over and he had lost, Nixon went into seclusion. Reportedly, Alexander Haig, his last chief of staff, oversaw the dismantling of the presidency. On August 8, 1974, wearing a blue suit with a blue tie and a flag pin in his lapel, Nixon announced his resignation. The following day, Vice President Gerald Ford was sworn in as president of the United States.

Elizabeth Purdy

SEE ALSO: *The* New York Times*; Vietnam; The* Washington Post.

BIBLIOGRAPHY

Barber, James David. *The Presidential Character: Predicting Performance in the White House*. Englewood Cliffs, NJ: Prentice-Hall, 1972.

Bernstein, Carl, and Bob Woodward. *All the President's Men*. New York: Simon & Schuster, 1974.

Fremon, David K. *The Watergate Scandal in American History*. Springfield, NJ: Enslow Publishers, 1998.

Genovese, Michael A. *The Watergate Crisis*. Westport, CT: Greenwood Press, 1999.

Kutler, Stanley I., and Richard M. Nixon. *Abuse of Power: The New Nixon Tapes*. New York: Free Press, 1997.

Lukas, J. Anthony. *Nightmare: The Underside of the Nixon Years*. New York: Viking, 1976.

Olson, Keith W. *Watergate: The Presidential Scandal That Shook America*. Lawrence: University Press of Kansas, 2003.

Schlesinger, Arthur M. *The Imperial Presidency*. Boston: Houghton Mifflin, 1973.

Schudson, Michael. *Watergate in American Memory: How We Remember, Forget, and Reconstruct the Past*. New York: BasicBooks, 1992.

White, Theodore H. *Breach of Faith: The Fall of Richard Nixon*. New York: Atheneum Publishers, 1975.

Woodward Bob, and Carl Bernstein. *The Final Days*. New York: Simon & Schuster, 1976.

Waters, Ethel *(1896–1977)*

Born in 1896 in Chester, Pennsylvania, Ethel Waters presided for nearly fifty years as one of America's most celebrated performers. She began her career as a singer in 1917 at the Lincoln Theatre in Baltimore, Maryland. Billed as "Sweet Mama Stringbean" during her early years as a shimmy dancer and robust singer of heartrending and sometimes naughty melodies, she worked in a variety of entertainment outlets, including vaudeville, stage, movie screen, radio, and television. Perhaps her most noteworthy achievement is her contribution to American music. Throughout the 1920s and 1930s she recorded with early jazz luminaries such as Fletcher Henderson, Coleman Hawkins, and Duke Ellington. For a time she even ran her own orchestra.

Some of Waters's memorable songs include "Get Up off Your Knees" (1928), "Am I Blue?" (1929), and "Birmingham Bertha" (1929). She appeared in numerous Broadway reviews and motion pictures. She starred in the stage and screen versions of *Cabin in the Sky* (1943) and *Member of the Wedding* (1952) and was nominated for an Academy Award for her performance in the 1949 film *Pinky*.

On television she earned the title role in the *Beulah* television series (1950–1953) but left the show after only one season. In her later years, after suffering failed marriages, complaints from the black community about appearing in stereotyped roles, and ill health, she turned to religion and was associated with evangelist Billy Graham until her death in 1977. In 1994 the U.S. Postal Service remembered Waters with a commemorative stamp.

Pamala S. Deane

SEE ALSO: *Academy Awards;* Beulah; *Broadway; Ellington, Duke; Graham, Billy; Hawkins, Coleman; Henderson, Fletcher; Hollywood; Jazz; Radio; Television; Vaudeville.*

BIBLIOGRAPHY

"Ethel Waters." Accessed December 2011. Available from http://www.pbs.org/jazz/biography/artist_id_waters_ethel.htm

"Ethel Waters." Red Hot Jazz Archive. Accessed December 2011. Available from http://www.redhotjazz.com/waters.html

Knaack, Twila. *Ethel Waters: I Touched a Sparrow*. Waco, TX: Word Books, 1978.

Waters, Ethel, and Charles Samuels. *His Eye Is on the Sparrow: An Autobiography*. New York: Pyramid, 1967.

Young, William C. *Famous Actors and Actresses on the American Stage*. New York: R. R. Bowker, 1975.

Waters, John *(1946–)*

Director John Waters earned the title "King of Bad Taste" in 1972 for *Pink Flamingos*, a raunchy film that makes a laughing matter of most every type of perversion. The film ushered in a new era for popular culture, in which the shocking and bizarre attract growing audiences and profits, penetrating every medium from mainstream newspapers to daytime television talk shows. Waters refined his obsession with *good bad taste*—a term he coined—over several decades, creating a new movie genre of the bizarre, according to director David Lynch.

Waters identifies himself as a writer foremost, but he is an example of an entrepreneur who uses many channels effectively. His witty essays have been collected in three volumes: *Shock Value: A Tasteful Book about Bad Taste* (1981), *Crackpot: The Obsessions of John Waters* (1983), and *Role Models* (2010). Collections of his screenplays and photographs also have been published. He has made a handful of cameo appearances in films and television programs, including the voice for a cartoon character in an Emmy-nominated episode of *The Simpsons*. In the 1990s he mounted a traveling exhibit of movie stills, and in the first decade of the 2000s he performed an autobiographical one-man show. A charming talk-show guest, Waters is in demand as a speaker at college campuses, film schools, and festivals.

Waters's success owes much to his abilities as a promoter.

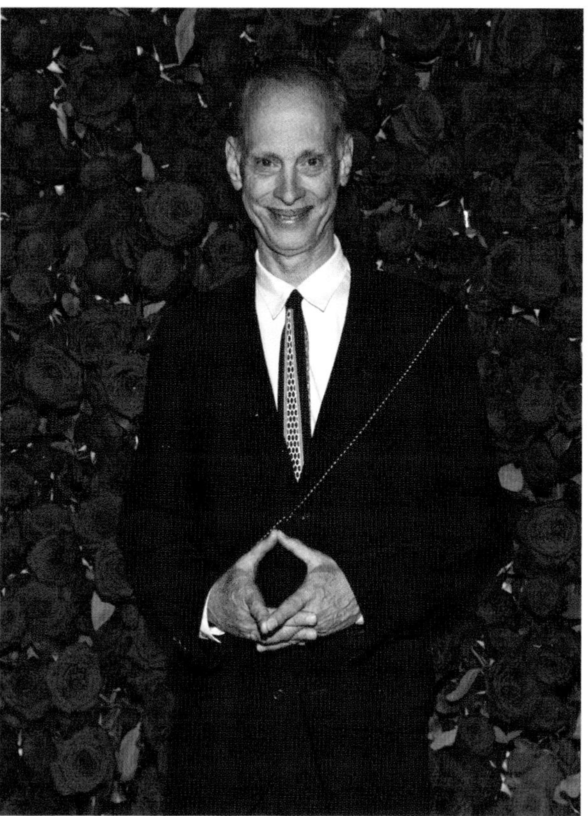

John Waters. *John Waters's movies have moved from cult to mainstream audiences while retaining their trademark "good bad taste."* CHARLES ESHELMAN/CONTRIBUTOR/FILMMAGIC/GETTY IMAGES.

Working from the trunk of his car in the early days, he persuaded East Coast theater owners to do midnight showings of *Pink Flamingos*, thus making money during hours when they normally would be closed. Through this stroke of marketing genius, he became an architect of the midnight cult-movie showing.

The director's oeuvre may be grouped into two periods. Following *Pink Flamingos*, his movies *Female Trouble* (1975), *Desperate Living* (1977), and *Polyester* (1981) have been described as "vulgar and cheerful nihilism," "blasphemous," "sophomoric," and "whimsical." Foul language and scatological visual and verbal references made these works unappealing to Middle America. Critics and audiences either hated his films or loved them, hailing him as an iconoclastic artist. His themes often presage cultural trends by decades. For example, in *Female Trouble*, the crazed heroine believes death in the electric chair for a life of crime is the equivalent of an Academy Award. Waters's loopy characterization antedated by nearly twenty years Oliver Stone's controversial treatment of warped lovers who go on a killing rampage to achieve media notoriety in *Natural Born Killers* (1994).

MOVE TO MAINSTREAM

In the 1990s Waters graduated from cult- and midnight-movie houses to suburban multiplexes with such films as *Hairspray* (1988), *Cry-Baby* (1990), *Serial Mom* (1994), *Pecker* (1998), and *A Dirty Shame* (2004). His second period continues his biting satire of American culture but without reference to such perversions as coprophagy, castration, necrophilia, and the gross visual images of the earlier films. A unifying theme of both periods is his focus on characters who are "insane but believe they are sane," Waters told National Public Radio interviewer Terry Gross. His films turn normative American values upside-down and champion outsiders.

Raised in an upper-middle-class family in Baltimore, Maryland, Waters, like many creative people, knew what he wanted to do early in life. He got his first subscription to *Variety* at age twelve and haunted the seedier movie theaters favoring horror films and "B" movies, especially admiring Russ Meyer. After Waters was dismissed from New York University's film school for smoking marijuana, he persuaded his father that financing a series of low-budget films would be cheaper than paying for his education. These early efforts include *Hag in a Black Leather Jacket* (1964); *The Diane Linkletter Story* (1969), a ten-minute exercise in bad taste about the LSD suicide of the daughter of a famous Hollywood entertainer; *Roman Candles* (1966), during which three short features are screened simultaneously on side-by-side screens; *Eat Your Make Up!* (1968), satirizing the modeling industry; *Mondo Trasho* (1969), a spoof of then-popular documentaries of the bizarre and pornographic around the world; and *Multiple Maniacs* (1971), which ends with the heroine being raped by a giant lobster. Most did not make it out of the church halls he rented for hometown showings.

Pink Flamingos brought Waters to the attention of the avant-garde artistic community. Andy Warhol—whose small-budget films such as *Sleep* convinced Waters that he, too, could make movies on a shoestring—reportedly advised Federico Fellini to see *Pink Flamingos*. Waters's work has been compared to that of the Italian master. One critic suggested that Waters had created a "Theater of Nausea," comparable to Antonin Artaud's "Theater of Cruelty" and Charles Ludlam's "Theater of the Ridiculous." *New York* magazine hailed *Pink Flamingos* as an American version of the Luis Buñuel and Salvador Dalí classic, *Andalusian Dogs*. *Pink Flamingos* was a commercial as well as an artistic success. Made for $12,000, it earned at least $2 million during the first few years after its release. His next movies were made with incrementally larger budgets and found growing audiences.

In the early films, Waters often took people on the margins of society and transformed them into "glamorous movie stars." He told the *Baltimore Sun* in 1978, "To me all those outrageous-looking people are beautiful. Because to me beauty is looks that you can never forget." It has been his life's work to ridicule the conventions of a society that ostracizes people who do not fit within its narrow standards of perfection and to exploit the potential of film to bring them the fame and success that, in his eyes, they deserve.

DIVINE CHARACTERS

The greatest of his on-screen creations was the metamorphosis of his friend Glenn Milstead into Divine, a 300-pound transvestite who vamped it up in the skintight gowns of Hollywood movie queens, with exaggerated makeup—including eyebrows that soared up his half-shaved head—and heavily bleached and teased blond hair. A charismatic performer, Divine took viewers by storm as the matriarch of a family of perverted criminals vying for the title of "Filthiest Family Alive" in *Pink Flamingos*. Mink Stole, a screen persona created for Waters's friend Nancy Stoll, played Divine's rival for the title, Connie Marble. Connie and her husband, Raymond (David Lochary), kidnapped and impregnated young women, chaining them in the basement of their suburban house of horrors, then sold the babies to lesbian couples. In a scene that may never be topped for grossness, Divine eats dog feces from the pavement to secure the title.

Hairspray, with Divine in a supporting role, marked Waters's transition into shopping mall theaters. The only shocking thing left for him to do, Waters had concluded, was to make a mainstream film. *Hairspray* is a lighthearted treatment of a serious issue—integration. The story is based on Baltimore's *Buddy Deane Show*, a teen dance showcase that was driven off the air in 1964 by the National Association for the Advancement of Colored People for segregating African American dancers to one program a month. In *Hairspray* teenagers defeat their parents' resistance to integration, and everybody dances together in the film's happy ending.

The story reflects the director's egalitarian sentiments. He praises Baltimore as the appropriate setting for his films because it is an "unholy mix" of old money and new immigrants, black and white poor, and a dirty industrial eastern seaport with the southern charm of the first city south of the Mason-Dixon Line. When it comes to nightlife, Waters told Richard Gorelick in a 1998 article in *Gay Life*, "I want to go somewhere where everyone is mixed—that's my ideal: rich, poor, black, white, gay, and straight, all together."

With the death of the irreplaceable Divine soon after the release of *Hairspray*, Waters's transition to the mainstream was virtually assured. *Cry-Baby*, an edgy *Bye-Bye Birdie* (1963), tells the story of a middle-class girl who longs to go bad and her romance with the leader of the Drapes, a rock-and-rolling, motorcycle-riding, black-leather-jacketed gang of juvenile delinquents. The freedom-loving Drapes prevail against the repressed and repressive clean-cut clique of upper-middle-class suburban kids. "My movies are very moral," says Waters, as quoted by Pat Aufderheide in a 1990 essay in *American Film*. "The underdogs always win. The bitter people are punished, and people who are happy with themselves win. They're all about wars between two groups of people, usually involving fashion, which signifies morals. It's part of a lifelong campaign against people telling you what to do with your own business."

STAR POWER

Johnny Depp as the title character in *Cry-Baby*—with a tattooed teardrop under one eye—guaranteed the film's box-office success. Waters turned to star power again in his next film, featuring Kathleen Turner as *Serial Mom*, a perfect suburban mother who just happens to be a serial killer. A prolific consumer of newspapers and magazines—he subscribes to more than eighty—Waters frequently pulls his inspiration from the headlines. *Pecker* (1998) pits the innocence of a young blue-collar Baltimore photographer who finds beauty everywhere against the exploitative glamour of the Manhattan art world. It features early work by then-rising talents Edward Furlong, Lili Taylor, and Christina Ricci. *A Dirty Shame* (2004)—with its NC-17 rating and raunchy sexual theme—marked Waters's return to more controversial work.

Adapting his writing to yet another medium, Waters created a photography exhibit, *Director's Cut*, that toured galleries in the 1990s, using frames isolated from others' films to author original storyboards. This technique illustrates the cultural phenomenon of bricolage, the art of recycling culture to create new works of art. Aufderheide sees the technique in Waters's films, commenting: "John Waters is the bard of a culture that creates itself out of commercial trash; he's a visionary of sorts, someone who discovers the bizarre in the everyday and the everyday in the bizarre."

Waters continued to explore other creative avenues in the first decade of the 2000s and the 2010s, including curating a typically idiosyncratic art museum exhibit in 2011, creating and performing his one-man show *This Filthy World* in 2006, and writing 2010's *Role Models*. Perhaps explaining his long absence from the silver screen, Waters said to the *New York Times* in 2011: "I make movies, but I couldn't get a movie made right now with the economy, so I wrote a book."

It is the ultimate accolade to Waters's cultural influence that he helped make the unspeakable acceptable, by making people laugh about the strange and sometimes repulsive truths of everyday existence. People who were marginalized as freaks during the early 1970s now routinely appear as guests on television talk shows. Jokes about flatulence and other bodily functions were taken up in films by such well-known humorists as Carl Reiner and the Monty Python troupe. In an article titled "Mr. Bad Taste Goes Respectable," *U.S. News & World Report* noted that it was increasingly difficult for Waters to retain his title when comedian Jim Carrey told butt jokes during a televised presentation of the Academy Awards.

BALTIMORE ESTABLISHMENT

Waters, who still lives in Baltimore and sets all of his movies there, is a local hero because his success brought the city's picturesque locales to the attention of other film crews and made the city a site for East Coast filmmaking. After such Hollywood luminaries as Alan Alda and Al Pacino arrived in town to make movies, the mayor established the city's Film Commission in 1980 to serve as a liaison for moviemakers seeking Baltimore locations. During the late 1960s and early 1970s, the group of self-styled juvenile delinquents and eccentrics that Waters gathered around himself evolved into Dreamland Studio, an ensemble production company. Reconciled with his family after years of rebellion and a proud homeowner who holds backyard barbecues for the Dreamland survivors, Waters told Aufderheide, "It's hilarious that in some ways I've become part of the establishment."

To his credit, Waters has never tried to top the vulgarity of *Pink Flamingos*, instead honing his talent to mock social intolerance, transvalue society's standards, and take every bizarre reality to its extreme. Long before radio shock jock Howard Stern came along, Waters was simultaneously offending people and making them laugh.

E. M. I. Sefcovic

SEE ALSO: *Alda, Alan; "B" Movies; Cult Films; Depp, Johnny; Divine; Fellini, Federico; Lake, Ricki; Linkletter, Art; Lynch, David; Pacino, Al; Shock Radio; Stern, Howard; Warhol, Andy.*

BIBLIOGRAPHY

Aufderheide, Pat. "The Domestication of John Waters." *American Film* 15, no. 7 (1990); 32–37.

Geier, Thom. "Mr. Bad Taste Goes Respectable." *U. S. News & World Report*, April 28, 1997, 16.

Gorelick, Richard. "John Waters' 'Pecker' Is His Gayest Film Ever, Mary." *Gay Life*, September 4, 1998, B6–B7.

Hirschey, Geri. "Waters Breaks." *Vanity Fair*, March 1990, 204–208, 245.

Hunter, Stephen. "A Good Place to Raise a Movie." *Washington Post*, September 27, 1998, G1, G6.

Mandelbaum, Paul. "Kinkmeister." *New York Times Magazine*, April 7, 1991.

Sefcovic, Enid. "Smutty Waters Just Keeps Rolling Along." *Extra*, April 20, 1975, 6, 10.

Sheets, Hilarie M. "John Waters, the Artful Dodger." *New York Times*, June 23, 2011, 21.

Waters, Muddy *(1915–1983)*

Muddy Waters's song title "The Blues Had a Baby and They Called It Rock and Roll" captures the link this seminal blues artist established between the two genres. The vocalist, guitarist, and songwriter was a major figure in the postwar Chicago blues scene. His impact on the conventional blues aesthetic, Chicago blues, and rock-and-roll music is unparalleled. Waters provided a model for scores of rock and blues musicians—including Mick Jagger, the Beatles, Mike Bloomfield, Paul Butterfield, Bob Dylan, James Cotton, and Johnny Winter; his 1950 composition "Rollin' Stone" inspired the name for Jagger's band.

Waters was born McKinley Morganfield on April 4, 1915, in Rolling Fork, Mississippi. His father was a farmer and part-time musician. When his mother died, Waters moved to Clarksdale to live with his grandmother. Early musical experiences included singing in the church choir and playing blues harmonica in juke joints and at suppers, picnics, and parties; he had taught himself to play the instrument. At the age of seventeen, he got hold of a guitar, soon earning the world-famous nickname Muddy Waters by performing "in the dirt" in and around the Delta. Alan Lomax, recording in Mississippi for the Library of Congress archives, taped Waters in 1941 on the Stovall plantation.

When the Mississippi blues traveled from the Delta to Chicago, it became louder, with amplified instruments and more forceful rhythms. Waters decided to move there, too, in 1943 and became a sideman for Mississippi harmonica player John Lee "Sonny Boy" Williamson at the Plantation Club. He was playing with pianist Sunnyland Slim, also from Mississippi, when he got his first commercial recording break. At the end of a session at the Aristocrat (later Chess) recording studio in 1948, Waters took advantage of some free time to record his first single, "Gypsy Woman." The record was successful enough to secure him another opportunity at the studio. In subsequent recordings of "(I Feel Like) Going Home," "Rollin' Stone," "I Can't Be Satisfied," and "Mannish Boy," Waters transformed his "down-home" country approach to an urbanized, raw Chicago-style blues.

Waters's vocal approach drew from the congregational song style of the southern black church. He often moaned or hummed the ends of phrases and, in recitative manner, slid upwards on certain syllables, incorporating shouts, vocal punches, and occasionally falsetto. His guitar style made extensive use of the slide or bottleneck technique, repetitive guitar phrases in response to his vocal line in a call-and-response fashion, and an uncompromising rough musical texture.

Starting his own band, Waters attracted some of the finest Chicago musicians, many of whom later formed bands themselves. In 1953 he assembled one of the best-ever Chicago blues groups: harmonica player Little Walter Jacobs, pianist Otis Spann, guitarist Jimmie Rodgers, and drummer Elgin Evans. With various personnel, the band toured the South, the rest of the United States, and eventually Europe. Willie Dixon, a celebrated singer, bassist, and composer in his own right, wrote a number of songs specifically for Waters that became hits, including "Hoochie Coochie Man" and "Same Thing." By 1958 Waters had scored fourteen Top 10 hits on the rhythm-and-blues charts. The same year, he and Spann toured the United Kingdom, but reviews were mixed; British audiences were accustomed to the music of such acoustic performers as Big Bill Broonzy, Sonny Terry, and Brownie McGhee.

As soul music gained favor in 1960s Chicago among black patrons, interest in the blues decreased, and consequently Waters's popularity began to wane. Fortunately, a blues revival was occurring elsewhere in the United States and in the United Kingdom, with other musicians emulating American blues. When groups began to acknowledge Waters's influence, attention to his music revived. He performed and recorded at the 1960 Newport Jazz Festival and collaborated with Johnny Winter successfully several times in the 1970s, fueling a rediscovery of his music by a largely white audience.

Waters continued to hit his artistic stride, gaining financial success. His band won the DownBeat Critics Poll for Best Rhythm and Blues Group in 1968 and a Grammy Award for Best Ethnic/Traditional Recording—*They Call Me Muddy Waters*—in 1971. In an interview Waters defined the music he played: "I think it's about tellin' a beautiful story . . . something about the hard times you've had." He died quietly in his sleep at his home in the Chicago suburb of Westmont on April 30, 1983.

Since his passing Waters's influence on popular music has expanded and solidified. Songs and albums by artists in a variety of genres make reference to the musician, covers and adaptations of his originals are common, and his works have been featured in several films. The releases of collections and live recordings, as well as remastered versions of his older albums, have introduced Waters to a new generation of blues fans. Notable among these releases are *The Essential Collection* (2000) and *Authorized Bootleg: Live at the Fillmore Auditorium November 4-6, 1966* (2009). In 2008 the film *Cadillac Records* brought the story of Chess Records to the big screen; Tony- and Emmy-winning actor Jeffrey Wright portrayed the blues star. Waters's substantial imprint on the sound and feel of American music will not be soon forgotten.

Willie Collins

SEE ALSO: *The Beatles; Blues; Dylan, Bob; Electric Guitar; Emmy Awards; Grammy Awards; Newport Jazz and Folk Festivals; Rhythm and Blues; Rock and Roll; Rodgers, Jimmie; The Rolling Stones; Soul Music; Tony Awards.*

BIBLIOGRAPHY

Krull, Bryan. *Lil' Choo-Choo Johnson, Bluesman.* Indianapolis: Dog Ear Publishing, 2010.

Rooney, James. *Bossmen: Bill Monroe & Muddy Waters.* New York: Dial Press, 1971.

Watson, Tom *(1949–)*

One of the greatest golfers of modern times, Tom Watson dominated his sport in the 1970s and 1980s. Watson is second only to Harry Vardon in British Open championships with five wins, and his performances in those victories led to his immense popularity with the British people. His eight major championship victories include two Masters titles and a dramatic victory in the 1982 U.S. Open at Pebble Beach. His fiery duels with Jack Nicklaus made for excellent television, and through them Watson contributed to the spread and popularity of golf. He was named player of the year for four consecutive years and won the Vardon Trophy for lowest scoring average three times.

Watson joined the Senior PGA Tour (later renamed the Champions Tour) in 1999 and found tremendous success, earning fourteen victories, including six major tournaments. With his dramatic near victory in the 2009 British Open at age fifty-nine, Watson again captivated golf fans.

Jay Parrent

SEE ALSO: *Golf; The Masters Golf Tournament; Nicklaus, Jack; Sports Heroes; Vardon, Harry.*

BIBLIOGRAPHY

Corcoran, Michael. *Duel in the Sun: Tom Watson and Jack Nicklaus in the Battle of Turnberry.* Edinburgh: Mainstream, 2002.

Feinstein, John. *A Good Walk Spoiled.* Boston: Little, Brown, 1995.

Peper, George; Robin McMillan; and James A. Frank, eds. *Golf* in America: The First One Hundred Years. New York: Harry N. Abrams, 1988.

Waxing

Waxing involves the rather abrupt removal of body hair by the application of hot wax or some other sticky compound, covered by a strip of cloth. When the wax has cooled, the salon specialist or home enthusiast tears it away, ripping hair out by the root and often causing a good deal of pain and rash as a result. Waxing lasts longer than shaving, so it needs to be done less often; however, it requires some growth (at least one-quarter inch) to give the wax a surface with which to bond. Waxing has come to be identified with the cleanliness, sexiness, and sleekly polished look that are expected of the young and hip. Favorite targets are the legs, armpits, chest, and genitals.

By 2012 the trend was considered an aesthetic ideal in popular culture, inspiring mostly funny scenes in TV shows such as *Sex and the City* and *Keeping Up with the Kardashians* and movies including *The 40-Year-Old Virgin* and *Friends with Benefits*—even though it was not an ideal that all people were willing to put into practice. Women's magazines, particularly *Cosmopolitan*, encouraged their readers to undertake this type of personal grooming as a way of making their bodies more appealing, though publications such as the *Village Voice* and Salon debated the advantages.

Some have argued that pornography is responsible for the new ideal. When the films became available on video for TV viewing in the 1980s, the smaller screen meant that bodies were less easy to see; thus, actors started removing hair in order to make camerawork easier. When interviewed, the performers often said the change was a matter of cleanliness—implying that what is more visible and less obscured by hair must naturally be cleaner and healthier.

Our culture aggressively markets the idea of hygiene and products associated with it, but the cleanliness claim is not always logical. Most doctors will say that genital hair is necessary as a screen to keep germs away from some of our most vulnerable spots (they do not make the same argument, of course, about chest and armpit hair). The violence of waxing and the rashes that result increase the chance of infection. And while many women and men prefer the waxed look in others, they are unwilling to view their own bodies as grounds that need "landscaping."

Popular magazines interested in self-empowerment and self-help encourage waxing as a way both to appeal to the opposite sex and to pamper oneself. Indeed, a group of men surveyed by *Cosmopolitan* fused the two concepts, saying that they like a woman who shaves or waxes, because of the very fact that she has decided to "lavish so much attention on herself." Thus cleanliness, pornography, self-actualization, and self-pampering are tied up in a lover's knot that keeps some of America's chests, legs, and genitals bare.

Susann Cokal

SEE ALSO: Cosmopolitan*; Manscaping; Pornography;* Sex and the City*;* Sex and the Single Girl*; Sexual Revolution.*

BIBLIOGRAPHY

Cokal, Susann. "Clean Porn: The Visual Aesthetics of Hygiene, Hot Sex, and Hair Removal." In *Pop(Porn): The Proliferation of Pornography*, ed. Mardia Bishop and Ann Hall. Westport, CT: Praeger/Greenwood, 2007.

Szuchman, Paula. "The History of Bikini Waxing: Hairstyles Come and Go—Even down below (Your Body)." *Cosmopolitan*, Summer–Fall, 2004, 90.

The Wayans Family

Continuing to make strong contributions to the U.S. comedy and entertainment scene, the Wayans family has been one of the most successful and influential African American families in show business. Of four actor-producer-comedian brothers, the eldest, Keenen Ivory Wayans, and his groundbreaking television show *In Living Color* (1990–1994) launched his siblings in show business. Damon Wayans has appeared on *Saturday Night Live* (1975–), *My Wife and Kids* (2001–2005), and a number of other television shows while maintaining a successful stand-up comedy career. The youngest brother, Marlon Wayans, appeared in a number of films in the late 1990s and starred with his brother Shawn Wayans on the television sitcom *The Wayans Brothers*, airing on the WB network from 1995 to 1999. Sister Kim Wayans also appeared on *In Living Color* and has many other credits in film and television.

The Wayans brothers are familiar faces in popular movie parodies, such as the *Scary Movie* series (2000, 2001, 2003, and 2006), and continue to be bankable and popular actors. Second generations of the Wayans family have started careers in comedy and television as performers, writers, and producers.

Jay Parrent

SEE ALSO: Saturday Night Live*; Sitcom; Stand-Up Comedy; Television.*

BIBLIOGRAPHY

Graham, Judith, ed. *Current Biography Yearbook, 1995.* New York: H.W. Wilson, 1995.

"Siblings Who Are Also Celebrities." *Jet*, January 19, 1998, 56–62.

Wayne, John *(1907–1979)*

To millions of people around the world, John Wayne has come to be more than just the single most recognizable screen actor in the history of film: John Wayne is America. From the late 1920s to the mid-1970s, Wayne played a cavalcade of heroes on screen, characters who were not always likable. They were almost never "politically correct"; they rarely had any sensitivity for the plight of those who opposed them, and they were often characterized by an overt jingoism. Nevertheless, they uniformly had one thing in common: they were stereotypically American.

As a result of this unifying trait Wayne himself became, in the world's eye, synonymous with the mythical American values of rugged individualism, bravery, loyalty, integrity, and courage. Despite playing a variety of roles, including soldiers, detectives, sailors, and football players, Wayne is best remembered for his Western heroes. As Garry Wills writes in *John Wayne's America*,

John Wayne. *John Wayne played cavalry officer Colonel Cord McNally in* Rio Lobo *in 1970.* SILVER SCREEN COLLECTION/CONTRIBUTOR/MOVIEPIX/GETTY IMAGES.

"the strength of Wayne was that he embodied our deepest myth—that of the frontier."

THE EARLY YEARS

John Wayne was born Marion Michael Morrison in Winterset, Iowa, on May 26, 1907. His mother, Mary (Molly) Brown Morrison, struggled to keep the family afloat in light of the shiftlessness of Wayne's father, Clyde Morrison. After a failed career as a druggist, Clyde decided to migrate to California in 1913 to be a farmer. His wife and two sons joined him a year later. Clyde, who had no experience as a farmer, made the misbegotten choice of Lancaster, which sits in the Antelope Valley, as his place of residence. The land's aridity, in addition to his inexperience, virtually assured Clyde's failure. Most historians believe Wayne developed his ironic lifelong dislike of horses while living in Lancaster, which appears to have stemmed from having to ride one daily from his father's farm to school.

After Clyde's inevitable failure as a farmer, he once again began working in a pharmacy, this time in the Los Angeles suburb of Glendale, where the family moved in 1916. It was here that Wayne first began to blossom. His family life was relatively unstable—he lived in several different homes in his nine years in Glendale, and his parents habitually fought, which ultimately resulted in their divorce. Nevertheless, by most accounts Wayne enjoyed his time in Glendale, especially his four years (1921–1925) at Glendale High, where he was immensely popular with his peers. He joined a number of social groups and was class vice president his sophomore and junior years and class president his senior year. In addition, he wrote for the school paper, participated as an actor and a stagehand in school productions, served on many social committees, and was a star guard on the football team.

Wayne's football ability, in combination with his high grades, earned him a scholarship to play football at the University of Southern California (USC) under legendary coach Howard Jones. In the fall of 1925, full of high hopes and promise, Wayne left Glendale for good, ostensibly headed toward a career as a football hero and then, after law school, a successful lawyer. When Wayne first arrived at USC, things went well for him. To augment his scholarship, he worked in the fraternities for extra money. He loved fraternity life and pledged Sigma Chi. He earned his letter on the freshman team and was poised to join the varsity squad at the start of his sophomore year.

It was at this point that things began to go awry. Wayne's size, 6 feet, 4 inches, made him a formidable and intimidating high school football player. However, in the college game, sheer size and strength were not enough to secure a position on the team. Just as important was speed, of which Wayne possessed none. After his sophomore year of college, Wayne lost his scholarship, thus ending his days at USC. In later years he would claim it was injury that cut short a promising career.

With his scholarship lost, he began working at Twentieth Century Fox in 1927. Although he occasionally appeared as an extra when needed and even had speaking roles in John Ford's *Salute* (1929) and *Men without Women* (1930), his main responsibility consisted of using his enormous strength to move props and equipment from set to set. In 1929 Wayne's manual labor caught the attention of Raoul Walsh, who didn't notice a lack of speed so much as a grace and fluidity of motion. Walsh immediately decided to make Wayne a star; from these inauspicious circumstances began the most culturally influential career in screen acting history.

Walsh's first, and perhaps most important, suggestion to Wayne was that he change his name. With that suggestion, Marion Morrison became John "Duke" Wayne. Although Ford is generally credited with "discovering" Wayne, he did not, nor was he initially responsible for, Wayne's becoming a major star. Wayne did not become larger than life all at once but cumulatively, after a long series of fits and starts. And more important perhaps than even *Stagecoach* (1939) was his long apprenticeship as a leading man in 1930s "B" Westerns, which began with his appearance in Walsh's epic *The Big Trail* in 1930.

THE MAKINGS OF A WESTERN HERO

For *The Big Trail* Wayne underwent a Hollywood makeover that would pervade his on-screen persona for the remainder of his life. He was taught to communicate with Native Americans via hand signals; wear the garb of a cowboy; and, perhaps most importantly, to properly ride a horse; Walsh transformed Wayne into a Western hero. In the early 1990s the Museum of Modern Art restored *The Big Trail* to its original form, which resulted in contemporary critics raising it to its rightful place in the pantheon of Hollywood's Western classics. However, at the time of its release *The Big Trail* was a financial failure.

This was disastrous for Fox studios, which had gambled its survival on the film's anticipated box-office success. Fox went into receivership, and Wayne was denied the studio buildup he would have received otherwise. Instead of becoming a major star, he was forced to scramble to find work at seven different studios over the next eight years. Nevertheless, the film convinced Hollywood that Wayne had potential as a Western hero.

From 1930 to 1939 Wayne appeared as the hero in some eighty films, the vast majority of which were Westerns. Although he was languishing financially, he was honing his craft; perfecting his famous walk, his economy of speech and movement; and learning, in his own words, to re-act rather than act—"How many times do I gotta tell you, I don't act at all, I *re*-act." Also important during this time was his relationship with Yakima Canutt, the famous Hollywood stuntman who profoundly influenced Wayne's career. Canutt was not only the toughest man on whatever set he happened to be working, he was also the most professional. Both traits rubbed off on Wayne. Many critics have poked fun at Wayne's sometimes stiff on-screen persona, especially during his later years when his work often seemed to unintentionally border on self-parody, but the fact of the matter is that under Canutt's influence in the 1930s, Wayne became a consummate student of film and remained so until the end of his life.

Despite his offscreen ribaldry, Wayne was always sober, prepared, intense, and by most accounts a generous actor when on set. That he survived the Depression as an actor is itself no small accomplishment, but he was still a minor figure in the landscape of Hollywood cinema. And then came 1939 and Ford's *Stagecoach*, the film that would begin to change Wayne's career.

STAGECOACH AND THE BEGINNING OF CULTURAL IMMORTALITY

By 1939 Wayne was a firmly established "B" Western movie star, but literally hundreds of actors were still better known. *Stagecoach* changed all that. Walter Wanger, the film's producer, urged Ford to cast Gary Cooper and Marlene Dietrich as the Ringo Kid and Dallas, but according to Tag Gallagher, Ford didn't want established stars and instead convinced Wanger that Wayne and Claire Trevor were right for the parts. He did so because casting Cooper and Dietrich would have led audiences to bring preconceived notions to the film. They were not only stars but "personalities" as well (especially Dietrich). In casting relative unknowns, Ford was able to ensure that audiences would be enthralled with the story and not the visual presence of big stars. For Wayne it was the film that began his climb toward cultural immortality.

Stagecoach's success helped Wayne in Hollywood, but he was still not quite the larger-than-life figure that he has since become. The final piece of that puzzle would not come until the release of Howard Hawks's *Red River* in 1948. Hawks saw in Wayne a man capable of better acting than had previously been required of him and cast him as Tom Dunson, a hard-driving authoritarian cattleman who was an older, darker, and much less sympathetic character than Wayne had previously played. His performance was brilliant, and other directors—the most important of whom was Ford—took note. Once it was discovered that Wayne not only looked the part of a hero but was a good actor as well, his career skyrocketed; he became a major Hollywood star at the age of forty.

From this point forward Wayne predominantly played the kinds of roles for which he is best remembered, what Wills calls "the authority figure, the guide for younger men, the melancholy person weighed down with responsibility." Perhaps the blueprint for the iconic Wayne character is his Sergeant Stryker from *Sands of Iwo Jima* (1949), who to this day is an enduring symbol for right-wing America. Stryker's cry of "Lock and load" has been used as a battle cry by many, including Oliver North; Pat Buchanan; and, more ironically, Sergeant Barnes, the villain of Oliver Stone's antiwar film *Platoon* (1986).

Wayne's on-screen persona became perhaps the only one in movie history that is hated or revered because of its perceived politics. A lot of people love Wayne simply because they love his movies, but seemingly just as many either like or dislike his films on the basis of the right-wing politics with which they have become inextricably associated. Clearly not all of Wayne's characters fit the right-wing stereotype with which they have been identified. However, beginning in the 1950s Wayne himself became increasingly political, which in turn affected the way people thought of his movies. Just as his on-screen persona came to be seen as representing American values, so too did he publicly begin to project the image of a superpatriotic ultra-American defender of the Old Guard. During the height of the McCarthy era, he helped form the Motion Picture Alliance for the Preservation of American Ideals, over which he eventually presided as president.

That he had this public persona apparently never struck Wayne as ironic, even though in his personal life he was both an active womanizer who married three times and a famously heavy drinker. In 1960 he directed and starred in *The Alamo*, which, despite some fine moments, is generally recognized as a mess. However, in the story of the siege of the Alamo, Wayne thought he saw a metaphor for all that was good in American character. Furthermore, he was a fundamentalist hawk who made the Vietnam War a personal crusade, which ultimately resulted in his both starring in and codirecting the excruciatingly propagandistic *The Green Berets* (1969). In the face of the seemingly senseless deaths of so many American youths in Vietnam, this film rubbed many the wrong way, especially because the varied reasons the pro-military Wayne offered for never having served in the armed forces himself were hazy at best.

Despite his success in other genres, Wayne was still the quintessential Western hero. After *Red River*, the primary reason for the perpetuation of Wayne's work in Westerns was a renewed working relationship with Ford, who saw in Wayne for perhaps the first time an actor capable of exuding the strength, confidence, and staunch independence typical of so many of Ford's heroes. The director saw Wayne as emblematic of the kind of hero he wanted in his films, and he was also able to get better work out of him than did any other director (with the notable exception of Hawks's *Red River* and *Rio Bravo* [1959]). This is perhaps because in films after *Stagecoach*, Ford cast Wayne in roles that were tailored to suit his particular talents. The result was a series of classic films, including the Cavalry Trilogy—*Fort Apache* (1948), *She Wore a Yellow Ribbon* (1949), and *Rio Grande* (1950)—and *The Quiet Man* (1952), an Irish love story that is perhaps both Wayne and Ford's best-loved film.

In Ford's later films he cannily chipped away at the veneer of Wayne's Western hero image. In films such as *The Searchers* (1956) and *The Man Who Shot Liberty Valance* (1962), Ford played on Wayne's cinematic iconography and increasing chronological age to re-create him as a far more complex, embittered figure than he was in the director's earlier work.

THE BIG C

After his work as Tom Doniphon in Ford's last masterpiece, *The Man Who Shot Liberty Valance*, Wayne starred in films that capitalized on his iconic stature as the quintessential Western hero. He repeatedly played individualistic tough guys with a strong personal code of morality. Although films such as *The Sons of Katie Elder* (1965), *Chisum* (1970), and *Big Jake* (1971) lacked the artistry of his earlier work with Ford and Hawks, they were nevertheless successful at the box office. In 1970 Hollywood finally awarded Wayne a long overdue Oscar, which he received for his performance as Rooster Cogburn, *True Grit*'s hard-drinking, eye-patch wearing, Western marshal. Offscreen Wayne had survived cancer in 1964, at which time he had a lung removed. He said he had "licked the Big C," but this was ultimately not the case.

In 1976 Wayne starred in *The Shootist*, the last of some 250 films and one that had haunting parallels with Wayne's real-life situation. In it Wayne plays J. B. Books, a reformed killer dying of cancer who is trying to live out his final days in peace. The film was not the celebratory cash cow that so much of his other work had been. Instead, it is a much more accurate depiction of the death of the West. It also contained an eerily prescient emotional resonance in its reflection of Wayne's off-screen battle with cancer. After its completion, Wayne underwent open-heart surgery in 1978. He then had his stomach removed in 1979. After a courageous battle, Wayne's cancer finally got the better of him on June 11, 1979.

During his lifetime, Wayne was Hollywood's biggest star, making the top ten in distributors' lists of stars with commercial appeal in all but one year from 1949 to 1974. Remarkably, death hasn't dimmed his stardom. In 1993 pollsters asked Americans "Who is your favorite star?" and Wayne came in second to Clint Eastwood, the same place he earned one year later when the poll was conducted again. In 1995 Wayne finished first. Even in death his cultural presence seems only to become more pervasive, continuing to flourish even in the late 1990s, an era in which most movie stars' time on top seemed to be more accurately measured in minutes than in years. Why does Wayne's popularity continue to grow? Perhaps Joan Didion said it best when she wrote that Wayne "determined forever the shape of certain of our dreams."

Early on in *Stagecoach*, there is a moment in which the stage encounters the Ringo Kid (Wayne) standing along the roadside, looking magnificent with his saddle slung over his left shoulder and his rifle, which he spins with graceful aplomb, in his right hand. Contemporary viewers can't help but think of Wayne, regardless of the particular character he is playing, as "The Duke." As historian Anne Butler writes in her essay in *The Oxford History of the American West*, "more than any other medium, film is responsible for the image of the West as a place locked in the nineteenth century and defined by stark encounters between whites and Indians, law and disorder. Although social trends have altered the content of Western films, the strong, silent man of action—epitomized by John Wayne—remains the central figure."

Wayne has come to stand for a particular kind of American, one who takes no guff and fights for what he knows is right, which often appears to be what is best for America as well, for no other reason than we cannot imagine Wayne, who in his personal life was far from an angel, as leading us down the wrong path. For better or worse the perception of John Wayne as the defining human symbol of America has become firmly ensconced in the collective global psyche.

Robert C. Sickels

SEE ALSO: *Academy Awards; "B" Movies; Cancer; Celebrity; College Football; Cooper, Gary; The Cowboy Look; Dietrich, Marlene; Eastwood, Clint; The Fifties; Ford, John; The Great Depression; Hawks, Howard; Hollywood;* The Man Who Shot Liberty Valance*; McCarthyism; Movie Stars;* Platoon*; Political Correctness;* The Searchers*;* She Wore a Yellow Ribbon*;* Stagecoach*; Stone, Oliver; Trevor, Claire; Vietnam; War Movies; The Western.*

BIBLIOGRAPHY

Butler, Anne M. "Selling the Popular Myth." In *The Oxford History of the American West*, ed. Clyde A. Milner, Carol A. O'Connor, and Martha A. Sandweiss. New York: Oxford University Press, 1994.

Cameron, Ian, and Douglas Pye, eds. *The Book of Westerns.* New York: Continuum, 1996.

Davis, Ronald L. *Duke: The Life and Image of John Wayne.* Norman: University of Oklahoma Press, 1998.

Didion, Joan. "John Wayne, a Love Song." *Slouching towards Bethlehem.* New York: Farrar, Straus & Giroux, 1968.

Kazanjian, Howard, and Chris Enss. *The Young Duke: The Early Life of John Wayne.* Guilford, CT: TwoDot, 2007.

Levy, Emanuel. *John Wayne: Prophet of the American Way of Life.* Metuchen, NJ: Scarecrow Press, 1988.

Munn, Michael. *John Wayne: The Man behind the Myth.* Waterville, ME: Thorndike Press, 2004.

Riggin, Judith M. *John Wayne: A Bio-bibliography.* New York: Greenwood Press, 1992.

Slotkin, Richard. *Gunfighter Nation: The Myth of the Frontier in Twentieth-Century America.* New York: Atheneum, 1992.

Wills, Garry. *John Wayne's America: The Politics of Celebrity.* New York: Simon & Schuster, 1997.

Wayne's World

The release of *Wayne's World* in 1992 marked the dawn of a new era of deliberately dumb comedies and ensured the production, if not the success, of a slew of other movies based on popular characters from the television show *Saturday Night Live. Wayne's World* was significant not only for its surprising popularity—it grossed more than $180 million worldwide—but also because its witty, self-conscious script and deliberately ludicrous jargon set a new standard for comedies aimed at a youth market in the 1990s.

Wayne's World was the first skit to be expanded from *Saturday Night Live* into a full-length feature since the very successful cult film *The Blues Brothers* was released in 1980. Like *The Blues Brothers*, the chemistry in *Wayne's World* lay in the rapport between two characters, Wayne Campbell and Garth Algar, played respectively by *Saturday Night Live* alumni Mike Myers and Dana Carvey. Myers developed the original characters and shared writing credits with Bonnie Turner for the final movie script, with *Saturday Night Live* producer Lorne Michaels retaining his duties for the film. A less likely member of the production team was director Penelope Spheeris who, although well respected, had built her reputation via a rather different take on youth culture with underground hits such as the dark *Suburbia* (1983) and *The Decline of Western Civilization Part II: The Metal Years* (1988), a documentary on the rise of heavy-metal bands in the early 1980s.

Beyond the good-natured simplicity of its plot, *Wayne's World* influenced the marketing strategies of future comedies. The promotional team took the unprecedented step of pouring the majority of their relatively small budget into buying advertising time on the youth-oriented cable music channel MTV, including sponsorship of an hour-long special on the film, and the bet paid off with huge box-office sales to the targeted youth audience. Cannily, the films had recognized that teenagers in the 1990s were increasingly cynical about exactly such marketing, and the plot of the film depicted a naive Wayne and Garth tempted by an unscrupulous television producer to include key products in their popular public access TV show.

In one memorable scene in the movie, Wayne and Garth balk at the suggestion that they sell out; standing in front of a loaded buffet table, the producer (played by Rob Lowe) tells them they have no choice. With a grin that lets audiences in on the spoof, Wayne responds by picking up a Pepsi and replying that, in fact, he does have a choice—and it is "the choice of a New Generation," Pepsi's current tagline. Similar overt references to other products are found throughout the movie, including spoofs on the campaigns for Doritos and Grey Poupon mustard.

In an ironic gesture befitting the movie, *Wayne's World* spun off a galaxy of commercial tie-ins, including a VCR board game, a Nintendo game, and a book cowritten by Myers, as well as the usual coffee mugs, T-shirts, and action figures. Perhaps the most unusual tie-in was a *Wayne's World*–themed amusement park section that opened in 1994 at Paramount's Kings Dominion (renamed Kings Dominion in 2007) in Virginia. There patrons could ride the Hurler roller coaster and pose next to Garth's Mirthmobile, a powder blue Pacer. (The attractions have since been revamped and stripped of most of the *Wayne's World* references).

The popularity of *Wayne's World* guaranteed a sequel, *Wayne's World 2*, released in 1993. Although both Myers and Carvey returned and the film was a commercial success, it received mediocre reviews from critics. Regardless, the *Wayne's World* movies are widely credited for leading the way for a new wave of comedy features starring television comics, including Jim Carrey's *Ace Ventura: Pet Detective* (1994), Adam Sandler's *Billy Madison* (1995), and Chris Farley's *Tommy Boy* (1995).

Deborah Broderson

SEE ALSO: *Advertising; The Blues Brothers; Farley, Chris; Heavy Metal; MTV;* Saturday Night Live*; Television.*

BIBLIOGRAPHY

Hamblin, Cory. *Serket's Movies: Commentary and Trivia on 444 Movies*. Pittsburgh, PA: Rosedog Books, 2009.

Myers, Mike, and Robin Ruzan. *Wayne's World: Extreme Close Up*. New York: Cader Books, 1992.

Rutter, Jason. "Stepping into *Wayne's World*: Exploring Postmodern Comedy." In *The Postmodern Presence: Readings on Postmodernism*, ed. Arthur Asa Berger. Walnut Creek, CA: AltaMira Press, 1998.

The Weathermen

Perhaps the Weathermen's greatest significance lay in their exploitation by President Richard Nixon's administration, which characterized them as typical protestors, despite their avowed goal to bring about a violent communist revolution in the United States. These few hundred extremists were used to represent the thousands constituting the antiwar movement, a strategy that allowed Nixon to offer the "silent majority" a clear choice: either his plan of gradual disengagement from the Vietnam War (called "Vietnamization") or the violent revolution supposedly espoused by all of the war's opponents.

ORIGIN OF THE WEATHERMEN

The Weathermen rose from the ashes of the Students for a Democratic Society (SDS), which self-destructed at its 1969 convention in a power struggle between the Progressive Labor (PL) Party—whose adherents were older, socialist, and principally interested in organizing workers to bring about social change—and the Revolutionary Youth Movement (RYM), younger, communist-oriented revolutionaries who saw armed struggle as the only viable political option. RYM's manifesto, distributed at the conference, was titled after a Bob Dylan lyric: "You don't need a weatherman to know which way the wind blows." The crisis came when Bernardine Dohrn, a leader of RYM and one of SDS's three national secretaries, gave a blistering speech that ended with her announcing the expulsion of PL from SDS. Many other members, adherents of neither faction, quit in disgust, leaving behind only the most radicalized element, RYM, which initially retained SDS's name but soon became known as Weatherman, the Weather Underground, or more commonly the Weathermen.

The new organization was small, so recruitment was deemed necessary before meaningful political activity could take place. The Weathermen believed that working-class white youths offered the best prospects for new members—these young people were already alienated from the system, it was reasoned, and would thus be eager recruits for the revolution. The effort was not a success. Some Weathermen tried to impress urban street kids with their toughness by challenging them to fight. Brawls were easy to find, but recruits were not. Other members invaded high schools in working-class areas, shouting "Jailbreak!" and disrupting classes, but most students were uninterested in the Weathermen's call to rise up against their teachers and the state.

VIOLENT PROTESTS

More dramatic action to garner attention and interest seemed called for, and the Weathermen's solution was the Days of Rage, a planned four-day series of demonstrations in Chicago in November 1969. The Weathermen chose Chicago partly in the hope of exacting revenge on the city's police, who had brutalized demonstrators during the 1968 Democratic National Convention, and partly because the leaders of those demonstrations—the so-called Chicago Seven—were facing trial on conspiracy charges there. The Weathermen wanted to protest the trial and also to take advantage of the presence of the national news media, which covered the proceedings.

Although the organizers of the Days of Rage predicted the attendance of thousands of protesters, only about 700 showed up. Over three days they demonstrated, rampaged through affluent downtown areas, and fought with the police. Many were arrested, with both police and protesters suffering injuries of varying severity. On balance, the Days of Rage were a failure. Chicago's working-class youth did not rally to the Weathermen's cause. Further, other organizations in the antiwar movement denounced the Weathermen's actions as counterproductive and cut off all ties with them. Even the Black Panthers, a militant group known for its defiant confrontations with authority, were critical of the Days of Rage.

The leaders of the Weathermen decided on a change of strategy. The most committed among them would drop out of public view, "go underground" in small groups, and strike out at the state with a coordinated program of bombings. The bombing went on for the next eleven months. The targets chosen were all politically symbolic, and the bombs were usually planted in retaliation for some action that the Weathermen perceived as oppressive: A bomb was set at the home of a New York City judge who was presiding over a trial of some Black Panthers. Another went off in a Pentagon lavatory after Nixon ordered increased bombing of North Vietnam. Still another bomb exploded at the office of the New York State Department of Corrections after the brutal suppression of the Attica prison riot.

END OF THE WEATHERMEN

Despite their reputation, as well as their violent rhetoric, the Weathermen were always careful to call in a bomb threat at least an hour before their bombs were timed to detonate. This allowed the target buildings to be evacuated, so no people were hurt in the blasts. The only fatalities that resulted from the Weathermen's bombs were three of their own members. On March 6, 1970, a town house in New York's Greenwich Village blew up. The owner, James Wilkerson, was away; he had allowed his daughter Cathy to stay there, little suspecting that she had joined the Weathermen, or that the place would be used as a bomb factory. Diana Oughton, Ted Gold, and Terry Robbins were killed in the blast.

The deaths of their comrades sobered the surviving Weathermen. They called off the bombing campaign and began to adopt more mainstream methods of persuasion. While still underground, they put out a number of publications espousing their political views and also gave interviews to counterculture publications such as the *Berkeley Tribe*. The Weathermen leaders, including Dohrn, even cooperated with director Emile de Antonio in the making of a documentary called *Underground.*

By 1975 the communist victory in Vietnam made the Weathermen passé. Internal squabbling soon put a finish to the organization, and its leaders eventually abandoned their fugitive lifestyle and rejoined the society they had claimed to so despise. *The Weather Underground*, a 2002 documentary about the group by Sam Green and Bill Siegel was nominated for an Academy Award and, combined with the controversy regarding then-presidential candidate Barack Obama's relationship with former Weatherman activist Bill Ayers, served to bring the group to the surface of the nation's collective memory, facilitating a number of books about the group and the period.

Justin Gustainis

SEE ALSO: *Academy Awards; Black Panthers; The Chicago Seven; Dylan, Bob; Obama, Barack; Protest Groups; Student Demonstrations; Students for a Democratic Society (SDS); Vietnam.*

BIBLIOGRAPHY

Berger, Dan. *Outlaws of America: The Weather Underground and the Politics of Solidarity.* Oakland, CA: AK Press, 2006.

Collier, Peter, and David Horowitz. *Destructive Generation.* New York: Summit Books, 1990.

Dohrn, Bernardine; Bill Ayers; and Jeff Jones, eds. *Sing a Battle Song: The Revolutionary Poetry, Statements and Communiqués of the Weather Underground.* New York: Seven Stories Press, 2006.

Jacobs, Harold. *Weatherman.* Berkeley, CA: Ramparts Press, 1970.

Jacobs, Ron. *The Way the Wind Blew: A History of the Weather Underground.* New York: Verso, 1997.

Rudd, M. *Underground: My Life with SDS and the Weathermen.* New York: HarperCollins, 2010.

Varon, Jeremy. *Bringing the War Home: The Weather Underground, the Red Army Faction, and Revolutionary Violence in the '60s and '70s.* Berkeley: University of California Press, 2004.

The Weather Underground. Directed by Sam Green and Bill Siegel. DVD. New York: New Video Group, 2003.

Wilkerson, Cathy. *Flying Close to the Sun: My Life and Times as a Weatherman.* New York: Seven Stories Press, 2007.

Weaver, Sigourney *(1949–)*

A tall, imposing actor who did not fit the mold of the glamorous Hollywood heroine, Sigourney Weaver has been most memorable in her roles as misfits and outsiders. Following more sedate beginnings on the live stage, Weaver exploded into fame in 1979 with the role of the gritty warrior Lieutenant Ellen Ripley in the horror film *Alien.* Independent and fierce, Ripley broke new ground for female protagonists and made *Alien* and its sequels into something unique in the horror-action genre. Weaver went on to play a wide variety of society's nonconformists, from a reclusive zoologist in *Gorillas in the Mist* (1988) to an isolated autistic woman in *Snow Cake* (2006). In the process she became a respected matriarch of the acting community and, though she was once called uncastable, one of the most authentic stars in Hollywood.

Weaver was born into entertainment aristocracy. Her father, Sylvester "Pat" Weaver, was an executive at the NBC television network, and her mother, Elizabeth Inglis, had been a respected stage and film actor in England before giving up her career to raise her family. Tall from an early age, Weaver learned young that a sense of humor could deflect unkind teasing. She became a class clown and then took to the stage, first in high school productions and then at Stanford University, where she developed an interest in Japanese Noh theater. After graduation she attended the Yale School of Drama, a painful experience (she was repeatedly told that she was too tall to be cast in leading female roles) that led to her developing the thick skin and inner confidence necessary for an acting career.

Besides a brief role in the NBC soap opera *Somerset*, most of Weaver's early work was in live theater, where she won a Drama Desk Award for her work in *Das Lusitania Songspiel*, which she cowrote with friend and colleague Christopher Durang. She first came to the notice of critics for a memorable six-second role at the end of Woody Allen's 1977 film *Annie Hall*, and in 1979 she was cast as the lead in the Ridley Scott blockbuster *Alien.* The role of Ripley, the tough warrant officer on a spaceship facing alien invasion, had originally been written for a man. Casting the tall, impressively built Weaver in the role gave Ripley a depth and authenticity unusual in a female protagonist and made *Alien* an instant hit. The film had an especially enthusiastic fan base of feminists and lesbians who welcomed the introduction of a competent and courageous proactive woman hero. *Alien* spawned four sequels, three of which starred Weaver as Ripley, and one, *Aliens* (1986), directed by James Cameron, was hailed as even better than the first film.

Once launched, Weaver's film career gained momentum, with acclaimed performances in Peter Yates's *Eyewitness* (1981) and Peter Weir's *The Year of Living Dangerously* (1982). In the 1984 Ivan Reitman comedy hit *Ghostbusters* she demonstrated the comic skill she had honed as a gawky adolescent. In 1988 Weaver took on the role of another independent woman; her portrayal of zoologist Dian Fossey in *Gorillas in the Mist* earned her a Golden Globe Award and an Oscar nomination for Best Actress. Having gained fame in roles that were neither glamorous nor traditional, Weaver proved she could also play high fashion as the villainous executive in the 1988 Mike Nichols comedy *Working Girl*, for which she once again won the Golden Globe and an Oscar nomination, this time for Best Actress in a Supporting Role.

Over the next two decades Weaver continued to demonstrate her star power and versatility in comedies such as the 1999 Dean Parisot outer space spoof *Galaxy Quest* and in intense dramas such as *Death and the Maiden* (directed by Roman Polanski; 1994). Continuing to choose unconventional and unexpected roles, she portrayed the isolating frustration and the humanity of autism in Marc Evans's *Snow Cake*, and in 2009 she took on the emotional role of a homophobic mother who drives her gay son to suicide before overcoming her prejudice in the Lifetime television movie *Prayers for Bobby*. Also in 2009 she reunited with Cameron for a major role in the 3-D science fiction blockbuster *Avatar*.

In addition to her prolific work in films, Weaver has occasionally been drawn back to the stage. In 1984 she was nominated for a Tony Award for her work in Nichols's *Hurlyburly*, and in 1996 she returned to Broadway in Durang's *Sex and Longing*. During the mid-1990s Weaver—with her husband, director Jim Simpson, and other theater professionals—founded the Flea Theater, a nonprofit off-Broadway venue for innovative drama.

In her sixties by the 2010s, Weaver remained an unconventional star, allowing her wrinkles and flaws to show, and she rejected the plastic surgery route to eternal youth. Like many of the strong heroines she portrayed, she kept her individuality in an industry that often demands conformity. In the process she added a number of iconic figures to the pantheon of pop culture film heroes, starting with Ripley, the alien fighter.

Christian L. Pyle

SEE ALSO: *Academy Awards;* Alien; *Allen, Woody;* Annie Hall; Avatar; *Broadway; Feminism; Hollywood; Lesbianism; Nichols, Mike, and Elaine May; Scott, Ridley; Tony Awards.*

BIBLIOGRAPHY

Hrabi, Dale. "Hail Mary." *Advocate*, February 2009, 81.

Maguffee, T. D. *Sigourney Weaver*. New York: St. Martin's Press, 1989.

Smith, C. Jason, and Ximena Gallardo C. *Alien Woman: The Making of Lt. Ellen Ripley*. New York: Continuum, 2004.

Waits, Donna. *The Sigourney Weaver Handbook—Everything You Need to Know about Sigourney Weaver*. Brisbane, Australia: Emereo, 2011.

The Weavers

Formed in 1948 by folksinger and banjoist Pete Seeger, the Weavers were considered the quintessential U.S. folk music group of its era, popularizing such classic tunes as "On Top of Old Smokey" and "Goodnight, Irene" before falling under the shadow of McCarthyism in the 1950s. When they began performing, the four members of the group had collectively amassed a repertoire of traditional ballads and folk songs; before disbanding in 1963, the Weavers had recorded many of these on popular albums, successfully bringing American folk music to the attention of a mass audience. Though their smooth, polished sound ruffled the feathers of a few folk-music purists, the Weavers have been credited for fueling the careers of numerous young performers who followed them, prompting the formation of the Newport Folk Festival series in the late 1950s and what would later be known as the American Folk Revival.

Unlike most popular folk-music performers of the mid-twentieth century, which included the Kingston Trio; Peter, Paul, and Mary; Bob Dylan; Joan Baez; the Clancy Brothers & Tommy Makem; and Canada's husband-and-wife team Ian & Sylvia, the members of the Weavers were significantly older than their fans (Seeger was born in 1919). Rather than their youth, it was their enthusiasm and folk-music credentials that earned the Weavers their legions of fans. Seeger, in particular, had ties to many folk performers of earlier decades, including the legendary Woody Guthrie, with whom he had performed as part of the Almanac Singers during the early 1940s.

The Weavers. *The members of the Weavers folk group were, clockwise from upper left, Pete Seeger, Ronnie Gilbert, Lee Hays, and Fred Hellerman.* © UNDERWOOD & UNDERWOOD/CORBIS.

The Weavers—Seeger, Lee Hays, Fred Hellerman, and female vocalist Ronnie Gilbert—debuted at New York City's Village Vanguard folk club in 1948. The Manhattan-born Seeger had abandoned a promising Harvard education to learn to play the long-necked banjo and hitchhike across the United States for the purpose of collecting the nation's folk songs. By contrast, Hays, with his deep, rumbling voice, had begun his career singing in the rural churches of his native Arkansas. The two younger members of the group, guitarist Hellerman and vocalist Gilbert, had become friends upon recognizing their common interest in folk music while working as summer-camp counselors in New Jersey.

The four musicians met during folk-music hootenannies in Greenwich Village during the mid-1940s and quickly decided that their combined vocals, backed by Seeger's banjo and recorder and Hellerman's acoustic guitar, made for a good mix. The foursome also received encouragement from folk-music fans wherever they performed. A six-month gig at the Village Vanguard, where such folkies as Burl Ives and Richard Dyer-Bennett had gotten their starts, allowed the group to perform its musical mix of everything from work-gang songs from the Old South to Indonesian lullabies.

Eventually the Weavers sparked the interest of Decca Records, which recorded two of the group's favorite songs: "Goodnight, Irene," by bluesman Leadbelly, and the Israeli hora "Tzena, Tzena, Tzena." Within a year both songs made the hit parade, with record sales to the college crowd cresting the million mark. The Weavers moved to Manhattan's Blue Angel nightclub and from there to Broadway's Strand Theater, where its take-home pay rose to $2,000 a week. The group was soon on its way to national prominence, with offers for bookings from venues in cities across the United States.

The Weavers' meteoric rise to national prominence abruptly ended in 1952, when Seeger's leftist leanings caused the group to fall under the shadow of the "Red Scare" that was fueled by Senator Joseph McCarthy and the House Un-American Activities Committee. Included among those entertainers suspected of procommunist sentiments, the group was blacklisted by theater owners and radio and television stations. Forced to return to the smaller folk clubs and coffeehouses where they had gotten their start, the Weavers continued their career in the folk community for another ten years before finally disbanding in 1963. During this period they recorded several albums for both Decca and Vanguard, among them *Weavers Almanac*, *Weavers on Tour*, *Travelling with the Weavers*, and *The Weavers at Carnegie Hall*—the last considered the group's finest album. Many of their songs continue to be available on album reissues.

While Seeger's political convictions may have ultimately ended the career of the Weavers—he was cited for contempt of Congress in 1961, although his conviction was ultimately overturned—he eventually emerged undaunted. Seeger has continued to entertain generations of Americans with songs that have become modern-day folk classics, as well as composing "If I Had a Hammer" and "We Shall Overcome," both of which became anthems of the civil rights movement of the 1960s.

Pamela L. Shelton

SEE ALSO: *Baez, Joan; Civil Rights Movement; Dylan, Bob; Folk Music; McCarthyism; Newport Jazz and Folk Festivals; Peter, Paul, and Mary; Seeger, Pete.*

BIBLIOGRAPHY

Cantwell, Robert. *When We Were Good: The Folk Revival.* Cambridge, MA: Harvard University Press, 1996.

Dicaire, David. *The Early Years of Folk Music: Fifty Founders of the Tradition.* Jefferson, NC: McFarland, 2010.

Lawless, Ray M. *Folksingers and Folksongs in America: A Handbook of Biography, Bibliography, and Discography.* New York: Duell, Sloan and Pearce, 1965.

"Out of the Corner." *Time*, September 25, 1950.

Willens, Doris. *Lonesome Traveler: The Life of Lee Hays.* New York: Norton, 1988.

Webb, Chick *(1902?–1939)*

With precise ensemble playing rather than standout soloists, drummer Chick Webb's orchestra regularly won big band jazz contests in the mid-1930s. Webb was born in Baltimore, Maryland, though the year of his birth remains in question: by some accounts it was 1902, while others place it at 1909. As an adult, Webb moved to New York City, and in 1926 he started a band that included star sax men Benny Carter and Johnny Hodges. Despite his diminutive stature, which was aggravated by a curved spine, Webb was a virtuoso drummer, anchoring his band's beat with impeccable taste. Starting in 1933 band member Edgar Sampson arranged such landmark numbers as "Stompin' at the Savoy." When Webb discovered the teenage Ella Fitzgerald in 1935, her singing led the band to new heights, with hit records for Decca and regular appearances at the Savoy Ballroom in Harlem, New York, broadcast nationally. After Webb died of spinal tuberculosis in 1939, Fitzgerald led the band for two years.

Benjamin Griffith

SEE ALSO: *Big Bands; Fitzgerald, Ella; Harlem Renaissance; Jazz; Savoy Ballroom.*

BIBLIOGRAPHY

Atkins, Ronald, ed. *All That Jazz.* New York: Smithmark, 1996.

Balliett, Whitney. *American Musicians.* New York: Oxford Press, 1986.

Otfinoski, Steven. *African Americans in the Performing Arts.* New York: Facts On File, 2003.

Simon, George T. *The Big Bands.* New York: Macmillan, 1974.

Webb, Jack *(1920–1982)*

Jack Webb's most famous public persona, Sergeant Joe Friday of the Los Angeles Police Department (LAPD), seemed to be a man with virtually no personality. Yet, paradoxically, this amazingly versatile actor-director-writer-producer-editor-executive was one of the most influential personalities to work in television during the 1950s and 1960s—the heyday of the Big Three networks and the formative period of the Media Age. He exerted his influence by speaking directly to the hitherto unexploited American appetite for unemotional professionalism. He was, as

Jack Webb. *Jack Webb portrayed Sgt. Joe Friday in* Dragnet *beginning in 1951.* SILVER SCREEN COLLECTION/CONTRIBUTOR/MOVIEPIX/GETTY IMAGES.

Norman Mailer said of the astronaut Neil Armstrong, "apparently in communion with some string in the universe others did not think to play." His not-so-secret weapon was an intense and exclusive focus on surface reality, a focus summed up in the most famous (and endlessly lampooned) line from his television series *Dragnet*: "Just the facts, ma'am."

Born April 2, 1920, in Santa Monica, California, John Randolph "Jack" Webb was educated at Belmont High School and served in the U.S. Army Air Force during World War II from 1942 to 1945. After his discharge, he joined the broadcast industry as a radio announcer in San Francisco. By the time he made his debut as a film actor—playing, significantly, a police detective in the film noir thriller *He Walked by Night* (1948)—Webb was well established as the lead in the radio dramas *Pat Novak for Hire* (1946) and *Johnny Modero, Pier 23* (1947).

DRAGNET

In 1949 he created the police series *Dragnet*. Although he continued to produce the radio version until 1955, he took the series to television as well in 1951, where it became one of the top-rated police dramas in broadcast history. He kept acting in other people's motion pictures though 1951, most memorably in Billy Wilder's *Sunset Boulevard* and in Fred Zinneman's *The Men*, both in 1950. After 1951 he acted only in movies he directed: *Dragnet* (1954), *Pete Kelly's Blues* (1955), *The D.I.* (1957), *-30-* (1959), and *The Last Time I Saw Archie* (1961). As a filmmaker, Webb was a genuine auteur, his directing style an extension of his television techniques.

Although Webb's movies rarely enjoyed much critical or popular success, they were nevertheless individually quite enjoyable—especially *Pete Kelly's Blues*, with its meticulous reconstruction of 1920s New Orleans and its shining performance by jazz singer Peggy Lee; *The D.I.*, about an unyielding drill instructor at the marine corps' Paris Island; and *-30-*, an exciting melodrama about a big-city newspaper. Judging his work by the exaggerated standards of Hollywood, critic Andrew Sarris says in *The American Cinema* that Webb's "style was too controlled for the little he had to say"—a clever formulation, and accurate enough to be worth repeating, but too dismissive. Webb's impact on American cinema was negligible, except that his 1954 film *Dragnet* was one of the first motion pictures to be derived from a television series.

Webb's impact on television was another matter. New episodes of *Dragnet* were produced from December 16, 1951, to September 6, 1959, and again from January 12, 1967, through September 10, 1970. By the time it finally went into syndication, *Dragnet* had become a significant presence in modern American folklore. Particularly striking were Walter Schumann's title theme; Webb's clipped, understated narration ("This is the city. Los Angeles, California. I work here. . . . I'm a cop."); the epilogue detailing the punishments imposed upon the evening's criminals; the sweaty, muscular forearms that chiseled the logo "Mark VII" (Webb's production company) into granite at the end of the program; and, of course, the quick, staccato, emotionless dialogue—an effect Webb sought deliberately and achieved by having his actors read their lines cold, from cue cards. Webb not only starred as Joe Friday but also produced all the episodes, wrote and directed most of them, and provided the voice-over narration. Before each episode of *Dragnet* was filmed, the script was submitted to the LAPD for approval and possible changes.

OTHER TV SERIES

Beginning in 1968, Webb created several other series, the most notable being *Adam 12* (1968–1975), about two LAPD officers in a patrol car, and *Emergency!* (1972–1979), which concerned the adventures of a mobile rescue unit. Though he did not appear in any of his other projects, each bore Webb's trademarks: they were about the lives of public service professionals, and the exclusive emphasis was on the characters' professional—not private—lives. Furthermore, the stories were told in Webb's patented low-key, obsessively factual, style—as if he were an engineer and making a television program was a dirty job but somebody had to do it.

Although he would undoubtedly have been horrified at the suggestion that he was "cool," Webb's laconic style was indeed a kind of cool, which is why it worked so well on the "cool" medium of television. He understood instinctively that histrionics and violent spectacle did not go over very well on television and could even be off-putting. What did go over well were close-ups of people talking to each other and a scrupulous, admirable record of people doing their jobs. His tremendous success was based upon his sure knowledge that, at any given moment in history, the squares outnumber the hipsters by about 500,000 to 1.

For example, Joe Friday was an archetypal stiff and proud of it, and his moral code was as simple and clear cut as his conception of his job as a cop: things were either right or wrong, as an act was either legal or illegal. It should not surprise anyone that Americans found this appealing—and Webb was able to reintroduce *Dragnet* at the height of the chaotic 1960s and keep it on the air, highly rated, through four complete seasons. Indeed, the people who welcomed *Dragnet* back on television in 1967 were the same people who elected Richard Nixon president in 1968.

Gerald Carpenter

SEE ALSO: *Film Noir; Lee, Peggy; Mailer, Norman; Radio; Radio Drama;* Sunset Boulevard*; Syndication; Television; Wilder, Billy; World War II.*

BIBLIOGRAPHY

Anderson, Christopher. *Hollywood TV*. Austin: University of Texas Press, 1994.

Hayde, Michael J. *My Name's Friday: The Unauthorized but True Story of* Dragnet *and the Films of Jack Webb*. Nashville, TN: Cumberland House, 2001.

Meyers, Richard. *TV Detectives*. San Diego, CA: A. S. Barnes, 1981.

Newcomb, Horace, ed. *Encyclopedia of Television*. Chicago: Fitzroy Dearborn Publishers, 1997.

Reed, Robert M., and Maxine K. Reed. *The Encyclopedia of Television, Cable, and Video*. New York: Van Nostrand Reinhold, 1992.

Sarris, Andrew. *The American Cinema: Directors and Directions, 1929–1968*. New York: E. P. Dutton, 1968.

Terrace, Vincent. *Encyclopedia of Television: Series, Pilots, and Specials*. New York: New York Zoetrope, 1985–1986.

Varni, Charles A. "Images of Police Work and Mass Media Propaganda: The Case of 'Dragnet'." PhD diss. Washington State University, Pullman, 1974.

Wedding Dress

The wedding dress is a costume or single-purpose article of clothing worn by a bride during the marriage ceremony. From antiquity, weddings have been highly regarded occasions. The clothing worn by the bride for her wedding has usually been distinguished from that of her daily wear. Symbolism may be attached to the dress, such as white for purity, and may be attached to items worn with the dress, such as something blue for luck. The symbolism associated with the wedding dress may have cultural, traditional, or personal significance.

HISTORIC WEDDING DRESSES

Colonial immigrants kept the marriage traditions of their homelands. Brides in the English Jamestown settlement likely wore the costumes of young country brides of the mid-Elizabethan period. Although records of the first American weddings do not describe clothing, it is known that English brides of this era wore dresses of russet, a woolen fabric of natural wool color or dyed a reddish brown with tree bark. They wore simple, fitted white caps on the head. Dresses and caps made for weddings were usually adorned with fine embroidery.

American wedding dresses evolved into more festive or elaborate versions of the usual dress worn by women of each subsequent era. The dress was considered a best dress to be worn for special occasions after the wedding. The dress was usually new, although laces and trimmings might be old and handed down from a family member. Beginning in the mid-1800s, wearing a mother's wedding dress became an acceptable sentimental option.

As the United States prospered, brides marked the occasion of their wedding by bedecking themselves in the finest and most becoming dresses of their day. They were influenced by the styles of Europe and news of royal marriages. Although white had been worn for Roman weddings, all colors were used for early American wedding attire. Though other colors were occasionally seen, white settled into vogue as the preferred choice of color after the immensely popular Queen Victoria of England wed in 1840 clad in white satin.

Since the Victorian era's hooped creations, the wedding dress has known countless variations on the style of the day. While some early dresses displayed a slight trail of fabric behind, the wedding dress with train came into vogue in the mid-1870s, as did the use of the flowing veil.

Elaborate fabrics, embroideries, laces, braids, and trimmings were used whenever possible. The laces Alencon, Venice, Honitan, and Chantilly were commonplace for wedding trims. The evolution of styles included the tubular skirts of the 1870s, the corset waists of the 1880s, the leg-o'-mutton sleeves of the 1890s, the bustles of the early 1900s, the ankle-length Gibson girl silhouette of the 1910s, and the short-skirted flapper look with accompanying long, full veil of the 1920s.

In the 1930s the wedding dress became known as the wedding gown, as the term *gown* denoted a luxurious dress worn in Depression-era America. Over the years hemlines varied in the

Wedding Dress Shopping. *A woman peruses the racks at a bridal salon in search of the perfect wedding dress.* CORBIS FLIRT/ALAMY.

daily style of dress, but beginning in the 1930s the majority of wedding dresses were designed floor length.

The 1940s war years' wedding gowns show an absence of elaborate laces and trims but an attention to tailoring detail with padded shoulders and belted waistlines. The prosperous 1950s ushered in a new era of extravagant wedding gowns with yards of gathered skirting, laces, sweetheart and off-the-shoulder necklines, and Peter Pan collars. Since it had become traditional for the groom to present his bride a gift of a single strand of pearls, much emphasis was placed on the neckline design to show off this gift.

MODERN STYLES

During the 1960s the prominence of traditional styles of wedding dresses decreased in favor of contemporary dress styles. Many brides wore floor-length flowered print dresses that were not significantly more elaborate than their usual mode of dress. By the late 1960s and early 1970s the hippie bride marrying in a meadow gave way to the miniskirted bride repeating vows before a justice of the peace.

As the 1970s progressed the traditional wedding gowns enjoyed a resurgence. Early baby boomers found meaning in unpacking, refitting, and wearing their mother's gowns of the 1940s and 1950s. For those not fortunate enough to have a gown from these periods, the bridal apparel industry was ready with fresh designs in polyester fabrics. Elaborate gowns of finer materials were still produced, and by the 1980s it had become customary for at least the dress bodice to be covered in beading and laces. A huge influence on the wedding dresses of the 1980s was the puff-sleeved, full-skirted, long-trained confection worn by Princess Diana at her 1981 wedding to Prince Charles of England. The dress was immediately copied and caused brides worldwide to want to "look like a princess" on their wedding day.

The 1990s wedding dress and its symbolism was a matter of individual taste. While many wedding dresses resurrected styles of the past, other styles continued evolving, such as the mermaid dress, a creation form-fitted to the knees with a flared skirt. The 1990s also saw the advent of high-fashion wedding dresses. Vera Wang, frustrated over her own inability to find a wedding dress with simple sophistication in 1989, decided to start her own line of bridal apparel. Her designs were sleek, sexy, and often strapless—and set a trend for the 1990s. Other designers entered the wedding business. Dresses could be designed with a skirted train, a detachable train, or a veil trailing beyond the hem of the dress simulating a train. Examples of wedding dresses with fine construction and beadwork continued to be made and preserved for wear by the next generation of brides. The majority of wedding dresses not designed for repeat wear might have had beading and trims glued to the dress instead of hand-sewn. These dresses were often boxed and kept for sentimental reasons. The practical bride may have chosen to rent a wedding dress.

The first two decades of the twenty-first century saw a much greater variety in wedding gowns and less of a dominant style than had been evident in previous decades. For example, when Kate Middleton married Princess Diana's son Prince William in 2011, she chose a traditional gown with a lace bodice, tight sleeves, and train. The gown was widely praised, and many expected that it would have a similar influence on fashion as Princess Diana's gown thirty years before, but by and large that did not happen. Instead, the brides of the 2010s were more interested in choosing dresses that reflected their own personal style rather than copying the gown of someone else, even a princess.

The modern wedding dress is steeped in tradition and history. The elaborateness of the design and the association of any cultural significance or traditional symbolism to the dress or to items worn with the dress remains the choice of the bride.

Taylor Shaw

SEE ALSO: *Baby Boomers; Diana, Princess of Wales; The Fifties; Flappers; Gibson Girl; The Great Depression; Hippies; Retro Fashion; World War II.*

BIBLIOGRAPHY

Ehrman, Edwina. *The Wedding Dress: 300 Years of Bridal Fashions.* London: V&A Publishing, 2011.

Haines, Frank, and Elizabeth Haines. *Early American Brides. A Study of Costume and Tradition, 1594–1820.* Cumberland, MD: Hobby House Press, 1982.

Khalje, Susan. *Bridal Couture: Fine Sewing Techniques for Wedding Gowns and Evening Wear.* Iola, WI: Krause Publications, 1997.

Murphy, Brian. *The World of Weddings, An Illustrated Celebration.* New York: Paddington Press, 1978.

Tasman, Alice Lea Mast. *Wedding Album. Customs and Lore through the Ages.* New York: Walker, 1982.

Weeds

Weeds is a popular and critically acclaimed dark comedy chronicling the life of Nancy Botwin, a recently widowed mom who begins selling marijuana to pay her bills and support her two sons. Created by Jenji Kohan and starring Mary-Louise Parker, the show first aired on August 7, 2005, on the Showtime cable network.

The first three seasons of *Weeds* take place in an upscale fictional California subdivision called Agrestic. The generic neighborhood could be any planned suburban community in the United States in the early twenty-first century. Many of the episodes satirize suburban culture by exposing the ugly underbelly of a supposed ideal community. One mom secretly feeds her overweight daughter chocolate laxatives, many of the parents in the community commit adultery, and there are enough marijuana-smoking accountants and lawyers to keep Botwin in business and to allow her to maintain her affluent lifestyle.

While Botwin's pot dealing is the primary story line of the series, the show is also about the Botwin family and her trials as a parent. At the outset of the series she struggles as a newly single and newly working parent, while also trying to conceal her marijuana-selling business from her sons, Shane and Silas (played by Alexander Gould and Hunter Parrish, respectively). As the boys age and as Botwin becomes increasingly involved in the drug industry, the young men join her in selling pot. Botwin's brother-in-law, Andy (Justin Kirk), serves as a surrogate father to her sons and provides comic relief.

While she has a knack for selling drugs, Botwin constantly finds herself in dire straits. Whether she is hiding heroin in her garage or discovering trafficked women, her job is never easy or safe. Botwin is frequently on the run from either law enforcement agents or competing drug dealers, occasionally both at the same time. Yet her defining characteristic is her ability to deftly maneuver out of desperate situations. Over the course of the series, the Botwins move around the United States as well as in and out of the country. In each new location, Botwin returns to selling marijuana to make ends meet, often with disastrous and comedic results.

Throughout its run, *Weeds* maintained a loyal following. It was Showtime's highest-rated show in its first season, and viewership grew steadily over the first four seasons, then leveled off, remaining one of the top shows throughout the first decade of the 2000s. The series was critically well received from the beginning and continued to be so in its later seasons. It received numerous Emmy Award nominations and wins, including the Emmy Award for Outstanding Comedy Series in 2009. For her performance as Nancy Botwin, Parker received Emmy Award nominations in 2007, 2008, and 2009 for Outstanding Lead Actress in a Comedy, and she received Golden Globe Award nominations in 2006, 2007, 2008, and 2009 for Best Performance by an Actress in a Television Series—Musical or Comedy, winning in 2006.

Jeff Merron

SEE ALSO: *Cable TV; Emmy Awards; Marijuana; Suburbia; Television.*

BIBLIOGRAPHY

Bolonik, Kera. *In the "Weeds."* New York: Simon & Schuster, 2007.

Clune, Richard. "The High Life: Mary-Louise Parker's Smoking New Series; Lighting up the Screen." *Sunday Telegraph* (Sydney), December 3, 2006.

Grant, Drew. "Nancy Botwin, TV's Worst Mom?" Salon, July 19, 2011. Accessed May 30, 2012. Available from http://www.salon.com/2011/07/19/nancy_botwin_weeds/

Pope, Kyle. "For Showtime, Suburban Angst Is Fast Becoming a Ratings Delight." *New York Times*, August 6, 2006. Accessed May 30, 2012. Available from http://www.nytimes.com/2006/08/06/arts/television/06pope.html

The Weekend

During the Great Recession, some experts proposed shortening the workweek by making Friday a half day or by implementing a four-day workweek. The thinking was that such a change would create jobs because existing workers would all produce a little less, so more workers would be needed. Those who saw their wages shrink because of the loss of hours would be compensated with that most precious of commodities: long weekends. Though this proposal did not take hold in most of the country, it can be seen as one more chain in the evolution of thinking about what constitutes the weekend. A thirty-hour workweek was a part of the "Share Our Wealth" Plan proposed by Senator Huey P. Long of Louisiana as he challenged President Franklin D. Roosevelt's "New Deal" in the early 1930s.

In contemporary American culture, the weekend generally signifies the end of the traditional workweek, or the period from

Friday night to Monday morning, a popular time for organized or unorganized leisure activities and for religious observances. Historically, the weekend was synonymous with the Sabbath, which, among European cultures, was marked on Sunday by Christians and on Saturday by Jews. To understand the weekend, some background on the origin of the week itself is helpful. Human time was first measured by nature's cycles, seasonal for longer units, and celestial for shorter ones (i.e., the rising and setting of the sun and the phases of the moon). This influence persists in the names of the days, which are derived from the ancient astrological seven-day planetary week: Monday, a corruption of the word *Moonday*, which in turn evolved from European derivations of the Latin word for *moon*, and Sunday, which has historically been considered the first day of the week but gradually has come to be perceived as the last day of the weekend.

The first calendar was devised by the Egyptians, who bequeathed it to ensuing civilizations. Egypt divided the years into three seasons, based on the cycles of the river Nile, and twelve months. The Egyptians' twenty-four-hour days were also grouped into weeklike ten-day periods (called "decades"). The Mesopotamian calendar was similar, but its months were divided by a special day, *shabattu*, perhaps the first manifestation of recurring intervals of time regularly punctuated by a special day devoted to leisure or celebration. The Roman calendar also established special days within its thirty- or thirty-one-day months, such as the Kalends, the Nones, and the Ides. The Ides fell on the thirteenth or the fifteenth day of the month and became part of the English language via William Shakespeare's famous warning in *Julius Caesar*: "Beware the Ides of March."

THE WEEKEND EVOLVES

In addition to the ancient Jewish Sabbath (and the Christian Sunday that evolved out of it), a later precursor of the modern weekend was the eighteenth-century European custom of Saint Monday, a weekly day of leisure. Saint Monday was gradually replaced by the Saturday holiday, which was first observed in Europe in the 1870s. In Britain and Ireland, shops often closed at midday on Wednesday, a custom observed in some American small towns until the 1950s. The custom of working half a day on Saturday took hold in the United States in the 1920s, with a full two-day "weekend off" soon following.

During the earlier era of the six-day workweek, conflict frequently arose between the Jewish Sabbath and the Christian Sunday, especially with shifts in European immigration patterns in the early 1900s, and the five-day workweek offered a convenient solution. In 1926 Henry Ford closed his factories all day on Saturdays, and in 1929 the Amalgamated Clothing Workers of America, composed primarily of Jewish employees, became the first union to propose a five-day workweek. While initially denounced in some quarters as bad economics and worse religion, the five-day Monday through Friday workweek soon became standard.

As the structure of the week/weekend cycle solidified over the years, cultural and capitalistic venues evolved with it. With the concept of personal leisure came a new "business of leisure," boosted by advertising venues, that soon began to promote leisure and the weekend not only as a pleasurable pastime but as an integral element of a thriving capitalistic society. The first Sunday paper, the (London) *Observer*, appeared in 1791; while a Sunday edition debuted in Baltimore, Maryland, in 1796, the American Sunday paper did not really catch on until the Civil War era.

The prototype U.S. Sunday newspaper was established by Joseph Pulitzer, whose *Sunday World* pioneered leisure-oriented articles geared to every member of the family: book and entertainment reviews, travel essays, women's and children's pages, and color comics and supplements. Prolific department store advertising helped make the *World* a moneymaking success as well, and voluminous ad inserts remain a major part of most Sunday editions. In addition to Sunday papers, the magazine, a product designed specifically for pleasure, first appeared in Georgian England, where the more substantial and time-consuming novel was also introduced in the 1740s.

TRADITIONAL WEEKEND ACTIVITIES

The first use of *week-end* appeared in England in an 1879 issue of the magazine *Notes and Queries*. British practice also laid the groundwork for most of the public leisure pursuits that have grown into the entertainment industries of today. Among these was commercial theater, with its playhouses for both affluent and general audiences. While most of today's modern theaters perform throughout the week, weekends remain peak box-office periods that sometimes command higher ticket prices, and community theaters often perform only on weekends.

Public concerts were given in London as early as 1672, and commercial musical venues developed in tandem with theater. Sports ran parallel in popularity and hand in hand with betting. Thus, with only a few innovations, public entertainments born in eighteenth-century England flourished into the twentieth and twenty-first centuries. The music hall, a popular Saturday night diversion in England, found its American counterpart in the vaudeville circuits that spread across the United States in the late 1800s.

The emergence of the cheap nickelodeon in turn-of-the-twentieth-century America established "going to the movies" as the preeminent American pastime—one that soon spread to Europe and beyond. The first storefront nickelodeons appeared in the major metropolitan areas of the East Coast and evolved into the movie palaces of the 1920s, where patrons could see a feature film, a variety of short subjects, and a spectacular live stage show with an orchestra or some other form of live music. Movies and the weekend developed independently but reinforced each other. Going to the movies became a major form of national recreation, and Saturday night became a favorite time for such an excursion—Saturday afternoon matinees were generally reserved for children.

"Going out on the town" for dancing or partying also became a popular Saturday night ritual that, with ironic connotations, was graphically explored in the popular 1977 film *Saturday Night Fever*, which also produced one of the best-selling soundtrack albums of the hedonistic disco scene in the 1970s. Even household routines had a particular weekend flavor: in the earlier part of the twentieth century, New Englanders traditionally sat down to a supper of baked beans on Saturday night. For others, especially in areas where water supplies were limited, the Saturday night bath was a familiar routine.

DAYS OF "REST"

Sunday was long considered a day of rest in Western Europe and America, after the account of creation in Genesis in which God rested on the seventh day. In Catholic Europe, church law prohibited "servile work" on Sunday, unless the work was devoted to the glory of God, such as a priest celebrating Mass, or to the relief of one's neighbor, as in tending to the sick. In the British Isles, Scotland especially, Sunday was a day of solemnity and restraint in which families were expected to be at church morning and evening and to engage in edifying pursuits during the day—Bible reading, hymn singing, or innocent pastimes like music or word games.

In some rural areas during the nineteenth century, zealous Sabbath observers tried to pass legislation prohibiting steam trains from operating on Sunday because they brought secularized passengers from the cities to disturb the holiness of the day with holiday frivolities. In some of the American colonies, especially Puritan New England and Pennsylvania, strict "blue laws" prohibited engaging in trade, dancing, playing games, or drinking on Sunday—laws that still survive in a number of places. It was not until the early 1970s, for example, that New York City boutiques and department stores were permitted to open on Sunday; many smaller jurisdictions still have old laws on the books that prohibit shopping on the Sabbath, except for small items such as essential groceries, newspapers, or toiletries.

School schedules in the industrialized world follow the same Monday-to-Friday regimen as the workweek. As Eviatar Zerubavel notes in *The Seven Day Circle—The History and Meaning of the Week*: "Much of the attractiveness of the weekend can be attributed to the suspension of work-related—or, for the young, school-related obligations." While clearly not a part of the actual weekend—after all, it is still a day on which one goes to work or school—Friday is nevertheless considered by many their favorite day of the week, because it promises the anticipation of the weekend, leading to the popular expression, "T.G.I.F.," for "Thank goodness (or God) it's Friday."

IN PURSUIT OF LEISURE

Transportation innovations revolutionized weekend possibilities. Prior to the introduction of railroads in the 1830s, methods of travel had been essentially unchanged since ancient times. The time and the expense involved made travel a luxury reserved for the moneyed classes. Cheap rail excursions began around the 1840s in England and soon achieved mass acceptance, especially among the working classes, who for the first time in history could avail themselves of quick and inexpensive travel. In the twentieth century the automobile and recreational vehicle did the same thing on an even broader scale. Weekend excursions to the seashore, to the mountains, or to leisure and gambling boomtowns such as Las Vegas, Nevada, and Atlantic City, New Jersey, revolutionized the tourist industry.

Post–World War II affluence brought significant changes to the structure and content of the American weekend. According to Zerubavel:

> While the dominant motif of the weekdays is production, that of the weekend is, in a complementary fashion, consumption. Middle-class Protestant youngsters of the late 1940s and early 1950s could (with the family) attend a movie on Friday evening and fall asleep blissfully secure in the knowledge that two full days of freedom and media-supplied diversion lay ahead. Saturday morning might be spent with a radio, where traditional shows such as "No School Today" or "Let's Pretend" were followed by such futuristic 1950s innovations as *Space Patrol*.

A movie matinee might be on the agenda after lunch, and if this happened to be at a first-run downtown theater, the afternoon might also be taken up with exploring nearby five-and-dime and department stores, where treasures such as comic books and movie magazines could be had for as little as a dime or fifteen cents. Saturday evening might have found the family again attending a movie, probably at one of the less expensive second-run neighborhood houses or at one of the popular drive-in theaters. Sunday continued with the same "special occasion" mood, but with a euphoria tempered by the bittersweet awareness that this period of freedom was destined to come to an end that evening.

After religious obligations were honored on Sunday morning—observant Jews, of course, attended synagogue or temple on Friday evening or Saturday morning—many families indulged in a special midday Sunday dinner, either at home or at a restaurant (perhaps a Howard Johnson's, splurging on one of its famous twenty-eight flavors of ice cream). Afternoons might be taken up with a Sunday drive or excursion to the country or to an amusement park, or to nowhere in particular. Radio could also occupy much of the afternoon and evening, and a light evening meal was sometimes enjoyed in the living room around the family radio. Beginning in the 1950s, when the concept of the frozen TV dinner entered the American culinary consciousness, television networks reserved their key programming for Sunday evenings.

MORE FRENZIED MODERN WEEKENDS

As malls, suburbs, and automobiles became pervasive facts of American life in the 1950s and beyond, the status of the American "downtown" began to decline as a focus of weekend activities. The weekly Friday evening excursion on foot to the modest neighborhood grocery store, brief enough to be followed by a trip to the movies, was replaced with an automobile excursion for a full evening at the shopping center or mall. Eventually movie theaters were added to the mall mix, hastening the decay of downtown as a space for social interaction.

The development of television together with antitrust suits in the 1950s caused movie chains to close their downtown outlets for good, further changing the American experience of the weekend as a time for leisure activity downtown. Still, weekend box-office takes for films have escalated to record highs. For example, in July 2011 *Harry Potter and the Deathly Hallows Part 2* took in $169 million on its first weekend. Likewise, college and professional sports events have become more important to the American weekend, particularly during football season in the fall, when college teams traditionally play on Saturday and professional teams on Sunday. The weekend of the Super Bowl has mushroomed into an event of national social and economic significance.

Analyzing the modern concept of the weekend, Witold Rybczynski writes in *Waiting for the Weekend*: "The weekend has imposed a rigid schedule on our free time. . . . The weekly rush to the cottage is hardly leisurely, nor is the compression of various recreational activities into the two-day break. The freedom to do something has become the obligation to do something." He concludes that "every culture chooses a different structure for its work and leisure, and in doing so it makes a profound statement about itself." The weekend "reflects the many unresolved contradictions in modern attitudes towards leisure. . . . We want the freedom to be leisurely, but we want it regularly, every week, like clockwork. . . . There is something mechanical about this oscillation, which creates a sense of obligation that interferes with leisure."

An interesting comment on the American view of weekend escape can be found in one of Walt Disney's Goofy cartoons, "Father's Week-end" (1953). After an exhausting weekend of battling crowded beaches and harrowing amusement parks; coping with screaming, tireless offspring; and fighting massive traffic gridlock at the end of it all, Goofy is finally seen blissfully setting off for work on Monday morning as voice-over narration declares, with obvious irony, that the harried Everyman may now finally relax again and rest up for another strenuous weekend of leisure.

In addition to *Saturday Night Fever*, movies and TV commercials have reflected a modern view of the weekend as a time when people can be prone to excess. The Academy Award–winning movie *The Lost Weekend* (1945), based on a novel of the same title by Charles R. Jackson, portrays the exploits of an alcohol-abusing writer. *Weekend at Bernie's* (1989) features two low-level insurance company employees who maintain the appearance that their deceased boss is alive while a party goes on at his mansion in the Hamptons. The movie was popular enough to spawn a sequel in 1993.

The weekend and partying have always seemed to go together. Anheuser-Busch ran a successful commercial for one of its brands through the late 1970s and early 1980s with the slogan, "Weekends are made for Michelob," and in 2012 Pepto-Bismol offered a solution to regretful partiers with its ad and slogan, "Here's to a long weekend and a short recovery. Wherever the weekend takes you, take Pepto-Bismol." Meanwhile, assaults on modern "blue laws" persist as states and counties nationwide look to tax alcohol sales traditionally banned on Sunday. Governor Dan Malloy in 2012 called for an end to such a sales ban in his state of Connecticut, one of fourteen states to ban Sunday sales as of 2011. Since 2002 fourteen states have repealed Sunday bans on alcohol sales.

Finally, experiments with a four-day workweek with three-day weekends have begun in the early 2010s, particularly as governments try to save their utility and fuel costs for employees. Utah mandated a four-day workweek in 2008 for more than 17,000 state employees but ended the practice in 2011. California Governor Jerry Brown called for an adoption of a four-day week for his state's employees in 2012.

Ross Care

SEE ALSO: *Advertising; Atlantic City; Broadway; Comic Books; Comics; Department Stores; Disco; Disney (Walt Disney Company); Drive-In Theater; Ford, Henry; Gambling; The Great Recession; Las Vegas; Leisure Time; Movie Palaces; The Musical; Nickelodeons; Radio;* Saturday Night Fever*; Sunday Driving; Super Bowl; Television; TV Dinners; Vaudeville.*

BIBLIOGRAPHY

Cross, Gary. *A Social History of Leisure since 1600.* State College, PA: Venture Publishing, 1990.

Cross, Gary. *Time and Money: The Making of Consumer Culture.* New York: Routledge, 1993.

Grover, Kathryn, ed. *Hard at Play: Leisure in America, 1840–1940.* Amherst: University of Massachusetts Press, 1992.

Meynell, Francis. *The Week-End Book.* New York: Overlook, 2006.

Murolo, Priscilla, and A. B. Chitty. *From the Folks Who Brought You the Weekend: A Short, Illustrated History of Labor in the United States.* New York: New Press, 2001.

Rybczynski, Witold. *Waiting for the Weekend.* New York: Viking, 1991.

Zelinski, Ernie J. *The Joy of Not Working.* Berkeley, CA: Ten Speed Press, 1997.

Zerubavel, Eviatar. *The Seven Day Circle—The History and Meaning of the Week.* New York: Free Press, 1985.

Weird Tales

J. C. Henneberger founded the American pulp magazine *Weird Tales* in 1923. It followed the success of titles by Rural Publications, which appeared in a variety of genres, notably *College Humor* and *Magazine of Fun. Weird Tales* was in publication until 1954 and was most successful during the 1930s under the editorship of Farnsworth Wright. During this period it published fiction by influential fantasy and horror writers H. P. Lovecraft, Robert E. Howard, Clark Ashton Smith, C. L. Moore, Edmond Hamilton, Robert Bloch, Manly Wade Wellman, and August Derleth.

Henneberger knew that there were talented writers who were unable to place their stories in the mixed-genre magazines of the early 1920s and presumed that there was an audience for stories that were weird and macabre. He established the character of the magazine through a policy of reprinting "weird" classics, such as Edward Bulwer Lytton's "The Haunted and the Haunters," Edgar Allan Poe's "The Murders in the Rue Morgue," and a later series of Mary Shelley's *Frankenstein.*

Weird Tales did not immediately attract a regular readership. In its first year Henneberger employed Harry Houdini as a writer, which resulted in the column "Ask Houdini" and the publication of stories (ghostwritten by Lovecraft) about supposed occurrences in Houdini's life. These adventures further established a fascination with Egypt, magic, and the supernatural. The oriental tales by Frank Owen and Seabury Quinn's long-running Jules de Grandin psychic detective series even furthered the magazine's popularity. Although it is notable that right from the first issue some of the bizarre events of the horror stories were explained in a rational scientific manner, the magazine achieved notoriety early on in its publishing history as it was allegedly banned from bookstalls in 1924 because it carried C. M. Eddy's "The Loved Dead," which had overtones of necrophilia.

After Wright and the Popular Fiction Publishing Company took over from Henneberger in 1924, the magazine offered stories in the range of weird scientific, horror, sword and sorcery, exotic adventure, and fantasy, and it maintained an audience even during the Great Depression. The magazine was especially congenial toward new writers. Howard published his first story in *Weird Tales* in 1925 and went on to publish the Conan the Barbarian series between 1932 and 1936. Lovecraft first appeared in the readers' letters column, "The Eyrie," commenting on stories from previous issues. He published most of his major works, especially those developing the Cthulhu Mythos series, in *Weird Tales.* Other writers who were particularly influenced by Lovecraft also wrote for the magazine. These included Bloch, who would go on to write *Psycho* in 1959; Henry Kuttner, who with his wife, Moore, would become prominent fantasy writers in the 1940s; and Derleth, who, as well as being a writer, became an influential anthologist and founded the publishing company Arkham House.

Some of the fiction published in *Weird Tales* was known for its relatively sophisticated sexual themes. Moore's first short story, "Shambleau," is a good example. She also published a fantasy series with the heroine Jirel of Joiry in the magazine. Along with Smith, Moore contributed to the magazine's fascination with a medieval setting and sword and sorcery theme as well as its acceptance of interplanetary locations.

The magazine's horror fiction tended to portray science as being out of control and subject to various representations of the mad scientist. It provided a niche for developing science fiction writers such as Hamilton, who was influential in the development of "space opera." His series Interstellar Patrol was published in *Weird Tales* from 1929 to 1930.

In the late 1930s the magazine changed its overall style with the deaths of Howard (1936) and Lovecraft (1937), the retirement of Smith in 1936, and Wright's relinquishment of the editorship in 1939 (he had been struggling with Parkinson's disease since 1921). The editorship was then taken over by Dorothy McIlwraith, an established magazine editor who stayed with *Weird Tales* until the publishing company went bankrupt in September 1954. Her editorial policy focused on supernatural fiction, especially occult detection, such as Wellman's Judge Pursuivant series published between 1938 and 1941. She also featured the work of Ray Bradbury and Fritz Leiber, but during this time *Weird Tales* was competing with a larger number of available outlets for fantasy writing. However, the pulp magazine's thirty-one years in publication and 279 issues were significant in supporting the careers of many initially underrated popular fiction writers.

In the decades after 1954 several unsuccessful attempts were made to restart the magazine. Finally in 1988 it resumed publication, surviving several changes of ownership and editorship. This recent version of the magazine published such authors as Tanith Lee, Ramsey Campbell, Thomas Ligotti, and Nina Kiriki Hoffman. As of 2012 *Weird Tales* was published by Betancourt's Wildside Press with Ann VanderMeer as editor-in-chief.

Nickianne Moody

SEE ALSO: *Bradbury, Ray; Derleth, August; Frankenstein; Houdini, Harry; Lovecraft, H. P.;* Psycho*; Pulp Magazines; Science Fiction Publishing.*

BIBLIOGRAPHY

Ashley, Michael, ed. *A History of the Science Fiction Magazine.* London: NEL, 1974.

Joshi, S. T. *H. P. Lovecraft: A Life*. West Warwick, RI: Necronomicon Press, 1996.

Joshi, S. T. *The Modern Weird Tale: A Critique of Horror Fiction.* Jefferson, NC: McFarland, 2001.

Weinberg, Robert E., ed. *The Weird Tales Story*. West Linn, OR: FAX Collector's Editions, 1977.

Weissmuller, Johnny *(1904–1984)*

Johnny Weissmuller first achieved fame as a freestyle swimmer, winning five Olympic gold medals and setting sixty-seven world records. However, he is best known for his film role as Tarzan, King of the Jungle, who had been orphaned in the African wild as an infant and raised by apes. Weissmuller starred in twelve *Tarzan* films between 1932 and 1948.

The Tarzan series, written by Edgar Rice Burroughs, became widely popular from the first book, *Tarzan of the Apes* (1914). More than twenty-five million copies of Burroughs's books sold worldwide as the public embraced the stories of an English nobleman's son who grew up to be the King of the Jungle. Weissmuller added to the popularity—and added to his own wealth—when his first Tarzan movie, *Tarzan the Ape Man*, was released in 1932, leading to spin-offs such as Tarzan radio programs and comic strips. The films costarred Maureen O'Sullivan as Jane and featured a combination of naive love interest with plenty of action, interspersed with the comic relief supplied by Cheetah the chimp.

The facts concerning Weissmuller's birth are the subject of some dispute. Official Olympic sources say he was born in Windber, Pennsylvania, on June 2, 1904, but there is credible evidence that he was born in Freidorf, near Timisoara, Romania, and immigrated with his parents to the United States as a young child. Biographer David Fury and others believe that Weissmuller's parents later switched his identity with that of his American-born brother in order to qualify him for the U.S. Olympic team. He attended school in Chicago through the eighth grade. His ability as an athlete led to his being trained in swimming as a teenager by the Illinois Athletic Club in Chicago.

In the 1920s Weissmuller participated as a member of several of the club's championship teams in relay and water polo events. He won twenty-six national championships in individual freestyle swimming in the 1920s in various events, including the 100 meters, 200 meters, 400 meters, and 800 meters, where he demonstrated his speed as well as stamina. At the 1924 Olympic Games in Paris, he broke three world records while winning three gold medals in the 100-meter and 400-meter freestyle and in the 800-meter relay. In the Olympic Games in Amsterdam in 1928 he added two more gold medals for the 100-meter freestyle and the 800-meter relay. When he turned professional in 1929, Weissmuller was unchallenged as the world's finest swimmer. His sports fame led to the production of several short films showing his aquatic prowess, bringing him to the attention of MGM (Metro-Goldwyn-Mayer), the studio that offered him the Tarzan role.

More than a dozen actors had played the part of Tarzan in silent films as well as talkies, including Buster Crabbe, Glenn Morris, Lex Barker, Gordon Scott, and Jock Mahoney, but the public considered them mere pretenders. No one else possessed the athleticism to skim through the alligator-filled rivers doing the Australian crawl or swing on a vine through the trees yelling his high-pitched, chest-thumping call. Of the twelve *Tarzan* films Weissmuller starred in, the most popular were the ones that included O'Sullivan as Jane. After making a hit in *Tarzan, the Ape Man* (1932), the couple continued to win fans in *Tarzan and His Mate* (1934), considered by many to be the best of the series; *Tarzan Escapes* (1936); *Tarzan Finds a Son!* (1939); *Tarzan's Secret Treasure* (1941); and *Tarzan's New York Adventure* (1942).

In the late 1940s and 1950s Weissmuller moved to Columbia Pictures for a series of movies with African settings in which he played Jungle Jim. These films were shot with low budgets as the lesser ends of double features and included *Jungle Moon Men* (1955).

Weissmuller was married and divorced five times. His third wife (from 1933 to 1938) was Lupe Velez, a star of silent films who played in "B" movies and early talkies as a tempestuous character known as "the Mexican Spitfire." After his retirement

Johnny Weissmuller. Johnny Weissmuller parlayed his success as a swimmer in the 1920s into a movie career. POPPERFOTO/CONTRIBUTOR/GETTY IMAGES.

from his swimming and film careers, Weissmuller returned to Chicago, where he opened a swimming pool company. He moved to Florida in the 1960s, serving as the curator of the Swimming Pool Hall of Fame in Fort Lauderdale. In 1973 he became a "greeter" for Caesars Palace Hotel in Las Vegas; a few years later he was hospitalized due to a stroke and died in 1984.

Benjamin Griffith

SEE ALSO: *Burroughs, Edgar Rice; Celebrity Couples; MGM (Metro-Goldwyn-Mayer); Movie Stars; Olympics; Tarzan; Velez, Lupe.*

BIBLIOGRAPHY

Behlmer, Rudy. "Johnny Weissmuller: Olympics to Tarzan." *Films in Review*, July/August 1996, 20–33.

Fury, David. *Kings of the Jungle: An Illustrated Reference to Tarzan on Screen and Television.* Jefferson, NC: McFarland, 1994.

Fury, David. *Johnny Weissmuller: "Twice the Hero."* Waterville, ME: Thorndike Press, 2001.

Halliwell, Leslie. *The Filmgoer's Companion.* New York: Hill and Wang, 1967.

Platt, Frank C., ed. *Great Stars of Hollywood's Golden Age.* New York: New American Library, 1966.

Shipman, David. *The Great Movie Stars: The Golden Years.* New York: Crown, 1970.

Welcome Back, Kotter

A popular ABC-TV sitcom from 1975 to 1979, *Welcome Back, Kotter* featured Gabe Kaplan in the title role of Gabe Kotter, a teacher who returns to his alma mater, Brooklyn's fictional James Buchanan High School, to instruct a bunch of remedial students known as the Sweathogs. Kaplan, who created the show with Alan Sacks, based *Welcome Back, Kotter* on his own real-life experiences in the Bensonhurst section of Brooklyn, New York, where he had himself been branded an "unteachable" student until inspired by a teacher named Miss Shepherd. Comedienne Janeane Garofalo once expressed relief that *Welcome Back, Kotter* was the fashion arbiter in her youth instead of *Beverly Hills, 90210* with its designer duds, because it was easier to live up to *Kotter*'s image of frizzy-haired students dressed in flared jeans and army jackets.

The Sweathogs were tough and streetwise, although their worst insult amounted to "up your nose with a rubber hose!" Kotter was hip to all their tricks, having pulled them all himself a decade earlier. Yet he was also still a rebel, flouting conventions and using humor to get his struggling students to learn something. Kaplan, a stand-up comedian with a bushy mustache and perpetual smirk, incorporated some of his material, sometimes awkwardly, into the beginning and end of the episodes but seemed a little less at ease as an actor carrying a sitcom. Luckily the Sweathogs picked up the slack.

The four main Sweathogs were Freddie "Boom Boom" Washington (Lawrence Hilton-Jacobs), a smooth African

American who called his teacher "Mr. Kot-*tair*"; Juan Epstein (Robert Hegyes), a Puerto Rican Jew who was always bringing in fake excuse notes from home and signing them "Epstein's mother" and whose delivery resembled that of Chico Marx; Arnold Horshack (Ron Palillo), a braying geek who screamed "Oh! Oh Oh!" when he raised his hand and snorted when he laughed; and Vinnie Barbarino (John Travolta), the hunky dim-witted leader of the group. Other regulars included Kotter's wife, Julie (Marcia Strassman), who had twins Robin and Rachel in 1977, and Kotter's nemesis, snotty vice principal Mr. Woodman (John Sylvester White).

A typical plot from early in the series: Washington, whose signature phrase was an ultra-slick "hi there," makes the varsity basketball team and decides he no longer needs to study. Mr. Kotter confronts the class and the basketball coach and threatens to fail Washington. In the end, Kotter teaches everyone about the importance of balancing education and sports.

Vinnie Barbarino proved the breakout role for Travolta, who soon launched his film career with *Saturday Night Fever* in 1977 and *Grease* in 1978. By that year, he was rarely seen on *Kotter* and was billed as a "special guest star."

The year 1979 marked the final season for *Welcome Back, Kotter*. That year, Kaplan chose to sit out many of the episodes due to creative differences with ABC, and he was rarely seen on television after that. The fact that Travolta was also making fewer appearances prompted the network to move the show to less desirable time slots and promote the show less vigorously. A slick southerner, Beau De Labarre, played by Stephen Shortridge, was brought in to replace the hunk void left by Travolta. Other character changes included the arrival—and quick departure—of Angie, the first female Sweathog, and the promotion of Kotter to vice principal and Woodman to principal.

Welcome Back, Kotter was used as a launching pad for other performers besides Travolta, although he is the only one for whom it really worked. A spin-off was attempted for the Horshack character and his family but was soon aborted. There was also the short-lived *Mr. T. & Tina*, based on another original *Kotter* character, which starred Pat Morita as a madcap Japanese inventor who moves his family from Tokyo to Chicago.

The show's hit theme song, "Welcome Back," was composed and performed by John Sebastian, of the Lovin' Spoonful. A radio staple in the 1970s, the song was later used to sell cold cuts and fast food. Years later, *Welcome Back, Kotter* enjoyed a revival on *Nick at Nite*.

Karen Lurie

SEE ALSO: Saturday Night Fever; *Sitcom; Stand-Up Comedy; Travolta, John.*

BIBLIOGRAPHY

Brooks, Tim, and Earle Marsh. *The Complete Directory to Prime Time Network and Cable TV Shows: 1946–Present*, 9th ed. New York: Ballantine Books, 2007.

Dalton, Mary M., and Laura R. Linder. *Teacher TV: Sixty Years of Teachers on Television*. New York: P. Lang, 2008.

McNeil, Alex. *Total Television: The Comprehensive Guide to Programming from 1948 to the Present*, 4th ed. New York: Penguin, 1996.

Tucker, Ken. "Welcome Back, Kotter." *Entertainment Weekly*, June 30, 1995, 88.

Welk, Lawrence *(1903–1992)*

For nearly three decades, Saturday night belonged to Lawrence Welk. The bandleader's television program, *The Lawrence Welk Show*, debuted on ABC in 1955 and was an immediate hit. The show remained on the air for twenty-seven years, making it the longest-running prime-time music program in television history. Welk's program highlighted conservative American values and provided good, wholesome entertainment that the entire family could enjoy.

Although he would one day become the second-most wealthy performer in the United States behind comedian and movie star Bob Hope, Welk never forgot his poor beginnings. He was born in 1903 in the small German-speaking town of Strasburg, North Dakota, the sixth of eight children of German immigrants Ludwig and Christina Welk. Young Welk had to drop out of school by the fourth grade to help on the family farm. His family's pre-Depression struggles were always with him and were partly responsible for his fierce loyalty to his band later in his life. His refusal to tip at restaurants could also be traced to his early struggles; instead of leaving money Welk would hand out penknives inscribed with his name.

As a young man, Welk learned to play the violin and then his father's accordion. He soon began performing with his father at local weddings, dances, and other social events to earn extra money for the family. In 1924, when Welk was twenty-one years old, he left home to pursue a career in music. He toured with a number of different bands and learned about show business. He then formed his own four-piece band, the Lawrence Welk Novelty Orchestra, and got a job playing for a South Dakota radio station, which led to more jobs throughout the Midwest.

In 1938 the now ten-piece band performed a concert in Philadelphia, where a listener complimented Welk's swinging dance music, saying it was like light, bubbly champagne. From then on Welk described his music as "champagne music," and he even changed the name of the band to the Champagne Music of Lawrence Welk. Starting in 1940 the band became the house orchestra for the Trianon Ballroom in Chicago, where they remained for the next ten years. In 1951 the band performed on a late-night television show broadcast from Los Angeles. The appearance led to more TV jobs, and in 1955 ABC offered Welk his own show.

THE LAWRENCE WELK SHOW

Welk's successful formula was short, tight musical and dance numbers and songs that people knew. He insisted that his show would "keep it simple, so the audience can feel like they can do it too." In addition to Welk's band and the regular singers and dancers, *The Lawrence Welk Show* had many guest stars, such as the Lennon Sisters, Joe Feeney, and Norma Zimmer. But no star was bigger than the bandleader, whose German accent and humble nature endeared him to millions.

Welk's TV program maintained clean-cut stability even as the popularity of rock and roll rose in the 1950s and the United States churned with the turmoil of the 1960s. As musical styles and tastes changed, Welk remained loyal to his champagne music. He justified his decision by noting that "champagne music puts the girl back in the boy's arms—where she belongs."

Welk also refused to incorporate the new styles associated with the beatnik poets or play any jazz or rock and roll, even when ABC and his band members made suggestions. He did not apologize for his tastes or opinions. For example, he did not like rock and roll and did not relate to the hippie culture. "It was always hard for me, for example, to understand the fad for patched-up jeans," he writes in his book, *Ah-One, Ah-Two!* "When I was a boy I had to wear them, much to my shame and embarrassment, and one of my earliest ambitions was to own a brand-new suit of clothes all my own." Because of Welk's clear vision, *The Lawrence Welk Show* remained a snapshot of a happy, booming middle America, frozen in a waltz and a smile.

Welk positioned himself as the conservative patriarch of his musical family. Women of all ages were his "girls," the players his "kids." He could be unforgiving when it came to his "kids," however. In 1959, at a time when publisher Hugh Hefner's *Playboy* magazine was bringing sex to the forefront of mainstream culture, Welk fired Alice Lon, one of the popular champagne ladies, when she flashed too much skin on camera. A few years later, in response to letters of protest, Welk gave the Lennon Sisters an earful after they wore one-piece bathing suits for a scene taped by a swimming pool and forbade the girls from wearing such things again on camera. For the band members, Welk's familial philosophy worked both ways. While he did not believe his crew should be paid any more than minimum union scale, they were able to participate in his profit-sharing plan.

LIFE AFTER ABC

ABC canceled *The Lawrence Welk Show* in 1971, and seventy-year-old Welk took the news hard, as if he had failed his first audition. "I felt just about as bad as a man can feel," he notes in *Ah-One, Ah-Two!* Initially deciding to put away his baton for good, Welk reconsidered when more than a million letters of support arrived, enough to convince him to syndicate the show himself. Eventually more than 250 stations picked up the show, giving the program airtime on more channels than during its ABC years. When Welk brought his show back to television, he did it his way. In the first show he made it clear that his style was the same. The broadcast featured "No, No, Nanette," "Tea for Two," and a group tap dance.

Welk retired in 1982 and last played with his band in 1989. He died of pneumonia on May 17, 1992, in Santa Monica, California. By the time of his death, Welk had amassed a business empire: a music library that includes all of composer Jerome Kern's work; resorts in Escondido, California, and Branson, Missouri; and the Welk Group, which includes several record labels.

Geoff Edgers

SEE ALSO: *The Great Depression; Hefner, Hugh; Hippies; Hope, Bob; Kern, Jerome;* Playboy; *Syndication; Television.*

BIBLIOGRAPHY

Floren, Myron, and Randee Floren. *Accordion Man.* Brattleboro, VT: S. Greene Press, 1981.

Sanders, Coyne Steven, and Ginny Weissman. *Champagne Music:* The Lawrence Welk Show. New York: St. Martin's Press, 1985.

Schwienher, William K. *Lawrence Welk, an American Institution.* Chicago: Nelson-Hall, 1980.

Welk, Lawrence, and Bernice McGeehan. *Ah-One, Ah-Two!: Life with My Musical Family.* Boston: G. K. Hall, 1974.

Welk, Lawrence, and Bernice McGeehan. *My America, Your America.* Englewood Cliffs, NJ: Prentice-Hall, 1976.

Welk, Lawrence, and Bernice McGeehan. *Lawrence Welk's Musical Family Album.* Englewood Cliffs, NJ: Prentice-Hall, 1977.

Welk, Lawrence, and Bernice McGeehan. *This I Believe.* Englewood Cliffs, NJ: Prentice-Hall, 1979.

Welk, Lawrence, and Bernice McGeehan. *You're Never Too Young.* Englewood Cliffs, NJ: Prentice Hall, 1981.

Welles, Orson *(1915–1985)*

Considered by many to be the most influential and innovative filmmaker of the twentieth century, Orson Welles made movies that were ambitious, original, and epic. This alone would qualify him as a popular culture icon, but when Welles's genius is considered in conjunction with his notorious life history, he becomes a singular legend. A child prodigy at age seven, Welles was Broadway's boy wonder by twenty-two, radio's enfant terrible at twenty-three, and Hollywood's hottest director at twenty-five. But by the 1940s his star had burned out, and even marriage to sex symbol Rita Hayworth wasn't enough to stop his decline. The forty years that followed were characterized by attempted comebacks, obesity, and maverick films. The life of Welles uniquely embodied the modern era.

Orson Welles. *Orson Welles peaked as an actor and director early in his career, never repeating the success he achieved as a young man in Hollywood.* MICHAEL OCHS ARCHIVES/GETTY IMAGES.

Born on May 6, 1915, George Orson Welles, the second son of a successful inventor and his pianist wife, spent his first six years in provincial Kenosha, Wisconsin, before moving to Chicago. Shortly thereafter his parents separated, and Orson's older brother, Richard, was sent to boarding school, leaving Orson alone with his mother, Beatrice, who soon commanded one of the city's most popular artistic and literary salons. Surrounded by actors, artists, and musicians and taken to the theater, symphony, and opera, the boy responded to this cultural deluge by becoming a prodigy. He learned Shakespeare soliloquies at seven, studied classical piano, and started to write plays at age eight. But when his mother died shortly after his ninth birthday, Welles's life changed drastically.

Welles spent two difficult years living with his alcoholic father, who exposed his son to his working-class artist and journalist friends. It was a relief when the eleven-year-old was sent to the Todd School for Boys, a rigorous college preparatory academy. There his precocious talents flourished. Welles wrote, directed, and starred in school theatricals and also studied painting. During summer vacations, father and son often traveled together, once taking a steamship as far as Shanghai. When Dick Welles died suddenly a few months before his son's sixteenth birthday, the boy was distraught but also relieved to no longer be burdened with the care of his alcoholic parent.

Six months after his father's death, Welles graduated from Todd and left for Ireland, planning to study painting. But after drifting around the country for a few months, he arrived in Dublin, where he began to haunt the local theaters. On his first visit to the experimental Gate Theatre, he decided to audition, touting himself as one of America's top young actors. Not surprisingly, the young self-promoter was hired and spent the next year learning his craft in the company of some of Ireland's cutting-edge actors and directors.

When he returned to America in 1932, Welles hoped to take Broadway by storm. But New York was singularly unimpressed, and the seventeen-year-old sheepishly returned to Chicago. Over the course of the next year and a half, he wrote plays, traveled to North Africa, and directed small productions before being hired by theatrical legends Katherine Cornell and Guthrie McClintic to join their Broadway company.

BROADWAY'S BOY WONDER

Welles made his Broadway debut at nineteen as Tybalt in *Romeo and Juliet*. A year later he met the man who would orchestrate his stardom, thirty-three-year-old director/producer John Houseman. Driven by the same high-flown theatrical goals, Houseman and Welles took part in the government-sponsored Work Projects Administration (WPA) Federal Theatre Project, where Welles directed an all-black, voodoo *Macbeth* to rave reviews. The two men soon formed their own repertory company, the Mercury Theatre, and in 1937 they took Broadway by storm with their production of *Julius Caesar*, set in fascist Italy. By age twenty-two Welles was world famous as Broadway's boy wonder.

The Mercury Theatre soon branched out into hour-long radio broadcasts, the most notorious of which was certainly Welles's October 30,1938, broadcast of H. G. Wells's *War of the Worlds*, which terrified a nation into believing that New Jersey was being invaded by Martians. Hollywood soon came to call. Hoping to exploit the hype around the brilliant enfant terrible, RKO offered Welles $225,000 to produce, direct, write, and act in two films. With total creative freedom and a percentage of the profits built into the contract, it was an offer Welles could not refuse.

CITIZEN KANE AND OTHER FILMS

Welles came out to Hollywood with the idea of filming Joseph Conrad's *Heart of Darkness*, but difficulties arose, and he decided to work with veteran screenwriter Herman J. Mankiewicz. Together they wrote a brilliant screenplay about an aging media tycoon dying in his Florida mansion. A thinly disguised biography of newspaper magnate William Randolph Hearst, *Citizen Kane* depicts Kane/Hearst as a tyrant who has alienated everyone who loves him. The film tells Kane's story from five different points of view.

With twenty-five-year-old Welles directing, producing, and starring in the title role, *Citizen Kane* broke new cinematic ground. As described in Baseline's *Encyclopedia of Film*, its innovations included:

> 1. composition in depth: the use of extreme deep focus cinematography to connect distant figures in space; 2. complex mise-en-scène, in which the frame overflowed with action and detail; 3. low angle shots that revealed ceilings and made characters, especially Kane, seem simultaneously dominant and trapped; 4. long takes; 5. a fluid, moving camera that expanded the action beyond the frame and increased the importance of off-screen space; and 6. the creative use of sound as a transition device . . . and to create visual metaphors.

The film featured a superb cast, which included Joseph Cotten and George Coulouris from the Mercury Theatre as well as Agnes Moorehead, Ruth Warrick, and Everett Sloane.

Citizen Kane was lauded by the critics, but it ran into trouble at the box office when Hearst refused to carry advertisements for the film in his newspapers and launched a smear campaign. Nominated for nine Academy Awards, Welles's masterpiece was snubbed by the Academy and only won one Oscar—Best Screenplay, shared by Mankiewicz and Welles. *Citizen Kane* has nonetheless come to be regarded as the greatest film ever made, ranking number one on the American Film Institute list of the top 100 movies of all time.

Welles's next film was an adaptation of the Booth Tarkington novel *The Magnificent Ambersons*. A somewhat more conventional film than *Citizen Kane*, *The Magnificent Ambersons* used many of the same experimental techniques to depict turn-of-the-twentieth-century America, but when Welles left the country, RKO edited more than forty minutes out of the film. It proved a commercial failure, losing more than half a million dollars, and Welles would never again be regarded as a bankable director.

A CAREER ON THE DECLINE

Welles married World War II cinematic sex symbol Rita Hayworth, but despite harnessing her star power to his marvelous 1948 film noir *The Lady from Shanghai*, his directorial career was on the decline. When his experimental film version of William Shakespeare's *Macbeth* failed at the box office a year later, the nails were all but in Welles's coffin. He left Hollywood for a self-imposed ten-year exile, returning in 1958 to direct and act in the classic *Touch of Evil* with his frequent costar Cotten.

In *Movie Magazine International*, Monica Sullivan wrote, "Orson Welles' early years were so spectacular that movie cultists might have preferred that he'd lived fast, died young and left a good-looking corpse." Indeed, although Welles returned to direct a few cinematic gems, his film career was uneven. As he grew older, he also gained weight, becoming a very obese man. Although he appeared on wine commercials and the occasional talk show, he became a somewhat tragic figure even as his status as filmmaking legend grew.

His final film, *The Other Side of the Wind*, a quasi-autobiographical tale of a famous filmmaker struggling to get his picture financed, remains unfinished. As noted in Baseline's *Encyclopedia of Film*, "As an unseen fragment, it was a sad and ironic end for a filmmaking maverick who set the standards for the modern narrative film and the man who was, in the words of Martin Scorsese, 'responsible for inspiring more people to be film directors than anyone else in the history of the cinema.'" Troubled though the life of Welles may have been—his potential as a director perhaps unfulfilled—his place in the pantheon of popular culture is ensured.

Victoria Price

SEE ALSO: *Academy Awards; Broadway;* Citizen Kane*; Community Theater; Cotten, Joseph; Halloween; Hayworth, Rita; Hearst, William Randolph; Hollywood; Radio; Scorsese, Martin; Sex Symbol;* War of the Worlds*; World War II.*

BIBLIOGRAPHY

Brady, Frank. *Citizen Welles*. New York: Scribner, 1989.

Callow, Simon. *Orson Welles: The Road to Xanadu*. New York: Viking Press, 1995.

Estrin, Mark W. *Orson Welles: Interviews*. Jackson: University Press of Mississippi, 2002.

Higham, Charles. *Orson Welles: The Rise and Fall of an American Genius*. New York: St. Martin's Press, 1985.

Kael, Pauline. *5001 Nights at the Movies*. New York: Henry Holt, 1991.

Kael, Pauline; Roger Ebert; James Monaco; et al. *Microsoft Cinemania 96*. Redmond, WA, 1995. CD-ROM.

Leaming, Barbara. *Orson Welles, a Biography*. New York: Viking Press, 1985.

Monaco, James, and the editors of Baseline. *Encyclopedia of Film*. New York: Perigee, 1991.

Sullivan, Monica. "Orson Welles." *Movie Magazine International*, May 1, 1991. Accessed January 2012. Available from http://www.shoestring.org/mmi_revs/welles-birthday.html

Wells, Kitty *(1919–2012)*

Kitty Wells was a demure housewife with three children when she recorded "It Wasn't God Who Made Honky-Tonk Angels," the first in a series of records she released during the 1950s that made her country music's first female superstar. Her success demonstrated to the conservative country establishment that women could profitably perform honky-tonk songs about controversial subjects such as infidelity and divorce. Wells became known as "the Queen of Country Music," and the songs she popularized gave listeners a woman's perspective on classic country themes. Her sharp nasal twang blazed a trail that would be followed by other "girl singers," as female country artists were known, including Patsy Cline and Loretta Lynn.

A native of Nashville, Tennessee, Wells was born Muriel Ellen Deason on August 30, 1919, into a family of singers and musicians. As a child she learned to play the guitar and sang gospel hymns with the church choir. While in her teens, she and her cousin performed on Nashville's WSIX as the Deason Sisters. Wells has said that the song they chose for their radio debut, "Jealous Hearted Me" by the Carter Family, contained a line that made the station's managers uncomfortable: "It takes the man I love to satisfy my soul." Fearing that the audience might be offended, the girls were cut off in mid-song. Listeners complained, however, and the Deason Sisters were given a short early morning program.

In 1937 Wells married Johnnie Wright, a cabinetmaker and musician. With Wright's sister Louise, the newlyweds performed on WSIX as Johnnie Wright and the Harmony Girls. By 1939 Wright and his friend Jack Anglin had a new act, Johnnie and Jack and the Tennessee Mountain Boys, while Wells occupied herself with the care of their first child. She made occasional appearances with her husband's group, using a stage name he gave her that came from an old folk song titled "Kitty Wells."

World War II dissolved the band, interrupting their progress for a few years, but by 1947 Johnnie and Jack had reunited and appeared for a brief time on WSM's *Grand Ole*

Kitty Wells. *Kitty Wells became a country superstar in the 1950s with her hit "It Wasn't God Who Made Honky-Tonk Angels," one of her many songs with an unwholesome subject matter that was in contrast to her demure image.* MICHAEL OCHS ARCHIVES/GETTY IMAGES.

Opry. The following year they joined a new hillbilly program, *Louisiana Hayride*, on Shreveport's KWKH. By this time Wells was a permanent part of their show, the girl singer who performed gospel and sentimental folk songs. Wells had the opportunity to record some of these songs for RCA Victor in 1949 after the label signed Johnnie and Jack. While their records made it onto the Billboard charts, with some reaching the Top 10, hers were barely noticed. RCA let her go, and she withdrew from the music industry to focus attention on her family.

CHEATIN' SONGS

In the spring of 1952, Paul Cohen of Decca Records suggested she record an answer song—one that responds to or continues the story of a previously released hit record—inspired by Hank Thompson's recent single "The Wild Side of Life." Wells was unenthusiastic about the song, but she agreed to return to the studio. Two months later "It Wasn't God Who Made Honky-Tonk Angels" was heading for the top of the country charts, and Wells was poised for stardom.

While "The Wild Side of Life" attacks "honky-tonk angels," implying that women are solely responsible for leading men astray, Wells's song proclaims "It's a shame that all the blame is on us women," noting that "married men [who] think they're still single" are also at fault. Though written by a man, the song offers a woman's point of view on "cheatin'," a common topic for country songwriters that had heretofore been strictly male territory. Initially, the song's controversial subject matter caused it to be banned by NBC radio and the *Grand Ole Opry* for being "suggestive." Fans embraced the record, however, and it remained on the charts for four months. Wells's Decca debut was followed by other popular answer songs as well as songs that became country classics, such as "Release Me" (1954) and "Makin' Believe" (1955).

According to Mary A. Bufwack and Robert K. Oermann, authors of *Finding Her Voice: The Saga of Women in Country Music*, Wells's body of work from the 1950s "essentially defin[ed] the postwar female style" in country music. After she achieved success, Wells continued to work package tours with her husband, who was told by *Grand Ole Opry* veteran Roy Acuff, "Don't ever headline a show with a woman. It won't ever work, because people just don't go for women." Most group shows during this era featured a single female performer, since promoters assumed that audiences would not tolerate more. Despite the prevalence of such prejudice throughout the music industry, Wright broke the rules and gave his wife top billing when they toured together. He also played an important role in her career, serving as her business manager, writing or choosing songs for her to record, and finding musicians for her recording sessions.

Two years after Wells's breakthrough single, the governor of Tennessee paid tribute to her music and her homemaking, calling her "an outstanding wife and mother, in keeping with the finest traditions of Southern womanhood." Although she married Wright shortly after she began her career, she was commonly introduced as "Miss Kitty Wells." As she sang of heartache and sin in a restrained voice, she put forth the public image of a devoted, well-behaved wife in gingham. Wells's popularity may have been largely due to the fact that she personally conformed to the mores of the 1950s, allowing her to dramatize unwholesome situations in her songs.

Wells won numerous awards during the first two decades of her career, and she continued recording into the 1970s. In the early 1980s she and her husband began operating their own museum outside Nashville. They continued performing together until a final show on December 31, 2000, after which they officially retired. Wells was inducted into the Country Music Hall of Fame, and she received a Grammy for Lifetime Achievement in 1991. Wright died on September 27, 2011, and Wells died the next year, on July 16.

Anna Hunt Graves

SEE ALSO: *The Carter Family; Cline, Patsy; Country Music; Grammy Awards;* Grand Ole Opry*; Lynn, Loretta; Radio; World War II.*

BIBLIOGRAPHY

Bufwack, Mary A., and Robert K. Oermann. *Finding Her Voice: The Saga of Women in Country Music*. New York: Crown, 1993.

Kingsbury, Paul, and Alan Axelrod, eds. *Country: The Music and the Musicians*, 314–341. New York: Abbeville Press, 1988.

Wolfe, Charles, and Kitty Wells. *The Queen of Country Music* (CD liner notes). Germany: Bear Family Records, 1993.

Wells, Mary *(1943–1992)*

The "First Lady of Motown," singer and songwriter Mary Wells launched Motown into the black with a succession of hits. As a teenager, Wells was the first Motown artist to have a Top 10 and number one single for the label. She was teamed with songwriter/producer Smokey Robinson, and their synergy produced the right combination of material and approach to showcase Wells's talent to the fullest. During her tenure with Motown, she had several hit songs in the R&B category and crossed over to have several in the pop category as well.

Mary Esther Wells was born in Detroit, Michigan, and grew up singing gospel music at her uncle's Baptist church; she had aspirations of becoming a songwriter. While she was in high school, Wells penned the gospel-inspired "Bye Bye Baby" (1960) with singer Jackie Wilson in mind. Songwriter Berry Gordy had written several hits for Wilson, and Wells sought out Gordy to listen to her new song. After hearing it, Gordy was convinced that the song wasn't for Wilson but instead was for Wells herself.

Gordy signed the seventeen-year-old Wells to his fledging Motown label. "Bye Bye Baby" climbed to number eight on the Billboard R&B chart. Following another hit single, "I Don't Want to Take a Chance" (1961), Motown placed Wells in the artistic care of Robinson. He and Wells represented Motown's first successful teaming of a songwriter/producer with an artist. Robinson encouraged Wells to veer away from blues- and gospel-inspired songs in favor of a sweet, girlish pop style, a natural for her innocent, sincere, and convincing voice.

"You Beat Me to the Punch" (1962) quickly climbed to number one on Billboard's R&B chart and crossed over to number nine on the pop chart. Wells was destined to ride the R&B and pop charts, and after several more hits, including "The One Who Really Loves You" (1962) and "Two Lovers" (1962), she recorded "My Guy" (1964). This, her greatest hit, shot to number one on the pop chart. It was also her last big pop hit, though she also recorded the duet "What's the Matter with You Baby" with Marvin Gaye the same year.

When Wells reached twenty-one, she was unsuccessful in renegotiating her contract with Motown and sued the company over the reported lack of royalties from her performances and songwriting. Prodded by her husband, former Motown artist Herman Griffin, Wells left Motown and succeeded in getting her contract declared null and void. This proved to be a disastrous move for her career, since she never was able to regain the success she had enjoyed with Motown and songwriter/producer Robinson. Wells signed with Twentieth Century Fox Records, which was a profitable arrangement, then with Atlantic/Atco, Jubilee, Reprise, and Epic.

Wells's professional career and her personal life seemed to slowly disintegrate. Her marriage to Griffin ended in divorce, and she married Cecil Womack, though that relationship also ended in divorce. Wells then shocked many by marrying Cecil's brother Curtis. She continued to perform her old hits until she was diagnosed with throat cancer in 1991.

With no medical insurance, evicted from her residence, and placed in a charity ward, Wells was destitute. The Rhythm and Blues Foundation came to her assistance by setting up a Mary Wells Fund. Several well-known artists contributed to the fund, including Bruce Springsteen, Rod Stewart, and Mary Wilson, as well as Motown entrepreneur Gordy. Wells had a choice to have a laryngectomy or radiation. She chose the latter, but the treatment was unsuccessful; she died July 26, 1992. Wells was inducted into the Michigan Rock and Roll Legends Hall of Fame in 2006.

Willie Collins

SEE ALSO: *Cancer; Gaye, Marvin; Gordy, Berry; Gospel Music; Motown; Pop Music; Rhythm and Blues; Robinson, Smokey; Springsteen, Bruce; Top 40.*

BIBLIOGRAPHY

Whitall, Susan. *Women of Motown: An Oral History.* New York: Avon Books, 1998.

Wertham, Fredric *(1895–1981)*

Although Fredric Wertham is remembered primarily as the author of *Seduction of the Innocent* (1954), an incisive, blistering attack on the violence and horror purveyed by the comic-book industry, his research took him through this era of crime comics to the culture that violent movies and television created. In 1966 Wertham wrote: "Television represents one of the greatest technological advances and is an entirely new, potent method of communication. Unfortunately as it is presently used, it does have something in common with crime comic books: the devotion to violence. In the School for Violence, television represents the classic course."

The climate of violence developing since this observation has, if anything, increased with the emergence of new technologies, such as the Internet and videos, and become more noxious. Competition for audience share, demand for advertising revenue, and misguided applications of constitutional rights have all encouraged aggressive displays of violent behavior to be broadcast. Though originally derided, Wertham's observations that the grammar of violence and its impact on the culture constitutes a public health issue have been sustained by the research of Leonard Eron, George Gerbner, and Albert Bandura. Nevertheless, Wertham was not a Luddite, opposed to technological advances, but a physician of wide and deeply humane interests, an advocate of social reform, and a defender of civil liberties.

INTELLECTUAL AWAKENING

Born March 20, 1895, in Nuremberg, Germany, Wertham was one of five children of Sigmund and Mathilde Wertheimer, nonreligious, assimilated middle-class Jews. As a young man, on the eve of World War I, Wertham spent several summers in England, where he found the environment there open and relaxed, a stark contrast to the rigid, disciplined, and intellectually pedantic German culture at home. During this period he explored Fabian socialism and the writings of Karl Marx and, more importantly, became an avid reader of Charles Dickens's writings on social reform.

When war broke out in 1914, Wertham, pursuing medical studies at King's College, London University, found himself stranded in England and, as a German national, was for a short time interned in a prison camp near Wakefield before being paroled. An admirer of British society, he remained in England during the war, reading medicine and literature. After the war he continued his studies at the Universities of Erlangen and Munich, obtaining an MD degree from the University of Würzburg in 1921. Paris and Vienna were additional venues of postgraduate study before he joined Emil Kraepelin's clinic in Munich.

Wertham left Germany in 1922 to work with Kraepelin's protégé Adolf Meyer at the Phipps Psychiatric Clinic at Johns Hopkins University in Baltimore, Maryland. During his years at Johns Hopkins, Wertham established a friendship with H. L. Mencken and worked with Clarence Darrow, becoming one of the first psychiatrists willing to testify on behalf of indigent black defendants. It was also during this period that he met and married Florence Hesketh, an artist doing biological research as a Charlton Fellow in Medicine at Johns Hopkins. Hesketh drew all the cell plate illustrations for *The Brain as an Organ: Its Postmortem Study and Interpretation* (1934), for which Wertham received the first psychiatric grant made by the National Research Council.

In addition, Wertham published the first study on the effects of mescaline and did pioneer work on insulin use in psychotherapy. He developed the mosaic test in which a patient manipulated small multicolored pieces of wood into a freely chosen design, which was evaluated for what it revealed about the patient's ego. Wertham's diagnostic technique was often used in conjunction with paintings by patients, such as the watercolors done by Zelda Fitzgerald when she was under treatment at the Phipps Clinic.

STUDY OF MURDER CASES

During the 1930s Wertham's expertise as a forensic psychiatrist became known to the general public. His involvement in a number of spectacular murder cases, which he discussed in *Dark Legend: A Study in Murder* (1941) and *The Show of Violence* (1949), led him to advocate the duty of a psychiatrist to bring the psychiatric background of murder into the relationship with the law and the society it represents. Wertham's support for an intelligent use of McNaughton's rule determining legal insanity, his understanding of how environmental forces shape individual responses, and his argument that violence and murder are diseases of society all persuaded him that violence is not innate and so could be prevented.

Dark Legend investigates the story of Gino, a seventeen-year-old Italian American who, commanded by the ghost of his dead father, murdered his promiscuous mother. Wertham's compelling narrative of his patient draws upon the myth of Orestes and the legend of Hamlet to explore matricide. The incisive analysis of matricide set out in *Dark Legend* prompted psychoanalyst Ernest Jones to remark, "Freud and I both underestimated the importance of the mother problem in Hamlet. You have made a real contribution." *Dark Legend* is significant because it ties an actual murder case to important psychological types in literature and supports a shift in an understanding of matriarchy among American psychiatrists.

In *The Show of Violence*, Wertham explains his theory of the Catathymic Crisis, in which "a violent act—against another person or against oneself—is the only solution to profound emotional conflict whose real nature remains below the threshold of the consciousness of the patient." He discusses his own role in several celebrated murder cases, including the pathetic Madeline, a young mother who killed her two children and then failed in her suicide attempt; the notorious child murderer Albert Fish; the "mad sculptor" Robert Irwin; and the professional gunman Martin Lavin. In each case Wertham probes the social background, the medical history, the political implications, and the legal response to uncover the effect societal forces had in the creation of the impulse to murder.

In 1932 Wertham moved to New York City, where he became a senior psychiatrist at Bellevue and organized for the Court of General Sessions the nation's first clinic providing a psychiatric screening for every convicted felon. Wertham became director of psychiatric services at Queens Hospital Center in 1940 and pioneered a clinic for sex offenders, the Quaker Emergency Service Readjustment Center, in 1947. With the encouragement of Earl Brown, Paul Robeson, Richard Wright, and Ralph Ellison, Wertham enlisted a multiracial, volunteer staff to establish in Harlem in 1946 a clinic dedicated to alleviating the "free-floating hostility" afflicting many in that community and to understanding the realities of black life in America. Named in memory of Marx's son-in-law, Dr. Paul Lefargue, the Lafargue Clinic became one of the most noteworthy institutions to serve poor Americans and to promote the cause of civil rights.

In order to prepare for discrimination cases in Delaware, attorneys Louis Redding, Jack Greenberg, and Thurgood Marshall needed medical testimony on the harm segregation caused children. Wertham's studies showed that the practice of racial separation "creates a mental health problem in many Negro children with a resulting impediment to their educational progress." Wertham's testimony was significant because his research was the first to examine both black and white children attending segregated schools. The evidence revealed the possibility that white children, too, may be harmed by school segregation. The Delaware cases became part of the legal argument used in the landmark school desegregation case, *Brown v. Board of Education of Topeka* (1954).

In addition to bringing psychotherapy to a neglected community, Wertham's work at the Lafargue Clinic led to the developments of his later ideas on the contribution horror and crime comic books made to a climate of juvenile violence. In 1948 he organized the first symposium dealing with media violence at the New York Academy of Medicine. Not only did Wertham identify media-induced violence as a public health issue, but he also challenged society "to overcome its own claustrophilia and take an interest in the social influences that bear on the individual." This research attracted widespread national attention, opening additional fora for Wertham to publicize his studies on the enigma of preventable violence. The quest to understand and prevent violence—the core of Wertham's psychiatric practice—shaped his thinking on how the mass media create a climate that both encourages and legitimizes violent antisocial acts.

THE ROSENBERG TRIAL

In the 1950s America faced two primary fears: communism and juvenile delinquency. The axis on which these two met found Wertham, whose studies probed the social dynamics that permitted the development of these fears and the underlying violence that inflamed their intensity. Attorney Emanuel Bloch believed that Wertham might be willing to appear for the defense in the espionage trial of Ethel Rosenberg and her husband, Julius. Convicted as members of a conspiracy to send stolen atomic-bomb secrets to Russia, the Rosenbergs nevertheless maintained their innocence and averred that they were victims of a U.S. government frame-up. Political passions, fears of the "red menace," and charges of treason and betrayal swirled at the time against a backdrop the Korean War and Soviet activity in Eastern Europe. Such circumstances persuaded many prominent individuals to keep a low profile in order not to be tainted by helping the Rosenbergs.

Although the court absolutely refused to allow Wertham direct access to Ethel, it gave him permission to testify in federal court under oath about her mental condition. Not only did this order deny her due process, but it also created the paradoxical situation of permitting Wertham to testify about the mental condition of a patient whom he was not allowed to examine. Using Bloch as an intermediary and relying on secondhand information, Wertham accepted these limitations and also braved a vicious and often improper cross-examination. Nevertheless, his understanding of the condition "prison psychosis" and his humanitarian concern for Ethel's health made his testimony compelling. Within a few days Washington reversed itself and moved Julius to Sing Sing, where husband and wife would be allowed to visit each other regularly. Moreover, Wertham was brought in to deal with the Rosenberg children, Michael and Robert, whom he advised and whose adoption by the Meeropol family he helped to make successful.

It was precisely Wertham's reputation for fearlessness and integrity that encouraged Senator Estes Kefauver to appoint him sole psychiatric consultant to the Senate Subcommittee for the Study of Organized Crime (1950). Wertham brought his expertise as a forensic psychiatrist to Kefauver's committee, and his experience in dealing with New York crime and governmental institutions made his observations particularly trenchant. The role organized crime played in American society was one that engendered fear, revulsion, cynicism, respect, and even admiration, especially for the way in which violent crime could be of service to politics. These televised hearings drew national attention, revealing the influence television had in shaping public opinion, and set the stage for the Senate Subcommittee to Investigate Juvenile Delinquency (1953–1956), which explored how juvenile delinquency led to adult crime.

VIOLENCE IN COMICS

A major theme of the investigation into juvenile delinquency was the impact the mass media exerted on youth and on a separate emerging youth culture. Wertham, who had published a series of articles and given lectures describing his research on the unhealthful effects of mass media violence, decided his work merited a book-length study aimed at the general public. In *Seduction of the Innocent* (1954), Wertham sets out his argument on the connection between the rise of juvenile delinquency and the role of crime comic books in promoting violent activity. The brutal and sadistic activity in these comics created a culture of violence and a coarsening of society. Such comic books routinely featured mutilation, gore, branding, blinding—so prominent as to receive its own classification of "eye-motif"—racism; bigotry; and, especially, crude sexual exploitation of women.

Wertham testified that these comics, so attractive and easily available to children, exploited them and harmed their development; he concluded that access to violent comics for children under fourteen years of age must be controlled. Although Wertham was maligned as a censor—a charge he vigorously denied—his work did stimulate the comic-book industry to adopt a code labeling the suitability of each comic-book published (the Code of the Comics Magazine Association of America, October 26, 1954).

Wertham's studies on juvenile delinquency led him to probe deeper into the role various media play in creating, perpetuating, and distorting the social problems of teenagers. Not only comic books but also mass news publications, television, and movies influenced behavior and distorted perceptions of teenagers and different ethnic groups. In *The Circle of Guilt* (1956), Wertham discovers the truth behind the death of "model boy" Billy Blankenship, murdered allegedly without provocation by Puerto Rican "hoodlum" Frank Santana in a New York City street fight. The paradigm of fear, racism, distrust, and prejudice many New Yorkers held conveniently fit Santana. Wertham, whose intuition told him that the case presented by the press reflected cultural prejudice rather than an understanding of the violent circumstances, agreed to investigate.

He discovered that Blankenship was active in teenage gang activities and that Santana had an undeveloped personality, one lacking in hostility, anger, or resentment. Despite Wertham's testimony, the court handed down a harsh sentence of twenty-five years to life for second-degree murder. His outrage at this sentence and at the prevailing climate of violence and prejudice compelled Wertham to write *The Circle of Guilt*, which exposes both failure and hypocrisy on the part of the legal system in complicity with the social service establishment. More importantly, this book reflects the violence afflicting society and the refusal to confront its own insidious cultural stereotyping.

HUMAN VIOLENCE

In 1966 Wertham published his major study on human violence, *A Sign for Cain: An Exploration of Human Violence*. To answer the paradoxical question "Can we abolish violence without violence?" Wertham stated "violence is becoming more entrenched in our society" than many believe and argued that if we are willing, it is within our capacity "to conquer and to abolish it." Essentially a sociological history of violence in Western culture, *A Sign for Cain* focuses on the effects of mass media exposure on the virulence of political tyrannies in the twentieth century, on the emergence of the legal and medical legitimization of violence, and on the willing acceptance of the value of violence.

Wertham's thinking on the nature of violence provokes controversy among social theorists who interpret scientific data in ways to explain away antisocial behavior. Although such theorists admit the existence of cultural shaping, they argue that an instinctive drive for aggression is present at birth. The widespread acceptance of this idea of "an inborn biologically fixed instinct of violence in man," Wertham argues, is "a theory that creates an entirely false and nihilistic destructive image of man." Violence may be the result of "negative factors in the personality and in the social medium where the growth of personality takes place." Indeed, Wertham avers that "the primary natural tendency [of man is] to maintain and care for the intactness and integrity of others. Man does not have an 'instinct' of violence; he has the *capacity* and the physiological apparatus for violence." To Wertham, humans have survived as a species not because of an instinct for violence but because people value cooperation.

His interest in youth and how communication by the young shapes the culture led Wertham to publish his last book, *The World of Fanzines: A Special Form of Communication* (1973). Arguing that fanzines—magazines created by fans of fantasy and science fiction—are a revealing form of communication because they are "free from outside interference, without control or manipulation from above, without *censorship*, visible or invisible," Wertham sees them as not just a product of our society but a reaction to it. Fanzines show the capacity of the individual fan to reshape violent material in a socially useful way. The paraculture that is the world of fanzines contains patterns of fantasy, art, and literature manifesting healthy creativity, independence, and social responsibility. The fan-produced magazine expresses a genuine voice wanting to be heard, defying the overpowering roar of the mass media. Since fanzine artists and writers stress the role of heroes who have "cleared their minds of cant," Wertham sees in the integrity of heroes and super-heroes "a message for our unheroic age."

The last years of Wertham's life were spent at his beloved Blue Hills, a former Pennsylvania Dutch farm near the Hawk Mountain Bird Sanctuary at Kempton. He died November 18, 1981.

James E. Reibman

SEE ALSO: *Comic Books; Comics Code Authority; Communism; Darrow, Clarence; Fan Magazines; Gangs; Mafia/Organized Crime; Mencken, H. L.; Robeson, Paul; Rosenberg, Julius and Ethel; Teenagers; Television; Wright, Richard.*

BIBLIOGRAPHY

Barker, Martin. *A Haunt of Fears: The Strange History of the British Horror Comics Campaign*. London: Pluto Press, 1984.

Barker, Martin. "Fredric Wertham—The Sad Case of the Unhappy Humanist." In *Pulp Demons: International Dimensions of the Postwar Anti-comics Campaign*, ed. John A. Lent, 215–233. Cranbury, NJ: Associated University Presses, 1999.

Beaty, Bart. *Fredric Wertham and the Critique of Mass Culture*. Oxford: University Press of Mississippi, 2005.

Gilbert, James. *A Cycle of Outrage: America's Reaction to the Juvenile Delinquent in the 1950s*. New York: Oxford University Press, 1986.

Kluger, Richard. *Simple Justice: The History of "Brown v. Board of Education" and Black America's Struggle for Equality.* New York: Vintage Books, 1977.

Reibman, James E. "The Life of Dr. Fredric Wertham." In *The Fredric Wertham Collection: Gift of His Wife Hesketh*, 11–22. Cambridge, MA: Busch-Reisinger Museum, Harvard University, 1990.

Reibman, James E. "Fredric Wertham: A Social Psychiatrist Characterizes Crime Comic Books and Media Violence as Public Health Issues." In *Pulp Demons: International Dimensions of the Postwar Anti-comics Campaign*, ed. John A. Lent, 234–268. Cranbury, NJ: Associated University Presses, 1999.

West, Jerry *(1938–)*

One of the greatest guards ever to play in the National Basketball Association (NBA), Jerry West was an all-star player during his NBA career in the 1960s and early 1970s and later served as head coach and general manager of the Los Angeles Lakers, one of the predominant teams of the 1980s. West's likeness is an icon to basketball fans and the general public as the silhouetted figure in the NBA's logo.

West might be described as an atypical basketball player. He weighed 185 pounds, and his 39-inch arms prompted some observers to comment on his ostrichlike appearance, but his competitive intensity and knack for sinking the last-second shot helped him overcome these deficiencies, earning for him his lifelong nickname, Mr. Clutch. A two-time All-American at the University of West Virginia, West later won a gold medal with the 1960 U.S. Olympic basketball team. He joined the Los Angeles Lakers the same year that another dynamic guard, Oscar Robertson, entered the NBA with the Milwaukee Bucks. During the 1960s the two men would emerge as the best shooters in basketball.

West averaged twenty-seven points per game and made the All-Star team every year he played. He averaged more than thirty points per game in four seasons. He saved his best work for the postseason, however, averaging 29.1 points in 153 playoff contests and winning or tying numerous games with critical buzzer-beating baskets. Yet the man who came to symbolize his sport spent much of his career beating back a reputation as a hard-luck player. Six times West led the Lakers to the NBA finals, only to lose to the Boston Celtics. Finally, in 1972 the team broke through, defeating the New York Knicks in the championship round. "The albatross around my neck," as West called the title drought, was lifted.

A pulled stomach muscle forced West to cut short his playing career in 1974. After a brief and unhappy retirement, he returned to the arena as Lakers head coach from 1976 to 1979. Despite some success, he clashed repeatedly with team owner Jack Kent Cooke and stepped out from behind the bench forever. New owner Jerry Buss convinced him to assume the post of general manager in 1982.

At the time, the Lakers were one of the NBA's premier teams. Star players Earvin "Magic" Johnson and Kareem Abdul-Jabbar led a potent offense, and head coach Pat Riley lent a Hollywood sheen to the proceedings with his slicked-back hair and expensive suits. Celebrities and swells flocked to the court-side seats at the Lakers' home gym, dubbed "the Fabulous Forum." As general manager, West developed a reputation as the league's most astute evaluator of talent. On numerous occasions he selected unheralded prospects from obscure colleges who quickly blossomed into productive NBA players. As one longtime friend of West's observed, "He's the only guy I know who went into oil for a tax loss and struck a gusher."

Under West the Lakers grew into an NBA powerhouse. They won championships for him in 1982, 1985, 1987, 1988, and 2000 and challenged for league supremacy several other years during West's tenure. The team's up-tempo style of play, dubbed "Showtime," proved an enormously popular marketing angle for the NBA worldwide. While the rivalry between the Boston Celtics' Larry Bird and the Lakers' Johnson has been widely credited with reviving public interest in professional basketball, it would be no exaggeration to say that West's careful nurturing of the Laker dynasty also contributed to that resurgence.

West's last year with the Lakers was 2000. He worked in the front office of the Memphis Grizzlies from 2002 to 2007, and in 2011 he became an adviser to the Golden State Warriors. West was awarded the NBA Executive of the Year Award in 1995 and 2004.

Robert E. Schnakenberg

SEE ALSO: *Abdul-Jabbar, Kareem; Basketball; Bird, Larry; The Boston Celtics; Johnson, Earvin "Magic"; The Los Angeles Lakers; National Basketball Association (NBA); The New York Knickerbockers; Olympics; Riley, Pat; Robertson, Oscar; Sports Heroes.*

BIBLIOGRAPHY

Deegan, Paul. *Jerry West.* Mankato, MN: Children's Press, 1974.

West, Jerry, and Bill Libby. *Mr. Clutch: The Jerry West Story.* Englewood Cliffs, NJ: Prentice-Hall, 1969.

West, Jerry, and Jonathan Coleman. *West by West: My Charmed, Tormented Life.* New York: Little, Brown, 2011.

West, Kanye *(1977–)*

Hailed as "the smartest man in pop music" in 2005 by *Time* magazine, Kanye West is a producer and rapper who has changed the face and image of contemporary hip-hop music. Known for his masterful use of samples and drum loops, West has a musical style that draws from a diverse palette of influences. His songs feature everything from sped-up classic soul and R&B to electronica, classical music, and indie rock. The results are poppy and popular tracks about topics such as dropping out of college. With his unabashedly preppy clothes and rhymes about middle-class life, West has broadened the stylistic and thematic scope of hip-hop.

EARLY INFLUENCES

West was an only child born to educated middle-class parents in Atlanta, Georgia. His father, Ray West, a former Black Panther who later became an award-winning photojournalist and marriage counselor, and his mother, Donda West, a college English professor, divorced when West was three. He began writing and rhyming in elementary school and soon after decided to become a rapper. Following that revelation he began creating beats. NO I.D., a Chicago producer, met West when he was fifteen and encouraged him to sample from R&B and classic soul songs and to remake them in an up-tempo, contemporary style. Acting on that advice, West purchased a sampling keyboard and began practicing with beats and songs. After graduating from high school in 1995, the aspiring musician attended the American Academy of Art in Chicago for a year and then transferred to Chicago State University to pursue a degree in English.

In college, West continued to pursue a career in music, but it took him years to prove he was more than a producer trying to rap. He had some success when he sold a beat to a Chicago rapper named Gravity for $8,000 in 1996. In 2002 West signed with Roc-A-Fella Records, where he did production work but was not initially allowed to record his own album. West always intended to be an artist in his own right after his career as a producer was established, but his image worked against him: record companies, including Roc-A-Fella, were unsure how to market him since his image, dress, and demeanor ran counter to expectations of what a rapper should be. West came from a middle-class family, attended good schools, did not wear baggy jeans, and never hustled or sold drugs. Contrary to the hustler persona popularized by Jay-Z and other rappers, West presented an alternative face of hip-hop, one dressed like a preppy in collared shirts, cardigan sweaters, and tight-fitting Italian suits.

West received production credit for several songs on Jay-Z's *The Blueprint* (2001), including "H to the Izzo," which did much to bolster his status as a top producer. In October 2002, overworked from hours in the recording studio, West wrecked his Lexus after falling asleep behind the wheel and almost lost his life. In the hospital with his jaw wired shut, he created a song about the accident titled "Through the Wire" that was built on Chaka Khan's "Through the Fire" (1984). "Through the Wire" was a precursor to the ambitious trio of concept albums that followed.

WORLDWIDE SUCCESS

College Dropout (2004), the first in a trilogy of college-themed concept albums, rated high in major critics' polls and earned ten Grammy nominations. The album boasted a wide range of listeners who found its lyrics and style immediately accessible. Notable songs from the album include the hit singles "Slow Jamz," "Through the Wire," and "Jesus Walks," the latter of which was cowritten with Rhymefest and saw regular rotation in clubs, on MTV, and on the radio. In promoting *College Dropout* West also introduced his iconic fashion sense to the public at large. With the second two installments in the trilogy—*Late Registration* (2005) and *Graduation* (2007)—West continued to refine both his musical and sartorial styles.

West's fourth album, *808s and Heartbreak* (2008), marked a departure from his previous albums. Notable for its extensive use of Autotune and its unique mix of electronic and R&B influences, *808s and Heartbreak* debuted at number one on the Billboard 200. West's fifth studio album, *My Beautiful Dark Twisted Fantasy* (2010), featured catchy melodies and sociopolitical messages. Standout tracks "Blame Game" and "Lost in the World" exude a joyous pain—a musical ethos that embodies West's modern take on the blues.

Arrogant and forthright, West is the only rapper who has garnered the contempt of two presidents. His statement "George Bush doesn't care about black people," made during a 2005 Red Cross fund-raising drive for the victims of Hurricane Katrina, famously angered President George W. Bush. In September 2009 President Barack Obama criticized West for upstaging pop star Taylor Swift's acceptance of the MTV Video Music Award for Best Female Video. Aware that his public image was taking a beating, West publicly acknowledged his regret for these acts and determined to reverse his negative image.

To project a more positive image, West used social media outlets to educate his audience about his music and philosophy. He explained his musical aesthetic via Twitter, and on "G.O. O.D. Fridays" he gave away free MP3 selections, including tracks from *My Beautiful Dark Twisted Fantasy*. The name of the weekly promotion references G.O.O.D. Music (an acronym for Getting Out Our Dreams), a record label and management firm founded by West. By appealing directly to his audience, West was able to quickly and effectively repair his public image. The 2011 album he made in collaboration with Jay-Z, *Watch the Throne*, debuted at number one on the Billboard 200 chart. The single "Otis," a duet with Jay-Z, won a Grammy for Best Rap Performance.

Willie R. Collins

SEE ALSO: *Autotune; Black Panthers; Grammy Awards; Hip-Hop; Hurricane Katrina; Indie Music; Jay-Z; MP3; MTV; Obama, Barack; Pop Music; Preppy; Radio; Rap; Rhythm and Blues; Soul Music; Swift, Taylor;* Time; *Twitter.*

BIBLIOGRAPHY

Brown, Jake. *Kanye West in the Studio: Beats Down! Money Up! (2000–2006).* Phoenix, AZ: Colossus Books, 2006.

Caramanica, Jon. "Kanye West, Still Unfiltered, on Eve of Fifth Album." *New York Times*, November 17, 2010.

Tyrangiel, Josh. "Why You Can't Ignore Kanye." *Time*, August 21, 2005.

West, Mae *(1893–1980)*

Writer, stage performer, screen actress, and nightclub entertainer Mae West emerged as a uniquely independent, outspoken, flamboyant, and humorously erotic woman. A ray of light during the Great Depression, she achieved legendary status in American show business folklore and won a wide international following. Rarely has a show business personality left so indelible a mark on American popular culture, influencing the laws of film censorship and bequeathing a series of outrageous ripostes and innuendoes to the language—most famously, "Why don't you come up sometime and see me?"—that were still being used in the early twenty-first century. During World War II Allied troops honored her hourglass figure by calling their inflatable life jackets "Mae Wests." Learning of this new meaning to her name, she commented: "I've been in 'Who's Who,' and I know what's what, but it's the first time I've been in a Dictionary."

EARLY CAREER

She began her stage career early, making her debut with Hal Clarendon's theatrical company in her hometown of Brooklyn, New York, in 1901. There she played such well-known juvenile roles as Little Eva, Little Willie, and even Little Lord Fauntleroy. By 1907, at the age of fourteen, she was a performer on the national vaudeville circuits with Frank Wallace and, in 1911, appeared as an acrobatic dancer and singer in the Broadway

Mae West. *Mae West's vampy style and skill at delivering a suggestive line earned her both fans and critics.* SILVER SCREEN COLLECTION/ CONTRIBUTOR/MOVIEPIX/GETTY IMAGES.

revue *À la Broadway and Hello, Paris*. She then began writing, producing, directing, and starring in her own plays on Broadway. Her first play, *Sex* (1926), starred West as Margie La Monte, a golden-hearted prostitute who wanders the wharves. The play ran for 375 performances and ended when she was jailed for ten days for obscenity and corruption of public morals. The publicity made her a national figure and added to the box-office success of her later plays, *Diamond Lil* (1928) and *The Constant Sinner* (1931).

A buxom blond with a feline purr, imported to Hollywood from Broadway, West's film career flourished from 1932 to 1940. She wrote the screenplays for all but the first of her nine films during this period and delivered her suggestive, sex-parodying lines to a variety of leading men, from Cary Grant to W. C. Fields. Paramount offered her the unheard-of sum of $5,000 for a minor role in her debut film, *Night after Night* (1932), and West, with her vampy posturing and sexual innuendo, stole the show. The film's star, George Raft, said later, "In this picture, Mae West stole everything but the cameras." Her entrance in this first of her films featured one of her most oft-repeated witticisms: when a hat-check girl, admiring Mae's bejeweled splendor, gushes, "Goodness, what beautiful diamonds!" the star responds with "Goodness had nothing to do with it, dearie." The joke was, of course, her own.

PARAMOUNT'S SAVIOR

Paramount offered West a contract, and she agreed on condition that her next picture was a film version of *Diamond Lil*. That film, released as *She Done Him Wrong* (1933) and costarring Grant, unveiled her trademark line, "Why don't you come up sometime and see me?" The film broke attendance records all over the world, and producer William Le Baron told exhibitors that *She Done Him Wrong* must be credited with having saved Paramount when that studio was considering selling out to MGM (Metro-Goldwyn-Mayer), and when Paramount theaters—1,700 of them—thought of closing their doors and converting into office buildings. She made *I'm No Angel*, again with Grant, the same year, by the end of which she was ranked as the eighth-biggest box-office draw of 1933. By 1935 her combination of glamour, vulgarity, and self-parody had made West the highest-paid woman in the United States.

Her success, however, based as it was on the risqué, brought a strong reaction from the puritanical wing. The Hays Office, charged with keeping movies wholesome in the wake of a succession of Hollywood sex scandals, was forced to bring in their new production code—the Hays Code—in 1934, expressly to deal with the Mae West problem. Her next film had the working title of *It Ain't No Sin*, but the Hays Office decreed that it be designated less provocatively as *Belle of the Nineties* (1934). West reached the peak of her popularity as a Salvation Army worker in *Klondike Annie* (1936), costarring Victor McLaglen. Posters for the movie announced, "She made the Frozen North Red Hot!" Another slogan used to publicize her movies was "Here's Mae West. When she's good, she's very good. When she's bad, she's better."

CAREER STRUGGLES

She costarred with Fields in 1940 in the comic Western *My Little Chickadee*, each of them writing their own lines, but with disappointing results. When she failed to persuade Paramount to let her play Catherine the Great, she took her script about the controversial Russian empress to Broadway in the mid-1940s, where it was staged as a revue called *Catherine Was Great*. Her success led to a tour of England with her play *Diamond Lil* in 1947–1948, and she took the play on a long tour of the United States for the next four years. With her film career over, she appeared in nightclubs and on television in an act with a group of young muscle men.

During the 1960s one of her few public appearances was in the 1964 TV series *Mister Ed* (1958–1966), but she made two last, disastrous screen appearances in the 1970s. She made a comeback as a Hollywood agent in the grotesque film version of Gore Vidal's sex-change comedy, *Myra Breckinridge* (1970), but despite the opprobrium heaped on the film (which starred Raquel Welch), West got most of the publicity, $350,000 for ten days' work and her own dialogue, and a tumultuous reception at the premiere from a new generation of fans. Then, aged eighty-six, the indomitable West starred in the lascivious and highly embarrassing *Sextette* (1978), adapted from her own play. Surrounded by a bevy of men, who included old-timers George Raft, Walter Pidgeon, Tony Curtis, George Hamilton, and Ringo Starr, it was an ignominious exit, but the legend lives on.

Benjamin Griffith

SEE ALSO: *Celebrity; Fields, W. C.; Grant, Cary; Hollywood; MGM (Metro-Goldwyn-Mayer);* Mister Ed*; Raft, George; Sex Symbol; Vidal, Gore; World War II.*

BIBLIOGRAPHY

Curry, Ramona. *Too Much of a Good Thing: Mae West as Cultural Icon*. Minneapolis: University of Minnesota Press, 1996.

Hamilton, Marybeth. *When I'm Bad I'm Better: Mae West, Sex, and American Entertainment*. New York: Harper-Collins, 1995.

Leonard, Maurice. *Empress of Sex*. New York: Birch Lane Press, 1991.

Watts, Jill. *Mae West: An Icon in Black and White*. New York: Oxford University Press, 2001.

West Side Story

When the curtain rose for the Broadway opening of the musical *West Side Story* on September 26, 1957, audiences were stunned and shaken by something new in American theater. Using a dynamic combination of classical theme and modern vernacular in script, music, and dance, the creators of *West Side Story* presented 1950s audiences with a disturbing, funny, and tragic look at what was happening in American society. Borrowing its plot from William Shakespeare's *Romeo and Juliet*, *West Side Story* replaces the rival families with rival street gangs and augments the theme of love defeated by a conflict-torn environment. The play ran for 732 performances on Broadway and was made into an award-winning film in 1961.

The plot of *West Side Story* is simple and familiar. Maria, newly arrived in New York from Puerto Rico, is expected to marry Chino, a nice Puerto Rican boy, but instead meets Polish-American Tony at a dance and they fall in love at first sight. But other forces are at work to keep them apart. Tony is one of the founders of the Jets, a street gang of white boys, and though he has drifted away from the gang and even gotten a job, he is still

West Side Story. *The Puerto Rican gang members and their girlfriends take to the dance floor in a scene from the 1961 film version of* West Side Story. ERNST HAAS/CONTRIBUTOR/GETTY IMAGES.

loyal to his "brothers" in the Jets. A new gang of Puerto Rican boys, the Sharks, led by Maria's brother Bernardo, is threatening the Jets supremacy on the streets, and the Jets are determined to hold on to their territory at all costs. The Sharks are equally determined to carve out a place for themselves in their new city, and the gangs scuffle regularly. Finally, Tony ends up involved in a rumble where his best friend is knifed, and in the ensuing melee, Tony accidentally kills Bernardo. Though grief-stricken, Maria forgives him, and they plan to leave the city and run together to somewhere peaceful and safe. Before they can escape, however, Maria's spurned boyfriend Chino finds Tony and kills him. Devastated, Maria accuses both the Sharks and Jets of killing Bernardo and Tony and, united for a moment at least, the rival gang members carry Tony's body away.

West Side Story was the brainchild of theatrical great Jerome Robbins. Robbins, often considered one of the greatest American choreographers as well as a producer and director, got the idea for the musical when a friend was cast to play Romeo in a production of the Shakespeare play. While trying to help his friend get a grasp on Romeo's character, Robbins began to envision Romeo in modern times, dealing with modern issues. The idea stuck with him, and he eventually gathered a distinguished group of artists to help him create a modern day *Romeo and Juliet* that would speak to the dilemmas of 1950s America. Famed composer Leonard Bernstein was recruited to write the score, with then-newcomer Stephen Sondheim for the lyrics. The book was to be written by Arthur Laurents. Robbins's original name for the piece was "East Side Story," and the star-crossed lovers were to be a Jew and a Catholic from New York's lower east side. Robbins, however, was looking for a new perspective, and he felt the conflict between Jews and Catholics had been documented in theater in plays such as *Abie's Irish Rose*. Taking note of the increased numbers of Puerto Rican immigrants to New York following World War II, he moved his play to the Upper West Side of Manhattan and staged his conflict between a gang of Puerto Rican boys and a gang of "American" boys, the sons of less recent immigrants.

While critics were somewhat bemused by the comic-tragic darkness of *West Side Story*, audiences were captivated. To a society striving to be "normal" while seething with angry undercurrents, *West Side Story* spoke with a hip, rebellious authority. The morality play plot fits well within an accepted 1950s genre that included films like *Rebel without a Cause*, but what made *West Side Story* different was its marriage of the classical and the hip. Bernstein's almost operatic score accentuates the incisive hard edged lyrics of Sondheim, and Robbins's baletic choreography stretches tautly over the angry grace of youth with nothing to lose. With words like "juvenile delinquent" and "street gang" beginning to pop up in the news media, *West Side Story* gave the delinquent a voice, a cool, powerful archetype of a voice.

Some have criticized the play for glamorizing gangs, and others have called its portrayal of Puerto Ricans racist. Indeed, both the Broadway play and movie were flawed by a lack of authentic Latin casting. Of the major cast members, only Chita Rivera in the play and Rita Moreno in the movie (both, coincidentally, playing Bernardo's girlfriend Anita) were Latina. In spite of these weak points, it remains one of the strongest popular statements about troubled youth and the devastating effects of poverty and racism. In the song "Gee, Officer Krupke!," the Jets stage a mock scenario where a delinquent is shunted from police to judge to psychiatrist to social worker, coming to the dismal conclusion that juvenile delinquency is an ailment of society and that "no one wants a fella with a social disease." The song is as explicit as a sociological treatise about the causes of many of the problems of urban youth, and its acute goofiness easily transcends decades of at-risk teenagers.

The Sharks' counterpoint to "Officer Krupke" is the song "America," sung by the Puerto Ricans about their new homeland. It is a bitter condemnation of the lie behind the "land of opportunity" couched in a rousing Latin rhythm and framed as an argument (in the play it is a debate among the girls; in the movie it is between the boys and the girls). "Here you are free and you have pride!" one side crows. "As long as you stay on your own side," the other counters. "Free to do anything you choose." "Free to wait tables and shine shoes." The song is a lively dance, showing the triumph of the spirit over the obstacles often faced by immigrants.

In contrast to the jubilantly angry mood of songs like "Officer Krupke" and "America," the song "Cool," sung by the leader of the Jets, seems to be ushering in a new age. Displacing the hotheaded cocky swagger of the 1950s, "Cool" ("Boy, boy, crazy boy, stay cool boy / Take it slow cause, daddy-o, you can live it up and die in bed") seems to point the way to the beatnik era of the 1960s, where rebellion takes a more passively resistant form.

On the cusp of the 1960s, American society, still recovering from the enormous upheaval of World War II, was seeking stability and control. American youth, particularly poor urban youth, rebelled against the falseness of this new American dream. *West Side Story* gave complacent 1950s audiences a taste of the bitter life on the streets, where working class youth had little opportunity in their future and "owning the streets," or controlling activity in their gang's territory, was their only way of claiming power. Since life for disadvantaged youth has changed little, the musical still speaks to audiences. Since its long Broadway run and its acclaimed film release, *West Side Story* has been widely revived as a play in theater companies across the United States and in many other countries. The soundtrack albums for both the play and movie rode the Billboard 200 chart for lengthy periods. There have been Japanese and Chinese versions of the Sharks and Jets. In the mid-1980s a recording of the score was released featuring world renowned opera singers, and in the mid-1990s one was released featuring current pop stars. Though *Romeo and Juliet* has been reprised many times, few productions have managed as well as *West Side Story* to so capture a moment in history, as well as the universality of the hopes of youth tangled in the violence of society.

Tina Gianoulis

SEE ALSO: *Bernstein, Leonard; Broadway; Moreno, Rita; The Musical; Rivera, Chita; Sondheim, Stephen; Wood, Natalie.*

BIBLIOGRAPHY

Bernstein, Leonard. *West Side Story.* New York: Random House, 1958.

Garesian, Keith. *The Making of West Side Story.* Toronto: LPC/Inbook, 1995.

Simeone, Nigel. *Leonard Bernstein, West Side Story.* Burlington, VT: Ashgate, 2009.

The West Wing

Airing on NBC from 1999 to 2006, *The West Wing* is an award-winning political drama created by Aaron Sorkin. The series is set in the tumultuous West Wing of the White House during the administration of Democratic President Josiah "Jed" Bartlet (Martin Sheen), who struggles to contain a number of political crises on both the domestic and international fronts. Sorkin imbued the series with a sense of realism by hiring a number of former White House staffers and speech writers to oversee script-writing, set design, and production, and the show was lauded by Washington insiders, television critics, and casual viewers alike for reviving a time-worn genre with an air of verisimilitude. *The West Wing* garnered more than eighty different awards in its seven-season run, including twenty-six Emmys (a record nine in its first season alone) and two Golden Globes.

Since the majority of the show is set in a relatively small and unchanging environment, Sorkin populated his West Wing with a group of actors capable of captivating viewers through dialogue alone, including stage veterans Allison Janney (as press secretary C. J. Cregg) and John Spencer (as chief of staff Leo McGarry); familiar screen actors like Rob Lowe (as deputy communications director Sam Seaborn) and Richard Schiff (as communications director Toby Ziegler); and relative newcomers such as Bradley Whitford (as deputy chief of staff Josh Lyman), Janel Moloney (as Lyman's assistant), and Dulé Hill (as the president's personal aide, Charlie Young). The chemistry of the cast, coupled with Sorkin's compelling scripts, helped to humanize the traditionally inaccessible world of the executive branch and earned the show's producers an Emmy Award for Outstanding Casting after the first season. Some complained that the characters, who often give impassioned speeches on behalf of their deeply held moral convictions, seem to represent an idealized version of American politics, but many credit *The West Wing*'s genuinely principled characters with initiating a new wave of political interest and involvement among young viewers.

The West Wing earned widespread praise for its interaction with and commentary on contemporaneous political events. The first few seasons of the show aired during the contentious final years of the Clinton administration, and they often depict Bartlet at odds with a Republican-controlled Congress over issues such as gun control, health care, gay marriage, and allegations of lying to the American people—each subject having real-life counterparts in the political news of the time. Later seasons dealt with the major political issues of the early twenty-first century, including the threat of terrorism, the appointment of new justices to the Supreme Court, immigration, genocide in Darfur, information leaks, and Social Security reform. If conservative commentators often took issue with the show's admittedly liberal viewpoint (Sorkin and Sheen are both prominent supporters of Left-leaning politicians), they just as frequently applauded its cerebral treatment of complex issues and lack of polemical rhetoric.

Most viewers agree that *The West Wing* went into general decline after its fourth season, following Sorkin's much-publicized departure from the show. Searching for new plot lines to reinvigorate their shrinking viewership, producers began to extend the action outside of the White House and to introduce new characters. The final seasons focus on the campaign to succeed President Bartlet between Democratic congressman Matt Santos (Jimmy Smits) and Republican senator Arnold Vinick (Alan Alda), who becomes secretary of state in the resulting Santos administration. *The West Wing* was canceled in May of 2006 amid faltering ratings but remains one of the most critically acclaimed shows to ever have aired on network television, having earned four consecutive Emmy Awards for Best Drama from 2000 to 2003.

Jacob Schmitt

SEE ALSO: *Alda, Alan; Emmy Awards; Smits, Jimmy; Television.*

BIBLIOGRAPHY

Crawley, Melissa. *Mr. Sorkin Goes to Washington: Shaping the President on Television's "The West Wing."* Jefferson, NC: McFarland, 2006.

Parry-Giles, Trevor, and Shawn J. Parry-Giles. *The Prime-Time Presidency: "The West Wing" and U.S. Nationalism.* Urbana: University of Illinois Press, 2006.

Rollins, Peter C., and John E. O'Connor. *"The West Wing": The American Presidency as Television Drama.* Syracuse, NY: Syracuse University Press, 2003.

The Western

Over the course of the twentieth century, the cultural significance of the Western has exceeded the borders of a simple film genre. The Western film's many incarnations remain the most obvious and popular frame for the mythos of the American frontier, but the Western itself is usefully conceptualized as a widely transitory aesthetic mode composed of recognizable conventions and icons that have spread across the face of international culture. From early-nineteenth-century examples such as Wild West shows, wilderness paintings, and dime novels to the legions of celluloid cowboys and Indians that ruled American movie houses from the 1930s through the 1960s, the full scope and majesty of the Western also made substantial contributions to radio dramas, television series, comic books, advertisements, rodeos, musicals, and novels.

As the Western's various forms continue to coat our cultural landscape, its apparently simple images have acquired a prolific range of meanings. Today, the Western constitutes a truly international entity, but its visual and ideological roots retain a distinctly American sense of rugged individualism and entrepreneurship. At the heart of its mythology of cowboys, Indians, horses, and six-guns, the Western can be read as a potent allegory for American society. All the hopes, triumphs, failures, and anxieties of American cultural identity are subtly written into the Western's landscape.

The primary colors of the Western palette are simple but bold. First, the Western's aesthetic foundations are consistently grounded in the south, west, or northwest portion of the American continents. Some Westerns, such as *The Treasure of the Sierra Madre* (1948) or *Butch Cassidy and the Sundance Kid* (1969) migrate as far as South America. The Lone Ranger enjoyed a brief sojourn fighting pirates on the Barbary Coast, and *Midnight Cowboy*'s (1969) Texan Hustler, Joe Buck, even immigrates to New York City. In every case, the Westerner always operates in a distinctly obvious fashion that effectively brings the West into foreign and exotic locales.

The Western mode is essentially a fusion of American history, myth, and art into a series of structuring tensions: between the individual and the community, between nature and culture, between freedom and restriction, and between agrarianism and industrialism. All are physically separated by the frontier between the West and the East. These differences may be manifested in conflicts between gunfighters and townspeople, ranchers and farmers, Indians and settlers, outlaws and sheriffs. But such are the complexities and richness of the material that the precise placing of any group or individual within these oppositions can never be predetermined. Indians may well signify savagery, but sometimes they stand for what is positive in the idea of "nature." Outlaws may be hostile to civilization; but Jesse James often represents the struggle of agrarian values against encroaching industrialization.

THE CLEAR-CUT WESTERN MAN

There is usually a man with a gun at the center of these continually shifting situations and conflicts. In any medium, from advertising to radio, the Western drama is rarely resolved without some use of, or reference to, masculine violence. The Western's "game" of binary conflicts also relies on an easily recognized hierarchy of standardized pawns. These stock characters comprise

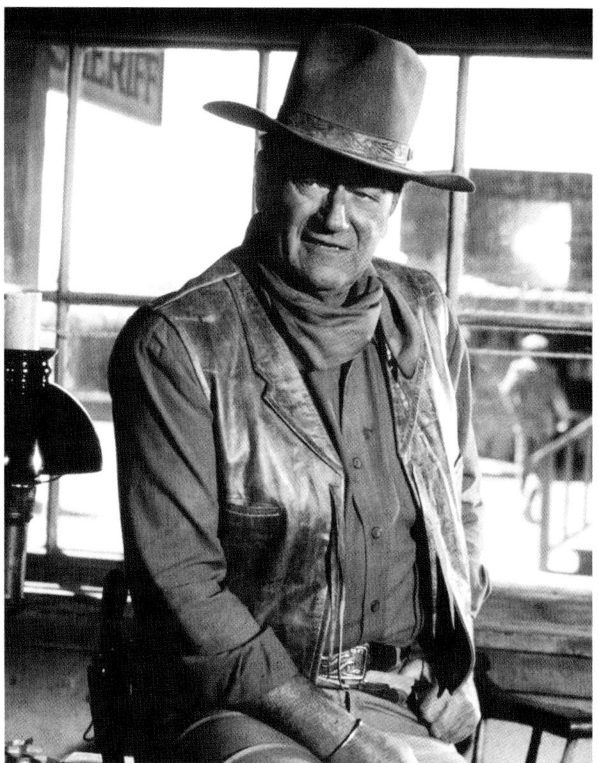

***John Wayne in* Chisum.** *John Wayne starred as John Chisum in the 1970 Western* Chisum. SILVER SCREEN COLLECTION/ CONTRIBUTOR/MOVIEPIX/GETTY IMAGES.

a profoundly limited cast of expressive icons headed by principal Westerners such as the cowboy, the gunslinger, the sheriff, the cavalry man, the outlaw, the rancher, and the farmer. These leading men are often accompanied by female companions and minor bourgeois players including the frontier wife, the saloon tart, the town drunk, the doctor, the mayor, the merchant, the gambler, the barber, the prospector, and the undertaker. Minorities such as Mexicans, Native Americans, and those pejoratively referred to as "half-breeds" tend to exist on the periphery as either obvious antagonists, faithful companions, or ambiguous alien influences.

Whatever their arrangement, this specialized cast populates a decidedly wild, moral universe that codifies the ethical complexities of a century that seeks order and peace through nostalgic backward glances at the untamed West. The form's continual preoccupation with the ghosts of the Civil War, the threat of Native American miscegenation, and the disappearance of the open plains all emphasize our wish to simplify or assuage a problem in American society through Western pageantry. Phil Hardy carefully delineates the cultural significance of the Western's therapeutic charms in *The Overlook Film Encyclopedia*: "In short, at a time when frustratingly complex issues like the Bomb, the Cold War, the House Un-American Activities Committee and Suez, were being raised, the Western remained a simple, unchanging, clear cut world in which notions of Good and Evil could be balanced against each other in an easily recognizable fashion."

This is not to say that good always triumphs or that good ever appears as constant and clear cut as the authors of Westerns might have wished. On the contrary, the evolution of the Western exhibits a tendency toward both pious optimism and depressed cynicism. For all the vibrant Americana celebrated in John Ford's *My Darling Clementine* (1946), Westerns such as William Wellman's *Ox-Bow Incident* (1943), Sam Fuller's *Run of the Arrow* (1957), and Robert Altman's *McCabe & Mrs. Miller* (1971) depict a decidedly pessimistic American milieu that turns on ruthless physical, racial, and economic violence such as lynching, massacres, and prostitution.

The majority of Western art obsesses over the stature of the "Westerner," the white male hero in arms. As is often expressed through the pedagogic interactions of men and children in films such as *Red River* (1948), *Shane* (1953), and *High Noon* (1952), boys, sons, and orphans idealize the resolute father figures that teach them how to think, work, and fight. In radio drama, most Western heroes had young apprentices such as the Lone Ranger's Dan Reed and Red Ryder's Little Beaver. Some Westerns, such as *Duel in the Sun* (1946), *Broken Lance* (1954), *The Searchers* (1956), and *The Shootist* (1976) would complicate this patriarchal formula with Oedipal and fraternal rebellions, but these conflicts usually resulted in an improvement or reevaluation of the original pedagogical perpetuation of male control.

SUPPORTING PLAYERS: WOMEN & MINORITIES

Although women and minorities often play crucial roles in the development of white Western identity, these groups are consistently relegated to marginal status in the traditional Western film. Forward, sensual Western women such as *My Darling Clementine*'s Chihuahua, *Duel in the Sun*'s Pearl, and *Destry Rides Again*'s (1939) Frenchy usually pay a deadly price for their sexual candor. A sexualized female finds comfort only in a Western scenario in which humble heroes such as *Stagecoach*'s (1939) Ringo Kid decide to ignore the tainted past of painted women such as Dallas or when Ransom Stoddard shuttles the illiterate Hallie back East in *The Man Who Shot Liberty Valance* (1962). Jane Russell's infamous portrayal of Rio in *The Outlaw* (1943) remains one of the more celebrated exceptions to this otherwise deadly standard. The tough but modest frontier wives like *Shane*'s Marian Starrett and *High Noon*'s Quaker bride, Amy Kane, refrain from blatant action until their husbands require such activity.

Male and female Mexicans and people of mixed race walk a grotesque line between hapless clowns à la *Stagecoach* and *The Magnificent Seven* (1960) or monstrous despots like the Rojos of *A Fistful of Dollars* (1964) and General Mapache in *The Wild Bunch* (1969). Native Americans generally signify the ethnic foil to white male order. This contrast can manifest itself as ravaging hordes in *Stagecoach* and *The Searchers*; as predictable savages in *Red River* and *The Naked Spur* (1953); or as noble alternatives to white hegemony in the Lone Ranger's Tonto, *Cheyenne Autumn* (1964), and *Dances with Wolves* (1990). Some revisionist Westerns such as *Soldier Blue* (1970), *Little Big Man* (1970), and *A Man Called Horse* (1970) exhibit a morbid fascination with the cultural conflicts between white and "red" men, but the majority of Western art continues to produce a very ambiguous mystification of Native American culture.

WESTERNS AS ENTERTAINMENT

Founded on a mixture of nineteenth-century American history, the melodramatic frontier fiction of James Fenimore Cooper (1789–1851) and James Oliver Curwood (1878–1927), and the Western visions of artists Frederic Remington (1861–1909), Charles Russell (1852–1916), and Jules Tavernier (1844–1889), the Hollywood Western film has become the most prevalent of all modern Wild West shows. In many ways, the Western and the movies have grown up together. Some of the earliest silent films, such as *The Great Train Robbery* (1903) and *The Squaw Man* (1914), clearly echo Western themes, although they were probably likened to contemporary crime thrillers at the time of their production. As silent film matured into an art form in the 1910s and 1920s, early cowboy heroes such as Broncho Billy Anderson, William S. Hart, Hoot Gibson, Harry Carey, Tom Mix, Buck Jones, and Tim McCoy initiated various flavors of Western entertainment. Whereas Anderson, Hart, and McCoy created what Edward Buscombe calls the realistic "good badman" whose natural roughness is accompanied by a heart of gold, Tom Mix and others opted to formulate a more fantastic Jazz Age cowboy whose rope tricks, fancy duds, and horseback stunts revived the Wild West Carnival aesthetics of Buffalo Bill Cody and Annie Oakley.

Later Western stars such as John Wayne and Gary Cooper would epitomize the rough benevolence of the good badman, until Clint Eastwood's cool "Man with No Name" popularized the image of the professional gunfighter in the mid-1960s. In later films, such as *The Magnificent Seven*, *The Wild Bunch*, and *The Long Riders* (1980), the gunfighter and the outlaw face a moral war between killing as a vocation and settling down on the frontier. Such films detail a world of lonely, desperate mercenaries and criminals whose worst enemy is the double-edged sword of their own profession.

TWO STRANDS OF WESTERN

Almost from the beginning, studios began to distinguish between prestigious "A" Westerns and the run-of-the-mill "B"-grade horse opera. Early studios such as Biograph and Bison churned out silent serial Westerns whose standardized melodramas became the basis for the subgenre of "B"-grade cowboy movies that would remain relatively unaltered well into the 1950s. By the mid-1930s, these series Westerns, produced predominantly by Herbert Yates's amalgamated Republic Pictures, had become an easily appreciated prefab package: There would be a fist fight within the first few minutes, a chase soon after, and inevitably a shoot-out at the end. Plots were usually motivated by some straightforward villainy, which could be exposed and decisively defeated by the hero. It was also common for footage to be reused. Costly scenes of Indian attacks or stampedes would reappear, more or less happily satisfying the demands of continuity in subsequent productions.

For all their apparent low budgets and simplicity, these assembly-line dramas prepared both the talent and the audience that would eventually propel the "A" Western into its own. Some prestige epics, such as *The Big Trail* (1930); *The Covered Wagon* (1923); and the Oscar-winning Best Picture of 1931, *Cimarron*, clearly invoked Western forms, but Westerns for the most part were considered second-tier kiddy shows until the unprecedented success of Ford's *Stagecoach* in 1939. *Stagecoach*'s microcosm of American society—complete with a hypocritical banker, an arrogant debutante, a southern gentleman, and the fiery youth of a suddenly famous Wayne—proved that Western scenarios could yield serious entertainment. Soon after, Hollywood's production of Westerns rose rapidly as both "A" and "B" Westerns thrived in the hands of the most talented Hollywood actors and auteurs.

Reaching its zenith in 1950, when 34 percent of all Hollywood films involved a Western scenario, the genre had developed a new energy and scope surrounding "A"- and "B"-level personalities such as Wayne, Henry Fonda, James Stewart, Audie Murphy, Roy Rogers, Gary Cooper, Randolph Scott, Ward Bond, and Joel McCrea. Amid the host of Western formula pictures, Hardy notes, were exciting innovations by Western directors such as Budd Boetticher, Ford, Anthony Mann, Delmer Daves, Allan Dwan, Samuel Fuller, Howard Hawks, Fritz Lang, Arthur Penn, Nicholas Ray, John Sturges, Jacques Tourneur, and Raoul Walsh, who produced individual masterpieces through their manipulation of popular narrative forms.

WESTERNS GO BEYOND CINEMA

Throughout the 1940s and 1950s, cinema remained the dominant showcase for Western drama, but other lesser Western media were also inundating American culture. While horses galloped across the silver screen, the roar of six-guns also glutted the airwaves as radio and TV shows brought the West into countless American living rooms. Between 1952 and 1970 no less than eleven Western TV series were on the air in any single year. The Lone Ranger, Matt Dillon, Hopalong Cassidy, and their lesser-known associates, including Straight Arrow; the Six-Shooter (played by Stewart); and Curly Burly, the Singing Marshal, offered a generation of children almost daily doses of Western idealism. Often, these heroes became highly merchandised icons, moving from pulp magazines into commercial radio, matinee serials, TV series, and comic books. Thus, *Gunsmoke*'s Matt Dillon and *Have Gun—Will Travel*'s Paladin became product-driven cowboy myths.

Most Western TV series, including *Rawhide*, *Gunsmoke*, *Bonanza*, *Maverick*, *The Big Valley*, and *The Wild, Wild West*, had their own tie-in comic book that lingered in young hands during the many hours between broadcasts. The Lone Ranger himself appeared in more than different comic series, the last appearing as late as 1994. The ten-cent comic market could even bear separate series for sidekicks Tonto and Little Beaver. For almost eight years, Dell comics exclusively devoted an entire series to the Lone Ranger's faithful stallion, Silver. Major Western stars such as Wayne, Tim Holt, Gabby Hayes, Andy Devine, Rogers, Dale Evans, and Hopalong Cassidy also bolstered their popularity through four-color dime comics, accentuating their already firm star image through the mass-market pantheon of Western characters such as the Ghost Rider, the Rawhide Kid, and Jonah Hex.

REEXAMINING THE GENRE

From the 1940s through the 1960s, while Mann twisted the genre with cynical stories of desperate and introspective Westerners and Ford began a series of bitter reexaminations of his earlier frontier optimism, another form of the self-conscious, aestheticized Western had emerged—the musical. Clearly indebted to early singing cowboys such as Gene Autry and Rogers, the new singing Western fused song-and-dance spectacle with honky-tonk themes and images. Songs such as Cole Porter's "Don't Fence Me In" and Jay Livingston and Ray Evans's Oscar-winning "Buttons and Bows" allowed popular vocalists a chance to dress up in silk bandannas, cowhide vests, and sequined Stetsons. Groups such as the Sons of the Pioneers and the Riders of the Purple Sage celebrated trendy cowboy fashions, and Hollywood's *Oklahoma!* (1955), *Red Garters* (1954), *Annie Get Your Gun* (1950), *Paint Your Wagon* (1969), and *Seven Brides for Seven Brothers* (1954) promoted melodious Western set pieces. Even the down-to-earth satirist Will Rogers's rope-tricking cowboy persona lent a humble quality to his jibes between numbers in the Ziegfield Follies.

Comedies and parodies also proliferated. Early Western clowning included Charles Laughton in *Ruggles of Red Gap* (1935) and Bob Hope in the *Paleface* films of 1948 and 1952. Among the most important later moments in Western comedy are Lee Marvin's Oscar-winning self-parody of a drunken gunfighter in *Cat Ballou* (1965); James Garner's send-up of *My Darling Clementine* in *Support Your Local Sheriff* (1969); and Mel Brooks's hugely successful black cowboy feature, *Blazing Saddles* (1974). Later films, such as *City Slickers* (1991), use a humorous cowboy milieu as a sort of moral high ground, teaching lessons of humility and conventional wisdom.

In the 1960s and 1970s, the traditionally conservative ideology of Western films fell prey to several new influences. The "international Western" reconfigured traditionally American material with an exaggerated European accent. The Italian-produced "spaghetti Westerns" of Sergio Leone, starring Clint Eastwood as the shrewd, silent, nameless mercenary, rejuvenated a genre that had become fairly exhausted in American hands. Leone revised tired gunfight scenarios through slow, tension-building showdowns composed of excruciatingly tight close-ups and split-second gun battles. Ennio Morricone's now-famous parodic scores also lent Leone's gory duels and forbidding scenery a fascinating, surreal atmosphere.

Leone's psychedelically violent images played alongside the American revisionist Westerns of Sam Peckinpah, Robert Altman, and Arthur Penn. *Little Big Man* (1970), *McCabe & Mrs. Miller* (1971), *Pat Garrett and Billy the Kid* (1973), and *Buffalo Bill and the Indians* (1976) deconstructed long-established

Western hierarchies, and Dennis Hopper's *Easy Rider* (1969) subtly defiled the cowboy image as his Buffalo Billy sold drugs, dropped acid, and toured America on a Harley. During the cultural upheaval of the 1960s, this trend toward the deconstruction of Western myths signified a popular cultural need to interrogate and explode previously accepted signs and images.

For all their gratuitous revision, however, the grim tales of drunks, swindlers, and psychopaths that dominate late 1960s and 1970s Westerns contributed a much-needed update to the general credibility and appreciation of Western forms. Of all these self-conscious filmmakers, only Eastwood continued as a popular Western actor and director; his *The Outlaw Josey Wales* (1976), *Pale Rider* (1985), and *Unforgiven* (1992) represent intense eulogies to older visions of the American West.

THE POSTMODERN WESTERN

The postmodern Western of the 1980s and 1990s sprouted into several fairly distinct branches. On the one hand, films such as *Silverado* (1985), *Young Guns* (1988), *Tombstone* (1993), *Posse* (1993), *Maverick* (1994), *Bad Girls* (1994), *The Quick and The Dead* (1995), and *Wild Wild West* (1999) used Western aesthetics as appropriated dramatic frames that emphasize their stars. More obviously expensive Western epics such as *Lonesome Dove* (1989), *Dances with Wolves* (1990), and *Wyatt Earp* (1994) attempted to re-create the spectacle of the great open plains. Along with these comprehensive Westerns, a noticeable cowboy strain leaked into blockbuster franchise films such as *Back to the Future III* (1990), unpopular "punk" odysseys such as *Straight to Hell* (1987) and *Dudes* (1987), neo-noir Westerns such as *Flesh and Bone* (1993) and *Red Rock West* (1993), and pastiche "cult" odysseys such as *The Adventure of Buckaroo Banzai in the 8th Dimension* (1984). Even the *The Muppet Movie* (1979) appropriates an old-fashioned Western showdown.

The 1990s also saw a revival of the contemporary Western. Art-house films such as *Lone Star* (1996), *Western* (1998), and *The Hi-Lo Country* (1999) find their roots in the well-named Hollywood epic *Giant* (1956) and its quieter companions *The Lusty Men* (1952), *Hud* (1963), *The Electric Horseman* (1979), and *Bronco Billy* (1980). These films are more concerned with describing the life of the modern West and the plight of the twentieth-century Westerner than in revising the myths of the old frontier. At the same time, however, each film offers sharp insight into how completely the Western and its heroes have shaped the popular appreciation of America's past.

Although Western films seemed to be on the wane as the century turned, Ang Lee's *Brokeback Mountain* (2005), the story of two cowboys struggling with their sexual identity in the Wyoming grasslands, brought the genre back into vogue. *Brokeback* was followed by a proliferation of traditional Westerns, including *The Assassination of Jesse James by the Coward Robert Ford* (2007), the story of the outlaw's last days and the dissolution of his band; and *Appaloosa* (2008), which featured the stock characters of old: lawmen versus ranchers. Several hit Westerns of yore were remade into fresh versions, including *3:10 to Yuma* (2007), with Russell Crowe and Christian Bale doing battle as outlaw versus rancher, respectively; and *True Grit* (2010), with Jeff Bridges playing the irascible Rooster Cogburn, a role originally inhabited by Wayne.

There Will Be Blood (2007), is more about businessmen and oil than cowboys, but its Western milieu lends a quiet desperation to the story line, while *No Country for Old Men* (2007), despite its modern-day setting, leans heavily on the idea of the lone cowboy in its portrayal of a variety of thieves on the run from each other and from the law. The Western expanded into science fiction both in terms of setting—*Cowboys & Aliens*, a 2011 big-budget blockbuster—and in terms of sensibility—Joss Whedon's space cowboys in TV's *Firefly* (2002–2003) and its cinematic follow-up *Serenity* (2005). A fresh female point of view was explored in Kelly Reichardt's *Meek's Cutoff* (2010), depicting a journey west along the Oregon Trail.

Westerns returned to the small screen as well in HBO's Western series *Deadwood* (2004–2006), pitting Timothy Olyphant as real-life lawman Seth Bullock against Ian McShane as Al Swearengen, the town's saloon owner and pseudo mob boss, as well as many other villains. Although the writers used many fictional elements, story lines, and characters, numerous historical Western figures appear throughout the series—Wild Bill Hickok, Wyatt Earp, and Calamity Jane, among others. As they did in the past, these modern interpretations all serve to further the mythos of the American West and to examine what Ryan Gilbey of *New Statesman* called "the complex relationship between Americans and the land beneath their feet."

Daniel Yezbick

SEE ALSO: *Academy Awards; Altman, Robert;* Annie Get Your Gun*; Autry, Gene; "B" Movies;* Back to the Future*; Blockbusters;* Bonanza*; Brooks, Mel;* Butch Cassidy and the Sundance Kid*; Cable TV; Cody, Buffalo Bill, and His Wild West Show; Comic Books; Cooper, Gary;* Deadwood*; Dime Novels; Eastwood, Clint;* Easy Rider*;* A Fistful of Dollars*; Fonda, Henry; Ford, John; Garner, James;* Giant*;* The Great Train Robbery*;* Gunsmoke*;* High Noon*; Hollywood; Hopalong Cassidy; Hope, Bob; Hopper, Dennis; Leone, Sergio; The Lone Ranger; Lynching;* The Magnificent Seven*;* Midnight Cowboy*; Mix, Tom; Movie Stars; The Muppets; The Musical;* My Darling Clementine*;* Oklahoma!*; Porter, Cole; Radio; Rodeo; Rogers, Roy; Rogers, Will; Russell, Jane; Scott, Randolph;* The Searchers*;* Shane*; Silent Movies; Spaghetti Westerns;* Stagecoach*; Stewart, Jimmy; Television;* The Treasure of the Sierra Madre*;* Unforgiven*; Wayne, John;* The Wild Bunch*;* The Ziegfeld Follies.

BIBLIOGRAPHY

Bazin, Andre. *What Is Cinema? Volume II.* Berkeley: University of California Press, 1971.

Buscombe, Edward, ed. *The BFI Companion to the Western.* New York: Da Capo Press, 1988.

Cameron, Ian, and Douglas Pye, eds. *The Book of Westerns.* New York: Continuum, 1996.

Frayling, Christopher. *Spaghetti Westerns.* London: Routledge & Kegan Paul, 1981.

Hardy, Phil, ed. *The Overlook Film Encyclopedia: The Western.* Woodstock, NY: Overlook Press, 1995.

Kitses, Jim. *Horizons West.* Bloomington: Indiana University Press, 1970.

MacDonald, J. Fred. *Don't Touch That Dial!: Radio Programming in American Life from 1920 to 1960.* Chicago: Nelson-Hall, 1996.

Mitchell, Lee Clark. *Westerns.* Chicago: University of Chicago Press, 1996.

Nachbar, Jack, ed. *Focus on the Western.* Englewood Cliffs, NJ: Prentice-Hall, 1974.

Newman, Kim. *Wild West Movies.* London: Bloomsbury, 1990.

Wharton, Edith *(1862–1937)*

Edith Wharton became one of the most successful American novelists of her time. She was perhaps best known for her many novels and short stories portraying the upper-class society in which she revolved, yet she also published travelogues, historical novels, and criticism.

Wharton's first novel was published in 1902, and by 1905 she was receiving both critical and audience acclaim with *The House of Mirth. Ethan Frome* (1911), which deals with working-class issues, cemented her reputation as a leading author of her day. Her wealthy background influenced much of her writing, including *The Age of Innocence* (1920), about upper-class New York society. This novel, which was turned into a movie in 1993, won a Pulitzer Prize. Wharton also became the first woman to receive the honorary Doctor of Letters from Yale University and the gold medal of the National Institute of Arts and Letters.

When discussing Wharton's work, critics have often overemphasized author Henry James's influence upon her—in part because of the belief that women writers of the time were capable only of imitating great male writing. Nevertheless, she has impacted American narrative in many ways, perhaps most notably in her treatment of gender issues and the supernatural.

Joe Sutliff Sanders

SEE ALSO: *Aykroyd, Dan; Pfeiffer, Michelle; Scorsese, Martin.*

BIBLIOGRAPHY

Killoran, Helen. *The Critical Reception of Edith Wharton.* Rochester, NY: Camden House, 2001.

Roillard, Douglas, ed. *American Supernatural Fiction: From Edith Wharton to the Weird Tales Writers.* New York: Garland, 1996.

Singley, Carol J. *Edith Wharton: Matters of Mind and Spirit.* New York: Cambridge University Press, 1995.

What Would Jesus Do?

SEE: *WWJD? (What Would Jesus Do?).*

What's My Line?

Aired on CBS from February 2, 1950, through September 3, 1967, the television panel game *What's My Line?* became an American favorite and remains the longest-running show of its type in prime-time television history. The premise was both rudimentary and clever. Contestants with uncommon occupations first signed their names on a blackboard and then whispered their "lines," or professions, to master of ceremonies John Daly and the viewers at home. Next, four panelists queried the contestants in order to ascertain their professions. Questions could be answered only with a simple "yes" or "no." For each "no" response, a contestant earned $5; after ten negatives, the game ended with the contestant pocketing $50. One participant each week was a "mystery guest," an easily identifiable celebrity. Here, out of necessity, the panelists donned masks, with the contestants responding to questions in distorted voices.

The show, a Mark Goodson–Bill Todman production, exuded a civilized, urbane Park Avenue/Fifth Avenue Manhattan air, which was established by Daly, the likable moderator. Daly's background was in journalism, and he hosted the show during its seventeen years on the air. He declined participation in the syndicated version, which was produced between 1968 and 1975 and hosted by Wally Bruner and Larry Blyden. In the early years of the show, Daly concurrently enjoyed a high profile at rival networks, anchoring the ABC evening news between 1953 and 1960, while also hosting *What's My Line?* for CBS.

The panelists on the debut broadcast were syndicated gossip columnist Dorothy Kilgallen (who participated in the show until her death in 1965), poet-critic Louis Untermeyer, former New Jersey Governor Harold Hoffman, and psychiatrist Richard Hoffman. The following week, actress Arlene Francis came on board and remained for the show's duration. Other regular panelists during the 1950s were television personality Steve Allen, comedian Fred Allen, and joke writer Hal Block. By the end of the decade, the group most often consisted of a set trio: Francis; Kilgallen; and writer, raconteur, and cofounder of Random House publishers Bennett Cerf, who joined the panel in 1951 and remained until the show went off the air. These three were supplemented with a celebrity guest panelist.

While watching *What's My Line?* and hearing the amusing and sophisticated banter of its panelists, one might have been eavesdropping on a chic and exclusive party whose guests included New York's wittiest intellectuals, peppered with celebrities from the world of entertainment, sports, and politics. The panelists, in fact, were personalities who exuded New York Upper East Side style, donning their masks as if preparing for a society costume ball.

The contestants on *What's My Line?* were awesome in their variety. Over the years they included oddball inventors, tugboat captains, pet cemetery grave diggers, pitters of prunes and dates, thumbtack makers, pigeon trainers, baseball stitchers, gas station attendants, and even a purveyor of fried chicken—who turned out to be none other than Colonel Harlan Sanders. As for the "mystery guests," writer/show business habitué Max Wilk once remarked that "it would be far more simple to list the names of the celebrities who have *not* appeared on the show over all these years than it would be to list those who did." Among them were athletes (Phil Rizzuto, who was the first *What's My Line?* mystery guest, and Ty Cobb); poets (Carl Sandburg); politicians (Eleanor Roosevelt, Estes Kefauver, and Everett Dirksen); and numerous movie and television personalities, from Gracie Allen to Warren Beatty, Ed Wynn to Ed McMahon, and Harold Lloyd to Howdy Doody.

The panelists on the final network telecast of *What's My Line?* were Francis, her actor husband Martin Gabel, Cerf, and Allen. The mystery guest, appropriately enough, was John Daly!

Rob Edelman

SEE ALSO: *Allen, Steve; Beatty, Warren; Cobb, Ty; Francis, Arlene; Game Shows; Goodson, Mark;* The Howdy Doody Show; *Sandburg, Carl.*

BIBLIOGRAPHY

Fates, Gilbert. What's My Line? *The Inside History of TV's Most Famous Panel Show*. Englewood Cliffs, NJ: Prentice-Hall, 1978.

McMahon, Ed, and David Fisher. *When Television Was Young: The Inside Story with Memories by Legends of the Small Screen*. Nashville, TN: T. Nelson, 2007.

Moran, Albert, and Justin Malbon. *Understanding the Global TV Format*. Bristol, UK: Intellect Books, 2006.

Wheel of Fortune

In 2009 America's most popular television game show, *Wheel of Fortune*, celebrated its twenty-sixth year in syndication by broadcasting its 5,000th episode. In the ubiquitous game created by executive producer Merv Griffin, popular hosts Pat Sajak and Vanna White have awarded contestants more than $190 million in cash and prizes for guessing the blank letters of mystery phrases, with the winning amounts determined by spins of a giant wheel. While the wheel spins it is traditional for contestants to scream "Big money!" and join the hosts in clapping hands. In fact, White was listed in the 1992 *Guinness Book of World Records* as television's most frequent hand-clapper, averaging 720 claps per show and 28,000 claps per season.

Wheel of Fortune. *Vanna White, left, and Pat Sajak take the stage at a taping of* The Wheel of Fortune *in 2008.* PAUL WARNER/STRINGER/WIREIMAGE/GETTY IMAGES.

The original *Wheel of Fortune* aired on NBC as a daytime game show on January 6, 1975, with hosts Chuck Woolery and Susan Stafford. Sajak made his debut on the show in December 1981, with Stafford continuing as cohost. White replaced Stafford in December 1982, and the show moved from network to syndication in 1983, placing it in prime-time slots and greatly increasing its audience. The easy camaraderie of the cohosts, known to audiences simply as Pat and Vanna, is often suggested as one of the secrets of the show's wide appeal.

HOSTS

Sajak has said he remembers sneaking out of bed at age eleven to watch Jack Paar host *The Tonight Show*; even then he aspired to host his own television show. He attended Columbia College in his native Chicago, majoring in broadcasting, before landing his first professional job as a newscaster on radio station WEDC in his hometown. The Vietnam War interrupted his career in 1968, and Sajak, then twenty-one, was assigned as morning disc jockey with Armed Forces Radio in Saigon. During his eighteen months in that post, Sajak opened his show with the words, "Gooood morrrning, Vietnaaam!"—a phrase later used by Robin Williams in the movie *Good Morning, Vietnam* (1987).

After his army discharge in 1970, Sajak worked briefly as a radio disc jockey in Kentucky and Washington, D.C., before landing his first television job as local weatherman on WSM-TV in Nashville, Tennessee. His relaxed style and sharp wit brought him additional assignments as host of a public affairs program as well as a talk show. In 1977 he was brought to Los Angeles to host KNBC's weekend public affairs program and to serve as the station's local weatherman. Four years later he was selected by Griffin to host *Wheel of Fortune*—a match made in television heaven.

Sajak has starred in many network and syndicated specials, briefly hosted a late-night talk show in 1989, and has appeared as a guest star on dozens of comedy, drama, and talk shows. He has won three Emmy Awards, a People's Choice Award, and an Excellence in Arts Award from the Vietnam Veterans of America and has been awarded a star on the Hollywood Walk of Fame. In 2011 Sajak and *Jeopardy!* (1964–) host Alex Trebek received lifetime achievement awards at the Daytime Emmy Awards, where their shows had just tied for Outstanding Game/Audience Participation Show. Sajak lives in Los Angeles with his wife, Lesly, and they have two children.

White, born in North Myrtle Beach, South Carolina, in 1957, attended the Atlanta School of Fashion Design and became a top model in that area before moving to Los Angeles to pursue an acting career. In 1982 she auditioned for the job as Sajak's cohost and was selected from a field of more than 400 letter-turning hopefuls. Although she has been called *Wheel of Fortune*'s "silent star," her weekly fan mail numbers in the thousands and she is a frequent guest on talk shows. Her autobiography, *Vanna Speaks* (1987), was a national best seller. Her fans enjoy her habit of making a different fashion statement for every show—she has worn more than 5,400 outfits at the puzzle board.

White has also made commercials, a nutritional video, and cameos in film and television shows. In 1988 she starred as Venus in the NBC made-for-television movie *Goddess of Love*. She is divorced and has two children, Nicholas and Giovanna.

KEEPING THE SHOW VITAL

One of the secrets of the ongoing success of *Wheel of Fortune* has been adding new features to the show's familiar format. In 1997 White's puzzle board received an update thanks to computer technology. Instead of turning letters, she now activates touch-sensitive membrane switches on a bank of fifty-two high-resolution Sony monitors. The update was more than cosmetic; the previous mechanical board required that each new puzzle be set by hand, slowing the momentum of the game. *Wheel of Fortune* has continued to keep up with technological and communication advances by designing digital formats for the game, both online and for mobile devices. In 2003 producers introduced the online Wheel Watchers Club, which provides a direct connection to the show's loyal fans. The first of its kind, the club allows viewers at home to play along with the televised game and earn points for prizes. By 2009 the club had five million members.

Interest in *Wheel of Fortune* was heightened by the introduction of special weeks that feature soap opera stars, best friends, celebrities and their moms, college students, and professional football players as contestants. In 1988 the show broadcast its first program from a remote location—Radio City Music Hall in New York. Since then the show has added fresh appeal by filming in nearly sixty remote locations, including New Orleans, Louisiana, days before Hurricane Katrina hit in 2005.

In 2007 *Wheel of Fortune* was once again renewed, this time through the 2013–2014 season. In 2009 the show celebrated its twenty-sixth season and 5,000th game with a cake in the shape of the number 5,000.

Benjamin Griffith

SEE ALSO: *Armed Forces Radio Service; Daytime Talk Shows; Disc Jockeys; Emmy Awards; Game Shows; Griffin, Merv; Hurricane Katrina;* Jeopardy!*; Made-for-Television Movies; Paar, Jack; Television;* The Tonight Show*; Vietnam.*

BIBLIOGRAPHY

Inman, David. *The TV Encyclopedia.* New York: Perigee Books, 1991.

"What Keeps *Wheel* on Fast Track?" *Television Week* 23, no. 3 (2004): 90.

White, Vanna. *Vanna Speaks.* New York: Warner, 1987.

Whisky a Go Go

Infused with the neon energy of the Sunset Strip, the Whisky a Go Go stands as Los Angeles's richest repository of rock-and-roll history. With the affluence of Beverly Hills and Malibu to its west; the fantasy of Hollywood to its east; West Hollywood's gay and lesbian influence directly south; and "the hills," home to the world's rich and famous, above it, the Whisky finds itself at the heart of a city in which anything can happen and often does. As its decades at the corner of Clark Drive and the famed Sunset Boulevard have proven, the Whisky's roster of rock performers chronicles the evolution of Los Angeles's highly influential music industry and its impact on popular culture at large.

Older than neighboring rock-and-roll haunts such as the Roxy and the Rainbow, the Whisky emerged onto Los Angeles's music scene in January 1964. Owners Elmer Valentine and Mario Maglieri transformed an old three-story bank building into a Parisian-inspired discotheque complete with female disc jockeys dancing in cages suspended above the stage. Hence, the term *go-go girl* was born.

The Whisky quickly became a breeding ground for the most influential musical talent of the mid- to late 1960s. Opening night featured Johnny Rivers, whose blues-inspired pop album titled *Johnny Rivers at the Whisky a Go Go* took him to the top of the charts. Johnny Carson, Rita Hayworth, Lana Turner, and Steve McQueen were just a few of the personalities who turned out to revel in Rivers's performance.

As the turbulent sociopolitical energy of the late 1960s gained momentum, so too did the influence of the Whisky. Bands such as the Doors and Buffalo Springfield brought revolutionary sounds to the music world and attracted the likes of John Belushi and Charles Manson to the venue. Guitar legend Jimi Hendrix dropped in on several occasions to jam with the Whisky's house bands, and rock's raspy leading lady, Janis Joplin, downed her last bottle of Southern Comfort at the Whisky before her death in 1970.

While the Whisky name is associated with some of the most significant performers of every rock era since the club's opening, it is the explosive decadence of the late 1960s that has most decisively defined the its place in the popular imagination. In his vivid film evocation of the period, *The Doors* (1991), Oliver Stone depicted one of the Doors' early performances on the Whisky stage to re-create the spirit of that era's radical, drug-fueled excess. The film, and other similar representations of the 1960s, affirm the Whisky's status as a potent emblem of the rebellious energy of a particular moment in music and pop culture history. "For much of the '60s and early '70s, . . . Whisky was the most important rock club in town," former *Los Angeles Times* pop music critic Robert Hilburn wrote in 1977. "It was an incubation spot for local bands and a showcase for highly touted visiting groups."

Despite its indisputable "hot spot" status during the 1960s, the Whisky's popularity waned in the early 1970s as a softer, more folk-inspired sound penetrated live music in Los Angeles. The Whisky nearly burned to the ground in 1971, and the club was forced to close for several months before reopening as a discotheque. With the buzz of the club's formative decade behind it, its producers sought out more economical performance ideas for the space, and operating a dance club appeared to be a cheaper, less troublesome alternative to the live music format. The venue also hosted minor theatrical performances such as *The Rocky Horror Picture Show* during this period, but no attempt to transform the Whisky attracted the kind of talent or intensity that the club had cultivated during the 1960s.

PUNK AND NEW WAVE

The rebirth of the Whisky as a rock club occurred in the late 1970s, when the embers of a punk scene in Los Angeles began to smolder. The influence of punk bands from London (the Sex Pistols, the Damned) and New York (Patti Smith, the Ramones) inspired Los Angeles groups such as the Runaways to bring a brash, do-it-yourself approach to music and to the Whisky. Kim Fowley, son of actor Douglas Fowley, hosted a "New Wave Rock 'N' Roll Weekend" at the Whisky in 1977 and introduced the likes of the Weirdos to the Sunset Strip scene. Shortly thereafter, the legendary Elvis Costello played his first Los Angeles gig at the club. The founders of the Whisky solidified their place in Los Angeles pop culture by opening Rainbow Bar & Grill and the Roxy Theater.

By the early 1980s rock once again ruled the Los Angeles music scene—and the Whisky—although this time in a much less lucrative fashion. No longer did the Whisky pay its bands for an evening's performance. Rather, upon reopening as a live venue—around the time that music mogul Lou Adler bought into the club—the musical acts themselves paid the Whisky for the opportunity to perform on its coveted stage. This new "pay to play" approach not only demonstrated how valuable the Whisky's reputation had become to up-and-coming talent, but it also confirmed the fact that the music business itself was changing. The tremendous popularity of rock music yielded a surplus of bands, which shifted the market in favor of clubs and promoters. Groups had to compete for stage space and ultimately finance (or hope that a record company would pay for) their own publicity.

Against this new economic backdrop, a number of hard rock and metal bands—including megastars Van Halen, Guns N' Roses, and Metallica—rose to prominence in the 1980s. While these glam bad boys went on to fill tens of thousands of seats in arenas all over the world, they could all point to the Whisky's stage as the site of some of their earliest live performances.

In the early 1990s the Whisky hosted a number of Seattle, Washington–based musicians who would later be dubbed "the godfathers of grunge." Bands such as Soundgarden, Nirvana, and the Melvins brought their guitar-laden, punk-loyal sound to Los Angeles in a very large, very loud way. Grunge maintained an anti-aesthetic that scoffed at the glam rock past of the 1980s and seemed, if only briefly, to speak to the fears of a generation of teenagers ravaged by divorce and a distinctly postmodern sort of uncertainty. Throughout this time, the Whisky continued to act as a touchstone for local and indie bands and as a familiar haunt for the occasional celebrity rocker, such as the band Black Sabbath, which used the club to announce its 2011 reunion tour. The punk and metal ethos merged in bands such as Death, while punk and rap came together with the Red Hot Chili Peppers; both bands cut their teeth at the Whisky.

Though the club's influence as a ground zero for cutting-edge trends in the music industry—and youth culture in general—has diminished considerably since its heyday, the Whisky remains an important Los Angeles landmark and offers a revealing window into some of the most crucial figures and movements of rock's history. The Whisky brand still carries weight: all sorts of artists, from country singer Vince Gill to death metal band Malevolent Creation, have released "Live at the Whisky" albums, while old recordings of Whisky gigs from artists as diverse as Humble Pie, X, and Alice Cooper have been released. As the son of cofounder Maglieri has noted: "The Whisky was on the forefront of every musical trend including Motown, rock and roll, heavy metal, punk and new wave. Because the Whisky . . . has held true to its original focus of nurturing emerging talent."

Jennifer Murray

SEE ALSO: *Belushi, John; Black Sabbath; Buffalo Springfield; Carson, Johnny; Cooper, Alice; Costello, Elvis; Disco; The Doors; Grunge; Hayworth, Rita; Hendrix, Jimi; Hollywood; Joplin, Janis; Manson, Charles; McQueen, Steve; New Wave Music; Nirvana; Punk; The Ramones; Rock and Roll;* The Rocky Horror Picture Show*; The Sex Pistols; Smith, Patti; Stone, Oliver;* Sunset Boulevard*; Turner, Lana; Van Halen.*

BIBLIOGRAPHY

Hoskyns, Barney. *Waiting for the Sun*. New York: St. Martin's Press, 1996.

Kamp, David. "Live at the Whisky." *Vanity Fair*, November 2000, 250.

Martin, Douglas. "Elmer Valentine, Owner of Rock Clubs, Dies at 85." *New York Times*, December 9, 2008, B14(L).

Quisling, Erick, and Austin Williams. *Straight Whisky: A Living History of Sex, Drugs, and Rock 'n' Roll on the Sunset Strip*. Chicago: Bonus Books, 2003.

Whistler's Mother

James Abbott McNeill Whistler's 1871 portrait of his mother, Anna Matilda McNeill, has crossed over from the realm of fine art to that of popular culture. Whistler (1834–1903), an expatriate American painter active in London and Paris, was one of a number of late nineteenth-century artists who downplayed subject matter and emphasized abstract values. People often refer to the painting as "Whistler's mother," but Whistler himself preferred to call it *Arrangement in Gray and Black*. Ironically, the painting is famous largely because of its subject. Recognized as a universal symbol of motherhood, Whistler's mother was featured, in 1934, on a U.S. postage stamp honoring Mother's Day. She has not, however, always been treated so reverently. The somber, seated figure, a familiar reference point in many countries, has been widely lampooned in the visual and popular performing arts.

Laural Weintraub

SEE ALSO: *Mother's Day.*

BIBLIOGRAPHY

Anderson, Ronald. *James McNeill Whistler: Beyond the Myth*. London: J. Murray, 1994.

Spencer, Robin. *Whistler*, rev. ed. London: Studio Editions, 1993.

White, Barry *(1944–2003)*

Barry White's immediately recognizable husky, bass-inflected voice, which obsessed over making love, was a staple on black radio during the 1970s. Songs such as "Your Sweetness Is My Weakness," "Can't Get Enough of Your Love, Babe," and the appropriately titled "Love Makin' Music" made the heavy-set man a sex symbol. Although his star did not shine as brightly through the 1980s and 1990s, he evolved into a popular culture icon, parodying himself on television shows such as *The Simpsons* (1989–).

Born in Galveston, Texas, White worked primarily out of Los Angeles and New York as a singer and musician. He began his music career at age eleven when he played piano on Jesse Belvin's hit single "Goodnight My Love." He recorded as a vocalist for a number of record labels in the early to mid-1960s and went on to work as an artists and repertoire (A&R) man for a small record label named Mustang. In 1969 he formed a female trio called Love Unlimited and a forty-piece instrumental group dubbed Love Unlimited Orchestra. The latter produced a number one pop single in 1973, "Love's Theme."

The period of 1973–1974 was a commercial highpoint for White. He performed on or produced a number of albums and singles that grossed a total of $16 million. Among his Top 10 pop singles were "I'm Gonna Love You Just a Little More Baby," "Never, Never Gonna Give Ya Up," "You're the First, the Last, My Everything," "What Am I Gonna Do with You?" and the number one 1974 smash "Can't Get Enough of Your Love, Babe."

Although all of his up-tempo dance numbers or slow jams tended to blend together, White was neither generic nor unoriginal. He had a distinct style that is best summed up in the lyrics of his song "Love Serenade": "Take it off / Baby, take it all off / I wanna see you the way you came into the world / I don't wanna feel no clothes / I don't wanna see no panties / Take off that brassiere, my dear." Hip-hop artists have sampled the drum breaks on such songs as "I'm Gonna Love You Just a Little More Baby," and arguably his spoken-word delivery has influenced rappers.

Throughout the 1980s and 1990s White's chart presence almost seemed contingent on collaborations with other artists. For instance, his 1990 hit "The Secret Garden (Sweet Seduction Suite)" featured singers and musicians such as Al B. Sure!, James Ingram, Quincy Jones, and El DeBarge. White also appeared on rapper Big Daddy Kane's 1991 rhythm-and-blues hit "All of Me," vocalist Lisa Stansfield's cover of "Never, Never Gonna Give You Up" (1997), and singer-songwriter Edie Brickell's "Good Times" (1994)—one of the strangest pairings of the 1990s. A 1999 solo effort paid off, and White's "Staying Power" earned him his only two Grammy Awards, including Best Male R&B Vocal Performance.

He enjoyed some exposure from the sitcom *Ally McBeal* (1997–2002), in which the character John Cage sings and dances to White's "You're the First, the Last, My Everything" to prepare himself for a date. After years of chronic high blood pressure, however, White's health began to fail in 2001. After a stroke, he officially retired from public life and died of kidney failure in July 2003 at age fifty-eight.

Kembrew McLeod

SEE ALSO: *A&R Men/Women;* Ally McBeal*; Grammy Awards; Pop Music; Rhythm and Blues; Sex Symbol;* The Simpsons.

BIBLIOGRAPHY

Vincent, Rickey. *Funk: The Music, the People and the Rhythm of the One*. New York: St. Martin's Griffin, 1996.

White, Barry, and Marc Eliot. *Love Unlimited: Insights on Life and Love*. New York: Broadway, 1999.

White, Betty *(1922–)*

Betty White was one of the first women to form her own television production company, and she also became one of TV's best-loved performers, whether her character was sweetly innocent or a harridan. Her early roles ranged from girl next door (*Life with Elizabeth*, 1952–1955) to screwball wife (*Date with the Angels*, 1957–1958), but it was as a man-crazy schemer on *The Mary Tyler Moore Show* from 1973 to 1977 that White became a household name. For her portrayal of predatory Sue Ann Nivens, White won back-to-back Best Supporting Actress Emmys (1975 and 1976), even though she appeared in less than half of the episodes in any given season. After *The Mary Tyler Moore Show* ended, she briefly hosted a game show called *Just Men!* and became the only woman to win an Emmy as best game show host (1983).

Two years later White returned to episodic television in the phenomenal hit *The Golden Girls* (1985–1992), in which she portrayed naive Rose Nylund, who never quite had the same conversations as those to whom she was talking and who often added seemingly unrelated comments dealing with life in her rural hometown, St. Olaf. A comedy that often placed four women—White, Estelle Getty, Rue McClanahan, and Bea Arthur—in outlandish situations, the series showed that older women could have active lives, and it helped to weaken the ageism that had been a hallmark of American popular culture. In 1995 White became the tenth woman to be inducted into the Television Hall of Fame.

White has continued to work steadily as a voice actor, writer of memoirs and advice books, and guest star on numerous television series; her role (as herself) on *The John Larroquette Show* earned her another Emmy in 1996. Her supporting role in *The Proposal* (2009)—starring Sandra Bullock and Ryan Reynolds—and her appearance in a Snickers ad during the 2010 Super Bowl thrust White back into the national spotlight. Fans started a campaign on Facebook to see White as a guest host on *Saturday Night Live*, and her appearance on the show that May earned her yet another Emmy: Best Guest Actress in a Comedy Series.

The TV Land sitcom *Hot in Cleveland* premiered in June 2010 with White in one of the lead roles, costarring with Valerie Bertinelli, Jane Leeves, and Wendie Malick. White was originally slated to appear only in the pilot but has appeared in the entire series. After winning a 2012 People's Choice Award for Favorite Cable TV Comedy and an Emmy for art direction, the show was renewed for a fourth season. Also in 2012 White celebrated her ninetieth birthday and introduced her new reality series, *Betty White's off Their Rockers*, which features senior citizens playing tricks on unsuspecting "youngsters."

Denise Lowe

SEE ALSO: *Arthur, Bea; Bullock, Sandra; Emmy Awards; Facebook; Game Shows;* The Golden Girls*;* The Mary Tyler Moore Show*;* Saturday Night Live*; Sitcom; Super Bowl; Television.*

BIBLIOGRAPHY

O'Dell, Cary. *Women Pioneers in Television*. Jefferson, NC: McFarland, 1997.

White, Betty. *Here We Go Again: My Life in Television*. New York: Scribner, 1995.

White, E. B. *(1899–1985)*

E. B. White's essays, poems, and children's stories have delighted people of all ages since the 1920s. He was among the early *New*

Yorker writers who helped the magazine build a reputation for elegant prose.

Elwyn Brooks White graduated from Cornell University, where he was the editor of the *Cornell Sun*. He worked as a journalist and a copywriter in an advertising agency before joining the *New Yorker* in its infancy in 1926. (The woman who hired him, Katharine Angell, later became his wife.) From 1938 to 1943 White also contributed a monthly column, "One Man's Meat," to *Harper's* magazine.

White's elegant yet informal, humorous, and humanitarian writing covered diverse subjects. Following the premature death of a pig in 1947 at the Whites' rural home in Maine, White said he wrote an essay "in grief, as a man who failed to raise his pig." This writing style is apparent in White's three classic children's books: *Stuart Little* (1945), about a mouse born to a human family and his adventures while searching for his best friend, a beautiful bird; *Charlotte's Web* (1952), in which a spider named Charlotte cleverly saves Wilbur the pig from death; and *The Trumpet of the Swan* (1970), featuring a mute trumpeter swan who tries to win the affection of the beautiful swan Serena.

In 1957 White published an essay praising his former Cornell English professor, William Strunk Jr., for his forty-three-page handbook on grammar. White lauded Strunk's attempt "to cut the vast tangle of English rhetoric down to size and write its rules and principles on the head of a pin." A publisher coaxed the ever-modest White into reviving and revising *The Elements of Style* (1959), known among its users as "Strunk and White," which has remained a fundamental text. White bolstered the original with an essay titled "An Approach to Style," which remains a timeless reflection on the virtues of good writing.

R. Thomas Berner

SEE ALSO: Harper's*; The* New York Times.

BIBLIOGRAPHY

Elledge, Scott. *E. B. White: A Biography*. New York: W. W. Norton, 1984.

Guth, Dorothy Lobrano, ed. *Letters of E. B. White*. New York: Harper & Row, 1976.

Hall, Katherine Romans. *E. B. White: A Bibliographic Catalogue of Printed Materials in the Department of Rare Books, Cornell University Library*. New York: Garland Publishing, 1979.

Root, Robert L., Jr., ed. *Critical Essays on E. B. White*. New York: G. K. Hall, 1994.

Russell, Isabel. *Katharine and E. B. White: An Affectionate Memoir*. New York: W. W. Norton, 1988.

Strunk, William, Jr., and E. B. White. *The Elements of Style*. New York: Macmillan, 1959.

Ward, S. *Meet E .B. White.*. New York: PowerKids Press, 2001.

White, E. B. *One Man's Meat*. New York: Harper & Row, 1942.

White, E. B. *Essays of E. B. White*. New York: Harper & Row, 1977.

White, Shaun *(1986–)*

Alternately known as the "Flying Tomato" (a reference to his long fire-red hair and stuntman mentality) and "Animal" (a comparison to the red-haired, wild-eyed drummer on *The Muppet Show*), Shaun White is an American snowboarding and skateboarding phenom. A two-time Olympic gold medalist, he is often credited with legitimizing snowboarding in the eyes of competitive sport purists.

Shaun Roger White was born in San Diego, California, on September 3, 1986. The youngest of three children, he suffered from a heart defect that limited the amount of oxygen in his blood and required two surgeries before age five. He grew up surfing and skiing and started snowboarding and skateboarding at age six. White won his first snowboard competition in 1993 and befriended skateboarding legend Tony Hawk on his way to winning five straight amateur national titles. He became a professional snowboarder at age thirteen and participated in his first X Games (an annual extreme sports competition sponsored by the television network ESPN) in 2000. In 2002 he won two silver medals at the X Games, and as of 2012 he has won at least one medal in every subsequent X Games competition.

White had a breakout year in 2003, winning two gold medals at the X Games, placing first in eight separate events at the U.S. Open Snowboarding Championships, and becoming the first athlete to appear in both the winter and summer X Games when he placed sixth in the skateboard vertical competition held in Los Angeles. He was named the Best Male Action Sports Athlete at the 2004 ESPY Awards and won gold at the 2003 Winter X Games for the slopestyle event before a knee injury forced him into rehabilitation for six months. In 2006 White became the first athlete to win four consecutive gold medals in a single X Games event when he once again captured the slopestyle championship in Aspen, Colorado. He also won his first skateboarding gold medal at the Panasonic Open in summer 2005 and went on to win a silver medal in the summer X Games vertical competition.

Having easily qualified for the 2006 Winter Olympics in Turin, Italy, White was the odds-on favorite to win the men's half-pipe event. Though he struggled in the early rounds of the competition, he wowed judges and spectators in the finals by performing back-to-back 1080s (three full spins in midair) and won the gold medal. White returned to the Olympics in 2010 and once again ran away with the half-pipe competition by performing a trick he called the Tomahawk: two full flips and three and a half spins. In 2012 he tallied the first-ever perfect score in the Superpipe event at the Winter X Games.

Perhaps the most recognizable action sports star in the world, White has been featured in a number of documentaries (*The Shaun White Album* [2004], *The Ultimate Ride—Shaun White* [2008], *Don't Look Down* [2009]), video games (Shaun White Snowboarding [2008], Shaun White Snowboarding: World Stage [2009], Shaun White Skateboarding [2010]), and a line of snowboards and sportswear from Burton Snowboards. In a short span White has amassed more medals and accolades than most athletes can dream of, and with decades of competition still ahead of him, the sky is (literally) the limit for what he can accomplish.

Jacob Schmitt

SEE ALSO: *ESPN; Extreme Sports; The Muppets; Olympics; Skateboarding; Snowboarding; Sports Heroes; Video Games; X Games.*

BIBLIOGRAPHY

Doeden, Matt. *Shaun White*, rev. ed. Minneapolis, MN: Lerner Publications, 2011.

Gitlin, Marty. *Shaun White: Snow and Skateboard Champion.* Berkeley Heights, NJ: Enslow Publishers, 2009.

Kennedy, Mike. *Shaun White.* Pleasantville, NY: Gareth Stevens Publishing, 2010.

White, Stanford *(1853–1906)*

On July 25, 1906, Harry Thaw walked into a fashionable New York cabaret restaurant—the Roof Garden at Madison Square Garden—and shot and killed architect Stanford White, who was dining with his lover, Mrs. Evelyn Nesbit Thaw. Thaw claimed he had been driven to the murder by the knowledge that White had "ruined" his wife, a twenty-two-year-old "Floradora" girl who had been involved in a sexual relationship with White since she was sixteen. After two sensational trials, Thaw (an heir to old Pittsburgh railroad money as well as a wife beater) was acquitted by a jury, which agreed that the cuckolded husband's murderous jealousy was justified.

The sensational story of the fatal Nesbit-White-Thaw love triangle was dramatized in a 1955 movie titled *The Girl in the Red Velvet Swing.* The title is derived from an infamous swing White kept in his studio to use in his well-orchestrated and numerous seductions.

Jackie Hatton

SEE ALSO: *Sex Scandals.*

BIBLIOGRAPHY

Craven, Wayne. *Stanford White: Decorator in Opulence and Dealer in Antiquities.* New York: Columbia University Press, 2005.

Lessard, Suzannah. *The Architect of Desire: Beauty and Danger in the Stanford White Family.* New York: Dial Press, 1996.

Mooney, Michael Macdonald. *Evelyn Nesbit and Stanford White: Love and Death in the Gilded Age.* New York: William Morrow, 1976.

White Castle

White Castle was the world's original fast-food restaurant chain. From humble beginnings in Wichita, Kansas, White Castle grew into a large-scale multistate operation that was copied by innumerable competitors. It began when Walter Anderson, a short-order cook, developed a process in 1916 for making the lowly regarded hamburger more palatable to a public still distrusting of ground beef in the wake of Upton Sinclair's *The Jungle.* Anderson soon had a growing business of three shops. In 1921 he took on a partner, Edward Ingram, a real estate and insurance salesman. Ingram came up with the name and image of "White Castle," with "'White' signifying purity and 'Castle' signifying strength, stability, and permanence," according to David Hogan's account in *Selling 'Em by the Sack.*

By 1931 there were 115 standardized White Castle outlets in ten states. Previously, only grocery or variety stores had used the chain system. By providing inexpensive food in a clean environment at uniform locations over a wide territory, White Castle helped shape the fast-food industry as it grew to have a strong influence on American life.

In the late twentieth century White Castle unexpectedly became a pop-culture icon. The restaurant chain was referenced by a number of bands and musicians in the 1980s and 1990s, most memorably by the Smithereens in their song "The White Castle Blues" and the Beastie Boys in five tracks in the seminal 1986 album *License to Ill.* In addition, several films have scenes that were shot in a White Caste or that have allusions to the restaurant. In the "stoner" comedy *Harold and Kumar Go to White Castle* (2004), Harold and Kumar are two friends who meet with misadventure as they search New Jersey for a White Castle restaurant. The film was so successful that it spawned two sequels and firmly established the chain as a fixture in the American cultural landscape.

Dale Allen Gyure

SEE ALSO: *Fast Food; Hamburger; McDonald's; Sinclair, Upton.*

BIBLIOGRAPHY

Hogan, David Gerald. *Selling 'Em by the Sack: White Castle and the Creation of American Food.* New York: New York University Press, 1998.

Ingram, Billy. *All This from a 5-Cent Hamburger!* New York: Newcomen Society in North America, 1975.

Jakle, John A., and Keith A. Sculle. *Fast Food: Roadside Restaurants in the Automobile Age.* Baltimore, MD: Johns Hopkins University Press, 2002.

White Flight

Urban flight, often called "white flight," refers to residential movement to avoid self-determined, unacceptable levels of racial integration. Scholars disagree on how much race acts as a singular factor in migratory decisions, many preferring a natural process called "ecological succession" in which older and less desirable housing stock filters down to lower-status classes. However, great episodes of neighborhood turnover in the United States after World War II prompted social scientists to focus specifically on race as a "tipping point" that stimulated white exodus to suburbs and newer suburban areas, a phenomenon that came to define urban life in the second half of the twentieth century.

MIGRATION TO THE NORTH

Urban flight began with the advent of large metropolitan areas in nineteenth-century America. Socially mobile whites in nineteenth-century New York, Philadelphia, Chicago, and similar cities followed mass transit and housing improvements into newly developed suburban areas. White flight was principally a twentieth-century phenomenon. Before 1900 approximately 90 percent of African Americans lived in the South. The few black populations in northern cities were small and highly centralized. Deteriorating social and economic conditions in the South, including lynchings, led to a mass exodus of African Americans to northern cities starting around World War I. These migrations increased the populations of African

Americans in such cities as Chicago from as little as 2 percent in 1910 to more than 30 percent by 1970.

At first, newer ethnic groups were the most affected. Around 1920 Jewish residents felt compelled to move from Chicago's Maxwell Street neighborhood and New York's Harlem area because of increasing numbers of blacks. The latter process contributed directly to the Harlem arts and cultural renaissance. Eventually threatened by the social and cultural disruptions portended by growing African American mobility, native-born whites lobbied politicians, bankers, developers, and real estate agents to restrict blacks to designated black neighborhoods, usually consisting of older housing stock.

In 1910 the Baltimore, Maryland, city council enacted an ordinance forbidding any black person from moving into a block where a majority of the residents were white, and a dozen other cities followed suit. The U.S. Supreme Court declared such residential segregation unconstitutional in 1917. When legal or extralegal exclusionary tactics failed to preserve such enclaves, whites resorted to outmigration, turning over a neighborhood to their former adversaries. Residential homogeneity could be based on such factors as class, religion, or ethnicity, but *white flight* came to be the term for relocation related to racial differences.

Housing demand, restricted by the Depression and the exigencies of World War II, exploded in the mid-twentieth century. New developments appeared almost overnight in outer-city and suburban areas, yet existing social standards continued to dictate settlement patterns based on racial considerations. The attractions of new suburbs, available only to middle-class and upper-class whites, and the growing housing needs of African Americans produced an era of unprecedented racial turnover in cities as neighborhoods, sometimes triggered by panic peddling or blockbusting—the intentional placing of an African American resident in a previously all-white neighborhood to create panic selling for profit—changed the neighborhoods' racial characteristics in short periods. Legal challenges to the status quo, judicial and legislative, contributed to the outmigration of whites from older urban areas. Although the white flight expanded areas for African Americans, it preserved traditional patterns of racial segregation.

SCHOOL DESEGREGATION

White flight reached its peak in the wake of school desegregation decisions in the 1960s and 1970s. The 1971 Supreme Court decision in *Swann v. Charlotte-Mecklenburg Board of Education* established a precedent that held that busing students was a legitimate and effective means to achieve desegregation. Following the decision, mandatory busing programs in such districts as Prince Georges County, Maryland, and Boston attempted to reconcile decades-old discriminatory housing patterns overnight. While some used the resulting outcry to argue against forced busing, others maintained that such metropolitan solutions were the only remedy for white flight. To a great extent, the debate over racial factors in changing school demographics mirrored the older debate about race and residence, with the same divergent results. As the debates intensified, the 1974 Supreme Court decision in *Milliken v. Bradley* qualified the early decision made in the *Swann* case. The court ruled that there was not sufficient evidence to suggest that the districts had been deliberately segregated and struck down a lower court's ruling that established a busing plan between suburban and urban schools. With its ruling, the court effectively endorsed white flight and removed a crucial tool from courts to integrate schools.

Such disputes continued until mandatory busing peaked and declined during the 1980s, and many districts were allowed to return to the de facto segregated status they had known before desegregation. The last third of the twentieth century saw a replication of urban white settlement patterns as middle-class African Americans began to suburbanize in so-called edge cities. In part, the outmigration involved aging inner-ring suburbs, which experienced the same type of ecological succession as inner-city neighborhoods did before and after World War II. However, enhanced personal incomes and job expectations, improved infrastructure, and cheap gasoline prices allowed increasing numbers of blacks to become suburban home owners. In some cases, suburban white flight was matched by equally affluent blacks interested in the same personal safety, good schools, and aesthetics. Overall the percentages of suburban blacks remained below urban averages, but African Americans became more of a factor in the suburbs than they ever had before.

TO THE SUBURBS

Demographic studies in the 1990s revealed another pattern of racial turnover in metropolitan areas. For the first time, more than half of all racial and ethnic groups residing in large metro areas lived in the suburbs. Such trends induced some observers to speculate that the radical racial changes of the postwar decades may have been temporary, especially in the older and larger northeastern and midwestern cities. Others theorized that small towns were benefitting from a different form of white flight as whites from large cities and their surrounding suburbs created a new rural renaissance. Los Angeles and New York City lost more than one million domestic migrants during the 1990s, while the greatest domestic migration gains during the decade occurred in predominately white, nonmetropolitan areas, such as the Mountain states, the south Atlantic states, Texas, and the Ozarks. Some scholars predicted that if the pattern continued, the city-suburb pattern of white flight might be replaced by an urban-rural model.

Instead, urban rather than white flight took center stage during the early twenty-first century because of continuing urban decay, called "blight flight"; a decreasing number of higher-paying industrial jobs in and near cities; and a disproportionate increase in the number of less financially stable "subprime" home loans. According to a Brookings Institution study, between 1999 and 2008 suburban poor grew by 25 percent, five times the rate of urban poor. For the first time, suburban poor came to outnumber their urban counterparts in Cleveland, Ohio; Minneapolis, Minnesota; Houston, Texas; Oklahoma City, Oklahoma; and Chicago. Meanwhile, decreasing crime levels and gentrification—the transformation from lower to higher property values—contributed to a lesser degree to "bright flight," a return of whites to formerly African American urban neighborhoods. Such cities as Washington, D.C.; Atlanta, Georgia; Portland, Oregon; Austin, Texas; and Los Angeles saw an increase in aspiring young adults seeking knowledge-based jobs and accompanying urban accouterments, such as public transportation and "ambiance."

Bucking both trends, the population of Detroit, Michigan, decreased from nearly two million in 1950 to 713,777 in 2010, the first example of large-scale "urban collapse" in American history, as African Americans and other minorities joined whites fleeing the city. A growing population of Middle Eastern immigrants failed to stem the tide. Detroit's ongoing demise contributed to a 0.6 percent drop in Michigan's overall population, making it the only state in the union to lose population between 2000 and 2010, a warning to other declining regions. Growing numbers of Hispanic and other immigrants, aging white populations, growing educational disparities, and income polarization suggest that similar urban flight patterns will continue and that governments may have to collaborate to develop unconventional solutions to defining city and county borders and administering urban and suburban resources and needs.

Richard Junger

SEE ALSO: *Harlem Renaissance; Lynching.*

BIBLIOGRAPHY

Anderson, Elijah, and Douglas S. Massey. *Problem of the Century: Racial Stratification in the United States.* New York: Russell Sage Foundation, 2001.

Avila, Eric. *Popular Culture in the Age of White Flight: Fear and Fantasy in Suburban Los Angeles.* Berkeley: University of California Press, 2004.

Bennett, Larry. *Fragments of Cities: The New American Downtowns and Neighborhoods.* Columbus: Ohio State University Press, 1990.

Bruegmann, Robert. *Sprawl: A Compact History.* Chicago: University of Chicago Press, 2005.

Clark, Thomas A. *Blacks in Suburbs: A National Perspective.* New Brunswick, NJ: Rutgers University Center for Urban Policy Research, 1979.

Dennis, Sam Joseph. *African-American Exodus and White Migration, 1950–1970.* New York: Garland, 1989.

Frey, William H.; Alan Berube; Audrey Singer; et al. *State of Metropolitan America: On the Front Lines of Demographic Transformation.* Washington, DC: Brookings Institution, 2010.

Hayden, Dolores. *Building Suburbia: Green Fields and Urban Growth, 1820–2000.* New York: Pantheon Books, 2003.

Kruse, Kevin M. *White Flight: Atlanta and the Making of Modern Conservatism.* Princeton, NJ: Princeton University Press, 2005.

Orser, W. Edward. *Blockbusting in Baltimore: The Edmondson Village Story.* Lexington: University Press of Kentucky, 1994.

Pais, Jeremy F.; Scott South; and Kyle Crowder. "White Flight Revisited: A Multiethnic Perspective on Neighborhood Outmigration." *Population Research Policy Review* 28 (2009): 321-346.

Rabinowitz, Alan. *Urban Economics and Land Use in America: The Transformation of Cities in the Twentieth Century.* Armonk, NY: M. E. Sharpe, 2004.

Rossell, Christine H. "School Desegregation and White Flight." *Political Science Quarterly* 90, no. 4 (1975–1976): 675–695.

Sugrue, Thomas J. *The Origins of the Urban Crisis: Race and Inequality in Postwar Detroit.* Princeton, NJ: Princeton University Press, 1996.

Teaford, Jon C. *The Metropolitan Revolution: The Rise of Post-Urban America.* New York: Columbia University Press, 2006.

White Supremacists

In a country of immigrants, white supremacy has been a curious and lasting preoccupation. Not just African Americans, but Catholics, Eastern Europeans, Italians, Jews, and all races not of Western European origin have been singled out as inferior at one time or another in U.S. history. But where did such behavior

American Nazi Rally. *A man wears a pendant made out of a bullet and a "White Power" T-shirt at an American Nazi rally in Chicago in 1978.* © OWEN FRANKEN/CORBIS.

come from, and why do so many continue to cling to such a backward creed? The simplest answer is that racism and racist organizations provide a comprehensive worldview in times of social turmoil, a way to interpret changes in social mores and often mystifying economic setbacks. But this is not enough. In virtually every country, bigotry exists, but in ostensibly egalitarian America, it remains one of the most paradoxical features of our social landscape.

Until recently, white supremacy was very much the norm. At the turn of the twentieth century, most labor unions were overtly racist, as were many social activists of a radical stripe. Author Jack London was both a socialist and a white supremacist, preaching the brotherhood of workers, provided they were lily white. It was London who first coined the term *great white hope* in articles beseeching a challenger to step forward against Jack Johnson, the black heavyweight boxing champion. In London's view—and he was regarded as a progressive—African Americans and Chinese ranked as hardly human. For the more conventional, the truth of white supremacy was hardly given a second thought; it was self-evident.

EARLY STAGES: 1920s

Like religious mania or consumer habits, white supremacy is not a constant but is inherently tied to historical conditions. It is a consolation in times of trouble and a rationale in times of prosperity. In the 1920s it was tied to the growing antipathy between city and country; during the Depression it became inextricably linked to anticommunism and opposition to Franklin Delano Roosevelt's New Deal. Father Coughlin, a virulent anticommunist radio personality, and William Pelley, leader of the fascist Silver Shirts, were both vocal enemies of the New Deal, and each embraced racist nationalism to explain the country's ills.

The worldwide Jewish conspiracy theory imported by Henry Ford in his *Dearborn Independent* had been integrated into supremacist beliefs during the 1920s. The next development was a theological justification for their beliefs. Soon after the conclusion of World War II, California preacher and Ku Klux Klansman Wesley Swift latched onto a racist Christian theology known as British Israelism. Swift renamed the theology Christian Identity. Exponents of British Israelism believe that the lost tribe of Israel immigrated to Britain; hence, Anglo Saxons were inherently superior and were in fact God's chosen people. Christian Identity proved to be a popular idea, and under Swift's tutelage the belief spread to Idaho, Michigan, and the South. Almost every supremacist group after World War II has in some way been influenced by Christian Identity, with Swift followers forming the Aryan Nation, Posse Comitatus, and the Minutemen, the most committed among the later waves of white supremacists.

RISE TO POWER: 1960s–1970s

By the 1960s white supremacy was a vigorous movement. Lurking behind the Senator Barry Goldwater Far Right, white supremacists wielded enormous influence and political power. Frightened by a world that appeared out of control, many Americans found solace in the strident rhetoric of the American Nazi Party or the Minutemen. The publications of the Liberty Lobby and the John Birch Society clearly explicated this dissatisfaction. The Ku Klux Klan mobilized visibly, and sometimes violently, against desegregation activists white and black alike; militia-like cells organized in the Midwest and the John Birch Society, while professing no racist sentiment, actively supported the supremacist ideology through their political activities. As manifested in the 1964 presidential campaign of Goldwater, the openly racist platform of Governor George Wallace in his 1968 and 1972 primary campaigns, and Ronald Reagan's 1966 gubernatorial race, white supremacy was a force to be reckoned with.

Political positions and economic conditions go hand in hand, as any student of Adolf Hitler's rise to power will attest. In 1970s America, a rash of bank foreclosures and declining agricultural prices sent tremors of fear across the heartland. In many places thus stricken, groups such as the Posse Comitatus, an organization vocally opposed to the federal government, often organized to combat what was perceived as unfair bank practices by rigging auctions and seizing land and equipment, sometimes provoking gun battles between law enforcement and farmers. In the declining industrial areas, the loss of lucrative union jobs swelled the ranks of the unemployed, mobilizing soldiers in a new racial movement; they called it the Fifth Era. Groups like WAR (White Aryan Resistance) mobilized around white unrest, often reaping a tidy profit with marketing schemes and paraphernalia.

Complete segregation was the goal most frequently advocated, and terrorism and paramilitary training the preferred method to attain it. Many groups published detailed maps that limited minorities to gerrymandered homelands. In Idaho, the quasi-military group the Order took a more direct approach, pulling off several profitable armed robberies (dispensing the proceeds among many supremacist groups) and murdering Denver talk-show host Alan Berg. The group was finally eradicated by the FBI, but not before they had distributed much of their illicit bounty, and there is evidence that their crimes have financed several campaigns and training camps.

Meanwhile, a new generation of disenchanted, working-class youth, having seen their parents lose a farm or well-paid factory job, had adopted the skinhead style and rhetoric of British youth, compensating for their helplessness with acts of racially motivated violence. For a time, skinhead gangs enjoyed high visibility, and just as quickly they learned the disadvantages of that conspicuity. Harassment by the police was a constant, and by the 1990s skinhead leaders were urging their dome-headed minions to grow their hair and recede quietly.

POLITICAL ASPIRATIONS

It is easy to picture white supremacy as a marginal ideology, but this would be a mistake. White supremacy is hydra-headed, springing up in unexpected places. Many supremacists, such as David Duke, for example, have tempered their rhetoric sufficiently to win public office. Other groups cloak their agendas under neutral-sounding names such as the Council of Conservative Citizens, who made headlines in 1998 after Republican Senator Trent Lott addressed the group on several occasions and then was forced to disassociate from the group and their openly racist agenda. While the constant splintering of the many organizations makes it difficult to ascertain how many active supremacists there are or how much political clout they wield, it can be safely asserted that white supremacy has become a permanent feature of the sociopolitical terrain.

The number of hate groups climbed dramatically during the first decade of the 2000s. In 2000 the Southern Poverty Law

Center (SPLC) documented 602 groups. As of 2011 SPLC estimated that 1,018 hate groups were active in the United States. Citing the election of Barack Obama, the poor state of the economy, and fears over immigration, the SPLC found that white extremist groups were developing an expansive platform from which to recruit. The National Socialist Movement and David Black, operator of a white nationalist website and a former grand wizard of the Ku Klux Klan, boasted that their numbers increased by the thousands after Obama was elected. Two weeks prior to the election, the FBI reported that it had prevented an assassination attempt by two skinheads.

Jack Levin, a criminologist who specializes in hate crimes, estimated that close to 50,000 people belong to white supremacy groups in the United States and that this number would likely continue to rise. Membership rose in the South, Texas, Arizona, and California; however, states such as Pennsylvania, Michigan, and Montana also saw their numbers increase. Following the deaths of major leaders like William Pierce, founder of the National Alliance, in 2002; David Lane, a member of the Order, in 2007; and Frank Roch of the Aryan Brotherhood and David Lynch of the skinhead group American Front in 2011, hate groups have continued to piece together a mainstream presence. As Levin explains, the organizers of the white power movements have dropped the telltale armbands and sheets in order to look more middle class. Following Duke's example, William Daniel Johnson and California State University psychology professor Kevin MacDonald formed the white nationalist political party the American Third Position (A3P). The group succeeded in getting twenty-three candidates on ballots nationwide for all levels of government. Although only Loy Mauch won his bid for election in Arkansas, other candidates also pulled in high vote percentages.

Michael Baers

SEE ALSO: *Coughlin, Father Charles E.; Ford, Henry; The Great Depression; John Birch Society; Johnson, Jack; Ku Klux Klan; London, Jack; New Deal; Obama, Barack; Reagan, Ronald.*

BIBLIOGRAPHY

Bello, Marisol. "White Supremacists Target Middle America." *USA Today*, October 21, 2008.

Bennett, David H. *The Party of Fear*. Chapel Hill: University of North Carolina Press, 1988.

Corcoran, James. *Gordon Kahl and the Posse Comitatus: Murder in the Heartland*. New York: Viking Penguin, 1990.

Dobratz, Betty A., and Stephanie L. Shanks-Meile. *"White Power, White Pride!": The White Separatist Movement in the United States*. Baltimore, MD: Johns Hopkins University Press, 2000.

Flint, Colin. *Spaces of Hate: Geographies of Discrimination and Intolerance in the U.S.A.* New York: Routledge, 2004.

Flynn, Kevin, and Gary Gerhardt. *The Silent Brotherhood: Inside America's Racist Underground*. New York: Free Press, 1989.

Higham, Charles. *American Swastika*. Garden City, NY: Doubleday, 1985.

Levin, Jack, and Gordona Rabrenovic. *Why We Hate*. Ann Arbor: University of Michigan Press, 2004.

MacCann, Donnarae. *White Supremacy in Children's Literature*. New York: Routledge, 2000.

Ridgeway, James. *Blood in the Face*. New York: Thunder's Mouth Press, 1990.

Rockwell, George Lincoln. *White Power*. Champaign, IL: John McLaughlin, 1996.

Southern Poverty Law Center. *Intelligence Report: The Year in Hate and Extremism*, 2012, 145.

Wade, Wyn Craig. *The Fiery Cross: The Ku Klux Klan in America*. New York: Simon & Schuster, 1987.

Whiteman, Paul *(1890–1967)*

Denver, Colorado–born bandleader Paul Whiteman is inseparable in American musical culture from George Gershwin's enduring classic "Rhapsody in Blue," which Whiteman famously commissioned, conducted at its sensational 1924 New York premiere, and recorded the same year. The most popular of all bandleaders prior to the big band era, Whiteman was called "the King of Jazz." However, this was not strictly accurate despite the jazz-based "Rhapsody in Blue," his association with several jazz musicians and vocalists, and his discovery and continued espousal of legendary trumpeter Bix Beiderbecke. Whiteman's disciplined arrangements left true jazz musicians little chance for improvisation, and as Wilder Hobson writes in *American Jazz Music* (1939), he "drew very little from the jazz language except for some of its simpler rhythmic patterns."

A former violin and viola player with the Denver and San Francisco Symphony orchestras, Whiteman formed his band in 1919 with pianist/arranger Ferde Grofe and trumpeter Henry Busse and, over the next couple of decades, unrolled a prodigious number of hits—well more than 200 by 1936. The band appeared in Broadway shows and films, the first of which, *King of Jazz* (1930), featuring "Rhapsody in Blue," was a creative landmark in the early history of the Hollywood musical. He hosted his own radio show in the 1930s and a television series in the 1950s. By 1954 Whiteman was ranked second only to Bing Crosby (with whom he worked and recorded) as a best-selling recording artist. Whiteman was eventually superseded by big band jazz artists such as Fletcher Henderson, but his Beiderbecke compilations, along with his Gershwin and Crosby recordings, remain his lasting memorials.

Benjamin Griffith

SEE ALSO: *Beiderbecke, Bix; Big Bands; Broadway; Crosby, Bing; Jazz; The Musical.*

BIBLIOGRAPHY

Berrett, Joshua. *Louis Armstrong & Paul Whiteman: Two Kings of Jazz*. New Haven, CT: Yale University Press, 2004.

DeLong, Thomas A. *Pops: Paul Whiteman, King of Jazz*. Piscataway, NJ: New Century Publisher, 1983.

Hobson, Wilder. *American Jazz Music*. New York: Norton, 1939.

Johnson, Carl. *A Paul Whiteman Chronology, 1890–1967*. Williamstown, MA: Whiteman Collection, Williams College, 1978.

Simon, George T. *The Big Bands*. New York: Macmillan, 1974.

Whiting, Margaret *(1924–2011)*

Margaret Whiting was a child of show business twice over. Her father was songwriter Richard Whiting ("Too Marvelous for Words," "On the Good Ship Lollipop"), and after he died when Whiting was a teenager, songwriter Johnny Mercer became her mentor. Signed to Mercer's Capitol label in the early 1940s, she had twelve gold records before the rock-and-roll era, including Mercer's "My Ideal" (1943) and her signature song, "Moonlight in Vermont" (1944). One of the first singers to cross Nashville, Tennessee, over into Tin Pan Alley, Whiting hit number one with "Slippin' Around" (1949), a duet with country star Jimmy Wakely.

A cabaret revival in the 1970s and 1980s gave Whiting a new career as one of New York's most beloved cabaret performers, on her own and as part of a revue, *4 Girls 4*, with Rosemary Clooney, Rose Marie, and Helen O'Connell. She also starred in a tribute to Mercer staged by her third husband, former gay porn star Jack Wrangler. Whiting toured the country with the production, called *I Remember Johnny*, for the decade leading up to her death in 2011.

Tad Richards

SEE ALSO: *Clooney, Rosemary; Country Music; Marie, Rose; Pornography.*

BIBLIOGRAPHY

Whiting, Margaret, and Will Holt. *It Might as Well Be Spring: A Musical Autobiography*. New York: William Morrow, 1987.

The Who

The Who were bold innovators who changed the face of popular music. Having planted the seeds of heavy metal, art rock, punk, and electronica, the Who are almost without peer in their range of influence. They boasted a dynamic singer and stage presence in Roger Daltrey, a powerful virtuoso bassist in John Entwistle, and one of the world's greatest drummers in the frenetic Keith Moon. However, the guiding genius of the Who was guitarist and songwriter Pete Townshend, who meticulously recorded the guitar, bass, drums, and vocals onto demos before presenting them to his bandmates to learn and perform. With the Beatles and the Rolling Stones, the Who form the "holy trinity" of English rock and roll. The Who melded the artistic leanings of the Beatles with the R&B drive of the Stones to create a unique sound that influenced everything from two-minute punk songs to hour-long rock operas.

SINGLES AND EARLY SUCCESS

Born in West London in 1945, Townshend attended Ealing Art College, where he learned about pop art and the merging realms of high and low culture. When he formed the Who, he found a suitable audience for this background among a youth subculture called the Mods, who wore pop art clothing and sought out stylish new music and amphetamine-driven dance styles. The Who's manager, Kit Lambert, encouraged the band to adopt the Mod look and write songs that would appeal to Mods. Their early hit "I Can't Explain" (1965) expresses adolescent frustration and was followed by the angst-ridden "My Generation" (1965), one of the great rock anthems of the period.

The Who were most famous for outrageous stage performances. Townshend specialized in "windmill" power chords, in which he would swiftly swing his arm 360 degrees before striking a chord. The group often smashed their instruments at the end of a show, with Townshend shoving his guitar through the amplifier and Moon kicking over his drum set. Despite their commercial success, the Who remained in debt until 1969 because of this expensive habit. Their performances on the TV show *The Smothers Brothers Comedy Hour* and in movies about the Monterey, Isle of Wight, and Woodstock music festivals are considered legendary.

The Who released their first album, *The Who Sing My Generation* in 1965. Like many bands, their focus was on hit singles, such as "Substitute" and "The Kids Are Alright." Their next album, *A Quick One* (1966, renamed *Happy Jack* in America) features a miniature "rock opera" on side two, a series of five songs narrating a tale of suburban infidelity. *The Who Sell Out* (1967) satirizes commercials, again revealing their interest in pop art. It contains their biggest-selling single, "I Can See for Miles," which Townshend later said was the best he could do writings pop songs. Spurred on by his manager, Townshend started thinking big. *Magic Bus* (1968) has the great title song and the masturbation ode "Pictures of Lily" but offers no hint of the grandeur of the group's next project, a full-scale rock opera.

TOMMY AND SUPERSTARDOM

The double album *Tommy* (1969) tells the story of a deaf, dumb, and blind boy who, after a miracle cure, becomes a cult leader. The work was influenced by Townshend's involvement with his guru, Meher Baba. If spirituality was an unexpected theme from the author of teen frustration and masturbation, the music was an equally bold advance, establishing Townshend as a versatile guitarist and ambitious composer. Nevertheless, responses to *Tommy* were mixed, partly due to the difficulty of following the story. Charges of pretentiousness were frequent. The artistic audacity of *Tommy* left the Who with a formidable dilemma: where could they go from there?

The Who followed up the rock opera with the raunchy, visceral *Live at Leeds* (1970), but soon Townshend grew ambitious again, formulating another opera, *Lifehouse*. Eventually the concept was abandoned, and the best songs written for the project were released as *Who's Next* (1971), which some critics regard as the greatest rock album ever made. Among its highlights are "Behind Blue Eyes," "Baba O'Riley," and the epic "Won't Get Fooled Again," a masterpiece of overwhelming power, featuring incredible performances by each band member. *Who's Next* made innovative use of synthesizers and sequencers, anticipating electronic music, and it established the Who as a major creative power in rock. The following year, Townshend released a solo album, *Who Came First*, devoted to Meher Baba.

QUADROPHENIA

Townshend then embarked upon yet another opera, based on the raw passions of youth rather than philosophical ideas. *Quadrophenia* (1973) depicts the Mods and their rival subculture, the Rockers. The story is simpler than that of *Tommy* but still rather confusing. However, the Who had grown musically since their first opera. Townshend was a more sophisticated arranger and made greater use of piano (which he played) and horns (played by Entwistle). *Quadrophenia* is regarded as Townshend's masterpiece, the definitive expression of adolescent angst, combining the ambitions of *Tommy* with the virtuosity and emotional power of *Who's Next.* Notable songs on the album include the driving "The Real Me" and the operatic "Love, Reign o'er Me."

The triumph of *Quadrophenia* left the Who in the same quandary that *Tommy* had: what next? They avoided the question with *Odds & Sods* (1974), a mixture of singles, B-sides, and leftovers from the *Lifehouse* project. For a hodgepodge, it is a fine album. *The Who by Numbers* (1975) is quieter, with thoughtful, introspective lyrics, while *Who Are You* (1978) finds the band delivering up-tempo rock again. The lengthy title song is a worthy follow-up to "Won't Get Fooled Again," and it gained renewed popularity in the first decade of the 2000s as the theme song for the television hit *CSI: Crime Scene Investigation.* The entire album is reminiscent of *Who's Next,* packed with powerful songs and showcasing synthesizers.

TRAGEDIES

Despite their artistic leanings, the Who became known as the world's loudest and most raucous live band, routinely filling football stadiums and arenas. They will be forever linked to a concert in Cincinnati, Ohio, on December 3, 1979, before which eleven people were trampled to death as fans raced to find seats. Before the band could tour to support *Who Are You,* Moon died from an overdose of an anti-alcoholic medication. He was replaced by former Small Faces drummer Kenney Jones, but for many fans, the Who were never the same on the road or in the studio after Moon's death. Whereas Townshend was the creative force, Moon was the engine that drove the band's music.

Following Moon's death, Townshend withdrew to record the fascinating *Empty Glass* (1980), his finest solo album. The Who recorded two albums with Jones, *Face Dances* (1981) and *It's Hard* (1982), before breaking up in 1982. Then came countless collections of rarities, outtakes, B-sides, demo tapes, and the like, which were testament to the Who's enduring popularity. However, critical respect for the group was compromised by the weakness of the post-Moon albums and by various uninspired reunion appearances, such as at Live Aid in 1985. Daltrey, Townshend, and Entwistle all embarked on solo music projects and other pursuits. For example, Daltrey acted, while Townshend published books. The Who toured again in 1996 and 1997, playing *Quadrophenia* with Ringo Starr's son, Zak Starkey, now on drums. Due to hearing loss, Townshend often played only acoustic guitar at these shows.

A RESURGENCE

If the tragedy of Moon's death all but shut down the band, another tragedy brought it back to life. In the wake of the September 11, 2001, attacks on the World Trade Center, the Concert for New York City was staged at Madison Square Garden. Although the Who were not the main act, they stole the show by all accounts. In particular, Daltrey's cathartic shout at the end of "Won't Get Fooled Again" captured the moment. Riding a new wave of popularity, the band faced another tragedy when Entwistle passed away in 2002. Once again, Daltrey and Townshend regrouped, continued to tour, and even released the Who's first studio album in more than twenty years, 2006's *Endless Wire.* The album features a mini-opera based on a Townshend novella. *Endless Wire* received favorable reviews, though nothing like previous works. It was as a live band that the Who could continue to excel, including in their halftime performance at the Super Bowl in 2010.

Other than playing sold-out shows, the Who mostly spent the years following Moon's death collecting honors. They were inducted into the Rock and Roll Hall of Fame in 1990 and the United Kingdom Music Hall of Fame in 2005. Additionally, they received the Grammy Lifetime Achievement Award in 2001 and became the first rock band to receive a lifetime achievement award from the Kennedy Center Honors in 2008. The Who also regularly appears near the top of various lists ranking the greatest rock-and-roll bands of all time.

All of these honors stem from the influence the Who have had on rock music. Punk bands such as the Clash, mod bands such as the Jam, and grunge bands such as Pearl Jam have all acknowledged that the Who paved the way for them. When inducting the group into the Rock and Roll Hall of Fame, U2 lead singer Bono said, "More than any other band, the Who are our role models." Every rock opera or musical harkens back to *Tommy,* and the Who's dynamic, instrument-destroying live performances are part of rock and roll lore. Movies enabled them to expand beyond music, including *Tommy* (1975) and *Quadrophenia* (1979) and the documentaries *The Kids Are Alright* (1979) and *Amazing Journey* (2007). As those two documentaries illustrate, the Who were more than just a band making music—they were bigger than the music itself.

The Who's Rock and Roll Hall of Fame biography sums it up best: "From Mod-era 'maximum R&B' to concept albums, rock operas and definitive classic rock tracks, the Who have reigned as one of rock's most powerful, energetic and literate rock bands. At their best, they've distilled the pent-up energy and chaos of rock and roll into its purest form while investing their songs with lyrical depth and visionary insight."

Douglas Cooke

SEE ALSO: *The Beatles;* CSI; *Grammy Awards; Heavy Metal; 9/11; Pearl Jam; Pop Art; Punk; Rock and Roll; The Rolling Stones; Stadium Concerts; U2; Woodstock.*

BIBLIOGRAPHY

Amazing Journey: The Story of the Who. DVD. Universal City, CA: Universal, 2007.

Barnes, Richard. *The Who: Maximum R&B.* London: Eel Pie, 1982.

Giuliano, Geoffrey. *Behind Blue Eyes: The Life of Pete Townshend.* New York: Dutton, 1996.

Marsh, Dave. *Before I Get Old: The Story of the Who.* New York: St. Martin's Press, 1983.

Neill, Andrew, and Matt Kent. *Anyway, Anyhow, Anywhere: The Complete Chronicle of the Who, 1958–1978.* New York: Michael Friedman Publishing, 2002.

Who Wants to Be a Millionaire

After its American debut on ABC in August 1999, *Who Wants to Be a Millionaire* revitalized one of television's oldest genres, the quiz show, for the twenty-first century. The show quickly became a national phenomenon, dominating prime-time ratings for two years. In an attempt to capitalize on its popularity, ABC began to broadcast multiple episodes per week, at one point airing the show nightly throughout the workweek. Ultimately, however, the strategy backfired. The show was overexposed, its ratings declined suddenly and precipitously, and it was canceled in June 2002 after its third season. Despite its fall, *Millionaire*, as the show was called by fans, produced a host of spin-offs and international variants throughout the world. The program was also famously used as the basis for the drama in *Slumdog Millionaire*, winner of the 2009 Academy Award for Best Picture.

The format for the *Millionaire* franchise was developed in England, where the program was first broadcast on the ITV network in September 1998. A contestant's journey to the million-dollar cash prize was straightforward: answer a series of fifteen multiple-choice questions worth an ascending amount of money. These questions, each with four possible answers, ranged from the easy $100 starter to the life-changing million-dollar finale. The original series provided several alternatives, called "Lifelines," for the contestant who was not quite sure of an answer. These Lifelines could be used only once during the game.

With the 50/50 Lifeline, two of the four possible answers would be eliminated, leaving the contestant with a 50 percent chance of answering the question correctly. The contestant could also ask the audience for their choice of the best answer and would be shown the percentage of people who had picked each option. The most popular Lifeline was Phone-a-Friend, which allowed the contestant to call a friend or relative who might be able to help them answer. Subsequent revivals and the syndicated versions added other Lifelines, including Jump the Question, Double Dip, and Ask the Expert.

The American version captivated audiences who were thrilled by the prospect of watching an ordinary person become a millionaire over the course of a half hour. After the August 1999 debut, the network spotlighted the show again in November, before launching it as a regular series in January 2000. Many credit veteran talk-show personality Regis Philbin, host of the prime-time American version of *Millionaire*, for the program's initial success. Typically dressed in dark, monochromatic clothes, he brought style and charm to the high-pressured proceedings and seemed unconcerned about the cash prize at stake and its capacity to alter the course of contestants' lives. Although the line was used by others before him, Philbin's unnervingly calm way of asking all contestants "Is that your final answer?" before revealing whether or not they had answered correctly turned the signature question into a popular American catchphrase.

The first contestant to win a million dollars was John Carpenter, who became an instant celebrity on November 19, 1999. Carpenter, a collection agent for the Internal Revenue Service, set the record for the biggest payday in quiz-show history. Other contestants answered all fifteen questions, but none attained the fame of Carpenter, who appeared on *Saturday Night Live* after his victory. He won the jackpot without assistance from the Lifelines. Prior to answering the final question, Carpenter did opt to use Phone-a-Friend, but rather than seeking help he merely assured his father that he was going to win.

At its peak during the first season, *Millionaire* set records for viewership. The top three shows of the 1999–2000 season were broadcasts of *Who Wants to Be a Millionaire* on three different evenings (Tuesday, Thursday, and Sunday), a feat unprecedented in the history of U.S. television. Ratings diminished considerably but remained respectable in the second season before plummeting in the third and final season. After its cancellation a syndicated version was launched in September 2002, with Meredith Vieira as the host. Airing five times a week, the daily version occasionally tweaks the game's format to maintain viewer interest. Through February 2012, Vieira had hosted more than 1,800 episodes and handed out $70 million in winnings, as well as receiving two Daytime Emmy Awards for her work.

ABC tried to bring back a revamped evening show, but with little success. In 2004 Philbin hosted a richer series, *Who Wants to Be a Super Millionaire*, in which contestants could win $10 million, and in August 2009 *Millionaire* celebrated its tenth anniversary with an eleven-night event. But in each case modest ratings indicated that the show's magic had dissipated.

Ron Simon

SEE ALSO: *Game Shows; Quiz Show Scandals; Television.*

BIBLIOGRAPHY

Carter, Bill. "Who Wants to Bury a Millionaire?" *New York Times*, May 20, 2002.

Marks, Peter. "Ride of Their Lives." *TV Guide*, January 15, 2000, 16–20.

Philbin, Regis. *Who Wants to Be Me?* New York: Hyperion, 2000.

"Who Wants to Be a Millionaire": The Official Book from the Hit TV Show. New York: Hyperion, 2000.

The Whole Earth Catalog

First published in 1968 by Stewart Brand, *The Whole Earth Catalog* introduced Americans to green consumerism and quickly became the unofficial handbook of the 1960s counterculture. Winner of the National Book Award and a national best seller, *TWEC* contained philosophical ideas based in science, holistic living, and metaphysics as well as listings of products that functioned within these confines. As many Americans sought to turn their backs on America's culture of consumption, *TWEC* offered an alternative paradigm based in values extending across the counterculture.

TWEC combined the best qualities of the *Farmer's Almanac* and a Sears catalog, merging wisdom and consumption with environmental activism and expression. The first page declared that "the establishment" had failed and that *TWEC* aimed to supply tools to help an individual "conduct his own education, find his own inspiration, shape his own environment, and share his adventure with whoever is interested." The text offered advice about organic gardening, massage, meditation, or do-it-yourself burial: "Human bodies are an organic part of the whole earth and at death must return to the ongoing stream of life." Many Americans used the resources and rationale within *TWEC* to live as rebels against the American establishment.

Interestingly, Brand did not urge readers to reject consumption altogether. *TWEC* helped create the consumptive niche known as green consumerism, which seeks to resist products contributing to or deriving from waste or abuse of resources, applications of intrusive technologies, or use of nonnatural raw materials. *TWEC* sought to appeal to this niche by offering products such as recycled paper and the rationale for its use. As the trendsetting publication of green consumption, *TWEC* is viewed by many Americans as having started the movement toward whole grains, healthy living, and the environmentally friendly products that continue to make up a significant portion of all consumer goods. Entire national chains have based themselves around the sale of such goods.

Even though green culture has infiltrated society, Whole Earth continues in the twenty-first century as a network of experts who gather information and tools in order to live a better life and, for some, to construct "practical utopias." *The Millennium Whole Earth Catalog* (1994), for instance, claims to integrate the best ideas since the 1970s with the best for the next twenty-five years, based on *TWEC* standards such as environmental restoration, community-building, whole systems thinking, and medical self-care.

The greatest tool in expanding green ideas, though, has clearly been the Internet. When Brand originally began publishing the catalog, his goal was to enable and equip an alternative consumer society. From its start, the Internet was built on a similar goal, enabling consumers to educate themselves and seek out the alternative products that specifically met their needs.

Brian Black

SEE ALSO: *Best Sellers; Consumerism; Environmentalism; Sears Roebuck Catalog.*

BIBLIOGRAPHY

Anderson, Terry H. *The Movement and the Sixties.* New York: Oxford University Press, 1996.

Kirk, Andrew. *Counter-Culture Green.* Lawrence: University of Kansas Press, 2011.

Rheingold, Howard. *The Millennium Whole Earth Catalog.* San Francisco: Harper, 1994.

Turner, Fred. *From Counterculture to Cyberculture.* Chicago: University of Chicago Press, 2008.

Wide World of Sports

"The thrill of victory and the agony of defeat" became one of the most familiar slogans on television, as popularized by the American Broadcast Company (ABC)'s *Wide World of Sports.* Beginning as a summer replacement in 1961, *Wide World of Sports* carried on into the 1990s, making a household name of original host Jim McKay, initiating ABC's dominance in sports television, and launching the career of future ABC Sports and News president Roone Arledge.

Arledge came up with the concept of packaging various sports under this umbrella title and sent McKay to anchor live coverage of two famed track meets—the Drake Relays from Des Moines, Iowa, and the Penn Relays from Philadelphia—for the inaugural broadcast of the program on April 29, 1961. *Wide World of Sports* survived its initial thirteen-week run and from then on the ninety-minute program was brought back every year in January, broadcast on Saturday afternoons and often on Sundays as well. The opening narration became famous: "Spanning the globe to bring you the constant variety of sport. The thrill of victory and the agony of defeat, the human drama of athletic competition. This is ABC's *Wide World of Sports.*"

Early on, *Wide World of Sports* covered many sports that later became their own live broadcast institutions, including tennis's Wimbledon, golf's British Open, and soccer's World Cup. But *Wide World* made its name with "nontraditional" sports, such as auto racing, boxing, swimming, diving, track and field, gymnastics, and figure skating. The particularly daring and unusual sports drew the most fans: surfing, bodybuilding, World's Strongest Man competitions, lumberjack contests, cliff divers from Acapulco, the Calgary Stampede rodeo, and most notably stunt motorcyclist Evel Knievel. Knievel dominated shows of the early 1970s, jumping barrels, cars, and buses and nearly making it across the Snake River Canyon on his motorcycle (and by rocket)—and breaking numerous bones in the process.

The program provided ABC Sports with sports coverage experience that it used to cover the Olympics. *Wide World* truly traveled the globe, covering events in Europe and Asia, even Cuba and China. Many of the events were broadcast live via satellite. The program developed a style that caused Americans to sit still and watch unfamiliar sports and foreign performers such as Russian gymnast Olga Korbut, Brazilian soccer star Pelé, and Russian weightlifter Vasily Alekseyev. The "up close and personal" features that detailed the life stories of the athletes grew out of *Wide World of Sports* and revolutionized sports coverage. Thanks to *Wide World,* sports coverage became storytelling rather than simply games, matches, scores, and stats. The success of its Olympics coverage propelled ABC out of its low ratings status into a respectable television network and earned Arledge the role of head of ABC Sports and ABC News.

During the 1970s *Wide World of Sports* became a brand name, and its most famous image was set: the "agony of defeat." While the "thrill of victory" changed almost every year, "the agony of defeat" was forever symbolized by hapless Yugoslavian ski jumper Vinko Bogataj, whose spectacular wipeout was taped in 1970. By the end of the 1980s *Wide World of Sports* lost its prominence as cable network ESPN became a superior ratings grabber and the ultimate sports show—twenty-four hours a day of the type of sports coverage that *Wide World* pioneered. The rise of ESPN was ironic, in that it was partly owned by ABC.

In the 1990s McKay left the role of studio host and was replaced by a succession of ABC Sports personalities that included Robin Roberts and Julie Moran. In 1998 *Wide World of Sports* was canceled. The hour-and-a-half program of all sorts of sports was replaced by a studio host introducing single-event broadcasts such as the Indy 500, horse racing's Triple Crown, and the national and world championships in figure skating. Eventually, the name was discontinued all together. One of the last appearances of the name and opening was when McKay died on June 7, 2008. The ABC announcement of his death aired during coverage of horse racing's Belmont Stakes (which was fitting, as McKay was a horse racing enthusiast and breeder and the founder of the Maryland Million day of racing).

The brand name "Wide World of Sports" lives on at the Walt Disney World Resort in Orlando. ESPN's Wide World of Sports has a baseball stadium, basketball courts, a track-and-field facility, playing fields for soccer, a tennis complex, an arena, and a restaurant.

Michele Lellouche

SEE ALSO: *Arledge, Roone; Disney (Walt Disney Company); ESPN; Knievel, Evel; Live Television; Olympics; Television; Wimbledon; World Cup.*

BIBLIOGRAPHY

The Best of ABC's Wide World of Sports, 3 vols. New York: CBS/Fox Video, 1990.

"Jim McKay." Archive of American Television. Accessed December 18, 2001. Available from http://www.emmytvlegends.org/interviews/people/jim-mckay

McKay, Jim, and Jim McPhee. *The Real McKay: My Wide World of Sports*. New York: Dutton, 1998.

Sugar, Bert Randolph. *Thrill of Victory: The Inside Story of ABC Sports*. New York: Hawthorn Books, 1978.

Wii

Released in the United States on November 19, 2006, Nintendo's Wii became the fastest-selling video-game console of its generation. Retailers could not keep it in stock, as the game repeatedly broke the record for most consoles sold in a single month. It was not until the summer of 2008 that supplies were generally able to keep up with demand.

The Wii's appeal centers on a motion sensor that allows players to mimic real-world actions using a remote dubbed the "Wii-mote." Popular in both schools and senior citizen centers, Wii caters to players of all ages. To continue reaching even more consumers, Nintendo promoted the notion of Wii-themed parties, for which groups would gather to play the game. This, of course, meant people had to buy more Wii-motes and other accessories. By March 2010 more than seventy million Wii consoles had been sold around the world.

INNOVATION

By allowing users to simulate actual activity, Wii introduced an element that was previously missing from video games. For example, with the game *Harry Potter and the Half-Blood Prince*, introduced in 2009, players can move the Wii-mote as if they are stirring a cauldron to make potions. When playing baseball or tennis in *Wii Sports*, users hold the Wii-mote as if it is a baseball bat or a tennis racquet. Popular Wii games that appeal to a broad spectrum of players include *The Legend of Zelda* series, the *Mario Brothers* series, *Xenoblade Chronicles*, *Monster Hunter Tri*, *Tales of Graces*, *Animal Crossing*, *Donkey Kong Country Returns*, *Call of Duty: Black Ops*, and *GoldenEye 007*.

Nintendo also introduced several unique features in Wii, such as the ability to create player avatars, or Miis, that mimic people's characteristics or represent their physical ideals. Some children like to create Miis that are as outlandish and as different from themselves as possible. The Wii also came with Wi-Fi capability, so players could connect to Wii channels that offered downloads of both new and classic games and video streams from services such as Netflix and Hulu.

As with other gaming technologies, the Wii had its share of problems. For example, new games were expensive and there was limited storage space on the system's hard drive. The most frustrating part of Wii gaming, however, was how often the remote lost contact with the sensor that was placed near the television to which the game was connected. Whenever that happened, the game temporarily stalled. An updated version of the game improved the ability of the Wii-mote to communicate with the sensor through Wii MotionPlus. Nintendo subsequently released Wii Remote Plus, which has a built-in censor and is not dependent on a separate device.

FITNESS AND HEALTH

Wii revolutionized the gaming industry, partially because of the physical aspect of mimicking real-life actions. Critics had long complained that video games led to a sedentary lifestyle. Nintendo resolved that problem not only with active games such as baseball, tennis, bowling, and boxing but also with the introduction of *Wii Fit* in 2008. Users could now establish fitness goals via such activities as blocking virtual soccer balls, swiveling their hips, and mimicking ski jumps.

Health experts touted *Wii Fit* as a way of helping patients with a variety of problems. In one study, the program was used with a group of African American women suffering from systemic lupus erythematosus and proved to produce significant benefits. Using *Wii Fit* for thirty minutes three times a week, patients lost weight, reduced disease-related fatigue, and experienced decreases in both pain and anxiety levels. The Wii has also been used in therapy and treatment for children and adolescents with cerebral palsy, and physicians have adopted the Wii to simulate surgical procedures.

However, the Wii has also been connected to user injuries, including hand lacerations, black eyes, forehead lacerations, and patellar (kneecap) dislocations. In the device's first year alone, 67 percent of Wii-related musculoskeletal injuries that were reported dealt with sprains and strains (29 percent) and ailments connected to repetitive motions (38 percent). These injuries, which often mimic the ones sustained from playing real sports, have become so common that they are called "Wii-itis" or "Nintendinitis." Wii-itis now refers to any type of acute inflammation associated with video gaming. Common subgroups of Wii-itis include "Wii shoulder," which involves the inflammation of upper-extremity muscles brought on by repetitive motions; "Wii knee," which is usually a dislocation of the kneecap from playing Wii bowling; and "Achilles Wii-itis," which involves the rupture of the Achilles tendon while engaged in virtual running or stretching.

Wii has maintained its popularity among families, although it has lost some of the appeal for hard-core gamers who prefer Sony's PlayStation 3 and Microsoft's Xbox 360. Both of those systems offer high-definition graphics and high-quality sound, and PlayStation 3 also serves as a Blu-ray player. Some observers question whether the Wii will survive now that both competitors have added motion-sensor accessories to their systems. The PlayStation Move, for example, has a video camera and a physical controller (wand) that detect motion. The sensor uses the earth's magnitude field to locate the controller at any given time. The Move, which requires a playing space of 5 to 9 feet, sold for $99 when it was first released in 2010. The Xbox Kinect turns the player's body into the controller and has image recognition, location identification, and voice recognition capabilities.

The competition from Sony and Microsoft, however, evidenced Wii's lasting effects on video-game culture. Nintendo's innovation incorporated social activity with gaming, effectively altering the way consoles were designed, manufactured, and marketed. Wii-themed parties became popular, and the intuitive technology helped Nintendo rebrand itself as a leader in the interactive gaming market.

Elizabeth Rholetter Purdy

SEE ALSO: *Computer Games; Hulu; Netflix; Video Games; Xbox Kinect.*

BIBLIOGRAPHY

Cogburn, Jon, and Mark Silcox. *Philosophy through Video Games*. New York: Routledge, 2009.

Foster, Derek. "'Wii're Here for a Good Time': The Sneaky Rhetoric of Wii-Themed Parties." *Journal of American Culture*, March 2010.

Greenwald, Will. "Kinect vs. PlayStation Move vs. Wii: Motion Control Showdown." *PC Magazine*, November 6, 2010.

"Reinventing Family Game Night." *PC World*, December 2011.

Sparks, Dorothy. "Did Too Much Wii Cause Your Patient's Injury?" *Journal of Family Practice*, July 2011.

Wesley, David, and Gloria Barczak. *Innovation and Marketing in the Video Game Industry: Avoiding the Performance Trap*. Burlington, VT: Ashgate, 2010.

Yuen, H.; K. Holthaus; D. L. Kamen; et al. "Using *Wii Fit* to Reduce Fatigue among African American Women with Systemic Lupus Erythematosus." *Lupus*, December 2011.

WikiLeaks

Founded in 2006, the website WikiLeaks has claimed responsibility for some of the most dramatic scoops and exclusive news stories in journalism history. Operated as a loosely organized nonprofit organization with no known physical headquarters, WikiLeaks provides classified, secret, and private documents from a variety of whistleblowers or anonymous sources to reveal diplomatic, military, government, and private sector misdoings. It is headed by Australian political activist Julian Assange and boasts a publicly available database of millions of documents. While it has been lauded by some as an Internet-era champion of free press and government openness, others have criticized WikiLeaks for trafficking in stolen property, endangering military safety and political security, and engaging in espionage.

A PRECEDENT FOR LEAKS

The verb form of *leak*, meaning to allow the disclosure of secret or confidential information, came into common usage around 1859, though the practice has been carried out for centuries. Benjamin Franklin leaked letters written by the Massachusetts royal governor in 1772 inciting colonists toward rebellion. *New York Herald* reporter John Nugent was arrested by the U.S. Senate in 1848 for publishing information on a secret treaty with Mexico. President Franklin Roosevelt leaked details of the Japanese Rape of Nanking in 1937 to bolster his efforts to expand the U.S. Navy.

President John F. Kennedy told reporters in an off-the-record comment in 1961 that the United States had a demonstrable strategic nuclear superiority over the Soviet Union, a comment that prompted Soviet leader Nikita Khrushchev to send nuclear missiles to Cuba. Antiwar activist Daniel Ellsberg leaked portions of a secret government study nicknamed the Pentagon Papers in 1971. Ellsberg subsequently became a volunteer for WikiLeaks, which has taken the concept of leaked information to an entirely new level.

EARLY EFFORTS

The Internet has made possible the mass distribution of information, especially digitized materials. That was the possibility Assange envisioned when he registered the domain name leaks.org in 1999 while working as an encryption technologist. When whistleblowers came forward looking for an outlet for their information following the 2003 American invasion of Iraq, Assange created WikiLeaks, which he termed "an open-source, democratic intelligence agency." Speaking to his motivation in a 2012 *Rolling Stone* interview, Assange said, "The Iraq War was the biggest issue for people of my generation."

Assange initially considered China, the former Soviet states, and some African nations as the most likely targets for disclosures but learned that most were linked to Western countries. In the West he discovered what he calls a shadow state of secret government agencies gathering and storing information without legal limitations. WikiLeaks asserts that it does not solicit information from such sources but will protect whistleblowers from exposure and retribution.

WikiLeaks distributed information about former Kenyan leader Daniel arap Moi and the Church of Scientology in 2008, but the website first attracted widespread American attention in late 2008 when it posted the contents of the Yahoo e-mail account of Republican vice presidential candidate Sarah Palin. The e-mails revealed that Palin had used her personal account to transact and keep official business from the public. A document related to the 2008 Icelandic banking crisis was made available the following year, and WikiLeaks released e-mails casting doubt on claims made by climate scientists. It also released the membership list of the Far Right British National Party.

THE MANNING MATERIALS

Assange personally unveiled video footage in April 2010 made by a U.S. helicopter crew of the 2007 shooting deaths of at least twelve people in Baghdad, including two Reuters news employees carrying cameras. The following July WikiLeaks released the Afghan War Diary, 92,000 low-level classified military documents on the Afghanistan war written by soldiers and intelligence officers between 2004 and 2009, including details on previously unreported incidents of covert operations against the Taliban and the killing of Afghan civilians by NATO assassination squads. The release was made to three international newspapers, including the *New York Times*, but many of the individual documents were incomplete or incorrect.

In October 2010 the site released the Iraq War Logs, some 392,000 military documents. The reports revealed that civilian casualties of the war in Iraq were greater and detainee abuse was more serious than previously known. Working with several mainstream news outlets, including the *New York Times*, in November 2010 WikiLeaks posted Cablegate, a collection of 250,000 American diplomatic cables to and from more than 150 countries. Revelations about the inner workings of corrupt Middle Eastern regimes were included in the disclosures, and some of the documents were credited with fueling the Arab Spring revolutions the following year.

In the wake of Cablegate, WikiLeaks's main Internet service provider dropped the website, although WikiLeaks had duplicate sites with other servers, and it was criticized by former supporters such as Amazon.com, Facebook, PayPal (and its parent company, eBay), and Wikipedia. Assange's personal assets were frozen by a Swiss bank, Master Card and Visa stopped processing donations, and Apple dropped WikiLeaks from its App Store. "I am concerned about the reports of pressure exerted on private companies, including banks, credit cards companies, and Internet service providers," United Nations High Commissioner for Human Rights Navanethem Pillay said in late 2010.

Meanwhile, U.S. Army Private Bradley Manning, an intelligence analyst with high security clearance who was deployed to Iraq in 2009, allegedly claimed credit for releasing secret materials to WikiLeaks used in the Afghan War Diary and Iraq War Logs, as well as video of Bagdad airstrikes. Manning allegedly downloaded materials to his personal computer using rewriteable CDs labeled "Lady Gaga." He was arrested by federal authorities in May 2010 and charged with numerous crimes under military law. Manning later claimed that he was mistreated while being held in a maximum security facility in Quantico, Virginia, in what was labeled by supporters as "no-touch torture." Under military law, Manning could be executed if he is found guilty, but prosecutors have said they would seek life imprisonment.

MORE RECENT EXPOSURES

In 2011 WikiLeaks released 779 U.S. Department of Defense documents related to detainees at the Guantánamo Bay detention camp in Cuba. The documents, published in the *New York Times* and other newspapers, revealed that more than 100 Afghans and Pakistanis had been held for years without being charged. The Spyfiles, first revealed in late 2011, showed the extent of the international private intelligence industry, with more than 160 contractors. In 2012 more than five million e-mails from Texas-based global intelligence company Stratfor were released on WikiLeaks. Among other things the documents purported that Pakistan's intelligence service knew the location of Osama bin Laden's safe house well before he was killed there by U.S. forces in 2011.

In 2010 newspapers reported that the United States had asked Great Britain, Germany, and Australia to consider criminal charges against Assange and to limit his international travel. That same year he was accused of criminal sexual conduct in Sweden. Assange was living in England at the time and asked authorities to deny extradition. His legal troubles may go even deeper: newspapers speculated in 2011 that U.S. authorities had a sealed grand jury indictment—perhaps for espionage, which could be punishable by death—against Assange for Cablegate and other releases.

Richard Junger

SEE ALSO: *Amazon.com; Apple Computer; eBay; E-mail; Facebook; The Internet; The* New York Times*; Palin, Sarah;* Rolling Stone*; Sex Scandals; War in Afghanistan; Watergate; Wikipedia.*

BIBLIOGRAPHY

Hastings, Michael. "Julian Assange: The *Rolling Stone* Interview." *Rolling Stone*, January 18, 2012.

Leigh, David, and Luke Harding. *WikiLeaks: Inside Julian Assange's War on Secrecy*. New York: Public Affairs, 2011.

Sifry, Micah L. *WikiLeaks and the Age of Transparency*. Berkeley, CA: Counterpoint, 2011.

"UN High Commissioner for Human Rights Navi Pillay Voices Concern at Reports of Pressure Being Exerted on Private Companies to Halt Financial or Internet Services for WikiLeaks." *Unifeed*, December 9, 2010.

Wikipedia

Wikipedia, the free Internet encyclopedia, bills itself as the world's largest online general reference resource. Its name is a combination of the words *wiki*, a type of collaborative website, and *encyclopedia*. Unlike a traditional encyclopedia, which features expert-reviewed content, Wikipedia's "crowdsourcing" approach means that articles can be written and edited by anyone—a fact that has made it a favorite target of many critics and satirists. Cofounder and Internet entrepreneur Jimmy Wales has described Wikipedia as "an effort to create and distribute a free encyclopedia of the highest possible quality to every single person on the planet in their own language."

As of March 2012, Wikipedia had more than twenty-one million articles in 284 languages, which may seem to prove that this colossal encyclopedia could actually reach Wales's lofty goal—but it is the word *quality* that continues to dog its efforts. Wikipedia had more than 400 million unique visitors per month as of February 2012, but critics of the site's populist approach continue to question whether anyone should consult this encyclopedia at all.

A COLLABORATIVE PROCESS

Wikipedia began its quest in 2001, building on Ward Cunningham's radical 1995 invention of a "wiki," a website that could be edited by anyone. This invention, along with the introduction in 1999 of Web 2.0 tools that allowed users to collaborate online, helped Wikipedia cofounders Wales and philosopher Larry Sanger realize their vision. Wikipedia did not start out in its current form, however. Wales, concerned that the Internet had not yet realized the promise of providing free access to high-quality information, hired Sanger in 1999 to create a free online encyclopedia called Nupedia. Unlike today's Wikipedia, Nupedia featured peer-reviewed articles, but the review process was slow, so Sanger suggested creating a companion site using Cunningham's wiki tool that would allow contributors to create articles without editorial review. The Wikipedia site went live in January 2001 and quickly surpassed Nupedia, generating more than 20,000 articles in eighteen languages by the end of the year. In 2003 Nupedia was shut down and its articles were added to Wikipedia.

Wales credits the collaborative process that he and Sanger created for Wikipedia's rise. "Wikipedia isn't a technological innovation at all; it's a social innovation," he says in the introduction to Andrew Lih's *The Wikipedia Revolution* (2009). "We had the Web already, but we discovered the basic idea of how to organize a community." Today Wikipedia is the most successful recent example of crowdsourcing—its articles are created by an all-volunteer force of more than thirty-one million registered users and countless anonymous users around the globe. While Wales might contend that this "open" approach has produced entries reflecting a more universal, populist perspective, critics have pointed to statistics from the nonprofit Wikimedia Foundation (Wikipedia's owner) that show most of the contributors have been white European and North American men with above-average education levels. To help correct at least some of this imbalance, the foundation's executive director, Sue Gardner, announced a goal in 2011 of increasing the share of female contributors to 25 percent by 2015.

The encyclopedia is primarily crowd-funded through donations to the Wikimedia Foundation. Each year, Wales's name and face are splashed across Wikipedia's pages during the foundation's annual appeal for donations. Some critics have questioned whether Wikipedia truly is a nonprofit venture, however, citing the large size of contributions made by such donors as venture capital firm Elevation Partners, which had donated $1 million to the foundation as of 2008, and Google, which donated $2 million to the foundation in 2010.

CRITICISMS

The questions about Wikipedia's funding, however, pale in comparison to criticisms of its content. Wikipedia places few restrictions on its articles, other than directing contributors to verify information, maintain a neutral point of view, and respect copyright law and the privacy of nonpublic figures. Wikipedia also requires that contributors supply known information, not original works or research. As part of its "open" editing model, no one owns a particular article—all articles can be edited by anyone, however they see fit. Edits show up immediately, without prior review, which means that errors, biases, or even nonsense can appear in an article until another editor comes along to fix the problem.

When disputes arise over edits, the editors involved discuss the changes and come to an agreement about how the article should read. It is this consensus approach that has drawn not only criticism, but ridicule as well, from Wikipedia's detractors. Comedian Stephen Colbert, host of the satirical late-night television program *The Colbert Report*, once, just for fun, urged viewers to alter a Wikipedia entry on African elephants to say that the population had tripled in a six-month period. He also coined the term *wikiality*, saying, "On Wikipedia, we can create a reality that we all agree on—the reality we just agreed on."

Perhaps cofounder Sanger found himself agreeing in part with the critics—in 2002, amid questions about the legitimacy of Wikipedia's articles, Sanger left to create a competing online encyclopedia called Citizendium, which has more rigorous criteria for contributors. Sanger has maintained in subsequent statements that Wikipedia does not have an accuracy problem; he has said it has an "anti-elitism" problem and an unwillingness to listen to expert opinions.

Wikipedia has also drawn fire for at least two cases of libelous comments being added to entries. In 2005 an entry ran uncorrected for more than 100 days stating falsely that John Seigenthaler Sr., assistant to Attorney General Robert Kennedy in the early 1960s, was thought for a time to have been involved in the assassinations of Robert and President John F. Kennedy. In 2008 literary agent Barbara Bauer sued Wikipedia over derogatory statements added to her entry about her intelligence and sales abilities. Despite these controversial cases, not everyone agrees that Wikipedia cannot be trusted. In 2005 a *Nature* magazine investigation found that Wikipedia's science articles came close to the level of accuracy of *Encyclopaedia Britannica*'s science articles (which *Britannica* disputes, however).

RESOLVING DISPUTES

To help ensure accuracy and respond to the problem of some contributors not following the rules, Wikipedia created a Wikipedia Arbitration Committee. This panel of volunteer editors (usually experienced Wikipedia editors) resolves disputes among contributing editors and determines which editors can have access to the CheckUser and Oversight tools that allow them to check Internet protocol (IP) addresses of other contributors and to delete content. Wikipedia has also limited the ability to edit some of its more popular articles—including President Barack Obama's page, which has a form to submit feedback instead of an edit button—to fight the criticism that articles are subject to "vandalism," or the intentional addition of erroneous information and offensive or biased language. Some Wikipedia editions, including the English-language edition, have decided to limit edits to registered users to help reduce such incidents. Ironically, it is these types of restrictions that have led critics to accuse Wikipedia of the very elitism and censorship that Wales set out to avoid and to question how "open" Wikipedia really is.

"DON'T CITE THE ENCYCLOPEDIA"

When Wikipedia first emerged, some expressed concerns that this free online encyclopedia might replace more traditional information resources. Others believe this will not be the case. *Wired* magazine editor-in-chief Chris Anderson, for example, wrote in *Nature* magazine that Wikipedia's "wisdom of crowds" approach would not replace scientific journals—with their rigorous review process—anytime soon. Still, Wikipedia continues to be one of the most visited sites on the Internet; in 2011, its traffic ranking was sixth among the world's websites. When the English-language site went "black" for twenty-four hours in January 2012 to protest proposed U.S. antipiracy laws, *BBC News Magazine* ran a column suggesting other ways Wikipedia visitors could find their facts that day—a nod to how many people have come to rely on the site for information.

Even educators are finding a way to somewhat peacefully coexist with Wikipedia. While many professors do not allow their students to include citations from Wikipedia, some concede that the website can serve as a starting point for more detailed research. Wales even seems to agree with this assessment. He said during a 2006 talk at the University of Pennsylvania that when he receives e-mails from students complaining that they received failing grades on papers because they cited Wikipedia, he tells them they got what they deserved: "For God sake, you're in college—don't cite the encyclopedia."

Sarah Roggio

SEE ALSO: *Colbert, Stephen; The Internet; Obama, Barack.*

BIBLIOGRAPHY

Anderson, Chris. "Technical Solutions: Wisdom of the Crowds." *Nature: International Weekly Journal of Science*, 2006. Accessed May 2012. Available from http://www.nature.com/nature/peerreview/debate/nature04992.html

Cohen, Noem. "Define Gender Gap? Look up Wikipedia's Contributor List." *New York Times*, January 20, 2011.

Hafner, Katie. "Seeing Corporate Fingerprints in Wikipedia Edits." *New York Times*, August 19, 2007.

Kelly, Jon. "Without Wikipedia, Where Can You Get Your Facts?" *BBC News Magazine*, January 18, 2012.

Lih, Andrew. *The Wikipedia Revolution: How a Bunch of Nobodies Created the World's Greatest Encyclopedia.* New York: Hyperion, 2009.

McHenry, Robert. "The Faith-Based Encyclopedia." Ideas in Action TV, November 15, 2004. Accessed May 2012. Available from http://www.ideasinactiontv.com/tcs_daily/2004/11/the-faith-based-encyclopedia.html

Rosen, Rebecca J. "Does Wikipedia Have an Accuracy Problem?" *Atlantic*, February 16, 2012.

Sanger, Larry. "Why Wikipedia Must Jettison Its Anti-elitism," IRC Network, December 30, 2004. Accessed May 2012. Available from http://www.kuro5hin.org/story/2004/12/30/142458/25

Seigenthaler, John. "A False Wikipedia *Biography*." *USA Today*, November 29, 2005. Accessed May 2012. Available from http://www.usatoday.com/news/opinion/editorials/2005-11-29-wikipedia-edit_x.htm

Young, Jeffrey R. "Wikipedia Founder Discourages Academic Use of His Creation." *Chronicle of Higher Education*, June 12, 2006.

The Wild Bunch

The definitive film, and only true epic, of director Sam Peckinpah's career, *The Wild Bunch* (1969) set the bar for movie violence higher than ever before. Earlier Westerns had good guys and bad guys as clearly demarcated as the sides in World War II, but *The Wild Bunch* came out during the Vietnam War, and it better reflected that war in both its complexity and carnage. Arthur Penn's *Bonnie and Clyde* (1967), which ended with its two protagonists being riddled by bullets, was the first major Hollywood film to show graphic violence—to suggest that shooting someone had consequences, that it was messy and painful—but nothing could have prepared 1960s audiences for the hundreds of deaths, for wave after wave of unrelenting carnage—shown in slow-motion and freeze-frame sequences—that climaxed *The Wild Bunch*.

Seven years before the film premiered, Peckinpah was deer hunting when he shot a buck and was struck by the fact that the bullet going in was the size of a dime, yet the blood on the snow was the size of a bowling ball. He concluded that was the way violence and death were and decided that was what he wanted to put on film. During filming Peckinpah had the technicians lay thin slices of raw steak across the bags of stage blood; when they exploded it looked like the bullets were ripping out of bodies mixed with blood and chunks of flesh. "Listen," Peckinpah said, "killing is no fun. I was trying to show what the hell it's like to get shot." He believed people would shun violence if he showed what violence was really like.

But violence in movies without flesh-and-blood characters (see almost any slasher film) is meaningless. Fortunately, Peckinpah had great characters, played by superb actors, in a strong story that was acted out before beautiful vistas and gorgeously photographed. As the movie opens the audience sees a tiny band of soldiers riding into a small town, then walking into the local railroad office, as scruffy, armed men flit back and forth on the rooftops overhead. It looks as though the bad guys are about to ambush the good guys, though the reverse is true. The railroad office manager asks the lead soldier, Bishop Pike (William Holden), "Yes, sir. Can I help you?" and Pike grabs the manager, pulls him out of his chair, shoves him and another against the wall, and tells the other soldiers, "If they move . . . kill 'em!" These aren't really soldiers at all, but the Wild Bunch in disguise, and the men on the roof are bounty hunters, there to ambush the outlaws and collect the prices on their heads.

Leading the bounty hunters is former Wild Bunch member Deke Thornton (Robert Ryan)—whose feud with Pike stems from the time they were busted by Pinkerton agents, with Thornton being shot and captured and Pike running away. Realizing they're about to be ambushed, the Wild Bunch times its departure to coincide with the passing of a parade of temperance marchers, and the resulting carnage is fairly intense.

The Wild Bunch. *Stars of* The Wild Bunch *included, from left, Ben Johnson as Tector Gorch, Warren Oates as Lyle Gorch, William Holden as Pike Bishop, and Ernest Borgnine as Dutch Engstrom.* SILVER SCREEN COLLECTION/CONTRIBUTOR/MOVIEPIX/GETTY IMAGES.

The gang escapes to Mexico, with the bounty hunters in hot pursuit. In the town of Agua Verde, they cross paths with Mapache, a ruthless general at war with revolutionary Pancho Villa, who has been oppressing the local natives—even murdering the father and stealing the fiancée of the Wild Bunch's one Mexican member, Angel. The gang agrees to rob a military supply train loaded with munitions for Mapache in exchange for gold, and the robbery itself is a slickly done caper, a Western *Topkapi!* Worried about helping Mapache get more guns, Angel agrees to participate if, instead of gold, he can take one case of guns for the revolutionaries. But Mapache finds out, and when the gang returns to Agua Verde to trade the arms for the gold, Mapache keeps Angel. At the end, the remaining outlaws decide to rescue Angel, and their fight against the soldiers provides the climactic bloodshed.

More complex than it first appears, *The Wild Bunch* is ultimately about redemption. Early in the film, Pike tells a gang member who wants to kill another, "We're gonna stick together, just like it used to be. When you side with a man you stay with him, and if you can't do that you're like some animal, you're finished!—we're finished. All of us." Yet Pike betrays this code again and again. During the original railroad office job, when Crazy Lee (Bo Hopkins) tells Pike he'll hold the hostages until Pike says different, Pike just leaves him behind to die. This is brought home when Pike's oldest friend, Sykes (Edmond O'Brien), tells Pike that Crazy Lee is his grandson. When another gang member is wounded and might slow them down, Pike shoots him; even Sykes himself is expendable when he becomes wounded.

At first, Angel is abandoned to Mapache and his men, but Pike has finally had enough, and, against impossible odds, he and the rest of the Wild Bunch decide to redeem themselves. They go down in a blaze of glory—and, joining the revolutionaries, the one remaining gang member and the one remaining bounty hunter ride off to fight the good fight.

Bob Sullivan

SEE ALSO: Bonnie and Clyde*; Gangs; Hollywood; Parades; Vietnam; The Western.*

BIBLIOGRAPHY

Bliss, Michael. *Justified Lives: Morality and Narrative in the Films of Sam Peckinpah.* Carbondale: Southern Illinois University Press, 1993.

Fine, Marshall. *Bloody Sam: The Life and Films of Sam Peckinpah.* New York: Donald I. Fine, 1991.

Hayes, Kevin J. *Sam Peckinpah: Interviews.* Jackson: University of Mississippi, 2008.

Seydor, Paul. *Peckinpah: The Western Films: A Reconsideration.* Urbana: University of Illinois Press, 1997.

Weddle, David. *If They Move . . . Kill 'Em!: The Life and Times of Sam Peckinpah.* New York: Grove Press, 1994.

Wild Kingdom

The first television program to help Americans visualize distant life and consider ways they might help protect it, *Wild Kingdom* became a crucial tool in the formation of America's environmental consciousness and particularly in the movement's shift toward global concerns. Mutual of Omaha's *Wild Kingdom* served as Americans' window into the exotic species of the natural world, starting in the 1960s and ending in 1971. In the tradition of *National Geographic,* host Marlin Perkins traveled throughout the world, sending back images of danger and intrigue. Perkins's pursuit of animals in their natural surroundings contributed to the interest in ecotourism, in which the wealthy travel to various parts of the world not to shoot big game but only to view it.

Wild Kingdom continues production and has spawned an entire genre of television, particularly for young viewers. When the program returned on Animal Planet in 2002, it entered a competitive marketplace of environmental programming.

Brian Black

SEE ALSO: National Geographic*; Television.*

BIBLIOGRAPHY

Dunaway, Finis. *Natural Visions.* Chicago: University of Chicago Press, 2008.

Mitman, Gregg. *Reel Nature.* Cambridge, MA: Harvard University Press, 1999.

The Wild One

The camera looks down a stretch of straight country highway, then the following appears in bold, white letters: "This is a shocking story. It could never take place in most American towns—but it did in this one. It is a public challenge not to let it happen again." The words fade away to be replaced by Marlon Brando's voice speaking in a southern drawl. "It begins here for me on this road," he says. "How the whole mess happened I don't know. But I know it couldn't happen again in a million years. Maybe I could have stopped it early. But once the trouble was on its way, I was just going with it." A crowd of leather-clad motorcyclists roars past the camera, and with the confident declaration that what follows is an aberration, Stanley Kramer launches *The Wild One* (1953). The truth of the matter is somewhat more complicated: not only did the film incite a rash of copycat behavior, but it may have had an effect on the Hells Angels' delectations a decade later.

The Wild One derives from a real riot, which followed a large motorcycle rally in the Northern California town of Hollister. According to witnesses, thousands of participants drag raced up and down the streets of Hollister; fist fights, lewd behavior, and vandalism were the norm, but the event was eventually dispatched by about forty police officers, and it ended without a single loss of life. The coverage in the July 1947 issue of *Life* magazine was sufficiently lurid and alarmist, and it inspired Frank Rooney to turn the incident into a short story, "The Cyclists' Raid." Rooney told the story from the point of view of Joel Bleeker, a hotel manager (and, significantly, a World War II veteran) who witnessed his daughter's death at the hands of the cyclists. Bleeker views the motorcyclists as inhuman quasi fascists, but in the story's transition to film, sympathies are switched. Johnny (Brando), leader of the Black Rebels Motorcycle Club, becomes the hero; he is sullen and incommunicative but also reserved, possessing a degree of chivalry lacking in his compatriots.

HOLLYWOOD VERSION

The rioting itself is transformed in typical Hollywood fashion into a Manichean contest between Johnny and his dissipated rival, Chino (Lee Marvin), who—to make matters perfectly clear—wears a horizontal-striped sweatshirt closely resembling prison garb. After gratuitously interfering in a local motorcycle race, the bikers proceed to the nearby town of Carbondale, where they cause all manner of havoc, prompted in part by the local saloon owner, who all but rubs his hands in excitement at the prospect of a bar full of hard-drinking motorcyclists.

The relationship between locals and bikers, already tense after a notoriously bad driver hits one of the bikers, is further challenged by the arrival of Chino and his cohorts. As the motorcyclists begin to run genuinely amuck, the town's craven police officer cowers in his office while his daughter, Kathie, is accosted by the bikers. She is rescued by Johnny, who drives off with her and is thus absent from the ensuing carnage. Nonetheless, as the leader, Johnny is blamed by the townspeople and is locked up. When he escapes, he is knocked off his motorcycle, accidentally killing an elderly man, whom he is unjustly accused of killing.

IMPACT

Despite the rather thin story line—*New Yorker* magazine called it "a picture that tries to grasp an idea even though the reach falls short"—*The Wild One* was an instant hit with young audiences. Theater owners throughout the country reported that teenage boys had taken to dressing in leather jackets and boots like Brando and were accosting passersby. The pioneering members of the Hells Angels (most of the group that later came to notoriety were children at the time) identified deeply with Brando. "Whadda ya got?" is Brando's insouciant reply to the famous question, "Hey Johnny, what are you rebelling against?" and it echoed in the real-life outlaws inchoate dissatisfaction. In *Hell's Angels, A Strange and Terrible Saga*, journalist Hunter S. Thompson quotes a founding member:

> We went up to the Fox Theater on Market Street. . . . There were about 50 of us, with jugs of wine and our black leather jackets. . . . We sat up there in the balcony and smoked cigars and drank wine and cheered like bastards. We could all see ourselves right there on the screen. We were all Marlon Brando.

Much of the lasting allure of *The Wild One* stems from Brando's lionization by not only the Hells Angels but also by countless teenagers. In "The Cyclists' Raid," Rooney writes: "They were all alike. They were standardized figurines, seeking in each other a willful loss of identity, dividing themselves equally among one another until there was only a single mythical figure, unspeakably sterile and furnishing the norm for hundreds of others." In light of the Hells Angels' response to *The Wild One* as quoted above, and considering the way Brando's image was disseminated on posters, in books, and turned into an archetype, it is no wonder many blamed *The Wild One* for the Hells Angels' excesses a decade later. Hollywood gossip columnist Hedda Hopper blamed Kramer entirely for the whole outlaw phenomenon, and Rooney might well have identified Brando as that "single mythical figure, unspeakably sterile and furnishing the norm for hundreds of others."

It would be simplistic to blame the filmmaker and leading man for a real-life contagion, but the suspicion remains to this day. Perhaps Thompson put it best when he wrote that the film "told the story that was only beginning to happen and which was inevitably influenced by the film. It gave outlaws a lasting, romance-glazed image of themselves, a coherent reflection that only a very few had been able to find in a mirror, and it quickly became the bike rider's answer to *The Sun Also Rises*."

Michael Baers

SEE ALSO: *Brando, Marlon; Drag Racing; Hells Angels; Hollywood;* Life*; The* New Yorker*; Thompson, Hunter S.; World War II.*

BIBLIOGRAPHY

Carey, Gary. *Marlon Brando: The Only Contender.* New York: St. Martin's Press, 1985.

Gabbard, Krin. *Black Magic: White Hollywood and African American Culture.* New Brunswick, NJ: Rutgers University Press, 2004.

Lewis, Jon. *The Road to Romance and Ruin: Teen Films and Youth Culture.* New York: Routledge, 1992.

Pettigrew, Terence. *Raising Hell: The Rebel in the Movies.* New York: St. Martin's Press, 1986.

Rooney, Frank. "The Cyclists' Raid." In *Stories into Film*, eds. William Kittredge and Steven M. Krauzer. New York: Harper & Row, 1979.

Shaw, Sam. *Brando in the Camera Eye.* New York: Exeter Books, 1979.

Spoto, Donald. *Stanley Kramer, Film Maker.* New York: Putnam, 1978.

Thomas, Tony. *The Films of Marlon Brando.* Secaucus, NJ: Citadel Press, 1973.

Thompson, Hunter S. *Hell's Angels, A Strange and Terrible Saga.* New York: Ballantine Book, 1967.

Wilder, Billy *(1906–2002)*

Born Samuel Wilder in an Austrian village, this six-time Academy Award–winning director, screenwriter, and producer was dubbed Billy after Buffalo Bill of the 1880s traveling Western show. That American nickname apparently foretold, in the wake of the Nazi rise to power, his 1934 immigration to Hollywood, where he joined fellow European exiles, learned English, and cultivated a legendary career that indelibly marked American movie history.

With partner Charles Brackett, Wilder cowrote acclaimed comedies such as *Ball of Fire* (1941) and then scripted, directed, and produced a string of hugely popular films, including the quintessential film noir *Double Indemnity* (1944) and *The Lost Weekend* (1945). Their alliance culminated with the savage portrayal of Hollywood in *Sunset Boulevard* (1950). With I. A. L. Diamond, Wilder created *Some Like It Hot* (1959) and *The Apartment* (1960). His self-produced works more flagrantly expressed his cynicism and penchant for vulgarity, with *Ace in the Hole* (1951) betraying a jaded sensibility ahead of its times.

Elizabeth Haas

SEE ALSO: *Academy Awards;* Double Indemnity*; Hollywood;* The Lost Weekend*;* Some Like It Hot*;* Sunset Boulevard.

BIBLIOGRAPHY

Lally, Kevin. *Wilder Times: The Life of Billy Wilder.* New York: Henry Holt, 1996.

McNally, Karen. *Billy Wilder, Movie-Maker: Critical Essays on the Films*. Jefferson, NC: McFarland, 2011.

Sikov, Ed. *On Sunset Boulevard: The Life and Times of Billy Wilder*. New York: Hyperion, 1998.

Zolotow, Maurice. *Billy Wilder in Hollywood*. New York: Putnam, 1977.

Wilder, Laura Ingalls *(1867–1957)*

One of the best-known children's authors, Laura Ingalls Wilder wrote the popular, autobiographical Little House novels about her late-nineteenth-century childhood on the American frontier. Published in the 1930s and 1940s, these eight books were considered classics of children's literature by the 1950s and have appealed to every succeeding generation of readers who thirsted for nostalgia.

The second of four daughters of Charles and Caroline Ingalls, a post–Civil War American pioneering family, Wilder began writing in childhood. She and her sisters penned poetry and compositions in the many homes the Ingalls family built in the wilderness. Her writing permitted her to have a voice, public and private, denied to many nineteenth-century women and provided a way to release her frustrations, disappointments, and

Laura Ingalls Wilder. Little House on the Prairie, *a popular television series adapted from the novels by Laura Ingalls Wilder, starred clockwise from upper left, Sidney/Lindsay Greenbush as Carrie, Michael Landon as Charles, Karen Grassle as Caroline, Melissa Gilbert as Laura, and Melissa Sue Anderson as Mary.* **SILVER SCREEN COLLECTION/CONTRIBUTOR/MOVIEPIX/GETTY IMAGES.**

enthusiasms during her life as pioneer, teacher, wife, mother, farmer, businesswoman, and author. Wilder continued her writing after she married her husband, Almanzo, in 1885. Keeping a travel diary of their 1894 trip to Mansfield, Missouri, Wilder submitted it for publication to the *De Smet News*, where both of her younger sisters worked as journalists. Distracted by farm duties and volunteer work in her community, Wilder did not write seriously until 1911 when she began preparing essays about farm life for the *Missouri Ruralist*.

The fictional Laura was adventurous and inquisitive yet compliant to the culture she lived in, obediently silencing herself and being still to please her Pa. She was predictable, providing steadiness to her readers. The real Laura craved such stability. Accustomed to economic and physical hardships, Wilder persevered despite her son's death, her husband's disability from disease, conflicts with her strong-willed daughter, crop failures and debt, and the misogyny and anti-intellectualism of her patriarchal community. Ambitious and intelligent, she ensured that the couple's farm, Rocky Ridge, survived while asserting her individuality.

Known as Bessie to her family, she became Laura Ingalls Wilder only in the last part of her life. This pen name represented a professional woman whom few people actually knew. The author Laura Ingalls Wilder answered fan mail, received awards, and signed books, while Bessie Wilder was an ordinary woman who performed her daily chores, read her Bible, attended club meetings, supported the local library, visited with friends, and cared for her ailing husband.

Wilder's daughter, Rose, an accomplished writer, encouraged her to write about her family's adventures on the frontier. Wilder completed her first attempt, *Pioneer Girl*, in 1930. In this novel, Laura narrated her story from childhood to marriage, but no publisher was interested. With Rose's help, Wilder rewrote her manuscript to meet literary expectations, dividing the novel into eight stories and presenting it in third person. Although the books were presented as based on Laura's experiences, the early stories about events during her infancy were obviously her parents' memories.

EARLY POPULARITY

Originally titled *When Grandma Was a Little Girl*, Wilder's first book, *Little House in the Big Woods*, was published in 1932 and was followed by *Farmer Boy* (1933), *Little House on the Prairie* (1935), *On the Banks of Plum Creek* (1937), *By the Shores of Silver Lake* (1939), *The Long Winter* (1940), *Little Town on the Prairie* (1941), and *These Happy Golden Years* (1943). (A manuscript for a story of Wilder's early years of marriage was found after her death. Edited by Roger Lea MacBride, *The First Four Years* was published in 1971.) Critics and readers immediately accepted her books, and the volumes sold well despite the Depression. The values of home, love, and personal courage formed an image of rural serenity that fulfilled readers' need for comfort and a connection to a past that they believed was simpler and happier than contemporary times.

Scholars noted the books' archetypes: Pa was the dreamer and provider, while Ma was the civilizer and stabilizer. Laura was a blend of her parents. The Ingalls were praised for being spiritual, hardworking, and resourceful, enduring tragedy while constantly moving in their covered wagon and homesteading virgin land. Aspects of nineteenth-century American culture were provided through the songs Pa sang, the items they purchased in stores, and the books and magazines the women read.

Scholars have criticized the patriarchal, domestic, and materialistic messages of Wilder's books and denounced the characters' racism toward Native Americans and minorities. The women were often isolated and confined to homes, while men were active participants with the outside world. Laura faced conflicts between her need for individual freedom and expression and self-sacrifice and obedience for the good of her family.

Wilder stressed that she wrote her stories to provide history lessons for new generations of children who no longer could experience the frontier and disappearing prairie that metaphorically offered hope, prosperity, and renewal. In so doing, she sparked a cultural phenomenon. Fans have dressed as Little House characters, collected memorabilia, and visited Laura Ingalls Wilder heritage sites. The Laura Ingalls Wilder–Rose Wilder Lane Home and Museum in Mansfield, Missouri, houses many items, such as Pa's fiddle, that are featured in the books. Bookstores sell adaptations of Wilder's stories, including series about Ma's and Rose's childhoods.

The commercialization of Laura Ingalls Wilder has meant that fans can buy Little House dolls, T-shirts, cookbooks, videos, diaries, and calendars. Wilder's books never have been out of print, and edited versions of her periodical writing and letters are also available. Foreign readers have also identified with Wilder's universal themes; her books have been published in forty languages, and websites connect Wilder fans around the globe.

The American Library Association initiated the Laura Ingalls Wilder Medal for accomplishments in children's literature in 1954. A television series, *Little House on the Prairie* (1974–1983), starred Michael Landon as Pa and Melissa Gilbert as Laura. The show offers an unrealistic portrayal of Wilder's life but was popular during an era when the Bicentennial and Alex Haley's book *Roots* revived Americans' interest in the past. A Broadway musical, *Prairie*, ran in 1982.

Elizabeth D. Schafer

SEE ALSO: *The Great Depression; Haley, Alex; Landon, Michael;* Roots.

BIBLIOGRAPHY

Anderson, William T. *Laura Ingalls Wilder: A Biography*. New York: HarperCollins, 2007.

Benge, Janet, and Geoff Benge. *Laura Ingalls Wilder: A Storybook Life.* Lynnwood, WA: Emerald Books, 2005.

Miller, John E. *Laura Ingalls Wilder's Little Town: Where History and Literature Meet.* Lawrence: University Press of Kansas, 1994.

Miller, John E. *Becoming Laura Ingalls Wilder: The Woman behind the Legend.* Columbia: University of Missouri Press, 1998.

Romines, Ann. *Constructing the Little House: Gender, Culture, and Laura Ingalls Wilder*. Amherst: University of Massachusetts Press, 1997.

Wilder, Thornton *(1897–1975)*

Thornton Wilder was an American novelist and playwright. His first novel, *The Cabala*, was published in 1926. His second novel, *The Bridge of San Luis Rey*, was published the very next year, and it was awarded the Pulitzer Prize in 1928. Five more novels followed: *The Woman of Andros* (1930), *Heaven's My Destination* (1934), *The Ides of March* (1948), *The Eighth Day* (1967), and *Theophilus North* (1973). Wilder also wrote a number of plays, including the Pulitzer Prize–winning *Our Town* (1938) and *The Skin of Our Teeth* (1942). One of his most popular plays was *The Matchmaker* (1954), which became the Tony Award–winning musical *Hello, Dolly!* (first produced in 1964) and an Academy Award–winning movie (1969) of the same name. In 1997, 100 years after his birth, cultural festivals throughout the United States celebrated the enormous talent of a man whose command of the classics was so great that he was nicknamed "The Library."

Joan Gajadhar

SEE ALSO: *Academy Awards; Broadway;* Hello, Dolly!*; The Musical; Streisand, Barbra; Tony Awards.*

BIBLIOGRAPHY

Burns, Edward, and Ulla Dydo. *The Letters of Gertrude Stein and Thornton Wilder*, ed. William Rice. New Haven, CT: Yale University Press, 1996.

Cunliffe, Marcus. *The Literature of the United States*. New York: Penguin Books, 1986.

Konkle, Lincoln. *Thornton Wilder and the Puritan Narrative Tradition*. Columbia: University of Missouri Press, 2006.

Will, George F. *(1941–)*

Political commentator, columnist, and amateur baseball historian, George F. Will is known for the way he imparts a conservative spin to his opinions about the intersection of American culture and politics in the late twentieth and early twenty-first centuries. Perhaps best known for his syndicated column in the *Washington Post*—for which he won the Pulitzer Prize for Commentary in 1977—and for his regular contributions to *Newsweek*, Will is also a frequent panelist on televised political commentary programs, such as ABC's *This Week*. As R. Emmett Tyrrell Jr. writes in his review of Will's collection of columns *The Leveling Wind: Politics, the Culture, and Other News, 1990–1994* (1994), "George F. Will has always been a sober, civilized man with serious political principles buttressed by wise historical thoughts."

Born in Champaign, Illinois, in 1941, Will received bachelor's degrees from Trinity College (1962) and Magdalene College of Oxford University (1964) and then obtained a master's degree and doctorate from Princeton University (1967). In 1974 he started his column in the *Washington Post* and, after achieving success, began to collect his newspaper and magazine columns and publish them as books. These collections include *The Pursuit of Happiness, and Other Sobering Thoughts* (1978), *The Pursuit of Virtue and Other Tory Notions* (1982), *The Morning After: American Successes and Excesses, 1981–1986* (1986), *Suddenly: The American Idea Abroad and at Home, 1986–1990* (1990), *With a Happy Eye But . . . : America and the World, 1997–2002* (2002), and *One Man's America: The Pleasures and Provocations of Our Singular Nation* (2008).

One of Will's biggest crusades has been against big government, notably as a supporter for term limitations for U.S. senators and representatives. Reflective of public frustration with the American political system during the 1980s and 1990s, he consistently pushed for term limits, believing, as Peter Knupfer notes in the *Journal of American History*, that these limits will "restore democratic institutions to deliberative processes and to leadership by public-spirited amateurs" who were more interested in the public good than in political careers. Will's writings on term limits are found in numerous columns and in one book, *Restoration: Congress, Term Limits, and the Recovery of Deliberative Democracy* (1992).

Although Will generally adopts a conservative position, he is by no means a typical Republican looking to either weaken government or weaken the Democratic Party. As a self-styled conservative, he has reshaped the way people view the spectrum of American political thought by insisting that conservatives move away from narrow self-interest toward an interest in the public good. Will's thought has urged conservatives to reconsider their assumptions and adopt ideas steeped in the "tradition of U.S. socio-political thought: the relation of individuals to the larger community, the ways of nurturing a dynamic democracy and the proper role of government," in the words of Marilyn Thie in *America*. From this position, Will has written many columns on what he sees as wasteful government spending, government inefficiency, and political gridlock. He has come to believe one of the biggest problems for American culture is the public's heavy reliance on—and demands on—its government. If the government is misfiring in itself, then its ability to serve the public is highly problematic, Will believes.

Will has continued his political commentary into the twenty-first century, though not without creating controversy over his views on social issues, the economy, and political candidates, both Democrat and Republican. Despite some criticism, he remains one of the most influential and popular journalists and political commentators of his time.

Beyond his primary focus on politics and American culture, Will has also written about a range of subjects, including pornography, journalistic ethics, advertising, the environment, and especially the game of baseball. Relating the myths of American life, such as the American dream and the great American pastime, to the realities of contemporary American life remains one of his contributions to cultural discourse. Besides several columns for a variety of periodicals, his book publications on the myths of American baseball include *Men at Work: The Craft of Baseball* (1990) and *Bunts: Curt Flood, Camden Yards, Pete Rose, and Other Reflections on Baseball* (1998).

Randall McClure

SEE ALSO: *Baseball;* Newsweek*; The* Washington Post.

BIBLIOGRAPHY

Chappell, Larry W. *George F. Will*. New York: Twayne, 1997.

Knupfer, Peter. Review of *Restoration: Congress, Term Limits, and the Recovery of Deliberative Democracy*, by George F. Will. *Journal of American History* 81, no. 1 (1994): 355–356.

Thie, Marilyn. "Suddenly: The American Idea Abroad and at

Home, 1986–1990 by George F. Will." *America*, June 8, 1991, 628–630.

Tyrrell, R. Emmett, Jr. "Alone Again, Naturally—*The Leveling Wind* by George F. Will." *National Review*, January 23, 1995, 64.

Will & Grace

The situation comedy *Will & Grace* ran on NBC from 1998 to 2006 and became the first successful mainstream American television series to feature openly gay characters. From 2001 to 2005 it was the highest-rated comedy in the coveted eighteen-to-forty-nine age group, drawing critical praise for its mixture of sophisticated banter, broad comedy, and creative characterization. At the same time, however, the show drew criticism from some in the gay community for its lack of political engagement.

Lead characters Will Truman (Eric McCormack) and Grace Adler (Debra Messing) began dating in college but broke off their relationship when Will revealed his homosexuality. As the series begins, they meet by accident, renew their friendship, and end up sharing a stylish New York City apartment. Despite their very different personalities—Will is a hyper-orderly attorney, Grace a messy, impulsive interior designer—the two share a deep connection. While that connection provides them both with emotional support and companionship, it also causes difficulty when they try to form other relationships.

Their lives are further complicated by the antics of two supporting characters: Will's best friend Jack (Sean Hayes), a flamboyantly gay, perpetually unsuccessful actor, and Grace's assistant Karen (Megan Mullally), a wealthy, jaded, and frequently outrageous substance abuser. Jack and Karen also develop a close friendship, often collaborating in a variety of schemes. Over the show's eight seasons, other friends—along with Will's parents, Grace's mother, and Karen's maid—move in and out of the story line. In the show's finale, it is revealed that Will and Grace will separate and marry other people, while Karen and Jack end up living together as friends.

Although Grace has a series of on-screen dating relationships, Will's romantic life is rarely depicted, leading to the criticism that his sexual orientation is marginalized. In a 2008 essay in *Rethinking Society in the 21st Century*, Karin Quimby suggested that the series is deliberately structured so that audiences can read Will and Grace "simultaneously as a gay man/straight woman dyad *and* as an ideal heterosexual couple." The comfort and trust they enjoy contrasts dramatically with Karen's marriage—a complicated mixture of mutual exploitation and dysfunctional affection. Quimby speculated that *Will & Grace* may reflect "straight women's dissatisfaction with the norms of masculinity and the kinds of relationships that such gendered conventions demand."

As Kathleen Battles and Wendy Hilton-Morrow pointed out in their piece in *Critical Studies in Media Communication*, *Will & Grace* made "the topic of homosexuality more palatable to a large, mainstream television audience by situating it within safe and familiar popular culture conventions, particularly those of the situation comedy genre." Some commentators have applauded this normalized depiction of gay characters, while others have criticized the series for avoiding issues such as gay marriage and homophobia. In the end, however, it was not social issues that made *Will & Grace* a classic of television comedy, but brilliant performances (all four principal actors earned Emmy Awards) and consistently clever writing.

Cynthia Giles

SEE ALSO: *Emmy Awards; Gay and Lesbian Marriage; Gay and Lesbian Press; Gay Liberation Movement; Gay Men; Sitcom; Television.*

BIBLIOGRAPHY

Battles, Kathleen, and Wendy Hilton-Morrow. "Gay Characters in Conventional Spaces: *Will & Grace* and the Situation Comedy Genre." *Critical Studies in Media Communication* 19, no. 1 (2002): 87–105.

Colucci, Jim. *Will & Grace: Fabulously Uncensored.* New York: Time Home Entertainment, 2004.

Quimby, Karin. "*Will & Grace*: Negotiating (Gay) Marriage on Prime-Time Television." In *Rethinking Society in the 21st Century: Critical Readings in Sociology*, ed. Michelle Webber and Kate Bezanson. Toronto: Canadian Scholars' Press, 2008.

will.i.am *(1975–)*

will.i.am is a rapper, singer, songwriter, producer, dancer, and actor who is best known as the front man and producer of the Black Eyed Peas, a wildly successful six-time Grammy Award–winning pop hip-hop group. The group is known for promoting a "don't worry, be happy" attitude through infectious electro-rap complemented by danceable urban pop beats. The Black Eyed Peas have sold more than 18 million albums worldwide, and will.i.am has also had a successful solo career.

Born William James Adams Jr. and raised in Estrada Courts, a public housing project in the largely Latino neighborhood of Boyle Heights in Los Angeles, will.i.am was encouraged to be an independent thinker by his mother, Debra Cain, a single parent. As a teenager, Adams attended Palisades Charter High School, one of the most highly ranked public high schools in the Los Angeles area. He began using the stage name Will 1X and performing in clubs with apl.de.ap (Allan Lindo) when he was a teenager. Augmented by three additional performers, Mookie Mook, DJ Motiv8 (Monroe Walker), and Dante Santiago, Will 1X and apl.de.ap formed the socially conscious rap group Atban Klann and soon caught the ear of Eazy-E, a Compton, California, rapper.

Eazy-E signed Atban Klann to his Ruthless Records label, and the group began working on an album called *Grass Roots*. Due to Eazy-E's untimely death in 1995, however, *Grass Roots* was never released. The group changed names twice, first to the Black-Eyed Pods and finally, in 1997, to the Black Eyed Peas. Four performers constituted the final incarnation of the Black Eyed Peas: will.i.am, apl.de.ap, Fergie, and Taboo.

After releasing two Black Eyed Peas albums—1998's *Behind the Front* and 2000's *Bridging the Gap*—will.i.am recorded his first solo release, 2001's *Lost Change. Lost Change* fuses aspects of jazz, electronica, funk, Caribbean, and trip-hop beats. As a solo performer will.i.am went on to release the albums *Must B 21* and *Songs about Girls* plus more than twenty singles featuring collaborations with a diverse group of artists ranging from Sergio Mendes to Snoop Dogg. "T.H.E. (The Hardest Ever)," featuring Mick Jagger and Jennifer Lopez, was the official lead single from *#willpower*, will.i.am's fourth solo album, released in 2012. In addition to his solo albums and collaborative singles, will.i.am also recorded "To Own It" as a promotional ad for the launch of Oprah Winfrey's OWN television network.

Throughout his musical career will.i.am has taken every opportunity to explore his lifelong interest in video games, robotics, and the relationship between music and technology. He served as game developer for *The Black Eyed Peas Experience*, a music video game featuring a number of hits by the Black Eyed Peas. It was released in 2011 to mixed reviews. In January 2011 will.i.am was appointed director of creative innovation at Intel Corporation. Soon after that he was selected as a top digital creative executive by *Advertising Age* in the magazine's annual digital innovators issue. He was also the creator and executive producer of *i.am FIRST: Science Is Rock and Roll*, a back-to-school primetime TV special that aired on ABC on August 14, 2011. Alongside his musical accomplishments and forays into the tech industry, will.i.am has landed numerous movie roles. His acting credits include *Rio*, *X-Men Origins: Wolverine*, and *Madagascar: Escape 2 Africa*.

While the Black Eyed Peas celebrate a positive message in their music, the group has never been overtly political. As a solo artist, however, will.i.am delved into sociopolitical themes in his music before and after the 2008 presidential election. Several tributes to Senator Barack Obama and his campaign to be elected the first African American president were composed by rappers, including Common's "The People" and Nas's "Black President," but will.i.am's support was unparalleled. He released five Obama-inspired singles before and after the election, including a track on the official inauguration album *Change Is Now: Renewing America's Promise*. One of the singles, "Yes We Can," featured a music video that showed the song's lyrics, which had been excerpted from a speech Obama had given on January 8, 2008. The video went viral and helped advance support for Obama. The subsequent four singles were "We Are the Ones," "It's a New Day," "America's Song," and "The Jackass Song," a collaboration with Kanye West. In 2011 the State Department tapped will.i.am to organize the 100,000 Strong Initiative Concert in Beijing to encourage cultural and educational exchanges between the United States and China.

will.i.am's generosity extends to a number of philanthropic causes. He created the i.am.scholarship in partnership with the College Track program, an academic mentoring program for high school students; he cofounded the Peapod Foundation with the Black Eyed Peas; he regularly performs benefit concerts for the Robin Hood Foundation; and he put on the TRANS4M Boyle Heights benefit concert to fund scholarships for students in Boyle Heights and other Los Angeles neighborhoods.

Willie R. Collins

SEE ALSO: *Black Eyed Peas; Grammy Awards; Hip-Hop; Lopez, Jennifer; Obama, Barack; Rap; Television; Video Games; West, Kanye; Winfrey, Oprah.*

BIBLIOGRAPHY

Chang, Jeff. "The Tipping Point." *Vibe*, November 2008, 91–97.

Hiatt, Brian. "Another Side of Will.i.am." *Rolling Stone*, November 1, 2007, 32.

Ratliff, Ben; Jon Pareles; Jon Caramanica; et al. "The Peas and What Follows 'E.N.D.'" *New York Times*, November 29, 2010.

Serpick, Evan. "Will.i.am." *Rolling Stone*, April 19, 2007, 20.

Williams, Andy *(1927–)*

One of the great middle-of-the-road singers of the mid-twentieth century, Andy Williams is among the few whose popularity survived the onset of rock and roll in the 1950s. Howard Andrew Williams was born in the small town of Wall Lake, Iowa. At age eight he joined his three brothers in the Williams Brothers Quartet. The group performed in the church choir before hitting it big with its first professional gig when Williams was in the third grade. After that, the brothers enjoyed success on the radio in nearby Des Moines, Iowa. The family relocated several times to facilitate the Williams Brothers' obtaining new radio contracts. At various times they lived in Des Moines; Chicago; Cincinnati, Ohio; and Southern California.

In 1947 the foursome teamed up with Kay Thompson. They played a wide variety of clubs over the next several years, including a tour of Europe, before disbanding in 1951. The brothers then went their separate ways professionally. Williams landed a regular job on Steve Allen's *The Tonight Show* in 1953, singing and taking part in Allen's manic clowning five nights a week. From 1962 to 1967 and again from 1969 to 1971, Williams had his own highly successful series on NBC called, fit-

Andy Williams. *Andy Williams's mellow voice and affable persona brought him success as a recording artist, television personality, and live performer.* MICHAEL OCHS ARCHIVES/GETTY IMAGES.

tingly enough, *The Andy Williams Show*. At various times his supporting cast included Dick Van Dyke, Jonathan Winters, Ray Stevens, and the Osmond Brothers. His program was noteworthy in that Williams was always willing to have competing singers—major personalities such as Bobby Darin or Robert Goulet—make guest appearances on his show.

Williams's recording career, benefiting from his national exposure on the *The Tonight Show*, was a hit from the start. He recorded for the Cadence label until 1962, when he switched to the larger Columbia Records. His recording career had actually started much earlier, however, in 1944, when he was picked to sing "Swingin' on a Star" with Bing Crosby. Williams had several hit singles in the 1950s, including "Canadian Sunset" and "The Hawaiian Wedding Song." His version of "Butterfly" was the number one record in America for three weeks in the spring of 1957.

The song most closely identified with Williams, 1961's "Moon River," was never a hit for him. However, it so perfectly suited his smooth voice and mellow delivery that it became his signature song and served as his television theme from 1962 onward. His popularization of the Henry Mancini–written "Moon River" (from *Breakfast at Tiffany's*) was not lost on the composer; Williams was invited to sing the theme for the 1963 film *Days of Wine and Roses*, another Mancini work. Williams's LP of the same name was a top-selling album of 1963. Major hits were rare for Williams after that year, his last being the theme from *Love Story* in 1970. His albums, television work, and live concerts all remained quite successful.

Williams became a noted collector of art in the late 1950s. He has built a well-regarded private collection of impressionist and modern paintings in his Manhattan home. In 1961 he married a nineteen-year-old Folies-Bergère showgirl, Claudine Longet. She unsuccessfully pursued careers in music and acting for years. The two separated in 1969 and divorced in 1975. The following year Longet fatally shot her longtime lover, professional skier Spider Sabich, in their Colorado home. Williams, who remained close to his ex-wife after the breakup of their marriage, was publicly supportive of Longet throughout her trial and the attendant media circus.

In addition to his highly rated variety program, Williams is known for hosting numerous seasonal television specials. He is an avid golfer and hosted the annual Andy Williams Open golf tournament for many years. In 1992 he opened his own theater, the Andy Williams Moon River Theatre, in Branson, Missouri. It is one of the more popular attractions in Branson, providing live music shows, including an annual Christmas show, for many of the millions of tourists who visit each year. In 2007 Williams opened the Moon River Grill restaurant in Branson.

David Lonergan

SEE ALSO: *Allen, Steve;* Breakfast at Tiffany's*; Crosby, Bing; Mancini, Henry; Stevens, Ray;* The Tonight Show*; Van Dyke, Dick; Winters, Jonathan.*

BIBLIOGRAPHY

Brooks, Tim, and Earle Marsh. *The Complete Directory to Prime Time Network and Cable TV Shows*, 6th ed. New York: Ballantine Books, 1995.

Hemming, Roy, and David Hajdu. *Discovering Great Singers of Classic Pop: A New Listener's Guide to the Sounds and Lives of the Top Performers and Their Recordings, Movies, and Videos*. New York: Newmarket Press, 1999.

LaBlanc, Michael, L. *Contemporary Musicians: Profiles of the People in Music, Vol. 2*. Detroit, MI: Gale Research, 1990.

Whitburn, Joel. *The Billboard Book of Top 40 Hits*, 6th ed. New York: Billboard Books, 1996.

Williams, Bert *(1874–1922)*

Known during his lifetime as "the funniest man in America," Egbert "Bert" Austin Williams enjoyed fame as the straight man and ballad singer of the African American comedy team of Williams and Walker. Together, the two men became one of the best-known acts of musical comedy during the early twentieth century.

Williams met his partner, George Walker, in San Francisco in 1893, when he began performing in order to finance his studies at Stanford University. They worked their way to New York, where in 1896 they appeared in Victor Herbert's *Gold Bug*. The two performed in such musical comedy hits as *The Sons of Ham* (1900), *In Dahomey* (1902), *Abyssinia* (1906), and *Bandanna Land* (1908). When Walker retired, Williams starred in *Mr. Lode of Koal* (1909), then performed with Florenz Ziegfeld's *Follies* from 1910 to 1919. In 1920 Williams joined fellow entertainer Eddie Cantor in *Broadway Brevities*.

Williams was admired for impeccable comedic timing and pantomimes. He died in 1922 after opening in *Under the Bamboo Tree*.

Susan Curtis

SEE ALSO: *Broadway; Cantor, Eddie; The Musical; Vaudeville; Walker, Aida Overton; Walker, George;* The Ziegfeld Follies.

BIBLIOGRAPHY

Charters, Ann. *Nobody: The Story of Bert Williams*. New York: Macmillan, 1970.

Phillips, Caryl. *Dancing in the Dark*. New York: Knopf, 2005.

Riis, Thomas L. *Just before Jazz: Black Musical Theater in New York, 1890–1915*. Washington, DC: Smithsonian Institution Press, 1989.

Smith, Eric Lidell. *Bert Williams: A Biography of the Pioneer Black Comedian*. Jefferson, NC: McFarland, 1992.

Williams, Hank, Jr. *(1949–)*

Perhaps no one has ever been simultaneously such a major star and so much in the shadow of his father as Hank Williams Jr. As an eight-year-old, Williams began his career as an imitator of his deceased father, who was still the biggest name in country music at the time. Ultimately trading on the fact that his name made it impossible for the country establishment to reject him, he became perhaps the most significant force in bringing rock music into country.

Williams was a prime example of an industry that has never been ashamed of exploitation. Between the ages of eight and fourteen, he played fifty shows a year, singing his father's songs. By the time he was in his midteens, he was signed to MGM Records, his father's old label, and he was recording overdubbed duets with his father; he even overdubbed the singing for George Hamilton in *Your Cheatin' Heart*, a movie biography of Hank Sr. By the time he was in his late teens, Williams was drinking heavily; he says he felt utterly trapped inside a musical world that was making less and less sense to him. He was listening to the rock and roll of his generation—Chuck Berry, Fats Domino, and Elvis Presley—and thinking about the kind of music he really wanted to play.

In 1974, with his first marriage breaking up, Williams attempted suicide. As part of his recovery, he left Nashville and moved to Alabama. He began to work seriously on developing his own music. In 1975, after finishing work on the landmark country rock album *Hank Williams, Jr. & Friends*, he took a vacation in Montana and suffered a devastating accident: a near-fatal fall down a mountain virtually tore his face off.

After extensive physical therapy and plastic surgery to reconstruct his face, Williams returned to music with an absolute determination to create his own rock-oriented sound. A new country audience—one that had opened up to the "outlaw" sounds of Willie Nelson and Waylon Jennings—was ready for him. After a few modest successes, the highest-charting being his cover version of Bobby Fuller's "I Fought the Law," he reached his stride in 1979 with a song that looked back at the past yet snarled with the beat and attitude of rock. The song was "Family Tradition," and it was highly autobiographical. In it Williams is asked, "Why do you drink / Why do you roll smoke / And why do you live out the songs that you wrote?" Williams responds that he is simply carrying on a family tradition.

"Family Tradition" proved to be a winning formula for Williams; many of his subsequent hits were autobiographical. In one, he asks an operator to put him through to Cloud Number Nine so he can talk to his father. In "All My Rowdy Friends Have Settled Down," he remembers the wildness of Nashville in the 1970s. Established as a major star in his own right by the mid-1980s, he was able to use his preoccupation with his father and his family history to successfully record Hank Williams Sr. hits like "Honky Tonkin'." In 1987 he even performed a duet with his father on a newly discovered unreleased recording of "There's a Tear in My Beer." Williams also released a video duet, in which his image is inserted into an old kinescope of his father. Since Williams Sr. had never performed "There's a Tear in My Beer" for the cameras, a film was used in which he sings "Hey, Good Lookin'" with his mouth electronically doctored to lip-synch the words of the other song.

Williams continued to be a major force in bringing rock into country and making it an important part of the new country sound. In his semi-anthemic 1988 hit "Young Country," he reminds his listeners that "We [the new generation of country performers] like old Waylon, and we know Van Halen." At the time this was a significant statement and one that it took a child of traditional country like Williams to make. A few years later the rockers themselves had become the country music establishment, with megastars like Garth Brooks modeling himself on arena rockers like Journey.

Williams seemed to settle into the role of middle-aged country establishment figure in the 1990s and the first decade of the 2000s. His theme song for *Monday Night Football* earned him four Emmy Awards and constant exposure. In 2011 Williams made news when he compared President Barack Obama to Adolf Hitler on national television. ESPN subsequently stopped using his theme song for *Monday Night Football*.

Tad Richards

SEE ALSO: *Alternative Country Music; Berry, Chuck; Brooks, Garth; Country Music; Domino, Fats; Emmy Awards; ESPN; Jennings, Waylon;* Monday Night Football*; Nelson, Willie; Obama, Barack; Presley, Elvis; Rock and Roll; Suicide; Van Halen; Williams, Hank, Sr.*

BIBLIOGRAPHY

Schick, Elizabeth A. *Current Biography Yearbook, 1999*. New York: H.W. Wilson, 1998.

Williams, Hank, Jr., and Michael Bane. *Living Proof: An Autobiography*. New York: Putnam, 1979.

Williams, Hank, Sr. *(1923–1953)*

Widely acknowledged as the father of contemporary country music, Hank Williams Sr. was a superstar at the age of twenty-five and dead at twenty-nine. Like Jimmie Rodgers, Williams had a short but highly influential career in country music. Though he never learned to read or write music, during his years of greatest commercial success Williams wrote and recorded more than 100 polished, unique, and lasting songs, releasing at least half a dozen hit records every year from 1949 until 1953. His direct, sincere, and emotional lyrics ("Your cheatin' heart / Will make you weep / You'll cry and cry / And try to sleep") set the stage for much of the country music that followed, and many of his songs, including "Cold, Cold Heart" and "Your Cheatin' Heart," have become classics.

Williams's ability to transfix his audiences is the stuff of legend. Chet Hagan's *Grand Ole Opry* offers the following assessments: Little Jimmy Dickens said that "You could hear a pin drop when Hank was working. He just seemed to hypnotize those people. It was simplicity, I guess. He brought his people with him. He put himself on their level." Minnie Pearl said, "He had a real animal magnetism. He destroyed the women in the audience. And he was just as authentic as rain." And according to Mitch Miller (a Columbia Records executive), "He had a way of reaching your guts and your head at the same time." Williams had the unique ability to connect with his audiences, composed primarily of poor, white southerners like himself, and, particularly in the early days, fist fights often broke out among his female fans.

HIS EARLY YEARS

Born and raised in Alabama, Williams got a guitar at the age of eight and learned to play and sing from a blues street performer known as "Tee Tot." This early exposure to African American blues styles shaped his own musical character, forming a key element of Williams's trademark honky-tonk, country-blues sound. When he was twelve years old Williams won $15 in a songwriting contest with his "WPA Blues." By fourteen he had organized his own band and had begun playing locally for hoedowns, square dances, and the like. In 1941 Williams and his band the Drifting Cowboys started performing at a radio station, most often covering the songs of other country artists, including Williams's hero, Roy Acuff. Despite attempts to make a name for himself and his band, his musical career stayed in a holding pattern for several years.

In 1946 Williams went to Nashville, Tennessee, with his wife and manager, Audrey, where a music publishing executive for Acuff-Rose Publishing set up a recording session for Williams with Sterling Records. The two singles he recorded then, "Never Again" (released in late 1946) and "Honky Tonkin'" (released in early 1947) were quite successful, rising to the top of the country music charts and breaking Williams's career out of its holding pattern. Williams signed the first exclusive songwriter's contract issued by Acuff-Rose Publishing, and he began a long and productive songwriting partnership with Fred Rose, with Williams writing the songs and Rose editing them.

In 1947 Williams won a contract with Metro-Goldwyn-Mayer (MGM) Records. "Move It on Over," his first MGM single, was a big hit, and Williams and the Drifting Cowboys began appearing regularly on *KWKH Louisiana Hayride*, a popular radio program. Several other releases followed, and Williams became a huge country music star. Already earning a reputation as a hard-drinking, womanizing man, he had trouble being accepted by the country music establishment, and Ernest Tubb's attempts to get the Grand Ole Opry to sign him on were initially rebuffed for fear that he would be too much trouble. He was finally asked to join the Opry in 1949 and earned an unprecedented six encores after singing the old country-blues standard "Lovesick Blues" at a 1949 Opry performance.

Strings of hit singles in 1949 and 1950 (including "Lovesick Blues," "Mind Your Own Business," and "Wedding Bells" in 1949 and "Long Gone Lonesome Blues," "Moaning the Blues," and "Why Don't You Love Me" in 1950) led to sellout shows for Williams and the reorganized Drifting Cowboys, earning Williams and the band more than $1,000 per performance. From 1949 through 1953 he scored twenty-seven Top 10 hits. During this period Williams began recording religious material (both music and recitations) under the name Luke the Drifter, and he managed to keep his drinking and womanizing in check.

CROSSOVER SUCCESS AND PERSONAL PROBLEMS

In 1951 Tony Bennett had a hit single with a cover of Williams's "Cold, Cold Heart," and other singers began recording (and having hits) with Williams's songs: Jo Stafford recorded "Jambalaya," Rosemary Clooney sang "Half as Much," and both Frankie Laine and Stafford covered "Hey Good Lookin'." As a result Williams began to enjoy crossover success on the popular music charts, appearing on the Perry Como television show and touring as part of a package group that included Bob Hope, Jack Benny, and Pearl. Though not all of his hit records were his own compositions, many of his best-known works were ones he wrote, and many of them seem to have an autobiographical bent.

Williams's professional success began to take a toll on his private life. His longtime tendency to drink to excess became full-blown alcoholism. Williams began showing up to concerts drunk and abusive. As a result he was fired from the Grand Ole Opry and told to return when he was sober. Rather than taking the Opry's action as a wake-up call, Williams drank even more heavily. An accident reinflamed an old back injury, and he began abusing the morphine he was prescribed to deal with back pain. His marriage fell apart, in part due to his drinking and drug abuse and in part due to his increasingly frequent dalliances with other women. In 1952, after divorcing Audrey, he quickly married a nineteen-year-old divorcée named Billie Jean, selling tickets to what was billed as a matinee "wedding rehearsal" and "actual wedding" that evening (both were frauds; Billie Jean and Williams had been legally married the previous day). Williams also came under the spell of a man calling himself "Doctor" Toby Marshall (actually a paroled forger), who often supplied him with prescriptions and shots for the sedative chloral hydrate, which Marshall claimed was a pain reliever.

In December 1952 Williams suffered a heart attack brought on by alcoholic cardiomyopathy (heart disease due to excessive drinking); found in the back seat of his car, he was rushed to the hospital but was pronounced dead on January 1, 1953. His funeral, held at a city auditorium in Montgomery, Alabama, was attended by more than 25,000 weeping fans. After his death his record company continued to issue a number of singles he had previously recorded, including what is probably his most famous song, "Your Cheatin' Heart." These singles earned a great deal of money for his record company and his estate, and artists as diverse as Johnny Cash and Elvis Costello have made their own recordings of Williams's songs. Many of those associated with Williams attempted to trade on his reputation after his death. Both of his wives went on tour, performing as "Mrs. Hank Williams." A supposedly biographical film, *Your Cheatin' Heart*, also exploited his fame and untimely death. Williams's children, Jett and Hank Jr., went into country music and have enjoyed some success (particularly Hank "Bocephus" Williams Jr.).

But it is Hank Sr. who left his mark on country music. Along with Rodgers and Fred Rose, he was one of the first inductees into Nashville's Country Music Hall of Fame, elected in 1961. In 2010 he received a posthumous Pulitzer Prize for his lifetime achievement as a songwriter. The award cited "his craftsmanship as a songwriter who expressed universal feelings with poignant simplicity and played a pivotal role in transforming country music into a major musical and cultural force in American life."

Deborah M. Mix

SEE ALSO: *Bennett, Tony; Benny, Jack; Cash, Johnny; Clooney, Rosemary; Como, Perry; Costello, Elvis;* Grand Ole Opry; *Hope, Bob; MGM (Metro-Goldwyn-Mayer); Pearl, Minnie; Rodgers, Jimmie; Williams, Hank, Jr.*

BIBLIOGRAPHY

Escott, Colin; George Merritt; and William MacEwen. *Hank Williams: The Biography*, rev. ed. New York: Back Bay Books, 2004.

Hagan, Chet. *Grand Ole Opry: The Complete Story of a Great American Institution and Its Stars.* New York: Holt, 1989.

Williams, Hank, Sr. *The Complete Hank Williams.* Polygram Records, 1998. Three discs.

Williams, Roger M. *Sing a Sad Song: The Life of Hank Williams.* Urbana: University of Illinois Press, 1981.

Williams, Robin *(1951–)*

With his manic versatility, comedic genius Robin Williams defined comedy during the late twentieth and early twenty-first centuries. Whether expressing himself as a stand-up comic or as an animated genie or a cross-dressing nanny, Williams was without equal in the field of American comedy. Much more

Robin Williams. *Robin Williams has parlayed his manic stand-up style and versatility as an actor into a successful television and film career.* HARRY LANGDON/GETTY IMAGES.

than a funnyman, however, he has been recognized for his fine work was a dramatic actor. He has brought humanity and warmth to a cast of characters ranging from a crazed widower in *The Fisher King* (1991) to a sad but optimistic psychiatrist in *Good Will Hunting* (1997), which won him an Academy Award for Best Supporting Actor. Williams remains one of the hardest-working entertainers in show business. He has expanded his range to include dark, unsympathetic characters, but it is his comedic roles that allow him to shine and provide him with opportunities for winning over a new generation of fans.

Williams was born on July 21, 1951, in Chicago, to a father who was a Ford Motor Company executive and a mother who was a former model engaged in charity work. While both parents had sons by previous marriages, Williams essentially grew up as an only child. In interviews he has described his childhood as lonely and himself as shy and chubby. His father was stern and distant, and his mother was charming and busy. While Williams was close to his mother, she was often absent, leaving him to roam their forty-room home for diversion. He turned to humor as a way to attract attention. His interest in comedy was aroused by hours spent in front of the television, and he was particularly enthralled by late-night shows, where he became a fan of Jonathan Winters, another comic who was known for his improvisational skills.

In 1967 Williams's family moved to Tiburon, an affluent suburb of San Francisco. In the less inhibited atmosphere of California, Williams blossomed. When his father steered him toward a career in business, Williams rebelled. His innate comedic skills were honed in college, but he chose to leave two schools without finishing. Receiving a scholarship, he then entered the prestigious Juilliard School in New York, where he roomed with actor Christopher Reeve, who remained a close friend until his death in 2004. While the other students found Williams's off-the-wall antics hilarious, his professors were unsure of how to handle such frenetic humor. Leaving Juilliard without graduating, Williams returned to California and appeared in comedy clubs such as the Improv and the Comedy Store.

MORK & MINDY

By the mid-1970s Williams had guest-starred on several television shows, including *Saturday Night Live*, *Laugh-In*, and *The Richard Pryor Show*. In 1978 a guest appearance on *Happy Days* as the alien Mork from the planet Ork propelled him to stardom. He reportedly won the role of Mork by showing up at his audition in rainbow suspenders and standing on his head when asked to sit like an alien. The appearance was so successful that the character of Mork was given his own show, *Mork & Mindy* (1978–1982), which costarred Pam Dawber as the earthling who took in the stranded alien.

In retrospect, it is perhaps unlikely that anyone else could have played Mork with such zany innocence. Each week the television audience discovered their own planet through Mork's reports to Orkean leader Orson at show's end. Even though the characters of Mork and Mindy predictably fell in love and married, the birth of their first child was anything but predictable: Jonathan Winters as Mearth, who aged backward, was the surprising result of this intergalactic coupling. Even though Williams had so much control over the content of the show that it became known informally as "The Robin Williams Show," he often felt stifled by the confines of network television as a medium. He claimed in a 1998 *TV Guide* interview that he found salvation in his Home Box Office (HBO) cable channel specials that aired without censorship, giving him freedom to expand as a comic and solidify his position as a top-notch performer.

BIG-SCREEN CAREER

In 1980 Williams lent his talent to the big screen with *Popeye*, based on the heavily muscled, spinach-eating sailor from the comic strip of the same name. It was a disappointing debut. His performance in *The World According to Garp* in 1982 was better received, but it was evident that Williams's vast talents were not being properly utilized outside of television. He managed to hit his stride with *Moscow on the Hudson* in 1984, playing a Russian defector. Perhaps the character who came closest to his own personality was that of an outrageous disc jockey in *Good Morning, Vietnam* (1987), a role that earned him his first Academy Award nomination for Best Actor.

Drawing on his cross-generational appeal, Williams appeared in a series of films aimed at family audiences, such as *Hook* (1991), in which he played Peter Pan. Although the movie was criticized by some reviewers, the role allowed Williams to display his own split personality—that of the child who never quite grew up in the body of an adult burdened by the everyday cares of his world. He followed *Hook* with a delightful performance as the voice of Batty Koda in the animated environmental film *FernGully: The Last Rain Forest*.

COMEDY ROLES

The enormity of Williams's comedic range was more evident, however, in Disney's *Aladdin* (1992). As Genie, he managed to make the character memorable. Refusing to be confined by his large-chested blue blob of a body, Williams's Genie metamorphosed into a Scotsman, a dog, Arnold Schwarzenegger, Ed Sullivan, Groucho Marx, a waiter, a rabbit, a dinosaur, William F. Buckley Jr., Robert De Niro, a stewardess, a sheep, Pinocchio, Sebastian from *The Little Mermaid*, Arsenio Hall, Walter Brennan, Ethel Merman, Rodney Dangerfield, Jack Nicholson, and a one-man band. There was talk of an unheard-of Academy Award nomination for Best Actor for the portrayal of an animated character. Williams did, in fact, win a special Golden Globe Award for his vocal work in *Aladdin*.

Even though *Toys* (1992) received little attention, Williams followed it up with the blockbuster *Mrs. Doubtfire* (1993), in which he played the estranged husband of Sally Field and cross-dressed as a nanny in order to remain close to his three children. *Jumanji* (1995), a saga of characters trapped inside a board game, demonstrated a darker side to Williams. He returned to Disney and reprised the role of the genie in the straight-to-video *Aladdin and the King of Thieves* in 1996. His zany side was again much in evidence in *Flubber* (1997), a remake of the Disney classic *The Absent Minded Professor*. Before *Flubber*, Williams had returned to adult comedy with his uproarious portrayal of a gay father whose son is about to be married in *The Birdcage* (1996).

DRAMATIC ROLES

While comedy is the milieu in which Williams excelled, his dramatic abilities also won critical acclaim. The role of Parry in *The Fisher King* introduced a side to Williams that stunned audiences and critics alike. After Parry's wife is murdered in a random shooting at a restaurant, he descends into insanity from which he only occasionally emerges to search for his personal Holy Grail with the help of costar Jeff Bridges. He was nominated for an Academy Award for his portrayal of John Keating, a teacher at a conservative prep school who attempts to open the eyes of his students to the world of poetry and dreams in *Dead Poets Society* in 1989.

The role of Dr. Malcolm Sayer, a dedicated physician who temporarily restores life to catatonic patients in *Awakenings*, again demonstrated Williams's enormous versatility. In 1998 he won an Academy Award for Best Supporting Actor in the Matt Damon/Ben Affleck film *Good Will Hunting*, leading Damon's character to awkward acceptance of his own reality and mathematical genius. Williams followed that success with back-to-back roles in *What Dreams May Come* and *Patch Adams* in 1998. Afterward, he expressed a desire to modify his busy schedule and perhaps return to a weekly series.

The turn of the twenty-first century saw Williams voicing Dr. Know in director Steven Spielberg's *A.I. Artificial Intelligence* (2001) and playing a villain opposite Al Pacino and Hilary Swank in *Insomnia* (2002). Over the next several years, Williams divided his time between drama and comedy. In 2002 he played the deranged host of a children's show in *Death to Smoochy* and a stalker in *One Hour Photo*. That same year he returned to comedy with *Robin Williams: Live on Broadway*, for which he earned two Emmy Award nominations. He entertained American soldiers in Iraq in 2004 and appeared in the thriller *The Final Cut*. Two years later he returned to the thriller genre in *The Night Listener*.

CHILDREN'S FILMS

Williams continued working on kids' movies, lending his voice to animated films such as *Robots* (2005), *Everyone's Hero* (2006), *Happy Feet* (2006), and *Happy Feet Two* (2011). He appeared as President Teddy Roosevelt in *Night at the Museum* (2006) and *Night at the Museum: Battle of the Smithsonian* (2009), as the father of a dysfunctional family in *RV* (2006), and as a wizard in *August Rush* (2007) before romping through *Old Dogs* (2009) with his friend John Travolta. Williams also performed in comedies aimed at a more mature audience, including *The Big White* (2005), *Man of the Year* (2006), and *License to Wed* (2007). He appeared in a Bobcat Goldthwait vehicle, *World's Greatest Dad*, in 2009 and planned to continue his career in the film industry.

Personally, Williams has had highs and lows. As a young performer, he was well known for his heavy consumption of drugs and alcohol. Williams was forced to reexamine his life when his friend and fellow comic John Belushi died after spending an evening with him. Another setback occurred when his first marriage fell apart amid tabloid reports that he had left his wife for his son's nanny, Marsha Garces. Williams insisted that the marriage was over before he became involved with Garces, whom he subsequently married. The couple, who had two children, divorced in 2010. The following year Williams married Susan Schneider. Along with friends Billy Crystal and Whoopi Goldberg, he continues to labor diligently for Comic Relief, a charity for the homeless.

Elizabeth Rholetter Purdy

SEE ALSO: *Academy Awards; Belushi, John; Buckley, William F., Jr.; Damon, Matt; De Niro, Robert; Disney (Walt Disney Company); Field, Sally;* Laugh-In*; The Marx Brothers;* Mork & Mindy*; Nicholson, Jack; Pacino, Al; Popeye; Pryor, Richard;* Saturday Night Live*; Schwarzenegger, Arnold; Spielberg, Steven; Stand-Up Comedy; Travolta, John; Winters, Jonathan.*

BIBLIOGRAPHY

Corliss, Richard. "Aladdin's Magic." *Time*, November 9, 1992, 74.

David, Jay. *The Life and Humor of Robin Williams: A Biography*. New York: William Morrow, 1999.

Dougan, Andy Y. *Robin Williams*. New York: Thunder's Mouth Press, 1998.

Weeks, Janet. "Face to Face with Robin Williams." *TV Guide*, November 14, 1998, 16–20.

Zoglin, Richard. *Comedy at the Edge: How Stand-Up in the 1970s Changed America*. New York: Bloomsbury, 2008.

Williams, Ted *(1918–2002)*

Ted Williams, "The Splendid Splinter," was one of the best hitters of all time and is the last baseball player to hit over .400 in a season. His scientific view of hitting changed the dynamics of the game forever. He was also probably the least celebrated modern-day baseball hero. While he had the makings of stardom, he was unable to cultivate the following enjoyed by less talented but more amiable players, such as his contemporary Joe DiMaggio.

On August 30, 1918, Theodore Samuel Williams was born in San Diego, California, into a lower-middle-class family. His parents worked constantly, leaving him plenty of time to play baseball. When he was seventeen he signed with the hometown San Diego Padres. But after only one year he was sold to the Boston Red Sox.

EARLY CAREER

Williams proved himself immediately when he started for the Red Sox in 1939. He led the league with 145 runs batted in (RBIs), the first rookie—and the second-youngest player in history—to do so. In 1941 his batting average topped .406. Going into the last day of the season, Williams's average was .39955, which in baseball terms is a .400 batting average. Manager Joe Cronin gave his star the option to sit out the doubleheader, but he decided to play and went six for eight, raising his batting average to an incredible .406. His 1942 campaign earned him his first Triple Crown by hitting .356 with 137 RBIs and 36 home runs. Though he won the Triple Crown, he did not win the Most Valuable Player (MVP) Award that year.

Williams interrupted his baseball career in 1943 to enlist during World War II, and he spent three years stateside as a pilot. When he returned to baseball in 1946, the Red Sox had a talented postwar team and Williams had another outstanding season, winning his first MVP. Baseball also encountered the "Williams Shift" in 1946. Cleveland manager Lou Boudreau pushed the infielders to the right side of the field, trying to force the left-handed Williams to hit the ball the opposite way, which he refused to do. That year he also led Boston to their only World Series during his career, but the Red Sox lost and Williams's hitting was criticized by the media.

Williams's relationship with the media, always tumultuous, turned ugly after the 1946 season. The Boston press and many fans felt disenchanted with the temperamental superstar. He often went public with his anger, liked to spit, never tipped his cap to the fans or came out for curtain calls after home runs, and was candid about his dislike of the Boston sportswriters, who in turn criticized him in print. Williams rebounded after the World Series, and in 1947 he won his second Triple Crown but lost the MVP to DiMaggio. He closed the decade by winning the batting title in 1948 and winning his second MVP in 1949 while leading the league in runs, walks, RBIs, and hitting.

BASEBALL AND BEYOND

The 1950s were less kind to Williams. In 1950 he missed half the season with a broken arm. In 1952 he was recalled to fight in the Korean War, in which he survived a fiery plane crash. He came back to baseball in 1954 and earned batting titles in 1957 and in 1958, making him the oldest player in baseball history to do so. A pinched nerve in his neck caused him to hit a career low .254 in 1959 and made fans and Red Sox owner Tom Yawkey push for his retirement. But Williams came back to finish his career in 1960, hitting .316 with twenty-nine home runs, including one in his final at-bat.

Williams finished his baseball career with a .344 lifetime batting average, the highest on-base percentage in history at .483, 521 home runs, and the second-highest slugging average at .634. The *Sporting News* named Williams its Player of the Decade for the 1950s. He was inducted into the National Baseball Hall of Fame in 1966.

After his playing days were over Williams worked as the manager of the Washington Senators from 1969 to 1972. He also worked periodically as a batting coach. During his retirement in Florida he spent time pursuing his second-favorite sport, fishing, and in 2000 he was inducted into the International Game Fish Association Hall of Fame.

Williams had the stuff heroes were made of, even though his contemporaries believed otherwise. He served his country in two wars and was the most prolific hitter of his era. He changed the face of baseball with his scientific approach to hitting and forcing opposing managers to move their fielders. And today, when any player chases .400, Williams is the man to beat.

In his autobiography, *My Turn at Bat*, Williams states that when he walked down the street he dreamed people would say, "There goes Ted Williams, the greatest hitter who ever lived." While a case could be made for such a claim, Williams is less remembered than other more charismatic players. But he did receive some belated recognition: in 1991 the Boston Red Sox commemorated the fiftieth anniversary of the year he batted .400 by holding a Ted Williams day; the slugger uncharacteristically tipped his hat to the cheering fans. And the Ted Williams Museum and Hitters Hall of Fame opened in Hernando, Florida, in 1994. (In 2006 it was moved to Tropicana Field, home of the Tampa Bay Rays.)

Williams died July 5, 2002, at age eighty-three. After his death two of his children had his body frozen at a cryogenics facility in the hope that a cure for the heart disease that killed him might be found. The eldest Williams daughter protested the move because her father's will requested that he be cremated. The story received wide coverage in the press and was revisited in 2009 amid sensational reports that Williams's corpse had been beheaded and abused at the facility. The man who made those allegations later recanted them. For sports fans everywhere the seedy publicity was a sad way to remember a baseball legend.

Nathan R. Meyer

SEE ALSO: *Baseball; Baseball Cards; Boston Red Sox; DiMaggio, Joe; Major League Baseball; The* Sporting News*; Sports Heroes; World Series; World War II.*

BIBLIOGRAPHY

Linn, Edward. *Hitter: The Life and Turmoils of Ted Williams.* San Diego, CA: Harcourt Brace, 1994.

Montville, Leigh. *Ted Williams: The Biography of an American Hero.* New York: Doubleday, 2004.

Williams, Ted, and John Underwood. *The Science of Hitting.* New York: Simon & Schuster, 1986.

Williams, Ted, and John Underwood. *My Turn at Bat: The Story of My Life.* New York: Simon & Schuster, 1988.

Wolff, Rick. *Ted Williams.* New York: Chelsea House, 1993.

Williams, Tennessee *(1911–1983)*

American playwright and screenwriter Tennessee Williams was regarded in his literary prime with equal measures of esteem and suspicion. Williams, along with Eugene O'Neill, was among the first playwrights to gain international respect for the emerging American dramatic genre. Williams excelled at creating richly realized characters imbued with humor and poignancy. Always casual with fact, the playwright shone in an era that adored celebrity and encouraged excess.

Tennessee Williams was born Thomas Lanier Williams on March 26, 1911, in Columbus, Mississippi. His mother, Edwina

Tennessee Williams. *Tennessee Williams poses in his office in 1956. Williams rose to international fame with the 1951 release of the film version of his stage play* A Streetcar Named Desire. ALFRED EISENSTAEDT/TIME LIFE PICTURES/GETTY IMAGES.

Dakin Williams, who was born in Ohio, imagined herself to be a southern belle. His father, Cornelius Coffin Williams, was a rough man with a fine southern pedigree. Cornelius was absent for long periods throughout Williams's childhood and repeatedly moved the family from town to town. Williams was sickly as a child and Edwina insisted that he focus on Shakespeare rather than sports, which fostered his interest in literature.

Tennessee Williams's work resonated deeply with the performing arts community of the 1940s. His complex characterization and difficult subject matter appealed to a new generation of actors. The 1947 Broadway production of *A Streetcar Named Desire* featured then-unknown actors Marlon Brando, Jessica Tandy, and Karl Malden, all of whom were trained in method acting, a new technique that stressed empathizing with one's character to create a realistic psychological portrayal. Actors trained in the method technique quickly discovered that Williams's work stripped bare an American culture of repression and denial. A close-knit circle of performers, directors, and writers gathered around the temperamental southern playwright. Williams preferred certain personalities to be involved with his projects, including actors Montgomery Clift and Maureen Stapleton, directors Elia Kazan and Stella Adler, and a cheerfully competitive group of writers including Truman Capote, Gore Vidal, and William Inge.

The 1951 film version of *A Streetcar Named Desire* brought both Williams and his actors instant fame. Lines from the film have entered into the popular lexicon, from Blanche's pitiful ironies ("I have always depended on the kindness of strangers") to Stanley's scream in the New Orleans night ("Stella!"). More than any other of Williams's screenplays, *A Streetcar Named Desire*'s lines resurface today in the most unlikely places, from advertisements to television sitcoms; the public often recognizes these phrases without having seen the production at all.

Williams's works pair misfortune and loneliness with gracefully lyrical speech and grapple with a repressed culture emerging from Victorian mores. Social commentary is present in most of his works, but the focus is on the poetry of human interaction, with its composite failings, hopes, and eccentricities. His early works, such as *Me, Vashya!*, whose villain is a tyrannical munitions maker, were bluntly political in nature. After *The Glass Menagerie*, however, Williams found he had a talent for creating real, vivid characters. Figures in his plays often struggle for identity and an awakened sense of sensuality with little to show for the effort. The roles of victim and victimizer are exchanged between intertwined couples, as with Alexandra and Chance in *Sweet Bird of Youth*. The paralyzing fear of mortality, so often an issue for his characters, plagues Mrs. Goforth of *The Milk Train Doesn't Stop Here Anymore*. Most significantly, perhaps, characters like Shannon of *The Night of the Iguana*, one of Williams's late plays, sometimes find peace of spirit after they can lose little else. Arthur Miller once declared Williams's most enduring theme to be "the romance of the lost yet sacred misfits, who exist in order to remind us of our trampled instincts, our forsaken tenderness, the holiness of the spirit of man."

The relationship between Williams's work and popular culture is long and varied. Many of his plays, including *The Glass Menagerie*, *A Streetcar Named Desire*, *Cat on a Hot Tin Roof*, *Sweet Bird of Youth*, and *The Night of the Iguana,* became major films of the 1950s and 1960s. These films were immediately popular with mainstream audiences despite their focus on the darker elements of American society, including pedophilia, venereal disease, domestic violence, and rape. Williams was one of the first American dramatists to introduce problematic and challenging content on a broad level. Some of the playwright's subplots border on sensationalism, with scenes of implied cannibalism and castration. Consequently Williams had the curious distinction of being one of the most-censored writers of the 1960s; *Baby Doll*, *Suddenly Last Summer*, and other films were thoroughly revised by producers before general release. The modern paradigm of film studios that celebrate their authors' fame while revising their content is embodied in Metro-Goldwyn-Mayer's treatment of Williams's work. The studio produced his films but at the same time censored him, fearing that audiences would find his subject matter too provocative.

Williams nurtured a public persona that gradually shifted from shy to flamboyantly homosexual in an era reluctant to accept gay men. Williams's fears of audience backlash against his personal life gradually proved groundless. Even late in life, however, Williams was reluctant to embrace a political agenda. *Gay Sunshine* magazine declared in 1976 that the playwright had never dealt openly with the politics of gay liberation, and Williams—always adept with the press—immediately responded, "People so wish to latch onto something didactic; I do not deal with the didactic, ever . . . I wish to have a broad audience because the major thrust of my work is not sexual orientation, it's social. I'm not about to limit myself to writing about gay people" (quoted in Leverich). As is so often the case with Williams, the statement is both true and untrue—his great midcareer plays focus upon relationships rather than politics, but the figure of the gay male appears in his characters both explicitly (Charlus in *Camino Real*) and implicitly (Brick in *Cat on a Hot Tin Roof*) throughout his works.

Williams was known for taking a casual approach toward the hard facts of his life. In the early period of his fame, Williams intrigued audiences by implying that characters like Tom (Thomas Lanier) in *The Glass Menagerie* represented his own experiences. Kazan, a director whose success was often linked to Williams, promoted the Williams myth once by declaring that "everything in his life is in his plays, and everything in his plays is in his life." Williams's connection with the outside world was often one of gentrified deceit, which began early in his life as the Williams family sought to hide his sister's schizophrenia and eventual lobotomy. Scholars including Lyle Leverich have documented the close blend of reality and art and the playwright's attachment to his sister, Rose Williams. The connection between Rose and Tennessee Williams was profound, and images of her mental illness and sexual abuse often surface in Williams's most poignant characters. Roses appear as a complex symbol in his plays, the flower indicative alternately of strength, passion, and fragility.

The 1970s saw a gradual decline in Williams's artistic skill, but he continued to tinker with the older plays and write new works until his death. He was highly prolific, crafting over forty plays, thirty screenplay adaptations of his work, eight collections of fiction, and various books of poetry and essays. He won the Pulitzer Prize twice, once in 1947 for *A Streetcar Named Desire* and again in 1955 for *Cat on a Hot Tin Roof.* In 1998 his play on prison abuses, *Not about Nightingales*, was staged in London for the first time, illustrating the continuing social relevance of his work.

Ryan R. Sloan

SEE ALSO: *Brando, Marlon; Capote, Truman; Gay Men;* The Glass Menagerie*; MGM (Metro-Goldwyn-Mayer);* A Streetcar Named Desire*; Vidal, Gore.*

BIBLIOGRAPHY

Gross, Robert F. *Tennessee Williams: A Casebook*. New York: Routledge, 2002.

Leithauser, Brad. "The Grand Dissembler: Sorting Out the Life, and Myth, of Tennessee Williams." *Time*, November 27, 1995.

Leverich, Lyle. *Tom: The Unknown Tennessee Williams*. New York: Crown, 1995.

Murphy, Brenda. *Tennessee Williams and Elia Kazan: A Collaboration in the Theatre*. New York: Cambridge University Press, 1992.

Phillips, Gene D. *The Films of Tennessee Williams*. Philadelphia: Art Alliance Press, 1980.

Savran, David. *Communists, Cowboys and Queers: The Politics of Masculinity in the Work of Arthur Miller and Tennessee Williams*. Minneapolis: University of Minnesota Press, 1992.

Spoto, Donald. *The Kindness of Strangers: The Life of Tennessee Williams*. Boston: Little, Brown, 1985.

"Tennessee Williams." In *American Writers: A Collection of Literary Biographies*, ed. Leonard Unger. 4 vols. New York: Scribner, 1974.

Williams, Venus and Serena

When the Williams sisters (Venus [1980–] and Serena [1981–]) burst onto the sedate women's tennis scene in the late 1990s, they brought a new power and speed to the game and a brash irreverent style that horrified the conservative establishment while winning over millions of fans. Though many prominent players and tennis commentators predicted failure for the unconventional pair, Venus and Serena Williams proved them all wrong as they forged record-breaking careers both individually and as doubles partners. As two of the very few African American players in a largely white, upper-class sport, the Williamses faced both overt and subtle prejudice from other players and white spectators, who sometimes greeted their success with hostility. However, the sisters relentless record of wins earned the respect of even their harshest critics, and their dynamic court presence revitalized the game of tennis, drawing in millions of new fans, among them large numbers of black fans who had previously had little interest in tennis.

WINNERS FROM THE START

By the standards of the tennis world, Venus and Serena have had unconventional careers. Two of five daughters of Richard Williams and Oracene Price, Venus Ebony Starr and Serena Jameka were born in 1980 and 1981, fifteen months apart, and spent their early years in the Compton, a city southeast of downtown Los Angeles. Having seen tennis matches with large cash prizes on television, Richard imagined that his daughters could be tennis stars, and he began training them early, braving drug dealers and gang members to take a four-year-old Venus to practice at their neighborhood court. Young Venus showed an immediate aptitude for the sport, and by the age of ten she had won thirty junior titles, becoming the number one player in the ten-to-twelve-year-old group. Venus's sister Serena was not far behind, winning tournaments and showing promise as an athlete.

Flouting the popular wisdom of the tennis establishment, Richard withdrew the girls from the junior tournament circuit, in part to ensure that they did not neglect their studies and in part to protect them from the racism and elitism of the country-club world of tennis. In 1991 the family moved to Florida, where Venus and Serena got a scholarship to the prestigious Rick Macci Tennis Academy.

Most tennis experts were convinced that playing the junior tour was necessary training for a successful tennis professional and that removing the girls from the tour would damage their future chances. Many also insisted that Richard's amateur coaching would hinder their careers in the sport. Venus and Serena spent the next two decades proving the experts wrong. In 1994, at the age of fourteen, Venus returned to professional tennis, and by 1997 she was ranked in the top 100. That same year she entered her first U.S. Open, where she won the crowd over with her powerful game and her indomitable attitude, becoming the second African American (after Althea Gibson in 1957) to make it to the finals. Though she did not win the title that year, her 119-mile-per-hour serve set a record for the tournament.

SUCCESS FROM THE OUTSET

Perhaps an even stronger player than her sister, Serena also joined the pro circuit as a teenager and began winning games immediately. At the age of seventeen she climbed from a ranking of 453 into the top twenty in only seven months. The sisters began systematically winning almost every important tournament in tennis, both in singles and as a doubles team. By 1999 Venus and Serena were ranked fifth and ninth, respectively, and they had the second- and third-highest earnings of any women's tennis pro.

In 1999 Serena won her first U.S. Open Singles championship, and in 2000 Venus won at the prestigious Wimbledon tournament. In 2001 they faced each other across the net for the first time in a Grand Slam final at the U.S. Open, and for several years both Wimbledon and the Open saw Williams versus Williams finals. By 2011 Venus had racked up forty-three singles titles and eighteen doubles, whereas her sister had earned thirty-nine singles championships and twenty doubles, these titles representing tens of millions of dollars in winnings. Both sisters became part of the U.S. Olympics tennis team; in 2000 Venus earned a gold medal in Sydney in women's singles. Together they won the gold in doubles. In 2008 they won their second gold medal in women's doubles in Beijing.

SISTERS AND FRIENDS

Venus and Serena have forged a special bond that has helped them remain best friends even when playing all out against each other in a tournament final. Venus has said, "Serena is my toughest opponent because she knows my game best. But we're a team no matter what happens on the court." In 2000 they moved into their own house in Palm Beach Gardens, Florida. Though they have always remained close, the sisters have different styles, on the court and off. Venus, more serious and introverted, is 6 feet, 1 inch tall and boasts an extended reach; she plays a fast, graceful game. The gregarious Serena, 4 inches shorter with muscular shoulders and legs, is a relentless powerhouse. Volatile and driven on the court, the sisters have also received criticism for their competitive attitude, and Serena has been fined twice for rude behavior during games.

Professional sports is a career for the young, and, encouraged by their parents, the two Williams sisters have always prepared themselves for a life outside tennis, using time sidelined by injuries to continue their studies and develop alternate business plans. In 2003 Venus launched an interior design firm called V Starr, and Serena markets her clothing designs under the name Aneres ("Serena" spelled backward). The two also have marketed their own brand of oxygenated water, SerVenRich, and an energy drink called Smash. They have written several books, including *How to Play Tennis* (2004) and *Venus and Serena: Serving from the Hip* (2005), an advice book for young people. In 2005 ABC aired several episodes of *Venus and Serena: For Real*, a reality show focused on the warm and supportive Williams family relationships and the irrepressible energy of Venus and Serena.

Perhaps because the color of their skin has always made them stand out in the overwhelmingly white world of professional tennis, the Williamses have never compromised their individuality. They have consistently challenged court conventions, even the rigid tennis dress code. Their trademark hairstyles of beaded braids and their stylish cutout tennis dresses have delighted their fans and dismayed the establishment throughout their careers. However, even those made uncomfortable by the sisters' unconventional flamboyance agree that they have made an unparalleled contribution to the popularity of women's tennis and women's sports in general.

Tina Gianoulis

SEE ALSO: *Ashe, Arthur; Gibson, Althea; Reality Television; Sports Heroes; Tennis; Wimbledon.*

BIBLIOGRAPHY

Bailey, Diane. *Venus and Serena Williams: Tennis Champions.* Sports Families. New York: Rosen Central, 2010.

Harris, Cecil, and Kyle-DeBose Larryette. *Charging the Net: A History of Blacks in Tennis from Althea Gibson and Arthur Ashe to the Williams Sisters.* Chicago: Ivan R. Dee, 2007.

Jenkins, Sally. "Double Trouble." *Women's Sports and Fitness,* November–December 1998, 102.

Willis, Bruce *(1955–)*

Bruce Willis rose to fame playing David Addison in the mid-1980s television show *Moonlighting*. With its appealingly eccentric mix of throwaway detective plots and screwball romantic comedy, the show was an ideal showcase for Willis's ironic tough-guy persona and launched his career as a wisecracking action star. His first two film roles, in *Blind Date* (1987) and *Sunset* (1988), both directed by Blake Edwards, highlighted his comic skills, but after his starring turn in *Die Hard* (1988), Willis became firmly established as one of the leading action stars of the 1990s. Though he remains the quintessential action hero, he has not allowed typecasting to prevent him from taking a wide range of roles, including several that spoof his hard-hitting film image.

As John McClane in the first *Die Hard* film, Willis seemed to embody a new, more human sort of action hero. Expertly directed by John McTiernan, *Die Hard* gave a new boost to action films, the rough-and-ready American hero fighting international terrorists in a disaster movie scenario that brought stylish action and violence to the genre, leading to at least four sequels and numerous imitations. In contrast to the robotic invincibility of Rambo and the Terminator, Willis's McClane was a vulnerable family man, up against high-tech criminals with nothing but his wits and a gun. Even after dispatching evildoers and uttering his cowboy catchphrase, "Yippee ki yay, motherfucker," he has real-life problems to face. Through the sequels, *Die Hard 2: Die Harder* (1990), *Die Hard with a Vengeance* (1995), and *Live Free or Die Hard* (2007), McClane struggles with marital problems and alcohol abuse as well as the bad guys. Willis's sarcastic cowboy cop set a standard for the genre that has not been matched.

Willis's early attempts to expand his range in such films as the Vietnam elegy *In Country* (1989) were not altogether successful. Critics were particularly harsh toward his work as Peter Fallow, the English journalist in Brian De Palma's adaptation of Tom Wolfe's *The Bonfire of the Vanities* (1990), and in the title role in *Hudson Hawk* (1991), an expensive box-office flop that Willis helped write. In order to focus more attention on his acting rather than his movie star status, Willis took on cameo roles in films such as *Billy Bathgate* (1991) with Dustin Hoffman and *Mortal Thoughts* (1991) with then-wife Demi Moore. The Willis action star image was a running joke in Robert Altman's 1992 film *The Player* (1992), which ended with Willis in a cameo send-up of the *Die Hard* series.

In 1994 Willis launched a more mature phase in his career as the boxer, Butch, in Quentin Tarantino's *Pulp Fiction*. Taking his place among an ensemble cast and latching onto Tarantino's hip dialogue, Willis pared down his usual smirks and steely stares, resulting in a notably different performance that was filled with internal rage and insecurity. Demonstrating his versatility, he interrupted his schedule of intense action films in 1996 to make an animated film and television series, *Bruno the Kid*, which followed the adventures of an eleven-year-old spy. The enormously popular 1999 M. Night Shyamalan film *The Sixth Sense* gave Willis a chance to demonstrate his abilities in a more understated part, and he won a People's Choice Award for the role of Malcolm Crowe, the ghostly psychologist.

Always equipped with an irreverent cynicism about his own status as an icon, Willis returned to television in 1997 to appear as himself in a cameo on the Paul Reiser/Helen Hunt sitcom *Mad about You*, once again spoofing his film persona as the star of the fictional film *Die Already*. In 2001 he was nominated for an American Comedy Award for Funniest Male Guest Appearance in a TV Series for a recurring role on the popular comedy show *Friends*. Sending up his tough-guy image, Willis played Paul, Rachel's (Jennifer Aniston) uptight older boyfriend, who could not stop crying once he finally opened up.

In his role as Frank Moses in the 2010 Robert Schwentke film *Red*, Willis plays one of a group of retired special agents who show they still have their fighting skills. Like the team of aging spies, he shows no sign of slowing. While maintaining his fast-paced film career, he is also an accomplished musician who performs with his rhythm-and-blues band, the Accelerators. He is also a restaurateur on the board of Planet Hollywood, a national chain of diners he opened in 1991 with fellow action stars Sylvester Stallone and Arnold Schwarzenegger.

In 2000 Willis and Moore divorced after thirteen years together. Though fans were disappointed by the end of their high-profile marriage, the couple has maintained a cordial relationship. Willis married model Emma Heming in 2009. He also worked with his daughter Rumer in the 2005 Florent-Emilio Siri film *Hostage*. Though he will probably be best remembered for his stunt-filled work in explosive action films, his easygoing stage presence and ironic humor have given Willis a unique place in the genre.

Stephen Keane

SEE ALSO: *Altman, Robert; Divorce;* Friends*; Hoffman, Dustin; Hollywood; Hunt, Helen;* Moonlighting*; Moore, Demi;* Pulp Fiction*; Rambo; Schwarzenegger, Arnold; Stallone, Sylvester; Tarantino, Quentin; Television;* The Terminator*; Wolfe, Tom.*

BIBLIOGRAPHY

Parker, John. *Bruce Willis: An Unauthorised Biography*. London: Virgin, 1997.

Quinlan, David. *Quinlan's Illustrated Directory of Film Stars*. London: Batsford, 1996.

Russell, Mike. "Willis Still Surprises as the Last Action Hero." *Oregonian*, March 11, 2005.

Vern. *Yippee Ki-Yay, Moviegoer: Writings on Bruce Willis, Badass Cinema, and Other Important Topics*. London: Titan Books, 2010.

Wills, Bob, and His Texas Playboys

Bob Wills pioneered "western swing," an upbeat style of country music that had a lasting impact on the industry. Wills, who grew up in the cotton fields of northern Texas during the World War I era, combined the blues of black sharecroppers with southern "hillbilly" music. In the mid-1930s he formed the Texas Playboys, a band using experienced swing and Dixieland jazz musicians that toured throughout the southwest to packed houses. Western swing became a national phenomenon after their 1940 hit "New San Antonio Rose," and Wills was inducted into the Country Music Hall of Fame in 1968. In 1999 Bob Wills and His Texas Playboys were inducted into the Rock and Roll Hall of Fame.

Jeffrey W. Coker

SEE ALSO: *Blues; Country Music; Dixieland; Rock and Roll; World War I.*

BIBLIOGRAPHY

Knowles, Ruth Sheldon. *Bob Wills: Hubbin' It*. Nashville, TN: Country Music Foundation Press, 1995.

Malone, Bill C. *Country Music USA*, rev. ed. Austin: University of Texas Press, 1985.

Townsend, Charles R. *San Antonio Rose: The Life and Music of Bob Wills*. Urbana: University of Illinois Press, 1986.

Wills, Rosetta. *The King of Western Swing: Bob Wills Remembered*. New York: Watson-Guptill Publications, 2000.

Wilson, Flip *(1933–1998)*

In the early 1970s, comedian Flip Wilson secured a place in television history as the first African American to headline a successful network variety series. Previous attempts by other black performers, such as Nat King Cole, Leslie Uggams, and Sammy

Davis Jr., had been ratings failures. From 1970 to 1974 *The Flip Wilson Show* presented comedy sketches, musical performances, and top Hollywood guest stars. The main attraction, however, was Wilson himself. He possessed a sharp yet nonconfrontational sense of humor that appealed to a diverse audience. During its first two seasons, *The Flip Wilson Show* was the second-highest-rated program on television, behind only *All in the Family*. The recurring characters created by Wilson drew the biggest laughs each week, particularly his sassy and liberated Geraldine Jones, who introduced the following catchphrase into the American lexicon: "What you see is what you get." Wilson proved that a mainstream American television audience would accept a black performer.

Clerow Wilson was born on December 8, 1933, in Jersey City, New Jersey, and raised in extreme poverty as one of eighteen children. He grew up in a series of foster homes and left school at age sixteen. During a four-year hitch in the air force, he traveled around the Pacific region, all the while entertaining his fellow enlisted men. Wilson was given the nickname "Flip" by the troops, who appreciated his flippant sense of humor. Upon being discharged from the service in 1954, Wilson spent the next decade honing his act in small nightclubs across America. His big break came with a 1965 appearance on *The Tonight Show Starring Johnny Carson*, which led to frequent guest spots on *The Ed Sullivan Show*, *Laugh-In*, and *Love, American Style*. In 1969, NBC signed the comedian to host an hour-long variety series.

Flip Wilson. *Flip Wilson's self-titled show, with its comedy sketches featuring a cast of characters played by Wilson himself, was the first successful variety series hosted by an African American on network television.* TIM BOXER/CONTRIBUTOR/ARCHIVE PHOTOS/GETTY IMAGES.

The Flip Wilson Show premiered on September 17, 1970. Unlike other programs of the variety genre, it did not feature chorus girls and large production numbers—rather, it was presented in a nightclub setting on a round stage that was surrounded by an audience. Wilson welcomed established stars such as John Wayne, Bing Crosby, Dean Martin, and Lucille Ball to his show, and he introduced audiences to musical guests such as Isaac Hayes, James Brown, and the Temptations. Wilson continued the variety-show tradition of portraying recurring characters, including Freddy the playboy, Sonny the White House janitor, Reverend LeRoy of the Church of What's Happening Now, and, of course, Geraldine Jones. Wilson played Geraldine in drag, and she became a national sensation with her wisecracks about her unseen, very jealous boyfriend, Killer. Said Wilson of her popularity: "The secret of my success with Geraldine is that she's not a putdown of women. She's smart, she's trustful, she's loyal, she's sassy. Most drag impersonations are a drag. But women can like Geraldine, men can like Geraldine, everyone can like Geraldine." Along with Geraldine's trademark line "What you see is what you get," Wilson popularized the phrases "The devil made me do it!" and "When you're hot, you're hot (and when you're not, you're not)." Although Wilson based many of his routines on ethnic humor and black stereotypes, he was rarely overtly political. In 1971, *The Flip Wilson Show* won the Emmy for Outstanding Variety Series-Musical and Outstanding Writing Achievement in Variety or Music. The show was canceled in 1974 due to strong competition from the CBS Depression-era drama *The Waltons*.

Wilson never again reached the heights he had with *The Flip Wilson Show*. He appeared in a handful of films, including *Uptown Saturday Night* and *The Fish That Saved Pittsburgh*, and made several guest appearances on television. In the mid-1980s, he starred in two short-lived TV series: the quiz show *People Are Funny* (1984) and the sitcom *Charlie & Company* (1985), a pale imitation of *The Cosby Show* in which singer Gladys Knight played his wife. Wilson then retired from show business to raise his family. In the late 1990s, Wilson resurfaced again with reruns of *The Flip Wilson Show* on the cable network TV Land. He died on November 25, 1998, of liver cancer.

As with Bill Cosby on the drama *I Spy* and Diahann Carroll on the sitcom *Julia*, Wilson is regarded as a pioneer who helped to destroy the color barrier on network television in the late 1960s and early 1970s. His ability to employ racial humor without demeaning its targets enabled him to provide network television with a black perspective that connected with mainstream America. In a *TV Guide* tribute shortly after Wilson's death, comedian Jay Leno wrote, "Flip was hip, but he made sure everybody could understand him and laugh. That's the sign of a great performer."

Charles Coletta

SEE ALSO: *Ball, Lucille; Brown, James; Cosby, Bill; Crosby, Bing;* I Spy; Julia; Laugh-In; *Leno, Jay; Martin, Dean; Stand-Up Comedy; Television; The Temptations;* TV Guide; The Waltons; *Wayne, John.*

BIBLIOGRAPHY

Andersen, Christopher P. *The New Book of People.* New York: Putnam, 1986.

Brooks, Tim. *The Complete Directory to Prime Time TV Stars.* New York: Random House, 1987.

Leno, Jay. "Flip Wilson." *TV Guide.* December 26, 1998, 9.

Sutherland, Meghan. *The Flip Wilson Show.* Detroit, MI: Wayne State University Press, 2008.

Wimbledon

The world-renowned British tennis tournament, Wimbledon, has become more than tradition, according to British journalist and author John Barrett: more than "just the world's most important and historic tennis tournament," having come to symbolize "all that is best about sport, royal patronage, and social occasion that the British do so well, a subtle blend that the rest of the world finds irresistible." Held in late June and early July, Wimbledon is the only one of the four Grand Slam tennis events that is still played on natural grass.

HISTORY OF THE CHAMPIONSHIP

The event started in 1877 as an amateur tournament called the Lawn Tennis Championships hosted at the England Croquet and Lawn Tennis Club (later renamed the All England Lawn Tennis Club). The only event was men's singles. Twenty-two players participated, and Spencer Gore won the final match, which spectators paid one shilling to watch. The women's singles event was instituted in 1884, when Maud Watson claimed victory over a field of thirteen. Previously played at Oxford, the men's doubles event was brought to Wimbledon in 1883. Over the years Wimbledon's popularity continued to grow steadily. By the mid-1880s permanent stands were in place for the crowds who were part of what Wimbledon historians refer to as the "Renshaw Rush," coming to see the British twins Ernest and William Renshaw win thirteen titles between them in both singles and doubles between 1881 and 1889.

By the turn of the twentieth century, Wimbledon had become an international tournament. U.S. player May Sutton won the women's singles title in 1905 to become Wimbledon's first overseas champion. About that time the royal family began its long association with Wimbledon when the Prince of Wales (subsequently George V) and Princess Mary attended the 1907 tournament, and the prince was named president of the club. In 1969 the Duke of Kent assumed the duty of presenting the winning trophy.

Play at Wimbledon was suspended during World War I, but the club survived on private donations. Tournament play resumed in 1919, with Suzanne Lenglen winning the women's and Gerald Patterson the men's titles. In 1920 the club purchased property on Church Road and built a 14,000-capacity stadium, which Wimbledon historians credit with playing a critical role in popularizing the event. World War II suspended play again, but the club remained open to serve various war-related functions, including a decontamination unit and fire and ambulance services. In 1940 a bomb struck Centre Court, demolishing 1,200 seats. Although the tournament's grounds were not fully restored until 1949, play resumed in 1946, producing men's champion Yvon Petra and women's champion Pauline Betz.

POSTWAR YEARS

The expansion of air travel in the 1950s brought even more international players to Wimbledon. This period also saw the domination of U.S. players at the tournament, with such champions as Jack Kramer, Ted Schroeder, Tony Trabert, Louise Brough, Maureen Connolly, and Althea Gibson (the first African American winner). Australian players Lew Hoad, Neale Fraser, Rod Laver, Roy Emerson, and John Newcombe then dominated the men's singles title from 1956 through the early 1970s.

In 1959 the club began considering a change in its amateur-only policy in light of the increasing number of players receiving financial assistance in excess of the limits set by the International Tennis Federation. It was not until 1967, however, that the Lawn Tennis Association voted to officially open the championship to both professionals and amateurs. At the first open tournament in 1968, Laver and Billie Jean King won the men's and women's singles titles, respectively.

In 1977 Wimbledon celebrated its centenary anniversary. In honor of the occasion, the Wimbledon Lawn Tennis Museum was opened at Wimbledon. The centenary of the women's singles event occurred in 1984. The tournament in the twenty-first century has five main events: men's and women's singles, men's and women's doubles, and mixed doubles. It also sponsors four events for juniors (eighteen and under) and invitation events for former players.

Each of the five main championships has a special trophy. The women's singles trophy, first presented by the All England Club in 1886, is a silver parcel gilt tray made by Elkington and Company in 1864. The men's singles trophy is a silver gilt cup and cover inscribed with the words "The All England Lawn Tennis Club Single Handed Championship of the World" and was first presented by the All England Club in 1887. The men's doubles trophy is a silver challenge cup, first presented in 1884. The women's doubles trophy is a silver cup and cover, known as the Duchess of Kent Challenge Cup, and was first presented in 1949 by Princess Marina, Duchess of Kent, then president of the All England Club.

Two important modernizations came to Wimbledon during the twenty-first century. In 2007 the championship began to offer equal prize money to both men and women for the first time in its history. By 2009 a retractable roof was installed over Centre Court, where championship matches are played; this made it possible to avoid rain delays, a common occurrence during the English summer.

THE PLAYERS

Roughly 500 players compete at Wimbledon each year. To participate, players have to submit an entry six weeks prior to the tournament. A management committee and a referee rank the entries and place players into three categories: accepted, need to qualify, and rejected. The committee then decides which wild cards to include in the draw. Wild cards are players who do not have a high enough international ranking to make the draw but are included by the committee on the basis of past performance at Wimbledon or popularity with British spectators. A qualifying tournament takes place a week before the championships at the Bank of England Sports Centre in Roehampton, and the winners in the finals of this tournament qualify to play at Wimbledon. Exceptions are players who lose in the final round of the qualifying tournament yet are still selected to play. Dubbed the "lucky losers" by tournament organizers, these players are chosen in order of their international ranking to fill any vacancies that occur after the first round of the draw.

To date, the youngest male champion was Boris Becker of Germany. In 1985 the seventeen-year-old won the men's singles championship. In 1996 Swiss player Martina Hingis became the youngest female champion at the age of fifteen. Other notable records include U.S. champion Martina Navratilova's unprecedented six-year reign on Centre Court as women's singles champion and her overall all-time record of nine singles titles. She also won many doubles titles at Wimbledon and became the oldest Grand Slam champion ever when she won the mixed doubles title in 2003 at the age of forty-six years, 261 days. Steffi Graf won the title seven times from 1988 to 1996. In the first decade of the 2000s the Williams sisters—African American players from the United States—dominated Wimbledon. By 2011 Venus had won five singles titles, while her younger sister Serena had won four; the Williams sisters also teamed up to take four doubles championships.

On the men's side, U.S. player Pete Sampras won the Wimbledon singles trophy seven times from 1993 to 2000. Three men have won the men's singles tournament five consecutive times: William Renshaw (1881–1886) of Britain, Björn Borg of Sweden (1976–1980), and Roger Federer of Switzerland (2003–2007). After losing to Spain's Rafael Nadal in 2008, Federer came back to win his sixth title in 2009.

Courtney Bennett

SEE ALSO: *Gibson, Althea; King, Billie Jean; Laver, Rod; Navratilova, Martina; Tennis; Williams, Venus and Serena; World War I; World War II.*

BIBLIOGRAPHY

Gorringe, Chris. *Holding Court.* London: Random House UK, 2010.

Medlycott, James. *100 Years of the Wimbledon Tennis Championships.* New York: Hamlyn, 1977.

Robertson, Max. *Wimbledon, Centre Court of the Game.* London: British Broadcasting Corporation, 1981.

Wade, Virginia, and Jean Rafferty. *Ladies of the Court: A Century of Women at Wimbledon.* New York: Atheneum, 1984.

Wimbledon Official Website. Accessed May 11, 2012. Available from http://www.wimbledon.com/

Winchell, Walter *(1897–1972)*

For almost forty years during the mid-twentieth century, Walter Winchell was thought to be the most powerful man in America. A former vaudevillian, Winchell's power came not from money, family connections, or politics—he was a gossip columnist. Indeed, it has even been said that Winchell invented gossip. Although this is clearly hyperbolic—gossip has always existed in some form—certainly he was the first member of the modern media to both understand its power and know how to wield it.

At the height of his influence, more than fifty million Americans, or two-thirds of the adult population of the country, either read his daily column or listened to his weekly radio program. His grasp of the potent uses to which gossip could be put changed the face of American culture and ultimately led to the overweening power held by the media in the early twenty-first century.

FROM VAUDEVILLE TO BROADWAY

The future gossip columnist was born Walter Winschel on April 7, 1897, in Harlem, New York. His grandfather was a Russian émigré who had come to America hoping for literary fame. His son, Walter's father, was similarly a man of high expectations and low achievement—a silk salesman who devoted much of his time to his mistresses. Because Walter received little attention at home, he sought it across the street at a local movie theater, where he and two other boys, one of whom was George Jessel, sang songs between movies for money. When they were spotted by a vaudeville talent scout, thirteen-year-old Walter left home to join the troupe, saying, "I knew what I didn't want . . . I didn't want to be hungry, homeless, or anonymous."

Walter spent his teenage years in vaudeville, and when he outgrew the boys act, he joined forces with another young vaudevillian, Rita Greene. Winchell (as he now called himself) and Greene continued to travel the country, performing their vaudeville act to surprising success. Booked to a two-year contract, in his free time Winchell began producing a vaudeville newsletter and sending in articles to *Billboard.*

After marrying Greene, he realized that his wife wanted to get out of show business, and so the couple moved back to New

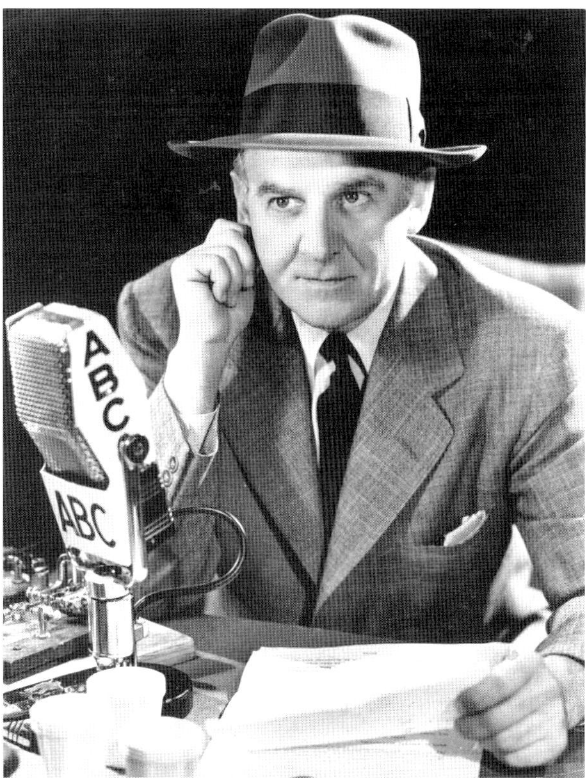

Walter Winchell. *Walter Winchell's radio broadcasts and newspaper columns pioneered the industry of celebrity gossip as entertainment.* KEYSTONE/STAFF/HULTON ARCHIVE/GETTY IMAGES.

York City, where he landed a job writing for the *Vaudeville News*. As Neal Gabler wrote:

> The twenty-three-year-old Winchell was columnist, office boy, deputy editor, part-time photographer, salesman, and general factotum. And he loved it, throwing himself into the job with desperate energy. Days he spent racing down Broadway, mingling, glad-handing, joking, collecting items for the column, making himself known. Nights he spent at the National Vaudeville Association Club on 46th Street, working the grill room and campaigning for himself as a Broadway figure.

Although Winchell's breakneck pace ultimately led to the dissolution of his marriage, it earned him a reputation as Broadway's man-about-town. And so, in 1924, when the young columnist heard that a new tabloid newspaper was being launched, he easily won the position of Broadway columnist and drama critic on the *New York Evening Graphic*.

THE GOSSIP COLUMNIST ASCENDANT

Winchell's column in the *Evening Graphic* was composed of Broadway news, jokes, and puns, and it was written in a catchy slang of Winchell's own invention. His unique linguistic twists captured the public's attention, but it was his brazen use of rumor, gossip, and innuendo in his column that made him famous. He saw himself as a maverick who had broken the cardinal rule of journalism by using unverified sources. He looked behind closed doors and reported what he saw—affairs, abortions, children out of wedlock—nothing was taboo to Winchell.

The public loved it, sensing that the formerly impenetrable walls between the powerful and the common man were being torn down by one of their own. Winchell, born into a lower-middle-class Jewish family, was daring to put the private lives of the rich and famous in print. And the rich and famous were duly shocked and alarmed. As Gabler observed, Winchell "understood that gossip, far beyond its basic attraction as journalistic voyeurism, was a weapon of empowerment for the reader and listener. Invading the lives of the famous and revealing their secrets brought them to heel. It humanized them, and in humanizing them demonstrated that they were no better than we and in many cases worse."

By 1928 Winchell's column was syndicated throughout the country, and the thirty-one-year-old was already one of the most influential public figures in America. The next year he moved to William Randolph Hearst's *Daily Mirror*, for which he wrote a daily column. By the early 1930s, when he began his weekly radio broadcast, Winchell wielded as much power with his pen as most politicians and public figures did with money and political clout. As Winchell himself put it, "Democracy is where everybody can kick everybody else's ass, but you can't kick Winchell's."

Throughout the 1930s Winchell's power continued to grow, extending beyond show business to politics and big business. Gabler wrote, "When Depression America was venting its own anger against economic royalists, Winchell was not only revealing the transgressions of the elites but needling industrialists and exposing bureaucratic cruelties so much that he became, in the words of one paper, a 'people's champion.'" Recognizing the extent of Winchell's influence, President Franklin D. Roosevelt invited the columnist to the White House not long after his first inauguration, thus initiating a relationship that would prove mutually beneficial to both men.

As Adolf Hitler's power grew in Germany during the mid-1930s, Winchell turned his attention to the international front, becoming one of the führer's most ardent and outspoken foes in America. In this task he had the full support of the Roosevelt administration, which grew to rely on Winchell's influence in encouraging the United States to enter the war. For Winchell, this foray into international politics was intoxicating. The former vaudevillian became a dedicated patriot, and once the United States entered the war, he devoted himself to supporting Roosevelt's wartime policies and keeping up the spirits of the soldiers overseas.

During the war Winchell was at the height of his power. As Gabler noted:

> If Winchell's career had ended then, he might have been regarded as the greatest journalistic phenomenon of the age: a colossus who straddled newspapers and radio, show business and politics. He almost certainly would have been remembered as a prime force in the public relations battle to boost America's home-front morale during World War II and as a defender of press freedom.

FALL FROM FAVOR

Following the war, however, Winchell's infatuation with politics led him to become involved in the McCarthy witch hunt as communism became the new target of his ire. The intellectual elite, who had tolerated Winchell as long as he was espousing liberal causes, were enraged, and they sought to bring him down. When the columnist became involved in a scandal involving African American singer Josephine Baker, who was not served at Winchell's favorite watering hole—the Stork Club—while the famed columnist was in attendance, the Left turned on Winchell, accusing him of racism.

In the ensuing battle between the media and the now right-wing Winchell, the gossipmonger ultimately lost. Over the course of the next two decades, Winchell would fall from his position as one of the most powerful men on the planet and become a relic of a distant era. As television became the main conduit for media, the man whom Winchell had once helped find a job, Ed Sullivan, would become an icon, while Winchell would fade into obscurity, eventually dying in Los Angeles in 1972.

Although it is perhaps now difficult to imagine the power once wielded by this man who gave rise to contemporary celebrity culture, Winchell was indeed once among the most influential men on the planet. Although his authority ultimately languished, he left the world a vastly changed place. By legitimizing the use of gossip in the mainstream media, he both paved the way for the extreme power now held by the media as well as laid the foundation for contemporary celebrity society.

Victoria Price

SEE ALSO: *Baker, Josephine; Broadway; Celebrity; Cold War; Communism; Gossip Columns; Hearst, William Randolph; Jessel, George; McCarthyism; Radio; Sullivan, Ed; Tabloids; Vaudeville.*

BIBLIOGRAPHY

Brodkey, Harold. "The Last Word on Winchell." *New Yorker*, January 30, 1995, 71–81.

Gabler, Neal. "Walter Winchell." *American Heritage*, November 1994, 96–105.

Gabler, Neal. *Winchell: Gossip, Power, and the Culture of Celebrity*. New York: Alfred A. Knopf, 1994.

Herr, Michael. *Walter Winchell: A Novel*. New York: Alfred A. Knopf, 1990.

Howard, Trustin. *Winchell and Runyon: The True Untold Story*. Lanham, MD: Hamilton Books, 2010.

Klurfeld, Herman. *Winchell: His Life and Times*. New York: Praeger, 1976.

Mosedale, John. *The Men Who Invented Broadway: Damon Runyon, Walter Winchell & Their World*. New York: R. Marek Publishers, 1981.

Weinraub, Bernard. "He Turned Gossip into Tawdry Power; Walter Winchell, Who Climbed High and Fell Far, Still Scintillates." *New York Times*, November 18, 1998.

The Windy City

One of Chicago's most enduring nicknames, "The Windy City" originally had nothing to do with the Illinois city's sometimes formidable atmospheric conditions but was coined by a nineteenth-century New Yorker to describe the city's loud, "windy" boosterism. For chilled Chicago Bears football fans at lakefront Soldier Field or for holiday shoppers on Michigan Avenue's famed Magnificent Mile, however, the nickname has had little to do with political opportunism.

Also known as the "Second City" because of its historical status as America's second-largest city behind New York, Chicago was praised loudly by business promoters who roamed up and down the East Coast throughout much of the nineteenth century touting the city's cosmopolitan character and excellent investment opportunities in an effort to lure capital needed for growth and expansion. Trying to debunk the popular image of their city as a cultural backwater and a "cow town," these boosters painted a picture of a midwestern mecca where there was boundless money to be made. Chicago had arisen from a swamp in just more than sixty years and had made a stunning rebound from the Great Fire of 1871. Engineers had reversed the flow of the polluted Chicago River to protect Lake Michigan, the source of the city's drinking water.

Detractors claimed that the boosters were full of hot air, and tension between backers of various cities came to its zenith in the race to host the 1893 World's Columbian Exposition in celebration of the 400th anniversary of Christopher Columbus's landing (one year late). City leaders in the early 1890s, hoping to establish their town as a world-class city, felt Chicago was an obvious choice to demonstrate American enterprise and ingenuity to the rest of the world. They organized a company to generate the necessary funds to underwrite the exposition. However, when Illinois Senator Shelby M. Cullom introduced a bill in the U.S. Congress in favor of federal support for the exposition, he neglected to specify that Chicago should play host. Immediately a vicious contest arose to obtain the event, with Chicago; New York; Washington, D.C.; and St. Louis, Missouri (which hosted a similar affair only ten years later), emerging as the major players.

Charles A. Dana, editor of the *New York Sun*, wrote an editorial snobbishly discounting the "nonsensical claims of that windy city . . . [whose] people could not build a world's fair even if they won it." According to most accounts, it is this editorial that popularized the Windy City nickname on a national basis. After New York was able to match Chicago's original $5 million bid, Chicago doubled it, and in April of 1890 President Benjamin Harrison announced that the blustering and confident midwestern city had won the exposition lottery. Three years later, the famous "white city" opened its gates. According to a contemporary city booster, "The Columbian Exposition was the most stupendous, interesting and significant show ever spread out for the public." With its imperial architecture, famous "midway," giant Ferris wheel, and exhibits of technology and science, the exposition continues to be remembered as one of the great defining moments in Chicago's history.

Though the Dana quotation was soon forgotten, the nickname stuck, having struck a nerve deeper than the rhetoric of boosterism. Over the course of the early twentieth century, the Windy City appellation came more and more to refer to Chicago's often severe weather. Chicago ranks fourteenth for wind velocity among American cities. Local weather reporters often talk of the "lake effect" in regard to conditions near Lake Michigan, where the water temperature tones down summer's extreme temperatures and the wind intensifies winter chills. With 29 miles of shoreline, and with many of the city's business, cultural, and residential centers located along the coast, the lake effect truly influences the city as a whole.

Moreover, Chicago's downtown streets have long been known as wind-swept corridors nestled among some of the world's oldest and tallest skyscrapers. It is this wind "having no regard for living things," not blustering political rhetoric of the nineteenth century, that Edgar Lee Masters credited in 1933, in the first pages of his city portrait, with giving the name of the Windy City to Chicago. Technically, consensus opinion holds Masters to be incorrect, but his error does demonstrate that by the third decade of the twentieth century at least, the original and the contemporary meaning of the nickname had diverged. As noted by Masters, winter winds coming off of Lake Michigan are blocked by Michigan Avenue's wall of buildings, "swirl down from the towers of the great city" and are diverted down the long, straight thoroughfares, making the Second City a very windy city indeed.

Chicago has a long history of African American culture. During the 1840s many fugitive slaves and freedmen established communities in Chicago, and during The Great Migration from 1910 to 1960, the African American population increased to 800,000. The migration birthed an influential musical and literary tradition and included jazz musician Louis Armstrong and poets Margaret Walker and Gwendolyn Brooks. One of the first African American newspapers, *The Chicago Defender* played an integral role in sparking The Great Migration and influenced Harry Truman to integrate the military in 1948. Since then Chicago has been home to numerous black intellectuals and celebrities, including Katherine Dunham, E. Franklin Frazier, Oprah Winfrey, and President Barack Obama.

Although the Windy City may have surpassed some of its perceived limitations, its sports teams were often the target of ridicule. A proud sports town, Chicago did not win a major national championship in over two decades until the Chicago Bears won Super Bowl XX in 1986, their first National Football

League (NFL) championship since 1963. Prior to the game, the team released a rap song and video, "The Superbowl Shuffle," selling more than 500,000 copies and hitting the Billboard Hot 100. In 1991 the Chicago Bulls, led by stars Michael Jordan and Scottie Pippen and coach Phil Jackson, began their dynasty that saw six championships in eight years. During baseball's early years, the White Sox were a perennial power, winning championships in 1906 and 1917. Eight members of the infamous 1919 "Black Sox" were banned for life from baseball for fixing the World Series. Chicago would not again be a Major League Baseball champion until 2005, when the White Sox, under the high-profile and verbose skipper Ozzie Guillen, swept the Houston Astros. One of the "Original Six" of hockey, the Chicago Blackhawks experienced more than a four-decade championship drought. Fueled by youthful forwards Jonathan Toews and Patrick Kane, the Blackhawks won the Stanley Cup in 2010 by defeating the Philadelphia Flyers. The Chicago Cubs, dubbed the "lovable losers" and known for their historical ballpark, Wrigley Field, entered the twenty-first century without having won a championship since 1908.

Throughout its history, the Windy City has been associated with high crime rates, and Chicago was a major gathering place for organized crime in the days of Prohibition. Al Capone moved there in 1919 to escape murder charges in New York and subsequently played a large part in the history of crime in the city. In 2003 the Windy City's history of crime received new attention when the long-running play *Chicago* was turned into a movie starring Renée Zellweger as Roxie Hart and Catherine Zeta-Jones as Velma Kelly. The plot focuses on Hart and Kelly becoming notorious in 1920s Chicago for murdering the men in their lives but avoiding conviction. The film won six Oscars, including Best Picture. The 1926 play by Maurine Watkins on which it was based had been modeled after two Chicago women accused of killing their lovers while they were under the combined influence of gin and jazz. Chicago's high crime rate is not limited to the movies or to the past. Gangs are a major problem, and the murder rate in 2011 (15.7 homicides per 100,000 residents) ranked second in the United States behind Philadelphia.

Steve Burnett

SEE ALSO: The Amos 'n' Andy Show; *Aparicio, Luis; Belushi, John; Black Sox Scandal; The Blues Brothers; Brooks, Gwendolyn; Butkus, Dick; Capone, Al; Caray, Harry; Century of Progress (Chicago, 1933); The Chicago Bears; The Chicago Bulls; Chicago Jazz; The Chicago Seven; Dillinger, John; Ditka, Mike; Durocher, Leo; Fey, Tina; Fisk, Carlton; Goodman, Benny; Halas, George "Papa Bear"; Hefner, Hugh; Hull, Bobby; Jackson, "Shoeless" Joe; Jordan, Michael; Kiwanis; Lollapalooza; Mamet, David; Murray, Bill; Newhart, Bob; Obama, Barack; Paretsky, Sara; Payton, Walter; Pippen, Scottie;* Playboy; *Race Riots; Royko, Mike; Sandburg, Carl; Savage, Dan; Sears Roebuck Catalog; Sears Tower; Second City; Skyscrapers; Soldier Field; Sosa, Sammy; Stagg, Amos Alonzo; Sunday, Billy; Terkel, Studs; Winfrey, Oprah; Wrigley Field.*

BIBLIOGRAPHY

Bone, Robert, and Richard A. Courage. *The Muse in Bronzeville: African American Creative Expression in Chicago.* New Brunswick, NJ: Rutgers University Press, 2011.

Cronon, William. *Nature's Metropolis: Chicago and the Great West.* New York: W. W. Norton, 1991.

Dedmon, Emmett. *Fabulous Chicago.* New York: Random House, 1953.

Gems, Gerald R. *The Windy City Wars: Labor, Leisure, and Sport in the Making of Chicago.* Lanham, MD: Scarecrow Press, 1997.

Hayes, Dorsha B. *Chicago: Crossroads of American Enterprise.* New York: Julian Messner, 1944.

Heise, Kenan, and Mark Frazel. *Hands on Chicago: Getting Hold of the City.* Chicago: Bonus, 1987.

Kingsbury, Alex. "Gangs in the U.S." *CQ Researcher* 20, no. 25 (2010).

Masters, Edgar Lee. *The Tale of Chicago.* New York: Putnam, 1933.

Miller, Donald L. *City of the Century: The Epic of Chicago and the Making of America.* New York: Simon & Schuster, 1996.

Tracy, Steven C. *Writers of the Black Chicago Renaissance.* Urbana: University of Illinois Press, 2011.

Winfrey, Oprah *(1954–)*

Oprah Winfrey, who began her career as a midwest talk show host in 1985, wielded such clout in the entertainment field in the early years of the twenty-first century that her participation in a project virtually guaranteed its success. During her years as host of *The Oprah Winfrey Show* (1985–2011), her strong identification with her audience could be witnessed again and again; when she did something as simple as starting a diet or as complex as taking a stand against social injustice, millions of people across the United States followed suit. Her considerable influence was neither happenstance nor opportunism. Her social and political views came from years of struggle and hardship that imbued her with a missionary zeal to get her message across.

OVERCOMING EARLY STRUGGLES

The television persona of "Oprah" is virtually inseparable from the person herself. She was born into poverty in 1954 in rural Mississippi and spent many of her formative years living in a Milwaukee, Wisconsin, ghetto with her divorced mother. As a teenager, her life began a downward spiral marked by sexual abuse and early signs of delinquency that were halted by the reappearance of her father, a Nashville, Tennessee, barber. He took custody of her, brought her to Tennessee, and placed her in a local high school, where she developed an interest in oratory. This experience led her to a student internship at a black radio station that sparked her interest in a career in journalism.

After graduation, she matriculated at Tennessee State University, where she garnered more experience in broadcast journalism but also competed for and won the "Miss Black Nashville" and "Miss Black Tennessee" titles. Despite her later pro-feminist stands on various issues, she harbored no regrets for cashing in on her physical beauty, saying that she won on "poise and talent." She later explained, "I was raised to believe that the lighter your skin, the better you were. I wasn't light skinned, so I decided to be the best and the smartest."

BREAKING INTO JOURNALISM

Her experience and poise also positioned her for a job as a "street reporter" at the CBS-TV affiliate in Nashville. She parlayed that job into a coanchor position at Baltimore, Mary-

Oprah Winfrey. *Oprah Winfrey ended her successful talk show in 2011 after twenty-five seasons to focus on other projects, including her OWN television network.* HINDUSTAN TIMES/CONTRIBUTOR/ GETTY IMAGES.

land's ABC outlet, where she ran into her first setback as a broadcaster. Her journalistic skills were undermined by her tendency to become emotional when hosting unpleasant stories, and questions were raised about her professional objectivity. ABC management thus decided to try her out on a morning talk program, where her emotionalism and penchant for becoming personally involved with her subject matter actually became a bonus.

After six years in Baltimore, Winfrey was hired in January 1984 to take over a faltering morning program on WLS-TV's *AM Chicago*, which had employed a succession of hosts only to finish dead last among the competition for the 9 a.m. ratings slot. Not the least of the show's problems was the fact that it was scheduled opposite *The Phil Donahue Show* (1970–1996), hosted by Chicago's favorite son and national ratings champ. Yet in Winfrey, WLS-TV found an engaging, personable host who had a "common touch" not possessed by the somewhat patrician-appearing Donahue. Her formula was simple: working with a studio audience and a number of guests in a classic town-hall format, she rose above the traditional moderator role by injecting both her persona and her life experiences into debates on failed relationships, sexual abuse, and weight-loss plans. Although her manner of interjecting her audience into the discussions by walking quickly through the crowd and jabbing the microphone into someone's face to get his or her point into play did not differ terribly much from Donahue's, she allowed herself to almost become part of her own audience in a way that her male counterpart did not.

A FILM ROLE BRINGS NATIONAL FAME

By 1985 the show had displaced *The Phil Donahue Show* at the top of the Chicago ratings, prompting the station management to expand the show to one hour and to take advantage of Winfrey's growing stardom by renaming it *The Oprah Winfrey Show* in 1985. When film composer Quincy Jones happened to turn on the show while on a visit to Chicago, he was so impressed that he mentioned Winfrey to director Steven Spielberg, who was beginning to cast roles for his film *The Color Purple*. Her performance as Sophia earned her an Academy Award nomination for Best Supporting Actress and transformed her into a household name. Within eighteen months, Winfrey had become a star in one medium and was standing on the threshold in another.

In 1986 WLS-TV began to syndicate the show nationally through King World, making Winfrey the first black woman to host her own show and become a millionaire by the age of thirty-two. At the same time, she formed her own production company, Harpo (her name spelled backward), and began to take a more active role in the creation of the show. Within its first five months, the show ranked number one among talk shows in 192 cities, forcing competitor Donahue to move his home base from Chicago to New York in an attempt to stay competitive.

THE BIRTH OF AN EMPIRE

When her contract expired in 1988, Winfrey threatened to leave in order to pursue other opportunities in film and television. This forced ABC, King World, and WLS-TV to guarantee her complete control of the show in return for her promise to stay on until 1993. Industry estimates at that time figured that Winfrey's company would garner more than $50 million for the 1988–1989 season alone. This cemented her position as the richest and most powerful woman on television and also freed her to pursue her own agenda without network interference.

Under her guidance, Harpo became a major player in prime-time dramatic programming with a miniseries, *The Women of Brewster Place*, in 1989 and the spin-off sitcom *Brewster Place* the following year. The company was also active in the TV documentary field during the early 1990s, with a number of special programs addressing social issues—particularly dealing with the topics of abused children and women's issues.

By the time Winfrey turned forty in 1994, *The Oprah Winfrey Show* was available in fifty-four countries and was reaching fifteen million viewers a day in the United States alone, the highest-rated show in syndication history. The host's personal fortune was an estimated $250 million. In 1996 Winfrey realized one of her long-held goals "to get America reading" by founding a book club segment on her show. The book club's first selection was first-time novelist Jacquelyn Mitchard's *The Deep End of the Ocean*, considered by many to be strictly a woman's romance. Winfrey discussed the book in a serious vein on her show and generated enough sales to make it the number one national best seller within four months of its publication, with sales of more than 850,000 hardcover copies. The phenomenon continued with the talk show host's next selection, Toni Morrison's nineteen-year-old *Song of Solomon*, which was being released in paperback. Between October 1996 and January 1997, the publisher reported more than 830,000 copies sold due to Winfrey's influence alone. By the end of the 2010 season, Oprah's Book Club had endorsed seventy books and had more than two million online members.

SOCIAL AWARENESS: FILMS AND PHILANTHROPY

The key to Winfrey's selection of projects, whether books or television, is the personal impact that the source material has made on her. If she likes a book, she will champion it; if she sees audience potential in it, she will produce it as a television program or a feature film. Under the banner *Oprah Winfrey Presents*, Harpo Productions has produced numerous television movies, including *Before Women Had Wings* (1997), which addressed the tragedy of domestic violence and child abuse; *David and Lisa* (a 1998 remake of the 1962 film), which portrayed two teens in a mental institution; and *Their Eyes Were Watching God* (2005), based on Zora Neale Hurston's novel about a black woman's search for identity in 1930s Florida.

Winfrey also made a return to acting in 1998 with a film version of Morrison's *Beloved*, which, while not terribly successful at the box office, spoke to several of her deeply held feelings about racism, slavery, and the power of a mother's love. "We look for projects that show individuals being responsible for themselves," she says. "It's all about seeing human beings as active creators of their lives rather than as passive victims." Many of Winfrey's most successful professional choices have been based on this philosophy, such as the critically acclaimed *Precious*, which she coproduced with Tyler Perry in 2009. Based on the novel *Push* by Sapphire, *Precious* tells a story deeply familiar to Winfrey, of a young African American girl who struggles to value herself when no one else seems to.

Winfrey carries her belief in nurturing potential and creativity over to her personal life as well. In 1997 she launched Oprah's Angel Network, which raised tens of millions of dollars in an ongoing campaign to spur her viewers into doing good works such as helping to build new houses for needy families. In 2005 the Angel Network added the Katrina Homes Registry, which helped hundreds of people displaced when Hurricane Katrina hit Louisiana's Gulf Coast. Education was the key to Winfrey's hope of a better life, and she has focused a large part of her philanthropy on providing access to education for those who need it the most. She has collaborated with A Better Chance, a Boston-based organization that works to improve educational opportunities for people of color, as well as endowing a number of individual scholarships at various institutions, including Morehouse College and her own alma mater Tennessee State University. In 2000, after visiting President Nelson Mandela in South Africa, Winfrey vowed to found a school for girls there, and in 2007 the Oprah Winfrey Leadership Academy for Girls opened its doors ,with a mission of developing a "new generation of dynamic women leaders."

The continuing success of *The Oprah Winfrey Show* made all of these endeavors possible by making Winfrey one of the wealthiest and most powerful people in the entertainment industry. In 1997 *Variety* reported that the show had surpassed *Saturday Night Live* as the best spot on television to generate music sales. The show thus became the first stop for mainstream artists to promote their latest releases. Performers such as Madonna, Rod Stewart, and Whitney Houston saw their albums experience significant sales gains following an appearance on *The Oprah Winfrey Show*. Stewart, for example, watched as his CD *If We Fall in Love Tonight* (1996) jumped twenty-five places on the sales charts within two days of his appearance, with sales of 40,000 units. This achievement extended Winfrey's clout to virtually all forms of media.

THE "OPRAH EFFECT"

The far-reaching impact of the show was also demonstrated in 1996 when Winfrey expressed her personal opinion on eating beef in a discussion of mad cow disease. Predictably, beef sales fell off a bit and a cattleman's association in Texas hauled her into court for defamation. After a two-month trial, she was vindicated, but no one would ever again doubt the pervasive influence of her show.

In 2008 she proved that the "Oprah effect," as media pundits have called her power to shape public opinion, reached into the political realm as well. In May 2007 she announced her endorsement of Democratic presidential candidate Barack Obama. Though Winfrey had never publicly backed a political candidate before, her audience of more than forty million viewers was thought to be a powerful asset—and certainly seemed to be, as Obama went on to win the election. A University of Maryland study estimated that Winfrey's endorsement might have swayed a million votes to Obama's side.

During its twenty-five year run, *The Oprah Winfrey Show* earned forty-seven Emmy Awards, including seven for its star. To keep the program fresh and vital, Winfrey continually incorporated new items of interest into the format. In the fall of 1998, for example, she took singing lessons and began to sing the theme song herself. She also created a segment called "Change Your Life TV," which assisted viewers in taking steps to reorder their bankbooks, their family life, and the clutter of their lives. Always generous with audience gifts, in 2004 she made headlines by giving each of the 270 audience members a new car.

Winfrey has continued to expand her media empire. In addition to her film and television productions, in 2000 she introduced *O: The Oprah Magazine*, a glossy monthly journal that features Winfrey on the cover of each issue. A South African version was published starting in 2002. Harpo Productions' online presence is a giant interactive website that offers ways for fans to connect with all of Winfrey's projects, from movies to health tips to philanthropy to product sales.

In 2009 Winfrey announced that she would end her long-running talk show in September 2011 and revealed plans for her new cable network, OWN (Oprah Winfrey Network). *The Oprah Winfrey Show* ended its twenty-five-year run with a three-show finale filled with tear-jerking remembrances and tributes to the show's host. Winfrey's new network, a joint project with Discovery Communications, featured a lineup of woman-centered programming, including her new talk show, *Oprah's Next Chapter*, which employs a traveling-interview format that highlights her empathetic conversational skills. Though the new network's first two years featured erratic ratings, Winfrey's confidence and indefatigable energy did not dim. She continued to behave as she had once told viewers at the end of her show: "The opportunity to have a voice and speak to the world every day is a gift."

Sandra Garcia-Myers

SEE ALSO: *Academy Awards; Beauty Queens; Best Sellers; Broadway; Daytime Talk Shows; Dieting; Donahue, Phil; Houston, Whitney; Hurricane Katrina; Hurston, Zora Neale; The Internet; Madonna; Morrison, Toni; Obama, Barack; Oprah's Book Club; Perry, Tyler;* Saturday Night Live*; Sitcom; Spielberg, Steven; Television; Television Anchors;* Variety.

BIBLIOGRAPHY

Berthed, Joan. "Here Comes Oprah! From *The Color Purple* to TV Talk Queen." *Ms.*, August 1986.

Cotton, Trystan T., and Kimberly Springer, eds. *Stories of Oprah: The Oprahfication of American Culture.* Jackson: University Press of Mississippi, 2009.

Flanagan, Caitlin. "The Glory of Oprah." *Atlantic*, December 2011.

Gillespie, Marcia Ann. "Winfrey Takes All." *Ms.*, November 1988.

Harris, Jennifer, and Elwood Watson, eds. *The Oprah Phenomenon.* Lexington: University Press of Kentucky, 2009.

Kinsella, Bridget. "The Oprah Effect." *Publishers Weekly*, January 20, 1997.

Mair, George. *Oprah Winfrey: The Real Story.* Secaucus, NJ: Carol, 1994.

Mascariotte, Gloria-Jean. "C'mon Girl": Oprah Winfrey and the Discourse of Feminine Talk." *Genders*, Fall 1991.

"Oprah Winfrey Reveals the Real Reason Why She Stayed on TV." *Jet*, November 24, 1997.

Randolph, Laura B. "Oprah Opens Up." *Ebony*, October 1993.

Sandler, Adam. "Warblers Warm Up at Oprah House." *Variety*, December 26, 1996–January 5, 1997.

Stodghill, Ron. "Daring to Go There." *Time*, October 5, 1998.

White, Mimi. *Tele-advising: Therapeutic Discourse in American Television.* Chapel Hill: University of North Carolina Press, 1992.

Winnie Winkle the Breadwinner

The comic strip *Winnie Winkle the Breadwinner* first appeared in newspapers on September 21, 1920. Created by former vaudevillian Martin Branner (1888–1970), it was the first of a genre of working-girl strips that later inspired imitators such as *Tillie the Toiler* (1921–1959).

A "new woman" of the 1920s, Winnie works in an office and provides for her parents and adopted brother Perry. As the strip evolved, Branner focused on Winnie's search for a husband, the strip's central running theme until she married William Wright in 1937. By 1955—with Mr. Wright killed in a mine accident in 1950 after several near mishaps during World War II—Winnie becomes the chief executive of a fashion house. Branner's strip criticizes the feminization of culture through the consumption of goods and services and the use of celebrity endorsements and laments the passing of vaudeville and its replacement by Hollywood movies. The last strip appeared on July 28, 1956.

Ian Gordon

SEE ALSO: *Comics; Vaudeville.*

BIBLIOGRAPHY

Gordon, Ian. *Comic Strips and Consumer Culture, 1890–1945.* Washington, DC: Smithsonian Institution Press, 1998.

Haugen, David M. *Comic Books.* Detroit: Greenhaven Press, 2005.

Winnie-the-Pooh

From educational videos to silk boxer shorts, from calendars to wristwatches, Winnie-the-Pooh has become as synonymous with Walt Disney as Mickey Mouse. The Bear of Very Little Brain enjoyed a renaissance in popularity in the 1990s and has parlayed his endearing befuddlement into a multimillion-dollar franchise. Pooh and his companions from the Hundred Acre Wood are icons of a gentler, simpler childhood, a childhood without games like Mortal Kombat and Duke Nukem.

HUMBLE BEGINNINGS

Alan Alexander Milne found inspiration for the Winnie-the-Pooh characters while watching his son Christopher Robin Milne at play; Pooh is based on a stuffed bear that Christopher received on his first birthday. Originally named Edward Bear, he was soon christened Winnie-the-Pooh, which is derived from Chris-

Winnie-the-Pooh. *A. A. Milne poses with son Christopher Robin and his toy stuffed bear, Winnie-the-Pooh, around 1930.* BOB THOMAS/POPPERFOTO/GETTY IMAGES.

topher's favorite bear in the London Zoo (named either Winnifred or Winnipeg, depending on the source) and a swan named Pooh. The stuffed menagerie grew to include a stuffed tiger, pig, and donkey. Milne introduced us to Pooh, Rabbit, Piglet, Eeyore, Owl, Tigger, Kanga, and Roo in his 1924 collection of verses *When We Were Very Young. Winnie-the-Pooh* was published in 1926, followed by *Now We Are Six* in 1927, and *The House at Pooh Corner* in 1928. All four volumes were enchantingly illustrated by Ernest H. Shepard.

The Pooh stories enjoyed early success on both sides of the Atlantic (and have since been translated into more than twenty-five languages). Winnie-the-Pooh became a favorite of Walt Disney's daughters, and he decided to bring Pooh to the American movie screens. Although Disney originally conceived the work as a feature-length film, he later decided that featurettes would introduce the beloved bear more slowly and better help to establish Pooh's recognition with American audiences. The first of the three featurettes, *Winnie-the-Pooh and the Honey Tree*, was released in 1966. The three shorts were connected and later reissued as *The Many Adventures of Winnie-the-Pooh*, Disney's twenty-second feature-length film, in 1977. It was rereleased in 1996 to celebrate the thirtieth anniversary of the original Pooh release. In 1997 *Pooh's Grand Adventure* resumed where the first film left off.

A CULTURAL PHENOMENON

Thanks to renewed popularity based on video sales and rentals of the rereleased movies, Disney found someone to rival Mickey Mouse as the face of Disney. Pooh and friends can be found on television in an animated cartoon series on ABC, in interactive stories and learning games for computers, and on educational videos, not to mention products such as pewter earrings and assorted neckties, which are targeted toward adult consumers.

Demand for Pooh merchandise stops just short of mania. When Disney stores released a limited-edition Beanie Pooh on November 27, 1998, merchants found customers lining up as early as 4 a.m. in order to improve their chances of purchasing the bear. These limited-edition bears were sold out nationally in a matter of hours. What makes Pooh marketing such a cultural phenomenon is the bear's broad appeal to all ages. Specifically, marketing is directed at two of the largest segments of society: the baby boomers and their children, Generation X.

These two distinct markets have created a split in Pooh's persona. For the comparatively more affluent boomers, there is a merchandising renaissance of the original Pooh as illustrated by Shepard. The Gund company markets stuffed versions modeled on the original ink and watercolor pictures found in the books, but these stuffed animals are not priced as items you would let a one-year-old drool on and play with. Shepard-inspired products also include decorative lamps, bookends, hatboxes, and charms—all valuable and collectible. These products are often found in larger, more upscale department stores, such as Dillard's and Macy's.

In contrast, Generation X is targeted with the "Disneyfied" Pooh. It is the round, yellow bear that is found on everything from watches and nightshirts to neckties and boxer shorts. While many such products are available only at Disney stores, far more are readily available (and affordable) at stores like Target and Wal-Mart. These products include many items directed at children: books, puzzles, games, educational toys, and durable stuffed animals.

Pooh's appearance, and significance, is in the eye of the beholder. For both Gen Xers and their parents, Pooh represents a childhood sense of safety and comfort. Pooh muddles through a world inevitably made more complex than necessary by his good friends Rabbit and Owl. Eventually, the bear whose head is "stuffed with fluff" figures out a simpler, and often gentler, way of solving the various problems of the Hundred Acre Wood. Not only does Pooh's gentleness of spirit triumph, but his other endearing attribute is the special bond of love and constancy between himself and Christopher Robin.

In a high-tech, high-speed, and high-violence world, Pooh and company provide a haven from the breakneck lunacy of everyday life. Pooh wonders where he will find his next "smackeral" of honey, not whether his 401k will lose value. Pooh does not stab anyone in the back while climbing the honey tree—honey trees are not corporate ladders. Pooh does not abandon Piglet, who, as a Small and Timid Animal, fails to be an adequate partner for material success. In the Hundred Acre Wood, the concerns of daily life are not today's priority issues; instead, love, loyalty, curiosity, generosity, companionship, and the celebration of the human spirit are Really Important Things.

AN ONGOING STORY

Winnie-the-Pooh's story has continued both on paper and on film. In 2009, author David Benedictus published *Return to the*

Hundred Acre Wood, a collection of new Pooh stories inspired by the A. A. Milne originals. Meanwhile, on the silver screen, Disney has continued to produce various animated versions of the Pooh story, with films such as *The Tigger Movie* (2000), *Piglet's Big Movie* (2003), and *Pooh's Heffalump Movie* (2005). In 2011, however, the company decided to give the franchise a rebirth with a new animated feature *Winnie the Pooh*. The Pooh theme song received an update from actress Zoey Deschanel, and Monty Python veteran John Cleese provided the narration, while some new voices also came into the mix, with Craig Ferguson, of TV's *The Late, Late Show* as Owl, for example. Some things were considered too classic to change, however, and the film features Pooh's traditional hand-drawn style as well as the voice of Jim Cummings as Pooh, a role he has been speaking since 1988.

The film was viewed favorably by many critics as a return to Pooh's beginnings, although it was criticized by some for its length—clocking in at only sixty-three minutes. Coinciding with the release of this nostalgic film, Disney also produced a more forward-looking installment of the series: an app for the Android mobile device, an interactive version of the children's book *Winnie the Pooh: What's a Bear to Do?*

Julie L. Peterson

SEE ALSO: *Animated Films; Baby Boomers; Consumerism; Disney (Walt Disney Company); Generation X; Hollywood; Macy's; Television; Toys; Video Games; Videos; Wal-Mart.*

BIBLIOGRAPHY

Hoff, Benjamin. *The Tao of Pooh*. New York: Dutton, 1982.

Hoff, Benjamin. *The Te of Piglet*. New York: Dutton, 1992.

Swan, T. B. *A. A. Milne*. New York: Twayne, 1971.

Thwaite, Ann. *The Brilliant Career of Winnie-the-Pooh: The Definitive History of the Best Bear in the World*. London: Dutton, 1992.

Williams, John Tyerman. *Pooh and the Philosophers*. London: Methuen, 1995.

Williams, John Tyerman. *Pooh and the Millennium: In Which the Bear of Very Little Brain Explores the Ancient Mysteries at the Turn of the Century*. New York: Dutton, 1999.

Winslet, Kate *(1975–)*

Award-winning actress Kate Winslet is known for her eclectic choices, seeking out interesting roles rather than large compensation. Often referred to as "The English Rose," a nod to her performance as Rose DeWitt in the blockbuster movie *Titanic* (1997), she has continued to connect with audiences in films both large and small throughout her career.

Born on October 5, 1975, in Reading, England, Winslet comes from an acting family, following in the footsteps of her father, uncle, and grandparents (as did two of her three siblings). She attended a local theater school, and her career started early with appearances in television commercials and television series dating back to the early 1990s. Her first real break came at the age of seventeen when Peter Jackson—who would later go on to direct the *Lord of the Rings* trilogy—cast her as one of the lead roles in *Heavenly Creatures* (1994), the story of two young girls whose obsessive friendship results in them committing a brutal murder. Her first Academy Award nomination would come just a year later for her supporting performance as Marianne Dashwood in Taiwan-born director Ang Lee's *Sense and Sensibility* (1995), in which she starred opposite Emma Thompson.

It was her performance as Rose DeWitt opposite Leonardo DiCaprio in director James Cameron's record-breaking *Titanic*, however, that brought her true commercial success and worldwide recognition (and another Oscar nomination). Yet, rather than moving on to more box-office bonanzas, she followed this up with smaller, quirky films such as *Hideous Kinky* (1998; where she met her first husband, assistant director Jim Threapleton); *Holy Smoke* (1999); and *Quills* (2000), where she played the Marquis de Sade's laundress, smuggling his illicit writings out of an insane asylum. In 2001 she had a Top 10 single in Britain with lead vocals in the song "What If" recorded for the animated feature *Christmas Carol*. That same year she also received an Oscar nomination for her work in *Iris*, starring as the young version of British novelist Iris Murdoch.

Throughout her career Winslet has chosen to work on interesting projects with renowned directors and actors, and her performances are notable for their versatility. Her characters range from the tomboyish Clementine, who dumps Jim Carrey in *Eternal Sunshine of the Spotless Mind* (2004), to the Victorian mother of four in *Finding Neverland* (2004), in which she starred opposite Johnny Depp as Scottish author J. M. Barrie. In the final months of 2006, she appeared in four different movies, the most unexpected of which was the romantic comedy *The Holiday*, starring Winslet and Cameron Diaz as lonely women in London and Los Angeles, respectively, who swap houses over Christmas vacation. Her second most commercial success at the time, it was her first role playing a contemporary Englishwoman. She voiced the part of Rita in *Flushed Away* and appeared in a remake of *All the King's Men*. Also released that year was the drama *Little Children*, where she plays an unhappy suburban mom who has an affair, a role Winslet says was perhaps her most difficult to relate to.

In 2008 Winslet lit up the screen with two films nominated for numerous awards: *The Reader*, where she plays a German woman who has an affair with a teenage boy and eventually finds herself on trial for murder as a Nazi guard, and *Revolutionary Road*, in which she reunites with DiCaprio to play a struggling 1950s suburbanite couple, directed by her then-husband Sam Mendes, known for the 1999 hit *American Beauty*. With her sixth Oscar-nominated role in *The Reader* (a Best Actress Oscar that she would go on to win), Winslet was the youngest actor to have received six Academy Award nominations—she was thirty-three years old at the time. She also won the Golden Globe for Best Actress for *Revolutionary Road* and the Golden Globe and the Screen Actors Guild (SAG) Award for Best Supporting Actress for *The Reader*.

In her next role Winslet returned to the small screen, turning in a Golden Globe–winning performance as the lead character *Mildred Pierce* (2011) in HBO's reinterpretation of the James M. Cain novel (formerly made into a movie released in 1945 with Joan Crawford in the lead). She was also awarded Emmy and SAG awards for this performance as a struggling single mother in Depression-era Los Angeles. Winslet had two 2011 releases: the big-budget, Steven Soderbergh–directed *Contagion*—by far her biggest box-office hit after *Titanic*—and the independently financed Roman Polanski piece *Carnage*, a film with only four actors and one set.

Known not only for her acting, Winslet has been outspoken in her defense of the female form, resistant to the diet and Botox trends that have swept through Hollywood. After narrating an Icelandic film, *A Mother's Courage: Talking Back to Autism* (2009), she cofounded the Golden Hat foundation to benefit children with autism. Despite her growing fame, she remained insistent that her most important role was as mother to daughter Mia and son Joe (children from her marriages to Threapleton and Mendes, respectively).

Carolyn Strug

SEE ALSO: *Academy Awards;* American Beauty*; Botox; Cable TV; Celebrity; Crawford, Joan; Depp, Johnny; DiCaprio, Leonardo; Emmy Awards; Hollywood;* Mildred Pierce*; Movie Stars; The* Titanic.

BIBLIOGRAPHY

Bailey, Sarah. "The Joy of Kate: One of the World's Most Compelling Actresses, Kate Winslet Reveals the Thrill of a Gold Handbag, How She Found Body Balance, and Why Domestic Bliss Is the Secret to Her Success." *Harper's Bazaar*, December 2005, 213+.

"Everything I've Ever Said: Kate Winslet." *Times* (London), January 28, 2012, 8.

Perrotta, Tom. "Kate Winslet." *New York Times Magazine*, February 8, 2009, 39.

Winslet, Kate; Keli Thorsteinsson; and Margret Ericsdottir. *The Golden Hat: Talking Back to Autism*. New York: Simon & Schuster, 2012.

Winston, George *(1949–)*

One of the torchbearers of New Age music, George Winston is known for his passion for the traditional and his ability to synthesize the elements of very different types of American music into his own style of "rural folk piano." Though some might sneer at his music as "easy listening," many welcome it as a deeply felt musical reminder of a simpler time, when life was tuned to the primal rhythm of the seasons.

As a child growing up in Montana, Mississippi, and Florida, Winston spent hours listening to pop music on the radio. He especially loved instrumentals and made sure to tune in each hour for the short piece of instrumental music that preceded the news. The bands he heard in those formative pop music decades of the 1950s and 1960s—the Ventures, Booker T. and the MG's, the Mar-Keys, Floyd Cramer—were his first musical inspirations. Winston began playing music after he graduated from high school in 1967. He began with the electric piano and organ, but by 1971 he was listening to the swing piano of Fats Waller and Teddy Wilson, and Winston switched to the acoustic piano, an instrument he has played ever since, with occasional forays into guitar and harmonica.

Also in the early 1970s, Winston met guitarist John Fahey, who became one of his mentors. Fahey was responsible for developing the "American primitive" style of guitar, and he and Winston shared a passion for nurturing and evolving traditional styles of music. In 1972 Winston released his first album, *Ballads and Blues*, on Fahey's Takoma label, but the album did not sell well, and he went back to doing odd jobs to make a living.

In 1979 Winston was introduced to the music of 1940s and 1950s progenitors of rhythm and blues such as Professor Longhair and James Booker. This music, especially Professor Longhair's "Rock 'n Roll Gumbo," inspired Winston anew. Able to find the common thread of earthy emotion in rural and urban traditional music, folk, jazz, and rhythm and blues, he created his own style: crystal clear, rhythmic, and sincere. In the materialistic atmosphere of the 1980s there arose a subculture seeking spirituality and a return to roots, and Winston's mellow music struck a chord. Those who sought more peaceful and traditional alternatives to a high-tech, fast-paced, hedonistic lifestyle turned to Eastern and other indigenous spiritual traditions for inspiration. They called their movement New Age, and they welcomed Winston's spare, gentle music as a part of its soundtrack.

Winston began to record again on Dancing Cat Records and became one of the anchors of William Ackerman's budding new age label, Windham Hill. This time there was no question of going back to odd jobs. Fans loved Winston's seasonal meditations, including *Autumn* (1980), *December* (1982), and *Winter into Spring* (1982). He also wrote and performed soundtracks for several animated children's videos, notably *The Velveteen Rabbit* (1984), *This Is America, Charlie Brown* (1988), and *Sadako and the Thousand Paper Cranes* (1995). His 1996 work *Linus and Lucy: The Music of Vince Guaraldi*, highlights the music of the little-known composer of such famous pieces as the 1960s classic "Cast Your Fate to the Wind" and many of the *Peanuts* television specials.

Winston released two albums, *Plains* (1999) and *Montana—A Love Story* (2004), inspired by his Montana childhood. In 2001 the pianist demonstrated his sense of responsibility to the larger community with *Remembrance—A Memorial Benefit*, an album for victims of the September 11, 2001, attacks, and in 2006 he released *George Winston: Gulf Coast Blues & Impressions—A Hurricane Relief Benefit*, to help those who were affected by Hurricane Katrina. He maintains an intensive concert schedule, playing more than 100 concerts and solo piano dances a year. Most are in the United States, though he has gained an international following as well and is especially popular in Japan and Korea.

Winston continues to seek inspiration in traditional and vintage music, and he has never ceased in his attempts to bring those kinds of music to the public attention. Along with his continued devotion to old-style New Orleans piano music, he has worked to bring attention to the traditional Hawaiian slack key guitar, a folk guitar style that originated in Hawaii in the early 1800s and inspired the modern steel guitar. An accomplished steel guitar player himself, he has devoted much energy to recording the masters of the Hawaiian guitar in an effort to preserve the dying traditional art.

Tina Gianoulis

SEE ALSO: *Booker T. and the MG's; Folk Music; Hurricane Katrina; Jazz; New Age Music; New Orleans Rhythm and Blues; 9/11;* Peanuts*; Pop Music; Rhythm and Blues.*

BIBLIOGRAPHY

Loder, Kurt. "Windham Hill's Left-Field Success." *Rolling Stone*, March 17, 1983, 41.

Milkowski, Bill. "George Winston: Mood Maker, Closet Rocker." *Down Beat*, March 1983.

Winters, Jonathan *(1925–)*

An improvisational comedian who brought a new kind of comedy to American television and films, Jonathan Winters has challenged his audiences over the years by allowing humor to happen spontaneously. He created such characters as Maude Frickert, Chester Honeyhugger, and Elwood P. Suggins, placing them in hilarious situations suggested by impromptu cues. The unpredictable comic appeared often on NBC's *The Tonight Show*, starring Jack Paar, who gave Winters free rein to extemporize and called him "pound for pound the funniest man on earth." His genius for mimicry allowed him to assume the character of anyone from a small lisping child to a large, wisecracking grandmother.

EARLY YEARS

Born in Dayton, Ohio, to an affluent family, Winters demonstrated early his talent for imitating sounds as he played with his toy automobiles and stuffed animals. When he was seven, his parents divorced, and his paternal grandfather—owner of the Winters National Bank—became the dominant male figure in his life. According to Winters, his grandfather was an irrepressible extrovert whose behavior was a strong influence on his grandson's comic talents.

Jonathan Winters. *Jonathan Winters performed on stage as a stand-up comic as well as on the big and small screens.* DONALDSON COLLECTION/CONTRIBUTOR/MICHAEL OCHS ARCHIVES/GETTY IMAGES.

In school Winters majored in being the class clown and told an interviewer, "I used to drive some of my teachers crazy." At seventeen he quit school and joined the U.S. Marine Corps, serving in combat in the Pacific during World War II. In his spare time he entertained his buddies with sidesplitting imitations of the officers. After the war he returned to finish high school and then drifted around the country, taking odd jobs picking apricots or working in factories, always adding to his store of interesting material that would find its way into comic routines. He decided on a career as a cartoonist and studied at the Dayton Art Institute for two and a half years, which he credits for increasing his power of observation as he later focused his wit on humorous characters and situations.

His future wife, a fellow art student, was entranced by Winters's talents as a comic improviser and persuaded him to enter a local contest for amateur entertainers, which he won. A Dayton radio station, impressed with his talents, hired him as an early-morning disc jockey. As Winters recalled to interviewer Alan Gill of *TV Guide* in 1964, "I couldn't entice one guest on the program that whole year. So I made up characters myself, drawing from the characters I'd observed over the years—the hip rubes, the Babbitts, the pseudo intellectuals, the little politicians." In 1950 he moved to a larger radio station in Columbus, Ohio, honing his talents there until 1953, when he left for New York City.

CAREER UPS AND DOWNS

Arriving in Manhattan with a total of $56.46 in his pocket, Winters began performing at the Blue Angel nightclub, where he met and impressed television personalities Arthur Godfrey, Paar, and Mike Wallace. All three found spots for him on their shows, and his career was launched. Particularly enthusiastic was Paar, who gave him a network audience on *The Morning Show*, which Paar emceed for CBS at that time. In the late 1950s Winters was a frequent guest on Paar's *The Tonight Show* (renamed *The Jack Paar Show* in 1958). He also occasionally filled in for the host, drawing rave reviews in newspapers all over the United States.

The comedian suffered a mental breakdown in May 1959, bursting into tears onstage in a San Francisco nightclub; a few days later, policemen took him in custody for climbing the rigging of an old sailing ship docked at Fisherman's Wharf. His wife transferred him to a private sanatorium, and after a month in analysis, Winters modified his work habits and lifestyle. He explained to Joe Hyams in an interview in the *New York Herald Tribune* in 1961, "I had a compulsion to entertain. Now I've found the button. I can push it, sit back, and let people come to me instead of going to them, as do most clowns like me who are victims of hypertension."

In the early 1960s Winters worked almost exclusively in television, playing dramatic roles on Shirley Temple's children's programs and comedy on variety shows hosted by Garry Moore and Paar. In May 1964 he signed an exclusive long-term contract with NBC calling for six television specials a season. He was already scheduled for a special with Art Carney called *A Wild Winter's Night* early in 1964, but the show disappointed both his fans and the critics, who found it too rigid in format for the freewheeling comedian. When Winters made an attempt to correct this problem in his six specials called *The Jonathan Winters Show*, critics found the shows too loose. Dennis Braithwaite of Toronto's *Globe and Mail* stated that Winters was better as an intruder on other people's shows as "a mocking corporeal wraith who comes ambling out of nowhere to delight and shock us awake and then retires to his tree." After one ill-fated season of the specials, NBC limited Winters to sporadic guest appearances.

BEYOND TELEVISION

One of Winters's major goals in the 1960s was to work in motion pictures. The most important films he appeared in were *It's a Mad, Mad, Mad, Mad World*; *The Loved One*; and *The Russians Are Coming*. He also starred in another medium: audio albums for Verve-MGM, including *The Wonderful World of Jonathan Winters*, *Down to Earth with Jonathan Winters*, and *Whistle-Stopping with Jonathan Winters*, a satire on politicians of all stripes. Making use of his cartooning talents, he created both the drawings and captions in the book *Mouse Breath, Conformity, and Other Social Ills*, published by Bobbs-Merrill in 1965.

In the 1980s he performed with Robin Williams as the baby in the *Mork and Mindy* series. Throughout the 1980s and 1990s, he appeared in TV movies, as well as doing voice-over work in both movies and episodic series, including a thirteen-episode stint on *The Completely Mental Misadventures of Ed Grimley*. He won an Emmy Award in 1991 for his supporting role on the TV series *Davis Rules* and a Grammy Award in 1995 for his comedy album *Crank Calls*. Winters was honored at the Kennedy Center for the Arts in 1999 where he was awarded with the center's Mark Twain Prize, which celebrates humor and its role in American life.

In 2011 Winters was the subject of a documentary *Certifiably Jonathan*, from director Jim Pasternak that featured many top comedians, including Williams, Howie Mandel, Jim Carrey, and Sarah Silverman. Winters continues to do voice-over work, including the voice of Papa Smurf in the 2011 *Smurfs* animated feature.

Winters is an entertainer with a rare and bountiful combination of talents. Director Stanley Kramer, who directed him in *It's a Mad, Mad, Mad, Mad World*, called him "the only genius I know."

Benjamin Griffith

SEE ALSO: *Animated Films; Disc Jockeys; Emmy Awards; Godfrey, Arthur; Grammy Awards; Made-for-Television Movies;* Mork & Mindy*; Paar, Jack; Radio; Silverman, Sarah; Stand-Up Comedy; Television; Temple, Shirley;* The Tonight Show*;* TV Guide*; Williams, Robin.*

BIBLIOGRAPHY

Aylesworth, Thomas G. *The World Almanac Who's Who of Film*. New York: World Almanac, 1987.

Braithwaite, Dennis. Interview with Jonathan Winters. *Globe and Mail* (Toronto), February 19, 1964.

Gill, Alan. Interview with Jonathan Winters. *TV Guide*, February 8, 1964.

Hyams, Joe. Interview with Jonathan Winters. *New York Herald Tribune*, March 5, 1961.

Inman, David. *The TV Encyclopedia: The Most Comprehensive Guide to Everybody Who Is Anybody in Television*. New York: Putnam, 1991.

Lackmann, Ron. *Remember Television*. New York: Putnam, 1971.

The Wire

The Wire, a multilayered police drama that ran on cable channel HBO from 2002 to 2008, provides a clear illustration of the contribution that premium cable networks can make to the artistic development of television programming. While other networks are often driven by ratings alone, subscription channels such as HBO already have a committed audience, which allows them to make bolder choices in the shows they develop. *The Wire*, with its innovative approach to storytelling, gritty realism, and complex characterizations, was just such a bold choice. Though the show did not attract record-breaking audiences and never won an Emmy Award (the traditional symbol of TV excellence), it did draw serious commendation from critics and became a weekly obsession for a committed and discerning audience.

From its beginnings *The Wire* (the name refers to electronic surveillance) took an innovative approach to telling its stories of law enforcement in the city of Baltimore, Maryland. Each multiple-episode season unfolds the details of a single case, giving time and space to develop characters and explore the complex mechanics of the systems that control their lives. Filmed in a starkly realistic style, the show makes the city of Baltimore as much a central character in the drama as its two detective leads, Jimmy McNulty and Shakima Greggs (played by Dominic West and Sonja Sohn, respectively). Like the grimly idealistic McNulty and the unflappable Greggs, the city is presented with a complex human face. Urban poverty, crime, and bureaucratic corruption are never shown simplistically but through the eyes of the people who struggle to build lives within their systems.

With Baltimore as a sort of Everycity, each season of *The Wire* centers on one particular aspect of the snarl of social structures that constitute modern urban life. The first season is an in-depth indictment of the war on drugs; the second focuses on the Baltimore waterfront and the struggles of the city's working class. The third season spotlights the corruption and machinations of city politics, the fourth the problems faced by impoverished children in the deeply troubled inner-city school system, and the fifth the inconsistencies of the press and the decline of newspapers. Within these broad outlines, *The Wire* tells the stories of small-time criminals, poor families, harried police, union officials, politicians, and judges—shattering stereotypes, revealing motivations, and making every character a believable person with flaws and virtues. The show also broke new ground by introducing fully developed gay characters, including Detective Greggs, an unapologetic African American lesbian.

The Wire's insider view of Baltimore police procedure was the result of the collaboration between a former crime reporter and a former detective. David Simon wrote about crime for the *Baltimore Sun* for thirteen years before distilling his experiences in *Homicide: A Year on the Killing Streets*, a nonfiction account of the life of city homicide detectives. NBC turned the book into its police procedural drama *Homicide: Life on the Street*, which ran from 1993 to 1999, with Simon as writer and producer. For his next book, *The Corner: A Year in the Life of an Inner City Neighborhood* (1997), Simon collaborated with Edward Burns, a retired Baltimore detective who had worked as a teacher in the city's inner-city school after twenty years on the police force. *The Corner* was adapted as a six-part HBO series in 2000.

Simon and Burns then proposed a new series to HBO, a crime drama that would present a complex and nuanced view of the problems facing all those who live in modern urban culture. *The Wire* debuted in 2002. Along with Simon and Burns, the new show featured a number of respected crime authors on its writing staff, including George Pelecanos and Richard Price, both authors of numerous detective novels.

Though *The Wire* quickly developed a loyal fan base and received recognition from critics for its innovative approach, quality acting, and excellent production values, it did not become a hit in the traditional sense. Overall the show received only two Emmy nominations, both for writing in 2008, though it did earn the prestigious Peabody in 2004 and won awards from the Writers Guild in 2008 and the Directors Guild in 2009. In an age of explosive action and fast-cut editing, *The Wire* seemed to demand more of its audience than the average cop show. Its one-case-per-season format meant that complex plots unfolded slowly, requiring patience and attention from viewers. In addition, *The Wire*'s unflinching realism meant that story lines often did not neatly wrap up every conflict and loose end but reflected the moral ambiguity of real-life situations. Though *The Wire* went off the air in 2008, it continued to gain fans through its release on DVD.

Tina Gianoulis

SEE ALSO: *Cable TV; Emmy Awards; Lesbianism; Television; War on Drugs.*

BIBLIOGRAPHY

Alvarez, Rafael, and David Simon. *The Wire: Truth Be Told.* New York: Grove Press, 2009.

Egner, Jeremy. "The Game Never Ends: David Simon on Wearying 'Wire' Love and the Surprising Usefulness of Twitter." *New York Times*, April 5, 2012.

Kamalakar, Anand. "HBO: Getting Wired." *World and I* 18, no. 6 (2003): 68.

Lowry, Brian. "The Wire." *Daily Variety*, September 8, 2006, 8.

Potter, Tiffany, and C. W. Marshall, eds. *Wire: Urban Decay and American Television*. New York: Continuum, 2009.

Walker, Jesse. "David Simon Says: The Creator of HBO's *The Wire* Talks about the Decline of Journalism, the Failure of the Drug War, and a New Kind of TV." *Reason*, October 2004, 56.

Wilson, Michael. "After *The Wire*, Moving on to Battles beyond the Streets." *New York Times*, July 6, 2008, AR1.

Wire Services

News was readily available from a variety of competing sources at the start of the twenty-first century: newspapers, magazines, radio, television, and the Internet. Yet many stories, no matter where they appeared, contained much of the same information, sometimes word for word. That is because most news organizations depend on wire services, collectives or for-profit companies that collect news stories, pictures and video; edit them to a standard style; and sell them to individual media. Called news agencies or wire services because of their early connection with the telegraph, organizations such as the Associated Press, Thomson Reuters, and Agence France-Presse provide standardized news at the most economical price.

STARTING OUT

Parisian advertising agent Charles-Louis Havas founded the oldest news agency, originally called Agence Havas, in 1835. In 1849 a onetime Havas employee named Bernhard Wolff started a wire service in Berlin, and another Havas ex-employee, Paul Julius Reuter, a saw an opportunity to exploit a gap in the telegraph lines the following year. He used carrier pigeons to transmit stock quotes between Aachen and Brussels before the telegraph finally connected the two cities in 1851. The following year, Reuter moved the company to London and began using the new Dover-Calais cable to communicate between the British and French stock markets. Reuters later expanded its content to include general news as well, and it managed to scoop other news bureaus with the first European reports of Abraham Lincoln's assassination in 1865.

In the United States, the Association of Morning Newspapers had been in operation in New York since 1820. Its main purpose was to coordinate the reporting of incoming news from Europe. There were other small local agencies as well. The Associated Press (AP) was formed in 1848, largely in response to the new technology of the telegraph, by a group of ten newspaper editors who had come to realize that pooling news gathering made more sense than competing for transmittal over wires already crowded with messages. It was not until six decades later that General George Owen Squier, the founder of Muzak, invented multiplexing. Included in the original consortium were the *Journal of Commerce* and New York's biggest dailies, the *Sun*, *Herald*, and *Tribune*. The first major story to be covered and distributed through AP was the 1848 presidential election, which Zachary Taylor won on the Whig ticket.

When Reuters and AP were first started, any exchange of news between Europe and America was dependent on dispatches carried by ships. One of the first joint ventures by the AP newspapers was a small, fast steamboat based in Halifax, Nova Scotia, Canada, whose crew raced out to meet passing vessels en route to the major East Coast seaports. The crew then sped back to harbor and telegraphed whatever news reports they carried, often beating by a day or more the reporters accustomed to waiting on the piers of Boston or New York for the transatlantic ships to arrive. On the other side of the ocean, as a boat from the United States came in sight of the British Isles at Crookhaven on the Irish coast, a Reuters launch came out to retrieve a hermetically sealed container thrown from the larger ship as it sailed past. Once back on shore, the wire service crew retrieved the dispatches inside and cabled their contents to London eight hours before the ship from the United States docked. This system remained in effect until the transatlantic cable came into permanent operation in 1866.

STANDARDIZATION

Although the first telegraph cable had been laid in 1857, it soon snapped, probably as a result of undersea earthquakes. It had, however, functioned long enough to bring the United States a report of the suppression of the Sepoy uprising in India. (That telegram's succinct forty-two words summarized five separate stories from the British press.) The expense and time of telegraphic transmission tended to force brevity on reporters, but the wire services in their earliest days did not necessarily sacrifice accuracy to terseness. For instance, AP correspondent Joseph L. Gilbert's on-the-spot transcription of Lincoln's Gettysburg Address was almost immediately accepted as authoritative and other reporters' variants soon forgotten. "My business is to communicate facts," wrote another veteran AP newsman, Lawrence A. Gobright, but readers had to plunge 200 words—about 5 column-inches—into his front-page story on the Lincoln assassination before reaching the statement that the president had been shot. It was not until the 1880s that AP mandated the so-called inverted pyramid structure for news stories familiar today, with the most important facts at the top and successive layers of elaboration down at the bottom.

The effect of standardized newspaper style on popular culture has been subtle but far reaching. Apart from the business correspondence and departmental memos encountered on the job, newspapers—or more often their online counterparts—remain in the twenty-first century a primary news source for many throughout the course of the average day, and it is not uncommon for people to consume an hour or more of leisure time reading the Sunday edition of their local daily. Moreover, many writers whose later works have attained the status of canonical literature, including Stephen Crane, Mark Twain, Jack London, and Ambrose Bierce, served apprenticeships in journalism.

Wire-service style manuals continue to play an important role in shaping other types of writing. AP's libel guidelines—a prominent section of their stylebook as a whole—also serve as the standard reference by which American journalists stay on the right side of the law, or at least flout the rules at their peril. Ian MacDowall (1935?–1991), a thirty-three-year Reuters veteran, summed up the goal of news copywriting in the introduction to that company's first and only printed manual as "simple, direct language which can be assimilated quickly, which goes straight to the heart of the story, and in which, as a general rule, facts are marshaled in logical sequence according to their relative importance."

This ideal fairly matched the aspirations of many twentieth-century writers in English—journalists, historians, novelists, essayists, even scientists—who wanted their words to be bought and their ideas assimilated by the ordinary reader. Such authors in turn helped to mold the public's taste toward an expectation of clarity, brevity, and pertinence in the popular press. While MacDowall's touch has been largely eliminated from the second edition (a free, online version of the handbook), many of the guidelines compiled by MacDowall are still germane, with several addendums pertaining to online publications.

VISUAL

Another way in which the wire services have made a lasting contribution to mass consciousness is through photographs. Starting with AP's first photos in 1927 (wire photos were introduced in 1935, at the then-astronomical research-and-development cost of $5 million), on-the-scene photographers have captured news events with images that have become cultural icons in their own right, integral elements of the American collective visual consciousness. These include the raising of Old Glory atop Mount Suribachi on Iwo Jima, caught on film by Joe Rosenthal in 1945, when American troops stormed the Pacific island in the final days of World War II and won it from its Japanese occupiers; a little girl, Phan Thi Kim Phuc, running naked, scorched, and screaming in terror toward photographer Huynh Cong (Nick) Ut with the smoke of her burning village behind her during the height of the Vietnam War in 1972; Murray Becker's stark and terrible photo of the dirigible airship *Hindenburg* burning after it exploded while landing in New Jersey in 1937; and Harry Truman snapped by Byron Rollins on election night in 1948 as the newly reelected president gleefully held aloft a newspaper with the premature and erroneous headline "Dewey Defeats Truman."

Video news agencies, such as AP Television News and Reuters TV, provide a continuous satellite feed of news and sports that many major television networks use for breaking worldwide coverage. Local, national, and cable television stations purchase the video news agency footage in a rough form with natural sound. The television stations edit the footage to suit their needs, add graphics and voice-overs, and transmit the finished product. This arrangement enables international rapid response video reporting of news through the combined efforts of agency crews, worldwide local crews, freelancers, and occasionally the public.

DISASTERS AND WARS

Rarely has so great a mistake as the Truman headline had so lasting a place in the public mind, but the need to make deadlines, however fragmentary the information available by press time, has sometimes led to educated guesses by editors who were proven horribly wrong by subsequent information. Initial reports of the sinking of the *Titanic* in 1912 reported that most if not all passengers had been rescued; only later was it learned that many passengers had in fact been lost, and it was several days before the full extent of the catastrophe was known and printed. Although accuracy and speed of publication often work at cross purposes, the wire services have attempted to reconcile the conflict throughout their history by enthusiastically embracing new technology, from Guglielmo Marconi's "wireless telegraphy" introduced in 1899 (its inventor held for a time a monopoly on radio news service to Europe), the teletype (1915), and the tape-fed teletypewriter machine (late 1940s) to communications satellites and computerized typesetting (1960s), computer-driven presses (late 1970s), fiber-optic cable networks (1980s), and reporters with laptop computers filing stories first by modem (1990s) and later through wireless Internet uploads (the first decade of the 2000s).

In wartime, at least, a second problem with accuracy in reporting has been military censorship, compounded by the need for the wire services to maintain a credible arm's-length relationship with government while remaining on friendly enough terms with officialdom to get the news at all. At the beginning of World War II the head of Reuters, Sir Roderick Jones, received an ominously enigmatic letter directing that the company and its officers "will at all times bear in mind any suggestion made to them on behalf of His Majesty's government as to the development or orientation of their news service or as to the topics or events which from time to time may require particular attention," a directive sufficiently vague that the wire service spent the duration of the war interpreting it as creatively as it dared.

During the Vietnam War, on the other hand, the U.S. military simply lied, with the connivance of President Lyndon Johnson's cabinet, pulling the wool over the eyes of Congress and press alike, as with the Gulf of Tonkin Resolution and the falsified count of enemy troops in the field, which allowed U.S. forces to be blindsided by the Tet offensive of 1968. Though the wire services for a time dutifully printed what they were given, the gap grew between official reports and the observations of reporters in the field, who began compiling reports that were increasingly skeptical. An additional spur may have been the small upstart Liberation News Service (LNS) run by young American leftists who fed information to a burgeoning alternative press. Information uncovered in this way included the LNS story on the 1967 protest march and police action at the Pentagon. It was carried by 100 such newspapers, and the information was often more accurate than anything included in a government press release.

The American government fought back by attempting to discredit the press. AP's Peter Arnett, reporting from South Vietnam's capital city of Saigon, was subjected to a smear campaign by the Federal Bureau of Investigation. In the end, the public sided with the wire services, and their photographs, film clips, and live reports flowing from the Southeast Asia war zone home to newspaper readers and television viewers in the United States played a crucial role in turning American popular sentiment against the war.

Although wire services have sometimes been criticized as exploiters of human suffering, especially when it comes to war coverage, such news is vital to investors and fascinating to most ordinary readers, as when the Reuters report of Napoleon III's speech in February 1859 ran in the London *Times*, giving Britons clear warning of France's impending entry into the Austro-Prussian war. On such occasions, an effective monopoly on news seems a blessing to subscribers, if a bane to the competition.

In fact, three years earlier, Reuters had signed a contract to share stock price news with Germany's Continental Telegraphen Compagnie, also known as the Wolff agency. The German agency had been founded in 1849, the same year Reuter's pigeons took wing. Reuters also shared information with the news company of Charles-Louis Havas in France (founded in 1835, later called l'Agence France-Presse, which remained, with Reuters and the Associated Press, a key player in world news at the beginning of the twenty-first century). In 1870 the three companies followed up with an agreement to carve up the world into exclusive news territories for each, in much the same manner as the spheres-of-influence diplomacy then fashionable among the major imperial powers. As a result, Reuters, Havas, and Wolff dominated international news gathering until World War I.

THE COMPETITION

Ironically, it had been World War I that brought the first serious competition in the Western Hemisphere to bear on the AP, at that time available only to its members and subscribers, who typically blocked rival dailies in their circulation areas from joining. In fact, AP had managed to coerce even its subscriber newspapers not to do business with rival news bureaus, until a court decision put a stop to the practice in 1915. In response to such tactics, several powerful newspaper companies formed their own agencies, including William Randolph Hearst's International News Service and the Scripps Howard chain's United Press Association. (The name was later changed to United Press International [UPI] when it merged with INS in 1958.) When World War I broke out, newspapers in Argentina, frustrated in their attempts to reach an agreement with either AP or Havas, turned to UPI, which soon came to dominate the South American news market as a result, an edge it held for most of the century.

Fortunately for UPI, an antitrust suit was successfully brought in the 1940s to force AP to let anyone subscribe who paid the fee. This did not have much effect on UPI's domestic market share at the time, as many newspapers in the postwar boom years subscribed to more than one wire service. Yet a generation later, several factors combined to weaken UPI's position, including the phenomenal growth of television news, with evening programs providing stiff competition for afternoon daily newspapers, forcing them to close or to transform into morning editions. In addition, the creation of news services by some of the larger chains, such as Knight-Ridder; Hearst; and, ironically, UPI's former owners, Scripps Howard, had prudently divested itself of the wire service in 1982. These new bureaus offered well-written supplemental news stories to fill in the gaps around AP's coverage and did so at much cheaper rates than UPI could offer. A series of bad managers also helped to cripple UPI, and it had ceased to be a significant player by 1990, leaving AP much as it had been at the beginning of the century: the dominant source for print news in the United States and one of a handful of major players across the globe.

In 1992, as UPI was going bankrupt, it was purchased by the London-based Middle East Broadcasting Center for $3.95 million. The company reorganized the agency into six bureaus and set about rebuilding its legitimacy. By 1996 UPI had begun focusing on broadcast and online services. News World Communications, owned by the Unification Church (a religious movement founded by Sun Myung Moon), purchased UPI in 2000 and consolidated the news agency further. As of 2012 UPI produced aggregated content on a narrow range of subjects, favoring niche markets over competition for major news organizations.

Even as UPI was failing, Reuters was enjoying unprecedented prosperity. In 1989, when UPI's staff had dwindled to 650 reporters and 30 photographers, for the first time more major daily newspapers in America were carrying Reuters than UPI. Reuters had never lost sight of its roots in the stock market, and it had also prudently diversified into television in 1985 by acquiring an international TV agency, Visnews, later renamed Reuters Television. Reuters had successfully broken into the Internet by supplying news to nearly 200 websites. By the end of the 1990s, it remained a robust source of financial news, obtaining quotes from more than 250 stock and commodities exchanges, disseminating financial data via a large cable network and its own synchronous-orbit communications satellites, and employing a staff of more than 16,000.

At the beginning of the twenty-first century, Reuters announced intentions to develop a substantial Internet presence and currently provides a wide arrange of online content. Information giant Thomson Company acquired Reuters in 2008, becoming Thomson Reuters Corporation. Throughout the first decade of the 2000s and 2010s the company continued to diversify through expansions and acquisitions in addition to its innovation in trading and financial data dissemination.

The world's oldest wire service, Agence Havas, signed an agreement with Paul Reuter and the Berlin-based Bernhard Wolff in 1852 to split Europe and much of the world into exclusive zones for the services, an arrangement that remained intact until the verge of World War II. During periods of international disagreements, the French government provided funding for the firm, as did the British for Reuters and Germans for Wolff. All three services served as propaganda agencies for their respective governments during and after World War I, and Britain's suppression of the Wolff service is considered one of the reasons the United States entered the war on its side and not the Germans. Following liberation from Nazi Germany in 1944, French journalists seized what was left of Havas, renaming it Agence France-Presse (AFP). It became a government-chartered public corporation in 1957, and the government remains its largest customer in spite of efforts to privatize it.

For Americans, AP remains the standard wire service. In *Flash! The Associated Press Covers the World*, an anthology of its photographers' work published in 1998, Arnett chronicles AP's accomplishments, stating that AP copy that year comprised as much as 65 percent of the news content of some American newspapers; 99 percent of American dailies and 6,000 broadcasters carried AP stories; the wire service employed more than 3,500 people in 236 bureaus, turning out millions of words of copy every day and hundreds of pictures; and employees had won forty-three Pulitzer Prizes. Despite revenue declines in 2010 and 2011, AP upheld its standing as the forerunner in American-based news services, employing more than 3,700 individuals in 300 locations and garnering a fiftieth Pulitzer Prize in 2012. The AP was also recognized for its advancements in social media, specifically its mobile phone access software, from which millions of users were able to get their daily news.

In the century and a half since AP was founded, nearly two dozen AP correspondents and photographers have died in the line of duty, ranging from reporter Mark Kellogg, who perished while covering Custer's Last Stand at the Little Bighorn River in June 1876; to photographer Huynh Thanh My, killed by the Viet Cong in October 1965; to photographer Ahmed Hadi Naji, killed in Iraq in 2007. Wire service reporters, Arnett argues, are ubiquitous; that's their job. Thus, when Mohandas Gandhi was discharged by the British viceregal government in India after serving one of his numerous jail terms for civil disobedience in the 1930s, he was driven to a remote village and let go. He immediately came face-to-face with AP reporter Jim Mills, who had gotten wind of where the illustrious prisoner was to be released and wanted to be on the spot to interview him. With wry amusement Gandhi declared, "I suppose when I go to the Hereafter and stand at the Golden Gate, the first person I shall meet will be a representative of the Associated Press!"

Over a century after its first scandal, wire services are still susceptible to criticism, specifically concerning the control they exercise over access to news and photographs that are published in newspapers around the world. A 2007 study defended the wire services, insisting that it is newspapers that have the final say over photographs that accompany a story and concluding that even when the same information and photographs are delivered to newspapers by a wire service, individual handling of stories results in vastly different stories.

THE INTERNET ERA

The twenty-first century brought with it nonstop access to information; whether the source was twenty-four-hour news television stations, the never-ending stream of content on online newspaper sites, or mobile phone software applications, news was everywhere. But this kind of coverage came at a cost. As more and more consumers received their news from the Internet and television, traditional print media was brought to near ruin. The development of streamlined and in-depth online newspapers have enabled news sources to keep pace with changing technology. Similarly, wire services have had to adapt to the same technologies. While the services continued to make the majority of their profits from major news subscribers, many also offered free content on their websites. Yet they have been eager to protect their legal status as timely, or "hot news," providers, which they argue has special protection under international copyright law from firms that copy or rereport nearly verbatim time-sensitive news reports.

In the 2010s Reuters, AP, and AFP were still key sources of general-interest news, and all three offered extensive real-time coverage. Both the AP and AFP offered mobile-phone access to their content as well. A continued commitment to objective and thorough reporting, as well as keeping up-to-date with evolving consumer habits and media platforms, has enabled the wire services to remain not only relevant but among the most trusted sources of news in the twenty-first century.

Nick Humez

SEE ALSO: *Alternative Press; Hearst, William Randolph; The* Hindenburg*; The Internet; London, Jack; Moonies/Reverend Sun Myung Moon; Muzak; Television; The* Titanic*; Twain, Mark.*

BIBLIOGRAPHY

Alabiso, Vincent; Kelly Smith Tunney; Chuck Zoeller; et al. *Flash! The Associated Press Covers the World.* New York: Associated Press and Harry N. Abrams, 1998.

Associated Press. *Charter and By-Laws of the Associated Press, Incorporated in New York, December 1, 1901.* New York: Associated Press, 1901.

Associated Press. *Member Editorials on the Monopoly Complaint Filed by the Government against the Associated Press on August 28, 1942.* New York: Associated Press, 1942.

Christian, Darrell; Sally Jacobsen; and David Minthorn, eds. *Associated Press 2009 Stylebook and Briefing on Media Law.* New York: Basic Books, 2009.

Collins, Henry M. *From Pigeon Post to Wireless.* London: Hodder and Stoughton, 1925.

Cook, Philip S.; Douglas Gomery; Lawrence W. Lichty; et al. *The Future of News: Television-Newspapers-Wire Services-Newsmagazines.* Washington, DC: Woodrow Wilson Center Press, 1992.

Diehl, Charles Sanford. *The Staff Correspondent: How the News of the World Is Collected and Dispatched by a Body of Trained Press Writers.* San Antonio, TX: Clegg Company, 1931.

Fahmy, S.; J. D. Kelly; and Y. S. Kim. "What Katrina Revealed: A Visual Analysis of the Hurricane Coverage by News Wires and U.S. Newspapers." *Journalism and Mass Communication Quarterly* 84, no. 3 (2007).

Gordon, Gregory, and Ronald Cohen. *Down to the Wire: UPI's Fight for Survival.* New York: McGraw-Hill, 1990.

Hannigan, William, and Ken Johnston. *Picture Machine: The Rise of American Newspictures.* New York: Harry N. Abrams, 2004.

Kirby, Jason, and Katie Engelhart. "Rupert Murdoch vs. the Internet." *Macleans*, January 8, 2010.

MacDowall, Ian, comp. *Reuters Handbook for Journalists.* Boston: Butterworth-Heinemann, 1992.

Mungo, Raymond. *Famous Long Ago: My Life and Hard Times with the Liberation News Service*. Amherst: University of Massachusetts Press, 2012

Read, Donald. *The Power of News: The History of Reuters, 1849–1989*. New York: Oxford University Press, 1992.

United Nations Educational, Scientific, and Cultural Organization (UNESCO). *News Agencies: Their Structure and Operation*. New York: Greenwood Press, 1969.

Wired Magazine

Dubbing itself the "*Rolling Stone* of technology," *Wired* magazine first hit newsstands in 1993. The first magazine to make digital technology seem hip to even those outside the "digerati," *Wired* promised not only to keep its readers informed about the latest tech tools but also to explain the implications of the digital revolution taking place at the end of the twentieth century. With its edgy award-winning approach to design—including splashes of neon, slanted text, and sometimes barely legible fonts—*Wired* itself seemed like some exciting new gadget. "At its height in the mid-1990s, *Wired* could be found in the lobbies of venture capitalists, on the light tables of designers, underneath the coffee cups of computer geeks and in the middle of the only conversation that seemed to matter," wrote David Carr in a *New York Times* review of the book *Wired: A Romance*, which chronicles the magazine's history. "It was, briefly, the coolest magazine on the planet."

This once-coolest magazine was the brainchild of journalist Louis Rossetto and his wife, former magazine advertising sales manager Jane Metcalfe, who wanted a way to document—and participate in—the digital revolution. (*Wired* has since expanded to include four editions: *Wired UK*, *Wired Italia*, *Wired Japan*, and *Wired Germany*.) Gary Wolf, *Wired* regular contributor and author of *Wired: A Romance*, calls Rossetto a larger-than-life personality and the "high priest" of this revolution. During the heady optimistic days of *Wired* magazine's founding, when investors were practically throwing money at every new Internet venture and computer technology was being hailed as the solution to all future problems, Rossetto's grandiose manifesto for the magazine—to foment "a revolution without violence that embraces a new, nonpolitical way to improve the future based on economics beyond macro control, consensus beyond the ballot box, civics beyond government and communities beyond the confines of time and geography"—seemed to fit right in.

While the degree to which *Wired* fostered the revolution is debatable, the magazine did help find the words to describe the revolution. During the late 1990s *Wired* published the *Wired Style Guide* to assist writers and editors struggling with new style questions, such as whether *Internet* should be capitalized and whether *website* should be one word or two. In 2006 *Wired* writer Jeff Howe coined the term *crowdsourcing* to describe the trend of companies paying amateurs (the crowd) little or no money for work once only assigned to professionals now that amateurs had the same access as professionals to such tech tools as product design software and digital video cameras. *Wired*'s "Geekipedia" section offers definitions of critical components of the digital world, ranging from angels (investors) to Zillow (the Internet app that provides estimates of real estate values).

Wired has not only helped document the present, but it has tried to foresee the technological future as well. From 2004 to 2008 it hosted an annual conference called NextFest, which focused on innovative products and technologies. The "Found: Artifacts from the Future" section on the last page of the magazine gives readers an imagined glimpse of the future with such images as the "Hitachi 2400 Smart Windshield," a computer-screen-like windshield complete with chat windows and weather data. One future event that *Wired* was not able to predict was the bursting of the technology stock market bubble in 2002. While the magazine survived, the *Wired* brand had already lost some of its cachet after a failed initial public offering of stock in 1996 and the sale of the magazine in 1998 to mainstream magazine publisher Condé Nast. Nonetheless, *Wired* has secured its place among the important objects of the digital revolution time capsule.

Sarah Roggio

SEE ALSO: *Apple Computer; Cell Phones; Condé Nast; Drudge, Matt; E-mail; E-Readers; Facebook; IBM (International Business Machines); The Internet; iPad; iPod / iTunes; Microsoft; MP3; Napster; Nerd Look; Netbooks; Netflix; Online Dating; Online Gaming; Online Shopping; Postsecret.com;* Rolling Stone*; Second Life; Skype; Smartphones; Stock Market Crashes; Twitter; Video Games; Viral Videos; WikiLeaks; Wikipedia; Y2K.*

BIBLIOGRAPHY

Carr, David. "The Coolest Magazine on the Planet." *New York Times*, July 27, 2003.

Flynn, Laurie. "*Rolling Stone* of Technology to Debut." *Seattle Times*, November 1, 1992.

Howe, Jeff. "The Rise of Crowdsourcing." *Wired*, June 2006.

Wolf, Gary. *Wired: A Romance*. New York: Random House, 2003.

Wister, Owen *(1860–1938)*

Owen Wister was among a long line of lawyer-writers in American literary history. This Pennsylvania-born, Harvard-educated patrician became one of America's first and most prominent writers of the Western genre. Popular in his own time, Wister developed his reputation as a short-story writer. He began to publish his Western stories in 1895 and was acclaimed by many, including Rudyard Kipling. In 1902 he wrote his most famous novel, one that is said by many to define the Western genre: *The Virginian: A Horseman of the Plains*.

Wister was the only child of Sarah Butler and Owen Jones Wister. His father was an intellectual; his mother was the daughter of actress Fanny Kemble, and his mother's family had many literary and musical connections in Europe. Wister, known as "Dan" to friends and family, went to a private school near his home and then to Harvard. There he continued a literary bent shown in earlier years by writing for the college paper, the *Crimson*, and dabbling in light opera. Although his mother encouraged his musical talents, she never seemed happy with his writing work. A review of Wister's correspondence reveals that neither parent ever seemed fully pleased with this capable, well-rounded Harvard Phi Beta Kappa.

After his 1882 graduation Wister studied music in Europe, and his piano virtuosity was touted by no less than composer

Franz Lizst. His father opposed the young man's love of music and pushed his own desire to see him established in a business career in Boston. Ever the obedient son, Wister returned to the United States. While the talented young man languished in his position at the Union Safe Deposit Vaults of Boston, he wrote a novel with a cousin but did not submit it for publication.

Although Wister formed many literary-minded friendships and enjoyed the men's clubs in Boston, his health began to deteriorate. In 1885, following the orders of his doctor, Wister summered in Wyoming. The clean air revived his physical powers and ignited a love of the West that would guide his future career. It was on the frontier that he found his métier, both creatively and spiritually. Wister once wrote: "One must come to the West to realize what one may have most probably believed all one's life long—that it is a very much bigger place than the East and the future of America is just bubbling and seething in bare legs and pinafores here—I don't wonder a man never comes back [East] after he has been here a few years."

According to biographer Darwin Payne, "Wister's deep sense of the antithesis between the civilized East and the untamed West was constant." He did return East to study and then practice law, but ever after he regularly vacationed in the West. Law school gave Wister a chance to renew old Harvard friendships: he corresponded with Robert Louis Stevenson and became close friends with Oliver Wendell Holmes. But none of his letters from that period seems to indicate any real interest in law, even after he began his practice as a member of the Pennsylvania bar in Philadelphia in 1890. The law seemed only something to do in between trips to the West.

Owen Wister. *Owen Wister's 1902 book* The Virginian *is considered by many to define the Western genre.* NEW YORK DAILY NEWS ARCHIVE/CONTRIBUTOR/NEW YORK DAILY NEWS/GETTY IMAGES.

SAGE OF THE WEST

In 1891, after an evening with friends lamenting that the American West was known in the East only through rough "dime" novels, Wister said that he regretted the lack of an American Rudyard Kipling to chronicle what he called "our sagebrush country." As they spoke Wister suddenly decided to take action himself and become that sage. He completed his first story that very night. Soon after he sent "How Lin McLean Went West" and "Hank's Woman" to *Harper's* magazine. "Hank's Woman" is the story of an Austrian servant girl who, fired during a visit to Yellowstone Park, marries a worthless man and is then driven to murder. The story of McLean describes a cowboy's return to Massachusetts, where his mean-spirited brother finds him an embarrassment. Both were published and found instant popular and critical acclaim.

These tales used the same style and formula that would characterize all of Wister's Western works. The stories were based on anecdotes he had heard, used vernacular language in dialogue-based actual speech (which he painstakingly recorded in his own notebooks), and were full of descriptions of the West. Others had already written Western tales, but it was Wister who defined the heroic, Arthurian character of the Western hero and gave him substance.

Wister's popularity and Western topics brought him into collaboration with Frederic Remington. The two worked together on a story for an 1895 issue of *Harper's* about the evolution of the cow puncher. Their friendship and collaboration was a "natural," since many critics both past and present felt that Remington expressed in bronze and with paint the same feeling about the West that Wister evoked with words. Harvard chum Theodore Roosevelt labeled Wister an "American Kipling" and arranged for him to meet Kipling, then a Vermont resident, in the spring of 1895. Upon meeting Wister, Kipling blurted out, "I approve of you thoroughly!" His approbation was great balm for Wister, who suffered much of his life without the approval of his parents—despite the fact that he now had a national reputation.

Not long after his father's death in 1896, Wister began to date a second cousin, Mary Channing "Molly" Wister. A practical young woman, Molly had a career in education under way when the couple married in 1898. For their honeymoon the Wisters toured the United States, making a long visit to Charleston, South Carolina, where Wister's grandfather had signed the U.S. Constitution, and trekking to the state of Washington so that Molly could see her "Dan" in his beloved West. Molly was supportive of his writing, and he supported her activities in education. Wister's writing flourished, and their family grew—they had three boys and three girls.

THE VIRGINIAN

Wister soon decided to write a longer work, and he began to study the art of the novel. In 1902 he published *The Virginian*, with its nameless hero; his schoolteacher sweetheart Molly; and the villain, Trampas. Payne reports that the *New York Times Saturday Review of Books*, in its review of *The Virginian* claimed:

"Owen Wister has come pretty near to writing the American Novel." Henry James wrote enthusiastically about the novel, which Wister had dedicated to his friend, Roosevelt. *The Virginian* was a financial, critical, and popular success. Wister himself turned it into a play, and it continued to be popular long after his death.

Four movies were made of the book: in 1914 (with a screenplay by D. W. Griffith), 1923, 1929, and 1946. Of the four movie versions, the best known was the 1929 version starring Gary Cooper in the title role and directed by Victor Fleming. Cooper seemed best to capture the near-mythic nature of Wister's hero. The nameless Virginian is an American knight—a soft-spoken gentleman who is ready and able to survive—even tame—the travails and splendid chaos of the West. Wister's novel defined the mythic Western hero as a quiet but volcanic strong man who plays by the rules. The story was also adapted for the small screen in a television series that ran from 1962 to 1966, as well as a cable TV film in 2000. *The Virginian* was thus one of the few stories that shaped Americans' understanding of the American West and of the place of individuals within it.

LATER FICTION

Most of Wister's later fiction deals with the conflict between the good and the bad within the West. According to Jane Tompkins in *West of Everything*, his work is realistic in setting, situation, and characters—more so than rival fiction of the period—but still tending toward the sentimental and melodramatic. Wister tried to expand his writing style by writing his own "novel of manners," modeled on Gustave Flaubert's *Madame Bovary* but set in genteel Charleston. The novel, *Lady Baltimore*, was not critically acclaimed and had moderate sales in its time.

In 1913 Wister's wife died and he stopped writing fiction. He began several projects before taking the path of political and nonfiction writing in the era just before World War I. His major post-*Virginian* achievement was a biography of his old friend Roosevelt and many articles about his past acquaintances and friendships. At the end of his life Wister was no longer remembered as a great literary figure. He died on July 21, 1938, just seven days after his seventy-eighth birthday. His reputation was resuscitated late in the twentieth century by the Western Writers of America, which named a major award after him, and by an increasing number of scholars willing to take his work seriously.

Joan Leotta

SEE ALSO: *Arthurian Legend; Cooper, Gary; Dime Novels; Griffith, D. W.;* Harper's; *Remington, Frederic; The Western.*

BIBLIOGRAPHY

Cobbs, John L. *Owen Wister*. Boston: Twayne, 1984.

Estleman, Loren D. *The Wister Trace: Classic Novels of the American Frontier*. Ottawa, IL: Jameson Books, 1987.

Folsom, James K., ed. *The Western: A Collection of Critical Essays*. Englewood Cliffs, NJ: Prentice Hall, 1979.

Payne, Darwin. *Owen Wister: Chronicler of the West, Gentleman of the East*. Dallas, TX: Southern Methodist University Press, 1985.

Soladay, James Richard. *Gone and Forgotten: American Novels and Illustration, 1901–1910*. San Diego: Aventine Press, 2005.

Tompkins, Jane. *West of Everything: The Inner Life of Westerns*. New York: Oxford University Press, 1992.

White, G. Edward. *The Eastern Establishment and the Western Experience: The West of Frederic Remington, Theodore Roosevelt, and Owen Wister*. New Haven, CT: Yale University Press, 1968.

Wister, Owen. *The Virginian: A Horseman of the Plains*. New York: Macmillan, 1902.

Wister, Owen. *Owen Wister's West: Selected Articles*, ed. Robert Murray Davis. Albuquerque: University of New Mexico Press, 1987.

Witherspoon, Reese *(1976–)*

Petite and blond, actor Reese Witherspoon could have spent her career playing spunky heroines in lightweight comedies. However, she has approached acting with a serious commitment and disarming intelligence that has added unexpected depth to her portrayals, and she has chosen her roles with discernment to embrace challenge and avoid stereotyping. By the second decade of the twenty-first century, Witherspoon was among the highest-paid female actors in the film industry and had a solid base of fans who felt they could depend on her for quality entertainment and high ethical standards.

Laura Jeanne Reese Witherspoon was born in New Orleans, Louisiana, in 1976. Descended from an old southern family that included a signer of the Declaration of Independence, young Reese was one of two children of John and Betty Witherspoon, a doctor and a registered nurse. Her father was a military surgeon during her childhood, and Witherspoon spent her early years at a U.S. military base in Germany before the family returned to the States and settled in Nashville, Tennessee. She began modeling when she was seven and later appeared in local television commercials and went to acting camp, where she learned to perform onstage.

Her first break in films came unexpectedly at the age of fourteen, when she auditioned for Robert Mulligan's 1991 coming-of-age drama, *The Man in the Moon*. Though only trying for a role as an extra, Witherspoon so impressed the director that he cast her in the lead. As Dani, a young tomboy confronting the intense changes of growing up, Witherspoon drew critical praise for her natural performance and her ability to carry such a central role. She soon got parts in other films, including a pivotal role in Mikael Salomon's *A Far Off Place* (1993), and in television shows such as the 1993 CBS miniseries *Return to Lonesome Dove*.

However, Witherspoon's parents were insistent that she finish her education, so she juggled acting roles and classes until her graduation from high school in 1994. She enrolled at Stanford University but left after a year to start her film career in earnest. Lead roles as a victim of domestic violence in James Foley's *Fear* and as a tough juvenile delinquent in Matthew Bright's *Freeway* in 1996 continued to prove Witherspoon's versatility and led to still more roles.

Between 1998 and 2000, she appeared in eight films and a number of television episodes, including a recurring role in 2000 on the NBC hit comedy *Friends* as Rachel's younger sister, Jill. However, it was her portrayal of Elle Woods, the frivolous sorority girl who aces Harvard Law School in Robert Luketic's 2001 film *Legally Blonde*, that made Reese Witherspoon a household name. The role of the perennially underestimated cute blond who triumphs over those who disrespect her seemed singularly appropriate for Witherspoon, and her star power made even the negligible *Legally Blonde 2: Red, White, and Blonde* a box-office hit.

The success of *Legally Blonde* made Witherspoon one of the most in-demand actors in Hollywood and one of the highest-paid. With more options than ever, she stepped away from the not-so-dumb blond image to take roles in more scholarly productions. She appeared in Oliver Parker's admired 2002 adaptation of Oscar Wilde's 1895 play *The Importance of Being Earnest*, and in 2004 she received warm reviews for showing the human side of classic literary villain Becky Sharp in *Vanity Fair*, Mira Nair's film of William Makepeace Thackeray's nineteenth-century novel.

In 2005 Witherspoon showed still another facet of her talent when she was cast to star opposite Joaquin Phoenix in the Johnny Cash/June Carter biopic *Walk the Line*, directed by James Mangold. Showing her ability to immerse herself in a character, Witherspoon reached back to her youth in Nashville's country music culture, learned to play autoharp and sing Carter's classic songs, and dyed her trademark blond hair dark for the role. Her sensitive, complex performance was hailed by critics and honored with an Academy Award for Best Actress.

After *Walk the Line*, Witherspoon's career lost momentum as she appeared in a number of critical flops, such as Gavin Hood's 2007 thriller *Rendition* and the 2012 McG comedy *This Means War*. However, she remained a bankable star and earned kudos for her work in the film adaptation of Sara Gruen's best-selling novel *Water for Elephants* (2011).

As her acting career progressed, Witherspoon noted the scarcity of vital, creative roles for women in the film industry. In an effort to gain more control of her own career and help improve options for women in movies, she launched her own production company, Type A productions, in 2000, producing such films as the 2006 modern fairy-tale *Penelope*, directed by Mark Palansky. In 2012 Witherspoon and producer Bruna Papandrea announced the merger of their two production companies to form Pacific Standard Productions, which continued to create innovative vehicles that represent women's experience.

Since her childhood, grounded by the support of her parents and grandparents, Witherspoon has always prioritized her family commitments. In 1999 she married fellow actor Ryan Phillippe and the couple had two children before their divorce in 2008. In 2011 she married talent agent Jim Toth, and as of 2012 they were expecting their first child together. Witherspoon is fiercely protective of her children and has worked with other actors to try to curb the aggressive tactics of paparazzi who follow the movements of her family.

Tina Gianoulis

SEE ALSO: *Academy Awards; Best Sellers; Broadway; Cash, Johnny; Celebrity; Celebrity Couples; Country Music; Divorce; Hollywood; Media Feeding Frenzies; Movie Stars; Sitcom; Television.*

BIBLIOGRAPHY

Bennetts, Leslie. "Regally Blonde." *Vanity Fair*, September 2004, 376.

Brown, Lauren. *Reese Witherspoon: The Biography*. Boston: Da Capo Press, 2007.

Coyne, Kate. "Really Reese." *Good Housekeeping*, December 2005, 118.

De Vries, Hilary. "Reese Witherspoon: What You Don't Know about Her *Imperfect* Life." *Marie Claire*, September 2005, 124.

Pesta, Abigail. "The Reinvention of Reese." *Marie Claire*, October 2011, 220.

Reed, Julia. "Straight from the Heart." *Vogue*, November 2005, 328.

The Wizard of Oz

The Wizard of Oz is a hugely popular and enduring movie. Released in 1939 by Metro-Goldwyn-Mayer (MGM) studios, it has been seen by more people than any movie ever made. Re-released in movie theaters in 1949, 1955, and 1998, the film began airing regularly on television in 1956, and in 1980 it was released on video. *The Wizard of Oz* was nominated for five Academy Awards, including Best Picture, and won two: for Best Original Score and for Best Song ("Over the Rainbow"). The American Film Institute ranks *The Wizard of Oz* as the sixth-greatest American movie of all time, following *Citizen Kane*, *Casablanca*, *The Godfather*, *Gone with the Wind*, and *Lawrence of Arabia*.

Based on the book *The Wonderful Wizard of Oz* (1900) by L. Frank Baum, *The Wizard of Oz* is about a young girl named Dorothy who is transported from Kansas to the magical, colorful Land of Oz by a tornado. Glinda, the Good Witch of the North, tells Dorothy to follow the yellow brick road to Emerald City, where she will find the Wizard of Oz, a mysterious person who can help her get home. Along the way Dorothy meets the Scarecrow, the Tin Man, and the Cowardly Lion, who join her in traveling to the Emerald City. Even though they are threatened by the Wicked Witch, the group makes it to the city, where Dorothy discovers that she had the power to return home all along.

Directed by Victor Fleming, *The Wizard of Oz* stars Judy Garland as Dorothy, Billie Burke as Glinda, Ray Bolger as the Scarecrow, Jack Haley as the Tin Man, Bert Lahr as the Cowardly Lion, Margaret Hamilton as the Wicked Witch, and Frank Morgan as the Wizard. From the beginning, it was a production beset by trouble: cast changes, director changes, injuries, and script rewrites kept cast and crew busy for twenty-three weeks, the longest shoot in MGM history.

The opening and closing scenes of the movie, which take place in Kansas, are in black and white, while the Oz scenes are in sumptuous (and expensive) Technicolor, a relatively new technology at the time. Dorothy's amazement at entering the world of color reflected the wonder experienced by the movie's early audiences. The importance of wonder did not stop there: Haley created the breathless, slightly stilted way he and Bolger speak to Dorothy as the Tin Man and Scarecrow. Haley told Fleming, "I want to talk the way I talk when I'm telling a story to my five-year-old son," and Bolger agreed, saying later, "I tried to get a sound in my voice that was complete wonderment."

Morgan, as the Wizard, perfectly embodied the harmless-trickster aspects of his character. Hamilton, as the Wicked Witch

***The Wicked Witch and Dorothy in* The Wizard of Oz.** *Margaret Hamilton, left, as the Wicked Witch menaces Judy Garland's Dorothy in the 1939 film version of* The Wizard of Oz. SILVER SCREEN COLLECTION/CONTRIBUTOR/MOVIEPIX/GETTY IMAGES.

of the West, scared many youngsters with her bright green skin and high-pitched cackle, even though Baum had wanted to create a fairy tale that eliminated "all the horrible and blood-curdling incidents" of traditional fairy tales, one that "aspires to being a modernized fairy tale, in which the wonderment and joy are retained and the heartaches and nightmares are left out."

BEYOND THE MOVIE

The songs in *The Wizard of Oz*, written by Harold Arlen and E. Y. Harburg, became immensely popular. "Over the Rainbow," Dorothy's plaintive song of a place where "the dreams that you dare to dream really do come true," became a jazz standard in the United States and an anthem of hope in England during World War II. Garland's version remains the most famous, but pop artists as diverse as Willie Nelson, Tori Amos, and Stevie Ray Vaughan have also recorded the song.

The Wizard of Oz spawned numerous remakes and sequels, including multiple animated cartoons, a Broadway show, an ice-skating show, the 1978 movie *The Wiz* (an all-black, urban revision starring Diana Ross as Dorothy and Michael Jackson as the Scarecrow), and the 2007 science fiction miniseries *Tin Man* (starring Zooey Deschanel). Many films, including *Zardoz* (1974), directed by John Boorman; *Star Wars* (1977), directed by George Lucas; and *Wild at Heart* (1990), directed by David Lynch, contain major allusions to *The Wizard of Oz*, and minor references to it are pervasive in American movies.

Dark revisionist fantasies of *The Wizard of Oz* appear in literature, including *Was*, a bleak Oz story written by Geoff Ryman that incorporates AIDS (acquired immunodeficiency syndrome), child abuse, and Garland's childhood; and *The Wicked Years* series written by Gregory Maguire. The first book in the series, *Wicked*, is an Oz prequel written from the Wicked Witch's point of view. It was later made into a highly successful Broadway musical of the same name. A song from that show, "Defying Gravity," features prominently in an early episode of the popular television series *Glee* (2009–).

The Wizard of Oz has also been influential in popular music. Singer Elton John titled an album *Goodbye Yellow Brick Road*; singer Ozzy Osbourne titled one of his albums *Blizzard of Oz*; and the rock group Electric Light Orchestra's *Eldorado* album cover features a pair of green hands reaching for Dorothy's ruby slippers.

The Wizard of Oz is part of everyday life in America in countless ways. Dunkin' Donuts restaurants named its donut-hole creations "Munchkins" after the little-people inhabitants of Munchkinland, where Dorothy's house lands in Oz. Quotes from the movie, such as "Toto, I've a feeling we're not in Kansas anymore"; "Lions and tigers and bears—oh my!"; and "Pay no attention to that man behind the curtain," were emblazoned on T-shirts. In 1990 the U.S. Postal Service released a twenty-five-cent stamp depicting Dorothy and Toto as one of four stamps honoring the fiftieth anniversary of classic, Academy Award–nominated movie.

References to *The Wizard of Oz* also appear in political cartoons, product advertisements, and greeting cards. There was an Oz theme park in North Carolina from 1970 to 1980, an Oz fan club, and a series of Oz conventions. During the Watergate scandal, President Richard M. Nixon was compared more than once to the humbug Wizard. The plot of the first episode of the children's television program *H.R. Pufnstuf* (1969) is unmistakably borrowed from *The Wizard of Oz*. In the late twentieth century, self-help gurus used the yellow brick road from the movie as a metaphor for the quest for self-knowledge.

MYTHS AND MEMORABILIA

Popular myths also sprang up about the movie, such as its supposed synchronicity with rock band Pink Floyd's *Dark Side of the Moon* album and exaggerated stories of the Munchkin actors' bad behavior on the set. A myth about a Munchkin suicide visible in the back of one scene persists despite being debunked numerous times.

The Wizard of Oz was originally released with the tagline "The Greatest Picture in the History of Entertainment," and MGM launched an aggressive merchandising campaign at the time. Objects from this campaign later fetched high prices as collectors' items. Memorabilia from the movie is also extremely valuable: one pair of Dorothy's ruby slippers is on permanent display at the Smithsonian Institution's National Museum of American History in Washington, D.C.; another pair was auctioned at Christie's auction house for $165,000 in 1988.

Film critic Roger Ebert has attempted to explain the movie's popularity: "*The Wizard of Oz* fills such a large space in our imagination. It somehow seems real and important in a way most movies don't. Is that because we see it first when we're young? Or simply because it is a wonderful movie? Or because it sounds some buried universal note, some archetype or deeply felt myth?" Ebert leans toward the last possibility, and indeed, Baum deliberately set out in 1900 to create a uniquely American fairy tale, one with timeless appeal to all the "young in heart." The film—and all that followed—made his dream come true.

Jessy Randall

SEE ALSO: *Academy Awards; Baum, L. Frank; Broadway;* Casablanca*;* Citizen Kane*; Garland, Judy;* Glee*;* The Godfather*;* Gone with the Wind*; Jackson, Michael; John, Elton;* Lawrence of Arabia*; MGM (Metro-Goldwyn-Mayer); Nelson, Willie; Osbourne, Ozzy;* Star Wars*; Television; Vaughan, Stevie Ray; Watergate; World War II.*

BIBLIOGRAPHY

Baum, Frank Joslyn, and Russell P. Macfall. *To Please a Child: A Biography of L. Frank Baum, Royal Historian of Oz.* Chicago: Reilly & Lee, 1961.

Baum, L. Frank. *The Wonderful Wizard of Oz.* Rockville, MD: Tark Classic Fiction, 2008.

Ebert, Roger. *The Great Movies.* New York: Broadway Books, 2002.

Fricke, John; Jay Scarfone; and William Stillman. *"The Wizard of Oz": The Official 50th Anniversary Pictorial History.* New York: Warner Books, 1989.

Harmetz, Aljean. *The Making of "The Wizard of Oz."* New York: Delta, 1989.

Hearn, Michael Patrick. *The Annotated "Wizard of Oz."* New York: Norton, 2000.

Rubin, Lawrence C., ed. *Popular Culture in Counseling, Psychotherapy, and Play-Based Interventions.* New York: Springer, 2008.

Shipman, David. *Judy Garland: The Secret Life of an American Legend.* New York: Hyperion, 1993.

Vare, Ethlie Ann, ed. *Rainbow: A Star-Studded Tribute to Judy Garland.* New York: Boulevard Books, 1998.

WKRP in Cincinnati

The sitcom *WKRP in Cincinnati* mirrored late-1970s American culture through the lives and antics of the employees of a small AM radio station. In its four-year run on CBS, from 1978 to 1982, *WKRP* developed one of the best ensemble casts on television and produced some of the more memorable scenes from the period. The show's ability to build contemporary issues into many of the stories makes it a time capsule for the era, as it dealt with topics such as alcoholism, race, urban renewal, drugs, infidelity, crime, guns, gangs, elections, and even other television shows. In a classic episode about a Thanksgiving promotion gone bad, newsman Les Nessman's report—a dead-on take from the *Hindenburg* disaster—and chief Arthur Carlson's trailing words—"As God is my witness, I thought turkeys could fly"—crackle with the show's characteristic intelligence and humor.

Frank E. Clark

SEE ALSO: *Sitcom; Television.*

BIBLIOGRAPHY

Brooks, Tim, and Earle Marsh. *The Complete Directory to Prime Time Network and Cable TV Shows, 1946–Present*, 6th ed. New York: Ballantine Books, 1995.

Kassel, Michael B. *America's Favorite Radio Station: WKRP in Cincinnati.* Bowling Green, OH: Bowling Green State University Popular Press, 1993.

McNeil, Alex. *Total Television: A Comprehensive Guide to Programming from 1948 to the Present*, 3rd ed. New York: Penguin Books, 1991.

Wobblies

A radical labor union committed to empowering all workers, especially the nonskilled laborers excluded from the American Federation of Labor (AFL), the Industrial Workers of the World (IWW), also known as the Wobblies, played a pivotal role in America's labor history. Believing that the nation's most exploited and poorest workers deserved a voice, the Wobblies called for "One Big Union" to challenge the capitalist system, first in the United States and later worldwide. In 1905 a group of 200 radical labor activists met in Chicago and formed the IWW. The group was overwhelmingly leftist and called for the ultimate overthrow of capitalism worldwide. Immediately feared by most and despised by AFL leader Samuel Gompers, the Wobblies challenged the status quo and fought for the rights of America's working poor. The Wobblies planned to do what no union had tried before: unite blacks, immigrants, and assembly-line workers into one powerful force.

IWW leaders included some of the most famous names in American labor history, such as Big Bill Haywood, head of the Western Federation of Miners; "Mother" Mary Jones; and Eugene V. Debs, the leader of the Socialist Party. Initially, the ranks of the IWW were filled with western miners under Haywood's control. These individuals became increasingly militant as they were marginalized by the AFL. Traveling by train, IWW organizers fanned out across the nation. Wobbly songwriters such as Joe Hill immortalized the union through humorous folk songs. The simple call for an inclusive union representing all workers took hold. At its peak, from 1912 to 1917, IWW membership approached 150,000, although only 5,000 to 10,000 were full-time members.

FIGHTING FOR WORKERS' RIGHTS

Long before the rise of the Bolsheviks in Russia, the courageous and militant Wobblies were calling for a socialist revolution and began organizing strikes around the nation as a prelude to a general worldwide strike among the working class. The Wobblies were nonviolent, but the strikes often turned bloody when business owners resisted IWW efforts. Despite brutal beatings and numerous arrests, the Wobblies continued to fight. They were attacked by the newspapers, the courts, the police, and goon squads formed to protect the interests of corporations. The IWW led important strikes at Lawrence, Massachusetts (1912); Paterson, New Jersey (1913); and Akron, Ohio (1913).

The Wobblies are best remembered for the Everett Massacre, which began in late October 1916. Everett Mill had refused to raise workers' pay as promised, and the Wobblies arrived in Everett, Washington, to bring public attention to the issue. They were arrested, tripped, and poked with cattle prods. On November 5, 250 Wobblies attempting to disembark from a boat were met by the local sheriff and 200 armed and angry citizens. Shots were fired, and seven people were killed. Although the Wobblies were charged with murder, they were later cleared.

As the Wobblies battled for free speech and higher wages across the nation, a legendary folklore developed regarding the union because of the violence and mayhem that seemed to follow them everywhere. The Wobblies became the scourge of middle-class America, especially in the highly charged atmosphere of World War I and the postwar Red Scare. The IWW, according to labor historian Melvyn Dubofsky in *We Shall Be All*, became "romanticized and mythologized." The reality was that the Wobblies mixed Marxism and Darwinism with American ideals to produce a unique brand of radicalism.

As the Wobbly "menace" became more influential, American leaders took action to limit the union's power. In an atmosphere where even criticizing the American government was made illegal, World War I provided the diversion the government needed to crush the IWW once and for all. Antilabor forces labeled the IWW subversive allies of Germany and Bolshevik Russia; one senator called the group "Imperial Wilhelm's Warriors." President Woodrow Wilson and his attorney general believed the Wobblies should be suppressed. On September 5, 1917, Justice Department agents raided every IWW headquarters in the country, seizing 5 tons of written material. By the end of September nearly 200 Wobbly leaders had been arrested on sedition and espionage charges.

In April 1918, 101 IWW activists were put on trial. That five-month trial became the nation's longest criminal trial to date. All the defendants were found guilty, and fifteen were sentenced to twenty years in prison, including Haywood, who jumped bail and fled to the Soviet Union, where he died a decade later.

The lasting importance of the IWW was in bringing unskilled workers into labor's mainstream. After the demise of the Wobblies, the AFL gradually became more inclusive and political. The Congress of Industrial Organizations, founded in 1935 by another mining leader, John L. Lewis, successfully organized unskilled workers. In 1955 the AFL and CIO merged to form the AFL-CIO, America's leading trade union throughout the second half of the century.

The heyday of the IWW lasted less than twenty years, but in that short span it took hold of the nation's conscience. Nearly forgotten today, the Wobbly spirit still can be found in novels by John Dos Passos and Wallace Stegner as well as in numerous plays and movies. By the 1950s and 1960s, IWW songs, collected in the famous *Little Red Song Book*, were rediscovered by a new generation of activists fighting for civil rights and an end to the Vietnam War.

Bob Batchelor

SEE ALSO: *Civil Rights Movement; Debs, Eugene V.; Labor Unions; Red Scare; Vietnam; World War I.*

BIBLIOGRAPHY

Berman, David R. *Radicalism in the Mountain West, 1890–1920: Socialists, Populists, Miners, and Wobblies.* Boulder: University Press of Colorado, 2007.

Carlson, Peter. *Roughneck: The Life and Times of Big Bill Haywood.* New York: W. W. Norton, 1983.

Conlin, Joseph R., ed. *At the Point of Production: The Local History of the IWW.* Westport, CT: Greenwood Press, 1981.

Dubofsky, Melvyn. *We Shall Be All: A History of the Industrial Workers of the World.* Chicago: University of Illinois Press, 1988.

Lynd, Staughton, and Andrej Grubacic. *Wobblies and Zapatistas: Conversations on Anarchism, Marxism, and Radical History.* Oakland, CA: PM Press, 2008.

Montgomery, David. *The Fall of the House of Labor: The Workplace, the State, and American Labor Activism, 1865–1925.* New York: Cambridge University Press, 1987.

Richardson, John G. "Mill Owners and Wobblies." *Social Science History* 33, no. 2 (2009).

Wodehouse, P. G. *(1881–1975)*

British author P. G. Wodehouse's best-known creations are upper-class incompetent Bertie Wooster and his capable servant, Jeeves, who first appeared in the story "Extricating Young Gussie" in 1917. Wodehouse's satirical view of the Jazz Age is both affectionate and incisive; he pokes fun at emblems of the interwar period such as flappers, gangsters, the fascist "Black Shirts," and the dreaded moralizing aunt.

Born Pelham Grenville Wodehouse in Guildford, Surrey, and educated at Dulwich College in London, Wodehouse moved to the United States in 1909 and obtained U.S. citizenship in 1955, after fleeing there to escape persecution in England for collaborating with the Nazis during World War II. It was not until 2011 that he was shown to be innocent of the charge. A journalist and writer of more than ninety books, he also worked as a lyricist and writer with such luminaries as Jerome Kern and George Gershwin. Age ninety-three, newly knighted, and with a waxwork of himself in Madame Tussaud's in London, he declared himself satisfied. He died the same year.

Chris Routledge

SEE ALSO: *Flappers; Kern, Jerome.*

BIBLIOGRAPHY

Connolly, Joseph. *Wodehouse.* London: Haus Publishing, 2004.

Green, B. *P. G. Wodehouse: A Literary Biography.* London: Pavilion Books, 1981.

Langley, William. "P. G. Wodehouse: Filthy Traitor or Frightful Ass?" *Daily Telegraph*, August 27, 2011.

McCrum, Robert. *Wodehouse: A Life.* London: Viking, 2004.

Wodehouse, P. G. *Over Seventy: An Autobiography with Digressions.* London: Jenkins, 1957.

Wolfe, Nero

SEE: *Stout, Rex.*

Wolfe, Tom *(1931–)*

Since the 1960s, American journalist Tom Wolfe has been one of the chief chroniclers of the times. Known for analyzing trends and exposing inherent cultural absurdities, Wolfe has coined terminology such as "radical chic" and "the Me decade." He has a knack for pinpointing an age, wrapping it up in vivid and readable prose, and presenting it back to society as a kind of mirror. Wolfe was one of the first in a cadre of writers—among them Jimmy Breslin, Truman Capote, Hunter S. Thompson, and Gay Talese—to adopt a style called New Journalism, the practice of writing nonfiction with many of the traditional sto-

Tom Wolfe. *Tom Wolfe's ability to chronicle the cultural details of American eras is evident in both his nonfiction and fiction works.* JEMAL COUNTESS/STAFF/WIREIMAGE/GETTY IMAGES.

rytelling elements of fiction. In addition, he distinguished himself by his frequent use of unorthodox punctuation and spelling and by peppering his text with interjections and onomatopoeia.

Some of Wolfe's most famous works include *The Kandy-Kolored Tangerine-Flake Streamline Baby* (1965), *The Electric Kool-Aid Acid Test* (1968), and *Radical Chic & Mau-Mauing the Flak Catchers* (1970). He was also applauded for his 1979 portrait of the early era of the American space program, *The Right Stuff*, and for his first novel, 1987's social satire *Bonfire of the Vanities*. More than a decade later, in late 1998, Wolfe again won warm critical reception with his second novel, *A Man in Full*, which shot to the top of the best seller lists. However, his next novel—2004's *I Am Charlotte Simmons*—met with mostly lackluster reviews. The novel explored—via its main character, a female scholarship student—class prejudice and sexual promiscuity at a prestigious American university.

Thomas Kennerly Wolfe Jr. was born on March 2, 1931, in Richmond, Virginia. In high school Wolfe was the editor of his student newspaper, and he went on to serve as sports editor of the campus paper at Washington and Lee University in Lexington, Virginia, where he also cofounded the literary quarterly *Shenandoah*. He received a bachelor's degree in English in 1951 and obtained a doctoral degree in American studies at Yale University in 1957. Eager to begin a professional writing career, he went to work at the *Springfield Union* in Massachusetts from 1956 to 1959 and then moved to the *Washington Post* in June 1959, winning awards for reporting and humor.

NEW JOURNALISM

In 1962 Wolfe began working at the *New York Herald Tribune*. There, he had the opportunity to contribute to its Sunday supplement, *New York*, which later became an independent magazine. During a newspaper strike, Wolfe landed an assignment for *Esquire* writing about the custom car craze in California. Though he was enamored of his subject matter—the chrome-laden, supercharged vehicles and their young enthusiasts—he told his editor that he could not manage to construct a story. He was told to type up his notes and send them in so that another writer could do the job. The editor was so taken with Wolfe's lengthy stream-of-consciousness descriptions and musings that he ran it unaltered. This became "There Goes (Varoom! Varoom!) That Kandy-Kolored Tangerine-Flake Streamline Baby," which Wolfe later included in his 1965 collection of essays, *The Kandy-Kolored Tangerine-Flake Streamline Baby*. The article's fertile detail, hip language, and unusual punctuation became Wolfe's trademarks.

Early on, Wolfe's style was characterized as gimmicky, but it was also applauded as the best way to approach some of the wacky topics he covered for his pieces. How better to record the rise in LSD and growth of the hippies than to use the language of the people about whom he wrote? Indeed, Wolfe eloquently outlined the 1960s drug era in *The Electric Kool-Aid Acid Test* in documenting the antics of novelist Ken Kesey and his Merry Pranksters, a group of LSD users on the West Coast who personified hippie culture. Subsequently, Wolfe delighted some and angered others in *Radical Chic & Mau-Mauing the Flak Catchers*, actually two separate long essays. *Radical Chic* was his bitingly humorous depiction of a fund-raising party given by the white bourgeois in support of the Black Panthers. His satiric observations cut too close to the bone for some white liberals and black activists; still others were appalled by his seemingly cruel mimicry. However, many critics praised his sharp eye and sociological approach.

BEST SELLERS

Wolfe toned down his style somewhat to pen *The Right Stuff* in 1979, a best seller explaining the rise of NASA and the birth of the program to send an American into space. Much of the book's focus was on the people involved, from Chuck Yeager, the air force pilot who first broke the sound barrier, to the *Mercury 7* astronauts and their families. It gave a personal, behind-the-scenes look at the lives affected by the space program, painting the men not only as heroes with the requisite "stuff" needed to fulfill such a duty but also as regular humans with failings and feelings as well. Wolfe's nonfiction throughout his career was as gripping as fiction because of his use of the genre's devices: dialogue, a shifting point of view, character development, and intensive descriptions of setting and other physical qualities in a scene.

He finally tried his hand at a novel in 1987, publishing the widely praised *Bonfire of the Vanities*, a keen and darkly witty profile of 1980s Americana, from the bottom social strata to the top. His second novel, *A Man in Full* (1998), dealt with similar themes of race and class in late-twentieth-century America, but it took place in the up-and-coming metropolis of Atlanta. *A Man in Full* was trademark Wolfe, featuring encyclopedic knowledge of a variety of subcultures and incisive observations about each. It, too, was a popular and critical success.

Being one of the most visible purveyors of the art known as New Journalism, Wolfe coedited and contributed to an anthology titled *The New Journalism* in 1973. A staple in some college journalism courses, the volume expertly collects some of the finest examples of the practice from top names in the field and explained the constructs involved. Though some of his novels have been considered fine achievements, his contribution to the field of literature generally rests on his nonfiction sociocultural examinations.

Geri Speace

SEE ALSO: *Black Panthers; Capote, Truman;* Esquire*; Hot Rods; Kesey, Ken; LSD; Me Decade; NASA; Thompson, Hunter S.; The* Washington Post.

BIBLIOGRAPHY

Bloom, Harold. *Tom Wolfe*. Philadelphia: Chelsea House Publishers, 2001.

Lounsberry, Barbara, "Tom Wolfe." *Dictionary of Literary Biography, Volume 152: American Novelists since World War II, Fourth Series*, ed. James Giles and Wanda Giles. Detroit, MI: Gale Research, 1995.

McKeen, William. *Tom Wolfe*. New York: Twayne, 1995.

Salamon, Julie. *The Devil's Candy: The Bonfire of the Vanities Goes to Hollywood*. Boston: Houghton Mifflin, 1991.

Scura, Dorothy M., ed. *Conversations with Tom Wolfe*. Jackson: University of Mississippi Press, 1990.

Shomette, Doug, ed. *The Critical Response to Tom Wolfe*. Westport, CT: Greenwood Press, 1992.

Wolfe, Tom, and E. W. Johnson, eds. *The New Journalism*. New York: Harper, 1973.

The Wolfman

The Wolfman—a bipedal, cinematic version of the werewolf archetype—dramatically embodies the Jekyll/Hyde (superego/id) dichotomy present in us all. The character has caught the imagination of numerous authors, artists, and actors throughout the twentieth and early twenty-first centuries.

The Wolfman first took center stage in Universal's *Werewolf of London* (1935) starring Henry Hull. Soon after, writer Curt Siodmak (*Donovan's Brain*, 1942) finished the screenplay for another Universal horror classic titled *The Wolf Man* (1941), directed by George Waggner. Lon Chaney Jr. starred as Lawrence Talbot, an American-educated Welshman who wants nothing more than to be cured of his irrepressible lycanthropy. Makeup king Jack Pierce devised an elaborate yak-hair costume for Chaney that would come to serve as the template for countless Halloween masks. Siodmak's story differs from previous werewolf tales in emphasizing the repressed sexual energy symbolically motivating Talbot's full-moon transformations.

Four more Chaney-driven Wolfman films came out in the 1940s; numerous imitators, updates, and spoofs have since followed, including *Wolf* (1994) starring Jack Nicholson and *The Wolfman* (2010) featuring Benicio Del Toro.

Steven Schneider

SEE ALSO: *Dr. Jekyll and Mr. Hyde; Horror Movies; Nicholson, Jack.*

BIBLIOGRAPHY

Skal, David. "'I Used to Know Your Daddy': The Horrors of War, Part Two." In *The Monster Show: A Cultural History of Horror.* New York: Norton, 1993.

Twitchell, James B. "Dr. Jekyll and Mr. Werewolf." In *Dreadful Pleasures: An Anatomy of Modern Horror.* New York: Oxford University Press, 1985.

Wolfman Jack *(1938–1995)*

With his trademark gravelly voice and howl, disc jockey Wolfman Jack became a cultural icon over the airwaves during the 1960s and was integral in popularizing rock music. The first radio personality to introduce rhythm-and-blues music to a mainstream audience, he opened the doors for African American artists to reach widespread success in the music world. The Wolfman did more than announce songs over the radio; his unique personality lent a context to the sound of a new generation and made him the undisputed voice of rock and roll.

Wolfman Jack was born Robert Weston Smith in Brooklyn, New York, on January 21, 1938, and grew up in a middle-class environment. Always fond of music, as a teenager he would pretend he was a disc jockey using his own stereo equipment. After some odd jobs selling encyclopedias and Fuller brushes, he attended the National Academy of Broadcasting in Washington, D.C. He got his professional start in 1960 at WYOU in Newport News, Virginia, a station that catered to a mostly black audience. There, the Wolfman began experimenting with on-air characters, while off the air he hosted dance parties. In 1962 he crossed the border to begin airing a show on Mexican radio's XERF, which held an extremely powerful 250,000-watt signal that reached across much of the continent. It was at this job that Bob Smith developed his Wolfman Jack persona.

Wolfman Jack's raspy voice and on-air howls and commands to "get nekkid" caught the attention of young music fans across the country. Unfortunately, the Federal Trade Commission was interested in his advertisements for an array of products announced on his show—including drug paraphernalia and sugar pills that supposedly helped with sexual arousal—which led to the demise of the station's profits. Meanwhile, however, the Wolfman became known for playing a range of black artists, including Ray Charles, Wilson Pickett, and Clarence Carter, leading to the crossover of African American artists into white culture. Though record company executives were pleased to see their markets broadening, not everyone was thrilled with the development, since integration was still a new concept. Later, when Wolfman Jack moved back to Louisiana and hosted racially mixed dances, the Ku Klux Klan burned crosses on his lawn. Subsequently, Bob Smith kept Wolfman Jack within the confines of the studio to avoid hostility.

In the mid-1960s Wolfman Jack moved to Minneapolis, Minnesota, where he ran a small local station and sent taped shows down to XERF. Wishing to resume live on-air performances, in 1966 he and a partner opened their own station on Sunset Strip in Los Angeles, which flourished until 1971. After that folded, he accepted a humble salary at KDAY and also began hosting the television show *Midnight Special* on NBC, which aired from 1972 to 1981. He appeared in most of the episodes. Wolfman Jack also had a part as himself in the hit George Lucas film *American Graffiti* (1973), a nostalgia movie about a group of teenagers in the early 1960s. The appearance finally put a face to the name for fans, who were reassured to discover that the Wolfman looked every bit the part, with bulging eyes and bushy hair, beard, and sideburns. Wolfman Jack used this publicity to land jobs on commercials and at concerts and conventions. He was also a guest on the game show *Hollywood Squares* and began working on WNBC in New York City hosting a radio show. In addition, he lent his voice to the rock song "Clap for the Wolfman" by the Guess Who.

Wolfman Jack. *Wolfman Jack hosted popular radio and television shows in the 1960s and 1970s that made him a rock music icon.* © MICHAEL OCHS ARCHIVES/GETTY IMAGES.

In the early 1990s Wolfman Jack flew from his home in North Carolina to Washington, D.C., each Friday to host the syndicated radio oldies program *Live from Planet Hollywood* on WXTR-FM. In 1995 he published his autobiography, which relates the ups and downs of his career, from hobnobbing with other celebrities to his battle with a cocaine addiction. Shortly after completing a twenty-day tour to promote the book, he died of a heart attack at his home in Belvidere, North Carolina, on July 1, 1995. He was survived by his wife of thirty-four years, Elizabeth "Lou" Lamb Smith, and his two children, Todd and Joy.

Geri Speace

SEE ALSO: American Graffiti; *Charles, Ray; Disc Jockeys;* Hollywood Squares; *Ku Klux Klan; Lucas, George; Radio; Rhythm and Blues; Rock and Roll.*

BIBLIOGRAPHY

Shannon, Bob. *Turn It Up! American Radio Tales 1946–1996.* Bainbridge Island, WA: Austrianmonk Publishing, 2009.

Stark, Phyllis. "Wolfman Dies on Cusp of Greatness." *Billboard,* July 15, 1995, 4.

Wolfman Jack, and Byron Laursen. *Have Mercy! Confessions of the Original Rock 'n' Roll Animal.* New York: Warner Books, 1995.

Woman's Day

Begun in the 1930s during the Great Depression, *Woman's Day* played a role in redefining American family life. The magazine began as a giveaway menu leaflet, the "A&P Menu Sheet," published and distributed to its customers by the Great Atlantic & Pacific Tea Company. The sheet was designed to teach women how to get the most out of the Depression-era dollar while still managing to provide family meals that were appetizing as well as nourishing. It included suggested menus for families with adequate budgets as well as for those with meager and less-than-meager spending money.

The menu sheet was successful, but it was also expensive to produce. As a result A&P executives Frank Wheeler and Donald P. Hanson developed plans to make a women's service magazine of the advice sheet. A subsidiary was founded, and in October 1937 the first 815,000 copies of *Woman's Day* were ready for sale for three cents in A&P grocery stores. Six of the thirty-two pages were devoted to recipes and menus. Other pages included advertising for products chiefly found at A&P, an article that told "What to Do about Worry," and another that asked "Is Football Worthwhile?" From its beginning the magazine contained how-to articles. Those articles were expanded in 1947 into a complete how-to section, "How to Make It—How to Do It—How to Fix It." By 1940 the magazine was able to guarantee advertisers a circulation of 1.5 million.

In 1943 Mabel Hill Souvaine began her fifteen-year tenure as editor, and under her management the magazine grew in circulation to nearly five million. By 1952 *Woman's Day* was distributed in 4,500 A&P stores and, like its archrival, *Family Circle,* was, as reported in *Business Week,* "hard on the heels of the big women's service magazines." In the 1950s *Woman's Day* told stores which dress patterns it would feature and then told readers which stores stocked fabrics appropriate for those patterns. In 1958, after a federal judge dismissed a suit brought by several food companies that alleged the magazine engaged in discriminatory practices that guaranteed it advertising revenues, A&P sold *Woman's Day* to the Fawcett Company.

Of the many store-distributed magazines founded in the 1930s, *Woman's Day* and *Family Circle* emerged as the hardiest and most prosperous. With a readership of nearly twenty million in the late 1980s, *Woman's Day* was a close competitor to *Family Circle,* known as the "world's largest women's magazine," which boasted a readership of twenty-nine million. In the 1990s *Woman's Day* continued to be one of the most popular sources of information designed specifically for women and their daily lives.

By the early twenty-first century, *Woman's Day* was feeling the pinch of a protracted economic downturn. At a time when all forms of print media were facing economic problems, the publication was being undercut by cheaper magazines such as *Woman's World* and *Real Simple,* which were also sold at supermarkets. After cutting the base rate guaranteed to advertisers from 4.1 to 4 million in 2005, *Woman's Day* was sold to Hearst Magazines in 2011, and the base rate was further slashed from 3.8 million to 3.25 million. Hearst also reduced the total number of issues sold each year from fifteen to twelve. Nevertheless, *Woman's Day* ranked ninth among the best-selling magazines in the United States.

Erwin V. Johanningmeier

SEE ALSO: Family Circle; *The Great Depression; Hearst, William Randolph.*

BIBLIOGRAPHY

Field, Douglas. *American Cold War Culture.* Edinburgh: Edinburgh University Press, 2005.

"Food-Store Magazines Hit the Big Time." *Business Week,* February 9, 1952.

Ives, Nat. "*Woman's Day* to Pare Rate Base to 3.8 Million." *Advertising Age,* July 10, 2006.

Taft, William H. *American Magazines for the 1980s.* New York: Hasting House Publishers, 1982.

Wood, James Playsted. *Magazines in the United States.* New York: Ronald Press, 1956.

Woodward, Helen. *The Lady Persuaders.* New York: Ivan Obolensky, 1960.

Wonder, Stevie *(1950–)*

In the 1970s, as pop music fractured into a thousand competing subgenres, Stevie Wonder blended pop, jazz, soul, rock, funk, and reggae without trivializing or parodying any of the styles. As he grew from child prodigy to music's foremost ambassador, he topped the charts while winning three consecutive Album of the Year Grammy Awards. A producer, an arranger, a composer, a singer, and a master of numerous instruments, Wonder also did more than anyone to tame the synthesizer, transforming it from special effect to musical instrument. Lyrically he addressed everything from social inequity to romance and heartbreak, from Plant Rights to the birth of his daughter—and he topped it all off with unrelenting good humor.

Stevie Wonder. *Stevie Wonder began his career as a child prodigy under the tutelage of Motown's Berry Gordy Jr.* MICHAEL OCHS ARCHIVES/GETTY IMAGES.

SUCCESS AT HIS FINGERTIPS

Born prematurely on May 13, 1950, Stevland Judkins (later Stevland Morris) lost his sight while in a hospital incubator. From his earliest years he demonstrated an aptitude for music, banging on anything he could get his hands on until his family managed, despite their poverty, to acquire some instruments for him to play. When he was ten years old a family friend introduced the boy to Motown founder Berry Gordy, who promptly signed the youth he soon renamed "Little Stevie Wonder." In addition to performing and recording, Wonder took music lessons from Motown's legendary studio band, the Funk Brothers. Though two early singles flopped, the boy's exuberance and showmanship came through on a 1963 live recording, "Fingertips Part Two," that soon became a number one single; the album, *Recorded Live—The Twelve Year Old Genius*, also rose to number one, a first for Motown.

A couple of lean years followed before Wonder displayed an ability to write his own songs: his 1966 composition "Uptight" became a major hit, and Gordy—who usually discouraged artists from writing their own material—assigned songwriters to help the budding genius. Over the next few years, hits included "For Once in My Life," "I Was Made to Love Her," and a cover of Bob Dylan's "Blowin' in the Wind" that marked Wonder's (and Motown's) first take on social themes. Wonder's "My Cherie Amour" was recorded in 1966 but saw release only in 1969 as a B-side; it proved Motown's Quality Control department wrong when it soared up the charts. As he developed Wonder became increasingly disenchanted with Motown's assembly-line approach to hit making, though he had more freedom than most of the label's artists. He was allowed to start producing some of his own music starting in 1968, and in 1970 won a Best R&B (rhythm and blues) Producer Grammy for *Signed, Sealed & Delivered.*

CONTROLLING HIS OWN MUSIC

But in 1971, when he reached the age of majority and received a ten-year backlog of royalties, he did not re-sign with the company. Instead, he invested much of his fortune in new synthesizers and devoted himself to recording at Electric Lady Studios, designed by fellow sonic explorer Jimi Hendrix. Shocked that Wonder would consider abandoning the Motown family, Gordy negotiated a new contract that gave the artist unprecedented artistic freedom, including his own music publishing company. Wonder responded with a run of the most innovative, popular, and critically praised albums in Motown history, starting with two albums in 1972: *Music of My Mind* and *Talking Book*, which spawned two number one singles, the ballad "You Are the Sunshine of My Life" and the funk tune "Superstition." The astonishing diversity of the material and the ear-opening range of synthesized sounds (programmed by associate producers Robert Margouleff and Malcolm Cecil) were to become trademarks of Wonder's adult career.

His next three albums, *Innervisions*, *Fulfillingness' First Finale*, and the double album *Songs in the Key of Life*, each won Album of the Year Grammies and contained hit singles such as "Livin' for the City," "You Haven't Done Nothin'," "I Wish," and "Sir Duke." The combination of trenchant political lyrics set to breathtaking melodies, unorthodox harmonies, and satisfying rhythms set a high-water mark for pop music; his positive, engaging manner kept the material from dragging the listener down.

Wonder was the foremost contributor to a trend in 1970s soul music (also upheld by Earth, Wind & Fire; the Isley Brothers; and War, among others) that shined a bright light on social problems but always with spirituality, a constructive attitude, and musical innovation. His do-it-yourself approach inspired a generation of artists who wrote and produced their own material (Prince being the most prominent example), and his unwillingness to take the easy way out has resulted in a book of compositions frequently played and recorded by top jazz musicians. Wonder's easy good cheer refuted the stereotype of the troubled, harassed superstar.

FADING MUSICAL SIGNIFICANCE

After *Songs*, however, Wonder's star began to fade. A 1979 soundtrack to the film version of the best-selling nonfiction book *The Secret Life of Plants* received mixed reviews from critics and record buyers alike, and Wonder rushed out *Hotter than July* in 1980 to reassure confused fans that he had not lost his mind. The new album focused on more traditional political issues, with "Happy Birthday" kicking off Wonder's ultimately successful campaign to make Martin Luther King Jr.'s birthday a national holiday. While his next album was in the works, a duet written by and performed with Paul McCartney, "Ebony and Ivory," kept Wonder in the public eye.

Then, in 1984, "I Just Called to Say I Love You" (from the movie *The Woman in Red*) became Wonder's best-selling single ever, but it had lasting negative consequences: the syrupy tune alienated many music critics, and Wonder became pigeonholed as a sappy balladeer. That opinion was bolstered by *In Square Circle* (1985) and its hit "Part Time Lover," which marked an end to Wonder's dominance of the pop charts. The 1987 follow-up, *Characters*, which sold relatively poorly, led off with the single "Skeletons," a hard funk groove with lyrics obliquely addressing the Iran-Contra affair. Despite the feel-good fund raising of mid-1980s events such as "We Are the World" and "That's What Friends Are For" (Wonder participated in both), social criticism with any sharpness had fallen out of favor in pop music. The 1991 soundtrack to Spike Lee's *Jungle Fever* also sank without an impact, though it contained some fine work.

But even as styles changed, Wonder's influence could still be heard all over the airwaves, as his distinctive vocal style inspired New Jack Swing and soul artists such as Boyz II Men, Mint Condition, and Jodeci. Later, in the mid-1990s, British retro outfit Jamiroquai rose to multiplatinum success by directly copying Wonder's landmark 1970s sound. Even with his career winding down, Wonder still won awards, capturing two Grammies in 1996 for his album *Conversation Peace*.

Wonder would go almost a decade before releasing another album, 2005's *A Time to Love*, which featured several guest musicians, including McCartney. He did not tour again until 2007, but he still performed at big events, such as the Super Bowl, a Capitol Fourth, and the 2008 Democratic Convention. Wonder also played at President Barack Obama's inaugural celebration in January 2009, and the next month was awarded by the president the Gershwin Prize from the Library of Congress. The Gershwin Prize recognizes "the profound and positive effect of popular music on the world's culture" and is given to songwriters who "exemplify the standard of excellence associated with the Gershwins."

CULTURAL SIGNIFICANCE

The Gershwin honor was just one of many Wonder has received over his long, illustrious career. He was inducted into the Songwriters Hall of Fame in 1983, the Rock and Roll Hall of Fame in 1989, and the Apollo Theater Hall of Fame in 2011. In 1996 he won a Grammy Lifetime Achievement Award and in 2010 was made a Commander of the Arts and Letters by French Culture Minister Frédéric Mitterrand. Wonder was honored by BET for his contribution to African American life in 2012. Wonder still performs at big events, and most recently he has been seen at the funerals of his contemporaries, such as Whitney Houston, Don Cornelius, and Michael Jackson.

Throughout his career Wonder has been more than just a musician. He has been an activist for causes such as the Martin Luther King Jr. holiday, and he joined the fight against apartheid in South Africa. He has raised funds for such causes as AIDS research, numerous children's and cancer charities, and disaster-relief fund-raising—for example the Hope for Haiti effort in 2010. For efforts such as these over many decades, in 2009 Wonder was named a Messenger of Peace by the United Nations.

David B. Wilson

SEE ALSO: *Funk; Gordy, Berry; Grammy Awards; Houston, Whitney; Jackson, Michael; Jazz; McCartney, Paul; Motown; Pop Music; Prince; Rhythm and Blues; Soul Music; Top 40.*

BIBLIOGRAPHY

Horn, Martin E. *Stevie Wonder: Career of a Rock Legend*. New York: Barclay House, 1999.

Lodder, Steve. *Stevie Wonder: A Musical Guide to the Classic Albums*. San Francisco: Backbeat, 2005.

Perone, James E. *The Sound of Stevie Wonder: His Words and Music*. Westport, CT: Praeger, 2006.

Ribowsky, Mark. *Signed, Sealed, and Delivered: The Soulful Journey of Stevie Wonder*. Hoboken, NJ: John Wiley, 2010.

Taylor, Rick. *Stevie Wonder: The Illustrated Disco/Biography*. London: Omnibus Press, 1985.

Werner, Craig Hansen. *Higher Ground: Stevie Wonder, Aretha Franklin, Curtis Mayfield, and the Rise and Fall of American Soul*. New York: Crown, 2004.

Wonder Woman

As America prepared to enter World War II and American women prepared to take on the roles of men at home, Wonder Woman became the first female superhero in the male-dominated world of comic books. Wonder Woman originally appeared in a nine-page spread in the December 1941 issue of DC Comics' popular *All Star Comics*. Her story was so well received that she was given a spot in DC's *Sensation Comics* in January 1942, and her own self-titled series debuted that summer. Strong, agile, intelligent, and brave, Wonder Woman challenged gender stereotypes, demonstrating that women, too, can rescue people from imminent danger and fight for justice.

Lynda Carter as Wonder Woman. *Lynda Carter brought the DC Comics character Wonder Woman to life in the television series of the same name, which ran from 1975 to 1979.* SILVER SCREEN COLLECTION/CONTRIBUTOR/MOVIEPIX/GETTY IMAGES.

Wonder Woman differed from her male counterparts in at least one important aspect: when she pursued her enemies—who were typically villains threatening America or seeking to subvert peace—she did so with an eye for reform rather than vengeance. Equipped with her golden lasso, bullet-deflecting bracelets, and Amazonian agility rather than guns or a propensity for violence, Wonder Woman was a role model for young women, encouraging them to compete and win in a man's world without ever surrendering their femininity.

A SUPER ROLE MODEL

Dreamed up by William Moulton Marston, who wrote under the pen name Charles Moulton, Wonder Woman was created to fill a void in the comic-book market. Marston, then employed as an educational consultant for Detective Comics Inc. (which later became DC Comics, then DC Entertainment), was the first to notice that the world of superheroes ignored an important demographic: girls. While young boys could pretend to be Batman, Superman, or the Green Lantern, young girls had to swap genders in order to participate in the role playing, a practice Marston perceived as damaging to their self-esteem. With the go-ahead from DC Comics head Max Gaines, Marston began work on the female superhero who was to become an American icon.

Marston's Wonder Woman was a kinder, gentler superhero than those who had come before her. Originally known as Princess Diana, she was raised as part of a hidden colony of Amazons who had fled Greece to escape male domination. From infancy, all of the Amazons were trained in Grecian contests of agility, dexterity, speed, and strength, enabling them to attain greater speed than Mercury and greater strength than Hercules. In addition, each possessed the wisdom of Athena and Aphrodite's ability to inspire love. The Amazons inhabited tiny Paradise Island, located in the Bermuda Triangle and surrounded by magnetic thought fields that prevented its detection.

But when Major Steve Trevor of American Intelligence crash-landed his plane there, the Amazons' lives changed. Diana found him and stayed by his side until he was well, falling in love with him in the process. When Major Trevor was well enough to be returned to the United States, Diana won permission to follow him and aid him in his battle for truth, justice, and the American way. Thus, Wonder Woman was born.

From the beginning, Wonder Woman's mission was one of peace, justice, and equality. While she did set out to capture criminals, she was never violent, nor did she use excessive force unless necessary. She did not carry a weapon but instead relied on her intelligence and agility to outwit and outmaneuver her opponents. She frequently encircled villains in her magic lasso, forcing them to reveal all of their evil secrets, and then delivered them to Transformation Island, a rehabilitation facility created by the Amazons of her native land. Many of her early foes were successfully reformed in this manner.

In addition to being a peaceful one, it is notable that Wonder Woman is a self-made superhero. Although changes made to the series in the 1950s and 1960s described her powers as a gift from the gods, the original story line attributed her superhero qualities to years of rigorous training and self-discipline. This concept, which was finally restored to the series in the late 1980s, suggested that young readers who worked hard enough could also achieve greatness. Or, as Wonder Woman herself said in one of her early comic strips in the 1940s, "Girls who realize woman's true powers can do greater things than I have done." In a time when millions of men were about to become heroes in World War II, Wonder Woman provided an ideal to which young girls could aspire and a vehicle through which they could find their own strength.

TELEVISION AND FILM

Wonder Woman has also had a life on the screen, although she has not had as much film exposure as some other superheroes. In 1974 ABC aired a made-for-TV movie featuring Cathy Lee Crosby as Wonder Woman. This was followed by an ABC action series from 1976 to 1977, starring Lynda Carter and set in the 1940s as the original comic had been. In 1977 CBS took over the series—with Carter still in the title role—set it in modern times, and changed the name to *The New Original Wonder Woman*. Wonder Woman was also animated on the ABC cartoon show *Super Friends*, which ran from 1973 to 1985.

In 2009 DC Comics parent company Warner Brothers took over the publishing company, changing its name to DC Entertainment and presiding over a complete reworking of its superhero comics. Wonder Woman was rebooted, as she had been several times before, with a new history and a new costume in an effort to attract a larger readership. Around the same time, writer and producer David E. Kelley began working on a new Wonder Woman television series. Kelley pitched a serious action series, devoid of the exaggerated campy plots and acting of the 1970s series. Though NBC expressed interest, and a pilot was made, the network rejected the show, leaving critics and fans to speculate about why, in an era when films are being made about many less well-known superheroes, there has been no Wonder Woman film or new TV series.

Wonder Woman has so captured the public imagination that many who have never read a single comic or seen an episode of the television series use "Wonder Woman" to describe a woman of achievement. In 1972 the first issue of the iconic feminist magazine *Ms.*, which sought to empower women, featured a larger than life cartoon of the comic heroine under the banner "Wonder Woman for President."

Belinda S. Ray

SEE ALSO: *Batman; Comic Books; DC Comics; Green Lantern; Kelley, David E.; Made-for-Television Movies;* Ms.*; Superman; Television; World War II.*

BIBLIOGRAPHY

Booker, M. Keith. *Encyclopedia of Comic Books and Graphic Novels.* Santa Barbara, CA: Greenwood Press, 2010.

Handy, Amy, and Steven Korté, eds. *Wonder Woman: Featuring over Five Decades of Great Covers (A Tiny Folio).* New York: Abbeville Press, 1995.

Marston, William Moulton, and H. G. Peter. *Wonder Woman Archives Vol. I.* New York: DC Comics, 1998.

Straczynski, J. Michael; Phil Hester; Don Kramer; et al. *Wonder Woman: Odyssey, Vol. 1.* New York: DC Comics, 2010.

Svetkey, Benjamin. "Wonder Woman: The Missing Superhero." *Entertainment Weekly*, November 19, 2010.

Wonderbra

The Wonderbra, a uniquely supportive and flattering model of brassiere, first appeared in Canada and the United States in the

1930s. By the 1970s it was popular in Canada but had not yet caught on elsewhere. That situation changed in 1991, when an innovative, controversial, and wildly successful advertising campaign relaunched the product in the United Kingdom.

The Wonderbra campaign in Britain presented the bra in a fresh, startling, sexy light. Referred to as the "Hello Boys" campaign, it featured the Czech model Eva Herzigová wearing only a Wonderbra and underwear and gazing down between her breasts. Sales skyrocketed. The success in Britain led to a Wonderbra relaunch in the United States in 1994 that used a nearly identical campaign and was just as successful. Offered at a suggested retail price of $26, one Wonderbra was sold every fifteen seconds in the first year of the campaign. First-year sales reached $120 million, and Wonderbra increased intimate apparel sales for the Sara Lee Corporation, which owned the design, by 14 percent.

As sales skyrocketed, demand exceeded production. Other companies vied for these new customers by offering their own versions of the Wonderbra. By the end of 1994, overall push-up bra sales had increased by 43 percent. Nevertheless, Wonderbra remained the undisputed Rolls-Royce of push-up bras. The Wonderbra design is based on an innovative three-part cup construction, with a precision-angled back and underwire cups. This design gives the brassiere its unique "plunge and push" effect. Removable, contoured pads and adjustable straps that help support the back complete the unique architecture of this undergarment.

Eventually Wonderbra, like Kleenex and Band-Aid before it, became a brand name that is synonymous with a generic product. The American Council of Fashion Designers recognized Wonderbra for "creating a phenomenon never before experienced in the industry." A later campaign for the Wonderbra attempted to re-create the success of "Hello Boys." A 2011 promotion for the "Ultimate Plunge" bra featured women bungee jumping off a building and before an enormous backdrop of an underwear model. The women slide down between her breasts before bouncing back up again. Though it had not yet recovered the momentum of those heady years in the 1990s, the Wonderbra continued to be popular in the 2010s.

Isabel Istanders

SEE ALSO: *Advertising; Bra; Frederick's of Hollywood; Supermodels; Victoria's Secret.*

BIBLIOGRAPHY

Farrell-Beck, Jane, and Colleen Gau. *Uplift: The Bra in America.* Philadelphia: University of Pennsylvania Press, 2002.

Prager, Emily. "Underwire Wars." *New York Times Magazine,* January 16, 1994.

Wong, Anna May *(1905–1961)*

Anna May Wong was the first Asian American actress to achieve Hollywood film star status and an early outspoken critic of Hollywood's racist attitudes. Born Wong Liu Tsong in Los Angeles, she was a third-generation Chinese American. Her first role was as an extra in *The Red Lantern* (1919), and her first lead was in the first Technicolor film, *The Toll of the Sea* (1922). Her most memorable part was in *Shanghai Express* (1932), which starred Marlene Dietrich.

Although she won critical acclaim for her acting in *The Thief of Bagdad* (1924), Wong grew tired of stereotyped casting and immigrated to Europe, where her stage and film work were well received. A gifted linguist, she played roles in several languages. After she returned to the United States, she declined, on principle, to consider playing the role of the concubine in *The Good Earth* (1937). In the early 1950s she starred in a short-lived television series. The last of the more than fifty films she appeared in was *Portrait in Black* (1960).

Yolanda Retter

SEE ALSO: *Dietrich, Marlene; Hollywood.*

BIBLIOGRAPHY

Parish, James Robert, and William T. Leonard, eds. *Hollywood Players: The Thirties.* New Rochelle, NY: Arlington House, 1976.

Hodges, Graham Russell. *Anna May Wong: From Laundryman's Daughter to Hollywood Legend.* New York: Palgrave Macmillan, 2004.

Zia, Helen, and Susan B. Gall, eds. *Notable Asian Americans.* New York: Gale Research, 1995.

Wood, Ed *(1924–1978)*

The director of some of filmdom's campiest flicks during the Tarnished Age of the "B" movie, the cross-dressing Edward D. Wood Jr. is remembered by a loyal cult following as the "worst director of all time" for such unforgettable creations as the transvestite epic *Glen or Glenda?* (1953) and the mock-serious science fiction drama *Plan 9 from Outer Space* (1959). Replete with bad dialogue, moralistic narration, infamously cheap special effects, and an eclectic group of Hollywood outcasts (including an aging Bela Lugosi), Wood's films rank among the most dreadful spectacles in cinematic history. His films moldered in relative obscurity for decades, known only to "B" film buffs, until the 1994 biographical comedy *Ed Wood* triggered a resurgence of interest in his work.

Born in 1924, Wood spent his formative years in New Jersey, cultivating his love of both Hollywood and angora sweaters. Although he was always a heterosexual, he admitted finding comfort in women's clothing. As a marine in World War II, he feared being injured in battle lest medics discover the bra and panties underneath his combat fatigues. In 1946, fresh from the service, Wood arrived in Hollywood with nothing but his unbreakable optimism and a change of lingerie. He spent a few years on the furthest of back lots, paying his dues, producing some short films, and planning his first major feature.

The opportunity finally came in 1953 when Wood released *Glen or Glenda?*, in which he starred as a cross-dressing businessman also known as Daniel Davis. It was during the filming that Wood met Lugosi, at that time an aging, drug-addicted actor desperate for the dignity of regular work. Enamored to have crossed paths with the star of *Dracula*, the 1931 horror classic, and desperate for publicity, Wood immediately invented a part for Lugosi. In the final scene of *Glen or Glenda?*, when Wood's character divulges his obvious secret to his girlfriend and she

Plan 9 from Outer Space. *Tor Johnson and Vampira play a scene from* Plan 9 from Outer Space *in 1959.* HULTON ARCHIVE/STRINGER/ARCHIVE PHOTOS/GETTY IMAGES.

dramatically hands him her prized angora sweater, Lugosi appears as an obviously out-of-place supreme being, inexplicably chanting "pull the string."

Over the next few years, Wood refined his unique style of moviemaking by working on several short films, including the high-camp horror flick *Bride of the Monster* (1955). With neither studio connections nor talented talent, Wood was forced to work entirely outside the Hollywood system, accepting financial backing from any willing sponsor and collecting old stock footage to fill screen time. He also assembled his own unusual Hollywood "family," including Loretta King; the morphine-addicted Lugosi; Criswell, a fake television psychic who once predicted an outbreak of cannibalism; Bunny Breckinridge, a drag queen; and Tor Johnson, a 300-pound Swedish wrestler turned actor. Despite the lack of production values, experienced actors, or quality scripts, Wood truly believed his pictures could make a difference, often relying on blatant narration to illustrate his point. Ever the optimist Wood never once did a second take, because in each instance, he truly believed the first take was perfect.

PLAN 9 FROM OUTER SPACE

In 1958 Wood released his most renowned film, *Plan 9 from Outer Space*, about aliens who transform the dead into killer zombies to teach the warmongers of Earth a lesson. Originally titled *Grave Robbers from Outer Space*, the film was renamed after Wood's unlikely sponsor, the First Baptist Church of Beverly Hills, opposed the original title for religious reasons. Lugosi died shortly after filming began, but rather than remove the only remotely marketable name from the marquee, Wood substituted his wife's chiropractor—who was a full foot taller—for Lugosi in the rest of the scenes. Wood "fans" have practically made an industry of ridiculing *Plan 9 from Outer Space* for the cheap sets; simplistic dialogue; and especially laughable special effects, such as the UFOs, which were nothing more than spinning hubcaps dangling from very visible strings. The film is Wood's true "masterpiece," a perpetual candidate for the worst film of all time.

Wood went on to direct several more movies, including *The Violent Years* (1956), a tale of the "untamed girls of the pack gang," and *Night of the Ghouls* (1959), a film that announced that it was "so astounding that some of you might faint." As low budget as they were, his films rarely made a cent. By the late 1960s Wood was broke and resorted to making soft-core pornography films and writing a few "adult books," including *Death of a Transvestite* (1967). He descended into alcoholism and died in 1978 at the age of fifty-four.

WORST DIRECTOR OF ALL TIME

A few months after his death, Wood was chosen the "worst director of all time" by the Golden Turkey Awards. Over the next decade his films appeared in "B" movie festivals around the world and gained a small cult following, which included director Tim Burton. In 1994 Burton released *Ed Wood*, a comedic tribute in which Johnny Depp was cast as the starry-eyed Wood. The film details Wood's life between 1952 and 1955, focusing on his relationship with Lugosi. Although it did not last long in theaters, the film drew considerable critical acclaim, making many critics' top-ten lists for 1994.

Rather than patronizing the obviously untalented director, Burton presents Wood as a naive and charismatic man with true affection for Lugosi and the rest of his coterie of "misfits and dope fiends." Martin Landau won the Oscar for best supporting actor for his mesmerizing portrayal of the drug-addicted Lugosi, bitter at the Hollywood world that had cast him aside. In the words of film critic Philip Wuntch of the *Dallas Morning News*, *Ed Wood* "succeeds as a salute to filmmaking and, on a personal level, as a valentine to the uncrushed human spirit."

Thanks to the 1994 film, the public gained some respect for the "worst director of all time." Many of his films became available on video, and Wood has become the center of a small but devoted cult following.

Simon Donner

SEE ALSO: *Academy Awards; "B" Movies; Camp; Cult Films; Depp, Johnny; Dracula; Drag; Hollywood; Lugosi, Bela.*

BIBLIOGRAPHY

Alexander, Scott, and Larry Karaszewski. *Ed Wood*. London: Faber, 1995.

Craig, Rob. *Ed Wood, Mad Genius: A Critical Study of the Films*. Jefferson, NC: McFarland, 2009.

Cross, Robin. *The Big Book of B Movies*. New York: St. Martin's Press, 1981.

Grey, Rudolph. *Nightmare of Ecstasy: The Life and Art of Edward D. Wood, Jr.* New York: Feral House, 1994.

Wood, Natalie *(1938–1981)*

Natalie Wood will always be remembered as the beautiful, sad little girl who learned to believe in Santa Claus in *The Miracle on 34th Street* (1947). In that movie, she was flanked by such outstanding talents as Edmund Gwenn and Maureen O'Hara, yet she held her own. Later, Wood proved her talents as an adult, starring in notable films such as *Rebel without a Cause* (1955), *West Side Story* (1961), and *Splendor in the Grass* (1961).

Born Natalie Zackharenko on July 20, 1938, to poor Russian immigrants, Wood was destined to become a star. Her mother was a classic stage mother, aggressive, obstinate, insistent, and convinced that others should recognize her daughter's beauty and talent. Although five-year-old Natalie failed to impress at her first screen test, her mother nevertheless convinced producer Irving Pichel to give her a part in his 1943 film *Happy Land*. In 1946 she had a small part in *Tomorrow Is Forever*, with veteran stars Claudette Colbert, Orson Welles, and George Brent, and one year later she starred in *Miracle on 34th Street*, launching her now legendary career.

Quickly becoming a seasoned performer, Wood made several films each year throughout her childhood. With *Rebel without a Cause*, she showed audiences that she was capable of more complex roles with her Academy Award–nominated performance, and this promise was borne out with another Oscar nod for *Splendor in the Grass*, in which she played a young woman whose parents' attempts to suppress her burgeoning sexuality result in her going mad. It was also in 1961 that she starred in the hugely successful *West Side Story*, completing her transition from child star to hardworking adult actress. Many critics consider her performance in *Love with the Proper Stranger* (1963) her finest.

Although her career was successful, Wood's personal life was frequently troubled. She married actor Robert Wagner in 1957, but the couple divorced five years later. In her search for love and stability, she engaged in a number of high-profile romances with such stars as James Dean, Elvis Presley, Dennis Hopper, and Warren Beatty. Her title role in the movie *Inside Daisy Clover* (1965) is considered to be somewhat autobiographical, with its portrayal of a young girl pushed so hard by her mother into becoming a singer that she loses control and blows up her own house. Daisy's attempt at suicide is comical, but Wood's was not. After a failed marriage and a number of failed romances, she decided to end her life. Fortunately, her attempt failed.

Wood continued working, but her career after 1963 was less distinguished. She tried her hand at comedy, most notably in the 1969 sex farce *Bob and Carol and Ted and Alice*, and later worked in television. In 1972 she remarried Wagner, and as the decade progressed, the couple came to symbolize that rare phenomenon: a truly successful Hollywood marriage. One of the many tragedies of the entertainment industry is that Wood died so soon after finding the stability and love for which she had searched her whole life.

On Thanksgiving weekend in 1981, Wood was killed while sailing with her husband and actor Christopher Walken, with whom she was making a film. The boat had been purchased after the remarriage and named the *Splendour* to commemorate their love and happiness. The coroner's report states that she accidentally drowned while attempting to either enter a dinghy tied to the boat or to stop the dinghy from banging against the bigger boat. She was dressed in a nightgown, a down jacket, and slippers. Reports indicated that Wood, Wagner, and Walken had been drinking, as had the boat's skipper, but the actual circumstances surrounding the event have always been spotty and have bred foul-play rumors for years. Indeed, the Los Angeles Police Department announced in late November 2011 that it would reopen the case; in January 2012, however, they declared that there was no new evidence of foul play.

Elizabeth Purdy

SEE ALSO: *Academy Awards; Beatty, Warren; Child Stars; Colbert, Claudette; Dean, James; Hollywood; Hopper, Dennis; Movie Stars; Presley, Elvis;* Rebel without a Cause*; Suicide; Welles, Orson;* West Side Story.

BIBLIOGRAPHY

Finstad, Suzanne. *Natasha: The Biography of Natalie Wood*. New York: Harmony Books, 2001.

Harris, Warren G. *Natalie Wood and R. J.: Hollywood's Star-Crossed Lovers*. New York: Doubleday, 1988.

Winton, Richard. "Detectives Find No Evidence of Foul Play in Natalie Wood's Death." *Los Angeles Times*, January 10, 2012. Accessed September 4, 2012. Available from http://latimesblogs.latimes.com/lanow/2012/01/detectives-find-no-evidence-of-foul-play-in-natalie-wood-probe.html

Wood, Lana. *Natalie: A Memoir by Her Sister*. New York: Chivers Press, 1986.

Wooden, John *(1910–2010)*

John Wooden coached the University of California at Los Angeles (UCLA) Bruins basketball team for twenty-seven years, ten of those years ending with the National Collegiate Athletic Association (NCAA) championship. Wooden won his first title in 1964 and won another in 1965. After a year out of the winner's circle, his teams won an unprecedented seven consecutive national titles (1967–1973). In 1975 the "Wizard of Westwood" (a nickname Wooden despised) won his last title.

Wooden finished his college coaching career with a .804 winning percentage. Included among his many accomplishments are an 88-game winning streak, 38 straight NCAA tournament wins, and 19 conference championships. He coached some of the best college players of their time, including Lew Alcindor (who later would be known as Kareem Abdul-Jabbar), Bill Walton, Sidney Wicks, and Walt Hazzard, as well as *Hill Street Blues* star Mike Warren.

Wooden's life started in the Midwest, in Martinsville, Indiana. It was there he met his beloved wife, Nellie, who died in 1985 after fifty-three years of marriage, leaving Wooden despondent for a long time. He dedicated his book *They Call Me Coach* to her, writing, "Her love, faith, and loyalty through all our years together are primarily responsible for what I am." Later in the book, reminiscing about Nellie again, he called her death "the ultimate tragedy."

Wooden was considered one of the greatest Indiana schoolboy players in history, quite an accomplishment considering the long history of great high school basketball in the Hoosier state. He had a brilliant athletic career as a guard at Purdue University, and he has been called at times the "Michael Jordan of his day" because of his accomplishments as a Boilermaker.

Wooden retired after the 1974–1975 season, recognizing that his professional responsibilities in addition to coaching, such as acting as liaison with athletic boosters, began to wear on him. He noted in *They Call Me Coach*, "As the years passed, . . . the pressure of the crowds at our regular season games and especially at our championship tournaments began to disturb me greatly. I found myself getting very uncomfortable and anxious to get away from it all."

His name was not forgotten after his retirement. The annual John Wooden Classic basketball game was established in 1994 to ensure that Wooden's legacy would not be forgotten. The strength of his talent in basketball was recognized again when he became the first man elected to the Naismith Memorial Basketball Hall of Fame as a player and as a coach. In addition, each year since 1977 the top college basketball player has been presented the John R. Wooden Award by the U.S. Basketball Writers Association. (One critical factor that Wooden demanded before he agreed to attach his name to the award was that the recipient be a good student, stressing that the primary reason athletes are in school is to earn an education.)

Through the end of 1990s Wooden remained active in basketball camps. He took particular pleasure in teaching kids the fundamentals of basketball. In *They Call Me Coach* Wooden notes that, during his camps, scrimmages are "the least important part of what we teach." Instead the camps emphasize complete attention to the fundamentals of the game. In Wooden's book *Wooden: A Lifetime of Observations and Reflections on and off the Court*, Denny Crum, a former UCLA player and assistant coach who went on to coach the University of Louisville to two NCAA championships, commented, "Coach Wooden was first of all a teacher. I believe he takes more pleasure from teaching than from all the recognition he amassed during his illustrious career."

Wooden's simple style and unique expressions became well known in the sports world. Some "Woodenisms" include "What is right is more important than who is right"; "Don't let making a living prevent you from making a life"; "Much can be accomplished by teamwork when no one is concerned about who gets credit"; "It is what you learn after you know it all that counts"; and "Discipline yourself and others won't need to."

Wooden received the Presidential Medal of Freedom in 2003. He passed away on June 4, 2010, four months shy of his 100th birthday.

D. Byron Painter

SEE ALSO: *Abdul-Jabbar, Kareem; Basketball;* Hill Street Blues*;* Hoosiers*; National Collegiate Athletic Association (NCAA); Walton, Bill.*

BIBLIOGRAPHY

Kirkpatrick, Curry. "Same as He Ever Was." *Sport*, January 1998, 70–76.

Williams, Pat, and Jim Denney. *Coach Wooden: The 7 Principles That Shaped His Life and Will Change Yours.* Grand Rapids, MI: Revell, 2011.

Wooden, John, and Jack Tobin. *They Call Me Coach.* Waco, TX: Word Books, 1972.

Wooden, John, and Steve Jamison. *Wooden: A Lifetime of Observations and Reflections on and off the Court.* Lincolnwood, IL: Contemporary Books, 1997.

Woods, Tiger *(1975–)*

Eldrick "Tiger" Woods is widely acknowledged as one of the greatest golfers in the history of the sport. Famous for his mastery of all facets of the game, as well as his fierce competitive drive, Woods single-handedly transformed professional golf in the early twenty-first century. He attracted legions of fans and helped drive Professional Golfers' Association (PGA) revenues to record levels. In 1997, at the age of twenty-one, he became the youngest golfer to win the Masters Golf Tournament. The victory also made him the first African American to claim a major golf title.

Over the next decade, he dominated the game. By 2008 he had won fourteen major titles, four shy of golf legend Jack Nicklaus's eighteen. In addition to his success on the fairway, he set a new standard for star power in professional sports, earning lucrative endorsement deals with such corporations as Nike, Rolex, and Gillette. At the peak of his career, he became the first professional athlete to achieve total career earnings of more than $1 billion.

In late 2009 his career entered an abrupt and unexpected tailspin amid revelations that he had engaged in a series of extramarital affairs. In the wake of the scandal, he lost a number of key endorsement deals. A highly publicized and messy divorce from his wife, Elin Nordegren, further tarnished his image, plunging his personal life into turmoil. At the same time, he suffered a string of major injuries, which posed a serious threat to his golfing career. In spite of these setbacks, he rededicated himself to regaining his former glory.

EARLY LIFE AND AMATEUR CAREER

Woods was born on December 30, 1975, in Cypress, California. His father, Earl, began teaching him the finer points of golf early in life. At six months the only child was watching his father take practice swings. By ten months—even before he had taken his first steps—he was swinging a club. He was on the practice green by his first birthday. When he was five, he appeared on the television show *That's Incredible!* and was featured in *Golf Digest*.

As Earl and mother Kultida nurtured their son's golf talents, they ingrained in him values of trust and respect. They kept him out of trouble, often by revoking his golf privileges or refusing to let him practice golf until he had completed his homework. Earl used his military training to prepare Tiger for the rigors of golf—for example, by intentionally distracting the young golfer as he prepared a shot. The training paid off. At fifteen Woods was the youngest golfer ever to win the U.S. Junior Amateur title, the first of three consecutive titles at that level. He went on to win three consecutive U.S. Men's Amateur titles, the only player in U.S. history to win both the Junior and Amateur titles.

Tiger Woods. *Tiger Woods hits a tee shot at a tournament in Thousand Oaks, California, in December 2011.* AP IMAGES.

PROFESSIONAL CAREER

In 1996 Woods became the National Collegiate Athletic Association (NCAA) golf champion. Bored with the college game, he decided to turn professional. In September 1996 he finished in a respectable sixtieth place at the Greater Milwaukee Open with a score of seven under par, earning $2,544 for his efforts. A few weeks later he won his first tournament in Las Vegas, Nevada, which ensured him a spot on the PGA Tour for 1997. After his fantastic start, *Sports Illustrated* named him Sportsman of the Year.

Woods's biggest accomplishment came in April 1997 at the Masters in Augusta, Georgia, where he shattered the tournament's record for largest margin of victory. After a rough start on the first nine holes, which left him at four over par, he made a subtle adjustment to his swing, according to father Earl. On the next sixty-three holes, he put on a show the likes of which the famed Augusta National Golf Club had never seen. He finished eighteen under par, winning by twelve strokes. Both feats set new records, and at twenty-one he became the youngest Masters champ in history, as well as the first African American to win the Masters.

In total, his performance broke twenty records almost fifty years to the day after baseball legend Jackie Robinson broke Major League Baseball's color barrier. Unfortunately, racially insensitive comments made by golfer Fuzzy Zoeller somewhat overshadowed the event. Although Zoeller immediately apologized for his remarks, the story persisted for several weeks. Some blamed Woods for the media attention because he was less than forgiving of Zoeller and did not return his phone calls.

Nevertheless, Woods quickly emerged as golf's most dominant player. He won the PGA Championship in 1999 and took three of four major titles in 2000. Among the most impressive performances of his career were at the 2000 U.S. Open, where he won by fifteen strokes, shattering a tournament record that had stood for 101 years. Between 2001 and 2008 he won three Masters titles, two British Open titles, two PGA championships, and two U.S. Open titles.

His 2008 U.S. Open win, a sudden-death victory over Rocco Mediate, was particularly impressive because he was battling serious knee issues throughout the tournament. Shortly after taking his third U.S. Open title, he elected to undergo reconstructive surgery, which kept him out of competition for the remainder of the year. He returned in 2009 to lead PGA golfers in total winnings, and his competitors voted him the year's top player for the tenth time in his career.

SCANDAL AND RECOVERY

Although his success had made him the most famous athlete in the world, his rise to fame came to an abrupt halt in November 2009 when police responded to a report that he had crashed his SUV into a fire hydrant near his home. Over the next several days, stories emerged claiming he had been fleeing his wife after a bitter fight. In the ensuing media frenzy, his involvement in a string of extramarital affairs surfaced. Although he announced he would be taking a hiatus from the game in order to repair his family life, the damage to his marriage proved too great. Elin filed for divorce a short time later, and he checked into a clinic to seek treatment for sex addiction in early 2010.

In the aftermath of the scandal, he struggled to regain his former status on the PGA Tour. In July 2011, amid his growing frustration with the declining quality of his game, he fired his longtime caddie, Steve Williams. The decision shocked the golf world, causing many to wonder if he would ever regain his former glory. Woods, however, remained focused on proving his doubters wrong. After undergoing a grueling rehabilitation and training regimen, with his personal troubles slowly fading into the background, he rededicated himself to chasing Nicklaus's major title record.

Woods is remarkable for the records he has set and his defiance of the image of traditional golf legends. For many years golf had been mostly an elitist white man's sport (through 1961 the constitution of the PGA of America contained a "Caucasian clause"). Because Woods came from a typical middle-class background and was the son of an African American father and a Thai mother, his success helped open up the game of golf to minorities, and many blacks picked up golf specifically because of him. Nevertheless, he has publicly grappled with his racial identity, stating he is Cablinasian—Caucasian, black, Indian, and Asian—and at times shunning the African American label (though he does not deny his father's African American roots). When he turned professional in 1996, he told *Newsweek*, "I don't see myself as the Great Black Hope. I'm just a golfer who happens to be black and Asian."

D. Byron Painter

SEE ALSO: *Divorce; Golf; The Masters Golf Tournament; Media Feeding Frenzies; National Collegiate Athletic Association (NCAA);* Newsweek*; Nicklaus, Jack; Nike; Robinson, Jackie; Sex Scandals; Sports Heroes;* Sports Illustrated.

BIBLIOGRAPHY

Abrahams, Jonathan. "Golden Child or Spoiled Brat?" *Golf Magazine*, April 1998, 56–65.

"Black America and Tiger's Dilemma: National Leaders Praise Golfer's Accomplishments and Debate Controversial 'Mixed Race' Issue." *Ebony*, July 1997, 28–33.

DiMeglio, Steve. "What's Next for Tiger?" *USA Today*, February 9, 2012.

Feinstein, John. "Tiger by the Tail." *Newsweek*, September 9, 1996, 58–61.

Feinstein, John. *The First Coming: Tiger Woods, Master or Martyr?* New York: Ballantine Publishing Group, 1998.

Mahler, Jonathan. "The Tiger Bubble." *New York Times*, March 28, 2010.

McCormick, John, and Sharon Begley. "How to Raise a Tiger." *Newsweek*, December 9, 1996, 52–57.

Strege, John. *Tiger: A Biography of Tiger Woods*. New York: Broadway Books, 1997.

Tigerwoods.com. Accessed March 2012. Available from http://web.tigerwoods.com

Woods, Earl. *Training a Tiger: A Father's Guide to Raising a Winner in Both Golf and Life*. New York: HarperCollins, 1997.

Woods, Earl. *Playing through: Straight Talk on Hard Work, Big Dreams, and Adventures with Tiger*. New York: HarperCollins, 1998.

Woodstock

In the 1960s the small town of Woodstock, New York, 90 miles north of New York City, nourished a small but growing community of folk musicians, including Bob Dylan, the Band, Tim Hardin, and John Sebastian. In 1969 Michael Lang, a young entrepreneur who had promoted the Miami Pop Festival the previous year, decided to open a recording studio for the burgeoning music community that would double as a woodland retreat for recording artists from New York City. Lang pitched his idea to Artie Kornfeld, a young executive at Capitol Records, and Joel Rosenman and John Roberts, two young entrepreneurs interested in unconventional business propositions. Together they formed a corporation, Woodstock Ventures, to create the studio and retreat center. They also decided to organize a Woodstock Music and Arts Fair to promote the opening of the studio.

As their festival plans grew more ambitious, the group realized that the small town could not accommodate such a festival, and a site in Wallkill, in the neighboring county, was chosen for the three-day-weekend event. Throughout the summer of 1969, the project snowballed as more and more artists were signed to perform. According to the plan, day one would feature folk-rock artists, day two would spotlight the burgeoning San Francisco scene, and day three would be saved for the hottest acts. By the time Jimi Hendrix agreed to play for $50,000, many of the foremost American bands had already signed on, as well as such major British groups as the Who and Ten Years After. The music soon eclipsed all other aspects of the festival, including the arts fair (which has been effectively forgotten) and the recording studio (which never materialized).

BRASS TACKS AND BETRAYALS

Woodstock Ventures spared no expense to cultivate a hip, counterculture image for their celebration of peace and music. They advertised the event through the underground press—which was rapidly mushrooming into a national network of antiestablishment groups—spreading the word that this was the happening event of the summer. Although they chose the Wallkill site for its rustic scenery and laid-back atmosphere, the name Woodstock was retained to convey the bucolic theme of the weekend. Throughout 1968 and 1969 the country-rock movement spearheaded by Dylan, the Band, and others reflected an emerging pastoral craze: "getting back to nature." Such films as *Easy Rider* (1969), which depicted hippies cruising across the country, living off the land (more or less), and visiting communes, celebrated the lure of the countryside.

Woodstock Ventures hired the Hog Farm, a New Mexico hippie commune, to prepare the festival campgrounds and maintain a free kitchen. The commune also set up a bad-trip shelter called the Big Pink for the drug freak-outs that were expected. An impromptu organization called Food for Love was engaged to run concession booths. The organizers enlisted Wes Pomeroy, renowned for his enlightened attitude toward youth and crowd control, as chief of security. Pomeroy recruited a nonaggressive, nonuniformed, unarmed security team—the "Peace Service Corps"—to unobtrusively dissuade undesirable behavior, such as riots, vandalism, and theft, while overlooking nonviolent activities, including drugs, sex, and nudity. Unfortunately, almost all of these suppliers eventually betrayed Woodstock Ventures.

A month before the scheduled weekend, the town of Wallkill voted to oust the festival. The organizers found a new site about 40 miles west in Bethel, New York, where they were able to overcome a lesser amount of resistance. Soon, they began to run into more alarming conflicts. The radical activist and showman Abbie Hoffman, a self-styled "cultural revolutionary" who had been charged (along with the rest of the Chicago Seven) with inciting riots at the 1968 Chicago Democratic Convention, threatened to sabotage the festival by using his influence over the underground press if Woodstock Ventures did not pay him $50,000. He claimed that the promoters were growing rich off the people and concluded that Woodstock should return the money by financing his own political mission, including his mounting legal debts. Hoffman also threatened to put acid in the water. The Woodstock promoters knew that Hoffman had the audacity and the power to arouse antiestablishment animosity toward the festival, so they paid him $10,000 to appease him. Many radical papers nevertheless portrayed Woodstock as a capitalist venture promoted by "straights" trying to profit from "the people."

FURTHER SETBACKS

Betrayals grew more frequent as the weekend approached. The day before the festival, the New York City police commissioner refused his officers permission to work at Woodstock. The officers then offered their services anonymously for extortionate wages. Thousands of tickets were sold, but since the gates were not built in time, droves of young people began streaming in days before the show. By Friday the promoters, having no way to collect tickets, had to declare Woodstock a free concert. Meanwhile, cars, vans, delivery vehicles, and masses of concertgoers clogged several miles of the New York State Thruway through the weekend, while acres of land rented for parking remained empty. State troopers arrested hippies on their way to the show, then danced naked on their patrol cars after drinking water laced with acid. Tons of supplies, and even some musicians, were stuck in the traffic jam and never made it to the site.

At the festival itself, the Hog Farm was proving to be opportunistic and irresponsible, stealing watches and wallets from the Woodstock staff and clashing with anyone they perceived as establishmentarian, including the medical staff. Food for Love threatened to quit during the festival, reneging on their prepaid $75,000 contract. A 40-foot trailer full of hot dogs rotted when refrigeration fuel ran out, and thousands of people endured the stench of rancid food while they went hungry. A rumor arose that Woodstock Ventures was bankrupt, and many bands refused to perform unless they were paid ahead in cash. Even the Grateful Dead, the most anticommercial band on the scene, demanded their fee, although two years earlier they had played for free outside the Monterey Pop Festival. Even Mother Nature refused to cooperate, assailing her hippie worshippers with two rainstorms that steeped the throng of 500,000 in mud. The revolving stage, designed to eliminate intermissions between acts, was the biggest and most expensive ever built, but once the equipment was loaded onto it, it refused to revolve (the only time it budged was when the mudslide hit it). Out in woods near the campgrounds a "pharmacy district" supplied illegal drugs.

NONVIOLENT BLISS

Woodstock was officially pronounced a disaster; a monument to faulty planning; a testament to the limitations and hypocrisies of hippie idealism; and a nightmare of absurdities, ironies, and incongruities. None of the pressures, however—bad press, bad weather, bad drug trips, technical problems, human error and duplicity—was enough to snuff the spirit of the crowd that had assembled for three days of peace and music. The most common feeling among all parties, including producers, musicians, audience, town, and nation, was the sense of history in the making. The festival had the largest group of young people ever gathered, drew the greatest roster of rock and folk musicians ever assembled, and became the defining moment of a generation. Initial media response tended toward panic, reporting the calamitous aspects of the event, but when riots failed to flare up, they recanted, reporting that Woodstock was a mass epiphany of goodwill and communal sharing.

On Sunday Max Yasgur, the dairy farmer who rented his 600 acres to the festival, took the stage and complimented the crowd, observing that the festival proved that "half a million kids can get together and have three days of fun and music, and have nothing BUT fun and music." The conspicuous absence Yasgur alluded to was violence. Rock festivals had become increasingly frequent since the Monterey Pop Festival in 1967, each one bigger and more riotous than the last. The assassinations of Martin Luther King Jr. and Robert Kennedy had also added a feeling of dread to all large gatherings. Woodstock promised nothing but disaster, then passed without a single act of violence; the relief that swept over the watching nation was almost intoxicating. It seemed like a miracle.

PULLING TOGETHER

Many commentators have since claimed that peace and goodwill arose at the event not in spite of disaster but because of it: that the hunger, rain, mud, and unserviced toilets conspired to create an adversity against which people could unite and bond. In "The Woodstock Wars," an article in the *New Yorker* magazine, Hal Espen observed that the communal spirit of the festival was typical of the group psychology of disasters: "What takes hold at the time is a humbling sense of togetherness . . . with those who shared the experience. What takes hold later is a privileged sense of apartness . . . from those who didn't." Espen explained that the memory of Woodstock led a generation to lay claim to "an epic and heroic youth culture" that subsequent generations could not match. Those who had been baby boomers now dubbed themselves "Woodstock Nation," an independent and enlightened subculture. Immediately after the concert Hoffman wrote a book of editorials (*Woodstock Nation*) contrasting the newly united masses with the "Pig Nation" of mainstream America.

It was not just the audience of hippies who bonded together in the face of adversity; community and nation joined in coming to their aid. The Red Cross, Girl Scouts, and Boy Scouts all donated food and supplies to the starving masses of concertgoers. Even local townspeople pardoned the havoc wrought upon their town and made sandwiches for the infiltrators. The youths who had fled from their parents in pursuit of utopian visions welcomed assistance from the very establishment that Woodstock symbolically rejected. They ultimately appreciated that these groups helped maintain the efficiency that got them out of their jam.

On the other side, many Bethel residents commented with surprise on the hippies' politeness and peaceful behavior. Mainstream America saw Yasgur's observation borne out: rock and violence were not inseparable, and perhaps the peace the hippies advocated was not such a delusion after all. In 1972 the Woodstock Nation repaid the compliment by nominating Yasgur for president of the United States.

REASSESSMENT

When the initial euphoria wore off, it became common to view Woodstock not as the beginning of a new era but as an ending, the high-water mark of the 1960s; at that point hippie freakdom reached critical mass and dissipated into the mainstream, and the establishment co-opted the diluted attitudes and fashions into a commodity. Much of the pride and idealism of the Woodstock Nation crumbled in the following years as their culture suffered devastating casualties. In December 1969 a spectator at the Rolling Stones' free concert at Altamont, California, was stabbed. The next year brought the student massacres at Kent State University, the breakup of the Beatles, and the deaths of Hendrix and Janis Joplin. In 1971 Jim Morrison died and Bill Graham closed down New York City's Fillmore Concert Halls; the following year Richard Nixon was reelected. Such defeats hastened the trend toward escapism. Rock and roll detoured into country music, singer/songwriters became apolitical, and youthful rebellion sank into the quagmire of narcissistic spiritual odysseys that signaled the "me decade."

In the wake of disillusionment, many claimed that the music was the most significant aspect of Woodstock and the only legacy successfully preserved. The documentary, *Woodstock: Three Days of Peace and Music* (1970), was enormously popular, providing vicarious excitement for the millions who were not there. Using split-screen technology to simulate the excitement of a live performance, the film won an Oscar for Best Documentary. The three-album soundtrack, *Woodstock: Music from the Original Soundtrack and More* (1970), also awoke nostalgia for the swiftly vanishing epoch. The arrangement of the music was jumbled, however, and many performers were omitted. A two-album sequel, *Woodstock Two* (1971), provided more songs by the artists already favored, but there were still notable absences.

In the minds of others, the recordings' inadequacies proved that the music was only a minor part of an essentially spiritual event that could not be captured on vinyl. Joplin and the Grateful Dead, emblems of the youth culture that had sprouted in San Francisco, reportedly delivered lackluster performances at the festival, while then-unknown acts such as Santana and Joe Cocker were among the highlights. A privileged few recall Joan Baez's performance at the free stage as a peak moment. The free stage had been built outside the festival fence so that those who did not have tickets could enjoy amateur bands and open mic. Even after the whole festival was declared free and the fence was torn down, however, the ever-valiant Baez, surveying the crowd of a half million people, perceived that the free stage would still be useful for entertaining those who could not get close to the main stage. She played to a fringe audience for forty minutes until her manager summoned her to her scheduled gig at the main stage. This touching moment was not captured on film or recorded.

TWENTY-FIVE YEARS LATER

In 1994 the twenty-fifth anniversary of Woodstock inspired a four-CD box set that includes most of the festival's performers and preserves the original chronological order (still omitting some performers, such as Ravi Shankar and the Incredible String Band, who have yet to appear on any Woodstock recording). The documentary was rereleased on video as a "Director's Cut" package, offering forty minutes of additional footage of Hendrix, Joplin, and Jefferson Airplane. A CD-ROM also appeared, boasting music, film clips, lyrics, hypertext biographies, and other features.

The most spectacular product of the twenty-fifth anniversary celebration was the Woodstock Two festival in Saugerties, New York. Plans for sequels had been brewing since 1970, but the original producers were in legal and emotional disarray. The occasion of the tenth anniversary in 1979 motivated a follow-up concert in New York City with many of the original players, but nostalgia for 1960s flower-power was at a low ebb, and the event was a disappointment. By the late 1980s and 1990s, however, reminiscences had been rekindled, and in 1994 the offspring of Woodstock Nation members were ready to prove that they could party like their parents.

Woodstock Two was a three-day music festival with a ticket price of $135 (the original Woodstock passes had sold for $18). It, too, generated a movie and soundtrack, and it was broadcast on pay-per-view television. The concert mainly featured popular 1990s bands, including the Cranberries and Green Day, with a few older bands such as Aerosmith. Dylan, the Woodstock resident who had missed the original festival, finally performed. Woodstock alumni Cocker and Crosby, Stills, and Nash joined in.

MONEY VERSUS POLITICS

Woodstock Two also mixed rock and advertising, charging corporations hefty fees for billboard space. Pearl Jam, Neil Young, and others refused to participate for this reason. The promoters rejected alcohol and tobacco sponsors, however, diverging from the pharmaceutical anarchy of the original Woodstock. The advertising slogan for the pay-per-view option was one of the worst ever conceived: "All you have to do to change the world is change the channel." The allusion was to John Lennon's line from the Beatles song, "Revolution" (1968), "We all want to change the world."

The ineptly chosen phrase did not necessarily represent the youth of the 1990s, however, who had lived through a revolution in the status of women, blacks, and gays. And the original Woodstock event did not necessarily reflect the political engagement associated with the 1960s. Beyond a few protest songs, Woodstock had been a largely apolitical event; when Hoffman attempted to make a speech about marijuana reform, Pete Townshend swatted him off the stage. Many forget that the original Woodstock was quite commercial, as Hoffman and others had observed at the time. Another common myth is that Woodstock was intended to be a free concert. Espen noted in the *New Yorker* that Woodstock is nostalgically eulogized as anticommercial, when in fact it was simply unsuccessfully commercial. Many of the innovations of Woodstock Two, such as the pay-per-view option, reflect improved technology and better planning as opposed to a greater emphasis on capitalism.

The Woodstock Two promoters, under the aegis of Woodstock Ventures (who retained the rights to the name), lost their credibility not through their commercialism but by suing a simultaneous festival called Bethel '94 planned at the original Woodstock site. The event was scheduled to include such veterans as Melanie, Country Joe McDonald, and Richie Havens. Woodstock Ventures, thwarted and sued by many during the first Woodstock, launched an $80 million lawsuit to prevent Bethel '94 from happening. Twelve thousand attended anyway, and Arlo Guthrie and others gave free impromptu performances. The litigation against Bethel '94 robbed Woodstock Two of any vestige of countercultural currency.

LONG-TERM LEGACY

In 1997 the original Woodstock site was sold to create the Bethel Woods Center for the Arts, which kicked off with a concert by Woodstock alumni Crosby, Stills, Nash, and Young in 2006. A museum dedicated to the festival opened there in 2008. On the festival's thirtieth anniversary, Rome, New York, hosted Woodstock '99, a weekend concert featuring a mix of rap and metal groups. The event was marked by violence, ending abruptly when concertgoers began setting fires, hurling bottles, and destroying the stage. The fortieth anniversary in 2009 brought a flood of books, a rerelease of the documentary on DVD, the feature film *Taking Woodstock* (directed by Ang Lee), and a three-CD set of the original music. Individual artists, such as Cocker, released CDs of their own performances at the festival. Although there was no huge festival, Bethel was a stop on the 2009 "Heroes of Woodstock" tour composed of groups such as Jefferson Starship, Ten Years After, and Canned Heat—albeit with few of the original members still onboard—as well as tribute groups.

Besides the dozens of histories and memoirs, Woodstock has inspired novels, stories, and songs. Its most famous anthem is Crosby, Stills, Nash, and Young's version of "Woodstock" from their album *Déja Vu* (1970). Joni Mitchell wrote the song and recorded it on her album *Ladies of the Canyon* (1970). A folk ballad, the song beautifully conveys the spirit—as well as the ironies—of the Woodstock Nation, with its theme of pastoral escape, the gathering of "half a million strong," the haunting subtext of Vietnam, and the poignantly passive dream of peace. Woodstock Ventures may retain its legal rights, but the memory of Woodstock belongs to the world, irrevocably embedded in American culture.

Douglas Cooke

SEE ALSO: *Academy Awards; Advertising; Aerosmith; Altamont; Alternative Press; Baby Boomers; Baez, Joan; The Beatles; Billboards; Boy Scouts of America; The Chicago Seven; Compact Discs; Consumerism; Country Music; Crosby, Stills, and Nash; Dylan, Bob;* Easy Rider*; Folk Music; Generation X; Girl Scouts; Graham, Bill; The Grateful Dead; Green Day; Guthrie, Arlo; Heavy Metal; Hendrix, Jimi; Hippies; Hoffman, Abbie; Jefferson Airplane/Starship; Joplin, Janis; Kent State Massacre; King, Martin Luther, Jr.; Lennon, John; LSD; Marijuana; Mitchell, Joni; The* New Yorker*; Pearl Jam; Pop Music; Rap; Rock and Roll; The Rolling Stones; Santana; Television; Vietnam; The Who; Young, Neil.*

BIBLIOGRAPHY

Espen, Hal. "The Woodstock Wars." *New Yorker*, August 15, 1994, 70–74.

Evans, Mike, and Paul Kingsbury, eds. *Woodstock: Three Days that Rocked the World.* New York: Sterling, 2009.

Hoffman, Abbie. *Woodstock Nation*. New York: Random House, 1969.

Lang, Michael, and Holly George-Warren. *The Road to Woodstock*. New York: Ecco, 2009.

Makower, Joel. *Woodstock: The Oral History*, 40th anniversary ed. Albany, NY: Excelsior Editions/State University of New York Press, 2009.

Pareles, Jon. "A Moment of Muddy Grace." *New York Times*, August 9, 2009, 1(L).

Reynolds, Susan. *Woodstock Revisited: 50 Far Out, Groovy, Peace-Loving, Flashback-Inducing Stories from Those Who Were There*. Avon, MA: Adams Media, 2009.

Spitz, Bob. *Barefoot in Babylon: The Creation of the Woodstock Music Festival, 1969*, rev. ed. New York: W. W. Norton, 1989.

Woolworth's

SEE: *Dime Stores/Woolworth's.*

Works Progress Administration (WPA) Murals

During the mid-1930s, in the midst of the Great Depression, the U.S. government initiated a series of programs that were meant to provide economic relief to unemployed visual artists. The first such program was the Public Works of Art Project (PWAP), a Treasury Department initiative under the direction of Edward Bruce. Launched in December 1933 and terminated the following spring, the PWAP was short-lived; even so, several hundred murals were completed under its auspices. In October 1934 the Treasury Department launched a second program, initially called the Section of Painting and Sculpture. Unlike the PWAP, which hired artists and paid them weekly wages, the new program sponsored competitions and awarded commissions to selected artists. More than 1,000 post office murals were commissioned by the Treasury Section between 1934 and 1943, the year of the program's demise.

The Federal Art Project (FAP) of the Works Progress Administration (WPA) was established in May 1935 and also survived until 1943. In addition to employing painters, sculptors, and graphic artists, the FAP provided funding for community art centers and exhibitions, operated a design laboratory, and supported indexing and bibliographic projects. Artists employed in the Mural Division were assigned projects in schools, hospitals, prisons, airports, public housing, and recreational facilities, and altogether produced more than 2,500 murals. Under a fourth program, the Treasury Relief Art Project (TRAP), in existence from July 1935 until June 1939, fewer than 100 murals were created.

PUBLIC MURALS WITH A MESSAGE

As a popular art form, mural painting was in its ascendancy in North America in the 1920s and 1930s. In the early 1920s the Mexican government began to subsidize the painting of murals celebrating Mexican history and the ideals of the Mexican Revolution. Artists such as Diego Rivera and José Clemente Orozco participated in this effort and later were privately commissioned to paint murals in the United States. Rivera, in particular, gained notoriety in the United States when, in 1933, he chose to include a portrait of Vladimir Lenin in a mural he had been invited to paint in the new Rockefeller Center in New York. John D. Rockefeller Jr., who had commissioned the mural, ordered the portrait removed. Rivera refused, and the mural was subsequently destroyed. The Rivera debacle, according to Karal Ann Marling in *Wall-to-Wall America*, forced painters, critics, and ordinary citizens "to weigh the principle of freedom of expression against the countervailing rights of a majority that did not share Rivera's communistic faith." Issues surrounding the mural artist's responsibility to the public versus his or her right to creative autonomy would surface frequently in discus-

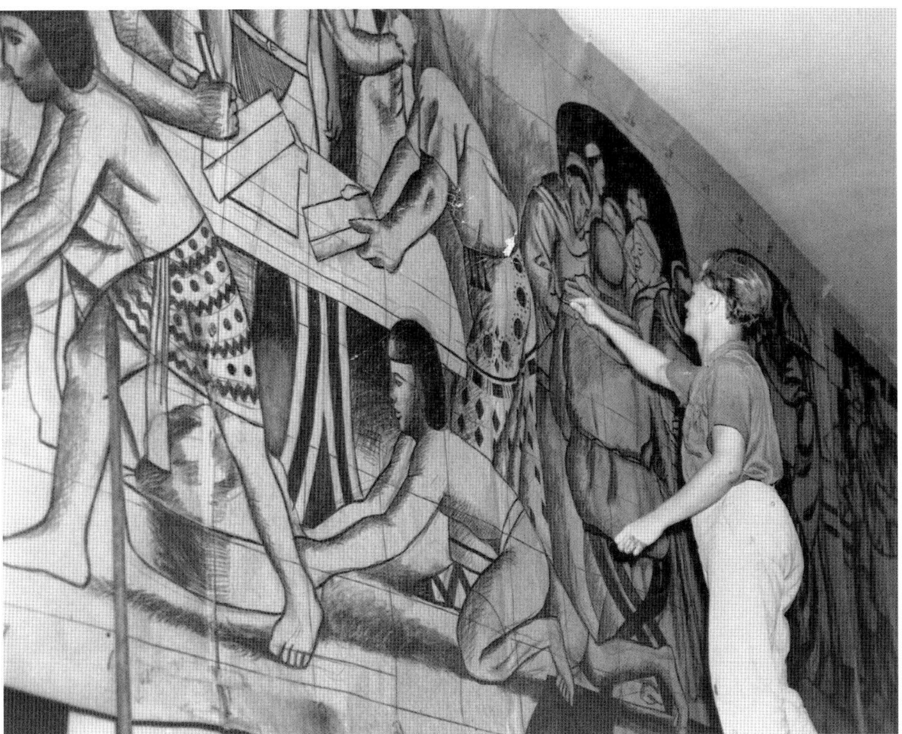

WPA Mural. *An artist with the Works Progress Administration works on one of the thousands of murals commissioned by government-sponsored programs in the 1930s and early 1940s.* © CORBIS.

sions of government-sponsored mural painting in the 1930s and 1940s.

STYLE AND SUBJECT MATTER

The government did not officially dictate the style of the murals it sponsored; however, it did encourage its artists to paint with the public in mind. An artist commissioned to paint a post office mural by the Treasury Section, in particular, was expected to spend time in the community for which the mural was destined and to solicit suggestions for themes from community members. Most of the government-sponsored murals were realistic in style. Several abstract murals were, however, sponsored by the FAP, including *Aviation: Evolution of Forms under Aerodynamic Limitations* by Arshile Gorky (1904–1948), which was installed at Newark Airport, in New Jersey, in 1937.

A typical mural reflected the influence of American Scene painting, a development in American art that emerged in the late 1920s as a reaction against European modern art and gained impetus in the 1930s. The most influential American Scene painter was Thomas Hart Benton (1889–1975), who painted *America Today* for the New School of Social Research in New York City and *The Social History of the State of Missouri* for the State Capitol Building in Jefferson City, Missouri, but never worked on any federally sponsored projects. American Scene paintings often depicted regional landscapes; local customs; and ordinary, hardworking people. This was exactly the sort of subject matter deemed appropriate by agency officials for government-sponsored murals.

In the murals produced, the settings were both contemporary and historical, but the values reflected in either case were traditional. Across the country, murals depicting Abraham Lincoln, the frontiersman Daniel Boone, the poet Carl Sandburg, the explorers Lewis and Clark, and the social reformer Jane Addams were produced. Often the subject chosen had local significance, as in the *Jane Addams Memorial* painted by Mitchell Siporin (1910–1976) for the Illinois FAP. This was also true of *The Role of the Immigrant in the Industrial Development of America* by Edward Laning (1906–1981), done under the auspices of the FAP for the dining room of Ellis Island. Subjects related to the processing and delivery of mail, both contemporary and historical, were frequently represented in post office murals: Philip Guston (1913–1980), for example, painted *Early Mail Service and the Construction of the Railroad* for the post office in Commerce, Georgia.

Although conservative opposition to the federal art projects had existed from the start, it increased throughout the 1930s, and by the start of World War II the nation's priorities began to shift. By 1943 the federal government had essentially ended its patronage of art. In slightly less than a decade it had sponsored some 4,000 murals, a large and diverse body of work that contributes to our enduring awareness of the value of public art.

Laural Weintraub

SEE ALSO: *Addams, Jane; The Great Depression; New Deal; Rivera, Diego; Sandburg, Carl.*

BIBLIOGRAPHY

Baigell, Matthew. *The American Scene: American Painting of the 1930s.* New York: Praeger, 1974.

Bustard, Bruce I. *A New Deal for the Arts.* Washington, DC: National Archives and Records Administration and University of Washington Press, 1997.

Grieve, Victoria. *The Federal Art Project and the Creation of Middlebrow Culture.* Urbana: University of Illinois Press, 2009.

Harris, Jonathan. *Federal Art and National Culture: The Politics of Identity in New Deal America.* Cambridge, UK: Cambridge University Press, 1995.

Marling, Karal Ann. *Wall-to-Wall America: A Cultural History of Post-Office Murals in the Great Depression.* Minneapolis: University of Minnesota Press, 1982.

McKinzie, Richard D. *The New Deal for Artists.* Princeton, NJ: Princeton University Press, 1973.

O'Connor, Francis V., ed. *Art for the Millions: Essays from the 1930s by Artists and Administrators of the WPA Federal Art Project.* Greenwich, CT: New York Graphic Society, 1973.

Park, Marlene, and Gerald E. Markowitz. *Democratic Vistas: Post Offices and Public Art in the New Deal.* Philadelphia: Temple University Press, 1984.

World Cup

The World Cup of football, or soccer, as the game is called in the United States, is the most popular sporting event in the world. For two years teams representing virtually every country in the world compete for the right to play in the summer tournament, which has been staged in different countries every four years since 1930. In front of a worldwide television audience, the winners claim the title of the best soccer team in the world. Although the U.S. team reached the semifinals of the tournament in its inaugural year, the World Cup and soccer have been slow to make an impact on American popular culture.

In the late nineteenth century soccer became a leading spectator sport in many major countries. Rules of the game were systematized, clubs were formed, and leagues were established. In 1900 the Olympic Games introduced soccer as one of its sports. In 1904 Robert Guerin of France assumed the presidency of the newly created world governing body of soccer, the Fédération Internationale de Football Associations (FIFA), with the intention of creating an international soccer tournament. However, the competition did not materialize for more than twenty years because of conflict among national federations over whether to allow only amateur players to compete, as in the Olympic Games, or to accept professional players, who were becoming more prevalent in Europe. Finally FIFA agreed to include professional players and to hold the tournament every four years, alternating with the Olympic Games.

FIFA selected Uruguay to host the first World Cup finals in 1930. Uruguay was chosen partly based on the country's dominance in capturing gold medals in the 1924 and 1928 Olympic Games and partly because no other viable candidate came forward. Only thirteen teams, including the United States, competed in the first World Cup tournament. Belgium, France, Romania, and Yugoslavia were the only Europeans to enter because of the three weeks it took to get to Uruguay by boat. The hosts beat Argentina 4–2 in the final in Montevideo to become the first winners of the FIFA world championship.

SOCCER IN THE UNITED STATES

Although the United States has never won the tournament, from 1930 to 2010 it qualified nine times, and its best finish was the semifinal in 1930. Soccer has, however, always played a shadowy existence in American popular culture. In the late nineteenth century immigrants from Europe formed soccer clubs and organized into local leagues, but as soccer flourished in Europe, U.S. political and business elites sought to create their own national identity in a land of immigrants by promoting American sports such as baseball. Soccer received no state support and was played in few U.S. colleges or schools. As Americanization movements increased at the turn of the twentieth century, more pressure was put on foreigners to assimilate by adopting American games such as baseball or gridiron football. Thus, the U.S. teams that competed in the World Cups of 1930, 1934, and 1950 consisted largely of immigrant players.

After World War II, soccer became the most popular sport on the planet. The sport produced international stars of the caliber of Pelé and great teams such as Brazil—which won the World Cup a record five times from 1958 to 2002—Argentina, Germany, and Italy. FIFA increased the number of teams competing in the World Cup from its original thirteen participants in 1930 to sixteen in 1958 and to twenty-four in 1982. Because of Cold War nationalism and the increase in television coverage of U.S. sports, however, the American public remained uninterested in soccer. In the 1950s baseball was still supreme, and American football began its rise to prominence. In the 1960s ice hockey and basketball captured a national television audience. Soccer, with its continuous forty-five minutes of play, was less suitable for commercial television and held little interest for the major television networks. From 1950 to 1990, the United States never qualified for the World Cup finals. In the 1970s the North American Soccer League operated, but this effort soon collapsed.

After the 1970s, however, the World Cup and soccer in general gained popularity with some sections of the American population. Relying more on skill than size or strength, soccer became a popular participatory sport among many American women and youth. In 1991 the U.S. women's team won the first ever FIFA Women's World Cup in China, a feat they repeated in the United States eight years later. At the same time FIFA, commercial sponsors, and television networks saw America as the last major market to be conquered by soccer. As a result, FIFA selected the United States to stage the World Cup finals for the first time in 1994.

The tournament was a great success, as it gained national television coverage and was played in packed stadiums, including more than 94,000 for the final in Los Angeles between Italy and the eventual winners, Brazil. Subsequently Major League Soccer was formed in America and began its first season in 1996. Women's Professional Soccer formed in 2007 and began playing in 2009; as of 2012 the league had five franchises. It remains to be seen whether these professional soccer leagues can continue to attract the attention of the American public and whether the United States can produce a team talented enough to mount a serious challenge for the World Cup.

The fan base in the United States does seem to be growing. About seventeen million U.S. viewers watched the 2006 World Cup final—and saw a controversial play of the type that ignites the passions of soccer fans worldwide. With just ten minutes to go in the final match of his career, legendary French player Zinedine Zidane head-butted Italian player Marco Materazzi. Zidane was ejected from the match, which Italy went on to win. The foul was reminiscent of other past plays that still cause heated arguments, such as the "hand of God" goal in the 1986 World Cup quarter finals, in which Diego Maradona scored by knocking the ball into the net with his hand; he got away with the illegal play because no officials saw it.

Even more than the occasional dirty play, true soccer fans love the athleticism of players such as the legendary Brazilian star Pelé, who played from 1956 through 1977, scoring more than 1,000 goals in his remarkable career and competing in four World Cups. German player Franz Beckenbauer was equally renowned, having represented his country on the soccer field 103 times, including in three World Cups.

With the continued popularity of youth, high school, and college soccer and the wider availability of soccer matches on cable television, an increasing number of Americans are becoming hooked on the drama that makes the World Cup so popular around the globe. The 2010 World Cup final between the Netherlands and Spain attracted a record number of U.S. viewers: 15.5 million viewers in English and an additional 8.8 million viewers in Spanish. This was more viewers than had watched the previous year's World Series.

John F. Lyons

SEE ALSO: *Pelé; Soccer; Sports Heroes.*

BIBLIOGRAPHY

Crouch, Terry, and James Corbett. *The World Cup: The Complete History*. London: Aurum Press, 2010.

Glanville, Brian. *The History of the World Cup*. London: Faber & Faber, 1980.

Murray, Bill. *Football: A History of the World Game*. London: Scolar Press, 1994.

World of Warcraft

SEE: *Computer Games; Online Gaming.*

World Series

Throughout much of the twentieth century and into the beginning decades of the twenty-first, the annual World Series baseball championship has consistently set standards for well-staged national sporting scenarios, earning its reputation as the Fall Classic. There have been heroes, villains, fools, and unknowns who have stolen the spotlight from superstars.

GETTING STARTED, SURVIVING SCANDAL

The term *World Series* was first coined for a nine-game series between the Boston Pilgrims and the Pittsburgh Pirates. The series was an informal outgrowth of a 1903 peace treaty signed between baseball's two competing major leagues, the twenty-seven-year-old National League (NL) and the upstart two-year-old American League (AL). The AL champion Pilgrims (later called the Red Sox) won, five games to three, to surprisingly good crowds and gate receipts. Yet the following year manager John McGraw and owner John Brush of the runaway NL champion New York Giants refused to face the repeating Boston club, stating publicly that such a meeting was beneath the quality of their team, which showcased future Hall of Fame pitcher Christy Mathewson. A less-publicized reason, however, was that they had objected to the growing popularity of the new AL franchise in New York City, the Highlanders (soon to be known as the Yankees).

Public and press outcry was so great against the Giants that Brush relented in 1905 and proposed a World Series (he proffered it as a seven-game affair) as a mandatory annual event. The Giants won easily that year (with Mathewson pitching the first three of his still-standing record four series shutouts), but the team would not prove to be as transcendent as Brush and McGraw believed, for they failed to win another series until 1921. A worse fate awaited the Chicago Cubs, another early dominating NL team. After winning the series in 1907 and 1908, they never won again, and never even reached another series after 1945. Starting in 1910 AL teams won eight out of the next ten series, establishing an edge over the NL that they have yet to relinquish.

The World Series soon gained formal acceptance, with President Woodrow Wilson attending the second game of the 1915 Boston Red Sox–Philadelphia Phillies series. The year 1915 also marked the series debut of Boston pitcher George Herman "Babe" Ruth. Ruth set a series record of 29 2/3 scoreless innings pitched, spanning Red Sox series championships in 1916 and 1918. After converting Ruth into an outfielder in 1919 and watching him shatter all previous home run (and league attendance) records, Red Sox owner Harry Frazee sold the Babe to the New York Yankees, on January 3, 1920, for $100,000 and a $300,000 loan to cover one of his Broadway shows. For Boston fans it became known as the Curse of the Bambino—after winning four series in the decade, the Red Sox went eighty-six years before winning another championship. The Yankees would be another story.

In 1919 the World Series endured one of its worst scandals in history. Many players had long felt the owners were denying them their fair share of club profits, and in no more obvious instance than in the World Series, where the triumphant owners were taking in record receipts and were rumored to have sold tickets to scalpers to make even more. The owners countered with rumors of their own, to the effect that players were being bribed to throw games by professional gamblers. Tensions had even precipitated a brief player's strike before the fifth game of the Red Sox–Cubs series in 1918, but the worst was yet to come.

Questionable betting patterns on the 1919 series, in which the Cincinnati Reds upset the Chicago White Sox, prompted a grand jury investigation. In 1920 eight White Sox players were indicted for taking bribes. Among them was "Shoeless" Joe Jackson, the star who legend has it was confronted on the courtroom steps by a young fan with the soon-to-be-famous line, "Say it ain't so, Joe!" The eight players were ultimately acquitted in court, but as a result of what was now known as the Black Sox scandal, they were subsequently banned from baseball for life in 1921. The rather draconian measure was enacted by the baseball commissioner, a post newly created by the owners to quickly restore baseball's image as well as maintain their own authority over the players.

THE BABE RUTH ERA

The World Series not only bounced back in the 1920s but also came to form the centerpiece of a new era of popularity and stability for baseball. Key factors were the rise of the New York Yankees and the coinciding development of radio as a mass medium. McGraw's Giants had returned to the World Series in 1921 to find they were in the first of thirteen Subway Series, facing their cotenants at the Polo Grounds, the Yankees, who now had the biggest star in sports, Ruth. In the first of their twenty-nine series appearances over the next forty-four years, the Yankees bowed to McGraw's veteran club. McGraw's pitchers kept throwing low curve balls to Ruth in 1922 as well, allowing the Giants to sweep the first World Series to be broadcast by radio (the announcer was Grantland Rice) and the last series triumph for their manager.

In 1923 Yankee Stadium was completed across the Harlem River in the Bronx, to be christened "the house that Ruth built," as all previous league attendance records were smashed. Ruth hit three homers in that year's rematch with the Giants, bringing the Yankees their first of twenty series victories in a forty-year span. By the time of their 1927 sweep, which was also the first World Series broadcast coast to coast, the Yankees had become America's team—setting a standard of excellence that McGraw and his Giants had never quite achieved—and they maintained a stranglehold on money and talent that most of the teams in the rest of the country could only admire from afar. All knew, however, that a victory over the Yankees in the series would assure their place in the annals of baseball. Such was the case when grizzled pitcher Grover Cleveland Alexander braved the Yankees "Murderers' Row" to preserve a 1926 series victory for the St. Louis Cardinals, a feat later to be immortalized on film (with Ronald Reagan playing Alexander).

Through the Great Depression and World War II radio provided the yearly vignettes about players both rough edged (Pepper Martin) and refined (Joe DiMaggio) that would cheer millions of Americans. However, one episode stood out particularly during this period. According to many accounts, in the 1932 Cubs–Yankees series, the faltering Ruth—brushing off slurs about his ancestry from the Cub bench and the hostile crowd at Chicago's Wrigley Field—paused to point to the center-field bleachers. He soon followed with his fifteenth and last World Series home run. The Yankees went on to sweep the series, but the "called shot" is what is still remembered and discussed today.

MAJOR CHANGES AND DRAMATIC HIGHLIGHTS

The climax of World War II brought with it the appearance of television and the breaking of the unofficial color line in baseball with Brooklyn Dodger star Jackie Robinson. The postwar years also marked the period of greatest dominance for the Yankees, who appeared in fifteen of eighteen series through 1964, winning ten (including five in a row from 1949 to 1953). The key components of that Yankee team were manager Casey Stengel and new stars Mickey Mantle, Yogi Berra, and Whitey Ford. The phrase "wait till next year" was made famous by Brooklyn fans as their "Bums" lost five series to the Yankees before winning in 1955, their only series championship before they relocated (along with the Giants) three years later to California.

Also in 1955 the World Series Most Valuable Player Award was initiated, won first by Johnny Podres of the Dodgers. Many call this baseball's and the series' golden era. The many highlights from this period include Willie Mays's incredible over-the-shoulder catch in his Giants' sweep of the Cleveland Indians in 1954, Yankee Don Larsen's perfect game over the Dodgers in 1956, and Pittsburgh Pirate Bill Mazeroski's series-winning home run in 1960.

A revamping of baseball's amateur draft rules, the sharing of network broadcast revenues among all franchises, and internal turmoil eventually restored mortality to the Yankees, and after 1964 they failed to appear in the postseason for eleven years. Apart from the flamboyant, mustachioed Swinging Oakland A's of 1972 to 1974, no team would again win more than two series in a row until the Yankees did it from 1998 to 2000. The advent of free agency allowed the players to get even (financially) with the owners, and exploding player salaries and bidding wars from the mid-1970s onward added some of the roster unpredictability of the early days to the game.

As television ratings came to be regarded as a measure of success, the series encountered increasingly stiff competition from the National Basketball Association championship, football's Super Bowl, and even its own playoff system, created in 1969. Yet the series has persevered, adding more classic moments for each generation: Carleton Fisk waving his homer fair in the sixth game of the 1975 Red Sox–Reds series; Reggie Jackson hitting three homers on three pitches off three different pitchers in the sixth game of the 1977 Yankees–Dodgers series, the New York crowd chanting "Reg-gie!"; the Curse of the Bambino willing New York Met Mookie Wilson's grounder through Red Sox first baseman Bill Buckner's legs in 1986; pinch-hitter Kirk Gibson homering off closer Dennis Eckersley to win the first game of the 1988 Dodgers–A's series; the faceoff of two 20-game winners—Roger Clemens and Curt Schilling—in the 2001 series between the Yankees and the Diamondbacks; Paul Konerko's grand slam in 2005 that helped the Chicago White Sox sweep the Astros to win their first World Series since 1917; and Albert Pujols becoming only the third player in history to hit three home runs in a World Series game in 2011.

Continuing animosity between the owners and players' union in 1994 caused what even two world wars could not: the cancellation of the World Series as the result of a strike. Through the efforts of many, including President Bill Clinton, the two sides declared a truce and the season and series were resumed in 1995. Well-played (and widely watched) seven-game series in 1996 and 1997 at least temporarily silenced the doomsayers predicting the coming end of the World Series as a marquee event.

INTO THE NEW MILLENNIUM

In 2003 Major League Baseball instituted a significant change to the World Series. The year before, the 2002 All-Star Game had ended in an extra-inning tie because the teams ran out of players. Alarmed that the All-Star Game was losing its significance, baseball decided that the outcome of what had been a meaningless exhibition would now determine which league had home-field advantage for the World Series. The decision was controversial when it was implemented and remained controversial for the next decade because it meant that the team with the best record might not receive the crucial advantage of hosting more games in the series.

The problem showed itself clearly in the 2011 series between the St. Louis Cardinals and the Texas Rangers. The Rangers had a .593 winning percentage and led their division for almost the entire season. The Cardinals had a lower .553 winning percentage and entered the playoffs as a wild-card team. Under the old rules the Rangers would have had home-field advantage, but because the National League had won the All-Star Game, St. Louis was given that privilege. The Cardinals won the series by taking the sixth and seventh games, played at their home park. As of 2012 the rule linking the All-Star Game and World Series remained in effect.

The World Series is a tradition rich in history, and during the first decade of the 2000s several significant achievements were reached. The Yankees' 2009 win gave them a record twenty-seven championship titles, more than double the eleven held by the second-place Cardinals. The Red Sox, the White Sox, and the Giants all ended droughts that had lasted more than fifty years. (The hapless Cubs, however, saw their drought pass the century mark.)

Alarmingly for Major League Baseball, television ratings for the 2008 and 2010 contests set all-time lows since records had been kept. However, some analysts have pointed out that the lower ratings were more a reflection of the decline of television's dominance rather than an indication of baseball's popularity. Despite the historically low number of viewers, the World Series was still the eighth-highest-rated show for the year—the same position it held in 1971. For all the dire predictions of the doomsayers, the series was holding its own with the American public. One proof of this was that viewership rose dramatically for the last two games of the thrilling seven-game contest between the Cardinals and the Rangers in 2011. For day-to-day sustained interest, capping a six-month-long season's endeavors, it is hard to imagine any other event in sports ever surpassing the intensity of World Series competitive drama.

C. Kenyon Silvey

SEE ALSO: *Baseball; Berra, Yogi; Black Sox Scandal; Boston Red Sox; The Brooklyn Dodgers; The Chicago Cubs; DiMaggio, Joe; Jackson, Reggie; Jackson, "Shoeless" Joe; Major League Baseball; Mantle, Mickey; Mays, Willie; The New York Yankees; Robinson, Jackie; Ruth, Babe; Sports Heroes; Stengel, Casey; Television.*

BIBLIOGRAPHY

Boswell, Thomas. *How Life Imitates the World Series.* New York: Doubleday, 1982.

Carney, Gene. *Burying the Black Sox: How Baseball's Cover-Up of the 1919 World Series Fix Almost Succeeded.* Washington, DC: Potomac Books, 2006.

Devaney, John, and Burt Goldblatt. *The World Series: The Complete Pictorial History.* New York: Rand McNally, 1972.

Schiffer, Don, ed. *World Series Encyclopedia.* New York: Thomas Nelson & Sons, 1961.

Schoor, Gene. *The History of the World Series.* New York: William Morrow, 1990.

Vaccaro, Mike. *The First Fall Classic: The Red Sox, the Giants, and the Cast of Players, Pugs and Politicos Who Re-invented the World Series in 1912.* New York: Doubleday, 2009.

World Trade Center

One of America's most identifiable icons, the World Trade Center stood for only a quarter of a century, but the buildings left an indelible mark on American culture. Originally conceived by the Port Authority of New York and New Jersey as a project to stimulate lower Manhattan economically and to promote international trade, the complex eventually grew to seven buildings. Twin towers—two 110-story skyscrapers standing next to each other at the edge of a five-acre public plaza—were the centerpiece of the project. Designed in the mid-1960s by architects Minoru Yamasaki and Associates, with Leslie E. Robertson Associates as the engineers, the buildings were constructed in the early 1970s. Instead of internal supports, the towers employed a tube-frame structural system that used rigid facades to carry the buildings' weights. Yamasaki and the engineers used closely spaced steel columns around the exterior, creating uninterrupted vertical lines that rose more than 1,300 feet to the roof and emphasized the buildings' tremendous heights. The twin towers surpassed the Sears Tower in Chicago to become the world's tallest buildings, while the complex as a whole became one of the largest ever built in the United States. Upon completion the World Trade Center held 13 million square feet of office space and could accommodate 50,000 workers on a daily basis.

The project as a whole, the choice of architect, and the massive twin towers all drew criticism from architects, planners, community activists, and New Yorkers upset that the beloved Empire State Building no longer reigned supreme on the city skyline. Opponents complained about a number of things, including the unnecessary addition of so much office space, as well as Yamasaki's lack of experience with the design of tall buildings and his status as an outsider to the East Coast architectural community. Some critics thought that the buildings had a "foreign" appearance—based on the pointed arches, a Yamasaki trademark, that appeared around the towers' bases—and some objected to the gargantuan scale that made the World Trade Center visible throughout the metropolitan area.

The towers opened in 1973. After a flurry of initial publicity, including a prominent appearance in the 1976 remake of the film *King Kong*, the World Trade Center began to fade into the urban fabric, failing to become the symbol of New York City that its developers had hoped. It did, however, become an icon of American economic might and of globalization and therefore a target for discontented groups. In February 1993 one of the towers was bombed by Islamic terrorists attempting to strike a blow at American society. The building survived without structural damage. Eight years later, however, another attack proved successful, when, on September 11, 2001, terrorists hijacked commercial airplanes and flew them into the towers. More than 2,750 people were killed, and both the twin towers and World Trade Center 7 were destroyed. The four other World Trade Center buildings later had to be demolished.

Ambitious rebuilding plans began to take shape just months after the tragedy, and an international competition was held to design the site. Daniel Libeskind's entry, which featured as its focal point a 1,776-foot Freedom Tower—its height meant to coincide with the date of the Declaration of Independence—was chosen over numerous other proposals. In addition to the Freedom Tower—or One World Trade Center—plans called for six other buildings of various sizes. The project soon became embroiled in political and financial controversy, however, and Libeskind and his design were replaced. The National September 11 Memorial & Museum, designed by Michael Arad and Peter Walker and Partners, was the first part of the rebuilding to be completed, occupying the site of the twin towers and highlighting their empty footprints.

Dale Allen Gyure

SEE ALSO: *Empire State Building;* King Kong*; 9/11; Sears Tower; Skyscrapers.*

BIBLIOGRAPHY

Darton, Eric. *Divided We Stand: A Biography of the World Trade Center*, 2nd ed. New York: Basic Books, 2011.

Douglas, George H. *Skyscrapers: A Social History of the Very Tall Building in America.* Jefferson, NC: McFarland, 1996.

Glanz, James, and Eric Lipton. *City in the Sky: The Rise and Fall of the World Trade Center.* New York: Times Books, 2003.

Goldberger, Paul. *The Skyscraper.* New York: Alfred A. Knopf, 1992.

Goldberger, Paul. *Up from Zero: Politics, Architecture, and the Rebuilding of New York.* New York: Random House, 2005.

Nobel, Philip. *Sixteen Acres: Architecture and the Outrageous Struggle for the Future of Ground Zero.* New York: Metropolitan Books, 2004.

Skinner, Peter, and Mike Wallace. *World Trade Center: The Challenge of the Future.* Vercelli, Italy: White Star Publishers, 2011.

World War I

The Great War (World War I), fought between 1914 and 1918, was one of the most decisive events of the twentieth century. The political and economic catastrophes in its wake led to another, even greater conflict, from 1939 to 1945. Some historians view the two world wars as aspects of the same struggle separated by an uneasy truce in the 1920s and 1930s. Certain ethnic and national-identity conflicts left unresolved at the Versailles peace conference of 1919 are still sources of tension and open hostility in the Balkans. It was in that fractious region of eastern Europe that World War I began when Serbian nationalists assassinated the heir to the throne of Austria-Hungary in the city of Sarajevo.

Uncle Sam Recruitment Poster. *Uncle Sam urges men to join the war effort in James Montgomery Flagg's recruitment poster.* UNIVERSALIMAGESGROUP/CONTRIBUTOR/GETTY IMAGES.

World War I required the unlimited commitment of all the resources of each warring society. Governments were forced to allocate human and natural resources, set economic priorities, and take measures to ensure the full cooperation of their citizens. Some societies cracked under the pressure. Monarchies collapsed in Russia, Germany, and Austria-Hungary. Even the victors, especially France and Belgium, were deeply scarred. The human sacrifices were appalling; the economic cost was overwhelming. World War I marked the decisive end of the old order in Europe, which, except for the Crimean War and the Franco-Prussian War and a few minor skirmishes, seemed to have weathered a century of relative peace after the Napoleonic wars that had ended 100 years earlier.

OUTBREAK OF WAR

The outbreak of the war had at first been greeted with jingoistic enthusiasm. It was not until the combatants experienced a tremendous loss of life in the trenches on the western front that this view was shattered. By the end of the war, pessimism and disillusion were endemic. For many in the West, the war denied the notion of progress. The same science and technology that had dazzled the nineteenth century with advances in medicine, communication, and transportation had produced poison gas, machine guns, and terror weapons. The Great War's legacy would include a deep pessimism, expressed in many forms, including antiwar literature that would be translated to the screen in the form of popular film.

World War I began when Serbian nationalists assassinated Archduke Francis Ferdinand, the heir to the throne of Austria-Hungary. Austria's attack upon Serbia on July 28 led to war with its protector, Russia. Prewar alliances ensured that Germany would declare war on Russia. When the French announced their intention to honor their commitments to Russia, Germany declared war on France. As the German armies passed through neutral Belgium to get at France, Britain declared war on Germany. Within a week of Austria's attack upon Serbia, the other four great European powers had gone to war over issues that few truly understood or, indeed, cared about. They seemed to have been swept along by their alliances in an inevitable cascade of falling dominoes over which humans had little control.

On the western front the German armies smashed through Belgium and into France, where they were halted 25 miles north of Paris. Both armies tried to get around the other in a "race to the sea." When they failed, the exhausted armies dug defensive positions. Two lines of trenches, 6 to 8 feet deep, zigzagged across northern France, from the Swiss border to the English Channel. The distance between the Allied trenches and those of the Germans depended on the terrain and ranged from 150 yards in Flanders to 500 yards at Cambrai. The great irony of warfare in the industrial age was that modern weapons forced the armies to live belowground and use periscopes to observe the other side. Steps in the sides of the trenches were used as

Wilson Declares War. President Woodrow Wilson asks Congress to declare war on Germany, April 2, 1917. UNIVERSALIMAGESGROUP/ CONTRIBUTOR/GETTY IMAGES.

platforms for firing at the enemy. The trench soldiers slept in sleeping holes dug into the sides of the trenches, where they suffered from rain, cold, poor sanitary facilities, lice, flies, trench foot, and a constant stench. Rats as big as small dogs fed on the dead. Of the casualties on the western front, 50 percent were directly attributable to conditions in the trenches.

In 1916 the major efforts to break the stalemate came at Verdun and on the Somme River. The Germans decided to attack Verdun, a historic city they knew the French would defend at all costs. The two sides fired more than 40 million artillery shells into a narrow front of less than 10 miles. When the firing ceased after 302 days, each side had suffered half a million casualties, with more than a hundred thousand dead. To relieve Verdun, the British opened an offensive on the Somme. An artillery bombardment of a million and a half shells was supposed to decimate the German positions. When the British army went "over the top" on July 1, however, they were cut down by German machine guns. On the first day of battle on the Somme, the British suffered 60,000 casualties, including 20,000 dead. After gaining 5 miles of territory, at the cost of 420,000 casualties, the British halted the offensive on November 13.

REALITIES OF WAR

When the war began, the common assumption was that it would be over within six months. In the prewar years many seemingly perceptive writers had written that modern economies were too integrated to accept a long war. There was also a general ignorance about what war in the industrial age would be like. There had not been a general European war since the defeat of Napoleon at Waterloo in 1815. Bourgeois middle-class life seemed boring and lacking in adventure. When World War I began, the armies marched to war with enthusiastic support. Intellectuals signed manifestos supporting the war. Sigmund Freud said, "All my libido is given to Austria-Hungary." Young men raced to the recruiting centers to sign up so they could be sure of getting into combat before the war was over. Fired by patriotism and by martial values of honor and glory, they were the first to be mowed down.

In "From 1914" English poet Rupert Brooke expressed his belief that his death in battle would sanctify a "foreign field" as "for ever England." The most popular poem of the war, John McCrae's "In Flanders Fields" appeared anonymously in *Punch* in December 1915. The poem may describe how "the poppies blow, / Between the crosses, row on row," but as Paul Fussell writes, the poem ends with "recruiting-poster rhetoric" demanding that others pick up the torch and not "break faith with us who die." These viewpoints changed with the reality of mass death and stalemate. Fussell observes that Edmund Blunden, Robert Graves, and Siegfried Sassoon came to an image of the war as lasting forever.

Trench warfare, in which neither side could gain the advantage, regardless of their courage, honor, and valor, suggested that humans had lost control of their history. Indeed, what did courage, honor, and valor have to do with modern war? In 1924 the German expressionist painter Otto Dix wrote thus of his trench experiences: "Lice, rats, barbed wire, fleas, shells, bombs, underground caves, corpses, blood, liquor, mice, cats, artillery, filth, bullets, mortars, fire, steel; that is what war is. It is the work of the devil."

To raise the large armies needed to continue the struggle, governments turned to the use of posters. The British Parliamentary Recruitment Committee commissioned a poster featuring Lord Kitchener's head and finger pointing at the viewer. The caption read "Your Country Needs You." As enlistments declined, the emphasis shifted to shaming those healthy young men still in Britain. The message was blunt in the poster "Women of Britain say, GO." A more subtle, but perhaps as effective, message was expressed in the British poster showing a little girl sitting on her father's knee, with an open book in her lap. The writing at the bottom of the poster asked the question, "Daddy, what did You do in the Great War?" At the father's feet was a little boy playing with a toy army and about to place a new soldier in the ranks. The committee would eventually commission 100 different posters, some of which were published in lots of 40,000. It is estimated that these posters generated one-quarter of all British enlistments. While most conscientious objectors accepted noncombatant alternatives, a hard core of 1,500 refused to accept any position that indirectly supported the war. They were sent to prison, where they suffered brutal treatment—70 of them died there. Poster art certainly contributed to the view that, in time of war, a man's place was in uniform.

The failure of the armies to achieve success led each side to seek new allies, open new fronts, resort to new military technologies, and engage in new forms of warfare. In 1915 Italy joined the Allies, and new fronts against the Austrians were opened in the Swiss Alps and on the Isonzo River. In the same year, the British opened a new front at Gallipoli, but after nearly a year of being pinned down on the beaches by Turkish guns, they were forced to withdraw. The Germans introduced gas warfare in 1915; the British introduced the tank in 1916. The romantic nature of air combat yielded to a more deadly form as machine guns were added to fighter aircraft. Germans bombed British cities; the British bombed German cities. The British mined German harbors and blockaded German ports; Germany responded with unrestricted submarine warfare. In the face of American protests, following the sinking of the *Lusitania*, the Germans suspended their attacks in 1915.

In Germany general rationing went into effect in 1916. The winter of 1916 to 1917, known as the "turnip winter," was particularly difficult. Bread riots, wage strikes, and a burgeoning black market that separated rich and poor threatened support for the war. There were also demands for political reform as a condition for continued support. In January 1917 the German government made the fateful decision to return to unrestricted submarine warfare with the full knowledge that this could lead to war with the United States. The German decision was predicated on the belief that Britain could be starved out of the war before the United States could train a large army and send it to Europe.

UNITED STATES JOINS ALLIES

Up to this point, the United States had been officially neutral during the war, keeping with its long tradition of avoiding "foreign entanglements." By 1917, however, its sympathies and economic interests had shifted to the Allied side. British propaganda had been highly effective in accusing Germans of atrocities in Belgium. President Woodrow Wilson resisted going to war because he feared what it would do to the progressive reforms of his administration and that war would release ugly patriotic excesses that would be difficult to control. His hand was forced by the sinking of American merchant ships and the Zimmerman telegram suggesting that, in return for a successful alliance, Germany would aid Mexico in its reacquisition of Arizona, Texas, and New Mexico. Finally, on April 6, 1917, Congress declared war on Germany, a move that Wilson promised would "make the world safe for democracy."

To raise a mighty army to fight in Europe, the U.S. government was forced to resort to locally supervised conscription. Unfortunately, these local boards often lacked objectivity. Not only was preference on exemptions given to family and friends, but African Americans were drafted in disproportionate numbers, and conscientious objectors without religious affiliations were either drafted or sent to prison. The government sought to encourage enlistments and discourage draft resisters by using British posters as a model. The Kitchener poster was deemed to be so effective that Americans substituted Uncle Sam's head and included the same caption: "Uncle Sam Wants You." The power of shame was also evident in the U.S. poster that featured a young woman dressed in a sailor's uniform with the caption, "Gee!! I Wish I Were a Man, I'd Join the Navy."

By 1917 all of the major belligerents had begun to regulate their industries and agriculture, borrow money to finance the war, ration food, and employ women in areas of the economy where they had not before worked. They also shaped consent for their policies and discouraged dissent. The War Industries Board, headed by Bernard Baruch, regulated American industries and set priorities. The Fuel Administration increased coal production by one-third and campaigned for heatless Mondays and gasless Sundays. The American Food Administration's appeal for food conservation included wheatless Mondays and Wednesdays, meatless Tuesdays, and porkless Thursdays and Saturdays. This voluntary conservation worked to such an extent that America was able to feed its armies and increase food exports to its allies by one-third without having to resort to rationing.

PATRIOTISM

Before radio and television, with film still in its infancy, the poster was a highly effective method of generating support. Posters were used to inspire industrial effort, urge citizens to conserve needed materials, and in general to support the war effort. Posters were also used extensively to gain support for the purchase of war bonds. While all the nations did this, none matched the American effort in this regard. For the third Liberty Loan drive, nine million posters were produced.

Voluntary sacrifices and poster art made everyone feel a part of the war effort, while also tending to generate emotional patriotic fervor. In America this reached heights of absurdity. High schools stopped teaching German, frankfurters became known as hot dogs, and orchestras stopped playing Brahms, Bach, and Beethoven. None of this was humorous to German Americans, who were attacked verbally and physically. These attacks seemed to have the support of the U.S. government.

The Committee of Public Information, directed by George Creel, not only kept the public informed about war news through films and pamphlets but also sent out 75,000 speakers to churches, schools, and movie theaters, where they lectured on war aims and German atrocities. The post office denied mail delivery of "radical," "socialist," and foreign-language newspapers and periodicals. The May 1918 Sedition Act made it a crime to speak about or publish anything disloyal. This could be and was used against those questioning U.S. participation in the war, the nation's war aims, and how it managed the war effort.

Hollywood producer Robert Goldstein was sentenced to ten years in prison because his film *The Spirit of '76* was not supportive of the British. The film, set in the period of the American Revolution, had shown British soldiers bayoneting civilians. Particularly vulnerable were Socialists such as Eugene Debs, who was sentenced to ten years, and leaders of the International Workers of the World (Wobblies), who were given twenty-year sentences. Their offenses stemmed more from their opposition to capitalism than to the war itself. The U.S. Justice Department brought charges of opposition to the war against 2,168 people, of whom 1,055 were convicted.

World War I brought forth great songs that would be sung long after the war was over. Many of these originated in London music halls, in French cabarets, and on Broadway. Some of America's greatest songwriters—including Jerome Kern, Irving Berlin, George M. Cohan, and George Gershwin—participated in this creative explosion. The most famous of these songs were the French "Madelon"; the British "Your King and Country Want You," "There's a Long, Long, Trail," "Roses of Picardy," and "It's a Long Way to Tipperary"; and the American "Pack Up Your Troubles in an Old Kit Bag," "Over There," "Keep the Home Fires Burning," "Goodbye Broadway, Hello France," "Mademoiselle from Armentieres," and "How Ya Gonna Keep 'em Down on the Farm?" These songs were sung at bond rallies but were also taught to the troops by official army song leaders. Most of the songs were comic, sentimental, and innocent. They were offered as a means to lift morale and provide a human respite for soldiers in an inhumane existence. Only the unofficial French song "La Chanson de Craonne," which declared soldiers doomed and victims of a wretched war, reflected the reality of the front.

WAR WEARINESS

What was most remarkable about the conflict until the end of 1916 was the willingness of European soldiers and civilians to accept the hardships the war demanded. Millions of soldiers had left home to face the horrors of modern war and to endure life in the trenches of the western front. This support collapsed in 1917. The German resumption of unrestricted submarine warfare reflected this change of mood. Most significant were the riots and insurrection in Petrograd, Russia, which led directly to the abdication of the Romanovs in March 1917. War weariness, the failure of Russian offensives in the summer of 1917, and the desertion of two million soldiers finally led to the October Bolshevik revolution and Russia's withdrawal from the war. In 1917 whole units of the French army refused to go to the front; those that did went chanting "baa baa baa"—the bleating of sheep being led to the slaughter. The British army's morale was close to the breaking point after the 1917 Flanders offensive resulted in what has been reported to be anywhere from 250,000 to 400,000 casualties for five captured miles of mud, in which thousands of these soldiers had drowned. At Caporetto, the Italian army reached its breaking point, and more than 275,000 Italian soldiers surrendered in a single day.

British and French generals desperately wanted American soldiers who would be merged into their own units. Wilson and his commander, John Pershing, were totally opposed to this. They wanted the United States to field its own independent army, with its own commanders, support forces, and separate sector of operations. Both recognized that unless a U.S. army fought as an independent entity, the United States would not be able to shape the peace. The United States would fight neither for the imperialistic aims of the great powers nor to restore the balance of power but instead "to make the world safe for democracy" by advocating self-determination, democratic government, the abolition of war, freedom of the seas, and an international organization to protect the peace. These lofty ideals were expressed in January 1918 in Wilson's Fourteen Points speech.

With Russia out of the war, Germany transferred its troops from the eastern front to the western front and launched its great offensive in the spring of 1918. As in 1914, the Germans were halted on the Marne River. American units put into battle at key places in the Allied lines fought well under French overall command. This time the German army did not settle into a trench line but was forced into a continuous retreat under the pressure of Allied armies. While the Germans were exhausted from four years of war, fresh American soldiers were arriving at the rate of a few hundred thousand per month and fighting as an independent army at Saint Mihiel and in the Argonne Forest. In other sectors, the Central powers collapsed. Turkey and Bulgaria were out of the war by October 1918. Austria-Hungary disintegrated, as the Hungarians sought a separate peace, and Slavs sought their own nations. Within Germany there were demonstrations at military bases and in Berlin. When the kaiser abdicated, the Germans asked for a peace based on what they had previously scorned, the Fourteen Points. The Germans signed the armistice, and at 11 a.m. on November 11, 1918, the guns went silent.

POSTWAR PESSIMISM

Four years of war had resulted in nine million deaths, one million of which were civilian. Many more millions of soldiers who lived through the war were crippled, mentally or physically. So many soldiers were facially disfigured that a new branch of medicine, plastic surgery, was developed. A great influenza pandemic resulted in thousands of civilian deaths in Europe and the United States. A deep pessimism settled over Europe.

Arnold Toynbee declared that the news from the front led him to believe that Western Civilization was following the same pattern that Classical Civilization had followed in its breakdown. His twelve-volume *A Study of History* would argue that World War I was to the West what the Punic Wars had been to the ancient world. Oswald Spengler's *Decline of the West* was even more pessimistic. W. B. Yeats's 1919 "Second Coming" saw anarchy "loosed upon the World" and the coming of another Dark Age. T. S. Eliot's "The Waste Land" expressed the despair and hopelessness felt by many. Freud admitted in *Civilization and Its Discontents* that it was the events of the war that led him to seek a second basic force at the core of human nature: the death instinct, in constant struggle against the life instinct.

Vera Britton's autobiographical *Testament of Youth* described the shattering impact of the war on her personal life. This pessimism shared the same viewpoint that was expressed by the war poets, such as Siegfried Sassoon and Wilfred Owen, who wrote their poetry and letters while at the front. David Kennedy has observed that he had not found this pessimism among American soldiers. Whereas the pessimism of the European writers came from the destructive impact of the war itself, American disillusionment came from the belief that America's entrance into the war had failed to create the new world of Wilson's vision. In addition, progressivism and protection of individual rights at home seemed to have been reversed, and the nation retreated into isolationism rather than follow Wilson's lead into the new League of Nations.

While the European and American reactions to the war were different, there is one area of popular culture where they seem to have coalesced. Following the war, outstanding antiwar books and films were written and produced in both Europe and the United States. The German film *Westfront 1918* (1930) depicted French and German soldiers dying without victory. Jean Renoir's *Grand Illusion* (1937) was another antiwar attack upon the European aristocracy that brought forth the horrors of World War I. Ludwig Renn wrote a critically acclaimed novel, *Krieg* (*War*), that was an impressive piece of literature but never achieved the popularity of Erich Maria Remarque's antiwar novel *All Quiet on the Western Front* (1929), which described the experiences of German youth who had gone to war as enthusiastic soldiers. The film by the same title, released in 1930, was so relentlessly antiwar that Remarque had to leave Germany. In 1930 the film received an Academy Award for Best Picture. Another antiwar book made into a film was Ernest Hemingway's *A Farewell to Arms* (1932), which describes the fate of an American ambulance driver who deserts the madness of the Italian retreat at Caporetto.

Two of the most powerful antiwar films done in the post–World War II period also dealt with specific events of World War I. Stanley Kubrick's *Paths of Glory* (1957), starring Kirk Douglas, was based on the mutinies in the French army. But it is Adolphe Menjou's depiction of a French general demanding the random selection and execution of three soldiers to cover his own failures that is the picture's most powerful image. Finally, Paramount's film *Gallipoli* (1981), appropriately starring the Australian actor Mel Gibson, faithfully describes what happened to those idealistic young Australian soldiers who went to war with enthusiasm and in search of adventure, only to be slaughtered like so many of their comrades on other fronts.

Thomas W. Judd

SEE ALSO: *Academy Awards; Berlin, Irving; Broadway; Cohan, George M.; Debs, Eugene V.; Freud, Sigmund; Gibson, Mel; Hemingway, Ernest; Kern, Jerome; Kubrick, Stanley; Plastic Surgery; Renoir, Jean; War Bonds; Wobblies; World War II.*

BIBLIOGRAPHY

Chambers, John. *To Raise an Army: The Draft Comes to Modern America.* New York: Free Press, 1987.

Ellis, John. *Eye-Deep in Hell: Trench Warfare in World War I.* Baltimore, MD: Johns Hopkins Press, 1976.

Fussell, Paul. *The Great War and Modern Memory.* New York: Oxford University Press, 1975.

Gilbert, Martin. *The First World War: A Complete History.* New York: Henry Holt, 1994.

Goldman, Dorothy, with Jane Gledhill and Judith Hattaway. *Women Writers and the Great War.* New York: Twayne, 1995.

Hardach, Gerd. *The First World War, 1914–1918.* Berkeley: University of California Press, 1977.

Harries, Meiron, and Susie Harries. *The Last Days of Innocence: America at War, 1917–1918.* New York: Random House, 1997.

Kennedy, David. *Over Here: The First World War and American Society.* New York: Oxford University Press, 1980.

Lyons, Michael. *World War I: A Short History.* Englewood Cliffs, NJ: Prentice Hall, 1994.

Marshall, S. L. A. *World War I.* Boston: Mariner Books, 2001.

Marshall Cavendish Corporation. *History of World War I.* 3 vols. Tarryson, NY: Marshall Cavendish, 2002.

Rochester, Stuart I. *American Liberal Disillusionment in the Wake of World War I.* University Park: Pennsylvania State University, 1977.

Roth, Jack J. *World War I: A Turning Point.* New York: Alfred A. Knopf, 1968.

Silkin, Jon, ed. *First World War Poetry.* London: Penguin Books, 1979.

Stromberg, Roland. *Redemption by War: The Intellectuals and 1914.* Lawrence, KS: Regents Press, 1982.

Timmers, Margaret. *The Power of the Poster.* London: V & A Publications, 1998.

Trask, David. *The AEF & Coalition Warmaking, 1917–1918.* Lawrence: University of Kansas Press, 1993.

Winter, Jay, and Blaine Baggett. *The Great War and the Shaping of the 20th Century.* London: Penguin Books, 1996.

World War II

Despite the Japanese invasion of China in 1937, most historians date the start of the World War II as September 1, 1939, the day German forces attacked Poland. Although Polish resistance was quickly overcome, treaty obligations brought Britain and France into the fray, and the war for Europe began in earnest. Strong isolationist sentiments, which were the aftermath of disagreements about the necessity for World War I, kept the United States out of the conflict until the Japanese bombed American naval forces anchored at Pearl Harbor in Hawaii on December 7, 1941. The surprise attack inflicted devastating losses on the U.S. fleet, and the next day, President Franklin Roosevelt asked for and received a congressional declaration of war on Japan. Three days later, Germany and Italy, which were bound to Japan by a mutual-defense treaty, declared war on the United States.

The fighting continued until August 1945, when Japan, the only Axis aggressor still fighting, finally surrendered after two American atomic bombs were dropped on the Japanese cities of Hiroshima and Nagasaki. The war affected every aspect of American life, including popular culture in all its forms. Some of this influence was the result of deliberate government propaganda, but much of it was simply the nation's response to the exigencies of life in wartime.

NEWSREELS AND PROPAGANDA

During the war American moviegoers were frequently exposed to a triple dose of messages. First, a newsreel showcased recent developments in the theaters of combat, along with pleasant feature stories unrelated to the conflict. An average newsreel ran about ten minutes and was changed twice each week. Although the typical moviegoer might not have known it, wartime newsreels were subject to indirect government censorship, with all film footage from overseas first passing through the government's hands. The content of newsreels was also subject to "guidance" from the Office of War Information (OWI), the government's propaganda bureau.

The newsreel was usually followed by one or more cartoons. Although many of the wartime versions were as innocuous as ever, quite a few leavened their laughs with propaganda. Porky Pig pokes fun at the Nazis in *Confusions of a Nutzy Spy* (1943), and Daffy Duck mocks the Third Reich in *Daffy—The Commando* (1943). Superman, America's favorite comic-book hero, took to the screen to thwart evil Japanese agents in *Japoteurs* (1942), while another cartoon, *Tokio Jokio* (1943), belittles the Japanese war effort by using blatantly racist stereotypes.

Then came the feature film, sometimes a documentary such as one of Frank Capra's *Why We Fight* series (1942–1945). Capra, already famous as a director, was drafted out of Hollywood, put in a major's uniform, and given the task of making films for new military recruits that would motivate them to fight in a war that not all of them understood. Relying mostly on seized Axis propaganda footage, Capra put together seven inspirational films covering different aspects of the global conflict. After a screening of the first, *Prelude to War*, President Roosevelt declared, "Every man, woman and child in America must see this film!" All seven were eventually shown in theaters, as well as in the boot camps for which they were originally intended.

Other notable Hollywood directors also made documentary films in support of the war effort. William Wyler directed *Memphis Belle* (1944), the saga of the last combat mission flown by an American bomber crew over Europe. John Huston helmed *The Battle of San Pietro* (1945), focusing on the bloody assault by American troops to capture an Italian town from the Germans, and John Ford brought his talents to *The Battle of Midway* (1942), which chronicles the first major American naval victory over the Japanese.

MOVIES AND POSTERS

Most films playing in neighborhood theaters during the war tell fictional stories, and about one-third of these deal with the war in one way or another. Many are combat films, often based on actual warfare. The first of these was *Wake Island* (1942), and it was followed by *Flying Tigers* (1942), *Bataan* (1943), *Destination*

Liberation of France. *Crowds line the Champs Élysées to view Allied tanks and half-tracks pass by after Paris was liberated in August 1944.* UNIVERSALIMAGESGROUP/CONTRIBUTOR/GETTY IMAGES.

Female Factory Worker during World War II. *During World War II, many American women on the home front took over jobs traditionally done by men.* UNIVERSALIMAGESGROUP/CONTRIBUTOR/GETTY IMAGES.

Tokyo (1943), *Gung Ho!* (1943), *Thirty Seconds over Tokyo* (1944), and *Objective, Burma!* (1945).

Other films offer intrigue, focusing on the shadowy worlds of spies, assassins, and double agents. These include *Sherlock Holmes and the Voice of Terror* (1942), *Nazi Agent* (1942), *Saboteur* (1942), and *They Came to Blow Up America* (1943). Still other productions glorify the heroic struggle of the citizens of occupied countries fighting against their Axis oppressors; *Hangmen Also Die* (1943), *Till We Meet Again* (1944), and *The Seventh Cross* (1944) are representative of this genre. Two-thirds of Hollywood films released during the war never mention the conflict at all. If such films have a subtext, it is that America is a place worth fighting for, a message that is conveyed subtly in such sentimental films as *Going My Way* (1944), *Meet Me in St. Louis* (1944), *Since You Went Away* (1944), and *An American Romance* (1944).

Film was certainly not the only medium to portray the war. Posters, for instance, could be found everywhere. Prominent artists and illustrators such as James Montgomery Flagg, Ben Shahn, Everett Henry, Stevan Dohanos, and John Atherton all created posters to encourage American citizens to support the war effort. Posters called men to military service; urged women to can food at home and consider getting a "war job"; and extolled everyone to hate the nation's ruthless and bestial foes, the Axis powers. Although Axis espionage never amounted to a serious threat to the United States, Americans on the homefront were nonetheless given a sense that they were helping to safeguard the nation when posters warned them not to discuss war information in public. The most famous of these admonitions was published by the Seagram Distillery Company. Below an illustration of a half-submerged freighter is the slogan "Loose lips might sink ships!" Even Norman Rockwell lent his distinctive vision of Americana to the war effort, with a series of four illustrations collectively titled *The Four Freedoms.*

RADIO

Radio was the principal entertainment medium for Americans during World War II. Although many people no doubt listened to the radio to escape the stress of the war, it was difficult to avoid the conflict for very long. President Roosevelt continued to give his "fireside chats," the tradition of informal-sounding speeches that he had begun during the 1930s. However, whereas the early addresses usually concerned the Depression and the president's efforts to alleviate it, the wartime broadcasts reflected the nation's principal preoccupation, which was the conflict itself. Roosevelt used these speeches to reassure his audience that the war was going well and that eventual victory was assured. He did this from the beginning of the war, even when such optimism was not shared by his advisers or justified by the military situation.

The government also used radio for propaganda in less obvious ways. William B. Lewis, head of the OWI's Domestic Radio Division, understood that people wanted entertainment from their radios, not heavy-handed propaganda. Lewis, a former vice president of CBS, worked out a rotation system (the Network Allocation Plan) wherein the existing radio dramas and comedies voluntarily took turns integrating government propaganda into their scripts, thus guaranteeing large audiences for the OWI's messages while also preserving radio's moneymaking programs. As a result, the popular comedy *Fibber McGee and Molly* justified the new gas rationing program by letting the character of Fibber, already established as a buffoon, complain about rationing, only to be set straight through the humor of the other characters. On another evening, *The Jack Benny Show* might feature America's most lovable tightwad finally getting rid of his ancient automobile by donating it to the War Salvage Drive. Benny's character has to be persuaded of the need for such a contribution, but he declares afterward that it was the right thing to do, indirectly encouraging his listeners to do likewise.

Radio also brought the news into American homes, and much of it came courtesy of a new kind of reporter: the on-air correspondent broadcasting live from the site of the story. Some World War II radio correspondents, such as William L. Shirer, Charles Collingwood, and Eric Sevareid, earned impressive reputations as journalists, but the dean of them all was Edward R. Murrow. Whether reporting from a London rooftop in the middle of an air raid or broadcasting a description of the Buchenwald concentration camp on the day it was liberated by the Allies, Murrow combined superb journalistic skills with a sonorous voice and a gift for near-poetic language to produce a series of radio programs that are still considered classics.

SONGS

Music has always been a mainstay of radio, and many of the songs that Americans listened to during the war reflected the era. The rousing "We Did It Before (And We Can Do It Again)" was penned by Charles Tobias and Cliff Friend immediately following the Japanese bombing of Pearl Harbor. It compares World War II with World War I and predicts the same outcome for the Allies. Irving Berlin's tune "Any Bonds Today?" was used by the government in a series of bond drives designed to raise money for the war effort. "I'll Walk Alone" by Sammy Cahn and Jule Styne promises every serviceman stationed overseas that his wife or girlfriend will still be waiting when he returns home. Louis Jordan, Antonio Casey, and Collenane Clark composed "Ration Blues" in 1943 as a good-natured lament over war-related shortages of material goods.

One of the most popular patriotic songs of the war was Kate Smith's rendering of "God Bless America." Although written by Berlin near the end of World War I, the song went unrecorded and forgotten until the next war. It became Smith's trademark, and she sang it frequently, especially at a series of hugely successful war bond rallies.

COMICS

The "funnies" (broadly defined) also helped the war effort. Many cartoons, comic books, and newspaper comic strips had their characters participating in the conflict. Bill Mauldin was the most famous of the war's cartoonists, although much of his work was initially drawn and published for a military audience (principally in the *Yank*, the armed forces newspaper). Mauldin's characters Willie and Joe, who can find grim humor in being wet, filthy, tired, and scared, represent a gritty and realistic portrayal of the average front-line existence of a "grunt." Virgil Partch II, who signed his cartoons "VIP," was a master of the grotesque and the absurd, and his work shows that the war contained no shortage of either one.

Comic books were an immensely popular entertainment medium in America during the 1940s. By the war's end, more than twenty million comics were sold every month. During the war years, dozens of comic-book characters participated in the struggle against fascism and militarism. A year before Pearl Harbor, the team of Joe Simon and Jack Kirby created Captain America, the first comic-book superhero to fight the Nazis. Captain Midnight, initially a hero of a radio drama in the 1930s, was put into comic books after America entered the war. Alan Armstrong, better known as Spy Smasher, foils Axis plots both at home and abroad. Wonder Woman, virtually the only female superhero of the era, is an Amazon warrior princess who possesses magic bracelets and a hatred of evil. Superman, the first popular comic superhero, spends the war at home in America, but he finds no shortage of Axis villains to defeat with his super powers.

The heroes of newspaper comic strips were also active in the war. According to a study conducted by the OWI, more than fifty regularly appearing strips used the war as part of their story lines. The first to "join up," in 1940, was the character Joe Palooka, a clean-cut professional boxer who enlists in the army. Milton Caniff's character Terry Lee (of *Terry and the Pirates*) joins the army after Pearl Harbor and spends the war flying missions against the Japanese. Little Orphan Annie's contributions to the war effort are mostly noncombatant, although she does on one occasion help blow up a German submarine. Other popular comic strip characters, such as Captain Easy, Smilin' Jack, Tillie the Toiler, and Snuffy Smith, do their part to make the world again safe for democracy.

POSTWAR LITERATURE

Many nonfiction books about the war sold well while the conflict raged, but there seemed to be little market for novels about it, with the exception of John Hersey's *A Bell for Adano*, the 1944 story of U.S. soldiers occupying a Sicilian town and the winner of the 1945 Pulitzer Prize. However, the war's end in August 1945 signaled the beginning of a flood of literary efforts, several of which proved to be of enduring significance. In 1948 Norman Mailer published *The Naked and the Dead*, which uses the motif of an American effort to take a Japanese-held Pacific island to discuss issues such as fascism, personal freedom, and individual-versus-group responsibility. The same year, Irwin Shaw's *The Young Lions* was published, a sweeping saga that examines the lives of three soldiers (two American and one German) against the backdrop of the European war's most momentous events.

Leon Uris's *Battle Cry* is one of the best novels about the U.S. Marines in the Pacific war. It follows a group of young men through basic training and into combat at Guadalcanal and, later, Tarawa. Although James Jones's celebrated novel *From Here to Eternity* (1951) is not really a war story (the Japanese attack on Pearl Harbor, where the novel is set, provides the climax), his next book, *The Thin Red Line* (1962), definitely can be classified as such. A grimly realistic story of a group of marines fighting to take Guadalcanal from the Japanese, the novel emphasizes the ugly, capricious, and ultimately pointless nature of war. The absurdity of war is also the theme of Joseph Heller's 1961 classic *Catch-22*. The protagonist, Yossarian, is an army air force bombardier based in Italy who knows that his chances of survival decrease with every mission he flies. There is a limit on the number of missions that a bomber crew can be sent on, but Yossarian's superiors keep raising the number. This darkly comic novel centers on Yossarian's efforts to stay alive in the midst of a system that seems determined to kill him.

Absurdity edges into surrealism in Kurt Vonnegut's *Slaughterhouse-Five* (1969), which mixes realism, science fiction, black comedy, and existentialism in the story of Billy Pilgrim, a man who "comes unstuck in time." He starts experiencing his life out of chronological sequence, and some of these temporal glitches take him back to his World War II days, when, as a prisoner of the Germans, he experienced the terrible Allied firebombing of Dresden.

POSTWAR COMICS

Comic-book publishers seemed to be almost as interested in the war after it ended as they had been during it. Several long-running comic series, most of which had begun during the war, outlasted the conflict and continued to provide drama and adventure through the perspective of fictional American heroes.

The most popular of these included *Gunner and Sarge* (marines fighting in the Pacific); *The Haunted Tank* (commanded by Lieutenant Jeb Stuart and protected by the ghost of the original Jeb Stuart of Confederate cavalry fame); and, the most famous of all, Sergeant Rock of Easy Company. Unlike most of his fellow comic warriors, Rock was not created until 1959, when he appeared in a DC Comics offering titled *Our Army at War*. Although most of the other World War II comics faded away in the 1960s, Sergeant Rock and his men marched on until 1988.

POSTWAR COMBAT FILMS

Hollywood's interest in World War II also continued long after the fighting ended. In fact, no other war has been the subject of so many films. The postwar movies dealing with the conflict can be discussed in terms of three broad categories: combat depictions, historical re-creations, and comedies. Combat films were a popular genre during the war itself, and they continued to be the most common type after 1945. One of the first was the John Wayne vehicle *Sands of Iwo Jima* (1949), which deftly integrates documentary footage of the actual landing with re-created elements. Marines are also the focus of 1955's *Battle Cry*, based on the popular novel. Mailer's book *The Naked and the Dead* was filmed in 1958, but it disappointed critics by leaving out most of the philosophical issues raised by the novel. *The Guns of Navarone* (1961), based on Alistair MacLean's novel, chronicles a commando raid designed to disable German cannons that control a strait vital to the Allies.

Featuring an all-star cast, *The Dirty Dozen* (1967) focuses on the efforts of a tough army major (Lee Marvin) as he struggles to turn a squad of condemned U.S. prisoners into a commando unit for a secret mission on the eve of D-day. *Castle Keep* (1969) is the surreal story of a group of army misfits relegated to duty in a Belgian castle that suddenly assumes strategic importance in the Battle of the Bulge. Samuel Fuller's *Samuel Fuller and the Big Red One* (1979) follows a squad of soldiers of the First Infantry Division as they fight their way across Europe.

Although the combat film languished throughout most of the 1980s and 1990s, two powerful examples were released near the end of the latter decade. Steven Spielberg's *Saving Private Ryan* (1998) stars Tom Hanks and is notable for the most realistically gruesome battle footage ever shown in a mainstream motion picture. *The Thin Red Line* (1998) is the second filmed version of Jones's classic novel and devotes as much time to moral issues as it does to combat.

A subgenre of the combat film involves stories focusing on prisoners of war, a category that includes some of the best movies made about World War II. *Stalag 17*, based on a popular play, is a comedy-drama about American prisoners held by the Germans. *The Bridge on the River Kwai* (1957), which won innumerable awards, tells the story of a group of British prisoners of war (POWs) in Burma who are forced by their Japanese captors to build a railroad bridge. *The Great Escape* (1963), based loosely on a true story, involves a German "escape-proof" prison camp and the Allied prisoners who break out of it. *Von Ryan's Express* (1965) stars Frank Sinatra as an American colonel who masterminds the hijacking of a German train by the Allied POWs it is transporting.

POSTWAR BATTLE RE-CREATION FILMS AND COMEDIES

Films that chronicle actual battles, campaigns, or leaders include *Battle of the Bulge* (1965) and *The Bridge at Remagen* (1969). *Patton* (1970) is George C. Scott's brilliant portrait of the general known to his troops as "Old Blood and Guts." *The Longest Day* (1962) is a sprawling, epic account of the D-day invasion, while *A Bridge Too Far* (1977) tells the story of a disastrous Allied plan to outflank the Germans that almost, but not quite, succeeds in ending the war a year early.

Comedies about World War II have been attempted with varying degrees of success. *Mister Roberts* (1955) focuses on sailors fighting boredom while stationed far from the combat. Cary Grant stars in *Operation Petticoat* (1959) as the commander of a submarine that takes on a bevy of beautiful nurses as passengers. Grant also stars in *Father Goose* (1964) as a coastwatcher who reluctantly helps a group of children escape internment by the Japanese. In *What Did You Do in the War, Daddy?* (1966), James Coburn plays the reluctant commander of a squad occupying an Italian village, and Spielberg had one of his few cinematic flops with the inane farce *1941* (1979).

POSTWAR TELEVISION

World War II was a fruitful subject for television programs well into the 1960s. One of the earliest TV shows to deal with the war was the documentary series *Battle Report* (1950–1952). Host Robert McCormick introduced a new "battle" each week, with film footage and interviews with surviving participants elucidating what had happened. Fictional programs began to appear in 1956 with *Combat Sergeant*, set against the backdrop of the battle for North Africa. The program lasted only a year, as did *O.S.S* (1957), featuring the espionage adventures of Frank Hawthorne, who operates behind enemy lines on behalf of the Office of Strategic Services.

Several years passed before the networks tried another World War II show. *The Gallant Men* (1962) tells the story of an infantry unit fighting its way through Italy. *Combat!* (1962–1967) is generally regarded as the best television drama about World War II, focusing on a U.S. infantry platoon in France (and later Germany) during the last two years of the conflict. The ensemble cast includes Rick Jason as Lieutenant Hanley and Vic Morrow as Sergeant Saunders. Well written and ably directed, *Combat!* never uses action as a substitute for human drama. In 1966 *The Rat Patrol* premiered, starring Christopher George as the leader of a four-man mechanized commando unit fighting the Germans in North Africa. The show lasted only two seasons. Another short-lived offering was *Garrison's Gorillas*

(1967–1968), a blatant attempt to cash in on the popularity of the film *The Dirty Dozen*.

World War II dramas largely disappeared from the airwaves until the arrival in 1976 of *Baa Baa Black Sheep* (retitled *Black Sheep Squadron* for its second, and last, season). Loosely based on a real marine aviation unit, the show stars Robert Conrad as Greg "Pappy" Boyington, who leads a group of misfit fighter pilots into aerial combat against the Japanese.

NOTABLE TV COMEDIES

Several television comedies have been based on the war, some of which have proved to be surprisingly popular, including *McHale's Navy* (1962–1966), starring Ernest Borgnine as Lieutenant Commander McHale. Meanwhile, a seagoing Sergeant Bilko cons his superiors in *The Phil Silvers Show* (1955–1959), ripping off the navy and striving to avoid combat with the Japanese. *The Wackiest Ship in the Army*, based on the 1960 film of the same name about a garbage scow, was launched in 1965 but sank at season's end. Jack Warden and Gary Collins star as officers commanding a mixed squad of soldiers and sailors that roams the South Pacific in an old wooden sailboat, attempting to gather intelligence about the Japanese forces in the area.

Perhaps the unlikeliest hit in the comedy category is *Hogan's Heroes* (1965–1971), set in a German POW camp for Allied prisoners. The show derives its humor from the abilities of the prisoners, led by Colonel Hogan (Bob Crane), to outsmart their German captors. So incompetent are the camp commander, Colonel Klink (Werner Klemperer), and his ranking noncom, Sergeant Schultz (John Banner), that the prisoners are able to run an espionage ring out of the camp, help downed Allied airmen return to England, and construct an elaborate underground complex directly under the camp itself. Despite the implausibility of both the premise and most of the scripts, the show ran for 168 episodes.

CULTURAL IMPACT

The aftermath of World War II redefined American culture in virtually every way, to the extent that the war is considered a dividing point in American history. The European powers that had been dominant before the war were economically and physically depleted after it. The United States, meanwhile, emerged relatively unscathed. The economic output during World War II signaled an end to the Great Depression, and the United States became the richest and most powerful nation in the world. Race relations also changed drastically, as African Americans who had fought for the United States refused to return to roles of subservience. This paved the way for the civil rights movement in the following decades. Women, who had filled in at jobs for the men who were off fighting, began to aim higher too. Resisting the push to become homemakers again, many women remained on the job while others opted for college. The result was the second wave of the women's rights movement in the 1960s and 1970s.

Politically, the Cold War that followed World War II shaped aspects of everything from the dawning of the space age to educational reforms that placed a new emphasis on science and mathematics to a slew of spy movies and novels. Nuclear weapons capable of destroying the world hastened an arms race that continued into the last decade of the twentieth century. Technologies used in the war led to products ranging from plastics to microwaves. The postwar baby boomers, born between 1945 and 1964, have had an enormous impact on all aspects of American culture. They continue to exert their influence as they reach retirement in the twenty-first century, redefining ideas about aging and shaping the health care industry.

THE GREATEST GENERATION?

In 1984 NBC correspondent Tom Brokaw was dispatched to Normandy, France, to report on the celebration of the fortieth anniversary of D-day. While there, Brokaw interacted with scores of veterans who were also in France for the celebration, leading him to write a book titled *The Greatest Generation* (1998). Within its first two years of publication, the book sold two million copies. The term *greatest generation* became part of the popular lexicon and generated a body of literature both agreeing and disagreeing with Brokaw's assessment. In *Myth of the Greatest Generation: A Social History of World War II*, for example, Kenneth D. Rose argues that the World War II generation was no greater than its predecessors. Rose points out that the World War II generation fell short regarding the inherent racism that led to the incarceration of Japanese Americans during the war and for expecting African American soldiers to fight for the United States in foreign countries while denying them civil rights at home.

World War II continues to fascinate authors. One of the most popular recent tomes on the subject is a children's book, *The Book Thief* (2006). Written by Australian author Markus Zusak, it chronicles the life of Liesel Meminger, a young German girl who cannot resist the lure of books, even when she has to steal them. British journalist Alan Pearce, the author of *Dunkirk Spirit* (2011), details the lives of both celebrated and ordinary British citizens during the war. In the United States, military historian Jeff Shaara introduced his World War II series in 2006 with *The Rising Tide*, which focuses on theaters in northern Africa and Sicily. The second installment, *The Steel Wave* (2008), chronicles the war in Europe. *No Less than Victory* (2009) starts with the Battle of the Bulge and ends with the fall of Adolf Hitler, and a fourth book, *The Final Storm* (2011), deals with the end of World War II.

Twenty-first-century filmmakers are also still finding rich material in World War II. *Enemy at the Gates* (2001) stars Jude Law and Ed Harris and depicts the Battle of Stalingrad. The following year, *Windtalkers* was released. Starring Nicolas Cage and Adam Beach, it tells the story of Navajo soldiers who use their native language to create an unbreakable radio cypher. Two movies released in 2006 by Clint Eastwood show the turning points of Iwo Jima from different perspectives: *Flags of Our Fathers* from that of the Americans and *Letters from Iwo Jima* from that of the Japanese. In 2009 Brad Pitt starred in *Inglourious Basterds*, a tale of Jewish American soldiers charged with instilling fear into the Third Reich. The coming years are sure to bring more films and literature centering on World War II. After all, it was a war that sharply defined what it means to be an American.

Justin Gustainis

SEE ALSO: *Baby Boomers; Benny, Jack; Berlin, Irving; The Bomb;* The Bridge on the River Kwai*; Brokaw, Tom; Capra, Frank; Captain America;* Catch-22*; Civil Rights Movement; Cold War; Comic Books; Comics; DC Comics;* The Dirty Dozen*; Eastwood, Clint;* Fibber McGee and Molly*; Ford, John;* From Here to Eternity*; Grant, Cary; The Great Depression;*

Hanks, Tom; Hogan's Heroes; *Huston, John; Japanese American Internment Camps; Little Orphan Annie; Mailer, Norman;* McHale's Navy; Meet Me in St. Louis; Patton; *Pitt, Brad; Radio; Rockwell, Norman; Sinatra, Frank; Smith, Kate; Spielberg, Steven; Superman; Television; Vonnegut, Kurt, Jr.; Wayne, John; Wonder Woman; World War I.*

BIBLIOGRAPHY

Blum, John Morton. *V Was for Victory: Politics and American Culture during World War II.* New York: Harcourt, Brace, Jovanovich, 1976.

Braverman, Jordan. *To Hasten the Homecoming: How Americans Fought World War II through the Media.* Lanham, MD: Madison Books, 1996.

Dick, Bernard F. *The Star-Spangled Screen: The American World War II Film.* Lexington: University Press of Kentucky, 1985.

Dower, John W. *Cultures of War: Pearl Harbor, Hiroshima, 9-11, Iraq.* New York: W. W. Norton, 2011.

Kruse, Kevin M., and Stephen Tuck, eds. *Fog of War: The Second World War and the Civil Rights Movement.* New York: Oxford University Press, 2012.

Miscamble, Wilson D. *The Most Controversial Decision: Truman, the Atomic Bomb, and the Defeat of Japan.* New York: Cambridge University Press, 2011.

Murray, Williamson. *War, Strategy, and Military Effectiveness.* New York: Cambridge University Press, 2011.

Rich, Don, and Kevin Brooks. *Glider Infantrymen: Behind Enemy Lines in World War II.* College Station: Texas A&M University Press, 2012.

Sparrow, James T. *State: World War II America and the Age of Big Government.* New York: Oxford University Press, 2011.

Waldmeir, Joseph J. *American Novels of the Second World War.* The Hague, Netherlands: Mouton Publishers, 1971.

Zeiler, Thomas W. *Annihilation: A Global History of World War II.* New York: Oxford University Press, 2011.

World Wrestling Federation

SEE: *WWE.*

World's Fairs

Modern world's fairs were events of the nineteenth and twentieth centuries. Whereas medieval fairs were concerned with the selling of goods, modern world's fairs were involved in the selling of industrial technology and industrial society; they fostered the idea that industrial development was to be equated with social progress. World's fairs not only furnished a place where the latest technological achievements could be presented to an international public, but they also provided an orientation to people confronting the vast and rapid changes of industrialism. They offered a story of past progress, a photograph of the present, and a vision of the future. But by the middle of the twentieth century, world's fairs had lost much of their importance and charm.

EARLY WORLD'S FAIRS

The first world's fair was held in London in 1851. Prince Albert, husband of Queen Victoria and president of the Royal Society of the Arts, wanted to go beyond the national industrial exhibitions that France had made famous and that Britain was ready to duplicate. After much discussion a building of glass, with iron and wood beams, was constructed in Hyde Park. This so-called Crystal Palace held all of the exhibits. Because it was built with prefabricated, interchangeable parts, the building could be constructed and taken down quickly, with little damage to the park. In fact, the building was actually constructed over ten large elm trees. During the 141 days it was open, more than six million people attended. The success of the Crystal Palace exhibition inspired other nations to hold international fairs.

Early world's fairs were often remembered by the products they introduced to the public. Americans were prominent in the Crystal Palace exhibition. Cyrus McCormick's reaper, Samuel Morse's telegraph, and Charles Goodyear's vulcanized rubber products were well received. Colt revolvers and Robbins & Lawrence rifles made with interchangeable parts were recognized as having revolutionized the making of firearms. At the New York World's Fair in 1853, Elisha Otis demonstrated his safety elevator. At the Philadelphia Exposition of 1876, Alexander Graham Bell introduced the telephone, and Thomas Edison gave his first public demonstration of the phonograph in Paris in 1889. Sound-synchronized movies, X-rays, and wireless telegraphy marked the 1900 Paris fair. The St. Louis World's Fair of 1904 introduced the safety razor, the ice cream cone, iced tea, and rayon. President Franklin D. Roosevelt's televised opening of the 1939 New York World's Fair inaugurated regular television broadcasting in the United States. Computer demonstrations by IBM (International Business Machines) educated visitors to the New York World's Fair of 1964–1965.

More important than the inventions were the industrial systems the fairs exhibited to the public. The Philadelphia Centennial Exposition of 1876 celebrated the age of steam. In Machinery Hall the giant Corliss steam engine, 40 feet high and with 2,520 horsepower, ran all of the machinery in the hall. There were also steam fire engines, steam locomotives, and steam pumps. By 1893 the Chicago World's Columbian Exposition was celebrating the age of electricity. At night the fair was lighted by thousands of incandescent lightbulbs. In the electrical building there were Edison and Westinghouse dynamos and electric motors that powered other machines. Transportation, however, was the theme in St. Louis in 1904. Trains, streetcars, and more than 160 motorcars were displayed. A major feature of the fair was the dirigible contest, in which a large cash prize awaited anyone who could pilot his airship over a prescribed route.

COMMEMORATIONS AND SOCIAL CHANGES

While world's fairs were held to celebrate historic milestones, contemporary concerns were also often in the minds of fair planners. The 1876 Philadelphia exposition recognized the centennial of the signing of the Declaration of Independence. The fair was also viewed as a means to remind Americans of their common ideals and thus to help heal the wounds of the Civil War. The 1889 world's fair in Paris celebrated the centennial of the French Revolution. The Chicago exposition of 1893 recognized the 400th anniversary of Christopher Columbus's discovery of America, and the St. Louis World's Fair of 1904 commemorated the centennial of the Louisiana Purchase. Both fairs were also seen as demonstrating the importance of the Midwest in the United States. The centennial of the founding of the city of Chicago was celebrated in a world's fair in 1933.

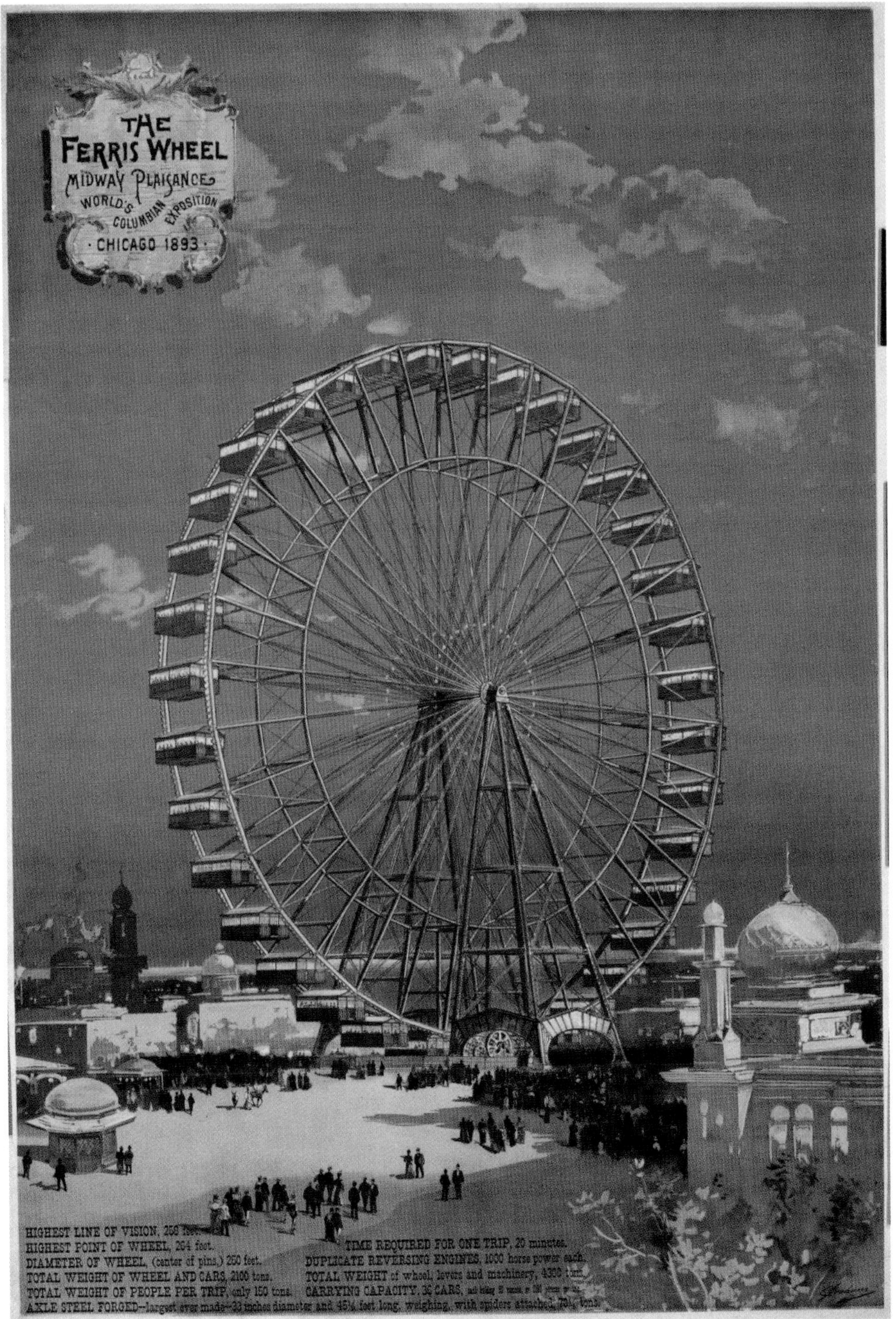

Ferris Wheel at Chicago Expo, 1893. *The world's first Ferris wheel was a featured attraction at the World's Columbian Exposition in Chicago in 1893.* CHICAGO HISTORY MUSEUM/GETTY IMAGES.

New York's World's Fair in 1939 celebrated the 150th anniversary of George Washington's inauguration. The purpose of the theme, "Building the World of Tomorrow," was to show how a well-planned democratic society would survive the world's turmoil. The outbreak of World War II, however, resulted in the new theme of "Peace and Freedom" for the 1940 opening.

The outside world had a way of impinging upon world's fairs. At the New York World's Fair of 1853, Susan B. Anthony led a demonstration for women's rights. At the Philadelphia Centennial Exposition in 1876, a building housed a display of inventions by women, along with photographs showing women working in a variety of occupations. Of particular note was Emma Allison, who operated a steam engine that ran six looms and a printing press. When a man asked her if the work was too demanding for someone of her sex, she replied, "It's easier than teaching, and the pay is better." At the Chicago World's Columbian Exposition of 1893, the women's building displayed a great collection of works by women. These included a library of 5,000 books, paintings, and sculptures, as well as mechanical devices invented by women. A careful selection of statistics from around the world showed the extent to which women were a part of the world economy. Anthony believed the women's building did more to raise the consciousness of women than had all the demonstrations of the nineteenth century.

ENTERTAINMENT AT WORLD'S FAIRS

At the Philadelphia Centennial Exposition of 1876, vendors and amusements were located outside the fairgrounds. The 1893 Chicago planners recognized, however, that a profit could be realized by bringing the amusements and vendors into the fair itself. One of the most popular of the Midway exhibits in Chicago was called the "streets of Cairo," featuring a belly dancer named Little Egypt. She also appeared at the 1904 St. Louis fair but was outdrawn there by Jim Key, the counting horse. The 1933 Chicago fair had a Midget Town and featured the fan dancer Sally Rand. The New York World's Fair of 1939 featured the synchronized swimming of the so-called Aqua girls in Billy Rose's Aquacade. The Eiffel Tower was a huge success at the 1889 Paris fair. For a generation that had not flown in an airplane, seeing the world from 985 feet was unlike anything they had ever experienced. The 1893 Chicago fair offered G. W. G. Ferris's great wheel: 40 cars, each carrying 36 passengers, moving to a height of 270 feet. Forty years later Chicago offered the 200-foot-high Sky Ride, across the second-longest suspension span in the United States. The parachute jump at the 1939 New York World's Fair attracted both thrill seekers and onlookers. Many world's fairs came to be remembered for their outstanding amusements.

Because world's fairs were international events, organizations often held their meetings at the fairs. For example, 127 international organizations met at the 1900 Paris fair. The second and third modern Olympic Games were held as part of the world's fairs in Paris (1900) and St. Louis (1904). Fairs also featured villages of peoples from around the world. Dressed in their native costumes, these villages were publicized as serving an educational function. The subtle message, however, was the ethnocentric view that celebrated Western progress by comparing the achievements shown at the fair with the backwardness of the native cultures. Following the Olympics, the St. Louis fair held three days of so-called anthropology games, in which native peoples were enticed to demonstrate their skills. Sioux participated in archery contests, Africans threw javelins, and seven-foot Patagonians tried the shot put. Their inability to match Western records not only confirmed the value of training but also suggested, to visitors at least, the superiority of Western civilization.

VISIONS OF THE FUTURE

Those people who went to world's fairs had their faith in Western industrial progress confirmed. In 1933, at the height of the Great Depression, for example, Chicago's Century of Progress assured visitors that science guaranteed a better future. The science building had a giant statue gently guiding a trembling man and woman into the future. The official guidebook to the fair stated, "Science Finds, Industry Applies, Man Conforms." By 1939, as fascism and Nazism were coming to dominate Europe, visitors to the New York's World Fair were given a powerful message of hope. The symbols of the fair, the Trylon and Perisphere, suggested that soaring human aspirations could be realized on the earth. Inside the sphere was a giant model city known as Democracity. This utopian city had Centerton as its business and cultural center, Millvilles of light industry, and Pleasantvilles that were exclusively residential. Democracity, with its defined zones and rational streets, carried the message that well-planned, livable cities were possible through democratic forms of government. Futurama, the General Motors exhibit, the most popular at the fair, presented a vision of the United States united by a 14-lane national highway in which radio-controlled automobiles moved at 100 miles per hour. With its green suburbs, industrial parks, productive farms, and high-rise urban centers, this vision of what the United States would be in 1960 offered an inspirational alternative to the chaos that the world was experiencing.

Over time, the expense of holding a world's fair requires corporate sponsorship, and the commercialization of the 1964–1965 New York World's Fair suggested that such affairs had become oriented toward selling products. The fair's Ferris wheel, for example, was a giant tire with the name of the company appearing in huge letters on the sides of the tires. Furthermore, people's attitude toward technology has changed. Many no longer accept the idea that simply because something can be done technologically it ought to be done. The 1964–1965 exhibit of General Motors, for example, demonstrated how humans might explore and colonize the oceans, the deserts, and the polar ice caps, but few people were inspired by the vision.

World's fairs have lost much of their importance as technical fairs and television have become a more effective means of presenting new technological developments to specialists and to the general public alike. Television and the Internet bring foreign cultures into people's homes, and air travel allows people to visit other cultures. Many international organizations are now connected with permanent agencies of the United Nations. Theme parks such as Disney World and Epcot Center provide the kinds of amusements and thrills that were once found at world's fairs.

While the world's fair large-scale exhibition model has fallen out of popularity and feasibility, such expositions continue to be held throughout the world. Because of the lack of interest and high cost, such demonstrations have met with varying degrees of success. Expo 2000, held in 2000 in Hannover, Germany, was a financial failure. However, Shanghai's Expo 2010, which cost more than $11 billion, saw record numbers of attendees. The exposition increased tourism and boosted revenue significantly for the city. In the twenty-first century, the purpose world's fairs once served may be obsolete, but the events can still be a source of income and pride for nations making their debut on the international stage.

Thomas W. Judd

SEE ALSO: *Alaska-Yukon Exposition (Seattle, 1909); Amusement Parks; Century of Progress (Chicago, 1933); Century 21 Exposition (Seattle, 1962); Feminism; Louisiana Purchase Exposition; Olympics; World War II.*

BIBLIOGRAPHY

Allwood, John. *The Great Exhibitions*. London: Studio Vista, 1977.

Badger, Reid. *The Great American Fair: The World's Columbian Exposition and American Culture*. Chicago: Nelson-Hall, 1979.

Briggs, Asa. *Iron Bridge to Crystal Palace: Impact and Images of the Industrial Revolution*. London: Thames and Hudson, 1979.

Burg, David. *Chicago's White City of 1893.* Lexington: University Press of Kentucky, 1976.

Findling, John E. *Chicago's Great World's Fairs.* Manchester, UK: Manchester University Press, 1994.

Geppert, Alexander C. T. *Fleeting Cities: Imperial Expositions in Fin-de-Siècle Europe.* New York: Palgrave Macmillan, 2010.

Harrison, Helen. *Dawn of a New Day: The New York World's Fair, 1939/40.* New York: New York University Press, 1980.

Luckhurst, Kenneth. *The Story of Exhibitions.* London: Studio Publications, 1951.

Mandell, Richard. *Paris, 1900: The Great World's Fair.* Toronto: University of Toronto Press, 1967.

Weimann, Jeanne. *The Fair Women: The Story of the Women's Building, World's Columbian Exposition, Chicago, 1893.* Chicago: Academy Chicago, 1981.

Wrangler Jeans

Wrangler jeans became the pant de rigueur for late twentieth-century country-and-western fashion. After their introduction in 1947, they became popular with midcentury rodeo riders because of their snug fit and boot-cut pant leg. Wranglers have since come to symbolize the free spirit and individualism embodied in the myths of the American frontier West. Although other brands, especially Levi's, became connected with urban chic, Wrangler focused its marketing almost exclusively on its western roots and association with rural authenticity.

As the jeans of choice for almost any star in the growing country music industry of the late 1980s and 1990s, Wranglers benefited from the resurgence of country music and the heavy advertising tie-ins associated with the music's rural and western image. Wrangler became culturally connected, and often financially intertwined, with rodeos, country music, competitive fishing, and pickup truck sales. In the early twenty-first century, legendary National Football League (NFL) quarterback Brett Favre became a spokesperson for the jeans. Wrangler also continued to maintain its western image by sponsoring rodeos and working to develop a better-fitting jean for riding.

Dan Moos

SEE ALSO: *Country Music; Jeans; Levi's; National Football League (NFL); Rodeo.*

BIBLIOGRAPHY

Gordon, Beverly. "American Denim: Blue Jeans and Their Multiple Layers of Meaning." *Dress and Popular Culture*, ed. Patricia A. Cunningham and Susan Voso Lab. Bowling Green, OH: Bowling Green State University Popular Press, 1991.

Sullivan, James. *Jeans: A Cultural History of an American Icon.* New York: Gotham, 2006.

Wray, Fay *(1907–2004)*

Despite a long career, versatile Canadian-born actress Fay Wray is indelibly etched on the public mind as the shrieking heroine in the grasp of a giant ape climbing the Empire State Building in the film *King Kong* (1933). For forty years she acted in more than seventy-five motion pictures as well as on the Broadway stage and television. She also coauthored a play with Nobel Prize winner Sinclair Lewis. Although Wray proved her acting ability in such films as *The Affairs of Cellini* (1934), opposite Fredric March, she was doomed to be typecast as the champion screamer and bedeviled heroine. In the 1950s she appeared in the television series *Pride of the Family* as the wife of Paul Hartman and mother of Natalie Wood. "When I'm in New York," she once said with a laugh, "I look at the Empire State Building and feel as though it belongs to me, or is it vice versa?"

Benjamin Griffith

SEE ALSO: *Broadway; Empire State Building;* King Kong*; Lewis, Sinclair; Television; Wood, Natalie.*

BIBLIOGRAPHY

Hodges, Ben, and John Willis. *Theatre World. Vol. 65, 2008–2009.* New York: Applause Theatre & Cinema, 2009.

Parish, James Robert, and William T. Leonard. *Hollywood Players: The Thirties.* New Rochelle, NY: Arlington House, 1976.

Ragan, David. *Movie Stars of the '30s: A Complete Reference Guide for the Film Historian or Trivia Buff.* Englewood Cliffs, NJ: Prentice-Hall, 1985.

Wright, Richard *(1908–1960)*

Richard Wright was once at the center of African American culture. In addition to being chosen as one of "twelve distinguished Negroes" of 1939 in a Schomburg Collection poll and receiving the Spingarn Medal in 1941 (then the highest award given by the National Association for the Advancement of Colored People), he mentored young black writers such as James Baldwin, Gwendolyn Brooks, and Ralph Ellison. In the decades that followed his death in 1960, however, Wright was viewed as an unpalatable novelist by readers and critics of his own race.

Born on a plantation in Roxie, near Natchez, Mississippi, Wright spent his childhood being shuttled from one relative to the next because his father had deserted the family and his mother was in ill health. In 1927 Wright moved to the South Side of Chicago, where he worked as a postal clerk and insurance policy vendor. While in Chicago, he joined first the John Reed Club and then the Communist Party, and he started to publish essays and poetry in leftist reviews such as *Midland Left, New Masses*, and *International Literature*. By 1936 Wright had become one of the principal organizers of the Communist Party, but his relationship with the party would always be strained, right up until his break with it in 1942.

A NEW VOICE EMERGES

In 1936 Wright's short story "Big Boy Leaves Home" appeared in the anthology *The New Caravan* and received critical praise in mainstream newspapers and magazines, marking a decisive step for his career as a writer. The following year Wright moved to New York, where he and Dorothy West launched the magazine *New Challenge* (which, lacking communist support, was short lived). In *New Challenge*, Wright published the influential essay "Blueprint for Negro Writing" (1937), in which he urged black writers to adopt a Marxist approach as a starting point in their analysis of society. He also encouraged black writers to consider as their heritage T. S. Eliot, Gertrude Stein, James Joyce, Marcel Proust, Ernest Hemingway, Sherwood Anderson, Henri Barbusse, Martin Andersen Nexø, and Jack London "no less than the folklore of the Negro himself"—a viewpoint that is considered problematic by contemporary black critics.

Wright's first novel, *Native Son* is based on a true story and describes the progressive entrapment and final execution of Bigger Thomas, a young African American chauffeur living in the Chicago slums who involuntarily kills the daughter of his boss. Published in 1940 by Harper, the novel sold 215,000 copies in its first three weeks and became a Book-of-the-Month Club selection, thus marking, as renowned academic Paul Gilroy points out in *The Black Atlantic*, an important change in the political economy of publishing black writers. The following year Orson Welles directed a successful stage version of *Native Son*. Two movie versions have been realized so far: the first in 1951 by Pierre Chenal starring Wright himself and the second in 1986 by Jerrold Freedman starring Victor Love, Matt Dillon, and Oprah Winfrey.

Native Son has had a great impact on successive generations of African American writers, who have either followed its "protest novel" pattern, as in the case of Anne Petry, Chester Himes, and William Gardner Smith (sometimes significantly grouped together as "the Wright school"), or have reacted to it very critically, as Baldwin does in his famous essay "Everybody's Protest Novel" (1949). In the essay, Baldwin states: "The failure of the protest novel lies in its rejection of life, the human being, the denial of his beauty, dread, power, in its insistence that it is his categorization alone which is real and which cannot be transcended."

Richard Wright. *Richard Wright rose to literary prominence with major works such as* Native Son *and* Black Boy, *which chronicled the black experience in America.* HULTON ARCHIVE/STRINGER/ ARCHIVE PHOTOS/GETTY IMAGES.

After the success of *Native Son*, Wright published with equal success and critical acclaim the folk history *12 Million Black Voices* (1941) and the first part of his autobiography, *Black Boy* (1945), which became another Book-of-the-Month Club selection. (The second part was published posthumously as *American Hunger* in 1977.) In 1945 Wright wrote the introduction to *Black Metropolis*, St. Clair Drake and Horace Cayton's classic sociological study of the black ghetto in Chicago.

WORLDWIDE ACCLAIM

Thanks to *Native Son* and *Black Boy*, which were translated into several languages, Wright was the first black writer to enjoy a global readership. However, *Black Boy* has attracted much criticism by contemporary African American scholars for Wright's depiction of black life in America as, to quote his own words, "bleak" and "barren." In *The Signifying Monkey*, for example, literary critic Henry Louis Gates Jr. finds that "Wright's humanity is achieved only at the expense of his fellow blacks . . . who surround and suffocate him," which makes Wright's autobiographical persona "a noble black savage, in the ironic tradition of *Oroonoko* and film characters played by Sidney Poitier—the exception, not the rule." Gilroy suggests a less disparaging, and ultimately more useful, perspective, describing Wright's work as fascinating precisely because "the tension of racial particularity on one side and the appeal of those modern universals that appear to transcend race on the other arises in the sharpest possible way."

In 1946 the French cultural attaché in Washington and famous anthropologist Claude Lévi-Strauss sent Wright an official invitation from the French government to visit Paris, where he was welcomed by prominent intellectuals such as Stein, Simone de Beauvoir, Jean-Paul Sartre, and André Gide. The following year Wright decided to settle permanently in Paris, where he started to work on his existentialist novel *The Outsider* (1953) and where he had an active role in several organizations, such as Sartre's Rassemblement Démocratique Révolutionnaire, Léopold Sédar Senghor and Aimé Césaire's Présence Africaine, and the Société Africaine de Culture. Wright's other books of this late period include a report on his travels in Africa (*Black Power*, 1954); an account, introduced by Swedish economist and sociologist Gunnar Myrdal, of the conference of nonaligned nations in Bandung, Indonesia (*The Color Curtain*, 1956); a collection of essays (*White Man, Listen!*, 1957); and two novels (*Savage Holiday*, 1954, and *The Long Dream*, 1958).

A TUMULTUOUS AFTERLIFE

Wright's last years were plagued by his progressive alienation from the African American community in Paris, which suspected Wright of being an agent for the FBI (in fact, evidence shows that the FBI monitored Wright's activities all his life), and by his increasing financial problems. Paradoxically and sadly for a writer who had to fight against white racism all his life and whose books were not allowed during his lifetime on the library shelves of several American towns, Wright has been held in contempt by influential black critics. They are disturbed by his unaffirmative portrayal of the African American community, by his controversial relationship with black culture, and by what many consider to be a stereotypical depiction of black women. It is hoped that critics and readers will find new and more inclusive strategies to recast Wright within the American and African American literary tradition.

Luca Prono

SEE ALSO: *Baldwin, James; Book-of-the-Month Club; Brooks, Gwendolyn; Civil Rights Movement.*

BIBLIOGRAPHY

Baldwin, James. *Notes of a Native Son*. Boston: Beacon Press, 1955.

Bloom, Harold, ed. *Richard Wright*. New York: Chelsea House Publishers, 1987.

Cappetti, Carla. *Writing Chicago: Modernism, Ethnography and the Novel*. New York: Columbia University Press, 1993.

Fabre, Michel. *The Unfinished Quest of Richard Wright*, tr. Isabel Barzun. New York: William Morrow, 1973.

Gates, Henry Louis, Jr. *The Signifying Monkey: A Theory of African-American Literary Criticism*. New York: Oxford University Press, 1988.

Gilroy, Paul. *The Black Atlantic: Modernity and Double Consciousness*. London: Verso, 1993.

Philipson, Robert. *The Identity Question: Blacks and Jews in Europe and America*. Jackson: University Press of Mississippi, 2000.

Sollors, Werner. "Modernization as Adultery: Richard Wright, Zora Neale Hurston and American Culture of the 1930s and 1940s." *Hebrew University Studies in Literature and the Arts* 18 (1990): 109–155.

Wrigley Field

Wrigley Field, the venerable home of the Chicago Cubs baseball team of the National League, sits at 1060 West Addison Street in Chicago. The field has played host to some of the most memorable incidents in the history of professional baseball. Opposing teams dread playing in "The Friendly Confines," as the park is known, because of the vicious winds that sometimes blow in from nearby Lake Michigan. The often raucous but always loyal fans turn out in droves to cheer on their beloved "Cubbies," even though they are one of the least successful teams in baseball history.

The field opened in March 1914 as the home of the Chicago Whales, a professional football team, and took the name Weeghman Park after the Whales's owner, Charles Weeghman. In 1916 Weeghman bought the Cubs and moved them to the park. Shortly afterward, the name was changed to Cubs Park. The Wrigley family (makers of chewing gum) bought the Cubs in 1920, and in 1926 the name was changed to Wrigley Field. Despite many changes throughout the years, Wrigley Field has preserved characteristics of old-time baseball, with the stadium, located in an urban residential neighborhood, surrounding a domeless field with real grass. In addition, there are 1930s-vintage amenities such as a hand-operated scoreboard, a beautiful ivy-covered outfield wall without advertising, and an infamous bleacher section often packed with "Bleacher Bums." With a seating capacity of only about 40,000, Wrigley Field remains unusually small for a major-league baseball park, which adds to the intimacy of watching a game within what is known as the stadium's "Friendly Confines." Under Wrigley ownership the Cubs also maintained a long-standing commitment to afternoon baseball games.

Among the more famous incidents in the history of Wrigley Field are Babe Ruth's "called shot" and the appearance of a black cat in 1969. The legend of Ruth's called shot in the third game of the 1932 World Series, in which he purportedly predicted the trajectory of one of his home runs, has achieved almost mythical status, despite evidence suggesting that the story was probably apocryphal. In the midst of the dramatic 1969 season, a black cat wandered into the Cubs dugout, supposedly contributing to the ultimately disastrous season that found the Cubs relinquishing a huge lead to New York's "Miracle Mets."

The Tribune Company, publishers of the *Chicago Tribune*, bought the Cubs in 1981 and made a concession to the modern age by installing lights for night baseball games. The first night game at Wrigley Field, on August 8, 1988, against the Philadelphia Phillies, was rained out, however. The Cubs completed its first official night game the next evening, defeating the New York Mets 6–4. Wrigley Field has continued to be an exception to the trend of selling corporations the naming rights to sporting venues. The Tribune Company, which owned the park until 2009, chose not to rename Wrigley Field, finding other ways to secure corporate sponsorship for the ballpark.

In the mid-1980s Anheuser-Busch was allowed to place Budweiser and Bud Light advertisements beneath the center-field scoreboard. The company's sponsorship went a step further in 2006, when the park's bleachers were renovated and officially dubbed the Bud Light Bleachers. Although owners had prohibited advertising within the walls of the park longer than any other club, by the early years of the twentieth-first century an electronic advertising screen was installed behind home plate. The screen was in the line of sight of the center-field television cameras, allowing rotating advertisements to be visible to television audiences; later the advertisements were also made visible to people in the park. In 2007 the first on-field advertising appeared since the park's early days.

Jason McEntee

SEE ALSO: *Baseball; Budweiser; The Chicago Cubs; Major League Baseball; Ruth, Babe.*

BIBLIOGRAPHY

Chicago Cubs Official Website. Accessed February 11, 2012. Available from http://chicago.cubs.mlb.com/index.jsp?c_id=chc

Golenbock, Peter. *Wrigleyville: A Magical History Tour of the Chicago Cubs*. New York: St. Martin's Press, 1994.

Hartel, William. *A Day at the Park: In Celebration of Wrigley Field*. Champaign, IL: Sagamore Publications, 1996.

Jacob, Marc; Stephen Green; and Ernie Franks. *Wrigley Field: A Celebration of Friendly Confines*. New York: McGraw-Hill, 2002.

Peterson, Paul Michael. *Chicago's Wrigley Field*. Charleston, SC: Arcadia Books, 2005.

Shea, Stuart. *Wrigley Field: The Unauthorized Biography*. Dulles, VA: Potomac Books, 2006.

Wuthering Heights

Emily Brontë's 1847 gothic novel about the brooding Heathcliff's passion for Cathy has become one of cinema's most enduring love stories. Director A. V. Bramble first brought *Wuthering Heights* to the screen, in a British silent production in 1920. However, Samuel Goldwyn's 1939 version, directed by William Wyler and starring Laurence Olivier and Merle Oberon, is considered to be the gold standard. (It also has been a source of much Hollywood lore, such as Goldwyn's postproduction decision to add a new "happy" ending, the now-famous scene, filmed with unknown actors, of the lovers walking together on the crag.) The many subsequent cinematic adaptations confirm the popularity of Brontë's tale. Some of these include director Luis Buñuel's *Abismos de Pasion* (1954), Robert Fuest's version (1970, starring Timothy Dalton), versions by the BBC (1948, 1953, 1962, 1967, and Peter Hammond's notable 1978 production), Jacques Rivette's *Hurlevent* (1985), Peter Kosminsky's *Emily Brontë's Wuthering Heights* (1992, starring Ralph Fiennes and Juliette Binoche), David Skynner's *Emily Brontë's Wuthering Heights* (1998), and Andrea Arnold's version (2011).

Barbara Tepa Lupack

SEE ALSO: *Goldwyn, Samuel; Olivier, Laurence.*

BIBLIOGRAPHY

Lupack, Barbara Tepa. *Nineteenth-Century Women at the Movies: Adapting Classic Women's Fiction to Film*. Bowling Green, OH: Bowling Green State University, 1999.

WWE

Exactly when professional wrestling transformed from a real athletic endeavor to a worked sports entertainment spectacle is unclear. What is known, however, is that one of the first promoters of the new slam-bang style in the 1920s was Toots Mondt, and by his side was Roderick "Jess" McMahon. Some sixty years later Jess's grandson Vincent Kennedy McMahon would be the dominant wrestling promoter not only in the United States but also in the world. The family-run business became a publicly traded company that began making money from wrestling as well as from the movies, merchandise, and media revolving around the performers and the events.

WORLD WIDE WRESTLING FEDERATION

With the advent of television in the late 1940s, professional wrestling experienced a resurgence in popularity. In 1953 Jess McMahon and Mondt formed Capitol Wrestling Corporation to promote wrestling on the East Coast. Shortly thereafter, however, McMahon died and was replaced by his son, Vincent James McMahon. The younger McMahon achieved great success by developing a simple formula: put an ethnic hero in the highest and most powerful position, that of champion. In the mid-1950s Italian-born Antonino "Argentina" Rocca became that hero.

Rocca soon gave way to "Nature Boy" Buddy Rogers, who was the National Wrestling Alliance (NWA) champ. Other NWA promoters wanted a different wrestler as champion, which led to McMahon breaking away from the NWA and starting the World Wide Wrestling Federation (WWWF) in 1963. Rogers snagged the new WWWF title but quickly lost it to Italian strongman Bruno Sammartino. Each month a new opponent would emerge as a threat to Sammartino, but he would eventually prevail. With Sammartino as his drawing card, McMahon expanded his territory to control all wrestling on the East Coast. Sammartino would be champion until a new ethnic hero, Puerto Rican–born Pedro Morales, took over in 1971. After Morales failed to attract fans from outside New York City, Sammartino came back for another run on top from 1973 to 1977. In 1979 the WWWF changed its name to the World Wrestling Federation (WWF).

During the 1970s McMahon pioneered the big event card, holding two successful shows at New York City's Shea Stadium, both headlined by Sammartino. By the early 1980s some sold-out wrestling events staged at Madison Square Garden in New York City would be broadcast via closed-circuit television to the adjacent Felt Forum, as it was then known. Also during this time McMahon's son, Vincent Kennedy McMahon, who had been working for his father as an announcer and promoting smaller towns, became more involved in the business. Eventually buying out his father's stock in the parent company, Capitol Wrestling Corporation, in 1982, Vincent changed the name to Titan Sports and proceeded to revolutionize wrestling.

WWF AND TITAN SPORTS

McMahon broke all the rules: he stole other promoter's talent, bought out their television time, signed exclusive agreements with their arenas, and scheduled shows opposite theirs. Soon the traditional wrestling territories started drying up. His new company, headlined by Hulk Hogan as lead hero and "Rowdy" Roddy Piper as lead villain, used the emerging cable television industry to market his promotion across the country. Shows such as *WWF Superstars* and McMahon's faux talk show *Tuesday Night Titans* were the top rated shows on cable. He also set up syndicated shows that became the highest rated in syndication.

Attracting mainstream press, using celebrities such as Cyndi Lauper; merchandising wrestlers as characters (the WWF would copyright and own each wrestler's gimmick); having wrestlers use entrance music; and, finally, making wrestling a true show thrust the WWF into the national consciousness. An exposé on the ABC newsmagazine *20/20*, which famously featured a WWF wrestler slapping reporter John Stossel when Stossel opined that wrestling was fake, created even more publicity. With Lauper, McMahon created a connection between rock and roll and wrestling, resulting in WWF matches setting a ratings record in 1985 on the then-fledgling MTV network.

McMahon's national expansion, however, was costing large amounts of money without enough revenue coming back. He risked everything on one show: WrestleMania in March 1985. He hired actor Mr. T to team with his superstar Hogan in the main event with former boxing champ Muhammad Ali as guest referee. The live event at Madison Square Garden was covered by hundreds of media outlets and shown across the country via closed-circuit TV. McMahon signed agreements for a cartoon show on CBS and inked a series of license agreements to create numerous products featuring the likenesses of his wrestlers, aiming his product at the family market. The WWF scored a coup in landing a monthly spot on network TV with *Saturday Night's Main Event* premiering on NBC in 1985 in a late-hour time slot. Forays into prime time began in 1988.

Success followed success as the WWF dominated in the United States. Events such as WrestleMania III (1987) drew more than 90,000 fans to the Pontiac Silverdome in Michigan, and wrestling became a profitable branch of the early pay-per-view industry. The WWF even exposed the wrestling industry in a hearing in New Jersey to rid itself of being taxed as a sport. A WWF official testified that wrestling was indeed fake, a headline that ended up in the *New York Times*. McMahon did not even attempt to enforce the facade any longer, telling *New York* magazine, "We're storytellers—this is a soap opera, performed by the greatest actors and athletes in the world. I'd like to say that it's the highest form of entertainment."

The WWF subsequently expanded to more than 1,000 events a year. When almost every other promotion went out of business, it became the dominant organization in U.S. wrestling, as McMahon took their TV slots, ran their arenas, and signed their best wrestlers. Already successful in Canada, in the late 1980s the WWF started broadcasting televised events all over the world and promoting live events in England, Germany, and Italy, and the Middle East. In 1992 more than 80,000 fans filled Wembley Stadium in England for the Summer Slam show, while events in other countries sold out both tickets and merchandise.

SCANDALS AND COMPETITION

While the success of the WWF was built on many factors, one of its main selling points was always the physique of its wrestlers. Hogan bragged about having the "largest arms in the world." McMahon marketed bodybuilders by developing the World Bodybuilding Federation in 1991, a huge, and expensive, failure. More bad times followed with the arrest of a WWF-affiliated doctor for trafficking in steroids. McMahon and the company itself were taken to court for distributing steroids in 1994 after a very public three-year investigation.

About the same time the steroid scandal broke, former WWF wrestlers and announcers were coming forth with stories of sex scandals involving WWF officials. The negative publicity from the scandals, coupled with the shrinking nature of the top wrestlers' physiques and the departure of top stars such as Hogan caused a downturn in business. The WWF tried its old tricks of involving celebrities—including Chuck Norris, Jenny McCarthy, Burt Reynolds, Pam Anderson, and National Football League Hall of Famer Lawrence Taylor—to wrestle in a WrestleMania main event, but fan interest was waning.

After dominating wrestling for more than a decade, the WWF faced its first serious competition in 1995 when media magnate Ted Turner's World Championship Wrestling (WCW) challenged the WWF directly by scheduling a show called *Monday Nitro* opposite the WWF's long-standing *Monday Night Raw*. Under new WCW President Eric Bischoff, WCW used McMahon's underhanded tactics against him and signed his former big stars Hogan, Randy "Macho Man" Savage, and Piper. A hot story line that turned Hogan into a villain leading the New World Order (NWO) faction led to huge ratings increases for WCW. Quickly losing talent, advertisers, and viewers, by 1997 the WWF was clearly rated the number two promotion.

RETURN TO THE TOP

To rebuild his brand, McMahon made several bold decisions. First, the WWF abandoned its family-friendly approach. It adopted a new hard-core edge and marketing campaign—"WWF attitude"—which featured lots of sex coupled with more violent wrestling and more outrageous story lines. Second, he moved out his dependable champion Bret Hart in favor of trash-talking middle-finger waving "Stone Cold" Steve Austin.

There was a problem, however: Hart was still the WWF champion and refused to drop the title in the ring as asked. To solve the problem, during a championship match in Montreal in November 1997, McMahon had the timekeeper ring the bell and declare Hart's opponent, Shawn Michaels, the winner and new champ. The controversy around the finish was so great that McMahon made another bold move: he turned himself into a wrestling character. As the evil Mr. McMahon, he became the promotion's number one villain when paired with new fan favorite Austin. Looking backward to his first success, McMahon paid former boxing champ Mike Tyson millions to get involved in the promotion, climaxing with Tyson holding up Austin's hand in victory at the end of WrestleMania XIV. The WWF and WCW battled back and forth for ratings in what became known as the Monday Night Wars.

With Austin on top and new stars such as Dwayne "The Rock" Johnson emerging, the WWF was regaining its status. As with the first wave of success, the WWF crashed into mainstream culture. Wrestlers such as Austin and The Rock appeared on numerous TV shows, including The Rock hosting *Saturday Night Live* shortly before WrestleMania 2000. MTV joined up with the WWF as Austin hosted the show *Celebrity Death Match* and even broadcast a match featuring The Rock during the 1999 Super Bowl halftime. Merchandising exploded as fans sold out arenas, ordered pay-per-view events, or watched the WWF on television. In 1999 McMahon created a new show, *SmackDown*, for the new UPN television network. With WCW collapsing, the WWF was big but about to get a whole lot bigger as McMahon took his company public in 1999. In March 2001 he bought out WCW and stood alone at the top of the wrestling world.

DEATH AND REBIRTH

The first death of a wrestler on McMahon's active roster occurred in 1997 when Brian Pillman passed away, his death in part attributed to painkiller and steroid abuse. In 1999 Bret Hart's brother Owen died when a stunt went horribly wrong. Later, the death of popular Eddie Guerrero in 2005 brought the high death toll of young wrestlers from drugs into the news. More tragedy followed. In June 2007 WWF wrestler Chris Benoit murdered his wife and young son, then took his own life. The case became a media circus when the tragedy was first linked to Benoit's alleged steroid use and then to repeated brain trauma sustained while wrestling.

In 2002 the WWF became World Wrestling Entertainment (later simplified to WWE, and in 2011 WWE was adopted as the organization's name) and split into two brands: Raw (for the lesser-known wrestlers) and SmackDown! (to showcase the more popular wrestlers). Both groups would have weekly shows on television and would, upon occasion, challenge each other. Crossover stars such as John Cena; hard-core wrestlers such as C. M. Punk; and icons such as The Rock, who returned to perform briefly, kept the audiences entertained. With a net worth of more than a billion dollars and millions of fans across the world, the WWE was set to remain on top of the wrestling world for a long time.

Patrick Jones

SEE ALSO: *Ali, Muhammad; Boxing; Cable TV; Hogan, Hulk; Lauper, Cyndi; Piper, "Rowdy" Roddy; Reynolds, Burt; Rock and Roll;* Saturday Night Live; *Savage, Randy "Macho Man"; Super Bowl; Television; Turner, Ted; Tyson, Mike.*

BIBLIOGRAPHY

Assael, Shaun, and Mike Mooneyham. *Sex, Lies, and Headlocks: The Real Story of Vince McMahon and the World Wrestling Federation.* New York: Crown, 2002.

Guttman, James. *World Wrestling Insanity: The Decline and Fall of a Family Empire.* Toronto: ECW Press, 2006.

Kerr, Peter. "Now It Can Be Told: Wrestling Is All Fun." *New York Times*, January 5, 1990, A1.

Maker, Elizabeth. "The Softer Side of Wrestling's Showman Extraordinaire." *New York Times*, March 2, 2008, 5(L).

WWJD? (What Would Jesus Do?)

The twentieth century perhaps saw no phrase so consistently popular among Protestants in the United States as "What Would Jesus Do?" What began as a series of evening story-sermons delivered by a Kansas preacher in 1896 became by the 1990s a billion-dollar industry as millions of people purchased bracelets, T-shirts, coffee mugs, and other paraphernalia with the acronym "WWJD?" inscribed upon them. For some the remarkable sales that the phrase engendered bespoke a hunger for the Christian gospel in the public sphere, but to others it showcased the ability of market-savvy capitalists to turn even the deepest religious impulses into profit-making ventures.

IN HIS STEPS

Charles M. Sheldon (1857–1946), a social gospel minister at the Central Congregational Church in Topeka, Kansas, landed on the idea of the story-sermon as a cure for chronically poor attendance at Sunday evening services. These serial messages would then be printed in the private weekly magazine, the *Advance*, and later compiled and released in book form. In 1896 the series he composed was titled *In His Steps*, recounting the experiences of the Reverend Henry Maxwell as he and his congregation discovered spiritual awakening and moral regeneration when they asked themselves "What would Jesus do?" in every situation they faced and sought to act accordingly.

The *Advance* series proved so popular that Sheldon decided to reissue the material as a book. When he applied for copyright protection, however, it was discovered that the original magazine series had not itself been copyrighted, and so the story was in the public domain. Thus, as the book began to sell, many firms

WWJD? Bracelet. *A young boy wears a WWJD? bracelet.* JOHN CHAPPLE/GETTY IMAGES.

other than the Advance Publishing Company rushed to meet the demand. By midcentury forty-one companies had published the book in the United States and fifteen in Great Britain, and the original text had been translated into twenty-six languages. The results of all this activity were mixed for Sheldon. He was catapulted to international fame, with his book selling no fewer than eight million copies and perhaps as many as thirty million, but Sheldon himself received very little in the way of royalties on the sales. Thus was born a mythology about *In His Steps*, the book that outsold all others save the Bible but whose author received not a penny in royalties.

TWENTIETH-CENTURY MARKETING

In His Steps has been continually in print since 1896, usually in more than one edition, but the end of the twentieth century saw an astonishing revival in its popularity. In 1989 Janie Tinklenberg, youth leader at the Calvary Reformed Church in Holland, Michigan, read Sheldon's book and discussed it with her youth group. Noticing that many of her kids were making friendship bracelets for one another, she hit upon the idea of creating a bracelet that would remind her charges to ask themselves what Jesus would do in a given situation. She contacted the Lesco Corporation, based in Lansing, Michigan, and had the company make a few hundred bracelets with the initialism "WWJD?" stitched into them.

Many of the students in Tinklenberg's group began explaining the message of Jesus Christ to their classmates, who would often themselves ask for a bracelet. The original supply was quickly depleted, and the phenomenon began to spread across the country. During the first seven years of marketing, Lesco sold 300,000 bracelets. In the spring of 1997, however, Paul Harvey mentioned them on his syndicated radio show, and sales skyrocketed. Fifteen million bracelets were sold by Lesco that year, and dozens of other corporations rushed to capitalize on the market craze.

Lesco quickly expanded its merchandising beyond the bracelets to include baseball caps, coffee mugs, key chains, jewelry, sweaters, and T-shirts, all sold by Christian bookstores around the country. An Indiana-based website was selling 300,000 bracelets a month by 1998. That same year several Christian publishing companies began compiling youth curriculum materials and offering inspirational publications using the same moniker. ForeFront Records released a WWJD? compact disc showcasing some of the most popular artists in contemporary Christian music, and publishing giant Zondervan issued the WWJD Interactive Devotional Bible. Most releases sold quite well. Some, including Beverly Courrege's *Answers to WWJD?*, became best sellers.

MAINSTREAM POPULARITY

By 1998 the fad had caught the attention of mainstream media outlets such that WWJD? materials could be purchased from high-profile stores such as Kmart, Wal-Mart, Hallmark, Barnes and Noble, and Borders Books and Music. The Christian press was astir with debate over whether Jesus himself would smile upon such vigorous marketing of his message, and controversy emerged over copyrights on the phrase itself. Fuel was added to the flames of controversy when it was found that some of the pewter jewelry bearing the WWJD inscription contained such high quantities of lead that children were contracting lead poisoning.

Spin-offs of the phrase—such as "Who Would Jesus Bomb?"—gained popularity, and the phrase was even adapted to advertising campaigns. For example, makers of fuel-efficient automobiles put the headline "What Would Jesus Drive?" on their ads. Even with such overuse, the slogan retained its hold on the popular imagination. In 2011 some of the Occupy protesters, a widespread and diverse popular movement of public demonstrations criticizing financial disparity and social injustice, displayed banners reading "What Would Jesus Do?" as a shorthand way of saying that Jesus had advocated for the poor. Such references made it clear that the message Sheldon had preached was still being heeded and put into practice more than 100 years later in a characteristically American blend of religious zeal and the entrepreneurial spirit.

Milton Gaither

SEE ALSO: *Contemporary Christian Music; Kmart; Religious Right; T-Shirts; Wal-Mart.*

BIBLIOGRAPHY

Cope, Mike, and Rubel Shelly. *What Would Jesus Do Today?* West Monroe, LA: Howard, 1998.

Miller, Timothy. *Following in His Steps: A Biography of Charles M. Sheldon*. Knoxville: University of Tennessee Press, 1987.

Sheldon, Charles M. *In His Steps; "What Would Jesus Do?"* Chicago: Advance Publishing, 1898.

Singleton, William C., III. "W.W.J.D. Fad or Faith?" *Homelife*, August 1998.

Smith, Michael R. "What Would Jesus Do? The Jesus Bracelet Fad: Is It Merchandising or Ministry?" *World*, January 10, 1998.

Wyeth, Andrew *(1917–2009)*

Realist painter Andrew Wyeth was the youngest of five children of artist/illustrator N. C. Wyeth, born in Chadds Ford, Pennsylvania. Wyeth learned to paint with the keen observation and drafting skills that his father passed on to him. His subjects, mainly nostalgic images of unpainted houses, austere New Englanders, and landscapes from his surroundings, became enormously popular after his first sold-out one-man show in New York in 1937. Like his father, he was offered the opportunity to paint covers for the *Saturday Evening Post*; unlike his father, he declined, preferring to pursue a free interpretative course in his art. Ironically, because of his ability to capture on canvas the American sense of courage and its triumph over the struggles and trials of life, Wyeth was the first artist to be featured on the cover of *Time* magazine.

Nearly all of Wyeth's paintings were executed in drybrush, watercolor, or egg tempera, a technique that allows for extreme precision. His subdued earth-tone palette, realistic style, and subject matter—often featuring a neighbor's farm in Chadds Ford and landscape scenes from his summers in Cushing, Maine—remained the same throughout his career. In the 1960s he began to paint portraits of his sister, Carolyn, which encouraged him eventually to embark on a series of nudes of Helga Testorf, one of his Chadds Ford neighbors.

An early Wyeth model, Christina Olson, was the subject of several of his portraits and one of his most famous paintings,

Christina's World (1948). The painting shows the crippled woman gazing back toward her house from a windswept, grassy pasture. An egg tempera work painted shortly after his father's death in a tragic railway accident, *Christina's World* emphasizes the somber introspection and sense of struggle for which Wyeth gained a great deal of notoriety. The Olson House, featured in *Christina's World*, was the first house listed in the National Historic Register of Places to become famous by being featured in a painting, attesting to the popularity of the artist's work.

From 1970 through 1985, Wyeth painted his popular "Helga" studies. These pictures were painted in secret and comprise 240 images of the artist's most mature works, featuring the same model in numerous environments and moods. A sense of moral dignity and courage is characteristic of the portraits in this series of paintings, which were exhibited at the National Gallery of Art in 1987 and were the first works by a living artist to be shown there. This exhibit came after Wyeth became the first living American artist to be given a retrospective at the New York Metropolitan Museum of Art, in 1976.

Imbuing his art with a sense of visual poetry, mysterious in its evocation of emotion, Wyeth's craft was developed independently of the modern and contemporary avant-garde movements.

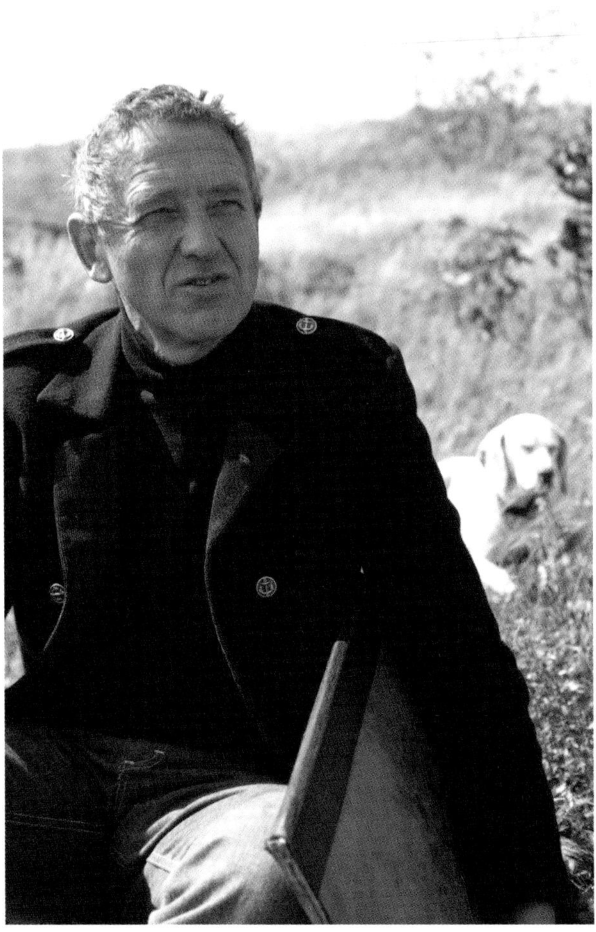

Andrew Wyeth. *Artist Andrew Wyeth is known for his realistic paintings of the landscape and people around him.* B. ANTHONY STEWART/CONTRIBUTOR/NATIONAL GEOGRAPHIC/GETTY IMAGES.

His apolitical, somewhat sentimental nature and keen sense of tenacity in subjects appeals to those who find beauty in the tangibly representational rather than the abstract. Wyeth, however, found that there was a kind of abstract discipline in utilitarian subjects that he was able to capture in paint, rendering image in a realistic style that appeared to reveal a basic truth to his viewers. His exhibitions drew record-breaking crowds and commanded some of the highest prices paid for the works of living American artists.

Wyeth's work depicts traditional values and grassroots images. He is quoted as stating, "I put a lot of things into my work which are very personal to me. So how can the public feel these things? I think most people get to my work through the back door. They're attracted by the realism and they sense the emotion and the abstraction—and eventually, I hope, they get their own powerful emotion."

Cheryl McGrath

SEE ALSO: *Metropolitan Museum of Art; The* Saturday Evening Post*;* Time*; Wyeth, N. C.*

BIBLIOGRAPHY

Canaday, J. *Works by Andrew Wyeth from the Holly and Arthur Magill Collection*. Greenville, SC: Greenville County Museum of Art, 1979.

Knutson, Anne Classen; Christopher Crosman; Kathleen A. Foster; et al. *Andrew Wyeth: Memory and Magic*. Atlanta, GA: High Museum of Art, 2005.

Wilmerding, John. *Andrew Wyeth: The Helga Pictures*. New York: H. N. Abrams, 1987.

Wyeth, N. C.; Andrew Wyeth; Jamie Wyeth; et al. *An American Vision: Three Generations of Wyeth Art*. Boston: Brandywine River Museum, 1987.

Wyeth, N. C. *(1882–1945)*

Indisputably one of the world's greatest illustrators, Newell Convers Wyeth is best known for adding a new and unforgettable dimension to dozens of classic adventure books—*Treasure Island* (1911), *The Boy's King Arthur* (1917), and *Robinson Crusoe* (1920) among them—in the early decades of the twentieth century. Combining skilled draftsmanship and a genius for light and color with the ability dictated by his teacher Howard Pyle to project himself into each painting, Wyeth succeeded brilliantly at evoking movement, mood, and the range of human emotions.

His prolific output, in addition to easel paintings and murals, included illustrations for hundreds of stories in periodicals from *McCall's* to the *Saturday Evening Post*, popular prints, posters, calendars, and advertisements. His early portrayals of the Old West reveal the influence of Frederic Remington, while much of his later work clearly made a strong impression on the art of his son, Andrew Wyeth, who, like his father, is one of America's most admired painters.

Craig Bunch

SEE ALSO: McCall's Magazine*; Remington, Frederic; The* Saturday Evening Post*; Wyeth, Andrew.*

BIBLIOGRAPHY

Allen, Douglas, and Douglas Allen Jr. *N. C. Wyeth: The Collected Paintings, Illustrations, and Murals.* New York: Crown, 1972.

Michaelis, David. *N. C. Wyeth: A Biography.* New York: Knopf, 1998.

Silvey, Anita. *The Essential Guide to Children's Books and Their Creators.* Boston: Houghton Mifflin, 2002.

Wynette, Tammy *(1942–1998)*

Often criticized for her conservative, traditional values, country vocalist Tammy Wynette became famous in the late 1960s for "Stand by Your Man," a hit single that made her an unintentional spokesperson for antifeminists. While she was known for her doormat songs, in which men treat women subserviently, much of her material offered valuable insights into the lives of working-class housewives and mothers. Her songs often exhibited an optimistic perseverance in a never-ending quest for love and happiness. Wynette expressed this attitude with a heartfelt sincerity, for even after she became a country superstar, her life was not easy.

Sometimes referred to as the Heroine of Heartbreak, she suffered from marital difficulties, drug addiction, financial troubles, and countless severe health problems. Although she was portrayed as an unhappy victim, Wynette was stronger than she appeared to be. As a woman in the male-dominated music industry of the 1960s, she held her own as a performer. During her 30-year career she sold more than 30 million records, had 39 Top 10 country hits, and received 3 Country Music Association awards.

Tammy Wynette. *Tammy Wynette became a country superstar singings songs from the point of view of working-class wives and mothers, including her signature hit, "Stand by Your Man."* CHARLIE GILLETT/REDFERNS/GETTY IMAGES.

BUILDING A BETTER LIFE

Born in Itawamba County, Mississippi, on May 5, 1942, Virginia Wynette Pugh was raised by her grandparents. As a child, she picked cotton on their farm, and this arduous and exhausting work made her determined to create a better life for herself. She learned to play the piano and the guitar, and she started singing in church. Accompanied by a female friend, she performed on local radio programs and in area talent competitions. In her autobiography, *Stand by Your Man* (1979), she recalled, "during my adolescence I daydreamed a lot about singing professionally."

In 1959, however, seventeen-year-old Wynette married Euple Byrd, and in 1961 their first child was born. One year later, after the birth of a second child, Wynette was training to become a licensed beautician. The family briefly lived in Memphis, Tennessee, where she worked as a barmaid in a beer joint, occasionally singing songs requested by the customers. In 1964, pregnant with their third child, she and her two daughters moved to Birmingham, Alabama. Born prematurely, her third daughter was diagnosed with spinal meningitis. Wynette divorced around that time but managed to support her family by working full time as a hairdresser and singing on a local early morning television show. She maintained her dream of being a professional country singer, and after attending a disc jockey convention in Nashville, Tennessee, she decided to move there and focus her efforts on landing a record deal.

Wynette auditioned unsuccessfully for several labels located in the part of Nashville known as Music Row. Eventually, she approached Bill Sherrill, a producer/songwriter with Epic Records. Recognizing her tremendous vocal capability, he agreed to record her. Within a few weeks he suggested that she call herself Tammy Wynette, and he chose "Apartment #9" as her first single. By December 1966 Wynette's debut release was on the country charts; less than a year later, her first album, *Your Good Girl's Gonna Go Bad*, reached the Top 10.

Despite this success, Wynette encountered further difficulties as she searched for a booking agency. According to her autobiography, one agent she approached expressed the opinion that women were "not worth the trouble" because of conflicting obligations to their families and careers. She managed to find an agent lacking this prejudice and began performing regularly as her next three singles became number one hits. About that time she married songwriter Don Chapel, but their marriage dissolved as she became involved with singer George Jones. By the time she married Jones in 1969, she was a full-fledged star known for the anthems "D-I-V-O-R-C-E" and "Stand by Your Man," which became one of the best-selling country songs ever recorded by a female artist.

PROBLEMS AND EARLY DEATH

As Jones's wife, Wynette was known as the first lady of country music, and together the couple performed and recorded duets that often reflected problems existing in their own relationship. Jones's legendary substance abuse and his tendency toward violence caused Wynette to seek a divorce in 1975. A year later she married for a fourth time, but the union lasted less than two months. Her fifth and final marriage took place in 1978 to George Richey, a songwriter she had known for several years. During the 1980s she began to be plagued by a variety of medical problems, many requiring operations, that continued up until her death. Her house in Nashville was broken into on fifteen separate occasions and mysteriously set on fire. In 1978 she was the victim of a bizarre kidnapping incident. By the late 1980s she had been treated for addiction to painkillers and had filed for bankruptcy. As a writer for *People* noted after her death, "in Tammy Wynette's world, something always seemed to go wrong."

As Wynette's career continued into the 1990s, so did her image as the devoted, subordinate wife. In 1992 Hillary Clinton made a condescending reference to Wynette on *60 Minutes*, but she quickly apologized at Wynette's insistence. That same year Wynette collaborated with the dance group KLF on "Justified and Ancient," which became a British club hit. An album she released in 1994 featured duets with noted singers such as Elton John, Smokey Robinson, and Sting, and the following year she and Jones were reunited on a new album, *One*, which would be her last. While the country industry essentially abandoned older artists like Wynette, the fans remained faithful. In spite of increasingly serious health problems, she persisted in performing up until a month before she died on April 6, 1998. Months later, artists from various musical genres recorded a tribute album of her songs titled *Tammy Wynette Remembered*.

Wynette's legacy endured after her death. She was elected to the Country Music Hall of Fame in 1998. In 2002 she was ranked second on a list of the forty greatest women in country music compiled by Country Music Television (CMT). The CD *Stand by Your Man: The Best of Tammy Wynette* was released in 2008, ten years after her death. Three years later the Library of Congress selected "Stand by Your Man" as one of the songs to be preserved in the National Recording Registry.

Anna Hunt Graves

SEE ALSO: *Country Music; Divorce; John, Elton; Jones, George;* People*; Robinson, Smokey;* 60 Minutes.

BIBLIOGRAPHY

Bufwack, Mary A., and Robert Oermann. *Finding Her Voice: The Saga of Women in Country Music*. New York: Crown, 1993.

Dew, Joan. *Singers and Sweethearts: The Women of Country Music*. Garden City, NY: Dolphin Books, 1977.

Gliatto, Tom. "Heroine of Hardship." *People*, April 20, 1998, 54–61.

McDonough, Jimmy. *Tammy Wynette: Tragic Country Queen*. New York: Viking, 2010.

Wynette, Tammy, and Joan Dew. *Stand by Your Man*. New York: Simon & Schuster, 1979.

X

X Games

The X Games bring together "extreme" athletes who compete in such sporting events as skateboarding, in-line skating, snowboarding, skysurfing, sport climbing, stunt bicycling, street luge, and barefoot water-ski jumping. The cable-TV sports network ESPN developed what it called the Extreme Games and first broadcast them in the summer of 1995. The name was changed to the X Games the following year, and the Winter X Games debuted in 1997.

Touted as an alternative Olympics, the X Games cater to youth culture (the name is an intentional reference to the term *Generation X*), and they popularize athletic risk taking. The popularity of the X Games has also helped commercialize and organize characteristically marginal and disorderly activities such as skateboarding and skydiving, calling into question whether these increasingly mainstream sports can still be considered extreme.

FITNESS EVOLUTION

Extreme sports are largely individualistic athletic activities that require participants to push themselves "to the extreme," often by defying not only gravity but also society's standards for reasonable risk. The emerging popularity of extreme sports in the 1990s reflected a shift in American fitness trends. The fitness craze of the 1980s inspired many otherwise inactive, nonathletic individuals to take up activities such as jogging and aerobics. Memberships at health clubs boomed. Health and fitness remained a big business into the 1990s, but advertisers and young adult consumers began to treat fitness as a lifestyle rather than just a periodic visit to the health club.

A cult of so-called adrenaline addiction infiltrated the rhetoric of youth culture and influenced the marketing strategies aimed at consumers of the extreme image. Sales of mountain bikes, in-line skates, and snowboards increased dramatically, as did the popularity of bungee jumping and skydiving. ESPN's X Games capitalized on this emerging fitness and consumer trend.

The X Games essentially codified activities that previously had no rules. By applying measurable performance criteria to such recreational pursuits as in-line skating, rock climbing, and snowboarding, ESPN was able to impose order and some measure of control over potentially chaotic sports. Because of their inherent physical dangers, extreme sports generally garnered society's disapproval, which consequently amplified their popularity in youth culture.

THE EXTREME BECOMES MAINSTREAM

The X Games assimilated extreme sports into an organized brand of Olympic-like games—including the awarding of gold, silver, and bronze medals. As a result, such activities became more respectable and organized, and the designation "extreme sports" became less clear. Extreme sports are a popular activity in part because of their marginality and perceived threat to the mainstream, but events such as the X Games render extreme sports less marginal and subsequently alter their meaning in popular culture.

One example of the growing influence of the X Games was the International Olympic Committee's decision to include snowboarding, beginning with the 1998 Winter Olympic Games. In 2002 the Winter X Games were held in Colorado only a few weeks before the Winter Olympics in Salt Lake City. The entire U.S. Olympic freestyle snowboarding team showed up to compete in the snowboard superpipe event in the X Games. In 2010 about one-half of the athletes in the Winter Olympics also competed in the Winter X Games.

Despite the increasing acceptance of extreme sports, they remain dangerous. In 2009 snowboarder Kevin Pearce suffered a traumatic brain injury during training. Three years later, only weeks before the Winter X Games of 2012, freestyle superpipe skier Sarah Burke, a four-time Winter X Games champion, died after crashing during a training run on the superpipe. Deaths have also occurred in the Olympic Games, as in the accident in which a luge competitor died during a training run in 2010. The reputation the X Games have of being more dangerous than other sporting events may be partly a perception based on the novelty of the sports involved.

GROWTH AND EXPANSION

The X Games have become increasingly commercial as they draw a growing number of spectators and home viewers. Over time the events themselves have been expanded and modified. In 2000 the half-pipe was changed to a superpipe with 22-foot sides for maximum "big air." In 2007 Mono Skier X—the first X event for disabled athletes—was added to the winter games. In 2010 an event called Real Street was added to the Summer X Games. It was a skateboarding event in which competitors submitted sixty-second videos of their skating on natural terrain—that is, on streets as opposed to skate parks or competitor arenas. In 2011 a similar snowboard event was added to the Winter X Games.

The X Games have come to represent far more than a sports competition. Mass marketing and media strategies tie in music, fashion, and product endorsements aimed at ESPN's mostly male, twelve- to thirty-four-year-old viewing audience. To continue drawing this audience the X Games have continued to evolve. Some of the original X Games sports—ice climbing, for example—were soon eliminated for not being visually engaging. Event sponsors have included makers of caffeinated colas, athletic shoes, and fast-food restaurants. The competition annually promotes related alternative music soundtracks and videos. ESPN launches a road show prior to the X Games, and the touring sports extravaganza spotlights the various events.

Though originally mocked by reporters and sports anchors, the X Games steadily grew more popular. Originally held only in the United States, X Games and qualifying matches began to be held in a variety of countries in Europe, Asia, South America, and the Middle East. Spectator attendance at the Winter X Games was up 36 percent year over year in 2011 (114,200 versus 84,100). Summer X Games 17, held in 2010, had 141,500 in attendance and was viewed by thirty-seven million people with round-the-clock international coverage. With this growth, ESPN expanded the number of major events held annually. In 2011 there were three main X Games competitions: Summer X in Los Angeles; Winter X in Aspen, Colorado; and Winter X Europe in Tignes, France. Plans were soon made for holding six annual stand-alone X Games in various cities around the world, each including cultural and other elements specific to its venue.

Adam Golub

SEE ALSO: *Bicycling; Cable TV; ESPN; Extreme Sports; Fast Food; Mountain Biking; Olympics; Rock Climbing; Skateboarding; Skating; Snowboarding.*

BIBLIOGRAPHY

Burke, Monte. "X-treme Economics: ESPN's X Games." *Forbes*, February 9, 2004.

"The End of Innocence: The Loss of Sarah Burke Has Shaken the Action Sports Community—Are the Athletes Being Pushed Too Far?" *Maclean's*, February 6, 2012, 24–25.

Youngblut, Shelly, ed. *Way inside ESPN's X Games*. New York: Hyperion, 1998.

Xbox Kinect

Microsoft's Xbox Kinect is widely proclaimed as the wave of the future in gaming and computers. Microsoft insists that the Kinect is "a family entertainment center" rather than a gaming device. Attached to an Xbox 360 gaming console, the Kinect allows a player's entire body to be used as a controller. It operates on the basis of motion capture, allowing a sensor to record and respond to every move a player makes.

The Xbox Kinect was released in November 2010; within sixty days, eight million units had been sold, making it the fastest-selling consumer electronics device in history. By January 2012 Microsoft had sold sixty-six million new Xboxes and eighteen million Kinect motion sensors. The main complaint is that the range of the Kinect sensor is limited to 6 to 8 feet.

Always adept at marketing, Microsoft introduced the Kinect as the 2010 holiday season began and used the child-oriented *Kinectimals* to promote the game for families. *Kinectimals* allows players to visit the islands of Lemuria and Mira and play with bear cubs. Windows phones are used to unlock additional cubs. A separate line of Kinectimals stuffed animals was sold, and those animals could be scanned and used on-screen. Microsoft also partnered with Build-a-Bear Workshop to offer additional animals for sale and scanning.

Initially the Kinect was available for approximately $150 as a stand-alone for consumers who already owned an Xbox 360. It was also packaged with an Xbox 360 and *Kinect Adventures* for around $300. When the Kinect launched in 2010, only seventeen games were available that were compatible with the new device, including *Kinect Adventures* and *Kinectimals*. Most other offerings were action oriented, involving dance, fitness, or sports. The only traditional games available were *Harry Potter and the Deathly Hallows, Part I*, and *Fighters Uncaged*.

Motion-capture technology did not originate with the Kinect, but it was Microsoft researchers who made the technology practical for common use. In earlier versions reflective markers were required for capturing human movements. Shortly after Microsoft began working on the Xbox Kinect, the company brought in a team of researchers at Microsoft Research in Cambridge in the United Kingdom. That five-person team helped to develop the human-motion technology used in the Kinect.

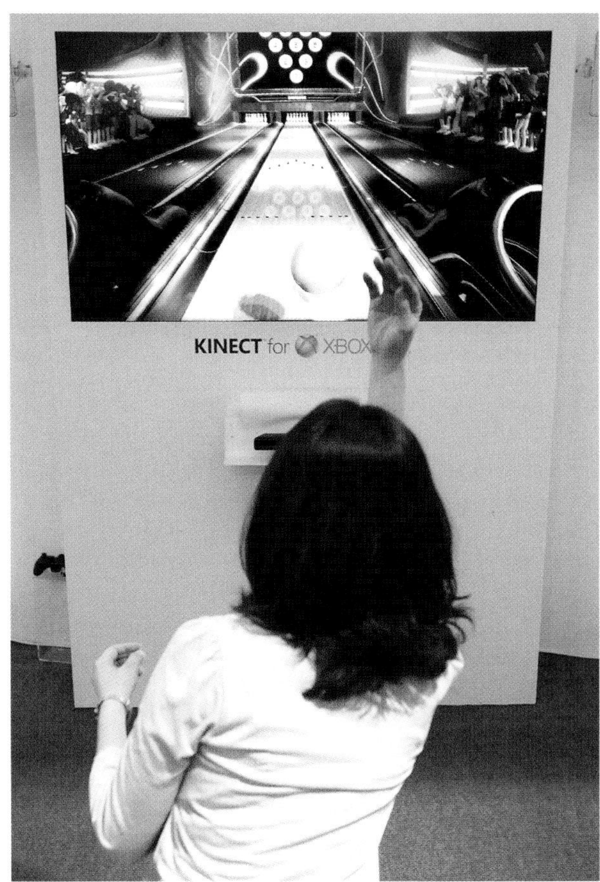

Xbox Kinect. *A visitor tests an Xbox Kinect game at the 2010 Tokyo Game Show, a showcase for soon-to-be-released gaming software and hardware.* KIYOSHI OTA/GETTY IMAGES.

The Kinect is operated by a sensor, which sends 3-D images of a player's body movements to software that analyzes them at a rate of thirty frames per second. Microsoft's Peter Molyneux previewed the Kinect with *Fable: The Journey*, a role-playing game, at the 2012 Xbox Spring Show in San Francisco, where one New Zealander called the technology "magic" upon finding that a horse could be healed by stroking it.

Working in conjunction with the Xbox 360, the Kinect can be used with streaming services such as ESPN and Netflix to institute functions by voice command. Televisions of the future are likely to use this same technology to create interactive experiences. It also has implications for revolutionizing technologies used in other fields, including entertainment, medicine, and engineering. A group of students at Warwick University have designed a robot that is operated with the Kinect, enabling it to map out and navigate three-dimensional spaces. Physical and occupational therapists are already using the Kinect to work with patients. Surgeons may use the technology to initiate hands-free computing to access radiological images directly from an operating room, allowing for the surgeon to reference important information without the risk of contamination or loss of time due to scrubbing in and out of the surgery.

Developmental researchers have incorporated the device in diagnosing autism, attention deficit disorder, and obsessive compulsive disorders, providing them with a more objective measure since the hands-free device removes intrusive sensors from their observations. Within a month of the Kinect's debut, researchers at the Georgia Institute of Technology had hacked the device to read a limited signing vocabulary using signs accepted by American Sign Language.

Elizabeth Rholetter Purdy

SEE ALSO: *Computer Games; Leisure Time; Microsoft; Video Games; Wii.*

BIBLIOGRAPHY

"Microsoft Xbox 360 Kinect." CNet, November 3, 2010. Accessed March 2012. Available from http://reviews.cnet.com/xbox-360-accessories/xbox-360-kinect/4505-9994_7-34182443.html#reviewPage1

Taylor, Matthew J. D.; T. Shawis; R. Impson; et al. "Activity Promoting Gaming Systems in Exercise and Rehabilitation." *Journal of Rehabilitation Research and Development* 48, no. 10 (2011): 1171–1186.

"Xbox Kinect: It's Kind of Magic." *New Zealand Herald*, March 8, 2012.

Xena, Warrior Princess

A 1996 *Ms.* magazine cover story lauded the television show *Xena: Warrior Princess* as a feminist and progressive retelling of Greek myth, as television notable for "breaking new ground in its treatment of sex." Broadcast in syndication from 1995 to 2001, the series chronicles the adventures of a sword-wielding princess seeking to atone for her violent past. Accompanied by her kind, naive sidekick, Gabrielle, Xena battles fickle gods, tyrants, slave traders, barbaric tribes, and other nemeses in a magical land that evokes ancient Greece and Rome. Filmed in New Zealand and produced by Renaissance Pictures in conjunction with MCA TV, the series offered a postmodern pastiche of classical mythology, characterized by hyperbolic violence and a slapstick, camp irony. At the same time, it managed to explore sexuality and ethical issues without losing its mass audience. Xena's sexually charged relationship with Gabrielle kept the series in vogue with lesbian audiences, among others.

Xena's impact is found in both popular culture and academe. The series spawned an animated film, *Hercules and Xena: The Battle for Mount Olympus* (1998), plus various comic-book spin-offs, video games, and novelizations. Xena's martial arts prowess arguably paved the way for all sorts of fighting female characters, such as the eponymous vampire slayer, Buffy. Scholars have debated the extent to which Xena's characterization is radical or conservative while using the series and its official and unlicensed derivatives to explore the relationship between media and fans. Not only have multiple doctoral dissertations and academic essays been written about Xena, a planet discovered in 2005 was named after her, together with its moon, dubbed Gabrielle.

Neal Baker

SEE ALSO: Buffy the Vampire Slayer*; Comic Books;* Hercules: The Legendary Journeys.

BIBLIOGRAPHY

Collier, Noelle R.; Christine A. Lumadue; and H. Ray Wooten. "*Buffy the Vampire Slayer* and *Xena: Warrior Princess*: Reception of the Texts by a Sample of Lesbian Fans and Web Site Users." *Journal of Homosexuality* 56, no. 5 (2009): 575–609.

Hayes, K. Stoddard. *Xena Warrior Princess: The Complete Illustrated Companion.* London: Titan, 2003.

Magoulick, Mary. "Frustrating Female Heroism: Mixed Messages in Xena, Nikita, and Buffy." *Journal of Popular Culture* 39, no. 5 (2006): 729–755.

Minkowitz, Donna. "Xena: She's Big, Tall, Strong—and Popular." *Ms.*, July/August 1996, 74–77.

The X-Files

When *The X-Files* premiered on the Fox network in the fall of 1993, no one predicted the degree of success that the show would eventually enjoy. After all, dramas in the fantasy and science fiction genres had not done well on TV for a decade (the *Star Trek* spin-offs excepted). However, there was considerable interest in unidentified-flying-object (UFO) phenomena in America, as evidenced by news accounts of alleged alien abductions, speculations about "crop circles," and sightings of supposed alien spacecraft streaking across the skies. For some Americans, belief in UFO visitations dovetailed with their mistrust of the U.S. government, which has consistently denied any knowledge of alien encounters.

Thus, when the show premiered, tales of visitors from space and government conspiracies to cover up those visits might find a ready audience—and *The X-Files* did. It finished its first season with respectable ratings, started the second season with an even larger audience, and continued for nine seasons. One of the few Fox programs to compete successfully with the major networks, the show became a massive hit with an almost cult following. Soon there were Golden Globe Awards, then Emmys,

The X-Files. *David Duchovny, left, starred opposite Gillian Anderson in* The X-Files. 20TH CENTURY FOX TELEVISION/THE KOBAL COLLECTION.

two full-length feature films, and a significant place in the public imagination.

A COMPLEX PARANORMAL UNIVERSE

The show's premise is that the Federal Bureau of Investigation (FBI) occasionally encounters cases that seem inexplicable in terms of science and logic—cases that are, in short, paranormal. Such investigations, designated "X-files," are referred to the show's two protagonists: Special Agent Fox Mulder (David Duchovny) and Special Agent Dana Scully (Gillian Anderson). Mulder tends readily to accept paranormal explanations for the cases that he and his partner investigate—partly because he believes that his sister, Samantha, who disappeared when they were children, was a victim of alien abduction. Scully, who earned a medical degree before joining the FBI, is usually a skeptic, positing rational explanations for phenomena that appear to defy reason. The two agents are supervised by FBI Assistant Director Walter Skinner (Mitch Pileggi). In the show's early years, Skinner tended to be suspicious of and sometimes hostile toward Mulder and Scully. By the fourth season, however, he appeared to have become their ally.

From the beginning, the show has had a recurring theme involving alien visitation, alien abductions, and the efforts of certain powerful groups to conceal or deny these sinister activities. The show's writers and producers refer to this story arc as "the mythology," although some fans call it "the conspiracy." The character most closely identified with the effort to cover up the alien presence is known only as "Cigarette Smoking Man" (William Davis), or CSM, a ruthless covert operator who has cold-bloodedly ordered the deaths of several people, including Mulder's father, who came too close to the truth.

The mythology is not the sum total of the series, however. In a typical season of *The X-Files*, about half the episodes deal with the ongoing struggle over the aliens, whereas the other shows find agents Mulder and Scully investigating other sorts of paranormal phenomena. Over the course of several seasons, the agents deal with zombies, werewolves, ghosts, vampires, demons, and witches, not to mention astral projection, precognition, reincarnation, and the transmigration of souls. A few of their cases have had no paranormal aspects at all, involving instead relatively mundane subjects, such as serial murder, psychological obsession, and genetic mutation.

In some of their cases involving the mythology, Mulder and Scully receive assistance from a group called "the Lone Gunmen"—an ironic reference to the Warren Commission's much-disbelieved conclusion that President John F. Kennedy was assassinated by a "lone gunman." These three men, identified only by their last names of Byers (Bruce Harwood), Langly (Dean Haglund), and Frohike (Tom Braidwood), are self-styled "conspiracy freaks" who once told Mulder that they help him because "You're more paranoid than we are."

ORIGIN OF THE SERIES

Chris Carter is the show's creator, producer, and principal writer. After some time spent writing for *Surfing* magazine, he married a television writer and soon began to turn out scripts of his own. He wrote for several TV series, acquiring the contacts that allowed him to sell *The X-Files* to the Fox network. Carter says that his idea for the show is derived from his memories of a short-lived TV series (lasting only the 1974–1975 season) called *Kolchak: The Night Stalker*. The show was based on two successful made-for-TV movies: *The Night Stalker* and *The Night Strangler*. The premise for the movies and the series was the same: the hard-bitten newspaper reporter Carl Kolchak (Darren McGavin), while covering the story of one or more bizarre crimes, comes to the conclusion that some supernatural creature is involved. Kolchak then researches the phenomenon (vampire, werewolf, witch, or whatever), learns how to kill the creature, and does so.

The 1998 feature film based on Carter's series, titled *X-Files: Fight the Future*, may be unique in one respect. Although it was not uncommon during the 1990s to see theatrical films based on popular TV shows, such films were invariably produced after the TV series that inspired them had gone off the air. The *X-Files* movie may be the only one to date to be based on a TV show still on the air with first-run episodes when the film was released. Indeed, *X-Files: Fight the Future* was tied into the last episode of the 1997–1998 season, its plot resolving several issues raised by the show's season-ending cliffhanger.

X-Files: Fight the Future earned a respectable $84 million at the box office, though some critics noted that it was more like an extended episode of the show than a developed full-length film. *X-Files* fans loved it, however, and the movie and the TV show boosted each other's popularity.

X-Files references and memorabilia spread throughout the popular culture. Animated versions of Mulder and Scully (voiced by Duchovny and Anderson) appeared in a 1997 episode of the popular Fox cartoon *The Simpsons*. Duchovny guest-hosted *Sat-*

urday Night Live several times, with skits parodying his series. *The X-Files* was also satirized on Fox's comedy show *Mad TV* in a skit about porn films called "The XXX Files." More respectful treatment has come from comic books and novels based on the series, video games, websites, chat rooms, fan clubs, and Fox-sponsored *X-Files* conventions. The show has also generated the usual ephemera associated with anything in popular culture with a devoted following—hats, T-shirts, posters, PC screen savers, and coffee mugs. In addition, episodes from the show became available on video and DVD about a year after airing.

Although the first five seasons of *The X-Files* were shot in Vancouver, British Columbia (to save on production costs), the show moved to Los Angeles beginning with the 1998–1999 season. The change was in response to a demand from Duchovny, who wanted to be nearer to his Los Angeles–based wife, the actress Téa Leoni. The Fox network's willingness to undergo the expense and inconvenience involved in the move was a testament to the popularity of the show and the network's high expectations for its future success.

THE X-FILES ENDS AND RESUMES

As the twenty-first century dawned, the *X-Files* juggernaut began to lose momentum. At the end of the 2000 season, Duchovny left to pursue a film career (Mulder was mysteriously abducted), and the show never recovered. The September 11, 2001, terrorist attacks in New York City and Washington, D.C., drastically altered the mood of the nation, and when *The X-Files* premiered in November 2001, audiences did not seem to find it quite as fun to be scared. The last season of the show averaged just more than nine million viewers, fewer than half of the viewers who had tuned in during its prime. *The X-Files* went off the air in 2002. Though there were rumors of a sequel to the *X-Files* movie in 2003, it was not until 2008 that *The X-Files: I Want to Believe* was released. Many fans and critics considered the film a disappointment, and it grossed less than $21 million.

Despite the cooling of the *X-Files* mania, the show was still in syndication as of 2012 and still very present in modern consciousness, with references to it—and the series catchphrase, "The truth is out there"—everywhere from headlines to cartoons. Carter's creation ushered in a new genre combining science fiction, horror, and police work. *The X-Files* inspired and was replaced by such paranormal series as *Medium* (CBS), *Lost* (ABC), *Heroes* (NBC), and *Fringe* (Fox).

Justin Gustainis

SEE ALSO: *Conspiracy Theories; Emmy Awards; FBI (Federal Bureau of Investigation); Horror Movies; Kennedy Assassination;* Lost; Saturday Night Live; *Serial Killers;* The Simpsons; *Syndication; Television; UFOs (Unidentified Flying Objects); Vampires.*

BIBLIOGRAPHY

Davis, William B. *Where There's Smoke . . . : Musings of a Cigarette Smoking Man.* Toronto: ECW, 2011.

Farrand, Phil. *The Nitpicker's Guide for X-Philes.* New York: Dell, 1997.

Genge, N. E. *The Unofficial "X-Files" Companion.* New York: Crown, 1995.

Lavery, David, and Angela Hague, eds. *"Deny All Knowledge": Reading the "X-Files."* Syracuse, NY: Syracuse University Press, 1996.

Lowry, Brian. *The Truth Is out There: The Official Guide to "The X-Files."* New York: HarperCollins, 1995.

Lowry, Brian. "Mostly for X-Philes." *Variety*, July 28, 2008, 23.

The X-Men

Flawed and complex, the mutant antiheroes known as the X-Men were the perfect comic-book champions for the disaffected youth of Generation X. Featuring an often-changing lineup of young mutant superheroes and unusually intricate story lines, the X-Men have found a consistently large and loyal audience of comic-book readers. Since 1980 only Spider-Man and Batman have rivaled them in popularity and sales. The X-Men's market clout has helped the publisher Marvel Comics remain the undisputed industry leader, and the series' formula has been widely imitated throughout the superhero genre. Few other comic-book series of recent decades have been as influential, and the X-Men film franchise, which started in 2000, has gained an even wider audience for the unconventional heroes.

X-Men's Wolverine. *Hugh Jackman played Logan/Wolverine in the 2000* The X-Men *movie based on the mutant Marvel Comics characters.* **20TH CENTURY FOX/MARVEL ENT GROUP/THE KOBAL COLLECTION.**

THE BIRTH OF THE SUPER TEAM

Marvel first published *The X-Men* in 1963. The concept devised by Stan Lee and Jack Kirby was an extension of the Marvel formula already realized in such characters as Spider-Man and the Fantastic Four. The X-Men were teenage, costumed superheroes who used their powers in the service of humanity, even though society at large misunderstood and feared them. Unlike their superhero peers, however, the X-Men had never even been human. As mutants, they were born with their special powers—usually as a consequence of parents exposed to radioactivity. This distinction left the X-Men especially alienated from human society and made them special victims of misplaced human anxieties. Lee and later writers would often use this premise to conceive stories critical of bigotry and racial persecution.

The first X-Men lineup consisted of Cyclops, with the power to project devastating "optic blasts"; the Beast, with the agility and strength of his namesake; the Angel, who could fly with the aid of natural wings; Iceman, with power over cold and ice; and Marvel Girl, with the mental ability to move objects. Their leader was the enigmatic Professor Xavier, who, though confined to a wheelchair, possessed an impressive variety of telepathic powers. Xavier recruited the teenage mutants to enroll in his private School for Gifted Youngsters, which was a front for the X-Men's training facility. The X-Men defended humanity against an array of evil mutants, the most formidable of whom was Magneto, "the master of magnetism." The heroes also had to fight in their own defense against the Sentinels—a series of mutant-hunting robots engineered by bigoted humans determined to resolve the "mutant question."

A modest-selling title, *The X-Men* did not achieve the spectacular commercial success enjoyed by most other Marvel comic books in the 1960s. By the early 1970s the series consisted only of reprinted stories and seemed doomed for cancellation. In 1975 Marvel revamped the series, keeping only Cyclops and Professor Xavier in the group and introducing a new lineup of international mutants. Created by the writer Len Wein and the artist Dave Cockrum, the new X-Men included Nightcrawler, a German with superhuman agility, the power of teleportation, and a horrifying demonic appearance; Colossus, a Russian—one of the first to be a hero in comic books—with extraordinary physical strength; Storm, an African princess with the ability to summon and control weather and the elements; and Wolverine, a hot-tempered Canadian armed with indestructible steel claws and the ferocious fighting tendencies of his namesake.

Between 1977 and 1981 writer Chris Claremont and writer-artist John Byrne transformed *The X-Men* from a second-tier title to the top-selling comic book on the market. As the lineup of the X-Men continued to evolve, the story lines became increasingly intricate and absorbing. The series offered something for most fans to enjoy. The interplay among the distinctive characters was exceptionally well developed and believable by comic-book standards. Wolverine's ethos of righteous morality backed up by violence made him one of the most popular superheroes of the Reagan-Rambo era. Such strong and complex female characters as Storm, Phoenix, and Rogue helped to make the X-Men one of the few superhero titles to win a significant following among teenage girls.

THE X-MEN INFLUENCE A GENERATION

The X-Men's fantastic commercial success predictably spawned a host of comic-book crossovers, spin-offs, and rip-offs throughout the 1980s and 1990s. There were titles devoted to adult mutants (*Excalibur*, *X-Factor*), adolescent mutants (*The New Mutants*, *Generation-X*), and even prepubescent mutants (*Power Pack*). The concept of the 1980s Teenage Mutant Ninja Turtles originated in part as a satire of the X-Men's overexposure (before itself graduating to overexposure). The first issue of a new X-Men title launched in 1991 set an industry record by selling more than eight million copies. An array of licensed products highlighted by the Fox network's successful *X-Men* animated series broadened the X-Men's market even further.

The consequences of this "X-Treme" mutant proliferation became a matter of some controversy among comic-book fans. While many welcomed the varieties of X-Men spin-offs and crossovers, others criticized them for being poorly conceived and confusing. Some fan critics charged Marvel with exploiting brand loyalty at the expense of good storytelling. To a large extent, the overexposure of the X-Men epitomized the problem of a saturated and shrinking market that plagued the comic-book industry as a whole in the mid-1990s.

The first feature-length, live-action X-Men film was released in 2000 with an unconventional advertising campaign that included a Mutant Watch 2000 website where visitors could turn in friends they thought had questionable super abilities. Directed by Brian Singer, the highly anticipated *X-Men* earned more than $100 million in its first four weeks. Singer also directed the first sequel, *X2* (2003), and Brett Ratner directed another sequel, *X-Men: The Last Stand* (2006). Further delving into the rich Marvel universe, filmmakers then produced two prequels, which give background information on the most popular heroes and villains: *X-Men Origins: Wolverine* (2009), directed by Gavin Hood, and *X-Men: First Class* (2011), directed by Matthew Vaughn.

In 2011 Marvel announced what it termed a "regenesis" of the X-Men universe. Beginning with a conflict between two of the strongest heroes, Cyclops and Wolverine, the team was to be torn in two, with each of the two antagonists leading a faction. What this development meant in the real world was two separate lines of X-Men comics, *Uncanny X-Men* and *Wolverine and the X-Men*. Though Marvel no doubt had hopes of doubling readership and profits, editors also felt that the separate story lines would enable writers to develop beloved characters more fully.

Though the apocalyptic plots and frenetic action are the undeniable center of the popularity of both the X-Men comics and the films, it is the subtext of the plight of society's outsiders that has kept the series fresh through the decades. The X-Men are an oppressed group, forced to hide what is most special about them in order to avoid condemnation by the mainstream. Though this theme has special appeal to those with minority status, such as people of color, gays, and women, almost everyone can relate to being an outsider, and almost everyone has imagined how powerful it would feel to be able to fight back like one of the X-Men.

Bradford Wright

SEE ALSO: *Batman; Comic Books; Comics;* The Fantastic Four; *Kirby, Jack; Lee, Stan; Marvel Comics; Rambo; Spider-Man.*

BIBLIOGRAPHY

Daniels, Les. *Marvel: Five Fabulous Decades of the World's Great-*

est Comic Book Heroes. New York: Harry N. Abrams, 1991.

Hudson, Laura. "Team Players: Freak Show." *Wired*, December 2011, 74.

Lee, Stan. *Son of Origins of Marvel Comics*. New York: Simon & Schuster, 1975.

Lee, Stan, and Marvel Comics Group. *The Uncanny X-Men*. New York: Marvel Comics, 1984.

Pappademas, Alex. "One Ridiculously Vast Cosmic Soap Opera about a Huge Cast of Characters Brawling." *New York Times Magazine*, July 31, 2011, 42.

Y

Yankee Doodle Dandy

In 1942 actor James Cagney starred in director Michael Curtiz's film *Yankee Doodle Dandy*, based upon the life of American composer and producer George M. Cohan. The title refers to Cohan's famous song, "I'm a Yankee Doodle Dandy," written for the Broadway play *Little Johnny Jones* in 1904. In the early Broadway musical hit, Cohan sang the lyrics that would remain popular into the twenty-first century: "I'm a Yankee Doodle Dandy, / A Yankee Doodle, do or die; / A real live nephew of my Uncle Sam / Born on the Fourth of July." It is one of several Cohan tunes that have been passed from generation to generation in celebration of the American spirit and history.

Released shortly after the Japanese attack on Pearl Harbor and the subsequent entry of the United States into World War II, *Yankee Doodle Dandy* was warmly received by American wartime audiences, who were particularly receptive to the patriotic songs in the film. Cagney won an Oscar for his performance, and the movie won Academy Awards for best sound recording and best scoring of a musical picture. On July 4, 1985, the Cagney film was rereleased as the first computer-colorized production by broadcasting entrepreneur Ted Turner. The National Film Preservation Board added *Yankee Doodle Dandy* to its National Film Registry in 1993 as an icon of American culture.

Sharon Brown

SEE ALSO: *Academy Awards; Cagney, James; Hollywood; The Musical; Turner, Ted; World War II.*

BIBLIOGRAPHY

McGilligan, Patrick. *Yankee Doodle Dandy*. Madison: University of Wisconsin Press, 1981.

"National Film Registry." Library of Congress, National Film Preservation Board. Accessed November 2011. Available from http://www.loc.gov/film/filmnfr.html

Yankee Stadium

Before occupying their new stadium in 2009, the New York Yankees had played in their original stadium for eighty-five years, since its opening in 1923. Considered a shrine to many baseball fans, the original stadium witnessed some of the game's most dramatic and historic moments. Not only was it one of the most hallowed of ballparks, haunted by the ghosts of baseball past, but it was also among the sport's grittiest, most plebeian arenas, famed around the major leagues for its rowdy, rough-house Bronx crowd.

THE ORIGINAL STADIUM

The original Yankee Stadium covered an area of approximately 11.6 acres in the South Bronx, with the playing field itself spanning 3.5 acres. Construction began on the park, designed as a permanent home for New York's American League baseball team, on May 5, 1922. On April 18 of the following year, Yankee Stadium opened to the public. Yankee right fielder Babe Ruth promptly delivered the edifice's first home run. Soon the park was renowned for its 296-foot "short porch" in right field, conducive to home runs by left-handed hitters. Righties were commensurately daunted by "Death Valley," a 457-foot expanse in left center, where sure home runs miraculously turned into fly-ball outs. With the advent of night baseball in 1946, a combination of 800 multivapor and incandescent lamps were installed to illuminate the field.

In 1932 the Yankees began to honor their greatest legends with the erection of monuments and plaques in the outfield section of the stadium. The first monument was dedicated to the memory of Miller Huggins, the manager who led the team to three world championships in the 1920s. Subsequent plaques and monuments have honored team captains Lou Gehrig and Thurman Munson, both of whom died tragically, as well as Hall of Fame players such as Ruth, Joe DiMaggio, and Mickey Mantle. Originally located on the playing field itself, the monuments posed a curious obstacle for outfielders, who often had to dodge the memorials to retrieve fly balls. Relocated in 1976 to a new area dubbed "Monument Park," the monuments were safely behind the outfield fences and available for viewing by the public.

In 1973, as the Yankees completed their fiftieth-anniversary season in what was now known as "The House That Ruth Built," Yankee Stadium was remodeled and renovated. While the two-year project was under way, the team played its home dates at nearby Shea Stadium. The remodeled Yankee Stadium opened on April 15, 1976, to mostly positive reviews. The building's distinctive Art Deco facade was retained in part and relocated to the centerfield bleachers.

NOTABLE EVENTS

The original Yankee Stadium played host to some of baseball's most historic moments. On September 30, 1927, Ruth clouted his record sixtieth home run there off Washington Senators pitcher Tom Zachary. Thirty-four years later, Yankee outfielder

Yankee Stadium. *With its rich and dramatic history, the original Yankee Stadium was considered hallowed ground by baseball fans.* CHRISTINA RICHARDS/SHUTTERSTOCK.COM.

Roger Maris eclipsed Ruth's record with his sixty-first homer off the Boston Red Sox Tracy Stallard, a mark that stood until St. Louis Cardinal Mark McGwire shattered it in 1998. The old stadium also provided the setting for some emotional farewells, from a dying Lou Gehrig's inspiring valedictory in 1939, when he told the world he was "the luckiest man on the face of the earth," to a cancer-ravaged Ruth's last salute in 1948.

In 1977 the Yankees celebrated their return to championship status, after a fifteen-year drought, by clinching a game that saw slugging outfielder Reggie Jackson club three home runs off three different Los Angeles Dodger pitchers. The following April, jubilant fans showered the field with "Reggie! Bars," a chocolate and peanut confection named for the hot-dogging star after he vowed he would become so famous "they'd name a candy bar after me."

Candy bars have not been the only objects to come flying out of the Yankee Stadium stands over the years. At various times, golf balls, shot glasses, batteries, assorted coins, and torrents of beer have been flung onto the field by jubilant, angry, or just plain inebriated fans looking to terrorize Yankee opponents. The prevailing air of rowdiness has occasionally taken a more endearing form, as when twelve-year-old Jeffrey Maier snatched a fly ball away from Baltimore Oriole right fielder Tony Tarasco during the 1996 American League Championship series, resulting in a game-tying Yankee home run.

A NEW STADIUM

In the 1990s Yankee Stadium suffered the ironic fate of becoming something of a political football when Yankee owner George Steinbrenner loudly threatened to move the team when its lease expired if he could not get a new stadium constructed with municipal assistance. New York politicians responded with recrimination and posturing. Several civic leaders called for a referendum aimed at keeping the team in the Bronx. Baseball purists and fans of the old building largely sided with them. The fact that the team's crosstown rivals—the New York Mets—played in Shea Stadium, a drab cookie-cutter facility, contributed to the glorification of "the Stadium" as one of baseball's high holy places.

Even as the Yankees won their twenty-fourth World Series in 1998, Steinbrenner continued to threaten to move the team if a new stadium was not built. Despite the structure's hallowed status, Steinbrenner's wish became a reality. When a beam fell from the roof during the 1997–1998 season (luckily when the stadium was empty), the urgency of the problem became apparent. In 2005 the Yankees announced plans to build a new stadium financed mostly by the team with the help of both taxable and tax-exempt bonds. Some public moneys were used for infrastructure and surrounding facilities.

The new Yankee Stadium opened in 2009. In keeping with the team's traditions, the dimensions of the playing field were kept the same as in the original. Monument Park was also retained. However, many new amenities were added to the ballpark, such as a huge video scoreboard and architectural features to improve accessibility. The team capped off the first season in the new stadium by winning its twenty-seventh World Series.

Robert E. Schnakenberg

SEE ALSO: *Baseball; Boston Red Sox; DiMaggio, Joe; Gehrig, Lou; Jackson, Reggie; Major League Baseball; Mantle, Mickey; Maris, Roger; McGwire, Mark; The New York Mets; The New York Yankees; Ruth, Babe; Steinbrenner, George.*

BIBLIOGRAPHY

Frommer, Harvey, and Bob Sheppard. *Remembering Yankee Stadium: An Oral and Narrative History of "The House That Ruth Built."* New York: Stewart, Tabori & Chang, 2008.

Gershman, Michael. *Diamonds: The Evolution of the Ballpark.* New York: Houghton Mifflin, 1995.

Lowry, Philip J. *Green Cathedrals: The Ultimate Celebration of All 271 Major League and Negro League Ballparks Past and Present.* Reading, MA: Addison-Wesley, 1992.

Robinson, Ray, and Christopher Jennison. *Yankee Stadium: 75 Years of Drama, Glamor, and Glory.* New York: Penguin Studio, 1998.

Santasiere, Al, and Mark Vancil. *Yankee Stadium: The Official Retrospective.* New York: Pocket Books, 2008.

Yankovic, "Weird Al" *(1959–)*

Rock and roll's top jester went by the name "Weird Al" Yankovic. Specializing in amusing parodies of popular rock tunes as well as humorous ditties written in generic song styles, Yankovic recorded albums and music videos, starred in his own television show, appeared in films, and performed comedic stage shows during a career that spanned more than three decades.

Yankovic was born Alfred Matthew Yankovic on October 23, 1959, in the Los Angeles suburb of Lynwood. His parents, Nick and Mary Yankovic, bought him an accordion from a door-to-door music school salesman, choosing that instrument because polka king Frankie Yankovic (no relation) also played the accordion. Hours watching television as a child would provide the inspiration for much of Yankovic's work (many of his songs centered on food or television shows). He became a fan of such musicians/comedians as Allan Sherman (who also specialized in creating song parodies) and Spike Jones while listening to the Dr. Demento radio show, which would later become a great source of publicity for Yankovic's own talents. His first song to be heard on radio, "Belvedere Cruising," was played on the Dr. Demento show in 1976.

After graduating from Lynwood High School as valedictorian, Yankovic attended California Polytechnic State University in San Luis Obispo to study architecture, a field he claimed he chose because it was listed first in the catalog. At college he earned the nickname "Weird Al" while hosting a radio show. In 1979 Yankovic recorded his first hit, "My Bologna," a parody of "My Sharona" by the Knack. Members of the Knack liked the song and convinced their label to release it as a single. The song came to be known as the "bathroom recording" because the original version was recorded in a men's room to achieve its acoustic effect.

Yankovic reached even wider public attention in 1984 with "Eat It," a spoof of Michael Jackson's hit "Beat It." His video of the song parodied the visuals of the Jackson video, resulting in valuable exposure on MTV. The single earned Yankovic his first Grammy Award, and the album, *"Weird Al" Yankovic in 3-D*, reached the Top 15. In the video for another song on the album, "I Lost on Jeopardy," based on a tune by the Greg Kihn Band, Yankovic re-created the set of the original *Jeopardy* TV series.

Yankovic was tapped to provide songs for films, including "This Is the Life" for *Johnny Dangerously* (1984) and "Dare to Be Stupid" for *Transformers: The Movie* (1986). He starred in his own film, *UHF* (1989), as George Newman, head of a beleaguered, small-time cable station, and he appeared in all three *Naked Gun* movies (1988, 1991, 1994), *Tapeheads* (1988), *Nothing Sacred* (2000), and *Desperation Boulevard* (1998). During the 1997–1998 television season, Yankovic starred in a Saturday morning program, *The "Weird Al" Show*, similar to the hit series *Pee-wee's Playhouse*. He played himself opposite a friend named Harvey the Wonder Hamster, with a collection of friends and regulars (including Stan Freberg) who dropped by to discuss that week's moral problem. Also included in the show

"Weird Al" Yankovic. *"Weird Al" Yankovic performs in Hollywood, Florida, in 2011.* LARRY MARANO/CONTRIBUTOR/FILMMAGIC/GETTY IMAGES.

was a series of "Fatman" animated cartoons (for which Yankovic supplied the voice) that featured a superhero version of the overweight character from Yankovic's "Fat" video.

His 1992 video "Smells Like Nirvana" poked fun at the video for Nirvana's "Smells Like Teen Spirit," lampooning the unintelligibility of the song's lyrics. Nirvana members said that they knew they had made it when Yankovic parodied their song. *Rolling Stone* listed the parody on its top 100 videos of all time. Yankovic's videos have been compiled into several collections, including *"Weird Al" Yankovic: The Ultimate Video Collection* (2003). On his album *Bad Hair Day* (1996), he featured a parody of Coolio's "Gangsta's Paradise" called "Amish Paradise." Coolio granted permission for the video but later condemned Yankovic's version. Yankovic's first Billboard Top 10 single, "White and Nerdy," was released in 2006.

As a director, Yankovic created a parody of Maurice Binder's James Bond opening titles for the film *Spy Hard* (1996). As Yankovic sings "Theme from *Spy Hard*," silhouetted overweight women swim by. In 2011 he conquered another form: his children's book reached number four on the *New York Times* bestseller list for children's picture books.

Dennis Fischer

SEE ALSO: *Grammy Awards; Jackson, Michael;* Jeopardy!*; MTV; Nirvana;* Pee-wee's Playhouse*;* Rolling Stone*; Television.*

BIBLIOGRAPHY

Insana, Tino, and Al Yankovic. *The Authorized Al.* Chicago: Contemporary Books, 1985.

Yanni *(1954–)*

Along with Slim Whitman, Ray Stevens, and Kenny G, New Age artist Yanni is one of those inexplicable music curiosities who rode to the top of the charts on a sea of critical incredulity. Dismissed by one reviewer as a "musical Fabio," Yanni is known not so much for the music he makes as the sensation he creates. His albums and videos have sold multiple millions worldwide, and he has personally saved more than a few public television stations with his prodigious pledge-drive potency.

Born Yanni Chryssomallis in Kalamata, Greece, the future New Age superstar was a national swimming champion in his teens. After immigrating to the United States in 1972 he passed up a career in clinical psychology to pursue his creative muse full time. A self-taught musician, Yanni began composing in his head, relying on collaborators to put his orchestrations down on paper. He released his first full-length album, *Keys to Imagination*, in 1986.

The "Yanni sound" changed very little over the next several years. Gauzy strains of synthesizer continued to waft insidiously down upon the listener, as vaguely Mediterranean-sounding hooks are stated and restated by various instruments. The music incorporated elements of classical, New Age, and world beat into a sonic mélange that one unfavorable reviewer called "aural wallpaper." Even Yanni himself often referred to the plastic arts when describing it. "Music is like creating an emotional painting," he explained. "The sounds are the colors." Colors derived from an irritatingly narrow spectrum, according to some critics, who found Yanni's repetition of musical themes numbingly aggravating. Despite these brickbats, however, the Greek tycoon's record sales climbed throughout the 1980s.

Yanni's live appearances became major moneymakers as well, as the mustachioed and classically handsome composer developed a large and devoted fan following. For concerts, Yanni assembled a multipiece orchestra with instrumentation culled from virtually every continent, over which he would preside beatifically from behind a stack of keyboards. Yanni often staged his appearances at major international landmarks such as the Taj Mahal and China's Forbidden City. These lavishly mounted productions generated enormous viewership for public television stations across the United States and were aired repeatedly during pledge weeks.

Befitting his superstar status, Yanni cultivated a personal life designed to keep him in the crosshairs of the paparazzi. In 1989 the then little-known Yanni began dating Linda Evans, star of TV's *Dynasty*. The flaxen-haired beauty reportedly was won over by the sinewy Greek's command of the music of the spheres. They would remain a couple until 1998, when conflicts over the directions of their respective careers compelled them to end the relationship.

Yanni. *Yanni performs with cellist Sarah O'Brien in Puerto Rico in 2011.* BOB GEVINSKI/CONTRIBUTOR/GETTY IMAGES ENTERTAINMENT/GETTY IMAGES.

Indeed, much of Yanni's success has been attributed to his appeal to women. But the New Age superstar has bristled at the suggestion that his cover-of-a-romance-novel appearance drove his record sales. He claimed the bulk of his fan mail comes not from sex-starved housewives but from the homebound and the infirm, who find his music soothing. Some have even ascribed healing powers to Yanni's compositions, a claim the composer modestly deflected. "I don't see myself as a peacemaker at all or anything like that," he told the *Orange County Register* in 1998. "I'm merely standing in one place saying it's possible for us to do this, for people of the world to share in my music. If I can play even a minute role in something like that in my lifetime, then I will have accomplished something special."

In early 1998 Yanni sold out an impressive ten dates at New York City's Radio City Music Hall. Burned out from a grueling concert schedule, the musician then took two years off from recording and touring. However, the twenty-first century has witnessed Yanni's resurgence. In the first decade of the 2000s he released two albums of new music and two live concert albums, the latter two ranking high on the Billboard New Age charts. He also published an autobiography in 2003, the *New York Times* best seller *Yanni in Words*. Into the second decade of the century, Yanni continued to have a prolific output and maintained a demanding tour schedule. While fans may have noticed a change to that distinctive Yanni sound, they continued to purchase albums and concert tickets in droves, ensuring his place at the top of the New Age ranks. Late in the first decade of the 2000s and in the early 2010s Yanni continued exploring new sounds in new albums as well as exploring new looks: gone were his signature long locks and luxurious mustache.

Robert E. Schnakenberg

SEE ALSO: Dynasty*; Fabio; New Age Music; Public Television (PBS); Stevens, Ray.*

BIBLIOGRAPHY

Ferguson, Andrew. "PBS: The Yanni State." *National Review*, May 2, 1994.

Wener, Ben. "Yanni, the World's Most Loved and Loathed Music Figure, Is Back." *Orange County Register*, March 4, 1998.

Yanni, and David Rensin. *Yanni: In Words*. New York: Miramax Books, 2003.

The Yardbirds

The backbone of the rock band the Yardbirds consisted of vocalist Keith Relf, rhythm guitarist Chris Dreja, bassist Paul Samwell-Smith, and drummer Jim McCarty. However, the band was most famous for their succession of luminary lead guitarists: Eric Clapton, Jeff Beck, and Jimmy Page. Under Clapton the Yardbirds played high-energy R&B with long improvisations called "rave-ups" in which they would alter tempo and volume, building to a climax before returning to the song. Although the recording technology is poor by today's standards, *Five Live Yardbirds* (1964) reveals a tight unit of talented musicians. Inspired by the phenomenal success of the Beatles, the Yardbirds then recorded the pop song "For Your Love," written by Graham Gouldman, and this became their first hit. The song featured a harpsichord and bongos but very little Clapton. Uncomfortable with the band's commercial direction, Clapton left to pursue pure blues in John Mayall's Bluesbreakers.

Guitar wizard Beck then joined the band and transformed the Yardbirds into trailblazing musical pioneers. Innovating with fuzztone, feedback, and harmonic sustain within the medium of Gouldman-penned pop songs, they produced classics such as "Evil Hearted You" and "Heart Full of Soul." Their first original studio album, *The Yardbirds* (1966, renamed *Over, Under, Sideways, Down* in the United States but commonly known as *Roger the Engineer* in either country) is a tour de force on Beck's part. When Samwell-Smith left the band, session musician Page was recruited as bassist until Dreja could learn the bass, and then Page moved up as second lead guitarist alongside Beck. The Beck-Page lineup recorded only three songs, one of them being "Stroll On" (a version of "Train Kept a-Rollin'"), which they performed in Michelangelo Antonioni's 1966 film *Blow-Up*, a cult classic of the "swinging London" scene.

When Beck left the group, Page introduced his own musical visions and recorded *Little Games* (1967). An odd mixture of pop songs and virtuoso guitar playing, this album is most intriguing as a document of Page's early development, displaying many riffs and effects that were later redeveloped in Led Zeppelin. Especially noteworthy is the instrumental "White Summer," later reworked as "Black Mountain Side," and the introduction of "Over the Hills and Far Away." When the remaining members left, Page recruited vocalist Robert Plant, bassist John Paul Jones, and drummer John Bonham and debuted the band as the New Yardbirds, later renamed Led Zeppelin.

In 1984 ex-Yardbirds Samwell-Smith, Dreja, and McCarty formed the band Box of Frogs (Relf had died in 1976, electrocuted by a guitar). Although some tracks from *Box of Frogs* (1984) and *Strange Land* (1986) featured guest guitarists Page and Beck, these heavy-metal offerings made little impact. The 1990s brought honors—introduction into the Rock and Roll Hall of Fame—and another version of the band with Dreja and McCarty. This unit would record the first Yardbirds studio album in thirty-five years with the 2003 release of *Birdland*. Composed of new songs and remakes, *Birdland* featured several guest artists, including Beck.

The Yardbirds are aptly called legendary, for although the band's recordings have lapsed into obscurity, their influence on guitar-driven rock is enduring and pervasive. Clapton, Beck, and Page gave rise to the "guitar hero," displacing the singer as the focal point of the rock-and-roll band, and a legion of 1970s guitarists cited the Yardbirds as a major influence. In spite of an uneven recording history, the Yardbirds' small, experimental body of work places the band just behind the Beatles, the Rolling Stones, and the Who as a major element of the British Invasion. Writing in the liner notes to a greatest hits collection, rock critic Parke Puterbaugh sums up the influence of the Yardbirds, noting that the "Yardbirds were the bridge between the tributary white R&B of early sixties London and the pastures of fuzz-toned psychedelia and power-chorded heavy metal plowed much later in the decade and throughout the seventies . . . the Yardbirds laid the groundwork for Rock Guitar As We Know It."

Douglas Cooke

SEE ALSO: *The Beatles; British Invasion; Clapton, Eric; Led Zeppelin; Rock and Roll; The Rolling Stones; The Who.*

BIBLIOGRAPHY

Clapton, Eric. *Clapton: The Autobiography*. New York: Broadway Books, 2007.

Clayson, Alan. *The Yardbirds: The Band That Launched Eric Clapton, Jeff Beck, Jimmy Page*. San Francisco, CA: Backbeat Books, 2002.

Mackay, Richard, and Michael Ober. *Yardbirds World*. N.p.: Author, 1989.

McStravick, Summer. *Blues-Rock Explosion*. Mission Viejo, CA: Old Goat Publishing, 2001.

Platt, John A. *The Yardbirds*. London: Sidgwick & Jackson, 1983.

Russo, Greg. *Yardbirds: The Ultimate Rave-Up*. Floral Park, NY: Crossfire Publishers, 1997.

Yastrzemski, Carl *(1939–)*

Nicknamed "Yaz," Carl Michael Yastrzemski of the Boston Red Sox epitomized the spirit of hard work and determination that made baseball players American heroes in the twentieth century. As a left fielder, Yastrzemski mastered the art of playing hits off Fenway Park's infamous "Green Monster" outfield wall, earning seven Gold Glove Awards during a major-league career that lasted from 1961 to 1983. He also was a consistently dangerous batter who had a flair for getting crucial hits in big games. Yastrzemski achieved the coveted Triple Crown for highest batting average (.326), most runs batted in (121), and most home runs (44) in 1967 en route to Boston's first American League pennant since 1946. By the time he retired, he had amassed 3,419 hits and 452 homers. Those numbers helped to earn him induction into the National Baseball Hall of Fame in 1989.

Susan Curtis

SEE ALSO: *Baseball; Boston Red Sox; Cooperstown, New York; Fenway Park; Major League Baseball; Sports Heroes.*

BIBLIOGRAPHY

Cressman, Mark. *The A-to-Z History of Baseball: Twentieth Century Baseball Players*. Philadelphia: Xlibris, 2008.

Yastrzemski, Carl, and Al Hirshberg. *Yaz: The Autobiography of Carl Yastrzemski*. New York: Viking Press, 1968.

Yearwood, Trisha *(1964–)*

A versatile performer with a powerful, sultry voice, Trisha Yearwood was the first woman in country music history to sell a million copies of her debut album, *Trisha Yearwood* (1991). The country singer subsequently became one of the most popular stars in Nashville, Tennessee, building a significant crossover audience through her work on film soundtracks. She also proved her acting skills on network television and became a best-selling cookbook author. In 2012 she entered yet another arena as the host of her own television cooking show on the Food Network.

Born in Monticello, Georgia, on September 19, 1964, Patricia Lynn Yearwood grew up listening to the passionate vocals of such modern country stars as Linda Ronstadt and Emmylou Harris. She set her sights on a music career and moved to Nashville, where she got a degree in business administration while interning at MTM Records. She began singing on demos for MTM and met another aspiring country singer, Garth Brooks. The two became friends, and, when Brooks's career took off, he offered Yearwood support and encouragement, having her sing backup on his 1990 album *No Fences*. He invited her to join his tour shortly afterward, giving a boost to Yearwood's first solo album.

The release of *Trisha Yearwood*, with its hit single "She's in Love with the Boy," propelled Yearwood to instant stardom. The 1990s were a decade of enormous growth in the popularity of country music, as a generation of clean-cut young stars modernized the look and sound of the genre with flashy music videos and an updated accessible sound. These artists included Clint Black, Shania Twain, Brooks, and Yearwood.

Yearwood's strong voice and vulnerable delivery gained her a wide range of fans as she sang about "the dreams of an average Jane," in the words of one of her biggest hits, "Walkaway Joe." In 1992 she recorded the Elvis Presley hit "Devil in Disguise" for the Andrew Bergman film *Honeymoon in Vegas*, after which she contributed to the soundtracks of a number of films and television shows. Her popularity continued as she released more than ten albums over the next two decades, winning three Grammys and a number of other awards. In 1998 she proved her talents extended beyond the soundstage when she got a recurring role in the CBS television crime drama *JAG*.

In 2005, after two divorces, Yearwood married Brooks, her old friend and mentor, and the two moved to Oklahoma. When a publisher suggested she write her autobiography, she countered by offering to write a cookbook based on the southern recipes of her childhood. The resulting book, *Georgia Cooking in an Oklahoma Kitchen* (2008), was a best seller, as was the follow-up, *Home Cooking with Trisha Yearwood* (2010). Combining her cooking skills with her stage presence, she premiered her own Food Network TV show, *Trisha's Southern Kitchen*, in the spring of 2012.

Tina Gianoulis

SEE ALSO: *Alternative Country Music; Black, Clint; Brooks, Garth; Country Music; Grammy Awards; Presley, Elvis; Television; Twain, Shania.*

BIBLIOGRAPHY

Holley, Debbie. "Trisha Yearwood's Fairy-Tale Rise to Fame." *Billboard*, July 27, 1991, 30.

Wolff, Kurt, and Orla Duane. "Hunks, Hat Acts, and Young Country Darlings: Nashville in the 1990s." In *Country Music: The Rough Guide*. London: Penguin Books, 2000.

Yearwood, Trisha. "Turning Points: Five Moments That Changed My Life." *Good Housekeeping*, May 2010, 141.

The Yellow Kid

The Yellow Kid by Richard Felton Outcault (1863–1928) is generally considered the character who gave birth to American comic strips. The Kid, later named Mickey Dugan by Outcault, is a smallish figure dressed in a nightshirt who roams the streets of New York City in company with other urchins. The Yellow Kid was not a comic strip; rather, he appeared as a character in a series of large single-panel color comic illustrations in Joseph

Pulitzer's *New York World* with the more or less continuous running title *Hogan's Alley*. The *World* published the first of these illustrations, *At the Circus in Hogan's Alley*, on May 5, 1895. The newspaper's readers, it seems, singled out the Kid as a distinctive character, and his popularity led other artists to create similar characters. In short succession these actions gave rise to the comic strip.

Outcault was born in Lancaster, Ohio, and studied design in Cincinnati before joining the laboratories of Thomas Edison as an illustrator in 1888. By 1890 he combined employment as an illustrator at *Electrical World*, a trade journal, with freelance cartoon work for illustrated humor journals such as *Puck*, *Judge*, *Life*, and *Truth*. The Kid's genesis lay in the genre of city urchin cartoons made popular by these journals. In particular, Outcault drew inspiration from Michael Angelo Woolf's work.

A prototype Yellow Kid showed up in Outcault's "Feudal Pride in Hogan's Alley," published in *Truth* on June 2, 1894. This small figure in a nightshirt cropped up in several other Outcault cartoons before blossoming into a larger, more familiar, as yet unnamed Kid in Outcault's "Fourth Ward Brownies," published in *Truth* on February 9, 1895, and reprinted in the *World* on February 17, 1895. The Kid appeared again in Outcault's "The Fate of the Glutton" in the *World* on March 10, 1895. In these two appearances the Kid's nightshirt has an ink-smudged handprint, a distinctive feature of the later *World* panels. The *World* published ten more "Hogan's Alley" panels in 1895. The Kid can be seen in them all. On January 5, 1896, the Kid is center stage in a yellow nightshirt and thereafter the focus of each panel.

MOVE TO HEARST'S *JOURNAL*

The Yellow Kid became the mainstay of the *World*'s comic supplement during 1896, but in mid-October Outcault moved his strip from the *World* to William Randolph Hearst's *New York Journal*. Hearst had infamously bought the talent of the *World* to staff the *Journal* and naturally enough poached Outcault for the launch of the comic supplement on October 18, 1896. Thereafter the Kid was shown in tabloid-page-size illustration under the running title "McFadden's Row of Flats" before departing on a world tour in 1897. Beginning on October 25, 1896, the Kid also began to appear in an occasional comic-strip-like series of panels under the running title of "The Yellow Kid," which was Outcault's first use of that name in a comic supplement. Outcault stayed with Hearst's *Journal* for a little more than a year. The last Yellow Kid comic feature can be found in the *Journal* on January 23, 1898. Outcault then returned to the *World*, producing a series of Hogan's Alley–like panels featuring an African American character.

Outcault's shift of the Yellow Kid from the *World* to the *Journal* raised issues of copyright. The *World* continued to publish a version of the Kid drawn by George Luks. Prior to leaving the *World*, Outcault had sought copyright protection for his creation in a letter to the Library of Congress on September 7, 1896. He had also attached the label "Do Not Be Deceived None Genuine without This Signature" above his signature in the *World*'s September 6, 1896, episode of "Hogan's Alley." Later advice from W. B. Howell of the Treasury Department, which policed copyright laws at that time, advised Outcault that he had failed to secure protection on the image of the Kid because he had included only one illustration instead of two in his application. Outcault did, however, secure protection for the title "The Yellow Kid."

Two minor controversies have marked the history of the Yellow Kid. Until the late 1980s, accounts of the origins of comic strips generally accepted that the Yellow Kid's nightshirt was colored yellow as a test of the ability of yellow ink to bond to newsprint. However, Richard Marschall argues in *America's Great Comic-Strip Artists* that this could not have been the case, as yellow ink had been used earlier. Similarly, Bill Blackbeard gives a detailed account of the *World*'s use of color in his introduction to *The Yellow Kid: A Centennial Celebration* that makes clear the "testing yellow ink theory" is incorrect.

Further, the Yellow Kid is often cited as the origin of the term *yellow journalism*. However, historian Mark Winchester has demonstrated that the term *yellow journalism* came into use during the Spanish-American War in 1898 to describe the war hysteria whipped up by Hearst and Pulitzer. The Yellow Kid was transformed into a symbol of yellow journalism during this campaign rather than giving his name to it. The distinction is subtle but crucial.

Ian Gordon

SEE ALSO: *Comics; Hearst, William Randolph.*

BIBLIOGRAPHY

Blackbeard, Bill; Martin Williams; and Smithsonian Institution. *The Smithsonian Collection of Newspaper Comics.* Washington, DC: Smithsonian Institution Press, 1977.

Gordon, Ian. *Comic Strips and Consumer Culture, 1890–1945.* Washington, DC: Smithsonian Institution Press, 1998.

Harvey, Robert C. *The Art of the Funnies: An Aesthetic History.* Jackson: University Press of Mississippi, 1994.

Howell, W. B. "Assistant Secretary, Treasury Department to W. Y. Connor, *New York Journal*, April 15, 1897." Reprinted in *Decisions of the United States Courts Involving Copyright and Literary Property, 1789–1909*, Bulletin 15: 3187–3188. Washington, DC: Library of Congress, 1980.

Marschall, Richard. *America's Great Comic-Strip Artists.* New York: Abbeville Press, 1989.

Olson, Richard D. *The Yellow Kid: America's First Comic Character Success Story.* New Orleans, LA: Author, 1993.

Outcault, Richard. *The Yellow Kid: A Centennial Celebration of the Kid Who Started the Comics.* Northampton, MA: Kitchen Sink Press, 1995.

Winchester, Mark D. "Hully Gee, It's a War! The Yellow Kid and the Coining of 'Yellow Journalism.'" *Inks* 2, no. 3 (1995): 22–37.

Yellowstone National Park

Comprising 2.2 million acres of northwest Wyoming, with slight incursions into Montana and Idaho, Yellowstone is the oldest national park in the United States. The park's unique sights originally inspired a nation that had not even fully conceived of what the term *national park* entailed. The park has evolved to stand as the preeminent symbol of the national park idea, whether inspiring the designation of other locations or revealing systematic flaws. Today, Yellowstone serves as an active battleground as Americans strive to define the meaning of preservation and wilderness in an era of budget constraints and increased fires.

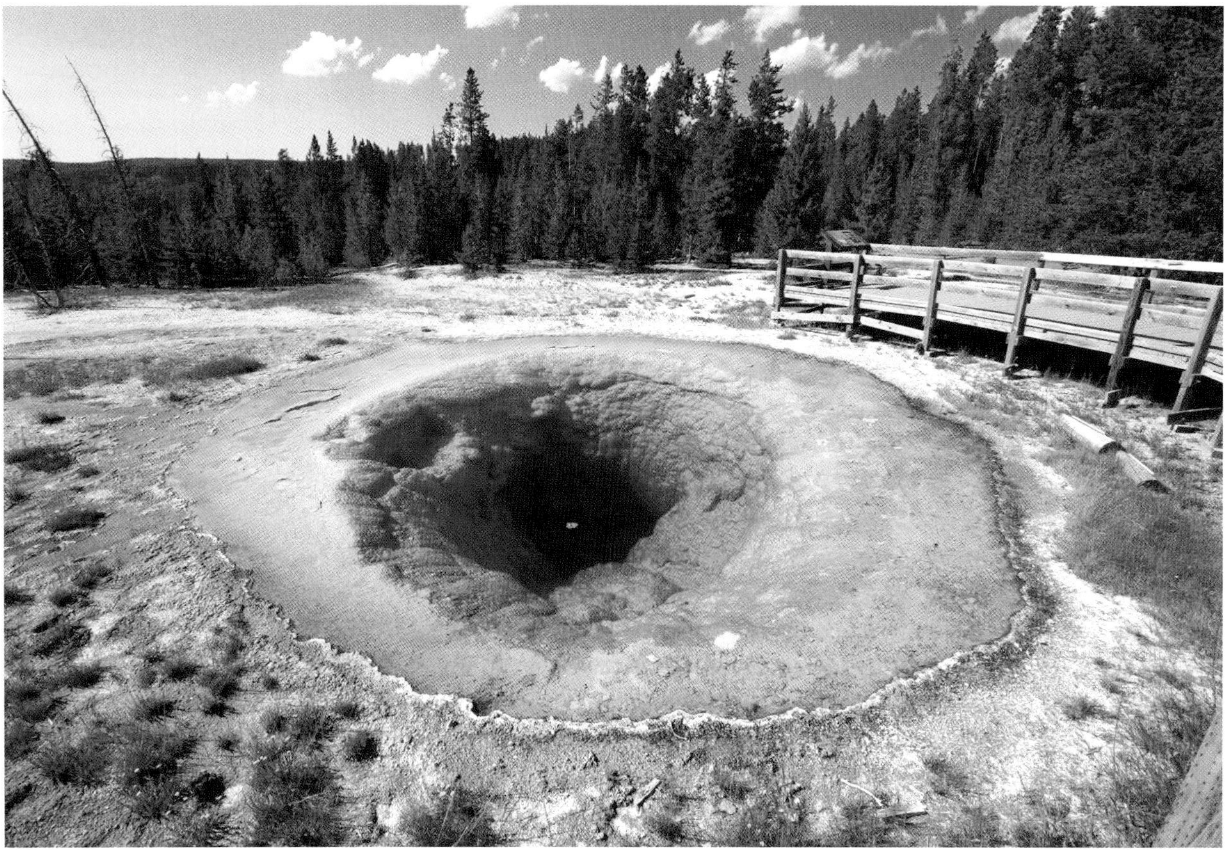

Yellowstone National Park. *The Morning Glory Pool is one of the many natural attractions at Yellowstone National Park.* JASON PATRICK ROSS/SHUTTERSTOCK.COM.

From the outset, Yellowstone's unique attraction derived from its natural oddities. The region was the stuff of rumors. The return of explorers from the northern Rockies in 1810 had piqued the public's attention with stories of odd natural occurrences: thermal phenomena, a beautiful mountain lake, and a magnificent canyon entered into the unconfirmed reports. "Could such a place exist?" Americans asked upon hearing descriptions of the park's bubbling cauldrons. In 1870 other expeditions set out to explore the sights, including the Hayden Survey in 1871. Overwhelmed by the majesty and oddity that they beheld, they were at once overcome by its beauty and potential for development. Such economic development, though, could exploit and ruin all that made the site peculiar. During this era of development and the massive harvesting of natural resources, these attributes were not sufficient to warrant preservation; the site also needed to be of no worth otherwise. The leader of the survey, Ferdinand Hayden, repeatedly assured Congress that the entire area was worthless for anything but tourism. Lurking behind such plans were railroad companies eager to find tourist attractions in the West.

The establishment of the park by President Ulysses S. Grant on March 1, 1872, rings hollow by the standards of modern environmentalism. In addition, today it is recognized that parks such as Yellowstone were created by displacing Native peoples from vast parts of the West. However, such designation, albeit under the jurisdiction of the U.S. Army until 1916, kept the area free of American settlement and development during some of the region's boom years. As an example, Yellowstone's herd of North American bison is given credit for the species' endurance. While hunters decimated the larger herd by 1880, the park offered sanctuary to at least a few bison. Today, the Yellowstone herd is considered an anchor for the entire species. The present herd, ironically, has also led to controversy as it creeps past park borders.

In 1916 President Woodrow Wilson signed the National Park Act, creating the National Park Service and initiating the search for the meaning of such designation. Tourism rose steadily through the war years, and Park Service Director Stephen T. Mather largely developed and linked the park system. With the Wilderness Act of 1964, the shared cause of the park system became the effort to preserve areas as unspoiled "wilderness." While it had originally been set aside due to geological oddities, Yellowstone became a primary illustration of one of the most unusual and secure ecosystems in the United States.

Yellowstone has proven to be an attraction of enduring proportions. Tourist visitation to the park has increased into the twenty-first century, with the park becoming an international attraction. Massive visitation rates, however, have taken a toll on the remaining wilderness within the park. Many environmentalists call overvisitation Yellowstone's major threat. In addition, fires have repeatedly torn through the park, forcing administrators to continually revisit their mandate. Proponents of wilderness argue that naturally occurring fires must be allowed to burn, whether or not they endanger tourists or damage park service property; administrators who see their responsibility to visitors argue for fire suppression. Such issues force Americans to consider what a national park seeks to accomplish and reidentify Yellowstone's position as the symbolic leader of the American system of national parks.

Brian Black

SEE ALSO: *Environmentalism; National Parks.*

BIBLIOGRAPHY

Louter, David. *Windshield Wilderness.* Seattle: University of Washington Press, 2006.

Runte, Alfred. *National Parks: The American Experience*, 4th ed. Lanham, MD: Taylor Trade, 2010.

Schullery, Paul. *Myth and History in the Creation of Yellowstone National Park.* Omaha, NE: Bison Books, 2011.

Spence, Mark David. *Dispossessing the Wilderness: Indian Removal and the Making of the National Parks.* New York: Oxford University Press, 2000.

Sutter, Paul. *Driven Wild.* Seattle: University of Washington Press, 2004.

Yes

Yes's combination of technical proficiency, enigmatic lyrics, and large egos captured the essence of the progressive rock movement. Formed in 1968, the British art rock band achieved international success with *The Yes Album* in 1971. Further success came with *Fragile* (1972) and its hit single "Roundabout" and *Close to the Edge* (1972), which is considered by many to be the band's masterpiece.

The band excelled in live shows and is known for its long-jamming songs, some of which are more than twenty minutes long. Lavish crystalline stage sets designed by the artist Roger Dean (who also drew the band's album covers) helped make for hugely successful live shows; in the late 1970s, Yes set a record for selling out New York's Madison Square Garden sixteen times. In 1983 the group released *90125*, which became their biggest-selling album, carried by their only American number one hit "Owner of a Lonely Heart."

Even though the members of the band have changed incessantly over the years, Yes has continued to tour and release new material through the 1980s, 1990s, and into the twenty-first century, with *The Ladder* (1999) often considered the band's best work since *90125*. Yes's exuberant, complex music and fusion of celestial, spiritual, and pastoral themes have influenced such bands as Genesis, King Crimson, and Rush and have made Yes a favorite for art rock fans worldwide.

David Elroy Goldweber

SEE ALSO: *Rock and Roll; Stadium Concerts.*

BIBLIOGRAPHY

Martin, Bill. *Music of Yes: Structure and Vision in Progressive Rock.* Chicago: Open Court, 1996.

Morse, Tim, ed. *Yesstories: Yes in Their Own Words.* New York: St. Martin's Press, 1996.

Snider, Charles. *The Strawberry Bricks Guide to Progressive Rock.* Chicago: Strawberry Bricks, 2007.

Welch, Chris. *Yes: Close to the Edge.* London: Omnibus, 2008.

Yippies

Forming one of the more outlandish and short-lived groups of the 1960s American counterculture, Yippies were members of the Youth International Party that was established in January 1968 by Abbie Hoffman and Jerry Rubin. The Yippies were an influential presence at some of the New Left's key later protests, notably the mass demonstrations at the Chicago Democratic Convention in August 1968. The Yippies were renowned for a surreal style of political dissent whose principal weapon was the public (and publicity-driven) mockery of institutional authority of any kind. Because of their countercultural spirit and the carnival ethic that infused their activism, the Yippies were frequently reviled by other New Left activist groups. The Yippies' departure from the radicalism of an earlier generation that led to the Civil Rights Act of 1964 helps illustrate the evolution of the American New Left movement during the 1960s as it subsided into factionalism and confusion over political objectives.

ORIGINS

The politics that Hoffman and Rubin brought to Yippie activism had its roots in the broad coalition of dissent that grew out of the civil rights movement of the early 1960s. Outside the South, the coalition initially grouped itself around Students for a Democratic Society (SDS). Hoffman had worked for a support group of the civil rights organization called the Student Nonviolent Coordinating Committee (SNCC) before the group abandoned its integrationist stance in 1966 and purged its white members. Rubin had enjoyed a high profile in the free speech movement (FSM) founded at the University of California at Berkeley in 1964. However, the presence of poets (such as Allen Ginsberg) and musicians (such as Country Joe and the Fish, Phil Ochs, and the Fugs) in the founding ranks of the Yippies shows how far the group's politics had shifted from the relatively orthodox activist strategies of the first-generation New Left.

In the place of politics, Yippie activism preached the political dimension of culture, stressing the subversive potential inherent in spontaneous acts of individual dissent exercised through the free play of imagination and the integration of an erotic theatricality into daily life. SDS itself may never have adhered to a coherent political agenda, but with Rubin and Hoffman, any attempt at sustaining a structured theoretical program was abandoned altogether. Separating itself abruptly from the early New Left's emphasis on community organizing and directed acts of protest, Yippie politics retained the New Left's pursuit of individual liberation.

Summarized by Ochs as "merely an attack of mental disobedience on an obediently insane society," the "cultural politics" of Yippies took American state capitalism and the Vietnam War as targets, with Rubin and Hoffman staging a range of theatrical street events in which the moral bankruptcy of "the system" was exposed or forced into exposing itself. As early as 1965, Rubin could be found rehearsing the Yippie ethos following his subpoena to appear before the House Un-American Activities Committee (HUAC). Summoned before the committee alongside a group of radicals drawn mainly from the Maoist

Progressive Labor Party (PL), Rubin arrived in full American Revolutionary War costume and stood stoned, blowing giant gum bubbles, while his cowitnesses taunted the committee with Nazi salutes. In 1967 Hoffman was among a group who scattered dollar bills from the balcony of the New York Stock Exchange as newspaper photographers captured the ensuing scramble for banknotes among the stockbrokers on the floor below. In October of the same year, he led a mass "exorcism of demons" during the March on the Pentagon.

THE 1968 DEMOCRATIC CONVENTION

Yippie tactics found their defining moment in Chicago during the Democratic Convention of August 1968. With the war in Vietnam dragging on and frustration mounting among the various different groupings of the New Left, a series of mass demonstrations was planned to coincide with the convention. From the very beginning, the lack of a coordinating voice or coherent agenda threatened to cause the demonstrations to collapse and bring violence to the streets of Chicago. The significant dissenting groups, with the exception of the SDS, agreed on the need for a large-scale protest, but each group had its own agenda. Dave Dellinger of National Mobilization Committee to End the War in Vietnam (MOBE) argued for a combination of routine speeches, marches, and picketing against the war. Representatives of the Progressive Labor Party, the Black Panther Party (BPP), and the New York anarchist group the Motherfuckers planned to attend in some capacity, and young Democrats sought to link a restrained demonstration to the proceedings of the convention itself.

The confusion was compounded by local Chicago residents, who turned out to stage a Poor People's March, and by a late change of heart by SDS to urge its members to attend. Against this backdrop, Chicago's Mayor Richard J. Daley announced that he would turn Chicago into an armed camp and made plans to call in the National Guard and the U.S. Army. It was the perfect scenario for the Yippies' own brand of chaotic theatrical dissent. With Hoffman and Rubin at the helm, the Yippies embarked on a campaign of maximum publicity and misinformation, first announcing that the Yippies would leave town for $200,000 and then spreading the word that the city's water supply was to be contaminated with LSD.

In Chicago's Lincoln Park the Yippies staged a freewheeling carnival called a "Festival of Life" (in opposition to what they called the convention's "Festival of Death"). The high point of the event was the nomination of a 150-pound pig named Pigasus as the Yippies' own presidential candidate (a direct reference to the figure of Pigasus in the International Dada Fair of 1920). The Festival of Life was broken up by violent police action, which escalated over the following two days. Hoffman and Rubin, together with protestors from the SDS, MOBE, and BPP, were arrested.

TRIAL AND AFTERMATH

Eight of the protestors arrested during the Chicago protests, including Hoffman and Rubin, were indicted and stood trial for conspiracy to incite a riot. During the trial, the number of defendants in the case was reduced to seven, who then became known in the press as the Chicago Seven. Hoffman and Rubin attempted to introduce Yippie politics into the judicial process, such as by appearing in court dressed in the robes of a judge.

The Yippies received a large amount of press coverage during and after the trial, and by the time Hoffman and Rubin were jailed in 1970, the pair had become international celebrities. Rubin's book *Do It!* and Hoffman's *Revolution for the Hell of It* subsequently became international best sellers. After appeal, both Hoffman and Rubin were released from prison in 1972.

Although an organization calling itself the Yippies continued to publish protest literature into the 1980s, the group was more or less finished as an activist political movement soon after the trial. The film *Steal this Movie!* (2000) portrays the life of Hoffman, including his conversion to activism and his role in forming the Yippies.

David Holloway

SEE ALSO: *Black Panthers; The Chicago Seven; Civil Rights Movement; Free Speech Movement; Ginsberg, Allen; LSD; New Left; Ochs, Phil; Students for a Democratic Society (SDS); Vietnam.*

BIBLIOGRAPHY

Albert, Judith Clavir, and Stewart Edward Albert. *The Sixties Papers: Documents of a Rebellious Decade.* New York: Praeger, 1984.

Caute, David. *Sixty-Eight: The Year of the Barricades.* London: Paladin, 1988.

Hayden, Tom. *Trial.* London: Jonathan Cape, 1971.

Hoffman, Abbie. *Revolution for the Hell of It.* New York: Dial Press, 1968.

Rubin, Jerry. *Do It!* New York: Simon & Schuster, 1970.

Steigerwald, David. *The Sixties and the End of Modern America.* New York: St. Martin's Press, 1995.

Yo Gabba Gabba!

On August 20, 2007, DJ Lance Rock stepped out onto an all-white set, dressed in what would become his trademark orange suit and fuzzy hat. He set down and opened up his large boom box radio, and *Yo Gabba Gabba!* came to life. Although this intro would remain the same for every episode, this decidedly off-kilter children's television show grew far beyond its modest beginnings, proving successful as a kids' show and a licensing powerhouse. It also developed a cult following among older, especially college-age, audiences. The show's origins are rather unusual, as it was created by Christian Jacobs and Scott Schultz, two Southern California fathers with limited television experience. The pilot episode was first circulated by the creators on the Internet until it caught the attention of Nickelodeon and was added to its lineup on Nick Jr.

In addition to DJ Lance Rock (Lance Robertson), the show features an array of strange, brightly colored creatures, who emerge from the boom box and drive the main plot, usually focused on a simple lesson for preschool children, such as self-confidence, interpersonal relationships, and hygiene. The characters, who are costumed actors, include Toodee, a blue cat-like creature; Foofa, who resembles a pink flower bulb; Plex, the yellow robot; and two monsters: the red cyclops, Muno, and the green, long-armed Brobee. Monstrous though these characters might be in form, they are presented as purely nonthreatening, as close friends to each other and to the audience.

The cast of characters has a decidedly retro quality to it, reminiscent of earlier shows such as *The Banana Splits Adventure*

Hour (1968–1970) and *New Zoo Revue* (1972–1977). In fact, the aesthetic of *Yo Gabba Gabba!* as a whole is strongly influenced by artifacts of past children's entertainment, likely shaped by what the creators would have been exposed to as children. Animated sequences often look as if they could have been produced in the 1970s or 1980s, and the computer graphics employed are deliberately primitive, hearkening back to the era of 8-bit video games.

The show also features many guest stars, and these have largely served to extend the popularity beyond its preschool base. Both creators had a background in music—Jacobs's band the Aquabats achieved some degree of success in alternative rock circles—so it is not surprising that music is a major component of the show. *Yo Gabba Gabba!* has incorporated performances by the Shins, My Chemical Romance, the Killers, Weezer, and others. Additionally, rapper Biz Markie makes regular appearances in a segment called "Biz's Beat of the Day," and Devo's Mark Mothersbaugh appears often, usually in a segment called "Mark's Magic Pictures." Like *Sesame Street*, *Yo Gabba Gabba!* brings in a number of other celebrities—Elijah Wood, Jack Black, and Tony Hawk all made appearances in the first season.

The extensive licensing of the show has resulted in not only DVD releases but also in books, toys, apparel, and other items. Notably, CDs featuring songs performed by both the cast and musical guests have been quite successful. A live *Yo Gabba Gabba!* show has also toured extensively. As with the TV program itself, these items and performances have found an eager audience among children as well as parents and college-age consumers.

Marc Oxoby

SEE ALSO: Barney and Friends*;* Dora the Explorer*;* Sesame Street*; Television; Toys.*

BIBLIOGRAPHY

Friedman, Emily. "Nickelodeon Cartoon Draws Unusual Fans." ABC News, May 7, 2008. Accessed May 21, 2012. Available from http://abcnews.go.com/Entertainment/Story?id=4799273

Garofoli, Joe. "Preschooler TV Goes Hip with 'Yo Gabba Gabba.'" *San Francisco Chronicle*, August 17, 2007. Accessed May 21, 2012. Available from http://www.sfgate.com/cgi-bin/article.cgi?f=/c/a/2007/08/17/DDL2RJTGF.DTL

Yo Gabba Gabba! Accessed May 21, 2012. Available from http://yogabbagabba.com

Yoakam, Dwight *(1956–)*

In 1986 Dwight Yoakam helped revitalize country music with his twangy debut album *Guitars, Cadillacs, Etc., Etc.* Recorded in Los Angeles, the album mixed classic country covers with Yoakam's own compositions. Born in Kentucky, Yoakam grew up in Ohio, where he attended college before moving to Southern California in the late 1970s. There he met his guitarist and producer Pete Anderson and developed an electric honky-tonk style derived from the early recordings of the country legend Buck Owens. Unable to break into Nashville, Tennessee's music scene, Yoakam found a niche playing to rock audiences in California. He recorded an extended play (EP) that caught the attention of record executives and launched his career.

By the early 1990s, he was creating his own unconventional country style and scoring hits with such songs as "A Thousand Miles from Nowhere." In the first decade of the 2000s he released *Population Me* (2003) and the self-produced *Blame the Vain* (2005). During the late 1990s and the next decade, he also demonstrated his acting talent in such films as *Sling Blade* (1996), *The Newton Boys* (1998), *Panic Room* (2002), *Wedding Crashers* (2005), and *Four Christmases* (2008).

Anna Hunt Graves

SEE ALSO: *Country Music; Owens, Buck; Rock and Roll.*

BIBLIOGRAPHY

Bego, Mark. *Country Hunks.* Chicago: Contemporary Books, 1994.

Kingsbury, Paul; Alan Axelrod; and Susan Costello, eds. *Country: The Music and the Musicians from the Beginnings to the '90s.* New York: Abbeville Press, 1994.

McCall, Michael; Dave Hoekstra; and Janet Williams. *Country Music Stars: The Legends and the New Breed.* Lincolnwood, IL: Publications International, 1992.

McLeese, Don. *Dwight Yoakam: A Thousand Miles from Nowhere.* American Music Series. Austin: University of Texas Press, 2012.

Yoga

Developed as an ancient Hindu spiritual discipline, the practice of yoga became prevalent in the late twentieth century in Western society. With celebrities such as Madonna and Jennifer Aniston touting its benefits, yoga has become trendy in America, especially among people looking for new ways to exercise and lose weight. Physicians and therapists recognize yoga as a sound means of maintaining one's physical and mental health.

The etymology of the word *yoga* can be traced to its Sanskrit origins. A literal translation of the word means "yoke," but the root *yuj* means to "join or unite," as in the body and the mind. Recognized as a mental, spiritual, and physical discipline, yoga sharpens the mind and strengthens the body. Various Eastern religions, such as Hinduism, Jainism, and Buddhism, incorporate aspects of yoga into their beliefs.

The Western world became marginally aware of yoga in 1946 when guru Paramahansa Yogananda published his *Autobiography of a Yogi*. The book sparked what would eventually become a cultural phenomenon in the West. Yoga was associated with the counterculture movement of the 1960s, then with the health consciousness of the 1980s. By this time yoga was seen less as a spiritual practice and more as an exercise routine, especially after Jane Fonda released a yoga workout video in 1993.

By the first decade of the 2000s millions of people in the United States alone were regular yoga practitioners. Many were using the *asanas* (poses) for yoga's physical benefits, such as toned muscles and greater flexibility. Still others focused on the spiritual aspects yoga offers with its emphasis on deep breathing and meditation. Health clubs and gyms began offering weekly classes in a variety of styles, including Bikram, vinyasa, and hatha, to accommodate this demand. A glut of yoga studios appeared across the country, providing retreats, study groups on the six branches of yoga, private lessons with gurus, and seminars. With the publication of Elizabeth Gilbert's successful memoir *Eat, Pray, Love* in 2006, yoga retreats became even more popular.

The prevalence of yoga in mainstream contemporary America met with some backlash from the Christian right. The Catholic Church took a public stance on yoga, stating that the practice was in conflict with Christian beliefs. Regardless, it has spawned a multibillion-dollar industry, and the manufacture of yoga-specific products such as mats, clothing, bags, and DVDs attests to the shift from spiritualism toward exercise.

An ancient practice and religious belief that promotes balance, calmness, and inner harmony, yoga became standard practice for many twenty-first-century exercise enthusiasts. As stars such as Lady Gaga, Sting, and Christy Turlington continued to advertise its benefits, yoga studios and classes became ubiquitous. The Mayo Clinic has stated, "Yoga can be an effective method to reduce stress and anxiety," and more doctors and health care professionals are recommending it to their patients. Dr. Richard Usatine, associate dean of medical education at Florida State University, prescribes specific yoga poses along with medication to treat conditions as diverse as asthma, depression, and migraines. Due to endorsements by celebrities and the medical community, yoga's popularity shows no sign of waning.

Jill Clever

SEE ALSO: *Fonda, Jane; Hippies; Lady Gaga; Madonna.*

BIBLIOGRAPHY

Broad, William J. *The Science of Yoga: The Risks and the Rewards.* New York: Simon & Schuster, 2012.

De Michelis, Elizabeth. *A History of Modern Yoga: Patãjali and Western Esotericism.* New York: Continuum, 2005.

Gray, Alexandra. *The Yoga Teacher.* New York: Grove Press, 2008.

McCall, Timothy. *Yoga as Medicine: The Yogic Prescription for Health and Healing.* New York: Bantam Books, 2007.

Schnabele, Verena. "Yoga in Modern Society." *International Journal of Yoga* 4 (2011): 102.

Singleton, Mark, and Jean Byrne, eds. *Yoga in the Modern World: Contemporary Perspectives.* New York: Routledge, 2008.

Young, Cy *(1867–1955)*

"Y is for Young/The magnificent Cy/People batted against him/But I never knew why." So wrote Ogden Nash about the man who won more Major League Baseball games than anyone in history—Denton True "Cy" Young. Young's 511 victories are nearly 100 more than the total of the nearest challenger (417, Walter Johnson). And though baseball historians have insisted that Johnson, Lefty Grove, and Roger Clemens were more skillful pitchers, they are confident that Young's record for wins, as well as his lifetime marks of 7,356 innings pitched and 749 complete games, will never be broken.

Young was born in Gilmore, Ohio, on March 29, 1867. He began his organized baseball career in nearby Canton, where he earned his nickname. Some baseball historians claim the moniker Cy is short for cyclone, referring to his fastball, while others say that Cy, like Rube, was a common nickname of the age for a naive, small-town ballplayer. Young began his major-league career in 1890 for the Cleveland Spiders of the National League, compiling an unimpressive 9–7 record as a rookie. Two seasons later, however, he went 36–12 for the Spiders. Young was so dominant that before the 1893 season, the major leagues moved back the pitcher's mound—from 50 feet from home plate to its current distance of 60 feet, 6 inches—to give batters a fighting chance. Yet despite those 10 extra feet, Young won thirty-four games in 1893 and thirty-five games in 1895.

After the 1898 season, Young was traded to the St. Louis Cardinals, for whom he won forty-five games over two seasons. In 1901, now in his mid-thirties, he jumped to the Boston Somersets (later the Red Sox) of the newly formed American League. He proceeded to win 193 games for Boston over the next eight years. In 1903 Young won twenty-eight games in leading Boston into the first modern World Series, where he notched two victories as his team upset Honus Wagner's Pittsburgh Pirates.

Young was the first major-league pitcher to throw three no-hitters during his career, a feat later matched by Bob Feller and surpassed by Sandy Koufax and Nolan Ryan. In May 1904 against the Philadelphia Athletics, Young pitched the twentieth century's first perfect game, meaning he didn't allow a single batter to reach base.

In 1909 Young was traded to the American League's Cleveland Naps (now the Indians), for whom he won his 500th

Cy Young. *Pitcher Cy Young won a record 511 Major League Baseball games.* © BETTMANN/CORBIS.

game in 1910. However, his efficiency was declining with the onset of age and an expanding waistline. Young admitted that he was unable to field bunts as he grew heavier, and batters took advantage of his lack of mobility. He ended his career in 1911 with the Boston Braves of the National League. In his final career start in September of that season, he lost 1–0 to Grover Cleveland Alexander, the rookie sensation for the Philadelphia Phillies who would go on to win 373 games in his lifetime.

Young returned to farming in Ohio and became a regular at major-league old-timer's games. When the National Baseball Hall of Fame elected its first induction class in 1936, Young narrowly missed out. (Voters had to select from a pool of nineteenth-century players and a pool of twentieth-century players, and Young's career spanned both eras.) Young was elected in 1937, and he attended the hall's inaugural induction ceremony in 1939 in Cooperstown, New York, where he posed for photographs with fellow greats Wagner, Babe Ruth, and Connie Mack. Young died on November 4, 1955, in Newcomerstown, Ohio, at the age of eighty-eight. In his honor the following year, Major League Baseball named its annual awards for the top pitchers, one American League and one National League, the Cy Young Award.

Andrew Milner

SEE ALSO: *Baseball; Boston Red Sox; Cooperstown, New York; Koufax, Sandy; Major League Baseball; Ruth, Babe; Ryan, Nolan; Wagner, Honus; World Series.*

BIBLIOGRAPHY

Browning, Reed. *Cy Young.* Amherst: University of Massachusetts Press, 2003.

James, Bill. *The Bill James Historical Baseball Abstract.* New York: Villard, 1986.

James, Bill. *Whatever Happened to the Hall of Fame? Baseball, Cooperstown and the Politics of Glory.* New York: Fireside, 1995.

Okrent, Daniel; Harris Lewine; and David Nemec. *The Ultimate Baseball Book.* Boston: Houghton Mifflin, 2000.

Thorn, John, and Pete Palmer, eds. *Total Baseball.* New York: Total Sports, 1999.

Young, Loretta *(1913–2000)*

In a career that lasted from the silent films to the 1980s, Loretta Young embodied the image of the eternal lady. She appeared as a child extra in early films before she received her first major film role in *Laugh Clown Laugh* (1928). Thereafter, she was invariably cast in roles as a young innocent. After winning an Academy Award for the film *The Farmer's Daughter* (1947), Young turned to television. Her anthology series, *The Loretta Young Show* (1953–1961), won her several Emmy Awards, although it was most notable for the fabulous costumes she wore. After Young's show went off the air, she continued to act on rare occasions, most notably in the television movie *Christmas Eve* (1986). Young died in 2000 at the age of eighty-seven.

Jill A. Gregg

SEE ALSO: *Academy Awards; Emmy Awards; Gable, Clark; Made-for-Television Movies; Silent Movies; Television.*

BIBLIOGRAPHY

Lewis, Judy. *Uncommon Knowledge.* New York: Simon & Schuster, 1994.

Morella, Joe. *Loretta Young: An Extraordinary Life.* New York: Delacorte Press, 1986.

Young, Neil *(1945–)*

Neil Young is a Canadian singer, guitarist, and songwriter who had modest commercial success in the late 1970s. His heavy rocking music had a profound impact on young musicians, who started a new movement called grunge rock in the 1990s, leading many to dub him the "godfather of grunge." From his beginnings in the mid-1960s rock band Buffalo Springfield to his intermittent stints as a 1970s acoustic singer-songwriter and hard rocker and on through his 1990s incarnation as grunge's guru, Young has spent his career ducking audience expectations. His idiosyncratic and sometimes perverse approach to music making has allowed him to be perhaps the only member of his

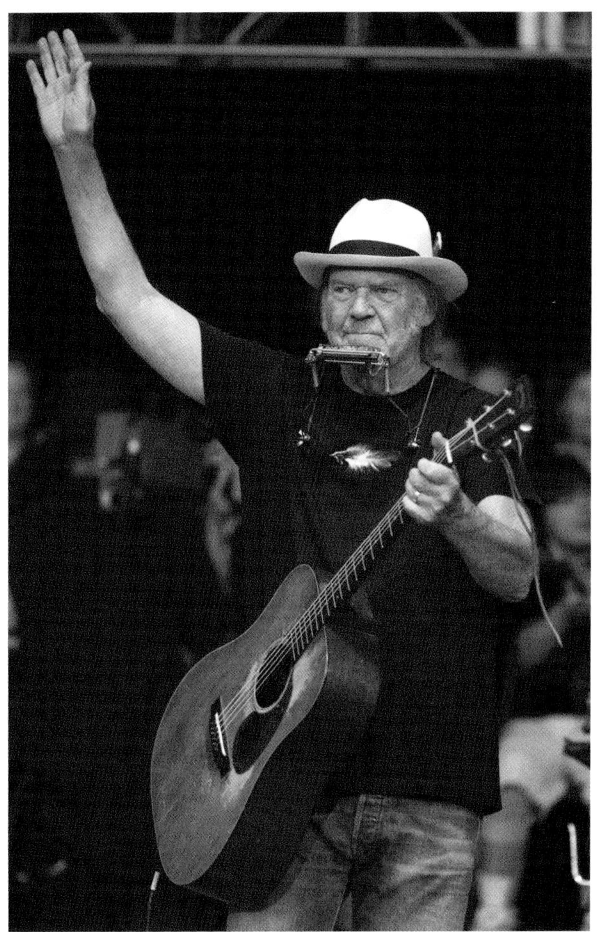

Neil Young. *Neil Young performs in Mountain View, California, in 2011.* STEVE JENNINGS/CONTRIBUTOR/WIREIMAGE/GETTY IMAGES.

generation to maintain critical respect years after most of his peers began treading water artistically.

On his varied and numerous albums Young wears many hats, including those of folk rocker, acoustic singer-songwriter, rockabilly artist, hard rocker, punk rocker, techno-dance artist, and blues guitarist. His body of work, which is matched in its depth and breadth only by Bob Dylan, is characterized by a sense of restlessness and experimentalism.

Buffalo Springfield disbanded in 1968. The following year Young released two solo albums that would set a pattern for the rest of his career. His self-titled debut album features country and folk-styled songs, utilizing acoustic guitars buffeted by lush string sections and tasteful female backing vocals. *Everybody Knows This Is Nowhere*, released a few months later, is a collaboration with garage band Crazy Horse, a group Young continued to record with throughout his career. This album shows off Young's hard-rocking, noisy side.

Most of Young's 1970s albums follow this pattern, with *Harvest* (1972) and *Comes a Time* (1978) filling his acoustic singer-songwriter shoes and *Tonight's the Night* (1975) and *Zuma* (1975) satisfying his craving for molten-hot guitar distortion. Young's artistic and commercial success reached its zenith with *Rust Never Sleeps* (1979), which incorporates both musical tendencies into one album.

During the 1980s Young's career faltered as he released a series of wildly varying albums that incorporated rockabilly, garage rock, electronic dance, folk, country, and blues. His records were not selling, and his new label, Geffen, sued him for not producing a consistent style. From 1983 to 1988 Young lost much of his audience, but with the release of *Freedom* in 1989 he began to regain the critical and commercial clout that had dissipated in the 1980s.

Another key to Young's career rejuvenation was the rise of alternative guitar rock during the late 1980s and early 1990s. One marker that signaled Young's reincarnation as the godfather of grunge was the release of *The Bridge* in 1989. This compilation album features covers of Young's songs by the likes of Soul Asylum, Flaming Lips, the Pixies, Sonic Youth, and Dinosaur Jr., all of whom became minor or major mainstream successes. By the early 1990s, groups such as Nirvana and Pearl Jam (who later played with Young) named Young as a main influence. Young cultivated this fandom by playing the most rocking, noisy music of his career and by taking guitar experimentalists Sonic Youth and grunge kings Pearl Jam on the road with him.

In 1994 Young's influence over young grunge musicians took a sad turn when Kurt Cobain, the lead singer and guitarist of Nirvana, committed suicide and left behind a note referencing a well-known Young lyric, stating, "it's better to burn out than to fade away," a line from the song "Hey Hey, My My (Into the Black)." Young reacted to this by recording *Sleeps with Angels* (1994), a mournful, low-key album filled with meditations on death and depression that served as Young's eulogy for Cobain. Throughout the rest of the 1990s, Young continued to release a series of solid but stylistically similar live and studio albums, primarily with his longtime band Crazy Horse.

Early in the first decade of the 2000s, Young built upon his renewed popularity by releasing a series of albums and concert films. In 2001 he recorded the single "Let's Roll" in tribute to the victims of the terrorist attacks on the United States on September 11, 2001, and covered songwriter and Beatle John Lennon's "Imagine" at the benefit concert America: A Tribute to Heroes. In 2005 Young had a major health scare when he was diagnosed with a brain aneurysm. He was successfully treated with surgery. Months later he released *Prairie Wind* (2005).

In 2006 Young released *Living with War*, exhibiting his activist sensibilities. Sparked by the 2003 U.S. invasion of Iraq, the album focuses on the human costs of war and exemplifies Young's emotional response to U.S. president George W. Bush's policies. Crosby, Stills, Nash & Young (a side project Young had first joined in 1969) reunited that year for the Freedom of Speech Tour '06, featuring Young's protest songs. Young followed the activist trend, releasing more ecologically centered material and even designing a hybrid car, the Lincvolt.

In 2010 Young performed with other artists in the Hope for Haiti Now telethon to raise money for the victims of the January 2010 Haiti earthquake. In addition to his philanthropic and commercial performances, Young released volumes of his Archive series and was featured in three documentary films directed by Jonathan Demme. The godfather of grunge remains a stalwart of the music world, winning multiple awards, including the 2011 Juno Artist of the Year award and a Grammy Award for Best Rock Song for "Angry World" in 2011.

Kembrew McLeod

SEE ALSO: *Alternative Rock; The Beatles; Buffalo Springfield; Crosby, Stills, and Nash; Dylan, Bob; Grammy Awards; Grunge; Hybrid Cars; Lennon, John; Nirvana; Pearl Jam; Rock and Roll.*

BIBLIOGRAPHY

Durchholz, Daniel, and Gary Graff. *Neil Young: Long May You Run: The Illustrated History*. Minneapolis, MN: Voyageur Press, 2010.

Heatley, Michael, and Neil Young. *Neil Young: In His Own Words*. New York: Omnibus Press, 1997.

McDonough, Jimmy. *Shakey: Neil Young's Biography*. New York: Random House, 2002.

Williams, Paul. *Neil Young: Love to Burn; Thirty Years of Speaking Out, 1966–1996*. New York: Omnibus, 1997.

Young, Robert *(1907–1998)*

Robert Young is best remembered for two successful television shows, *Father Knows Best* (1954–1960) and *Marcus Welby, M.D.* (1969–1976), that earned him a total of three Emmy awards. He began his career in motion pictures in the 1930s and 1940s, invariably playing the amiable, dependable guy who loses the girl. Young made his film debut opposite Helen Hayes in *The Sin of Madelon Claudet* (1931), and he appeared in classics such as *Secret Agent* (1936) and *The Enchanted Cottage* (1945) before turning to television.

In 1933 Young married Betty Henderson. They had four daughters and remained married until her death in 1994. As for his TV persona, he made an indelible impression on American culture as everyone's favorite father figure.

Jill A. Gregg

SEE ALSO: *Emmy Awards;* Father Knows Best*;* Marcus Welby, M.D.*; Television.*

BIBLIOGRAPHY

Leibman, Nina Clare. *Living Room Lectures: The Fifties Family in Film and Television.* Austin: University of Texas Press, 1995.

Parish, James Robert, and Ronald L. Bowers. *The MGM Stock Company: The Golden Era.* New Rochelle, NY: Arlington House, 1973.

Parish, James Robert, and Gregory W. Mank. *The Hollywood Reliables.* Westport, CT: Arlington House, 1980.

The Young and the Restless

When *The Young and the Restless* premiered on March 26, 1973, it revolutionized the entire concept of the soap opera. Historically, the format reflected its roots in radio, and despite its jump to television, it was still an aural medium with its primary emphasis on dialogue and story content. *The Young and the Restless*, however, placed a premium on shadowy, sensuous lighting, intriguing camera angles, and production values that provided a lavish romanticism that appealed to female viewers and, by eroticizing the genre, changed forever the way that "soaps" were photographed.

However, the series did not rely on style alone. Building from the typical soap opera structure of two intertwining families—the wealthy Brooks family, who owned the city newspaper, and the not-so-rich Foster family—the show featured the inevitable star-crossed romance. The show also ventured into new areas, providing the first soap opera treatment of an extended rape sequence and the aftermath of a trial. It also dealt with such issues as euthanasia, drugs, obesity, eating disorders, mental illness, and problems of the handicapped. In the 1980s the show once again revolutionized the genre by shifting its focus away from its original core families to an entirely new set of younger characters. During the 1990s it continued to introduce new characters while maintaining the consistency of its vision and of its story lines, a remarkable feat for the genre, allowing it to keep pace with its traditional competitors and the new programs that debuted during the decade.

Throughout its history, *The Young and the Restless* has won more than 100 Daytime Emmy Awards, including seven for Outstanding Drama. Even in the early twenty-first century, when soaps that had been on the air since the days of radio were being canceled, *The Young and the Restless* managed to survive. It was contracted to be on the air through at least 2013.

Sandra Garcia-Myers

SEE ALSO: *Emmy Awards; Radio; Radio Drama; Soap Operas; Television.*

BIBLIOGRAPHY

Brunsdon, Charlotte. *The Feminist, the Housewife, and the Soap Opera.* New York: Clarendon Press, 2000.

Ford, Sam; Abigail De Kosnik; and C. Lee Harrington, eds. *The Survival of Soap Opera: Transformations for a New Media Era.* Jackson: University Press of Mississippi, 2011.

LaGuardia, Robert. *Soap World.* New York: Arbor House, 1983.

Schemering, Christopher. *The Soap Opera Encyclopedia.* New York: Ballantine Books, 1985.

Spence, Louise. *Watching Daytime Soap Operas: The Power of Pleasure.* Middletown, CT: Wesleyan University Press, 2005.

Youngman, Henny *(1906–1998)*

Regardless of the time devoted to working on an act and the energy put into a stage performance, a comic's material is the key to success or failure—a truism perhaps no comedian understood better than the "King of the One-Liners," Henny Youngman. For more than seventy years he entertained audiences as the quintessential Catskills comedian. His rapid-fire delivery, in which he could tell a half dozen wisecracks in sixty seconds, was filled with timeless bits that drew as many groans as laughs. Youngman's theory of comedy was to keep his jokes simple and compact. Beginning in the mid-1920s and extending into the 1990s, he repeated countless gags that could be immediately understood by everyone. Among his most famous lines are such comic gems as: "I just got back from a pleasure

Henny Youngman. *Henny Youngman was known as the "King of the One-Liners" throughout a career that spanned seventy years.* HULTON ARCHIVE/STRINGER/ARCHIVE PHOTOS/GETTY IMAGES.

trip. I drove my mother-in-law to the airport"; "The food on the plane was fit for a king. Here, King!"; and "A man goes to a psychiatrist, 'Nobody listens to me!' The doctor says, 'Next!'" In 1991 Youngman commented on his act's enduring popularity when he wrote, "Fads come and go in comedy. But the one-liner always remains sacred. People laughed at these jokes when I told them at Legs Diamond's Hotsy Totsy Club sixty years ago—and they're still laughing at these same one-liners at joints I play today."

Born on March 16, 1906, in England to Russian Jewish immigrants who later settled in New York, Henry Youngman harbored dreams of entering show business from an early age. His first taste of success came as a bandleader for a quartet known as the Swanee Syncopaters. By the mid-1920s the group became a regular presence in the Borscht Belt, an area in the Catskill Mountains filled with private summer resorts that catered to a predominantly Jewish clientele. At the Swan Lake Inn Youngman played with his musical group, while between sets he acted as the hotel's "tummler"—a job that consisted of walking around the resort to make sure all the guests were having a good time. The tummler would often schmooze the male guests, dance with any unattached female patrons, and even serve as an unofficial matchmaker. To keep the guests amused, a tummler had to have many jokes for practically any situation at his fingertips. Youngman recalled his days in the Catskills and their influence on his comedic style when he stated, "I'm quite sure my love of one-liners came from this mountain laboratory. You had to be able to rat-a-tat-tat them out, on all subjects, to all kinds of people, every hour, day or night."

Youngman quit the Swanee Syncopaters for the life of a stand-up comedian when a nightclub owner asked him to fill in for an act that failed to show. His comedy routine, honed from his days as a tummler, was a great hit. He soon came to the attention of a rising comedy headliner named Milton Berle (1908–2002), who was impressed with Youngman's delivery and helped him get stand-up gigs at small clubs and bar mitzvahs. By the mid-1930s the former tummler had become the featured comedian on radio's *Kate Smith Show*. For two years he had a regular six-minute spot during which he told his one-liners and played the violin. It was during this period that Youngman acquired his signature joke: When his wife, Sadie, arrived at the show with several friends, the nervous comedian wanted her to sit in the audience so he could prepare. He grabbed an usher and told him, "Take my wife, please." The comic incorporated the humorous ad-lib into his act and continued to use the line even after his wife died in 1987.

Youngman spent the greatest portion of his career touring throughout the world with his unvarying act. He was proud to say he had performed before both Queen Elizabeth II (1926–) and the gangster Dutch Schultz (1902–1935). No matter the audience or setting, he would take to the stage with his prop violin and still-humorous lines. Jokes such as "My doctor told me I was fat. I said I wanted a second opinion. He said, 'Okay, you're ugly, too'" were repeated for years to audiences long familiar with Youngman's routine. He also frequently appeared on television talk and variety shows into his eighties. However, his attempts to become a regular TV performer were less successful. The summer of 1955 saw the failure of *The Henny and Rocky Show*, which paired him with former middleweight boxing champion Rocky Graziano (1919–1990). In 1990 he made a brief appearance as the emcee at the Copacabana in the mobster epic *Goodfellas* by Martin Scorsese (1942–). Youngman died in New York on February 24, 1998.

Audiences laughed at Youngman's nearly endless supply of one-liners because they were instantly funny and recognizable to almost everyone. He did not offer long comic monologues, controversial humor, or provocative social satire but rather provided funny gags for anyone who has ever had to deal with life's more mundane occurrences, such as bad drivers, unhelpful doctors, drunken husbands, and mothers-in-law. Furthermore, his longevity allowed younger audiences to experience a still-vital performer with roots in vaudeville. He proved that even the most well-worn jokes, such as "One fellow comes up to me and says he hasn't eaten in three days. I say, 'Force yourself!'" are still funny.

Charles Coletta

SEE ALSO: *Borscht Belt;* GoodFellas; *Scorsese, Martin; Stand-Up Comedy; Vaudeville.*

BIBLIOGRAPHY

Youngman, Henny. *Take This Book, Please*. New York: Gramercy Publishing, 1984.

Youngman, Henny, and Neal Karlen. *Take My Life, Please!* New York: William Morrow, 1991.

Your Hit Parade

A landmark musical variety series on both radio (1935–1953) and television (1950–1959, 1974), *Your Hit Parade* was one of the first and most important manifestations of the musical countdown or survey. Unlike later variations of this format, on *Your Hit Parade* the songs were performed live by a regular cast of singers, some of them famous (such as Frank Sinatra, Doris Day, and Dinah Shore). The television version of *Your Hit Parade* has been cited, somewhat implausibly, as a forerunner of music video and MTV.

RADIO YEARS

The radio series *Lucky Strike Hit Parade* debuted on the NBC radio network on April 20, 1935. During the next two years both NBC and CBS carried the program from time to time, until in 1937 it found its "home" in the Saturday evening schedule on CBS, where it remained until 1947, when it moved back to NBC. The TV version premiered in 1950 as a simulcast of the radio series. This arrangement lasted until 1953, at which point the radio series was canceled. *Your Hit Parade* continued on NBC until 1958, then moved back to CBS and was canceled in 1959. A revival on CBS in 1974 lasted less than a year and is notable mainly for employing future *Love Connection* host Chuck Woolery as a singer.

The show's cast of singers and orchestra leaders changed frequently, especially during its radio years. The TV cast was more stable and included singers Dorothy Collins, Snooky Lanson, Gisele MacKenzie, and Russell Arms; bandleader (and future electronic music pioneer) Raymond Scott; and announcer Andre Baruch. The most memorable feature of the series is probably its opening, which consists of the sound of a tobacco auctioneer; in the television version there are also pictures of animated dancing cigarettes. As Philip Eberly points out in *Music in the Air*, *Your Hit Parade* was one of a multitude of musical programs sponsored by tobacco companies during the golden age of American radio.

The idea behind *Your Hit Parade* was simple yet novel for the 1930s. Each week the program's house orchestra and featured singers performed the week's most popular songs. The number of songs in the "hit parade" varied from seven to fifteen. The American Tobacco Company owned and sponsored the program, and the company's "dictatorial" president, George Washington Hill, "personally controlled every facet of the program," according to Arnold Shaw's account in *Let's Dance*. The ranking of songs was determined by a secret methodology administered by the company's advertising agency—at first, Lord and Thomas; later, Batten, Barton, Durstine & Osborne. The hit parade placed songs in competition with each other, and the unveiling of each week's number one song became an eagerly awaited event.

DECIDING WHAT IS POPULAR

The TV program's opening announcement asserted that the hit parade was an "accurate, authentic tabulation of America's taste in popular music," based on sheet-music sales, record sales, broadcast airplay, and coin-machine play. The most important factor, at least until the mid-1950s, was radio airplay—and, as Shaw notes, *Your Hit Parade* itself helped to establish radio as the major venue for American popular music.

Your Hit Parade remained rooted in Tin Pan Alley—the slang term for the music publishing district in 1890s Manhattan and the name that eventually came to symbolize the (white) mainstream in American popular music. Tin Pan Alley stood for the primacy of songs (as opposed to records) and for a highly conventionalized song structure and performance style (usually a verse-chorus structure, romantic or novelty lyrics, smooth singing or "crooning," and orchestration). The prevalence of songs over records allowed *Your Hit Parade* to showcase its own performers along with the week's hits. A song would often remain on the survey for several weeks, so, for variety's sake, the song would be handed off from one singer to another from week to week.

***Frank Sinatra at Rehearsal for* Your Hit Parade.** *Frank Sinatra rehearses for his appearance on* Your Hit Parade. © BETTMANN/CORBIS.

The advent of the television series prompted an additional attempt at variety—each week the song would receive a new "visualization." Rather than delivering a straight performance into the camera, singers were placed in a fictional and dramatic context ostensibly inspired by the title or lyrics of the song. For example, in a 1952 episode Lanson portrayed a customer singing "Slow Poke" to the back of a female customer at a diner. In this case, as in most others, the visualization had only a tenuous and forced connection with the text of the song—a "slow poke" sandwich appeared on the diner's menu, and the female customer kept Lanson waiting for a seat while he sang lyrics that complained about "you" (presumably his lover) keeping him waiting. As unremarkable as the song itself was, the visualization managed to trivialize it by converting it from a love song into an imaginary monologue about Lanson's lunch.

Contrary to Michael Shore's contention in *The Rolling Stone Book of Rock Video* that "*Your Hit Parade* was a pathfinder in the conceptualization of music video," the program in fact was a clumsy attempt to import the dramatic premise and visual splendor of musical films into the more frantic production context of live TV. Most music videos, even if they have a dramatic premise, use a prerecorded soundtrack and show the singer lip-synching directly into the camera. Thus, the typical music video is quite different from the standard visualization on *Your Hit Parade*. This is one reason why the TV series, when viewed today, seems unique and old-fashioned.

The reason for the show's demise, however, has as much to do with sound as with image. As the 1950s progressed, Tin Pan Alley gradually lost ground to rock and roll, and records became the predominant medium in the music industry. Radio lost much of its audience to television and soon discovered the Top 40 format as one of the best ways to stay in business. Top 40, of course, is much like a hit parade but ranks recordings (as performed by a specific singer) rather than songs (as performed by anybody). Lanson performed "Heartbreak Hotel" on *Your Hit Parade* in 1956, but the song was so definitively associated with Elvis Presley that the version by crooner Lanson lacked credibility. This sort of incongruity became more and more common on *Your Hit Parade* as the decade wore on, and the program's contrived and corny "visualizations" only underscored the series' irrelevance.

Despite belated attempts to make the program more contemporary, *Your Hit Parade* could not survive the ascendance of rock and roll and the triumph, in both radio and TV, of recording over live performance. The look of the future in musical TV programs was *American Bandstand*, which rose just as *Your Hit Parade* was falling, and which remained dominant in its field until MTV supplanted it in the 1980s.

Gary Burns

SEE ALSO: American Bandstand*; Cigarettes; MTV; Pop Music; Radio; Top 40.*

BIBLIOGRAPHY

Brooks, Tim, and Earle Marsh. *The Complete Directory to Prime Time Network and Cable TV Shows, 1946–Present*, 6th ed. New York: Ballantine Books, 1996.

Burns, Gary. "Visualising 1950s Hits on *Your Hit Parade*." *Popular Music* 17, no. 2 (1998): 139–152.

Eberly, Philip K. *Music in the Air: America's Changing Tastes in Popular Music, 1920–1980.* New York: Hastings House, 1982.

Elrod, Bruce C. *Your Hit Parade.* Columbia, SC: Colonial Printing, 1977.

Sanjek, Russell. *American Popular Music and Its Business, the First Four Hundred Years: Volume III, from 1900 to 1984.* New York: Oxford University Press, 1988.

Shaw, Arnold. *The Rockin' '50s: The Decade That Transformed the Pop Music Scene.* New York: Hawthorn Books, 1974.

Shaw, Arnold, and Bill Willard. *Let's Dance: Popular Music in the 1930s.* New York: Oxford University Press, 1998.

Shore, Michael. *The Rolling Stone Book of Rock Video.* New York: Quill, 1984.

Super, John C., ed. *Fifties in America.* Pasadena, CA: Salem Press, 2005.

Your Show of Shows

A 1950s variety program, *Your Show of Shows* (1950–1954) distinguished itself with its artful satire and parody performed by an ensemble led by Sid Caesar. Caesar was blessed with a stable of young writers that included, at one time or another, Neil Simon, Woody Allen, Mel Brooks, Carl Reiner, and Larry Gelbart.

The program took advantage of television's ability to be topical. It was live television at its best, and Caesar and his partner, Imogene Coca, could parody recent films—including foreign films—at will. However, because of the dangers of McCarthyism, they could not parody politics. There were no retakes in live television, so the performers' ability to ad lib was essential to the show's success and soon became a secret to its popularity.

Caesar was born in Yonkers, New York, in 1922. He entered show business as a Juilliard-trained saxophonist and enjoyed success in a number of famous big bands. During his army service, Max Liebman, who would later become his producer on *Your Show of Shows*, noticed Caesar's ability to make his fellow band members laugh. He decided to feature Caesar as a comedian in future productions. In 1949, after appearing in nightclubs and on Broadway, Caesar began his television career in *Admiral Broadway Revue*, the forerunner of *Your Show of Shows*.

The program took six days to put on, from writing to performing. In an interview for the *Saturday Evening Post*, Caesar noted the difference between *Your Show of Shows* and television in the late twentieth century: "I didn't come in and have a script handed to me. Never happened. The show took six long days to write, and I was there on Monday morning, working with the writers, putting in the blank sheet of paper. See, the show had to be written by Wednesday. Thursday we put it up on its feet. Friday we went over it with the technicians and Saturday was the show—live."

Your Show of Shows ran for ninety minutes and was number one for four years. NBC soon began plans for two programs that would be highly rated, and *Caesar's Hour* and *The Imogene Coca Show* were born. *Caesar's Hour* was highly rated for a time, but Caesar's descent into alcoholism and pill-taking finally took its toll. Its fourth season was its last.

Although Caesar eventually had a number of female partners on his various shows, Coca is the one best remembered by fans. She began acting at the age of eleven and had a long career before joining Caesar on *Your Show of Shows*. Leonard Sillman drafted Coca and Henry Fonda into doing comedy bits for scene changes for his Broadway production, *New Faces*. Prior to that Coca had been noted for her singing, dancing, and acting. Eventually, she so impressed the critics that she became hailed as the next great comedienne. In 1949 she joined Caesar in the *Admiral Broadway Revue*. Coca left to do her own television program after the 1954 season. The program, however, failed, and so did her reunion with Caesar in 1958.

Your Show of Shows paved the way for *Saturday Night Live* and other similar live revues such as Second City. It has remained

Your Show of Shows. *Sid Caesar and Imogene Coca appear in costume for a skit on their popular 1950s comedy/variety television series* Your Show of Shows. NBC TELEVISION/HANDOUT/HULTON ARCHIVE/GETTY IMAGES.

popular on PBS and in video sales. The movie *10 from* Your Show of Shows, featuring ten of its classic skits, also did well commercially and is still available on video.

Frank A. Salamone

SEE ALSO: *Allen, Woody; Big Bands; Broadway; Brooks, Mel; Coca, Imogene; Fonda, Henry; Live Television; McCarthyism; Public Television (PBS); Reiner, Carl; The* Saturday Evening Post; Saturday Night Live; *Second City; Simon, Neil.*

BIBLIOGRAPHY

Gold, Todd. "Sid Caesar's New Grasp on Life." *Saturday Evening Post,* January 1986, 64–66.

Oder, Norman. "Caesar's Writers: A Reunion of Writers from 'Your Show of Shows' and 'Caesar's Hour'?" *Library Journal* 121, no. 16 (1998): 146.

Sennett, Ted. *Your Show of Shows.* New York: Applause Theatre & Cinema Books, 2002.

Youth International Party

SEE: *Yippies.*

The *Youth's Companion*

For just over a century, from 1827 to 1929, a monthly periodical called the *Youth's Companion* dispensed moral education, information, and fiction to generations of young people. By 1885 the periodical was claiming that 385,000 copies were printed each week, making it the most widely circulated journal of its day, largely because of the premiums and prizes it offered for new subscriptions.

The *Youth's Companion* was founded in Boston in 1827 by Nathaniel Willis and Asa Rand as a Sunday school organ in the tradition of Boston Congregationalism, one that would "warn against the ways of transgression, error and ruin, and allure to those of virtue and piety." The classic children's bedtime prayer "Now I Lay Me Down to Sleep" appeared in its first issue. Rand left the venture after three years, and Willis remained as editor until he sold the paper in 1857 to John W. Olmstead and Daniel Sharp Ford. Ford, who was known to his readers as "Perry Mason" because he called his company the Perry Mason Company, remained as editor until his death in 1899. During his editorship, he completely revamped its content and format, making the *Youth's Companion* into a well-respected publication of high literary merit. By publishing serial and scientific articles and puzzles, by soliciting articles from readers, and by including contributions from notable writers such as Harriet Beecher Stowe, Rudyard Kipling, Thomas Hardy, and Jack London, Ford was able to increase the circulation tenfold within a decade and to nearly half a million by 1899. The magazine survived until the onset of the Great Depression, when, as a victim of financial woes and changing tastes, it folded and merged with *American Boy.*

Edward Moran

SEE ALSO: *London, Jack.*

BIBLIOGRAPHY

Tebbel, John. *The American Magazine: A Compact History.* New York: Hawthorn Books, 1969.

Tebbel, John, and Mary Ellen Zuckerman. *The Magazine in America: 1741–1990.* New York: Oxford University Press, 1991.

YouTube

Debuted in 2005, YouTube is a website that permits viewers to upload, view, and share shorter-form videos in dozens of languages through individually tagged videos or channels of like material. It was the first successful website to provide video content without editing, preparation, or fact-checking, other than for illegal activities; copyright violations; and sexually explicit, graphic, violent, and crude content. In doing so, it has promulgated decidedly American perspectives and standards. YouTube's universal content has generated criticism for encouraging lowbrow entertainment in place of more polished, better edited, and less error-prone content. For instance, "Charlie Bit My Finger—Again!" a 2007 baby video said to be one of the site's most popular, has been accused of putting a premium on popularity rather than good judgment and taste.

PRE-YOUTUBE VIDEO

YouTube made the shorter-form video popular, but it did not introduce the art form. With the development of 8-millimeter film by the Eastman Kodak Company in 1932, hobbyists had a medium to capture and preserve personal, shorter-length motion pictures. Expensive technology initially kept 8-millimeter film from the middle classes, but cheaper, foreign-made cameras and projectors and the introduction of magnetic sound stripes and wider-format Super 8 film in the 1960s made it possible for most Americans to shoot and show their own home movies.

Video recorders and players, introduced by Sony and JVC in the mid-1970s, lowered the cost and made video technology, introduced commercially in 1951, commonly accessible. EMTV, which first appeared in 1981, featured shorter shots and disjunctive editing in its music videos, influencing shorter-form video. When the U.S. Supreme Court ruled in 1984 that all videotaping was legal for personal use, it made it possible for nearly everyone to "be world-famous for 15 minutes," as artist Andy Warhol had predicted in 1968. All that was lacking was an effective platform to share the results. Smaller magnetic video recorders and cameras, digital video cameras including the Flip (introduced in 2006), and digital editing software enabled more shorter-form video production.

There were various visions offered before YouTube. In the 1985 film *Max Headroom: 20 Minutes into the Future,* producer George Stone demonstrated Blipverts, concentrated three-second television commercials that supposedly made channel changing impossible. The Master-Lock company showed a one-second TV commercial (called a "blink ad") in 1998, as did General Electric and Miller Brewing during the first decade of the 2000s. TV commercials, many uploaded to YouTube, have generally shrunk in length from one minute to as low as ten or fewer seconds since the 1980s.

Evolutionary biologist Richard Dawkins introduced the concept of memes in 1976, and the term came to include cultural ideas or concepts spread repeatedly via the Internet. One of the first popular Internet video memes was the Dancing, or Oogachaka, Baby, a 1996 animation that also appeared on a popular television show *Ally McBeal*. With the introduction of Web 2.0's concept of peer-to-peer website interactivity in the late 1990s, early Internet memes such as "Hamsterdance Song" (1998) and "Star Wars Kid" (2002) were widely shared. They were duplicated so quickly and so many times that they were said to have "gone viral," a concept applied to computers for the first time in the 1992 novel *Snow Crash*.

THE YOUTUBE COMPANY

The exact genesis of YouTube remains in doubt, even if the site's success has not. PayPal employee Steve Chen told a newspaper reporter in 2006 that he and fellow employee Chad Hurley came up with the idea for the site in early 2005, after they had discovered that there was no way to share online a dinner-party video they had made. The role of a third cofounder, Jawed Karim, is more controversial. Karim has claimed that the idea for the site was his and that Chen and Hurley have since tried to deny or diminish his role in founding the site. Chen and Hurley maintain that Karim had the idea to do a video version of HOTorNOT.com, a dating website developed in 2000 that compared voluntarily submitted photographs. Karim said he was interested in the site "because it was the first time that someone had designed a website where anyone could upload content that everyone else could view." Hurley's father-in-law, James Clark, was the creator of the first Web browser, the 1994 Mosaic Netscape, and the media-sharing site Shutterfly in 1999. All have played down Clark's role in YouTube.

Regardless, the domain name YouTube was registered by Chen, Hurley, and Karim on February 15, 2005, and the first video, the nineteen-second "Me at the Zoo," which featured Karim, was uploaded April 23. A beta version of the site appeared the following month, and a working version came online in November 2005, using an $11.5 million start-up investment from a company with ties to Sequoia Capital.

There were video-sharing sites before YouTube, including Vimeo, Google Video, Revver, blip.tv, and Phanfare, which charged a subscription fee, but none achieved the same level of popularity as YouTube. Observers have said the site grew in number of users based on its quirky name, simple logo, and slightly forbidden underground appeal. Computer engineer Chen recognized the need to be able to upload, retrieve, and play videos seamlessly and with as few technical errors as possible. More than 65,000 videos were uploaded daily in 2006, with more than a million daily views. By 2012 sixty hours of new videos were being uploaded every minute, with more than fourteen million videos viewed each month. YouTube estimated that 30 percent of the site's videos accounted for 99 percent of the views.

The three inventors shared $1.65 billion in stock when Google purchased YouTube in October 2006 and remained involved in the site until 2010, even as Google treated the website as a profit loser. YouTube was quick to implement new trends in video technology, including offering a smartphone format in 2007, widescreen 16:9 aspect ratio in 2008, 1080p HD in 2009, and updated 3-D technology in 2011. By 2012 YouTube was providing more than four billion views per day. Part of that experience included prerolls—commercials that started as soon as the site opened—along with in-stream advertising and overlay banners, all designed to help the site's profitability.

YouTube launched a new version of its home page in late 2011 that was more similar to social networking sites. The introduction of channels, along with longer-length videos (ten hours for select users compared to fifteen minutes for everyone else) and more commercially produced content, marked a dramatic shift from a social to a mass medium. Celebrities such as Madonna and Jay-Z helped finance the change, along with media companies such as the *Wall Street Journal* and the *Onion*. It set the stage for YouTube to compete with online video providers such as Netflix and Hulu Plus, cable and satellite providers, and broadcast television networks.

YOUTUBE HITS AND CULTURAL CONTRIBUTIONS

Some of YouTube's more popular videos, such as "Hyperactive—Lasse Gjertsen" (2006) and "Where the Hell Is Matt?" (2008), have pushed the boundaries of the shorter-video art form, but most have gone viral based on their predictability. For instance, "Keyboard Cat" (2007) helped inspire a host of like-minded online pet and animal videos. Few baby videos surpassed the popularity of one of the originals, "Charlie Bit My Finger—Again!" but many have tried. "Flea Market Montgomery" (2006) and Rebecca Black's "Friday" (2011) are only two of millions of YouTube videos that made brief celebrities of otherwise unmemorable people. Stunts such as Judson Laipply's "Evolution of Dance" (2006), "Diet Coke + Mentos" (2006), and "Real Estate Downfall" (2008) attracted viewers much like fender-bender traffic accidents. They were in contrast to real-life "rubbernecker" events such as "Don't Tase Me, Bro!" (2007) and "Iranian Woman Killed in Protests" (2009). YouTube quickly became a platform for commercial speech as well, from cutting-edge TV commercials such as "Kenwood—Staying Alive" (2006) to immensely popular music videos like Justin Bieber's "Baby ft. Ludacris" (2010).

YouTube has been lauded for changing the core conversations that people have from older cultural forms such as network television or MTV, just as it has been celebrated for advancing video and film education and production. As early as 2006 educators saw the value of selected YouTube videos as part of their teaching to generations brought up on video. YouTube gave users a chance to escape from the anonymity of modern life, even as it created the idea that being on a screen was the only significant form of self-validation. At the same time, videos remain harder to search than text for specific content, reducing their usefulness in scholarly and other endeavors. And critics have faulted YouTube and similar websites for dumbing down American and Western culture. "Never work with children or animals" was a remark attributed to twentieth-century vaudevillian and comedian W. C. Fields, who believed they diverted an audience's attention. To many, YouTube remains the twenty-first century incarnation of that comment.

Richard Junger

SEE ALSO: *Facebook; Fields, W. C.; Hulu; The Internet; Jay-Z; Madonna; Netflix; New 3-D; Social Media; Twitter; Videos; Viral Videos.*

BIBLIOGRAPHY

Cloud, John. "The YouTube Gurus." *Time*, December 25, 2006.

Grossman, Lev. "The Beast with a Billion Eyes." *Time*, January 30, 2012.

Keen, Andrew. *The Cult of the Amateur: How Today's Internet Is Killing Our Culture.* New York: Doubleday, 2007.

Learmonth, Michael. "Lowered Expectations: Web Redefines 'Quality.'" *Business Insider*, February 22, 2010.

Terese, Adam. "Former U. Illinois Students Develop Successful Internet Business." *Daily Illini*, February 3, 2006.

Winograd, Morley, and Michael D. Hais. *Millennial Makeover: MySpace, YouTube, and the Future of American Politics.* New Brunswick, NJ: Rutgers University Press, 2008.

Yo-Yo

In the 1920s a Filipino immigrant, Pedro Flores, introduced a Philippine hunting weapon named yo-yo, translated in English as "come back," to the United States. Donald Duncan bought the rights to the name (and, ultimately, the toy) in 1929. He created the Duncan Imperial and the well-known Butterfly yo-yos. Tricks done with the toy include "walk the dog" and "around the world." The yo-yo became a fad again during the 1960s and surged in popularity in 1962.

Beginning in the yo-yo's early years, tournaments in which contestants could display their well-practiced tricks were popular in the United States. Such tournaments have enjoyed popularity throughout the early twenty-first century, in part because of the continued development in both design and materials of the yo-yo and because of the increased connectivity of yo-yo enthusiasts through forums and social networks on the Internet. The National Yo-Yo Museum opened in Chico, California, in 1993, and in 1999 the yo-yo's induction into the National Toy Hall of Fame commemorated the toy's lasting popularity.

S. Naomi Finkelstein

SEE ALSO: *The Internet; Leisure Time; Social Media; Toys.*

BIBLIOGRAPHY

Duncan, Donald F. *How to Master Championship Yo-Yo Tricks.* Whitefish, MT: Kessinger Publishing, 2010.

Duncan Toy Company. *The Original Duncan Yo-Yo and Spin Top Trick Book.* Middlefield, OH: Author, 1985.

National Yo-Yo Museum. Accessed January 2012. Available from http://nationalyoyo.org/

Skolnik, Peter. *Fads: America's Crazes, Fevers and Fancies.* New York: Crowell, 1978.

Y2K

The expression *Y2K*, shorthand for the year 2000 (*Y* equals *year*; 2 equals *two*; *K* equals the symbol for 1,000), helped define the

Clinton Promises No Disruption to Social Security Payments. *President Bill Clinton promises Americans that Y2K would not delay Social Security payments during a ceremony at the White House in December 1998.* © CYNTHIA JOHNSON/GETTY IMAGES NEWS/GETTY IMAGES.

closing days of the twentieth century by spotlighting some pitfalls of the computer age. Y2K represented a major problem caused mainly by older computers whose programmers and software designers failed to foresee what could happen in 2000. Often called the "Y2K bug" or the "millennium bug," this problem came about because early computer designers used only a two-digit year, dropping the "19" that stands at the beginning of every year from 1900 to 1999. What most designers failed to consider—the designers of the Apple Macintosh were an exception—was the problem posed by 2000. Computer logic meant that machines would translate the numbers 00 not as 2000 but as 1900. In the closing days of the century, the world was put on notice that computers using the two-digit formulation could malfunction because of this inability to distinguish years belonging to different centuries. As it turned out, billions of dollars were spent on fixing the bug, and there were no major problems reported.

Because by 1999 computers had become intertwined with almost every facet of life in the United States and the rest of the developed world, some doomsayers predicted that if Y2K struck, banks would fail, military systems would become paralyzed, planes would fall out of the sky, elevators would stop, stock exchanges would collapse, and life in general would be dramatically disrupted. Although the problem had been known about for years, businesses and governments delayed dealing with it. It was not until September 1997 that the Securities and Exchange Commission (SEC), the U.S. government watchdog over the stock exchange markets, issued a notice to investors to pressure investment companies to make their computers "Y2K compliant"—a phrase meaning that computers had been checked and fixed, if necessary, to avoid any problems when the clock struck midnight on December 31, 1999.

With great fanfare, U.S. President Bill Clinton announced in December 1998 that the Social Security Administration, which then handled some tens of millions of checks each month for pensioners, disabled people, and widows, was Y2K compliant. Nevertheless, some Republicans took issue with the Democratic president's claims that checks would go out on time, noting that some banks that received checks for recipients and that were vital to the system might be noncompliant.

Later the agriculture secretary, Dan Glickman, announced at a Senate hearing on the Y2K problem that there would not be widespread food shortages in the United States because of the millennium bug. "There are some fear-mongers out there," Glickman said, as he urged people to avoid stockpiling or hoarding food as 2000 approached. Glickman conceded, however, that although he did not see major food shortages, "there will be some glitches" and disruptions in the marketplace.

In November 1999 the *Washington Post* reported that U.S. businesses and the government had spent at least $100 billion in dealing with the Y2K bug and declared it "the most expensive peacetime catastrophe in modern history." Worldwide the figure is thought to be more than $300 billion. While American businesses and local, state, and federal governments were spending billions of dollars to correct the problem with computers, some developing countries lagged. The World Bank reported that some areas, notably sub-Saharan Africa, could run into major problems with electricity, food, and health care. In early 1999, with less than a year to go before the 2000 bug might hit, the bank found in a survey of 139 countries that only twenty-one had taken major steps to solve the problem, although fifty-four had some kind of national policy to deal with the bug.

By the end of 1999, observers hoped that the steps taken by companies and governments would prevent Y2K from causing any major disasters, and in the end the date passed with no major problems. Critics of the drive to fix the bug argued that the problem had been overblown and that the whole affair had been a moneymaking scheme by computer consultants looking for a quick profit. While there is no doubt that some unscrupulous businesses made money from the fear of Y2K rather than from the bug itself, in many cases the Y2K panic gave companies an opportunity to upgrade their antiquated systems. The drive to test, fix, and update old machines, which companies should have been doing anyway, helped avoid a major problem.

In the long run, the effect on the information technology industry was to make updating software and hardware a more pressing issue; the crisis also deflated the esteem some held for the early designers of software and computers, who had been looked upon as geniuses and had become millionaires and billionaires virtually overnight. It opened up a whole new opportunity for computer services consultants, and since it happened alongside a growing software market, it probably helped inflate the dot-com boom of the early twenty-first century.

Michael Posner

SEE ALSO: *Apple Computer; IBM (International Business Machines); Stock Market Crashes.*

BIBLIOGRAPHY

Chandrasekaran, Rajiv. "$100 Billion Price Tag for Y2K Fix." *Washington Post*, November 18, 1999.

De Jager, Peter, and Richard Bergeon. *Countdown Y2K: Business Survival Planning for the Year 2000.* New York: John Wiley, 1999.

Mitchell, Robert L. "Y2K: The Good, the Gad, and the Crazy." *Computerworld*, December 28, 2009.

Yuppies

Coined during the 1980s, the term *yuppie* refers to *y*oung *u*rban *p*rofessionals from the Reagan era who took high-paying white-collar jobs and, rather than assuming the traditional responsibilities of marriage and child rearing, chose to frequent the single scene and lead a life characterized by the acquisition of expensive material goods. Typically from middle- and upper-middle-class backgrounds, many of the yuppies who were establishing themselves in successful mainstream careers in the 1980s had participated in the countercultural movement of the 1970s when they were in college.

Uninterested in the moral and political seriousness espoused by large segments of the American population during the 1960s and 1970s, yuppies began to spend their money on themselves, often going into debt to purchase high-priced status symbols and expensive adult playthings. Rolex watches, designer fashions, trendy gourmet foods, and BMW cars came to represent the self-indulgent lifestyle of the wealthy young professionals. Snob appeal became the measuring stick for purchases. Yuppies were also associated with drug use—not the bohemian marijuana of the hippies but cocaine, the expensive drug of the jet set.

"Whoever dies with the most toys, wins" and "Who says you can't have it all?" became the catchphrases of the day.

THE ME GENERATION

Yuppies soon came to symbolize everything the media found to criticize in the 1980s. Calling the 1980s the "me generation" and the "greed decade," media pundits lambasted yuppie swingers as they had their hippie counterparts. Books such as Jay McInerney's *Bright Lights, Big City* (1984) and Tom Wolfe's *The Bonfire of the Vanities* (1987) chronicled the self-aggrandizing decadence of the yuppie life, and films such as Oliver Stone's *Wall Street* (1987) explored the culture of greedy acquisition.

In reality the economic boom of the early 1980s contributed to rising consumption throughout middle-class America, and the well-educated young elite were merely particularly well positioned to take advantage of it. They had been raised with a sense of their own importance and entitlement, which was reinforced by the jobs and salaries they had been given. Their lifestyle values were the opposite of those of their parents, the conservative children of the Great Depression. Professional life seemed merely like a step beyond college parties, and the fun was less limited. Profitably employed married couples without children were given the name "dinks" (for "double income, no kids") by the press, which showed a liking for catchy acronyms. Dinks had unprecedented disposable income, and in an increasingly consumer society, it was easy to spend.

Those young professionals who did have families tried as best they could to fit them into the yuppie status-symbol mold. Two-career households necessitated nannies and housekeepers. Young couples began to search for the "right" schools, while their children were still babies. Along with the expensive party lifestyle came pressure to keep up appearances and to keep making money. As Stan Schultz, a cultural historian at the University of Wisconsin has described it, "We are terribly busy souls, doing important things that no one else can do."

Internal conflicts began to emerge, because yuppies' liberal ideologies started to conflict with their economic conservatism. The 1980s was the Reagan era in U.S. politics, and new advantages were being doled out to the rich and the corporations at the expense of social services. Yuppies found themselves on an uncomfortable side of this dichotomy. Jerry Rubin, once a leader of the famous radical group the Yippies, was one of those who traded in his revolutionary politics for economic security—"Money in my pockets mellowed out my radicalism," he said.

Of course, frenzied spending has its price, and the yuppies soon found themselves in deep debt. As long as high-salaried jobs were available, the debt was not a problem, but toward the late 1980s the economic boom began to end. In 1987 the stock market crashed, and its effects were felt in every societal stratum. Many of the previously secure young professional found themselves "downsized," laid off from jobs or forced to take great cuts in salary.

So many defaulted on credit-card payments that bankers coined the term *yuppie bill syndrome* to describe them. New "yuppie pawnshops" sprang up, not the sad, dark hock shops of the inner city but upscale shops with bright lighting in middle-class shopping areas so that yuppies could cash in some of their costly toys to help cover more necessary expenses. *Downscale chic* was the term used to describe the return to simpler consumption—jeans and T-shirts instead of designer clothes.

DEATH AND REBIRTH

Receiving less attention in the media than the maligned yuppies were the working class and poor, whose circumstances were less improved by the 1980s boom. The working class also had two-income families—not to create a pool of disposable income but to try to cover their bills. The working class had little sympathy for overextended yuppies, who were seen as exemplifying the waste and irresponsibility of the upper classes.

Just as the yuppies themselves had been part of a backlash, they caused their own backlash. Redefining the word *yuppie* to mean "young unhappy professionals," some young professionals began to look for a new way of life. Some dubbed "domos" (for "downwardly mobile professionals"), dropped out of the fast-paced life of the urban professional by choosing a simpler life and perhaps moving to the country. One exodus took many former yuppies to Montana to seek a bucolic freedom from stress in the mountains. Other yuppies did not drop out but instead changed their focus to making money by doing work they could believe in, such as environmental protection work or fighting cancer. *The Artist's Way* by Julia Cameron (1992) and *Getting a Life* (1998) by Jacqueline Blix describe the joys of trading the consumer rat race for a more fulfilling life by making a dramatic lifestyle change.

As the upper-middle-class professionals of the baby boom generation began to reach middle age, the press began to announce the "death of the yuppie." Rebellious youth of the 1990s phrased it more harshly, putting "Die, yuppie scum!" on T-shirts and placards. Although some young people of the post-Reagan years embraced unambitious "slacker" values in reaction to the striving yuppie lifestyle, consumerism as a staple of modern society was here to stay.

Self-indulgent luxury commodities, such as coffee grinders, Cuisinarts, BMWs, and sushi, once deemed the province of the yuppie, have quietly remained the hallmark of the hip young professional into the twenty-first century. Long-running television shows such as NBC's *Frasier* (1993–2004) and HBO's *Sex and the City* (1998–2004) both gently mocked and normalized the effete self-involvement of yuppie life.

Each economic boom has led to a frantic wave of conspicuous consumption relying heavily on credit, and yuppies were a manifestation of the economic boom of the 1980s. The term *yuppie* has been widely used—many say overused—by the media to describe a certain privileged segment of the baby boom generation at a particular time in the lives of its members. Though the term has become somewhat dated, it is still descriptive of a lifestyle and ethos that remains very much alive in the twenty-first century.

Tina Gianoulis

SEE ALSO: *Baby Boomers; Cocaine/Crack; Coffee; Consumerism; Environmentalism;* Frasier*; The Great Depression; Hippies; Marijuana; Me Decade; Reagan, Ronald;* Sex and the City*; Stone, Oliver; Wolfe, Tom; Yippies.*

BIBLIOGRAPHY

Adler, Jerry. "The Rise of the Overclass." *Newsweek*, July 31, 1995, 32.

Frank, Robert. *Luxury Fever: Weighing the Cost of Excess.* Princeton, NJ: Princeton University Press, 2010.

Gordinier, Jeff. "The Return of the Yuppie." Details, November

2006. Accessed May 17, 2012. Available from http://www.details.com/culture-trends/critical-eye/200611/the-return-of-the-yuppie?currentPage=1

Shapiro, Walter. "The Birth and—Maybe—Death of Yuppiedom: After 22,000 Articles, Is This Truly the End?" *Time*, April 8, 1991, 65.

Yuppies and Baby Boomers: A Benchmark Study from Market Facts, Inc. Chicago: Market Facts, 1985.

Z

Zanuck, Darryl F. *(1902–1979)*

Darryl F. Zanuck ranks as one of Hollywood's most famous and long-lived movie moguls. He oversaw scores of popular films and created many film stars. Many of these movies and their stars were tremendously popular at the time and remain so today. He also revived and created Twentieth Century Fox, functioning as its chief of production from the mid-1930s through the mid-1950s. Three of the films Zanuck produced received Academy Awards: *How Green Was My Valley* (1941), *Gentleman's Agreement* (1947), and *All about Eve* (1950). He created several stars; child star Shirley Temple and Betty Grable (World War II's "pin-up girl") made his Twentieth Century Fox into a true powerhouse.

After the war, Zanuck produced a series of films that dealt with social issues, including racism and mental illness. These postwar films, including *Gentleman's Agreement, The Snake Pit* (1948), and *Pinky* (1949), proved tremendously popular money-makers for the studio. Upon returning to Fox in the early 1960s, Zanuck worked with his son Richard and produced one major hit, *The Sound of Music* (1965). Zanuck was a brilliant producer who possessed the unequaled ability to detect potential in screenplays and screen actors.

Liza Black

SEE ALSO: *Academy Awards;* All about Eve*; Child Stars; Grable, Betty;* The Sound of Music*; Temple, Shirley.*

BIBLIOGRAPHY

Behlmer, Rudy, ed. *Memo from Darryl F. Zanuck: The Golden Years at Twentieth Century Fox.* New York: Grove Press, 1993.

Custen, George. *Twentieth Century's Fox: Darryl F. Zanuck and the Culture of Hollywood.* New York: Basic Books, 1997.

Eagan, Daniel, and National Film Preservation Board (U.S.). *America's Film Legacy: The Authoritative Guide to the Landmark Movies in the National Film Registry.* New York: Continuum, 2010.

Zap Comix

Considered by pop-culture critics to be the quintessential underground comic book of the 1960s, *Zap Comix* came out of the San Francisco Bay counterculture scene late in that decade. Three men were chiefly responsible for the *Zap Comix* phenomenon: Don Donahue and Charles Plymell were instrumental in securing the money and arranging the distribution of the early issues, while visionary cartoonist Robert Crumb assumed editorial control. Crumb, a Philadelphia native with no formal art training, was to become one of underground comics' most influential creators. Although there are no records on its circulation numbers, *Zap Comix* is now estimated to have millions of copies in print, including such classics as the sexually explicit "Fritz the Cat" series and the trippy "Mr. Natural" books.

In the 1960s Crumb, a onetime illustrator for the American Greeting Card Company, began doing freelance work for *Help* magazine, a publication by *MAD Magazine*'s cocreator Harvey Kurtzman. Crumb's experimentation with LSD and other drugs inspired him to create ever more bizarre situations and characters; he created "Fritz the Cat" and "Mr. Natural" during this acid-soaked period. His best early work was published in the pages of underground newspapers like New York's *East Village Other*.

In 1967 Crumb moved to San Francisco, where he hooked up with a community of artists and writers who shared his countercultural sensibility. Donahue and Plymell soon enlisted him to take the reins of *Zap* as a vehicle for his unique talents. The first issue of *Zap*, numbered zero, hit the streets in February 1968. Dubbed "the comic that plugs you in," the cover featured a Crumb drawing of an embryonic figure with its umbilical cord plugged into an electrical socket. The comic quickly became a forum for some of the most prominent underground cartoonists of the time, many of them influenced by the early *MAD Magazine*. *Zap* featured illustration work by the likes of S. Clay Wilson, Spain Rodriguez, and Gilbert Shelton.

Zap's content ranged widely, from instructions on how to smoke a joint to quasi-pornographic features like "Wonder Wart-Hog," in which the eponymous swine overcomes his impotence by using his snout. The pages of *Zap Comix* offered readers an explicit panorama of the sex, drugs, and revolution ethos of the 1960s, subjects never before seen in comic books. *Zap Comix* was often sold in head shops, sharing counter space with bongs and roach clips. It was the unofficial bible of the tuned-in, turned-on generation of hippies and other countercultural folk.

With the success of *Zap*, Robert Crumb became an icon of the underground. The hip cachet of his comics allowed him to triumph over his own sexual frustration. As he explained later in an autobiographical cartoon story, "I made up for all those years of deprivation by lunging maniacally at women I was attracted to . . . squeezing faces and humping legs . . . I usually got away with it . . . famous eccentric artist, you know." Occasionally, however, Crumb's commitment to exploring his own personal sexual obsessions got him and the comics in hot water. In 1969 Crumb's incest-themed story "Joe Blow" in *Zap* number 4 sparked obscenity busts at several bookstores.

Attention to Crumb and *Zap* would return in the 1990s with the acclaimed documentary *Crumb*. The film outlines Crumb's life and career and highlights members of his family. It won awards at the Sundance Film Festival and was named the best film of the year by several critics, including the influential Gene Siskel. In 2008 *Entertainment Weekly* named *Crumb* the fourteenth-best film of the past twenty-five years.

In 2011 the Seattle-based comics publisher Fantagraphics announced it would reprint all sixteen *Zap* issues in two hardback volumes scheduled to be released in 2012. When announcing the deal, Fantagraphics publisher Gary Groth noted that *Zap* was "one of the most significant comic series ever published and for an unusual reason. Because not only is it a cultural landmark like Superman or Batman or Spider-Man but also based purely on its artistic merits it's a significant comic series."

While *Zap* can trace its own genealogy back to the publication of Jack "Jaxon" Jackson's *God Nose* in 1963, it has itself served to inspire others. The daring style and content of *Zap Comix* paved the way for a generation of cartoonists, both mainstream and underground, who felt comfortable tackling previously taboo, adult-themed subjects. "To say [*Zap*] made a deep impression is an understatement," said Alan Moore, the comics writer who created the popular *Watchmen* title of the 1980s. Author Trina Robbins described reading *Zap* for the first time as "probably a lot like what discovering Jesus is to 'born-again' Christians. In a way, knowing that I could do a comic book was very much like being 'born again.'" *Zap* led the way for adult graphic novels such as Harvey Pekar's *American Splendor* in the 1970s and *Love and Rockets* by the Hernandez brothers in the 1980s. Today's readers can also thank *Zap* for the plethora of alternative comics in print and on the Web. As publisher Groth has noted, the significance of *Zap* "cannot be overstated relative to where we are today."

Robert E. Schnakenberg

SEE ALSO: *Batman; Crumb, Robert;* Entertainment Weekly; *Hippies;* MAD Magazine; *Siskel and Ebert; Spider-Man; Sundance Film Festival; Superman; Tijuana Bibles; Underground Comics.*

BIBLIOGRAPHY

Crumb, Robert. *The Complete Crumb Comics.* Seattle: Fantagraphics, 1988.

Danky, James Philip. *Underground Classics: The Transformation of Comics into Comix.* New York: Abrams, 2009.

Hatfield, Charles. *Alternative Comics: An Emerging Literature.* Jackson: University Press of Mississippi, 2005.

Sabin, Roger. *Comics, Comix & Graphic Novels: A History of Graphic Novels.* New York: Phaidon Press, 2001.

Zappa, Frank *(1940–1993)*

Few rock-and-roll icons can match the innovation and prolific output of Frank Zappa. His synthesis of blues, rock, jazz, doo-wop, classical, and avant garde, combined with irreverent lyrics and politically oriented stage theatrics, expanded the range of popular music. From his work with seminal 1960s freak band the Mothers of Invention to the numerous albums released posthumously in the decades following his death in 1993, Zappa made music according to his own iconoclastic and fiercely original standards, rewriting the rules of the music industry in the process.

THE TEEN MUSICIAN

Frank Vincent Zappa was born December 21, 1940, in Baltimore, Maryland. The Zappa family moved often, as his father followed wartime civil service employment, until settling in 1956 in Lancaster, California, north of Los Angeles. Zappa's main interests during his formative years were chemistry (specifically explosives), drums, and the dissonant music of Edgard Varèse, a modern composer who worked with sound effects, electronics, and large percussion sections. This was an important influence on young Zappa, as it introduced him to unconventional musical forms before the advent of rock and roll.

Bored with high school, Zappa taught himself to read and write twelve-tone symphonic music and began composing his own. After graduation he worked as a rhythm guitarist in vari-

Frank Zappa. *Frank Zappa performs in the Netherlands in 1988.* FRANS SCHELLEKENS/CONTRIBUTOR/REDFERNS/GETTY IMAGES.

ous lounge cover bands, when it became clear that merely composing would not pay the bills. In 1963, however, at age twenty-two, he scored the soundtrack for a low-budget film and acquired a homemade recording studio in downtown Cucamonga, California. Unfortunately, Studio Z had a brief life. Trouble with the locals culminating in a ten-day jail sentence, along with impending urban development, forced Zappa to move to Los Angeles, where he found gigs for his proto-rock-and-roll band, the Mothers.

After "perfecting" their artsy, improvisational live show, the Mothers recorded *Freak Out!* (1966), the first rock double album. Out of necessity, though, the band became the Mothers of Invention, as record executives objected to the original name. *Freak Out!* was a landmark in musique concrète, as pop music and was a bracing satire on the hippie culture oozing into Southern California. The follow-up album, *Absolutely Free* (1968), intensified these themes, laying the groundwork for much of Zappa's future lyrical and compositional endeavors. Later he created the cult film *200 Motels* (1971), named for the estimated number of dives the band had stayed in during its five-year life span. Dissonant and self-consciously weird, *200 Motels* foreshadowed the music video even as it lampooned life inside a touring rock-and-roll band, incorporating ballet, opera, and Zappa's dizzying orchestrations to make its acidic point. As freaky as Zappa was, though, he was an adamant teetotaler, which caused tension among fellow musicians. This, combined with low pay and bad reviews, ultimately led to the breakup of the Mothers of Invention. Zappa, however, was just getting started.

AN INTERNATIONAL SENSATION

Throughout the 1970s Zappa's reputation grew, especially in Eastern Europe. He also became known for his prowess with a guitar, while his lyrics became more surreal and confrontational. His attempts at "serious" music, however, were thwarted, beginning with contractual disputes stemming from the *200 Motels* sessions with the Royal Philharmonic and continuing every time he tried to hire an orchestra. Zappa still considered himself primarily a composer—an odd vocation for a subversive rock musician, but as he remarked, "Apart from the snide political stuff, which I enjoy writing, the rest of my lyrics wouldn't exist at all if it weren't for the fact that we live in a society where instrumental music is irrelevant."

In 1977 Zappa became embroiled in lawsuits involving ownership of his early albums. During this litigious period (and in an effort to fulfill remaining contracts) he released as many as four albums a year and toured relentlessly, while another self-referential work, called *Joe's Garage* (1979), achieved mainstream popularity with its Orwellian plot and scatological humor. Eventually Zappa became the owner of his entire back catalog and an eponymous record label, as well as a new recording studio in the basement of his Los Angeles home.

The establishment began to recognize Zappa in the 1980s, and his Billboard-charting single, "Valley Girl" (1982), was a fluffy parody of Southern California teen pop culture, featuring the voice of his daughter Moon. In 1985 Zappa testified before a Senate committee and denounced legislation calling for explicit-content warning labels on albums. He later became close friends with then president of Czechoslovakia, Václav Havel, and was nearly appointed ambassador of trade and culture to that country. Zappa also received a Best Instrumental Album Grammy Award in 1986 for *Jazz from Hell*, which was conceived on the Synclavier, an electronic device allowing him to play his most difficult compositions note for note.

LATER YEARS

In 1990 Zappa was diagnosed with prostate cancer. Between debilitating treatments he produced a live program of his orchestral works called *The Yellow Shark* (1993), which was performed by ardent fans, the renowned German Ensemble Modern. He also set up the Zappa Family Trust, placing total creative and financial control of his successful niche-market mail-order business in the hands of his partner and wife, Gail. Zappa died on December 4, 1993. He was inducted into the Rock and Roll Hall of Fame in 1995 and received a lifetime achievement Grammy Award two years later.

The years following Zappa's death also saw the appearance of a number of previously unreleased recordings. In 1996 his family put out *Frank Zappa Plays the Music of Frank Zappa: A Memorial Album.* Other posthumous releases include *Everything Is Healing Nicely* (1999), a collection of additional tracks from the 1993 *Yellow Shark* sessions, and *Imaginary Diseases* (2007), a sampling of live performances from 1972 featuring Zappa's relatively obscure Petite Wazoo band. In 2010 his native city of Baltimore unveiled a commemorative bust of the musician outside the Enoch Pratt Free Library. That same year the London Contemporary Orchestra conducted a revival concert in honor of Zappa's seventieth birthday.

The legacy of Frank Zappa lives on in every outspoken, self-made rock star, in every do-it-yourself basement recording and autobiographical music video montage. He rescued the stodgy reputation of the serious orchestral composer by marrying it to the lifestyle of a hard-touring rock band, creating some of the most challenging and defiant music of the twentieth century. He also pioneered recording technologies, stretching the boundaries of what popular music could be. Zappa is known worldwide for his irreverent attitude and masterful musicianship, proving that, as he often quoted Varèse, "The present day composer refuses to die!"

Tony Brewer

SEE ALSO: *Ballet; Blues; Cancer; Doo-wop Music; Grammy Awards; Hippies; Jazz; Pop Music; Rock and Roll; Top 40.*

BIBLIOGRAPHY

Hall, Chris. "Zappa: 'You Still Sense Frank Here—There's Electricity in the Air.'" *Guardian* (London), October 30, 2010.

Roura, Phil. "Zapping a Few Myths." *New York Daily News*, October 28, 2007.

Walley, David. *No Commercial Potential: The Sage of Frank Zappa*, rev. ed. New York: Da Capo Press, 1996.

Watson, Ben. *Zappa: The Negative Dialectics of Poodle Play.* New York: St. Martin's Press, 1995.

Zappa, Frank. *Them or Us.* Los Angeles: Barfko-Swill, 1984.

Zappa, Frank, and Peter Occhiogrosso. *The Real Frank Zappa Book.* New York: Poseidon Press, 1989.

The Ziegfeld Follies

Brainchild of Broadway impresario Florenz Ziegfeld and his first wife, European singer Anna Held, *The Ziegfeld Follies* dominated

Ziegfeld Follies. *Cyd Charisse and Fred Astaire appear in a number in the 1946 film* Ziegfeld Follies. © SUNSET BOULEVARD/CORBIS.

the American theatrical revue scene from 1907 until the late 1920s and early 1930s, when the popularity of vaudeville began to diminish. Featuring scores of women in elaborate costumes and boasting the debut of some of the country's most popular songs, such as "Shine on Harvest Moon," the *Follies* started as an American version of satiric French cabaret acts whose sophistication Ziegfeld hoped to evoke in order to appeal to a high-hat audience. Ziegfeld's attempt at continental appeal, however, could not match the flamboyance and over-the-top glitz his own personal flair lent to his works. Thus *The Ziegfeld Follies* offered a hybrid: highbrow artistic endeavor reflected, for example, in the Art Nouveau sets, and near vulgarity evidenced by skimpy, even gaudy, costuming.

Though *The Passing Show*, which debuted in 1894, was the very first American revue, Ziegfeld's combination of dance routines, still tableaux, stand-up comedy, political satire, one-act plays, and optical illusions became the most well known, an emblem of its era and the quintessential revue. The spectacle was what critic Marjorie Farnsworth calls "a feast of desire," and it reflected what F. Scott Fitzgerald called the Jazz Age and its celebration of economic prosperity and hedonism.

The key to *The Ziegfeld Follies'* extraordinary popularity and influence lay in Ziegfeld's appreciation for the revue staple, the chorus girl. Where other revue shows at the time typically used around twenty chorus girls and perhaps two or three costume changes a show, Ziegfeld arrayed 120 girls before his audiences. He dressed them in imported fabrics of tremendous extravagance and his own outrageous design, giving them five or six wardrobe changes an evening. He famously handpicked not only his fabrics but his chorus line as well, selecting only those he considered the most beautiful women of the day.

Based on his connoisseurship of women and his role in launching the Broadway musical *Glorifying the American Girl*, Ziegfeld became known as "the Glorifier." He adored women and had numerous affairs with his employees, but he also viewed them as art objects to sculpt and perfect. He wrote newspaper columns outlining his specifications for the perfect female figure. In the mid-1920s he declared the tall, statuesque look "out" and the shorter, more vivacious figure "in." His aim was to create a fantasy world of radiant women with perfect figures whose beauty and allure transcended anything any spectator could have ever before witnessed.

The *Follies* offered outlandish dance numbers, including one in which the chorines dressed as taxicabs and moved across a darkened stage, their headlamps the only light. Ziegfeld also billed optical illusions that played off the encroaching movie industry. In one, he displayed a film of a featured performer running down a path. At the end of the path there suddenly appeared the actress herself, the screen apparently disappearing behind her. In another famous routine, "Laceland," the dancers wore glow-in-the-dark painted costumes and dressed as milliner objects—scissors, thimble, needle, etc.—and danced around a woman tatting lace. As early as 1909 Ziegfeld rigged his theater ceiling to "fly" performer Lillian Lorraine above audience's heads while she sang, "Up, Up, Up in My Aeroplane." Ziegfeld is also credited with the idea of a chorine or featured female performer entering the stage by descending a staircase. This image was later picked up and magnified by musical choreographer Busby Berkeley in movies such as his Gold Digger series, all of which were influenced by *The Ziegfeld Follies*.

The *Follies* chorus became known as Ziegfeld Girls. Discussed in gossip columns as public personalities, Ziegfeld Girls were precursors to movie stars, both figuratively and literally. Before them, chorus girls were anonymous, everyday women. After Ziegfeld promoted them, they became celebrities, and many of them then went on to become famous film stars. That list includes Barbara Stanwyck; Paulette Goddard; and Ziegfeld's last wife, Billie Burke.

The Ziegfeld Follies launched a number of other famous personalities. Among the male comedians to take their first bow on Ziegfeld's stage were Bert Lahr; Eddie Cantor; and the well-loved humorist Will Rogers, who began his career with Ziegfeld by making fun of politicians and satirizing news of the day. His style was folksy, but his humor had a contemporary edge. The comedian Fanny Brice also made her name as a long-running performer in *The Ziegfeld Follies*, as did legendary songwriters Irving Berlin, Jerome Kern, and Oscar Hammerstein.

The Ziegfeld Follies' vaunted showgirl lives on in the nightclub acts of Las Vegas and Atlantic City, but she's lost the lavish, individualized attention Ziegfeld bestowed upon her. His own legend survives in films based on his career and the dizzying, singular history of the *Follies*. These include 1941's *Ziegfeld Girl*, directed by Busby Berkeley and featuring Jimmy Stewart and Lana Turner, and *Ziegfeld Follies* (1946), directed by Vincente Minnelli and starring William Powell as Ziegfeld. Brice's life and career became the subject of the 1964 play *Funny Girl*, made into a film in 1968 and for which actress and singer Barbra Streisand won an Academy Award. A follow-up, *Funny Lady* (1975), was also based on Brice and again featured Streisand. In the early 1990s Broadway staged *The Will Rogers Follies*, a Tony Award–winning musical billed as "paying tribute to two American legends—Will Rogers and *The Ziegfeld Follies*."

Elizabeth Haas

SEE ALSO: *Berkeley, Busby; Berlin, Irving; Brice, Fanny; Cantor, Eddie; Kern, Jerome; Lahr, Bert; Minnelli, Vincente; Powell, William; Rodgers and Hammerstein; Rogers, Will; Stanwyck, Barbara; Stewart, Jimmy; Streisand, Barbra; Turner, Lana; Vaudeville.*

BIBLIOGRAPHY

Cantor, Eddie, and David Freedman. *Ziegfeld: The Great Glorifier*. New York: A. H. King, 1934.

Carter, Randolph. *The World of Flo Ziegfeld*. New York: Praeger, 1974.

Farnsworth, Marjorie. *The Ziegfeld Follies*. New York: Bonanza Books, 1956.

Higham, Charles. *Ziegfeld*. Chicago: Henry Regnery, 1972.

Mizejewski, Linda. *Ziegfeld Girl: Image and Icon in Culture and Cinema*. Durham, NC: Duke University Press, 1999.

Zines

Zines are nonprofessional, anticommercial, small-circulation magazines produced, published, and distributed by their creators themselves. Composed and formatted on home computers, zines are reproduced on copiers or printers, assembled on kitchen tables, and sold or swapped through the mail or made available at small book or music stores. It is estimated that between 10,000 and 20,000 zines circulate in the United States and in other countries throughout the world. With names like *Dishwasher*, *Temp Slave*, *Pathetic Life*, *Practical Anarchy*, *Punk Planet*, and *Slug & Lettuce*, zines have a subject matter that ranges from the sublime to the ridiculous and sometimes the unfathomable. What binds these publications together is the prime directive "do-it-yourself." Zines advocate that people stop shopping for culture and create their own.

THE ORIGIN OF ZINES

Zines have been shaped by a long history of alternative presses in the United States. In fact, zine editor Gene Mahoney calls Thomas Paine's revolutionary pamphlet *Common Sense* "the zine heard 'round the world." As a distinct medium, however, zines first appeared in the 1930s. It was then that fans of science fiction, often through the clubs they had founded, began producing what they called "fanzines" as a way of sharing science-fictional stories and commentary. Although it is difficult to be certain of anything about a cultural form as ephemeral as zines, it is generally accepted that the first fanzine was the *Comet*, published by the Science Correspondence Club in May 1930. More than four decades later, in the mid-1970s, another type of zine appeared as fans of punk rock, ignored by and critical of the mainstream music press, began printing fanzines about their music and cultural scene. The first punk zine, appropriately named *Punk*, appeared in New York City in January 1976.

Factsheet Five and its creator, Mike Gunderloy, were central in the history of zines. The zine was in part the accidental offspring of a letter sent to a dozen friends and in part a conscious plan to "connect up the various people who were exercising their First Amendment rights in a small, non-profit scale [so] . . . they could learn from each other . . . and help generate a larger alternative community." Gunderloy began *Factsheet Five* in May 1982 by printing reviews and contact addresses for all zines sent to him. The result was a cross-fertilization of the two major types of zines, science fiction and punk. They were joined by smaller numbers of publications created by fans of other genres, disgruntled self-publishers, and what remained of political dissent from the 1960s. A genuine subculture of zines developed over the next decade as the prefix "fan" was, by and large, dropped from "zine," and their number increased exponentially. For many years *Factsheet Five* continued to function as the center of the geographically dispersed zine world.

TRADITIONAL ZINES

Zines are, first and foremost, about the individuals who create them. Zinesters use their zines to unleash an existential howl: "I exist, and here is what I think." While their subject matter varies from punk music to Pez candy dispensers to anarchist politics, it is the authors and their own personal perspective on the topic that defines the editorial rants, essays, comics, illustrations, poems, and reviews that make up the standard fare of zines. Consider the prominent subgenre of "perzines," that is, personal zines that read like the intimate diaries usually kept hidden safely in the back of a drawer. Here personal revelation outweighs rhetoric, and polished literary style takes a back seat to honesty. Unlike most personal diaries, however, these intimate thoughts, philosophical musings, or events of the day are written for an outside audience.

The audience for zines is, by and large, other zine editors. While the practice has changed somewhat and selling zines has become more commonplace, it is traditional practice to trade one zine for another zine. By the 1980s and 1990s those doing the selling and trading were predominantly young, white, and middle-class. Raised in a relatively privileged position within the dominant society, zinesters embarked on lives that moved them to the margins. They embraced downwardly mobile careers, unpopular musical and artistic tastes, transgressive ideas about sexuality, and a politics resolutely outside the status quo, more often to the left but sometimes to the right. In short, they became what used to be called "bohemians." But rather than being in Paris, there were small subcultures in cities and in small towns and suburbs. Zines thus became a way to share, define, and hold together a culture of discontent, a virtual bohemia. "Let's all be alienated together in a newspaper," zine editor John Klima of *Day and Age* has said, only half in jest.

One of the things that keeps such alienated individuals together is the shared ethic and practice of do-it-yourself. Zines are a response to a society in which consuming culture and entertainment that others have produced is the norm. By writing about the music, sports, literature, and other activities that are so central to their lives, fans use their zines to forge a personal connection with what is essentially a mass-produced product. Zines also constitute a reaction to living in a consumer society, for publishing a zine is an act of creating one's own culture. As such, zine writers consider what they do as a small step toward reversing the traditional role of a cultural consumer to that of a cultural producer. Deliberately low-tech, the medium is one that anyone can use. "The scruffier the better," Michael Carr, one of the editors of the punk zine *Ben Is Dead*, has argued, because "they look as if no corporation, big business or advertisers had anything to do with them." The amateur ethos of the zine world is so strong that writers who dare to move their projects into profitability—or at times even popularity—are accused of "selling out."

CHANGES IN THE ZINE WORLD

For more than fifty years zines were unknown outside their small circles. But this changed in the late 1980s and the early 1990s when those who had been born in the 1960s and 1970s, called Generation X, came of age. The discovery of a white, alternative youth culture was fueled in part by the phenomenal success of the postpunk grunge band Nirvana in 1991, but it was also influenced by the apprehension on the part of businesses that a $125 billion market was passing them by. In December 1992 *Business Week* voiced these fears in a cover story: "Grunge, anger, cultural dislocation, a secret yearning to belong: they add up to a daunting cultural anthropology that marketers have to confront if they want to reach twentysomethings. But it's worth it. Busters do buy stuff." As the underground press of this generation, zines were discovered by big business. *Time*, *Newsweek*, the *New York Times*, the *Washington Post*, and *USA Today* all ran features on zines. Trying to connect with the youth market, advertisers began to borrow the look of the zines and the lingo of zine culture. Some went as far as to produce faux fanzines. The Alternative Marketing division of Warner Records, for example, produced a "zine" titled *Dirt*, Nike created *U Don't Stop*, and the chain store Urban Outfitters printed *Slant*, including a punk rock issue.

As zines became more popular, new ideas made their way into the zine world, and its norms and mores were challenged. For some, the disdain for commercial and professional culture was supplanted by the realization that zines could be a stepping stone into mainstream publishing. For others, however, the reaction was the opposite. To separate themselves from the mainstream, some writers searched for more and more obscure topics and used ever more complex layers of irony. Accusations of selling out became commonplace in zines.

The attention span of the culture industry can be fleeting, but what motivates people to write and share their writing endures. The renewal of zine culture in the twenty-first century seems to confirm this. Thus, zines have endured, with publications continuing at a healthy pace, even though the medium has to some extent changed. With the rise of the Internet, and the lowering of financial and technical barriers to its use, zines have been migrating steadily to the Web. At the same time there may always be a place for traditional zines on paper. In a sense the medium does not matter, for zines are less about the material form and more about a persistent desire to be creative and to communicate. Meanwhile, zines on paper have found archival homes in libraries and institutes throughout the world, ensuring that their unique history will not be lost to a digital generation.

Stephen Duncombe

SEE ALSO: *Alternative Press; Fan Magazines; Generation X; Grunge; Nirvana; Punk; Science Fiction Publishing.*

BIBLIOGRAPHY

Bartel, Julie. *From A to Zine: Building a Winning Zine Collection in Your Library.* Chicago: American Library Association, 2004.

Duncombe, Stephen. *Notes from Underground: Zines and the Politics of Underground Culture.* New York: Verso, 1997.

Friedman, R. Seth. *The Factsheet Five Zine Reader.* New York: Three Rivers Press, 1997.

Gunderloy, Mike, and Cari Goldberg Janice. *The World of Zines: A Guide to the Independent Magazine Revolution.* New York: Penguin, 1992.

Piepmeier, Alison. *Girl Zines: Making Media, Doing Feminism.* New York: New York University Press, 2009.

Rowe, Chip. *The Book of Zines.* New York: Henry Holt, 1997.

Taormino, Tristan, and Karen Green. *A Girl's Guide to Taking Over the World: Writings from the Girl Zine Revolution.* New York: St. Martin's Press, 1997.

Vale, V., ed. *Zines!* Vol. 1. San Francisco: V/Search, 1996.

Watson, Esther, and Mark Todd. *Whatcha Mean, What's a Zine?* Boston: Graphia, 2006.

Wertham, Fredric. *The World of Fanzines.* Carbondale: Southern Illinois University Press, 1973.

Zippy the Pinhead

Known for its nonlinear style, quirky dialogue, experimental graphics, and social satire, the *Zippy the Pinhead* comic strip has entertained and engaged a loyal following of readers since its inception in 1970. Created by Bill Griffith, the strip revolves around the non-sequitur-spouting microcephalic Zippy and his small circle of friends. These friends include Griffy, the creator's alter ego; Shelf-Life, the manic observer of marketing trends; Claude Funston, the trailer-inhabiting good ol' boy; and Mr. Toad, whose violent impulses create an occasional bit of suspense within the strip. The exploits of this fivesome have cultivated the loyalty of an intensely specified audience that continues to identify with the strip's counterculture worldview.

To appreciate Zippy, and to understand his value as an agent of satire, one must know a bit about the world of Griffith. Zippy was shaped in part by several meetings that Griffith had in the early 1970s with microcephalics, in whose disconnected impulses and childlike personalities he found appropriate material for a comic strip. Zippy's first appearance was in an underground comic book called *Real Pulp* that was published in October 1970. Soon the character had enough of a following to merit his own comic venue, *Yow! Comics*, and he attained a measure of mainstream status when the strip became nationally syndicated in 1976. The strip then appeared regularly in both weekly and daily newspapers in cities such as Boston; Detroit, Michigan; Washington, D.C.; Los Angeles; and Phoenix, Arizona, appealing to a small circle of followers that loudly protested any efforts to remove it.

Because of its nonlinear narrative structure and quirky, non-sequitur dialogue, the strip has been criticized by detractors who don't "get" its humor. Its fans, however, admire the astute social commentary that Zippy offers through his childlike perspective on current fads and issues, as well as the way he illustrates to viewers the strangeness of modern culture. The style of *Zippy*'s social commentary is inspired by the absurdity of crass consumerism, though its real roots are perhaps located in Griffith's suburban upbringing in Levittown, New York, which he describes in a 1997 *Boston Globe* interview as a "surreal space." Griffith's sense of absurdism is attributable to many childhood influences, but two that are addressed regularly in *Zippy* are the comic strip *Nancy* by Ernie Bushmiller and the TV show *Sgt. Bilko*.

Zippy began to take shape during Griffith's tenure at a Brooklyn art college from 1962 to 1964, when he took an interest in the sideshow microcephalics, or "pinheads," portrayed in the 1932 movie *Freaks*. A connection with a famous Barnum & Bailey pinhead, "Zip the What-Is-It" (1842–1926), solidified the character. Zip the What-Is-It's real name, William H. Jackson, is also the name of Griffith's great-grandfather. Griffith's own full name is William H. Jackson Griffith, which he describes in a 1981 interview as being "a bit unnerving."

True to its absurdist roots, the strip chooses not to give its main character any set origins. In one series, Zippy's parents, Eb and Flo, are introduced. His depressed brother Lippy, dressed in trademark black suit, makes an occasional visit. His family, including wife, Zerbina and children, Fuelrod and Meltdown, also appear sporadically. Zippy is a regular in Laundromats, where the workings of the washing machine unfailingly fascinate him. He is intensely loyal to donut shops and even more so to Hostess products, which he is drawn to because of the many preservatives they contain, particularly polysorbate 80. Ultimately, the comic strip's commentaries on consumerism mirror Griffith's own immersion in it; in the same 1981 interview, Griffith claims to have "absorbed the characters and plotlines of 10,000 sitcoms, "B"-movies, and talk shows. Doing comics gives me a way to re-channel some of this nuttiness so it doesn't back up on me like clogged plumbing."

Zippy is best known for his famous question, "Are we having fun yet?" The strip's unofficial slogan, it has worked its way into *Bartlett's Familiar Quotations* and is also embedded in the national consciousness as a cliché that describes any surreal moment one might encounter in a postmodern, consumption-driven world. While many people lay claim to initiating the question, Griffith explained in a National Public Radio interview on *Fresh Air* in 1995 that Zippy first posed it on the cover of a comic book in 1976 or 1977. In the context of that particular scene, Griffith noted, "it just seemed like the right existential thought at the moment . . . if you have to ask it, I guess you aren't, or maybe you are. Or are you questioning the very nature of fun? It seemed like the right question to ask. And his devotees believe that the microcephalic social critic is just the one to ask it."

Warren Tormey

SEE ALSO: *Comic Books; Comics; Consumerism;* Freaks*; Levittown; Suburbia.*

BIBLIOGRAPHY

Griffith, Bill. *The Zippy Annual: October 2002–October 2003*. Seattle, WA: Fantagraphics Books, 2003.

"An Interview with Bill Griffith." In *Zippy Stories*, 4th ed., 6–8. San Francisco: Last Gasp, 1986.

McIntyre, Tom. "Zippy's Roots in . . . Levittown? Community Was Both 'Wonderland' and Dullsville, Artist Griffith Says." *Boston Globe*, October 5, 1997, E3.

Zoos

Collecting and displaying live animals, often from exotic locales and faraway continents, has been part of human life for at least 4,500 years. Originally featured in royal or imperial parks and pleasure gardens, upon the rise of bourgeois culture, such animal collections opened to the public and became known as zoological gardens, or zoos, where visitors could contemplate "the wild" and its relationship to human civilization. By the end of the twentieth century, a zoo visit had become one of the rituals of modern life, particularly during childhood; according to a study by the American Association of Zoological Parks and Aquariums, 98 percent of all American and Canadian adults had been to a zoo by 1987, and one-third of them had paid a visit in the last year. About the same time, the legitimacy of collecting and displaying animals became hotly debated, with some people arguing that putting animals in any kind of cage or enclosure was inhumane, and others pointing out that zoos and captive breeding programs offered many species their only hope of survival. In any event, by the turn of the millennium, modern zoos seemed to be focusing (somewhat desperately) on animal welfare and conservation, combined with human education, rather than on entertaining visitors at the expense of inmates.

LIVING CONDITIONS OF ZOO ANIMALS

Zoos have traditionally been dispersal points for information about the relationship between humanity and nature—information deliberately shaped by the owners and/or caretakers of the

Central Park Zoo Polar Bear. A polar bear greets a visitor at New York's Central Park Zoo. DAVID HANDSCHUH/NY DAILY NEWS ARCHIVE VIA/GETTY IMAGES.

animals, whose decisions have in turn been guided (at least in the last hundred years or so) by what research shows the zoo-goers want to see. In any collection, the animals have been essentially packaged—made into products filtered by human minds—and placed in surroundings that say something about the beauty of Creation, the dominance of humankind over nature, or the need for environmental economy and sensitivity. Whether enclosed in cages or moated "environments," the collected creatures usually seem to do no work (unlike farm animals), earning their keep simply by *being* and by being looked at—only passively conveying their controllers' subliminal messages to viewers.

For most of the history of zoos, this perceived limited utilitarian function resulted in cramped quarters, poor diets, depression, and early death for the animals. In an era when animals' value was measured by the physical work they did or the food they produced, perhaps it was reasoned that if the animals served a merely decorative function—as most zoo owners and visitors seemed to have felt they did—they were not entitled to comfortable environments and interesting daily activities. In the twentieth century, studies proved again and again that for most animals a caged life was a short and unhappy one.

To begin with, for many species (including *Homo sapiens*), a stare is received as a threat. Bored and depressed animals might fill the hours with repetitive behaviors known as stereotypy: masturbating to a danger point, pacing their paws raw, or—like many chained elephants—swaying endlessly from side to side. Some chimpanzees developed bulimia, and scientists documented psychosis in a baboon kept on Cyprus. While some people were concerned about these conditions over the years, few took it upon themselves to do much more than decry them; the zoos were not there for the animals but for the people who might have emotional reactions to them.

SYMBOLS OF POWER

Over the years, animal collections and their subliminal significance evolved from the huge local antelope assemblages in Saqqara, Egypt, through signs of imperial power in ancient China and Rome, to the living museums of the current century. In ancient times, a large collection of exotics made a fine testament to royal or imperial power, demonstrating a warrior's ability to bring natural (and, by extension, human) populations under control.

Egyptian, Greek, and Persian rulers were avid collectors, and the Hebrew Bible attributes a substantial menagerie to King Solomon in the tenth century BCE. In the early Common Era, Roman emperors kept lions, tigers, crocodiles, elephants, and other impressive animals; the public could view these exotics in between triumphal imperial processions and spectacular gladiatorial exhibitions in which the animals were, by and large, massacred—occasionally by the thousand. Medieval European nobles and monarchs assembled private menageries that testified to the owners' social position; they often exchanged exotic animals as gifts and tokens of esteem. Lions and leopards were considered particularly valuable.

Indeed, from the Middle Ages to the nineteenth century, Europeans were more interested in the animals of Africa and the Far East than in those of the New World. Meanwhile, European voyagers were discovering the same passion for exotic animals in other cultures. In the thirteenth century Marco Polo marveled at Chinese emperor Kublai Khan's extensive menagerie, including leopards, tigers, elephants, and hunting birds, while in 1519 Hernando Cortés reported that Aztec emperor Montezuma employed hundreds of gardeners and animal keepers for his collections (300 worked in the aviaries alone).

PUBLIC FASCINATION AND ENTERTAINMENT

As cities developed in the modernizing world, zoos became increasingly attractive and accessible to the public. Humankind was moving away from daily contact with nature, and even locally occurring animals were exoticized by urban living. Commoners—most of whom had no opportunity to travel to distant locales—were just as interested in exotic collections as their rulers were. Ancient Greeks paid to see certain bird collections, and starting in 1252 the subjects of Henry III of England could visit his menagerie in the Tower of London for a small fee.

During the Renaissance, some enterprising men toured menageries around smaller towns and villages. With the industrial revolution and its attendant notions of educating and "re-creating" the worker, zoos (like other large urban parks) became truly widespread and available to the masses. A stroll through a zoological garden, it was believed, was an opportunity for relaxation, play (visitors were usually encouraged to feed the animals), and useful contemplation of the wild and exotic.

Zoos were never more popular than in the late nineteenth and early twentieth centuries. The Philadelphia Zoo, the first to be founded (though not the first to be opened) in the United States, welcomed its first visitors in 1874; that year 200,000 people paid 10 or 25 cents, depending on age, to see more than 250 exotics. In an era when a bear cub could cost only $10, the Central Park and Lincoln Park Zoos weren't far behind; the National Zoo opened in 1889, closely associated with the Smithsonian Museum of Natural History. In fact, although there was some emphasis on educating and enriching the common mind, such a relationship between living and taxidermied museums was not uncommon; many zoos were founded as a response to taxidermists' and scientists' clamoring for live models. In the early 1800s the nascent Zoological Society of London declared its intention to bring together animals "from every part of the globe, to be applied either to some useful purpose, or as objects of scientific research, not of vulgar admiration."

Yet vulgar admiration could be said to have carried the day. Trained by television and amusement parks, the majority of twentieth-century zoo-goers went for cotton candy and sea lion stunt shows, elephant feedings and monorail rides. Education—about habitat destruction, the human value of the rain forest, the life cycle of the koala bear—was largely incidental, though it did eventually become the administrators' battle cry.

NATURALISM AND EDUCATION

To visit a typical modern zoological garden is to step into an exotic realm, from the African village-style gateway to the far reaches of the polar bear environment and the ubiquitous jungle-themed trading posts and snack bars. But immersion in an exotic environment had rarely been part of the original zoo experience. Until well into the twentieth century, stacks of cages and gloomy indoor display areas (some of them located in the upper stories of warehouses) were considered acceptable; after all, the public was coming to see the animals, not how the animals lived in the wild. The London Zoo, for example, was famous for housing its collection in buildings that would be considered stylish for human inhabitants, but those buildings were not necessarily the most healthful or comfortable for the exotic species.

Plants were not part of a typical exhibit until France's Louis XIV established what is considered the first real zoological *garden* at Versailles. His design was revolutionary in that it displayed animals (222 species) and plants together—rather than animals in cages and plants outside. In 1907 German maverick Carl Hagenbeck opened the first barless zoo, whose enclosures incorporated plant life along with animals. Until the end of the twentieth century, however, indoor barracks and outdoor cages were the norm, and an effort toward naturalism might mean someone had painted an iceberg on the wall of the polar bear exhibit. To avoid harmful drafts, animals were often denied any form of fresh air; in *Animal Gardens*, historian Emily Hahn writes that in 1902 the cats, monkeys, and parrots in London's Regent's Park zoo were even kept from oxygen. To keep an animal alive under these conditions was nearly miraculous—and, again, made another neat statement about the powers of its possessor.

In 1993 Stephen St. C. Bostock, author of a book on zoos and animal rights, pointed out that zoo animals were not really prisoners, largely because they showed no consciousness of imprisonment; nonetheless their status was debated, with the result that many of the conditions in which they lived underwent radical change. In his 2010 book, *Zoo Story*, former administrator Thomas French, for example, refers to his old zoo as a "Garden of Captives." The newly documented stereotype led zookeepers to try sometimes radical treatments. A few animals were given the antidepressant Prozac, with surprisingly positive results; however, the cost of dosing a multiton elephant was prohibitive, and in any case drugs were usually a last resort. It was generally considered more desirable to enrich animals' lives through stimulating activities, such as searching for food, and through more naturalistic environments. Landscape architects and contractors with truckloads of faux rock moved in and remade one zoo after another with cinematic realism.

The more dangerous and exotic an animal was perceived to be, the more popular it was, and hence the more money and attention lavished on its environment. Lions, tigers, giant pandas, koalas, and gorillas were among the first to benefit from new-generation treatment. In the 1980s, according to a *Newsweek* estimate, 143 American zoos spent $1 billion on enriching their animals' lives. Much of that sum went toward creating new naturalistic environments with record-setting price tags, such as Zoo Atlanta's $4.5 million rain forest and the Bronx Zoo's $9.5 million Jungleworld. Most spending was on a more modest scale, but administrators discovered that the animals tended to be happier in their new environments—or at least the animal lovers were happier thinking about the creatures in them.

Even these attempts at creating natural environments might disappoint their inhabitants. A heap of Gunite boulders, for example, probably does not feel like the real thing to a lion-tailed macaque. Moreover, only the parts of an exhibit visible to visitors were likely to be redesigned; the night cages, where the animals sleep, generally did not change. One administrator declared an intention to "mold an exhibit that would provide zoo guests with an experience as natural as possible"; accordingly, most redesigns still kept in mind the zoo-goer rather than the inhabitant. Studies did in fact show that zoo-goers (all television-trained by this point) tended to think animals displayed in natural environments were more active and attractive, whereas those in cages were more passive and less interesting. But all that planning and work was, in the end, lavished on a fleeting experience. A 1987 American Association of Zoological Parks and Aquariums (later the Association of Zoos and Aquariums) study found that most visitors stayed at an exhibit for only one to three minutes.

CONSERVATION AND CRYOGENICS

Hand in hand with redesign came an interest in conservation, most of it dependent on highly developed technologies. In fact, zoos already had a long history as breeding grounds for scientific discovery and research. In the eighteenth century visits to the Swedish royal menagerie inspired Carolus Linnaeus to develop the Latinate system of binomial nomenclature by which animals and plants have been classified ever since, and post–industrial revolution zoos were considered valuable resources for natural historians and taxidermists.

In the mid-twentieth century, as human concern for the environment mounted, zoo animals took on a new function, as agents of global salvation. By means of captive breeding programs, including cryogenically frozen eggs and sperm, zoos set out to become latter-day arks, saving species from what many people saw as inevitable extinction due to expanding industrialism and consequent environmental catastrophe. There was also a concern with preserving not just an animal's body but also its natural behaviors (including mating, predation, foraging, and leisure activities). These new interests, similar to the surge in redesign, were perhaps the indirect result of the technology used in television's nature programs and cinema's special effects. Zoos had to become more "authentic" too.

This emphasis on conservation was seen by some as ironic, given the depredations that had taken place as industrial-era zoos were first stocked. Until the Endangered Species Act was passed in 1973, famous animal suppliers such as Frank Buck regularly ventured into the wild to slaughter adult animals and bring the babies back alive. But by the turn of the millennium there seemed to be little doubt that preservation of individuals and conservation of species, as well as enrichment of captive lives, were high priorities.

Accredited zoos joined a worldwide breeding network; under the Species Survival Plans, sperm and eggs were frozen, and live animals shipped from one end of the globe to the other in order to mate. Some embryos of rare animals, such as zebras, were gestated inside more common species, such as domestic horses. Yet even with their best efforts and most sophisticated technology, zoo administrators estimated that they could save only about 900 of the 2,000 vertebrate species expected to go extinct by 2000. The current success rate is impossible to determine, but most admit that, for example, the African elephant will almost certainly be extinct by 2020, with just a few elderly specimens languishing in zoos that cannot provide the conditions in which they might reproduce successfully.

With the cryogenic zoo, humankind has become more than ever the race that has mastered all others. Even as most zoological gardens attempt to educate visitors about the beauty and importance of wild animals and plants, other workers behind the scenes are manipulating nature with their test tubes and psychotropic medications. Zoos are thus a combination of television-era entertainment, light news, and science fiction.

It must be emphasized that most scientists and keepers—and many fee-paying visitors—are indeed motivated by high ideals, such as respect for other species, rather than the appetite for self-aggrandizement that marked the owners of older zoos. But the desire to rescue those species nonetheless may be said to stem from the old impulse to control nature and make use of it as something both antithetical and complementary to human civilization. In *New Worlds, New Animals*, Michael H. Robinson, onetime director of the Smithsonian Institution's National Zoological Park, places the drive to collect living things and "alter . . . them for our benefit" at the origin of civilization. As the twenty-first century advances, the contemporary zoo, similar to its predecessors, is a living (though increasingly frozen) embodiment of that drive.

Susann Cokal

SEE ALSO: *Amusement Parks; Central Park; Leisure Time; Smithsonian Institution; Television;* Wild Kingdom.

BIBLIOGRAPHY

"African Elephants Face Extinction by 2020, Conservationists Warn." *Telegraph*, August 4, 2008. Accessed December 12, 2011. Available from http://www.telegraph.co.uk/earth/earthnews/3348683/African-elephants-face-extinction-by-2020-conservationists-warn.html

Bartlett, Abraham Dee, and Edward Bartlett. *Wild Animals in Captivity*. London: Chapman and Hall, 1899.

Bostock, Stephen St. C. *Zoos and Animal Rights: The Ethics of Keeping Animals*. London: Routledge, 1993.

Croke, Vicki. *The Modern Ark*. New York: Scribner, 1997.

French, Thomas. *Zoo Story: Life in the Garden of Captives*. New York: Hyperion, 2010.

Hahn, Emily. *Animal Gardens*. Garden City, NY: Doubleday, 1967.

Hancocks, David. *A Different Nature: The Paradoxical World of Zoos and Their Uncertain Future*. Berkeley: University of California Press, 2002.

Hanson, Elizabeth. *Animal Attractions: Nature on Display in American Zoos*. Princeton, NJ: Princeton University Press, 2004.

Hoage, R. J., and William A. Deiss, eds. *New Worlds, New Animals*. Baltimore, MD: Johns Hopkins University Press, 1996.

Livingston, Bernard. *Zoo Animals, People, Places*. New York: Arbor House, 1974.

Ritvo, Harriet. *The Animal Estate: The English and Other Creatures in the Victorian Age*. Cambridge, MA: Harvard University Press, 1989.

Zuckerman, Lord, ed. *Great Zoos of the World: Their Origins and Significance*. Boulder, CO: Westview Press, 1980.

Zoot Suit

The zoot suit was a style of clothing popularized by young male African Americans, Filipino Americans, and Mexican Americans during the 1930s and 1940s. A zoot suit had very baggy, high-waisted pants, pegged around the ankles, and a long jacket that came to below the knee. The jacket had high, wide shoulder pads that jutted out from the shoulder, giving the wearer a broad look. A long chain dangled from the belt, and the outfit was trimmed with thick-soled shoes and a wide-brimmed hat. The style of very hip "cats," it is believed to have been created in the African American community, although stories abound as to the zoot suit's exact origins.

In the urban jazz culture of Harlem, New York, the word *zoot* meant something exaggerated, either in style, sound, or performance. The style of dress was an extravagant one, out of proportion to the norm, and it later came to be known as the zoot suit, which consisted of "a killer-diller coat with a drape-shape, reat-pleats and shoulders padded like a lunatic's cell." The suit was for having fun, with the baggy pants made for dancing the jitterbug and the long coat and wide-brimmed hat giving the wearer a grown-up look.

One theory of the origins of the zoot suit was that it was an imitation of the suit worn by Clark Cable in the movie *Gone with the Wind*. In fact, some people called zoot suits "Gone with the Wind suits." Another possibility is that big-band leader and clothier Harold C. Fox designed the first zoot suit. He claimed that he copied the fashions of ghetto-dwelling teenagers to create the zoot suit for musicians who wanted an "eye-poppin' style." When Fox died in 1996 at the age of eighty-six, he was buried in a lavender zoot suit.

The most believed story about the zoot suit's origins is one published in the *New York Times* in 1943—during the zoot suit riots in Los Angeles—that stated that a young African American busboy from Gainesville, Georgia, placed an order with a tailor for what would be the "first zoot suit on record." Clyde Duncan ordered a suit with a 37-inch-long coat and with pants 26 inches in circumference at the knees and 14 inches at the ankle. Once the suit was made, the tailor took Clyde's picture and sent it to *Men's Apparel Reporter*, where the photo was printed.

Many famous black entertainers and musicians wore the zoot suit. Duke Ellington performed at the Orpheum Theatre in Los Angeles in 1941 with a musical number called "Jump for Joy," and all his performers wore zoot suits. Cab Calloway wore a zoot suit in the 1943 film *Stormy Weather*.

On the West Coast, the suit came to be identified with young Mexican Americans, known as *pachucos*. They were mostly second-generation Mexican Americans, the sons of working-class immigrants who settled in Los Angeles. Pachucos created a subculture with a mysterious argot that incorporated archaic Spanish, modern Spanish, and English slang words. They dressed in zoot suits, creating a distinct style that identified them as neither Mexican nor American but that emphasized their social detachment and isolation.

After the United States entered World War II in 1941, and fabric as well as other materials needed to be conserved, wearing the zoot suit was considered an unpatriotic act. In the summer of 1943, while the whole country watched, gangs of sailors and zoot-suiters fought in the streets of Los Angeles. Outraged at the zoot suit style, sailors chased the zoot suiters through the streets and unclothed them. It is unclear if this was a race riot or a riot of patriotism by the sailors who attacked, beat, and stripped young Mexican Americans, whom they perceived to be disloyal immigrants.

Zoot Suit. *A man models a zoot suit, complete with oversized bow tie, elongated chain, and suspenders, in a clothing store in 1942.* MARIE HANSEN/TIME LIFE PICTURES/GETTY IMAGES.

The zoot suit received wide attention and recognition in the 1970s with the production of the play *Zoot Suit*, written and produced by Luis Valdez. It was performed in Los Angeles and New York. A film of the play, with the same name, was released in 1981 with performances by actors Daniel Valdez and Edward James Olmos.

In the late 1990s the zoot suit had a brief rebirth with the revival of swing music, together with imitations of Calloway, the zoot suit, and jump-dance steps. From Chicago to San Francisco, twenty-somethings danced to big bands—including the Mighty Blue Kings, the Big Six, Bag Bad Voodoo Daddy, and Indigo Swing—that played swing music from the 1930s and 1940s. Part of the fun of this music was dancing at big clubs and wearing the clothes to match. By the end of the twentieth century, the revival had lost its mainstream appeal, and the popularity of the zoot suit faded once again.

Rafaela Castro

SEE ALSO: *Big Bands; Calloway, Cab; Ellington, Duke; Gable, Clark;* Gone with the Wind*; The* New York Times*; Olmos, Edward James; Pachucos; Swing Dancing; Valdez, Luis; World War II.*

BIBLIOGRAPHY

Peiss, Kathy. *Zoot Suit: The Enigmatic Career of an Extreme Style*. Philadelphia: University of Pennsylvania Press, 2011.

Rourke, Mary. "A Suitable Enterprise for the Counterculture: Reflections on the Zoot Suit." *Los Angeles Times*, August 5, 1996.

Tyler, Bruce. "Zoot-Suit Culture and the Black Press." *Journal of American Culture* 17 (1994): 21–33.

White, Shane, and Graham White. *Stylin': African American Expressive Culture from Its Beginnings to the Zoot Suit*. Ithaca, NY: Cornell University Press, 1998.

Zorro

Zorro, the sword-wielding, black-clad avenger, is one of the most influential fictional characters of twentieth-century literature. By day he was Don Diego, a respected nobleman of nineteenth-century California. By night, however, he cut a much more dashing figure as "The Fox"—El Zorro. Dressed completely in black with a mask and wide-brimmed hat to conceal his identity, Zorro battled evildoers with the aid of his whip and sword and made fast getaways on his black steed, Tornado. He was a superbly talented fencer—only Cyrano de Bergerac, D'Artagnan, and the Three Musketeers challenge him for the title of fiction's most popular swordsman. No matter where he went, he always signed his work with a distinctive *Z*, often cut into the clothing or skin of his enemies.

BEGINNINGS

Zorro's adventures have been chronicled in many different media. Created by writer Johnston McCulley in 1919 for "The Curse of Capistrano," which was serialized in the pulp magazine

Antonio Banderas as Zorro. *Antonio Banderas portrayed the title character in the 2005 film* The Legend of Zorro. COLUMBIA PICTURES/SPYGLASS/THE KOBAL COLLECTION/COOPER, ANDREW.

All-Story Weekly, Zorro is the oldest of the modern superheroes. McCulley would write a total of sixty-five adventures of the black-clad avenger over the next thirty-nine years. Since Zorro's introduction, countless characters have been created using the same basic theme: a normally law-abiding individual who is faced with great injustice and takes up a mask and secret identity to right wrongs and protect the innocent. Moreover, Zorro's devil-may-care attitude, mastery with the sword, daring escapes, and tendency to laugh in the face of authority have become common traits of swashbuckling heroes.

Though he began as a pulp-magazine character, Zorro soared to popularity in film. In all, he has been featured in dozens of movies, plus a number of Republic serialized adventures. Zorro's first foray onto the big screen came when popular actor Douglas Fairbanks Sr., on his honeymoon with Mary Pickford, read "The Curse of Capistrano." He and Pickford chose that story to kick off their new film studio, United Artists, and in 1920 released it as *The Mark of Zorro*. Zorro remained a popular film character in the decades that followed. Tyrone Power took up the sword and mask in *The Mark of Zorro* (1940).

A 1950s Disney television show, *Zorro*, starred Guy Williams in the title role. the program was, at the time, the highest-budgeted Western on television. Many more movie and television adaptations of Zorro's adventures were made in the 1960s, 1970s, and 1980s. They included films from Europe and an animated series, *The New Adventures of Zorro*, which ran from 1981 to 1983.

RENEWED INTEREST

Zorro experienced another resurgence in popularity in the 1990s with a live-action television series that ran for eighty-eight episodes. A new animated series debuted in 1992, and a 1995 stage musical opened to critical acclaim. The year 1998 saw the release of *The Mask of Zorro*, starring Antonio Banderas as the protégé of Anthony Hopkins' Don Diego. The film was a great success, collecting almost $95 million at the box office, the highest total for any Zorro film, and it led to a sequel in 2005 titled *The Legend of Zorro*. Yet another animated series was unveiled around the same time, along with a line of Zorro toys.

Zorro has also seen his share of caricature. In the early 1980s the television series *Zorro and Son* took a comedic approach toward his adventures, and the 1981 film *Zorro, the Gay Blade* featured George Hamilton as an effeminate relative of Zorro who fought injustice in a pink leather costume, complete with Zorro's trusty whip.

In 2008 *Zorro the Musical* opened in London. The script by playwright Stephen Clark was based on novelist Isabel Allende's 2005 fictional biography *Zorro*, and the music was written by the well-known pop group the Gypsy Kings. The show's London run lasted until March 2009, which was followed by a worldwide tour, with U.S. shows beginning in 2012.

Much of Zorro's continued resurgence is a result of the efforts of Zorro Productions, a company formed by John Gertz in the 1970s to promote the fictional hero. The company has produced many of the movie and TV versions of the story, and it also promotes Zorro in other industries. There are Zorro-licensed slot machines and a Zorro-branded tequila, for example, as well as Zorro merchandising lines for costumes, home decor, and other items.

WHY THIS HERO?

Zorro was one of the earliest of many successful twentieth-century characters who tapped into the frustration of readers. People were afraid: afraid of crime, afraid of war, afraid of oppressive governments. El Zorro and his dashing adventures allowed them to imagine a world where wrongs could be righted, not through a system that was often slow and corrupt but one that was swift and sure. His sword and whip attacked villains whom justice could not touch—sometimes the villains were themselves the supposed guardians of justice.

Zorro is also the consummate romantic, a combination of Latin lover, gentleman bandit, and charming rogue. Even as enemy forces closed in from all sides, he often found the time to give his leading lady a passionate kiss before he executed another daring escape.

Another important component of Zorro's appeal lies in his near-supernatural ability to defy the odds. No matter how great the challenge or powerful the enemy, Zorro always comes out on top to set things right. He was the underdog who could even the odds with a stroke of his blade, taking down the powerful and arrogant by several notches. Whenever a screen swashbuckler defies a sputtering tyrant, or a grim, black-clad comic-book vigilante stalks the night seeking criminal prey, both are following in the footsteps of El Zorro and the ideals that made him popular through generations of fans.

Paul F. P. Pogue

SEE ALSO: *Disney (Walt Disney Company); Fairbanks, Douglas, Sr.; Pickford, Mary; Pulp Magazines; Television; Toys; United Artists; The Western.*

BIBLIOGRAPHY

Curtis, Sandra R. *Zorro Unmasked: The Official History.* New York: Hyperion, 1998.

Hutchison, Don. *The Great Pulp Heroes.* Buffalo, NY: Mosaic Press, 1996.

McCulley, Johnston. *The Mark of Zorro.* New York: American Reprint, 1976.

Toth, Alex. *Zorro: The Complete Classic Adventures.* Forestville, CA: Eclipse Books, 1988.

Zydeco

Zydeco is a unique blend of African American and African French musical traditions that developed amid the prairie landscapes of southwestern Louisiana. Born out of close interaction between the Cajun (white) and Creole (black) French-speaking cultures, zydeco's current popularity as an infectious dance music is directly tied to the past when house dances were the primary form of entertainment and interaction for the rural Creole population. The music played for these gatherings was called "la-la" and was the immediate precursor to modern zydeco. From this hearth area the music spread to other regions, at first associated with the outmigration patterns of Creoles to east Texas and Southern California. The availability of this music in recorded form has enabled people everywhere to listen to the sounds of southwestern Louisiana. Following zydeco's commercial success, many groups have toured extensively, both nationally and internationally, and zydeco has become popular in other parts of the world.

"Buckwheat Zydeco." *Stanley "Buckwheat Zydeco" Dural performs during the 2011 New Orleans Jazz & Heritage Festival.* JEFFREY UFBERG/STRINGER/WIREIMAGE/GETTY IMAGES.

BEGINNINGS OF A TRADITION

The origin of the term *zydeco* is most often attributed to the folk expression "les haricots ne sont pas salés" (the beans are not salted), a saying that reflects those hard times when people could not even afford to put salt pork in their pot of beans. The name found its way into popular culture in the 1950s, when folk music field recording anthologist Mack McCormick spelled out the word for the first time. The proper pronunciation is with the accent on the first syllable. Early forms of zydeco used the same instruments as Cajun music. The fiddle, which came to Louisiana from Canada after 1755 by way of the Acadian migration, was the standard lead instrument. During the mid-1800s the accordion was adopted and soon replaced the fiddle as the lead; the typical configuration was a diatonic accordion with a single or double row of buttons.

A unique rhythm instrument—the *frottoir*, or rubboard—is the signature instrument of zydeco, and no band is deemed complete without one. Its antecedents most likely are the rasped or notched gourds common to African and African Caribbean traditions, though it also has connections to the old-fashioned washboards once used to scrub laundry. The modern instrument, made out of corrugated sheet metal, is worn over the shoulders like a breastplate and played with a pair of spoons or old-style bottle openers. The zydeco pioneer Clifton Chenier was fond of telling the story of how he first traced out the design for the contemporary frottoir in the sand of an oil refinery yard. Zydeco's spreading popularity led to the marketing of a novelty "zydeco tie," a mini-rubboard that could be worn as a necktie and played with thimbles by armchair zydeco musicians.

During the first several decades of the twentieth century, when social events were still strictly segregated in Louisiana, the most influential Creole musician was Amédé Ardoin, who was a much-sought-after performer at both white and black dances. The effect of his accordion playing and plaintive singing on audiences is the stuff of legend. A grimmer remembrance concerns the career-ending incident in which he was brutally assaulted while walking home after a dance for allegedly accepting a white woman's handkerchief to wipe off his sweaty brow.

As with other aspects of popular culture in America, the zydeco landscape experienced rapid changes after World War II. The house dances faded away, to be replaced by the dance halls and clubs that hosted a variety of music in vogue with black audiences, although zydeco bands still formed a major component of the bookings. Despite a more commercial, adult-oriented setting, many of the clubs retained something of a family atmosphere. Instrumentation responded to the popularity of other musical forms and the newer, more spacious venues, becoming a fuller sound with the addition of drums, electric guitars, and even saxophones.

As the music became influenced by an urbanized blues and other commercially recorded styles of the 1940s and 1950s, the piano accordion replaced the Cajun button accordion within zydeco. The emerging genre was best personified by Chenier, the undisputed king of zydeco, who was born in 1925 near Opelousas, in the very heart of Louisiana's Creole country. In 1947 he moved to Lake Charles, Louisiana, and then to Port Arthur, Texas. In 1958 he moved to Houston, Texas, where his playing became influenced heavily by the urban blues scene. It was Chenier who popularized the term *zydeco* and specifically linked it to his music, which ranged from blues sung in either French or English and backed by a full ensemble to more traditional African French songs accompanied only by an accordion and a frottoir.

THE MAINSTREAM DISCOVERS ZYDECO

Other prominent musicians have helped to guide the development of zydeco and to place it in a more accessible position within the wider arena of popular culture. Another early pioneer, Boozoo Chavis, after cutting a few records during the 1950s, actually stopped playing music publicly for more than twenty years. In 1984 he emerged from relative obscurity in a joyous comeback. Still playing the older button accordion, which he preferred for its raw energy and more traditional sound, Chavis remains the favorite zydeco performer of many devoted fans even after his death in 2001.

Queen Ida Guillory, originally from Lake Charles but living for many years in the San Francisco Bay Area, began playing for the displaced Louisiana Creoles who had migrated to the West and were holding traditional house dances in their basements or at Catholic church halls. As her music gained fans among the general population, she began touring and was the first zydeco artist to play in Japan. In 1983 she also became the first zydeco musician to receive a Grammy Award, for her album *Queen Ida on Tour*. In 2009 Guillory received the National Endowment for the Arts National Heritage Fellowship, the nation's highest honor for folk artists. Other notable musicians of corresponding vintage include several who have died, including Alton "Rockin' Dopsie" Rubin Sr., John Delafose, and Clarence "Gatemouth" Brown.

Certain performers have deliberately sought a wider audience for zydeco, either by touring extensively or by blending more rock and soul influences into their sound; these include Terrance Simien and the Zydeco Experience, who won a 2008 Grammy Award for their album *Live! Worldwide*, and Stanley "Buckwheat" Dural Jr.

An accordionist, Dural was especially influential in the spread of zydeco into mainstream culture. Once part of Chenier's band, Dural began using the name Buckwheat Zydeco and formed the Ils Sont Partis Band, named for the announcer's call at the beginning of horse races at Evangeline Downs in Lafayette in the heart of French-speaking Louisiana. The first zydeco musician to sign with a major record label (Island Records in 1986), Dural has received Grammy nominations. He played at both inaugural celebrations for President Bill Clinton (1993 and 1997) and performed at the 1996 Summer Olympics in Atlanta, Georgia. Dural became known for his innovative renditions of unlikely popular music in zydeco style, such as his children's album *Bayou Boogie* (2010), which features rousing zydeco versions of such favorites as "Hokey Pokey."

During the 1990s a new generation emerged in Louisiana to carry the tradition into the future. Dubbed "zydekids" by some, they played a "nouveau zydeco," which drew on the earlier French "la-la" music rather than the previous attempts at crossover appeal. Foremost among that trend, Beau Jocque began playing accordion after a painful industrial accident in 1987 left him temporarily paralyzed. Until his death in 1999 he was widely acclaimed as the leader of the new zydeco sound, which featured simplified accordion chords; a deeper, more powerful bass; and a catchy dance rhythm from the drums known as "double clutching." Among others pursuing a revitalized zydeco were Keith Frank; Jo Jo Reed; and a pair of traditionalist women accordion players, Ann Goodly and Rosie Ledet.

FROM THE DANCE HALL TO THE RADIO

Perhaps the most effective carrier for diffusion of this music to other places has been its commercial recording and widespread distribution on records, tapes, and CDs. Early zydeco recordings by Douglas Bellard, Ardoin, and others were strictly for regional release. Clarence Garlow of Beaumont, Texas, had a few minor hits in the early 1950s, paving the way for two back-to-back releases that began the commercial success of recorded zydeco: "Paper in My Shoe" by Chavis in 1954 followed by Chenier's "Ay-Tete-Fee" in 1955. Before national record labels began capitalizing on the growing popularity of this music, the commercial recording and distribution of most zydeco records were shepherded by two independent labels: Chris Strachwitz's Arhoolie Records in El Cerrito, California, and Floyd Soileau's Maison de Soul in Ville Platte, Louisiana. In 1982 Rockin' Sidney Simien's hit single "My Toot-Toot" became an international sensation, and, with more than a million copies sold, it is still among the best-selling records in zydeco history.

The popularity of zydeco has continued to grow and spread. New digital formats, such as YouTube, have made access to the greats of the genre easier than ever, and cajunradio.org offers a comprehensive guide to Louisiana's traditional music, with an emphasis on the Baton Rouge area. In response to zydeco's growing audience, in 2007 the Grammy Awards added a separate category for Best Zydeco or Cajun Music Album, although the category was eliminated in a 2011 revamp. The Disney animated film *The Princess and the Frog* (2009) is set in New Orleans and features a zydeco-inspired original soundtrack by the award-winning songwriter Randy Newman.

Like many traditional genres, zydeco is very much a generational music, with children and grandchildren following their parents in performing groups. For example, Alphonse "Bois Sec" Ardoin, cousin of the zydeco pioneer Amédé Ardoin, was an acclaimed accordionist from the mid-1940s into the first decade of the 2000s, some of that time with the Ardoin Family Orchestra. During the 1970s, three of Bois Sec's sons—Morris, Lawrence, and Gustave—joined the zydeco scene as the Ardoin Brothers, and by the late 1990s his grandsons Chris and Sean had formed their own zydeco bands. As these new generations of zydeco musicians emerge, they continue the development of the genre by adding modern influences of funk, rock, and hip-hop.

Zydeco clubs remain active throughout the Lafayette-to-Houston corridor and heartily welcome people of all races who want to hear the music in its original setting. Since 1982 the tiny crossroads community of Plaisance plays host each year to the Southwest Louisiana Zydeco Festival. This event showcases the leading zydeco musicians in the world and consists of a full roster of entertainment, with bands taking the stage one after another in a twelve-hour-long continuous celebration. In 2007 the New Orleans Jazz and Heritage Foundation introduced an annual Louisiana Cajun-Zydeco Festival in New Orleans. Although still identified with Creole culture in its home territory, zydeco has become a popular style of dance music around the world.

Robert Kuhlken

SEE ALSO: *Blues; Chavis, Boozoo; Chenier, Clifton; Disney (Walt Disney Company); Folk Music; Funk; Grammy Awards; Hip-Hop; Rhythm and Blues; Rock and Roll; YouTube.*

BIBLIOGRAPHY

Ancelet, Barry. "Zydeco/Zarico: Beans, Blues, and Beyond." *Black Music Research Journal* 8 (1988): 33–49.

Brasseaux, Ryan André. *Cajun Breakdown: The Emergence of an American-Made Music.* New York: Oxford University Press, 2009.

Broven, John. *South to Louisiana: The Music of the Cajun Bayous.* Gretna, LA: Pelican Publishing, 1983.

DeWitt, Mark F. *Cajun and Zydeco Dance Music in Northern California: Modern Pleasures in a Postmodern World.* Jackson: University Press of Mississippi, 2008.

Gould, Philip, and Barry Jean Ancelet. *Cajun Music and Zydeco.* Baton Rouge: Louisiana State University Press, 1992.

Kuhlken, Robert, and Rocky Sexton. "The Geography of Zydeco Music." In *The Sounds of People and Places: A Geography of American Folk and Popular Music,* 3rd ed., ed. G. Carney. Lanham, MD: Rowman & Littlefield, 1994.

Nyhan, Patricia; Brian Rollins; and David Babb. *Let the Good Times Roll! A Guide to Cajun & Zydeco Music.* Portland, ME: Upbeat Books, 1997.

Sandmel, Ben. *Zydeco!* Jackson: University Press of Mississippi, 1999.

Tisserand, Michael. *The Kingdom of Zydeco.* New York: Arcade Publishing, 1998.

ZZ Top

From respected roots rockers to bearded icons of the music-video age, this Texas band maintained a consistently successful career throughout the 1970s and 1980s, embracing many new trends that crossed its path. Although not as active in the early twenty-first century as they were in their prime, ZZ Top's three members (Billy Gibbons, Dusty Hill, and Frank Beard on guitar, bass, and drums, respectively) remain one of the few groups to retain all its original members after forty years. Existing in the 1970s as a critically acclaimed, popular Texas blues-boogie band, the band updated its sound to include propulsive synthesizer rhythms. Further, ZZ Top was one of the first pre-music-video rock bands to immediately take advantage of the advent of MTV.

In the late 1960s Gibbons played in the Texas psych-punk band the Moving Sidewalks, and Hill and Beard were the rhythm section for American Blues. Future ZZ Top manager Bill Ham brought the three together in 1970 and, because of Ham's scheme of constant recording and ceaseless touring, by the end of the decade the group had carved out a sizable niche as a popular blues-boogie band. In 1970 ZZ Top released *ZZ Top's First Album,* and by the band's third album it struck gold with its first major hit and concert staple, "La Grange," a tribute to an infamous whorehouse. "La Grange" (whose signature riff was based on the John Lee Hooker song "Boogie Chillen") set the fire that would culminate in one the 1970s most successful tours, the year-and-a-half-long "Worldwide Texas Tour."

Even though the group's string of hits continued through the end of the 1970s and into the early 1980s, it was the 1983 *Eliminator* album that propelled ZZ Top to superstardom. The group's adoption of synthesizers and drum machines to augment their sound helped explain its success, but what perhaps was the most important element was the band's videos. With sunglasses and long beards, ZZ Top had a distinctive made-for-music-video image, and they filled the videos with scantily clad, sexy women—a perfect formula for early MTV success. *Eliminator* contained a number of hit singles and videos, including "Legs," "Sharp Dressed Man," and "Gimme All Your Lovin'." Choosing not to disrupt their successful formula, the group made their 1985 *Afterburner* in the image of their multiplatinum predecessor, and the album spawned the hits "Sleeping Bag," "Velcro Fly," "Rough Boy," and "Stages." The group applied its "if it ain't broke don't fix it" philosophy to *Afterburner*'s videos as well.

The commercial peaks of its mid-1980s period behind it, the band remained a big concert draw and its albums continued to sell respectably. The 1996 release of *Rhythmeen,* a back-to-basics album, cleared the table of the high production sheen and synthesizers that characterized their *Afterburner* and *Eliminator* period. The album was critically acclaimed and demonstrated that Gibbons was certainly one of the most talented white blues guitarists this side of Stevie Ray Vaughan. ZZ Top released *Mescalero* in 2003, the band's last studio album as of 2012. They were inducted into the Rock and Roll Hall of Fame in 2004 and have continued to record and play live for a whole new generation of fans through the early part of the new millennium.

Kembrew McLeod

SEE ALSO: *Blues; Hooker, John Lee; MTV; Punk; Rock and Roll; Videos.*

BIBLIOGRAPHY

Blayney, David. *Sharp-Dressed Men: ZZ Top behind the Scenes from Blues to Boogie to Beards.* New York: Hyperion, 1994.

Gibbons, Billy; David Perry; and Tom Vickers. *Billy F. Gibbons: Rock and Roll Gearhead.* St. Paul, MN: MBI Publishing, 2005.

Sinclair, David. *The Story of ZZ Top: Tres Hombres.* London: Virgin, 1986.

Reading List

The following reading list is meant as a supplement to the bibliographies included in the entries. It includes two types of works: those that explain the long-term, historical development of popular culture in the United States and those that discuss the academic study of popular culture. Among the latter are both theoretical explications and reference works.

Ashplant, T. G. *Explorations in Cultural History*. Sterling, VA: Pluto Press, 2001.

Barthes, Roland. *Mythologies*, tr. Annette Lavers. New York: Noonday Press, 1972.

Benshoff, Harry, and Sean Griffin. *America on Film: Representing Race, Class, Gender, and Sexuality at the Movies*, 2nd ed. Malden, MA: Wiley-Blackwell, 2009.

Bigsby, C. W. E., ed. *Approaches to Popular Culture*. Bowling Green, OH: Bowling Green State University Popular Press, 1976.

Bluestein, Gene. *Poplore: Folk and Pop in American Culture*. Amherst: University of Massachusetts Press, 1994.

Bode, Carl. *The Anatomy of American Popular Culture, 1840–1861*. Berkeley: University of California Press, 1960.

Bordo, Susan. *Unbearable Weight: Feminism, Western Culture, and the Body*. Berkeley: University of California Press, 1993.

Browne, Ray B. *Popular Culture and the Expanding Consciousness*. New York: Wiley, 1973.

Browne, Ray B., and Ronald J. Ambrosetti, eds. *Continuities in Popular Culture: The Present in the Past and the Past in the Present and Future*. Bowling Green, OH: Bowling Green State University Popular Press, 1993.

Browne, Ray B., and Marshall Fishwick, eds. *Preview 2001+: Popular Culture Studies in the Future*. Bowling Green, OH: Bowling Green State University Popular Press, 1995.

Browne, Ray B., and Marshall Fishwick, eds. *Symbiosis: Popular Culture and Other Fields*. Bowling Green, OH: Bowling Green State University Popular Press, 1988.

Browne, Ray B.; Marshall W. Fishwick; and Kevin O. Browne, eds. *Dominant Symbols in Popular Culture*. Bowling Green, OH: Bowling Green State University Popular Press, 1990.

Browne, Ray B., and David Madden. *The Popular Culture Explosion*. Dubuque, IA: W. C. Brown, 1972.

Browne, Ray B., and Michael T. Marsden, eds. *Pioneers in Popular Culture Studies*. Bowling Green, OH: Bowling Green State University Popular Press, 1999.

Buhle, Paul, ed. *Popular Culture in America*. Minneapolis: University of Minnesota Press, 1987.

Cantor, Norman F., and Michael S. Werthman, eds. *The History of Popular Culture*. New York: Macmillan, 1968.

Carter, Steven. *Leopards in the Temple: Studies in American Popular Culture*. San Francisco: International Scholars Publications, 1997.

Cullen, Jim. *The Art of Democracy: A Concise History of Popular Culture in the United States*. New York: Monthly Review Press, 1996.

Dale, Timothy M., and Joseph J. Foy, eds. *Homer Simpson Marches on Washington: Dissent through America Popular Culture*. Lexington: University Press of Kentucky, 2010.

Denney, Reuel. *The Astonished Muse*. Chicago: University of Chicago Press, 1974.

Denning, Michael. *The Cultural Front: The Laboring of American Culture in the Twentieth Century*. New York: Verso, 1998.

Douglas, Susan. *Where the Girls Are: Growing Up Female with the Mass Media*. New York: Times Books, 1994.

Elledge, Jim, ed. *Queers in American Popular Culture*. Santa Barbara, CA: Praeger, 2010.

Fishwick, Marshall W. *Common Culture and the Great Tradition: The Case for Renewal*. Westport, CT: Greenwood Press, 1982.

Fishwick, Marshall W. *Parameters of Popular Culture*. Bowling Green, OH: Bowling Green State University Popular Press, 1974.

Fiske, John. *Understanding Popular Culture*. Boston: Unwin/Hyman, 1989.

Flaherty, David H., and Frank E. Manning, eds. *The Beaver Bites Back?: American Popular Culture in Canada*. Montreal: McGill-Queen's University Press, 1993.

Gans, Herbert J. *Popular Culture and High Culture: An Analysis and Evaluation of Taste*. New York: Basic Books, 1974.

Geist, Christopher D., and Jack Nachbar, eds. *The Popular Culture Reader*. Bowling Green, OH: Bowling Green State University Popular Press, 1983.

Geist, Christopher D.; Michael T. Marsden; Ray B. Browne, et al., eds. *The Directory of Popular Culture Collections*. Phoenix, AZ: Oryx Press, 1989.

Gibian, Peter, ed. *Mass Culture and Everyday Life*. New York: Routledge, 1997.

Giroux, Henry A. *Disturbing Pleasures: Learning Popular Culture*. New York: Routledge, 1994.

Gordon, Mark, and Jack Nachbar, eds. *Currents of Warm Life: Popular Culture in American Higher Education*. Bowling Green, OH: Bowling Green State University Popular Press, 1980.

Gournelos, Ted, and Viveca Greene, eds. *A Decade of Dark Humor: How Comedy, Irony, and Satire Shaped Post-9/11America*. Jackson: University Press of Mississippi, 2011.

Guins, Raiford A., and Omayra Zaragoza Cruz, eds. *Popular Culture: A Reader*. Thousand Oaks, CA: Sage Publications, 2005.

Hall, Stuart, and Paddy Whannel. *The Popular Arts*. New York: Pantheon, 1965.

Hinds, Harold E., Jr.; Angela Nelson; and Marilyn F. Motz. *Popular Culture Theory and Methodology: A Basic Introduction*. Madison: University of Wisconsin Press/ Popular Press, 2006.

Hoffmann, Frank W. *American Popular Culture: A Guide to the Reference Literature*. Englewood, CO: Libraries Unlimited, 1995.

Hollows, Joanne, and Rachel Moseley eds. *Feminism in Popular Culture*. New York: Berg, 2006.

Inge, M. Thomas, ed. *Handbook of American Popular Culture*, 2nd ed. Westport, CT: Greenwood Press, 1989.

Inge, M. Thomas, ed. *Concise Histories of American Popular Culture*. Westport, CT: Greenwood Press, 1982.

Ingraham, Chrys. *White Weddings: Romancing Heterosexuality in Pop Culture*, 2nd ed. New York: Routledge, 2008.

Laforse, Martin W., and James A. Drake. *Popular Culture and American Life: Selected Topics in the Study of American Popular Culture*. Chicago: Nelson-Hall, 1981.

Landrum, Larry N. *American Popular Culture: A Guide to Information Sources*. Detroit: Gale Research, 1982.

Levine, Lawrence W. *The Opening of the American Mind: Canons, Culture, and History*. Boston: Beacon Press, 1996.

Levine, Lawrence W. *The Unpredictable Past: Explorations in American Cultural History*. New York: Oxford University Press, 1993.

Levine, Lawrence W. *Highbrow/Lowbrow: The Emergence of Cultural Hierarchy in America*. Cambridge, MA: Harvard University Press, 1988.

Lipsitz, George. *Time Passages: Collective Memory and American Popular Culture*. Minneapolis: University of Minnesota Press, 1990.

Lowenthal, Leo. *Literature, Popular Culture, and Society*. Englewood Cliffs, NJ: Prentice-Hall, 1961.

Lynes, Russell. *The Tastemakers*. New York: Harper, 1954.

MacDonald, Dwight. *Against the American Grain*. New York: Random House, 1962.

Maltby, Richard, ed. *The Passing Parade: A History of Popular Culture in the Twentieth Century*. New York: Oxford University Press, 1989.

Milestone, Katie, and Anneke Meyer. *Gender and Popular Culture*. Malden, MA: Polity Press, 2012.

Motz, Marilyn F.; John G. Nachbar; Michael Marsden; et al. *Eye on the Future: Popular Culture Scholarship into the Twenty-First Century in Honor of Ray B. Browne*. Bowling Green, OH: Bowling Green State University Popular Press, 1994.

Mukerji, Chandra, and Michael Schudson, eds. *Rethinking Popular Culture: Contemporary Perspectives in Cultural Studies*. Berkeley: University of California Press, 1991.

Nachbar, Jack, and Kevin Lause, eds. *Popular Culture: An Introductory Text*. Bowling Green, OH: Bowling Green State University Popular Press, 1992.

Norton, Anne. *Republic of Signs: Liberal Theory and American Popular Culture*. Chicago: University of Chicago Press, 1993.

Nye, Russel B., ed. *New Dimensions in Popular Culture*. Bowling Green, OH: Bowling Green State University Popular Press, 1972.

Nye, Russel B. *The Unembarrassed Muse: The Popular Arts in America*. New York: Dial Press, 1970.

Petracca, Michael, and Madeleine Sorapure, eds. *Reading Popular Culture*. Boston: Prentice Hall, 2011.

Radway, Janice. *Reading the Romance: Women, Patriarchy, and Popular Literature*. Chapel Hill: University of North Carolina Press, 1984.

Root, Robert L. *The Rhetorics of Popular Culture: Advertising, Advocacy, and Entertainment*. Westport,

CT: Greenwood Press, 1987.

Ross, Andrew. *No Respect: Intellectuals and Popular Culture*. New York: Routledge, 1989.

Russo, Vito. *The Celluloid Closet: Homosexuality in the Movies*, rev. ed. New York: Harper & Row, 1987.

Schroeder, Fred E. H., ed. *Twentieth-Century Popular Culture in Museums and Libraries*. Bowling Green, OH: Bowling Green State University Popular Press, 1981.

Seldes, Gilbert. *The Seven Lively Arts*. New York: Harper and Brothers, 1924.

Smith, Henry Nash. *Virgin Land: The American West as Symbol and Myth*. New York: Vintage, 1957.

Stanton, Frank Nicholas. *Mass Media and Mass Culture*. New York: Columbia Broadcasting System, 1962.

Storey, John. *Cultural Theory and Popular Culture: An Introduction*, 6th ed. Harlow, UK: Pearson, 2012.

Susman, Warren. *Culture as History: The Transformation of American Society in the Twentieth Century*. New York: Pantheon, 1984.

Takacs, Stacy. *Terrorism TV: Popular Entertainment in Post-9/11 America*. Lawrence: University Press of Kansas, 2012.

Toll, Robert C. *The Entertainment Machine: American Show Business in the Twentieth Century*. New York: Oxford University Press, 1989.

Ulanov, Barry. *The Two Worlds of American Art: The Private and the Popular*. New York: Macmillan, 1965.

Urish, Ben, ed. *Ray Browne on the Culture Studies Revolution: An Anthology of His Key Writings*. Jefferson, NC: McFarland, 2010.

Warshow, Robert. *The Immediate Experience: Movies, Comics, Theatre, and Other Aspects of Popular Culture*. Garden City, NY: Doubleday, 1964.

Wertheim, Arthur Frank, ed. *American Popular Culture: A Historical Bibliography*. Santa Barbara, CA: ABC-Clio Information Services, 1984.

White, David Manning, and John Pendleton, eds. *Popular Culture: Mirror of American Life*. Del Mar, CA: Publisher's Inc., 1977.

Whiting, Cecile. *A Taste for Pop: Pop Art, Gender, and Consumer Culture*. Cambridge, UK: Cambridge University Press, 1997.

Williams, Martin T. *Hidden in Plain Sight: An Examination of the American Arts*. New York: Oxford University Press, 1992.

Williams, Raymond. *Culture and Society, 1780–1950*. London: Chatto and Windus, 1960.

Wilmeth, Don B. *American and English Popular Entertainment: A Guide to Information Sources*. Detroit: Gale Research, 1980.

Woodward, John Donald, ed. *Popular Culture: Opposing Viewpoints*. Detroit: Thomson/Gale, 2005.

Notes on Advisers and Contributors

ABRAMS, Nathan. Independent scholar. Editor of *Containing America: Cultural Production and Consumption in Fifties America.*

ALDAMA, Frederick Luis. Distinguished Professor of Arts & Humanities, Ohio State University. Coeditor of *Cognitive Approaches to Literature and Culture* series.

ALVAREZ, Roberto. Freelance writer.

ANDERSON, Byron. Associate professor and head of reference, University Libraries, Northern Illinois University. Compiler and editor of *Alternative Publishers of Books in North America*, 4th edition.

ANDREWS, Carly. Freelance writer.

APARICIO, Frances R. Professor of Spanish and Portuguese and director of the Latina and Latino Studies program, Northwestern University. Author, *Listening to Salsa: Gender, Latin Popular Music, and Puerto Rican Cultures* (1998) and coeditor of various critical anthologies, including *Tropicalizations: Transcultural Representations of Latinidad* (1997).

APPEL, Jacob M. Author, bioethicist, and social critic. Writer of short stories in numerous journals, including *Iowa Review*, *Prairie Schooner*, and *Threepenny Review*.

ARNOLD, Tim. Member of English Department, University of Kentucky.

ASHDOWN, Paul. Professor of journalism, University of Tennessee. Editor of *James Agee: Selected Journalism* and contributor of articles to scholarly journals.

ATTIAS, Bernardo Alexander. Professor and chair, Department of Communication Studies, College of Arts, Media, and Communication, California State University, Northridge.

AUGUSTYN, Frederick J., Jr. Cataloger, Library of Congress. PhD in American history, University of Maryland, College Park.

BADIKIAN-GARTLER, Beatriz. Lecturer in literature, creative writing, and women's studies, Roosevelt University, Chicago, Illinois; Northwestern University, Evanston, Illinois; and the Newberry Library, Chicago. Author of several essays on popular culture, including film and travel literature.

BAERS, Michael. Freelance writer. Contributor to *LA Weekly*, *Glue Magazine*, and other publications.

BAKER, Neal. Humanities and languages librarian, Earlham College, Richmond, Indiana.

BANE, S. K. Assistant professor of history and director of Honors Program, Arkansas Tech University. Editor of *American Personalities.*

BARBAS, Samantha. Associate professor, State University of New York at Buffalo Law School.

BARKSDALE, J. Allen. Freelance writer.

BARTEL, Pauline. President and CEO, Bartel Communications, Inc. Author of *Amazing Animal Actors*, *Reel Elvis*, and *The Complete* Gone with the Wind *Trivia Book.*

BATCHELOR, Bob. Assistant professor, School of Journalism, Kent State University. Member of editorial review board, The *Journal of Popular Culture* and *Journal of American Culture.*

BEATTY, Greg. Freelance writer, Bellingham, Washington. Award-winning writer of science fiction.

BELL, Vance. Freelance art, film, and new media critic. Editor-in-chief, *Other Voices: The Journal of Cultural Criticism* at the University of Pennsylvania.

BELLMAN, Samuel I. Professor emeritus of English, California State Polytechnic University, Pomona. Author of two biographies in the G.K. Hall/Twayne United States Authors Series (*Marjorie Kinnan Rawlings* and *Constance Mayfield Rourke*), editor of *The College Experience* and *Survey and Forecast*, and author of numerous poems, short stories, reviews, and articles in journals and reference books.

BELPEDIO, James R. Professor of history, government, and humanities, Becker College, Worcester, Massachusetts.

BENNETT, Courtney. Freelance writer. Contributor of articles to scholarly journals.

BERG, Timothy. Assistant professor, Department of History, Ball State University, Muncie, Indiana.

BERGERON-DUNCAN, Lisa. Instructor of psychology and sociology, Ouachita Technical College, Malvern, Arkansas.

BERNARDI, Daniel. Professor and chair of the Cinema Department, San Francisco State University. Author of *Star Trek and History: Race-ing toward a White Future* and editor of *Classic Whiteness: Race and the Emergence of U.S. Cinema.*

BERNER, R. Thomas. Professor of journalism and American studies, Pennsylvania State University. Author of *The Literature of Journalism: Text and Context.*

BEVIS, Charlie. Member of Society for American Baseball Research. Author of *Mickey Cochrane: The Life of a Baseball Hall of Fame Catcher.*

BICKELL, Lara. Freelance writer. Contributor, *American West.*

BINKLEY, Sam. Associate professor of sociology, Emerson College, Boston, Massachusetts.

BLACK, Brian. Professor of history and environmental studies, Pennsylvania State University, Altoona. Author of *Petrolia: The Landscape of the First Oil Boom.*

BLACK, Liza. Member of visiting faculty, theatre arts, Cornell University, Ithaca, New York.

BLANKENSHIP, Bethany. Associate professor and chair of English Department, The University of Montana Western, Dillon. Author of "Visualizing Voice: Popular Songs in the Composition Course," *Washington English Journal.*

BLUSTEIN, Rebecca. Freelance writer.

BODROGHKOZY, Aniko. Assistant professor of film and media studies, University of Virginia. Author of *Groove Tube: Sixties Television and Youth Rebellion.*

BOND, Gregory. Freelance writer. PhD in American history, University of Wisconsin–Madison.

BONE, Martyn. Associate professor of English, University of Mississippi.

BOOTH, H. Austin. Vice provost for University Libraries, State University of New York at Buffalo.

BOWLER, Gerry. Professor of history, University of Manitoba.

BREMSETH, Marlena E. Adjunct professor, Black Studies Program, The College of William & Mary, Williamsburg, Virginia.

BRENNAN, Carol. Freelance writer.

BREWER, Tony. Actor, writer, lyricist, musician, and sound effects artist.

BRODERSON, Deborah. Freelance writer.

BRODY, Michael. Freelance writer.

BROESKE, Pat H. Coauthor of *Howard Hughes: The Untold Story* and *Down at the End of Lonely Street: The Life and Death of Elvis Presley.*

BROWN, Robert J. Associate professor of history, Daniel Webster College, Nashua, New Hampshire. Author of *Manipulating the Ether: The Power of Broadcast Radio in Thirties America* and of numerous articles on the history of broadcasting.

BROWN, Sharon. Instructor in American literature, State University of New York at Stony Brook. Author of *American Travel Narratives as a Literary Genre from 1542–1832: The Art of a Perpetual Journey.*

BUHLE, Paul. Senior lecturer, history and American civilization, Brown University, Providence, Rhode Island. Written or edited thirty books, including *Popular Culture in America* (University of Minnesota Press, 1987), *Tender Comrades: A Backstory of the Hollywood Blacklist* (St. Martin's, 1997), and *From the Lower East Side to Hollywood: Jews in American Popular Culture* (Verso, 2004). Frequent contributor to *Journal of American History*, *Village Voice*, and the *Nation.*

BUNCH, Craig. Librarian, Coldspring-Oakhurst C.I.S.D., Texas. Former review editor, *Popular Culture in Libraries.*

BURNETT, Stephen. Professor of history, Roosevelt University, Chicago, Illinois.

BURNS, Gary. Professor of communication, Northern Illinois University. Editor of the journal *Popular Music and Society.* Coeditor of *Making Television.*

BURNS, Margaret E. Freelance writer, Bloomington, Indiana.

CABRERA, Manuel V., Jr. Freelance writer.

CAMPANA, Joseph. Project editor, Thomas Riggs & Company, Missoula, Montana.

CARE, Ross. Freelance composer and author. Writer of music for theater and films. Contributor to *Scarlet Street*, *Sight and Sound*, *Film Quarterly*, and *Performing Arts: Motion Pictures.*

CARPENTER, Gerald. Contributing editor, *Santa Barbara Independent*, and lifestyle editor, *Goleta Valley Voice.* PhD in French history, University of California.

CAST, Anthony. Instructor of rhetoric, University of Illinois at Urbana-Champaign.

CASTRO, Rafaela. Humanities/social sciences librarian, Shields Library, University of California, Davis. Author of "Latino Literature" in *What Do I Read Next? Multicultural Literature* and *Dictionary of Chicano Folklore.*

CHAMBERS, Jason. Associate professor of communications, University of Illinois at Urbana-Champaign.

CHANDLER, Chris. Award-winning broadcast journalist and broadcast historian and collector.

CHAPMAN, Michael K. Freelance writer.

CHAPMAN, Roger. Assistant professor of history, Palm Beach Atlantic University, West Palm Beach, Florida.

CHIASSON, Lloyd, Jr. Professor, Department of Mass Communications, Nicholls State University. Coauthor of *Reporter's Notebook*, a journalism interactive computer textbook. Editor and coauthor of *The Press in Times of Crisis, The Press on Trial*, and *Three Centuries of American Media*.

CIASULLO, Ann M. Assistant professor of English, Gonzaga University, Spokane, Washington.

CLARK, Dylan. Lecturer in anthropology, University of Toronto.

CLARK, Frank. Freelance writer. Presenter at Northeast Popular Culture Association meetings.

CLARK, Randall. Freelance writer.

COBANE, Craig T. Professor of political science, Western Kentucky University. Contributor to *PS: Political Science and Politics*, *International Journal*, and *Journal of Criminal Justice Education*.

COFFEY, Dan. Associate professor and subject librarian, social sciences and humanities, Iowa State University.

COHEN, Adam Max. Associate professor of English, University of Massachusetts, Dartmouth. Author of "The Nature of Genius: Blake, Einstein, and Theories of Relativity," *Wordworth Circle*.

COHEN, Toby Irene. Retired teacher.

COKAL, Susann. Professor of creative writing, Virginia Commonwealth University. Author of *Breath and Bones* and *Mirabilis*.

COKER, Jeffrey W. Professor of history, Belmont University, Nashville, Tennessee.

COLETTA, Charles A., Jr. Professor of popular culture, Bowling Green State University, Bowling Green, Ohio.

COLLINGS, Michael R. Professor of English, director of creative writing, and poet-in-residence, Seaver College, Pepperdine University, Malibu, California. Author of multiple volumes of scholarship, criticism, bibliography, and poetry.

COLLINS, Willie. Cultural specialist and CEO of the Consortium for California Cultural Conservation, Oakland, California. Contributor of articles on African American music and culture to scholarly journals.

CONSALVO, Mia. Graduate instructor, School of Journalism and Mass Communication, University of Iowa. Author of "Hegemony, Domestic Violence and Cops: A Critique of Concordance," *Journal of Popular Film & Television*.

COOKE, Douglas. Freelance writer.

COOPER, B. Lee. Author of many books, including *Images of American Society in Popular Music* (Nelson-Hall, 1982), *A Resource Guide to Themes in Contemporary American Song Lyrics, 1950–1985* (Greenwood Press, 1986), *Popular Music Perspectives* (Popular Press, 1991), and *Rock Music in American Popular Culture*, 3 volumes (Haworth Press, 1995, 1997, 1999). Contributor of articles and reviews to *Popular Music and Society*, *Journal of American Culture*, *Rock and Blues News*, and other scholarly journals and music magazines.

CORONADO, ViBrina. Clothing designer and researcher. PhD candidate in theater.

COTTRELL, Robert C. Professor of history and American studies, California State University, Chico. Author of *Izzy: A Biography of I. F. Stone* and *The Social Gospel of E. Nicholas Comfort: Founder of the Oklahoma School of Religion*.

CRAGIN, Becca. Assistant professor of popular culture, Bowling Green State University, Ohio. Author of "Noirish Inversions: Investigation and Victimization in *The Silence of the Lambs* and *Basic Instinct*," *Americana: The Journal of American Popular Culture*, "Lesbians and Serial TV: *Ellen* Finds Her Inner Adult" in *The New Queer Aesthetic on Television: Essays on Recent Programming*, and other articles.

CREEKMUR, Corey K. Associate professor of English, University of Iowa. Coeditor of *Out in Culture: Gay, Lesbian, and Queer Essays on Popular Culture*. Author of essays and reviews in *The Road Movie Book*, *Oscar Micheaux and His Circle*, *Film Quarterly*, *Wide Angle*, the *Hitchcock Annual*, *Discourse*, and other publications.

CREPEAU, Richard C. Professor of history, University of Central Florida. Specializes in sports in America.

CULLEN, Jim. Chair of History Department, Ethical Culture Fieldston School, Bronx, New York. Author of *The Civil War in Popular Culture: A Reusable Past*; *The Art of Democracy: A Concise History of Popular Culture in the United States*; and *Born in the U.S.A.: Bruce Springsteen and the American Tradition*.

CURTIS, Susan. Professor of history and director of the American Studies Program, Purdue University, West Lafayette, Indiana. Author of *A Consuming Faith: The Social Gospel and Modern American Culture*; *Dancing to a Black Man's Tune: A Life of Scott Joplin*; and *The First Black Actors on the Great White Way*.

DAVIS, Glyn. Academic coordinator of postgraduate

studies, The Glasgow School of Art. Author of *Queer as Folk*; *Superstar: The Karen Carpenter Story*; and *Far from Heaven*.

DAVIS, Janet. Associate professor of American studies, University of Texas at Austin.

DAVIS, Stephen P. Freelance writer.

DEANE, Pamala S. Independent writer and scholar.

DECHERT, S. Renee. Associate professor of English, Northwest College, Powell, Wyoming. Author of *Larry McMurtry and the Western: The Rhetoric of Novelization.*

DEITRICK, John R. Freelance writer.

DEMLER, Mariel. Freelance writer.

DiMAURO, Laurie. Writer and editor specializing in biographical and literary reference.

DOHERTY, John J. Librarian and freelance writer.

DOMINA, Thurston. Freelance writer.

DONLON, Jon Griffin. Director and coordinator, Center for the Study of Controversial Leisure, University of Southwestern Louisiana. Fellow, Royal Geographic Society.

DONNER, Simon. Freelance writer and environmental scientist.

DOSSEY, Lauren. Attorney. Member of California State Bar.

DUNCAN, Randy. Professor of communication, Henderson State University, Arkadelphia, Arkansas. Cofounder, Comic Arts Conference.

DUNCOMBE, Stephen. Associate professor of media and cultural studies, Gallatin School, New York University. Author of *Notes from Underground: Zines and the Politics of Alternative Culture.*

DuPELL, Eugenia Griffith. Freelance writer.

DYER, Stephanie. Associate professor of American history, Hutchins School of Liberal Studies, Sonoma State University, Rohnert Park, California.

EDELMAN, Rob. Film journalist and historian. Contributing editor, *Leonard Maltin's Movie & Video Guide.* Author of *Great Baseball Films* and *Baseball on the Web*, and coauthor of *Angela Lansbury: A Life on Stage and Screen* and *Meet the Mertzes.*

EDGERS, Geoff. Reporter for the Living/Arts section of the *Boston Globe*. Author of *The Midnight Hour: Bright Ideas for after Dark* and contributor to *Details*, *Spin*, the *New York Times Sunday Magazine*, *Salon*, and the *Boston Phoenix.*

EMBRY, Jessie L. Associate director, Charles Redd Center for Western Studies, and instructor in history, Brigham Young University, Provo, Utah. Author of articles on aviation in the West with Roger D. Launius.

ESCOFFIER, Jeffrey. Author of *American Homo: Community and Perversity.*

EVANS, Cindy. Manager of retail education, TruServ Corporation. PhD in anthropology. Author of training programs in customer satisfaction, personnel selection, and orientation.

EVANS, Sean. Collection documenter, Cline Library, Northern Arizona University. Avid Route 66 traveler and researcher.

EVERETT, William A. Associate professor of music history, Conservatory of Music, University of Missouri, Kansas City. Author of articles on musical theater and other topics.

FALWELL, Alyssa L. Public relations consultant.

FEINBERG, Richard A. Professor, Department of Consumer Sciences and Retailing. Director, Center for Customer-Driven Quality, Purdue University. Seminar presenter, consultant, and expert witness. Coauthor of *Customer Relationship Management* and of numerous research and trade articles.

FINCHUM, G. Allen. Associate professor of geography, Oklahoma State University. Editor of *Sport Place: An International Journal of Sports Geography.*

FINKELSTEIN, S. Naomi. Antipoverty activist, writer, and radical historian. Contributor to *Bridges*, *Sinister Wisdom*, and *Gay Community News.*

FISCHER, Dennis. Author of *Horror Film Directors* and *Science Fiction Film Directors*. Contributor to *American Film*, *Movieline*, *Cinefantastique*, *Starlog*, *The Aliens Story*, *The Kung Fu Book*, *Bela Lugosi*, *Backstory II*, and *Backstory III.*

FREIND, Bill. Professor of English, Rowan University, Glassboro, New Jersey. Author of two collections of poetry, *American Field Couches* and *An Anthology.*

FREIRE-MEDEIROS, Bianca. Freelance writer. PhD in history and theory of art and architecture, State University of New York at Binghamton.

FRENTNER, Shaun. Freelance writer.

FRIEDMAN, James. Manager, University of California at Los Angeles Film and Television Archive Research and Study Center.

FURNESS, Adrienne. Freelance writer and reference librarian, Rochester, New York.

GAFFNEY, Paul. Associate professor of English, Hiram College, Hiram, Ohio.

GAITHER, Milton. Associate professor of education, Messiah College, Mechanicsburg, Pennsylvania.

GAJADHAR, Joan. Communications lecturer, Open Polytechnic of New Zealand, Lower Hutt, Wellington. Author (with Jim Sinclair) of "A Modern Detective Fiction" in *Encyclopedia of British Culture*, as well as "Plagiarism and the Internet" in *Ultibase*, an online journal for tertiary education.

GALLEY, Catherine C. Architect and urban designer.

GAMSON, Joshua. Chair, Sociology Department, University of San Francisco, California. Author of *Claims to Fame: Celebrity in Contemporary America* (University of California Press, 1994), *Freaks Talk Back: Tabloid Talk Shows and Sexual Nonconformity* (University of Chicago Press, 1998), *The Fabulous Sylvester: The Legend, the Music, the Seventies in San Francisco* (Holt, 2005), and numerous scholarly and nonscholarly articles on media, social movements, popular culture, and sexuality.

GANNON, Caitlin L. Freelance writer and teacher of communications and software. Owner and editor, Javelina Books, a women's press in Tucson, Arizona.

GARCIA-MYERS, Sandra. Director, The David L. Wolper Center for the Study of the Documentary, University of Southern California.

GARD, Greta. Project editor, Thomas Riggs & Company, Missoula, Montana. PhD candidate in English, Indiana University, Bloomington.

GARMAN, Bryan. Head of School, Wilmington Friends, Wilmington, Delaware. PhD in American studies, Emory University, Atlanta, Georgia. Author of *A Race of Singers: Whitman's Working Class Hero from Guthrie to Springsteen.*

GARROUTTE, Eva Marie. Associate professor of sociology, Boston College. Contributor of articles to scholarly journals.

GATEWARD, Frances. Assistant professor of media theory and criticism, University of California, Northridge. Author of essays published in journals and in the anthologies *Still Lifting, Still Climbing* and *Ladies and Gentlemen, Boys and Girls: Gender in Film at the End of the Twentieth Century.*

GEORGE, Jason. History teacher, The Bryn Mawr School, Baltimore, Maryland.

GIANOULIS, Tina. Freelance writer and lesbian activist.

GILES, Cynthia. Freelance writer. PhD in interdisciplinary humanities, University of Texas at Dallas. Former editor-in-chief, Saybrook Publications.

GILES, James R. Professor of English, Northern Illinois University. Author of several books, including *Understanding Hubert Selby, Jr.* and *The Naturalistic Inner-City Novel in America.*

GOLDIN, Milton. Fund-raising counsel and writer. Member of National Coalition of Independent Scholars. Author of *The Music Merchants* and *Why They Give.*

GOLDMAN, Ilene S. Independent film scholar. Contributor of articles and reviews to *Jump Cut, Journal of Film and Video, Latin American Research Review,* the *Chicago Tribune*, and *Spectator*, as well as essays on contemporary Latin American cinema in *The Ethnic Eye: Latino Media Arts* and *Framing Latin American Cinema: Contemporary Critical Perspectives.*

GOLDSTEIN, Dayna. Professor of composition, Georgia Southern University.

GOLDSTEIN, Matthew Mulligan. Freelance writer.

GOLDWEBER, David Elroy Goldweber. Adjunct professor of English, San Francisco area. Author of *Claws & Saucers: Science Fiction, Horror, and Fantasy Film: A Complete Guide: 1902–1982.* Contributor of articles to scholarly journals.

GORDON, Ian. Professor of American studies, National University of Singapore. Author of *Comic Strips and Consumer Culture, 1890–1945.*

GORDON, W. Terrence. Professor of French, Italian, and linguistics, Dalhousie University, Halifax, Canada. Author of *McLuhan for Beginners* and *Marshall McLuhan: Escape into Understanding. A Biography.*

GOULART, Ron. Freelance writer. Author of *The Funnies* and *Groucho Marx, Private Eye.*

GRAINGE, Paul. Associate professor of film studies, University of Nottingham, United Kingdom.

GRANGER, Brian. Author-composer, *Deirdre*, a musical. Member and composer for a nationally performing a cappella group.

GRAVES, Anna Hunt. Freelance writer. Author of *Folk.*

GRAVES, Steve. Professor of geography, California State University, Northridge.

GREGG CLEVER, Jill. Reference librarian, Toledo-Lucas County Public Library, Toledo, Ohio.

GRIFFITH, Benjamin. Emeritus professor of English and dean of the Graduate School, University of West Georgia. Author of numerous books on language and literature and contributor of articles to scholarly journals.

GROSSMAN, Perry. Project Manager, NMR Group, Inc. Author of "Identity Crisis: The Dialectics of Punk, Rock, and Grunge," *Berkeley Journal of Sociology.*

GUSTAINIS, Justin. Professor of communication, State University of New York at Plattsburgh. Author of *American Rhetoric and the Vietnam War.*

GYURE, Dale Allen. Associate professor, College of

Architecture and Design, Lawrence Technological University, Southfield, Michigan.

HA, Kristine. Freelance writer.

HAAS, Elizabeth. Freelance writer.

HABERSKI, Ray, Jr. Associate professor of history, Marian University, Indianapolis, Indiana.

HAINES, Laurel. Project manager, Kaplan Publishing.

HALL, Jeanne. Associate professor of communications, Pennslvania State University. Author of essays on film history and criticism. Coauthor of "Beat the Press" (monthly column), *Voices.*

HANSON, Steve. Director, Cinema-Television Library and Archives of Performing Arts, University of Southern California. Humanities biographer, University of Southern California. Coauthor of *Lights, Camera, Action: A History of the Movies in the Twentieth Century, Sourcebook for the Performing Arts, Film Review Index 1950–1985*, and *Film Review Index (1882–1949).* Film reviewer, *Screen International*, and feature writer, *Stills.* Associate editor of *Magill's Survey of Cinema* (series I, II, III) and *Magill's Bibliography of Literary Criticism.*

HATTON, Jackie. PhD, Cornell University.

HAVEN, Chris. Professor of creative writing, Grand Valley State University, Allendale, Michigan.

HAY, Ethan. Educational specialist, Sausalito, California. Freelance writer, illustrator, and editor. Contributing writer and illustrator of *The Learn 2 Guide: How to Do Almost Anything* and *Birth of a Notion.*

HEER, Jeet. Toronto-based journalist who focuses on arts and culture. Articles have appeared in the *National Post, Slate.com*, the *Boston Globe*, and other publications.

HEINZE, Andrew R. Playwright and independent scholar. Author of *Jews and the American Soul* and *Adapting to Abundance: Jewish Immigrants, Mass Consumption and the Search for American Identity.*

HESS, Mary. Freelance writer.

HIRSCH, Joshua. Freelance writer. Author of *Afterimage: Film, Trauma, and the Holocaust.*

HIXSON, David L. Freelance writer.

HOFFMAN, Scott W. Independent scholar. Author of "Holy Martin: The Overlooked Canonization of Dr. Martin Luther King," *Religion and American Culture: A Journal of Interpretation*, and "How Do You Solve a Problem Like Maria? St. Maria Goretti in the Post-Countercultural World," the *Critic.*

HOLCOMB, Briavel. Professor of urban studies and geography, Rutgers University. Coauthor of *Revitalizing Cities* and *The United States: A Contemporary Human Geography.*

HOLLORAN, Peter C. Professor of history, Bentley College, Waltham, Massachusetts. Executive secretary, Northeast Popular Culture/American Culture Association.

HOLLOWAY, David. Lecturer in American studies, University of Derby, United Kingdom. Author of a number of articles on American novelist Cormac McCarthy.

HOLLOWAY, Kimberley. Associate professor of English and technical communication, director of the Writing Center, King College, Bristol, Tennessee.

HORTON, Ron. Freelance writer. Travel writer, *PDX Magazine.* Author of *Awesome Athletes, Extreme Athletes*, and *Weekend Rock Oregon.*

HOVDE, Karen. Reference librarian, University Libraries, Northern Illinois University.

HOWLEY, Kevin. Associate professor, media studies, Depauw University, Greencastle, Indiana.

HUMEZ, Nick. Silversmith. Former principal music reviewer for the *Maine Sunday Telegram* and its associated daily, the *Portland Press Herald.* Coauthor of books on romance philology and its cultural corollaries, including *Latin for People/Latina pro Populo.*

ISAKSEN, Judy L. Associate professor of communication, High Point University, High Point, North Carolina.

ISTANDERS, Isabelle. Freelance writer.

JANKAUSKAS, Jennifer. Curator of art, Montgomery Museum of Fine Arts, Montgomery, Alabama.

JOHANNINGMEIER, Erwin V. Freelance writer. Author of *Equality of Educational Opportunity and Knowledgeable Human Capital: From the Cold War and Sputnik to the Global Economy and No Child Left Behind.*

JONES, Patrick. Librarian. Author of *What's So Scary about R. L. Stine?*

JONES, Patrick D. Professor of history, Institute for Ethnic Studies, University of Nebraska, Lincoln.

JONES, Preston Neal. Writer and film historian. Contributor to *Cinefantastique Magazine, American Art Review*, and the *Library of Congress Performing Arts Annual.*

JOSEPH, Mark. President of MJM Entertainment Group, Los Angeles, California. Author of *Out of This World: Why People of Faith Abandoned Rock and Roll, Why They're Coming Back.*

JUDD, Thomas W. Freelance writer.

JUNGER, Richard. Professor of communications and English, Western Michigan University. Author of books and articles on mass media and popular culture in American history.

KALLINEY, Peter. Associate professor of English, University of Kentucky, Lexington.

KANELLOS, Nicolás. Brown Professor of Hispanic Literature, University of Houston. Author of various reference books and histories of Hispanic culture.

KARNEY, Robyn. Editor and writer specializing in film subjects. Editor-in-chief, *Chronicle of the Cinema*. Author of biographies of Audrey Hepburn and Burt Lancaster, coauthor of *The Foreign Film Guide*, and editor of *Crown Series of Hollywood Studio Histories*.

KEANE, Stephen. Lecturer in film studies, Bretton Hall College, University of Leeds, United Kingdom. Teaching and research interests include modernism, postmodernism, critical theory, and popular culture.

KEELINE, James D. Freelance writer and independent scholar. Area chair, Popular Culture Association section on Dime Novels, Pulps, and Series Books. Author of *Stratemeyer Syndicate* and numerous articles for scholarly and genre periodicals.

KEELINE, Kimberlee Diane. Freelance writer. PhD candidate in English, University of Southern California.

KELLERMAN, Max. Freelance writer.

KEMPCKE, Ken. Information coordinator, Lethbridge College, Lethbridge, Alberta.

KENNEDY, Kerri. Freelance writer and editor.

KENNY, Stephen C. Lecturer in nineteenth- and twentieth-century North American history, University of Liverpool, United Kingdom.

KERCHER, Stephen. Professor of history, University of Wisconsin Oshkosh. Author of *Revel with a Cause: Liberal Satire in Postwar America*.

KERR, Matt. Freelance writer.

KIBLER, M. Alison. Department chair, Associate professor of American studies and women and gender studies, Franklin & Marshall College, Lancaster, Pennsylvania. Author of *Rank Ladies: Gender and Cultural Hierarchy in American Vaudeville*.

KILLMEIER, Matthew A. Associate professor of communication and media studies, University of Southern Maine.

KING, Jason. Assistant professor, The Clive Davis Department of Recorded Music, Tisch School of the Arts, New York University.

KLINKOWITZ, Jerome. Professor of English and university distinguished scholar at the University of Northern Iowa. Author of forty books on modern and contemporary culture, including *Literary Disruptions*, *Listen: Gerry Mulligan*, and *Writing Baseball*.

KLINKOWITZ, Jon. Journalist, *Iowa City Press-Citizen*. Professional blues guitar player.

KNIGHT, Judson. Freelance writer. Author, *Abbey Road to Zapple Records: The Beatles Encyclopedia*.

KONICKI, Leah. Historic preservation officer, city of Covington, Kentucky. Author of various articles on Sears and catalog houses.

KOTOK, Steven. Publisher, DDM Press, New York City.

KUHLKEN, Robert. Cultural geographer on the faculty of Central Washington University. Author of numerous journal articles on subjects ranging from agricultural history to zydeco music.

KUNKA, Andrew J. Associate professor of English, University of South Carolina, Sumter.

KUPFERBERG, Audrey E. Film and video archivist and appraiser. Lecturer in film history at the State University of New York at Albany. Coauthor of *Angela Lansbury: A Life on Stage and Screen* and *Meet the Mertzes*.

KUPPERS, Petra. Associate professor of English, University of Michigan, Ann Arbor.

LAMBERT, Emma. Contributor to *49th Parallel: An Interdisciplinary Journal of North American Studies*.

LANE, Christina. Associate professor, School of Communication, University of Miami.

LAUSE, Kevin. Freelance writer. Coauthor of *Popular Culture: An Introductory Text*.

LEAVELL, Nadine-Rae. Research coordinator and information specialist, Summerland Information Services, Buffalo, New York.

LELLOUCHE, Michele. Assistant general counsel, SunGard Relius, Jacksonville, Florida. Contributor to *History of the Modern Olympic Movement*.

LENT, Robin. Lecturer in creative writing and library sciences, University of New Hampshire, Durham.

LEOTTA, Joan. Freelance journalist specializing in business, history, education, and travel.

LEVINE, Richard. Freelance writer.

LIMSKY, Drew. Executive editor, *Story*, New York City. Cultural criticism and fiction contributor, the *Washington Post*, the *Los Angeles Times*, *Genre*, *His 2*, and *His 3*.

LINDLEY, Daniel. Freelance writer and editor, Eugene, Oregon. Author of *Ambrose Bierce Takes on the Railroad*.

LINEHAN, Joyce. President, Ashmont Media, Dorchester, Massachusetts.

LITTON, Margaret. Freelance writer.

LLOYD, James H. Library director, Cincinnati Christian University.

LONERGAN, David. Reference librarian, Northern Illinois University. Research interests in popular music, especially rock and roll.

LONGLEY, Eric. Freelance writer.

LOTT, Rick. Professor of English, Arkansas State University, Jonesboro, Arkansas. Author of poems widely published in magazines, as well as articles in *Journal of Popular Culture, University of Mississippi Studies in English*, and *Clues: A Journal of Detection*.

LOVETT-GRAFF, Bennett. Senior acquisitions editor, Scarecrow Press.

LOWE, Denise. Academic conference and seminar presenter throughout the United States.

LUDWIG, Jenny. Freelance writer.

LUPACK, Barbara Tepa. Editor and publisher, Round Table Publications. Author of numerous books on American literature and culture, including *Illustrating Camelot, Critical Essays on Jerzy Kosinski, King Arthur in America, Arthurian Literature by Women*, and *Nineteenth-Century Women at the Movies*.

LURIE, Karen. Author of numerous publications about television and popular culture, including *TV Chefs: The Dish on the Stars of Your Favorite Cooking Shows*.

LUTES, Michael A. Reference and government documents librarian, University of Notre Dame. Contributor to *Encyclopedia of AIDS, Gay and Lesbian Biography, Gay and Lesbian Literature* (Vols. 1 and 2), and *Gay and Lesbian Literary Companion*. Reviewer for *Library Journal* and *Choice*.

LYONS, James. Senior lecturer in English, University of Exeter, United Kingdom.

LYONS, John F. Associate professor, Joliet Junior College, Joliet, Illinois.

MACEK, Steve. Associate professor of speech and communication at North Central College, Naperville, Illinois.

MACOR, Alison. Freelance writer. PhD in radio-TV-film, University of Texas at Austin. Author of *Chainsaws, Slackers, and Spy Kids: Thirty Years of Filmmaking in Austin, Texas*.

MARC, David. Writer and editor, Syracuse University and CNY Writing Consultants. Visiting professor and Steven H. Scheuer Scholar in Television Studies, S.I. Newhouse School of Public Communications, Syracuse University. Author of *Comic Visions*, a history of American television comedy.

MARKOWITZ, Robin. PhD lecturer in sociology, California State University, Long Beach. Editor and founder, *Cultural Studies Central*, an electronic clearinghouse of cultural studies resources and original analysis.

MARSH-FITZPATRICK, Tilney. Freelance writer.

MARTIN, Richard. Curator, The Costume Institute, The Metropolitan Museum of Art, New York City. Adjunct professor of art history and archaeology, Columbia University, and adjunct professor art, New York University. Author of *Fashion and Surrealism, Cubism and Fashion*, and *The Ceaseless Century: Three Hundred Years of Eighteenth-Century Costume*, as well as hundreds of essays and dozens of exhibition catalogs.

MARTIN, Sara. Senior assistant teacher, Universitat Autonoma de Barcelona, Spain. Cofounder of S.I.N.P.L.I. (Spanish Association for the Study of Popular Texts in English).

MARTINDALE, Linda Ann. Program assistant for the Foreign Language Department and language testing coordinator, Elon University, Elon, North Carolina. Author of "Why Should I Worry about HIV?," "Being HIV Negative," and "Being HIV Positive" in *Human Sexuality: Biological, Psychological, and Cultural Perspectives*.

MATTSON, Kevin. Professor of history, Ohio University, Athens. Author of *Rebels All!: A Short History of the Conservative Mind in Postwar America* and numerous other books, essays, and reviews.

McCLURE, Randall. Professor of writing and linguistics, Georgia Southern University.

McCRACKEN, Allison. Associate professor and codirector, American studies, DePaul University, Chicago.

McDAID, Jennifer Davis. Historical archivist, Norfolk Southern Corporation, Norfolk, Virginia.

McDERMOTT, Theodore. Assistant editor, Thomas Riggs & Company, Missoula, Montana.

McENTEE, Jason. Associate professor of English, South Dakota State University, Brookings.

McGRATH, Cheryl. Instructor of art history, North Central Texas College.

McHONE-CHASE, Sarah. Librarian, Northern Illinois University, DeKalb.

McLENDON, Jacquelyn Y. Associate professor of English and director of black studies, College of William & Mary. Author of *Phillis Wheatley: A Revolutionary Poet* and *The Politics of Color in the Fiction of Jessie Fauset and Nella Larsen*.

McLEOD, Kembrew. Associate professor of popular culture, University of Iowa. Contributor to the *Village Voice, Raygun*, and *SonicNet*. Author of "Authenticity within Hip-Hop and Other Cultures Threatened with Assimilation," *Journal of Communication*.

McQUAIL, Josephine A. Associate professor of English, Tennessee Technological University, Cookeville.

MEDEIROS, Alex. Freelance writer.

MELTON, Brad. Coauthor of *Arizona Goes to War: The Home Front and the Front Lines during World War II.*

MENDIBLE, Myra. Professor, contemporary literary and cultural studies, Florida Gulf Coast University. Contributor of articles to scholarly journals and academic conferences.

MERRON, Jeff. Freelance writer.

MERTZ, Thomas J. Freelance writer.

MEYER, Nathan R. Secondary educator and historical researcher.

MEYER, Stephen. Freelance writer.

MIDDLEBROOK, Jonathan. Professor of English, San Francisco State University. Author of *Mailer and the Times of His Time*, as well as various articles, scholarly and popular.

MILLARD, Andre. Professor of history, University of Alabama at Birmingham. Author of *Beatlemania: Technology, Business, and Teen Culture in Cold War America.* Contributor to *National Academy of Recording Arts and Sciences Journal.*

MILLER, Jeffrey S. Assistant professor of English and journalism, Augustana College, Sioux Falls, South Dakota. Author of *Something Completely Different: British Television and American Culture.*

MILLER, Karen. Freelance writer.

MILLER, P. Andrew. Lecturer in creative writing, Northern Kentucky University. Member of Science Fiction and Fantasy Writers of America.

MILLS, Dorothy Jane. Freelance writer and baseball researcher. Author of *Chasing Baseball: Our Obsession with Its History, Numbers, People, and Places*; *The Labyrinth*; and *The Sceptre.*

MILNER, Andrew. Critic, *Philadelphia City Paper.* Contributor to *Spy Magazine* and *Stephen Sondheim: A Casebook.*

MINTZ, Lawrence E. Associate professor, American studies, University of Maryland. Former director, Art Gliner Center for Humor Studies. Editor of *Humor: International Journal of Humor Research* and author of numerous articles, book chapters, reviews, and conference papers on popular culture, particularly American humor.

MIX, Deborah M. Visiting assistant professor, Department of American Thought and Language, Michigan State University.

MOODY, Nickianne. Principal lecturer, media and cultural studies, Liverpool, John Moores University.

MOODY, Rick. Professor of film studies, Utah Valley State College and Salt Lake Community College. Author of *Introduction to Media Art* and contributor of articles to scholarly journals.

MOORE, Charles F. Member of staff, Center for Appalachian Studies and Services, East Tennessee State University. Editor of *Asunaro: Living in the Mountains of Japan.*

MOORE, Leonard N. Associate professor of history, Louisiana State University. Specializes in African American and urban history.

MOOS, Dan. Freelance writer.

MORACE, Robert A. Professor of English, Daemen College, Amherst, New York. Author of *Irvine Welsh*, *Irvine Welsh's Trainspotting*, and *The Dialogic Novels of Malcolm Bradbury and David Lodge.* Contributor to journals and collections, including *The Chippewa Landscape of Louise Erdrich.*

MORAN, Edward. Associate editor, *Random House Dictionary of the English Language* and H.W. Wilson's *World Authors* and *World Musicians* reference series. Writes about American cultural and literary history of the twentieth century.

MORRIS, Barry. Associate professor of speech communication, Pace University, New York City. Contributor of articles on rhetoric, politics, and culture to the *Quarterly Journal of Speech* and other publications.

MULLANE, Janet. Freelance writer. Tutor of English as a second language, OneWorld Language Solutions.

MURPHY, Michael J. Assistant professor, Women and Gender Studies Department, University of Illinois, Springfield.

MURRAY, Jennifer A. Freelance writer.

MURRAY, Susan. Associate professor of media, culture, and communication, New York University.

MUSCOREIL, Debra Lucas. Research and technical consultant, freelance writer, and contributor to newspapers, newsletters, and books.

MVUYEKURE, Pierre-Damien. Professor of English and African American Literature, University of Northern Iowa, Cedar Falls.

NAJJAR, Michael. Assistant professor, Department of Theatre Arts, University of Oregon, Eugene. Founding artistic director, Riverside Repertory Theatre.

NASH, Ilana. Associate professor of gender and women's studies, Western Michigan University, Kalamazoo. Author of *American Sweethearts: Teenage Girls in Twentieth-Century Popular Culture.*

NEMANIC, Mary Lou. Associate professor of communications, Pennsylvania State University, Altoona. Contributor to *Biographical Encyclopedia of Indoor Sports* and codirector of documentaries.

NEWMAN, Scott A. Professor of history, Loyola University, Chicago.

NIBLOCK, Eliot. Freelance writer.

NICKS, Joan. Adjunct professor of film studies and popular culture, Brock University, St. Catharines, Ontario. Author of chapters in *Documenting the Documentary* and *Gendering the Nation: Canadian Women's Cinema*. Contributor of articles to scholarly journals.

NORDEN, Martin F. Professor of communication, University of Massachusetts, Amherst. Author of *The Cinema of Isolation: A History of Physical Disability in the Movies* and *John Barrymore: A Bio-bibliography*. Editor of *The Changing Face of Evil in Film and Television*.

NORDSTROM, Justin. Professor of history, Pennsylvania State University, Hazelton.

NOTARO, Anna. Professor of English, University of Nottingham, United Kingdom.

OCKERSTROM, Lolly. Professor of English, Park University, Parkville, Missouri.

O'CONNOR, William F. Professor, School of Liberal Arts, Asia University, Tokyo. Coeditor of *The Kenkyusha Dictionary of English Collocations*.

O'HARA, S. Paul. Assistant professor of history, Xavier University, Cincinnati, Ohio.

O'NEAL, Angela. Director of Collections Services, National Digital Newspaper Program, Ohio Historical Society.

O'SHEA, Christopher D. Professor of history, Wilfrid Laurier University, Waterloo, Ontario.

OWENS, Kerry. Professor, Communication and Media Studies Department, University of Mary Hardin-Baylor, Belton, Texas.

OXOBY, Marc. Lecturer, Core Humanities Program, University of Nevada, Reno.

PAINO, Troy. Professor of history and president, Truman State University, Kirksville, Missouri. Contributor of articles and book reviews about sports in American culture.

PAINTER, D. Byron. Freelance writer.

PALLADINO, Grace. Former codirector, The Samuel Gompers Papers, University of Maryland, College Park. Author, *Teenagers: An American History* (Basic Books, 1996) and books on working-class history.

PARATTE, Henri. Professor, Acadia University. Specializes in translation, cultural studies, and Acadian studies. Author of ten books and numerous articles in journals, magazines, and newspapers in Canada, the United States, and Europe.

PARIS, Leslie. Professor of history, University of British Columbia, Vancouver. Author of *Children's Nature: The Rise of the American Summer Camp*.

PARRENT, Jay. Dean of student affairs, Madisonville Community College, Madisonville, Kentucky.

PAXTON, Felicity H. Director, Penn Women's Center, Philadelphia, Pennsylvania.

PENDERGAST, Sara. President, Full Circle Editorial, Inc. Editor, *Contemporary Designers* (3rd edition), and coeditor, *U-X-L Graphic Novelists: Profiles of Cutting Edge Authors and Illustrators*, *Gay and Lesbian Literature* (Vol. 2), *St. James Guide to Children's Writers* (5th edition), and *St. James Guide to Young Adult Writers* (2nd edition).

PENDERGAST, Tom. Principal, Full Circle Editorial, Inc. PhD in American studies, Purdue University. Author of *Consuming Men: Masculinity, Race, and American Magazines, 1900–1950*, and coeditor, *U-X-L Graphic Novelists: Profiles of Cutting Edge Authors and Illustrators*, *Gay and Lesbian Literature* (Vol. 2), *St. James Guide to Children's Writers* (5th edition), and *St. James Guide to Young Adult Writers* (2nd edition).

PENDRAGON, Jana. Writer, teacher, and critic. Author of a published thesis titled "The Use of King Arthur as an Icon in Popular American Culture."

PETERSON, Geoff. Chair and professor of political science, University of Wisconsin, Eau Claire.

PETERSON, Kurt W. Assistant professor of history, Judson College, Marion, Alabama.

PETTIGREW, Emily. Communications coordinator, Ernst & Young.

PHILIPPON, Daniel J. Associate professor of rhetoric, University of Minnesota, Twin Cities. Editor, *Our Neck of the Woods: Exploring Minnesota's Wild Places*.

PHILO, Simon. Lecturer in American studies, University of Derby, United Kingdom. Author of chapters and articles on *The Simpsons*, MTV, American youth television, and the literature of the Vietnam War.

PHY-OLSEN, Allene. Professor of English and director of honors program, Austin Peay State University, Clarksville, Tennessee.

PIETERS, Jürgen. Professor of literary theory, University of Ghent, Belgium.

POGUE, Paul F. P. Writer and photographer at *NUVO* magazine.

POHLAD, Mark B. Associate professor, Department of

Art and Art History, DePaul University, Chicago. Teaches and publishes in American art and the history of photography.

POSNER, Michael L. Retired correspondent for Reuters and United Press International.

PRICE, John A. Freelance writer.

PRICE, Victoria. Freelance writer and lecturer. Author of *Vincent Price: A Daughter's Biography*. PhD in American studies, University of New Mexico.

PRONO, Luca. Freelance writer. PhD University of Nottingham, United Kingdom.

PURDY, Elizabeth Rholetter. Independent scholar. Contributor to various scholarly works on political science and women's issues. Editor of *Celebrating Women in American History*.

PYLE, Christian L. Freelance writer.

RABINOVITZ, Lauren. Professor of American studies and film studies, University of Iowa. Author of *Memory Bytes: History, Technology, and Digital Culture*, as well as *Yesteryear's Wonderlands: Introducing Modernism to America*.

RANDALL, Jessy. Curator of special collections, Colorado College. Author, *Injecting Dreams into Cows* and *The Wandora Unit*.

RAVID, Taly. Freelance writer.

RAY, Belinda S. Author of *Sweet Valley High #138* and *Sweet Valley High: Senior Year #5*.

RAYKOFF, Ivan. Associate professor of the arts, The New School, New York. Coeditor of *A Song for Europe: Popular Music and Politics in the Eurovision Song Contest*.

REAVES, Wendy Wick. Curator of prints and drawings, National Portrait Gallery, Smithsonian Institution. Author of *Celebrity Caricature in America*. Coauthor of *Eye Contact: Modern American Portrait Drawings*.

REED, T. V. Lewis E. and Stella G. Buchanan Distinguished Professor of English and American Studies, Washington State University, Pullman. Author of *Fifteen Jugglers, Five Believers: Literary Politics and the Poetics of American Social Movements* (University of California Press, 1992) and *The Art of Protest* (University of Minnesota Press, 2005). Author/manager of the website culturalpolitics.net, which includes sites on Popular Culture, Digital Cultures, Social Movement Cultures, Environmental Justice Cultural Studies, and Interdisciplinary Cultural Theory.

REIBMAN, James E. Adjunct professor, Northampton Community College, Allentown, Pennsylvania. Author of *My Brother's Keeper: The Life of Fredric Wertham, M.D.* Coeditor of *A Fredric Wertham Reader*. Author of numerous articles and book chapters on legal writers of the Scottish Enlightenment, law and literature, Samuel Johnson and his circle, and popular culture.

RETTER, Yolanda. Former librarian, International Gay and Lesbian Archives, Los Angeles, and manager, Lesbian History Project website. Contributor to various anthologies and reference works.

REVELS, Tracy J. Associate professor of history, Wofford College, Spartanburg, South Carolina. Author of *Mostly Parodies*, *Grander in Her Daughters: Florida's Women during the Civil War*, and *Watery Eden: A History of Wakulla Springs*.

RHOLETTER, Wylene. Instructor, Department of English, Auburn University, Auburn, Alabama. Author of poems published in *Caesura*, *Chattahoochee Review*, and other literary magazines and of papers delivered at various conferences, including SAMLA and NCTE.

RICHARDS, Tad. Instructor, State University at New York at New Paltz. Author of *My Night with the Language Thieves: Collected Poems*. Coauthor, with Melvin B. Shestack, of *The New Country Music Encyclopedia*.

RIDINGER, Robert. Full professor, University Libraries, Northern Illinois University. Author of *The Gay and Lesbian Movement* and *References and Resources*. Contributor to *St. James Press Gay and Lesbian Almanac* and *Gay and Lesbian Biography*.

RIOUX, Anne Boyd. Professor of English and women's and gender studies, University of New Orleans. Author of *Writing for Immortality: Women and the Emergence of High Literary Society in America*.

RITTER, Jeff. Associate professor and chair, Department of Communication, Media, and Technology, La Roche College, Pittsburgh. Producer and writer in a variety of media, including video, radio, and the Internet.

ROBERTSON, Thomas. Associate professor of American studies, Worcester Polytechnic Institute. Author of *The Malthusian Moment: Global Population Growth and the Birth of American Environmentalism*.

ROBINSON, Arthur. Adjunct professor of American culture, Diablo Valley College, Pleasant Hill, California, and Santa Rosa Junior College, Santa Rosa, California. Author of "Teaching about Social Unrest: The 1992 L.A. Uprising as a Text in the Critical Thinking Classroom," *Inside English*.

ROGGIO, Sarah. Freelance writer.

ROSA, Todd Anthony. Teaching fellow, George Washington University.

ROSE, Ava. Social worker specializing in trauma survivors. Has taught college courses, published articles, and presented conference papers on film and television theory, culture studies, feminism, and psychoanalysis.

ROUTLEDGE, Chris. Professor of English, University of Liverpool, United Kingdom.

ROY, Abhijit. Associate professor of marketing, University of Scranton, Pennsylvania. Author of articles in *MIT Sloan Management Review*, *Journal of International Business Studies*, *Journal of Consumer Marketing*, *Journal of Direct Marketing*, *Journal of Product and Brand Management*, and *Journal of Services Marketing*.

RUSSELL, Adrienne. Assistant professor, Department of Media, Film, and Journalism Studies, University of Denver.

RUSSELL, Dennis. Associate professor, Walter Cronkite School of Journalism and Mass Communication, Arizona State University. Author of articles published in *Popular Culture Review*, *Studies in Popular Culture*, *Popular Culture Review*, and *Southwestern Mass Communication Journal*.

SAGOLLA, Lisa Jo. Adjunct assistant professor, Columbia University Teachers College. Author of *Rock 'n' Roll Dances of the 1950s* and *The Girl Who Fell Down: A Biography of Joan McCracken*.

SALAMONE, Frank A. Emeritus professor, Department of Sociology, Iona College, New Rochelle, New York. Author of books on Africa, religion, and missions, as well as articles on jazz and popular culture.

SANDERS, Joe Sutliff. Assistant professor of English, Kansas State University. Author of articles in *The Rise of the American Comics Artist: Creators and Contexts*; *Teaching African-American Women's Writing*; *The Lion and the Unicorn*; *Extrapolation*; and the *Children's Literature Association Quarterly*.

SARGENT, Andrew. Assistant professor of English, West Chester University, West Chester, Pennsylvania.

SCELFO, Julie. Reporter and writer, *New York Times*.

SCHAFER, Elizabeth D. Independent scholar. PhD in American history, Auburn University, Auburn, Alabama. Author, *Auburn: Plainsmen, Tigers, and War Eagles*. Coauthor, *Women Who Made a Difference in Alabama* and "'I'm Gonna Glory in Learnin': Academic Aspirations of African-American Characters in Children's Literature," *African American Review* 32.

SCHEEDER, Louis. Director of the Classical Studio, New York University.

SCHIFF, James. Associate professor, University of Cincinnati. Author of *Updike in Cincinnati: A Literary Performance*, *Updike's Version: Rewriting "The Scarlet Letter," Understanding Reynolds Price*, and *John Updike Revisited*. Editor of *Critical Essays on Reynolds Price*.

SCHMITT, Jacob. Research editor, Thomas Riggs & Company, Missoula, Montana.

SCHNAKENBERG, Robert E. Freelance writer. Author of numerous books, including *Sci-Fi Baby Names*, *Christopher Walken A to Z*, and *Secret Lives of the Supreme Court*.

SCHNEIDER, Steven. Producer of numerous films, including *Paranormal Activities*, *Insidious*, *The Bay*, and *The Devil Inside*. Author of articles in *Paradoxa: Studies in World Literary Genres* and *Other Voices: A Journal of Critical Thought*.

SCHRUM, Kelly. Associate professor and director of educational projects, George Mason University, Fairfax County, Virginia. Author of *World History Matters: A Student Guide to History Online*, *Some Wore Bobby Sox: The Emergence of Teenage Girls' Culture, 1920–1950*, and *U.S. History Matters: A Student Guide to History Online*.

SCHURK, William L. Sound recordings archivist, Bowling Green State University, Bowling Green, Ohio. Coauthor, *Tarnished Gold* (Transaction, 1986). Served as editorial board member of *Popular Music and Society*, *Journal of Popular Culture*, *Journal of American Culture*, and *Popular Culture and Libraries*.

SCODARI, Christine. Associate professor of communication, Florida Atlantic University. Author of numerous scholarly articles related to popular culture.

SCOTT, Alison M. Head of collection development, George Washington University Libraries, Washington, D.C. Coeditor, *The Writing on the Cloud: American Culture Confronts the Atomic Bomb* (University Press of America, 1997), and author of articles on popular culture in libraries and the history of the book.

SCOTT, Randall W. Popular culture, radicalism, and comic art bibliographer, original catalog librarian, and assistant head, Special Collections Division, Michigan State University Libraries, East Lansing. Author, *A Subject Index to Comic Books and Related Material* (Michigan State University Libraries, 1975), *Comic Books and Strips, an Information Sourcebook* (Oryx Press, 1988), *Comics Librarianship, a Handbook* (McFarland, 1990), *The Comic Art Collection Catalog* (Greenwood Press, 1993), and *European Comics in English Translation: A Descriptive Sourcebook* (McFarland, 2002).

SEARS, Ann. Professor of music, Wheaton College, Norton, Massachusetts. Review editor, College Music Society Journal Symposium. Contributor of articles to scholarly journals.

SEFCOVIC, E. M. I. Editor and publisher, Fashion after 50.com. Professor, adjunct faculty, Keiser University and Broward College, Fort Lauderdale, Florida. Author of academic publications and conference papers on labor rhetoric and culture, as well as women's aging and health issues.

SEGAL, Eric J. Harn Curator of Academic Programs, Samuel P. Harn Museum of Art, University of Florida, Gainesville.

SENF, Carol A. Professor and associate chair, School of Literature, Communication, and Culture, Georgia Institute of Technology, Atlanta. Author of *Science and Social Science in Bram Stoker's Fiction*, *Dracula: Between Tradition and Modernism*, *The Critical Response to Bram Stoker*, and *The Vampire in Nineteenth-Century British Fiction.*

SEUL, Tim. Associate professor of political science, Waseda University, Tokyo.

SHASHKO, Alexander. Lecturer in African-American Studies, University of Wisconsin–Madison.

SHAUF, Michele S. Learning Strategist, Invesco Ltd., Atlanta. Editor of *Computers, Ethics, and Society.*

SHAW, Taylor. Freelance writer.

SHEEHAN, Anne. Freelance writer.

SHEEHAN, Steven T. Associate professor of history, University of Wisconsin–Fox Valley, Menasha.

SHELTON, Pamela L. Freelance writer. Editor of *Feminist Writers* and *Contemporary Women Poets.*

SHERMAN, Sandra. Freelance writer.

SHINDO, Charles J. Professor of history, Louisiana State University, Baton Rouge. Author of *Dust Bowl Migrants in the American Imagination.*

SHUPP, Mike. Former aerospace engineer. Author of *With Fate Conspire*, *Morning of Creation*, *Soldier of Another Fortune*, *Death's Gray Land*, and *The Last Reckoning.*

SICKELS, Robert C. Associate professor of rhetoric and film studies, Whitman College, Walla Walla, Washington. Author of *American Film in the Digital Age* and *American Culture through History: The 1940s.*

SILVEY, C. Kenyon. Contributor to *SF Weekly*, *Penthouse*, *High Times*, and *Lounge.*

SIMON, Ron. Curator, Paley Center for Media. Author and curator of *World's without End: The Art and History of the Soap Opera*, *Jack Benny: The Radio and Television Work*, and *Witness to History.*

SIMPSON, Philip L. Professor of communications and humanities, Brevard Community College, Palm Bay, Florida. Author of *Psycho Paths: Tracking the Serial Killer through Contemporary American Film and Fiction*, as well as numerous essays on contemporary film and literature.

SKAINE, Rosemarie. Author of *Female Suicide Bombers*; *Female Genital Mutilation: Legal, Cultural, and Medical Issues*; and *The Women of Afghanistan under the Taliban.*

SLOAN, Ryan R. Freelance writer.

SLONIOWSKI, Jeannette. Associate professor of popular culture and film, Brock University, St. Catharines, Ontario. Coeditor of *Candid Eyes: Essays on Canadian Documentaries*, *Slippery Pastimes: A Canadian Popular Culture Reader*, *Canadian Communications: Current Issues in Media and Culture*, and *Documenting the Documentary: Close Readings of Documentary Film and Video.*

SMITH, Cheryl A. Associate director of publications, Denver Seminary. Author of *A Tertium Quid: The Interactive Dualism of Thomas Aquinas* and *The Falcon and the Serpent*, as well as numerous articles on popular culture.

SMITH, Erin. Associate professor of American studies and literature, University of Texas at Dallas. Author, *Hard-Boiled: Working-Class Readers and Pulp Magazines* (Temple University Press, 2000), and contributor of articles to scholarly journals.

SMITH, Kyle. Freelance writer.

SMOLENSKI, John. Associate professor of history, University of California–Davis. Author of *Friends and Strangers: The Making of a Creole Culture in Colonial Pennsylvania.* Coeditor of *New World Orders: Violence, Sanction, and Authority in the Colonial Americas.*

SOCHEN, June. Professor of history, Northeastern Illinois University, Chicago.

SOLOMON, Irvin D. History program director, Florida Gulf Coast University. Author of *Feminism and Black Activism in Contemporary America: An Ideological Assessment*, 2nd edition.

SPEACE, Geri. Freelance writer.

SPIELDENNER, Andrew. Director of Programs, National Association of People with AIDS. Contributor to *Queer P.A.P.I. Porn*; *Names We Call Home: Autobiography on Racial Identity*; *Voices of Identity, Rage and Empowerment*; and the Vietnamese magazine *Doi Dien.*

STABIN, Tova. Diversity coordinator, Lane Community College, Eugene, Oregon. Editor, poet, researcher, and photographer. Contributor to many journals, magazines, and anthologies.

STABLER, Scott. Associate professor of history, Grand Valley State University, Allendale, Michigan. Former coach, teacher, and professional baseball umpire.

STERNGRASS, Jon. Freelance writer.

STRUG, Carolyn. Freelance writer. Former vice president, supervisory analyst, Barclays Capital.

STUMP, Roger W. Professor of geography, State University of New York at Albany. Author of *Boundaries of Faith: Geographical Perspectives on Religious Fundamentalism.*

SULLIVAN, Bob. Screenwriter. Film reviewer, *Los Angeles Free Press.* Author of screenplay for *Clonus.* Editor of *Helicon.*

SYKES, Marc R. Adjunct professor of history, Rutgers, The State University of New Jersey.

TAKAGI, Midori. Associate professor of history, Fairhaven College, Western Washington University, Bellingham. Author of *Rearing Wolves to Our Own Destruction: Slavery in Richmond, Virginia, 1782–1865.*

TAYLOR, Candida. Freelance writer. Author of "Zoot Suit: Parading UnAmericanism," *Containing America: Cultural Production and Consumption in Fifties America.*

THILL, Scott. Editor, Morphizm.com. Contributor to *Salon, XLR8R, Wired,* and other publications.

THOMPSON, Robert. Trustee professor of television and popular culture, S.I. Newhouse School of Public Communications, Syracuse University, Syracuse, New York. Founding director, Bleier Center Television and Popular Culture.

THOMPSON, Stephen L. Reference/collection development librarian, John D. Rockefeller, Jr., Library, Brown University, Providence, Rhode Island.

THOMSON, Rosemarie Garland. Professor of women's studies, Emory University, Atlanta. Author of *Staring: How We Look* and *Extraordinary Bodies: Figuring Physical Disability in American Literature and Culture.* Editor of *Freakery: Cultural Spectacles of the Extraordinary Body.*

TOBEY, Daryna M. Freelance writer.

TODD, Jan. Professor, Department of Kinesiology and Health Education, University of Texas at Austin. Curator, Todd-McLean Physical Culture Collection. Author of *Physical Culture and the Body Beautiful: Purposive Exercise in the Lives of American Women.* Coeditor of *Iron Game History: The Journal of Physical Culture.*

TODD, Terry. Senior lecturer, Department of Kinesiology and Health Education, University of Texas at Austin. Director, Todd-McLean Physical Culture Collection. Coeditor of *Iron Game History: The Journal of Physical Culture.*

TOMASIC, John. Freelance writer.

TORMEY, Warren. Professor, Department of English, Middle Tennessee State University, Murfreesboro.

TRACEY, Grant. Professor, University of Northern Iowa. Teaches film theory, popular culture, and creative writing. Author, *Parallel Lines and the Hockey Universe.* Fiction editor, *North American Review.*

TREVIÑO, David. Professor of history, Ohio Northern University.

TREVIÑO, Marcella Bush. Instructor of history, Texas A&M University, Kingsville.

TRIBBLE, Scott. Senior associate director for digital strategy, Denison University, Granville, Ohio. Author of *A Colossal Hoax: The Giant from Cardiff That Fooled America.*

TRINCHERA, Tom. Reference librarian, Dutchess Community College, Poughkeepsie, New York.

TURSE, Nicholas A. Associate editor, Nation Institute's Tomdispatch.com. Author of *The Complex: How the Military Invades Our Everyday Lives,* as well as articles in the *Village Voice, Los Angeles Times, Atlanta Journal-Constitution,* and other publications. Editor of *The Case for Withdrawal from Afghanistan.*

UBELHOR, Anthony. Instructor of English, University of Kentucky.

UMBERGER, Daryl. Freelance writer. Web Content Specialist, Geographic Solutions, Tampa/St. Petersburg, Florida.

VAN KRANENBURG, Rob. Chair, Working Group Society, IoT Forum (Internet of Things Forum). Author of *The Internet of Things.*

VARGAS, Colby. U.S. history and popular culture teacher, New Trier High School, Winnetka, Illinois.

WALKER, Sue. Stokes Distinguished Professor of Creative Writing, University of South Alabama, Mobile.

WALTERS, Lori C. Assistant professor of history, University of Central Florida.

WANG, Nancy Lan-Jy. Freelance writer. Winner of the 1997 Ina Coolbrith Memorial Poetry Contest. Contributor of poetry to the *Los Angeles Times.*

WATHEN, Adam. Collections development manager, Johnson County Library, Overland Park, Kansas.

WEINTRAUB, Laural. Art historian. Adjunct assistant professor, history of art, Fashion Institute of Technology

WEISBERGER, Jon. Vice chair, International Bluegrass Music Association. Producer, Blue Side of Town. Proprietor, Use Your Words Music, Nashville, Tennessee.

WELKY, David B. Associate professor of history, University of Central Arkansas, Conway. Contributor to *Journal of Sport History* and *Culture, Sport, Society.*

WELLS, Christopher W. Professor of history, Macalester College, St. Paul, Minnesota.

WHITE, Celia. Head of cataloging, D'Youville College, Buffalo, New York.

WILSON, Christopher S. Visiting instructor, Faculty of Fine Arts, Design and Architecture, Bilkent University, Ankara, Turkey.

WILSON, David B. Computer programmer. Associate editor, *Weekly News Update on the Americas.*

WILSON, Kristi M. Professor of English, Soka University of America, Aliso Viejo, California. Coeditor of *Film and Genocide* and *Italian Neorealism and Global Cinema.*

WILTSE, Jeff. Associate professor of history, University of Montana.

WOLOSON, Wendy. Researcher, Library Company of Philadelphia. PhD in American civilization, University of Pennsylvania.

WOODARD, David E. Professor of history, Concordia University, St. Paul, Minnesota. Contributor to *Civil War History, Transactions of the Illinois State Historical Society, Gulf Coast Historical Review, American National Biography*, and *Teaching History: A Journal of Methods.*

WRIGHT, Bradford W. Adjunct associate professor of history, University of Maryland University College Europe. Author of articles on comic books and American history.

YABLON, Sharon. Playwright, director, and writer.

YEZBICK, Daniel. Assistant professor of English, Peninsula College, Port Angeles, Washington.

YOUNGKIN, Stephen D. Freelance writer. Archivist, Utah State Historical Society. Author of *The Lost One: A Life of Peter Lorre.* Coauthor of *The Films of Peter Lorre* and *Peter Lorre: Portrait des Schauspielers auf der Flucht.*

ZOOK, Kristal Brent. Associate professor and director, MA Journalism Program, Hofstra University, Hempstead, New York. Author of *I See Black People: The Rise and Fall of African-American Owned Television and Radio, Black Women's Lives: Stories of Pain and Power*, and *Color by Fox: The Fox Network and the Revolution in Black Television.*

Time-Frame Index

1900–1909

1910–1919

1920–1929

1930–1939

1940–1949

1950–1959

1960–1969

1970–1979

1980–1989

1990–1999

2000–2009

2010–

Subject Index

Boldface page numbers (e.g., 3:**437–439**) refer to the main entry on the subject. Page numbers in *italics* refer to illustrations. This index is sorted alphabetically word by word.

C

Subject Index

Subject Index

Subject Index

Subject Index

G

Subject Index

H

I

Subject Index

J

Subject Index

K

L

M

Subject Index

N

Q

R

Subject Index

Subject Index

Subject Index

T

V

X

Y

Subject Index